CANADIAN

ORGANIZATIONAL BEHAVIOUR

THIRD EDITION

STEVEN L. McSHANE

ORGANIZATIONAL BEHAVIOUR

THIRD EDITION

STEVEN L. McSHANE

Toronto New York Burr Ridge Bangkok Bogotá Caracas
Lisbon London Madrid Mexico City Milan New Delhi
Seoul Singapore Sydney Taipei

McGraw-Hill
Ryerson Limited

*A Subsidiary of The **McGraw·Hill** Companies*

Canadian Organizational Behaviour
Steven L. McShane
Third Edition

CANCOPY

ISBN: 0-07-560316-0

3 4 5 6 7 8 9 10 GTC   7 6 5 4 3 2 1 0 9

Printed and bound in Canada

SENIOR SPONSORING EDITOR: Evelyn Veitch
ASSOCIATE EDITOR: Elke Price
DEVELOPMENTAL EDITOR: Karina TenVeldhuis
PRODUCTION EDITOR: Geraldine Kikuta
COPY EDITOR: Liba Berry
PRODUCTION CO-ORDINATOR: Nicla Dattolico
COVER & TEXT DESIGN: Dave Murphy/ArtPlus Limited
COVER ILLUSTRATION/PHOTO: Art Wolfe/Tony Stone Images
PAGE MAKE-UP: Valerie Bateman/ArtPlus Limited
PRINTER: Transcontinental Group

Canadian Cataloguing in Publication Data

McShane, Steven Lattimore
    Canadian organizational behaviour

3rd ed.
Includes index.
ISBN 0-07-560316-0

1. Organizational behaviour. 2. Organizational behaviour — Canada I. Title

HD58.7.M32 1998   658.3   C97-932693-1

Dedicated with love and devotion to Donna,
and to our wonderful daughters,
Bryton and Madison

About the Author

Steven L. McShane is Professor and Director of Graduate Programs in SFU's Faculty of Business Administration. He is a Past President of the Administrative Sciences Association of Canada, has been Organizational Behaviour Division Chair in that association, and was recently a visiting scholar at the University of Western Australia.

Along with writing *Canadian Organizational Behaviour*, 3rd ed., Steve has published numerous research articles on wrongful dismissal, pay equity, business media representativeness, labour union participation, and related topics. Steve is also a frequent commentator in the media on organizational behaviour and human resource management issues.

Steve earned his Ph.D. at Michigan State University, a Master of Industrial Relations from the University of Toronto, and a Bachelor of Arts from Queen's University. He lives in the Vancouver area with his wife and two daughters.

CONTENTS IN BRIEF

Preface   xxix

Part 1   Introduction   1

  1   Introduction to the Field of Organizational Behaviour   2

Part 2   Individual Behaviour   27

  2   Individual Behaviour and Learning in Organizations   28
  3   Foundations of Employee Motivation   58
  4   Applied Motivation Practices   84
  5   Stress Management   116

Part 3   Individual and Interpersonal Processes   143

  6   Perception and Personality in Organizations   144
  7   Emotions and Values in the Workplace   172
  8   Communicating in Organizational Settings   198

Part 4   Team Processes   229

  9   Team Dynamics   230
  10   Employee Involvement and Quality Management   258
  11   Decision Making in Organizations   284
  12   Organizational Power and Politics   312
  13   Organizational Conflict and Negotiation   336
  14   Organizational Leadership   360

Part 5   Organizational Processes   389

  15   Organizational Change and Development   390
  16   Organizational Culture   416
  17   Employment Relationship and Career Dynamics   436
  18   Organizational Structure and Design   460

Additional Cases   490

Appendix A   Theory Building and the Scientific Method   505

Appendix B   Vroom-Jago Decision Tree   514

Appendix C   Answers to Practice Session Questions   516

Glossary   520

Indexes   588

CONTENTS

Preface xxix

PART 1
INTRODUCTION   1

Chapter 1   Introduction to the Field of Organizational Behaviour   2

The Field of Organizational Behaviour   4
  What are Organizations?   4
  Why Study Organizational Behaviour?   5
    Satisfying the need to predict   5
    Adopting more accurate theories of reality   5
    Controlling organizational events   5
  Emerging Trends in Organizational Behaviour   6
    The changing workforce   6
    The "new deal" employment relationship   7
    Teams, teams, and more teams   8
    Computer technology and OB   9
The Five Anchors of Organizational Behaviour   9
  The Multidisciplinary Anchor   9
  The Scientific Method Anchor   11
  The Contingency Anchor   11
  The Multiple Levels of Analysis Anchor   11
  The Open Systems Anchor   11
Organizational Knowledge and Learning   13
  Perspective 1.1   British Airways Flies High With Systems Thinking   14
  Organizational Learning   15
  Knowledge Acquisition   15
    Individual learning   16
    Environmental scanning   16
    Grafting   16
    Experimentation   16
  Knowledge Dissemination   17
  Knowledge Utilization   17
  Organizational Memory   17
  Perspective 1.2   City of Ottawa Loses Some Organizational Memory   18
Organization of This Book   19
Chapter Summary   21
Discussion Questions   22
Chapter Case   An Untimely Incident at Ancol Ltd.   23
Experiential Exercise   It All Makes Sense?   24

Practice Session for Part 1   25

PART 2
INDIVIDUAL BEHAVIOUR   27

Chapter 2   Individual Behaviour and Learning in Organizations   28

Model of Individual Behaviour and Performance   30
    Employee Motivation   31
    Ability   31
    Role Perceptions   32
    Situational Contingencies   33
    Perspective 2.1   Situational Contingencies Reduce Waste at Bell Canada   33
    Types of Work-Related Behaviour   33
        Joining the organization   33
        Remaining with the organization   34
        Maintaining work attendance   35
        Performing required tasks   35
        Exhibiting organizational citizenship   35
Learning in Organizations   36
    Learning Explicit and Tacit Knowledge   37
    Perspective 2.2   Kao Infosystems Canada Boosts Productivity
                      Through Continuous Learning   37
OB Modification: Learning Through Reinforcement   38
    A-B-Cs of OB Modification   38
    Contingencies of Reinforcement   39
        Comparing reinforcement contingencies   40
    Schedules of Reinforcement   41
    Shaping Complex Behaviour   43
    OB Mod in Practice   43
    Limitations of OB Mod   43
    Perspective 2.3   Marine Atlantic Sails Through Rough Waters with
                      OB Mod and Feedback   44
Learning Through Feedback   44
    Feedback Sources   45
    Giving Feedback Effectively   46
    Seeking Feedback   47
    Ethics of Employee Monitoring   47
Social Learning Theory: Learning by Observing   48
    Behavioural Modelling   48
        Behaviour modelling and self-efficacy   49
    Learning Behaviour Consequences   49
    Self-Reinforcement   49
Learning Through Experience   50
Practising Learning Through Experience   51
Chapter Summary   51
Discussion Questions   52
Chapter Case   Pushing Paper Can Be Fun   53
Experiential Exercises
    Task Performance Exercise   54
    Assessing Your Self-Efficacy   56

Chapter 3 Foundations of Employee Motivation 58

Content Theories of Motivation *60*
    Maslow's Needs Hierarchy Theory *60*
    Alderfer's ERG Theory *61*
    McClelland's Theory of Learned Needs *62*
        Learning needs 63
    Practical Implications of Content Motivation Theories *63*
    Perspective 3.1 Motivating Generation-X 64
Process Theories of Motivation *64*
Expectancy Theory of Motivation *64*
    Expectancy Theory Model *65*
        E→P expectancy 65
        P→O expectancy 65
        Outcome valences 66
    Predicting Work Effort: An Organizational Example *66*
    Perspective 3.2 Pacing Yourself at Saskatoon's Department of Parks and Relaxation 67
    Expectancy Theory in Practice *67*
        Increasing E→P expectancies 68
        Increasing P→O expectancies 69
        Increasing outcome valences 69
    Does Expectancy Theory Fit Reality? *69*
Equity Theory *70*
    Outcome/Input Ratio *70*
    Comparison Other *71*
    Equity Evaluation *71*
    Consequences of Inequity *71*
    Equity Theory in Practice *73*
Goal Setting *73*
    Perspective 3.3 Fair Pay in the Executive Suite 74
    Characteristics of Effective Goals *75*
        Specific goals 75
        Results-oriented goals 75
        Challenging goals 75
        Goal Commitment 76
        Participation in goal formation (sometimes) 77
        Goal feedback 77
    Goal-Setting Applications and Limitations *77*
Comparing Motivation Theories *77*
Are Motivation Theories Culture Bound? *77*
Chapter Summary *79*
Discussion Questions *80*
Chapter Case Steelfab Ltd. 80
Experiential Exercise Bonus Decision-Making Exercise 81

Chapter 4 Applied Motivation Practices 84

Reward Systems *86*
    Membership and Seniority-Based Rewards *87*
        Advantages and disadvantages 87

Job Status-Based Rewards   *87*
   Advantages and disadvantages   87
Competency-Based Rewards   *88*
   Advantages and disadvantages   88
Performance-Based Rewards   *89*
   Individual rewards   89
   Team rewards   90
Perspective 4.1   Campbell Soups Up Its Team Rewards   90
   Organizational rewards   91
The Trouble with Rewards   *92*
   Measure performance accurately   93
   Recognize and adjust for situational contingencies   93
   Use team rewards for interdependent jobs   93
   Ensure rewards are valued   94
   Watch out for unintended consequences   94
Job Design   *94*
Job Design and Work Efficiency   *95*
   Perspective 4.2   When Rewards Go Wrong   95
Scientific Management   *96*
Problems with Job Specialization   *97*
Job Design and Work Motivation   *98*
   Core Job Characteristics   *99*
   Critical Psychological States   *100*
   Individual Differences   *100*
Inreasing Work Motivation Through Job Design   *100*
   Job Rotation   *100*
   Job Enlargement   *101*
   Job Enrichment   *102*
      Empowering employees   102
   Perspective 4.3   Empowering Staff at Dufferin Game Room   103
      Forming natural work units   103
      Establishing client relationships   104
Job Design Prospects and Problems   *104*
   Obstacles in Job Design   *104*
Motivating Yourself Through Self-Leadership   *105*
   Personal Goal Setting   *105*
   Constructive Thought Patterns   *106*
      Self-talk   106
      Mental imagery   107
   Designing Natural Rewards   *107*
   Self-Monitoring   *108*
   Self-Reinforcement   *108*
   Self-Leadership in Practice   *108*
Chapter Summary   *109*
Discussion Questions   *109*
Chapter Case   Vêtements Ltée   110
Experiential Exercises
   Is Student Work Enriched?   111
   Assessing Your Self-Leadership   113

Chapter 5   Stress Management   116

What is Stress?   *118*
    General Adaptation Syndrome   *119*
        Alarm reaction   119
        Resistance   119
        Exhaustion   119
Stressors: The Causes of Stress   *120*
    Physical Environment Stressors   *120*
    Role-Related Stressors   *120*
    Interpersonal Stressors   *121*
    Perspective 5.1   Lean Production: Management by Stress at CAMI   122
    Organizational Stressors   *122*
    Work-Family Stressors   *122*
        Time-based conflict   123
    Perspective 5.2   Canadian Women Face Stress of the "Second Shift"   123
        Strain-based conflict   123
        Role behaviour conflict   124
    Stress and Occupations   *124*
Individual Differences in Stress   *125*
    Type A/Type B Behaviour Pattern   *125*
Consequences of Stress   *126*
    Physiological Consequences   *126*
    Behavioural Consequences   *126*
        Workplace aggression   127
    Psychological Consequences   *127*
        Job burnout   127
Managing Work-Related Stress   *128*
    Removing the Stressor   *129*
        Family-friendly workplaces   129
    Withdrawing from the Stressor   *130*
        Temporary withdrawal strategies   130
    Changing Stress Perceptions   *131*
    Controlling the Consequences of Stress   *132*
    Fitness and Lifestyle Programs   *132*
    Employee Counselling   *132*
    Perspective 5.3   Meditation and Relaxation Become Mantras for Executive Stress   133
    Social Support   *133*
Chapter Summary   *134*
Discussion Questions   *134*
Chapter Case   Jim Black — Sales Representative   135
Experiential Exercise   Behaviour Activity Profile — The Type A Scale   136

Practice Session for Part 2   *140*

PART 3
INDIVIDUAL AND INTERPERSONAL PROCESSES 143

Chapter 6 Perception and Personality in Organizations 144

The Perceptual Process *146*
    Selective Attention *146*
        Characterisics of the perceiver 147
    Perceptual Organization and Interpretation *148*
        Perceptual grouping 148
        Mental models 149
Social Identity Theory *149*
    Perceiving Others Through Social Identity *150*
Stereotyping in Organizational Settings *151*
    Problems with stereotyping 152
    Perspective 6.1 Bank of Montreal Employees Discover the Person,
                Not the Stereotype 152
    Ethical Problems with Stereotyping *153*
    Stereotyping and Workplace Harassment 153
    Perspective 6.2 Imperial Oil Clears Up Cross-Cultural Misunderstanding 154
Attribution Theory *155*
    Consequences of Attribution *155*
    Attribution Errors *155*
Self-Fulfilling Prophecy *156*
    Self-Fulfilling Prophecies in Organizations *157*
Other Perceptual Errors *158*
    Halo Effect *158*
    Primacy Effect *158*
    Recency Effect *159*
    Projection Bias *159*
Improving Perceptions *160*
    Increase Awareness of Perceptual Biases *160*
    Empathize With Others *160*
    Perspective 6.3 Increasing Empathy by Being There 161
    Postpone Impression Formation *161*
    Compare Perceptions with Others *162*
    Know Yourself: Applying the Johari Window *162*
        Johari Window in practice 163
Personality in Organizations *164*
    Biology or Environment? *165*
    "Big Five" Personality Dimensions *165*
    Personality and Organizational Behaviour *166*
        Limitations of personality traits 166
Other Personality Traits *167*
    Locus of control 167
    Self-monitoring 167
Chapter Summary *168*
Discussion Questions *168*
Chapter Case Nupath Foods Ltd. 169
Experiential Exercise Perceptions in a Diverse Workforce: The Royal Bank of
                Canada Vignettes 170

Chapter 7 Emotions and Values in the Workplace 172

Emotions in the Workplace   174
   Emotions and Personality   175
   Emotions, Attitudes, and Behaviour   175
      Three components of attitudes   176
      Linking beliefs and feelings   177
      Linking emotions to behaviour   177
      Cognitive dissonance   177
   Perspective 7.1   Brewing with Attitude at Labatt's   178
Job Satisfaction   178
   Job Satisfaction in Canada   179
   A Model of Job Satisfaction   179
   Job Satisfaction and Work Behaviours   181
      Job satisfaction and job performance   182
Organizational Commitment   182
   Consequences of Organizational Commitment   183
   The Decline of Organizational Commitment   184
   Building Organizational Commitment   184
   Perspective 7.2   Ontario Hydro's New Employment Deal Threatens Loyalty   185
Managing Emotions   186
   Problems with Emotional Labour   186
   Supporting Emotional Labour   186
      Emotional intelligence   188
Values at Work   188
   Cultural Differences in Values   189
      Cultural values in aboriginal organizations   190
   Ethical Values   191
   Perspective 7.3   Tough Choices at Sunnybrook Health Sciences Centre   191
   Supporting ethical values in organizations   192
Chapter Summary   193
Discussion Questions   193
Chapter Case   Rough Seas on the LINK650   194
Experiential Exercise   Ethical Dilemmas in Employment   196

Chapter 8 Communicating in Organizational Settings 198

A Model of Communication   200
Communication Barriers (Noise)   201
   Perceptions   201
   Filtering   202
   Language   202
      Jargon   202
      Ambiguity   202
   Information Overload   203
Communication Channels   204
   Perspective 8.1   Chrysler Revs Up Communication Channels   204
   Oral and Written Communication   205
   Electronic Mail   205
      Problems with e-mail   205
   Other Computer-Mediated Communication   207

Nonverbal Communication   *207*
    Emotional contagion   208
Choosing the Best Communication Channels   *208*
    Media Richness   *209*
    Symbolic Meaning of the Medium   *210*
Communicating in Organizational Hierarchies   *210*
    Employee Surveys   *210*
    Distributing News Down the Hierarchy   *210*
    Perspective 8.2   Straight Talk for BC Telecom Employees   211
    Visible Leadership   *211*
    Perspective 8.3   Nigel Fast Freight Keeps Communication Lines Open   212
    Improving Communication Through Workspace Design   *213*
        Nonterritorial offices   213
Communicating Through the Grapevine   *214*
    Grapevine Characteristics   *214*
    Grapevine Advantages and Disadvantages   *215*
Cross-Cultural and Gender Communication   *216*
    Verbal Differences   *216*
    Nonverbal Differences   *216*
        Silence and conversational overlaps   217
    Gender Differences in Communication   *217*
    Perspective 8.4   Coca-Cola Executive Learns That
                    Noise to Some is Music to Others   218
Improving Interpersonal Communication   *219*
    Getting Your Message Across   *219*
    Active Listening   *219*
Persuasive Communication: From Understanding to Acceptance   *220*
    Communicator Characteristics   *220*
    Message Content   *221*
    Communication Medium   *221*
    Audience Characteristics   *221*
Chapter Summary   *222*
Discussion Questions   *222*
Chapter Case   Sea Pines   223
Experiential Exercises
    Cross-Cultural Communication: A Not-So-Trivial Trivia Game   225
    Communication, Feedback, and the Manager Exercise   225

Practice Session for Part 3

PART 4
TEAM PROCESSES   229

Chapter 9   Team Dynamics   230

What Are Teams?   *232*
    Formal Work Teams   *232*
        Team-based organizations   234
Cross-functional Teams   *235*
        Virtual teams   235

Perspective 9.1   Virtual Teams at Sun Microsystems   236
Informal Groups   *236*
 Why informal groups exist   237
A Model of Team Dynamics and Effectiveness   *237*
Team Context and Design   *238*
 Organizational Environment   *238*
 Task Characteristics   *239*
 Team Size   *240*
 Team Composition   *240*
  Team diversity   240
Team Development   *241*
 Forming   *241*
 Storming   *242*
 Norming   *242*
 Performing   *242*
 Adjourning   *242*
Team Norms   *243*
 Conformity to Team Norms   *243*
 How Team Norms Develop   *243*
 Changing Team Norms   *244*
Team Cohesiveness   *245*
 Causes of Team Cohesiveness   *245*
  Member similarity   245
  Member interaction   246
  Team size   247
  Somewhat difficult entry   247
  Team success   247
  External competition and challenges   247
 Consequences of Team Cohesiveness   *247*
  Cohesiveness and team performance   248
 Perspective 9.2   Armstrong World Industries Builds Cohesiveness
    Through Team Expo   248
The Trouble With Teams   *248*
  Social loafing   249
  Minimizing social loafing   250
Team Building   *250*
 Types of Team Building   *251*
  Role definition   251
  Interpersonal process   251
  Goal setting   252
  Problem solving   252
 Is Team Building Effective?   *252*
 Perspective 9.3   Action Adventure Team Building   252
Chapter Summary   *254*
Discussion Questions   *254*
Chapter Case   The "No Martini" Lunch   255
Experiential Exercises
 Team-Trust Exercise   256
 Wrapping Presents: A Team Exercise   257

Chapter 10   Employee Involvement and Quality Mangement   258

Employee Involvement   *260*
    Forms of Employee Involvement   *260*
        Representative participation   261
    Levels of Employee Involvement   *262*
        Perspective 10.1   Democratic Participation at Windsor Factory Supply   262
        Open book management   263
        High involvement   264
Self-Directed Work Teams (SDWTs)   *264*
    Sociotechnical Design Theory   *265*
Potential Benefits of Employee Involvement   *266*
    Decision Quality   *266*
    Perspective 10.2   Unleashing Better Decisions Through Employee Involvement   266
    Decision Commitment   *267*
    Employee Satisfaction and Empowerment   *268*
    Employee Development   *268*
Barriers to Employee Involvement   *268*
    Cultural Differences   *268*
    Management Resistance   *269*
    Labour Union Resistance   *270*
Quality Management   *270*
    Quality Awards and ISO Certification   *271*
Quality Management Principles   *272*
    Customer Focus   *272*
    Employee Involvement for Quality   *273*
    Continuous Improvement   *273*
    Perspective 10.3   Standard Aero Ltd. Flies Higher with Quality Management   274
    Defect Prevention   *275*
    Performance Measurement   *275*
    Continuous Learning   *276*
Quality Management Tools   *276*
    Benchmarking   *276*
    Concurrent Engineering   *277*
Limitations of Quality Management   *278*
Chapter Summary   *280*
Discussion Questions   *280*
Chapter Case   Employee Involvement Cases   281
Experiential Exercise   Winter Survival Exercise   282

Chapter 11   Decision Making in Organizations   284

A General Model of Decision Making   *286*
Individual Problems in Decision Making   *287*
    Problems with Identifying Problems   *287*
        Perceptual biases   288
        Poor diagnostic skills   288
    Perspective 11.1   Famous Missed Opportunities   288
    Problems with Choosing the Best Solution   *289*
        Problems with goals   290
        Problems with information processing   290

Problems with maximization   290
Problems with Evaluating Decision Outcomes   *290*
Postdecisional justification   290
Escalation of Commitment   *291*
Causes of escalating commitment   291
Team Problems in Decision Making   *292*
Time Constraints   *292*
Evaluation Apprehension   *292*
Conformity to Peer Pressure   *293*
Groupthink   *293*
Group Polarization   *294*
Improving Decision Making   *295*
Decision Support Systems   *296*
Perspective 11.2   Great Lakes Power Uses Technology for More Accurate Decisions   296
Improving Team Dynamics   *297*
Creativity in Decision Making   *297*
Creativity Model   *297*
Conditions for Creativity   *298*
Creativity Training   *299*
Divergent thinking strategies   299
Team Structures for Creativity and Decision Making   *300*
Constructive Controversy   *300*
Perspective 11.3   Mavericks Like Randy Powell Create Constructive Controversy   301
Brainstorming   *302*
Electronic Brainstorming   *303*
Effectiveness of electronic brainstorming   303
Nominal Group Technique   *305*
Chapter Summary   *306*
Discussion Questions   *306*
Chapter Case Eastern Province Light and Power   307
Experiential Exercises
Hopping Orange Exercise   310
Creativity Brainbusters Exercise   310

Chapter 12   Organizational Power and Politics   312

The Meaning of Power   *314*
A Model of Power in Organizations   *315*
Sources of Power in Organizations   *315*
Legitimate Power   *316*
Reward Power   *316*
Coercive Power   *317*
Perspective 12.1   The Power of Peer Pressure   317
Expert Power   *318*
Referent Power   *318*
Information and Power   *318*
Control over information flow   318
Coping with uncertainty   319
Contingencies of Power   *320*
Substitutability   *320*

Centrality   *322*
Discretion   *322*
Perspective 12.2   Centrality and Power in a Major League Baseball Strike   322
Visibility   *323*
Consequences of Power   *323*
Sexual Harassment: An Abuse of Power   *324*
Organizational Politics   *325*
Perspective 12.3   Organizational Politics at Bow Valley   326
Organizational Politics: Good or Bad?   *327*
The ethics of organizational politics   327
Types of Political Activity   *328*
Attacking or Blaming Others   *328*
Selectively Distributing Information   *329*
Controlling Information Channels   *329*
Forming Coalitions   *330*
Cultivating Networks   *330*
Creating Obligations   *331*
Managing Impressions   *331*
Conditions for Organizational Politics   *331*
Personal Characteristics   *331*
Gender differences in organizational politics   332
Controlling Political Behaviour   *332*
Chapter Summary   *333*
Discussion Questions   *333*
Chapter Case   Analyzing Political Behaviour in Organizations   334
Experiential Exercise   Power Relations in a Loonie Organization   335

Chapter 13 Organizational Conflict and Negotiation   336

What Is Conflict?   *338*
Task-Related Versus Socio-Emotional Conflict   *338*
Conflict escalation cycle   338
Consequences of Organizational Conflict   *339*
*Perspective 13.1   Revenge of the Andons: Conflict at CAMI
and Subaru-Isuzu   340*
Sources of Conflict in Organizations   *340*
Goal Incompatibility   *340*
Differentiation   *341*
Task Interdependence   *342*
Scarce Resources   *343*
Ambiguity   *343*
Communication Problems   *343*
Interpersonal Conflict Management Styles   *344*
Cultural and Gender Differences in Conflict Management Styles   *345*
Structural Approaches to Conflict Management   *346*
Emphasizing Superordinate Goals   *346*
Reducing Differentiation   *346*
Perspective 13.2   Colour-Coded Conflict   347
Improving Communication and Understanding   *348*
Intergroup mirroring   348

Reducing Task Interdependence   *348*
Increasing Resources   *349*
Clarifying Rules and Procedures   *349*
Perspective 13.3   Armstrong and Booz Allen Sort Out Their Differences   349
Resolving Conflict Through Negotiation   *350*
Bargaining Zone Model of Negotiations   *350*
Situational Influences on Negotiations   *351*
Location   351
Physical setting   352
Time passage and deadlines   352
Audience characteristics   352
Negotiator Behaviours   *353*
Third-Party Conflict Resolution   *353*
Types of Third-Party Intervention   *354*
Choosing the Best Third-Party Intervention Strategy   *355*
Chapter Summary   *356*
Discussion Questions   *357*
Chapter Case   Maelstrom Communications   357
Experiential Exercise   Ugli Orange Role Play   359

Chapter 14   Organizational Leadership   360

Perspectives of Leadership   *362*
Trait Perspective of Leadership   *363*
Limitations of the Trait Perspective of Leadership   *365*
Behavioural Perspective of Leadership   *365*
The "Hi-Hi" Leadership Hypothesis   *366*
Limitations of the Behavioural Leadership Perspective   *367*
Contingency Perspective of Leadership   *368*
Path-Goal Theory of Leadership   *368*
Perspective 14.1   The Trials of Practising Contingency Leadership   368
Leadership styles   369
Contingencies of Path-Goal Theory   *370*
Skill and experience   370
Locus of control   371
Task structure   371
Team dynamics   371
Recent Extensions of Path-Goal Theory   *371*
Evaluating Path-Goal Theory   *372*
Other Contingency Theories   *372*
Changing the situation to match the style   373
Leadership substitutes   373
Transformational Perspective of Leadership   *374*
Transformational versus Transactional Leadership   *374*
Transformational versus Charismatic Leadership   *375*
Features of Transformational Leadership   *376*
Creating a strategic vision   376
Communicating the vision   376
Modelling the vision   377
Building commitment toward the vision   377
Evaluating the Transformational Leadership Perspective   *377*

Romance Perspective of Leadership   378
    Attributing Leadership   378
    Stereotyping Leadership   378
    Need for Situational Control   379
    Gender Issues in Leadership   379
    Perspective 14.2   Do Women Lead Differently?   380
Chapter Summary   381
Discussion Questions   382
Chapter Case   Leadership in Whose Eyes?   383
Experiential Exercise   Leadership Diagnostic Analysis   384

Practice Session for Part 4   385

PART 5

ORGANIZATION PROCESSES   389

Chapter 15   Organizational Change and Development   390

Forces for Change   392
    Computer Technology and Organizational Change   392
Resistance to Change   393
Supporting Organizational Change   394
    Unfreezing the Status Quo   395
        Creating an urgency for change   396
        Communication   396
        Training   398
        Employee involvement   398
        Stress management   399
    Perspective 15.1   Richmond Savings Gets Everyone Involved in Change   399
        Negotiation   400
        Coercion   400
    Refreezing the Desired Conditions   400
    Diffusion of Change   401
    Perspective 15.2   Diffusing Change at Schneider's   401
Organization Development   402
    The Client-Consultant Relationship   403
    Diagnose the Need for Change   403
    Introduce the OD Intervention   404
    Evaluate and Stabilize Change   405
Emerging Trends in Organization Development   405
    Parallel Learning Structures   406
    Appreciative Inquiry   406
Effectiveness of Organization Development   408
    Cross-Cultural Concerns with OD   408
    Ethical Concerns with OD   408
    Perspective 15.3   Organization Development Behind Closed Doors at SaskTel   409
Chapter Summary   410
Discussion Questions   411
Chapter Case   Eastern Provincial Insurance Corporation   412
Experiential Exercise   Force Field Analysis   414

Chapter 16   Organizational Culture   416

What Is Organizational Culture?   *418*
    Artifacts of Organizational Culture   *419*
    Perspective 16.1   DuPont Canada's Fanatical Safety Culture   419
    Organizational Culture Content   *420*
    Strength of Corporate Culture   *421*
Organizational Culture and Performance   *421*
    Organizational Subcultures   *422*
Communicating Organizational Culture   *423*
    Organizational Stories   *423*
    Rituals and Ceremonies   *423*
    Organizational Language   *424*
    Physical Structures and Space   *424*
    Perspective 16.2   Transmitting Cultural Values Through Design   425
Merging Organizational Cultures   *425*
    Strategies to Merge Different Organizational Cultures   *426*
        Assimilation   426
        Deculturation   427
        Integration   427
        Perspective 16.3   Abitibi and Stone Consolidated Merge Cultures
                          Through Integration   427
        Separation   428
Strengthening Organizational Culture   *428*
    Actions of Founders and Leaders   *429*
    Introducing Culturally Consistent Rewards   *429*
    Maintaining a Stable Workforce   *429*
    Managing the Cultural Network   *429*
    Selecting and Socializing Employees   *430*
Chapter Summary   *430*
Discussion Questions   *431*
Chapter Case   Hillton's Transformation   432
Experiential Exercise   Organizational Culture Assessment Exercise   434

Chapter 17   Employment Relationship and Career Dynamics   436

The Psychological Contract   *438*
    Types of Psychological Contracts   *438*
    Trust and the Psychological Contract   *439*
    Psychological Contract Dynamics   *440*
    Perspective 17.1   Rethinking the Psychological Contract at Petro-Canada   441
Organizational Socialization   *442*
Stages of Socialization   *443*
    Stage 1: Pre-Employment Socialization   *443*
        Conflicts when exchanging information   443
        Postdecisional justification   444
    Stage 2: Encounter   *445*
    Stage 3: Role Management   *445*
Managing the Socialization Process   *446*
    Realistic Job Previews   *446*
    Socialization Agents   *446*

Organizational Careers   447
   Perspective 17.2   Separating the Steam from the Haze   447
   Career Anchors and Career Stages   448
   Lateral Career Development   450
   Perspective 17.3   Lateral Career Development at Japan's Mitsui Group   450
     Encouraging lateral career development   451
Contingent Workforce   451
   Why Contingent Work Is Growing   452
   Types of Contingent Workers   453
   Contingent Workforce Concerns   454
     Job performance of contingent workers   454
   Adjusting to a Contingent Workforce   455
Chapter Summary   456
Discussion Questions   456
Chapter Case   Quantor Corp.'s Contingent Workforce   457
Experiential Exercise   Organizational Socialization Diagnostic Exercise   459

Chapter 18   Organizational Structure and Design   460

Division of Labour and Coordination   462
   Division of Labour   462
   Coordinating Work Activities   462
Elements of Organizational Structure   463
   Span of Control   463
     Tall and flat structures   464
   Centralization and Decentralization   465
   Formalization   465
     Problems with formalization   466
   Mechanistic Versus Organic Structures   466
Traditional Forms of Departmentation   466
   Simple Structure   467
   Functional Structure   468
     Advantages and disadvantages   468
   Divisional Structure   468
     Advantages and disadvantages   470
     Perspective 18.1   Creating "Mini-Mobils" Around the World   470
   Matrix Structure   471
     Advantages and disadvantages   472
   Hybrid Structure   473
Emerging Forms of Departmentation   473
   Team-Based (Lateral) Structure   473
   Perspective 18.2   Oticon Holding A/S Turns to Spaghetti   476
     Advantages and disadvantages   476
   Network Structure   476
     Virtual corporations and affiliate networks   478
     Perspective 18.3   The Network Structure of Emergex Planning Inc.   478
     Advantages and disadvantages   479
Contingencies of Organizational Design   479
   Organizational Size   479
   Technology   479

External Environment   *480*
Organizational Strategy   *481*
Chapter Summary   *482*
Discussion Questions   *483*
Chapter Case   The Rise and Fall of PMC AG   484
Experiential Exercise   Words in Sentences Company   486

Practice Session for Part 5   *488*

Additional Cases   490

Case 1   Arctic Mining Consultants   491
Case 2   A Window on Life   493
Case 3   Cantron Ltd.   494
Case 4   Jersey Dairies Ltd.   496
Case 5   Pamela Jones, Former Banker   498
Case 6   Perfect Pizzeria   499
Case 7   Treetop Forest Products Ltd.   501
Case 8   Western Agencies Ltd.   502

Appendix A   Theory Building and the Scientific Method   505

Theory Testing: The Deductive Process   *505*
Defining and measuring constructs   506
Testing hypotheses   507
Using the Scientific Method   *507*
Selected Issues in Organizational Behaviour Research   *507*
Sampling in Organizational Research   *508*
Causation in Organizational Research   *509*
Ethics in Organizational Research   *510*
Research Design Strategies   *510*
Laboratory Experiments   *510*
Advantages of laboratory experiments   511
Disadvantages of laboratory experiments   511
Field Surveys   *511*
Advantages and disadvantages of field surveys   512
Observational Research   *512*

Appendix B   Vroom-Jago Decision Tree   514

Appendix C   Answers to Practice Session Questions   516

Glossary   *520*
Notes   *530*
Indexes   *588*

Virtual teams. "New deal" employment relationships. Intellectual capital. Computer-based information technology. Emotional intelligence. Contingent workforce. Nonterritorial offices. These are a few of the dramatic, exciting, and sometimes disturbing changes that are occurring in today's workplace. *Canadian Organizational Behaviour*, Third Edition helps you ride this wave of change by discussing these emerging issues as well as their theoretical foundations. This book also provides detailed descriptions of other theories that help you understand and influence behaviour in organizations.

Canadian Organizational Behaviour has become the most widely read organizational behaviour textbook in Canada. Instructors and reviewers say that this textbook keeps students informed and interested. Organizational behaviour concepts are presented clearly and concisely. The book provides a distinctly Canadian orientation and connects organizational behaviour concepts with reality through meaningful examples. The third edition of *Canadian Organizational Behaviour* continues to embrace the following four philosophies: a Canadian orientation, theory-practice link, OB knowledge for everyone, and contemporary theory foundation.

Canadian Orientation

Canadian Organizational Behaviour, Third Edition, has been written specifically for the Canadian audience, although it may be used effectively in other countries (just as American texts have been used in Canada and elsewhere for so many years). This book includes several Canadian cases and makes solid use of Canadian scholarship in organizational behaviour. The Canadian orientation is most apparent in the Canadian examples that appear throughout the book. For example, you will read about organizational memory loss at the city of Ottawa, improving customer service at Canadian Pacific Hotels and Resorts Ltd., goal setting at Kanke Restaurants, employee loyalty at WestJet Airlines, self-directed work teams at Pratt & Whitney Canada's Halifax plant, organizational politics at Intercontinental Packers, and shifting to a "new deal" employment relationship at Petro-Canada Ltd.

Without losing its Canadian orientation, *Canadian Organizational Behaviour*, Third Edition, also provides more international material than in previous editions. For instance, you will learn about communicating change at CEMEX in Mexico, practising action learning at Britvic in the United Kingdom, team building among Coca-Cola executives in Mainland China, forming a team-based structure at Oticon Holding A/S in Denmark, conflict following a merger of two banks in Japan, job design at Kellogg's in Australia, and managing stress at securities firm Phatra Thanakit in Thailand.

Theory-Practice Link

Canadian Organizational Behaviour, Third Edition, relies on real-life examples to help students understand organizational behaviour concepts more easily. Along with Perspectives, this edition applies the theory-practice link with more in-text anecdotes and captioned photos. The value of this theory-practice link philosophy is well known among educators and trainers. Anecdotes effectively communicate the relevance and excitement of this field by bringing abstract concepts closer to reality. The stories found throughout this book also make interesting reading, such as how all 400 employees at Richmond Savings Credit Union were able to participate in a week-long organizational change session, how SaskTel employees rebelled when an organization development intervention got too personal, and how employee involvement at Windsor Factory Supply is so strong that employees even vote for the company president!

Organizational Behaviour Knowledge for Everyone

A distinctive feature of *Canadian Organizational Behaviour*, Third Edition, is that it is written for everyone in organizations, not just traditional "managers." The philosophy of this book is that everyone who works in and around organizations needs to understand and make use of organizational behaviour knowledge. The new reality is that people throughout the organization — systems analysts, production employees, accounting professionals — are assuming more responsibilities as companies remove layers of bureaucracy and give teams more autonomy over their work. This book helps every employee make sense of organizational behaviour, and gives them the tools to work more effectively within organizations.

Contemporary Theory Foundation

The first two editions of *Canadian Organizational Behaviour* were respected for their solid foundation of contemporary organizational behaviour scholarship. By thoroughly searching the recent literature on every major OB topic, the third edition has maintained those standards. As you can see in the notes, each chapter is based on dozens of articles, books, and others sources, a large percentage of them published within the past five years. This literature update has produced numerous content changes throughout *Canadian Organizational Behaviour*, Third Edition, which we describe next.

Changes to the Third Edition

Canadian Organizational Behaviour, Third Edition, has been substantially changed and improved. The first thing that might catch your eye is that this edition of the book is in full colour. In fact, *Canadian Organizational Behaviour*, Third Edition, is the first all-Canadian OB textbook published in colour, thereby continuing the textbook's history of breaking new ground. (*Canadian Organizational Behaviour* was the first all-Canadian organizational behaviour textbook [1992] and apparently the first OB textbook anywhere to include a full PowerPoint® presentation package [1995].) Although we like to think that the content of this book keeps students interested, the colourful graphics and photographs in this edition will certainly help convey the excitement of this field of study.

Instructors will notice that several chapters have been reorganized so that the book is more closely aligned with their preferred sequence of topics. For instance, organizational culture now has its own chapter. Individual and team decision making have been combined, as have the topics of employee involvement and quality management. Every chapter has been substantially updated with new conceptual and anecdotal material. All of the chapter-opening vignettes and over one-half of the Perspectives are new. Several dozen new photographs appear throughout the textbook to further illustrate organizational behaviour concepts and issues.

Based on a substantial literature search, *Canadian Organizational Behaviour*, Third Edition, includes numerous content changes and significantly updated references in every chapter. The following are some of the emerging concepts and issues introduced or expanded in this edition:

- *Chapter 1: Introduction to the Field of Organizational Behaviour* Intellectual capital and organizational learning are fully described. Several emerging trends in OB — changing workforce, new employment relationship, work teams, and computer technologies — are introduced.

- *Chapter 2: Individual Behaviour and Learning in Organizations* Expanded coverage of individual learning through reinforcement, feedback, social learning, and experiential learning. Implicit learning and action learning are briefly introduced.

- *Chapter 3: Foundations of Employee Motivation* New issues in goal setting are covered. More discussion of cultural issues with motivation.

- *Chapter 4: Applied Motivation Practices* Includes a new section on the emerging concept of self-motivating, including self-talk and mental imagery. Fuller discussion on the trouble with reward systems. Agency theory is briefly introduced.

- *Chapter 5: Stress Management* New material on family-friendly workplace practices. Brief discussion of workplace aggression and stress.

- *Chapter 6: Perception and Personality in Organizations* Full discussion of social identity theory, which has become the prominent theory of social perception. New or expanded information on the "Big Five" personality dimensions, mental models, and ethical issues with stereotyping.

- *Chapter 7: Emotions and Values in the Workplace* Work attitude material has been updated to reflect current OB writing on workplace emotions. The emerging topics of emotional labour and emotional intelligence are described. Updated coverage of organizational commitment as well as cross-cultural values.

- *Chapter 8: Communicating in Organizational Settings* Expanded discussion of electronic mail and other computer-mediated communication. Concepts of emotional contagion and nonterritorial offices are introduced.

- *Chapter 9: Team Dynamics* The emerging concept of virtual teams is introduced. Fuller discussion of the trouble with teams.

- *Chapter 10: Employee Involvement and Quality Management* Open book management is described. Expanded discussion of benchmarking, concurrent engineering, the limitations of quality management, and cross-cultural issues with employee involvement.

- *Chapter 11: Decision Making in Organizations* Creativity in decision making receives expanded coverage. Individual and team decision-making concepts are integrated into one chapter. Updated material on brainstorming and electronic brainstorming.

- *Chapter 12: Organizational Power and Politics* Gender differences in organizational politics, as well as sexual harassment as an abuse of power, are briefly discussed. Revised discussion of forms of organizational politics.

- *Chapter 13: Organizational Conflict and Negotiation* New material is presented on cultural and gender differences in conflict management styles. Clarification of task-oriented versus socio-emotional conflict.

- *Chapter 14: Organizational Leadership* This edition provides a more critical evaluation of path-goal and transformational leadership theories. Recent extensions to path-goal theory are introduced.

- *Chapter 15: Organizational Change and Development* Cross-cultural concerns with organization development are discussed more fully. The change process model now includes discussion on the need to create an urgency for change.

- *Chapter 16: Organizational Culture* This edition provides a separate chapter on organizational culture. The process of merging two corporate cultures receives expanded coverage.

- *Chapter 17: Employment Relationship and Career Dynamics* This edition adds a new section on the psychological contract, including the emerging "new deal" relationship of employability. Another new section discusses OB issues surrounding the contingent workforce.

- *Chapter 18: Organizational Structure and Design* The section on network organizational structures is expanded, including brief coverage of affiliate networks.

Along with these changes, *Canadian Organizational Behaviour*, Third Edition, expands gender and cross-cultural issues in organizational behaviour. For instance, we examine gender differences in communication, organizational politics, and conflict management styles. Cross-cultural issues are found in the discussion of employee motivation, employee involvement, conflict management styles, and organization development practices. This edition continues to recognize ethical issues in various organizational behaviour topics, such as monitoring employee performance, stereotyping employees, using peer pressure, engaging in organizational politics, and applying organization development practices.

Learning Elements

Canadian Organizational Behaviour, Third Edition, supports employee learning through several innovative pedagogical practices. We believe that these learning elements will make reading this book more enjoyable, and make the OB material more memorable.

Photos and Cartoons Dozens of colourful photographs and cartoons have been carefully selected and placed throughout so that organizational behaviour concepts are brought to life (with a little humour here and there). Each photograph includes a caption to describe how it relates to the text. A photograph also accompanies the opening vignette to each chapter to give it more visual meaning.

Perspectives and In-Text Examples Each chapter includes Perspectives — stories that describe specific organizational incidents in Canada and elsewhere. These anecdotes are strategically placed near the relevant organizational behaviour concepts, and the text clearly links them to these concepts. The text of each chapter also includes numerous real-life examples to further strengthen the theory-practice link.

Practice Sessions New to this edition, a practice session at the end of each part of the book gives students the opportunity to practise true-false, multiple-choice, and written-answer questions. These questions are similar to those found in the test bank. Appendix C provides answers to all five practice sessions.

Margin Notes and End-of-Text Glossary The book tries to avoid unnecessary jargon, but the field of organizational behaviour (as with every other discipline) has its own language. To help you learn this language, key terms are highlighted in bold print and brief definitions appear in the margin. These definitions also appear in an alphabetical glossary at the end of the book.

Cases and Experiential Exercises   Every chapter includes one case and at least one experiential exercise. Several additional cases appear at the end of the book. The cases encourage you to use organizational behaviour knowledge as a tool to diagnose and solve organizational problems. The experiential exercises involve you in activities where you either experience organizational behaviour or practise your OB knowledge in entertaining and informative ways.

Graphic Exhibits   Colourful graphic exhibits created with recent computer technologies are placed throughout each chapter to help you visualize key elements of OB models or integrate different points made in the text.

Indexes   A corporate index, name index, and subject index are included at the end of the book to help you search for relevant information and make *Canadian Organizational Behaviour* a valuable source for years to come.

Chapter Summary and Discussion Questions   Each chapter closes with a summary and list of discussion questions. The chapter summary highlights important material, while the discussion questions help you to check your understanding of key points in the chapter.

Learning Objectives and Chapter Outline   Several learning objectives and an outline of the main topic headings are listed at the beginning of each chapter to guide you through the key points of the material to follow.

Supplementary Materials

Canadian Organizational Behaviour, Third Edition, includes a variety of supplemental materials to help instructors prepare and present the material in this textbook more effectively.

PowerPoint® Presentations   Instructors who adopt *Canadian Organizational Behaviour*, Third Edition, receive, on request, a PowerPoint presentation package. This package includes a complete file of PowerPoint "slides" for each chapter, as well as a PowerPoint Viewer software to display this colourful material on your microcomputer. Each PowerPoint file has several overheads relating to the chapter, complete with builds and transitions. Most files include one or more photographs from the textbook.

Instructor's Manual   The *Instructor's Manual* includes a wealth of information for instructors. Each chapter in the manual presents the learning objectives, glossary of highlighted words, a chapter summary, complete lecture outline (in larger typeface!), solutions to the end-of-chapter discussion questions, notes for the case and experiential exercises, one or more supplemental lectures, summary sheets for the PowerPoint file, and a list of related video programs. The *Instructor's Manual* also includes a very large set of transparency masters, some cases and exercises not found in the textbook, and notes for the end-of-text cases.

Computerized Test Bank   A computerized test bank includes dozens of multiple-choice and true-false questions for each chapter. It also includes several essay questions. Instructors receive special software that lets them design their own examinations from the test bank questions. It also lets instructors edit test items and add their own questions to the test bank.

Video Package   We live in the age of television, so it isn't surprising that students appreciate video programs to punctuate the lectures, cases, and other pedagogical devices used in the organizational behaviour class. McGraw-Hill Ryerson has several organizational behaviour video programs in its library, copies of which are available to adopters of *Canadian Organizational Behaviour*, Third Edition Several Canadian videos have also been developed or selected specifically for this book.

Canadian Organizational Behaviour Web Site   Students and instructors can visit this web site to gain access to a variety of aids and support.

Acknowledgements

Next to a supportive family, the most important ingredient for writing a textbook is the support, guidance, and friendship of colleagues. I am fortunate to have colleagues at Simon Fraser University who continually teach me new ideas and support me in my writing projects. I would especially like to thank my organizational behaviour colleagues in the Faculty of Business Administration: Mark Wexler, Rosalie Tung, Dean Tjosvold, Larry Pinfield, Stephen Havlovic, Carolyn Egri, and Gervase Bushe. I also owe a special debt of gratitude to former dean Stan Shapiro for being a superb role model, and to incoming dean John Waterhouse for continuing to provide this support and patience.

Several colleagues from other colleges and universities across Canada provided valuable feedback and suggestions as reviewers of *Canadian Organizational Behaviour*, Third Edition. Their comments significantly improved the quality of the final product: Robert Cameron, Lakehead University; Joan Condie, Sheridan College; Claude Dupuis, University of Calgary; Susan FitzRandolph, Ryerson Polytechnic University; Kristi Harrison, Centennial College; Barbara Shannon, Seneca College; Verlie Thomas, Mount Royal College; Pat Sniderman, Ryerson Polytechnic University; and Judith Zacharias, University of Manitoba.

I would also like to extend my gratitude to the following colleagues who provided valuable input in the previous two editions of this book: Brenda Bear, Northern Alberta Institute of Technology; Donna Bentley, Northern Alberta Institute of Technology; Ron Burke, York University; Richard Foggo, Southern Alberta Institute of Technology; Beth Gilbert, University of New Brunswick, Saint John; Brian Harrocks, Algonquin College; Jack Ito, University of Regina; Jacques Plamondon, Northern Alberta Institute of Technology; Anwar Rashid, Ryerson Polytechnic University; John Redston, Red River Community College; Pat Sniderman, Ryerson Polytechnic University; Paul Tambeau, Conestoga College; Judy Wahn, University of Saskatchewan.

The students in my BUS272 classes deserve special mention. They have been very supportive as I lectured on new OB concepts, introduced new cases and exercises, tested new examination questions, and experimented with computer-based overheads. My BUS272 class typically has more than 200 people who come from all age groups and walks of life. I could not ask for a better setting to put this book to the test. Through their enthusiasm for this project and favourable ratings of the book, BUS272 students have doubled my energy.

Canadian Organizational Behaviour, Third Edition, is very much a team effort. I would like to extend my appreciation to Yvonne Chan and Patti Moen for tracking down research articles and to Andrew Rae for scouting for photographs. The efforts of Lenard Reid, who worked on the first two editions of the book, are still apparent and I am grateful for the opportunity to work with him. Other research assistants who contributed to previous editions include Michelle Berner, Anne Courtney, Tammi Mason, Henrick Jorgennsen, and Karim Karmali. Sadly, Anne Courtney passed away recently. She will be very much missed, but never forgotten.

Evelyn Veitch (Senior Sponsoring Editor), Karina TenVeldhuis (Developmental Editor), Elke Price (Associate Editor), Geraldine Kikuta (Production Editor), and Liba Berry (Copy Editor) provided excellent service and support throughout this third edition. Evelyn had the vision to see new directions for the textbook. Karina has the most incredible diplomatic skills for keeping textbook authors on schedule. Liba's keen copy-editing skills made *Canadian Organizational Behaviour,* Third Edition, the most error-free book I have written. Geraldine and Elke kept the production process flowing smoothly toward the publication date. Thanks to you all! I would also like to extend my continued thanks to Rod Banister for planting the original seed that resulted in the first edition of *Canadian Organizational Behaviour.*

Finally, I am forever indebted to my wife and best friend, Donna McClement, and to our wonderful daughters, Bryton and Madison. Their love and support give special meaning to my life. I dedicate this book to them.

PART 1

Introduction

CHAPTER 1
Introduction to the Field of Organizational Behaviour

Introduction to the Field of Organizational Behaviour

CHAPTER OUTLINE

The Field of Organizational Behaviour

The Five Anchors of Organizational Behaviour

Organizational Knowledge and Learning

Organization of This Book

Chapter Summary

Discussion Questions

LEARNING OBJECTIVES

After reading this chapter, you should be able to:

- Identify three reasons for studying organizational behaviour.

- List four emerging trends in organizational behaviour.

- Discuss ways in which computer technology has influenced organizational behaviour.

- Diagram an organization from an open systems perspective.

- Define intellectual capital.

- Identify four common ways that organizations acquire knowledge.

- Explain how companies can minimize organizational memory loss.

Manitoba Premier Gary Filmon sits behind the wheel of a Motor Coach Industries Renaissance bus. Motor Coach relied on organizational behaviour concepts and practices to design and build this successful touring coach.

"Has this thing got a Detroit Diesel engine in it?" drawled a cowboy-hatted customer. "Yes," came the reply. Nodding approvingly, the customer responded: "I'll take five of them." Over $2 million worth of luxurious new Renaissance tour buses had just been ordered from Winnipeg-based Motor Coach Industries (MCI).

Three years ago, some people doubted that MCI's Winnipeg facility would be manufacturing any buses, let alone something as elegant as the Renaissance. MCI's familiar commercial buses still dominated the North American market, but they were quickly losing ground to new competitors. Also, the company had been bought by a Mexican consortium and there were fears production would move south. "We're in a global market," explains MCI chief executive officer Jim Bernacchi. He adds that developing and manufacturing the Renaissance in Winnipeg was a careful decision "because the competition is pretty fierce out there."

MCI radically changed the way employees designed buses. Product development staff were organized into teams around each part of the Renaissance. They worked in an open area around tables rather than at desks in cubicles. This ensured that everyone could communicate without physical barriers and that problems could be solved through spontaneous meetings.

Teams set performance goals by benchmarking competing buses and interviewing everyone from bus passengers to tow-truck operators. Important dates and targets were painted on the walls of MCI's open design studio so that employees would keep focused on these goals. Teams devised subtle ways to motivate themselves toward goal accomplishment. For example, one goal was to reduce vehicle weight, so a "Golden Anvil" award was jokingly given each week to the employee who did the least toward this goal. It was an award no one wanted on his or her desk!

The result was a high-performance group of employees that created a leading-edge product. "It is the most modern product in the industry today," beams MCI's Jim Bernacchi.[1]

The Renaissance is considered an engineering marvel, but it is really about the marvels of organizational behaviour. More than ever, Canadian organizations are relying on organizational behaviour concepts to remain competitive. For example, Motor Coach Industries leveraged the power of team dynamics. The company redesigned the workplace to improve communication and problem solving. Goal setting and rewards were introduced to bolster employee motivation and job performance. Employees were empowered with new autonomy and responsibilities to get the work done. And MCI likely took the right steps to manage the change process and create an organizational culture that supports this innovative work environment.

This book is about people working in organizations. Its main objective is to help you understand behaviour in organizations and to help you work more effectively in organizational settings. Organizational behaviour knowledge is not only relevant for managers and leaders. It is useful to anyone who works in and around organizations. In this chapter, we introduce you to the field of organizational behaviour, outline the main reasons why you should know more about it, describe the fundamental anchors behind the study of organizations, and introduce the concept that organizations are knowledge and learning systems. We conclude with a summary of the organization of this book.

The Field of Organizational Behaviour

Organizational behaviour
The study of what people think, feel, and do in and around organizations.

Organizational behaviour (OB) is the study of what people think, feel, and do in and around organizations. OB researchers systematically study individual, team, and structural characteristics that influence behaviour within organizations. Through their research, OB scholars try to predict and understand how these behaviours influence organizational effectiveness.

When we say that organizational behaviour is a field of study, we mean that experts have been accumulating a distinct knowledge about behaviour within organizations — a knowledge base that has become the foundation of this book. Most OB texts discuss similar topics, which shows that OB has evolved into a reasonably well-defined field of inquiry. This is remarkable considering that OB is still in its infancy. It emerged as a distinct field in the 1930s or 1940s, and continues to evolve as new perspectives and theories emerge or are imported from other disciplines.

What are Organizations?

Organizations are as old as the human race. Archaeologists have discovered massive temples dating to 3500 B.C. that were constructed through the organized actions of many people. The fact that these impressive monuments were built suggests not only that complex organizations existed, but that they operated reasonably well.[2]

We have equally impressive examples today of what organizations can do. Consider Hibernia Management and Development Co., the consortium that oversaw development of the 1.2 million tonne oil platform situated off the coast of Newfoundland. Construction of the $5.8 billion platform required more than six years and employed 5,000 people on three continents. The platform base, which is the size of two football fields across, was built, for the most part, just offshore. At one point, 2,000 workers were ferried each day to the platform, which was surrounded by a flotilla of 40 barges. Elsewhere, five supermodules constructed in Taiwan, Italy, and Newfoundland were carefully pieced together to form the topside of the platform. "I don't think that a more complicated civil-construction project will ever be built," says Hibernia's construction general manager, Henck van Zante.[3]

Organizations Groups of people who work interdependently toward some purpose.

So, what are **organizations**? They are groups of people who work interdependently toward some purpose.[4] Organizations are not buildings or other physical structures. In fact, organizations don't really need bricks or mortar. Instead, they are people who interact to achieve a set of goals. Employees have structured patterns of interaction, meaning that they expect each other to complete certain tasks in a coordinated way — in an organized way.

Organizations have a purpose, whether it's building an oil platform or curing cancer. Some organizational behaviour scholars are skeptical about the relevance of goals in a definition of organizations.[5] They argue that an organization's mission statement may be different from its true goals. They also note that not all organizational members believe in the same goals. These points may be true, but organizations do have a collective sense of purpose, even though it may not be fully understood or agreed upon.

Why Study Organizational Behaviour?

1. predict + understand organizational ev
2. adopt more accurate theory of reali
3. control organizational events

In all likelihood, you are reading this book as part of a required course in organizational behaviour. Apart from degree or diploma requirements, why should you learn the ideas and practices discussed here? There are three main reasons: (1) to predict and understand organizational events; (2) to adopt more accurate theories of reality; and (3) to control organizational events more effectively.

Greg Locke. Used with permission.

The Hibernia rig in Newfoundland illustrates the marvels of organizations. The rig's construction required more than six years and employed 5,000 people on three continents. "I don't think that a more complicated civil-construction project will ever be built," says Hibernia's construction general manager, Henck van Zante.

Satisfying the need to predict and understand

We have an inherent need to know about the world in which we live. This is particularly true of organizations, because they have a profound effect on our lives. We want to predict and understand organizational events to satisfy our curiosity and to map out life's events more accurately.[6] The field of organizational behaviour uses scientific research to discover systematic relationships. And by learning about these relationships, you will gain a better understanding of organizational life.

Adopting more accurate theories of reality

Through personal observation and learning from others, you have already formed numerous personal theories about the way people behave. Some of these may be quite accurate and predict behaviour in many situations. The theories and concepts presented in this book will further clarify or crystallize these personal views of the world. Of course, not all of our personal theories of organizational life are accurate, even though many appear to be common sense. The field of organizational behaviour uses methods and applied logic to test the accuracy of personal theories in organizational settings. The knowledge you will gain by reading this book will help you to confirm and challenge your personal theories, and will give you new perspectives of reality.

Controlling organizational events

Perhaps the most practical reason for learning about organizational behaviour is that it has direct implications for controlling organizational events. Through OB research, we now understand how to improve employee performance, communicate with oth-

ers, manage conflict, make better decisions, structure organizations, build commitment, and help work teams operate more effectively.

This book takes the view that organizational behaviour knowledge is for everyone —
not just managers. Indeed, as organizations reduce layers of management and delegate
more responsibilities to employees, the concepts described in this book will become
increasingly important for anyone who works in and around organizations. We all need
to master the knowledge and skills required to control organizational events.

Although organizational behaviour takes a prescriptive view, it does so in the context
of theory and research. OB scholars use scientific research to build strong theory, which
then provides the foundation for effective practice. In other words, the best organizational practices are those built on sound organizational behaviour theory and research.[7]

Emerging Trends in Organizational Behaviour

There has never been a better time to learn about organizational behaviour. The pace
of change is accelerating, and most of the transformation is occurring in the workplace. Let's take a brief tour through a few of the emerging organizational behaviour
issues that are discussed in this textbook.

The changing workforce

diversity
- women
- Education

Canada's workforce is becoming more diverse.[8] Consider the following: Nearly one-
half of all immigrants today arrive from Asian and Middle Eastern countries, compared to only 3 percent a few decades ago. As we see in Exhibit 1.1, the percentage of

---

EXHIBIT 1.1: Increasing Participation of Women in the Canadian Labour Force

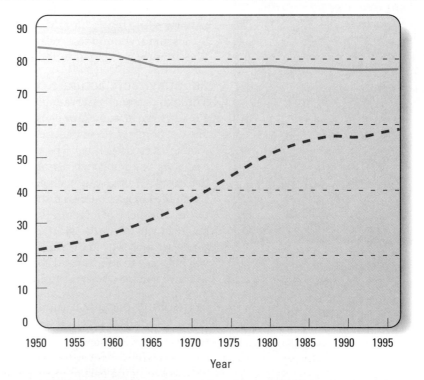

Year

Source: Statistics Canada, *The Labour Force* (Ottawa: Minister of Supply and Services Canada, various years).

Steven L. McShane.

Organizations have been adjusting to Canada's more diverse workforce by increasing awareness of cultural diversity, providing more family-friendly work arrangements, and giving employees autonomy and responsibility.

women in the paid labour force has increased dramatically. At the same time, the percentage of men working has dropped. Today, employees are more likely than ever to have spouses in the workforce. Employees are also more likely to have some postsecondary education.

The result of these changes is that the typical employee is no longer a white male with a wife at home. Organizations have been adjusting to these realities by increasing awareness of cultural diversity, providing more family-friendly work arrangements, and giving employees more autonomy and responsibility. "If a company is to be successful in today's business environment, it must develop policies and practices in step with an increasingly diverse workforce," says Bernard F. Isautier, CEO of Calgary-based Canadian Occidental Petroleum Ltd. (CanOxy). Proactive firms also view Canada's diversity as a competitive advantage in the global marketplace. Bell Canada, CanOxy, and other organizations increasingly work with clients around the world, and they require people who have diverse backgrounds to fulfil those work requirements.

Another form of workforce diversity is represented by the emerging values and needs of younger Canadians entering the workforce. While baby boomers are starting to think about retirement, Generation-X employees are seeking out meaningful career opportunities. So far, Canadian companies don't seem to be adjusting fast enough. Only 58 percent of Gen-X employees are somewhat or very satisfied with their jobs, compared with over 90 percent of baby boomers. Only 2 percent of the younger generation feel that their work provides an opportunity to get ahead.[9]

genx want meaningful jobs.

Some organizational behaviour scholars suggest that Gen-Xers bring a new set of values that require companies to rethink how employees are "managed." For example, one researcher frequently heard Gen-Xers say, "We are not living to work but working to live, choosing a life that we want to have as opposed to just bringing home a paycheque."[10] Consider 25-year-old Ivan Pulleyn, who was interviewed for a software developer's job at Electronic Data Systems Corp. (EDS). When Pulleyn caught a glimpse of the rows of cubicles and people tapping robotically on PCs, he knew the EDS job wasn't for him. "I walked into EDS and it felt like the Death Star," Pulleyn recalls. Although EDS offered him the job, Pulleyn accepted a lower-paying position with a company that was more in tune with his needs.[11]

The "new deal" employment relationship

Canada's workforce isn't the only thing that's changing. After more than 100 years of stability, employment relationships are being redefined. In the wake of downsizing, restructuring, and contracting out non-core activities, many Canadian organizations are reluctant to hire people for the long term. Replacing the job-for-life contract is a "new deal" called employability. Employees perform a variety of work activities rather than hold specific jobs, and they are expected to continuously learn skills that will keep them employed. Terry Albert, a manager at Windsor Casino, sums up this new employment deal: "Nothing is forever anymore. We are all temporarily employed. It's a fact of business life. Downsizing is a part of today's reality. It affects everyone."[12]

The sharp tone of Albert's statement reveals that the emerging employment relationship creates a new set of organizational behaviour concerns, including misaligned career patterns, increased stress, and declining organizational loyalty.[13] At the same time, a new breed of "free agents" is emerging.[14] Self-employment in Canada has increased to over 12 percent of the workforce. And although a large percentage of these people might prefer stable, well-paying jobs, many are finding new freedom in being their own boss.

Teams, teams, and more teams

Organizational behaviour scholars have long argued that in many situations teams can be more effective than individuals working alone. For example, a diverse work group can potentially resolve complex problems more creatively than if those team members had worked individually. Moreover, by giving teams direct responsibility for coordination and control of work activities, companies can increase responsiveness and remove unnecessary layers of management.

Companies are now discovering the power of teams.[15] Motor Coach Industries, described at the beginning of the chapter, relied on teams to design the Renaissance tour bus. DuPont Canada Ltd. and several other firms have created cross-functional teams to solve problems and discover more efficient uses of its resources. Shell Chemicals in Sarnia, Ontario, and GE Canada's plant in Bromont, Quebec, among others, have introduced self-directed work teams that manage entire work processes.

Courtesy of DuPont Canada.

DuPont Canada cut layers of management to increase its competitiveness. The chemical company now relies on cross-functional work teams to solve problems and improve work efficiency.

These firms are moving toward the team-based organizational structure. As with any organizational behaviour application, teams are not appropriate in every situation. Later in the book, we will learn that there are costs and problems associated with team-based work.

Computer technology and OB

When Bombardier Inc. developed Global Express, the world's most advanced business jet, it leveraged more than just the power of teamwork. The Montreal-based transportation manufacturer also made use of the latest computer systems to design the aircraft. Paper-based blueprints were replaced by a complete digital prototype modelled almost to the last rivet. This computer model was constantly updated, so everyone from engineers to machinists could have the latest plans instantly and simultaneously.[16]

Computer technology is having a revolutionary effect on the way people perform their tasks and the way they work with each other. When properly configured with employees in mind, computer systems can increase job enrichment and improve communication across work units. At Bombardier, employees became "virtual teams," working on or working from the same computer model at different physical locations. Virtual teams operate across space, time, and organizational boundaries with members who communicate mainly through electronic technologies.[17] For example, a Buckman Labs employee in Australia might post an electronic question to co-workers throughout the world. Within a few hours, the employee has an answer from people in five different countries, working at several levels in the hierarchy.[18]

One step beyond virtual teams is the "virtual corporation." This represents an emerging organizational form in which a company instantaneously reorganizes itself to create a product or provide a service in real time, at the moment the customer needs it. How does it reorganize itself? Mainly by forming relationships with other businesses that provide part of the service. The last chapter examines how virtual corporations are associated with the trend toward outsourcing non-core work units in the organization. This virtual structure is made possible by linking people through efficient information technologies.

The Five Anchors of Organizational Behaviour

A changing workforce, new employment relationships, work teams, and computer technologies are only a few of the issues and topics that this book covers. For these and other topics, organizational behaviour scholars rely on a set of basic beliefs or knowledge structures. These conceptual anchors represent the way that OB researchers think about organizations and how they should be studied. Let's look at each of these five conditions that anchor the study of organizational behaviour.

The Multidisciplinary Anchor

Organizational behaviour is anchored around the idea that it should draw on knowledge from other disciplines rather than just its own isolated knowledge base.[19] In other words, OB should be multidisciplinary. Exhibit 1.2 highlights the main disciplines that have had the greatest impact on organizational behaviour knowledge. The field of psychology has aided our understanding of motivation, stress, perceptions, attitudes, and other individual and interpersonal behaviour. The field of sociology helps us study organizations as social systems, as sociologists generally research the areas of team dynamics, organizational socialization, work/nonwork roles, communication, organizational power, leadership, and organizational structure.

Research and concepts from anthropology have laid the foundation for our knowledge of organizational culture as well as cross-cultural relations. Political science research has aided OB knowledge primarily in the areas of intergroup conflict, power, political behaviour, and decision making.[20] The field of engineering has contributed to organizational behaviour in the areas of work efficiency, productivity, and work measurement. Economists influenced early OB writing on organizational power, negotiations, and decision making. Some economic concepts have recently found their way into organizational behaviour writing about employment relationships (transactional costs) and reward systems (agency theory). However, some scholars warn that economics offers only one of many ways to view organizations.[21]

The true test of OB's multidisciplinary anchor will occur as the field matures and develops its own models and theories. Will OB scholars forget that new ideas are also emerging in other disciplines that may be relevant to OB? Or, while refining their own theories, will OB scholars continue to scan other disciplines for innovative perspectives? History suggests that OB's multidisciplinary anchor may lose out to a more inward focus.[22] This would be unfortunate, because divergent knowledge in sociology, psychology, information systems, communication, and other fields would benefit our understanding, prediction, and control of what goes on in organizations.

EXHIBIT 1.2: Multidisciplinary Anchor of Organizational Behaviour

Discipline	Research Emphasis	Relevant Topics
Psychology	Individual behaviour	Motivation, perception, attitudes, personality, job stress, job enrichment, performance appraisals, leadership
Sociology	Interpersonal relations and social systems	Team dynamics, work/nonwork roles, organizational socialization, communication patterns, organizational power, status systems, organizational structure
Anthropology	Relationship between social units and their environments	Corporate culture, organizational rituals, cross-cultural aspects of OB, organizational adaptation
Political Science	Individual and group behaviours within political systems	Intergroup conflict, coalition formation, organizational power and politics, decision making, organizational environments
Economics	Rational behaviour in the allocation of scarce resources	Decision making, negotiation, organizational power, agency theory
Industrial Engineering	Efficient operation of physical human behaviour	Job design, productivity, work measurement

multidisciplinary [handwritten]

The Scientific Method Anchor

Scientific method A set of principles and procedures that help researchers to systematically understand previously unexplained events and conditions.

A second anchor of organizational behaviour relates to the way we study organizations. For the most part, OB researchers test their hypotheses about organizations by collecting information according to the **scientific method**. The scientific method is not a single procedure for collecting data; rather, it is a set of principles and procedures that help researchers to systematically understand previously unexplained events and conditions. Appendix A summarizes the main elements of the scientific method, as well as various ways to conduct research.

The Contingency Anchor

Contingency approach The idea that a particular action may have different consequences in different situations; that no single solution is best in all circumstances.

"It depends" is a phrase that OB scholars often use to answer a question about the best solution to an organizational problem. The statement may frustrate some people, yet it reflects an important way of understanding and predicting organizational events, called the **contingency approach**. This anchor states that a particular action may have different consequences in different situations. In other words, no single solution is best in all circumstances.

Many early OB theorists have proposed universal rules to predict and explain organizational life, but there are usually too many exceptions to make these "one best way" theories useful. For example, in Chapter 14 we will learn that leaders should use one style (e.g., participation) in some situations and another style (e.g., direction) in other situations. Thus, when faced with a particular problem or opportunity, we need to understand and diagnose the situation, and select the strategy most appropriate *under those conditions.*[23]

Although contingency-oriented theories are necessary in most areas of organizational behaviour, we should also be wary about carrying this anchor to an extreme. Some contingency models add more confusion than value over universal ones. Consequently, we need to balance the sensitivity of contingency factors with the simplicity of universal theories.

The Multiple Levels of Analysis Anchor

organization
team
individual [handwritten]

team = way ppl interact [handwritten]

individual - characteristics behaviours of employees [handwritten]

Organizational events can be studied from three levels of analysis: individual, team, and organizational (see Exhibit 1.3). The individual level includes the characteristics and behaviours of employees as well as the thought processes that are attributed to them, such as motivation, perceptions, personalities, attitudes, and values. The team level of analysis looks at the way people interact. This includes team dynamics, decisions, power, organizational politics, conflict, and leadership. At the organizational level, we focus on how people structure their working relationships and on how organizations interact with their environments.

Although an OB topic is pegged into one level of analysis, it usually relates to all three levels.[24] For instance, communication includes individual behaviours and interpersonal (team) dynamics. It also relates to the organization's structure. Therefore, think about each OB topic at the individual, team, *and* organizational levels, not just at one of these levels.

The Open Systems Anchor

Phil Carroll likes to think of himself as an ecologist for the organization. In fact, the chief executive officer of Shell Oil believes that all executives should take this

EXHIBIT 1.3: Three Levels of Analysis in Organizational Behaviour

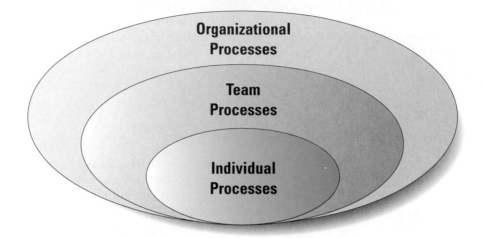

view because they are responsible for organizations and their interactions with the environment. "Perhaps my real job [as CEO] is to be the ecologist for the organization," Carroll explains. "We must learn how to see the company as a living system and to see it as a system within the context of the larger systems of which it is a part."[25]

Open systems
Organizations and other entities with interdependent parts that work together to continually monitor and transact with the external environment.

Phil Carroll is describing the fifth anchor of organizational behaviour — the view that organizations are **open systems**. This means that organizations consist of interdependent parts that work together to continually monitor and transact with the external environment.[26]

Exhibit 1.4 presents a simplified image of organizations as open systems. An organizational system acquires resources from its external environment, including raw materials, employees, information, financial support, and equipment. Technology (such as equipment, work methods, and information) transforms these inputs into various outputs that are exported back to the external environment. The organization receives feedback from the external environment regarding the use of these outputs and the availability of future inputs. It also receives more resources in return for its outputs. This process is cyclical and, ideally, self-sustaining, so that the organization may continue to survive and prosper.

To understand the open systems anchor better, think about its opposite: closed systems. A closed system exists independent of anything beyond its boundaries. It has all the resources needed to survive indefinitely. Organizations are never completely closed systems, but those operating in very stable environments tend to become relatively closed by ignoring their surroundings for long periods of time.

Companies develop systems thinking by making employees more aware of the different products or services that are provided. Gould Shawmut Ltd. has taken this approach through product-awareness training for its 220 employees. A cross-functional team helped design the training program, and classes were conducted in-house by an engineer. Production supervisor Rosalia Fonseca says that classes improved product quality because employees became more aware of the seriousness of making a mistake in their work. The knowledge also increased company pride, particularly when staff learned that their fuses are used in SkyDome's scoreboard and in the CN Tower.[27]

EXHIBIT 1.4: Open Systems View of Organizations

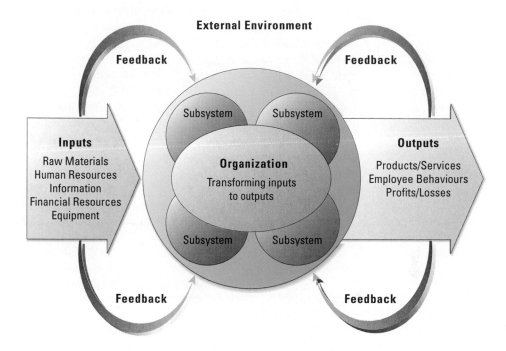

So far, we have described organizational systems in terms of their external environments. But the open systems anchor also recognizes that organizations have many parts (called subsystems) that must coordinate with each other in the process of transforming inputs to outputs. To achieve their objectives, firms must monitor the relationships among these subsystems and take corrective actions whenever friction occurs. Of course, even the best-laid plans are paved with unintended consequences. This occurs because subsystem interdependence is so complex that an event in one department may ripple through the organization and affect other subsystems. Making employees aware of this fact can minimize problems. British Airways used some innovative approaches to teach employees this open systems view, as we see in Perspective 1.1.

Open systems thinking is an important anchor in how we view organizations. More recently, organizational behaviour scholars have added to this view the notion that organizations are systems of knowledge and learning. Let's examine this emerging view of organizations more closely.

Organizational Knowledge and Learning

There is a story about a factory engineer who became a consultant after being laid off by his employer. A year later, the plant manager where the consultant had worked called him in to fix a broken piece of equipment. As his former boss anxiously looked on, the consultant scratched his head, looked carefully at the machine from different angles, and thought for a moment. He then reached for a small hammer and tapped

PERSPECTIVE 1.1

British Airways Flies High With Systems Thinking

British Airways is a vanguard organization in the application of open systems thinking. One of the airline's innovative ways to teach employees about open systems is by encouraging departments to host "A Day in a Life" seminars. People from other parts of the company attend these sessions that describe a department's activities. For example, the reservations group might give pilots a tour of the reservations system. Flight attendants might help accountants learn more about working on an aircraft.

Another open systems learning tool at British Airways is Domino, an interactive computer simulation. This simulation challenges employee teams to get "Granny" on a flight from London, England, so that she can visit her new grandchild in Toronto. The trick is to make Granny a happy British

Airways passenger without disrupting other areas of the company.

When Domino participants select a course of action, the computer shows the impact of this decision on other departments in the organization. For example, if participants decide to lure Granny to a particular flight with bonus air miles, the computer explains that the marketing department must now decide how to communicate the bonus plan to Granny and other potential customers.

Few companies have gone as far as British Airways in helping employees develop an open systems perspective. The results are apparent. As one employee commented, British Airways has been transformed from a "bloody awful" government-controlled company to "the world's favourite airline."

Source: E. P. Lima, "Pioneering in People," *Air Transport World*, April 1995, pp. 51-54; "British Airways Encourages Employees to Be Conceited," *Travel Weekly*, Oct. 8, 1992, pp. 41, 42; K. Macher, "Creating Commitment," *Training and Development Journal*, April 1991, pp. 45-52.; J. Aspery, "British Companies Meet the Challenge of Change," *ABC Communication World* 7, December 1990, pp. 39–41.

twice at a particular spot. The lights came back on and the machine sprang to life. When the engineer presented an invoice for $1,000, the irate plant manager demanded that the bill be itemized. The consultant took the invoice and wrote: "Tapping machine with hammer, $1. Knowing where to tap, $999."[28]

As this story illustrates, brains have replaced brawn as the primary source of corporate-wealth creation. According to some estimates, nearly 80 percent of North American jobs involve knowledge work rather than manual labour. "All companies have a great deal of critical knowledge that resides with the employees," explains Tim Casgrain, one of Canada's most experienced turnaround or "workout" managers and a managing partner with Edper Group Ltd.[29]

Intellectual capital The knowledge that resides in an organization, including its human, organizational, and customer capital.

The knowledge that resides in an organization is called its **intellectual capital**. Intellectual capital is the sum of an organization's human capital, organizational capital, and customer capital.[30] *Human capital* refers to the knowledge that employees possess and generate. *Organizational capital* is the knowledge captured in an organization's systems and structures. *Customer capital* is the value that customers perceive from doing business with the organization.

An organization's knowledge — its intellectual capital — is the main source of competitive advantage for most companies. Software companies, for example, have few assets other than the knowledge held by their employees. Some firms, including CIBC and Northern Telecom, realize that intellectual capital does not show up in financial statements, so they try to measure it in some way. This isn't easy, however. "Intellectual capital is by nature dynamic, so parts of it may always be hard to measure with precision," says Claude Balthazard, a CIBC consultant. "We are finding that the most meaningful measurements involve a degree of subjectivity either in their derivation or in their interpretation."[31]

[handwritten margin note: intellectual capital = knowledge that resides in an organization. H.C C.C O.C]

Whether or not accountants will be able to quantify the value of a company's knowledge, organizational behaviour scholars are beginning to understand the process of acquiring, disseminating, and utilizing intellectual capital. This process is called organizational learning, which we discuss next.

Organizational Learning

Organizational learning
An organization's capacity to acquire, disseminate, and apply knowledge for its survival and success.

[handwritten margin note: 1. Knowledge acquisition 2. disem 3 utilization — survival success]

Organizational learning refers to the capacity of an organization to acquire, disseminate, and apply knowledge for its survival and success.[32] This "capacity" to learn means that companies have established systems, structures, and organizational values that support the learning process, as well as the application of knowledge for more effective employee behaviours. Organizational learning is an extension of open systems theory because it recognizes that firms need to learn about their internal and external environments in order to survive and succeed through adaptation.[33]

Organizational learning has three main elements: knowledge acquisition, knowledge dissemination, and knowledge utilization.[34] Each element includes a variety of strategies, as illustrated in Exhibit 1.5.

Knowledge Acquisition

Knowledge acquisition includes the organization's ability to extract information and ideas from its environment as well as through insight. Four common ways organiza-

EXHIBIT 1.5: Elements of Organizational Learning

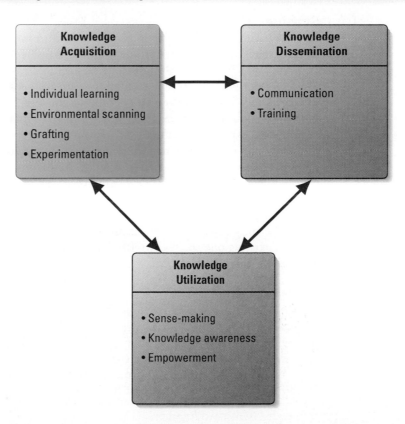

Organizational learning [handwritten]

acquisition [handwritten]

tions acquire knowledge are through individual learning, environmental scanning, grafting, and experimentation.

Individual learning

Organizations learn through individuals, so knowledge acquisition requires the processes used by individual employees to acquire knowledge. Since this is a vital topic in organizational behaviour, Chapter 2 examines how individual employees learn through reinforcement, feedback, observation, and experience. The quality management practices of benchmarking and continuous improvement, described in Chapter 10, also involve individual learning. The main point here is that organizations acquire knowledge more effectively by assisting the process of individual learning.

Environmental scanning

Environmental scanning
Receiving information from the external and internal environments so that more effective strategic decisions can be made.

Environmental scanning involves receiving information from the external and internal environments so that more effective strategic decisions can be made. Environmental scanning helps build new perspectives of the world, called mental models, which are described in Chapter 6. There are many forms of environmental scanning. Price Waterhouse Limited uses a computer program to identify newspaper articles that mention its clients, then sends those clippings to partners currently working with the mentioned clients.[35] Telephone companies employ people whose main goal is to continuously monitor government activities that may result in changing telecommunications policy. CIBC, Xerox Canada, and other companies regularly survey customers to determine what market changes are likely to occur. For internal scanning, many firms survey employees, as we discuss in Chapter 8.

Grafting

Microsoft Corporation has an incredible amount of organizational knowledge that it has translated into successful products and services. However, did you know that some of Microsoft's best-known products were acquired rather than developed in-house? For example, PowerPoint™ presentation software became a Microsoft product after the company bought its creator, Forethought Inc., in the 1980s. More recently, Microsoft acquired Vermeer Technologies Corp. so that it could quickly add the Web editor Frontpage to its product list.[36]

Grafting The process of acquiring knowledge by hiring individuals or buying entire companies.

The process of acquiring knowledge by hiring individuals or buying entire companies is called **grafting**.[37] Microsoft is not unique in acquiring information through grafting. Every company hires new employees who bring fresh ideas as well as technical knowledge with them. Mergers and acquisitions are classic examples of grafting, particularly in software and other knowledge-based industries where intellectual capital is the only resource worth acquiring. Of course, grafting an acquired company onto an existing one creates problems with merging different organizational cultures, as we shall learn in Chapter 16.

Experimentation

The previous three activities primarily collect information from elsewhere. However, knowledge acquisition also comes from within the person through insight. This insight is the result of experimentation and creative processes.[38] Through creative thinking as well as trial and error, employees find new ways to complete their work or make use of organizational resources. Creativity is an important part of decision making, so we discuss it more fully in Chapter 11.

Knowledge Dissemination

A major customer of a mid-sized Canadian firm went into receivership, leaving its accounts unpaid. When executives looked for ways to minimize unpaid accounts in the future, they discovered that their own truck drivers knew the customer was in trouble. The drivers had heard the customer's employees worrying about job security, saying that their payroll had been missed for two weeks in a row. Unaware of any problems, the executives had extended the customer's credit amount, which resulted in higher losses than would have otherwise occurred.[39]

This true story illustrates the point that many organizations are reasonably good at acquiring knowledge but waste this resource by not effectively disseminating it. As one Canadian study revealed, knowledge dissemination is usually the weakest link in organizational learning.[40] "We create way too much knowledge," says Arian Ward, an organizational learning champion at Hughes Space & Communications Co. "We have to start learning how to reuse."[41]

How do companies disseminate knowledge? Many corporate executives tend to think of training as the first answer. In fact, some believe that training is the main element of organizational learning. However, this overstates the role of training. Formal training is useful for some forms of knowledge transfer, but most knowledge dissemination occurs in more spontaneous and timely ways.[42]

Communication is probably the most vital tool for knowledge dissemination. Organizations are traditionally "silos of knowledge." They are divided into distinct units that consciously or unwittingly hoard information rather than send it out to others. Learning organizations introduce more efficient and effective communication systems so that employees can quickly and fluidly share that knowledge. For instance, Ault Foods uses a computer network so that employees can efficiently distribute information that they acquire. It ensures that the right information gets to the right people at the right time.[43] Chapter 8 is devoted to the topic of communication, and includes a discussion of emerging electronic technologies. As we learn in Chapters 9, 10, and 11, teams also provide a communication channel for organizational learning.[44]

Knowledge Utilization

Organizational learning occurs when companies make use of knowledge. This involves making sense of the information received and applying it to employee behaviours either directly or through organizational systems and structures. It seems obvious that useful information should be applied, but several conditions need to exist. First, employees need to realize that they possess information to potentially improve customer service or product quality. This requires clear role perceptions, which we discuss in Chapter 2. Second, employees need to have the freedom to apply their knowledge. Thus, knowledge utilization requires employee empowerment, which we discuss in Chapter 4.

Organizational Memory

When NASA officials went to the United States Congress to fund its next-generation launch vehicle, someone asked why the space agency didn't simply rebuild its successful Saturn 5 rocket. NASA had invested $50 billion in that rocket, which had carried the *Apollo* space capsule and astronauts to the moon. NASA officials investigated this option, but they soon discovered that the agency didn't have a complete set of plans, tools, or dies for the rocket. Moreover, most engineers in the Saturn project had since retired or died.[45]

Organizational memory
The storage and preservation of the organization's knowledge (i.e., its intellectual capital).

NASA learned an expensive lesson — that intellectual capital can be lost as quickly as it is acquired. Corporate leaders need to recognize that they are the keepers of an **organizational memory**. This unusual metaphor refers to the storage and preservation of intellectual capital. Organizational memory includes information that employees possess as well as knowledge embedded in the organization's systems and structures. It includes documents, objects, and anything else that provides meaningful information about how the organization should operate. In other words, organizational memory is the stock of knowledge an organization possesses at any given time. NASA is certainly not alone in its loss of organizational memory. As we see in Perspective 1.2, the City of Ottawa suffered significant memory loss when one-third of its finance staff left due to a corporate downsizing.

PERSPECTIVE 1.2

City of Ottawa Loses Some Organizational Memory

Ottawa's City Hall is suffering from a bout of collective amnesia. Three years of employee buyouts have left the municipality without some of the organizational knowledge it needs to function properly.

The collective memory loss problem became apparent when the city's budget overlooked a $1.4 million debt that it owed to the Province of Ontario. This "oversight" forced city politicians to reopen budget-spending estimates to make up for the loss.

A senior finance manager was demoted for the incident. However, a consultant's audit later concluded that the problem occurred because one-third of the finance department's employees had taken the early-retirement package, leaving the unit with large gaps in its collective knowledge. In particular, the employees who knew about the provincial government agreement when it was signed two years earlier were gone when the unused funds were due.

"The trouble with early-retirement packages is that it's voluntary and you don't get to choose who leaves," acknowledges an Ottawa city councillor.

The consultant's report also noted that city councillors received numerous complaints during the previous winter about snowplough operators who damaged homeowners' lawns with their equipment. This occurred because several experienced employees had taken early retirement without teaching rookie snowplough operators about snow removal on specific streets in Ottawa.

"When the city loses a long-term employee, it loses a piece of its corporate memory," said the audit report.

Ottawa City Hall lost valuable knowledge when several of its finance department employees took early retirement.

Source: Based on R. Eade, "Errors Traced to Staff Cuts, Audit Revealed," *Ottawa Citizen*, August 2, 1996, p. B6.

How do organizations retain intellectual capital? One way for an organization to hold on to knowledge is by keeping good employees and systematically transferring their knowledge when they leave. Documentation is another obvious solution. Documentation is more than writing down facts. It includes bringing out hidden knowledge, organizing it, and putting it in a form that can be available to others.[46] Patents represent a clear example of this, but any practice that assists the organization can be documented. As we shall learn in Chapter 10, quality management experts recognize the importance of documentation to maintain consistency and retain intellectual capital.

Successful companies also unlearn. Sometimes it is appropriate for organizations to selectively forget certain knowledge.[47] This means that they should cast off the routines and patterns of behaviour that are no longer appropriate. Employees need to rethink their perceptions, such as how they should interact with customers and which is the "best way" to perform a task. As we shall discover in Chapter 15, unlearning is essential for organizational change.

Organization of This Book

This concludes our opening discussion of the organizational behaviour field. Now let's introduce you to the rest of this book. *Canadian Organizational Behaviour,* Third Edition, is organized into five parts, including this introduction (see Exhibit 1.6).

Part 2 examines the dynamics of individual behaviour, with particular emphasis on learning and motivation. Chapter 2 introduces a model of employee behaviour, and introduces several forms of individual learning. Chapter 3 presents the main content and process theories of motivation. Chapter 4 discusses three applied motivation practices in organizational settings: rewards, job design, and self-leadership. The dynamics of stress and stress management practices are found in Chapter 5.

Part 3 discusses other individual and interpersonal processes. This begins in Chapter 6 with a look at perception and personality in organizations. Chapter 7 examines emotions and values in the workplace, including the issue of emotional labour. In Chapter 8, we learn about the dynamics and practices of interpersonal and organizational communication.

Part 4 examines team processes in organizations. In Chapter 9, we look at the dynamics and effectiveness of work teams. Chapter 10 describes the forms and levels of employee involvement, as well as quality management practices. Chapter 11 integrates decision-making concepts, ranging from perceptual issues to team dynamics in the decision process. Chapter 12 investigates the factors that influence individual power, as well as the sources of and remedies for political behaviour in organizations. We learn about the dynamics of organizational conflict and negotiation in Chapter 13. Chapter 14 presents several perspectives of leadership, with particular emphasis on the emerging model of transformational leadership.

The final section of this book, Part 5, focuses on organizational-level activities. We learn about organizational change and development in Chapter 15, including strategies to reduce resistance to change and organization development interventions. Chapter 16 discusses organizational culture, including how its dominant values are maintained or strengthened. In Chapter 17, we look at the changing employment relationship, including the psychological contract, socialization, careers, and the contingent workforce. Chapter 18, the final chapter of the book, examines the different forms of organizational design, and the contingencies that affect the best structural configuration in a particular environment.

EXHIBIT 1.6: Organization of This Book

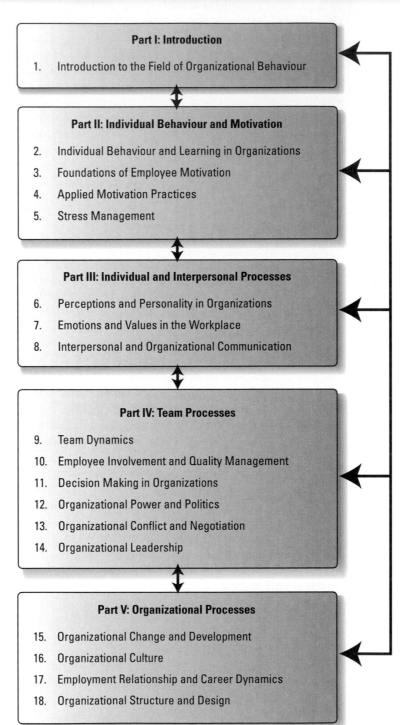

Part I: Introduction

1. Introduction to the Field of Organizational Behaviour

Part II: Individual Behaviour and Motivation

2. Individual Behaviour and Learning in Organizations
3. Foundations of Employee Motivation
4. Applied Motivation Practices
5. Stress Management

Part III: Individual and Interpersonal Processes

6. Perceptions and Personality in Organizations
7. Emotions and Values in the Workplace
8. Interpersonal and Organizational Communication

Part IV: Team Processes

9. Team Dynamics
10. Employee Involvement and Quality Management
11. Decision Making in Organizations
12. Organizational Power and Politics
13. Organizational Conflict and Negotiation
14. Organizational Leadership

Part V: Organizational Processes

15. Organizational Change and Development
16. Organizational Culture
17. Employment Relationship and Career Dynamics
18. Organizational Structure and Design

Chapter Summary

- Organizational behaviour is a relatively young field of inquiry that studies what people think, feel, and do in and around organizations. Organizations are groups of people who work interdependently toward some purpose.

- OB concepts help us to predict and understand organizational events, adopt more accurate theories of reality, and control organizational events more effectively. They let us make sense of the work world, test and challenge our personal theories of human behaviour, and understand ways to manage organization activities.

- There are several emerging issues and changes in organizational behaviour. The workforce is becoming increasingly diverse. Companies are replacing the job-for-life with an employment relationship based on employability. Employees are expected to work in teams rather than alone. Computer technology has created virtual teams and virtual corporations.

- Organizational behaviour scholars rely on a set of basic beliefs to study organizations. These anchors include beliefs that OB knowledge should be multidisciplinary and based on scientific method, that organizational events usually have contingencies, that organizational behaviour can be viewed from three levels of analysis (individual, team, and organizational), and that organizations are open systems.

- Intellectual capital is knowledge that resides in an organization, including its human capital, organizational capital, and customer capital. It is a firm's main source of competitive advantage. Organizational learning refers to the capacity of an organization to acquire, disseminate, and apply knowledge for its survival and success.

- Knowledge acquisition occurs through individual learning, environmental scanning, grafting, and experimentation. Knowledge dissemination occurs mainly through communication and training. Knowledge utilization is more effective when employees are aware that they have certain knowledge, are able to make sense of that knowledge, and have sufficient freedom to apply that knowledge. Organizational memory refers to the storage and preservation of intellectual capital.

Discussion Questions

1. A friend suggests that organizational behaviour courses are only useful to people who will enter management careers. Discuss the accuracy of your friend's statement.

2. Look through the list of chapters in this book and discuss how computer technology could influence each organizational behaviour topic.

3. "Organizational theories should follow the contingency approach." Comment on the accuracy of this statement.

4. Describe and diagram your college or university in terms of an open system. Your answer should indicate the main inputs, transformation processes, outputs, and forms of feedback.

5. Employees in the City of Calgary's water distribution unit were put into teams and given orders to find ways to improve efficiency. The teams boldly crossed departmental boundaries and areas of management discretion in search of problems. Employees working in other parts of the City of Calgary began to complain about these intrusions. Moreover, when some team ideas were implemented, the city discovered that a dollar saved in the water distribution unit may have cost the organization two dollars in higher costs elsewhere. Use the open systems concept to explain what happened at the City of Calgary.

6. Fully describe intellectual capital, and explain how an organization can retain this capital.

7. BusNews Inc. is the leading stock market and business news service in North America. Over the past two years, BusNews has experienced increased competition from other news providers. These competitors have brought in Internet and other emerging computer technologies to link customers with information more quickly. There is little knowledge within BusNews about how to use these computer technologies. Based on the knowledge acquisition processes for organizational learning, explain how BusNews might gain the intellectual capital necessary to become more competitive in this respect.

8. Of what importance is communication in organizational learning?

Chapter Case

An Untimely Incident at Ancol Ltd.*

Paul Simard was delighted when Ancol Ltd. offered him the job of manager at its Jonquiere, Quebec, plant. Simard was happy enough managing a small metal-stamping plant with another company, but the headhunter's invitation to apply for the plant manager job at one of Canada's leading metal-fabrication companies was irresistible. Although the Jonquiere plant was the smallest of Ancol's 15 operations across Canada, the plant manager position was a valuable first step in a promising career.

One of Simard's first observations at Ancol's Jonquiere plant was that relations between employees and management were strained. Using what he had learned at a recent executive seminar on building trust in the workplace, Simard ordered the removal of all time clocks from the plant. Instead, the plant would assume that employees had put in their full shift. This symbolic gesture, he believed, would establish a new level of credibility and strengthen relations between management and employees.

Initially, the 250 employees at the Jonquiere plant appreciated their new freedom. They felt respected and saw Simard's gesture as a sign of position change from the new plant manager. Two months later, however, problems started to arise. A few people began showing up late, leaving early, or taking extended lunch breaks. Although this represented only 5 percent of the employees, others found the situation unfair. Moreover, the increased absenteeism levels were beginning to have a noticeable effect on plant productivity. The problem had to be managed.

Simard asked supervisors to observe and record when the employees came or went and to discuss attendance problems with those abusing their privileges. But the supervisors had no previous experience with keeping attendance and many lacked the necessary interpersonal skills to discuss the matter with subordinates. Employees resented the reprimands, so their relations with supervisors deteriorated. The additional responsibility of keeping track of attendance also made it difficult for supervisors to complete their other responsibilities.

After only a few months, Ancol found it necessary to add another supervisor position and reduce the number of employees assigned to each supervisor.

But the problems did not end there. Without time clocks, the payroll department could not deduct pay for the amount of time that employees were late. Instead, a letter of reprimand was placed in the employee's personnel file. However, this required yet more time and additional skills from the supervisors. Employees did not want these letters to become a permanent record, so they filed grievances with their labour union. The number of grievances doubled over six months, which required even more time for both union officials and supervisors to handle these disputes.

Nine months after removing the time clocks, Paul Simard met with union officials, who agreed that it would be better to put the time clocks back in place. Employee-management relations had deteriorated below the level when Simard had started. Supervisors were burnt out from overwork. Productivity had dropped due to poorer attendance records and increased administrative workloads.

A couple of months after the time clocks were put back in place, Simard attended an operations meeting at Ancol's headquarters in Toronto. During lunch, Simard described the time-clock incident to Liam Jackson, Ancol's plant manager in northern British Columbia. Jackson looked surprised, then chuckled. He explained that the previous B.C. plant manager had done something like that with similar consequences six or seven years ago. The manager had left some time ago, but Jackson heard about the B.C. time-clock incident from a supervisor during his retirement party two months earlier.

"I guess it's not quite like lightning striking the same place twice," said Simard to Jackson. "But it sure feels like it."

---

*This case is based on actual events, but names and some facts have been changed to provide a fuller case discussion. © Copyright 1998. Steven L. McShane.

Experiential Exercise

It All Makes Sense?

Purpose: This exercise is designed to help you understand how organizational behaviour knowledge can help you adopt more accurate theories of reality.

Instructions: Read each of the statements below and circle whether each statement is true or false, in your opinion. The instructor might put you in groups to compare results and reach agreement on the correct answer. The class will consider the answers to each question and discuss the implications for studying organizational behaviour. After reviewing these statements, the instructor will provide information about the most appropriate answer.

1. True   False   A happy worker is a productive worker.

2. True   False   Decision makers tend to continue supporting a course of action even though information suggests that the decision is ineffective.

3. True   False   Organizations are more effective when they prevent conflict among employees.

4. True   False   It is better to negotiate alone than as a team.

5. True   False   Companies are most effective when they have a strong corporate culture.

6. True   False   Employees perform better when they don't experience stress.

7. True   False   The best way to change an organization is to get employees to identify and focus on its current problems.

8. True   False   Female leaders involve employees in decisions to a greater degree than do male leaders.

9. True   False   Male business students today have mostly overcome the negative stereotypes of female managers that existed 20 years ago.

10. True   False   Top-level executives tend to exhibit a Type A behaviour pattern (i.e., hard-driving, impatient, competitive, short-tempered, strong sense of time urgency, rapid talkers).

11. True   False   Employees usually feel overreward inequity when they are paid more than co-workers performing the same work.

Practice Session For Part 1

The true-false, multiple-choice, and written-answer questions presented here are based on information in Part 1 of this book (Chapter 1). These questions can help test your knowledge of material in this chapter. If your instructor uses the test bank for this textbook, these questions also give you an opportunity to practise for examinations in this course. The answers to these questions are found in Appendix C.

True–False

1. T F   The new employment relationship has resulted in stronger organizational loyalty, reduced stress, and clearer career patterns.

2. T F   Organizational behaviour topics are usually studied from these three levels of analysis: input, throughput, and output.

3. T F   The process of acquiring, disseminating, and utilizing intellectual capital is called organizational learning.

Multiple-Choice

1. Which of the following does NOT represent a belief that anchors organizational behaviour? (a) OB should view organizations as open systems; (b) OB should assume that employees are more effective in teams; (c) OB should draw on knowledge from other disciplines; (d) OB should rely on the scientific method to generate knowledge; (e) OB topics can be studied from multiple levels of analysis.

2. As part of the organizational learning process, environmental scanning mainly affects: (a) measuring intellectual capital; (b) knowledge acquisition; (c) organizational memory; (d) knowledge dissemination; (e) unlearning.

Written-Answer Question

1. Identify three ways in which organizational behaviour can potentially benefit students.

PART 2

Individual Behaviour and Motivation

CHAPTER 2
Individual Behaviour and Learning in Organizations

CHAPTER 3
Foundations of Employee Motivation

CHAPTER 4
Applied Motivation Practices

CHAPTER 5
Stress Management

Individual Behaviour and Learning in Organizations

CHAPTER OUTLINE

Model of Individual Behaviour and Performance

Learning in Organizations

OB Modification: Learning Through Reinforcement

Learning Through Feedback

Social Learning Theory: Learning by Observing

Learning Through Experience

Chapter Summary

Discussion Questions

LEARNING OBJECTIVES

After reading this chapter, you should be able to:

- Describe the four factors that influence individual behaviour and performance.

- Identify five types of work-related behaviour.

- Describe the A-B-C model of organizational behaviour modification.

- Compare and contrast the four contingencies of reinforcement.

- Explain how feedback influences individual behaviour and performance.

- Identify five elements of effective feedback.

- Describe the three features of social learning theory.

- Discuss the value of learning through experience.

Canadian Pacific Hotels & Resorts Ltd. depends on Fred Zammit and other employees to provide exceptional guest service.

A s doorman, Fred Zammit is one of the first people guests meet at Toronto's Royal York Hotel. A 15-year employee, Fred offers the level of service excellence that strengthens guest loyalty to Canadian Pacific Hotels and Resorts Ltd., which owns the Royal York.

CP Hotels uses a Service Plus program to ensure that employees provide superb guest service. "If you don't invest in people, your other investments are for naught," says Carolyn Clark, CP Hotels' vice-president of human resources.

Since CP Hotels hires people with a customer orientation, a 65-question interview carefully screens applicants with this and other competencies. Next, employees participate in Service Plus 2000, a training program that clarifies the importance of guest service and teaches specific behaviours for better guest service.

The third element of Service Plus is a reward-and-recognition program that motivates employees to provide exceptional guest service. This reward program, called SHARE Team, pays employees of CP Ltd. common shares based on guest service ratings, corporate profitability, and the specific hotel's health and safety record over the previous year.

Carolyn Clark explains that with the SHARE Team Program, "employees have an increased interest in overall hotel performance, and in what they can do to help improve guest service and profitability."[1]

At CP Hotels, individual behaviour is the foundation of customer service, profitability, and other indicators of the company's success. Its employees engage in desired behaviours because they understand their roles and have the ability and motivation to fulfil corporate objectives. CP Hotels also provides the resources necessary for people to do their jobs effectively.

This chapter introduces the dynamics of individual behaviour and learning in organizations. We begin by introducing a model of individual behaviour and performance as well as the main types of work-related behaviour. Most elements of the individual behaviour model are influenced by individual learning, so the latter part of the chapter discusses the concept of learning and describes four perspectives of learning in organizational settings: reinforcement, feedback, observation, and experience.

Model of Individual Behaviour and Performance

The Royal York Hotel depends on Fred Zammit to perform his job in a way that satisfies customers and fulfils other organizational objectives. Why does Zammit provide better customer service than many other people? And how can organizations ensure that all employees provide exceptional customer service and fulfil their other work obligations? The model of individual behaviour and performance shown in Exhibit 2.1 provides a good place to start to answer these questions. As illustrated, four factors directly influence an employee's voluntary behaviour and performance: motivation, ability, role perceptions, and situational contingencies.

The model also shows that these four factors have a combined effect on behaviour and performance. If any one factor weakens, employee performance will decrease. For example, highly qualified salespeople who understand their job duties and have sufficient resources will not perform their jobs as well if they aren't motivated to market the company's products or services. Let's briefly examine these four influences on individual behaviour and performance.

EXHIBIT 2.1: Model of Individual Behaviour and Performance

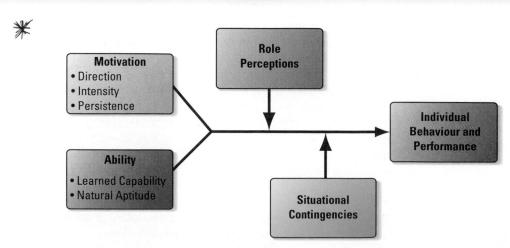

Employee Motivation

Motivation The internal forces that affect the direction, intensity, and persistence of a person's voluntary choice of behaviour.

Opel, General Motors' German subsidiary, recently announced that employee motivation is essential for its long-term success: "Employee motivation represents one of our largest competitive reserves and is therefore a key element for increasing the international competitiveness of German automobile manufacturers."[2] **Motivation** represents the forces within a person that affect his or her direction, intensity, and persistence of voluntary behaviour.[3] *Direction* refers to the fact that motivation is goal-oriented, not random. People are motivated to arrive at work on time, finish a project a few hours early, or aim for many other targets. *Intensity* is the amount of effort allocated to the goal. For example, two employees might be motivated to finish their project a few hours early (direction), but only one of them puts forth enough effort (intensity) to achieve this goal. Finally, motivation involves varying levels of *persistence*; that is, continuing the effort for a certain amount of time. Employees sustain their effort until they reach their goal or give up beforehand.

Ability

Ability The natural aptitudes and learned capabilities required to successfully complete a task.

A second influence on individual behaviour and performance is the person's ability. **Ability** includes both the natural aptitudes and learned capabilities required to successfully complete a task. *Aptitudes* are the natural talents that help employees learn specific tasks more quickly and perform them better. For example, people with finger dexterity tend to quickly learn how to manipulate small objects using their fingers. You cannot learn finger dexterity; rather, some people have a more natural ability than others to adeptly manipulate small objects with their fingers. There are many different physical and mental aptitudes, and our ability to acquire skills is affected by these aptitudes.

Competencies The abilities, individual values, personality traits, and other characteristics of people that lead to superior performance.

Learned capabilities refer to the skills and knowledge that people have actually acquired. This includes the physical and mental skills they possess as well as the knowledge they acquire and store for later use. A related concept that has caught the interest of many Canadian organizations is employee **competencies** — the characteristics of people that lead to superior performance.[4] Competencies include natural and learned abilities, but many practitioners also include the individual's values and personality traits as competencies required for a job. Canadian Occidental Petroleum Ltd. (CanOxy), a Calgary-based energy company, has identified adaptability/managing change, effective communications, global cultural sensitivity, initiative, leadership, and teamwork as competencies required for all of its employees.[5] Notice that some competencies identified at CanOxy are mainly learned capabilities (e.g., communicating effectively), while others are personality traits or personal values (e.g., initiative).

There are three ways to match an individual's abilities with those needed to perform the assigned work.[6] One strategy is to select applicants whose existing abilities best fit the required tasks. A second approach is to redesign the job so that employees are given tasks only within their capabilities. For instance, new employees might initially be assigned to clients with less complex problems or requests. This is usually a temporary strategy, although jobs may be permanently changed to provide reasonable accommodation for employees with disabilities. Training, the third strategy, is one of the most effective ways to improve employee performance. Studies confirm that employees provide significantly better customer service after they receive appropriate technical and customer values training.[7] Training also increases employee flexibility through *multiskilling*. This means that employees acquire the abilities to perform several different tasks and can therefore be moved to different jobs as work demands require.

Role Perceptions

During a recent safety exercise, the crew of a BC Ferries vessel was so disorganized that it couldn't find a simulated fire, let alone put it out! One ship's mate heard the fire alarm and ran to the alarm station, but didn't look for the fire. A catering attendant knew the fire's location, but stood there watching the drill without saying anything. "The drill was so poorly conducted that I considered detaining the vessel until proficiency could be shown," wrote the officer inspecting the fire drill.[8]

BC Ferries normally has a very good safety record, but this incident illustrates how **role perceptions** affect job performance. Role perceptions are a person's beliefs about what behaviours are appropriate or necessary in a particular situation. Employees have accurate role perceptions when they understand the specific tasks assigned to them, the relative importance of those tasks, and the preferred behaviours to accomplish those tasks. Some employees in the BC Ferries exercise had poor role perceptions because they didn't understand what they had to do in case of fire. The ship's mate didn't realize that he had to look for the fire. The catering attendant didn't know that it was part of her job to advise others where the fire was located. In a real fire, these misperceptions would have potentially fatal consequences.

Inaccurate role perceptions cause employees to exert effort toward the wrong goals, and ambiguous role perceptions lead to lower effort.[9] These misperceptions occur when employees receive conflicting information about task responsibilities and the relative importance of those responsibilities. More accurate role perceptions develop when the required tasks are described clearly, employees are trained in the most appropriate way to accomplish those tasks, and they receive frequent and meaningful performance feedback.

Role perceptions A person's beliefs about what behaviours are appropriate or necessary in a particular situation, including the specific tasks that make up the job, their relative importance, and the preferred behaviours to accomplish those tasks.

Ron Long. Courtesy of Simon Fraser University.

The crew of a BC Ferries vessel recently performed a safety exercise so poorly that the officer inspecting the fire drill considered detaining the vessel from service. The problem was that several crew members didn't know which tasks they should perform — they had poor role perceptions — during a shipboard fire or emergency.

Situational Contingencies

Situational contingencies
Environmental conditions beyond the employee's immediate control that constrain or facilitate employee behaviour and performance.

Job performance depends not just on motivation, ability, and role perceptions. It is also affected by **situational contingencies**. Situational contingencies are the environmental conditions — time, people, budget, and physical work facilities — that constrain or facilitate employee behaviour and performance.[10] They are beyond the individual's control, at least in the short term.

Some situational contingencies — such as the economy and consumer preferences — interfere with employee performance and are mainly beyond the control of both employees and the organization. For instance, a sales representative may have more difficulty selling the product or service when the economy enters a recession or when a sales area includes fewer people who would purchase the item. Other situational contingencies can be altered by the organization to redirect individual behaviour and performance. Bell Canada successfully used this strategy to reduce wasteful behaviour among its employees. As we see in Perspective 2.1, the telecommunications company encouraged more environmentally friendly behaviours by removing resources that supported wasteful behaviour and by introducing resources that supported desired behaviours.

Types of Work-Related Behaviour

People engage in many different types of behaviour in organizational settings. Exhibit 2.2 highlights five types of behaviour discussed most often in the organizational behaviour literature: joining the organization, remaining with the organization, maintaining work attendance, performing required tasks, and exhibiting organizational citizenship.

Joining the organization
Organizations need to attract qualified people to accomplish their goals and serve stakeholders. Some companies try to motivate qualified applicants to accept employment

---

PERSPECTIVE 2.1

Situational Contingencies Reduce Waste at Bell Canada

It's never easy to change old habits. So when it came to reducing waste, Bell Canada used situational contingencies that forced employees to change their wasteful behaviour.

Bell Canada's Zero Waste program was successful, in part, because it created barriers to wasteful behaviour. Paper towels were replaced with electric hand dryers in the washrooms. Disposable cups were replaced with reusable mugs at each employee's desk. Metal garbage cans at each workstation were replaced with plastic recycling bins. Employees were left with tiny reusable bags to carry nonrecyclables to specially marked bins located elsewhere in the building.

These situational contingencies forced employees to perform new behaviours that are less wasteful. But the dramatic change did not come easily. One employee explains: "It's hard to get people to change the way they've done things; to think about, when they're going to put something in the pail: 'Oh, can this be recycled?'"

"It was different, unusual," recalls a Bell Canada manager about the first week of the Zero Waste program. "You're walking around with garbage in your hands, not sure where to put it."

Nevertheless, employees broke old habits and the daily garbage levels dropped by more than 90 percent. Zero Waste is now in place at other Bell Canada buildings.

Source: J. Mills, "Bell Sets Example with 'Zero Waste' Program," *Montreal Gazette*, February 14, 1993, p. C3; C. Mahood, "Bell Zeros in on Waste," *Globe & Mail*, May 4, 1992, pp. B1, B2; "Bell Canada," *Inside Guide*, January 1993, pp. 46–48.

EXHIBIT 2.2: Types of Work-Related Behaviour

offers through signing bonuses or larger paycheques.[11] Others use the World Wide Web, to make job opportunities more widely known to applicants. Mississauga-based Nortel receives more than 125,000 "hits" (Web-page viewers) at its job listings Web site *each month*, and gets about 500 electronic résumés each month. Mitel Corp. of Kanata, Ontario, and Royal Bank of Canada have Web sites that guide applicants through the challenges of writing a résumé and preparing for the interview.[12]

Remaining with the organization

After hiring qualified people, organizations usually try to keep them. Low turnover translates into better-qualified employees with a more thorough understanding of the organization. Digital Equipment Corporation selected its Kanata, Ontario, plant as one of the company's premier manufacturing facilities partly because employee turnover is only 2 percent. This kind of stable, skilled workforce keeps defect rates low, reduces recruitment and training costs, and improves on-time delivery. In contrast, Digital's Mexican production facility was recently shut down

because turnover exceeded 15 percent. Excessive turnover resulted in high training costs and low product quality, easily offsetting Mexico's low-wage advantage.[13]

Motivation plays a central role in employee turnover. Employees become dissatisfied with their employment relationship, which motivates them to search for and join another organization with better conditions.[14] Some scholars have recently identified career values as another motivational influence on employee turnover. They refer to a "hobo phenomenon" in which some people have short employment patterns because they reject the idea that long-term employment with one organization is a sign of career success.[15]

Maintaining work attendance

Absenteeism affects the ability of organizations to operate and compete. Not long ago, absenteeism at Cape Breton Development Corp. (Devco) was so bad that its president warned employees: "No company can stand these numbers of absentees and stay competitive."[16] On any given day, about 300 of the 2,300 employees scheduled to work at the government-owned mining company would be off sick. Statistics Canada reports that most companies have more moderate absenteeism rates. Canadians miss 9.1 days of scheduled work each year, on average. Two-thirds of this absenteeism is due to illness or disability, and the remaining one-third is due to personal or family responsibilities.[17]

What causes people to be absent from work? Situational contingencies, such as poor weather, family responsibilities, and transportation problems certainly influence work attendance.[18] Ability is also a factor, such as when a person is incapacitated by illness or injury. Employee motivation to attend is a third factor. Attendance motivation mainly explains why absenteeism is higher in companies with generous sick-leave benefits and among those who are dissatisfied with their jobs or experience a lot of work-related stress. For these people, taking time off is a way to temporarily withdraw from stressful or dissatisfying conditions.[19]

Performing required tasks

Task performance Goal-directed activities that are under the individual's control.

People are hired to perform tasks above a minimum standard. **Task performance** refers to goal-directed activities that are under the individual's control.[20] These include physical behaviours as well as mental processes leading to behaviours. For example, foreign-exchange traders at the Bank of Montreal make decisions and take actions to exchange funds. These traders have certain *performance standards;* that is, their behaviours and the outcomes of those behaviours must exceed a minimum acceptable level.

In most jobs, employees are evaluated on several performance dimensions.[21] Foreign-exchange traders, for example, must be able to identify profitable trades, work cooperatively with clients and co-workers in a stressful environment, assist in training new staff, and work on special telecommunications equipment without error. Each of these performance dimensions requires specific skills and knowledge. Some dimensions are more important than others, but only by considering all performance dimensions can we fully evaluate an employee's contribution to the organization.

Exhibiting organizational citizenship

Rick Boomer, head porter at the Empress Hotel in Victoria, B.C., happened to be in the hotel on his day off when a tour left for Whistler, leaving behind 100 pieces of luggage. Rick rented a one-ton truck, loaded it himself, took the 90-minute ferry ride across Georgia Strait, fought Vancouver's rush-hour traffic, negotiated twisting mountain roads, and delivered the luggage to Whistler Mountain. He took a quick nap, then returned to Victoria for his regular work shift![22]

Rick Boomer's extraordinary actions extend well beyond required job duties. They represent a set of behaviours collectively known as **organizational citizenship**. Organizational citizenship behaviours include avoiding unnecessary conflicts, helping others without selfish intent, gracefully tolerating occasional impositions, being involved in organizational activities, and performing tasks that extend beyond normal role requirements.[23] For example, good organizational citizens work cooperatively with co-workers and share resources. They forgive others for mistakes and help co-workers with their problems.

For the past 50 years, management writers have known that an organization's success depends on organizational citizenship.[24] This view is echoed by today's corporate leaders. "The issue is not that employees are not getting their work done," explains Federal Express Canada vice-president Jon Slangerup. "It's a matter of discretionary effort — having employees do things above and beyond the call of duty every single day. To me, that is the difference between a great company and a good one."[25]

How do employees become good organizational citizens? Awards and other forms of special recognition may be useful, but research has identified two fundamental conditions. One of these is the perceived fairness of the company's treatment of employees.[26] Organizations encourage organizational citizenship by correcting perceptions of injustice in the workplace. The second condition is the degree to which employees hold strong ethical values, particularly a sense of social responsibility or conscientiousness.[27] The social responsibility norm exists when employees are willing to assist others, even when they are aware that this assistance will never be repaid. It is a value learned through lifelong socialization, so organizations might try to hire people with this value.

The model of individual behaviour and performance, as well as the five types of behaviours described above, will be mentioned throughout this book. However, probably the most important influence on this model is individual learning because it affects employee ability, role perceptions, and motivation. The rest of this chapter examines learning in organizational settings.

Organizational citizenship Employee behaviours that extend beyond the usual job duties. They include avoiding unnecessary conflicts, helping others without selfish intent, gracefully tolerating occasional impositions, being involved in organizational activities, and performing tasks that extend beyond normal role requirements.

Learning in Organizations

Learning A relatively permanent change in behaviour (or behaviour tendency) that occurs as a result of a person's interaction with the environment.

Learning is a relatively permanent change in behaviour (or behaviour tendency) that occurs as a result of a person's interaction with the environment.[28] Behaviour change is our only evidence of learning. For example, if a team leader had a tendency to be blunt or rude toward co-workers but doesn't act this way anymore, we say that he or she has learned to interact with others more effectively. Learning occurs when behaviour change is due to interaction with the environment. This means that we learn through our senses, such as through study, observation, and experience. Learning requires a relatively permanent behaviour change. This distinguishes learning from situational contingencies that cause short-term behaviour changes.

Learning influences ability, role perceptions, and motivation in the model of individual behaviour and performance. Learned capabilities, including many of the competencies that companies want employees to possess on the job, are developed through formal and informal learning processes. Employees also clarify role perceptions through learning. At Bell-Northern Research Ltd., for example, employees use a template called NERV (needs, expectations, rights, values) that helps them learn what they need, expect, value, and have a right to receive from each other. Through this learning process, employees at the Ottawa-based research and development centre develop clearer role perceptions by sharing their beliefs and resolving discrepancies.[29]

Lastly, learning is a basic assumption behind many theories of motivation. For example, employees learn to expect certain rewards (or less favourable outcomes) following their behaviour and performance. They develop or lose confidence by learning whether their effort results in desired performance. Feelings of accomplishment and other forms of need fulfilment would be difficult or impossible if employees did not receive information about their work and reactions from co-workers.

Organizational learning
An organization's capacity to acquire, disseminate, and apply knowledge for its survival and success.

Along with its role in individual behaviour, individual learning is essential for **organizational learning**. As explained in Chapter 1, organizational learning is the firm's capacity to acquire, disseminate, and apply knowledge for its survival and success.[30] Through individual learning and other knowledge-acquisition strategies, firms develop **intellectual capital** — the knowledge that resides in the organization. Successful organizations leverage this acquired knowledge by disseminating and fully utilizing it. Perspective 2.2 describes how Kao Infosystems Canada Inc. has become one of the world's most productive manufacturers of computer disks by developing intellectual capital through individual learning.

Intellectual capital The knowledge that resides in an organization, including its human, organizational, and customer capital.

Learning Explicit and Tacit Knowledge

When employees learn, they acquire both explicit and tacit knowledge. Explicit knowledge is organized and can be communicated from one person to another. The information you receive in a lecture is mainly explicit knowledge because the instructor packages

---

PERSPECTIVE 2.2

Kao Infosystems Canada Boosts Productivity Through Continuous Learning

Brian Dyer can operate a dozen different types of production equipment at computer-diskette manufacturer Kao Infosystems Canada Inc. The senior manufacturing technician also understands magnetic theory, digital electronics, and computer-aided design.

Yehiel Sobol, Kao Infosystem Canada's president, explains that an ideal operator-technician at the Arnprior, Ontario, plant "can run the operation and do basic repair on the equipment, deal with suppliers, give customer tours, and make presentations to senior management. We won't have as many of them per unit produced, but they'll be multiskilled and well paid."

Kao has created a learning culture in which employees are motivated to continuously learn new competencies.

"Training is not an option here," says Sobol. "If you want a salary increase, you have to study." In fact, up to 25 percent of the employees' pay is tied to their ability to pass training courses and demonstrate higher productivity on the job.

Kao Corp., the Japanese soap-making giant that owns Kao Canada, isn't complaining about the cost of training and other forms of learning at its Arnprior facility. Kao has tripled its output of computer diskettes with only 20 percent more employees. The company is now spending millions to enter the CD-manufacturing business. But to make the technology work, Kao needs a multiskilled workforce. "We need production-level people who have good technical skills and a solid knowledge base," says Yehiel Sobol.

Source: M. Salter, "Not-So-Smart Technology," *Canadian Business,* Technology Issue (May 1995), p. 62; J. Bagnall, "Kao Now: Why This Diskette Maker Is a Training Success," *Financial Times of Canada,* November 28, 1992, pp. 1, 4, 6; and "Canadian Disk Maker Expands," *Winnipeg Free Press,* November 24, 1992, p. B10.

and consciously transfers it to you. Explicit knowledge can be written down and given to others. However, explicit knowledge is really only the tip of the knowledge iceberg.

Tacit knowledge Subtle information, acquired through observation and experience, that is not clearly understood and therefore cannot be explicitly communicated.

Most of what we know is **tacit knowledge**.[31] Tacit knowledge is subtle information acquired through observation and experience, that is not clearly understood and therefore cannot be explicitly communicated. You have probably said to someone: "I can't tell you how to do this, but I can show you." The knowledge and skills you want to give to others are complex and not completely understood. Consequently, tacit knowledge is acquired through observation and direct experience.[32] For example, airline pilots do not learn how to operate a commercial jet simply by being told how to do it. They master the necessary skills by watching the subtle details as others perform the tasks, and by directly experiencing this complex interaction of behaviour with the machine's response.

Learning occurs in many ways. The discussion that follows identifies four perspectives of learning: reinforcement, feedback, social learning (observation), and direct experience. These activities are not completely different (for example, feedback can be viewed as a form of reinforcement). Rather, they provide different views of the learning process and, by understanding each of these perspectives, we can more fully appreciate the dynamics of learning.

OB Modification: Learning Through Reinforcement

Organizational behaviour modification A theory that explains learning in terms of the antecedents and consequences of behaviour.

Behaviourism A perspective that focuses entirely on behaviour and observable events, rather than on a person's thoughts.

One of the oldest, and arguably the most radical, perspectives of learning in organizational settings is **organizational behaviour modification** (OB Mod).[33] OB Mod emphasizes the environment, rather than human thought, as the source of all learning. It does not question the existence of human thoughts, but views them as unimportant intermediate stages between behaviour and the environment. Because it focuses on behaviour without reference to human thoughts, OB Mod is called a theory of **behaviourism**.

A-B-Cs of OB Modification

The OB Mod process is easy to remember with the help of the A-B-C model shown in Exhibit 2.3. The central objective of OB Mod is to change behaviour (B) by managing its antecedents (A) and consequences (C).[34]

Antecedents are events preceding the behaviour, informing employees that certain behaviours will have particular consequences. An antecedent may be an e-mail advising you about a new incentive program, or it may be a request from your supervisor to complete a specific task by tomorrow. These events are antecedents because they are cues. They signal employees to establish certain behaviours in order for certain consequences to occur.

Although antecedents are important, OB Mod mainly focuses on the consequences of behaviour. *Consequences* are events following a particular behaviour that influence its future occurrence. This concept is based on the law of effect. If a behaviour is followed by a pleasant experience, the person is more likely to repeat the behaviour. If the behaviour is followed by an unpleasant experience or by no response at all, the person is less likely to repeat it.

With its purely behaviourist approach, OB Mod is admittedly a narrow perspective of learning. However, it has a lot to say about how environmental conditions influence learning and behaviour. OB Mod is particularly useful for identifying four types of consequences and the five schedules to administer these consequences discussed below.

EXHIBIT 2.3: A-B-Cs of OB Modification

OB Mod Steps

Examples

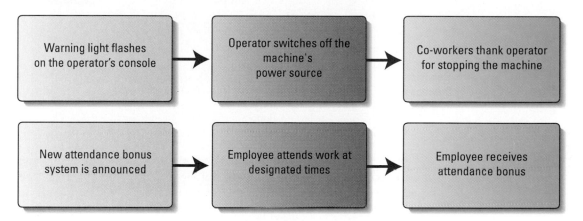

Source: Adapted from T.K. Connellan, *How to Improve Human Performance*, (New York: Harper & Row, 1978), pg. 50; F. Luthans and R. Kreitner, *Organizational Behaviour Modification and Beyond*, (Glenview, Ill.: Scott, Foresman, 1985), pp. 85–88.

Contingencies of Reinforcement*

Positive reinforcement
Occurs when the introduction of a consequence increases or maintains the frequency or future probability of the behaviour preceding that event.

Extinction Occurs when the removal or withholding of a consequence decreases the frequency or future probability of the behaviour preceding that event.

Punishment Occurs when the introduction of a consequence decreases the frequency or future probability of the behaviour preceding that event.

OB Mod identifies four types of consequences, collectively known as the *contingencies of reinforcement*, that strengthen, maintain, or weaken behaviour. As we see in Exhibit 2.4, these contingencies are positive reinforcement, extinction, negative reinforcement, and punishment.[35]

- *Positive reinforcement* **Positive reinforcement** occurs when the *introduction* of a consequence *increases or maintains* the frequency or future probability of a behaviour. A compliment from a co-worker on your presentation would be positive reinforcement if it increases the probability that you use those behaviours in the future.

- *Extinction* **Extinction** occurs when a consequence is *removed, withheld,* or *terminated* and this *decreases* the frequency or future probability of a behaviour. For example, if your performance slips and you stop receiving a bonus, then you are less likely to do things that caused your performance to slip (such as taking long lunches, talking too much with co-workers, etc.). Behaviour that is no longer reinforced tends to disappear or be extinguished. In this respect, extinction is a do-nothing strategy.[36]

- *Punishment* **Punishment** occurs when the *introduction* of a consequence *decreases* the frequency or future probability of a behaviour. An example would be warning someone that he or she will be fired if job performance does not improve.

EXHIBIT 2.4: Contingencies of Reinforcement

	Consequence is Introduced	Consequence is Removed or Withheld
Behaviour Increases or is Maintained	Positive Reinforcement Example: A co-worker compliments you on your presentation.	Negative Reinforcement Example: Supervisor stops criticizing you when your job performance improves.
Behaviour Decreases	Punishment Example: You are warned that you will be fired if your job performance remains substandard.	Extinction Example: You stop receiving a bonus after your job performance slips.

Negative reinforcement
Occurs when the removal or termination of a consequence increases or maintains the frequency or future probability of the behaviour preceding that event.

- *Negative reinforcement* **Negative reinforcement** occurs when the *removal or termination* of a consequence *increases or maintains* the frequency or future probability of a behaviour. Supervisors apply negative reinforcement when they stop criticizing employees whose substandard performance has improved. By withholding the criticism, employees are more likely to repeat behaviours that improved their performance.[37]

Negative reinforcement and punishment are easy to mix up. As we see in Exhibit 2.5, punishment occurs when you receive a negative consequence, such as having your boss criticize you for serving customers too slowly. Negative reinforcement removes negative consequences, such as occurs when your boss stops criticizing you. Punishment reduces the frequency or likelihood of a behaviour. For instance, after your boss criticizes your performance, you are less likely to do things (such as chatting with co-workers) that cause slow service. Negative reinforcement, on the other hand, increases the frequency or likelihood of a behaviour. Thus, you are more likely to repeat the behaviours that provide speedier customer service.

Comparing reinforcement contingencies

All four reinforcement contingencies are found in organizations, but which is best? Conventional wisdom suggests that we should follow desired behaviours with positive reinforcement and follow undesirable behaviours with extinction (removing or withholding the positive reinforcer). This may work for most behaviours, but not all. Few companies would merely withhold an employee's bonus if he or she

EXHIBIT 2.5: Comparing Punishment with Negative Reinforcement

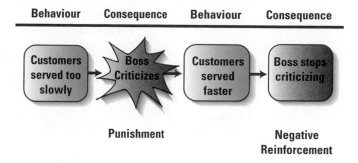

seriously hurt a co-worker or was caught stealing inventory. For these extreme behaviours, some form of punishment (dismissal, suspension, demotion, etc.) seems more likely.

Some theorists suggest that punishment is a necessary part of organizational life because it maintains a sense of equity.[38] Research indicates that employees who are disciplined believe this action maintains justice in the workplace. Co-workers are often eager to hear about an employee's punishment through the grapevine because it fulfils their need for social justice.

Unfortunately, organizations tend to be inconsistent in their administration of punishment, so justice through discipline is an elusive goal.[39] Moreover, punishment is usually an emotionally charged event that creates negative feelings and undermines the employee's ability to learn from the punishment.[40] In extreme cases, employees develop hostilities toward the organization that may result in aggression and other forms of dysfunctional behaviour. This happened at a Frito-Lay plant where managers fired 58 of the 210 employees in less than one year. The remaining employees retaliated by putting obscene messages on the potato chips they packaged.[41]

Schedules of Reinforcement

Along with the types of consequences, OB Mod identifies the timetable or schedule that should be followed to maximize the reinforcement effect. In fact, there is some evidence that scheduling the reinforcer affects learning more than the size of the reinforcer.[42]

OB Mod theorists have identified five schedules of reinforcement. One of these is **continuous reinforcement** — reinforcing every occurrence of the desired behaviour. This produces the most rapid learning of the targetted behaviour. When the reinforcer is removed, extinction also occurs very quickly. Continuous reinforcement is most effective for employees learning new behaviours. When practising new skills, trainees might receive immediate reinforcement from the computer whenever they perform the correct action.

The other four schedules of reinforcement are intermittent because reinforcement does not occur every time or with every behaviour. Instead, intermittent schedules apply the reinforcer after a fixed or variable time (interval) or number of target behaviours (ratio). As illustrated in Exhibit 2.6, a fixed schedule means that the reinforcer is introduced after the same number of behaviours or time units, whereas a variable schedule means that the reinforcer varies randomly around an average number of behaviours or time units.

Continuous reinforcement
A schedule that reinforces behaviour every time it occurs.

EXHIBIT 2.6: Schedules of Reinforcement

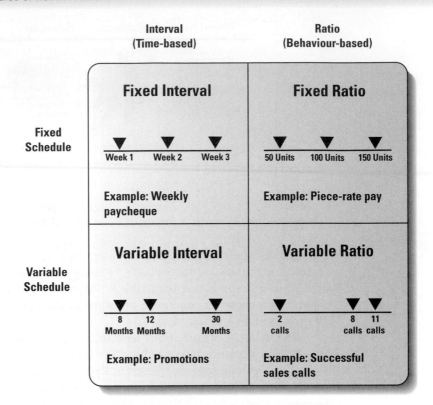

Fixed interval schedule
A schedule that reinforces behaviour after it has occurred for a fixed period of time.

Variable interval schedule A schedule that reinforces behaviour after it has occurred for a variable period of time around some average.

Fixed ratio schedule A schedule that reinforces behaviour after it has occurred a fixed number of times.

Variable ratio schedule A schedule that reinforces behaviour after it has occurred a varying number of times around some average.

The **fixed interval schedule** occurs when behaviour is reinforced after a fixed period of time. Most people get paid on a fixed interval schedule because their paycheques are received every week or two weeks. As long as the job is performed satisfactorily, a paycheque is received on the appointed day. The **variable interval schedule** involves administering the reinforcer after a varying length of time. Promotions typically follow this schedule because they occur at uneven time intervals. The first promotion might be received after two years of good performance, the next after four years, and the third after 18 months, and so on. Promotions are interval-based because they are typically received after a period of time rather than after a desired number of behaviours.

The **fixed ratio schedule** reinforces behaviour after it has occurred a fixed number of times. Some piece-rate systems follow this schedule where employees get paid after they produce a fixed number of units. The **variable ratio schedule** reinforces behaviour after it occurs a varying number of times. Salespeople experience variable ratio reinforcement because they make a successful sale (the reinforcer) after a varying number of client calls. They might make four unsuccessful calls before receiving an order on the fifth one. This is followed by 15 unsuccessful sales calls before another sale is made. One successful sale might be made after 10 calls, on average, but this does not mean that every tenth call will be successful. Behaviour that has been reinforced with a variable ratio schedule is highly resistant to extinction. This schedule is also cost-effective because employees are rewarded infrequently using a random timetable.

Shaping Complex Behaviour

Ideally, people are reinforced only when they exhibit desired behaviour, but many tasks are very complex or difficult to master. Without some early reinforcement, employees become frustrated as they continually fail to produce the ideal behaviour.

The solution to this dilemma is to initially reinforce crude approximations of the ideal behaviour, then increase the reinforcement standard until only the ideal behaviour is rewarded. This process, called **shaping**, directs employee behaviour from crude approximations to the ideal form through continuous reinforcement.[43] For instance, a trainee might be praised initially for backing a dump truck anywhere near the desired dump location. As the trainee improves, the supervisor would provide praise only as the truck is placed close to the dump location and eventually only when the vehicle is driven to the ideal location.

Shaping The strategy of initially reinforcing crude approximations of the ideal behaviour, then increasing reinforcement standards until only the ideal behaviour is rewarded.

OB Mod in Practice

Organizational behaviour modification has been widely used in industry as a formal process of learning and behaviour change. For example, one recent study demonstrated how OB Mod reduced labour costs of a roofing crew by 64 percent. A second intervention resulted in significantly improved compliance with safe behaviours. When OB Mod practices were applied to banquet staff at a hotel, the group's performance on a quality measure (setting up completely and on time) jumped from 68.8 to more than 99 percent. OB Mod has also been applied with favourable results in a Russian cotton mill.[44]

In Canada, OB Mod principles have been successfully applied at Marine Atlantic, the federally owned Crown corporation that operates ferry services in the Atlantic provinces. Perspective 2.3 describes some of these OB Mod practices and how they improved Marine Atlantic's productivity, putting the ferry service in a better position for the challenges that lie ahead.

Limitations of OB Mod

OB Mod isn't always cost-effective, and it certainly has a number of limitations.[45] Here are its main problems:

- *Can't reinforce nonobservable behaviour*   OB Mod may work with easily observed behaviours, such as work attendance, but it's more difficult to reinforce conceptual activities, such as making good decisions.

- *Reinforcer tends to wear off*   OB Mod programs often suffer from "reward inflation," in which the reinforcer either is quickly forgotten or is eventually considered an entitlement. In other words, a bonus that was once an unexpected surprise becomes an expected part of the employment relationship. Removing the reinforcer may represent extinction, but it feels like punishment![46]

- *Variable ratio schedule is a form of gambling*   The variable ratio schedule may be best for maintaining behaviour, but it also resembles a lottery. Some people worry about the ethical nature of this schedule because employees are essentially betting that they will receive a reinforcer after the next behaviour. A forest products firm that tried a variable ratio schedule discovered that some of its employees who held strong anti-gambling beliefs were repulsed by these OB Mod practices.[47]

PERSPECTIVE 2.3

Marine Atlantic Sails Through Rough Waters with OB Mod and Feedback

Marine Atlantic Inc., the Moncton-based Crown corporation that runs ferry services in Atlantic Canada, was heading into rough waters during the early 1990s. Customer service was poor, government funding was threatened, and the risk of competition was increasing. When Terry Ivany was hired as Marine Atlantic's chief executive officer, one of his first tasks was to apply organizational behaviour modification and feedback practices to improve efficiency and customer service.

Important information about each department's past performance is posted so that employees can discover ways to become more efficient and effective. Ivany explains: "The idea is for each supervisor and employee or team of employees to identify what is important, to put in place a data system to measure performance, to provide detailed feedback in graph form, to positively reinforce success, and to celebrate the achievement of measurable results."

For example, with the aid of charts showing how much it costs to run the cafeteria, kitchen-staff members aboard each ferry learned how to reduce those costs. This feedback was further supported by a new service-excellence program that taught supervisors how to create measurement and feedback systems, give positive reinforcement, facilitate consensus decision making, and deal with conflict.

Marine Atlantic's application of OB Mod and feedback paid off in many ways. Customer satisfaction ratings soared. Employees significantly cut costs in most areas of the organization, saving Canadian taxpayers millions of

Courtesy of Marine Atlantic.

Marine Atlantic Inc. relied on OB Mod and feedback to improve customer service and work efficiency.

dollars in annual operating subsidies. These successes also gave the Canadian government a better opportunity to consider privatizing Marine Atlantic rather than impose further cuts.

Source: J. Schilder, "White Water, Safe Passage," *Human Resource Professional*, June 1993, pp. 13–16; K. Cox, "A Drifting Crew Finds an Anchor," *Globe & Mail*, March 23, 1993, p. B22; "Smooth Sailing," *Commercial News*, September 1992, pp. 22–23.

- *Ethical concerns about perceived manipulation*   Some critics say that OB Mod tries to manipulate employee behaviour and treat people as animals with low intelligence.[48] This perception occurs largely because OB Mod holds a behaviourist perspective and tends to ignore human thoughts. In response, OB Mod experts point out that any attempt to change employee behaviour is a form of manipulation. No matter how valid this counterargument, OB Mod has an image problem that will remain for some time to come.

Learning Through Feedback

Feedback Any information that people receive about the consequences of their behaviour.

When the Conference Board asked human resource executives to identify the primary causes of poor performance, the top-ranked problem was poor or insufficient feedback to employees.[49] **Feedback** is any information that people receive about the consequences of their behaviour. Feedback may be an antecedent or a consequence, if we look at it from an OB Mod perspective. However, our discussion of learning through feedback will take a broader view by considering the effects on employee thoughts as well as behaviours.

As with other forms of learning, feedback has a powerful effect on behaviour and job performance by improving role perceptions, ability, and motivation.[50] With respect to role perceptions, feedback lets people know what behaviours are appropriate or necessary in a particular situation.[51] For example, your boss might remind you to spend more time on a certain activity and less on another. Feedback improves employee ability by frequently providing information to correct performance problems.[52] Employees develop better skills and acquire job-related information by watching instrument dials or nonverbal cues from customers. This is known as *corrective feedback* because it makes people aware of their performance errors and helps them correct those errors quickly.

Feedback is a source of motivation. As we shall learn in Chapter 3, positive feedback fulfils personal needs and makes people more confident that they are able to accomplish certain tasks. Connectix, Inc. (maker of RamDoubler) uses feedback in this way. The software company distributes letters from happy customers to employees who have worked on those projects. This customer feedback has a powerful effect on employee motivation. Whenever a difficult problem arises, the letters boost a product team's confidence and drive to get the job done.[53]

Feedback Sources

Feedback can originate from social or nonsocial sources. Social sources include supervisors, clients, co-workers, and anyone else who provides information about the employee's behaviour or results. BC Gas, Consumers Gas Co. Ltd., Nortel, and Aetna Life Insurance are some of the firms that use multisource feedback, in which employees receive performance feedback from several people.[54] This is often called **360-degree feedback** because feedback is received from a full circle of people around the employee (see Exhibit 2.7). At Pepsi-Cola Company, managers receive feedback from five salespeople, three managers at their level, and their immediate supervisor. Multisource feedback may be received directly and anonymously, or indirectly through the employee's supervisor in a single performance review.[55]

The main reason for implementing multisource feedback is that supervisors usually do not observe employees on all performance dimensions. Subordinates may have the best information about the employee's leadership and interpersonal skills. Supervisors may have the best view of the employee's task orientation. Customers provide the best information about the individual's service orientation. By receiving feedback from a representative sample of these people, the employee gets more accurate and complete feedback.

Along with social sources, employees usually receive nonsocial sources of feedback. With the click of a computer mouse, a marketing manager at Xerox Canada can look at the previous day's sales and compare them with the results from any other day over the previous year. At Carpenter Technology, Inc., a computer monitoring system lets any employee receive feedback on the productivity of any machine and the status of any work order going through the specialty metals plant.[56] The job itself can also be a source of feedback. Many employees see the results of their work effort by looking directly at the finished product.

The preferred feedback source depends on the purpose of the information. To learn about their progress toward goal accomplishment, employees usually prefer nonsocial feedback sources, such as computer printouts or feedback directly from the job.[57] This is because information from nonsocial sources is considered more accurate than from social sources. Corrective feedback from nonsocial sources is also less

360-degree feedback
Performance feedback is received from a full circle of people around the employee.

EXHIBIT 2.7: 360-Degree Feedback

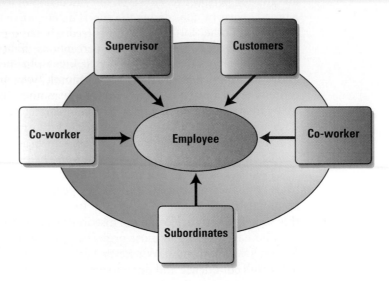

damaging to self-esteem. This is probably just as well because social sources aren't very accurate when communicating negative feedback. They tend to delay negative information, leave some of it out, and distort the bad news in a positive way.[58]

When employees want to improve their self-image, they seek out positive feedback from social sources. It feels better to have co-workers say that you are performing the job well than to discover this from a computer printout.[59] Positive feedback from co-workers and other social sources motivates mainly because it fulfils social (relatedness) as well as growth needs (see Chapter 3).

Giving Feedback Effectively

Whether feedback is received from a supervisor or statistical control system, it should be specific, sufficiently frequent, timely, credible, and relevant.

- *Specific feedback* Feedback should include specific information such as "you exceeded your sales quota by 5 percent last month" rather than subjective and general phrases such as "your sales are going well." This helps employees redirect their effort and behaviour more precisely and gives them a greater sense of accomplishment when the feedback is positive.

- *Frequent feedback* Feedback should be continuously available to employees from nonsocial sources so they can adjust the feedback frequency to suit their needs. If feedback must be provided by someone else, the optimal frequency depends on the task cycle (how long until the task is completed) and task uniqueness. Cashiers and assembly-line workers have very short cycles (they finish working with a customer or product unit in a few minutes), so they should receive feedback more often than people with long cycles (executives, salespeople). Employees working on unique tasks should also receive more frequent feedback because they require more behaviour guidance and reinforcement.

- *Timely feedback* Feedback should be available as soon as possible so that employees see a clear association between their behaviour and its consequences.[60] Computers and other electronic monitoring systems can sometimes provide timely feedback, but usually only for routine behaviour.

- *Credible feedback*   Employees are more likely to accept feedback (particularly corrective feedback) from trustworthy and credible sources.[61] Multisource feedback has higher credibility because it comes from several people. Employees are also more likely to accept corrective feedback from nonsocial sources (e.g., computer printouts, electronic gauges) because it is not as judgmental.

- *Relevant feedback*   Feedback must relate to the individual's behaviour rather than to conditions beyond the individual's control. This ensures that the feedback is not distorted by situational contingencies.[62] Feedback is also relevant when it is linked to goals. Goals establish the benchmarks (i.e., what ought to be) against which feedback is judged.

Seeking Feedback

So far, we have presented the traditional view that supervisors and others give feedback to employees. However, employees do not just passively receive feedback; they actively seek it.[63] The most obvious way to do this is through *inquiry* — asking other people about our performance and behaviour. This feedback-seeking tactic tends to be used when individuals have high self-esteem, expect to receive positive feedback, and work in an organization that values openness.

The main problem with direct inquiry is that it can create awkward moments for both the sender and receiver. Imagine watching a co-worker perform a task badly, and then have the person proudly ask you, "How am I doing?" As we noted earlier, supervisors and co-workers tend to provide inaccurate feedback when the information is negative. Moreover, it is more difficult to save face when receiving negative feedback in response to a direct request. A third problem is that inquiry is only possible when someone else is available and has time to answer questions.

Thus, employees often use other feedback-seeking tactics. The most common of these is *monitoring*. This involves scanning the work environment and the behaviour of others for information cues. Monitoring occurs in various ways. Salespeople monitor the nonverbal cues of customers during a transaction. Executives monitor corporate data to determine whether their strategies have worked. Monitoring avoids problems with saving face because it usually comes from a nonsocial source or nonverbal cues of a social source. Also, monitoring can usually occur at any time and is quite efficient. For instance, instrument dials can help production employees monitor the quality of their work quickly and without bothering others.

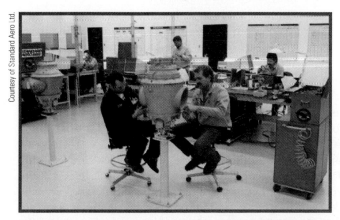

Courtesy of Standard Aero Ltd.

These employees at Standard Aero Ltd. in Winnipeg receive feedback directly by observing the results of their work. By using their senses, they can quickly detect and correct errors while working on this aircraft engine.

Ethics of Employee Monitoring

One of the more contentious issues in feedback management is monitoring employee performance.[64] According to one study, most of Canada's service firms monitor employee transactions, mistakes, keystrokes, completion time, or other forms of performance either through supervisors or computers.[65] Air Canada managers listen to conversations between customers and reservation agents. TD Greenline managers monitor how quickly employees answer customer calls. Some Canadian food retailers electronically monitor cashier performance. Transit companies time bus drivers along their routes. An extreme example is found at a U.S.-based company that processes direct-mail ad responses. Eight TV cameras can zoom in on a desk at any time. Employees must make 8,500 keystrokes an hour, and any failure to achieve this norm is electronically noted and punished.[66]

Critics view employee monitoring as a repressive management-control practice and an invasion of employee privacy.[67] For instance, some physicians were appalled when the University of Alberta Hospitals installed a computer system to monitor each patient's length of hospital stay and other expenses. "Some doctors were upset that we were keeping track of them to that extent," recalls the head of the surgery department.[68]

Companies argue that workplace monitoring gives employees more accurate feedback to improve product or service quality. It also protects company assets and provides a safer workplace.[69] Some studies confirm that employees see monitoring as a necessary evil. They are worried about invasion of privacy, but are willing to be monitored when the information only provides developmental feedback.[70]

Social Learning Theory: Learning by Observing

Social learning theory A theory stating that learning mainly occurs by observing others and then modelling the behaviours that lead to favourable outcomes and avoiding behaviours that lead to punishing consequences.

Feedback and organizational behaviour modification mainly consider learning through direct experience with the environment. However, we also learn by observing the behaviours and consequences of other people. **Social learning theory** states that much learning occurs by observing others, then modelling the behaviours that lead to favourable outcomes and avoiding behaviours that lead to punishing consequences.[71] There are three related features of social learning theory: behavioural modelling, learning behaviour consequences, and self-reinforcement.

Behavioural Modelling

People learn by observing the behaviours of a role model on the critical task, remembering the important elements of the observed behaviours, and then practising those behaviours.[72] Behavioural modelling works best when the model is respected and the model's actions are followed by favourable consequences. For instance, recently hired college graduates should learn by watching a previously hired college graduate who successfully performs the task.

Behavioural modelling is a valuable form of learning because tacit knowledge and skills are mainly acquired from others in this way. Earlier in the chapter, we explained that tacit knowledge is the subtle information about required behaviours, the correct sequence of those actions, and the environmental consequences (such as a machine response or customer reply) that should occur after each action. The adage that a picture is worth a thousand words applies here. It is difficult to document or verbally explain how a master baker kneads dough better than someone less qualified. Instead, we must observe these subtle actions to develop a more precise mental model of the required behaviours and the expected responses.

Behavioural modelling also guides role perceptions. Leaders model the behaviour that they expect from others, for example. Procter & Gamble relied on this form of learning to ensure that employees wear protective eyewear in a hazardous work area. Managers were told always to wear safety glasses in the area in order to convey the importance of safety. This practice, along with a large sign asking employees to wear safety equipment at this site, resulted in a dramatic increase in compliance.[73]

Behaviour modelling and self-efficacy

A third reason behavioural modelling is effective is that it enhances the observer's **self-efficacy**. Self-efficacy refers to a person's belief that he or she has the ability, motivation, and situational contingencies to complete a task successfully.[74] People with high self-efficacy have a "can-do" attitude toward a specific task and, more generally, with other challenges in life.

Behavioural modelling increases self-efficacy because people gain more self-confidence after seeing someone else perform the task than if they are simply told what to do. This is particularly true when observers identify with the model, such as someone who is similar in age, experience, gender, and related features. They form a "can-do" attitude when it becomes apparent that others who are similar to them are able to perform the task.

Self-efficacy is also affected by initial experiences when practising the previously modelled behaviour. Observers gain confidence when the environmental cues follow a predictable pattern and there are no unexpected surprises when practising the behaviour.[75] For example, computer trainees develop a stronger self-efficacy when they click the mouse and get the same computer response as the model did when performing the same behaviour. The expected response gives trainees a greater sense of control over the computer because they can predict what will happen following a particular behaviour.

Learning Behaviour Consequences

A second element of social learning theory says that we learn by observing the *consequences* that other people experience following their behaviour. Whereas OB Mod says that our future behaviour is reinforced by our own past behaviour consequences, social learning theory says that we also learn to *anticipate* these consequences by observing the experiences of other people. Consider the employee who observes a co-worker receiving a stern warning for working in an unsafe manner. This event would reduce the observer's likelihood of engaging in unsafe behaviours because he or she has learned to anticipate a similar reprimand following those behaviours.[76]

Self-Reinforcement

Social learning theory recognizes that we often engage in *self-reinforcement*. Self-reinforcement occurs whenever an employee has control over a reinforcer but doesn't "take" the reinforcer until completing a self-set goal.[77] You might have authority to take a break from work at any time, but you don't use this privilege until a certain amount of work is completed. The work break is a form of positive reinforcement that is self-induced. You use the work break to reinforce completion of a task. Numerous consequences may be applied in self-reinforcement, including congratulating yourself for completing the task.[78] Self-reinforcement has become increasingly important because employees are given more control over their working lives and are less dependent on supervisors to dole out positive reinforcement and punishment.

Self-efficacy A person's belief that he or she has the ability, motivation, and situational contingencies to complete a task successfully.

Learning Through Experience

The classroom is surrounded by trees at International Forest Products Ltd. (Interfor). The Canadian forest products company introduced a peer trainer program in which specially trained employees provide hands-on, just-in-time learning to co-workers right in the forest. Rather than going to off-site lectures, Interfor employees can now learn a new skill on the job when they need it (i.e., just-in-time) from a peer trainer. Interfor has less down time and its employees receive a more thorough understanding of the training topic.[79]

Interfor and other organizations are discarding the notion that learning is measured by the number of hours employees spend in the classroom. Instead, most learning occurs when employees directly interact with their environment, whether it is experimenting with a new software program or learning better forestry practices on-site from a trained co-worker. "The more you separate learning from the job, the less effective and competitive you're going to be," says Lucy Carter, Apple Computer's training director.[80]

Implicit learning The experiential phenomenon of acquiring information about relationships in the environment without any conscious attempt to do so.

Learning through experience is important because tacit knowledge and skills are acquired through experience as well as observation. Thus, much of our learning takes place while practising new behaviours and watching the environmental responses to our actions. This also relates to the concept of **implicit learning**. Implicit learning occurs when we acquire information about relationships in the environment without any conscious attempt to do so.[81] In other words, we aren't even aware of much of the information we acquire. Most implicit learning occurs when we interact with the environment, such as when we work with customers or operate a machine. Less implicit learning occurs off the job because knowledge about the environment is indirect.

Courtesy of International Forest Products Ltd.

At International Forest Products Ltd., employees learn in the woods, not just in the classroom. Peer trainers provide on-site instruction and practice so there's less down time and employees receive a more complete understanding of the training topic.

Practising Learning Through Experience

Learning by doing must occur within a learning culture. In other words, the organization or immediate work unit must value the process of individual and team learning. It does this by establishing an environment that rewards experimentation and recognizes mistakes as a natural part of the learning process. Without these conditions, mistakes are hidden and problems are more likely to escalate or re-emerge later.[82] Coca-Cola recently *celebrated* the tenth anniversary of the launch of New Coke to demonstrate the value of making mistakes. "We celebrated the failure because it led to fundamental learning and showed that it's okay to fail," explains Neville Isdell, president of Coca-Cola's Greater Europe Group. Mistakes are thoroughly studied so that Coke employees learn from them, but the errors are viewed as part of the experiential learning process.[83]

Along with a learning culture, learning through experience is nurtured through structures that support an ongoing learning process. The peer training system at Interfor is one such example. Vancouver City Savings Credit Union (VanCity) has also introduced this form of hands-on just-in-time training. Employees are placed into learning teams and a system is implemented whereby team members learn specific skills and knowledge from each other on the job. The team is assigned responsibility for the learning process, including the need to put any theory into practice.[84]

Action learning A form of on-site, experiential-based learning in which participants investigate an organizational problem or opportunity and possibly implement their solution.

Action learning is another form of on-site, experiential-based learning. Action learning typically involves the formation of cross-functional teams that investigate an organizational problem or opportunity, write up their recommendation, and meet with senior executives to discuss their results. In some cases, the teams are asked to help implement the recommendation. Britvic, a leading British soft drink manufacturer, recently applied this learning strategy with 30 employees across the organization. The teams identified changes that eventually saved Britvic more than $6 million. More than 50 percent of the employees in Britvic's action learning pilot program were subsequently promoted.[85]

Chapter Summary

- Individual behaviour is influenced by motivation, ability, role perceptions, and situational contingencies. Motivation consists of internal forces that affect the direction, intensity, and persistence of a person's voluntary choice of behaviour. Ability includes both the natural aptitudes and learned capabilities to perform a task. Role perceptions are a person's beliefs about what behaviours are appropriate or necessary in a particular situation. Situational contingencies are environmental conditions that constrain or facilitate employee behaviour and performance. These four factors influence various types of behaviour, including joining the organization, remaining with the organization, maintaining work attendance, performing required job duties, and exhibiting organizational citizenship.

- Learning is a relatively permanent change in behaviour (or behaviour tendency) that occurs as a result of a person's interaction with the environment. Learning influences ability, role perceptions, and motivation in the model of individual behaviour. The four main perspectives of learning in organizations are reinforcement, feedback, social learning, and direct experience.

- OB Mod is a behaviourist view of learning based on the law of effect. According to this view, behaviour change occurs by altering its antecedents and consequences. Antecedents are environmental stimuli that provoke (not necessarily cause) behaviour. Consequences are events following behaviour that influence its future occurrence. Consequences include positive reinforcement, negative reinforcement, punishment, and extinction. The schedules of reinforcement also influence behaviour.

- Feedback is any information that people receive about the consequences of their behaviour. It affects role perceptions, learning (through corrective feedback), and employee motivation. Employees prefer nonsocial sources of feedback to learn about their goal progress. They prefer positive feedback from social sources to improve their self-image. Effective feedback is specific, frequent, timely, credible, and relevant. Employees seek out feedback rather than passively receive it. Although employee monitoring is sometimes necessary for feedback, it raises ethical concerns.

- Social learning theory states that much learning occurs by observing others, then modelling those behaviours that seem to lead to favourable outcomes and avoiding behaviours that lead to punishing consequences. It also recognizes that we often engage in self-reinforcement. Behavioural modelling is effective because it transfers tacit knowledge and enhances the observer's self-efficacy.

- Many companies now use peer trainers, action learning, and other experiential-based methods of employee learning. Learning through experience is an effective way of acquiring tacit knowledge and skills and is consistent with the implicit learning process.

Discussion Questions

1. An insurance company has high levels of absenteeism among the office staff. The head of office administration argues that employees are misusing the company's sick-leave benefits. However, some of the mostly female staff members have explained that family responsibilities interfere with work. Using the model of individual behaviour and performance, as well as your knowledge of absenteeism behaviour, discuss some of the possible reasons for absenteeism in this company and suggest ways how it might be reduced.

2. Contrast organizational citizenship behaviour with job performance.

3. You notice that the sales representative for Eastern Ontario made 20 percent fewer sales to new clients over the past quarter than salespeople located elsewhere in Canada. Use the model of individual behaviour to explain why his or her performance was lower than the performance of other salespeople.

4. What are the A-B-Cs of OB modification?

5. When do employees prefer feedback from nonsocial rather than social sources? Explain why nonsocial sources are preferred under those conditions.

6. Explain why behaviour modelling is often more effective than direct reinforcement for helping employees learn new behaviours.

7. The person responsible for training and development in your organization wants to build a new training centre where all employees can receive instruction in new skills and knowledge. Why might this idea be an ineffective approach to learning?

8. Describe action learning and explain what benefits it provides over classroom training.

Chapter Case

Pushing Paper Can Be Fun

A large metropolitan city government was putting on a number of seminars for managers of various departments throughout the city. At one of these sessions the topic to be discussed was motivation—how we can get public servants motivated to do a good job. The plight of a police captain became the central focus of the discussion. He explained:

"I've got a real problem with my officers. They come on the force as young, inexperienced rookies, and we send them out on the street, either in cars or on a beat. They seem to like the contact they have with the public, the action involved in crime prevention, and the apprehension of criminals. They also like helping people out at fires, accidents, and other emergencies.

"The problem occurs when they get back to the station. They hate to do the paperwork, and because they dislike it, the job is frequently put off or done inadequately. This lack of attention hurts us later on when we get to court. We need clear, factual reports. They must be highly detailed and unambiguous. As soon as one part of a report is shown to be inadequate or incorrect, the rest of the report is suspect. Poor reporting probably causes us to lose more cases than any other factor.

"I just don't know how to motivate them to do a better job. We're in a budget crunch and I have absolutely no financial rewards at my disposal. In fact, we'll probably have to lay off some people in the near future. It's hard for me to make the job interesting and challenging because it isn't—it's boring, routine paperwork, and there isn't much you can do about it.

"Finally, I can't say to them that their promotions will hinge on the excellence of their paperwork. First

of all, they know it's not true. If their performance is adequate, most are more likely to get promoted just by staying on the force a certain number of years than for some specific outstanding act. Second, they were trained to do the job they do out in the streets, not to fill out forms. All through their career it is the arrests and interventions that get noticed.

"Some people have suggested a number of things, like using conviction records as a performance criterion. However, we know that's not fair—too many other things are involved. Bad paperwork increases the chance that you lose in court, but good paperwork doesn't necessarily mean you'll win. We tried setting up team competitions based upon the excellence of the reports, but the officers caught on to that pretty quickly. No one was getting any type of reward for winning the competition, and they figured why should they bust a gut when there was no payoff.

"I just don't know what to do."

Discussion Questions

1. What performance problems is the captain trying to correct?

2. Use the model of individual behaviour and performance to diagnose the possible causes of the unacceptable behaviour.

3. Has the captain considered all possible solutions to the problem? If not, what else might be done?

Source: T. R. Mitchell and J. R. Larson, Jr., *People in Organizations*, 3rd ed. (New York: McGraw-Hill, 1987), p. 184. Used with permission.

Experiential Exercise #1

Task Performance Exercise

Purpose: This exercise is designed to help you understand how specific behaviours are associated with job performance and how people may have different standards or expectations about which behaviours constitute good performance.

Instructions: The instructor will identify a job that all students know about, such as a bank teller or course instructor. Students will focus on one performance dimension, such as service skills among cafeteria cashiers, technical skills of computer lab technicians, or lecture skills of professors. Whichever performance dimension or job is chosen for your team, the following steps apply:

Step 1:   Students are placed into teams (preferably four or five people).

Step 2:   Working alone, each student writes down five specific examples of effective or ineffective behaviour for the selected job and performance dimension. Each incident should clearly state the critical behaviour that made it effective or ineffective (e.g., "Instructor sat at desk during entire lecture;" "Bank teller chewed gum while talking to client"). The statements should describe behaviours, not attitudes or evaluations.

Step 3:   Members of each team jointly number each statement and delete duplicates. Each behaviour statement is read aloud to the team and, without any discussion, each team member privately rates the statement using the 7-point behaviourally anchored rating scale accompanying this exercise. When all statements have been rated, the ratings for each statement are compared. Discard statements about which team members significantly disagree (such as when ratings are 2 or 3 points apart).

Step 4:   Average the ratings of the remaining statements and write them at the appropriate location on the accompanying 7-point behaviourally anchored rating scale. An arrow or line should point to the exact place on the scale where the statement's average score is located. (You may want to put the 7-point rating scale and your results on an overhead transparency or flip chart if your results will be shown to the class.)

Step 5:   Each team presents its results to the class and describes areas of disagreement. Other class members will discuss their agreement or disagreement with each team's results, including the quality of the statements (e.g., behaviour-oriented) and their location on the performance scale.

Performance Rating Scale

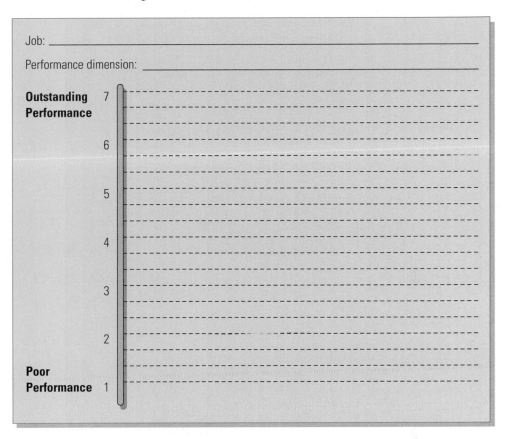

Experiential Exercise #2

Assessing Your Self-Efficacy Scale

Purpose: This exercise is designed to help you understand the concept of self-efficacy and to estimate your general self-efficacy.

Overview: Self-efficacy refers to a person's belief that he or she has the ability, motivation, and situational contingencies to complete a task successfully. Self-efficacy is usually conceptualized as a situation-specific belief. You may believe that you can perform a certain task in one situation, but are less confident with that task in another situation. However, there is also evidence that people develop a more general self-efficacy that influences their beliefs in specific situations.

Instructions: Read each of the statements below and circle the response that best fits your personal belief. Then use the scoring key to calculate your results. This exercise is completed alone so that students assess themselves honestly without concerns of social comparison. However, class discussion will focus on the meaning of self-efficacy, how this scale might be applied in organizations, and the limitations of measuring self-efficacy in work settings.

General Self-Efficacy Scale

To what extent does each statement describe you? Indicate your level of agreement by circling the appropriate response on the right.

	Strongly Agree	Agree	Neutral	Disagree	Strongly Disagree
1. When I make plans, I am certain I can make them work.	❑	❑	❑	❑	❑
2. One of my problems is that I cannot get down to work when I should.	❑	❑	❑	❑	❑
3. If I can't do a job the first time, I keep trying until I can.	❑	❑	❑	❑	❑
4. When I set important goals for myself, I rarely achieve them.	❑	❑	❑	❑	❑
5. I give up on things before completing them.	❑	❑	❑	❑	❑
6. I avoid facing difficulties.	❑	❑	❑	❑	❑
7. If something looks too complicated, I will not even bother to try it.	❑	❑	❑	❑	❑
8. When I have something unpleasant to do, I stick to it until I finish it.	❑	❑	❑	❑	❑
9. When I decide to do something, I go right to work on it.	❑	❑	❑	❑	❑
10. When trying to learn something new, I soon give up if I am not initially successful.	❑	❑	❑	❑	❑
11. When unexpected problems occur, I don't handle them well.	❑	❑	❑	❑	❑
12. I avoid trying to learn new things when they look too difficult for me.	❑	❑	❑	❑	❑
13. Failure just makes me try harder.	❑	❑	❑	❑	❑
14. I feel insecure about my ability to do things.	❑	❑	❑	❑	❑
15. I am a self-reliant person.	❑	❑	❑	❑	❑
16. I give up easily.	❑	❑	❑	❑	❑
17. I do not seem capable of dealing with most problems that come up in life.	❑	❑	❑	❑	❑

Source: M. Sherer, J. E. Maddox, B. Mercandante, S. Prentice-Dunn, B. Jacobs, and R. W. Rogers, "The Self-Efficacy Scale: Construction and Validation," *Psychological Reports* 51 (1982), pp. 663–71.

Scoring Key for General Self-Efficacy Scale

To calculate your score on the general self-efficacy scale, assign the appropriate number to each question from the scoring key below. Then add up the numbers.

For statement items 1, 3, 8, 9, 13, 15:	For statement items 2, 4, 5, 6, 7, 10, 11, 12, 14, 16, 17:
Strongly Agree = 5 Agree = 4 Neutral = 3 Disagree = 2 Strongly Disagree = 1	Strongly Agree = 1 Agree = 2 Neutral = 3 Disagree = 4 Strongly Disagree = 5

CHAPTER 3

Foundations of Employee Motivation

CHAPTER OUTLINE

Content Theories of Motivation

Process Theories of Motivation

Expectancy Theory of Motivation

Equity Theory

Goal Setting

Comparing Motivation Theories

Are Motivation Theories Culture Bound?

Chapter Summary

Discussion Questions

LEARNING OBJECTIVES

After reading this chapter, you should be able to:

- Discuss the practical implications of content motivation theories.

- Explain how each component of expectancy theory influences work effort.

- Discuss the management implications of expectancy theory.

- Explain how employees react to inequity.

- Describe the characteristics of effective goal setting.

Staff at Joe Fortes and The Fish House restaurants in Vancouver are motivated through "stretch" goals and rewards for good service.

A t Joe Fortes Seafood Restaurant in downtown Vancouver, manager Christine Penner tells servers to imagine that they are each running a small business. "For the next five hours, these tables are your shop. Show me what you've got," she says.

To add substance to this image, servers are rewarded beyond their minimum wage with incentives based on sales at their tables. Top performers are further rewarded with free meals and weekend getaways to Vancouver Island.

Kanke Seafood Restaurants Ltd., which owns Joe Fortes and The Fish House in Vancouver, knows how to motivate employees. Bud Kanke, who founded Kanke Restaurants in the 1980s, believes that effective motivation strategies are essential in today's competitive environment. "The restaurant business has never been more sophisticated than it is today," notes Mr. Kanke.

Mr. Kanke's company doesn't rely on incentives alone to motivate staff. In fact, he believes that recognition is far more important than money. Instead, he talks a lot about "stretching" his 250 staff members by setting challenging goals. For example, each of the company's 30 managers and chefs fill out a two-page goal planner that motivates them to achieve corporate goals.

"Setting and achieving goals is the highest and most effective form of self-motivation that exists," says Mr. Kanke. Reaching your goals, he states, generates self-satisfaction and confidence, which spills over to co-workers.[1]

Bud Kanke and other corporate leaders know that motivation is one of the key ingredients in employee performance and productivity. Even when people have clear work objectives, the right skills, and a supportive work environment, they won't get the job done without sufficient motivation to achieve those objectives. **Motivation** refers to the forces within a person that affect his or her direction, intensity, and persistence of voluntary behaviour.[2] Motivated employees are willing to exert a particular level of effort (intensity), for a certain amount of time (persistence), toward a particular goal (direction).

Motivating employees has never been more challenging than it is today.[3] One reason is that massive restructuring, re-engineering, and downsizing have significantly damaged the levels of trust and commitment necessary for employees to put out effort beyond the minimum requirements. Some organizations have completely given up on motivation from the heart and, instead, rely on pay-for-performance and layoff threats. These strategies may have some effect (both positive and negative), but they do not capitalize on the employee's motivational potential.

A second problem is that organizations have flattened their hierarchies to reduce costs. Consequently, there aren't enough supervisors around to practise the old "command-and-control" methods of motivating employees. This is probably just as well, because direct supervision is incompatible with the values of today's educated workforce. Still, many businesses have not discovered other ways to motivate employees.

Lastly, as explained in Chapter 1, the workforce is changing. Generation-X employees bring different needs and expectations to the workplace than their baby-boom counterparts. There is some evidence that companies have not yet realigned their motivation strategies with these needs.[4] Meanwhile, baby boomers' needs are shifting as they enter new stages of their lives. Companies must realign their sources of motivation with these changes.

In this chapter, we look at the foundations of employee motivation. Motivation theories fall into two main categories: content theories and process theories. **Content theories of motivation** explain the dynamics of employee needs, such as why people have different needs at different times. By understanding an employee's needs, we can discover the conditions that motivate that person. **Process theories of motivation** do not directly explain how need deficiencies emerge. Instead, they describe the processes through which need deficiencies are translated into behaviour. Specifically, process theories explain why someone with a particular need deficiency engages in a particular direction, intensity, and persistence of effort to reduce the need tension.

Motivation The internal forces that affect the direction, intensity, and persistence of a person's voluntary behaviour.

Content theories of motivation Theories that explain the dynamics of employee needs, such as why people have different needs at different times.

Process theories of motivation Theories that describe the processes through which need deficiencies are translated into behaviour.

Content Theories of Motivation

Needs Deficiencies that energize or trigger behaviours to satisfy those needs.

Most contemporary theories recognize that motivation begins with individual needs. **Needs** are deficiencies that energize or trigger behaviours to satisfy those needs. At some point in your life, you might have a strong need for food and shelter. At other times, your social needs may be unfulfilled. Unfulfilled needs create a tension that makes us want to find ways to reduce or satisfy those needs. The stronger your needs, the more motivated you are to satisfy them. Conversely, a satisfied need does not motivate.

Maslow's Needs Hierarchy Theory

Needs hierarchy theory Maslow's content motivation theory of five instinctive needs arranged in a hierarchy, whereby people are motivated to fulfil a higher need as a lower one becomes gratified.

One of the earliest and best-known content theories to explain why people have different needs at different times is the **needs hierarchy theory**, developed by psychologist

Abraham Maslow. Maslow condensed the many needs into five basic categories and placed them in a hierarchy.[5] At the bottom are *physiological needs*, which include the need to satisfy biological requirements for food, air, water, and shelter. Next are *safety needs* — the need for a secure and stable environment and the absence of pain, threat, or illness. *Belongingness* includes the need for love, affection, and interaction with other people. *Esteem* includes self-esteem through personal achievement as well as social esteem through recognition and respect from others. At the top of the hierarchy is *self-actualization*, which represents the need for self-fulfilment — a sense that the person's potential has been realized.

Maslow recognized that an employee's behaviour is motivated simultaneously by several need levels, but one need level dominates over the others at any given time. As the person begins to satisfy the dominant need, the next higher need in the hierarchy slowly becomes the most important. This is known as the **satisfaction-progression process**. Physiological needs are initially the most important and people are motivated to satisfy them first. As physiological needs become gratified, safety needs emerge as the strongest motivator. As safety needs are satisfied, belongingness needs become most important, and so forth. The exception to the satisfaction-progression process is self-actualization; as people experience self-actualization, they desire more rather than less of this need.

Maslow's needs hierarchy is one of the best-known organizational behaviour theories, but the model is much too rigid to explain the dynamic and unstable characteristics of employee needs.[6] Researchers have found that individual needs do not cluster neatly around the five categories described in Maslow's model. Moreover, gratification of one need level does not necessarily lead to increased motivation to satisfy the next higher need level. Although Maslow's model may not predict employee needs as well as scholars initially expected, it provides an important introduction to employee needs and it laid the foundation for Alderfer's ERG theory which has better research support.

Alderfer's ERG Theory

ERG theory was developed by organizational behaviour theorist Clayton Alderfer to overcome the problems with Maslow's needs hierarchy theory.[7] ERG theory groups human needs into three broad categories: existence, relatedness, and growth. (Notice that the theory's name is based on the first letter of each need.) As we see in Exhibit 3.1, **existence needs** correspond to Maslow's physiological and physically related safety needs. **Relatedness needs** refer to Maslow's interpersonal safety, belongingness, and social-esteem needs. **Growth needs** correspond to Maslow's self-esteem and self-actualization needs.

ERG theory states that an employee's behaviour is motivated simultaneously by more than one need level. Thus, you might try to satisfy your growth needs (such as by serving a client exceptionally well) even though your relatedness needs aren't completely satisfied. However, ERG theory applies the satisfaction-progression process described in Maslow's needs hierarchy model, so one need level will dominate a person's motivation more than others. As existence needs are satisfied, for example, relatedness needs become more important.

Unlike Maslow's model, however, ERG theory includes a **frustration-regression process** whereby those who are unable to satisfy a higher need become frustrated and regress to the next lower need level. For example, if existence and relatedness needs have been satisfied, but growth need fulfilment has been blocked, the individual will become frustrated and relatedness needs will again emerge as the dominant source of motivation.

Satisfaction-progression process A process whereby people become increasingly motivated to fulfil a higher need as a lower need is gratified.

ERG theory Alderfer's content motivation theory of three instinctive needs arranged in a hierarchy, in which people progress to the next higher need when a lower one is fulfilled, and regress to a lower need if unable to fulfil a higher need.

Existence needs A person's physiological and physically related safety needs, such as the need for food, shelter, and safe working conditions.

Relatedness needs A person's need to interact with other people, receive public recognition, and feel secure around people (i.e., interpersonal safety).

Growth needs A person's self-esteem through personal achievement as well as self-actualization.

Frustration-regression process Process whereby people who are unable to satisfy a higher need become frustrated and regress to the next lower need level.

EXHIBIT 3.1: ERG Theory and Needs Hierarchy Theory Compared

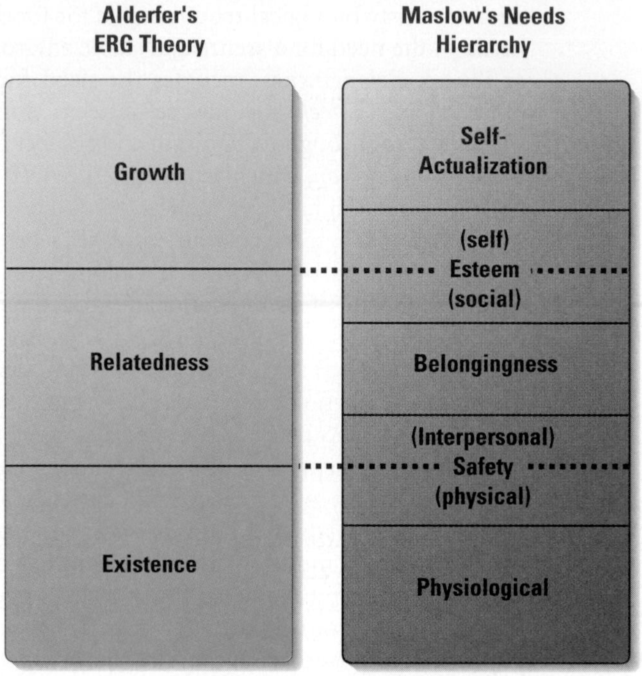

Although not fully tested, ERG theory seems to explain the dynamics of human needs in organizations reasonably well.[8] Human needs cluster more neatly around the three categories proposed by Alderfer than the five categories in Maslow's hierarchy. The combined processes of satisfaction-progression and frustration-regression also provide a more accurate explanation of why employee needs change over time. Overall, ERG theory seems to come closest to explaining why employees have particular needs at various times.

McClelland's Theory of Learned Needs

Maslow's needs hierarchy and Alderfer's ERG theory assume that needs are instinctive and therefore fixed for life. However, people also have secondary needs or drives that are learned and reinforced through children's books, parental styles, and social norms. Psychologist David McClelland has devoted his career to studying three secondary needs that he considers particularly important sources of motivation:[9]

- *Need for achievement*   Need for achievement refers to a desire to accomplish moderately challenging performance goals, be successful in competitive situations, assume personal responsibility for work (rather than delegating it to others), and receive immediate feedback.

- *Need for power*   Need for power refers to a desire to control one's environment, including people and material resources. Some people have a high *socialized power* need in which they seek power to help others, such as improving society or increasing organizational effectiveness. Those with a strong *personal power* need seek power so that they can revel in their power and use it to advance their career and other personal interests.

- *Need for affiliation* Need for affiliation refers to a desire to seek approval from others, conform to their wishes and expectations, and avoid conflict and confrontation. People with a strong affiliation need want to form positive relationships with others, even if this results in lower job performance.

Men and women with a high need for achievement make better entrepreneurs because they establish challenging goals for themselves and thrive on competition.[10] Recent research at Pepsi Cola Company suggests that people with a high need for achievement also perform well in subsidiaries of large organizations where they face competition and have few layers of management.[11] However, senior executives in large corporations should have a somewhat lower need achievement orientation and a moderately high need for socialized power because they must delegate work and build support (characteristics not usually found in high-need achievers). Senior executives also must have a fairly low need for affiliation so that their decisions and actions are not biased by a personal need for approval.[12]

Learning needs

McClelland argued that achievement, power, and affiliation needs are learned rather than instinctive. Accordingly, he developed training programs that strengthen these needs. In his achievement motivation program, trainees review imaginative stories written by high-achievement-need people and then practise writing their own achievement-oriented stories. They practise achievement-oriented behaviours in business games and examine whether being a high achiever is consistent with their self-image and career plans. Trainees also complete a detailed achievement plan for the next two years and form a reference group with other trainees to maintain their new-found achievement-motive style.[13]

These programs seem to work. For example, need-achievement course participants in India subsequently started more new businesses, demonstrated greater community involvement, invested more in expanding their businesses, and employed twice as many people as nonparticipants. Research on similar achievement-motive courses for North American small-business owners reported dramatic increases in the profitability of the participants' businesses.

Practical Implications of Content Motivation Theories

Content theories of motivation suggest that different people have different needs at different times. Some employees are ready to fulfil growth needs, whereas others are still struggling to satisfy their minimum existence needs. Needs change as people enter new stages of their lives. Moreover, different generations of employees bring a unique set of needs that have been influenced by experiences while they were growing up. As we see in Perspective 3.1, Generation-X employees tend to have a different combination of needs than their baby-boom co-workers. Companies must realign their motivational practices to fit these changing needs.

Most organizations distribute the same reward, such as a salary increase or paid time off, to all employees with good performance. But, as we will discuss in Chapter 4, rewards that motivate some people will have little effect on those with different needs. Thus, content motivation theories advise organizations to offer employees their choice of rewards. Those who perform well might trade part of the bonus for extra time off. The result of a flexible reward system is that employees can create a reward package with the greatest value to them. This principle is also found in flexible benefits systems, in which employees alter their pensions, vacation time, and other benefits to match their particular needs.

PERSPECTIVE 3.1

Motivating Generation-X

Robert Barnard hates the label Generation-X. Yet the 29-year-old and his three partners in Toronto-based D-Code Inc. spend all of their time helping companies figure out what motivates people in this age group (25 to about 35 years old).

"[Generation-X employees] are more media-savvy, techno-literate, educated, worldly and more skeptical than any previous generation," says Mr. Barnard. "Unlike the boomers, money is not their driving force."

Although young people want good pay, they seem to place more emphasis on work that fits their lifestyle. One 20-something employee summed up Gen-X motivation this way: "We can work harder than anybody — just ask Microsoft — but we need to know you care, we need to know what's in it for us, and we need to have a decent time while we're at it."

Bruce Tulgan, who wrote a book on managing Gen-Xers, believes that many companies have complained about Gen-X employees mainly because they don't know how to motivate these people. "The greatest obstacle preventing Xers from giving our best in the workplace is that we are severely misunderstood," complains Tulgan.

For example, Gen-Xers aren't arrogant; they are just more individualistic and entrepreneurial than baby boomers. They want to be challenged and participate in organizational change. "Managers need to remember that Xers are the latchkey kids — we are used to taking care of ourselves," Tulgan explains. He adds that Gen-Xers are voracious learners who enjoy sorting through and digesting massive amounts of information.

Companies that understand Gen-X needs have the upper hand at motivating them to join and work for the organization. Royal Bank of Canada improved its campus recruiting after D-Code identified information that young people look for in a job. "We hire about 3,000 people a year and probably one-third of that is done from campus recruitment for entry-level management jobs," explains Michael Kavanagh, Royal Bank's manager of recruitment strategies. "D-Code's staff . . . show us how to make ourselves look more mobile, exciting, and different from other large organizations."

Source: A. Fisher, "Readers Sound Off: Are Gen-Xers Arrogant Or Just Misunderstood?" *Fortune*, February 17, 1997; G. MacDonald, "The Eyes and Ears of a Generation," *Globe & Mail*, February 4, 1997, p. B11; B. Tulgan, "Correcting the 'Slacker Myth': Managing Generation X in the Work Place," *Manage* (July 1996), pp. 14–16.

Another important lesson from content theories of motivation is that organizations should not rely too heavily on financial rewards as a source of employee motivation.[14] The reason is that financial rewards correspond to lower-level needs, whereas growth needs represent the most powerful and sustaining sources of employee motivation. Margot Franssen, president of The Body Shop Canada, echoes this point: "The amount of time and effort put into thinking up new schemes to attract, motivate, and keep employees through money and things would be laughable if it were not so very sad," she says.

Process Theories of Motivation

At the beginning of the chapter we distinguished the content theories presented above from process theories of motivation. Content theories explain why people have different needs at different times, whereas process theories describe the processes through which need deficiencies are translated into behaviour. Three of the most popular process theories of motivation are expectancy theory, equity theory, and goal setting.

Expectancy Theory of Motivation

Expectancy theory A process motivation theory stating that work effort is directed toward behaviours that people believe will lead to desired outcomes.

Expectancy theory is a process motivation theory based on the idea that work effort is directed toward behaviours that people believe will lead to desired outcomes.[15] Through experience, we develop expectations about whether we can achieve various levels of job performance. We also develop expectations about whether job performance and work behaviours lead to particular outcomes. Finally, we naturally direct our effort toward outcomes that help us fulfil our needs.

Expectancy theory emerged from the writings of Kurt Lewin and other social psychologists in the 1930s.[16] Victor Vroom is generally credited with introducing expectancy theory to organizational settings in 1964, although his version of the model is unnecessarily complex and often described incorrectly. The version of expectancy theory presented in this book was developed by Edward E. Lawler and is easier to understand, yet equally effective at explaining employee motivation.[17]

Expectancy Theory Model

Lawler's expectancy theory model is presented in Exhibit 3.2. The key variable of interest in expectancy theory is *effort* — the individual's actual exertion of energy. An individual's effort level depends on three factors: effort-to-performance (E→P) expectancy, performance-to-outcome (P→O) expectancy, and outcome valences (V). Employee motivation is influenced by all three components of the expectancy theory model. If any component weakens, motivation weakens.

According to Margot Franssen, president of The Body Shop Canada, companies cannot rely on financial rewards alone to motivate employees. "The amount of time and effort put into thinking up new schemes to attract, motivate, and keep employees through money and things would be laughable if it were not so very sad," she says.

E→P expectancy

Effort-to-performance (E→P) expectancy An individual's perceived probability that a particular level of effort will result in a particular level of performance.

The **effort-to-performance (E→P) expectancy** is the individual's perception that his or her effort will result in a particular level of performance. Expectancy is defined as a *probability*, and therefore ranges from 0.0 to 1.0. In some situations, employees may believe that they can unquestionably accomplish the task (a probability of 1.0). In other situations, they expect that even their highest level of effort will not result in the desired performance level (a probability of 0.0). In most cases, the E→P expectancy falls somewhere between these two extremes.

P→O expectancy

Performance-to-outcome (P→O) expectancy An individual's perceived probability that a specific behaviour or performance level will lead to specific outcomes.

The **performance-to-outcome (P→O) expectancy** is the perceived probability that a specific behaviour or performance level will lead to specific outcomes. In extreme cases, employees may believe that accomplishing a particular task (performance) will *definitely* result in a particular outcome (a probability of 1.0), or they may believe that this outcome will *definitely not* result from successful performance (a probability of 0.0). More often, the P→O expectancy falls somewhere between these two extremes.

EXHIBIT 3.2: Expectancy Theory of Motivation

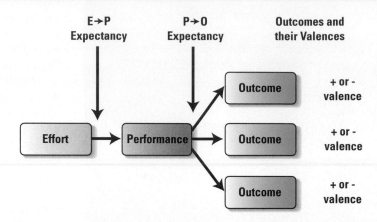

One important issue in P→O expectancies is which outcomes do we think about? We certainly don't evaluate the P→O expectancy for every possible outcome. There are too many of them. Instead, we only think about outcomes that are of interest to us at the time. One day, your motivation to complete a task may be fuelled mainly by the likelihood of getting off work early to meet friends. Other times, your motivation to complete the same task may be based more on the P→O expectancy of a promotion or pay increase. The main point is that your motivation depends on the probability that a behaviour or job performance level will result in outcomes that you think about.

Outcome valences

Valence The anticipated satisfaction or dissatisfaction that an individual feels toward an outcome.

The third element in expectancy theory is the **valence** of each outcome that you consider. Valence refers to the anticipated satisfaction or dissatisfaction that an individual feels toward an outcome. It ranges from negative to positive. (The actual range does not matter; it may be from −1 to +1, or from −100 to +100.) An outcome valence is determined by the strength of the person's basic needs that are associated with the outcome. Outcomes have a positive valence when they directly or indirectly satisfy the person's needs, and a negative valence when they inhibit the person's need fulfilment. If you have a strong social need, for example, then outcomes that likely fulfil that need will have a strong positive valence to you. Outcomes that move you further away from fulfilling your social need will have a strong negative valence.

Notice that some outcomes directly fulfil personal needs, whereas other outcomes indirectly fulfil those needs. You might be motivated to achieve the highest sales in your company this month because "it feels great." This is the direct outcome of growth need fulfilment. At the same time, you might want to be the top salesperson because you will be mentioned in the company magazine, thereby indirectly fulfilling your social needs.

Predicting Work Effort: An Organizational Example

The amount of effort that we exert toward a task depends on all three components of the expectancy model. Let's see how these three components work in reality. Perspective 3.2 describes how Jack Wong's motivation to perform his job at the City of Saskatoon's Parks and Recreation Department diminished over time. Expectancy theory can help explain why this occurred.

PERSPECTIVE 3.2

Pacing Yourself at Saskatoon's Department of Parks and Relaxation

It didn't take long for Jack Wong to work more slowly for the City of Saskatoon's Parks and Recreation Department. Soon after he was hired as a seasonal employee, Jack heard a co-worker jokingly refer to the work unit as the department of "Parks and Relaxation."

The title was quite appropriate. A few days later, while working at a pace normal to most human beings, Wong was scolded by a "lifer" (a lifetime city employee) for going too fast. Wong was told to pace himself so that the job wasn't completed so quickly.

Jack Wong soon learned that this was useful advice. There were no rewards in finishing a job early. If the work crew got the job done faster than expected, the foreman would often have nothing else for them to do. This frustrated the foreman and left employees with the painful duty of trying to look busy for the rest of the day.

"Unfortunately, I was a bad actor," admits Wong. "I couldn't look busy even if my life depended on it. Every year during my year-end evaluation, my foreman told me: 'You stand around and wait too much to be told what to do.'" So to avoid warnings from lifers and poor evaluations from his supervisor, Wong tried his best to adopt a more leisurely pace of work.

Another deterrent to working hard was that Wong and other seasonal employees would be laid off each summer after their assigned projects were completed or the department's budget for summer help was spent. The employees didn't want to get laid off early, and the department managers didn't want a budget surplus because City Hall might cut the extra money from next year's budget. So everyone was quite happy to see Wong and others working slowly and taking longer coffee breaks until the budget was spent.

Eventually, Jack Wong managed to slow down his work effort. But now that he no longer works summers at the City of Saskatoon's Parks and Recreation Department, he has trouble getting motivated for jobs that require real work effort. "I work at a slower pace than the living dead," he complains. "And I can't dig a hole unless five guys are watching me. Who should I blame for this sorry state?"

Source: Based on J. Wong, "Nice Work if You Can Get It (And You Can Get It if You Don't Try)," *Globe & Mail*, December 31, 1993, p. A18.

Let's start with the outcomes that Jack seems to be thinking about, and the valences of these outcomes. The three work-performance outcomes that Jack mentions are: being scolded by co-workers, getting laid off early, and trying to look busy. Jack dislikes (negative valences) all three outcomes, so he tries to avoid them.

Regarding his P→O expectancies, Jack clearly believes that he will get scolded by co-workers, get laid off early, and have to look busy if he gets his work done quickly. In other words, he has high P→O expectancies that each of these outcomes will occur if he reaches a high level of job performance. If he works slowly, on the other hand, Jack probably will not get scolded or laid off early, and will not have to pretend that he is busy. By multiplying these P→O expectancies with the valences of the three outcomes, we can see that Jack prefers completing his work slowly.

Lastly, we need to consider the E→P expectancies of getting his work done quickly or slowly. Jack knows that he can get the job done quickly, and he is quite confident that he can work slowly. In expectancy theory language, he has high E→P expectancies for both performance levels. Now, put this information together with the P→O expectancies and outcome valences. You can understand why Jack is more motivated to work slowly than quickly for Saskatoon's Parks and Recreation Department.

Expectancy Theory in Practice

One of the appealing characteristics of expectancy theory is that it provides clear guidelines for increasing employee motivation by altering the person's E→P expectancies, P→O expectancies, and/or outcome valences.[18] Several practical implications of expectancy theory are listed in Exhibit 3.3 and described below.

EXHIBIT 3.3: Practical Applications of Expectancy Theory

Expectancy Theory Component	Objective	Applications
E→P Expectancies	To increase the belief that employees are capable of performing the job successfully	• Select people with the required skills and knowledge. • Provide required training and clarify job requirements. • Provide sufficient time and resources. • Assign simpler or fewer tasks until employees can master them (shaping). • Provide examples of similar employees who have successfully performed the task. • Provide counselling and coaching to employees who lack self-confidence.
P→O Expectancies	To increase the belief that good performance will result in certain (valued) outcomes	• Measure job performance accurately. • Clearly explain the outcomes that will result from successful performance. • Describe how the employee's rewards were based on past performance. • Provide examples of other employees whose good performance has resulted in higher rewards.
Valences of Outcomes	To increase the expected value of outcomes resulting from desired performance	• Distribute rewards that employees value. • Individualize rewards. • Minimize the presence of countervalent outcomes.

Increasing E→P expectancies

E→P expectancies are based on self-esteem and previous experience in that situation.[19] Consequently, employees should be given the necessary abilities, clear role perceptions, and favourable situational contingencies to reach the desired levels of performance so that they form higher E→P expectancies.

Employee abilities must be matched with job requirements, or the job should be changed to fit the incumbent's existing abilities. For example, the Insurance Corporation of British Columbia assigns relatively simple automobile accident cases to newly hired adjusters. After a few months, when the adjuster feels confident with these files, more challenging cases are assigned. Even with the requisite abilities, some employees may have low E→P expectancies because they lack self-confidence. Counselling and coaching may be advisable so that employees develop confidence that they already possess the skills and knowledge to perform the job.

We must also keep in mind that E→P expectancies are learned, so the learning practices described in Chapter 2 should be applied. For instance, feedback will help employees perceive that they are capable of performing the assigned tasks effectively.[20] Shaping and behavioural modelling also tend to increase E→P expectancies in many situations.

© 1992 Farcus Cartoons/dist. by Universal Press Syndicate   WAISGLASS/COULTHART

Bob finally gets the recognition he deserves.

Increasing P→O expectancies

The most obvious ways to improve P→O expectancies are to measure employee performance accurately and distribute more valued rewards to those with higher job performance. This is not as easy as it may sound. As we shall see in Chapter 4, reward systems sometimes have little effect on employee motivation or, worse, may inadvertently motivate undesirable behaviours.

P→O expectancies are perceptions, so employees should *believe* that higher performance will result in higher rewards. Having a performance-based reward system is important, but this fact must be communicated. When rewards are distributed, employees should understand how their rewards have been based on past performance. More generally, companies need to regularly communicate the existence of a performance-based reward system through examples, anecdotes, and public ceremonies.

Increasing outcome valences

Performance outcomes influence work effort only when they are valued by employees.[21] This brings us back to a conclusion of the content theories of motivation; namely, that companies must pay attention to the needs and reward preferences of individual employees. They should develop more individualized reward systems so that employees who perform well are offered a choice of rewards.

Finally, expectancy theory emphasizes the need to discover and neutralize countervalent outcomes. This refers to the situation in which some outcomes of good job performance have negative valences, thereby reducing the effectiveness of existing reward systems. Earlier, in Perspective 3.2, we saw how Jack Wong's work effort was curtailed by pressures from co-workers and his immediate supervisors. Although the City of Saskatoon may want motivated employees, the countervalent forces in its Parks and Recreation Department easily offset any outcomes that encourage higher work effort.

Does Expectancy Theory Fit Reality?

Expectancy theory has been a difficult model to test because it must recognize almost every possible performance level and outcome that employees could imagine. Most of the early studies also suffered from measurement and research design problems.[22] Some critics suggest that expectancy theory is an imperfect theory because it doesn't predict spontaneous behaviours (such as making a rude remark to a co-worker).[23] One could argue that expectancy theory accounts for spontaneous behaviours because they are learned from past experience, but expectancy theory needs further clarification on this point.

In spite of its limitations, expectancy theory offers one of the best models available for predicting work effort and motivation. For example, recent studies show that expectancy theory predicts a person's motivation to use a decision support system, leave the organization, and work with less effort in a group setting.[24] All three components of the model have received some research support. There is particularly good evidence that P→O expectancies influence employee motivation.

Equity Theory

When four Halifax hospitals recently merged into the Queen Elizabeth II Health Sciences Centre, senior executives had much more to worry about than shuttling patients into new beds. The mega-merger also created strong feelings of inequity. Nurses who worked at Victoria General Hospital earn $4,300 more than those from another merged hospital, yet a government-imposed wage freeze prevented the QEII administration from creating a fairer pay structure. "How can nurses . . . be expected to work side by side when there are such glaring differences?" asks a representative of the Nova Scotia Government Employees Union.[25]

Equity theory A process motivation theory that explains how people develop perceptions of fairness in the distribution and exchange of resources.

Equity theory explains how people develop perceptions of fairness in the distribution and exchange of resources. As a process theory of motivation, it explains what employees are motivated to do when they feel inequitably treated. There are four main elements in the equity process: outcome/input ratio, comparison other, equity evaluation, and consequences of inequity.[26]

Outcome/Input Ratio

Inputs include skills, effort, experience, amount of time worked, performance results, and other employee contributions to the organization. Employees see their inputs as investments into the exchange relationship. Outcomes are the things employees receive from the organization in exchange for the inputs, such as pay, promotions, recognition, or an office with a window.

Both inputs and outcomes are weighted by their importance to the individual. These weights vary from one person to the next. To some people, seniority is a valuable input that deserves more organizational outcomes in return. Others consider job effort and performance the most important contributions in the exchange relationship, and give seniority relatively little weight. Similarly, equity theory recognizes that people value outcomes differently because they have different needs. For example, it accepts that some employees want time off with pay whereas others consider this a relatively insignificant reward for job performance.

When four Halifax hospitals recently merged into the Queen Elizabeth II Health Sciences Centre, nurses from some hospitals found themselves working beside higher-paid nurses from other hospitals. A provincial government wage freeze prevented senior management from resolving these feelings of inequity.

Comparison Other

Equity theory states that we compare our situation with a comparison other.[27] However, the theory does not tell us who the comparison other is in a particular situation. It may be another person, group of people, or even yourself in the past. It may be someone in the same job, another job, or another organization. People tend to compare themselves with others within the same organization rather than with people in other organizations. One reason is that employees develop firm-specific skills and attachments that limit their likelihood of looking beyond the organization in which they are currently employed (i.e., the internal labour market). Another reason is that co-workers are similar to the employee and it is easier to get information about co-workers than from people working elsewhere. Some research suggests that employees frequently collect information on several referents to form a "generalized" comparison other.[28] For the most part, however, the comparison other is not easily identifiable.

Equity Evaluation

According to equity theory, employees form an outcome/input ratio and compare this with the ratio of the comparison other. This evaluation is shown in Exhibit 3.4 with three different comparison situations. The first comparison illustrates the *equity condition* in which the person's outcome/input ratio is the same as the comparison other's ratio. The amount of inputs and outcomes must be proportional. For instance, we feel equitably treated when we work harder than the comparison other and receive proportionally higher rewards as a result.

Inequity feelings emerge when the person's ratio is significantly different from the comparison other's. People tend to ignore minimal differences, but inequity occurs when the difference in ratios exceeds a threshold level. *Underreward* inequity occurs when the person's ratio is significantly lower than the comparison other's. This may occur when two people provide the same inputs to the organization but the other person receives more outcomes, as the second comparison in Exhibit 3.4 illustrates. Underreward inequity may also occur when the outcomes are the same but the comparison other's inputs are lower, or in any other situation in which the person's ratio is lower than the comparison other's.

Overreward inequity occurs when the person's ratio is significantly higher than the comparison other's. As the third comparison in Exhibit 3.4 illustrates, overreward inequity would occur when the person receives more outcomes than the comparison other, even though the inputs are the same. Overreward inequity would also occur when the person's inputs are lower than the comparison other's but both receive the same outcomes, or in any other situation in which the person's ratio is higher than the comparison other's.

Consequences of Inequity

Feelings of inequity manifest themselves in many ways. For example, when SaskPower's managers received salary increases averaging 8 percent, the company's technical employees were so incensed that they refused to work overtime. They claimed that the increases were unfair, particularly since their pay was frozen for three years.[29]

Employees are motivated to reduce or eliminate their feelings of inequity by correcting the inequitable situation. By refusing to work overtime, SaskPower's technical employees were trying to reduce inequity by receiving pay increases similar to management or (less likely) by reducing management's raises. There are six possible ways to reduce feelings of inequity.[30] Notice, however, that the strategy used depends on the person's past experience as well as whether they are under- or overrewarded.

EXHIBIT 3.4: Equity Theory Model

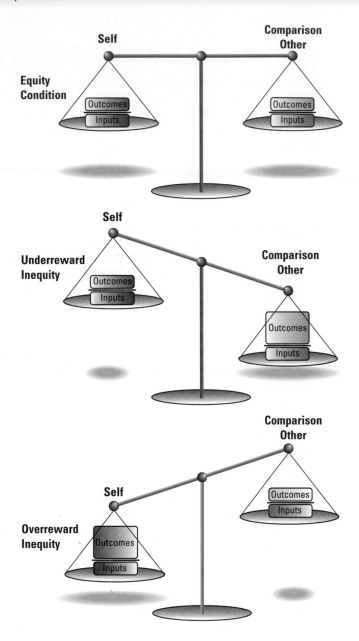

1. *Changing inputs* Underrewarded workers tend to reduce their effort and performance if these outcomes don't affect their paycheque. Overpaid workers sometimes
   (but not very often) increase their inputs by working harder and producing more.

2. *Changing outcomes* People with underreward inequity might ask for more
   desired outcomes, such as a pay increase. If this does not work, some are motivated
   to join a labour union and demand these changes at the bargaining table.[31] Others
   misuse sick leave for more paid time off. At the extreme, some people steal company property or use facilities for personal use as ways to increase their outcomes.[32]

3. *Changing perceptions* Employees may distort inputs and outcomes to restore equity feelings.[33] Overrewarded employees typically follow this strategy because it's easier to increase their perceived inputs (seniority, knowledge, etc.) than to ask for less pay! As Canadian author Pierre Burton once said: "I was underpaid for the first half of my life. I don't mind being overpaid for the second half."[34]

4. *Leaving the field* Some people try to reduce inequity feelings by getting away from the inequitable situation. Thus, equity theory explains some instances of employee turnover and job transfer. This also explains why an underrewarded employee might take more time off work even though he or she is not paid for this absenteeism.

5. *Acting on the comparison other* Equity is sometimes restored by changing the comparison other's inputs or outcomes. If you feel overrewarded, you might encourage the referent to work at a more leisurely pace. If you feel underrewarded, you might subtly suggest that the overpaid co-worker should be doing a larger share of the workload.

6. *Changing the comparison other* If we can't seem to alter the outcome/input ratio through other means, we might eventually replace the comparison other with someone who has a more compatible outcome/input ratio. As mentioned earlier, we sometimes rely on a generalized comparison other, so feelings of inequity may be reduced fairly easily by adjusting the features of this composite referent.

Equity Theory in Practice

Feelings of inequity are all around us. Consider the issue of executive salaries in Canada's financial services industry, described in Perspective 3.3. On the one hand, many employees and shareholders believe that Canada's bank CEOs are paid far too much. Some have even gone to court to try to limit executive pay so that it seems more equitable. Yet what is fair to employees and shareholders may not be fair to bank executives. They compare themselves to CEOs in the United States who make more money. Eventually, some executives may leave Canada to correct feelings of inequity if their pay levels are cut.

Equity theory has received considerable support in research and practice. The model helps us to understand why baseball players change teams, why employees steal from their employer, why people become hostile at work, and why employees enact numerous other behaviours.[35] One of the clearest lessons from equity theory is that we need to continually treat people fairly in the distribution of organizational rewards. If feelings of inequity are sufficiently strong, employees may put less effort into the job, leave the organization, steal resources or time (e.g., absenteeism), or join a labour union to correct these inequities.

Unfortunately, maintaining feelings of equity is not an easy task. Employees have different opinions regarding which inputs should be rewarded (e.g., seniority versus performance) and which outcomes are more valuable than others.[36] We can try to improve equity perceptions by telling employees how rewards are distributed, but we also need to understand the inputs and outcomes that are most important to people.

Goal Setting

When Soren Gyll became chairman of Volvo, he gave each of his senior executives a watch with three numbers stamped on the straps: 25, 50, and 100. The numbers represented the goals that Gyll expected them to achieve: 25 percent return on assets, 50 percent reduction in project time, and 100 percent attainment of corporate vision. "If you set objectives and go for things," says Gyll, "you can accomplish goals the books say are impossible."[37]

PERSPECTIVE 3.3

Fair Pay in the Executive Suite

Yves Michaud is fed up with exorbitant salaries among Canada's bank executives. For three years, the retired journalist and Quebec politician has tried to let Royal Bank and National Bank shareholders vote on his proposal to limit executive pay to 20 times the average bank employee. The banks had blocked this vote, but Michaud's perseverance paid off when a Quebec court ordered the banks to put his idea forward to shareholders. Michaud's proposal, which was subsequently rejected by shareholders, would have cut Royal Bank chairman John Cleghorn's $2.3 million paycheque to about $900,000.

What is a fair level of pay for corporate executives? Plato, the Greek philosopher, felt that no one in a community should earn more than five times the lowest-paid worker. In the 1970s, management guru Peter Drucker suggested that 20 times the lowest worker's earnings was more reasonable. Bankers cherish Drucker's wisdom on many issues, but not on fair pay. Bank of Montreal CEO Matthew Barrett recently earned $3.8 million, putting his compensation level at 100 times the average (not the lowest) bank employee.

Although limiting executive compensation may help employees and shareholders reduce their feelings of inequity, bankers and consultants warn that this action will increase feelings of inequity among executives. The result is that top performers will leave for higher-paying jobs in the United States.

"On a global scale . . . we'll be attracting some of the weakest banking talent in the world, or underpaying some of the best talent," complains Mark Maxwell, an analyst at CIBC Wood Gundy Securities Inc. CIBC chairman Al Flood, whose $2.9 million salary is threatened by another shareholder proposal, warns: "You would put [Canada] at a disadvantage if you start putting artificial and arbitrary ranges around compensation."

These warnings may not be supported in practice. Herman Miller, the successful furniture manufacturer, restricts CEO pay to 20 times the average worker and has been able to recruit top-quality executive talent. Moreover, when the company was looking for a new CEO, none of the eight shortlisted candidates objected to the salary cap. In fact, the person hired for the job later told the executive compensation committee that there is no reason to change this compensation strategy.

Source: T. Fennell, "Battling the Banks," *Maclean's*, January 27, 1997, p. 52; A. Gibbon, "CIBC Opposes Executive Pay Limit," *Globe & Mail*, January 17, 1997, p. B4; J. McFarland, "Higher U.S. Pay Triggers Concern," *Globe & Mail*, November 6, 1996, p. B17; R. Gibbons and R. Blackwell, "Banks Bow to Shareholder," *Financial Post*, January 16, 1997, pp. 1, 2; A. J. Vogl, "Risky Work," *Across the Board*, July/August 1993, pp. 27–31; G. S. Crystal, *In Search of Excess: The Overcompensation of American Executives* (N.Y.: W.W. Norton & Co., 1991).

Goals The immediate or ultimate objectives that employees are trying to accomplish from their work effort.

Goal setting The process of motivating employees and clarifying their role perceptions by establishing performance objectives.

Management-by-objectives (MbO) A formal, participative goal-setting process in which organizational objectives are cascaded down to work units and individual employees.

Goal setting is one of the most widely practised theories of motivation in organizations.[38] **Goals** are the immediate or ultimate objectives that employees are trying to accomplish from their work effort. **Goal setting** is the process of motivating employees and clarifying their role perceptions by establishing performance objectives. Notice that goal setting potentially improves employee performance in two ways: (1) by stretching the intensity and persistence of effort, and (2) by giving employees clearer role perceptions so that their effort is channelled toward behaviours that will improve work performance.

Almost every organization in Canada tries to motivate employees through goal setting. Kanke Seafood Restaurants Ltd., described at the beginning of this chapter, involves most of its employees in goal setting. Some companies also apply goal setting through a formal process known as **management-by-objectives** (MbO). There are a few variations of MbO programs, but they generally identify organizational objectives, then cascade them down to work units and individual employees.[39] The employee is actively involved with his or her supervisor in goal formation as well as clarifying the means to reach the agreed-upon goals. MbO also includes periodic review and feedback. Although the process frequently creates too much paperwork, MbO can be an effective application of goal setting in some parts of the organization.

Characteristics of Effective Goals

Goal setting is more complex than simply telling someone to "do your best." Instead, organizational behaviour scholars have identified five conditions, diagrammed in Exhibit 3.5, that are necessary to maximize task effort and performance.[40]

Specific goals

Employees put more effort into a task when they work toward specific goals rather than "do-your-best" targets. A specific goal would include a quantitative level of change over a specific time, such as "reduce scrap rate by 7 percent over the next six months." Specific goals communicate more precise performance expectations, so employees can direct their effort more efficiently and reliably.

Results-oriented goals

Results-oriented goals improve work performance more than process-oriented goals. A results-oriented goal directly refers to the person's job performance, such as number of customers served per hour. Process-oriented goals refer to the work processes used to get the job done. An example of a process-oriented goal would be finding one way to reduce the time for customers to describe their problems. Research indicates that process-oriented goals encourage employees to think about different ways to get the job done, but they seem to block employees from choosing one method and getting on with the job. Therefore, results-oriented goals tend to be more effective.

Challenging goals

Employees tend to have more intense and persistent work effort when they have challenging rather than easy goals. Challenging goals also increase the person's growth-need fulfilment when the goal is achieved.[41] Some organizations, such as General Electric and Chrysler, like to use "stretch" goals — goals that are challenging enough to stretch the employee's abilities and motivation toward peak performance. Stretch goals are effective if employees receive the necessary resources to accomplish them and do not become overstressed in the process.[42]

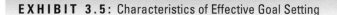

EXHIBIT 3.5: Characteristics of Effective Goal Setting

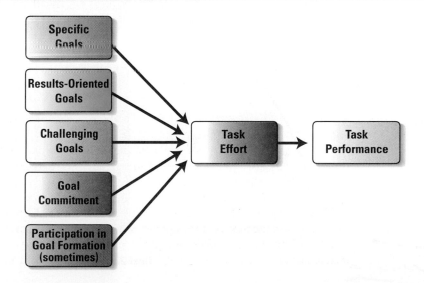

Of course, there are limits to challenging goals. At some point, a goal becomes so difficult that employees will reject it. At that point, work effort falls dramatically, as we see in Exhibit 3.6. Therefore, the optimal level of goal difficulty is the area in which it is challenging but still acceptable. The problem with finding this optimal level is compounded by the fact that most of us have several work-related goals. Recent evidence suggests that we naturally tend to prioritize these goals, with the easiest ones at the top of the list. Unless employees experience some pressure (such as friendly reminders from the boss) to complete the most difficult goals, these challenging assignments tend to get put aside indefinitely.[43]

Goal commitment

Goal setting will only work if employees accept the goal.[44] One influence on goal commitment is the person's belief that he or she has sufficient ability and resources to accomplish the goal. This is the same as the E→P expectancy that we learned about in the section on expectancy theory.[45] The higher the E→P expectancy that the goal can be accomplished, the more committed (motivated) the employee is to the goal. The Nova Scotia government discovered this when it gave highways employees targets for reducing highway deaths. Employees didn't think they could affect the number of highway fatalities because management, not the employees, decide when to salt and shovel the roads.[46]

Self-efficacy A person's belief that he or she has the ability, motivation, and situational contingencies to complete a task successfully.

Another influence on goal commitment is the employee's **self-efficacy**. Recall from Chapter 2 that high self-efficacy employees have a "can-do" attitude. They are confident that they can perform the tasks facing them. Recent evidence suggests that high self-efficacy employees are more likely to accept their goals because they believe they can choose successful strategies to reach those goals.[47] Those with low self-efficacy, on the other hand, tend to be in a panic when given a unique goal where the means to achieve that goal isn't obvious.

EXHIBIT 3.6: Effect of Goal Difficulty on Performance

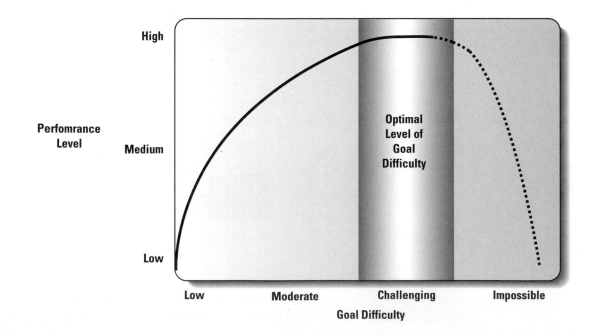

Participation in goal formation (sometimes)

Involving employees in the goal-setting process, rather than assigning the goal to them, is sometimes necessary.[48] One reason is that participation in goal formation tends to increase goal commitment. Participation may also improve goal quality, because employees have valuable information and knowledge. However, participation may not be necessary when employees will be committed to assigned goals and those who decide the goals have sufficient information.

Goal feedback

Feedback is another necessary condition for effective goal setting. As discussed in Chapter 2, feedback is a powerful source of learning. In terms of goal setting, feedback lets us know whether we have achieved the goal or are properly directing our effort toward it. Feedback is also an essential ingredient in motivation because growth-need strength can't be satisfied unless we receive information on goal accomplishment.

Goal-Setting Applications and Limitations

Goal setting does not work for everyone in every situation. When goals are tied to monetary incentives, some employees are motivated to select easy rather than difficult goals.[49] In some cases, employees have negotiated goals with their supervisor that have already been completed! Employees with high self-efficacy and need for achievement tend to set challenging goals whether or not they are financially rewarded for their results, but the general consensus is that reward-based goal setting creates problems.[50]

Another problem with goal setting is that it can interfere with job performance on new or complex tasks.[51] The best explanation we have for this is that working on a new or complex task requires a large amount of **implicit learning** (as discussed in Chapter 2). We use our unconscious learning strategies to sort out the best work processes for these tasks. Unfortunately, goal setting interferes with implicit learning by shifting our attention to more explicit (and cumbersome) learning processes. Goal setting is effective for simple or routine tasks, on the other hand, because the best work processes are already known or are quickly learned without much thought.[52]

Implicit learning The experiential phenomenon of acquiring information about relationships in the environment without any conscious attempt to do so.

Comparing Motivation Theories

Exhibit 3.7 summarizes the central ideas behind the three content and three process theories of motivation presented in this chapter. As you can see, each of the process theories provides a unique perspective of employee motivation. Each looks at different variables in the workplace and the minds of employees. As for the content theories, Alderfer's ERG theory builds on Maslow's needs hierarchy theory. McClelland's learned needs theory is somewhat different because it suggests that some needs are acquired (learned) rather than instinctive.

Are Motivation Theories Culture Bound?

Are the motivation theories presented throughout this chapter relevant across cultures? A few scholars don't think so. They argue that most theories of motivation were developed by American scholars and tested on Americans, so they reflect the values of Americans and don't readily apply in cultures with different values.[53]

Some of this criticism has focused on older content theories (e.g., Maslow's needs hierarchy) that were rejected by organizational behaviour theorists long ago. It doesn't

EXHIBIT 3.7: Comparing Employee Motivation Theories

Motivation Theory	Type	Central Idea
Maslow's Needs Hierarchy	Content	People try to satisfy higher need when lower need is fulfilled (satisfaction-progression).
Alderfer's ERG Theory	Content	Satisfaction-progression (above) and people focus on lower need if unable to satisfy higher need (frustration-regression).
McClelland's Learned Needs	Content	Some needs are learned rather than instinctive.
Expectancy Theory	Process	Motivation is determined by perceived expectancies, outcome values, and a rational decision-making process.
Equity Theory	Process	Perceived equity is formed from outcome/input ratios with a comparison other, and people are motivated to reduce perceived inequities.
Goal Setting	Process	Clear, relevant goals increase motivation and performance by stretching the intensity and persistence of effort and by clarifying role perceptions.

make sense to complain about the relevancy of motivation theories abroad if they don't work in North America, either. Another criticism has been that people in other cultures have different needs. However, research has revealed that feelings of achievement and interesting work are the two most important motivating factors in several cultures (China, Germany, United States, etc.) Employees in different cultures may have different absolute levels of need for achievement, for example, but their relative strength is similar. Moreover, the conceptual structure of need for achievement is consistent across several different cultures, suggesting that its meaning is relevant in other societies.[54]

Expectancy theory has also been criticized as culture bound because it assumes that people act rationally to control their environment.[55] This feeling of personal control is strong in American culture, but not in countries where people believe that the consequences of their actions are largely preordained by God or some other external force. However, expectancy theory does not assume that people feel in control; on the contrary, the E→P expectancy directly varies with the employee's perceived control over the work situation. Research indicates that expectancy theory predicts employee motivation in different cultures.[56]

Equity theory also allows for individual differences and, consequently, seems to apply equally well to other cultures. We know that feelings of inequity vary somewhat across cultures, but they exist in everyone. Equity theory also allows for the fact that the most important inputs and outcomes can vary from one culture to the next.[57]

The debate over the cross-cultural relevance of motivation theories will continue for some time. Certainly, we must not automatically assume that a theory successfully tested in Canada will apply equally well in other societies. We need to continuously evaluate motivation theories and other organizational behaviour concepts in other cultures. Hopefully, future research will throw more light on the topic by evaluating the cross-cultural relevance of expectancy, goal setting, and other contemporary motivation theories. In the meantime, it is not clear (at least, not as clear as the critics believe) that contemporary motivation theories are culture bound.

Chapter Summary

- Work motivation refers to the forces within a person that affect his or her direction, intensity, and persistence of voluntary behaviour in the workplace. Companies need to rethink their motivational practices because of corporate downsizing, flatter organizations, and a changing workforce.

- Content theories of motivation explain why people have different needs at different times. Process theories of motivation describe the processes through which needs are translated into behaviour. Alderfer's ERG theory is a content motivation theory that groups human needs into a hierarchy of three broad categories: existence, relatedness, and growth. McClelland studied three needs that are learned rather than instinctive: need for achievement, need for power, and need for affiliation.

- Expectancy theory states that work effort is determined by the perception that effort will result in a particular level of performance (E→P expectancy), the perception that a specific behaviour or performance level will lead to specific outcomes (P→O expectancy), and the valences that the person feels for those outcomes.

- The E→P expectancy increases by improving the employee's ability and confidence to perform the job. The P→O expectancy increases by measuring performance accurately, distributing higher rewards to better performers, and showing employees that rewards are performance-based. Outcome valences increase by finding out what employees want and using these resources as rewards.

- Equity theory explains how people develop perceptions of fairness in the distribution and exchange of resources. The model includes four elements: outcome/input ratio, comparison other, equity evaluation, and consequences of inequity. The theory also explains what people are motivated to do when they feel inequitably treated.

- Goal setting is the process of motivating employees and clarifying their role perceptions by establishing benchmarks against which growth needs are fulfilled. Goals are more effective when they are specific, results-oriented, challenging, accepted by the employee, and accompanied by meaningful feedback. Participative goal setting is important in some situations. Goal setting is usually less effective when tied to financial rewards and when applied to new or complex tasks.

- We must not automatically assume that an employee motivation theory successfully tested in Canada will apply equally well in other cultures. However, there is increasing support for the cross-cultural relevance of the motivation theories described in this chapter.

Discussion Questions

1. The chapter begins by saying that motivating employees has never been more challenging. Describe three reasons why this might be true.

2. How does McClelland's needs theory differ from Alderfer's ERG theory?

3. As a team leader, you notice that one employee isn't putting a lot of effort into the team project because she doesn't believe she has the ability to contribute anything valuable. Using your knowledge of expectancy theory's E→P expectancy, identify four ways that you might increase this person's motivation to contribute to the team.

4. Use all three components of expectancy theory to explain why some employees are motivated to show up for work during a snowstorm, whereas others don't make any effort to leave their home.

5. Last year, Prairie Cellular Ltd. introduced a goal-setting program to improve motivation and performance among its salespeople. In January each year, salespeople are assigned a set of specific goals to improve work processes (e.g., submitting sales notes on time; say the customer's last name in conversations, etc.) After the first year, however, senior management decided to cancel the goal-setting program because sales did not improve even though competitors did well. Use your knowledge of the characteristics of effective goals to explain why goal setting may not have been effective at Prairie Cellular.

6. How does an employee's self-efficacy affect goal setting?

7. The five service representatives are upset that the newly hired representative with no previous experience will be paid $1,000 per year above the usual starting salary on the pay range. The department manager explained that the new hire would not accept the entry-level rate, so the company raised the offer by $1,000. All five reps currently earn salaries near the top of the scale ($10,000 higher), although they all started at the minimum starting salary a few years earlier. Use equity theory to explain why the five service representatives feel inequity in this situation.

8. Why is it difficult to maintain feelings of equity among employees?

Chapter Case

Steelfab Ltd.

Jackie Ney was an enthusiastic employee when she began working in the accounting department at Steelfab Ltd. In particular, she prided herself on discovering better ways of handling invoice and requisition flows. The company had plenty of bottlenecks in the flow of paperwork throughout the organization, and Jackie had made several rec- ommendations to her boss, Mr. Johnston, that would improve the process. Mr. Johnston acknowledged these suggestions and even implemented a few, but he didn't seem to have enough time either to thank her or explain why some of her suggestions could not be implemented. In fact, Mr. Johnston didn't say much to any of the other employees in the department about anything they did.

At the end of the first year, Jackie received a 6 percent merit increase based on Mr. Johnston's evaluation of her performance. This increase was equal to the average merit increase among the 11 people in the accounting department and was above the inflation rate. Still, Jackie was frustrated by the fact that she didn't know how to improve her chances of a higher merit increase the next year. She was also upset that another new employee, Jim Sandu, received the highest pay increase (10 percent) even though he was not regarded by others in the finance department as a particularly outstanding performer. According to others who worked with him on some assignments, Jim lacked the skills to perform the job well enough to receive such a high reward. However, Jim Sandu had become a favoured employee to Mr. Johnston and they had even gone on a fishing trip together.

Jackie's enthusiasm toward Steelfab Ltd. fell dramatically during her second year of employment. She still enjoyed the work and made friends with some of her co-workers, but the spirit that had once carried her through the morning rush-hour traffic had somehow dwindled. Eventually, Jackie stopped mentioning her productivity-improvement ideas. On two occasions during her second year of employment, she took a few days of sick leave to visit friends and family in New Brunswick. She had used only two sick days during her first year and these were for a legitimate illness. Even her doctor had to urge Jackie to stay at home on one occasion. But by the end of the second year, using sick days seemed to "justify" Jackie's continued employment at Steelfab Ltd. Now, as her second annual merit increase approached, Jackie started to seriously scout around for another job.

Discussion Questions

1. What symptoms exist in this case to suggest that something has gone wrong?

2. What are the root causes that have led to these symptoms?

3. What actions should the organization take to correct these problems?

© Copyright. Steven L. McShane.

Experiential Exercise

Bonus Decision-Making Exercise

Purpose: This exercise is designed to help you understand the elements of equity theory and how people differ in their equity perceptions.

Instructions: Four managers in a large national insurance company are described below. The national sales director of the company has given your consulting team (first individually, then together) the task of allocating $60,000 in bonus money to these four managers. It is entirely up to your team to decide how to divide the money among these people. The only requirements are that all of the money must be distributed and that no two branch managers can receive the same amount. The names and information are presented in no particular order. You should assume that economic conditions, client demographics, and other external factors are very similar for these managers.

Step 1:   Students will form teams of four or five people. Working alone, read information about the four managers. Then fill in the amount you would allocate to each manager in the "Individual Decision" column on page 83.

Step 2:   Still working alone, fill in the "Equity Inputs Form" (page 83). First, in the "Input Factor" column, list in order of importance the factors you considered when allocating these bonus amounts (e.g., seniority, performance, age, etc.). The most important factor should be listed first and the least important last. Next, in the "Input Weight" column estimate the percentage weight that you assigned to this factor. The total of this column must add up to 100 percent.

Step 3: After individually allocating the bonus money and determining the input factors and weights, team members will compare their results and note any differences. Then, for each job, team members will reach a consensus on the bonus amount that each manager should receive. These amounts will be written in the "Team Decision" column.

Step 4: The instructor will call the class together to compare team results and note differences in inputs and input weights used by individual students. Discussion of these results in terms of equity theory will follow.

Manager Profiles

Bob B.   Bob has been in the insurance business for more than 27 years and has spent the past 21 years with this company. A few years ago, Bob's branch typically made the largest contribution to regional profits. More recently, however, it has brought in few new accounts and is now well below average in terms of its contribution to the company. Turnover in the branch has been high and Bob doesn't have the same enthusiasm for the job as he once had. Bob is 56 years old and is married, with five children. Three children are still living at home. Bob has a high school diploma as well as a certificate from a special course in insurance management.

Edward E.   In the two years that Edward has been a branch manager, his unit brought in several major accounts and now stands as one of the top units in the country. Edward is well respected by his employees. At 29, he is the youngest manager in the region and one of the youngest in the country. The regional director initially doubted the wisdom of giving Edward the position of branch manager because of Edward's relatively young age and lack of experience in the insurance industry. Edward received an undergraduate business degree from the University of Prince Edward Island and worked for five years as a sales representative in Kitchener, Ontario, before joining this company. Edward is single and has no children.

Lee L.   Lee has been with this organization for seven years. She spent the first two years as a sales representative in the office that she now manages. According to the regional director, Lee rates about average as a branch manager. She earned an undergraduate degree in geography from the University of Calgary and worked in Alberta as a sales representative for four years with another insurance company before joining this organization. Lee is 40 years old, divorced, and has no children. She is a very ambitious person but sometimes has problems working with her staff and other branch managers.

Sandy S.   Sandy is 47 years old and has been a branch manager with this company for 17 years. Seven years ago, her branch made the lowest contribution to the region's profits, but this situation has steadily improved and her branch is now slightly above average. Sandy seems to have a mediocre attitude toward her job but she is well liked by her staff and other branch managers. Her experience in the insurance industry has been entirely with this organization. She previously worked in non-sales positions, and it is not clear how she became a branch manager without previous sales experience. Sandy is married and has three school-aged children. Several years ago, Sandy earned a diploma in business from a nearby community college by taking evening courses.

BONUS ALLOCATION FORM

Name	Individual Decision	Team Decision
Bob. B.	$ _____	$ _____
Edward E.	$ _____	$ _____
Lee L.	$ _____	$ _____
Sandy S.	$ _____	$ _____
TOTALS:	$ 60,000	$ 60,000

EQUITY INPUTS FORM

Input Factor*	Input Weight**
_____	_____ %
_____	_____ %
_____	_____ %
_____	_____ %
_____	_____ %
TOTAL:	100%

* List factors in order of importance, with the most important factor listed first.
** The weight of each factor is a percentage ranging from 1 to 100. All factor weights together must add up to 100 percent.

CHAPTER 4

Applied Motivation Practices

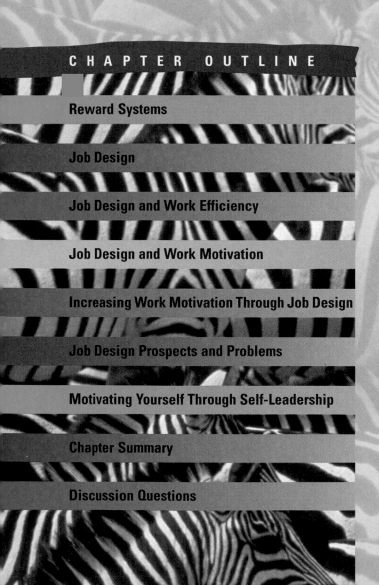

CHAPTER OUTLINE

Reward Systems

Job Design

Job Design and Work Efficiency

Job Design and Work Motivation

Increasing Work Motivation Through Job Design

Job Design Prospects and Problems

Motivating Yourself Through Self-Leadership

Chapter Summary

Discussion Questions

LEARNING OBJECTIVES

After reading this chapter, you should be able to:

- Discuss the advantages and disadvantages of the four types of rewards.

- Give an example of an individual, team, and organizational-level performance-based reward.

- Describe Kohn's five main concerns with rewards in organizations.

- Discuss the advantages and disadvantages of job specialization.

- Diagram the job characteristics model of job design.

- Identify three strategies to enrich jobs.

- Describe the five elements of self-leadership.

- Explain how mental imagery improves employee motivation.

Hewlett-Packard (Canada) Ltd.'s Beatrice Masini believes that her company has the right formula for motivating salespeople.

S elling computer hardware is a cut-throat business. The field is crowded and the competition is merciless. Hewlett-Packard (Canada) Ltd. knows this and has found ways to reward salespeople who make the difference. "We have a sales organization, and we like to recognize everybody in the organization that is helping the company achieve success," says Beatrice Masini, H-P Canada's manager of marketing and distribution.

H-P's top salespeople, along with their companions, are invited to the annual High Achievers Club meeting at a popular vacation spot. The real motivation is bragging rights. High Achievers have stars put on their name tags for each year they are members of this respected club.

"It certainly is a status symbol for somebody to be there with seven stars or eight stars on their name tag," says Gary Cooper, H-P's director of total quality management. "It indicates that they have been a High Achiever for that many years running."

The High Achievers Club is respectable, but Hewlett-Packard's sales elite get treated like conquering heroes if they become members of the President's Club. The President's Club is hosted by the president of Hewlett-Packard Worldwide at an exotic resort. People are selected by senior management based on their teamwork, customer satisfaction, and sales performance. "Typically, there will be only four people from Canada," says Cooper.

"The High Achievers and the President's Club definitely do [keep them motivated]," says Beatrice Masini. "What encourages the sales force is a lot of face-to-face recognition, constant feedback. Constant positive reinforcement, encouraging them face-to-face when they are doing well, gets them motivated a long way."[1]

W hether it's Hewlett-Packard's President's Club, IBM's One Hundred Percent Club, or American Express's Centurion Program, travel and recognition rewards have been incredibly successful. They motivate employees by fulfilling their social-esteem needs, and build loyalty by forming a social bond with other top performers in the company.

This chapter begins by introducing the different reward systems in organizations, and by considering some of their problems. But reward systems are not the only way to motivate employees. This chapter also examines the dynamics of job design, specific job design strategies to motivate employees, and the effectiveness of recent job design interventions. Then we turn to the emerging concept of self-leadership. This final section explains how employees motivate themselves through personal goal setting, constructive thought patterns, designing natural rewards, self-monitoring, and self-reinforcement.

Reward Systems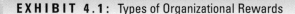

Rewards are a fundamental part of the employment relationship.[2] Organizations distribute money and other benefits in exchange for the employee's availability, competencies, and behaviours. The main idea behind these financial rewards is to ensure that individual goals are linked to corporate goals. You may have heard someone say: "This job is so much fun, I can't believe I'm being paid for it." However, some form of financial compensation is usually necessary to ensure that employees perform the work needed to serve customers, improve shareholder value, and satisfy government obligations. This concept of economic exchange can be found across cultures. The word for "pay" in Malay and Slovak means to replace a loss; in Hebrew and Swedish it means making equal.[3] No matter which culture, a paycheque means giving back or rebalancing the employee's contribution to the employer.

Exhibit 4.1 identifies the four main types of organizational rewards. Although Western culture dominates current thinking on reward systems, these rewards exist to varying degrees across cultures. For example, there is increasing evidence that individuals across cultures value some amount of performance-based pay rather than a completely fixed salary. A recent survey found that about 65 percent of large employers throughout Asia already use some form of performance-based reward system. Incentives were most popular in Thai companies and least likely to be found in Indonesian firms.[4]

Ethical values influence which type of reward dominates. Most Canadian companies provide long-term disability (LTD) insurance for ethical reasons. LTD insurance

EXHIBIT 4.1: Types of Organizational Rewards

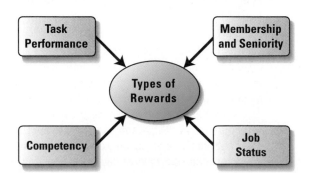

is a reward because employees usually value LTD when they need it, but it seldom motivates people to join an organization or put more effort into their work. Instead, this insurance satisfies the organization's moral obligations by ensuring that employees do not suffer financially if they become disabled and can no longer work.[5]

Membership and Seniority-Based Rewards

Most Canadians in paid employment receive hourly wages or fixed salaries and have the same benefits as their co-workers. Other rewards increase with seniority, such as the amount of paid vacation time. Some employees receive seniority-based pay increases; they progress one step through the pay range for each year in the job. Even merit systems have a large seniority component, because employees must spend time in the job before receiving an increase.[6] Company pension plans also emphasize seniority, because those who leave within the first two years of employment (or longer in some provinces) forfeit the pension money that the company has contributed on their behalf.

Advantages and disadvantages

Membership-based rewards may attract job applicants, particularly when the size of the reward increases with seniority. Seniority-based rewards reduce turnover because the cost of quitting increases with the employee's length of service. One problem with membership-based rewards is that they do not directly motivate job performance. For many years, Shell Canada Ltd. offered a generous pension plan and other membership-based rewards, but the company had lacklustre performance until it shifted to competency- and performance-based pay. Another problem is that membership-based rewards discourage poor performers from leaving voluntarily because they seldom have better job offers. Instead, the good performers are lured to better-paying jobs.

Job Status-Based Rewards

Job evaluation
Systematically evaluating the worth of jobs within the organization by measuring their required skill, effort, responsibility, and working conditions. Job evaluation results create a hierarchy of job worth.

Reward systems in Canada still rely on job status, particularly the use of job evaluation systems, to determine the size of a person's paycheque. **Job evaluation** systematically evaluates the worth of each job within the organization by measuring its required skill, effort, responsibility, and working conditions.[7] Job evaluation results create a job hierarchy that becomes the basis for pay differentials. A senior engineer would be assigned more job evaluation points and therefore be placed in a higher pay grade than an administrative assistant, because the engineer's job requires more skill, effort, and responsibility, and/or may have more challenging working conditions.

Some perquisites are also based on job status. For instance, senior executives at the Canadian Imperial Bank of Commerce have exclusive access to a private dining room. Procter & Gamble Canada and Amoco Canada assign larger offices with better furniture to people holding higher positions.

Advantages and disadvantages

Job evaluation systems are used in almost every large Canadian company because they try to maintain pay equity. Job evaluation systems are also used to identify cases of pay discrimination — situations in which women are paid less than men performing work of comparable value to the organization.[8] More generally, job status–based rewards motivate employees to compete for positions farther up the organizational hierarchy.

Despite these advantages, job evaluation systems have received much criticism for their subjectivity and tendency to justify the existing job hierarchy. Moreover, they motivate employees to increase their job's worth by exaggerating job duties and hoarding resources. These political behaviours may help employees move into a higher pay rate, but they don't help the organization.[9] Job status–based rewards also increase resistance to change and cause employees to focus on narrowly defined tasks rather than on broader organizational citizenship and customer service behaviours.

Job status–based benefits, such as executive dining rooms and golf-club memberships, create a psychological distance between employees and management, thereby inhibiting communication across these groups. Some companies have tried to minimize these problems by closing executive dining rooms and removing other status-based perquisites. However, the most recent trend is to shift the emphasis from job status to competencies, as we learn next.

Competency-Based Rewards

Competencies The abilities, individual values, personality traits, and other characteristics of people that lead to superior performance.

In Chapter 2, we defined **competencies** as the underlying characteristics of people that lead to superior performance.[10] Competency-based rewards pay employees for their skills, knowledge, and traits that lead to desired behaviours. Employees are expected to have several competencies, and these competencies are evaluated by observing specific behaviour patterns.

For instance, providing superior customer value is one of several competencies that employees are expected to possess at Bell Sygma (a subsidiary of Bell Canada). The company uses 360-degree feedback (Chapter 2) and other means to assess how well each employee identifies customer requirements, meets commitments on schedule, is responsive to customer problems, and provides quality products and services.[11] Employees who meet or exceed expectations on providing customer value receive higher pay.

Competency-based pay typically relies on *broadbanding*. Broadbanding reduces the number of pay grades in the organization and widens the range of pay that people might receive within their pay grade.[12] A company might have only 7 pay grades with wide ranges, rather than 30 pay grades with narrow ranges. In a broadbanded pay grade, employees move up the range of pay based on their level of competency. This compares with traditional status-based pay systems in which employees increase their pay mainly by being promoted into a new job and pay grade.

Skill-based pay (SBP)
Pay structures in which employees earn higher pay rates with the number of skill modules they have mastered, even though they perform only some of the mastered tasks in a particular job.

Skill-based pay (SBP) plans represent another variation of competency-based pay. In SBP plans, employees earn higher pay rates with the number of skill modules they have mastered.[13] Through special training and job rotation, employees learn how to operate another machine or complete another set of tasks. When the new skill module is mastered, their pay rate increases. Employees typically perform only one skill area at a time, but their pay rate is based on the number of areas for which they are currently qualified. Several Canadian firms use this reward system for production employees, including Northern Telecom, Shell Canada, Westinghouse Canada, and GE Canada Inc.

Advantages and disadvantages

Competency-based rewards, particularly skill-based pay plans, have been praised because they develop a flexible, multiskilled workforce. This ensures that employees can be moved around to fill labour shortages or satisfy immediate customer needs. Product or service quality tends to improve because multiskilled employees are more likely to know where problems originate. Moreover, employees find it easier to discover ways to improve the work process as they learn more skills and tasks in that process.[14]

Competency-based rewards are also consistent with the emerging view that people are hired into organizations, not into specific jobs. Rather than paying people for their ability in a specific job, these rewards ensure that the best-paid employees are those who can adjust to new situations because they possess the capabilities across jobs and circumstances.

However, competency-based rewards have their limitations. Competencies are supposed to be measured by assessing the employee's specific behaviours, but some critics argue that this can deteriorate into subjective personality assessments by co-workers and team leaders.[15] Unfortunately, as we will see in Chapter 6, it is difficult to measure personality traits and equally difficult to justify that they affect job performance.

Skill-based pay systems measure specific skills, so they are usually more objective and accurate than the broader competency approach. However, SBP plans are expensive because they motivate employees to spend time learning new tasks. Also, it's not uncommon to have most employees eventually reach the highest pay rate because there is no mechanism to reduce pay rates when employees get rusty on specific skills.

Performance-Based Rewards

One hundred years ago, Timothy Eaton awarded bonuses to clerks with the highest monthly sales. Many years before that, the Hudson's Bay Company paid voyageurs based on distance travelled rather than a fixed rate. This motivated them to accept the arduous task of crossing the Canadian wilderness for the company.[16] Today, performance-based rewards are found in most organizations, from entry-level employees to the executive suite. Performance-based rewards are not new to Canadian industry, but they now come in more flavours than ever before. Exhibit 4.2 lists the most common types of performance-based pay in each of the three levels of analysis.[17]

Individual rewards

Individual rewards have existed since Babylonian days in the twentieth century B.C.[18] The oldest of these is the *piece rate*, which calculates pay by the number of units an employee produces. For instance, employees at Stratton Knitting Mills in Toronto receive higher earnings if they sew more sweaters.[19] *Commissions* are similar to piece rates, except that earnings are based on sales volume rather than units produced. Many real-estate personnel and automobile salespeople are paid straight commission.

EXHIBIT 4.2: Types of Performance–Based Rewards

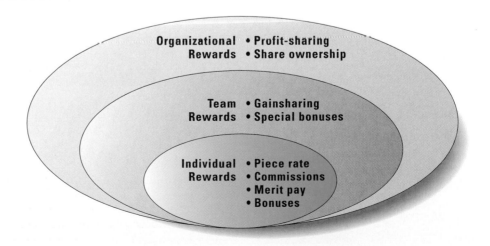

Organizational Rewards	• **Profit-sharing** • **Share ownership**
Team Rewards	• **Gainsharing** • **Special bonuses**
Individual Rewards	• **Piece rate** • **Commissions** • **Merit pay** • **Bonuses**

Many people receive *merit pay* — pay increases based on performance appraisal results in the previous year. However, firms are replacing merit increases with re-earnable *bonuses* for accomplishing specific tasks or achieving certain goals. Companies are discovering that gifts can also be effective individual rewards. Consumers Gas Co. in Toronto gives managers a budget to award ball-game or theatre tickets to individual employees who do something beyond normal requirements. Continental Airlines takes this one step further by providing its frequent customers with special certificates, and asking them to give the certificates to particularly helpful employees. Employees who receive these certificates redeem them for merchandise.[20]

Team rewards

The popularity of team-based rewards has soared, mainly because many companies are moving toward team-based structures.[21] Some team incentives take the form of bonuses

---

PERSPECTIVE 4.1

Campbell Soups Up Its Team Rewards

Campbell Soup Co. Ltd. wanted a reward system for its distribution employees that supports the company's team-based culture. The task of designing the reward system was given to one of the best distribution teams who, in turn, selected three members. This task force proposed a unique team-based reward system that has since been adopted across Campbell Soup's Canadian operations.

The team decided on three incentives: the Exceptional Teamwork Award, the Total Team Incentive Award, and the King Damage Award. The Exceptional Teamwork Award is given to the team member who consistently displays teamwork. The entire team receives the Total Team Incentive Award, based on exceeding budget expectations.

Award recipients receive a team barbecue, and may earn a leather Campbell Soup jacket if team performance is high enough. Phil Drouillard, Campbell Soup's human resources manager, says that it's important for employees to receive rewards that they really want. "They really wanted leather jackets, which they couldn't buy in the Campbell's store," Drouillard explains. "The jackets are special."

And what about the King Damage Award? This incentive, which is also called the "Skunk Trophy," is given to the person who damages the most soup cans each month during the distribution process. "The Skunk Trophy is a way to have fun with the plan," explains Drouillard. Of course, the objective is to *avoid* being a recipient of the King Damage Award.

Ron Chown, one of the three employees who designed the team reward system, has noticed that the plan has

Campbell Soup introduced a reward system that strengthens team dynamics among its distribution employees.

improved team behaviours. "People pay more attention to their work and are more willing to help each other out. In the Distribution Centre, we all want a leather jacket."

Source: Adapted from "Dream Teams," *Human Resources Professional*, November 1994, pp. 17–19.

or gifts. Health Care Diaper uses this approach to maintain product quality. Each week, the Richmond, British Columbia, manufacturer inspects a random case of disposable diapers and gives every production employee on that work shift a $10 bonus if the quality meets standards. If there is a quality problem or a customer complaint can be traced back to that work shift, the group loses its bonus for the week.[22] As we see in Perspective 4.1, Campbell Soup Co. Ltd. rewards teams for work quality. Individuals are also recognized for their teamwork.

Another type of team reward, called the **gainsharing plan**, motivates team members to reduce costs and increase labour efficiency. These plans calculate cost savings and pay out the same bonus to all team members using a predetermined formula. MacMillan Bloedel has gainsharing in several of its Western Canadian sawmills, where 10 percent of an employee's paycheque would be a gainsharing bonus in a typical year. Gainsharing plans are also found in service work. At University Hospital in Edmonton, the clerical support group shares a gainsharing bonus for suggestions that reduce waste.[23]

Gainsharing plans A reward system usually applied to work teams that distributes bonuses to team members based on the amount of cost reductions and increased labour efficiency in the production process.

Organizational rewards

Some rewards are based on indicators of the organization's performance. **Profit-sharing** plans are found in many Canadian companies, particularly firms that use teams and face plenty of competition.[24] Profit sharing includes any arrangement in which a designated group of employees receives a share of corporate profits. Although profit-sharing tries to motivate employees to reduce waste and improve performance, its clearest benefit is to automatically adjust employee wages with the firm's prosperity, thereby reducing the need for layoffs or negotiated pay reductions during recessions.[25]

Employee share ownership plans (ESOPs) encourage employees to buy shares of the company. Approximately one-third of publicly traded firms in Canada have some form of ESOP.[26] The employee-owned company is an extreme variation of share ownership. In several cases, such as Toronto Sun Publishing Co. and Algoma Steel Inc., employees have bought the company when it was about to be sold or closed down.[27] They receive shares of the company, and the value of those shares is affected by the company's prosperity.

Profit-sharing A reward system in which a designated group of employees receives a share of corporate profits.

Employee share ownership plan (ESOP) A reward system that encourages employees to buy shares of the company.

Ottawa Sun. Used with permission.

Ottawa Sun publisher John Paton acknowledges some of the paper's owners — its employees. Staff at the *Ottawa Sun*, three other Sun newspapers, and the *Financial Post* bought the Toronto Sun Publishing Corp. from Rogers Communications for $410 million.

The Trouble with Rewards

Canadian companies are using performance-based rewards more than ever. Yet, this does not mean that incentives are always good for business. One strong critic of workplace rewards is Alphie Kohn, an educational researcher and writer.[28] Kohn argues that rewards undermine employee motivation and end up costing more than they're worth.

Although Kohn identifies many different concerns, he takes direct aim at the organizational behaviour modification problems that we discussed in Chapter 2. For example, he argues that incentives lose their value over time. He even suggests that praise is unhealthy when applied as an OB Mod reinforcer. Kohn's five main arguments against the use of performance-based rewards are as follows:

- *Rewards punish*   Kohn suggests that there are punitive features built into every reward. First, when rewarding someone, we are also demonstrating our control over them. This can eventually assume a punitive quality by making the reward recipient feel subservient. Second, after being rewarded, employees come to expect that reward in the future. If their expectation is not met, they feel punished.

- *Rewards rupture relationships*   Kohn complains that individual rewards create jealousies and competition. Team rewards aren't any better, because they encourage peer pressure. Rewards also create a psychological distance between the person giving and receiving the reward. Taken together, rewards disrupt the collaboration needed for organizational learning.

- *Rewards ignore reasons*   Employers need to spend time discovering the cause of behaviour problems. Instead, according to Kohn, they use incentives as quick fixes. We can see this in situations where companies use incentives for the most trivial reasons. For example, an Arizona company hands out cash to employees who arrive early at company meetings and fines those who arrive late.[29] The company would be better off identifying the causes of lateness and changing the conditions, rather than using money to force a solution to the problem.

- *Rewards discourage risk taking*   Kohn cites evidence that rewards motivate people to do exactly what is necessary to get the reward, and nothing more. Incentives dampen creativity because employees no longer explore new opportunities outside the realm of rewarded behaviour or results. In other words, rewards motivate employees to get rewards, not to discover better ways to help the organization.

- *Rewards undermine intrinsic motivation*   Kohn's greatest concern with reward systems is that they kill a person's motivation found in the work itself. This intrinsic motivation relates to fulfilling growth needs, which are the most powerful and sustaining sources of motivation (see Chapter 3). Several studies report that employees are less intrinsically motivated to perform a task after they have received an extrinsic reward for performing the task.[30]

Agency theory An economic theory that assumes company owners (principals) and employees (agents) have different goals and interests, so rewards and other control systems are required to align the agent's goals with those of the principals.

Should we abandon rewards, based on Alphie Kohn's arguments? Probably not. Organizational behaviour scholars have known for years that performance-based rewards are imperfect, but when implemented properly, they serve an important purpose. The strongest argument for performance-based rewards comes from the economic concept called **agency theory**.[31] According to agency theory, company owners (principals) and employees (agents) have different goals and interests. For example, companies typically want to provide a good return on investment to shareholders, serve customers effectively, and meet government obligations. Reward systems are designed to successfully align employee goals and actions with these interests.

Although agency theory may not appreciate that employees are motivated by the work itself, Kohn and other critics of rewards do not recognize that employees also need some alignment through incentives, praise, and other reward practices. At the same time, we need to avoid the problems that often plague performance-based reward systems in organizational settings. Here are some of the more important strategies.

Measure performance accurately

Rewards won't work unless companies learn how to measure employee performance and tie that information to the reward. This connection strengthens the low P→O expectancy that we learned about in Chapter 3. Unfortunately, one recent survey reported that only 36 percent of Canadian employees believed top performers receive more money and recognition than average or poor performers.[32] This occurs partly because it is difficult to measure the many elements of job performance and organizational citizenship. Moreover, evidence suggests that performance pay decisions are biased by organizational politics. Employees with organizational connections (e.g., friendships with senior management) tend to receive higher increases.[33]

Recognize and adjust for situational contingencies

Reward systems need to correct for circumstances where superior or inferior performance is caused by situational contingencies rather than the employee's ability or motivation. MacMillan Bloedel experienced this problem with its gainsharing plan. Employees enjoyed an unexpectedly large bonus because a falling Canadian dollar suddenly improved the gainsharing results. The plan was intended to reward employees for their personal productivity improvements, not for windfall gains in exchange rates.[34]

Use team rewards for interdependent jobs

Companies need to use team (or organizational) rewards rather than individual rewards when employees work in highly interdependent jobs. One reason for team rewards in team settings is that we can't identify or measure individual contributions very well in these situations. For example, you can't see how well one employee in a chemical-processing plant contributes to the quality of the liquid produced. It is a team effort. A second reason is that team rewards tend to make employees more cooperative and less competitive. People see that their bonuses or other incentives depend on how well they work with co-workers, and they act accordingly.

A third reason for having team rewards in team settings is that they influence employee preferences for team-based work arrangements. This was found in a recent study of Xerox customer service representatives. The Xerox employees assigned to teams with purely team bonuses eventually accepted and preferred a team structure, whereas those put in teams without team rewards did not adapt as well to the team structure.[35]

Ensure rewards are valued

Employers often introduce a reward without considering whether employees really value it. This point relates to the valence concept in expectancy theory. If reward valence is low, then motivation is low. Campbell Soup Co., described earlier, appreciated this issue and therefore relied on employees to identify valued rewards, such as leather jackets. A related issue is whether any positive value of the reward is offset by countervalent forces. Consider the experience of a British firm that asked employees to choose an employee-of-the-month. Everyone thought that the incentive was so tacky they chose the worst employees for the award. "The company was surprised at the choices," explains a consultant familiar with the case, "but it didn't dawn on them what was going on."[36] Employees may have appreciated praise, but the "uncool" nature of this reward easily offset its benefits.

Watch out for unintended consequences

Performance-based reward systems sometimes influence different behaviours than we intend. One such example was the pizza company that decided to reward its drivers for on-time delivery. The plan got more hot pizzas to customers, but it also caused drivers to drive recklessly.[37] Perspective 4.2 describes a few other examples where reward systems had unintended consequences. Systems theory explains why these problems occur. In Chapter 1, we learned that organizations are open systems with many interdependent parts. This makes it very difficult to predict the possible consequences of organizational actions, such as the introduction of a performance-based reward system.

Job Design

Job design The process of assigning tasks to a job and distributing work throughout the organization.

Job design involves assigning tasks to a job and distributing work throughout the organization. Some jobs have very few tasks, each requiring limited skill or effort. Other jobs include a very complex set of tasks and can be accomplished by only a few highly trained tradespeople or professionals.

The tasks that people perform are constantly changing. Computer technology often affects job duties, although management can influence the way jobs are designed around this technology.[38] Organizational restructuring has resulted in a shift away from job-based employment. Instead, many employees are hired into generic positions (associates, team members) and are expected to perform a variety of tasks. "Employees today perform tasks, not jobs, and they can do a multiplicity of things," says Rod Seiling, president of the Ontario Hotel/Motel Association.[39]

Job design is important because of its influence on employee attitudes, motivation, and performance. As we shall see, job design often produces an interesting conflict between the employee's motivation and ability to complete the work. To understand this issue more fully, we begin by describing early job design efforts aimed at increasing work efficiency through job specialization.

Job Design and Work Efficiency

Mary Strang sees plenty of windshields, about 72 of them every hour. Mary and her assembly-line partner mount one windshield onto a Chrysler Neon every 45 seconds. That's more than 500 windshields on each work shift, five days each week, plus a couple of Saturdays every month.[40]

Job specialization The result of division of labour in which each job now includes a narrow subset of the tasks required to complete the product or service.

Mary works in a job with a high degree of **job specialization**. Job specialization occurs when the work required to build a Neon car — or any other product or service — is subdivided into separate jobs assigned to different people. The resulting jobs each include a very narrow subset of tasks and usually require a short "cycle time." A cycle time is the time required to complete the task before starting over with a new work unit. For Mary, the cycle time is less than a minute.

The economic benefits of job specialization were popularized more than 200 years ago by Adam Smith in his famous example of pin manufacturing.[41] According to Smith, there are several distinct operations in pin manufacturing, such as drawing out the wire, straightening it, cutting it, sharpening one end, grinding the other end, putting on the head, and whitening the head. In one factory where these tasks were

---

PERSPECTIVE 4.2

When Rewards Go Wrong

There is an old saying that "What gets rewarded gets done." But what companies reward isn't always what they had intended for employees to do. Here are a few dramatic examples:

- Donnelly Mirrors, the automobile parts manufacturer, introduced a gainsharing plan that motivated employees to reduce labour but not material costs. Employees knew that their work took longer as the diamond grinding wheels started to wear down, so they reduced labour costs by replacing the expensive wheels more often. This action reduced labour costs, thereby giving them the gainsharing bonus, but labour savings were easily offset by much higher costs for diamond grinding wheels.
- An insurance company wanted salespeople to contact potential clients, so it devised an incentive that rewarded them based on the number of telephone calls made each month to prospective clients. The salespeople made significantly more calls under this plan, but they didn't sell any more insurance policies. In fact, the company had fewer sales and a much larger telephone bill.
- Productivity bonuses have been used in the Canadian mining industry for many years. However, some claim that

miners are more likely to bypass safety procedures under this reward system so that they get a larger bonus. One tragic example involved Richard Kerr, a miner at Inco Ltd.'s Garson mine who died while installing roof supports. Kerr's work significantly affected everyone's safety (the supports prevented the mine from caving in), yet an inquiry learned that nearly half of his paycheque was based on bonuses for working faster. The company did not have a bonus for proper construction of the roof supports.

- Like many automobile companies, Toyota rewards its dealerships based on customer-satisfaction surveys, not just car sales. What Toyota discovered, however, is that the system motivates dealers to increase satisfaction scores, not customer satisfaction. One Toyota dealership received high ratings because it offered free detailing to every customer who returned a "Very Satisfied" survey. The dealership even had a special copy of the survey showing clients which boxes to check off. At another dealership, a recently hired salesperson was found pleading with customers to give him a good rating so that he didn't lose his job. This increased customer ratings, but not customer satisfaction.

Sources: Adapted from F. F. Reichheld, *The Loyalty Effect* (Boston, MA: Harvard University Press, 1996), p. 236; D. R. Spitzer, "Power Rewards: Rewards That Really Motivate," *Management Review*, May 1996, pp. 45–50; E. E. Lawler III, *Strategic Pay* (San Francisco: Jossey-Bass, 1990), p. 120; T. Pender, "Miners' Bonus Wage System Comes Under Ontario Scrutiny," *Globe & Mail*, August 25, 1986, p. A16.

divided among 10 people, Smith reported that the work team could produce almost 4,800 pins per day. But if the same 10 people made their own pins separately and independently, they would produce only 100 to 200 pins per day!

Why does job specialization potentially increase work efficiency? One reason is that employees have fewer tasks to juggle and therefore they spend less time changing activities. A second explanation is that employees require fewer physical and mental skills to accomplish the assigned work, so less time and resources are needed for training. A third reason is that employees practise their tasks more frequently with shorter work cycles, so jobs are mastered quickly. Lastly, work efficiency increases because employees with specific aptitudes or skills can be matched more precisely to the jobs for which they are best suited.[42]

Adam Smith was mainly writing about *horizontal job specialization*, in which the basic physical behaviours required to provide a product or service are divided into different jobs (see Exhibit 4.3). *Vertical job specialization*, on the other hand, refers to separating physical tasks from the administration of these tasks (planning, organizing, scheduling, etc.). In other words, vertical job specialization divorces the "thinking" job functions from the "doing" job functions.

Scientific Management

Scientific management
The process of systematically determining how work should be partitioned into its smallest possible elements and how the process of completing each task should be standardized to achieve maximum efficiency.

One of the strongest advocates of job specialization was Frederick Winslow Taylor, an industrial engineer who introduced the principles of **scientific management** in the early 1900s.[43] Taylor described scientific management as a revolutionary way for management and workers to view their respective roles. In practice, it involves systematically determining how work should be partitioned into its smallest possible elements and how the process of completing each task should be standardized to achieve maximum efficiency.

Taylor advocated vertical job specialization so that detailed procedures and work practices are developed by engineers, enforced by supervisors, and executed by employees. In Taylor's words: "All possible brain work should be removed from the shop floor and centred in the planning and laying out department."[44] He also applied horizontal job specialization, such as specializing the supervisor's role so that one person manages operational efficiency, another manages inspection, and another is the disciplinarian.

EXHIBIT 4.3: Horizontal and Vertical Job Specialization

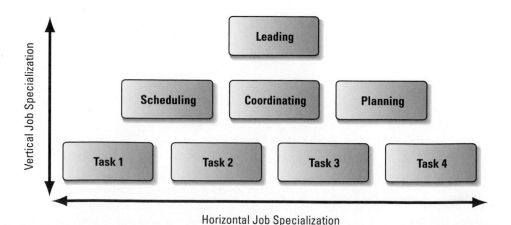

Methods-time measurement The process of systematically observing, measuring, and timing the smallest physical movements to identify more efficient work behaviours.

Scientific management ideas can be found throughout industry today. Goal setting, employee training, incentive systems, and other practices described in this book were popularized by Taylor. **Methods-time measurement** also developed out of scientific management. Methods-time measurement involves systematically observing, measuring, and timing physical movements to identify more efficient work behaviours. Industrial engineers use these practices to identify the best way to lay bricks, prepare hamburgers in fast-food restaurants, or engage in any other observable behaviour. For example, Canada Post uses methods-time measurement on letter carrier routes to improve productivity. National Sea Products Ltd. in Nova Scotia has done the same in its fish processing plants.[45] In fact, many companies rely on these practices, although consultants often use trendier names.

There is ample evidence that scientific management has improved efficiency in many work settings. One of Taylor's earliest interventions was at a ball-bearing factory where 120 women each worked 55 hours per week. Through job specialization and work efficiency analysis, Taylor increased production by two-thirds using a workforce of only 35 women working fewer than 45 hours per week. Taylor also doubled the employees' previous wages. No doubt, some of the increased productivity can be credited to improved training, goal setting, and work incentives, but job specialization has also contributed to the success of scientific management.

Scientific management was also successful in Canada. In 1927, an American industrial engineer was hired by York Knitting Mills in Toronto to increase productivity through methods-time measurement and wage incentives. The results were so dramatic that Douglas Woods (York's owner) and two colleagues formed their own consulting firm to practise a variation of scientific management known as the "York Plan."[46] Woods' company later became one of Canada's largest consulting firms (Woods Gordon).

Problems with Job Specialization

Job specialization tries to increase work efficiency, but it doesn't necessarily improve job performance. The problem is that this practice ignores the effects of job content on employees.[47] Highly specialized jobs are tedious, trivial, and socially isolating. These conditions lead to worker alienation, whereby employees feel powerlessness and meaninglessness in their work lives, as well as increasing removal from social norms, and a psychological separation of oneself from the activities being performed.[48]

Job specialization was supposed to let companies buy cheap, unskilled labour. Instead, many companies must offer higher wages — some call it *discontentment pay* — to compensate for the job dissatisfaction of narrowly defined work.[49] Labour unions have also been effective at organizing and negotiating higher wages for employees in specialized, short-cycle jobs. Job specialization also costs more in terms of higher turnover, absenteeism, sabotage, and mental health problems.

Work quality has become another major concern. Employees in specialized jobs usually see only a small part of the process, so they can't identify with the customer's needs. As one observer of General Motors' traditional assembly line reported: "Often [workers] did not know how their jobs related to the total picture. Not knowing, there was no incentive to strive for quality — what did quality even mean as it related to a bracket whose function you did not understand."[50]

Perhaps the most important reason job specialization has not been as successful as expected is that it ignores the motivational potential of jobs. As Exhibit 4.4 illustrates, job specialization may have a curvilinear effect on job performance. As jobs become specialized, the work tends to become easier to perform, but it is less moti-

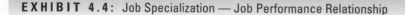

EXHIBIT 4.4: Job Specialization — Job Performance Relationship

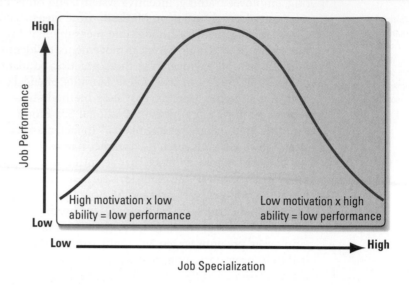

High motivation x low
ability = low performance

Low motivation x high
ability = low performance

Job Specialization

vating. As jobs become more complex, work motivation increases, but the ability to master the job decreases. Maximum job performance occurs somewhere between these two extremes, where most people can eventually perform the job tasks efficiently, yet the work is interesting.

Job Design and Work Motivation

Industrial engineers may have overlooked the motivational effects of job characteristics, but it is now the central focus of most job design interventions.[51] In the 1950s, Frederick Herzberg proposed that employees are primarily motivated by characteristics of the work itself, such as recognition, responsibility, advancement, achievement, and personal growth. These factors are called *motivators* because employees experience job satisfaction when they are received and are therefore motivated to obtain them. In contrast, job security, working conditions, company policies, co-worker relations, supervisor relations, and other factors extrinsic to the work, called *hygienes*, affect the extent that employees feel job dissatisfaction. Improving hygienes will reduce job dissatisfaction, but they will have almost no effect on job satisfaction or employee motivation.[52]

Herzberg's work was significant because few writers had previously addressed the idea that employees may be motivated by the work itself. This shift in thinking has led to considerable study into the motivational potential of jobs.[53] Out of that research has emerged Hackman and Oldham's **job characteristics model**. This model, shown in Exhibit 4.5, details the motivational properties of jobs as well as specific personal and organizational consequences of these properties.[54] The job characteristics model identifies five core job dimensions that produce three psychological states. Employees who experience these psychological states tend to have higher levels of internal work motivation (motivation from the work itself), job satisfaction (particularly satisfaction with the work itself), and work effectiveness.

Job characteristics model A job design model that relates five core job dimensions to three psychological states and several personal and organizational consequences.

EXHIBIT 4.5: The Job Characteristics Model

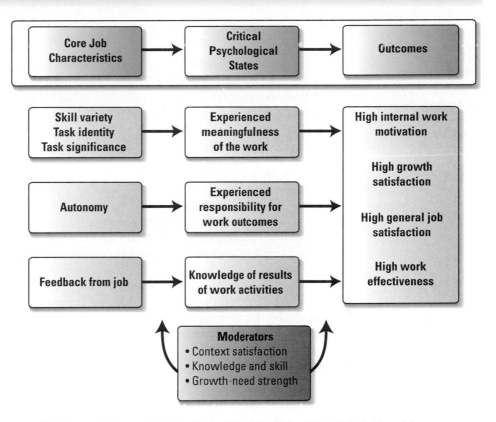

Source: J. R. Hackman and G. Oldham, *Work Redesign* (Reading, MA: Addison-Wesley, 1980), p. 90. Used with permission.

Core Job Characteristics

Hackman and Oldham, along with earlier researchers, have identified five core job characteristics (see Exhibit 4.5). Desirable work outcomes increase when jobs are redesigned such that they include more of the following characteristics:

Skill variety The extent to which a job requires employees to use different skills and talents to complete a variety of work activities.

- *Skill variety* **Skill variety** refers to using different skills and talents to complete a variety of work activities. For example, sales clerks who normally only serve customers might be assigned the additional duties of stocking inventory and changing storefront displays.

Task identity The degree to which a job requires completion of a whole or identifiable piece of work.

- *Task identity* **Task identity** is the degree to which a job requires completion of a whole or identifiable piece of work, such as doing something from beginning to end, or where it is easy to see how one's work fits into the whole product or service. An employee who assembles an entire computer modem rather than just solders in the circuitry would develop a stronger sense of ownership or identity with the final product.

Task significance The degree to which a job has a substantial impact on the organization and/or larger society.

- *Task significance* **Task significance** is the degree to which the job has a substantial impact on the organization and/or larger society. For instance, Canadian Coast Guard radio operators would have a high degree of task significance because the quality of their work affects the safety of others.

Autonomy The degree to which a job gives employees the freedom, independence, and discretion to schedule their work and determine the procedures to be used to complete the work.

Job feedback The degree to which employees can tell how well they are doing based on direct sensory information from the job itself.

- *Autonomy* Jobs with high levels of **autonomy** provide employees with freedom, independence, and discretion in scheduling the work and determining the procedures to be used to complete the work. In autonomous jobs, employees make their own decisions rather than rely on detailed instructions from supervisors or procedure manuals.

- *Job feedback* **Job feedback** is the degree to which employees can tell how well they are doing based on direct sensory information from the job itself. Airline pilots can tell how well they land their aircraft and physicians can see whether their operations have improved the patient's health.

Critical Psychological States

The five core job characteristics discussed above affect employee motivation and satisfaction through three critical psychological states.[55] One of these is *experienced meaningfulness* — the belief that one's work is worthwhile or important. Skill variety, task identity, and task significance directly contribute to the job's meaningfulness. If the job has high levels of all three characteristics, employees are likely to feel that their job is highly meaningful. Meaningfulness drops as the job loses one or more of these characteristics.

Work motivation and performance increase when employees feel personally accountable for the outcomes of their efforts. Autonomy directly contributes to this feeling of *experienced responsibility*. Employees must be assigned control of their work environment to feel responsible for their successes and failures. The third critical psychological state is *knowledge of results*. Employees want information about the consequences of their work effort. Knowledge of results can originate from co-workers, supervisors, or clients. However, job design focuses on knowledge of results from the work itself.

Individual Differences

Job redesign increases work motivation only under certain conditions. One condition is that employees must have the required skills and knowledge to master the more challenging work. Otherwise, job redesign tends to increase stress and reduce job performance. A second condition is that employees must be reasonably satisfied with their work environment (e.g., working conditions, job security, salaries) before job redesign affects work motivation.

A third condition is that employees must have strong growth needs. As we learned in Chapter 3, these people have satisfied their relatedness or existence needs, and are looking for challenges from the work itself. In contrast, people who are primarily focused on existence or relatedness needs will be less motivated by job design.[56]

Increasing Work Motivation Through Job Design

Three main strategies potentially increase the motivational potential of jobs: job rotation, job enlargement, and job enrichment. As we will learn in this section, there are also several ways to implement job enrichment.

Job Rotation

Job rotation Moving employees from one job to another for short periods of time.

Job rotation is the practice of moving employees from one job to another, as shown in Exhibit 4.6. This form of job redesign is widely practised in North America, particularly in the manufacturing sector.[57] Binney and Smith, the manufacturer of Crayola Crayons, encourages job rotation at its Lindsay, Ontario, plant to reduce the boredom

EXHIBIT 4.6: Job Rotation and Job Enlargement

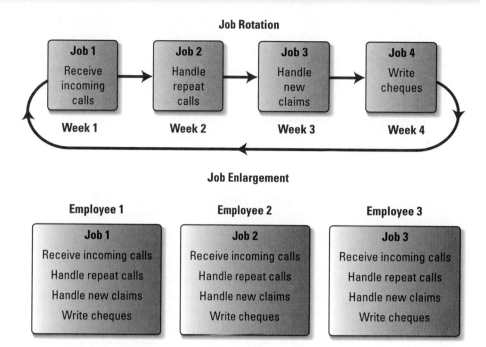

of repeating the same short-cycle tasks all day. Although some employees were initially reluctant, most enjoy the increased skill variety by rotating from fork lifts to hexagonal crayon mold machines.[58]

The main reason many companies have introduced job rotation isn't to reduce boredom. Rather, they want to develop a multiskilled workforce. Job rotation helps employees learn other tasks and thereby increase their ability to move to jobs where they are needed. At Memorial Medical Centre in Las Cruces, New Mexico, cooks are expected to do catering and pot-washers do some cooking. Costs are reduced because multiskilled workers can cover for each other's absences and thereby minimize labour shortages in food preparation. "Some employees don't like switching around like this and some have left the department because of it," explains Memorial Medical Centre's manager in charge of food services. "But we have to do [job rotation] to build in flexibility."[59]

A third objective of job rotation is to reduce the incidence of repetitive strain injuries. Snap-On Tools of Canada Ltd. relies on job rotation for this reason. The company experienced high injury rates at its Newmarket, Ontario, plant because employees were using the same muscles in their narrowly defined jobs. Job rotation, along with better workplace design, significantly reduced these soft-tissue injury rates.[60]

Job Enlargement

Job enlargement
Increasing the number of tasks employees perform within their job.

Job enlargement involves increasing the number of tasks employees perform *within* a job (see Exhibit 4.6). This increases skill variety and lengthens the work cycle so that tasks are repeated less frequently. Job enlargement is sometimes called *horizontal job loading* because it reverses horizontal job specialization.

A recent example of job enlargement can be found at the Windsor, Ontario, affiliate of the Canadian Broadcasting Corporation (CBC), where "video journalists" serve as camera operators as well as TV reporters.[61] Although Citytv in Toronto has been doing the same thing for several years, this is a dramatic change in an industry that takes job specialization to an extreme. To give you a contrast, the employees who design graphics throughout the CBC are usually different from those who print the names of people appearing on-screen. The Windsor TV station also combined those tasks into one job.

Some companies, including NCR Canada and GTE Canada, have reported improved product quality when job enlargement is introduced.[62] This might occur because giving more tasks to fewer workers reduces coordination problems. However, recent information suggests that simply giving employees more tasks won't affect motivation, performance, or job satisfaction. Instead, these benefits result only when skill variety is combined with more autonomy and job knowledge.[63] In other words, employees are motivated when they have a variety of tasks *and* the freedom and knowledge to structure their work to achieve the highest satisfaction and performance. Increasing job autonomy is at the heart of job enrichment, which we discuss next.

Job Enrichment

Job enrichment
Assigning responsibility for scheduling, coordinating, and planning work to employees who actually make the product or provide the service.

Job enrichment is based on the idea that motivation increases when the job provides opportunities for recognition, responsibility, advancement, achievement, and personal growth. The responsibility for scheduling, coordinating, and planning work is assigned to the employees who make the product or provide the service. Job enrichment is sometimes called *vertical job loading* because it reverses vertical job specialization.

How do you enrich jobs? Generally, job enrichment includes any strategy that increases one or more of the core job characteristics (skill variety, task identity, task significance, autonomy, feedback.)[64] For example, employees have more enriched jobs if they get direct feedback about their work. This feedback may occur by performing an entire task and seeing the results, or with the assistance of gauges and other instruments to monitor production results. Although there are numerous ways to enrich jobs, three of the most popular methods include empowerment, forming natural work units, and establishing client relationships.

Empowering employees

At the heart of job enrichment is the idea of vertically loading the job; that is, giving employees control over scheduling, coordinating, and planning their work. In practice, vertical loading involves letting job holders decide work methods, check quality, establish work schedules, decide how to solve problems, and even have knowledge of and control over financial budgets. In short, employees are given more autonomy over the work process.

Empowerment The feeling of control and self-efficacy that emerges when people are given power in a previously powerless situation.

Many organizations apply a form of vertical job loading called **empowerment**. Empowerment refers to a feeling of control and self-efficacy that emerges when people are given power in a previously powerless situation.[65] Empowered employees are given autonomy — the freedom, independence, and discretion over their work activities. They are assigned work that has high levels of task significance — importance to themselves and others. Empowered employees also have control over performance feedback that guides their work. Also notice from the definition that empowered employees have feelings of self-efficacy; that is, they believe that they are capable of successfully completing the task.[66]

Empowerment has become such a popular practice in Canadian organizations that it is in danger of being labelled a trendy fad. Indeed, many companies claim that they practise empowerment, but haven't introduced the changes necessary to make this a

---

PERSPECTIVE 4.3

Empowering Staff at Dufferin Game Room

Customer satisfaction isn't good enough at Dufferin Game Room Store Ltd. Instead, the Canadian retail chain that sells playing cards, pool tables, and other game accessories wants to amaze its customers. To achieve this daunting goal, Dufferin empowers its employees and supports their performance with valued incentives.

"[Employees] could do anything, anywhere, any time, any way it took, no matter what the cost, to amaze our customers," says Phillip Adsetts, Dufferin's vice-president of operations. For example, unlike many other retailers, Dufferin employees can decide without management approval whether to accept returned items that have been opened or where the receipt is lost.

When Dufferin gave employees this autonomy, the only problem was that they didn't know how to handle it. "It scared the heck out of them," recalls Adsetts. So Dufferin introduced training programs that show staff how to make decisions that serve customers wisely. "[We] empower our front lines, but also educate them how to use the empowerment," says Adsetts.

Dufferin's sales staff also receive special incentives to support their empowerment. Employees receive "Dufferin Dollars" for exceptional customer service, sales, or store displays. Dufferin Dollars can be redeemed for selected merchandise from the company. Top-selling stores also receive "party packages" containing everything they need to celebrate their success.

Dufferin's application of empowerment and rewards has paid off. Shrinkage (lost or stolen inventory) is less than one-quarter of what it was a few years ago. Moreover, employees are challenged by the enriched jobs and meaningful rewards. "I have part-time staff that really work their hearts out because of the positive motivation," says Bruce Hovey, manager of a Dufferin Game Room store in Barrie, Ontario.

Source: Adapted from C. Knight, "Sales Training in Which the Customer is Everything," *Canadian HR Reporter*, September 9, 1996, p. 2.

---

reality. This may explain why some studies in Canada and elsewhere have not found any improvements after corporate leaders have allegedly "empowered" employees.[67]

Fortunately, we have many examples of companies that have truly implemented empowerment. Highland Valley Copper in British Columbia is one example. Supervisors and managers went through nearly two years of daily coaching by a consulting firm to learn how to give employees more power over their work. It was a dramatic shift from the militaristic culture that previously existed at the company. "We want to get away from kick-butt-style management," explains Rod Killough, Highland Valley's industrial relations manager. "We want to see supervisors and crews working on their own initiative."[68] Perspective 4.3 illustrates how empowerment works at Dufferin Game Room Store Ltd., and how this form of job enrichment can potentially reap rewards for both employees and the company.

Forming natural work units

Another way to enrich jobs is to group tasks into a logical set. A natural grouping might refer to completing a whole task, such as assembling an entire toaster rather than just some parts of it. Or it might involve assigning employees to a specific client group, such as managing entire portfolios for specific clients rather than taking random client calls from a customer service pool.

By forming natural work units, job holders develop a sense of responsibility for an identifiable body of work. They feel a sense of ownership and, therefore, tend to increase job quality. Forming natural work units increases task identity and task significance because employees make a complete product or perform a complete service and can more readily see how their work affects others.

Establishing client relationships

As mentioned, some natural work units assign employees to a specific client group. Establishing client relationships takes this one step further by putting employees in *direct contact* with their client group rather than using the supervisor as a go-between. The key factor is direct communication between the employee and the client. The client submits work and provides feedback directly to the employee rather than through a supervisor.[69]

Nova Scotia Power Inc. applies this form of job enrichment in its rural districts. At one time, installing and disconnecting service, reading meters, and collecting over-due accounts were assigned to people in different jobs. Now, one employee completes all of these tasks for the same client and works directly with the client. By being directly responsible for specific clients, employees have more information and can make decisions affecting those clients. Louis Comeau, Nova Scotia Power's CEO, explains: "The customer receives first-class service, employees enjoy more variety, wider responsibility and greater job satisfaction, and the company reduces its costs."[70]

Job Design Prospects and Problems

Job design has become tremendously popular in recent years. Only 2 percent of Canadian firms had job design interventions before 1960, compared with somewhere between 30 to 50 percent today. These interventions also have a much higher survival rate than most work interventions.[71]

But to what extent does job enrichment improve employee and organizational effectiveness? Employees with high growth needs whose jobs are enriched have higher job satisfaction, higher work motivation, lower absenteeism, and lower turnover. Productivity is also higher when task identity and job feedback are improved.[72] Error rates, number of defects, and other quality indicators tend to improve, because job enrichment increases the job holder's felt responsibility and sense of ownership over the product or service. Quality improvements in production and service are particularly evident when the job enrichment intervention involves completing a natural work unit or establishing client relationships.[73]

Obstacles in Job Design

Job design is not easy to implement. One concern is that it is difficult to accurately measure the core job characteristics.[74] Consequently, firms have trouble pinpointing which jobs require changing and how well job design interventions are working. Another problem is that many work settings require team-based job redesign because the technology is fixed or the work cycle is too complex for one person to handle alone. For example, one employee would not make an entire automobile or operate an entire petrochemical process. Although much of the job design literature has concentrated on changing individual jobs, more focus is needed on self-directed work teams and related team-based job design interventions.[75] We will discuss these practices in Chapter 10 after introducing team dynamics in Chapter 9.

Job design interventions also face resistance to change. Some supervisors don't like job redesign interventions because they change the supervisors' roles and may threaten job security.[76] Labour union leaders have been bitter foes of job specialization and scientific management, yet they complain that job enrichment programs are management ploys to get more work out of employees for less money. Unskilled employees may lack the confidence or growth-need strength to learn more challenging tasks. Skilled employees are known to resist job redesign because they believe the intervention will undermine their power base and force them to perform lower-status work.[77]

Kellogg's, the U.S.-owned cereal company, recently experienced this problem at its production plant in Australia. The company wanted to enlarge and enrich jobs for a multiskilled workforce, but maintenance employees refused to let production employees do simple maintenance tasks. "We had negotiated to lift the skill levels of operators through a comprehensive multiskilling program, only to have the maintenance unions continually renege on that," says Clyde Morgan, Kellogg's Australian human resources manager. To remove this barrier, the company contracted out the entire maintenance work.[78]

An ongoing dilemma with job design is finding the ideal balance between job enrichment and specialization. There are several competing factors to consider. Specialized jobs may improve work efficiency, but job performance may decline as employee motivation falls. Job enrichment may increase motivation, but performance may fall if employees lack the skills necessary to complete more challenging tasks. Job enrichment may increase recruiting and training costs, whereas job specialization may increase compensation costs if companies provide discontentment pay to entice people into boring jobs.[79] Job enrichment improves product quality, but error rates may increase when tasks become so challenging that employees lack the necessary skills or experience stress.[80] Of course, job specialization also increases stress if employees do not make effective use of their talents in narrowly defined jobs, as we will learn in Chapter 5.

Motivating Yourself Through Self-Leadership

Most of the literature on workplace motivation assumes that companies must do things to motivate employees. Yet these practices overlook the fact that employees motivate themselves most of the time. They engage in specific behaviours to strengthen their work effort without direct intervention from external conditions. In fact, with leaner, flatter structures, companies must increasingly rely on employees who can motivate themselves to get the work done.

Self-leadership The process of influencing oneself to establish the self-direction and self-motivation needed to perform a task. This includes personal goal setting, constructive thought patterns, designing natural rewards, self-monitoring, and self-reinforcement.

Self-leadership is an emerging organizational behaviour concept that captures this overlooked perspective of employee motivation and performance. Self-leadership refers to the process of influencing oneself to establish the self-direction and self-motivation needed to perform a task.[81] This concept includes a tool kit of behavioural activities borrowed from social learning theory (Chapter 2) and goal setting (Chapter 3). It also includes constructive thought processes that have been extensively studied in sports psychology. Overall, self-leadership takes the view that individuals mostly regulate their own actions through these behavioural and cognitive (thought) activities.

Although we are in the early stages of understanding the dynamics of self-leadership, Exhibit 4.7 identifies the five main elements of this process. These elements, which generally follow each other in a sequence, include personal goal setting, constructive thought patterns, designing natural rewards, self-monitoring, and self-reinforcement.[82]

Personal Goal Setting

The first step in self-leadership is to set goals for your own work effort. This applies the ideas we learned in Chapter 3 on goal setting, such as identifying goals that are specific, results-oriented, and challenging. The only difference between personal goal setting and our previous discussion is that goals are set alone rather than assigned by or jointly decided with a supervisor.[83] According to the self-leadership literature, effective organizations establish norms whereby employees have a natural tendency to set their own goals to motivate themselves.[84]

EXHIBIT 4.7: Elements of Self-Leadership

Constructive Thought Patterns

Before beginning a task and while performing it, employees should engage in positive (constructive) thoughts about that work and its accomplishment. In particular, employees are more motivated and better prepared to accomplish a task after they have engaged in self-talk and mental imagery.

Self-talk

Self-talk Talking to yourself about your own thoughts or actions, for the purpose of increasing self-efficacy and navigating through the decisions required to get the job done effectively.

Do you ever talk to yourself? Most of us do, although perhaps not out loud. **Self-talk** refers to any situation in which a person talks to him- or herself about his or her own thoughts or actions.[85] The statements that we make to ourselves affect our self-efficacy, which, in turn, can influence our behaviour and performance in a particular situation.[86] In other words, self-talk creates a "can-do" belief and thereby increases motivation by raising our E→P expectancy. We often hear that professional athletes "psyche" themselves up before an important event. They tell themselves that they can achieve their goal and that they have practised enough to reach that goal.

Self-talk also affects how well we figure out the best way to accomplish new or complex tasks. People who tell themselves "I can do this job well; I've got the necessary skills!" are more effective at navigating through the decisions required to get the job done effectively. In contrast, people who make negative self-statements tend to have more difficulty deciding how to complete new or complex tasks.[87] Thus, increased self-efficacy seems to improve not only a person's motivation to accomplish a task, but also how to determine the best way to accomplish that task.

Les Bazso. With permission of the *Vancouver Province.*

With the guidance of a sports psychologist, Theo Fleury (left) and other members of the Calgary Flames hockey team use mental imagery and other self-leadership practices to win games. Self-leadership has been popular with sports professionals for many years, and it is now being discovered by organizations in other industries to increase employee motivation.

Mental imagery

You've probably heard the phrase "I'll cross that bridge when I come to it!" Self-leadership takes the opposite view. It suggests that we need to mentally practise a task and imagine successfully performing it beforehand. This process is known as **mental imagery**.[88]

Mental imagery Mentally practising a task and visualizing its successful completion.

As you can see from this definition, mental imagery has two parts. One part involves mentally practising the task, anticipating obstacles to goal accomplishment, and working out solutions to those obstacles before they occur. By mentally walking through the activities required to accomplish the task, we begin to see the problems that may occur. We can then imagine what responses would be best for each contingency.[89] For example, imagine yourself meeting with a difficult customer. You would think about things to say and how the customer might react to those statements. This mental rehearsal works best on thinking tasks (probably because the imagery is closer to the true task activity) than for physical tasks. However, mental practice may also improve some physical activities, such as lifting objects or speaking to an audience.

The other part of mental imagery involves visualizing successful completion of the task. We imagine the experience of completing the task and the positive results that follow. Everyone daydreams and fantasizes about being in a successful situation. You might imagine yourself being promoted to your boss's job, receiving a prestigious award, or taking time off work. This visualization increases goal commitment and motivates us to complete the task effectively.

Designing Natural Rewards

Self-leadership recognizes that employees can find ways to make the job itself more motivating.[90] One way is to think about how the work affects co-workers, customers, and others. Production employees who mount wheels on new cars might keep in mind that mounting wheels properly ensures customer safety. By consciously thinking about the effects of one's work, employees can increase the perceived task significance of their work.

There are other ways to build natural rewards into the job. One strategy is to alter the way a task is accomplished. People often have enough discretion in their jobs to make slight changes to suit their needs and preferences. For instance, you might prefer to drop by a co-worker's office to discuss an issue rather than send that person an e-mail. The visit fulfils your social needs and is a natural reward of performing the task. Another example would be trying out a new software program to design an idea, rather than sketch the image with pencil. By using the new software, you are adding challenge to a task that may have otherwise been mundane.

Self-Monitoring

Self-monitoring is the process of keeping track of one's progress toward a goal. In the section on job design, we learned that feedback from the job itself communicates whether we are accomplishing the task successfully. Self-monitoring includes the notion of consciously checking that naturally occurring feedback at regular intervals.

Self-monitoring also includes designing artificial feedback where natural feedback does not occur. Salespeople might arrange to receive monthly reports on sales levels in their territory. Production staff might have gauges or computer feedback systems installed so they can see how many errors are made on the production line.

Self-Reinforcement

Self-leadership includes the social learning theory concept of self-reinforcement. Recall from Chapter 2 that self-reinforcement occurs whenever an employee has control over a reinforcer but doesn't "take" the reinforcer until completing a self-set goal.[91] A common example is taking a break after reaching a predetermined stage of your work. The work break is a self-induced form of positive reinforcement.

Self-reinforcement also occurs when you decide to do a more enjoyable task after completing a task that your dislike. For example, after slogging through a difficult report, you might decide to spend time doing a more pleasant task, such as scanning Web sites for information about competitors.

Self-Leadership in Practice

Does self-leadership improve employee motivation and performance? It's too early to say that every component of the model is useful, but the overall results are impressive.[92] For instance, one recent study reported that newcomers in a Canadian organization who practised self-set goals and self-reinforcement had higher internal motivation than others.

Studies of self-talk and mental imagery, most of which are in sports psychology, indicate that constructive thought processes improve individual performance. For example, research on young Canadian skaters found that those who received self-talk training improved their performance one year later.[93] Recent evidence suggests that self-talk and mental imagery are also effective in organizations. Employees at America West Airlines who received constructive thought training experienced better mental performance, enthusiasm, and job satisfaction than co-workers who did not receive this training. This self-leadership training was particularly useful because America West was under bankruptcy protection at the time of the study.

Employees with a high degree of conscientiousness have a more natural tendency to apply self-leadership strategies, compared to people with lower conscientiousness scores. Conscientiousness is a personality trait (Chapter 6) and one of the key elements of organizational citizenship behaviour (Chapter 2). People with a high degree of conscientiousness are meticulous, careful, organized, responsible, and self-disciplined. However, one of the benefits of self-leadership is that it can be learned. Training programs have effectively improved self-leadership skills in those with lower conscientiousness scores.[94] Overall, self-leadership promises to be a valuable concept and practice for improving employee motivation and performance.

Chapter Summary

- Organizations reward employees for their membership and seniority, job status, competencies, and performance. Competency-based and performance-based rewards are increasingly popular in Canadian firms. Job status–based rewards are becoming less important because they are inconsistent with flatter organizational structures and the need for a flexible workforce.

- There are many types of individual, team, and organizational rewards. However, these performance-based rewards have also been criticized for doing more damage than good to employee motivation. Performance-based rewards tend to work better when companies measure performance accurately, recognize and adjust for situational contingencies in job performance, use team rewards for interdependent jobs, ensure rewards are valued, and minimize unintended consequences.

- Job design involves assigning tasks to a job and distributing work throughout the organization. Job specialization subdivides work into separate jobs for different people. This increases work efficiency because employees master the tasks quickly, spend less time changing tasks, require less training, and can be matched more closely with the jobs best suited to their skills. However, job specialization may reduce work motivation, create mental health problems, lower product or service quality, and increase costs through discontentment pay, absenteeism, and turnover.

- Contemporary job design strategies reverse job specialization through job rotation, job enlargement, and job enrichment. Hackman and Oldham's job characteristics model is the most popular foundation for recent job redesign interventions because it specifies core job dimensions, psychological states, and individual differences. Companies often enrich jobs through empowerment, forming natural work units, and establishing client relationships.

- Self-leadership is the process of influencing oneself to establish the self-direction and self-motivation needed to perform a task. This includes personal goal setting, constructive thought patterns, designing natural rewards, self-monitoring, and self-reinforcement.

- Constructive thought patterns include self-talk and mental imagery. Self-talk refers to any situation in which a person talks to him- or herself about his or her own thoughts or actions. Mental imagery involves mentally practising a task and imagining successfully performing it beforehand.

Discussion Questions

1. Shell Canada was once a bureaucratic company that valued long service and promotions through a steep hierarchy. After several years of difficult change, it is now a much flatter organization that places more responsibility with self-directed work teams. Explain what changes Shell Canada probably made (or should have made) to align its reward system with this new corporate philosophy.

2. Compare and contrast gainsharing with profit-sharing plans.

3. Educational researcher Alphie Kohn claims that rewards punish. Describe two ways that this may be true.

4. Lunenberg Widgets Ltd. has redesigned its production facilities around a team-based system. However, the company president believes that employees will not be motivated unless they receive incentives based on their individual performance. Give three explanations why Lunenberg Widgets should introduce team-based, rather than individual rewards in this setting.

5. Under what conditions would job specialization be most appropriate?

6. Explain what job design changes occur when companies provide more empowerment to employees.

7. Tomorrow, you present your first report to senior management to extend funding for your unit's special initiative. All of the materials are ready for the presentation. Following the five steps in self-leadership, describe how you can prepare for that meeting.

8. Several elements of self-leadership are derived from concepts presented earlier in this book. Identify those concepts and explain how they are applied in self-leadership.

Chapter Case

Vêtements Ltée

Vêtements Ltée is a chain of men's retail clothing stores located throughout the province of Quebec. Two years ago, the company introduced new incentive systems for both store managers and sales employees. Store managers receive a salary with annual merit increases based on sales above targetted goals, store appearance, store inventory management, customer complaints, and several other performance measures. Some of this information (e.g., store appearance) is gathered during visits by senior management, while other information is based on company records (e.g., sales volume).

Sales employees are paid a fixed salary plus a commission based on the percentage of sales credited to that employee over the pay period. The commission represents about 30 percent of a typical paycheque and is intended to encourage employees to actively serve customers and to increase sales volume. Because returned merchandise is discounted from commissions, sales staff are discouraged from selling products that customers do not really want.

Soon after the new incentive systems were introduced, senior management began to receive complaints from store managers regarding the performance of their sales staff. They observed that sales employees tended to stand near the store entrance waiting for customers, and would occasionally argue over "ownership" of the customer. Managers were concerned that this aggressive behaviour intimidated some customers. It also tended to leave some parts of the store unattended by staff.

Many managers were also concerned about inventory duties. Previously, sales staff would share responsibility for restocking inventory and completing inventory reorder forms. Under the new compensation system, however, few employees were willing to perform these essential tasks. On several occasions, stores have faced stock shortages because merchandise was not stocked or reorder forms were not completed in a timely manner. Potential sales have suffered from empty shelves when plenty of merchandise was available in the back storeroom or at the warehouse. The company's new automatic inventory system could reduce some of these problems, but employees must still stock shelves and assist in other aspects of inventory management.

Store managers have tried to correct the inventory problem by assigning employees to inventory duty, but this has created resentment among the employees selected. Other managers have threatened sales staff with dismissals if they do not do their share of inventory management. This strategy has been somewhat effective when the manager is in the store, but staff members sneak back onto the floor when the manager is away. It has also hurt staff morale, particularly relations with the store manager.

To reduce the tendency of sales staff to hoard customers at the store entrance, some managers have assigned employees to specific areas of the store. This has also created some resentment among employees stationed in areas with less traffic or lower-priced merchandise. Some staff have openly complained of lower paycheques because they have been placed in a slow area of the store or have been given more than their share of inventory duties.

Discussion Questions

1. What symptoms exist in this case to suggest that something has gone wrong?

2. What are the root causes that have led to these symptoms?

3. What actions should the organization take to correct these problems?

© Copyright. Steven L. McShane.

Experiential Exercise #1

Is Student Work Enriched?

Purpose: This exercise is designed to help students learn how to measure the motivational potential of jobs and to evaluate the extent that jobs should be further enriched.

Instructions: Being a student is like a job in several ways. You have tasks to perform and someone (such as your instructor) oversees your work. Although few people want to be students most of their lives (the pay rate is too low!), it may be interesting to determine how enriched your job is as a student.

Step 1: Students are placed into teams (preferably 4 or 5 people).

Step 2: Working alone, each student completes both sets of measures in this exercise. Then, using the guidelines below, they individually calculate the score for the five core job characteristics as well as the overall motivating potential score for the job.

Step 3: Members of each team compare their individual results. The group should identify differences of opinion for each core job characteristic. They should also note which core jobs characteristics have the lowest scores and recommend how these scores could be increased.

Step 4: The entire class will now meet to discuss the results of the exercise. The instructor may ask some teams to present their comparisons and recommendations for a particular core job characteristic.

JOB DIAGNOSTIC SURVEY

Circle the number on the right that best describes the job you are assessing.	Very Little ▼		Moderately ▼			Very Much ▼	
1. To what extent does student work permit you to decide on your own how to go about doing the work?	1	2	3	4	5	6	7
2. To what extent does student work involve doing a whole or identifiable piece of work, rather than a small portion of the overall work process?	1	2	3	4	5	6	7
3. To what extent does being a student require you to do many different things, using a variety of your skills/talents?	1	2	3	4	5	6	7
4. To what extent are the results of your work as a student likely to significantly affect the lives and well-being of other people (e.g. within the school, your family, society)?	1	2	3	4	5	6	7
5. To what extent does working on student activities provide direct information about your performance?	1	2	3	4	5	6	7

Circle the number on the right that best describes the job you are assessing.	Very Inaccurate ▼		Uncertain ▼			Very Accurate ▼	
6. Being a student requires me to use a number of complex and high-level skills.	1	2	3	4	5	6	7
7. Student work is arranged so that I do NOT have the chance to do an entire piece of work from beginning to end.	7	6	5	4	3	2	1
8. Doing student work itself provides many chances for me to figure out how well I am doing.	1	2	3	4	5	6	7
9. The work of a student is quite simple and repetitive.	7	6	5	4	3	2	1
10. The work of a student is one where a lot of other people can be affected by how well the work gets done.	1	2	3	4	5	6	7
11. Student work denies me any chance to use my personal initiative or judgment in carrying out the work.	7	6	5	4	3	2	1
12. Student work provides me the chance to completely finish the work I begin.	1	2	3	4	5	6	7
13. Student work itself provides very few clues about whether or not I am performing well.	7	6	5	4	3	2	1
14. As a student, I have considerable opportunity for independence and freedom in how I do the work.	1	2	3	4	5	6	7
15. The work I perform as a student itself is NOT very significant or important in the broader scheme of things.	7	6	5	4	3	2	1

Adapted from the Job Diagnostic Survey, developed by J. R. Hackman and G. R. Oldham. The authors have released any copyright ownership of this scale (see J. R. Hackman and G. Oldham, *Work Redesign* (Reading, MA: Addison-Wesley, 1980), p. 275).

Calculating The Motivating Potential Score of Student Work

Scoring Core Job Characteristics
Use the following set of calculations to estimate the motivating potential score for the job of being a student. Use your answers from the Job Diagnostic Survey measures that you completed above.

Skill Variety (SV) $\qquad \dfrac{\text{Question } 3 + 6 + 9}{3} \qquad = \underline{\hspace{2cm}}$

Task Identity (TI) $\qquad \dfrac{\text{Question } 2 + 7 + 12}{3} \qquad = \underline{\hspace{2cm}}$

Task Significance (TS) $\qquad \dfrac{\text{Question } 4 + 10 + 15}{3} \qquad = \underline{\hspace{2cm}}$

Autonomy $\qquad \dfrac{\text{Question } 1 + 11 + 14}{3} \qquad = \underline{\hspace{2cm}}$

Job Feedback $\qquad \dfrac{\text{Question } 5 + 8 + 13}{3} \qquad = \underline{\hspace{2cm}}$

Calculating the Motivating Potential Score (MPS)
Use the following formula and the results above to calculate the motivating potential score. Notice that skill variety, task identity, and task significance are averaged before being multiplied by the score for autonomy and job feedback.

$$\left(\frac{\text{SV} + \text{TI} + \text{TS}}{3} \right) \times \text{Autonomy} \times \text{Feedback}$$

$$\left(\frac{\underline{\hspace{1cm}} + \underline{\hspace{1cm}} + \underline{\hspace{1cm}}}{3} \right) + \underline{\hspace{1cm}} + \underline{\hspace{1cm}} = \underline{\hspace{1cm}}$$

Experiential Exercise #2

Assessing Your Self-Leadership

Purpose: This exercise is designed to help you understand self-leadership concepts and to assess your self-leadership tendencies.

Instructions: Read each of the statements below and circle the response that you believe best reflects your position regarding each statement. Then use the scoring key to calculate your results. This exercise is completed alone so that students assess themselves honestly without concerns of social comparison. However, class discussion will focus on the meaning of each self-leadership concept, how this scale might be applied in organizations, and the limitations of measuring self-leadership in work settings.

SELF-LEADERSHIP QUESTIONNAIRE

Circle the number that best reflects your position regarding each of these statements.	Describes Me Very Well ▼	Describes Me Well ▼	Describes Me Somewhat ▼	Does Not Describe Me Very Well ▼	Does Not Describe Me At All ▼
1. I try to keep track of how I am doing while I work.	1	2	3	4	5
2. I often use reminders to help me remember things I need to do.	1	2	3	4	5
3. I like to work toward specific goals I set for myself.	1	2	3	4	5
4. After I perform well on an activity, I feel good about myself.	1	2	3	4	5
5. I seek out activities in my work that I enjoy doing.	1	2	3	4	5
6. I often practise important tasks before I do them.	1	2	3	4	5
7. I usually am aware of how I am performing an activity.	1	2	3	4	5
8. I try to arrange my work area in a way that helps me positively focus my attention on my work.	1	2	3	4	5
9. I establish personal goals for myself.	1	2	3	4	5
10. When I have successfully completed a task, I often reward myself with something I like.	1	2	3	4	5
11. When I have a choice, I try to do my work in ways that I enjoy rather than just trying to get it over with.	1	2	3	4	5
12. I like to go over an important activity before I actually perform it.	1	2	3	4	5
13. I keep track of my progress on projects I am working on.	1	2	3	4	5
14. I try to surround myself with objects and people that bring out my desirable behaviours.	1	2	3	4	5
15. I like to set task goals for my performance.	1	2	3	4	5
16. When I do an assignment especially well, I like to treat myself to something or an activity I enjoy.	1	2	3	4	5
17. I try to build activities into my work that I like doing.	1	2	3	4	5
18. I often rehearse my plan for dealing with a challenge before I actually face the challenge.	1	2	3	4	5

The scale presented here excludes the self-punishment dimension found in the SLQ1 instrument because it is not calculated in the SLQ1 total score. The designing natural rewards dimension presented here is measured by items in the third dimension of the SLQ1 instrument.

Source: C. C. Manz, *Mastering Self-Leadership: Empower Yourself for Personal Excellence* (Englewood Cliffs, N.J.: Prentice-Hall, 1992). Used with permission of the author.

Scoring Key for Self-Leadership Questionnaire

To calculate your score on the Self-Leadership Questionnaire, assign the appropriate number to each question from the scoring key below. Then add up the numbers for that dimension. The self-leadership total score is calculated by adding up all dimensions.

Self-Leadership Dimension	Calculation	Your Score
Personal Goal Setting	Item 3 + Item 9 + Item 15 =	_____
Mental Practice*	Item 6 + Item 12 + Item 18 =	_____
Designing Natural Rewards	Item 5 + Item 11 + Item 17 =	_____
Self-Monitoring**	Item 1 + Item 7 + Item 13 =	_____
Self-Reinforcement	Item 4 + Item 10 + Item 16 =	_____
Cueing Strategies***	Item 2 + Item 8 + Item 14 =	_____
Self-Leadership Total	Add up all dimension scores =	_____

* Mental practice is similar to constructive thought patterns, but does not represent self-talk and mental imagery quite as clearly.

** Self-monitoring is called "Self-Observation" in the SLQ1.

** Cueing strategies represent activities that help us behave in certain ways. Although not explicitly described in Chapter 4, it is similar to "antecedents" in the A-B-C model of organizational behaviour modification described in Chapter 2. The only difference is that these antecedents are self-developed or self-controlled rather than introduced and controlled by others.

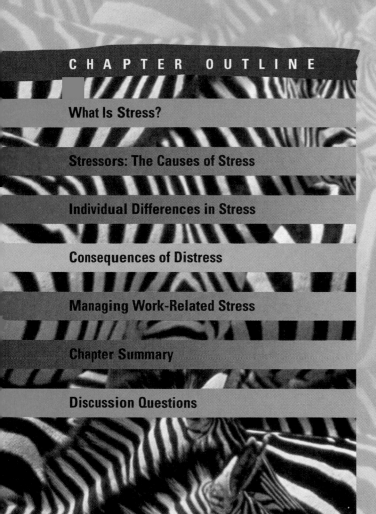

CHAPTER 5

Stress Management

CHAPTER OUTLINE

What Is Stress?

Stressors: The Causes of Stress

Individual Differences in Stress

Consequences of Distress

Managing Work-Related Stress

Chapter Summary

Discussion Questions

LEARNING OBJECTIVES

After reading this chapter, you should be able to:

- Describe the stress experience.

- Outline the stress process from stressors to consequences.

- Discuss four types of role-related stressors.

- Explain how work and family demands may become stressors.

- Explain why a stressor might produce different stress levels in two people.

- Identify five ways to manage workplace stress.

- Explain why social support may reduce work-related stress.

"Teachers look like they have been hit with a bucket of water," says Grade 5 teacher Karen Minish. More than 600 Manitoba teachers are receiving stress counselling.

Sandra Johannson never thought teaching would put her in the hospital. But it did. After 10 years of working under increasingly difficult conditions, the Riverton, Manitoba, schoolteacher was so stressed-out that she suffered physical pain.

"My body was aching," she recalls. "It was intense pains through the shoulder area and the lower back. It was because of the stress." When Johannson visited her doctor to discuss her pain, she broke down and couldn't stop crying.

"Right then you knew you were at the end of the line. The tank was empty. There was nothing left to give." Johannson was put in hospital for two weeks and didn't return to school until the next fall.

Karen Minish, a Grade 5 teacher in Winnipeg, says teachers are stressed-out because they try to absorb the staff cuts and student behaviour problems that have plagued schools in recent years. "Teachers look like they have been hit with a bucket of water," she says. Minish has first-hand experience. Her school cut three teachers this year. A few years ago, she was pushed and then punched in the face by a 12-year-old boy.

"You enjoy the kids, but we're people, not machines," says Sandra Johannson. "There's just so much to do. It's almost like you don't have a life. When you get home, you don't want to go out or visit with anybody. You just want to sit on your couch and catch your breath. We're burning out fast. It's just horrible."[1]

The stress-related problems that Sandra Johannson and Karen Minish describe are widespread. Currently, more than 600 of Manitoba's 13,000 teachers are receiving stress counselling. Among Saskatchewan teachers, stress is the primary factor in 28 percent of disability claims and is the secondary cause in another 44 percent of claims. And in Calgary, a report concluded that stress and job burn-out are widespread among teachers and other staff throughout the city.[2]

Teachers are not the only people experiencing stress at work. One-third of Canadians say they feel constantly stressed; the same percentage has health problems caused by work-related stress. Work-related stress costs Canadian businesses more than $20 billion each year in lower productivity and higher absenteeism, turnover, alcoholism, and medical costs. It can also cost employers in arbitration awards, court decisions, and occupational health and safety premiums. Canadian insurance companies report that more than one-quarter of current disability claims are stress-related. But perhaps most troubling is that people born after 1955 are up to three times as likely to experience stress-related disorders as were their grandparents.[3]

Not all stress is bad. In fact, a certain level of stress is a necessary part of life. "Stress is much like water," writes Canadian Auto Workers (CAW) health and safety director Cathy Walker. "Take it away completely and we die of thirst; give us the right amount and we are healthy; immerse us in too much and we drown."[4] The problem is that many Canadians are drowning in stress at work.

In this chapter, we look more closely at the dynamics of work-related stress and how to manage it. The chapter begins by describing the process of experiencing stress. Next, the causes and consequences of stress are examined, along with the factors that cause some people to experience stress when others do not. The final section of the chapter looks at ways to manage work-related stress from either an organizational or individual perspective.

Stress An individual's adaptive response to a situation that is perceived as challenging or threatening to the person's well-being.

What Is Stress?

Stress is an adaptive response to a situation that is perceived as challenging or threatening to the person's well-being.[5] Stress has both psychological and physiological dimensions. Psychologically, people perceive a situation and interpret it as challenging or threatening. This cognitive appraisal leads to a set of physiological responses, such as higher blood pressure, sweaty hands, and faster heartbeat.

We often hear about stress as a negative consequence of modern living. People are stressed from overwork, job insecurity, competition, and the increasing pace of life. These events produce *distress* — people experiencing stress beyond their capacity to resist the stressful conditions. There is also a positive side of stress, called *eustress*, that refers to relatively low levels of stress over a short time. Eustress is necessary to activate and motivate people to achieve goals, change their environments, and succeed in life's challenges. However, most research focuses on distress, because it is a significant concern in organizational settings.[6] Employees frequently experience enough stress to hurt their job performance and increase their risk of mental and physical health problems. Consequently, our discussion will focus more on distress than on eustress.

STRESS MANAGEMENT

WAISGLASS/COULTHART   © 1993 Farcus Cartoons/dist. by Universal Press Syndicate

"...now let's see how you react to scenes of your employees leaving early."

General adaptation syndrome. A model of the stress experience, consisting of three stages: alarm reaction, resistance, and exhaustion.

General Adaptation Syndrome

The stress experience was first documented by Dr. Hans Selye, a Montreal-based pioneer in stress research. Selye wrote that the stress experience occurs in three stages: alarm, resistance, and exhaustion. This process, illustrated in Exhibit 5.1, is called the **general adaptation syndrome.**[7]

Alarm reaction

In the alarm reaction stage, the perception of a threatening or challenging situation causes the brain to send a biochemical message to various parts of the body, resulting in increased respiration rate, blood pressure, heartbeat, muscle tension, and other physiological responses. Initial exposure to the stressor reduces the person's survival capabilities and, in extreme circumstances, may cause death due to shock. In most situations, the alarm reaction alerts the person to the environmental condition and prepares the body for the resistance stage.

Resistance

The resistance stage involves introducing various biochemical, psychological, and behavioural mechanisms to deal with the stressor. For example, as adrenaline increases, you may try to overcome or remove the stressor. However, this resistance is directed to only one or two stressors, so that you become more vulnerable to other stressors. This explains why people are more likely to catch a cold or other illness when they have been working under pressure.

Exhaustion

People have a limited resistance capacity and, if the stressor persists, they will eventually move into the exhaustion stage as this capacity diminishes. In most work situations, the general adaptation syndrome process ends long before total exhaustion. Employees resolve tense situations before the destructive consequences of stress become manifest, or they withdraw from the stressful situation, rebuild their survival capabilities, and return later to the stressful environment with renewed energy. However, people who frequently experience the exhaustion stage have increased risk of long-term physiological and psychological damage.

The general adaptation syndrome describes the stress experience, but this is only part of the picture. To effectively manage work-related stress, we must understand its causes and consequences as well as individual differences in the stress experience.

EXHIBIT 5.1: Selye's General Adaptation Syndrome

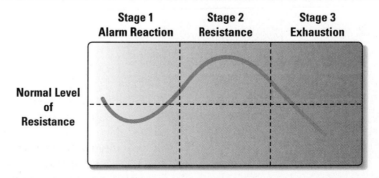

Source: Adapted from J. L. Gibson, J. M. Ivancevich, and J. H. Donnelly, *Organizations: Behavior, Structure, Processes*, 7th ed. (Burr Ridge, Ill.: Richard D. Irwin, 1994), p. 265.

Stressors: The Causes of Stress

Stressor Any environmental condition that places a physical or emotional demand on the person.

Stressors, the causes of stress, include any environmental conditions that place a physical or emotional demand on the person.[8] There are numerous stressors in organizational settings and other life activities. Exhibit 5.2 lists four types of work-related stressors: physical environment, role-related, interpersonal, and organizational stressors.

Physical Environment Stressors

Some stressors are found in the physical work environment, such as excessive noise, poor lighting, and safety hazards. For example, a recent study of textile workers who worked in a noisy plant found that their levels of stress measurably decreased when they were supplied with ear protectors.[9] Logging truck drivers in Western Canada wear mouthguards because they would otherwise grind their teeth down from stress while driving the fully loaded rigs along treacherous mountain roads.

Role conflict A situation whereby people experience competing demands, such as having job duties that are incompatible with their personal values, or receiving contradictory messages from different people.

Role-Related Stressors

Role-related stressors include conditions under which employees have difficulty understanding, reconciling, or performing the various roles in their lives. Four particularly important role-related stressors are role conflict, role ambiguity, work overload or underload, and task characteristics.

People experience **role conflict** when they face competing demands.[10] One form of role conflict, called *person-role conflict*, occurs when organizational values and

---

EXHIBIT 5.2: Causes and Consequences of Stress

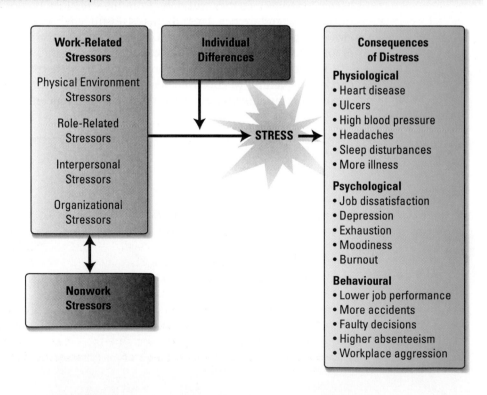

work obligations are incompatible with personal values. Many employees experience person-role conflict when they must demonstrate emotions (e.g., compassion) toward a client even though they do not actually feel these emotions toward the person. Others face this stressor when their personal values are incompatible with the organization's dominant values.[11] *Intrarole conflict* occurs when the individual receives contradictory messages from different people. This stress is particularly strong when the role sender (your boss, for instance) has power over you.[12] Labour union stewards are frequently exposed to this stressor because they must deal with competing demands from different union members and the local union executive.[13]

Role ambiguity
Uncertainty about job duties, performance expectations, level of authority, and other job conditions.

Role ambiguity exists when employees are uncertain about their job duties, performance expectations, level of authority, and other job conditions. This tends to occur when people enter new situations, such as joining the organization or taking a foreign assignment, because they are uncertain about task and social expectations.[14] They cannot rely on past routines (e.g., how to greet people) so they concentrate on their actions and carefully monitor responses from others.

Work underload and overload represent another form of role-related stressor. Work underload occurs when employees receive too little work or are given tasks that do not make sufficient use of their skills or knowledge. Work overload occurs when employees cannot keep up with deadlines or are given work that is beyond their abilities. Work overload appears to be a major source of stress today as employees are expected to perform more tasks in less time and with fewer resources. For example, Royal Canadian Mounted Police (RCMP) officers in Kelowna, British Columbia, say they are stressed out by staff shortages due to underfunding. At times, the entire region is monitored by only four officers. "It's not so much that we're angry as just plain tired . . . exhausted," says one officer.[15]

Lean production The practice of continuously pushing for more output with less human effort, less equipment, less time, and less space.

Task characteristics represent another type of role stressor. Tasks are most stressful when they involve decision making, monitoring equipment, or exchanging information with others. Lack of control over work activities and environment also falls into this category.[16] **Lean production** practices seem to increase stressful task activities by restricting employee time and control. The philosophy of lean production is to accomplish more output with less human effort, less equipment, less time, and less space.[17] It typically includes *kaizen*, the practice of continuous improvement that is part of quality management (Chapter 10). In practice, employees are expected to perform more tasks with less time and resource flexibility. Perspective 5.1 describes how lean production has increased stress levels in Canadian industry.

Interpersonal Stressors

Interpersonal stressors include ineffective supervision, office politics, and other conflicts we experience with people. In the opening story, we read how student behaviour problems have become interpersonal stressors among Canadian teachers. Customer service representatives and call centre operators face similar interpersonal stressors because they work with abusive callers. A recent study of call centre employees in New Brunswick reported that most employees in these jobs feel stressed from dealing with uncooperative customers while facing high productivity quotas. "Two hundred and sixty calls a day from rude and angry people . . . it's hard to deal with at times," concludes one call centre employee.[18]

Sexual harassment is a serious interpersonal stressor, particularly for women. Nearly one-quarter of all Canadian women have been sexually harassed on the job, mostly by co-workers and supervisors. An internal RCMP report recently revealed that 60 percent of female officers have experienced some form of sexual harassment at work. Stress is such a powerful outcome of harassment that it is now considered a

PERSPECTIVE 5.1

Lean Production: Management by Stress at CAMI

According to a recent study by the Canadian Auto Workers (CAW) union, Canadian automobile assembly employees are dispirited and stressed-out. The study is particularly critical of General Motors of Canada, where employees feel the most stressed. The reason, according to the CAW, is that GM has pushed lean production more than any other automotive company.

In lean production, employees continuously reduce time, space, and effort *(kaizen)* to improve work efficiency. The problem is that these changes usually result in less time to complete tasks and correct mistakes. The job becomes so standardized that tools must be placed precisely and every second is devoted to a specific task element. There is little flexibility but plenty of stress.

At CAMI Automotive Inc. — the General Motors–Suzuki plant in Ingersoll, Ontario — the effects of lean production are well known. "The [CAMI] plant is actually set up — I mean the equipment is actually designed — to be called management by stress," explains Rob Pelletier, a former CAMI employee. "They [CAMI management] adjust the line

speed . . . and when everybody is starting to feel a little more comfortable, what happens? They turn the line speed up again."

Cathy Austin, a CAMI employee, says that the pressure to constantly improve becomes overpowering. "I can remember dreaming at night," she says, "trying to figure out how I can cut seconds out of the process."

Toyota Motor Company, which introduced lean production nearly 40 years ago, has started to investigate how much fatigue is caused by each job. If unacceptable levels of fatigue and stress are identified, the work team is supposed to *kaizen* the jobs to reduce those problems. However, critics claim that *kaizen* produces the stress in the first place, so it is unlikely to provide a solution.

Cathy Austin points out that lean thinking is so powerful that employees buy into the fast-paced, low-control work until they are stressed-out. "[I first thought] we have to run, run, run because our lives depend on it in the automotive industry," she recalls. "I went out and I tried it . . . until I woke up to the fact that this isn't humanly possible."

Source: "Autoworkers Dispirited and Tired," *Canadian Press Newswire*, June 3, 1996; J. P. Womack and D. T. Jones, *Lean Thinking* (N.Y.: Simon & Schuster, 1996); P. Kraft, "To Control and Inspire: US Management in the Age of Computer Information Systems and Global Production," in M. Wardell, P. Meiksins, and T. Steiger (eds.), *Labor and Monopoly Capital in the Late Twentieth Century: The Braverman Legacy and Beyond.* (Albany, N.Y.: SUNY Press); J. Rinehart, C. Huxley, and D. Robertson, "Worker Commitment and Labour Management Relations Under Lean Production at CAMI," *Relations Industrielles* 49 (1994), pp. 750–75; Canadian Auto Workers, *Working Lean Video* (Toronto: CAW, 1993); D. Robertson, J. Rinehart, C. Huxley, and CAW Research Group on CAMI, "Team Concept and *Kaizen*: Japanese Production Management in a Unionized Auto Plant," *Studies in Political Economy* 39 (Autumn 1992), pp. 77–107.

health and safety issue. For example, an African-Canadian employee at Colgate Palmolive Canada Inc. was racially and sexually harassed to the point where she had a nervous breakdown. An African-Canadian teacher in Quebec took long periods of sick leave because his school did not correct intolerable levels of racial harassment that students exhibited toward him.[19]

Organizational Stressors

As we shall learn in Chapter 15, organizational change is a stressor for most employees, and this stress must be managed in order for change to occur more effectively. For example, the shift toward flatter, team-based companies is an organizational stressor. Mergers, acquisitions, and privatization also create numerous stressors, particularly related to job insecurity, revised work demands, and interpersonal conflicts.[20]

Work-Family Stressors

For many employees, the most persistent stressors occur from the interface between work and family roles. Almost 50 percent of the Canadian workforce experiences some type of work-family stressor. There are three work-family stressors: time-based, strain-based, and role behaviour–based conflict.[21]

Time-based conflict

A recent survey of Maritime Life employees in Halifax found that 78 percent feel challenged to balance the demands of work with family and other nonwork activities.[22] These people are experiencing *time-based conflict* because the time required for work obligations conflicts with the time required for family and other nonwork obligations. This explains why stress increases with the number of hours of paid employment and the amount of business travel or commuting time. Inflexible work schedules and rotating-shift schedules can also take a heavy toll because they prevent employees from effectively juggling work and family duties.[23]

Time-based conflict is more acute for women than for men. As we see in Perspective 5.2, the problem is that housework and childcare represent a "second shift" for many women in dual-career families. One estimate is that working mothers devote 79 hours each week to paid employment, childcare, household chores, and personal chores, whereas working fathers spend 69 hours on these activities. The difference occurs because women have 31 hours of childcare and household work, whereas men have only 15 hours each week.[24] Until men increase their contribution to homemaking, and business learns to accommodate the new social order, many of these "supermoms" will continue to experience superstress.

Strain-based conflict

Strain-based conflict occurs when stress from one domain spills over to the other. The death of a spouse, financial problems, and other nonwork stressors produce tension and fatigue that affect the employee's ability to fulfil work obligations. This problem works the other way as well. Stress at work spills over to an employee's home life and often becomes the foundation of stressful relations at home. Several Canadian studies

---

PERSPECTIVE 5.2

Canadian Women Face Stress of the "Second Shift"

Diane Stang's life would leave anyone feeling wrung-out. In a typical day, she gets her kids up and fed, then drives them to school in Bolton, where she teaches Grade 1. Stang also handles the school's computer programs, and often stays for other duties after class ends. Her evenings are devoted to driving her children to dance classes and gymnastics, helping them with homework, and doing laundry or other chores. Any spare time is spent catching up on her school work.

"Sometimes I wonder how I got myself into this," sighs Stang. "I have to orchestrate the whole thing and I feel as if everybody needs a piece of me. Sometimes I'm so tired I just feel like a vegetable."

Diane Stang and many other women in the labour force experience stress due to work-family conflict. Although women are accepting increasing responsibility in employment, their male counterparts are not embracing the role of homemaker quite as readily. This leaves working women with a "second shift" — performing household chores — as well as their paid-employment tasks.

Many women admit that it is not easy to be everything to everyone. Kathleen Christie, of Deloitte & Touche management consultants, was able to have two children and develop her career until she was made partner in charge of the Toronto consulting practice. However, her children demanded more of her time when they reached the ages of four and seven.

"It just got to the point where the hours and the demands of the job were greater than I was prepared to give, and I give a lot." Fortunately, the firm agreed to give Christie a six-month sabbatical to catch up on family life.

Until men increase their contribution to homemaking and business learns to accommodate the new social order, many women will experience frustration and stress.

Source: P. Chisholm, "Coping with Stress," *Maclean's*, January 8, 1996 pp. 32–36; A. Kingston, "Beyond the Fantasy of the Supermom," *Financial Times of Canada*, September 10, 1990, p. 13; and B. Dalglish, "Having It All," *Maclean's*, September 3, 1990, pp. 32–35.

have recently looked at this issue. One reported that the stresses of work spill over to home life more than vice versa. Another study found that fathers who experience stress at work engage in dysfunctional parenting behaviours which, in turn, explain their children's behaviour in school. A third Canadian study suggests that Canadian female managers are more likely to experience work-family stress due to strain-based conflict than to other work-family stressors.[25]

Role behaviour conflict

A third work-family stressor, called *role behaviour conflict*, occurs when people are expected to enact incompatible emotional roles at work and at home. People who act logically and impersonally at work have difficulty switching to a more compassionate role at home. For example, one study found that police officers were unable to shake off their professional role when they left the job. This was confirmed by their spouses, who reported that the officers would handle their children in the same manner as they would people in their job.[26]

Stress and Occupations

Several studies have attempted to identify which jobs have more stressors than others.[27] Not everyone has the same "high-stress" and "low-stress" lists, but Exhibit 5.3 identifies the jobs most commonly found in each category. You should view this information with some caution, however. One problem with rating the stress of occupations is that task characteristics and job environments differ considerably for the same job in different organizations and societies. A police officer's job may be less stressful in a small town, for instance, than in a large city where crime rates are higher and the organizational hierarchy is more formal.

Another important point to remember when looking at Exhibit 5.3 is that a major stressor to one person is insignificant to another. In this respect, we must be careful not to conclude that people in high-stressor occupations actually experience higher stress than people in other occupations. They are exposed to more serious stressors, but careful

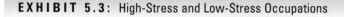

EXHIBIT 5.3: High-Stress and Low-Stress Occupations

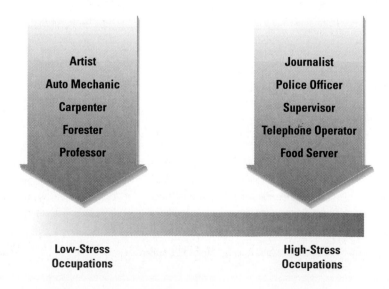

Low-Stress Occupations	High-Stress Occupations
Artist	Journalist
Auto Mechanic	Police Officer
Carpenter	Supervisor
Forester	Telephone Operator
Professor	Food Server

selection and training can result in stress levels no different from those experienced by people in other jobs. The next section discusses individual differences in stress.

Individual Differences in Stress

Individual differences represent another element in the relationship among stressors, stress, and stress consequences. As illustrated in Exhibit 5.2, individual characteristics moderate the extent to which different people experience stress or exhibit a specific stress outcome in a given situation. Two people may be exposed to the same stressor, such as the threat of job loss, yet they experience different stress levels or different stress symptoms.

Individual factors affect the stress experience in at least three ways. First, employees experience different stress levels because they perceive the situation differently. For instance, those with high self-efficacy are less likely than those with low self-efficacy to view new employment situations and other stressors as a threat.[28] Second, people have different threshold levels of resistance to a stressor. Younger employees generally experience fewer and less severe stress symptoms than older employees because the former have a larger store of energy to cope with high stress levels.

A third reason people may experience the same level of stress and yet exhibit different stress outcomes is that they use different coping strategies.[29] Employees with long job tenure tend to ignore the stressor, hoping that it will go away. This is usually an ineffective approach, which would explain why they experience higher stress levels. There is some evidence (although still inconclusive) that women cope with stress better than their male counterparts. Specifically, women are more likely to seek emotional support from others in stressful situations, whereas men try to change the stressor or use less effective coping mechanisms.[30] However, we must remember that this is not true for all women or all men.

Type A behaviour pattern
A behaviour pattern of people with high risk of premature coronary heart disease; Type A's tend to be impatient, lose their temper, talk rapidly, and interrupt others.

Type A/Type B Behaviour Pattern

One of the most frequently cited individual differences is the Type A/Type B behaviour pattern. In the 1950s, two cardiologists noticed that patients with premature coronary heart disease exhibited common behaviours that were collectively labelled a **Type A behaviour pattern**. Type A people are hard-driving, competitive individuals

---

EXHIBIT 5.4: Characteristics of Type A and Type B Behaviour Patterns

Type A Behaviour Pattern	Type B Behaviour Pattern
Talks rapidly	Handles details patiently
Devoted to work	Less competitive with others
Highly competitive	Contemplates issues carefully
Struggles to perform several tasks	Low concern about time limitations
Strong sense of time urgency	Doesn't feel guilty about relaxing
Impatient with idleness	Relaxed approach to life
Easily loses temper	Works at a steady pace
Interrupts others	Not easily angered

with a strong sense of time urgency. They tend to be impatient, lose their temper, talk rapidly, and interrupt others during conversations (see Exhibit 5.4).[31]

Type B behaviour pattern
A behaviour pattern of people with low risk of coronary heart disease; Type B's tend to work steadily, take a relaxed approach to life, and be even–tempered.

In contrast, those with a **Type B behaviour pattern** are less competitive and less concerned about time limitations. Type B people may be just as ambitious to achieve challenging tasks, but they generally approach life more casually and systematically than do Type A people. They tend to work steadily, take a relaxed approach to life, and be even-tempered. The important distinction, however, is that Type B people are less likely than Type A people to experience distress and its physiological symptoms (such as heart disease) when exposed to a stressor. For example, a study of Montreal nurses reported that Type A nurses experienced significantly greater job stress, role ambiguity, conflict, and overload than Type B nurses.[32]

Regarding job performance, Type A people tend to work faster than Type B people, choose more challenging tasks, have higher self-motivation, and are more effective in jobs involving time pressure. On the other hand, Type A people are less effective than Type B people in jobs requiring patience, cooperation, and thoughtful judgment.[33] Type A people tend to be irritable and aggressive, so they generally have poorer interpersonal skills. Studies report that middle managers tend to exhibit Type A behaviours, whereas top-level executives tend to have Type B behaviours.[34] One possible explanation is that Type B people receive more promotions due to their superior human relations skills.

Consequences of Distress

At the beginning of the chapter, we said that not all stress is bad. Eustress gives people the energy to meet the challenges of everyday life. However, high levels of stress or prolonged periods of stress diminish the individual's resistance, resulting in adverse consequences for both the employee and the organization. This distress often creates a vicious cycle whereby stress leads to a dysfunctional consequence (such as alcoholism), which becomes a stressor leading to further dysfunctional consequences. Some of the more common outcomes or symptoms of work-related stress were listed earlier in Exhibit 5.2 and are discussed here.

Physiological Consequences

Stress takes its toll on the human body.[35] Approximately 10 percent of the Canadian workforce has ulcers and other digestive system diseases. Up to one-third have hypertension (high blood pressure). Both ulcers and hypertension often result from anxiety and worry. Coronary heart disease is one of the most disturbing effects of stress in modern society. This disease, including strokes and heart attacks, was virtually unknown a century ago but is now the leading cause of death among Canadian adults. Recent physiological problems, such as fibromyalgia, also seem to be caused or aggravated by stress.[36]

Behavioural Consequences

How does stress affect employee behaviour? When stress becomes distress, job performance falls and workplace accidents are more likely to happen. A high stress level impairs our ability to remember information, make effective decisions, and take appropriate action.[37] You have probably experienced this in an exam or emergency work situation. You forget important information, make mistakes, and otherwise "draw a blank" under intense pressure.

Overstressed employees also tend to have higher levels of absenteeism. One reason, as we saw with Sandra Johannson at the beginning of the chapter, is that people become sick from stress. The physical symptoms of stress cause people to take sick leave and sometimes wind up in hospital. The other reason is that absenteeism is a coping mechanism. At a basic level, we react to stress through fight-or-flight. Absenteeism is a form of flight — temporarily withdrawing from the stressful situation so that we have an opportunity to re-energize. Companies may try to minimize absenteeism, but it sometimes helps employees avoid the exhaustion stage of the stress experience (see Exhibit 5.1).[38]

Workplace aggression

Workplace aggression — including verbal abuse, harassment, and assault — is an increasingly worrisome symptom of workplace stress. Aggression represents the "fight" (instead of flight) reaction to stress. In its mildest form, employees engage in verbal conflict. They "fly off the handle" and are less likely to empathize with co-workers. Occasionally, the combination of an individual's background and workplace stressors escalate this conflict into more dangerous levels of workplace hostility.

The murders of four Concordia University professors is a widely reported, although still rare display of workplace aggression in Canada. More frequent examples of workplace aggression are harassment and assaults.[39] The Workers' Compensation Boards in Ontario and British Columbia each receive more than 1,200 cases of work-related aggression each year. Although many acts of violence are caused by customers and criminals, evidence from the United States estimates that 30 percent of workplace attacks and 43 percent of violent threats are committed by co-workers, bosses, or former employees (rather than criminals or customers).[40]

Experts often focus on the characteristics of aggressive employees (eg., white, male, middle-aged, loner). While certain people are more likely to be aggressive, we must also remember that workplace stressors usually trigger these aggressive acts. Moreover, stress can lead to aggression in employees who have no previous behaviour problems. In other words, employee aggression is a consequence of extreme stress, not just the temperament of certain individuals.[41]

Psychological Consequences

There are several psychological symptoms of work-related stress. Probably the most common of these is job dissatisfaction. Stressed-out employees are less satisfied with their jobs and work environment. Employees with a high level of stress also tend to be moody and depressed. Emotional fatigue is another psychological consequence of stress. This symptom is usually a feature of job burnout, which we discuss next.

Job burnout

Job burnout The process of emotional exhaustion, depersonalization, and reduced personal accomplishment resulting from prolonged exposure to stress.

Job burnout is a phrase often heard today, yet it was coined 30 years ago. Job burnout refers to the process of emotional exhaustion, depersonalization, and reduced personal accomplishment resulting from prolonged exposure to stress.[42] It is a complex process that includes the dynamics of stress, coping strategies, and stress consequences. Burnout is caused by excessive demands made on people who serve or frequently interact with others. In other words, burnout is mainly due to interpersonal and role-related stressors.[43] For this reason, it is most common in helping occupations (e.g., nurses, teachers, police officers).

Exhibit 5.5 diagrams the relationship among the three components of job burnout. *Emotional exhaustion* represents the first stage and plays a central role in the burnout process.[44] It is characterized by a lack of energy and a feeling that one's emotional resources are depleted. Emotional exhaustion is sometimes called compassion

EXHIBIT 5.5: The Job Burnout Process

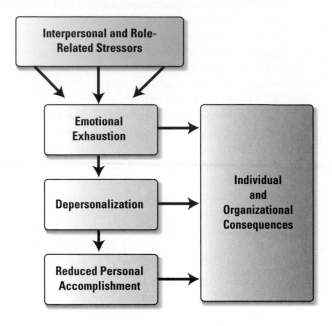

fatigue because the employee no longer feels able to give as much support and caring to clients. Sandra Johannson, who we met in the opening story to this chapter, identified this condition when she said: "There was nothing left to give."

Depersonalization follows emotional exhaustion and is identified by the treatment of others as objects rather than people. Burned-out employees become emotionally detached from clients and cynical about the organization. This detachment is to the point of callousness, far beyond the level of detachment normally required in helping occupations. For example, a burned-out nurse might coldly label a patient as "the kidney in room 307." Depersonalization is also apparent when employees strictly follow rules and regulations rather than try to understand the client's needs and search for a mutually acceptable solution.

Reduced personal accomplishment, the final component of job burnout, refers to the decline in one's feelings of competence and success, and is observed by feelings of diminished competency. In other words, the person's self-efficacy declines (Chapter 2). In these situations, employees develop a sense of learned helplessness as they no longer believe that their efforts make a difference. Sandra Johannson experienced this when she broke down in the doctor's office. As we read in the opening story, she felt that there was so much to do and that she no longer had the capacity to accomplish those impossible tasks.

Managing Work-Related Stress

Alain LeBlanc nearly burned out at the age of 35. Fortunately, his employer, Hewlett-Packard (Canada) Ltd., had introduced several stress management strategies after learning that stress was the number-one concern among employees. LeBlanc completed a stress self-assessment and discovered that he was in trouble. "I was a bit shocked by the result," he says. "I had to make a move, and a serious one, really quickly. I didn't think I'd survive if I didn't." LeBlanc changed jobs within H-P Canada and received some advice from the employee assistance program on managing stress. He also joined the company's fitness centre to rebuild his physical stamina and take an occasional break from work.[45]

Everyone needs to manage stress, but not everyone handles the problem as well as Alain LeBlanc did. Sandra Johannson tried to deny the stress until it was too late. This avoidance strategy creates a vicious cycle because the failure to cope with stress becomes another stressor on top of the one that created the stress in the first place.

The solution is to fully understand the tool kit of effective stress management strategies presented in this section, and to determine which ones are best for the situation.[46] Exhibit 5.6 identifies the different approaches to stress management. As we look at each approach, keep in mind that effective stress management often includes more than one of these strategies.

Removing the Stressor

Some writers argue that the *only* way to manage stress effectively is to remove the stressors that cause unnecessary tension and job burn-out. For example, the Canadian Auto Workers union has argued that "work causes stress," and that we must therefore minimize these work stressors, not simply give employees seminars on how to cope with them. Other stress management strategies may keep employees "stress-fit," but they don't solve the fundamental causes of stress.[47]

There are many ways to remove stressors in the workplace. One of the most powerful solutions is to give employees more control over their work and work environment. This would include empowering employees and establishing self-directed work teams (Chapter 9) with greater autonomy over their work processes.[48] Role ambiguity and uncertainty can be reduced by improving organizational communications and clarifying work duties. Noise and safety risks are stressful, so improving these conditions would also go a long way to minimize stress in the workplace.

Family-friendly workplaces
Organizations that try to minimize work-family time conflict by offering flexible work arrangements, job sharing, telework, family leave, and childcare facilities.

Family-friendly workplaces

Companies that try to create **family-friendly workplaces** are mainly removing the stressors that cause time-based conflict. Flexible work arrangements, job sharing, telework,

---

EXHIBIT 5.6: Types of Stress Management Interventions

Royal Bank of Canada's Work-Family Life program now includes nearly 1,000 job-sharing arrangements across Canada. Job sharing splits a career position between two people so they experience less time-based stress between work and family.

family leave programs, and childcare facilities help parents perform their jobs with less worry about being in two places at the same time.[49] Let's look at each of these family-friendly strategies that minimize time-based conflict:

- *Flexible work arrangements*   Companies are breaking out of the traditional "9-to-5" schedule so that employees can fit family obligations into their work lives. Many firms let employees decide when to begin and end their workday. For instance, employees at CIBC's Gold VISA Card office must work 150 hours each month, but they can work as few as six hours on a given day. "This arrangement gives employees greater control over their lives and their jobs," explains Dan McCabe, the centre's senior manager.

- *Job sharing*   Job sharing is an increasingly popular activity in which two people share the same job. They typically work different parts of the week with some overlapping work time in the weekly schedule to coordinate activities. Royal Bank of Canada successfully launched job sharing with its Work-Family Life program in 1990 and now has nearly 1,000 job-sharing arrangements across Canada.[50]

- *Telework*   Companies allow or encourage some employees to work at home or at satellite offices some days of the week. These telework arrangements present several benefits and challenges to employees and employers. One benefit is that telework avoids the stress of commuting home in time to meet the kids at the end of their schoolday. For some, telework also allows some flexibility between work and household chores throughout the day.[51] Unfortunately, a common misperception is that telework allows employees to watch the kids while working. This is usually an impossible combination.

- *Family-leave programs*   Maternity and paternity leaves give employees several weeks of partially paid or unpaid leave to care for a new family. Some companies offer personal leave so that employees can take time off to provide eldercare or other obligations.

- *Childcare facilities*   On-site childcare centres have existed since World War II, when women worked in defence plants. In 1964, Toronto's Riverdale Hospital became one of the first organizations during the post-war era to have a childcare centre. Soon after opening the centre, the number of female applicants jumped 40 percent and absenteeism dropped significantly. Today, childcare facilities are found at National Bank of Canada, Husky Injection Molding Systems, and many other companies.[52]

Withdrawing from the Stressor

If the stressor can't be removed from the work environment, organizations should permanently or temporarily remove employees from the stressor. One permanent approach is to transfer employees to jobs for which they are better suited. Alain LeBlanc, the Hewlett-Packard (Canada) team leader described at the beginning of this section, followed this stress management strategy. A more drastic action is to have the employee leave the organization if a suitable position is not available.

Temporary withdrawal strategies

Temporarily withdrawing from stressors is how employees most frequently manage stress. We do it every day through short work breaks, finding a quiet place to enjoy a

Don Tracy, Courtesy of Cigna Corp.

Cigna Corp. encourages employees to take 15-minute "Fast Breaks" during the day to combat work-related stress. Employees at the Philadelphia-based insurance company choose from seven programs, such as "Move to Music," "Tackle Tension," and "Sanity Stretch" (shown in photo).

cup of coffee, or simply closing the office door for a few minutes. In Philadelphia, Cigna Corp. is trying to apply this stress-relief practice through a program called "Fast Break." The program encourages groups of employees to take healthy breaks of up to 15 minutes during the workday, during which they engage in stress-busting activities such as the Sanity Stretch and Tackle Tension.[53]

Vacations represent another form of temporary withdrawal from workplace stressors. Similarly, Toronto Sun Publishing Corp., the City of Toronto, and a few other Canadian firms offer paid sabbaticals to help long-term employees restore their capacity to cope with stressful work experiences. As one *Toronto Sun* employee confirms: "Taking (a sabbatical leave) is so therapeutic, it's unbelievable. When I came back, if there was a deadline on something, I didn't let it give me anxiety attacks!"[54]

Employees typically experience stress when living and working in another culture. Lacking common assumptions and expectations, expatriates must pay constant attention to how others react to their behaviours. For example, expatriates say that Vietnam is the most stressful Asian nation to live and work in because it is difficult to communicate and understand each other's goals. To manage this stress, some expatriates retreat into a stabilization zone — anyplace similar to the home country where they can rely on past routines to guide behaviour.[55] These may include attending a "Canadian night" at a club in the foreign country or having dinner with friends from the home country.

Changing Stress Perceptions

Employees often experience different levels of stress in the same situation because they perceive it differently. Consequently, stress can be minimized by changing perceptions of the situation. This does not mean that people should ignore risks or other stressors. Rather, companies can help employees strengthen their self-efficacy and self-esteem so that job challenges are not perceived as threatening.

Several elements of self-leadership described in Chapter 4 can alter employee perceptions of job-related stressors. Positive self-talk, for example, is a method of increasing self-efficacy. Mental imagery can reduce the uncertainty of future work activities. A recent study of newly hired Canadian accountants reported that personal goal-setting and self-reinforcement can reduce the stress that people experience when they enter new work settings.[56]

Controlling the Consequences of Stress

Relaxation and meditation programs manage stress by controlling its physiological consequences. In relaxation training, employees practise muscle relaxation, breathing exercises, and visualization. The objective is to achieve a relaxation response in which heart rate, blood pressure, muscle tension, and breathing rate decrease. Relaxation is best achieved in a quiet location, sitting in a comfortable chair, with eyes closed.

T'ai chi, the ancient Chinese mind-body exercise, is a form of relaxation activity in which individuals slowly act out a pattern of behaviours. According to its advocates, T'ai chi reduces stress by emphasizing breath control, balance, and mind-body coordination. Employees at Qantas Airlines and BC Telecom have practised T'ai chi exercises to reduce stress.[57] The mayor of Toronto and the president of the Industrial Accident Prevention Association recently led a T'ai chi demonstration in Nathan Phillips Square as part of the city's "stress-down day."

Meditation is a variation of relaxation involving a specific sitting position and special repetitive chant. This may include removing oneself from any distractions, such as visiting a retreat for a few days. Research suggests that relaxation and meditation programs are effective, particularly in reducing blood pressure levels and muscle tension.[58] As we see in Perspective 5.3, many companies are adopting these practices to minimize workplace stress.

Fitness and Lifestyle Programs

Corporate fitness programs have probably received more financial resources from Canadian business than any other strategy to combat work-related stress. Physical exercise helps employees lower their respiration, muscle tension, heartbeat, and stomach acidity, thereby reducing the physiological consequences of stress. Lifestyle programs train employees and reinforce their behaviour in better nutrition and fitness, regular sleep, and other good health habits. For example, Labatt Breweries recently introduced a lifestyle program in which employees learn how to balance their lives. Husky Injection Molding Systems Ltd. has a fitness centre and naturopathic adviser to help employees live a healthier lifestyle.[59] There is increasing evidence that fitness and lifestyle programs help employees control the dysfunctional consequences of stress.[60]

Employee Counselling

Employee assistance programs (EAPs)
Counselling services that help employees cope with personal or organizational stressors and adopt more effective coping mechanisms.

Employee assistance programs (EAPs) are counselling services that help employees overcome personal or organizational stressors and adopt more effective coping mechanisms. One estimate suggests that one-third of Canadian companies offer some form of EAP. Most EAPs in Canada started as alcoholism treatment programs, but most are now "broad-brush" programs that counsel employees on work or personal problems. Family problems often represent the largest percentage of EAP referrals, although this varies with industry and location. For instance, all of Canada's major banks provide post-trauma stress counselling for employees after a robbery, particularly when a weapon was visible.[61]

Meditation and Relaxation Become Mantras for Executive Stress

On his daily GO-train commute, George sits up comfortably, closes his eyes, and meditates. Unbeknownst to other commuters, the Toronto investment company president has moved into a state of deep relaxation. "People sleep on the train all the time, so I don't look at all unusual," George explains.

George doesn't want to overstate the benefits of meditation, but he claims that it has made him more relaxed, more alert, and more creative. "I can't imagine not doing it," he says.

Around the world, organizations have discovered the potential stress-busting benefits of meditation and relaxation. Many Japanese companies have corporate meditation programs. McDonald's Restaurants and Levi Strauss in the United States also have meditation rooms where employees chant mantras to release pent-up tension. Alcan

Aluminum, Canada's largest metal producer, brought a Benedictine monk into its Montreal head office to counsel managers on the value of reflection. British Steel managers have learned yoga and meditative exercises to manage their stress levels.

Phatra Thanakit, one of Thailand's top finance and securities companies, sends stressed-out staffers to a one-week retreat in a Buddist monastery. The monastic setting cuts employees off from contact with the outside world, while they take courses in meditation, contemplation, breathing, and basic Buddhism. "In our kind of work, if you have excessive greed it becomes troublesome for your colleagues, and for the firm as well," says managing director Sripop Sarasan. Sripop is convinced that too much greed eventually leads to stress, poor working relations, and job burnout.

Source: Adapted from P. Janssen "Refresher Course At Temple," *Asian Business*, August 1995; J. Turner, "Executive Meditation," *Toronto Star*, May 24, 1993, pp. B1, B2; F. S. Heilbronn, "The Use of Hatha Yoga as a Strategy for Coping with Stress in Management Development," *Management Education and Development* 23 (Summer 1992), pp. 131–39.

Social Support

Social support from co-workers, supervisors, family, friends, and others is one of the more effective stress management practices.[62] Social support refers to the person's interpersonal transactions with others and involves providing either emotional or informational support to buffer the stress experience. Organizations can increase the level of social support by providing opportunities for social interaction among employees as well as their families. Managers should also adopt a supportive leadership style when employees work under stressful conditions and need this social support. Mentoring relationships with senior managers may also help junior employees cope with organizational stressors.[63]

Social support reduces stress in at least three ways.[64] First, employees improve their perception that they are valued and worthy. This, in turn, increases their self-esteem and perceived ability to cope with the stressor (e.g., "I can handle this crisis because my colleagues have confidence in me"). Second, social support provides information to help employees interpret, comprehend, and possibly remove the stressor. For instance, social support might reduce a new employee's stress because co-workers describe ways to handle difficult customers. Finally, social support can help buffer the stress experience directly when the employee perceives that he or she is not facing the stressor alone. This last point reflects the idea that "misery loves company." People seek emotional support from others when they face threatening situations.[65]

Chapter Summary

- Stress is an adaptive response to a situation that is perceived as challenging or threatening to the person's well-being. Distress represents high stress levels that have negative consequences, whereas eustress represents the moderately low stress levels needed to activate people. The stress experience, called the *general adaptation syndrome*, involves moving through three stages: alarm, resistance, and exhaustion.

- Stressors are the causes of stress and include any environmental conditions that place a physical or emotional demand on the person. Stressors are found in the physical work environment, the employee's various life roles, interpersonal relations, and organizational activities and conditions. Conflicts between work and family obligations represent a frequent source of employee stress.

- Two people exposed to the same stressor may experience different stress levels because they perceive the situation differently, they have different threshold stress levels, or they use different coping strategies. Employees with Type A behaviour patterns tend to experience more stress than those exhibiting Type B behaviours.

- High levels of prolonged stress can cause physiological symptoms, such as high blood pressure, ulcers, sexual dysfunction, headaches, and coronary heart disease. Behavioural symptoms of stress include lower job performance, poorer decisions, more workplace accidents, higher absenteeism, and more workplace aggression. Psychologically, stress reduces job satisfaction and increases moodiness, depression, and job burnout. Job burnout refers to the process of emotional exhaustion, depersonalization, and reduced personal accomplishment resulting from prolonged exposure to stress. It is mainly due to interpersonal and role-related stressors and is most common in helping occupations.

- Many interventions are available to manage work-related stress. Some directly remove unnecessary stressors or remove employees from the stressful environment. Others help employees alter their interpretation of the environment so that it is not viewed as a serious stressor. Fitness and lifestyle programs encourage employees to build better physical defences against stress experiences. Social support provides emotional, informational, and material resource support to buffer the stress experience.

Discussion Questions

1. Two recent graduates join the same major newspaper as journalists. Both work long hours and have tight deadlines to complete their stories. They are under constant pressure to scout out new leads and be the first to report new controversies. One journalist is increasingly fatigued and despondent, and has taken several days of sick leave. The other is getting the work done and seems to enjoy the challenges. Use your knowledge of stress to explain why these two journalists are reacting differently to their jobs.

2. Describe the general adaptation syndrome process.

3. Sally works as a corporate law specialist for a leading Winnipeg law firm. She was married a few years ago and is currently pregnant with her first child. Sally expects to return to work full-time a few months after her baby is born. Describe two types of work-family conflict that Sally will likely experience during the first year after her return to work.

4. Police officer and food server are often cited as high-stress jobs, whereas professor and mechanic are low-stress jobs. Why should we be careful about describing these jobs as high- or low-stress?

5. Do people with Type A personalities make better managers? Why or why not?

6. A friend says that he is burned-out by his job. What questions might you ask this friend to determine whether he is really experiencing job burnout?

7. How might fitness programs help employees working in stressful situations?

8. A senior official at the Canadian Auto Workers union recently stated: "All stress management does is help people cope with poor management. [Employers] should really be into stress reduction." Discuss the accuracy of this statement.

Chapter Case

Jim Black: Sales Representative

Jim Black impatiently drummed the steering wheel and puffed a cigarette as his car moved slowly northbound along the Don Valley Parkway. Traffic congestion was normal in the late afternoon, but it seemed much heavier today. In any event, it was another irritation that was going to make him late for his next appointment.

As a sales representative at Noram Canada Ltd., Jim could not afford to keep clients waiting. Sales of compressed oxygen and other gases were slower during this prolonged recession. Other compressed-gas suppliers were eager to grab new accounts and it was becoming more common for clients to switch from one supplier to another. Jim pressed his half-finished cigarette against the ashtray and accelerated the car into another lane.

Buyers of compressed gases knew that the market was in their favour and many were demanding price discounts and shorter delivery times. Earlier in the week, for example, one of Jim's more demanding customers telephoned for another shipment of liquid oxygen to be delivered the next morning. To meet the deadline, Jim had to complete an expedited delivery form and then convince the shipping group to make the delivery in the morning rather than later in the day. Jim disliked making expedited delivery requests, even though this was becoming increasingly common among the reps, because it often delayed shipment of Noram's product to other clients. Discounts were even more troublesome because they reduced his commission and, except for very large orders, were frowned upon by Noram management.

Meanwhile, at Noram Canada's headquarters in nearby Brampton, senior managers were putting more pressure on sales reps to produce. They complained that the reps weren't aggressive enough and area supervisors were told to monitor each sales rep's monthly numbers more closely.

Jim fumbled for another cigarette as the traffic stopped momentarily.

Two months ago, the area sales supervisor had had "a little chat" (as he called it) with Jim about the stagnant sales in his district and loss of a client to the competition. It wasn't exactly a threat of being fired — other reps also received these chats — but Jim felt nervous about his work and began having sleepless nights. He began making more calls to potential clients, but was only able to find this time by completing administrative paperwork in the evenings. The evening work wasn't helping relations with his family.

To make matters worse, Noram's parent company in New York announced that it planned to sell the Canadian operations. Jim had heard rumours that a competitor was going to purchase the firm, mainly to expand its operations through Noram's Western Canadian sales force and production facilities. The competitor was well established in Ontario and probably wouldn't need a larger sales force here, so Jim's job would be in jeopardy if the acquisition took place. Jim felt another headache coming on as he stared at the endless line of red taillights slithering along the highway ahead.

Even if Jim kept his job, any promotion into management would be a long way off if the competitor acquired Noram Canada. Jim had no particular desire to become a manager, but his wife was eager for him to receive a promotion because it would involve less travel and provide a more stable salary (less dependent on monthly sales). Business travel was a nuisance, particularly for out-of-town appointments, but Jim felt less comfortable with the idea of sitting behind a desk all day.

The loud honk of another car startled Jim as he swerved into the exit lane at Eglinton Avenue. A few minutes later, he arrived at the client's parking lot. Jim rummaged through his briefcase for some aspirin to relieve the headache. He heaved a deep sigh as he glanced at his watch. Jim was 15 minutes late for the appointment.

Discussion Questions

1. What stress symptoms is Jim experiencing?

2. What stressors can you identify in this case?

3. What should Jim do to minimize his stress?

Experiential Exercise

Behaviour Activity Profile — The Type A Scale

Purpose: This exercise is designed to help you estimate the extent to which you follow a Type A behaviour pattern. It also shows you specific elements of Type A patterns in various life events.

Instructions: This is a self-diagnostic exercise to be completed alone. Each of us displays certain kinds of behaviour — thought patterns of personal characteristics. For each of the 21 sets of descriptions below, circle the number that you feel best describes where you are between each pair. The best answer for each set of descriptions is the response that most nearly describes the way you feel, behave, or think. Answer these in terms of your regular or typical behaviour, thoughts, or characteristics.

1. I'm always on time for appointments.   7 6 5 4 3 2 1   I'm never quite on time.

2. When someone is talking to me, chances are I'll anticipate what they are going to say, by nodding, interrupting, or finishing sentences for them.   7 6 5 4 3 2 1   I listen quietly without showing any impatience.

3. I frequently try to do several things at once.   7 6 5 4 3 2 1   I tend to take things one at a time.

4. When it comes to waiting in line (at banks, theatres, etc.), I really get impatient and frustrated.   7 6 5 4 3 2 1   Waiting in line doesn't bother me.

5. I always feel rushed.   7 6 5 4 3 2 1   I never feel rushed.

6. When it comes to my temper, I find it hard to control at times.   7 6 5 4 3 2 1   I don't seem to have a temper.

7. I tend to do most things like eating, walking, and talking rapidly.   7 6 5 4 3 2 1   I tend to do most things slowly.

Total score 1-7 _____ = S

8. Quite honestly, the things I enjoy most are job-related activities.   7 6 5 4 3 2 1   Leisure-time activities are what I most enjoy.

9. At the end of a typical workday, I usually feel like I needed to get more done than I did.   7 6 5 4 3 2 1   I accomplished everything I need to.

10. Someone who knows me very well would say that I would rather work than play.   7 6 5 4 3 2 1   I'd rather play than work.

11. When it comes to getting ahead at work nothing is more important.   7 6 5 4 3 2 1   Many things are more important than work.

12. My primary source of satisfaction comes from my job.   7 6 5 4 3 2 1   I regularly find satisfaction in nonjob pursuits, such as hobbies, friends, and family.

13. Most of my friends and social acquaintances are people I know from work.   7 6 5 4 3 2 1   Most of my friends are not connected with my work.

14. I'd rather stay at work than take a vacation.   7 6 5 4 3 2 1   Nothing at work is important enough to interfere with my vacation.

Total score 8-14 _____ = J

15. People who know me would describe me as hard-driving and competitive.   7 6 5 4 3 2 1   Most people would describe me as relaxed and easygoing.

16. In general, my behaviour is governed by a desire for recognition and achievement.   7 6 5 4 3 2 1   What I want to do — not by trying to satisfy others.

17. In trying to complete a project or solve a problem, I tend to wear myself out before I'll give up on it.   7 6 5 4 3 2 1   I tend to take a break or quit if I'm feeling fatigued.

18. When I play a game (tennis, cards, etc.) my enjoyment comes from winning.   7 6 5 4 3 2 1   My enjoyment comes from the social interaction.

19. I like to associate with people who are dedicated to getting ahead.   7 6 5 4 3 2 1   I like people who are easygoing and take life as it comes.

20. I'm not happy unless I'm always doing something.   7 6 5 4 3 2 1   Frequently, "doing nothing" can be quite enjoyable.

21. What I enjoy doing most are competitive activities.   7 6 5 4 3 2 1   Noncompetitive pursuits are what I most enjoy.

Total score 15-21 _____ = H

Impatience (S)	Job Involvement (J)	Hard Driving and Competitive (H)	Total Score (A) = S + J + H

The *Behaviour Activity Profile* attempts to assess the three Type A coronary-prone behaviour patterns, as well as provide a total score. The three a priori types of Type A coronary-prone behaviour patterns are shown:

Items	Behaviour Pattern		Characteristics
1–7	Impatience	(S)	Anxious to interrupt Fails to listen attentively Frustrated by waiting (e.g., in line, for others to complete a job)
8–14	Job involvement	(J)	Focal point of attention is the job Lives for the job Relishes being on the job Immersed by job activities
15–21	Hard driving/ competitive	(H)	Hardworking, highly competitive Competitive in most aspects of life, sports, work, etc. Racing against the clock
1–21	Total score	(A)	Total of S + J + H represents your global Type A behaviour

Score ranges for total score are:

Score	Behaviour Type
122 and above	Hard-core Type A
99–121	Moderate Type A
90–98	Low Type A
80–89	Type X
70–79	Low Type B
50–69	Moderate Type B
40 and below	Hard-core Type B

PERCENTILE SCORES

Now you can compare your score to a sample of over 1,200 respondents

Percentile Score	Raw Score	
Percentage of Individuals Scoring Lower	Males	Females
99%	_____ 140	_____ 132
95	_____ 135	_____ 126
90	_____ 130	_____ 120
85	_____ 124	_____ 112
80	_____ 118	_____ 106
75	_____ 113	_____ 101
70	_____ 108	_____ 95
65	_____ 102	_____ 90
60	_____ 97	_____ 85
55	_____ 92	_____ 80
50	_____ 87	_____ 74
45	_____ 81	_____ 69
40	_____ 75	_____ 63
35	_____ 70	_____ 58
30	_____ 63	_____ 53
25	_____ 58	_____ 48
20	_____ 51	_____ 42
15	_____ 45	_____ 36
10	_____ 38	_____ 31
5	_____ 29	_____ 26
1	_____ 21	_____ 21

Practice Session For Part 2

The true-false, multiple-choice, and written-answer questions presented here are based on information in Part 2 of this book (Chapters 2 to 5). These questions can help test your knowledge of material in these chapters. If your instructor uses the test bank for this textbook, these questions also give you an opportunity to practise for examinations in this course. The answers to these questions are found in Appendix C.

True-False

1. T F Competencies refer to an individual's skills and knowledge, but not personal values and personality traits.

2. T F Tacit knowledge about operating a computer program is more likely to be received by a trainee when observing a role model than by listening to a lecture about that topic.

3. T F Alderfer's ERG theory provides a more accurate and less rigid explanation than Maslow's Needs Hierarchy regarding the dynamics of human needs.

4. T F According to expectancy theory, employees are motivated by their expectation of receiving more outcomes than a comparison other related to their level of inputs.

5. T F Mental imagery refers to any situation in which a person talks to himself or herself about his or her own thoughts or actions.

6. T F The general adaptation syndrome describes the stress experience.

Multiple-Choice

1. When the president of XYZ Corp. says that he/she wants more organizational citizenship in the company, the president is mostly likely saying that: (a) the organization needs to identify itself more with its home country rather than act as a "global entity"; (b) employees need to spend more time helping co-workers; (c) the organization needs to take on more obligations to help society; (d) employees should have the right to elect their supervisor; (e) none of the above.

2. The main reason for having 360-degree feedback is that: (a) employees usually want to tell co-workers what they really think of them; (b) in most organizations, employees no longer have supervisors; (c) people other than the immediate supervisor are in a better position to observe the individual's performance on some dimensions; (d) all of the above; (e) none of the above.

3. Which of the following is a competency-based reward? (a) gainsharing; (b) pay increase resulting from a promotion; (c) skill-based pay plan; (d) merit increase based on performance appraisal results; (e) additional week of paid vacation after completing five years of service with the company.

4. Two employees perform the same work at XYZ Corp. and dislike their current job because of the same low pay and boring job tasks. One employee is motivated to quit because he/she believes there is a strong chance of finding a better job elsewhere,

whereas the other isn't motivated to quit because he/she believes the chances of alternate employment are low. According to expectancy theory, these employees have different levels of motivation to quit mainly because they differ in their: (a) $E{\rightarrow}P$ expectancy; (b) $P{\rightarrow}O$ expectancy; (c) comparison other; (d) outcome valences; (e) both a and b.

5. Which of the following practices relies on constructive thought patterns? (a) scientific management; (b) self-leadership; (c) job rotation; (d) status-based rewards; (e) job enrichment.

6. Which of the following activities tries to manage stress by controlling its consequences? (a) improved person-job matching; (b) work breaks; (c) meditation and relaxation; (d) seminars that increase self-esteem; (e) all of the above.

Written-Answer Questions

1. The deputy minister of labour in a provincial government is excited about the benefits of job enrichment and wants to apply it to the ministry construction inspectors located in four regional offices. Inspectors currently receive assignments from their supervisor and file their reports with the supervisor when the inspection is completed. These inspectors were construction workers in their younger years and now enjoy the easier life of a desk job. The deputy minister wants inspectors to perform more tasks previously assigned to their supervisor, such as receiving all work orders, scheduling inspection, and dealing directly with contractor complaints and inquiries. (Contractors don't always agree with the ministry's inspection reports.) What advice would you give the deputy minister before this job enrichment intervention begins?

2. Comment on the accuracy of the following statement: "According to goal-setting theory, performance increases when employees participate in setting the goals."

PART 3

Individual and Interpersonal Processes

CHAPTER 6
Perception and Personality in Organizations

CHAPTER 7
Emotions and Values in the Workplace

CHAPTER 8
Communicating in Organizational Settings

CHAPTER 6

Perception and Personality in Organizations

CHAPTER OUTLINE

The Perceptual Process

Social Identity Theory

Stereotyping in Organizational Settings

Attribution Theory

Self-Fulfilling Prophecy

Other Perceptual Errors

Improving Perceptions

Personality in Organizations

Chapter Summary

Discussion Questions

LEARNING OBJECTIVES

After reading this chapter, you should be able to:

- Describe the perceptual process.

- Explain how we perceive ourselves and others through social identity.

- Discuss how stereotyping influences discrimination and sexual harassment.

- Describe two attribution errors.

- Diagram the self-fulfilling prophecy process.

- Explain how the Johari Window can help improve our perceptions.

- Identify the "Big Five" personality dimensions.

Christine Cushing recalls how female chefs were stereotyped when she started in this profession: "My confidence kept being attacked by people who didn't see me as being capable."

When Barbara Gordon makes her rounds through Toronto's Boba Restaurant, customers sometimes ask why she is dressed like a chef. The reason for the outfit is that Gordon *is* pastry chef as well as co-owner of the restaurant.

Women still face gender stereotypes and misperceptions in Canada's food-service industry. This is particularly true of female chefs in large hotels. Few women choose to apprentice in hotels because the regimented kitchen environment tends to uphold gender stereotypes. The locker-room mentality and incidents of sexual harassment in some kitchens is also a problem. As a result, female executive chefs are almost completely absent from major Canadian hotels.

Christine Cushing has noticed fewer incidents of stereotyping and prejudice than in the early 1980s when she became a chef. "It was very difficult," recalls the owner of Toronto's Chez Toi cooking school. "My confidence kept being attacked by people who didn't see me as being capable."

Laura Prentice agrees that conditions have improved. "People don't treat me as a piece of fluff now," says the chef and business partner of the Pan restaurant in Toronto and Lola restaurant in Port Dalhousie, Ontario.

Lynn Heard, head chef and owner of Edmonton's Unheard Of Restaurant, has also noticed that female chefs are more accepted today, but some perceptual biases and harassment still exist. "We're worlds away in terms of where women have gone and can go," she says.[1]

The Greek philosopher Plato wrote that we see reality only as shadows reflecting against the rough wall of a cave.[2] In other words, reality is filtered through an imperfect perceptual process. **Perception** is the process of receiving information about and making sense of the world around us. It involves deciding which information to notice, how to categorize this information, and how to interpret it within the framework of our existing knowledge. As we saw in the opening vignette, the perceptual process often leads to misperceptions and inaccurate assumptions. These, in turn, affect our behaviour toward other people. As the workforce becomes increasingly diverse, we need to pay closer attention to the perceptual process to minimize these problems.

This chapter begins by describing the perceptual process; that is, the dynamics of selecting, organizing, and interpreting external stimuli. Social identity theory is introduced, including how this process influences our self-perceptions and the perceptions of others. Social identity theory lays the foundation for the discussion of stereotyping, prejudice, and discrimination. The perceptual processes of attribution and self-fulfilling prophecy are described next, followed by an overview of strategies to minimize perceptual problems. Our perception of others, as well as most other organizational behaviour processes, are influenced by personality. The final section of the chapter introduces this important concept and its relevance to organizational behaviour.

The Perceptual Process

As Exhibit 6.1 illustrates, the perceptual process begins when environmental stimuli are received through our senses. Most stimuli are screened out; the rest are organized and interpreted based on various information-processing activities. The resulting perceptions influence our emotions and behaviour toward those objects, people, and events.[3]

Selective Attention

Our five senses are constantly bombarded with stimuli. Some things get noticed, but most are screened out. A nurse working in post-operative care might ignore the smell of recently disinfected instruments or the sound of co-workers talking nearby. Yet, a small flashing red light on the nurses' station console is immediately noticed because it signals that a patient's vital signs are failing. This process of filtering information received by our senses is called **selective attention**.

One influence on selective attention is the size, intensity, motion, repetition, and novelty of the target (including people). The red light on the nurses'-station console receives attention because it is bright (intensity), flashing (motion), and a rare event (novelty). As for people, we would notice two employees having a heated debate if co-workers normally don't raise their voices (novelty and intensity).

Notice from the example of two people arguing that selective attention is also influenced by the context in which the target is perceived. We probably wouldn't notice two people arguing in a noisy bar, but they stand out in a quiet office. Similarly, you might be aware that a client has an Australian accent if the meeting takes place in Fredericton, but not if the conversation takes place in Melbourne, Australia, particularly if you'd been living there for some time. On the contrary, it would be your Canadian accent that others would notice!

EXHIBIT 6.1: Model of the Perceptual Process

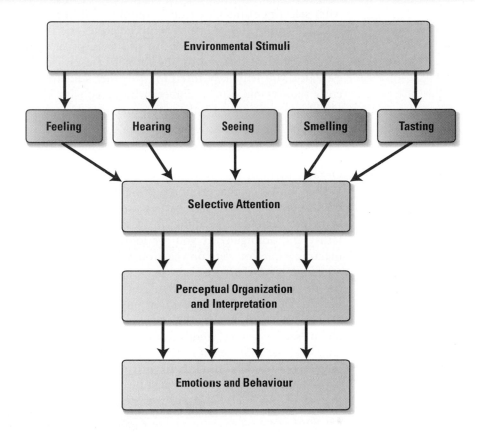

Characteristics of the perceiver

Selective attention is influenced by the perceiver's emotions and expectations. With respect to emotions, we tend to remember information that is consistent with our attitudes and ignore information that is inconsistent. For example, interviewers who develop positive feelings toward a job applicant early in the interview tend to subsequently screen out negative information about that candidate.[4] In extreme cases, our emotions screen out large blocks of information that threaten our beliefs and values. This phenomenon, called **perceptual defense**, protects our self-esteem and may be a coping mechanism to minimize stress in the short run.[5]

Our expectations, which are shaped by stereotypes and other preconceived perspectives of the world, condition us to be "ready" for certain events and to ignore others.[6] If we believe that professors are forgetful, for instance, then we notice information that confirms this belief and tend to screen out contradictory evidence.

Cultural conditioning also influences our expectations of others.[7] In a conversation between a Canadian and an Egyptian, the Canadian may notice and even feel uncomfortable by the close physical distance between them. In contrast, the Egyptian is accustomed to smaller personal space in social interactions and, therefore, does not notice the physical distance. Only when the Canadian steps back to a more comfortable distance does the Egyptian suddenly notice that they are too far apart.

Perceptual defense A defensive psychological process that involves subconsciously screening out large blocks of information that threaten the person's beliefs and values.

Perceptual Organization and Interpretation

After selecting stimuli, we usually simplify and "make sense" of it. This involves organizing the information into general categories and interpreting it. Our emotions and needs play an important role in this perceptual process. Suppose that you and another student disagree on the format of a project for this course. If the conflict escalates, you will likely interpret the other student's statements and actions differently than would team members who agree with your opponent's position. As we shall learn in Chapter 13, the perceptual distortion that occurs during conflicts tends to cause that conflict to further escalate.

Perceptual grouping

Perceptual grouping The perceptual organization process of placing people and objects into recognizable and manageable patterns or categories.

Organizing information mainly occurs through the process of **perceptual grouping**. We rely on perceptual grouping principles to organize people and objects into recognizable and manageable patterns or categories (see Exhibit 6.2). One grouping principle is closure — filling in missing information so that we minimize uncertainty and ambiguity. If you are told that the president of your company held a meeting while you were on vacation, you would likely make assumptions about who attended, what was said, and where the meeting was held. These assumptions fill in the missing information so that you can minimize ambiguity and categorize the meeting more easily with previous meetings.

Another perceptual grouping principle is identifying trends. Marketing analysts try to "see" consumer trends from seemingly random information. Sometimes, they later discover that the information *was* random! A third grouping principle is based on a target person's similarity or proximity to others. We might assume that a particular employee is inefficient because he or she works in a department where employees tend to be inefficient. Another example would be our tendency to label someone by their appearance because they "look like" people in that social category.

Perceptual grouping helps us to make sense of the workplace, but it can also inhibit creativity and open-mindedness. It puts blinders on our ability to organize and interpret people and events differently. Perceptual grouping is influenced by our broader perspectives of the world in which we live. These are known as mental models, which we discuss next.

EXHIBIT 6.2: Forms of Perceptual Grouping

Mental models

Marshall McLuhan once wrote that people wear their own set of idiosyncratic goggles. In his colourful way, McLuhan was saying that each of us holds a unique view of what the world looks like and how it operates. These idiosyncratic goggles are known as **mental models**.[8] Mental models are the broad world-views or "theories-in-use" that people rely on to guide their perceptions and behaviours. Mental models develop from our experiences and values. They create the screens through which we select information, the boxes we use to contain that knowledge, and the assumptions we use to interpret events. In other words, mental models have large-scale and long-term effects on how we manage our perceptual environment.

Mental models The broad world-views or "theories-in-use" that people rely on to guide their perceptions and behaviours.

Although the mental models we adopt help guide our perceptions, they also blind us to alternative and potentially better perspectives of the world. Mental models that give us a rich or efficient understanding of one environment may cause us to screen out or ineffectively organize information for another environment.[9] A well-known example of this occurred in the automobile industry. For many years, automobile executives judged their products by styling rather than quality or reliability. At one time, styling was a useful measure of excellence, but the executives were slow to change their thinking when customers changed their expectations and values. The result was a significant loss of market share to European and Japanese automakers who had already adopted mental models that emphasize quality.[10]

The important point here is that employees need to make room for new mental models. They need to be mentally flexible enough to perceive the world in different ways as their current perspective becomes outdated.

Social Identity Theory

Social identity theory A model that explains self-perception and social perception in terms of our unique characteristics (personal identity) as well as membership in various social groups (social identity).

The perceptual process is more than just placing other people into groups. It is an interactive dynamic between our self-perceptions and perceptions of others. **Social identity theory** has become the prominant model of social perception to explain this process.[11] According to social identity theory, self-perceptions are anchored along a continuum, from personal identity at one end to social identity at the other end. *Personal identity* includes the individual's unique characteristics and experiences, such as physical appearance, personality traits, and special talents. For example, you might have an unusual achievement that distinguishes you individually from other people. This becomes a personal characteristic with which you partially identify yourself.

Social identity, on the other hand, refers to the individual's self-identity in terms of membership in various social groups. For example, your self-perception might be based on your identity as a Canadian, a graduate of the University of New Brunswick, and an employee at Acme Widget Company. This social categorization process helps us to locate ourselves within the social world (see Exhibit 6.3).

Some scholars argue that self-concepts are derived totally from our interaction with others.[12] However, the more conservative view is that people adopt degrees of personal and social identity, depending on the situation. If your organizational behaviour class is well represented by both genders and students from different fields (marketing, finance, etc.), then you would tend to identify yourself in terms of personal identity characteristics in that context (e.g., "I'm probably the only one here who kayaked across Georgia Strait!"). On the other hand, if you are one of the few computer science students in a class with business students, then your group membership — your social identity — would dominate your self-perception. In

EXHIBIT 6.3: Self-Perception and Social Perception Through Social Identity

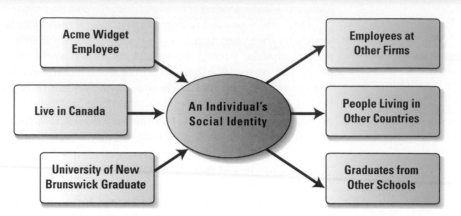

this situation, you would define yourself more by your field of specialization ("I'm from computer science") than by any personal identity characteristics. As your distinguishing social identity becomes known to others, they, too, would likely identify you by that feature.

People tend to perceive themselves as members of several groups, not just one or two. In this respect, social identity is a complex combination of many memberships determined by personal priorities. Also, we are motivated to create and present a positive self-image. According to social identity theory, this occurs by identifying ourselves with groups that have a positive public reputation. This explains why medical doctors almost always define themselves in terms of their profession, whereas people in low-status jobs are less likely to do so. Also, we tend to highlight the positive features of our group and ignore the negative features.

Perceiving Others Through Social Identity

Along with self-perception, social identity theory explains how and why we categorize others into homogeneous and often less favourable groups. Social identity is a *comparative* process, meaning that we define ourselves in terms of our differences with people who belong to other groups. To simplify this comparison process, we tend to *homogenize* people within social categories. Specifically, we think that people within our group share certain traits, and people in comparison groups share a different set of traits. This may be partly true, but we further exaggerate these differences. For example, you might hear students from one college or university describing students from a rival school as though the latter think and act differently.

Comparison and homogenization explain why we perceptually group other people and overgeneralize their traits. However, we also tend to develop less positive (or sometimes downright negative) images of people outside our social identity group. This occurs because, as mentioned earlier, we usually construct favourable images of our own social identity group and, by default, less favourable images of people belonging to other social categories.

To summarize, the social identity process explains how we perceive ourselves and others. We partly identify ourselves in terms of our membership in social groups. This comparison process includes creating a homogeneous image of our own social groups and different homogeneous images of people in other groups. We also tend to assign more favourable features to our groups and less favourable features to other groups. This perceptual process makes our social world easier to understand. However, it also becomes the basis for stereotyping and, potentially, discrimination and prejudice, which are discussed next.

Stereotyping in Organizational Settings

Stereotyping The process of using a few observable characteristics to assign people to a preconceived social category, and then assigning less observable traits to those persons based on their membership in the group.

Stereotyping is an extension of the social identity process. It generally refers to the process of assigning traits to people based on their membership in a social category.[13] For example, professors might be stereotyped as being absent-minded. Stereotyping economizes mental effort. It is much easier to remember categories of people than to store information on each person we meet. Stereotyping also fills in the missing information when we lack the opportunity or motivation to directly know others.[14]

Exhibit 6.4 illustrates the three steps in the stereotyping process. First, we develop social categories and assign traits that are difficult to observe (e.g., intelligent, absent-minded) to each category. We identify these unobservable traits from personal experiences, although direct experience is often overshadowed by images from movie characters and other public characterizations.

Second, people are identified with one or more social category based on easily observable information about them, such as gender, occupation, and race. Observable features allow us to assign people to a social group quickly and without much investigation. Third, the cluster of traits linked to the social category is assigned to people identified as members of that group. For example, we develop a generalized set of beliefs about professors (e.g., absent-minded). When we enter college or university, these traits are subconsciously assigned to the professors we meet, at least until we know them better.

EXHIBIT 6.4: The Stereotyping Process

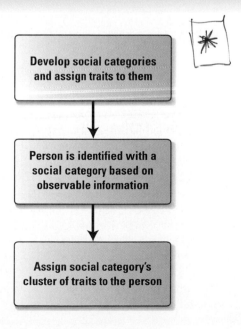

Problems with Stereotyping

Everyone engages in some degree of stereotyping, but we need to be aware that it frequently results in incorrect perceptions. One problem is that stereotyped traits do not accurately describe every person in that social category. Although it may be true that some professors are absent-minded, many are not. Another concern is that widely held stereotypes include inaccurate traits. For example, professors might be quite punctual, on average, even though popular stereotypes suggest otherwise. This inaccuracy may occur because we don't interact often enough with professors, or the public images of people in this social group overpower our personal experiences.

A third problem with stereotyping is that we subconsciously maintain our stereotypic expectations by ignoring or misinterpreting information that is inconsistent with the stereotype.[15] Stereotypes are notoriously easy to confirm because they include abstract personality traits that are supported by ambiguous behaviours. Moreover, conflicting evidence may appear consistent with the stereotype by making external attributions. If we meet a professor who is punctual, for example, we might assume that a helpful assistant, rather than the professor's own ability or motivation, caused this inconsistent behaviour.

Relying on inaccurate stereotypes is a common problem when interacting with people who are physically challenged.[16] Studies suggest that we tend to stereotype people who are confined to a wheelchair, have limited sight, or experience other physical challenges. For example, research has found that people with physical challenges are described as quiet, gentle-hearted, shy, insecure, dependent, and submissive. Yet these beliefs are grossly overgeneralized and probably not representative of the average person with a physical challenge. As we see in Perspective 6.1, employees at a branch of the Bank of Montreal had to deal with their stereotypes as they anticipated the branch's first hearing-impaired employee.

PERSPECTIVE 6.1

Bank of Montreal Employees Discover the Person, Not the Stereotype

Employees at a Bank of Montreal branch in Vancouver were a little worried when they learned that William Ko would be working with them. It wasn't just that Ko was a new recruit. It was that he was deaf.

"We were a little upset," admitted one employee. "Like, why us? Why were we singled out to have a deaf employee?"

"I had reservations — big time!" recalls Elaine Collins, assistant manager at the Bank of Montreal branch where Ko is employed. "I just could not envision how this was going to work. I had concerns about how we were going to train him . . . how he would interact toward other staff, and also how our customers would react to him."

Like most of us, these employees relied on their stereotypes to form initial expectations about working with a hearing-impaired person. Aside from the logistics of communicating, employees formed initial expectations about what William Ko would be like and how he would interact with others. However, staff members at the branch quickly learned that Ko is a highly qualified and motivated employee.

"I wanted to show that working one-on-one with customers is something that I could obtain," says Ko. "One of my personal goals is to learn as much as I can regarding all of the departments within the bank and to work my way up [at] the bank. It's been a great opportunity."

"William has been incredible," exclaims Terry Miller, Bank of Montreal's senior customer service manager. "Customers have really taken to William, even some of our more demanding commercial account–type clients."

"All [our] fears were allayed within three months," says Elaine Collins. "William's personality came out very strongly." It shows that knowing the person is better than knowing the stereotype.

Source: Bank of Montreal, "Challenging Perceptions," *875 Live* (Employee Video Magazine), Spring 1994.

Ethical Problems with Stereotyping

Stereotyping is an essential way for us to organize our social world, but we should also be aware that potentially it becomes the foundation for the ethical problems of prejudice and harassment. Recall from social identity theory that our perceptions of another group are often less favourable than beliefs about our own group. Consequently, we sometimes form negative emotions, known as **prejudice**, toward people in the stereotyped group based on inaccurate perceptions about people in that group. Prejudice can lead to employment discrimination by preventing qualified people in identifiable groups from having equal employment opportunities because of their membership in that group. For example, the opening story to this chapter described how traditional stereotypes of chefs may have limited the employment opportunities of women in this field.

Prejudice Negative emotions toward people belonging to a particular stereotyped group based on inaccurate perceptions about people in that group.

We occasionally hear about incidents of overt sexism and racism, but it is probably fair to say that most Canadians try to avoid discriminatory behaviours in the workplace. They support the notion of equality and try to act consistently with this equality value. People tend to monitor their own emotions and suppress prejudices arising from ingrained stereotypes, although recent studies suggest that some people are better than others at containing their prejudices.[17]

Even if we suppress our prejudices, subtle discrimination occurs because we rely on stereotypes to establish notions of the "ideal" person in specific roles.[18] One concern among organizational behaviour scholars is how we stereotype successful middle managers.[19] According to recent studies (two of them Canadian), male business students continue to hold a masculine stereotype of successful middle managers.[20] The risk is that women in these jobs might be evaluated less favourably than men in these jobs. In contrast, female students and female managers no longer stereotype managerial jobs. Instead, they perceive women as more likely to hold some traits necessary for managerial success, while men hold others; neither has a competitive advantage.[21] Stereotyping managerial jobs affects how women are perceived as leaders, which we will discuss in Chapter 14.

Subtle stereotyping can also affect the decision to hire someone. As we read in Perspective 6.2, Imperial Oil Ltd. realized that some managers were relying on stereotypes of the "ideal" job candidate that limited the employment opportunities of Asian applicants. The company introduced diversity-awareness training so that decision makers would recognize that their stereotypes did not work for people from different cultures.

Stereotyping and workplace harassment

Before leaving the topic of stereotyping and prejudice, we should note that these perceptual problems are partly responsible for workplace harassment. **Harassment** is broadly defined as unwelcome conduct that detrimentally affects the work environment or leads to adverse job-related consequences for the victims of harassment.[22] What constitutes harassment is a subjective and contentious issue. The Supreme Court of Canada has concluded that sexual harassment — the most frequently reported form of workplace harassment — covers a variety of behaviours, ranging from posting pornographic material, leering, and making unwanted sexual comments, to unwanted touching and demanding sexual favours.[23]

Harassment Unwelcome conduct that detrimentally affects the work environment or leads to adverse job-related consequences for the victims of harassment.

As we will discuss in Chapter 12, harassment is almost always explained in terms of the harasser's power over the victim.[24] As an example, when male physicians sexually harass their patients, we are quick to explain that they are abusing

Imperial Oil Clears Up Cross-Cultural Misunderstanding

While recruiting new employees for Imperial Oil's information technology area, Al Chan noticed that Asians were receiving fewer job offers than Caucasians, even though many Asians were interviewed. Chan, a chemical engineer with 20 years of service at Imperial Oil, presented his concerns to management and was asked to investigate.

"I think one of the reasons [for the discrepancy] is a significant difference in the way Westerners and Asians view authority," explains Chan. "Westerners are assertive and will challenge the leader. Generally, Asians do not — they perceive that it is their role to listen to the experienced, more senior person. In the workplace this can be misinterpreted as passiveness."

The solution, says Chan, is greater awareness of our perceptual biases. "Encouraging greater awareness is vital because the essential issue is how to get people to be more tolerant of differences. I say, 'Don't judge me on who I am; please look at the results of my work.'"

Along with Chan's observations, a group of Asian employees told senior management that they believed they were being negatively stereotyped and that they were missing out on promotions. To explore these perceptual problems further, several dozen Imperial Oil executives attended workshops on the importance of valuing diversity. Among other things, they learned that stereotyping people and making superficial judgments about them is harmful to organizations and individuals alike. The work-

Courtesy of Imperial Oil Ltd.

"Don't judge me on who I am; please look at the results of my work," says Imperial Oil's Al Chan.

shops were so enlightening that managers throughout Imperial Oil now participate in them.

Imperial Oil president Ron Brenneman believes that his company's journey toward a truly multicultural workforce demands changing perceptions. "We must deepen our understanding of our own biases," says Brenneman. "Shouting from the top isn't what will change things — learning and awareness will."

Source: Adapted from J. Finlayson, "Balancing Act," *Imperial Oil Review* 77 (Summer 1993), pp. 20–23.

their position of power. However, power does not completely explain why two-thirds of female physicians in Ontario report that patients have sexually harassed *them*.[25] Similarly, it does not sufficiently explain why an African-Canadian teacher in Quebec experienced racial harassment from his students to the point that he required stress-related medical leave.[26] Clearly, another factor is also responsible for workplace harassment.

The second factor in harassment is stereotyping and the resulting prejudices against the victim. According to recent writing on this topic, sexual harassment is more prevalent where the harasser (typically a man) holds benevolent sexist motives based on paternalism and gender stereotyping.[27] In other words, harassment is more likely to occur among people who stereotype the victim as subservient and powerless. It is less common among those who perceive others as equals. The main point here is that harassment is not just about power; it is also a function of how we perceive others and how we act on those perceptions.

Attribution Theory

Attribution process A perceptual process whereby we interpret the causes of behaviour in terms of the person (internal attributions) or the situation (external attributions).

Much of this chapter has focused on the dynamics of grouping, including social identity and stereotyping. A different perceptual activity, called the **attribution process**, helps us to understand the world in a different way. The attribution process involves deciding whether an observed behaviour or event is largely due to internal or external causes.[28] Internal causes refer to conditions under the person's control, such as ability and motivation. We make an internal attribution by believing that an employee is late for work because that person is lazy. External causes refer to conditions beyond the individual's control, such as luck and other situational contingencies. An external attribution would occur if we believe that the employee is late because the public transit system broke down.

How do we decide whether to make an internal or external attribution about a co-worker's excellent job performance or a supplier's late shipment? Basically, we figure out whether the target person has acted this way in the past and in other situations, and whether other people act similarly in this situation. For example, if an employee is producing several poor-quality products on a machine one day, we would probably conclude that there is something wrong with the machine (an external attribution) if the employee has made good-quality products on this machine in the past and on other machines, and if other employees have recently had quality problems on this machine.

Consequences of Attribution

Attributing behaviour to internal versus external factors affects our subsequent reactions to that event.[29] One study reported that grievance arbitration outcomes largely depend on the arbitrator's attribution of causality or responsibility for the wrongdoing. In particular, arbitration decisions favour the employee when other employees have committed the same error and the employee has not been guilty of the wrongdoing before.[30]

Attribution decisions also affect the implications of performance feedback and reward allocation. Employees receive larger bonuses or pay increases when decision makers attribute good performance to the employee's ability or motivation.[31] Employees also develop a stronger self efficacy and tend to have higher job satisfaction when they believe positive feedback relates to events within their control rather than to external causes.[32]

Attribution Errors

Actor-observer error An attribution error whereby people tend to attribute their own actions to external factors and the behaviour of others to internal factors.

Self-serving bias A perceptual error whereby people tend to attribute their own success to internal factors and their failures to external factors.

The attribution process is far from accurate. Two common attribution errors are actor-observer error and self-serving bias. **Actor-observer error** is the tendency to make external attributions about our own behaviour and internal attributions about the behaviour of other people. We conclude that employees arrive late for work due to their lack of effort because the situational factors influencing this behaviour are not easily seen. In contrast, we see that our own lateness is due to road-construction delays or other external causes because we are more aware of them. In organizational settings, this can lead to conflict between supervisors and employees over the degree to which employees should be held responsible for their poor performance or absenteeism.[33]

Self-serving bias is the tendency to attribute our favourable outcomes to internal factors and our failures to external factors. Simply put, we take credit for our successes and blame others or the situation for our mistakes. The existence of self-serving bias in corporate life has been well documented. In a unique study of corporate annual reports, researchers discovered that organizational successes were typically explained by internal attributions such as management strategy, workforce qualities, and research/development efforts. But when explaining corporate problems, the annual reports relied more on external attributions such as bad weather, strong competition, and inflationary pressures.[34]

Aside from these two errors, attributions vary from one person to another based on personal values and experiences. For instance, one recent study reported that female managers are less likely than male managers to make internal attributions about their job performance.[35] Attributions also vary across cultures. Japanese and Chinese employees are less likely to engage in self-serving bias than North American employees. In collectivist cultures, where a person's attachment to a group is important (Chapter 7), individuals try to maintain harmony among group members, so they make more external attributions about another employee's poor performance.[36] Overall, we need to be careful about personal and systematic biases in the attribution process within organizations.

Self-Fulfilling Prophecy

For the past 35 years, Ottawa restaurant owner David Smith has known that employees will achieve remarkable performance levels when their boss believes they can do it. "When you show people you believe in them, it's amazing what can happen," advises Smith. As owner of Nate's Deli, Smith has seen his high expectations make some employees confident enough to take on more challenging assignments in the organization. "I've put busboys into tuxedos," he says.[37]

Self-fulfilling prophecy
A phenomenon in which an observer's expectations of someone causes that person to act in a way consistent with the observer's expectations.

David Smith has been practising a powerful perceptual process called **self-fulfilling prophecy**. Self-fulfilling prophecy occurs when our expectations about another person cause that person to act in a way that is consistent with those expectations.[38] In other words, our perceptions can influence reality. If a supervisor believes a new employee won't be able to perform the job, this expectation influences the supervisor's behaviour toward the employee and, without realizing it, may cause the recruit to perform the job poorly. Consequently, the supervisor's perception, even if originally incorrect, is confirmed. Exhibit 6.5 illustrates the four steps in the self-fulfilling prophecy process using the example of a supervisor and subordinate.[39]

1. *Expectations formed*   The supervisor forms expectations about the employee's future behaviour and performance. These expectations are sometimes inaccurate, because first impressions are usually formed from limited information.

2. *Behaviour toward the employee*   The supervisor's expectations influence his or her treatment of employees.[40] Specifically, high-expectancy employees (those expected to do well) receive more emotional support through nonverbal cues (e.g., more smiling and eye contact), more frequent and valuable feedback and reinforcement, more challenging goals, better training, and more opportunities to demonstrate their performance.

3. *Effects on the employee*   The supervisor's behaviours have two effects on the employee. First, through better training and more practice opportunities, high-expectancy employees learn more skills and knowledge than low-expectancy

EXHIBIT 6.5: The Self-Fulfilling Prophecy Cycle

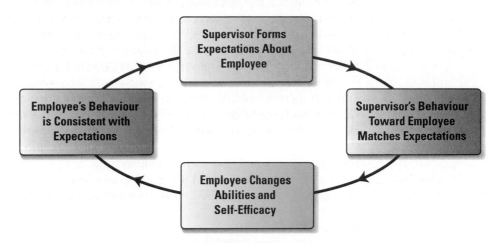

Self-efficacy A person's belief that he or she has the ability, motivation, and situational contingencies to complete a task successfully.

employees. Second, the employee develops a stronger **self-efficacy**.[41] Recall from Chapter 2 that high-self-efficacy employees believe that they have the ability, motivation, and situational contingencies to complete a task successfully.[42] This results in higher motivation because employees develop stronger effort-to-performance expectancies and set more challenging goals for themselves.

4. *Employee behaviour and performance*   With higher motivation and better skills, high-expectancy employees are more likely to demonstrate desired behaviours and better performance. This is observed by the supervisor and reinforces the original perception.

The self-fulfilling prophecy effect extends beyond supervisor-subordinate relationships. Some of the earliest research reported that teacher expectancies influenced the subsequent behaviour and performance of elementary-school children. Courtroom research has found that judges influence jury decisions by nonverbally communicating their expectations. And while self-fulfilling prophecy is an interpersonal effect, it also operates at a macro level in the stability of financial institutions. The stability of a bank, for instance, depends on the public's expectation that it will be stable. As soon as people begin to doubt this belief, the financial institution has a "run on the bank" that threatens its survival.[43]

Self-Fulfilling Prophecies in Organizations

In organizational settings, employees are more likely to be victims of negative self-fulfilling prophecy than benefactors of positive self-fulfilling prophecy.[44] This is unfortunate because, as restaurant owner David Smith knew, self-fulfilling prophecy is a potentially valuable strategy to maximize employee performance and satisfaction. Researchers have reported, for example, that hard-core unemployed trainees were more likely to find work and poor-performing sailors in the United States Navy were more likely to improve their performance when instructors or supervisors formed positive expectations about them.[45]

One of the best examples of self-fulfilling prophecy took place in an Israeli Defense Force combat command course. Course instructors were told that one-third of the incoming trainees had high command potential, one-third had normal potential, and the rest had unknown potential. The trainees had been randomly placed into these categories by the researchers, but the instructors were led to believe that this was accurate information. As predicted, high-expectancy soldiers performed significantly better by the end of the course than did others. They also had more favourable attitudes toward the course and the instructor's leadership effectiveness.[46]

How can organizations harness the power of positive self-fulfilling prophecy? Supervisors must exhibit more contagious enthusiasm and, although providing accurate feedback, continue to express hope and optimism in each employee's potential.[47] In some situations, researchers have found that these positive expectations spread from one or two employees to the entire group. To block negative self-fulfilling prophecy, companies need to help employees to fight negative stereotypes and avoid first impressions. They should also develop more objective performance measures and provide fair access to challenging assignments and training opportunities.

Other Perceptual Errors

Perception is an imperfect process. This is already apparent from our discussion of stereotyping, attribution, and self-fulfilling prophecy. Some of the other troublesome errors that distort our ability to perceive people and events include halo, primacy, recency, and projection.

Halo Effect

Halo effect A perceptual error whereby our general impression of a person, usually based on one prominent characteristic, biases our perception of other characteristics that person possesses.

Halo effect occurs when our general impression of a person, usually based on one prominent characteristic, colours our perception of other characteristics of that person.[48] If we meet a client who speaks in a friendly manner, we tend to infer a host of other favourable qualities about that person. If a colleague doesn't complete tasks on time, we tend to view his or her other traits unfavourably. In each case, one trait important to the perceiver forms a general impression, and this impression becomes the basis for judgments about other traits. Halo effect is most likely to occur when concrete information about the perceived target is missing or we are not sufficiently motivated to search for it.[49] Instead, we use our general impression of the person to fill in the missing information.

Halo effect has received considerable attention in research on performance appraisal ratings.[50] Consider the situation in which two employees have the same level of work quality, quantity of work, and customer relations performance, but one tends to be late for work. Tardiness might not be an important factor in work performance, but the supervisor has a negative impression of employees who are late for work. Halo effect would cause the supervisor to rate the tardy employee lower on *all* performance dimensions because the tardiness created a negative general impression of that employee. The punctual employee would tend to receive higher ratings on *all* performance dimensions even though his or her performance level is really the same as that of the tardy employee. Consequently, halo effect distorts our judgments and can result in poor decision making.

Primacy Effect

Primacy effect A perceptual error in which we quickly form an opinion of people based on the first information we receive about them.

Primacy effect relates to the saying that "first impressions are lasting impressions." It is our tendency to quickly form an opinion of people based on the first information we receive about them. This rapid perceptual organization fulfils our need to make sense of others and provides a convenient anchor to integrate subsequent information about them. For example, if we meet a new employee who avoids eye contact and speaks softly, we quickly conclude that the person is bashful. It is easier to remember the person as bashful than to recall the specific behaviours exhibited during the first encounter.

Unfortunately, first impressions tend to result in perceptual errors because they are formed with little information. Moreover, subsequent information about the person is given less attention and contradictory information is ignored. In fact, if the contradictory information is ambiguous, we often believe that it is consistent with the first impression.[51] Thus, the person we think is bashful will have difficulty shaking this first impression.

Recency Effect

Recency effect A perceptual error in which the most recent information dominates our perception about the person.

The **recency effect** occurs when the most recent information dominates our perception of others.[52] This effect is stronger than the primacy effect when the first impression is formed long before the person is evaluated. In other words, the most recent information has the greater influence on our perception of someone when the first impression has worn off with the passage of time.

The recency effect is found in performance appraisals, for which supervisors must recall every employee's performance over the previous year. Recent performance information dominates the evaluation because it is the most easily recalled. Some employees are well aware of the recency effect and use it to their advantage by getting their best work on the manager's desk just before the performance appraisal is conducted.

Projection Bias

Projection A perceptual error in which we tend to believe that other people hold the same beliefs and attitudes that we do.

Projection bias occurs when we believe other people have the same beliefs and behaviours that we do.[53] If you are eager for a promotion, you might think that others in your position are similarly motivated. If you are thinking of quitting your job, you start to believe that other people are also thinking of quitting.

Projection bias is usually a defence mechanism to protect our self-esteem. If we break a work rule, projection justifies this infraction by claiming that "everyone does it." We feel more comfortable with the thought that our negative traits exist in others, so we are quick to believe that others also have these traits. Similarly, projection maintains the credibility of our goals and objectives. When we want an organizational policy changed, we tend to believe that others also have this goal.

DILBERT

Courtesy of Digital Equipment Corp.

Digital Equipment Corp. has been a leader in diversity awareness with its "Valuing Differences Program." Core groups of employees from different cultural backgrounds are formed to discuss and learn to appreciate one another's differences.

Improving Perceptions

We may not be able to bypass the perceptual process, but there are ways to make it less distorted. Five strategies to improve our perceptions include the following: increasing awareness of perceptual biases; learning to empathize with others; postponing our impression of others; comparing our perceptions with others; and becoming more aware of our values, beliefs, and prejudices.

Increase Awareness of Perceptual Biases

The journey toward improving perceptions begins by making employees aware of their perceptual biases. The Bank of Montreal followed this approach by forming a task force to dispel myths about women in management. The task force reported that female employees have longer service records than men at almost every level, thereby refuting the myth that women are less committed to their careers. The task force also reported that women at the bank are more likely to receive the top two performance appraisal ratings, thus shattering the myth that women don't have the "right stuff" to compete with men for more senior jobs.[54]

Stereotypes are difficult to change simply by having employees read more accurate information about social groups. As a result, many Canadian firms, including CIBC, Bank of Montreal, Colgate Palmolive, and Digital Equipment Corp. have diversity awareness programs.[55] These programs usually begin by describing the benefits of diversity, such as improved decision making and better customer service. Then participants learn through experiential activities about stereotypes and prejudices that may undermine these benefits of diversity.

In Imperial Oil's diversity awareness workshop, for example, managers learn how their norms and preconceptions may differ from those of employees raised in other cultures. Digital Equipment Corp.'s "Valuing Differences Program" sets up small, ongoing discussion groups consisting of employees from different cultural backgrounds. Through open dialogue, these employees test their stereotypes and assumptions about group members from other cultures.[56]

Federal Express has applied a more dramatic experiential day-long program in which managers teamed up with blind people to complete a series of tasks. At the end of the day, the blind participants gave feedback about their partner's management style. The Federal Express managers also discovered their perceptual limitations. Said one manager: "It was easy to see how I made bad assumptions about the people I work with and I grossly underestimate their abilities."[57]

Empathize with Others

Empathy　A person's ability to understand and be sensitive to the feelings, thoughts, and situation of others.

Empathy refers to a person's ability to understand and be sensitive to the feelings, thoughts, and situation of others. This is particularly useful for reducing actor-

PERSPECTIVE 6.3

Increasing Empathy by Being There

Hyundai Motor Co. president Chon Sung-Won recently made history by removing his tie, donning coveralls, and hunching over the fender of an Excel. It was the first time any executive at the Korean automobile company had crossed the line to perform blue-collar work. Chon is trying to mend years of conflict between management and employees by improving empathy between the two groups. "Mutual understanding, respect, and trust are the keys," explains Chon.

Many executives are bringing their perceptions back into focus by working alongside front-line employees. At Continental Airlines, senior management become flight attendants and reservation agents every three or four months. At Quebec City's Château Frontenac hotel, managers switch roles with front-line employees for one day each month. "I will certainly appreciate the amount of work [employees] are doing after this," says Château Frontenac's guest services manager after helping to serve some of the 500 breakfasts in the hotel's restaurant.

Holger Kluge, president of the CIBC's Personal and Commercial Bank division, agrees. He has spent a few days each year behind the counter at CIBC branches, learning first-hand from the bank's customers and front-line employees about their needs and concerns. "You can really only understand a job if you do it," says Kluge. "You have to feel it."

One of the most enthusiastic supporters of having executives work in front-line jobs is William Malec, chief financial officer of the Tennessee Valley Authority. Malec devotes one day each month to scrubbing toilets, sorting mail, or performing other nonmanagement jobs while hearing the concerns of employees who work in that department.

A vivid illustration of his perceptual awakening came one day when Malec delivered mail to a manager who was always sugary-sweet when Malec was in his chief financial officer job. But the manager didn't recognize Malec in his temporary role as mailroom employee, and rudely snubbed him. The incident helped Malec realize that it isn't easy to see reality when you're looking from the top of the corporate ladder. The abrupt manager also learned in his next performance review how to improve his behaviour toward employees.

Source: A. Gibbon, "The Onion-Busting Boss," *Globe & Mail*, June 13, 1995, p. B10; O. Gadacz, "Korean Executives Work on Assembly Line," *Automotive News*, May 30, 1994, p. 48; J. M. Feldman, "Structure," *Air Transport World*, November 1994, pp. 30–38; T. Gutner, "Meeting the Boss," *Forbes*, March 1, 1993, p. 126; "The Common Touch," *Maclean's*, October 19, 1992, p. 11.

observer attribution errors because empathy makes us more sensitive to external causes of the employee's performance and behaviour.[58]

Putting yourself in the other person's shoes is easy to recommend, but not so easy to implement. The best way to increase empathy is to spend time participating in the employee's work environment. As Perspective 6.3 describes, several executives are increasing their empathy of employees and clients by "walking in their shoes."

Postpone Impression Formation

It is very tempting to categorize people into boxes as soon as possible. After all, the sooner we have labelled them, the sooner we can simplify the world and reduce the tension of uncertainty. Unfortunately, this practice of forming impressions with limited information forces us to rely on inaccurate and overgeneralized stereotypes. It is much better to postpone forming impressions and avoid making stereotyped inferences until more information is received. When working with people from different cultural backgrounds, for instance, you should constantly challenge your stereotypic expectations and actively seek out contrary information. By blocking the effects of stereotypes, first impressions, and other perceptual blinders, you are better able to engage in a developmental learning process that forms a better understanding of others.[59]

Compare Perceptions with Others

Another useful way of reducing perceptual bias is to compare your perceptions with the perceptions other people have about the same target. By sharing perceptions, you learn different points of view and potentially gain a better understanding of the situation. If your colleagues have different backgrounds but similar perceptions of the situation, then there is reason to be more confident in your interpretation. Of course, there is no way to know for sure that your perceptions are correct, but they are less likely to be wrong if people with different backgrounds have the same general interpretation of the situation.

Know Yourself: Applying the Johari Window

How do you get ahead in a corporation? According to Paul Houston, CEO of Scott's Restaurants, Inc. in Markham, Ontario, you start by knowing yourself and getting straight talk from a trusted source. "Be as brutally frank with yourself as you can be," says Houston. "[Get] somebody who will close the door to their office and say, 'Listen . . . here's the reality.'"[60]

Knowing yourself — becoming more aware of your values, beliefs, and prejudices — is a powerful way to improve your perceptions.[61] For example, suppose that you dislike a particular client who treated you badly a few years ago. If the client meets with you to re-establish the relationship, you might be more open-minded about this business opportunity if you are conscious of these emotions. If you act harshly to the client, your colleagues are likely to understand the reason for your behaviour and draw this to your attention.

The **Johari Window** is a popular model for explaining how co-workers can increase their mutual understanding.[62] Developed by Joseph Luft and Harry Ingram (hence the name *Johari*), this model divides information about yourself into four "windows" — open, blind, hidden, and unknown — based on whether your own values, beliefs, and experiences are known to you and to others.

Johari Window A model of personal and interpersonal understanding that encourages disclosure and feedback to increase the open area and reduce the blind, hidden, and unknown areas of oneself.

EXHIBIT 6.6: Johari Window

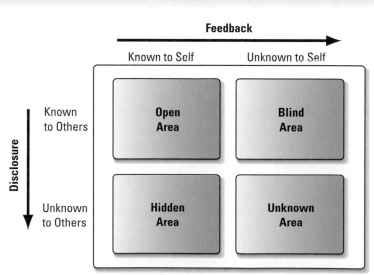

Source: Based on J. Luft, *Group Processes* (Palo Alto, Calif.: Mayfield, 1984).

As we see in Exhibit 6.6, the *open area* includes information about you that is known both to you and others. For example, both you and your co-workers may be aware that you don't like to be near people who smoke cigarettes. The *blind area* refers to information that is known to others but not to yourself. For example, your colleagues might notice that you are embarrassed and awkward when meeting someone confined to a wheelchair, but you are unaware of this fact. Information known to you but unknown to others is found in the *hidden area*. We all have secrets about our likes, dislikes, and personal experiences. Finally, the *unknown area* includes your values, beliefs, and experiences that aren't known to you or others.

The main objective of the Johari Window is to increase the size of the open area so that both you and your colleagues are aware of your perceptual limitations. This is partly accomplished by reducing the hidden area through *disclosure* — informing others of your beliefs, feelings, and experiences that may influence the working relationship. Disclosure must be reciprocal among team members. Fortunately, self-disclosure by one person tends to cause others to make a self-disclosure.[63] The open area also increases through *feedback* from others about your behaviours. This information helps you to reduce your blind area because co-workers often see things in you that you do not see. Finally, the combination of disclosure and feedback occasionally produces revelations about information in the unknown area.

Johari Window in practice

The Johari Window can be found in diversity awareness programs, such as Federal Express's program where managers receive feedback after working with people who are blind. It is also evident in 360-degree performance feedback systems (Chapter 2). Jane Haberbusch, a manager at Toronto-based Consumers Gas Co. describes such an incident. "Someone wrote [on the 360-degree feedback form] that I interrupted people when I spoke and that I was coming across as impatient. Actually, it was just enthusiasm, but it made me aware of how others perceived me and I was able to change."[64]

Swedbank used some aspects of Johari Window to improve mutual understanding among its executives. Consultants helped the executive team to increase their level of openness through ongoing discussion. Although initially reluctant to give each other feedback, the executives eventually engaged in open debates about the strengths and weaknesses of executives in the group.[65]

The Johari Window may work well in some situations, but the model ignores culture differences in openness, egalitarianism, and face-saving. The model is more difficult to implement in Asia, for example, where feedback and self-disclosure is less acceptable than in Canada. Similarly, some colleagues from Mexico may have difficulty with the Johari Window because of their stronger cultural norm of saving face. Lastly, in any country, we must remember that everyone needs to have a hidden self. As we will learn in Chapter 15, some organization development programs cross ethical boundaries by trying to invade that private space.

No matter which steps are taken to improve the perceptual process, we need to recognize that our perceptions of the world are partly structured by our personality. In fact, an individual's personality traits play a pervasive role in almost every aspect of organizational behaviour, from learning processes to one's willingness to adopt a company's cultural values. Let's now turn to the topic of personality in organizations.

Personality in Organizations

Stewart Allen is a personality to reckon with in the bottled water business. His determination, achievement orientation, and sociable style turned Halifax-based Sparkling Spring Water Ltd. into a $45 million operation with 400 employees. Allen's personality also helped to double sales at Canadian Springs Water Co. Ltd. in Burnaby, British Columbia, which he purchased in 1996. "I've known Stu for eight years and he's a man on a mission," says an executive at Sobey Stores. A colleague at Pepsi-Cola Ltd. adds: "Stewart is incredibly passionate about the work he does, and that's infectious. He's very dynamic and a self-made man."[66]

Personality The relatively stable pattern of behaviours and consistent internal states that explain a person's behavioural tendencies.

It is difficult to describe Stewart Allen — or anyone else — without referring to the concept of **personality**. Personality refers to the relatively stable pattern of behaviours and consistent internal states that explain a person's behavioural tendencies.[67] This definition recognizes that personality has both internal and external elements. The external traits are the person's social reputation — the observable behaviours that we rely on to identify someone's personality. For example, we can observe Stewart Allen's sociability by how often he interacts with other people and how comfortable he acts in those social settings. The internal states represent the thoughts, values, and genetic characteristics that we infer from the observable behaviours.

An individual's personality is relatively stable. If it changes at all, it is only after a very long time or as the result of traumatic events. Also, we say that personality

Dominic Schaefer. Used with permission.

Stewart Allen's personality is a driving force behind the success of his bottled water businesses in Nova Scotia and British Columbia. "Stewart is incredibly passionate about the work he does," says a colleague at Pepsi-Cola Ltd.

explains behavioural tendencies because a person's behaviour is influenced by the situation as well as by personality traits. For example, talkative people spend much of their time in conversations when free to do so, but not in situations in which they are explicitly told to keep quiet. Thus, personality mainly affects behaviour in "weak" situations — environments that do not constrain the person's natural dispositions and tendencies. In "strong" situations (in which social norms and reward systems constrain our behaviour), people with different personalities act very much the same.[68]

Biology or Environment?

An individual's personality is both inherited and shaped from the environment.[69] Our personality is partly inherited genetically from our parents. However, these genetic personality characteristics are altered somewhat by life experiences. Stewart Allen's personality is partly handed down genetically from his parents, but it has also been shaped by a variety of life experiences, such as early friendships, interactions with parents, and traumatic events.

"Big Five" Personality Dimensions

"Big Five" personality dimensions The five abstract personality dimensions under which most personality traits are represented: extroversion, agreeableness, conscientiousness, emotional stability, and openness to experience.

Extroversion A "Big Five" personality dimension that characterizes people who are outgoing, talkative, sociable, and assertive.

About 100 years ago, scholars began cataloguing different personality traits used to describe people. They identified thousands of words in *Roget's Thesaurus*, and later in *Webster's* dictionary, that describe personality traits. These words were aggregated into 171 clusters, then further shrunk down to five abstract personality dimensions. Scholars recently reconfirmed the same five dimensions — known as the **"Big Five" personality dimensions** — using more sophisticated techniques.[70] As Exhibit 6.7 shows, these five dimensions include:

- *Extroversion* **Extroversion** characterizes people who are outgoing, talkative, sociable, and assertive. The opposite is introversion, which characterizes people who are quiet, shy, and cautious.

- *Agreeableness* This includes the traits of being courteous, good-natured, trusting, cooperative, empathic, and caring. Some scholars prefer the label "friendly compliance" for this dimension, with its opposite being "hostile noncompliance."

EXHIBIT 6.7: The "Big Five" Personality Dimensions

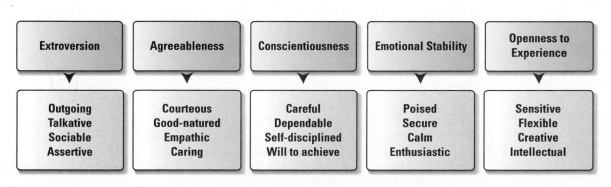

Extroversion	Agreeableness	Conscientiousness	Emotional Stability	Openness to Experience
Outgoing Talkative Sociable Assertive	Courteous Good-natured Empathic Caring	Careful Dependable Self-disciplined Will to achieve	Poised Secure Calm Enthusiastic	Sensitive Flexible Creative Intellectual

Conscientiousness
A "Big Five" personality dimension that characterizes people who are careful, dependable, and self-disciplined.

- *Conscientiousness*   **Conscientiousness** refers to people who are careful, dependable, and self-disciplined. Some scholars argue that this dimension also includes the will to achieve, rather like the need for achievement described in Chapter 3.

- *Emotional stability*   People with high emotional stability are poised, secure, calm, and enthusiastic. At the other extreme are people who tend to be depressed, anxious, indecisive, and tense.

- *Openness to experience*   This dimension is the most complex and least agreed upon. It generally refers to the extent to which people are sensitive, flexible, creative, and intellectual.

Personality and Organizational Behaviour

We use personality traits to make sense of people in organizational settings, anticipate their future behaviour, and possibly increase their satisfaction and performance through better person-job matching. The effectiveness of some job design strategies and leadership styles is contingent on employee personalities. Champions of organizational change (people who effectively gain support for new organizational systems and practices) seem to be placed along the positive end of the five personality dimensions described above. Personality traits affect the types of jobs in which people are interested. In fact, some vocational interest tools are based on personality concepts.[71]

The nagging question in personality research is whether certain personality traits predict job performance. At one time, it seemed obvious that people needed to have certain personalities to perform the job well. By the 1950s, many companies in Canada and the United States were giving personality tests to job applicants. Then, in the 1960s, researchers reported that there is a very weak relationship between personality and job performance.[72] They cited problems with measuring personality traits and explained that the connection between personality and performance exists only under very narrowly defined conditions. This finding coincided with the emerging notion that behaviour is better than abstract concepts at predicting future behaviour. In other words, why rely on personality traits when we can learn about a job applicant's past job performance or see how that person performs on a work sample?[73]

In the past few years, personality has regained some of its credibility as a predictor of job performance.[74] Conscientiousness has taken centre stage as the most valuable personality trait for predicting job performance in almost every job group.[75] Conscientious employees set higher personal goals for themselves and have higher performance expectations than employees with low levels of conscientiousness. Moreover, as we learned in Chapter 2, high-conscientiousness employees tend to engage in more organizational citizenship behaviours. Conscientious employees are necessary for emerging organizational structures that rely on empowerment rather than the traditional "command and control" system. This personality trait also plays an important role in customer service, along with agreeableness and emotional stability.[76]

Limitations of personality traits

While personality traits seem to predict job performance, these findings do not suggest that we should replace current hiring practices with personality tests. Rather, specific personality measures might supplement current selection methods. One problem with this approach is that personality tests are usually weaker than other predictors of job performance (work experience, aptitudes, work-sample performance, etc.). Also, some scholars complain that the Big Five dimensions are too broadly defined to be useful in employment selection.[77] A third concern is that it is difficult to measure personality well enough in organizational settings.

Finally, we must be careful about using personality traits to oversimplify a more complex world. These labels can become perceptual blinders that label people even after their personal dispositions have changed.[78] Too often, we see problems as "personality clashes" rather than diagnosing the situation to discover the underlying causes. Nobel Prize–winning scholar Herbert Simon warns that the concept of personality is unfortunately abused as "a magical slogan to charm away the problems that our intellectual tools don't handle."[79]

Other Personality Traits

The Big Five personality dimensions don't capture every personality trait. A few others are frequently cited in the organizational behaviour literature, such as the Type A and Type B behaviour patterns described in Chapter 5 and the learned needs introduced in Chapter 3. Two other personality traits that you should know about are locus of control and self-monitoring.

Locus of control

Locus of control A personality trait that refers to the extent that people believe what happens to them is within their control; those who feel in control of their destiny have an internal locus, whereas those who believe that life events are controlled by fate or luck have an external locus of control.

Locus of control refers to a generalized belief about the amount of control people have over their own lives. Individuals who feel that they are very much in charge of their own destiny have an *internal locus of control;* those who think that events in their life are due mainly to fate or luck have an *external locus of control.* Of course, externals believe that they control many specific events in their lives — such as opening a door or serving a customer — but they have a general belief that outside forces guide their fate. This is particularly apparent in new situations in which the person's control over events is uncertain.

People perform better in most employment situations when they have a moderately strong internal locus of control. They tend to be more successful in their careers and earn more money than their external counterparts. Internals are also more satisfied with their jobs, cope better in stressful situations, and are more motivated by performance-based reward systems.[80]

Internals are particularly well suited to leadership positions and other jobs requiring initiative, independent action, complex thinking, and high motivation. Two studies reported that Canadian firms led by internals pursued more innovative strategies than firms led by executives with a more external locus of control. The internals invested more in research and development, introduced new products more quickly than the competition, and made more drastic product-line changes. They also pursued more aggressive strategies and planned further into the future.[81]

Self-monitoring

Self-monitoring A personality trait that refers to the extent that people are sensitive to situational cues and can readily adapt their own behaviour appropriately.

Self-monitoring refers to an individual's level of sensitivity and ability to adapt to situational cues. High self-monitors can adjust their behaviour quite easily and, therefore, show little stability in other underlying personality traits. In contrast, low self-monitors are more likely to reveal their moods and personal characteristics, so it is relatively easy to predict their behaviour from one situation to the next.[82]

The self-monitoring personality trait has been identified as a significant factor in many organizational activities. Employees who are high self-monitors tend to be better conversationalists, better organizational leaders, and better in boundary-spanning positions (in which incumbents work with people in different departments or organizations). One study of Canadian business students also reported that high self-monitors experienced better job interview success and higher starting-salary levels.[83]

Chapter Summary

- Perception involves selecting, organizing, and interpreting information to make sense of the world. Selective attention is influenced by characteristics of the target, the target's setting, and the perceiver. Perceptual grouping principles organize incoming information. This is also influenced by our emotions and existing mental models.

- According to social identity theory, people perceive themselves by their unique characteristics and membership in various groups. They also develop homogeneous, and usually positive, images of people in their own groups, and usually less positive homogeneous images of people in other groups. This leads to overgeneralizations and stereotypes.

- Stereotyping is the process of assigning traits to people based on their membership in a social category. Stereotyping economizes mental effort and fills in missing information, but often results in incorrect perceptions about others. These misperceptions may lead to prejudice, employment discrimination, and harassment.

- The attribution process involves deciding whether the behaviour or event is largely due to the situation (external attributions) or personal characteristics (internal attributions). Two attribution errors are actor-observer error and self-serving bias. Self-fulfilling prophecy occurs when our expectations about another person cause that person to act in a way that is consistent with those expectations.

- We can improve our perceptions in organizational settings by increasing awareness of our perceptual biases, learning to empathize with others, postponing our impression of others, comparing our perceptions with others, and becoming more aware of our values, beliefs, and prejudices.

- Personality refers to the relatively stable pattern of behaviours and consistent internal states that explain a person's behavioural tendencies. It is shaped by both heredity and environmental factors. Most personality traits are represented within the "Big Five" personality dimensions: extroversion, agreeableness, conscientiousness, emotional stability, and openness to experience. Two other traits are locus of control and self-monitoring.

- Personality traits are important for some job design activities, for championing organizational change, and for matching people to jobs. However, some concerns remain about relying too heavily on personality traits to understand and predict behaviour in organizations.

Discussion Questions

1. You are part of a task force to increase worker responsiveness to emergencies on the production floor. Identify four factors that should be considered when installing a device that will get every employee's attention when there is an emergency.

2. Use social identity theory to explain why we tend to develop overgeneralized beliefs about, and usually less favourable attitudes toward, people in other social groups.

3. During a diversity awareness session, a manager suggests that stereotypes are a necessary part of working with others. "I have to make assumptions about what's in the other person's head, and stereotypes help me do that," he explains. "It's better to rely on stereotypes than to enter a working relationship with someone from another culture without any idea of what they believe in!" Discuss the merits and problems of the manager's statement.

4. Define sexual harassment and explain how the harasser's perceptions contribute to this unwanted behaviour.

5. At the end of an NHL hockey game, the coach of the losing team is asked what happened. "I dunno," he begins. "We've done well in this rink over the past few years. Our busy schedule over the past two weeks has pushed the guys too hard, I guess. They're worn-out. You probably noticed that we also got some bad breaks on penalties tonight. We should have done well here, but things just went against us." Use attribution theory to explain the coach's perceptions of the team's loss.

6. Explain how self-fulfilling prophecies affect employee performance.

7. You are the leader of a newly formed project team that will work closely together over the next three months. The seven team members are drawn from as many worldwide offices. They do not know each other and come from different professional specializations. Describe the activities of a one-day retreat that would minimize perceptual errors and potential communication problems among the team members.

8. Western Widgets Ltd. wants to hire employees for its new production plant. Employees will have a high degree of autonomy because the plant uses self-directed work teams. The work also requires employees who are careful because the materials are sensitive to mishandling. Identify one personality trait from the Big Five that may be appropriate for selecting people in these jobs, describe the trait, and fully explain your answer.

Chapter Case

Nupath Foods Ltd.

James Ornath read the latest sales figures with a great deal of satisfaction. The vice-president of marketing at Nupath Foods Ltd. was pleased to see that the marketing campaign to improve sagging sales of Prowess cat food was working. Sales volume of the product had increased 20 percent in the past quarter compared with the previous year, and market share was up.

The improved sales of Prowess could be credited to Denise Roberge, the brand manager responsible for cat foods at Nupath. Roberge had joined Nupath less than two years ago as an assistant brand manager after leaving a similar job at a consumer products firm. She was one of the few women in marketing management at Nupath and had a promising career with the company. Ornath was pleased with Roberge's work and tried to let her know this in the annual performance reviews. He now had an excellent opportunity to reward her by offering her the recently vacated position of market research coordinator. Although technically only a lateral transfer with a modest salary increase, the marketing research coordinator job would give Roberge broader experience in some high-profile work, which would enhance her career with Nupath. Few people were aware that Ornath's own career had been boosted by working as marketing research coordinator at Nupath several years before.

Denise Roberge had also seen the latest sales figures on Prowess cat food and was expecting Ornath's call to meet with her that morning. Ornath began the conversation by briefly mentioning the favourable sales figures, and then explained that he wanted Roberge to take the marketing research coordinator job. Roberge was shocked by the news. She enjoyed brand management and particularly the challenge involved with controlling a product that directly affected the company's profitability. Marketing research coordinator was a technical-support position — a "backroom" job — far removed from the company's bottom-line activities. Marketing research was not the route to top management in most organizations, Roberge thought. She had been sidelined.

After a long silence, Roberge managed a weak "Thank you, Mr. Ornath." She was too bewildered to protest. She wanted to collect her thoughts and reflect on what she had done wrong. Also, she did not know her boss well enough to be openly critical. Ornath recognized Roberge's surprise, which he naturally assumed was her positive response to hearing of this wonderful career opportunity. He, too, had been delighted several years earlier about his temporary transfer to marketing research to round out his marketing experience. "This move will be good for both you and Nupath," said Ornath as he escorted Roberge from his office.

Roberge had several tasks to complete that afternoon, but was able to consider the day's events that evening. She was one of the top women in brand management at Nupath and feared that she was being sidelined because the company didn't want women in top management. Her previous employer had made it quite clear that women "couldn't take the heat" in marketing management and tended to place women in technical-support positions after a brief term in lower brand-management jobs. Obviously Nupath was following the same game plan. Ornath's comments that the coordinator job would be good for her was just a nice way of saying that Roberge couldn't go any further in brand management at Nupath. Roberge was now faced with the difficult decision of confronting Ornath and trying to change Nupath's sexist practices or submitting her resignation.

Discussion Questions

1. What symptoms exist in this case to suggest that something has gone wrong?

2. What are the root causes that led to these symptoms?

3. What actions should the organization take to correct these problems?

Experiential Exercise

Perceptions in a Diverse Workforce: The Royal Bank of Canada Vignettes

Purpose: This video exercise is designed to help you understand perceptual issues when working in a diverse workforce.

Instructions: The instructor will play a few vignettes from the video that portray actual events at the Royal Bank of Canada. For each vignette, the class will likely follow these steps (although the instructor may present the video in other ways):

Step 1:   Watch the vignette, keeping in mind the questions presented below.

Step 2:   The instructor will stop the videotape at the appropriate place and the class will discuss the vignette, guided by the following questions (the instructor may ask additional questions).
(a) What is your reaction to this incident?
(b) What is the main issue in this vignette?
(c) What perceptual problems might exist here?
(d) What solutions, if any, would you recommend?

Step 3:   After discussing the vignette, the instructor will play the video follow-up so that the class can hear what the Royal Bank of Canada recommends in this situation.

CHAPTER 7

Emotions and Values in the Workplace

CHAPTER OUTLINE

Emotions in the Workplace

Job Satisfaction

Organizational Commitment

Managing Emotions

Values at Work

Chapter Summary

Discussion Questions

LEARNING OBJECTIVES

After reading this chapter, you should be able to:

- Distinguish emotions from moods and attitudes.

- Discuss the linkages between emotions and behaviour.

- Explain the weak relationship between job satisfaction and performance.

- Describe five strategies to increase organizational commitment.

- Outline the dimensions of emotional intelligence.

- Define the five main values that vary across cultures.

Flight attendant Yvette Landry is one of WestJet's 250 "fun and friendly" employees. The discount airline relies on employee loyalty and friendly customer service to remain competitive.

One hundred and fourteen passengers aboard WestJet Airlines Flight 115 applauded and sang "Happy Birthday" to a flight attendant. They chortled over a joke that was announced over the public address system. And all this happened *before* the flight left Calgary for Vancouver. "We get the passengers involved early," explains Yvette Landry, the WestJet flight attendant who celebrated her birthday that day.

WestJet Airlines doesn't provide meals or reserved seating, but it tries to make up for that with plenty of fun and friendly employees. Employees at the Calgary-based discount carrier enjoy working for the fledgling airline. Eventually, they hope that their positive emotions will produce healthy bonuses from the company's profit-sharing program.

"I like this job. It's very enjoyable," says Cindy Pawluk, a WestJet flight attendant from Edmonton. Pawluk spent 11 years as an X-ray technician and prefers serving passengers than patients. "It's a more positive environment working with passengers, rather than with people who are ill all the time. The stress factor is less."

Along with job satisfaction, WestJet CEO Clive Beddoe claims that the company's 250 employees demonstrate an incredible level of loyalty. This loyalty was unexpectedly tested when the Canadian government shut down the airline for 17 days because it used different maintenance manuals. WestJet engineers worked 18-hour days converting maintenance records, while pilots and flight attendants handled calls from perplexed customers. "I've never seen anything like it," exclaims Beddoe. "Every single employee came through in an incredible display of company loyalty."[1]

WestJet Airlines depends on the emotions, attitudes, and values of its employees to serve customers and fulfil other important tasks. This chapter explores the dynamics of these three concepts. We begin by learning about emotions in the workplace and their relationship to attitudes and individual behaviour in the workplace. This discussion also covers a basic model of work attitudes. We then look at two work attitudes — job satisfaction and organizational commitment — with particular emphasis on their implications for organizational behaviour. Our attention then turns to the emerging organizational behaviour topic, managing emotions. We consider the implications of emotional labour as well as the concept of emotional intelligence. The final section of the chapter introduces individual values at work, including five values that differ across cultures and three values that guide ethical behaviour.

Emotions in the Workplace

Emotions permeate organizational life.[2] A team leader is alarmed that critical supplies have not yet arrived. A new employee feels proud when telling a friend about being hired by ABC Corp. A nurse feels sympathy for a patient whose family has not visited her in hospital. In each scenario, someone has experienced one or more emotions. Scholars have organized emotions into the six categories shown in Exhibit 7–1.[3]

Emotions Feelings experienced toward an object, person, or event that create a state of readiness.

Emotions are feelings experienced toward an object, person, or event that create a state of readiness.[4] Although scholars don't fully agree on the meaning of emotions, this definition includes the most widely held views. Emotional episodes are communications to ourselves.[5] They make us aware that events have occurred that may affect important personal goals. In fact, strong emotions demand our attention and inturrupt our train of thought. They also create a state of readiness to respond to those events. In other words, they generate the motivation to act toward the object of our attention.

Emotions are experienced through our thoughts, behaviours, and physiological reactions. A person may experience fear in a stressful situation by mentally sensing it, showing it through facial expressions, and developing a higher heartbeat. Facial

EXHIBIT 7.1: Types of Emotions in the Workplace

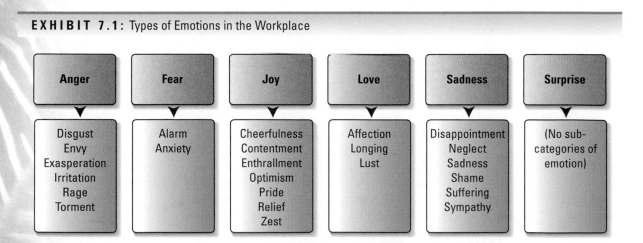

Anger	Fear	Joy	Love	Sadness	Surprise
Disgust	Alarm	Cheerfulness	Affection	Disappointment	(No sub-categories of emotion)
Envy	Anxiety	Contentment	Longing	Neglect	
Exasperation		Enthrallment	Lust	Sadness	
Irritation		Optimism		Shame	
Rage		Pride		Suffering	
Torment		Relief		Sympathy	
		Zest			

Source: Based on in H. M. Weiss and R. Cropanzano, "Affective Events Theory: A Theoretical Discussion of the Structure, Causes, and Consequences of Affective Experiences at Work," *Research in Organizational Behavior* 18 (1996), pp. 1–74; P. Shaver, J. Schwartz, D. Kirson, and C. O'Conner, "Emotion Knowledge: Further Exploration of a Prototype Approach," *Journal of Personality and Social Psychology* 52 (1987), pp. 101–86.

expressions and other behaviours play an interactive role in the emotional experience. For example, you tend to smile when feeling joyful, and this smiling reinforces your feeling of joyfulness. Similarly, your sense of fear is maintained when you notice your heart thumping.

Emotions are directed toward someone or something. For example, we experience joy, fear, and other emotional episodes toward tasks, customers, public speeches we present, a software program we are using, and so on. This contrasts with **moods**, which are emotional states that are not directed toward anything in particular.[6] You may be in a cheerful mood, but you don't know why you have this emotion. Your cheerfulness may be caused by something at work or elsewhere, but you aren't consciously aware of this.

Moods Emotional states that are not directed toward anything in particular.

Emotions and Personality

Have you ever noticed how some co-workers seem upbeat most of the time while others are almost never happy about anything? To some extent, a person's emotions are influenced by his or her personality, not just by workplace experiences. Two personality traits that affect emotions are positive and negative affectivity.

Positive affectivity (PA) is the tendency to experience positive emotional states, whereas **negative affectivity** (NA) is the tendency to experience negative emotional states.[7] PA is closely associated with the **extroversion** personality trait, which we described in Chapter 6 as a characteristic of people who are outgoing, talkative, sociable, and assertive. Employees with high NA, on the other hand, tend to be more distressed and unhappy because they focus on the negative aspects of life.

Positive affectivity (PA) The tendency to experience positive emotional states.

Negative affectivity (NA) The tendency to experience negative emotional states.

Extroversion A "Big Five" personality dimension that characterizes people who are outgoing, talkative, sociable, and assertive.

To what extent do these personality traits influence emotions? Some research indicates that a person's level of personal affectivity can help us to predict how he or she will feel about work two years from now. Studies of twins raised apart conclude that a person's heredity influences emotions and judgments about work. However, other evidence suggests that the effects of PA and NA are relatively weak.[8] Overall, it seems that PA and NA influence emotions and judgments in the workplace, but their effects are not as strong as situational factors.

Emotions, Attitudes, and Behaviour

Emotions are related to the broader concept of **attitudes**. Attitudes represent the cluster of beliefs, assessed feelings, and behavioural intentions toward an object.[9] They are *judgments* about the attitude object. The joy we experience when we receive a promotion is an emotion. Our attitude toward promotions is more complex and long-lasting. It includes your perceptions about promotions (e.g., promotions indicate that senior management values your abilities), your assessed feelings (i.e., promotions are good), and your intentions to receive promotions (e.g., you intend to work hard to get a promotion). As we shall see below, attitudes develop from two sources: (1) our emotional experiences, and (2) our perceptual process.

Attitudes The cluster of beliefs, assessed feelings, and behavioural intentions toward an object.

Emotions affect attitudes, but the two concepts are different (see Exhibit 7.2). As just noted, emotions are experiences, whereas attitudes are judgments. This is the basic distinction between feeling and thinking. We *feel* emotions, whereas we *think about* attitudes. Moreover, emotions can be brief, whereas attitudes are more stable over time. For example, the joy experienced when hearing about your promotion may last a few minutes or hours, whereas your attitude toward promotions can be stable for weeks, months, or even years.

Three components of attitudes

Our definition of attitudes and the illustration in Exhibit 7.2 indicate that this concept has three components. The first component, *feelings,* represents a positive or negative assessment of our emotional experiences relating to the attitude object. We experience many emotional episodes in the workplace. Today, for example, you may have been frustrated with a troublesome customer, proud that you completed a difficult task, and anxious that your boss might not support your suggestions on a particular issue. These emotions are experienced, and they shape your assessment about your job or some other attitude object. Over time, you develop a more general positive or negative feeling toward the attitude object based on these emotional experiences.[10]

The second component of attitudes, *beliefs,* provides the connection between attitudes and our perceptions. As we learned in Chapter 6, we select, organize, and interpret information through our perceptual process. This results in a set of beliefs about the world around us. The statement "The CEO of this company values ideas from employees" is a belief because it describes a perceived characteristic of the company's top executive (the attitude object). This belief develops over time through direct experience, although it is also influenced by what others tell us.[11]

The third component of attitudes, *behavioural intentions,* represents a motivation to engage in a particular behaviour. You might hear people say that they are willing to wear their safety glasses. Others intend to complain to management about the poor dental plan. These are examples of the behavioural intentions component of attitudes. Returning to Exhibit 7.2, we can see that behavioural intentions are formed from a person's beliefs and feelings. We intend to quit our jobs, for example, *because* we believe that the boss is unfair and *because* we feel frustration when performing the work.

EXHIBIT 7.2: Model of Attitudes and Behaviour

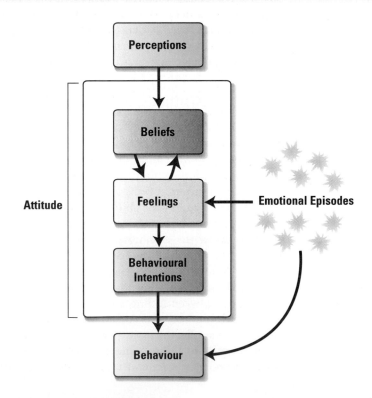

Linking beliefs and feelings

Beliefs and feelings influence each other, as Exhibit 7.2 illustrates.[12] First, beliefs create feelings about something or someone. For instance, you have a positive feeling about the CEO because you believe that he or she values your ideas. This positive feeling results from this and other beliefs about the CEO. Second, feelings can influence beliefs. You may feel frustrated in a work situation without knowing why, so you rationalize this feeling. In other words, people find reasons (beliefs) to explain why they have certain emotional episodes. In this case, your emotions and feelings precede your perceptions of the situation.

Notice that emotions can occur independently of any conscious beliefs.[13] You may feel uncomfortable working with a co-worker, even though you can't think of any rational reason for this feeling. In this case, your emotions create negative feelings, whereas your beliefs have a neutral or positive effect on your feelings toward the person. This may create ambivalent feelings, or your emotions may dominate your rational thoughts.

Linking emotions to behaviour

How are emotions and attitudes related to behaviour in the workplace? For the most part, a person's beliefs and feelings influence that individual's behavioural intentions which, in turn, influence behaviour. For example, suppose an employee believes that his or her pay is too low and does not like low pay. These beliefs and assessed feelings may produce a desire to leave the organization. This is a behavioural intention, which is a motivation to leave the organization. Thus, behavioural intentions are the best predictors of behaviour. We can be more certain that a person will leave the organization if we know he or she intends to do so than if we only know that he or she is dissatisfied with low pay.[14]

But behavioural intentions are not perfectly related to behaviour. The reason, as we learned in Chapter 2, is that behaviour depends on more than the individual's motivation to engage in the behaviour. You may intend to have no absenteeism during the next month, but illness or something beyond your control prevents that intention from coming true. You may intend to serve customers well, but you lack the skills or knowledge necessary to achieve this goal. Thus, we need to consider the person's ability, role perceptions, and situational contingencies to understand whether intentions will result in the expected behaviour.[15]

We have described behaviours as conscious and logical actions based on emotions and attitudes. If we believe and feel that our job is boring, then we deliberately leave this organization. However, Exhibit 7.2 reveals that emotions can directly influence behaviour — the situation in which people react to their emotions rather than their judgments (attitudes). When upset, an employee might stomp out of a meeting, bang a fist on the desk, or break into tears. When overjoyed, an employee might embrace a co-worker or break into a little dance. These behaviours are not carefully thought out or planned. Instead, they are automatic emotional responses that serve as coping mechanisms in that situation.[16]

Cognitive dissonance

Cognitive dissonance A state of anxiety that occurs when an individual's beliefs, attitudes, intentions, and behaviours are inconsistent with one another.

Behaviours sometimes influence beliefs and feelings rather than vice versa. This occurs when you engage in a behaviour that you subsequently realize is inconsistent with your previous attitudes (such as representing your firm on public television even though you don't like your employer). This situation creates an uncomfortable tension called **cognitive dissonance,** because your behaviour (publicly representing your company) is inconsistent with your attitude toward the organization.

PERSPECTIVE 7.1

Brewing with Attitude at Labatt's

Nancy More enjoys her job as head brewmaster at Labatt Breweries. "There's a real feeling of pride when you go out for lunch in a restaurant and see people enjoying the fruits of your labour," she says. "It's never boring. We're really allowed to make anything we want out of our jobs. We're encouraged to take risks."

More became head brewmaster at Labatt's plant in Saint John, New Brunswick. This marked the first time a female had held such a position with a major brewery in North America. Her route to this prestigious position included working in virtually every job in the brewery, from running kettles to cleaning equipment.

Labatt believes that job satisfaction and employee commitment are important attitudes. The company regularly surveys employee attitudes and tries to help workers feel satisfied with their jobs. However, Labatt and other companies are rethinking how to build a loyal workforce. "The old model of once you join a company you work there for your entire career is really dead," explains More. "So building employee loyalty is a much more complex issue.

Tri-City News. Used with permission.

Labatt and other companies are rethinking how to build a loyal workforce, explains head brewmaster Nancy More.

"Now, employees and employers have to be honest with each other about what their intentions are, what the contract is between them, what the company is willing to give to the employee, and what the employee is willing to give back to the company."

Source: "Nancy More" (McGraw-Hill/Irwin video program, 1995); R. Dal Monte, "Progress Is Brewing," *Tri-City News* (Vancouver), April 5, 1992, pp. B1, B3.

To reduce this dissonance, people tend to realign their attitudes with their behaviours.[17] This is because it is easier to change beliefs about something than to change past behaviour toward it, particularly when the behaviour is known to everyone, was done voluntarily, and can't be undone. In the example above, publicly representing your employer would likely change your negative attitude about the company to a more favourable one.

Two of the most important attitudes that organizations need to consider are job satisfaction and organizational commitment. As Labatt Breweries head brewmaster Nancy More describes in Perspective 7.1, job satisfaction is experienced in many ways. She also notes that companies and employees are rethinking ways to maintain a loyal workforce. The next two sections examine the concepts of job satisfaction and organizational commitment.

Job Satisfaction

Job satisfaction A person's attitude (beliefs, assessed feelings, and behavioural intentions) regarding the job and work context.

One of the most important and widely studied work attitudes is job satisfaction. **Job satisfaction** represents a person's evaluation of his or her job and work context.[18] In other words, job satisfaction is an *appraisal* of the perceived job characteristics and an employee's emotional experiences at work. Satisfied employees have a favourable evaluation of their job, based on their observations and emotional experiences.

Consider the statements made by WestJet flight attendant Cindy Pawluk at the beginning of the chapter. She stated that she enjoys her job because of the positive work environment. Pawluk is providing an evaluation based on her perceptions of the work environment as well as her emotional experiences on the job.

Job satisfaction is really a collection of attitudes about specific facets of the job.[19] Employees can be satisfied with some elements of the job while simultaneously dissatisfied with others. For example, an employee might be satisfied with supervision but somewhat dissatisfied with working conditions or pay level. Different types of satisfaction will lead to different intentions and behaviour. An employee might complain to the supervisor when dissatisfied with low pay, but not complain with regards to co-worker dissatisfaction. Overall job satisfaction is a combination of the person's feelings toward the different job satisfaction facets. Satisfaction with the work itself is usually an important component of overall satisfaction, but this can vary from one person to the next.

Job Satisfaction in Canada

How satisfied are Canadians with their jobs? According to a recent survey, 90 percent of Canadians have a positive overall attitude toward their jobs.[20] Unfortunately, public surveys tend to present inflated estimates of job satisfaction because they typically use a single direct question, such as "How satisfied are you with your job?" Many dissatisfied employees are reluctant to reveal their feelings in a direct question because this is tantamount to admitting that they made a poor job choice and are not enjoying life.

This inflated estimate is apparent when the same employees are asked about specific facets of their jobs. Although most people claim to be satisfied overall with their jobs, satisfaction with specific elements of the job is almost always lower. As shown in Exhibit 7.3, only 58 percent of Canadians are satisfied with pay, 51 percent are satisfied with job security, and only 36 percent like the company's career advancement opportunities.

Although Canadians might not be quite as satisfied with their jobs as some surveys suggest, they do seem to be more satisfied than employees in other countries. One study reported that Canadian employees are more satisfied than Americans with their personal accomplishment at work, resources to perform their work, and other conditions of work. Seventy-six percent of Canadians say that they would recommend their company to a close friend as a good place to work, whereas only 66 percent of Americans agreed with this statement.[21]

Another survey recently estimated that Canadians enjoy the highest levels of job satisfaction among people in 13 countries, followed by employees in Finland, Spain, and the United States. Employees from Asia, Germany, and the United Kingdom report the lowest job satisfaction levels.[22] Although cultural values influence the degree of reported job satisfaction in different countries, the 97-item questionnaire revealed a sufficiently wide spread in job satisfaction scores to suggest that Canadians really do have a better working life than people in many other countries.

A Model of Job Satisfaction

What determines an employee's level of job satisfaction? The best explanation is provided by a combination of **discrepancy theory** and **equity theory**.[23] Discrepancy theory states that the level of job satisfaction is determined by the discrepancy between

Discrepancy theory A theory that partly explains job satisfaction and dissatisfaction in terms of the gap between what a person expects to receive and what is actually received.

Equity theory A process motivation theory that explains how people develop perceptions of fairness in the distribution and exchange of resources.

EXHIBIT 7.3: Job Satisfaction in Canada

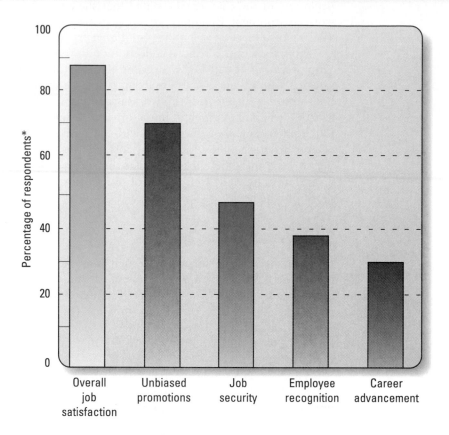

* Indicates percentage of employees who thought their companies were good or excellent in the category indicated.

Source: Based on results from Angus Reid Group survey of 693 Canadian employees, conducted for Royal Bank of Canada in 1996. Reported in M. Gibb-Clark, "Workers Pinpoint Bosses' Flaws," *Globe & Mail*, October 18, 1996; A. Chamberlain, "Workers Not so Happy about Bosses," *Toronto Star*, October 18, 1996, p. E3.

what people expect to receive and what they experience.[24] As Exhibit 7.4 illustrates, job satisfaction or dissatisfaction results from a comparison of the amount the employee expects to receive and the perceived amount received. Job dissatisfaction occurs when the received condition is noticeably less than the expected condition. Job satisfaction improves as the person's expectations are met or exceeded (up to a point).

Equity theory is also built into Exhibit 7.4. Recall from Chapter 3 that equity occurs when you and your comparison other have similar outcome/input ratios. This is relevant to job satisfaction, because the amount we expect to receive is partly determined by our comparison with the amount received by other people. For instance, the level of pay we expect to receive depends not only on how hard we work, but also on how hard other people work in this job compared to their level of pay.

Equity theory also explains why job satisfaction does not always continue to increase as the received condition exceeds expectations. As people receive much better outcomes than they expect, they typically develop feelings of guilt and a belief that management practices are unfair to others. At first, employees adjust their expectations upward when they are overrewarded. However, if the overreward is so large that

EXHIBIT 7.4: A Model of Job Satisfaction

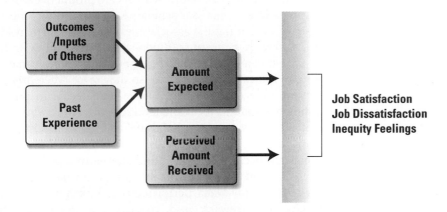

Source: Based on E. E. Lawler III, *Motivation in Work Organizations* (Monterey, Calif.: Brooks/Cole, 1973), p. 75.

it cannot be justified, then feelings of inequity persist and dissatisfaction with management practices may result.

In summary, discrepancy and equity theories predict that as reality meets and exceeds expectations, job satisfaction will increase. However, when the perceived job situation is so much better than expected that the overreward creates a feeling of guilt or unfairness, job satisfaction begins to decrease.

Job Satisfaction and Work Behaviours

When Northern Telecom recently changed its corporate codes of conduct, it outlined what employees should expect from the company, not just what the company should expect from employees. Senior executives at the Mississauga, Ontario, company now include a number of specific employee-satisfaction objectives that will affect an employee's performance rating and bonus.[25]

Nortel and other companies pay attention to job satisfaction because this work attitude is related to many work behaviours. Employees with higher levels of job satisfaction, particularly satisfaction with the work itself, are less likely to quit, be absent, and experience mental or physical health problems.[26] Federal government employees have had very low morale over the past few years due to pay freezes and limited promotions. Morale is so low that government leaders underestimated the number of people who were willing to accept the standard buyout packages when they were offered.[27]

Joining a labour union and going on strike are usually associated with job dissatisfaction. However, not all forms of dissatisfaction lead to these behaviours.[28] For instance, people are more likely to go on strike because they dislike their level of pay or working conditions than if they dislike their co-workers. Dissatisfied employees are also more likely to steal, particularly to correct feelings of inequity.[29] This occurred at Canada's External Affairs department, where more than a dozen staff members were caught filing bogus travel claims. Some experts explained that these employees were illegally compensating for overwork and abysmal morale problems.[30] Indeed, dissatisfied employees have sabotaged company products and equipment in retaliation to management practices. In the United States, several dissatisfied employees have engaged in acts of violence against their supervisor or co-workers.[31]

Job satisfaction and job performance

It seems obvious that happy workers are productive workers. Yet, for the past 30 years, organizational behaviour scholars have warned that job satisfaction has a statistically insignificant or modest association with job performance.[32] There are three reasons for this difference between common sense and research findings.

First, general attitudes don't predict specific behaviours very well. People have unique values and experiences, so they react differently to the same level of job satisfaction. One dissatisfied employee may decide to put in less work effort, whereas another maintains the same level of work effort while looking for employment elsewhere. As noted earlier, situational contingencies also prevent behavioural intentions from becoming behaviours. For instance, some employees may hate their jobs, but don't quit because they can't find alternative employment.

A second explanation is that job performance leads to job satisfaction (not vice versa), but only when performance is linked to valued rewards. Higher performers receive more rewards and, consequently, are more satisfied than low-performing employees who receive fewer rewards. The connection between job satisfaction and performance is weak because many organizations do not reward good performance.[33]

Third, the weak relationship between job satisfaction and performance may occur because satisfied employees engage in more **organizational citizenship** behaviours but not in higher levels of traditional job performance.[34] Recall from Chapter 2 that organizational citizenship behaviours include working beyond required job duties, such as assisting others with their tasks and promoting a positive work environment. Satisfied employees might be more likely to help the company beyond their normal job duties because they feel a higher sense of obligation or reciprocity to the organization.

Aside from the issue of job satisfaction and job performance, there is increasing evidence that more satisfied employees provide better customer service.[35] Corning Glass is so convinced of this that it measures satisfaction as part of its quality service management program. One reason satisfied employees likely provide better customer service is that job satisfaction affects a person's general mood: employees who are in a good mood are more likely to communicate friendliness and positive feelings, which customers appreciate. A second reason is that satisfied employees are less likely to quit their jobs, which allows companies to provide more consistent service (customers get the same employees to serve them) and employees have more experience and better skills to serve clients.

Organizational citizenship Employee behaviours that extend beyond the usual job duties. They include avoiding unnecessary conflicts, helping others without selfish intent, gracefully tolerating occasional impositions, being involved in organizational activities, and performing tasks that extend beyond normal role requirements.

Organizational Commitment

During the mid-1800s, Samuel Cunard founded Cunard Lines, the greatest steamship line ever to cover the Atlantic Ocean. The energetic Nova Scotian was able to make ship transportation dependable and safe, long before it was thought possible, by employing the best ships, officers, and crew. Cunard insisted on safety before profits and, by listening to his technical experts, he was able to introduce into his company the latest innovations. Above all, Cunard had the quaint notion that if you picked people well, paid them well, and treated them well, they would return the favour with loyalty and pride.[36]

Nearly 150 years later, Samuel Cunard's assumptions about the benefits of **organizational commitment** have found strong support in organizational behaviour research. Organizational commitment is a set of attitudes regarding an individual's relationship with the organization and his or her motivation to remain with the organization.[37]

Organizational commitment A complex attitude pertaining to the strength of an individual's identification with and involvement in a particular organization; it includes a strong belief in the organization's goals, as well as a motivation to work for and remain a member of the organization.

Organizational commitment includes three components: affective, normative, and continuance. Although these commitments can be targeted to the local work group, company owners, and others in the organization, we will concentrate mainly on the employee's overall commitment to the organization.[38]

Affective commitment is the employee's emotional attachment to, identification with, and involvement in a particular organization.[39] Affective commitment comes closest to what we commonly call employee loyalty.

Normative commitment refers to employee feelings of obligation to remain with the organization. For example, employees feel that they need to repay the company through hard work and continued employment for the company's investment in them. Normative commitment is closely related to the ethical norm of reciprocity.

Continuance commitment is the degree that employees believe it is in their own personal interest to remain with the organization. Continuance commitment is a calculative bond with the organization. For example, you may have met people who do not particularly enjoy working for a company but feel bound to remain there because it would be too costly to quit. Continuance commitment is this motivation to stay because of the high cost of leaving.[40]

Consequences of Organizational Commitment

Samuel Cunard wanted a loyal workforce because he believed that it would benefit his organization. Today, we know that his assumptions are mostly true. Employees with high levels of affective and normative commitment are less likely to quit their jobs and be absent from work. This, in turn, improves customer service, because employees with longer service have better knowledge of work practices. Also, clients like to do business with the same employees because transactions are predictable.[41]

Employees with high affective commitment are motivated to work harder. This translates into higher job performance if they possess the necessary abilities, role perceptions, and situational contingencies. Employees with strong affective and normative commitment to the organization are also more likely to engage in organizational citizenship behaviours.[42]

When RBC Dominion Securities bought brokerage firm Richardson Greenshields, it relied on continuance commitment to prevent Richardson's brokers from leaving. Brokers who quit within two years after the acquisition would lose a large part of a stock payment that RBC was offering.[43] These "golden handcuffs" tie employees financially to the organization, but they also create problems. Evidence suggests that employees with high levels of continuance commitment have lower performance ratings and are *less* likely to engage in organizational citizenship behaviours.[44] To build an effective workforce, employers must win employees' hearts (affective commitment) rather than tie them financially to the organization (continuance commitment).

Affective commitment can also cause behaviour problems if employees become too dedicated to the organization. One potential problem is that a highly committed workforce may have such low turnover that the organization stagnates. Another concern is that highly committed employees may put the organization above society's standards of ethical conduct. They are less likely to report wrongdoing in the organization (i.e., less whistle-blowing) and may be more likely to break laws to aid the company. For example, the president of a Montreal dredging company destroyed documents connected with a case that the RCMP was investigating. When asked why he had done this illegal act, the president replied: "For 22 years I put the company ahead of myself. I came second."[45]

© 1997 Farcus Cartoons/dist. by Universal Press Syndicate   WAISGLASS/COULTHART

"It makes you miss the good ol' days when they at least pretended to value employees."

The Decline of Organizational Commitment

Given that moderately strong levels of loyalty benefit organizations, business leaders should be interested in cultivating and maintaining this attitude. Some companies do take organizational commitment seriously. Four Seasons Hotels Inc. carefully monitors affective commitment through regular employee surveys. A dedicated workforce is also important at Sun Microsystems Canada Ltd. "The only way you grow is with committed employees," says a Sun Microsystems executive.[46]

But these two companies may be exceptions. There is overwhelming evidence that organizational commitment has declined over the past couple of decades.[47] Two recent surveys reported that about 25 percent of working Canadians and 29 percent of their American counterparts feel less loyal to their employer today than a few years ago. Another survey found that 86.7 percent of managers in the United States felt there was less loyalty between companies and their employees compared to five years earlier.

Much of the decline in loyalty is due to the "new employment deal," which is discussed more fully in Chapter 17.[48] This trend has shifted the emphasis from affective to continuance commitment. Companies no longer protect employee jobs, and they no longer expect loyalty in return. "The strong sense of loyalty and belief in the company is eroding," says Lowell Hoffman, an employee who left IBM as part of a buyout package. "I used to believe the mission statement of IBM. But IBM is no different than any other company, and when things go rough, they lay off people just like anyone else."[49]

Building Organizational Commitment

How do you build and maintain a dedicated workforce?[50] A general answer is to practise the recommendations in this and other organizational behaviour textbooks. Organizational commitment is influenced by many experiences in the workplace, but the following activities have been most prominent in the literature.

- *Fairness and satisfaction*   The most important ingredients for a loyal workforce are positive and equitable work experiences. New employees must believe that the company is fulfilling its obligations and not violating the psychological contract (see Chapter 17).[51] Problems with organizational commitment occur as people face increased workloads while their companies make record profits and senior executives earn lucrative bonuses.

- *Job security*   Employees need to feel some permanence and mutuality in the employment relationship. Lifetime employment guarantees aren't necessary, although Federal Express Canada, Canada Post, and Cadet Uniforms have maintained such policies. Rather, there should be enough job security to nurture a relationship in which employees believe their efforts will be rewarded eventually. Job insecurity, on the other hand, fosters a more formal contractual relationship, with minimal feelings of mutuality.[52] Thus, it's not surprising that layoff threats

PERSPECTIVE 7.2

Ontario Hydro's New Employment Deal Threatens Loyalty

For several months, Martin Scheller organized scores of going-away parties for colleagues who were cut loose from Ontario Hydro's payroll. Then Scheller received his own surplus notice, which meant that he had to find another job within Hydro that would match his 16 years of mechanical-drafting experience.

To stem huge financial losses, Ontario Hydro cleared out nearly 7,000 employees within a few months. The 22,000 people who chose to stay faced the unsettling experience of having to reapply for their own position — if it still existed — and compete with co-workers to get it back.

"People feel incredibly beaten up by the process of having to reapply for their jobs when there was no indication they were doing badly," says a senior Ontario Hydro manager. "You see people in their offices and you can tell all they are doing is waiting for the phone to ring. . . . It's killing people's self-esteem. Productivity is in the dumpers."

Senior executives at the electrical utility acknowledge that organizational loyalty has also suffered. "The psychological contract for many Hydro employees was: 'I will give you loyalty and you will give me security,'" says Dane MacCarthy, Ontario Hydro's vice-president of Human Resources. "But that security and loyalty thing, in terms of the economic situation we are in, is no longer a viable contract."

Allan Kupcis, Ontario Hydro's CEO [at the time], claims that his company has replaced the old entitlement culture with an earning culture. This means that the corporation helps employees with continuous training, but it no longer offers 40 years of job security. "That's not easy," Kupcis says. "There's a huge shift that has to be made in how you treat employees, what their expectations are and what their rewards are in the new environment."

Source: "Why Profitable Firms Lay Off Workers," *Financial Post*, April 20–22, 1996, p. 32; V. Galt, "Musical Chairs a Crying Game," *Globe & Mail*, November 13, 1993, pp. B1, B2; and M. Gibb-Clark, "High-Voltage Pain at Hydro," *Globe & Mail*, July 14, 1993, pp. B1, B12.

are one of the greatest blows to employee loyalty, even among co-workers whose jobs are not immediately at risk.[53] As Perspective 7.2 describes, Ontario Hydro faces the challenge of rebuilding employee loyalty following its massive restructuring.

- *Organizational comprehension* Affective commitment is a person's identification with the company, so it makes sense that this attitude is strengthened when employees have a solid comprehension of the company. Employees should be regularly informed about organizational activities and should personally experience other parts of the company. At Finning International's Vancouver headquarters, secretaries have an opportunity to ride Caterpillar tractors to better understand the product their company sells and services. British Airways has introduced a similar program, called "Day in the Life," that introduces employees to other parts of the company they would not normally see.[54]

- *Employee involvement* Employees feel that they are part of the organization when they make decisions that guide the organization's future.[55] Through participation, employees begin to see how the organization is a reflection of their decisions. Edson Packaging Machinery Ltd. in Hamilton, Ontario, follows this strategy by involving its 63 employees in strategic planning and major purchasing decisions. "You lose some predictability," says Edson's president, "but you gain a workforce in which people feel part of the organization." Employee involvement also builds loyalty because giving this power is a demonstration of the company's trust in its employees.

Trust Positive expectations about another party's intentions and actions toward us in risky situations.

- *Trusting employees* **Trust** occurs when we have positive expectations about another party's intentions and actions toward us in risky situations.[56] Trust means putting faith in the other person or group. It is also a reciprocal activity: in order to receive trust, you must demonstrate trust. "If they don't trust that I'm really giving them [employees]responsibility and the authority, and I don't trust they can make the decisions, this is never going to work," admits Stan Jacobson, general manager of Domtar's corrugated packaging division.[57] Trust is important for organizational commitment because it touches the heart of the employment relationship (Chapter 17). Employees identify with and feel obliged to work for an organization only when they trust its leaders.

Managing Emotions

Employees at Earl Industries, Inc. had gone out of their way to put together a proposal for a customer who was in a pinch, but the client changed its mind about what it wanted. Jerrold L. Miller, president of the Portsmouth, Virginia, ship-repair company blew up at the client's representatives. "I just had a shouting match with my best customer," says Miller. "I can't believe I talked to those people like that." Later, Miller called to apologize for his outburst. "I think I was right, but I didn't present it properly," he says.

Like Jerrold Miller, we are sometimes overcome by our emotions. It may be expressed by a spontaneous outburst of laughter or the banging of a fist on the desk. However, employees are expected to manage their emotions. **Emotional labour** refers to the effort, planning, and control needed to express organizationally desired emotions during interpersonal transactions.[58] When interacting with co-workers, customers, suppliers, and others, employees are expected to abide by *display rules*. These rules are norms requiring employees to display certain emotions and withhold others. Jerrold Miller's outburst clearly violated organizational display rules. Even as company president, Miller is expected to follow a set of norms regarding the emotions presented to customers.

All employees at Walt Disney World are told to think of themselves as actors. Whether their role is a ticket seller or Mickey Mouse, they act it out to satisfy the customer and their fellow employees. In a somewhat different role, bill collectors have display rules that vary with the debtor's emotional condition. They are expected to show warmth to anxious first-time debtors. For indifferent debtors — those who don't seem to care if they ever pay off their debts — bill collectors are supposed to show irritation without yelling or exhibitions of uncontrolled anger.[59]

Emotional labour The effort, planning, and control needed to express organizationally desired emotions during interpersonal transactions.

Problems with Emotional Labour

Comedian George Burns once said: "The secret to being a good actor is honesty. If you can fake *that*, you've got it made." Burns's humour highlights an important reality in emotional labour; namely, that it is very difficult to hide true emotions in the workplace. Usually, they "leak" out as voice intonations, posture, and in other subtle ways.[60]

True emotions are most likely to leak out when they conflict with prescribed emotions toward a particular client. If you are angry with a client, but are supposed to show patience, some of your anger will likely spill out. This is particularly true of anger, which is one of the most difficult emotions to control. This role conflict between required and true emotions is a significant cause of stress and job burnout, as we learned in Chapter 5.[61] Emotional labour can also create a sense of emotional numbness, particularly where employees are expected to display the same emotion to many clients each day.

We also need to be sensitive to different cultural norms of emotional labour.[62] When McDonald's opened operations in Moscow, employees were taught to smile at customers. However, this norm did not exist in Russia, so some customers thought the employees were mocking them. Hong Kong–based Cathay Pacific Airlines also trained employees to smile while helping customers. The staff members loved the role-play exercise, but didn't smile as much on the job as hoped because people are not expected to smile so often in that culture. Moreover, training staff discovered that employees and their supervisors were worried that excessive smiling caused wrinkles!

Supporting Emotional Labour

Organizations use various tactics to ensure that employees follow prescribed emotional display rules. As noted above, many companies provide extensive training, so employees learn the subtle behaviours necessary to express appropriate emotions. At Delta Airlines, employees act out their roles in training programs, then receive feedback from instructors while watching the video playback of their behaviours. On the job, many firms monitor employee behaviours. For instance, Air Canada supervisors listen to conversations between customers and reservations agents to ensure that agents use appropriate language and voice intonations.

A number of companies, including Four Seasons Hotels and Resorts and Cadet Uniforms, have moved toward the "hire for attitude, train for skills" approach. This means that people are hired who have attitudes consistent with the job requirements. Isadore Sharp has one explanation for the superb service at Four Seasons hotels. "You can train them to do any job," says the Four Seasons CEO, "but employees must bring the right attitude with them."[63]

Courtesy of Four Seasons Hotels and Resorts.

Four Seasons Hotels and Resorts "hires for attitude, trains for skills." The company philosophy is that employees must possess the emotional intelligence needed to interact effectively with guests in different situations.

Emotional intelligence

Emotional intelligence
The ability to monitor your own and others' emotions, to discriminate among them, and to use the information to guide your thinking and actions.

One characteristic that employers may look for in job applicants is their degree of **emotional intelligence (EI)**. Emotional intelligence is the ability to monitor your own and others' emotions, to discriminate among them, and to use the information to guide your thinking and actions.[64] EI has its roots in social intelligence, a concept which was introduced more than 75 years ago. Scholars spent most of this time focused on cognitive intelligence, but many are now realizing that emotional intelligence is just as important for an individual's success at work and in other social environments.

Emotional intelligence has five dimensions. The first, and, arguably, the most important dimension is *self-awareness*, which involves monitoring and being conscious of your emotional experiences. Notice that this (as well as some other EI domains described here) is similar to the **self-monitoring personality** concept described in Chapter 6.

Self-monitoring A personality trait referring to the extent that people are sensitive to situational cues and can readily adapt their own behaviour appropriately.

Managing emotions is a second dimension of emotional intelligence. This involves finding ways to direct the energy from your emotions so that they are expressed appropriately. For example, rather than yell at a client, you manage to remain calm and later "talk out" the emotion to a co-worker.

Motivating yourself is a third dimension. This involves stifling impulses, directing emotions toward personal goals, and delaying gratification. This overlaps with the self-reinforcement and constructive-thought concepts covered in the discussion of self-leadership in Chapter 4.

Empathy, defined in Chapter 6 as the ability to understand and be sensitive to the feelings, thoughts, and situation of others, is a fourth dimension of emotional intelligence.

The fifth dimension is *handling relationships*. This refers to the ability to manage the emotions of other people. It requires social competence and skills to guide the way other people act.

There is still much to learn about emotional intelligence, such as how robust these five dimensions are and how they relate to self-monitoring personality. Some companies now use tests that select applicants with high emotional intelligence, although it isn't clear how well these tests work. Also, we need to learn whether people with high emotional intelligence are better at coping with the role conflict created by emotional labour requirements in service jobs.

Values at Work

Values Stable, long-lasting beliefs about what is important to the individual.

Earlier in the chapter, we said that beliefs are perceptions about an attitude object. We also have a higher-order set of beliefs, called **values**. Values represent stable, long-lasting beliefs about what is important to the individual. They define what is right or wrong, or good or bad, in the world.[65] Some people value the practical, whereas others value the aesthetic. Some people value frugality, whereas others value generosity. Values differ from attitudes. Values are generalized conceptions of the world, whereas attitudes are directed toward specific objects, events, or people. Of course, values influence our attitudes toward those attitude objects.

Values are gaining prominence in organizational behaviour.[66] Personal values influence a person's decisions and actions. Scholars have described more than 100 personal values.[67] Organizational culture values, which are discussed in Chapter 16, shape the behaviours of employees aligned with those values. Cross-cultural values, which are examined next, affect our ability to understand and get along with people from different countries. Ethical values, which are discussed in the last section of the chapter, lay the foundation for the appropriateness of our actions.

Cultural Differences in Values

Oki Poki Designs Inc., a Montreal manufacturer of children's clothing, missed an entire shipment of spring clothes from its Mexican subcontractor. When the Montreal office called the Mexican company, they were told, "*No problema, no problema*, we'll put them on the next plane." When the shipment still didn't arrive, the Montreal office called again, only to learn that the subcontractor's owner was out of town. "We have had a very bad experience with the mentality of the people," says Oki Poki's owner, referring to his Mexican business associates. "They don't respect what they say or write."[68]

Tensions between Oki Poki and the Mexican subcontractor likely occurred because of differences in values across the two cultures. In particular, time is less precise to many people in Latin America. It isn't unusual for Latin Americans to arrive half an hour late for a meeting. This contrasts with Germany, where temporal precision is highly valued. Canada fits somewhere between these two. A second explanation for this conflict is that many Mexicans place a high value on saving face. In this incident, saving face meant avoiding acknowledging that production was late.

We need to understand cultural value differences to avoid unnecessary conflicts and subtle tensions between people from different cultures. This is particularly true when a company opens operations in another country. Five values account for a large portion of the differences in orientations across cultures.[69] Exhibit 7.5 shows how Canadian societal values compare to other cultures on these five dimensions. This information must be treated with some caution because it is based on limited samples (IBM employees and college students). However, it provides a preliminary comparison of these values across cultures.

Individualism-collectivism The degree that people value their individual versus group goals. Collectivists respect and value their membership in the group to which they belong, whereas individualists tend to give low priority to group interests.

- *Individualism-collectivism* **Individualism-collectivism** refers to the degree that people value their individual versus group goals. Individualists look after themselves and tend to give low priority to group interests. Collectivists, on the other hand, respect and value their membership in the group to which they belong. They tend to treat people within the group differently from people outside the group. Collectivists also emphasize harmony over self-expression and experience more socially based emotions (indebtedness, friendliness) rather than socially disengaged emotions (pride, anger).[70]

Power distance The extent that people accept unequal distribution of power in a society.

- *Power distance* **Power distance** is the extent that people accept unequal distribution of power in a society. Those with high power distance accept and value unequal power, whereas those with low power distance expect relatively equal power sharing. In high power distance cultures, employees expect to receive commands from their superiors, and conflicts are resolved through formal rules and authority. In contrast, participative management is preferred in low power distance cultures, and conflicts are resolved more through personal networks and coalitions.[71]

Uncertainty avoidance The degree to which people tolerate ambiguity (low uncertainty avoidance) or feel threatened by ambiguity and uncertainty (high uncertainty avoidance).

- *Uncertainty avoidance* **Uncertainty avoidance** is the degree to which people tolerate ambiguity (low uncertainty avoidance) or feel threatened by ambiguity and uncertainty (high uncertainty avoidance). Employees with high uncertainty avoidance value structured situations where rules of conduct and decision making are clearly documented. They prefer direct rather than indirect or ambiguous communications. There are exceptions, however. The Japanese culture has very high uncertainty avoidance, yet, as we learn in Chapter 8, it relies on ambiguous and indirect communication. This occurs because there is a high power distance and collectivism in Japan. High power distance makes it less appropriate to speak forthrightly to those with higher status. The collectivist culture discourages direct communication, which can potentially disrupt harmonious relations within the group.[72]

Masculinity-femininity
The degree to which people value assertiveness, competitiveness, and materialism (masculinity) versus relationships and the well-being of others (femininity).

- *Masculinity-femininity*   **Masculinity-femininity** is a complex value. Generally, people in masculine cultures value assertiveness, competitiveness, and materialism. In feminine cultures, the emphasis is more on relationships and the well-being of others.

- *Long-term orientation*   People tend to have a long- or short-term orientation. Those with a long-term orientation anchor their thoughts more in the future than in the past and present. They value thrift, savings, and persistence, whereas those with a short-term orientation place more emphasis on the past and present, such as respect for tradition and fulfilling social obligations.

Cultural values in aboriginal organizations

Cultural differences exist *within* Canada as well as across countries. Cultural differences (and tensions) have existed among English and French Canadians for centuries.[73] Aboriginal people in Canada have a unique set of cultural values that has recently caught the attention of researchers. Although there are several aboriginal cultures in Canada, research indicates that most Native companies have a strong collectivist value, low

EXHIBIT 7.5: Cultural Differences in Values

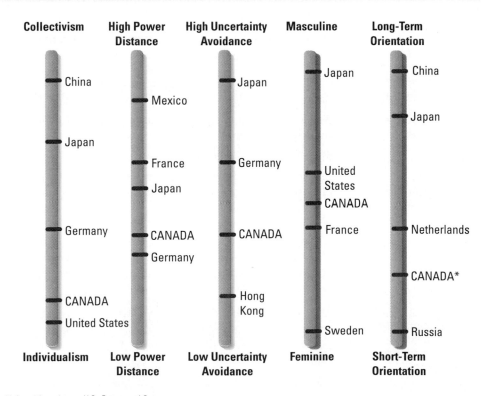

*Inferred from data on U.S., France, and Germany

Note: Ratings are from IBM employees in these countries. Germany refers only to the former West Germany.

Source: Based on G. Hofstede, "Cultural Constraints in Management Theories," *Academy of Management Executive* 7 (1993), pp. 81–94; G. Hofstede, "The Cultural Relativity of Organizational Practices and Theories," *Journal of International Business Studies* 14 (Fall 1983), pp. 75–89.

power distance, low uncertainty avoidance, and a relatively feminine value orientation.[74] The long-term orientation value has not yet been explored.

The strong collectivist orientation is based on traditional Native ideals regarding survival of the small group. Low power distance is apparent by the culture's preference for consensus-oriented decision making and selection of people based on their expertise rather than position. People in aboriginal organizations seem to have a lower uncertainty avoidance value than those in nonaboriginal Canadian companies, as indicated by the lack of formal rules and procedures in aboriginal companies and the preference for internalized beliefs about respect, sharing, and wholeness to guide employee behaviour. Finally, there is evidence that Native firms adopt a relatively feminine value orientation. This is manifested by the emphasis on the well-being of co-workers and maintenance of positive relationships among them. There is decidedly less emphasis on material gain and goal accomplishment compared to non-Native organizations.

Ethical Values

Ethical values Beliefs about whether certain actions are good or bad, directing them to what is virtuous and right.

Ethical values are beliefs about whether certain actions are good or bad. People continually rely on their ethical values to make morally correct decisions. This is not as easy as it may seem, as Perspective 7.3 illustrates. Should the Sunnybrook Health Science Centre's head of pharmacy buy an expensive drug for one person even though this won't leave enough money to save seven future cancer patients?

Canadians value companies and their leaders with ethical values. "Consumers are demanding ethical behaviour, and choosing to do business with those companies they perceive as ethical," says John Belcher, president of Calgary-based Hughes Aircraft of Canada. "They want to have confidence in your products, services, and behaviour."[75]

PERSPECTIVE 7.3

Tough Choices at Sunnybrook Health Science Centre

Patricia M. left Sunnybrook Health Science Centre in North York, Ontario, more than a year ago, but head pharmacist Tom Paton remembers her well. Not her name, or her face — he didn't actually meet her. What he remembers is the $63,000 price tag for an intravenous drug that saved her life.

"The AmBisome case," says Paton, referring to the high-priced antifungal drug that Patricia received after her heart-valve replacement surgery. Patricia was a Jehovah's Witness and would not authorize a blood transfusion. Fungizone, a less costly antifungal drug, would lower her blood count to the point that she would not survive open heart surgery. AmBisome was Patricia's only hope. The medicine worked, but at a whopping cost of $900 per day compared to $112 for Fungizone.

The moral dilemma that Paton faced was that Sunnybrook's $5.5 million budget for drugs must be shared by more than 17,000 inpatients each year. Now Paton was asked to spend more than 1 percent of that budget to save a single life.

The $63,000 spent on Patricia M. could have bought six courses of Neupogen — another high-priced drug — for each of seven cancer patients. The dilemma was complicated by uncertainties about the consequences of giving Neupogen to cancer patients. How many of the seven cancer patients would live? For how long? How do you perform a cost-effectiveness analysis with such imponderables?

"If I had the money available," says Paton, "I could say in those iffy cases, 'I think we should try this.' And maybe it would work." In the meantime, for Paton and pharmacists at other Canadian hospitals, scarce resources will continue to bring tough moral choices.

Source: Adapted from I. Shapiro, "Is There an Auditor in the House?" *Report on Business Magazine* (November 1993), pp. 86–102.

An early example of ethical values in business is Timothy Eaton, founder of Eaton's department stores. Eaton launched his enterprise in 1869 with a stern warning that clerks should not deceive customers or sell them goods they did not need.[76]

Unfortunately, some corporate leaders have violated ethical values. A few years ago, the head of Canadian Tire's automotive parts division was secretly demanding kickbacks from suppliers. Long-term suppliers who refused to participate in the scam eventually told the company's senior management about the problem. The manager was fired and later convicted on six charges of accepting secret commissions. At the Westray coal mine in Nova Scotia, senior management placed the short-term goals of investors ahead of Canadian ethical values. As a result, 26 miners lost their lives in a powerful explosion.[77]

What are the ethical values upon which we should base our actions? Scholars have identified three basic principles: utilitarianism, individual rights, and distributive justice.[78] All three values should be considered together because actions that rely solely on one principle may be inappropriate. Also, we need to keep in mind that different cultures emphasize each ethical value to a different degree.[79]

Utilitarianism A moral principle stating that decision makers should seek the greatest good for the greatest number of people when choosing among alternatives.

- *Utilitarianism*   **Utilitarianism** advises us to seek the greatest good for the greatest number of people. In other words, we should choose the option that provides the highest degree of satisfaction to those affected. Unfortunately, utilitarianism can occasionally result in unethical choices because it judges morality by the results, not the means to attaining those results. Moreover, it accepts situations in which a few people may be severely oppressed to benefit others.

- *Individual rights*   This ethical value is the belief that everyone has entitlements that let them act in a certain way. For example, Canadians believe that everyone has the right to free speech. In fact, we have enshrined this right in the Canadian Charter of Rights and Freedoms. Unfortunately, there may be times when certain individual rights conflict with others. For example, the shareholders' right to be informed about corporate activities may ultimately conflict with an executive's right to privacy.

- *Distributive justice*   This is the ethical value of fairness. It suggests that inequality is acceptable if (1) everyone has equal access to the more favoured positions in society, and (2) the inequalities are ultimately in the best interest of the least well off in society. The first part means that everyone should have equal access to higher-paying jobs and other valued positions in life. The second part says that some people can receive greater rewards than others if this benefits those less well off. Employees in risky jobs should be paid more if this benefits others who are less well off. The problem with this principle is that society can't seem to agree on what activities provide the greatest benefit to the least well off.

Supporting ethical values in organizations

Approximately 75 percent of large firms in Canada have introduced safeguards to ensure that employee behaviours are consistent with society's ethical values.[80] The most common of these is to provide employees with a code of ethical conduct. New employees at Imperial Oil read the 20-page corporate code of ethics and sign a statement confirming their understanding of and compliance with those values.[81]

Ethics training is another popular way to instill ethical values. Bell Canada recently introduced ethics training after it was accused by the press of anti-competitive practices. Every Bell employee will eventually participate in the seminar, which covers Canada's competition laws. Hughes Aircraft of Canada provides ongoing training by publishing bulletins of case studies, holding quarterly focus groups, and distributing pamphlets to keep employees informed about ethical conduct.[82]

Chapter Summary

- Emotions are feelings experienced toward an object, person, or event that create a state of readiness. They differ from moods, which are not directed toward anything in particular. To some extent, a person's emotions can result from his or her personality, not just from workplace experiences.

- Attitudes represent the cluster of beliefs, feelings, and behavioural intentions toward an object. Beliefs are a person's perceptions about an attitude object. Feelings are judgments about our emotional experiences associated with the target. Behavioural intentions represent a motivation to engage in a particular behaviour with respect to the target. Emotions can occur independently of our beliefs. They influence our behaviour directly as well as indirectly through attitudes.

- Job satisfaction represents a person's evaluation of his or her job and work context. Satisfaction occurs when expectations are met. Dissatisfaction occurs either when expectations are not met or are conspicuously excessive, resulting in feelings of inequity. Job dissatisfaction tends to increase turnover, absenteeism, physical or mental ailments, militancy, and deviant behaviours. Employees with high job satisfaction tend to provide better customer service and demonstrate organizational citizenship, but not necessarily other indicators of job performance.

- Organizational commitment is a set of attitudes regarding the individual's relationship with the organization and his or her motivation to remain with the organization. The three dimensions of commitment — affective, normative, and continuance — have different effects on employee behaviour. Companies build loyalty through fairness and satisfaction, some level of job security, organizational comprehension, employee involvement, and trust.

- Companies expect emotional labour from their employees, particularly those in service roles. This means that employees are expected to abide by a set of display rules that communicate certain emotions. One problem is that employees' true emotions tend to leak out, and conflicts between expected and true emotions causes stress and burnout. Employees with a high level of emotional intelligence are able to monitor their own and others' emotions, to discriminate among them, and to use the information to guide their thinking and actions.

- Values represent stable, long-lasting beliefs about what is important to us. They influence our decisions and interpretation of what is ethical. Five values that differ across cultures are individualism-collectivism, power distance, uncertainty avoidance, masculinity-femininity, and long/short-term orientation. Three values that guide ethical conduct are utilitarianism, individual rights, and distributive justice.

Discussion Questions

1. After a few months on the job, Susan has experienced several emotional episodes ranging from frustration to joy toward the work she is assigned. Use the attitude model to explain how these emotions affect Susan's level of job satisfaction with the work itself.

2. Explain how an employee's attitudes might be affected by cognitive dissonance.

3. The latest employee attitude survey in your organization indicates that employees are unhappy with some aspects of the company. However, management tends to pay attention to the single-item question asking employees to indicate their over-all satisfaction with the job. The results of this item indicate that 86 percent of staff are very or somewhat satisfied, so management concludes that the other results refer to issues that are probably not important to employees. Explain why management's interpretation of these results may be inaccurate.

4. Universal Broadcasting Corp. is concerned about losing some of its best technical staff to competitors. Senior executives have decided that the best way to build a loyal workforce is to introduce a deferred profit-sharing plan. Employees would receive half of each year's profit share at the end of the year, but the other half would be paid out over the next two years as trailers. Anyone who leaves, other than due to retirement or layoffs, would forfeit some or all of the deferred payments. Explain what effect this plan may have on organizational commitment and employee behaviours.

5. Give two reasons why employee involvement tends to increase organizational commitment.

6. If a co-worker told you that he or she had a high level of emotional intelligence, what would you look for to confirm that statement?

7. Your company is beginning to expand operations in Japan and wants you to form working relationships with Japanese suppliers. Considering only the values of individualism and uncertainty avoidance, what should you be aware of or sensitive to in your dealings with these suppliers? You may assume that your contacts hold typical Japanese values along these dimensions.

8. Compare and contrast the ethical values of individual rights and distributive justice.

Chapter Case

Rough Seas on the LINK650*

Professor Suzanne Baxter was preparing for her first class of the semester when Shaun O'Neill knocked lightly on the open door and announced himself: "Hi, Professor, I don't suppose you remember me?" Professor Baxter had large classes, but she did remember that Shaun was a student in her organizational behaviour class two years earlier. Shaun had decided to work in the oil industry for a couple of years before returning to school to complete his diploma.

"Welcome back!" Baxter said as she beckoned him into the office. "I heard you were on an East coast oil rig. How was it?"

"Well, Professor," Shaun began, "I had worked two summers in Alberta's oil fields, so I hoped to get a job on the LINK650, the new CanOil drilling rig that arrived with so much fanfare in St. John's two years ago. The LINK650 was built by LINK, Inc., in Dallas, Texas. A standard practice in this industry is for the rig manufacturer to manage its day-to-day operations, so employees on the LINK650 are managed completely by LINK managers with no involvement from CanOil. No one has forgotten the *Ocean Ranger* tragedy, but drilling-rig jobs pay well and offer generous time off. The newspaper said that nearly one thousand people lined up to complete job applications for the 50 nontechnical positions. I was lucky enough to get one of those jobs.

"Everyone hired on the LINK650 was enthusiastic and proud. We were one of the chosen few and were really pumped up about working on a new rig that had received so much media attention. I was quite impressed — so were several other hires — with the recruiters because they really seemed to be concerned about our welfare out at sea. I later discovered that the recruiters came from a consulting firm that specializes in hiring people. Come to think of it, we didn't meet a single LINK manager during that process. Maybe things would have been different if some of those LINK supervisors had interviewed us.

"Working on LINK650 was a real shock, even though most of us had some experience working along the Newfoundland coast. I'd say that none of the 50 nontechnical people hired in St. John's was quite prepared for the brutal jobs on the oil rig. We did the dirtiest jobs in the biting cold winds of the North Atlantic. Still, during the first few months most of us wanted to show the company that we were dedicated to getting the job done. A couple of the new hires quit within a few weeks, but most of the people hired in St. John's really got along well — you know, just like the ideas you mentioned in class. We formed a special bond that helped us through the bad weather and gruelling work.

"The LINK650 supervisors were another matter. They were tough SOBs who had worked for many years on oil rigs in the Gulf of Mexico or North Sea. They seemed to relish the idea of treating their employees the same way they had been treated before becoming managers. We put up with their abuse for the first few months, but things got worse when the LINK650 was brought into port twice to correct mechanical problems. These setbacks embarrassed LINK's management and they put more pressure on the supervisors to get us back on schedule.

"The supervisors started to ignore equipment problems and pushed us to get jobs done more quickly without regard to safety procedures. They routinely shouted obscenities at employees in front of others. Several of my work mates were fired and a few more quit. I almost

lost my job one day just because my boss thought I could secure a fitting faster. Several people started finding ways to avoid the supervisors and get as little work done as possible. Many of my co-workers developed back problems. We jokingly called it the 'Hibernia backache' because some employees faked their ailment to leave the rig with paid sick leave.

"On top of the lousy supervisors, we were always kept in the dark about the problems on the rig. Supervisors said that they didn't know anything, which was partly true, but they said we shouldn't be so interested in things that didn't concern us. But the rig's problems, as well as its future contract work, were a major concern to crew members who weren't ready to quit. Their job security depended on the rig's production levels and whether CanOil would sign contracts to drill new holes. Given the rig's problems, most of us were concerned that we would be laid off at any time.

"Everything came to a head when Bob MacKenzie was killed because someone secured a hoist improperly. You probably read about it in the papers around this time last year. The government inquiry concluded that the person responsible was not properly trained and that employees were being pushed to finish jobs without safety precautions. Anyway, while the inquiry was going on, several employees decided to call the Seafarers International Union to unionize the rig. It wasn't long before most employees on LINK650 had signed union cards. That really shocked LINK's management and the entire oil industry because it was, I think, just the second time that a rig had ever been unionized in Canada.

"Since then, management has been doing everything in its power to get rid of the union. It sent a 'safety officer' to the rig, although we eventually realized that he was a consultant the company hired to undermine union support. One safety meeting with compulsory attendance of all crew members involved watching a video describing the international union president's association with organized crime. Several managers were sent to special seminars on how to manage under a union workforce, although one of the topics was how to break the union. The guys who initiated the organizing drive were either fired or given undesir-able jobs. LINK even paid one employee to challenge the union certification vote. The labour board rejected the decertification request because it discovered the company's union-busting tactics. Last month, the labour board ordered LINK to negotiate a first contract in good faith.

"So you see, Professor, I joined LINK as an enthusiastic employee and quit last month with no desire to lift a finger for them. It really bothers me, because I was always told to do your best, no matter how tough the situation. It's been quite an experience."

Discussion Questions

1. Use the job satisfaction model to explain why the LINK650 employees were dissatisfied with their work.

2. Identify the various ways that employees expressed their job dissatisfaction on the LINK650.

3. Shaun O'Neill's commitment to the LINK organization dwindled over his two years of employment. Discuss the factors that affected his organizational commitment.

© Copyright 1995. Steven L. McShane. This case is based on actual events, although names and some information have been changed.

Experiential Exercise

Ethical Dilemmas in Employment

Purpose: This exercise is designed to help you apply ethical principles to real moral dilemmas that employers and employees have faced in Canada.

Instructions: The following incidents are adapted from real events and ultimately require someone to make a decision with strong moral implications. For each incident, indicate what you would do and identify one of the three ethical principles described in this chapter to explain your decision.

When everyone is done, students will form small teams and compare their decisions and justifications for each incident. If possible, try to reach a consensus on the appropriate action for each incident, but leave enough time to discuss each incident. Finally, the class will discuss each incident, beginning by tallying the actions that each student initially wrote down as well as the group results. The subsequent discussion should look at the ethical principle that dominated over others, as well as the role of personal values in ethical decision making.

The Case of the Illegal Application Form

You want to apply for a professional job at a mid-sized manufacturing company. As part of the hiring process, you are given an application form that asks, among other things, about your age and marital status. Requesting this information is a clear violation of human rights in every Canadian jurisdiction. If you bring this fact to the employer's attention, however, there is a concern that the employer might think you won't be a loyal employee or that you aren't a team player. If you leave those sections blank, the employer might come to the same conclusion or think that you have something to hide. You don't know much about the quality of the employer, but getting this job would be important to your career. What would you do?

The Case of Questionable Objectivity

You are the owner of a highly rated talk radio station in Atlantic Canada. The popular radio personality on the morning phone-in show, Judy Price, is married to John Price, a lawyer who entered provincial politics a few years ago. Last month, John Price became leader of the Official Opposition. There is increasing concern from the board of directors that the radio station's perceived objectivity would be compromised if Ms Price remains on air as a news commentator while her husband holds such a public position in the region. Some co-workers doubt that Judy Price would publicly criticize her husband or his party's policies, although they don't know for certain. Ms Price says that her job comes first and that any attempt to remove her would represent a form of discrimination on the basis of marital status. There are no other on-air positions available for her at this station. What would you do?

The Case of the Awkward Office Affair

As head of Human Resources, you have learned from two employees that one of the office administrators, Sandi, is having an affair with Jim, an employee in Shipping and Receiving. Jim is single, but Sandi is married and her husband also works in the company's Shipping and Receiving department. You have spoken privately to Sandi, who admits to the affair but doesn't think that her husband knows about it. Moreover, she retorted that the company has no right to snoop into her private life and that she will hire a lawyer if the company does anything to punish her. So far, there haven't been any signs of office disruption because the handful of employees who know about the affair have not communicated it through the grapevine. However, morale problems could develop if the news spreads. The two employees who initially told you about the affair believe strongly in marital fidelity and feel that Jim, Sandi, or both should leave the company. Finally, there is the concern that Sandi's husband might have an altercation with Jim, and that the company could be liable for the consequences. What would you do?

CHAPTER 8

Communicating in Organizational Settings

CHAPTER OUTLINE

A Model of Communication

Communication Barriers (Noise)

ommunication Channels

Choosing the Best Communication Channels

Communicating in Organizational Hierarchies

Communicating Through the Grapevine

Cross-Cultural and Gender Communication

Improving Interpersonal Communication

Persuasive Communication:
From Understanding to Acceptance

Chapter Summary

Discussion Questions

LEARNING OBJECTIVES

After reading this chapter, you should be able to:

- Diagram the communication process.

- Identify common sources of noise in communication.

- Describe problems when communicating through electronic mail.

- Identify the conditions requiring high data-carrying capacity media.

- List three visible leadership practices.

- Describe characteristics of the organizational grapevine.

- Discuss how men tend to communicate differently from women.

- Summarize the key features of persuasive communication.

CAE Electronics relies on surveys, town-hall meetings, and employee task forces to facilitate communication throughout the company.

C AE Electronics is one of Canada's leading high-technology companies and the home to thousands of talented employees. So when a survey revealed that employees of CAE Inc.'s Montreal-based subsidiary were concerned with some company practices, senior management responded quickly.

To begin the process, executives met face-to-face with all 3,400 employees. Management rented a large hall close to the plant, and people were bussed over in groups of 300. In each session, the executive team went through the survey results, question by question. Employees were then given up-to-date information about the company's finances and corporate strategies.

Eight task teams were created to analyze and recommend improvements to the issues identified by the survey results. The task team responsible for communication recommended introducing computer-mediated communication systems that would attract people to the information. They also recommended an "automatic reflex to communicate," meaning that CAE should encourage employees to ask themselves automatically whether information they receive should be communicated to others.

"Communication is not just about more bulletin-board announcements and reports from management," says CAE president John Caldwell. "It's about sharing information so we can all better serve our customers and improve the way we work. Communication is also about obtaining points of view from others and not only listening, but hearing what others say."[1]

At the beginning of the book, we said that organizations are people who interact with each other to achieve some purpose. Employees are the organization's brain cells, and communication represents the nervous system that carries this information and shared meaning to vital parts of the organizational body. Large organizations, such as CAE, require innovative strategies to keep the communication pathways open. Smaller organizations may have fewer structural bottlenecks, but they, too, can suffer from subtle communication barriers.

Communication refers to the process by which information is transmitted and *understood* between two or more people. We emphasize the word *understood* because transmitting the sender's intended meaning is the essence of good communication. Corporate leaders spend almost 80 percent of their day communicating, so it isn't surprising that leadership performance is closely related to their communication skills.[2] The three main purposes of workplace communication are to coordinate work activities, allow more informed decisions, and fulfil individual relatedness needs.

- *Coordination* Employees communicate with each other to coordinate work activities.[3] This involves interacting on mutual tasks as well as sharing mental models — working models of the world (Chapter 6). By forming common mental models, employees synchronize their work activities through common expectations and assumptions.[4]

- *Decision making* Decision makers depend on effective communication for information to identify problems and choose the best solutions. For example, Canon's recent Tsushin Corporate Plan emphasizes "heart-to-heart and mind-to-mind communication." The idea is for employees worldwide to share information on customers and products so that they can make more informed choices about corporate actions.[5]

- *Relatedness needs* Employees fulfil their relatedness needs (the need to be with and recognized by other people) by communicating with them. Moreover, employees identify more with the organization when they feel connected to co-workers and receive information about their organization.[6] Communication is also the basis for social support, which eases work-related stress (Chapter 5).[7]

This chapter begins by presenting a model of the communication process and discussing barriers that create "noise" in this process. Next, the different types of communication channels, including computer-mediated communication, are described, followed by factors to consider when choosing a communication medium. The chapter then presents some options for communicating in organizational hierarchies and describes the pervasive organizational grapevine. The latter part of the chapter examines cross-cultural and gender differences in communication and strategies to improve interpersonal communication and persuasive communication.

A Model of Communication

The communication model presented in Exhibit 8.1 provides a useful "conduit" metaphor for thinking about the communication process.[8] According to this model, communication flows through channels between the sender and receiver. The sender forms a message and encodes it into words, gestures, voice intonations, and other symbols or signs. Next, the encoded message is transmitted to the intended receiver through one or more communication channels (media). The receiver senses the

Communication The process by which information is transmitted and understood between two or more people.

EXHIBIT 8.1: The Communication Process Model

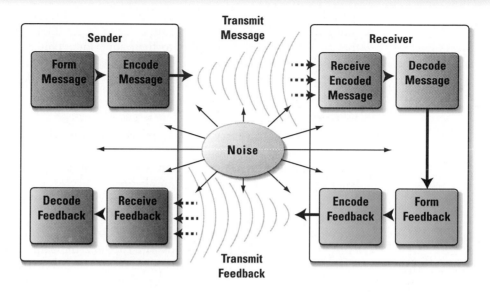

incoming message and decodes it into something meaningful. Ideally, the decoded meaning is what the sender had intended.

In most situations, the sender looks for evidence that the other person received and understood the transmitted message. This feedback may be a formal acknowledgement, such as a "Yes, I know what you mean," or indirect evidence from the receiver's subsequent actions. Notice that feedback repeats the communication process. Intended feedback is encoded, transmitted, received, and decoded from the receiver to the sender of the original message.

This model recognizes that communication is not a free-flowing conduit.[9] Rather, the transmission of meaning from one person to another is hampered by *noise* — the psychological, social, and structural barriers that distort and obscure the sender's intended message. If any part of the communication process is distorted or broken, the sender and receiver will not have a common understanding of the message.

Communication Barriers (Noise)

In spite of the best intentions of sender and receiver to communicate, several types of "noise" inhibit the effective exchange of information. Four common communication barriers are perceptions, filtering, language, and information overload.

Perceptions

As we learned in Chapter 6, the perceptual process determines what messages we select or screen out, as well as how the selected information is organized and interpreted. This can be a significant source of noise in the communication process if the sender's and receiver's perceptions are not aligned. E-mail messages sometimes suffer from this problem. The sender does not intend an e-mail message to show anger or upset, but the receiver interprets the message this way because he or she currently feels these emotions toward the sender due to an earlier conflict.

Filtering

Some messages are filtered or stopped altogether on their way up or down the organizational hierarchy. Employees and supervisors might filter upward communication so that they look more favourable to their superiors. This occurs most commonly in organizations that emphasize status differences and that tolerate high levels of political behaviour, as well as among employees with strong career-mobility aspirations.[10]

Language

Words and gestures carry no inherent meaning with them. Instead, the sender must ensure that the receiver understands these symbols and signs. In reality, lack of mutual understanding is a common reason why messages are often distorted. Two potential language barriers are jargon and ambiguity.

Jargon

Jargon Technical language of a particular occupational group or recognized words with specialized meaning in specific organizations or social groups.

Jargon can be technical language of a particular occupational group (such as medical or legal terms) or recognized words with specialized meaning in specific organizations or social groups. Jargon potentially increases communication efficiency when both sender and receiver understand this specialized language, and it can be a powerful element in shaping and maintaining an organization's cultural values.[11]

However, jargon becomes noise in the communication process when the receiver doesn't understand this specialized language. For example, employees at Wacker Siltronic Corp. were breaking saw blades and causing a high rate of product defects after new machinery was introduced. Management eventually discovered that the manuals were written for engineers, and that employees were guessing (often incorrectly) at the meaning of the jargon. Productivity improved and machine costs dropped after the manuals were rewritten with the jargon removed.[12]

Ambiguity

Ambiguous language is often a problem in communication because the sender and receiver interpret the same word or phrase differently. If a co-worker says, "Would you like to check the figures again?," the employee may be politely *telling* you to double-check the figures. But this message is sufficiently ambiguous that you may think the co-worker is merely *asking* if you want to do this. The result is that meaning is not transferred and both parties become frustrated by the communication failure.

Ambiguous language is not always a problem, however. Euphemisms are often ambiguous, yet they minimize the emotions conveyed by more direct language. For instance, brokerage firms sometimes use euphemisms such as "swap" or "avoid" rather than the direct "sell" word to avoid upsetting clients. One New York investment firm advised individual investors that a particular bank stock was "long-term attractive," meaning that the investors should

"That's what we like about you, sir — there are no gray areas."

sell it immediately. The bank was one of the investment firm's clients, and it didn't want to offend the bank's executives with a "sell" recommendation.[13]

Ambiguous language is also necessary where the event or object being described is ill-defined or lacks agreement.[14] Effective leaders use metaphors such as "laying pipe" or "wild geese" to describe complex organizational values so that they are interpreted broadly enough to apply to diverse situations. Scholars also rely on metaphors because they convey rich meaning about complex ideas. For example, organizational behaviour scholars often describe organizations as "machines" or "organisms" to reflect their complex nature.[15]

Information Overload

Employees have a certain *information processing capacity;* that is, the amount of information that they are able to process in a fixed unit of time. At the same time, jobs have a varying *information load;* that is, the amount of information to be processed per unit of time.[16] If information load exceeds information processing capacity, then employees experience **information overload**, as we see in Exhibit 8.2.

Information overload A condition in which the volume of information received by an employee exceeds that person's ability to process it effectively.

Information overload is a serious problem for many people due to increasing workloads and more efficient electronic communication systems. This may result in lost information, poorer decisions, and stressed-out employees. To minimize information overload, we can try to increase the employee's information-processing capacity and reduce the job's information load.[17]

We can increase our information-processing capacity by learning to read faster, scanning documents more efficiently, and removing distractions that slow information-processing speed. Time management also increases information-processing capacity. When information overload is temporary, we can increase information-processing capacity by working longer hours.

EXHIBIT 8.2: Dynamics of Information Overload

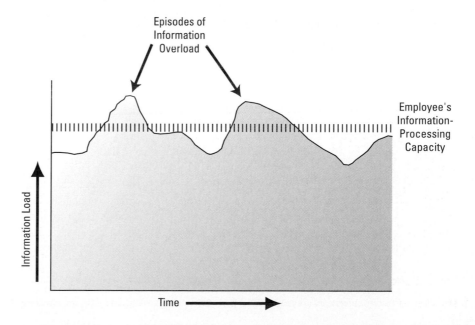

We can reduce information load by omitting, summarizing, or buffering the information. One increasingly popular omitting activity is to activate filtering algorithms in e-mail software so that junk mail from unwanted addresses is automatically deleted. Summarizing reduces information load by condensing information into fewer words. For instance, we rely on abstracts and executive summaries before deciding to read an entire document. Buffering occurs when assistants screen messages and forward only those considered essential reading. Microsoft's Bill Gates and other CEOs depend on these buffers to handle the large number of e-mail messages they receive each day.[18]

Perceptions, filtering, language, and information overload are not the only sources of noise in the communication process, but they are probably the most common. Noise also occurs when we choose an inappropriate channel through which the message is sent. The next section takes a closer look at communication channels.

Communication Channels

A critical part of the communication model are the channels through which information is transmitted. Generally, communication channels fall into two categories: verbal and nonverbal. *Verbal communication* includes any oral or written methods of transmitting meaning through words. *Nonverbal communication*, which we discuss later in the chapter, is any part of communication that does not use words. To remain competitive, companies rely on many different communication channels. An example of such a company is Chrysler Corp. As Perspective 8.1 describes, the automaker has dramatically expanded the use of computer-mediated and videoconferencing

PERSPECTIVE 8.1

Chrysler Revs Up Communication Channels

When Chrysler Corp. manager William DeRosa wants to find out when a particular production schedule is due, he simply clicks a button on his Web browser and downloads the schedule to his screen. He does the same thing to check regulatory procedures for certain product models.

Chrysler Corp. has discovered the power of communication. From Web-accessible databases to more face-to-face dialogue, the automaker wants to improve organizational learning by ensuring that communication flows openly across units and levels.

At Chrysler Canada's minivan plant in Windsor, Ontario, production and quality-assurance managers hold a series of short meetings with employees throughout the manufacturing process to identify problems and hear employee solutions. A 30-minute meeting, called the Tire Kick, is held at

the end of each day with 50 managers and employees representing all areas of the plant.

To further strengthen communication links with employees, the production manager has moved his desk from the executive offices to the same floor as the production facilities. "You have to show that you are part of the team," he says. "You have to find out what employees are thinking."

Chrysler has also set up a satellite-linked video network so that people at the Windsor plant can communicate in real time with their counterparts at minivan plants in St. Louis and in Europe. In fact, the Windsor plant has 54 communication posts connected to the video system. In this way, technical specialists at each plant can share innovations and jointly work out problems.

Source: J. B. White, "Chrysler's Intranet: Promise v. Reality," *Globe & Mail*, May 13, 1997, p. B11; E. Heinrich, "Keep the Minivan in the Fast Lane," *Financial Post*, September 9, 1995, pp. 6–7; A. Vido, "Chrysler and Minivans: Are We There Yet?" *CMA Magazine* 67 (November 1993), pp. 11–16; C. G. Johnston and C. R. Farquhar, *Empowered People Satisfy Customers* (Ottawa: Conference Board of Canada, 1992), p. 12; and G. Brockhouse, "Can This Marriage Succeed?" *Canadian Business*, October 1992, pp. 128–36.

Norm Betts. Used with permission of the *Toronto Sun.*

Toronto Sun Publishing Corp. CEO Paul Godfrey (front) and chairman Lionel Schipper met directly with *Toronto Sun* and *Financial Post* employees to tell them that the company had been put up for sale. Communicating dramatic news directly to a large gathering of employees lends emotional support to the event.

technologies throughout North America. Chrysler has also provided more opportunities for face-to-face meetings across organizational levels. In this section, we investigate some of these channels of communication and discuss their merits.

Oral and Written Communication

Oral communication, particularly face-to-face interaction, is usually better than written methods for transmitting emotions and persuading the receiver. This is because nonverbal cues accompany oral communication, such as voice intonations and the use of silence. Moreover, in face-to-face settings, the sender receives immediate feedback from the receiver and can adjust the emotional tone of the message accordingly. This is why Toronto Sun Publishing Corp. CEO Paul Godfrey and chairman Lionel Schipper relied on a large face-to-face gathering to inform employees that the company was for sale.[19] This news was an emotional event, so they used oral communication to transmit their emotional support as well as the factual content of the message.

Written communication is more appropriate for recording and presenting technical details. Employees receiving written information tend to have a higher comprehension of the material than when they receive it verbally.[20] Traditionally, written communication has been slow to develop and transmit, but electronic mail and other computer-mediated communication channels have significantly improved written communication efficiency.[21]

Electronic Mail

Electronic mail (e-mail) is revolutionizing the way we communicate in organizational settings.[22] E-mail users can quickly form, edit, and store messages. Information can be appended and transmitted quickly to many people with the simple click of a computer mouse. E-mail is asynchronous (messages are sent and received at different times), so there is no need to coordinate a communication session. This technology also allows fairly random access of information; you can select any message in any order and skip to different parts of a message.

When companies introduce e-mail, communication patterns change in several ways. E-mail tends to increase the frequency of communication within the organization.[23] It replaces some face-to-face and telephone communication, but also expands communication patterns across work units. Some social status differences still exist with e-mail, but they are less apparent than in face-to-face or telephone communication.[24] This explains why communication to higher levels in the organization increases when e-mail is introduced. E-mail tends to be the preferred medium for coordinating work (e.g., confirming a co-worker's production schedule) and for sending well-defined information for decision making.

Problems with e-mail

Anyone who has used e-mail knows that it has several problems and limitations. Perhaps the most obvious of these is that e-mail contributes to information overload. E-mail messages can be written quickly, and they can be copied to thousands of people through group mailbox systems. Consequently, surveys indicate that many e-mail users are overwhelmed by hundreds of messages each week, most of which are irrelevant to them. Consider Ron Hulse, an executive at Compaq Canada. He arrives at the office by 6:30 a.m. most mornings, attacking his e-mail for an hour or more before scrambling through the day's tasks. At this rate, he almost dreads the thought of returning from vacation. "If I go away for a week's vacation, I come back to 300 messages," he complains.[25]

Flaming Sending an emotionally charged electronic mail message.

A second concern is that e-mail increases the frequency of **flaming**. Flaming is the act of sending an emotionally charged message to others. This occurs because people can post e-mail messages before their emotions subside, whereas the sender of a traditional memo or letter would have time for sober second thoughts. Presumably, flaming and other communication problems will become less common as employees learn the unique dynamics of e-mail.[26]

A third problem is that the emotional tone of an e-mail message is sometimes difficult to interpret. One scholar recently quipped that the result "of new information technologies within organizations has not been better communication, only faster misunderstandings."[27] For example, it is extremely difficult to convey sarcasm by e-mail because the verbal message requires contrasting nonverbal cues. E-mail aficionados try to clarify the emotional tone of their messages by combining ASCII characters to form graphic faces. An entire lexicon of faces has developed, such as those illustrated in Exhibit 8.3. Less sophisticated users, on the other hand, are unaware that people interpret emotions from the form of the e-mail message. For example, they innocently write an e-mail message in CAPITAL LETTERS, not realizing that this is often interpreted as anger.

Another concern is that e-mail lacks the warmth of human interaction. It is clearly inappropriate to fire or lay off an employee through e-mail (although some managers have done this), because this medium does not effectively communicate empathy or social support. As employees increasingly cocoon themselves through their computers

---

EXHIBIT 8.3: Icons of Emotion in E-Mail Messages

Icon	Meaning
:-)	Happy
:-}	Smirk
:-(	Unhappy
<:-)	Dumb question
:-j	Tongue in cheek
:-p	Tongue sticking out
:-x	OOPS!
{}	Hug
12x—<—@	12 Dozen Roses

Source: Cited in R. Weiland, "The Message is the Medium," *Incentive*, September 1995, p. 37.

and other forms of information technology, they lose the social support of human contact that potentially keeps their stress in check. As one computer consultant warns: "People are finding themselves spending a major portion of their day surrounded by machines and communicating through machines, and they feel hungry for human connection and warmth and perspective and wisdom."[28]

Other Computer-Mediated Communication

Computer-mediated communication systems play a central role in today's hyperfast world of corporate information sharing.[29] With a mouse click, employees can gain access to information created a few minutes ago in another part of the world. This communication is made possible through networks connecting the individual's computer to clusters of powerful computers and storage systems elsewhere in the organization. Bank of Montreal, Hewlett-Packard, and Apple are some of the companies that have opened their information systems to employees.[30]

Internet and Intranet networks are blossoming throughout Canadian industry. These networks use browser software that allow employees to view text, graphics, and live video from other sites.[31] For instance, Northern Telecom has thousands of Web site "pages" with information for its employees. Nortel has also been experimenting since the early 1990s with Intranet videoconferencing using CU-SeeMe (developed by Cornell University) and other software. Other companies are trying out multimedia training programs that "stream" the information through the Intranet to the user in a seamless presentation.

Ault Foods, CIBC, and Price Waterhouse use interactive software that lets several users work on the same document or post ideas to a common electronic blackboard. At AGF, a Toronto-based mutual fund company, computer systems retrieve images of paper forms to anyone with access. Emerging software provides sophisticated "data mining"; that is, it searches corporate databases and organizes the requested information in a presentable way.[32]

Nonverbal Communication

Although most attention these days focuses on computer-mediated communication, the most powerful communication channel is nonverbal. By most estimates, over two-thirds

Nonverbal communication is an important part of transmitting meaning to others, such as at this Battlefords Credit Union meeting in New Battlefords, Saskatchewan.

of all information in face-to-face meetings is communicated nonverbally.[33] Nonverbal communication includes facial gestures, voice intonation, and even silence.

Nonverbal communication differs from verbal communication in two ways. First, we normally know what words we say or write, whereas nonverbal cues are typically automatic and subconscious. A second distinction is that nonverbal communication is less rule bound than verbal communication. We receive a lot of formal training on how to understand spoken words, but very little to understand the nonverbal signals that accompany those words. Consequently, nonverbal cues are more ambiguous and more susceptible to misinterpretation.

Nonverbal communication also plays an important role in emotional labour. Recall from Chapter 7 that **emotional labour** refers to the effort, planning, and control needed to express organizationally desired emotions.[34] Employees make extensive use of nonverbal cues to transmit prescribed feelings to customers, co-workers, and others. Delta Airlines carefully trains flight attendants in their use of facial expressions and physical movement. Trainers videotape flight simulations so that employees can see how their nonverbal behaviours communicate prescribed or undesirable messages to customers.[35]

Emotional labour The effort, planning, and control needed to express organizationally desired emotions during interpersonal transactions.

Emotional contagion

What happens when people see a co-worker accidentally bang his or her head against a file cabinet? Chances are, they wince and put their hand on their own head as if they had hit the cabinet. This automatic and subconscious tendency to mimic and synchronize our nonverbal behaviours with other people is called **emotional contagion**.[36]

We tend to "catch" other people's emotions by continuously mimicking their facial expressions and nonverbal cues. For instance, listeners smile more and exhibit other emotional displays of happiness while hearing someone describe a positive event. Similarly, listeners will wince when the speaker describes an event in which he or she was hurt.

Emotional contagion The automatic and subconscious tendency to mimic and synchronize our nonverbal behaviours with other people.

Emotional contagion serves three purposes. First, mimicry provides continuous feedback, communicating that we understand and empathize with the sender. To consider the significance of this, imagine if employees remain expressionless after watching a co-worker bang his or her head against a file cabinet! The lack of parallel behaviour conveys a lack of understanding or caring.

Second, mimicking the nonverbal behaviours of other people seems to be a way of receiving emotional meaning from those people. If a co-worker is angry with a client, your tendency to frown and show anger while listening helps you share that emotion more fully. In other words, we receive meaning by expressing the sender's emotions as well as by listening to the sender's words.

Third, emotional contagion is a type of "social glue" that bonds people together. Social solidarity is built out of each member's awareness of a collective sentiment. Through nonverbal expressions of emotional contagion, people see others share the same emotions that they feel. This strengthens team cohesiveness by providing evidence of member similarity.

Choosing the Best Communication Channels

Employees perform better if they can quickly determine the best communication channels for the situation and are flexible enough to use different methods as the occasion requires.[37] But which communication channels are most appropriate? We partly answered this question above, in our evaluation of the different communication channels. However, two additional contingencies worth noting are media richness and symbolic meaning.

Media Richness

Media richness The data-carrying capacity of a communication medium; the volume and variety of information that it can transmit.

Communication channels can be organized into a hierarchy based on their **media richness**. This refers to their *data-carrying capacity*; that is, the volume and variety of information that can be transmitted.[38] Face-to-face interaction has the highest data-carrying capacity because the sender can simultaneously transmit verbal and nonverbal signals, the receiver can provide immediate feedback, and the information exchange can be customized to suit the situation. In contrast, financial reports and other impersonal documents represent the leanest media because they allow only one form of data transmission (e.g., written), the sender does not receive timely feedback from the receiver, and the information exchange is standardized for everyone.

As Exhibit 8.4 illustrates, the most appropriate medium depends on whether the situation is nonroutine and ambiguous. Nonroutine situations require rich media because the sender and receiver have little common experience and, therefore, need to transmit a large volume of information. During emergencies, for instance, face-to-face meetings should be used to coordinate work efforts quickly and minimize the risk of misunderstanding and confusion. Lean media may be used in routine situations because the sender and receiver have common expectations through shared mental models.

EXHIBIT 8.4: A Hierarchy of Media Richness

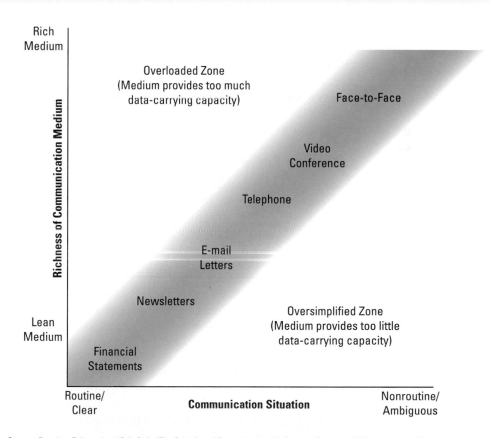

Source: Based on R. Lengel and R. L. Daft, "The Selection of Communication Media as an Executive Skill," *Academy of Management Executive* 2, no. 3 (August, 1988), p. 226; R. L. Daft and R. H. Lengel, "Information Richness: A New Approach to Managerial Behavior and Organization Design," *Research in Organizational Behavior*, 1984, p. 199.

Ambiguous situations also require rich media because the parties must share large amounts of information to resolve multiple and conflicting interpretations of their observations and experiences.[39] The early stages of a project require rich media communication because team members need to resolve different interpretations of the project task, each member's role, and the parameters of acceptable behaviour.[40]

Symbolic Meaning of the Medium

"The medium is the message."[41] This famous phrase by communications guru Marshall McLuhan means that the sender's choice of communication channel transmits meaning beyond the message content. For example, a personal meeting with an employee may indicate that the issue is important, whereas a brief handwritten note may suggest less importance.

The difficulty we face when choosing a communication medium is that its symbolic meaning may vary from one person to the next. Some people view e-mail as a symbol of professionalism, whereas others see it as evidence of the sender's efficiency. Still others might view an e-mail message as a low-status clerical activity because it involves typing.[42] Overall, we must be sensitive to the symbolic meaning of the selected communication medium to ensure that it amplifies rather than contradicts the meaning found in the message content.

Communicating in Organizational Hierarchies

Organizations need to support practices that facilitate communication flow. Otherwise, work units become "silos of knowledge," in which information becomes isolated and underutilized. In Chapter 1, we explained that organizational learning occurs when firms are able to disseminate knowledge to those who need it for decision making. In this section, we consider some of the more popular or emerging approaches to communicating up, down, and across the organization.

Employee Surveys

Traditionally, medium and large Canadian organizations have used employee surveys to monitor employee morale. Today, surveys are mainly used to provide feedback to decision makers on organizational practices, involve employees in decisions about proposed changes, and create benchmark measures of executive and corporate performance.[43] As we read in the opening story to this chapter, CAE Inc. surveys employees to evaluate corporate practices. James MacLaren Industries, a pulp and paper company in Buckingham, Quebec, also surveys its 1,800 employees to assess the need for change.[44]

Federal Express has a regular survey called Survey-Feedback-Action that benchmarks corporate performance and evaluates management as part of 360-degree feedback (Chapter 2). "The first survey is always an experience for new managers," explains a Federal Express executive. "But they soon realize they need it. Good communication increases the morale — and the productivity — of the group." If a manager's rating falls below 40 percent on the survey ratings, he or she is transferred until performance improves.[45]

Distributing News Down the Hierarchy

Until recently, medium and large firms would either send employees a quarterly newsletter or keep them completely in the dark about corporate activities. While

---

PERSPECTIVE 8.2

Straight Talk for BC Telecom Employees

BC Telecom's bimonthly employee magazine, *Perspectives*, may have been glossy and colourful, but an employee survey revealed that it delivered old news.

"The information in [*Perspectives*] was always way out-of-date and there was no way we could use it for fast-breaking news," explains Catherine Aberlee, BC Telecom's employee communications manager. The glossy magazine was also very labour-intensive and expensive to produce.

Based on the survey results, BC Telecom replaced *Perspectives* with a weekly black-and-white, two-sided news sheet. This dramatically reduced costs and got information to employees faster. With a black-and-white format, the news sheet would be faxed and was easy to transfer to the company's electronic bulletin-board system.

"We also realized that not everyone is print-oriented," says Aberlee. "We should be providing [communication] vehicles that people feel comfortable accessing, and if I prefer to listen to something rather than read it, in this company I now have that option."

BC Tel's nonprint option is Straight Talk, an interactive telephone information line that employees can access toll-free across North America. Straight Talk is updated weekly, with late-breaking information added during the week. News items are professionally produced with items of interest to listeners.

Straight Talk is also highly interactive. Employees can voice their opinions on any of the news items using one of the options in the telephone system. "Employees want to have a say," explains Dianne Bentley, BC Telecom's communication manager responsible for Straight Talk. "[Straight Talk] is a tool for employees to have their say, and they are using it."

Source: "Improving Employee Communications at B.C. Telecom" (Video) and interviews with Catherine Aberlee and Dianne Bentley.

---

newsletters are still popular, they are being replaced by more contemporary methods. As we see in Perspective 8.2, BC Telecom stopped producing its long-running *Perspectives* magazine because employees were reading old news by the time they received a copy. Instead, the telecommunications company is experimenting with more efficient and timely media.

Bank of Montreal, Fletcher Challenge, Canada Trust, and other Canadian firms produce video magazines that supplement or replace hard-copy newsletters. The advantage of video is that it makes employees feel somewhat closer to top executives who appear in these programs. Canada Trust's video program encourages employees to submit video materials from their branches. Without creating a "home video syndrome," this idea has strengthened the bond among the thousands of people who work in this financial institution.[46]

Electronic mail and Intranet Web sites are starting to replace hard-copy newsletters and magazines. AT&T was one of the first companies to send daily or weekly e-mail bulletins to all employees, supplementing the organization's hard-copy publications.[47] A few companies have introduced Intranet-based *e-zines* (electronic magazines). These Web sites keep employees updated within minutes and use colourful text and graphics at a much lower cost than traditional hard copy. Moreover, e-zines can include video clips, thereby combining the benefits of video magazines.

Visible Leadership

Elliot Dary can remember when executives in Canada's banking industry didn't communicate very much with their employees. "One guy had a light installed outside his office, and you couldn't go in when it was on," chuckles Dary, who manages a CIBC branch in Winnipeg. "In those days, the manager was God."[48]

Times have changed. Today, corporate leaders are expected to communicate through **visible leadership** (also known as management by wandering around). They must get out of their offices and communicate face-to-face with employees throughout the organization.[49] Perspective 8.3 describes how Nesel Fast Freight, Inc., a trucking firm in Mississauga, Ontario, uses regular meetings, line-of-sight, and other forms of direct communication to keep the information flowing between management and employees.

Nesel Freight can rely on direct communication because it is a relatively small organization. But how do you apply visible leadership in corporations with thousands of employees? One solution is the town-hall meeting in which executives meet with employees in a large lecture or forum arrangement. The opening story to this chapter described an example of this practice at CAE. Groups of 300 employees listened to executives talk about the employee survey, update them on company news, and answer questions from the audience.

Champion Road Machinery Ltd. also applies this town-hall method to maintain face-to-face communication between executives and the company's 600 employees. "I'm a great believer in communicating with the employees," explains Arthur Church, CEO of the road-grader manufacturer in Goderich, Ontario. "We have full employee briefings in groups of 85 to 90 every three months. We lay the whole picture out for them, give them a chance to ask the tough questions."[50] Another form of visible management involves senior executives meeting with small groups of employees to hear their views on organizational issues.[51] Toronto's Hospital for Sick Children holds open forums in which randomly selected employees discuss their concerns with the president.

These visible leadership activities seem to work well in Canada, but would they be equally successful in other cultures? Maybe not. As we learned in Chapter 7, some cultures emphasize power distance between employees and their superiors. In those countries, executives who try to bypass the hierarchy or try to be equals with employees are

Visible leadership A management practice of having frequent face-to-face communication with employees so that managers are better informed about employee concerns and organizational activities.

PERSPECTIVE 8.3

Nesel Fast Freight Keeps Communication Lines Open

Times have been tough in Canada's trucking industry, but Nesel Fast Freight, Inc. is surviving the competitive onslaught. Even when the economy faltered a few years back, Nesel's employees were willing to sacrifice their driving bonuses to save jobs and make ends meet. What is Nesel's secret to this loyalty? Keep employees informed and listen to their concerns.

"When we get into a crunch situation, it is part of the culture of this company to talk about it," says Katherine McWilliams, Nesel's president.

Employee meetings are a regular event at Nesel, including quarterly get-togethers with drivers, monthly meetings with warehouse staff, and weekly management meetings. Daily communication with the boss is also the norm, thanks in part to McWilliams's open-door policy and line-of-sight office setting. A large window allows truckers in the dispatch area to see McWilliams directly. This gives Nesel's president the opportunity to encourage employees who seem to want to talk.

However, McWilliams warns that being visible is more than line-of-sight and talking to employees. Executives must also be willing to listen with interest. "Sit down and listen and allow the employee to do the talking," she advises. "People know the difference between when they're being listened to and when they're being humoured."

Source: C. Knight, "Employee Relations at Family-run Nesel: 'For the Good of the Whole,'" *Canadian HR Reporter*, June 3, 1996, pp. 1, 2; D, Estok, "The High Cost of 'Dumbsizing,'" *Maclean's*, June 3, 1996, pp. 28–29.

not necessarily viewed as favourably as their counterparts in Canada. One scholar recently described an unwritten rule in Singapore that upward communication must go through the immediate supervisor. This norm is so strong that some Singaporean workers have been known to avoid senior management so that they do not inadvertently communicate new information to them.[52]

Improving Communication Through Workspace Design

There's nothing like a wall to prevent employees from talking to each other. That's why Northern Telecom recently transformed its old manufacturing facility in Bramalea, Ontario, into a faux cityscape for 1,300 headquarters employees. The building has a main street, side streets and crossroads (instead of corridors), and several parks with potted trees. Offices are temporarily separated by dividers (not walls), but even the dividers will go when employees feel more comfortable with the open setting. The governing metaphor here is to break down the walls that isolate employees from each other. "It takes walls down literally and makes managers more accessible to people," says a Nortel employee.[53]

Nortel is the latest company to improve communications through more open office design, but it is not alone. Winnipeg-based Precision Metalcraft, Inc. converted their executive offices into a storage area, and moved managers' desks onto the shop floor beside the machines.[54] At Toyota Motor Company's headquarters in Cambridge, Ontario, staff share a common open-office with the company president. "The fact that there are no barriers is a tangible example of how Japanese look at communication," explains a company spokesperson. "If I want to see the vice-president of administration, I just look up and see if he's at his desk. I don't have to phone his secretary and make an appointment to see him."[55]

This line-of-sight principle is also applied on the plant floor. Toyota production areas typically consist of U-shaped subassembly cells so that everyone on the line can coordinate their work and solve problems more quickly through direct communication. This contrasts with the traditional I-shaped or L-shaped lines at General Motors of Canada, which make it difficult for employees to communicate with each other.[56]

Other companies are discovering that employee creativity increases when the building's physical design allows spontaneous, horizontal communication.[57] When Corning Glass learned that its engineers acquired 80 percent of their ideas from face-to-face discussions with colleagues, the company moved employees into a low-rise building with informal meeting places and easy access to all areas. Engineering productivity increased by more than 10 percent in the new building. 3M's building in Austin, Texas, also has several interaction areas, with blackboards, couches, and coffee machines, where employees can hold spontaneous gatherings to share knowledge.

Nonterritorial offices

Nonterritorial offices
Office arrangements in which employees work at any available workstation and are not assigned to specific desks, offices, or workspaces.

Oticon A/S in Denmark, TBWA Chiat/Day in Toronto, and AGI in Illinois have taken the open-workspace concept one step further by creating **nonterritorial offices**.[58] Nonterritorial office arrangements — also called free-address, hot-desking, hotelling, and virtual space — do not assign people to specific desks, offices, or workspaces. Instead, employees take their work from a storage area to any available location. At advertising agency TBWA Chiat/Day, employees can set up their portable computers in the "Club House" or join their team members in one of the many "war rooms." At Oticon, a Danish hearing-aid manufacturer, employees keep their belongings in a cart that they can move around the building.[59]

In theory, nonterritorial offices improve communication and facilitate team dynamics. The idea is that employees work together and share ideas more freely than

Employees at TBWA Chiat/Day's offices in Toronto can set up their portable computers in the "Club House" (shown) or anywhere else in the nonterritorial office setting. The advertising agency made these changes to encourage better communication and creativity amongst employees.

if they work in an isolated office space. We know that physical structures influence communication.[60] However, it is too early to say how well the nonterritorial-office concept will improve communication. One concern is that companies with nonterritorial offices may be ignoring the occasional need for private communication. Chiat/Day discovered that some private space was needed when employees were found making telephone calls in bathroom stalls and under their desks.

Communicating Through the Grapevine

When St. Luke's Medical Center radically redesigned nursing duties, the change team knew that the organizational grapevine would go into overdrive. Team members at the Chicago hospital also knew that a fair amount of that information would be erroneous, so a 24-hour rumour hotline was set up and responses were reported in regular newsletters to employees. Even with this intensive communication strategy, the rumour mill continued to buzz.[61]

No matter how carefully and efficiently companies design formal communication structures, employees receive a considerable amount of information through the informal communication network known as the **grapevine**. The grapevine is an unstructured network founded on social relationships rather than organizational charts or job descriptions. Employees often receive news from the grapevine before they hear about it through formal channels. For example, one survey reported that 45 percent of Canadian employees first hear about layoffs through the grapevine.[62]

Grapevine The organization's informal communication network that is formed and maintained by social relationships rather than the formal reporting relationships.

Grapevine Characteristics

The grapevine has several unique features.[63] It transmits information very rapidly in all directions throughout the organization. According to one estimate, more than 75 percent of grapevine news is relatively accurate, possibly because the parties tend to use media-rich communication channels (e.g., face-to-face) and are motivated to communicate effectively. Nevertheless, the grapevine also distorts information by deleting fine details of the story and exaggerating key points. It transmits kernels of

EXHIBIT 8.5: Transmission Pattern of Grapevine Communication

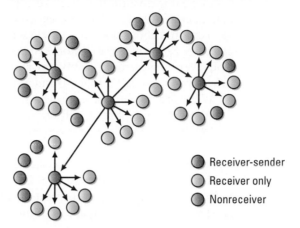

Receiver-sender
Receiver only
Nonreceiver

truth with several embellishments and, consequently, should not be viewed as the definitive source of organizational news.

The grapevine typically transmits information through the *cluster chain* pattern illustrated in Exhibit 8.5. Senders transmit grapevine information only to people they know and believe are interested. Some employees rarely receive grapevine information because they are not integrated with the organization's social network.

The grapevine relies on social relations, so it is more active where employees have homogeneous backgrounds and are able to communicate easily with each other. It is most active when employees are anxious about an issue and information from formal channels does not satisfy their need to know.[64] Even when the formal network provides some information about a particular situation, employees will participate in the grapevine because social interaction relieves some of their anxiety.

This explains why the hotline at St. Luke's Medical Center did not wither the informal grapevine. The Royal Bank of Scotland also discovered this when it conducted a full-scale review of its branch banking system. Senior management knew that the review would increase employee anxiety, so it used newsletters and other formal communications to describe the project. Yet a company survey revealed that employee reliance on the grapevine *increased* rather than decreased during the review period.[65]

Grapevine Advantages and Disadvantages

Should the grapevine be encouraged, tolerated, or quashed? The difficulty in answering this question categorically is that the grapevine has both advantages and disadvantages. First, let's discuss its advantages.

One benefit is that the grapevine helps employees make sense of their workplace when the information is not available through formal channels.[66] It is also the main conduit through which organizational stories and other symbols of the organization's culture are communicated (Chapter 16). Along with its informational value, the grapevine is an important social process that bonds people together and fulfils their need for affiliation.[67] Finally, because it is most active when employees are worried about an issue, the grapevine is a valuable signal for managers to take appropriate action. This may include resolving the problems behind the rumours, or communicating more fully through formal networks.

Now let's examine the disadvantages of the grapevine. Morale tumbles when management is slower than the grapevine in communicating information because it suggests management's lack of sincerity and concern for employees. Moreover, grapevine information may become sufficiently distorted that it escalates rather than reduces employee anxieties. For example, when Dominion Insurance was put up for sale, rumours about potential purchasers ran through the grapevine with disturbing regularity. Some of these rumours increased employee stress, such as the story that a Vancouver construction group was about to buy the Waterloo, Ontario, insurance company to use it as a money-laundering front for the Mafia![68]

What should companies do about the grapevine? Some managers try in vain to stop the grapevine, but it will always exist. Others try to send messages down to employees through the grapevine, but this overlooks the problem that the grapevine has a selective audience and may distort important facts. A better strategy, as mentioned earlier, is for managers to listen to the grapevine as a signal of employee anxiety, then correct the root cause of this anxiety. BC Tel, St. Luke's Medical Center, and the Royal Bank of Scotland also treat the grapevine as a competitor against which their newsletters and other formal communication programs are judged.

Cross-Cultural and Gender Communication

A culturally diverse workforce potentially improves organizational effectiveness through better decision making, greater creativity and innovation, and more successful marketing to different types of consumers.[69] But to realize these benefits, employees must become more sensitive and competent in cross-cultural communication. They must also overcome their reluctance to communicate with co-workers from other cultural groups. These communication competencies are also gaining importance as companies increasingly work with clients, suppliers, and joint-venture partners from other countries.

Verbal Differences

Language is the most obvious (although not necessarily the most serious) problem we face when communicating with people from other cultures. One study of cultural diversity in Toronto's major hotels reported that language barriers made it difficult for managers to give non-English employees meaningful feedback to help them improve their jobs. As one Toronto hotel manager explained: "If communication is difficult because of a language barrier, many supervisors don't bother to try. Messages go uncommunicated, and staff members do not get the feedback or the praise."[70]

Nonverbal Differences

Even when people from different cultures have mastered the same language, communication problems may occur when interpreting voice intonation.[71] A deep voice symbolizes masculinity in Canada, but African men often express their emotions using a high-pitched voice. Middle Easterners sometimes speak loudly to show sincerity and interest in the discussion, whereas Japanese people tend to speak softly to communicate politeness or humility. These different cultural norms regarding voice loudness may cause one person to misinterpret the other.

Aside from voice intonation, Canadians tend to rely on written or spoken communication as the source of true meaning. In contrast, people in Japan interpret more of a message's meaning from nonverbal cues, even when the verbal cues send a conflicting message. To avoid offending or embarrassing the receiver (particularly outsiders), Japanese people will often say what the other person wants to hear (called *tatemae*) but send more subtle nonverbal cues indicating the sender's true feelings (called *honne*).[72] A Japanese manager might politely reject your business proposal by saying "I will think about that," while sending nonverbal signals that he or she is not really interested.

This difference explains why Japanese employees may prefer direct conversation to e-mail and other media that lack nonverbal cues. "When you talk to someone in person, you can tell if there is real understanding," explains Chikako Lane, a Japanese-born manager at Calsonic North America, a subsidiary of the Nissan Group. "Our Japanese engineers dislike e-mail so much that I have to track them down every couple of days and remind them to read their messages."[73]

Most nonverbal cues are specific to a particular culture and may have a completely different meaning to people raised in other cultures.[74] For example, Canadians shake their head from side to side to say "No," but this means "I understand" to some people from India. Filipinos raise their eyebrows to give an affirmative answer, yet Arabs interpret this expression (along with clicking one's tongue) as a negative response. Canadians are taught to maintain eye contact with the speaker to show interest and respect, yet this is considered rude to some Asian and Middle Eastern people, who are taught to show respect by looking down when a supervisor or older person is talking to them.

Even the common handshake communicates different meaning across cultures. Canadians tend to appreciate a firm handshake as a sign of strength and warmth in a friendship or business relationship. In contrast, many Asians and Middle Easterners favour a loose grip and regard a firm clench as aggressive. Germans prefer one good handshake stroke, whereas anything less than five or six strokes may symbolize a lack of trust in Spain. If this isn't confusing enough, people from some cultures view any touching in public, including handshakes, as a sign of rudeness.

Silence and conversational overlaps

People from different cultures must also learn to correctly interpret and tolerate different lengths of silence and conversational overlap. In Japan, people tend to remain silent for a few seconds after someone has spoken, as a sign of respect, to contemplate what has just been said.[75] To them, silence is an important part of communication (called *haragei*) because it preserves harmony and is more reliable than talk. Silence is shared by everyone and belongs to no one, so it becomes the ultimate form of interdependence. Moreover, Japanese people value empathy, which can only be demonstrated by understanding others without using words. In contrast, Canadians view silence as a lack of communication and often interpret long breaks as a sign of disagreement.

Conversational overlaps — when two or more people speak at the same time — are considered rude in Canada, but are the cultural norm in Brazil and other Latin American countries. Canadians usually stop talking when they are interrupted, whereas Brazilians typically continue talking over the other's speech. Perspective 8.4 describes how one Coca-Cola executive discovered cultural differences in conversational overlap during his assignment in Puerto Rico.

Gender Differences in Communication

When Monica McCandless became a vice-president at Campbell Soup Co. Ltd. in Toronto, she noticed that male colleagues were asserting their power and status in the executive meetings. Campbell Soup's CEO called it "normal male rutting behaviour," but McCandless pointed out that this behaviour wasn't helping social relations or teamwork among executive members.[76]

McCandless's observations reveal communication differences between men and women in organizational settings. Some research shows that men tend to view

PERSPECTIVE 8.4

Coca-Cola Executive Learns That Noise to Some Is Music to Others

George Gourlay, a senior executive at the Coca-Cola Company, recalls a meeting in Puerto Rico, attended mostly by Puerto Ricans, in which everyone seemed to be speaking at once. This seemingly incoherent babble made Gourlay uncomfortable and confused, so he used his managerial prerogative to force order in the meeting. Gourlay thought the meeting was now going well, until he noticed that the others appeared uncomfortable.

By coincidence, Gourlay took a course over the next three days in Puerto Rican culture. During the training program, the Coca-Cola manager learned that the noisy exchange with conversational overlaps in the earlier meet-

ing was the natural way for Puerto Ricans and other Hispanics to communicate. It is normal for them to start talking while the other person is still speaking. Three or four people might talk at the same time, creating a noisy discourse to the uninitiated. By contrast, people from Germany, Canada, and a few other countries prefer a more orderly communication exchange, in which it is impolite to speak until the other person has finished speaking.

With this knowledge in hand, Gourlay decided to adapt his style during his meetings in Puerto Rico. "I am still uncomfortable, but meetings are more productive," he admits.

Source: Based on G. Gourlay, "Quality's Cultural Foundation," in *Making Total Quality Happen*, ed. F. Caropreso (New York: Conference Board, 1990), pp. 71–74.

conversations as negotiations of relative status and power.[77] Men assert their power by giving advice to others' problems and using direct statements such as "You should do the following." They interrupt women far more often than vice versa. Moreover, in conversations between men and women, men dominate the talk time. Men are reluctant to seek advice from others because this threatens their status. For example, some men will drive around for nearly an hour looking for a location rather than stop to ask for directions.

Men tend to engage in "report talk," in which the primary function of the conversation is impersonal and efficient information exchange. Women also engage in report talk, particularly when conversing with men. But conversations among women tend to have a higher incidence of relationship building through "rapport talk." Women's preference for building rapport rather than asserting status is also apparent when giving advice. Women might say, "Have you considered . . . ?" or some other indirect approach that doesn't assert their superiority. Similarly, women apologize more often and seek advice from others more quickly than do men. Finally, research confirms that women are more sensitive than men to nonverbal cues in face-to-face meetings.[78]

After reading some popular-press books, you would think that men and women come from different planets (Mars and Venus, respectively) and require United Nations translators![79] This is not so. Men and women mostly overlap in their communication styles. Some men are very passive conversationalists, and some women are aggressive. Moreover, we know that women (and, to a less extent, men) vary their communication styles with the situation.

Both men and women usually understand each other, but there are irritants. For instance, Monica McCandless felt uncomfortable with the "male rutting behaviour" at executive meetings. Female scientists in Canada have similarly complained that adversarial interaction among male scientists makes it difficult for women to participate in meaningful dialogue.[80]

Another irritant occurs when women seek empathy but receive male dominance in response. Specifically, women sometimes discuss their personal experiences and problems to develop closeness with the receiver. They look for expressions of understanding, such as "That's the way I felt when it happened to me." But when men hear problems, they quickly suggest solutions because this asserts their control over the situation. Not only does this frustrate a woman's need for common understanding, but the advice actually says: "You and I are different; you have the problem and I have the answer." Meanwhile, men become frustrated because they can't understand why women don't appreciate their advice.

Improving Interpersonal Communication

Effective interpersonal communication depends on the sender's ability to get the message across and the receiver's performance as an active listener. In this section, we outline these two essential features of effective interpersonal communication.

Getting Your Message Across

This chapter began with the statement that effective communication occurs when the other person receives and understands the message. To accomplish this difficult task, the sender must learn to empathize with the receiver, repeat the message, choose an appropriate time for the conversation, and be descriptive rather than evaluative.

- *Empathize*   Put yourself in the receiver's shoes when encoding the message. For instance, be sensitive to words that may be ambiguous or trigger the wrong emotional response.

- *Repeat the message*   Rephrase the key points a couple of times. The saying "Tell them what you're going to tell them; tell them; then tell them what you've told them" reflects this need for redundancy.

- *Use timing effectively*   Your message competes with other messages and "noise," so find a time when the receiver is less likely to be distracted by these other matters.

- *Be descriptive*   Focus on the problem, not the person, if you have negative information to convey. People stop listening when the information attacks their self-esteem. Also, suggest things the listener can do to improve, rather than point to him or her as a problem.

Active Listening

Listening is at least as important as talking. As one sage wisely wrote: "Nature gave people two ears but only one tongue, which is a gentle hint that they should listen more than they talk."[81] But listening is more than just being quiet; it is an active process that requires more effort than most people realize. The main elements of active listening are illustrated in Exhibit 8.6. Please remember that these guidelines apply to Canadian society and might be contrary to communication norms in some other cultures.[82]

One of the most important features of active listening is to avoid interrupting the speaker. Give the other person an opportunity to complete the message, and allow a brief pause before responding. While listening, try to empathize with the speaker so that you decode the verbal and nonverbal cues from the other person's point of view. As with any behaviour, active listening requires motivation. Try to maintain interest by taking the view — probably an accurate one — that there is always something of value in a conversation. Also, postpone your evaluation of the message until the speaker has finished.

Listeners process information three times faster than the average rate of speech, so active listening involves concentrating on what the speaker is saying and regularly organizing the information into key points. It is also important to motivate the

EXHIBIT 8.6: Elements of Active Listening

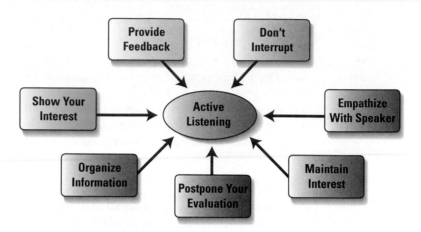

speaker by showing your interest in the conversation. This feedback is communicated through eye contact and back-channel signals such as "Oh, really!" and "I see" during appropriate breaks in the conversation. Finally, active listeners provide feedback by rephrasing the speaker's ideas at appropriate breaks ("So you're saying that . . . ?"). This further demonstrates your interest in the conversation and helps the speaker determine whether you understand the message.

Persuasive Communication: From Understanding to Acceptance

Persuasive communication The process of having listeners accept rather than just understand the sender's message.

This chapter has focused on how to get people to receive and understand messages. However, we usually want others to *accept* our information, not just *understand* it. People understand your message when they perceive the same meaning that you intended. They accept your message when it becomes part of their belief system and changes their opinions. The elements of **persuasive communication** include characteristics of the communicator, message content, communication medium, and the audience being persuaded.[83]

Communicator Characteristics

What makes one person more persuasive than another? One important factor is the communicator's perceived expertise on the topic. In this regard, listeners mainly consider the speaker's credentials and experience, but speech pattern also influences perceived expertise. Specifically, people seem to have expertise when they talk confidently and relatively quickly, use some technical language, and avoid pauses ("um," "uh") and hedges ("you know," "I guess").[84]

Communicators are more persuasive if they are trustworthy. Thus, employees are more likely to accept a new policy if it is communicated and supported by a respected peer. Trustworthiness also exists when communicators do not seem to profit from the persuasion attempt and state a few points against their position. For example, the effective persuader will acknowledge that an opposing position has one or two positive elements.

Finally, people who are physically attractive or similar to us tend to be more persuasive because we tend to think they have expertise and trustworthiness.[85]

Message Content

We are persuaded more by the communicator's characteristics when we don't consider the issue extremely important. When the issue is important, however, the message content becomes the critical feature of persuasive communication. The best strategy is to present all sides of the argument. Begin by introducing facts sympathetic to the audience's viewpoint, then shift into the theme of your position. Discussing only one point of view reduces your perceived trustworthiness and gives listeners the feeling of being cornered. When this happens, they react by rejecting your information.[86]

Your message should be limited to a few strong arguments, because listeners are more likely to remember these points. These arguments should be repeated a couple of times, but not to the extent that you are battering listeners over the head with them.[87]

Is it better to be logical or emotional when communicating information? The general conclusion is that people are more strongly persuaded by emotional appeals if they are accompanied by specific recommendations to overcome the threat. In a safety campaign, for example, employees are more persuaded by graphic pictures of accident victims than by a lecture on recent accident statistics, but only if they are given explicit steps to avoid the danger.[88]

Inoculation effect A persuasive communication strategy of warning listeners that others will try to influence them in the future and that they should be wary about the opponent's arguments.

Finally, persuasive communicators use the **inoculation effect** to ensure that listeners are not influenced by other points of view. This involves warning listeners that others will try to influence them in the future and that they should be wary about the opponent's arguments. This inoculation causes listeners to generate counterarguments to the anticipated persuasion attempts. For instance, a coalition that wants the company to purchase new production equipment might warn senior management about arguments the finance department will use to try to convince them otherwise. This tends to make the finance department's subsequent persuasion attempts less effective.

Communication Medium

Earlier in this chapter we recommended using two-way verbal communication to persuade or motivate the listener. The personal nature of this medium seems to increase the credibility of the information. Furthermore, it is easier for the sender to determine whether the persuasive message is having the desired effect. Two-way communication also increases the receiver's active participation in the process. As long as this participation does not involve presenting defensive statements, the receiver is more likely to be involved in the conversation and to internalize some of the information presented.

Persuasion may require written documentation, however, when dealing with technical issues. Whenever written communication is necessary for this purpose, it should be combined with direct discussions for the greatest persuasive effect. The verbal exchange could repeat highlights of the report and provide graphic images for the listener, thereby adding emotional appeal to an otherwise logical message.

Audience Characteristics

Not everyone is equally persuaded by the strategies and conditions described above. For example, it is more difficult to persuade people who have high self-esteem.[89] And, as mentioned, it is very difficult to persuade those who have been inoculated against your persuasive intent.

Chapter Summary

- Communication coordinates work activities, aids decision making, and fulfils relatedness needs. The communication process involves forming, encoding, and transmitting the intended message to a receiver, who then decodes the message and provides feedback to the sender. Effective communication occurs when the sender's thoughts are transmitted to and understood by the intended receiver.

- Common barriers to effective communication include perceptions, filtering, language, and information overload.

- Communication channels are either verbal or nonverbal. Electronic mail (e-mail) and other computer-mediated communication methods have dramatically altered communication in organizations, and have created new problems. Nonverbal communication transmits more information than verbal communication in face-to-face conversations, and is an important part of emotional labour and emotional contagion.

- The most appropriate communication medium depends on its data-carrying capacity (media richness) and its symbolic meaning to the receiver. Nonroutine and ambiguous situations require rich media.

- To facilitate communication flow, many organizations rely on employee surveys, downward news vehicles, and visible-leadership practices. Some firms have redesigned workspaces and create nonterritorial offices to improve communication flow. In any organization, employees rely on the grapevine, particularly during times of uncertainty.

- We need to be aware of cross-cultural and gender differences in communication. Voice intonation, silence, and other nonverbal cues have different meaning and importance in different cultures. Some writers have exaggerated communication differences between men and women, but there are a few gender distinctions that create irritants.

- Effective interpersonal communication depends on the sender's ability to get the message across and the receiver's performance as an active listener. Persuasive communication attempts to have listeners accept rather than just understand the message.

Discussion Questions

1. A Canadian city intends to introduce e-mail for office staff at its three buildings located throughout the city. Describe two benefits that the city will likely experience from this medium, as well as two potential problems that it may face.

2. Under what conditions is ambiguity good in the communication process? Under what conditions is it bad?

3. Marshall McLuhan coined the popular phrase "The medium is the message." What does this phrase mean, and why should we be aware of it when communicating in organizations?

4. What channel of communication does emotional contagion mainly rely on?

5. Should companies try to eliminate grapevine communication? Explain your answer.

6. The Bank of Western Ontario (BWO) has just moved into one of the tallest skyscrapers in downtown Toronto. Senior management is proud of its decision,

because each department is neatly located on its own floor with plenty of closed offices. BWO executives have a breathtaking view from their offices on the top floor. There is even a large BWO branch at street level. Unfortunately, other tenants occupy some floors between those leased by BWO. Discuss the potential effects of this physical structure on communication at BWO.

7. Explain why men and women are sometimes frustrated with each other's communication behaviours.

8. This chapter makes several distinctions between communication in Japan and Canada. Discuss three distinctions between communication in these two cultures.

Chapter Case

Sea Pines

The coastal town of Sea Pines, Nova Scotia, retained a Toronto consulting engineer to study the effect of greatly expanding the town's sewage system and discharging the treated waste into the harbour. At that time, fishermen in the town were experiencing massive lobster kills in the harbour and were concerned that the kills were caused by the effluent from the present Sea Pines sewage treatment plant. They were convinced that any expansion of the plant would further aggravate the problem. The fishermen invited Tom Stone, the engineer, to the monthly meeting of the local fishermen's organization to discuss their concerns. On the night of the meeting, the Legion Hall was filled with men in blue jeans and work jackets, many of whom were drinking beer. An account of this meeting follows, with Fred Mitchell, a local fisherman, speaking first.

Mitchell: Well, as you all know, Mr. Stone has been kind enough to meet with us tonight to explain his recommendations concerning the town's sewage-disposal problem. We're all concerned about the lobster kills, like the one last summer, and I for one don't want to see any more sewage dumped into that harbour. [Murmurs of assent are heard throughout the hall.] So, Mr. Stone, we'd like to hear from you on what it is you want to do.

Stone: Thank you. I'm glad to get this opportunity to hear your concerns on the lobster situation. Let me say from the outset that we are still studying the problem closely and expect to make our formal recommendation to the town about a month from

now. I am not prepared to discuss specific conclusions of our study, but I am prepared to incorporate any relevant comments into our study. As most of you are probably aware, we are attempting to model mathematically, or simulate, conditions in the harbour to help us predict the effects of sewage effluent in the harbour. We . . .

Mitchell: Now wait a minute. I don't know anything about models except the kind I used to make as a kid. [Laughter.] I can tell you that we never had lobster kills like we have now until they started dumping that sewage into the harbour a few years back. I don't need any model to tell me that. It seems to me that common sense tells you that if we've got troubles now in the summer with the lobster, increasing the amount of sewage by 10 times the present amount is going to cause 10 times the problem.

A Fisherman: Yeah, you don't need to be an engineer to see that.

Stone: Although it's true that we're proposing to extend the sewage system in town, and that the resulting sewage flow will be about 10 times the present flow, the area of the sewage discharge will be moved to a larger area of the harbour, where it will be diluted with much more sea water than is the present area. In addition, if the harbour is selected for the new discharge, we will design a special diffuser to mix the treated sewage effluent quickly with ocean water. As I indicated, we are attempting to use data on currents and water quality that we collected in the harbour and combine it with some mathematical equations in our computer to help us predict what the quality in the harbour will be.

Mitchell: I don't understand what you need a computer to tell you that for. I've been fishing in this area for over 35 years now, and I don't need any computer to tell me that my lobsters are going to die if that sewage goes into the harbour.

Stone: Let me say before this goes too far that we're not talking about discharging raw sewage into the harbour. The sewage is treated and disinfected before it is discharged.

Mitchell: Isn't the sewage that's being dumped into the harbour right now being treated and disinfected, Mr. Stone?

Stone: Yes, it is, but . . .

Mitchell: The lobsters still die, so it's clear to me that "treated and disinfected" doesn't solve the problem.

Stone: Our model will predict whether the treatment provided will be sufficient to maintain the water quality in the harbour at the province's standard for the harbour.

Mitchell: I don't give a damn about any provincial standard. I just care about my lobsters and how I'm going to put bread on the table for my kids! You engineers from Toronto can come out here spouting all kinds of things about models, data, standards, and your concern for lobsters, but what it really comes down to is that it's just another job. You can collect your fees for your study, go back to your office, and leave us holding the bag.

Stone: Now wait a minute, Mr. Mitchell. My firm is well established in Canada, and we didn't get that way by giving our clients that fast shuffle and making a quick exit out of town. We have no intention of leaving you with an unworkable solution to your sewage problem. We also will not solve your sewage problem and leave you with a lobster-kill problem. Perhaps I have given you the wrong impression about this modelling. We regard this as one method of analysis that may be helpful in predicting future harbour conditions, but not the only method. We have over 40 years' experience in these harbour studies, and we fully intend to use this experience, *in addition* to whatever the model tells us, to come up with a reasonable solution.

Mitchell: Well, that's all well and good, but I can tell you, and I think I speak for all the lobstermen here, that if you recommend dumping that sewage into the harbour, we'll fight you all the way down the line! [Shouts of agreement.] Why can't you pipe the sewage out to the ocean if you're so concerned about dilution? I'm sure that your model will tell you there's enough dilution out there.

Stone: I agree that the ocean will certainly provide sufficient dilution, but the whole purpose of this study is to see if we can avoid a deep ocean outfall.

Mitchell: Why?

Stone: Because the cost of constructing a deep ocean outfall in this area is very expensive — say about $500 per metre. Now, if the length of the outfall is 2,000 metres, don't you think that it makes good sense to spend a few thousand dollars studying the harbour area if we can save you millions?

Mitchell: All that money that you're going to save the town doesn't do much for the lobster trappers who'll be put out of business if that sewage goes into the harbour.

Stone: As I said, we wouldn't recommend that if we thought, based on our modelling and our experience in this area, that the quality of water in the harbour would kill any lobster or any other aquatic life.

Mitchell: Well, I'm telling you again, if you try to put that stuff in our harbour, we'll fight you all the way. I think we've made our position clear on this thing, so if there are no further comments, I vote that we adjourn the meeting. [Seconded.]

When the meeting ended, the fishermen filed out, talking heatedly among themselves, leaving Mr. Stone standing on the platform.

Discussion Questions

1. What symptoms exist in this case to suggest that something has gone wrong?

2. What are the root causes that have led to these symptoms?

3. What actions should Stone and his firm take to correct these problems?

Source: This case was written by Terence P. Driscoll.

Experiential Exercise #1

Cross-Cultural Communication: A Not-So-Trivial Trivia Game

Purpose: This exercise is designed to develop and test your knowledge of cross-cultural differences in communication and etiquette.

Instructions: Each student chooses or is assigned a partner. Each pair of students is then matched with another pair. The instructor will hand each group of four people a stack of cards with the multiple-choice questions face down. These cards contain questions and answers about cross-cultural differences in communication and etiquette. No books or other aids are allowed.

The exercise begins with a member of Team 1 picking up one card from the top of the pile and asking the question on that card to both people on Team 2. The information given to Team 2 includes the question and all alternatives listed on the card. Team 2 has 30 seconds to answer and earns one point if the correct answer is given. If Team 2's answer is incorrect, however, Team 1 earns that point. (Correct answers to each question are indicated on the card and, of course, should not be revealed until the question is correctly answered or time is up.)

Next, one member from Team 2 picks up the next card on the pile and asks it to both members of Team 1. This procedure is repeated until all of the cards have been read or time has elapsed. The team receiving the most points wins the experiential exercise.

Note: The textbook provides very little information pertaining to the questions in this exercise. Rather, you must rely on past learning, logic, and luck to win.

Experiential Exercise #2

Communication, Feedback, and the Manager Exercise

Purpose: The purpose of this exercise is to demonstrate the effect of feedback on the communication process.

Instructions for Part One: This exercise comprises two parts. In Part One, the instructor or a student from the class will read aloud a set of instructions. You are asked to follow these instructions by drawing a specific configuration of objects on a piece of blank paper.

You are not allowed to ask questions or talk to others while completing this task. The reader will not stop reading or repeat any information. This is the so-called "easy task."

After instructions have been read, you will be asked to *predict* how many objects in your drawing are oriented correctly. Next, you will be shown the correct results and asked to report how many objects *actually* are oriented correctly. Write this information in the "Results" exhibit below. The instructor will solicit your reactions and comments.

Instructions for Part Two: In Part 2 of this exercise, the instructor or a student will read a set of instructions to the class. You are asked to follow these instructions by drawing a specific configuration of objects on a piece of blank paper.

In addition, a volunteer from the class will draw his or her objects on the blackboard, flip chart, or other means that will be displayed to the class. This student can ask any questions to the person reading the instructions, and the reader of the instructions is required to answer these questions. No one else is allowed to ask or answer questions.

After the instructions have been read, you will be asked to *predict* how many objects in your drawing are oriented correctly. Next, you will be shown the correct results and asked to report how many objects *actually* are oriented correctly. Write this information in the results table below. The instructor will solicit your reactions and comments.

RESULTS TABLE

Part 1 Results	Information	Part 2 Results
	Reading Time	
	Objects Predicted Correct	
	Objects Actually Correct	
	Student Comments	
	Presenter Comments	

Source: This exercise was developed by Michael Piczak, and is reproduced here with his permission. Credit is also given to McMaster University and Mohawk College.

Practice Session For Part 3

The true-false, multiple-choice, and written-answer questions presented here are based on information in Part 3 of this book (Chapters 6 to 8). These questions can help test your knowledge of material in these chapters. If your instructor uses the test bank for this textbook, these questions also give you an opportunity to practise for examinations in this course. The answers to these questions are found in Appendix C.

True-False

1. T F   According to social identity theory, people simplify perceptions by thinking that people within their group share common traits.

2. T F   The halo effect refers to our tendency to believe that positive events are caused by our own motivation or ability, whereas negative events are caused by circumstances or other people.

3. T F   Job satisfaction is a collection of attitudes about specific facets of the job.

4. T F   Power distance is the extent that people accept unequal distribution of power in a society.

5. T F   Emotional contagion provides continuous feedback to the speaker in a conversation, thereby communicating that the listener understands and empathizes with the speaker.

6. T F   Media richness refers to the cost and convenience of using a particular communication medium relative to others.

Multiple-Choice

1. Stereotyping is an extension of: (a) perceptual defence; (b) attribution theory; (c) social identity theory; (d) Johari Window; (e) projection. *perc. group > simp > "making" sense*

2. Which of the following is an example of perceptual organization and interpretation? (a) You recognize that a problem exists with the production process because the warning light flashes; (b) You believe that the older man wearing the suit is the store manager; (c) The employment interviewer notices from the résumé that an applicant was raised in the same town as the interviewer; (d) all of the above; (e) none of the above.

3. Emotions are _____, whereas attitudes are _____. (a) experienced feelings, judgments; (b) perceptions, values; (c) fictitious, real; (d) thoughts, behavioural tendencies; (e) real, fictitious.

4. Which of the following actions is most likely to increase continuance commitment? (a) Keep employees informed of organizational events; (b) Offer employees large stock options that pay out only after a long period of service; (c) Involve employees in organizational decisions; (d) Ensure that the employee's psychological contract is not violated; (e) Demonstrate that management trusts its employees.

5. Electronic mail tends to: (a) reduce the likelihood of information overload; (b) reduce the risk of sending emotionally charged messages to other people; (c) increase the likelihood that the receiver will correctly interpret the emotional meaning of the sender's message; (d) transmit messages faster than traditional written media; (e) do all of the above.

6. Reading summaries of large reports rather than the entire document reduces information overload by: (a) increasing information processing capacity; (b) increasing information load; (c) reducing information processing capacity; (d) reducing information load; (e) doing both a and d.

Written-Answer Questions

1. You have been asked to hire several customer service representatives for a financial institution, and senior management is keen on employing people with high levels of emotional intelligence. Describe this concept and discuss the ways that you might identify in an employment interview people with high emotional intelligence.

2. Discuss the effect of actor-observer on the perceptions of co-workers who see an employee show up late for work.

PART 4

Team Processes

CHAPTER 9
Team Dynamics

CHAPTER 10
Employee Involvement and Quality Management

CHAPTER 11
Decision Making in Organizations

CHAPTER 12
Organizational Power and Politics

CHAPTER 13
Organizational Conflict and Negotiation

CHAPTER 14
Organizational Leadership

CHAPTER 9

Team Dynamics

CHAPTER OUTLINE

What Are Teams?

A Model of Team Dynamics and Effectiveness

Team Context and Design

Team Development

Team Norms

Team Cohesiveness

The Trouble With Teams

Team Building

Chapter Summary

Discussion Questions

LEARNING OBJECTIVES

After reading this chapter, you should be able to:

- Distinguish departmental teams from team-based organizations.

- Explain why virtual teams are becoming more common.

- Outline the model of team dynamics and effectiveness.

- Describe the five stages of team development.

- Identify four factors that shape team norms.

- List six factors that influence team cohesiveness.

- Explain how companies minimize social loafing.

- Summarize the four types of team building.

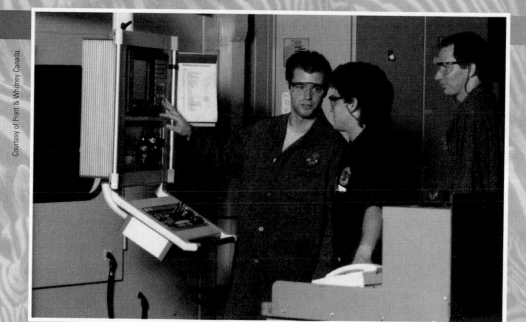

Pratt & Whitney Canada's Halifax plant is a leading example of the emerging team-based organization. "The Halifax plant is absolutely unique," says plant general manager Peter Wressell.

In the 1980s, Pratt & Whitney Canada (P&W) set out to build a utopian plant, one that would be entirely team-based and run mainly by employees. The few managers at the site would set goals and facilitate the team. This ideal concept took shape in a wooded area near Halifax airport, and is now the centrepiece of P&W's thrust toward the use of teams throughout the organization.

"The Halifax plant is absolutely unique," says the plant's general manager Peter Wressell. The facility has no middle managers, no supervisors, no executive washrooms, no executive parking spaces, and no fancy job titles. Instead, a team of six managers sets overall plant objectives, and self-directed work teams decide how best to meet them.

The 450 employees are assigned to teams that are almost completely responsible for manufacturing turbine blades and related aircraft-engine parts. For example, one team saved the company $750,000 when it bought a special machine from a surplus list in the United States and rebuilt it for use at the Halifax facility. Special task forces are also established at the Halifax plant to review plant rules and evaluate job applicants.

The team-based organization is still a new concept for many employees, and the change has required a period of adjustment. Says one Pratt & Whitney veteran of 35 years: "I knew about this idea and the way this plant would be set up before I came to Halifax, but it still took some time for me to get used to it." Still, the movement to teams has made P&W's Halifax plant a world leader. Together with extensive use of robotics technology, team practices have dramatically improved operating efficiency, job satisfaction, and admiration from others in the industry.[1]

T eams are replacing individuals as the basic building blocks of organizations. Companies are discovering that teams potentially make more creative and informed decisions and coordinate work without the need for close supervision. When Asea Brown Boveri Canada (ABB) moved its distribution switchgear division to a new building in Milton, Ontario, employees were placed into autonomous teams responsible for different work processes in the plant. At Vancouver City Savings Credit Union, special peer-learning teams meet regularly to help each other develop skills for the future. And at Nova Scotia Power Inc., employees participated in several cross-functional teams that radically re-engineered the organization.[2]

This chapter looks at the dynamics and effectiveness of formal work teams as well as informal groups in organizations. We begin by introducing the different types of teams in organizational settings, and then outlining a basic model of team dynamics and effectiveness. Most of the chapter examines each part of this model, including team context and design, team development, norms, and cohesiveness. The chapter concludes by surveying the strategies to build more effective work teams.

What Are Teams?

Team Two or more people who interact and mutually influence each other to achieve common goals.

Teams (as well as informal groups) consist of two or more people who interact and mutually influence each other to achieve common goals.[3] A team may comprise only two people or it may comprise hundreds, although a large team has more difficulty maintaining meaningful interaction among its members. All groups require some form of communication so that members can coordinate and share common meaning.

All groups exist to fulfil some purpose. Members of formal work teams might share the common goal of assembling a product, providing a service, or making an important decision. An informal group might exist so that its members can enjoy each other's company. In every type of group, members are dependent on each other because their goals require collaboration with others. Finally, group members influence each other so that their effort is directed toward the group's objectives. Everyone on the team has influence, although some members are typically more powerful than others.

Formal Work Teams

Formal work teams are responsible for a specific set of tasks in the organization. Departments may represent formal teams, although this is not always so.[4] Departments lack a team structure when employees work alone and report individually to the immediate supervisor. This individualistic department structure is illustrated in Exhibit 9.1(a). Not long ago, Honeywell Ltd.'s plant in Scarborough, Ontario, had this departmental structure. Employees were expected to take directions from the supervisor and do their work without talking to co-workers.[5]

A department becomes a formal work team when employees are encouraged to interact directly and coordinate work activities with each other, as we can see in Exhibit 9.1(b). The supervisor still serves as central coordinator and conduit to higher levels in the organization, but employees share information to get the work done.

EXHIBIT 9.1: Formal Work Teams

(a) Individual-Oriented Department

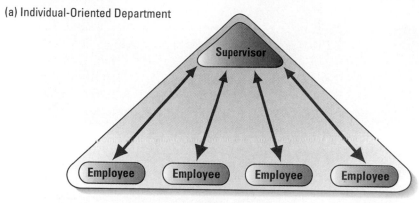

Department A

(b) Team-Oriented Department

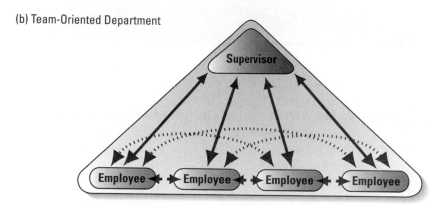

Department A

(c) Team-Based Organization

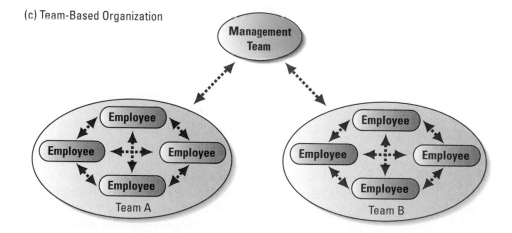

Courtesy of GE Canada.

GE Canada's Bromont, Quebec, plant includes a senior management team, an "A" team of support people, and eight "B" teams. Each production team has almost complete responsibility for a specific production process.

Team-based organizations

Team-based structure A type of departmentation with a flat span of control and relatively little formalization, consisting of self-directed work teams responsible for various work processes.

Self-directed work team (SDWT) A work group that completes an entire piece of work requiring several interdependent tasks and has substantial autonomy over the execution of these tasks.

As illustrated in Exhibit 9.1(c), a **team-based organization** relies on **self-directed work teams (SDWTs)** rather than functional departments as the core work units.[6] SDWTs (also known as *self-managing work teams*) are described more fully in the next chapter because they represent the highest level of employee involvement. SDWTs are highly autonomous work units. Almost all day-to-day decisions are made by team members rather than by someone further up the organizational hierarchy.

Team-based organizations typically form teams around work processes rather than functional departments. Teams are responsible for developing, producing, or maintaining an entire product or service, whereas traditional departmental teams provide one skill (e.g., painting, purchasing, maintenance) for the product or service. Another feature of team-based organizations is that the supervisory role is almost completely delegated to the team by having members take turns as the coordinator. The teams are fairly autonomous, as indicated by the dashed lines in Exhibit 9.1(c), so there is less need for someone to report continuously to management. We will look more closely at this emerging team-based structure in Chapter 18.

Pratt & Whitney's Halifax plant, which was described in the opening story, operates as a team-based organization. So does GE Canada's jet engine plant in Bromont, Quebec. The Bromont plant consists of a small senior management team, an "A" team of support people, and eight "B" teams (a maintenance team, a tooling team, a warehouse team, and five production teams). Each production team has approximately 80 people who are continuously responsible for a specific production process. This includes maintaining production schedules, setting employee schedules, undertaking training, maintaining product quality, hiring new employees, and coordinating with other teams. One member of each team is selected by the others to coordinate the team for six months.[7]

Cross-Functional Teams

Cross-functional teams are temporary or permanent groups that overlay a more permanent structure (usually functional departments).[8] Employees remain members of their units, but participate in the cross-functional team. *Task forces* are cross-functional teams that investigate a particular problem and disband when the solution or decision is made. For instance, Toronto's Sunnybrook Health Science Centre used a task force of nurses and other professionals to develop a new chart system for medical/surgical records.[9]

   Skunkworks are typically cross-functional teams formed spontaneously to develop products or solve complex problems. They are initiated by an innovative employee (a *champion*) who borrows people and resources (called *bootlegging*) to help the organization.[10] They are typically isolated from the rest of the organization and are able to ignore the more bureaucratic rules governing other organizational units. For example, Ford's popular Mustang was designed in the 1960s by a team of people that Lee Iacocca pulled together from design, marketing, and public relations. The group, called the Fairlane Committee, met regularly at a hotel of the same name rather than at Ford headquarters so that it could operate without corporate interference.[11]

Virtual teams

Information technology has dramatically altered the way people interact in organizational settings. Rather than visiting a co-worker's office on another floor of the building, you send an e-mail or call the person on the telephone. Many companies are now taking the next step by forming **virtual teams** — cross-functional teams that operate across space, time, and organizational boundaries with members who communicate mainly through electronic technologies.[12] Virtual teams are usually temporary task forces or product development groups, which explains why their members may be located in different cities or countries. Less often, these teams are formed from intact work units where some members switch to telework or are constantly in the field (such as salespeople).

   Virtual teams communicate through any number of media. E-mail seems to be the most common, although telephone conferences, computer-based videoconferences, electronic bulletin boards (e.g., Lotus Notes, FirstClass), and Intranet sites are increasingly used. Sun Microsystems has moved quickly toward virtual team projects. Perspective 9.1 describes one virtual team at Sun Microsystems that operated without a single face-to-face meeting of all its members, yet was able to accomplish a complex project in seven months.

   Why are virtual teams becoming more common? Like Sun Microsystems, many companies are now recognizing the potential benefits of having employees work together rather than alone, particularly on complex tasks and decisions. Second, by adopting the learning organization philosophy, corporate leaders are realizing that corporate assets are locked in the heads of their employees (Chapter 1). Forming virtual teams is a powerful way to leverage this intellectual capital.

   A third reason we will see more virtual teams in the future is that information technology has come closer to the "look and feel" of face-to-face communication. For example, Northrop Grumman recently introduced electronic communication

PERSPECTIVE 9.1

Virtual Teams at Sun Microsystems

Sun Microsystems did something unusual when it designed a new electronic customer-order system. The 15 project team members who created the system came from three different companies and three different countries, yet they completed the project in just seven months without ever meeting face-to-face. "We never had the entire team in the room at the same time," says Bill Crowley, one of the team's two co-leaders.

Sun Microsystems has leapt into the world of virtual teams. After Sun's corporate leaders discovered the power of teams at Motorola and Xerox, they encouraged employees to form cross-functional teams to solve problems and build better products. Teams were encouraged to use the Internet, videoconferencing, and other communication media so that anyone from anyplace could be involved.

The SunTeam that created the electronic customer-order system was as diverse and dispersed as a team can get. Bill Crowley and several other Sun employees at the company's Massachusetts business unit joined forces with co-workers from Japan, Holland, and the company's global headquarters in California. A representative from Motorola's operations in Texas provided a customer perspective, and Sun's major warehouse management supplier from Illinois was added to the group.

The Sun Microsystems team relied most heavily on e-mail, supplemented by weekly two-hour telephone conference calls. Videoconferencing was avoided because it was too structured for such a small group. However, the weekly telephone conferences kept everyone focused by establishing deadlines and goals for the following week. "Our strategy was that we did the work during the week outside the meeting and then came to the meeting prepared to talk about updates or problems," explained Crowley. "In retrospect, we realized that we had a formula for success."

Source: Adapted from J. Lipnack and J. Stamps, *Virtual Teams: Reaching Across Space, Time, and Organizations with Technology* (New York: John Wiley & Sons, 1997), pp. 11–13, 160–67.

systems that incorporate live videoconferencing, graphical interfaces, and three-dimensional engineering drawings. With these media, the Los Angeles–based aircraft manufacturer expects engineers at different sites to work together as virtual teams on product designs and manufacturing projects.[13]

Informal Groups

Informal group Two or more people who group together primarily to meet their personal (rather than organizational) needs.

Along with formal teams, organizations consist of **informal groups** that exist primarily for the benefit of their members.[14] Informal groups are not specifically formed by organizational decision makers, although their structure may be influenced by the existence of formal teams. They shape communication patterns in the organization, particularly the grapevine described in Chapter 8. Informal groups can also interfere with the formal team because members might resist their formal team's activities that conflict with the informal group's values.

Exhibit 9.2 illustrates how members of a formal team may belong to different informal groups. Some informal groups, such as the group you meet for lunch, might overlap with the formal team. These groups form out of convenience and the need for affiliation. Other groups are bound together for reasons other than social needs. For instance, you might belong to an informal group that shares a car pool and another group that plays together on the company's sports team.

Coalition An informal group that attempts to influence people outside the group by pooling the resources and power of its members.

A **coalition** is an informal group that attempts to influence people outside the group by pooling the resources and power of its members. By banding together, coalition members have more power than if each person worked alone to influence others.

EXHIBIT 9.2: Informal Groups in Organizations

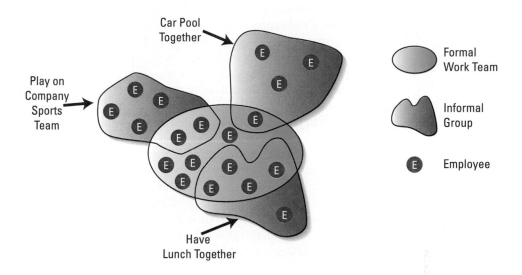

They also reinforce each other and further mobilize support for their position.[15] The coalition's mere existence can be a source of power by symbolizing the importance or level of support for the issue.

Why informal groups exist

Why do people join informal groups in organizational settings? One reason is that group membership fulfils relatedness needs (Chapter 3). We join friends for lunch or stop by their work areas for brief chats because this interaction fulfils this need. Similarly, as discussed in Chapter 6, we define ourselves by our group affiliations. If we belong to work teams or informal groups that are viewed favourably by others, we tend to view ourselves more favourably. We are motivated to become members of groups that are similar to ourselves because this reinforces our social identity.[16]

Some groups form because they accomplish tasks that cannot be achieved by individuals working alone. While this certainly explains why formal teams exist, it also explains the formation of coalitions and other task-oriented informal groups. When these groups are successful, it is easier to attract new members to the group. Lastly, informal groups tend to form in stressful situations because we are comforted by the physical presence of other people and are therefore motivated to be near them.[17] This explains why soldiers huddle together in battle, even though they are taught to disperse under fire. This also explains why employees tend to congregate when hearing the organization may be acquired or that some people may be laid off.

A Model of Team Dynamics and Effectiveness

What are the characteristics of effective teams? Why do some groups have a strong team spirit while other groups barely survive? These questions have interested organizational theorists for some time and, as you might expect, numerous models of team effectiveness have been proposed over the years.[18]

Team effectiveness The extent to which the team achieves its objectives, achieves the needs and objectives of its members, and sustains itself over time.

Team effectiveness refers to how the group affects the organization in which it exists, its individual members, and the group's existence.[19] First, most groups exist to serve some purpose relating to the organization or other system in which the group operates. Production teams at Pratt & Whitney's Halifax plant are given the challenge of continually improving the quality and efficiency of manufacturing aircraft turbines and other parts. Many informal groups also have task-oriented goals, such as a coalition that wants to persuade senior management to change a corporate policy.

Second, our definition of team effectiveness considers the satisfaction and well-being of its members. People join groups to fulfil their personal needs, so it makes sense that effectiveness is partly measured by this need fulfilment. Finally, team effectiveness refers to the group's ability to survive. It must be able to maintain the commitment of its members, particularly during the turbulence of the team's development. Without this commitment, people leave and the group will quickly fall apart.

Exhibit 9.3 presents the model of team dynamics that will be described over the next several pages. We begin by looking at the team's context and design, including the internal and external environment, the task that the team wants to accomplish, team size, and team composition. Next, we consider the team's structure and processes, including its development, norms, and cohesiveness.

Team Context and Design

Our discussion of team dynamics and effectiveness logically begins with the contextual factors that influence group structure and processes. These inputs include the organization's environment, task characteristics, team size, and team composition.

Organizational Environment

There are many environmental factors that influence team effectiveness. Teams are more effective when they have supportive leadership and organizational values, and receive sufficient resources to perform the work. External competition, resource availability, and physical layout of the work area also influence team dynamics, such as cohesiveness and coordination.

EXHIBIT 9.3: A Model of Team Dynamics

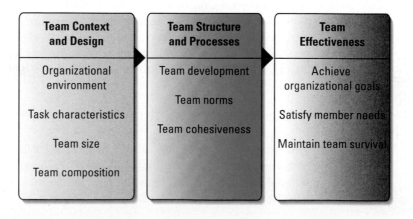

Team Context and Design	Team Structure and Processes	Team Effectiveness
Organizational environment	Team development	Achieve organizational goals
Task characteristics	Team norms	Satisfy member needs
Team size	Team cohesiveness	Maintain team survival
Team composition		

Reward systems must be realigned to be more consistent with team dynamics. One recent survey found that companies with the best team dynamics are more likely to have team-based rewards, merit increases partly determined by the individual's team contribution, and 360-degree feedback systems (Chapter 2).[20] Team members can still receive some pay based on their individual performance, but team-based rewards support the interdependence of effective teams.

Communication systems are becoming an important factor in team success.[21] This is particularly true for virtual teams, because their existence depends on information technologies to keep team members linked together. An inappropriate configuration of communication systems may bog down a virtual team's progress, or result in information overload. The key is to fit the communication system with the type of team that will be using it. Telephone conferences worked well for Sun Microsystem's order-system development team, described earlier. On the other hand, videoconferences and electronic chalkboards may have been too cumbersome.

Task Characteristics

Teams are generally more effective when tasks are clear and easy to implement, because team members can learn their roles more quickly.[22] In contrast, teams with ill-defined tasks require more time to agree on the best division of labour and the correct way to accomplish the goal. These are typically more complex tasks requiring diverse skills and backgrounds, which further strain the team's ability to develop and form a cohesive unit.

Another important task characteristic is **task interdependence**. High task interdependence exists when team members must share common inputs to their individual tasks, need to interact in the process of executing their work, or receive outcomes (such as rewards) that are partly determined by the performance of others.[23] Teams are well suited to highly interdependent tasks because people coordinate better as teams than

Task interdependence
The degree to which the task requires collective action. High task interdependence exists when team members must share inputs or outcomes, or need to interact while executing their work.

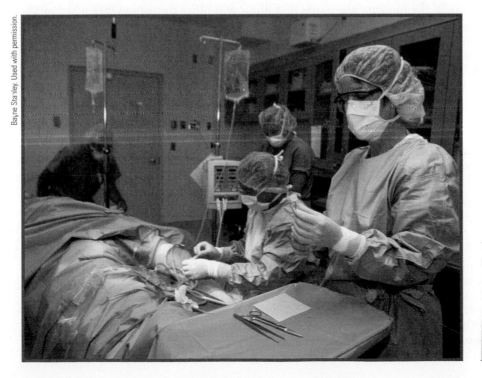

This surgical team in a Vancouver hospital has a high degree of task interdependence. Each team member's performance, and the overall success of the operation, depends on the performance of other team members.

when they work separately. This is why Sun Microsystems has encouraged employees to form teams when creating new products or services (such as the on-line ordering system described earlier). The design, marketing, and technical elements of the project are highly interdependent, so a cross-functional team coordinates the work more efficiently than individuals working in separate functional departments.

Team Size

What is the best size for a work team or informal group? Some say the optimal number is five people, give or take one or two. Others suggest an upper limit of 20 team members. The general rule is that teams should be large enough to provide the necessary competencies and perspectives to perform the work, yet small enough to maintain efficient coordination and the meaningful involvement of each member.[24]

Larger teams are typically less effective because members consume more time and effort coordinating their roles and resolving differences. Individuals have less opportunity to participate and, consequently, are less likely to feel that they are contributing to the team's success. Larger work units tend to break into informal subgroups around common interests and work activities, leading members to form stronger commitments to their subgroup than to the larger team. For instance, although GE Canada's Bromont plant has teams of 80 people, each team would have several informal groups based on common interests or work hours.

Team Composition

When Pfizer, Inc. tried to get everyone working in teams, some employees weren't too eager. Many were near retirement and had always worked by themselves. One burly operator in his fifties said to a Pfizer team trainer: "Look, lady, we barely tolerate each other here. You're out of your mind if you think you're going to get us to work in these teams you're talking about."[25]

One of the fundamental issues that Pfizer and other companies face when establishing teams is whether employees possess the necessary motivation *and* competencies to work together. On the first point, every member must be motivated to perform the task in a team environment. Specifically, team members must be motivated to agree on their goals, work together rather than alone, and abide by the team's rules of conduct. Employees with a collectivist orientation — those who value group goals more than their own personal goals (Chapter 7) — tend to perform better in work teams, whereas those with a strong individualist orientation tend to perform better alone. For this reason, Shell Canada, Anchor Hocking, and other companies are more carefully selecting job applicants with the motivation and ability to work in teams.[26]

The second point is that employees must possess the skills and knowledge necessary to accomplish the team's objectives.[27] Each person needs only to possess some of the necessary skills, but the entire group must have the full set of competencies. Moreover, each team member's competencies need to be known to other team members. At Digital Equipment Corporation, one team took the time and effort to develop a skills inventory. This inventory helped everyone to know who had expertise about specific issues. By generating an understanding of each member's knowledge, the team was able to increase revenue by 56 percent within four months.[28]

Team diversity

Homogeneous teams
Formal or informal groups whose members have similar technical expertise, ethnicity, experiences, or values.

Another issue to consider in team composition is the diversity of its members.[29] **Homogeneous teams** include members with common technical expertise, ethnicity,

Heterogeneous teams
Formal or informal groups whose members have diverse personal characteristics and backgrounds.

experiences, or values, whereas **heterogeneous teams** have members with diverse personal characteristics and backgrounds. Employees experience higher satisfaction, less conflict, and better interpersonal relations when their team members have similar backgrounds. Consequently, homogeneous teams tend to be more effective on tasks requiring a high degree of cooperation and coordination, such as emergency-response teams or string quartets.[30]

Heterogeneous teams experience more interpersonal conflict and take longer to develop, but they are generally more effective than homogeneous teams on complex projects and problems requiring innovative solutions.[31] This is because people from different backgrounds see a problem or opportunity from different perspectives. Heterogeneous team members also solve complex problems more easily because they usually have a broader knowledge base. Finally, a team's diversity may give it more legitimacy or allow its members to obtain a wide network of cooperation and support in the organization.

Team Development

Team members must resolve several issues and pass through several stages of development before emerging as an effective work unit. They must get to know each other, understand their respective roles, discover appropriate and inappropriate behaviours, and learn how to coordinate their work or social activities. This is an ongoing process because teams change as new members join and old members leave. Tuckman's five-stage model of team development, shown in Exhibit 9.4, provides a general outline of how teams evolve by forming, storming, norming, performing, and eventually adjourning.[32]

Forming

The first stage of team development is a period of testing and orientation in which members learn about each other and evaluate the benefits and costs of continued membership. People tend to be polite during this stage and will defer to the existing authority of a formal or informal leader who must provide an initial set of rules and structures for interaction. Members experience a form of socialization (Chapter 17) as they try to find out what is expected of them and how they will fit into the team.

EXHIBIT 9.4: Stages of Team Development

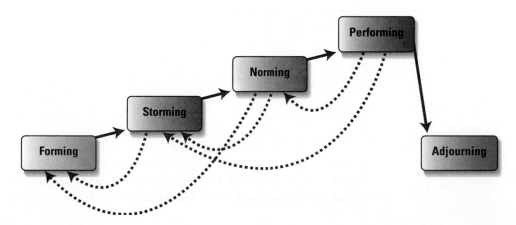

Storming

During the storming stage of team development, individual members become more proactive by taking on specific roles and task responsibilities. This stage is marked by interpersonal conflict as members compete for leadership and other positions in the team. Coalitions may form to influence the team's goals and means of goal attainment. Members try to establish norms of appropriate behaviour and performance standards. This is a tenuous stage in the team's development, particularly when the leader is autocratic and lacks the necessary conflict-management skills.

Every formal team and informal group has two sets of roles — behaviours and expectations assigned to a particular position — that help it to survive and be more productive. One set of roles helps focus the team on its objectives, such as giving and seeking information, elaborating ideas, coordinating activities, and summarizing the discussion or past events. The other set of roles tries to maintain good working relations among team members. These socioemotional roles include resolving conflicts among team members, keeping communication channels open, reinforcing positive behaviours of other team members, and making team members aware of group process problems when they emerge.[33] During the storming stage, team members begin to sort out the specific features of these roles as well as identify the members responsible for each role.

Norming

During the norming stage, the team develops its first real sense of cohesion as roles are established and a consensus forms around group objectives. Members have developed relatively similar mental models, so they have common expectations and assumptions about how the team's goals should be accomplished.[34] This common knowledge structure allows them to interact more efficiently so they can move into the next stage, performing.

Performing

The team becomes more task-oriented in the performing stage because it shifts from establishing and maintaining relations to accomplishing its objectives. Team members have learned to coordinate their actions and to resolve conflicts more efficiently. Further coordination improvements must occasionally be addressed, but the greater emphasis is on task accomplishment. In high-performance teams, members are highly cooperative, have a high level of trust in each other, are committed to group objectives, and identify with the team.[35]

Adjourning

Most work teams and informal groups eventually end. Task forces disband when their project is completed. Informal work groups may reach this stage when several members leave the organization or are reassigned elsewhere. Some teams adjourn as a result of layoffs or plant shutdowns. Whatever the cause of team adjournment, members shift their attention from task orientation to a socioemotional focus as they realize that their relationship is ending.

Tuckman's model is a useful framework for thinking about how teams develop. In fact, Gil Amelio relied on it to turn around ailing National Semiconductor.[36] However, we must keep in mind that the model is not a perfect representation of the dynamics of team development.[37] It does not explicitly show that some groups remain in a particular stage longer than others, and two stages of development may overlap. Moreover, the model does not recognize that team development is a continuous process. As membership changes and new conditions emerge, teams need to cycle back to earlier stages in the developmental process to regain the equilibrium or balance lost by the change.

Team Norms

Norms Informal rules and expectations that groups establish to regulate the behaviour of their members.

Have you ever noticed how employees in some departments almost run for the exit the minute the workday ends, whereas people in the same jobs elsewhere almost seem to be competing for who can stay at work the longest? These differences are partly due to **norms** — the informal rules and expectations that groups establish to regulate the behaviour of their members. Norms apply only to behaviour, not to private thoughts or feelings. Moreover, norms exist only for behaviours that are important to the team.[38]

Norms guide the way team members deal with clients, how they share resources, whether they are willing to work longer hours, and many other behaviours in organizational life. Some norms ensure that employees support organizational goals, whereas other norms might conflict with organizational objectives. For example, the level of employee absence from work is partly influenced by absence norms in the workplace. In other words, employees are more likely to take days off if they work in teams that support this behaviour.[39]

Conformity to Team Norms

Everyone has experienced peer pressure at one time or another.[40] Co-workers grimace if we are late for a meeting or make sarcastic comments if we don't have our part of the project completed on time. In more extreme situations, team members may temporarily ostracize deviant co-workers or threaten to terminate their membership. These actions are forms of coercive power (Chapter 12) that teams use to enforce their norms.

Norms are also directly reinforced through praise from high-status members, more access to valued resources, or other rewards available to the team.[41] But team members often conform to prevailing norms without direct reinforcement or punishment because they identify with the group and want to align their behaviour with the team's values. This effect is particularly strong in new members because they are uncertain of their status and want to demonstrate their membership in the team.

The power of conformity to team norms is revealed in the classic story of a pyjama-factory employee assigned to work with a small group of pressers.[42] The group had informally established a norm that 30 units per hour was the upper limit of acceptable output. As Exhibit 9.5 illustrates, the newcomer quickly reached this level and soon began to exceed it. By Day 12, co-workers were making sarcastic remarks about her excessive performance, so the employee reduced her output to a level acceptable to the team. On Day 20, the work group was disbanded and everyone except the new employee was transferred to other jobs. With the others gone and the team norm no longer in effect, the employee's performance in the pressing room nearly doubled within a few days. For the next 20 days, she maintained a performance level of 92 units per hour compared with 45 units in the presence of co-workers.

How Team Norms Develop

Norms develop as team members learn that certain behaviours help them function more effectively.[43] Some norms develop when team members or outsiders make

EXHIBIT 9.5: Influence of Team Norms on Individual Behaviour

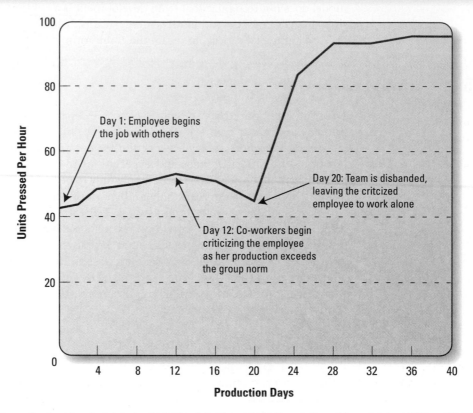

Source: Based on information in L. Coch and J. R. P. French, Jr., "Overcoming Resistance to Change," *Human Relations* 1 (1948), pp. 512–32.

explicit statements that seem to aid the team's success or survival. For example, the team leader might frequently express the importance of treating customers with respect and courtesy. A second factor triggering the development of a new norm is a critical event in the team's history. A team might develop a strong norm to keep the work area clean after a co-worker slips on metal scraps and seriously injures herself.

A third influence on team norms is the team's early experiences.[44] The way members of a newly formed team initially greets each other, where they locate themselves in a meeting, and so on, sets the tone for future behaviours. A fourth influence on team norms is the beliefs and values that members bring to the team. For example, bargaining groups develop norms about appropriate bargaining behaviour based on each member's previous bargaining experience.[45]

Changing Team Norms

Although many team norms are deeply anchored, there are ways to change or make them less influential on employee behaviour. One approach is to introduce performance-oriented norms as soon as the team is created. Digital Equipment Corporation asks members of newly formed teams to think about a peak learning experience, and to reflect on the norms that contributed to it. The team discusses these experiences and selects those norms that would enable the team to be more effective. Team members then formally agree to hold themselves and each other accountable for those norms.[46]

Another strategy is to select members who will bring desirable norms to the group. For example, if the organization wants team norms to emphasize safety, team members who already value this standard should be selected. Selecting people with positive norms may be effective in new teams, but not when adding new members to existing teams with counterproductive norms. A better strategy for existing teams is to explicitly discuss the counterproductive norm with team members using persuasive communication tactics (Chapter 8).[47]

Team-based reward systems can sometimes weaken counterproductive norms. Unfortunately, the pressure to conform to the counterproductive norm is sometimes stronger than the financial incentive.[48] For instance, employees working in the pyjama factory described earlier were paid under a piece-rate system. Most individuals in the group were able to process more units and thereby earn more money, but they all chose to abide by the group norm of 50 units per hour.

Finally, a dysfunctional norm may be so deeply ingrained that the best strategy is to disband the group and replace it with people who have more favourable norms. Companies should again seize the opportunity to introduce performance-oriented norms when the new team is formed, and select members who will bring desirable norms to the group.

Team Cohesiveness

Cohesiveness The degree of attraction that members feel toward their team and their motivation to remain members.

An important characteristic of any work team is its level of cohesiveness. **Cohesiveness** — the degree of attraction people feel toward the team and their motivation to remain members — is usually recognized as an important factor in a team's success.[49] Logically, employees feel cohesiveness when they believe the team will help them achieve their personal goals, fulfil their need for affiliation or status, or provide social support during times of crisis or trouble. However, cohesiveness is an emotional experience, not just a calculation of whether to stay or leave the team. Cohesiveness is the glue or *esprit de corps* that holds the group together and ensures that its members fulfil their obligations.[50]

Causes of Team Cohesiveness

The main factors influencing team cohesiveness are identified in Exhibit 9.6. For the most part, these factors reflect the individual's identity with the group and beliefs about how team membership will fulfil personal needs.[51] Several of these factors are related to our earlier discussion of the attractiveness and development of teams. Teams become more cohesive as they reach higher stages of development and are more attractive to potential members.

Member similarity

Homogeneous teams become cohesive more easily than heterogeneous teams. For example, a recent study reported that Canadian business-school graduates have poor work-group integration when they are dissimilar to other team members in terms of age, education, and lifestyle.[52] Generally, team members feel more cohesive in homogeneous groups because it confirms their perspective of reality and they eventually attach their self-identity to the group (Chapter 6). Moreover, people who think alike find it easier to agree on team objectives, the means to fulfil those objectives, and the rules applied to maintain group behaviour. This, in turn, leads to greater trust and less dysfunctional conflict within the group — two desirable qualities for its members.[53]

EXHIBIT 9.6: Factors Contributing to Team Cohesiveness

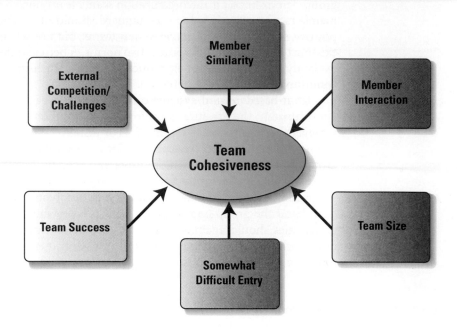

To build a more cohesive team, then, you would enlist employees with similar backgrounds. However, this may pose a dilemma because, as we explained earlier, heterogeneous teams are best for complex tasks or problems requiring creative solutions. Under these conditions, you need a heterogeneous team with either diverse skills or different perspectives of reality. Thus, we face a trade-off between the benefits of heterogeneity and homogeneity in team dynamics.[54]

Member interaction

Team cohesiveness increases when members perform highly interdependent tasks, are co-located (reside physically near each other), and work under other conditions that encourage direct interaction.[55] This raises some concerns about cohesiveness in virtual teams, or in situations where some members participate in telework. The lack of face-to-face interaction makes it difficult for team members to feel a common bond, even when they work effectively over the Internet. The problem may be worse for teleworking employees, because they are physically removed from other team members who have frequent contact. In the long run, the distant workers may feel left out of an otherwise cohesive team.[56]

Even when team members work in the same area, physical structures may interfere with their level of interaction. This is why Nortel, TBWA Chiat/Day, and other firms are introducing open and nonterritorial office designs. As we mentioned in Chapter 8, these arrangements encourage communication and team cohesiveness. Oticon Holding A/S has perhaps taken this idea to its extreme by having employees assigned to movable carts rather than fixed desks. When a new team is formed, employees at the Danish hearing-aid manufacturer move their rolling workstations to a common area where they can interact in close proximity. This practice has made Oticon a more flexible, team-oriented organization.[57]

Team size

Smaller teams tend to be more cohesive than larger teams because it is easier for a few people to agree on goals and coordinate work activities. This does not mean that the smallest teams are the most cohesive, however. Having too few members may prevent the team from accomplishing its objectives. Continued failure may undermine cohesiveness as members begin to question the team's ability to satisfy their needs. Thus, team cohesiveness is potentially greatest when teams are as small as possible, yet large enough to accomplish the required tasks.

Somewhat difficult entry

Teams tend to be more cohesive when it is *somewhat* difficult to become a member. Notice the emphasis on the word *somewhat* — severe initiations can do more damage than good to bonding the individual to the group. Somewhat difficult entry occurs, for example, when applicants must pass through several interviews and selection tests before being accepted into the group. When entry to the team is somewhat difficult, teams are perceived as more prestigious to those within and outside the team. Moreover, existing team members are more willing to welcome and support new members after they have "passed the test," possibly because they have shared the same entry experience.[58]

Team success

Cohesiveness increases with the team's level of success.[59] Individuals are more likely to attach their social identity to successful teams than to those with a string of failures. Moreover, team members are more likely to believe the group will continue to be successful, thereby fulfilling their personal goals (continued employment, pay bonus, etc.) Team leaders can increase cohesiveness by regularly communicating and celebrating the team's successes.

External competition and challenges

Team cohesiveness increases when members face external competition or a challenging, yet valued, objective. This might include the threat from an external competitor, or it could be the result of friendly competition from other teams. Many corporate leaders try to focus employees on external competitors in order to strengthen their collective solidarity. Motorola has discovered that friendly competition among its total customer-satisfaction teams can improve cohesiveness within the team and boost work performance.[60] As described in Perspective 9.2, Armstrong World Industries, Inc. has applied a similar cohesion-building activity, called Team Expo.

Why does competition increase cohesiveness? When external threats are serious (e.g., executives under siege from the media), team membership serves an important socioemotional function. A second reason is that employees feel more dependent on the group to overcome the threat or competition if they can't solve the problem individually. Of course, teams remain cohesive only when members believe that working together is more effective than working alone to overcome the challenge. Teams quickly fall apart otherwise.

Consequences of Team Cohesiveness

Every team must have some minimal level of cohesiveness to maintain its existence.[61] In high-cohesion teams, members are motivated to maintain their membership and to help the team work effectively. Compared to low-cohesion teams, people in high-cohesion teams spend more time together, share information more frequently, and are

PERSPECTIVE 9.2

Armstrong World Industries Builds Cohesiveness Through Team Expo

When Armstrong World Industries introduced process improvement teams a few years ago, it wanted to strengthen team cohesiveness and emphasize the importance of continuous improvement. The U.S.-based manufacturer of floor, ceiling, and insulation products found an answer in the form of Team Expo.

Team Expo is an annual competition to find the most successful process improvement team among the hundreds of such teams in Armstrong's plants around the world. Process improvement teams (also called corrective action teams) operate within each plant to identify and correct quality problems.

In the first stage of Team Expo, all process improvement teams within a plant are invited to compete with each other against a 100-point standard. The standard identifies specific points on which teams are judged for the project or process selected, analysis techniques, solution determination, teamwork, implementation, presentation, and results. Teams participate in plant heats to become finalists. The plant is closed on the day when the finalists give their presentations. This is also a social event with free meals, drinks, and entertainment following the presentations.

The winning process improvement team in each Armstrong plant goes on to compete in the divisional finals in Florida, French Mediterranean, or other destinations. The company pays all expenses for the dozen or so teams that make it to the divisional events. Along with the competition events, the company provides two days of celebration and recognition for its process improvement teams.

Source: Adapted from "Business Excellence at Armstrong World Industries," *IRS Employment Review*, October 1996, pp. 13–16.

more satisfied with each other. They are generally more sensitive to each other's needs and develop better interpersonal relationships, thereby reducing dysfunctional conflict. When conflict does arise, members of high-cohesion teams seem to resolve these differences swiftly and effectively. They also provide each other with better social support in stressful situations.[62]

Cohesiveness and team performance

With better cooperation and more conformity to norms, high-cohesion teams usually perform better than low-cohesion teams.[63] However, the relationship is a little more complex. As we see in Exhibit 9.7, the extent that cohesiveness results in higher team performance depends on the extent that team norms are consistent with organizational goals. Cohesive teams will likely have lower task performance when norms conflict with organizational objectives, because cohesiveness motivates employees to perform at a level more consistent with group norms. In our earlier example of the pyjama factory, the new employee maintained low output because group norms discouraged high performance. If the group had low cohesiveness, she would have performed at a higher level because group norms would be less important to her.

The Trouble With Teams

With so much hoopla over the advantages of teams, it is easy to lose sight of the reality that teams aren't always needed.[64] While consensus and involvement have certain advantages (Chapter 10), there are also times when quick, decisive action by one person is more appropriate. Similarly, some tasks can be performed just as easily by one person as by a group. "Teams are overused," admits Philip Condit, president of Boeing, Inc.[65] The Seattle-based aircraft manufacturer makes extensive use of teams, but knows that they aren't necessary for everything that goes on in organizations.

EXHIBIT 9.7: Effect of Team Cohesiveness on Task Performance

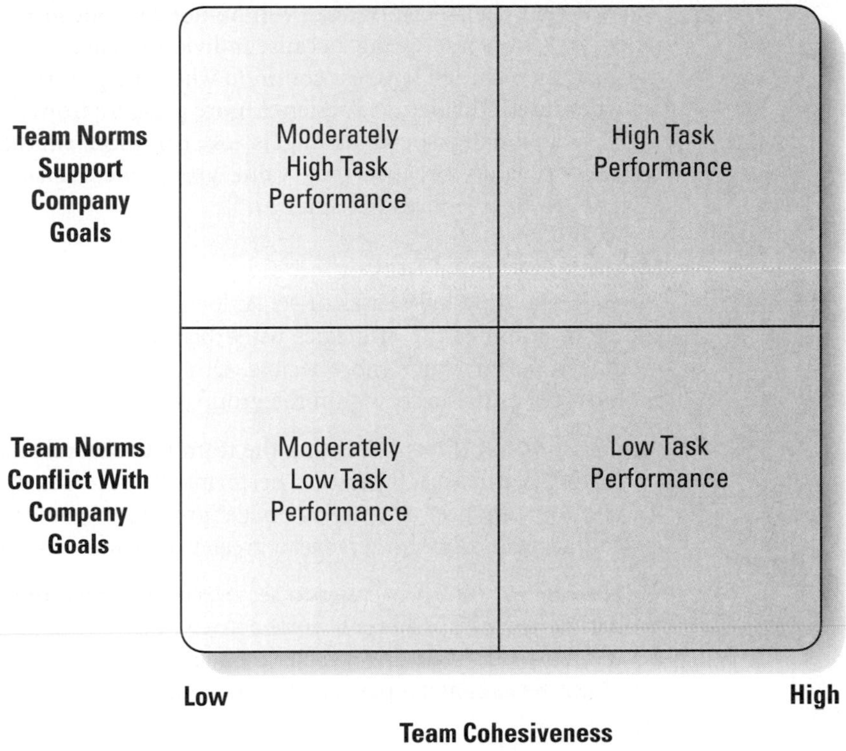

	Low ← Team Cohesiveness → High	
Team Norms Support Company Goals	Moderately High Task Performance	High Task Performance
Team Norms Conflict With Company Goals	Moderately Low Task Performance	Low Task Performance

Low   **High**

Team Cohesiveness

Process losses Resources (including time and energy) expended toward team development and maintenance rather than toward the task.

A second problem is that teams take time to develop and maintain. Scholars refer to these hidden costs as **process losses** — resources (including time and energy) expended toward team development and maintenance rather than applied to the task.[66] It is much more efficient for an individual to listen to and agree with him- or herself than to discuss these issues with other people. Individuals have to resolve internal conflicts regarding future decisions and actions; these pale in comparison to resolving differences among team members. Researchers point out that the cost of process losses may be offset by the benefits of teams. Unfortunately, few companies conduct a cost-benefit analysis of their team activities.[67]

A third problem is that many companies don't create an environment that allows teams to flourish. As we learned earlier in the chapter, some work environments support team dynamics, whereas other conditions do not. If companies simply put people in teams without considering the environmental factors, the effort will often be wasted.

Social loafing

Social loafing The situation in which people perform at a lower level when working in groups than when working alone.

Perhaps the best-known limitation of teams is the risk of productivity loss due to **social loafing**. Social loafing occurs when people exert less effort (and usually perform at a lower level) when working in groups than when working alone.[68] Some scholars question whether social loafing is very common, but students can certainly report many instances of this problem in their team projects!

Social loafing is most likely to occur in large teams where individual output is difficult to identify. This particularly includes situations in which team members work alone toward a common output pool (i.e., they have low task interdependence). Under these conditions, employees have a lower evaluation apprehension — they aren't as worried that their performance will be noticed. Social loafing is less likely to occur when the task is interesting, because individuals have a higher intrinsic motivation to perform their duties. It is less common when the group's objective is important, possibly because individuals experience more pressure from other team members to perform well. Finally, social loafing is less common among members with a strong collectivist value, because they value group membership and believe in working toward group objectives (Chapter 8).[69]

Minimizing social loafing

By understanding the causes of social loafing, we can identify ways to minimize this problem. Some of the strategies listed below reduce social loafing by making each member's performance more visible. Others increase each member's motivation to perform his or her tasks within the group.[70]

- *Form smaller teams*   Splitting the team into several smaller groups reduces social loafing because each person's performance becomes more noticeable and important for team performance. A smaller group also potentially increases cohesiveness, so that would-be shirkers feel a greater obligation to perform fully for the team.

- *Specialize tasks*   It is easier to see everyone's contribution when each team member performs a different work activity. For example, rather than pooling their effort for all incoming customer inquiries, each customer service representative might be assigned a particular type of client.

- *Measure individual performance*   Social loafing is minimized when each member's contribution is measured, such as using cash register systems to record the number of items that each grocery-store cashier has scanned over a fixed time. Of course, individual performance is difficult to measure in some team activities, such as problem-solving projects in which the team's performance depends on one person discovering the best answer.

- *Increase job enrichment*   Social loafing is minimized when team members are assigned more motivating jobs, such as requiring more skill variety or having direct contact with clients. This minimizes social loafing only if members have a strong growth-need strength (Chapter 4). Generally, however, social loafing is less common among employees who enjoy the assigned work.

- *Select motivated employees*   Social loafing can be minimized by carefully selecting job applicants who are motivated by the task and have a collectivist value orientation. Those with a collectivist value are motivated to work harder for the team because they value their membership in the group.

Team Building

Team building Any formal intervention directed toward improving the development and functioning of a work team.

When Standard Aero Ltd. created teams to improve production efficiency and product quality, the Winnipeg-based aircraft-engine repair company had employees spend dozens of hours in team-building sessions. **Team building** is any formal intervention directed toward improving the development and functioning of a work team. It is the most common form of organizational development (Chapter 15). Most team-building activities accelerate the team development process, which, in turn, might reshape team norms or strengthen cohesiveness. Team-building interventions are sometimes applied to newly established teams, but they are more common among existing teams that have regressed to earlier stages of team development. Team building is therefore most appropriate when the team experiences high membership turnover or members have lost focus of their respective roles and team objectives.[71]

Types of Team Building

There are four main types of team building: role definition, interpersonal processes, goals setting, and problem solving. A typical team-building intervention includes two or more of these.[72]

Role definition

The role-definition perspective examines role expectations among team members and clarifies their future role obligations to each other. Participants typically describe perceptions of their own role as well as the role expectations they have of other team members. After discussing these perceptions, team members revise their roles and present them for final acceptance.[73] This process determines whether individuals have the same role expectations that others assume of them. For example, Human Resource Development Canada (the federal government department responsible for employment insurance) held a team-building retreat that included a "stop, start, continue" activity. Team members were asked to tell each other what behaviours they can stop, start, and continue to make the team function better.[74]

Interpersonal process

Interpersonal process interventions try to build trust and open communications among team members by resolving hidden agendas and misperceptions. One popular interpersonal process activity is Outward Bound and related programs, in which teams are placed in wilderness settings to face special challenges and threats.[75] By solving problems in unfamiliar settings, team members learn more about each other's strengths and weaknesses, and discover how interpersonal relations at work can limit each person's potential.

There are many types of team-building interventions that emphasize interpersonal process. As we see in Perspective 9.3, team building in the woods, paintball wars, and obstacle-course challenges can be fun while bringing home the message that trust and respect are important elements of effective teams. Notice that these exercises also help teams develop other abilities, such as improved decision making. However, some of these fun events were designed for personal growth, not team development. Consequently, they may improve individuals, but not team dynamics.[76]

Dialogue A process of conversation among team members in which they learn about each other's mental models and assumptions, and eventually form a common model for thinking within the team.

Another interpersonal process intervention, called **dialogue**, helps team members learn about the different mental models and assumptions that each person applies when working together. Recall from Chapter 6 that mental models are working models of the world or "theories-in-use" that arise from our experiences and values. Dialogue is based on the idea that a team develops a "wholeness" or sense of unity when its members continually engage in conversations to understand each other. As they gain awareness of each other's models and assumptions, members eventually begin to form a common model for thinking within the team.[77]

Goal setting

As a team-building strategy, goal setting involves clarifying the team's performance goals, increasing the team's motivation to accomplish these goals, and establishing a mechanism for systematic feedback on the team's goal performance. This is very similar to individual goal setting described in Chapter 3, except that the goals are applied to teams. Consequently, team dynamics must be addressed, such as reaching agreement on goals. Evidence suggests goal setting is an important dimension of team building.[78]

Problem solving

This type of team building examines the team's task-related decision-making process and identifies ways to make it more effective.[79] Each stage of decision making, which we describe in Chapter 11, is examined, such as how the team identifies problems and searches for alternatives. To help them improve their problem-solving skills, some teams participate in Gold of the Desert Kings and other simulation games that require team decisions in hypothetical situations.[80] Some of the team-building games described in Perspective 9.3 improve team problem solving as well as interpersonal processes.

Is Team Building Effective?

Team building can be costly and time-consuming, so we need to know whether the time and money are well spent. So far, the answer is an equivocal "maybe." There are plenty of anecdotal accounts of satisfied customers of team-building interventions.

Gold of the Desert Kings is one of the most popular team-building simulations and games in North America. Developed and conducted by Eagle's Flight, Inc. in Guelph, Ontario, this exercise places participants in a desert where they mine for gold and try to return within a certain number of days. Each day is a few minutes in the game.

TEAM BUILDING COURSE

WAISGLASS/COULTHART   © 1997 Farcus Cartoons/dist. by Universal Press Syndicate

"Let's agree to blame this on Filmore from accounting."

More recent empirical studies suggest that some team-building interventions are successful, but just as many fail to improve team effectiveness.[81]

Too often, team building is ineffective because it is applied incorrectly.[82] One problem with team-building interventions is that they are introduced without anyone looking at the team's needs. As we learned above, different team-building interventions serve different purposes. Yet, many companies make the unfortunate assumption that "one size fits all" in team building. A related contingency is the type of team that will receive the team building. Many formal work teams require a lot of coordination, so interpersonal process development may be most important. Cross-functional teams, on the other hand, often exist for a limited time to solve problems, so problem-solving interventions may be most appropriate.

A third problem is that companies tend to view team-building interventions as medical inoculations that every team should receive when the team is formed. Team building is an ongoing process, not a three-day jump-start. Some experts suggest, for example, that wilderness experiences often fail because this team-building process rarely includes follow-up consultation to ensure that what team members learned during the intervention is transferred back to the workplace.[83] Real team development requires members to frequently return to the developmental issues and learnings. We must also remember that team building occurs on the job, not just in Algonquin Park. Organizations should encourage team members to reflect on their work experiences and to experiment with just-in-time learning for team development.

Finally, there is the potential problem that team building is too effective. The intervention may encourage team members to become more loyal to the team than to the larger organization.[84] Although the team process may improve, the high cohesiveness may result in dysfunctional conflict between the team and others in the organization. Few team-building efforts seem to have had this effect, but the risk is always present.

Chapter Summary

- Work teams and informal groups consist of two or more people who interact and mutually influence each other to achieve common goals. A team-based organization relies on self-directed work teams rather than functional departments as the core work units. Cross-functional teams are temporary or permanent groups that overlay a more permanent structure. Virtual teams operate across space, time, and organizational boundaries with members who communicate mainly through electronic technologies. Informal groups exist primarily for the benefit of their members and are not specifically formed by the organization.

- Team effectiveness includes the group's ability to survive, achieve its system-based objectives, and fulfil the needs of its members. Team effectiveness is partly affected by the team's context and design, including a supportive environment, interdependent and well-defined tasks, and optimal team size. The team's members should be motivated to work in groups and have the breadth of competencies required for the task.

- Teams develop through the stages of forming, storming, norming, performing, and eventually adjourning. They develop norms to regulate and guide the behaviours of their members. These norms may be influenced by critical events, explicit statements, initial experiences, and members' pregroup experiences.

- Cohesiveness is the degree of attraction people feel toward the team and their motivation to remain members. Cohesiveness increases with member similarity, degree of interaction, smaller team size, somewhat difficult entry, team success, and external challenges. Teams need some level of cohesiveness to survive, but high cohesive units have higher task performance only when their norms do not conflict with organizational objectives.

- Teams are not necessary for all organizational activities. Moreover, they have hidden costs, known as process losses, and require particular environments to flourish. Social loafing is another potential problem with teams. This is a tendency for individuals to perform at a lower level when working in groups than when working alone. Social loafing can be minimized by making each member's performance more visible and increasing each member's motivation to perform tasks within the group.

- Team building is any formal intervention directed toward improving the development and functioning of a work team. Four team-building strategies are role definition, interpersonal process, goal setting, and problem solving. Some team-building interventions succeed, but companies often fail to consider the contingencies of team building.

Discussion Questions

1. During an organizational behaviour course, the instructor states that the concept of "virtual teams" is just a fad that doesn't deserve any attention in this class. Explain to the instructor why this statement about the future of virtual teams may be incorrect.

2. If you were randomly assigned with four other students to complete a group project, what team-related problems might you experience? Describe the positive characteristics of student teams in this situation.

3. You have been put in charge of a cross-functional task force that will develop Internet banking services for retail customers. The team includes representatives

from marketing, information services, customer service, and accounting, all of whom will move to the same location at headquarters for three months. Describe the evidence or behaviours that you might observe during each stage of the team's development.

4. You have just been transferred from the Regina office to the Saskatoon office of your company, a Canada-wide sales organization of electrical products for developers and contractors. In Regina, team members regularly called customers after a sale to ask whether the products arrived on time and whether they are satisfied. But when you moved to the Saskatoon office, no one seemed to make these follow-up calls. A recently hired co-worker explained that other co-workers discouraged her from making those calls. Later, another co-worker suggested that your follow-up calls were making everyone else look lazy. Give three possible reasons why the norms in Saskatoon might be different from those in the Regina office, even though the customers, products, sales commissions, and other characteristics of the workplace are almost identical.

5. "Ideally, all work teams should have five members, give or take one or two." Discuss the accuracy of this statement.

6. The CEO of Eastern Railway Corp. wants employees throughout the organization to perform their work in teams. According to the CEO, "Teams are our solution to increasing competition and customer demands." Discuss three problems with teams that Eastern Railway's CEO may not be aware of.

7. The Johari Window, described in Chapter 6, is sometimes used as the foundation of team building. Explain what type of team building is most likely served by Johari Window interventions.

8. What is a "dialogue" intervention, and how does it build more effective teams?

Chapter Case

The "No Martini" Lunch

Jim Lyons had just completed his second month as manager of an important office of a nationwide sales organization. He believed that he had made the right choice in leaving his old company. This new position offered a great challenge, excellent pay and benefits, and tremendous opportunity for advancement. In addition, his family seemed to be adjusting well to the new community. However, there was one very serious problem that Jim believed must be confronted immediately or it could threaten his satisfaction in the long run.

Since taking the job, Jim had found out that the man he'd replaced had made an institution of the hard-drinking business lunch. He and a group of other key executives had virtually a standing appointment at various local restaurants. Even when clients were not present, they would have several drinks before ordering their lunches. When they returned, it was usually well into the afternoon and they were in no condition to make the decisions or take the actions that were often the pretext of the lunch in the first place. This practice had also spread to the subordinates of the various executives, and it was not uncommon to see various groups of salespersons doing the same thing a few days each week. Jim decided that he wanted to end the practice, at least for himself and members of his group.

Jim knew this was not going to be an easy problem to solve. The drinking had become institutionalized, with a great deal of psychological pressure from a central figure — in this case, the man he had replaced. He decided to plan the approach he would take and then discuss the problem and his approach for solving it with his superior, Norm Landy.

The following week Jim made an appointment with Norm to discuss the situation. Norm listened intently as Jim explained the drinking problem, but did not show any surprise at learning about it. Jim then explained what he planned to do.

"Norm, I'm making two assumptions on the front end. First, I don't believe it would do any good to state strong new policies about drinking at lunch, or lecturing my people about the evils of the liquid lunch. About all I'd accomplish there would be to raise a lot of latent guilt that would only result in resentment and resistance. Second, I am assuming that the boss is often a role model for his subordinates. Unfortunately, the man I replaced made a practice of the drinking lunch. The subordinates close to him then conformed to his drinking habits and exerted pressure on other members of the group. Before you know it, everyone was a drinking buddy and the practice became institutionalized, even when one member was no longer there.

"Here is what I intend to do about it. First, when I go to lunch with the other managers, I will do no drinking. More important, however, I am going to establish a new role model for the members of my group. For example, at least once a week we have a legitimate reason to work through lunch. In the past, everyone has gone out anyway. I intend to hold a business lunch and have sandwiches and soft drinks sent in. In addition, I intend to make it a regular practice to take different groups of my people to lunch at a no-alcohol coffee shop.

"My goal, Norm, is simply to let my subordinates know that alcohol is not a necessary part of the workday, and that drinking will not win my approval. By not drinking with the other managers, I figure that sooner or later they too will get the point. As you can see, I intend to get the message across by my behaviour. There will be no words of censure. What do you think, Norm?"

Norm Landy pushed himself away from his desk and came around and seated himself beside Jim. He then looked at Jim and whispered, "Are you crazy? I guarantee you, Jim, that you are going to accomplish nothing but cause a lot of trouble. Trouble between your group and other groups if you succeed, trouble between you and your group, and trouble between you and the other managers. Believe me, Jim, I see the problem, and I agree with you that it is a problem. But the cure might kill the patient. Will all that conflict and trouble be worth it?"

Jim thought for a moment and said, "I think it will be good for the organization in the long run."

Discussion Questions

1. What is Jim Lyons fundamentally trying to do in this case?

2. Do you agree with Norm Landy or Jim Lyons? Why?

3. What other strategies, if any, might achieve Jim's goals?

Source: J. L. Gibson, J. M. Ivancevich, and J. H. Donnelly, Jr., *Organizations: Behavior, Structure, Processes*, 9th ed. (Burr Ridge, Ill.: Irwin, 1997), pp. 220–21.

Experiential Exercise #1

Team-Trust Exercise*

Purpose: This exercise is designed to help you understand the role of interpersonal trust in the development and maintenance of effective teams.

Instructions: Students are divided into teams of approximately 10 people. Each team receives 15 objects from the instructor. The same 15 objects are arranged in a specific way on a table at the front of the room (or elsewhere, as designated by the instructor). The table is behind a screened area so that the arrangements cannot be seen by participants from their work areas.

The goal of each team is to duplicate the *exact* arrangement (e.g., location, overlap, spacing) of the objects on the table, using its own matching set of objects, within 20 minutes (or other time limit given by the instructor). Participants are allowed one 30-second opportunity at the beginning of the exercise to view the screened table. They may not write, draw, or talk while viewing the screened table.

Each team will have up to *two saboteurs.* These are people who have been selected by the instructor (either before the exercise or through notes distributed to all participants). Saboteurs will use any reasonable method to prevent the team from producing an accurate configuration of objects in their work area. They are forbidden from revealing their identities.

At the end of the time limit, the instructor will evaluate each team's configuration and decide which one is the most accurate. The class members will then evaluate their experience in the exercise in terms of team development and other aspects of team dynamics.

*This exercise is based on ideas discussed in G. Thompson and P. Pearce, "The Team-Trust Game," *Training and Development*, May 1992, pp. 42–43.

Experiential Exercise #2

Wrapping Presents: A Team Exercise

Purpose: This exercise is designed to help students understand the importance of team development and to experience team development stages.

Instructions: Form teams with four students on each team. Several students should be assigned as judges to evaluate the results produced by each team. Observers time the performance of each team and record the team's results for each of the three task activities described below.

Each team should receive one pair of scissors, one roll or dispenser of tape, one bow (optional), and wrapping paper. (Newspaper or plain paper may substitute, but they aren't as pretty.) Each team also receives a mid-sized box, such as the boxes department stores provide when you buy clothing as a gift.

Each team's objective is to wrap the box as quickly and professionally as possible. However, all team members will have their hands tied behind their backs throughout this exercise. The box will be wrapped three times with the following conditions:

First Task: With hands tied behind their backs, team members wrap the present using only the materials provided. They are allowed to talk throughout this task. Judges record the completion time when they (the judges) are satisfied with the wrapping quality. The team then removes and discards the wrapping paper and other materials from the box.

Second Task: With hands tied behind their backs *and no talking allowed*, team members wrap the present using only the materials provided. Team members must use new materials (i.e., can't reuse wrapping paper from the first task.) Judges record the completion time when they (the judges) are satisfied with the wrapping quality. The team then removes and discards the wrapping paper and other materials from the box.

Third Task: This is identical to the second task — team members have hands tied behind their backs and are not allowed to talk. Judges record the completion time when they (the judges) are satisfied with the wrapping quality.

Source: The origin of this exercise is unknown. A group of students in an organizational behaviour class at Simon Fraser University presented it in a tutorial assignment. The author thanks Eleanor MacDonald for describing this exercise.

CHAPTER 10

Employee Involvement and Quality Management

CHAPTER OUTLINE

Employee Involvement

Self-Directed Work Teams (SDWTs)

Potential Benefits of Employee Involvement

Barriers to Employee Involvement

Quality Management

Quality Management Principles

Quality Management Tools

Limitations of Quality Management

Chapter Summary

Discussion Questions

LEARNING OBJECTIVES

After reading this chapter, you should be able to:

- Describe the different forms and levels of employee involvement.

- Outline the main features of self-directed work teams.

- Discuss the potential benefits of employee involvement.

- Identify the reasons managers and unions resist employee involvement.

- List the six quality management principles.

- Summarize the key features of concurrent engineering.

Engineering vice-president David Ross (left) and marketing vice-president Jay Roszell stand in front of Champion Road Machinery Ltd.'s Series IV grader, the result of a journey toward quality.

C hampion Road Machinery Ltd.'s spartan yet rugged road graders are ideal for government purchases. But the Goderich, Ontario, manufacturer's future depends on private contractors who are willing to pay premium prices for more sophisticated and comfortable equipment.

To meet this challenge, Champion developed the Series IV grader with the help of employee involvement, concurrent engineering, and quality management. David Ross, Champion's engineering vice-president, explains: "Design it right from the outset; get manufacturing, engineering, design, and other departments involved from the outset; identify customer requirements; and use those findings to drive the development process."

The Series IV project team gathered ideas from customers, dealers, employees, and service people. Based on this information, the project was divided into five key areas to keep the issues focused and manageable. "Don't get everyone from welders and vendors into a room and ask how they would design this or that product, because they won't know," says Ross. "But they do know about specific issues involving welding or pumps."

Champion's Series IV team also focused on the key elements of quality improvement, such as detecting errors before they became costly problems. "As soon as you are aware of a defect, stop, review, and correct it," warns Ross. "We found a number of holes in our methods and continually updated our product-development process guidelines."

By involving employees and focusing on customer needs, Champion's new Series IV grader has won many kudos. Even skeptical contractors are quickly won over. "After we take them out to our test site and let them try the Series IV for an hour, I have to flag them down to get them out," say Ross.[1]

C hampion Road Machinery has leveraged the knowledge potential of its workforce through employee involvement and quality management. This chapter discusses both topics because, as the opening story reveals, quality management goes hand in hand with employee participation in corporate decisions.[2] We begin by describing the forms and levels of employee involvement, including a detailed discussion of self-directed work teams. This is followed by discussions of the potential benefits and limitations of employee involvement. The latter part of the chapter introduces quality management. We learn about the main principles (including employee involvement) behind quality management, the emerging certification standards, and two quality-management practices: benchmarking and concurrent engineering. The chapter closes with a critical assessment of the limitations of quality management.

Employee Involvement

Employee involvement
The degree to which employees share information, knowledge, rewards, and power throughout the organization.

Employee involvement (also called participative management) refers to the degree that employees share information, knowledge, rewards, and power throughout the organization.[3] Employee involvement extends beyond controlling resources for one's own job; it includes the power to influence decisions in the work unit and organization. Employees have some level of activity in making decisions that were not previously within their mandate. The higher the level of involvement, the more power they have over the decision process and outcome. Involved employees also receive information and possess the knowledge required to make a meaningful contribution to this decision process.

Employee involvement is not new to Canada. In 1942, Prime Minister William Lyon Mackenzie King called for the establishment of labour-management committees in every industry. By the end of World War II, more than 1,000 committees had been created.[4] These committees were designed to advance cooperation between management and labour union leaders, as well as to boost productivity for the war effort.

After the war, the Canadian government continued to encourage employee involvement through these committees so that Canada would remain economically competitive with other nations. A few firms began to experiment with advanced forms of employee involvement. At the Lever Brothers plant in Toronto, corporate leaders viewed employees as expert consultants whose ideas would improve productivity.[5] Another company, Kitchen Overall & Shirt Company in Brantford and Simcoe, Ontario, experimented with team-based structures and reward systems.

Today, most companies apply some form and level of employee involvement. For example, Placer Dome's Sigma gold mine in Val d'Or, Quebec, holds consensus meetings in which miners, supervisors, and technical staff discuss mining plans and agree on future schedules. Employees at Palliser Furniture Ltd. in Winnipeg are responsible for planning budgets and establishing production quotas with their team members. And at the Edmonton operations of Schneider Canada, employees made a series of cost-saving recommendations that improved productivity and avoided a permanent plant closure.[6]

Forms of Employee Involvement

Employee involvement exists in many forms, as we see in Exhibit 10.1.[7] Formal participation activities, such as the self-directed teams at Pratt & Whitney's Halifax facility (Chapter 9), are founded on codified policies and institutionalized practices. Informal

EXHIBIT 10.1: Forms of Employee Involvement

Form of Involvement	Description	Example
Formality		
Formal	Participation is codified policy or institutionalized practice	Self-directed work teams at Pratt & Whitney
Informal	Casual or undocumented activities at management's discretion	Employee on the shop floor makes a suggestion to the supervisor
Legal Mandate		
Statutory	Government-legislated activities	Joint health and safety committees at DuPont Canada
Voluntary	Any participation activity without force of law	Manitoba Telephone System involves employees in work reorganization
Directness		
Direct	Employees are personally involved in decisions	Placer Dome's miners discuss mining plans directly with supervisors and technical specialists
Representative	Employees participate through representation of peers	Algoma employees have four representatves on the board of directors

participation is influenced by management style and the organization's value system, such as an employee's ability to approach a supervisor with an idea or suggestion.

Many employee-involvement activities are voluntary, meaning that companies implement them without any statutory requirement. Other forms of employee involvement are legally mandated. *Joint health and safety committees* (JHSCs) and *works councils* are two legally required forms of employee involvement. Every jurisdiction in Canada requires JHSCs in high-risk industries and some provinces (e.g., Ontario) require them in almost every industry. JHSCs have equal numbers of management and employee representatives and provide health and safety recommendations to management.[8] Works councils are legally mandated throughout continental Europe. These employee-representation committees must be kept informed of financial performance and employment decisions within the organization. In Sweden, these groups are given the power to veto layoffs and other employment decisions.[9]

Employee involvement also varies to the extent that it is direct or representative. Direct participation occurs when employees personally influence the decision process, such as Placer Dome's consensus meetings in which all miners in a work area discuss mining plans with supervisors and technical staff. Representative participation occurs when employees are represented by elected peers, such as occurs in JHSCs and works councils.

Representative participation

In a few North American firms, employees are represented by their peers on the company's board of directors. In the United States, Republic Steel's 13-member board includes four union employees, four management representatives, and five people outside the company. The company also has structures to "drive information down through the company" so that employees have meaningful information to participate in corporate decisions. For instance, all meetings, whether corporate or crew level, publish minutes. Some meetings are videotaped for all employees to view.[10]

A similar arrangement exists at Algoma Steel Inc. in Canada, where five of the 13 board of director positions represent employees. These seats were given to employees in return for concessions during the early 1990s. Canadian Airlines International (CIA) and parent company PWA Corp. also have employee representation on the board of directors.[11] However, one of the most democratic examples of representative employee involvement exists at Windsor Factory Supply in Windsor, Ontario. As Perspective 10.1 describes, employees not only decide future corporate strategy, they also vote on who will run the organization.

✓Levels of Employee Involvement

There are different levels of employee involvement. These levels reflect both the degree of power over the decision and the number of decision steps over which employees can apply that power.[12] The lowest level of involvement is selective consultation, in which employees are individually asked for specific information or opinions about one or two aspects of the decision. They do not necessarily recommend solutions and might not even know details of the problem for which the information will be used.

A moderate level of employee involvement occurs when employees are more fully consulted either individually or in a group. They are told about the problem and offer their diagnosis and recommendations, but the final decision is still beyond their control. **Quality circles** fall into this middle level of employee involvement.[13] Quality circles are small teams of employees who meet for a few hours each week to identify quality and productivity problems, propose solutions to management, and monitor

Quality circles Small teams of employees who meet for a few hours each week to identify quality and productivity problems, propose solutions to management, and monitor the implementation and consequences of these solutions in their work area.

PERSPECTIVE 10.1

Democratic Participation at Windsor Factory Supply

Windsor Factory Supply has taken employee ownership the entire journey through to democratic management. Based in Windsor, Ontario, all 140 employees at the tool supply company vote on the nine people who will become the board of directors. When elected, the board then elects the company president.

This unique arrangement started decades ago when two owners decided to sell out to employees. Although a novel idea back then, it seemed more appropriate to leave the company to its employees than to sell to an outsider.

Windsor's employee ownership and involvement system allows anyone in the company to play an active role in corporate decisions. Wes Delenea, for example, came up

from the position of truck driver to become Windsor's current president.

"We are different from an ESOP [employee share ownership plan] because our owners are active in management," says Delenea. "We have no hierarchy. No employee can hold more than 6 percent of the shares. And I have no office. Our books are open to everyone."

Has Windsor Factory Supply's unique form of employee involvement paid off? Several factors suggest that it has. "We are a cash-intensive business," explains Delenea, "yet we have not been to the bank in 30 years and we have almost no bad debts. That is almost unheard of in this business."

Source: "Employee Share Ownership Can Pay Big Dividends," *Globe & Mail*, March 14, 1997, p. C7.

Courtesy of Canadian Airlines International.

Employees at Canadian Airlines International (CAI) have representative involvement in corporate decisions by nominating one director to the eight-member CAI board and two directors to the board of CAI's parent company, PWA Corp. These directors regularly communicate with employees through a specially incorporated company, the Council of Canadian Airlines Employees.

Gainsharing plans A reward system usually applied to work teams that distributes bonuses to team members based on the amount of cost reductions and increased labour efficiency in the production process.

the implementation and consequences of these solutions in their work area. For example, 250 employees have volunteered to participate in more than 30 quality circles at CAE Electronics in Saint-Laurent, Quebec. Over the past five years, these teams have presented 44 major proposals to reduce costs and improve quality.[14]

Gainsharing programs, which we introduced in Chapter 4, also require a moderate level of participation. Gainsharing programs calculate cost savings and pay out the same bonus to all team members using a predetermined formula. Employee participation is an essential ingredient for the success of gainsharing programs because cost saving comes from the ideas that employees recommend.[15] The earliest form of gainsharing, called the Scanlon Plan, emphasized information sharing and ensured that employees learned about the financial aspects of the units or organizations. In this respect, gainsharing is similar to the recent practice of open book management, which we discuss next.

Open book management

Another activity that represents a moderate level of employee involvement is *open book management*.[16] Open book management primarily involves sharing financial information with employees and encouraging them to recommend ideas that improve those financial results. Employees receive monthly or quarterly financial data and operating results so they can keep track of the organization's performance. For instance, all 2,300 Amoco Canada employees receive monthly updates via e-mail of the company's financial performance.

However, few employees can read financial statements, so companies must provide training to improve financial literacy. Employees learn the meaning and implications of income statements, balance sheets, and cash-flow statements. Moreover, they learn how their work activities (unused scrap, shipment delays, etc.) influence these financial indicators. Wascana Energy Inc. walks its employees through an oil company's first three years of operation so that they learn about financial statements, royalties, depletion expenses, and the like. The Regina-based energy firm then has employees apply this knowledge in a computer game that simulates running an exploration and recovery business.[17]

A unique element of open book management is that the training program encourages employees to think of financial performance as a game that they can play and win. Employees and management are on the same team. Employees learn the rules of the game and their roles and responsibilities to help the team win. With their financial training and game-oriented perspective, employees are more likely to make meaningful recommendations that will improve the company's financial performance.

Norwest Soil Research Ltd. practises this gamelike orientation each month. Managers at the Edmonton-based testing laboratory convene every month to talk about the company's finances. At the end of the month, they meet again to compare projections with actual results. Each manager then conducts a "posthuddle" meeting with staff to develop strategy and find ways to improve, meet, or exceed forecasts.[18] Notice that this represents a moderate level of employee involvement. Employees know the problem and are informed of the situation, but management retains control of approving ideas.

High involvement

So far, we have given examples of low and moderate levels of employee involvement. The highest level of employee involvement occurs when employees have complete power over the decision process. They discover and define problems, identify solutions, choose the best option, and monitor the results of their decision. This is most apparent in team-based organizations, which are sometimes known as *high involvement* organizations (Chapter 9).[19] Team-based organizational structures rely on self-directed work teams, which we discuss next.

Self-Directed Work Teams (SDWTs)

When Bayer Inc. consolidated five companies in four years, the health-care and chemical company decided it was time to restructure its Canadian warehouse operations into self-directed work teams. All warehouse employees now work in a team-based environment and have the same job title — warehouse operator. They are expected to share work activities by learning the four skill levels representing the previous job categories (e.g., picker, forklift operator). "It took nearly two years to develop and institute this transformation, but it has been worth it," says Harold Mueller, Bayer's director of logistics. "From the outset, employees took ownership of their respective jobs [and] supported the warehouse team concept."[20]

Self-directed work teams (SDWTs) are work groups that complete an entire piece of work requiring several interdependent tasks (such as operating a warehouse) and have substantial autonomy over the execution of these tasks. By most estimates, almost half of the medium and large organizations in North America use SDWT structures

Self-directed work team (SDWT) A work group that completes an entire piece of work requiring several interdependent tasks and has substantial autonomy over the execution of these tasks.

Courtesy of Shell Canada.

Shell Canada has been a leader in implementing self-directed work teams. This packaging team at Shell's lubricants plant in Brockville, Ontario, is completely responsible for decisions in this work process.

for part of their operations.[21] SDWTs are the core operating units of the team-based organizations described in Chapter 9.

Although SDWTs vary somewhat from one firm to the next, most have the following features: SDWTs decide their own work activities as well as the pace of work. They are responsible for most support tasks (quality control, maintenance, and inventory management) along with the core production activities (manufacturing a product, serving a client). They order supplies, maintain equipment, check quality standards, and hire new co-workers with little or no outside direction. Some teams are responsible for addressing problems of poor performance among team members, but many employees want management to keep this role.

You may have noticed from this description that members of SDWTs have enriched and enlarged jobs. The team's work is horizontally loaded because it includes all the tasks required to make an entire product or provide a service. It is also vertically loaded because the team is mostly responsible for scheduling, coordinating, and planning these tasks.[22]

Self-directed work teams were initially designed around production processes, but they are now entering administrative and service areas of the organization. GE Capital Fleet Services in Richmond Hill, Ontario, organized its 100 head-office staff members into self-directed work teams. Banff Springs Hotel assigned housekeeping staff members to self-directed teams and gave them responsibility for supervising each other, checking their own work, and writing their own work orders. These situations are well suited to self-directed teams because members have interdependent tasks, and decisions are frequently made that require the employee's knowledge and experience.[23]

✓Sociotechnical Design Theory

Sociotechnical design A theory stating that every work site consists of a social system and a technological system, and that organizations are most effective when the two systems are compatible with each other.

Self-directed work teams evolved from the **sociotechnical design** theory that Eric Trist and his colleagues at Britain's Tavistock Institute introduced in the 1950s.[24] Sociotechnical design theory states that every work site consists of two interdependent parts: (1) the social system of individual skills, needs, and interpersonal relations, and (2) the technological system of machines, tools, and production processes.

Sociotechnical design advocates a team-based structure in which employees have sufficient autonomy to manage the work process. In other words, the technological system should encourage team dynamics, job enrichment, and employee well-being. This requires more than simply putting employees in groups and giving them some team building. Such actions may adjust the social system, but the technical system may be incompatible. Instead, companies need to diagnose the technological structure to see whether it supports a team-based work environment. A balance must be struck between production demands and employee needs to maximize the operation's productivity.[25] In other words, sociotechnical design is effective when both the social and technical systems are compatible with each other.

Shell Chemical's plant in Sarnia, Ontario, was one of the first companies in Canada to restructure the technical system and social system for optimal design.[26] In a traditional chemical plant, employees are assigned to specialized departments, such as polypropylene extrusion, warehousing, and quality control. In contrast, Shell Canada's chemical plant functions as a single department operated by a 20-person process team. Traditional plants have two separate control centres for processing polypropylene and isopropyl alcohol. Instead, Shell designed a single control system for both processes so that team members can work together. Finally, Shell's computer system directly provides team members with all available chemical and financial information, so that they make decisions without intervention from someone further up the organization. In traditional plants, employees do not directly receive enough information to be autonomous decision-making units.

The problem with sociotechnical design is determining the optimal alignment of the social and technical system. Volvo's Kalmar and Uddevalla plants in Sweden may have demonstrated this point.[27] Volvo's Kalmar plant was built in the early 1970s and was one of the earliest sociotechnically designed plants; the Uddevalla plant opened in the late 1980s. These plants replaced the traditional assembly line with fixed workstations at which teams of approximately 20 employees assemble and install components in an unfinished automobile chassis. This technological structure creates a strong team orientation, but productivity at the two Volvo plants is among the lowest in the automobile industry because the technological design is not sufficiently flexible. In other words, in its attempt to accommodate the social system, Volvo may have compromised technological efficiency beyond an optimal level.

Potential Benefits of Employee Involvement

For the past half century, organizational behaviour scholars have advised that self-directed work teams and other forms of employee involvement offer potential benefits for both employees and the company.[28] These benefits include improved decision quality, decision commitment, employee satisfaction and empowerment, and employee development.

Decision Quality

Perhaps the central reason companies encourage employee involvement is that it can potentially improve corporate decisions. This is particularly true for complex decisions where employees possess relevant information.[29] Employees are closer to customers and

---

PERSPECTIVE 10.2

Unleashing Better Decisions Through Employee Involvement

There are fascinating examples of employee involvement that have helped companies to identify problems or opportunities, and to identify sound solutions. Here are two Canadian examples:

- Operators at one of PanCanadian Petroleum's Alberta oil and gas sites knew that their gas field had additional reserves. They assumed that management knew about this, but didn't say anything until management decided to increase productivity through employee involvement. When given the opportunity, the employees asked management why it wasn't using the resource. Management acted on this information, which resulted in a dramatic increase in gas production and profits at PanCanadian.

- Moses Waldner, an underground diamond driller, had been having problems with his drill. He was convinced that the machine was ineffective and that more cost-effective equipment was available. Waldner's employer, the Manitoba Division of Inco Ltd., fully supported employee involvement for quality improvement. Waldner was allowed to analyze the drilling process and make a case to senior management. His solution has reduced the cost of drilling by approximately 53 percent, and reduced the cost of drill bits to just one-third of the previous amount. Inco also saves on the cost of a repair mechanic, because the new equipment that Waldner recommended allows him to repair the machine himself.

Source: C. G. Johnston and B. L. Chartrand, *Quality in a Unionized Organization* (Ottawa: Conference Board of Canada, 1994), p. 9; C. Motherwell, "PanCanadian Uncaps the Enthusiasm of Guys Like Ed," *Globe & Mail,* August 25, 1992, p. B20.

production activities, so they often know where the company can save money, improve product or service quality, and realize unused opportunities. Perspective 10.2 highlights two dramatic examples where employee involvement helped to identify problems and their solutions.

Employee involvement may improve the quality of decisions in three ways, as Exhibit 10.2 illustrates. First, it may lead to a more accurate definition of the problem. Employees are, in many respects, the sensors of the organization's environment. When the organization's activities become misaligned with customer expectations, employees are usually the first to know. Employee involvement ensures that everyone in the organization is quickly alerted to these problems.

Synergy People working together and building on each other's strengths can potentially generate more and better solutions than if these people worked alone.

Second, employee involvement can potentially improve the number and quality of solutions generated to organizational problems. In a well-managed meeting, team members create **synergy** by pooling their knowledge to form new alternatives that no one would have designed alone. In other words, several people working together and building on each other's strengths can potentially generate more and better solutions than if these people worked alone.

Third, involving employees in decisions increases the likelihood that the best option will be selected. This occurs because the decision is reviewed by people with diverse perspectives and a broader representation of values than if one executive made the choice alone. In other words, there is less chance that a grossly inaccurate solution will be selected when knowledgeable people are involved.

Decision Commitment

An old maxim says that the best person to put in charge of a problem is the one most directly affected by the outcome.[30] If employees are expected to implement organizational decisions, they should be involved in making them. This participation creates psychological ownership of the decision. Rather than viewing themselves as agents of someone else's decision, staff members feel personally responsible for its success. Consequently, they tend to exhibit less resistance to change and are more motivated to implement these decisions.[31]

Employee involvement can also increase the sense of fairness that people feel about an organizational decision.[32] If a company begins a gainsharing plan or some

---

EXHIBIT 10.2: How Employee Involvement Improves Decision Making

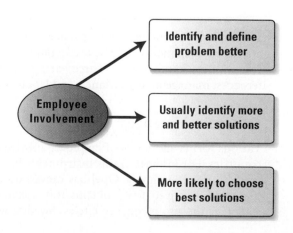

- Identify and define problem better
- Employee Involvement
- Usually identify more and better solutions
- More likely to choose best solutions

other reward system (Chapter 4), an individual is more likely to believe that the reward distribution is fair if he or she has had the opportunity to influence the rules for distributing those rewards. This may occur even when the reward distribution does not favour the employee.

Employee Satisfaction and Empowerment

Employees generally express a higher degree of work satisfaction when they are involved in decisions about work methods. This is particularly true where employees are involved in decisions about work methods rather than whether to launch a new product and other strategic issues.[33]

A related benefit of employee involvement is that it potentially gives employees a feeling of **empowerment**. Recall from Chapter 4 that empowerment refers to a feeling of control and self-efficacy that emerges when people are given power in a previously powerless situation.[34] Empowerment increases job satisfaction because employees feel less stress when they have some control over life's events. It also includes feelings of self-efficacy — the "can-do" belief that people have toward a specific task and, more generally, with other challenges in life.[35]

Of course, we can't expect all employees to suddenly become happier when they are given more freedom to make decisions. Some employees may dislike employee involvement because they have individualistic values that are incompatible with participative work activities.[36] Employee involvement is a form of job enrichment, so we also need to consider the contingency factors discussed in Chapter 4. Specifically, employee involvement is more likely to increase satisfaction when employees receive adequate training and resources and are sufficiently satisfied with their work context. We also need to recognize that some people have a low growth-need strength, so they won't be as satisfied with higher employee involvement.[37]

Empowerment The feeling of control and self-efficacy that emerges when people are given power in a previously powerless situation.

Employee Development

Many forms of involvement give employees the opportunity to develop better decision-making skills and prepare themselves for higher levels of responsibility. Team decision making may offer the additional benefits of fostering teamwork and collegiality as co-workers learn more about each other and come to appreciate each other's talents.[38]

Barriers to Employee Involvement

Employee involvement is not a panacea for all organizational problems. In some situations, participation would be useful but resistance to it could threaten the company's effectiveness in other ways. Three barriers to employee involvement are cultural differences, management resistance, and labour union resistance.

Cultural Differences

Various forms and levels of employee involvement have been implemented in many countries. For instance, Texas Instruments has successfully implemented self-directed work teams in Malaysia. Opel has moved quickly toward a high-involvement workplace with relatively few problems at its German automobile plants. Japan has been a leader in the use of quality circles. Sweden was one of the first countries to apply

Individualism-collectivism The degree to which people value their individual versus group goals. Collectivists respect and value their membership in the group to which they belong, whereas individualists tend to give low priority to group interests.

Power distance The extent to which people accept unequal distribution of power in a society.

sociotechnical design practices.[39] In spite of these international applications of employee involvement, it would be folly to assume that every employee-involvement initiative will be successful in every culture. As with so many other aspects of organizational behaviour, we need to consider the contingencies of the situation.[40]

Interpersonal or team-based employee involvement seems to be adopted most readily in cultures with high **collectivism**. Recall from Chapter 7 that collectivist cultures emphasize harmony over self-expression. People with a collectivist value appreciate and support their membership in the group to which they belong. Consequently, they work more comfortably in teams. For example, most aboriginal organizations in Canada have a consensual decision-making style in which each person's views are heard and respected.[41] This reflects the collectivist value held by many Native Canadians.

Most forms of employee involvement require low **power distance** because power is shared with employees. Power distance refers to the extent that people accept unequal distribution of power in a society. Employees with low power-distance values expect to be involved in corporate decisions, whereas those in high power-distance cultures expect to receive commands from their superiors and may view participative management as a sign of weak leadership. This may explain why employee involvement has been successful in North America. Although we tend to be individualistic, we also have low power distance. In other words, many employees in Canada and the United States expect to be involved in corporate decisions to some degree.

Management Resistance

For 25 years, Durata Massa's supervisor at National Rubber didn't want to hear his ideas. "If I had an idea, all he would say is 'Do it how I tell you!'" recalls Massa. If the boss did listen to an idea, he would later claim it was his own. Now employee involvement is the norm rather than the exception at the Toronto rubber-recycling plant. Even Massa's supervisor has changed. "Now the super talks better to me," he says. "I tell him what I want to do, and he says go ahead and do it. If I have an idea . . . he will tell [management] that it is my idea."[42]

Durata Massa's supervisor may have adjusted to increased levels of employee involvement, but many people in management positions have difficulty with this transition.[43] Their main worry is that they will necessarily lose power when employees gain power through participation. Some are concerned that their jobs will lose value, whereas others believe that they will not have any jobs at all. This problem occurred at General Electric Canada's plant in Airdrie, Alberta. When production employees were put into self-directed work teams, supervisors began complaining that their days with the company were numbered. "They had to send out a vice-president promising job security before things settled down," recalls the Airdrie plant manager.[44]

Another problem is that supervisors do not know how to become "hands-off" facilitators of several work teams rather than "hands-on" supervisors of several employees.[45] Many slip back into their command-oriented supervisor styles because they are still ultimately responsible for the team's success. Litton Systems Canada Ltd. faced this problem when it introduced self-directed work teams in the late 1980s. Several supervisors at the Etobicoke, Ontario, high-technology company were reluctant to adopt the facilitator style because they felt responsible for the results in their area and believed that their experience gave them a wealth of knowledge to direct the work teams. Only after many training sessions did the supervisors begin to accept the facilitator role and allow work teams the autonomy that the company had intended.[46]

Labour Union Resistance

Labour unions have been strong advocates of joint health and safety committees, but they are often skeptical of other forms of employee involvement. In fact, these programs are usually introduced in unionized settings only when external competitive threats force union leaders into productivity bargaining. Specifically, unions agree to employee involvement and team-based structures in return for temporary job security when there is otherwise a perceived risk of job loss.[47]

Without external pressure, some unions have resisted employee involvement. In the United States, some labour unions used labour relations legislation dating back 50 years to block companies from creating self-directed work teams. For instance, the United Brotherhood of Carpenters complained that team practices interfered with its ability to unionize employees at Efco Corp., which builds windows and doors in Monett, Missouri. A DuPont plant in New York State stopped putting its unionized employees in teams when the union local complained that this adds new tasks for which employees are not paid.[48] (The U.S. government has since changed the legislation to permit teams in union and nonunion businesses.)

Labour union leaders have three main concerns about employee involvement.[49] First, they are concerned that employee involvement programs improve productivity at the price of higher stress levels among employees. Second, higher levels of employee involvement promote flexibility by reversing work rules and removing job categories that unions have negotiated over the years. Labour union leaders are therefore concerned that it will be a difficult battle to regain these hard-fought union-member rights. Finally, a few union leaders believe that companies use employee involvement programs as a subtle strategy to bypass the union and thereby weaken its power in the workplace. The president of an International Woodworkers Union local in Vancouver sums up this concern: "There is no question the employer has done an end run around the union in going to the crews and getting their support for these things."[50]

These union fears are troublesome because employee involvement programs require union support and partnership where employees are represented by a labour union.[51] Union support tends to speed up the diffusion of employee involvement throughout the plant and to other operations. Union officials can influence employee reactions to these initiatives and can provide valuable ideas when deciding ways to adapt employee involvement practices to the workplace. Finally, union support can increase the chances that employee involvement will continue long after the original management champion has left the organization.

Quality Management

"Quality is Job 1!" "Quality Means the World to Us!" "Leadership Through Quality!" These are just some of the slogans that Canadian companies have been proclaiming to highlight their dedication to the quality movement.[52] Two decades ago, quality was rarely mentioned and almost never studied in organizational behaviour. Today, many companies consider quality to be the driving force for competitive advantage.

Quality refers to the value that the end user perceives from the product or service. A product or service has quality when its features satisfy and anticipate customer needs and expectations. This also implies reliability or conformance to a standard, because people expect the product or service to be consistently good. Quality must be defined in terms of "value" because the benefits of a product or service must be assessed against its price to the consumer. The quest for quality is a journey rather

Quality The value that the end user perceives from the product or service, including satisfying customer needs or expectations and conforming to a standard.

EXHIBIT 10.3: Sand Cone Model of Quality

than a fixed goal, and the challenge is for organizations to provide products or services that meet (or preferably surpass) customer needs and expectations at the lowest possible cost, the first time and every time.

Quality management (also known as total quality management) is a philosophy and a set of guiding principles to continuously improve the organization's product or service quality.[53] Quality management also rests on the idea that it is possible to simultaneously improve quality, dependability, speed/flexibility, and cost/efficiency. In other words, making a higher-quality product or service does not necessarily require higher cost or lower efficiency. As Exhibit 10.3 illustrates, quality should be viewed as the foundation on which companies build dependability, speed/flexibility, and cost-efficiency. This sand cone model, as it is called, implies that to increase cost-efficiency, organizations need to increase (not decrease) the quality component of its operations.[54]

Quality Awards and ISO Certification

Customer loyalty is the driving force behind quality management, but it is not the only force. Many companies also strive for government-sponsored quality awards. The Canadian government introduced the Canada Awards for Business Excellence in 1984. These annual awards include categories for quality, as well as for innovation, productivity, and entrepreneurship. There are also quality awards in the United States, Europe, Australia, and other jurisdictions. Companies apply for these awards and are judged on several criteria, such as customer focus, employee development, and process optimization. Award winners receive favourable public recognition.

Although quality awards are valued, most Canadian companies today are introducing quality management practices to achieve one of the three ISO 9000 series certifications from the International Standards Association. ISO 9000 certification is an international standard that indicates the company performs above a minimum level of quality and competence.[55] "It's your admission ticket to international markets," says Denton Grenke, manager at Ford's Oakville, Ontario, automobile assembly plant.[56] ISO certification is so cherished in Canada that companies raise large banners proudly identifying their ISO status. Law firms, advertising agencies, educational institutions, and other non-manufacturing organizations have also received ISO 9000 registration.[57]

ISO 9000 certification is primarily a documentation and auditing procedure. Companies write down how they conduct business at each step of the entire process. They execute every procedure exactly as documented. They provide objective documented evidence to an independent auditor every three years that the company's quality system meets ISO 9000 standards. After receiving certification, companies are expected to thoroughly assess their procedures annually or more often to ensure their quality system remains effective. Les Knebl, quality assurance manager at Thomas J. Lipton's Brampton, Ontario, plant views the ISO documentation as an integral part of the business. "It is a working document which we refer to daily," he says. "As such, it has enabled us to operate our business in a superior fashion and deliver higher-quality final product to our customers."[58]

ISO 9000 registration requires documentation of quality processes, but this standard does not explicitly require continuous improvement, benchmarking, and other quality management principles and tools described later in this chapter. Consequently, General Motors of Canada, Ford Motor Company of Canada, and Chrysler Corp. jointly developed a set of quality standards, called QS 9000, for suppliers in the automobile industry.[59] These standards include elements of ISO 9000 as well as explicit quality management practices.

Quality Management Principles

It is difficult to find complete agreement on the principles of quality management. In fact, some well-known writers (e.g., Deming, Juran, Crosby) have conflicting views on how quality should be achieved. Nevertheless, the six principles shown in Exhibit 10.4 appear in most discussions of this topic.

Customer Focus

Quality is always defined in terms of customers — anyone outside or inside the organization to whom the employee supplies products, services, or information.[60] Some organizations like to say that they follow the "voice of the customer" in their quality management practices. For manufacturers, this voice comes from retailers and end users. Consulting firms listen to clients. Medical professionals have patients.

EXHIBIT 10.4: Quality Management Principles

Notice that customers also exist *within* the organization. Any employee who receives work or services from another employee is a customer for that person. For instance, employees at Toyota Canada's Cambridge plant identify the next person on the assembly line as their customer. By being close to internal and external customers, employees feel a stronger sense of responsibility to ensure that the product or service is defect-free. Moreover, recent evidence indicates that employees who receive high-quality services from others within the organization tend to provide better service to external customers.[61]

Although it is useful to think about co-workers as customers, all employees must remain focused on their external customers because they establish the true value of the work performed. This customer focus involves more than just satisfying customers. Many quality-oriented companies prefer to "delight" and "surprise" their customers with high-quality products and services. They anticipate rather than react to their customers' needs. "The new quality imperative also goes beyond simply satisfying the customer," warns Diane McGarry, CEO of Xerox Canada. "That word 'satisfy' is to me a prescription for mediocrity."[62]

Companies focus on external customers through surveys, focus groups, and other marketing practices. As we learned in Chapter 8, some corporate executives also keep in touch with customers by occasionally working the front lines, such as by answering customer complaint lines and directly serving customers. A few companies send employees to customer locations for a few weeks to better understand their needs. Many firms invite primary customers to participate in product or service development. When developing the Boeing 777 aircraft, for example, Boeing, Inc. worked closely with airlines that had placed advance orders.

Employee Involvement for Quality

Quality is the responsibility of all employees in everything they do, so employee involvement is an integral part of quality management. This employee involvement comes in many forms, but the trend is distinctly moving toward self-directed work teams.[63] These team-based structures, which were described earlier in the chapter, give employees enough autonomy to reduce waste and improve product or service quality without the bureaucratic hurdles of lower forms of employee involvement.

Whether or not companies introduce self-directed work teams, any level of employee involvement is important for quality management because employees have the best information to identify quality problems and take corrective actions.[64] Quality management is also a process of continual change, so employee involvement becomes an important factor in minimizing resistance to that change. Lastly, as a form of job enrichment, employee involvement may increase employee motivation and performance which, in turn, improves customer satisfaction.[65]

Continuous Improvement

Quality management is a never-ending process of continually improving processes that create the company's products and services. This continuous improvement process, known as *kaizen*, focuses employees on the need to eliminate scrap, time, distance, space, and other forms of waste in work processes. Waste exists when employees need to move raw materials long distances throughout the work facility. It exists when parts or work-in-progress is idle inventory. It exists when workstations are poorly configured, leaving large spaces and confusing arrangements for work flows.

Freudenberg-NOK General Partnership's (FNGP) plant in Indiana illustrates the power of continuous improvement. Employees at this seal and gasket plant made 55 units per employee before *kaizen*. Three years later, they made 600 units per employee — a productivity increase of 991 percent! Moreover, the amount of space needed was reduced by 48 percent.[66] Steelcase, the office equipment manufacturer, discovered that parts in one plant travelled 50 kilometres around the plant for 28 days. Continuous improvement reduced this to less than 300 metres with a completion time of less than one week.[67] Another dramatic example of a company engaged in continuous improvement is Standard Aero Ltd. As we read in Perspective 10.3, the Winnipeg-based aircraft-engine repair company redesigned work processes so that production required fewer steps, a much shorter distance, less space, and less time.

Notice that Standard Aero's continuous improvement process began by physically moving work activities from functional departments (welding, painting, etc.) into work process flows. This strategy of redesigning production around flows rather than

PERSPECTIVE 10.3

Standard Aero Ltd. Flies Higher with Quality Management

Quality management has transformed Winnipeg-based Standard Aero Ltd. from a sleepy 50-year-old collection of machine shops into one of the top three aircraft-engine repair companies in the world. At the heart of Standard Aero's philosophy is its focus on customer expectations and continuous improvement of work processes. "The idea is to make engines good, fast and cheap, and to continually do that," explains Standard Aero's president, David Shaw.

Standard Aero began quality management with an employee task force that visited customers and potential customers in five countries. The survey results helped the company set tough goals and begin the process of continuous improvement. One competitor claimed that it could repair the T56 Allison turboprop engine (the major repair line at Standard Aero) in 30 days, far below the industry average of 75 days. So Standard Aero aimed for — and eventually achieved — the impossible: It now repairs the T56 engine in 15 days.

As part of the continuous improvement process, employees reviewed every activity involved with repairing the T56 engine. They grouped workstations into natural clusters and posted charts around every work area to give teams feedback on their performance. Employee suggestions also produced some very impressive ways to redesign the work process.

For example, a T56 gearbox previously required 213 steps and travelled 4,200 metres throughout the plant.

Courtesy of Standard Aero.

Quality management has transformed Winnipeg-based Standard Aero Ltd. into one of the top three aircraft-engine repair companies in the world.

Today, it takes just 66 steps and travels less than 900 metres. These improvements were so astounding that when Standard Aero bid for a United States military contract, officials were incredulous. Only after they personally visited Standard Aero's facilities did these officials understand the company's success with continuous improvement.

Source: A. Allentuck, "Standard Aero: Designing Credibility into Engines," *Trade and Commerce*, October/November 1996, pp. V1–X2; M. McNeill, "Standard Revs Its Engines," *Winnipeg Free Press*, September 26, 1995, p. B4; T. Wakefield, "No Pain, No Gain," *Canadian Business* 66 (January 1993), pp. 50–54; J. Cook, "Standard Aero Intensifies Quality Commitment," *Canadian Machinery & Metalworking* 86 (November 1991), pp. 15, 18; and P. A. Sharman, "World-Class Productivity at Standard Aero," *CMA Magazine* 65 (April 1991), pp. 7–12.

functional departments has become an important part of continuous improvement. It significantly reduces time and distance, and makes it easier for employees to identify work practices that do not add value to customers. Xerox Canada regularly trains its work teams in process flow mapping, a flow chart methodology that maps out and streamlines work processes.[68] Chrysler Corp. has also been focusing on this aspect of quality improvement. "We're working on putting more value-added content into our operations by eliminating waste," explains Dennis Pawley, Chrysler's executive vice-president of manufacturing. "There are still people on the floor in Windsor walking 25 to 30 miles a day doing their job."[69]

Many organizations are streamlining work processes by physically moving work-stations so that everyone can see the entire process. This "line of sight" reduces space and time between work activities; equally important, it helps employees visibly see how they are working together toward a final product or service.[70] This increases task identity and task significance (Chapter 4), resulting in higher quality as employees realize how their particular activity influences the entire production cycle. Line of sight is also a better environment for verbal and nonverbal communication.

One final observation about continuous improvement is that it works best in learning organizations.[71] Information must flow easily to any employee so that improvements are more quickly identified and solved. Employees must learn through experience where work processes may be improved. They also study other organizations to discover better ways to improve work efficiency. Companies also train employees in various statistical control methodologies and decision-making techniques so that continuous improvement may be monitored.

Defect Prevention

Quality management is built on the adage that "a stitch in time saves nine." A defect or error should stop at its source, because the cost of repair increases exponentially as the defect moves further along the process.[72] Thus, a central tenet of quality management is "Do it right the first time." The only way to prevent defects or errors is to make every employee responsible for quality rather than letting defects persist until detected by inspectors or customers. The quality philosophy also pushes toward zero defects, because even the smallest defect rate may have sizable consequences.

Cadet Uniform Services in Toronto is fiercely committed to the motto "do it right the first time, every time." One reason is that Cadet president Quentin Wahl is an amateur mountain climber. In that sport, making mistakes isn't an option. "You don't get to make mistakes in mountain climbing," say Wahl, "and I don't think business should be any different." To prevent mistakes (such as sending the wrong uniform to a customer), Cadet employees use leading-edge tracking technology, receive extensive training, and are rewarded for error-free, first-time performance.[73]

Performance Measurement

Performance measurement is the main driver for continuous improvement and defect prevention. By measuring the efficiency of work processes and organizational outcomes, quality problems become apparent and employees can see how their efforts are reducing these problems.[74] This is consistent with the trend toward *fact-based management*; that is, using objective rather than subjective information to assess quality and make corporate decisions.

Performance measurement occurs through standardized quality control data, but many companies are training employees in statistical control methods so that they have information for defect prevention and continuous improvement. At Xerox, performance measurement activities extend up to the executive level. Trained in quality assessment, managers throughout the organization conduct annual quality self-assessments across 43 different quality practices. The assessors provide each unit with a detailed picture of where it stands, what needs to be improved, and some insight into how to get at the root causes of any shortfalls.[75]

Continuous Learning

Employee involvement, continuous improvement, and other aspects of quality management require knowledgeable employees who are able to work in teams and adapt to new work environments. Thus, quality management requires a heavy investment in employee training and a cultural value in continuous learning. This is also consistent with our earlier connection between continuous improvement and organizational learning. Employees must continually acquire and apply knowledge to improve product and service quality.

Alcan Cable's LaPointe Works in Jonquiere, Quebec, has improved the quality of its products through the principle of continuous learning. Since the early 1990s, the aluminum rod manufacturing facility has spent $750,000 training its 65 employees in quality improvement. Operators learn all aspects of the operation and study procedures for quality improvement. New employees receive seven weeks of training to develop a practical and theoretical understanding of the production process. Gaston Bessette, manager of the LaPointe Works, says that the investment has paid off. "As an example, chemical composition of each batch is now accurate every time," he notes. "The first time is the right time, without errors."[76]

Quality Management Tools

Quality management is both a philosophy and a set of tools to improve product and service quality. In this section, we look at two of these practices: benchmarking and concurrent engineering.

Benchmarking

Benchmarking A systematic and ongoing process of improving performance by measuring a product, service, or process against a partner that has mastered it.

Benchmarking is a systematic and ongoing process of improving performance by measuring a product, service, or process against a partner that has mastered that product, service, or process.[77] Benchmarking begins by identifying and measuring performance levels of the product, service, or process to be benchmarked, then finding benchmark companies or work units to compare these data. The comparison is usually "best in class," so that the benchmark offers the highest standard of comparison. However, some experts argue that poorly performing organizations should use less extreme benchmarks.

Benchmarked partners may include other operating units within the organization (internal benchmarking), other organizations that compete in the same product/service market (competitive benchmarking), or other organizations that are the best in a particular functional process whether or not they are competitors (functional benchmarking). Benchmarking usually involves visiting a benchmark partner to observe how a product is made or a service provided. For example, when Florida Power and Light wanted to improve reliability of its distribution system, it visited Philips Petroleum to study how the firm distributed oil from wellhead to tankcars. Benchmarking can also occur without the target company's knowledge. One common practice is reverse engineering, in which a competitor's product is taken apart and analyzed.

Benchmarking was developed by Xerox in 1979 and has been widely adopted by other organizations. There are at least four reasons for its popularity. First, benchmarking is consistent with performance measurement and fact-based management. It provides objective rather than subjective standards against which to evaluate your own organization. Second, benchmarking is a form of goal setting with continually moving targets (Chapter 3). For this reason, corporate leaders sometimes refer to benchmarked information as stretch goals.[78] Third, benchmarking is part of the continuous learning process. By visiting other firms, employees learn new practices through observation. This encourages them to continuously question their current work practices and to seek out new practices. Fourth, benchmarking reduces employee resistance to change because the benchmarked companies provide visible evidence that a higher standard of performance is both necessary and achievable. These role models provide a more powerful force for change than a CEO who lectures employees about distant threats of competition.[79]

Concurrent Engineering

Concurrent engineering
The integration and concurrent development of a product or service and its associated processes, usually guided by a cross-functional team.

The quality management philosophy of "doing it right the first time" has been applied to product and service development through the process of **concurrent engineering**. Concurrent engineering (also called *platform teams* or *parallel processing teams*) refers to the cross-functional integration and concurrent development of a product or service and its associated processes.[80] Generally, this occurs by assigning product development to a cross-functional project team consisting of people from marketing, design, manufacturing, customer service, and other areas.

Concurrent engineering is a dramatic shift from the serial process traditionally used to develop a product or service. As illustrated in Exhibit 10.5 (a), the marketing department traditionally develops a strategy or product concept, which is passed "over the wall" to the design engineers. These designs are then sent to manufacturing engineers who figure out how to make the product or service efficiently. The manufacturing designers usually require the product designers to make several changes to standardize parts and minimize custom tooling. The customer service department is brought in at some later date to consider product repair and parts replacement issues. Customers and suppliers are rarely involved at all.

In contrast, concurrent engineering creates a cross-functional project team — often including customers and suppliers — that simultaneously works on several phases of product or service development. Design and manufacturing engineers begin work *while* the marketing people are creating the product or service idea. Primary customers and suppliers provide suggestions *during* the design rather than later. Exhibit 10.5 (b) illustrates the most common form of concurrent engineering, in which the different development phases are combined. Concurrent engineering also occurs where employees from different product groups form a common team to coordinate their designs. Microsoft used this approach to ensure that its Excel, Word, and Powerpoint software development groups created better compatibility and interfaces.

One of the main arguments for concurrent engineering is that products and services are too complex for designers to create alone. As we learned in the opening story to this chapter, this is why Champion Road Machinery Ltd. relied on concurrent engineering practices to develop a superior road grader. Asea Brown Boveri (ABB) also switched to concurrent engineering to improve quality. Engineers at its Guelph, Ontario, business had been working alone, designing transformer products that looked great on paper but had a high failure rate in the field. One year after ABB introduced concurrent engineering, the product failure rate had fallen by 50 percent.[81]

EXHIBIT 10.5: Traditional and Concurrent Product Development

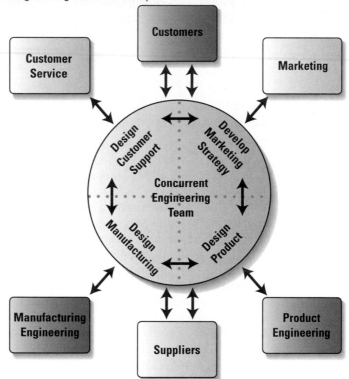

a) Traditional Serial Product Development

b) Concurrent Engineering Product Development

A second benefit of concurrent engineering is improved communication. Team members are usually "co-located"; that is, they work together in the same physical space. Co-location results in richer and more timely face-to-face communication, thereby minimizing costly errors early in the design process. When this is combined with people working concurrently on different phases of the project, concurrent engineering can dramatically reduce the time required to send the product or service to market. Pratt & Whitney Canada of Longueuil, Quebec, discovered this when it formed a concurrent engineering team to design the PW500 turbofan engine. The team completed the project in less than 12 months, whereas a traditional development process would have taken almost two years.[82]

Limitations of Quality Management

Quality management has been very successful in many organizations, but a closer look reveals that this approach also has its limitations. One major concern is that the narrow interpretation of quality management ignores stakeholders other than customers.

Laura Arsie. LA Photography. Used with permission.

This concurrent engineering team at Pratt & Whitney Canada designed the PW500 turbofan engine in less than 12 months — a process that would require nearly two years without concurrent engineering.

Employees are expected to continuously improve production efficiency, yet companies tend to overlook the adverse effects this has on stress and employee health (Chapter 5). Shareholders may also be forgotten in the quest for quality. Several companies have discovered that quality may rise, but profits may simultaneously fall if they invest in quality management practices without considering shareholder return on investment. Realizing this, Federal Express and AT&T now invest only in quality management initiatives that provide a sufficient return on investment.[83]

A second reason some quality management interventions have failed is that they require more commitment and dedication from executives and employees than some companies assume. According to one estimate, nearly three-quarters of quality management initiatives fail to produce meaningful results, mostly for this reason.[84] With so many management fads passing through organizations, it is not surprising that employees have viewed quality management as another quick fix. This problem is confirmed by studies that report weak commitment by many corporate leaders who introduce quality management practices.[85] At the same time, these change agents have applied quality management with high expectations that these initiatives will provide quick and dramatic improvements.

Finally, some quality management initiatives, such as ISO 9000 certification, can degenerate into paperwork bureaucracies that undermine organizational flexibility. Consider Montreal ad agency 3H Communications. The company recently achieved ISO 9000 registration partly because it requires employees to document every step in the design of an advertisement. If a logo on a piece of artwork is moved, the employee must fill out a form. If someone calls a client in another city, another form must be filled out. Staff members now use 10 more forms to document their work activities than they did before ISO 9000 registration.[86] Some of these documents provide valuable information later for billing and the like, but we must also consider the time consumed preparing all of these pieces of paper.

Overall, quality management may establish a new way of thinking about how organizations should operate. It certainly clarifies employee and organizational goals, and leverages the benefits of employee involvement. At the same time, we must neither underestimate the challenges of implementing quality management nor ignore its potential limitations.

Chapter Summary

- Employee involvement (or participation) refers to the degree to which employees share information, knowledge, rewards, and power throughout the organization. It may be formal or informal, direct or representative, and voluntary or legislated. The level of participation may range from an employee providing specific information to management without knowing the problem or issue, to complete involvement in all phases of the decision process.

- A few companies have representative participation, in which employee representatives make corporate decisions on behalf of all employees. Open book management involves sharing financial information with employees and encouraging them to recommend ideas that improve those financial results.

- Self-directed work teams are groups of employees assigned almost total responsibility for managing a specific work process, including most support tasks. They evolved from sociotechnical design theory that states that the organization's social and technical systems must be compatible with each other, and should encourage team dynamics, job enrichment, and employee well-being.

- Employee involvement may lead to higher decision quality, decision commitment, employee satisfaction and empowerment, and employee development in decision-making skills. Three barriers to some forms of employee involvement are cultural differences, management resistance, and union resistance.

- Quality refers to the value that the end user perceives from the product or service. Quality management tries to continuously improve the organization's product or service quality. It rests on the idea that it is possible to simultaneously improve quality, dependability, speed/flexibility, and cost-efficiency. Government awards and ISO certification objectives have encouraged many firms to implement quality management.

- The main quality management principles include customer focus, employee involvement, continuous improvement, defect prevention, performance measurement, and continuous learning. Two popular quality management tools are benchmarking and concurrent engineering.

- One problem with quality management is that it tends to overlook the needs of stakeholders other than customers. Companies typically underestimate the amount of time and effort required to implement quality management. Also, some quality management standards may degenerate into paperwork bureaucracies, thereby offsetting the potential advantages of quality management.

Discussion Questions

1. When Great West Life Assurance Co. decided to build a new headquarters in Winnipeg, it formed a task force of employees representing different areas of the organization. The group's mandate was to identify features of the new building that would help employees do their jobs more effectively and work more comfortably. Describe the forms and level of employee involvement in this task force.

2. Describe the characteristics of a typical self-directed work team.

3. Northern Chicken Ltd. wants to build a new chicken-processing plant in Quebec that represents a sociotechnically designed operation. In a traditional chicken-processing plant, employees work in separate departments — cleaning and cutting, cooking,

packaging, and warehousing. The cooking and packaging processes are controlled by separate workstations in the traditional plant. Describe the general changes to the social and technical systems that may be required to ensure that Northern Chicken's plant is sociotechnically designed.

4. Discuss three ways that employee involvement potentially improves decision quality.

5. Central River Wheat Pool's management wants employees to form continuous improvement teams that recommend ways to increase productivity and product quality, but the local labour union opposes this idea. Discuss two possible reasons why the union's leadership might be against this form of employee involvement.

6. Describe any four of the six quality management principles identified in this chapter.

7. Why is employee involvement an integral part of quality management?

8. Eastern Canadian Bank Corp. has been trying to develop new services involving Internet banking. However, the development requires people from several departments in Toronto and Montreal who seem to have difficulty working in a traditional development process. Describe how concurrent engineering can be applied to improve efficient service development in this situation.

Chapter Case

Employee Involvement Cases

Case 1: New Machines Decision Problem
You are a manufacturing manager in a large electronics plant. The company's management is always searching for ways to increase efficiency. The company has recently installed new machines and put in a new simplified work system, but to the surprise of everyone, including yourself, the expected increase in productivity was not realized. In fact, production has begun to drop, quality has fallen off, and the number of employee separations has risen.

You do not believe that there is anything wrong with the machines. You have had reports from other companies using them that confirm this opinion. You have also had representatives from the firm that built the machines go over them, and they report that the machines are operating at peak efficiency.

You suspect that some parts of the new work system may be responsible for the change, but this view is not widely shared among your immediate subordinates, who are four first-level supervisors, each in charge of a section, and your supply manager. The drop in production has been variously attributed to poor training of the operators, lack of an adequate system of financial incentives, and poor morale. Clearly, this is an issue about which there is

considerable depth of feeling among individuals and potential disagreement among your subordinates.

This morning you received a phone call from your division manager. He had just received your production figures for the last six months and was calling to express his concern. He indicated that the problem was yours to solve in any way that you thought best, but that he would like to know within a week what steps you plan to take.

You share your division manager's concern over the falling productivity and know that your people are also disturbed. The problem is to decide what steps to take to rectify the situation.

Case 2: Coast Guard Cutter Decision Problem
You are the captain of a 72-metre Canadian Coast Guard cutter, with a crew of 16, including officers. Your mission is general at-sea search and rescue. At 2:00 a.m. this morning, while en route to your home port after a routine 28-day patrol, you received word from the nearest Canadian Coast Guard station that a small plane had crashed 100 kilometres offshore. You obtained all the available information concerning the location of the crash, informed your crew of the mission, and set a new

course at maximum speed for the scene to commence a search for survivors and wreckage.

You have now been searching for 20 hours. Your search operation has been increasingly impaired by rough seas, and there is evidence of a severe storm building to the southwest. The atmospherics associated with the deteriorating weather have made communications with the Coast Guard station impossible. A decision must be made shortly about whether to abandon the search and place your vessel on a northeasterly course to ride out the storm (thereby protecting the vessel and your crew, but relegating any possible survivors to almost certain death from exposure) or to continue a potentially futile search and face the risks it would entail.

Before losing communications, you received an update advisory from Atmospheric Environmental Services concerning the severity and duration of the storm. Although your crew members are extremely conscientious about their responsibility, you believe that they would be divided on the decision of leaving or staying.

Discussion Questions (for both cases)

1. To what extent should your subordinates be involved in this decision? (Note: You may assume that neither case has time constraints that would prevent the highest level of participation.) Please choose one of the following:

AI. You make the decision alone with no employee involvement.

AII. Subordinates provide information that you request, but they don't offer recommendations and they might not be aware of the problem.

CI. You describe the problem to relevant subordinates individually, getting their information and recommendations. You make the final decision, which does not necessarily reflect the advice that subordinates have provided.

CII. You describe the problem to subordinates in a meeting in which they discuss information and recommendations. You make the final decision, which does not necessarily reflect the advice that subordinates have provided.

GII. You describe the problem to subordinates in a meeting. They discuss the problem and make a decision that you are willing to accept and implement if it has the entire team's support. You might chair this session, but you do not influence the team's decision.

2. What factors led you to choose this alternative rather than the others?

3. What problems might occur if less or more involvement occurred in this case (where possible)?

Source: Adapted from V. H. Vroom and A. G. Jago, *The New Leadership: Managing Participation in Organizations* (Englewood Cliffs, N.J.: Prentice Hall, 1988).© 1987 V. H. Vroom and A. G. Jago. Used with permission of the authors.

Experiential Exercise

Winter Survival Exercise

Purpose: This exercise is designed to help you understand the potential advantages of team decision making compared with individual decision making.

Situation: You have just crash-landed somewhere in the woods of southern Manitoba or possibly northern Minnesota. It is 11:32 a.m. in mid-January. The small plane in which you were travelling crashed on a small lake. The pilot and co-pilot were killed. Shortly after the crash, the plane sank completely into the lake with the pilot's and co-pilot's bodies inside. Everyone else on the flight escaped to dry land and without serious injury.

The crash came suddenly, before the pilot had time to radio for help or inform anyone of your position. Since your pilot was trying to avoid the storm, you know the plane was considerably off course. The pilot announced shortly before the crash that you were 70 kilometres northwest of a small town that is the nearest known habitation.

You are in a wilderness area made up of thick woods broken by many lakes and rivers. The snow depth varies from above the ankles in windswept areas to more than knee-deep where it has drifted. The last weather report indicated that the temperature would reach minus 10 degrees Celsius in the daytime and minus 35 degrees at night. There is plenty of dead wood and twigs in the area around the lake. You and the other surviving passengers are dressed in winter clothing appropriate for city wear — suits, pantsuits, street shoes, and overcoats. While escaping from the plane, your group salvaged the 12 items listed in the chart below. You may assume that the number of persons in the group is the same as the number in your group, and that you have agreed to stay together.

Instructions: Your task is to rank the 12 items shown in the chart below according to their importance to your survival. In the "Individual Ranking" column, indicate the most important item with 1, going through to 12 for the least important. Keep in mind the reasons each item is or is not important. Next, the instructor will form small teams (typically five members) and each team will rank order the items in the second column. Team rankings should be based on consensus, not simply averaging the individual rankings.

When the teams have completed their rankings, the instructor will provide the expert's ranking, which can be entered in the third column. Next, each student will compute the absolute difference (i.e., ignore minus signs) between the individual ranking and the expert's ranking, record this information in column four, and sum the absolute values at the bottom of column four. In column five, record the absolute difference between the team's ranking and the expert's ranking, and sum these absolute scores at the bottom. A class discussion of the merits of individual versus team decision making will follow.

Source: Adapted from "Winter Survival" in D. Johnson and F. Johnson, *Joining Together*, 3rd ed. (Englewood Cliffs, N.J.: Prentice Hall, 1984).

WINTER SURVIVAL TALLY SHEET

Items	Step 1 Your Individual Ranking	Step 2 Your Team's Ranking	Step 3 Survival Expert's Ranking	Step 4 Difference between Steps 1 and 3	Step 4 Difference between Steps 2 and 3
Ball of steel wool					
Newspapers					
Compass					
Hand axe					
Cigarette lighter					
.45-calibre pistol					
Sectional air map					
Canvas					
Shirt and pants					
Shortening					
Whiskey					
Chocolate bars					
Total					

(The lower the score, the better)   Your score   Team score

CHAPTER 11

Decision Making in Organizations

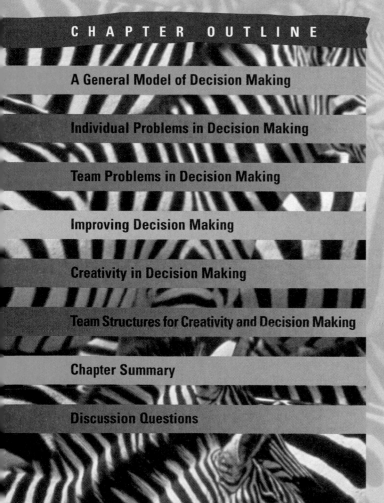

CHAPTER OUTLINE

A General Model of Decision Making

Individual Problems in Decision Making

Team Problems in Decision Making

Improving Decision Making

Creativity in Decision Making

Team Structures for Creativity and Decision Making

Chapter Summary

Discussion Questions

LEARNING OBJECTIVES

After reading this chapter, you should be able to:

• Diagram the general model of decision making.

• Explain why people have difficulty identifying problems.

• Identify three problems with choosing the best alternative.

• Outline the causes of escalation of commitment to a poor decision.

• Identify five problems facing teams when making decisions.

• Discuss three strategies to improve creativity in decision making.

• Describe the main conditions for constructive controversy.

• Contrast brainstorming with electronic brainstorming.

Behind CBC's "The National" smooth presentation is a day full of tough decisions and frantic last-minute choices.

"Tonight: Albertans are going to the polls!" announces Canadian Broadcasting Corporation (CBC) news anchor Peter Mansbridge. Behind this opening teaser for "The National" is a day of tough choices and decisions.

During the mid-morning meeting, "The National's" executive producer Tony Burman and his news team evaluate last night's lead story showing seals being bludgeoned by hunters. It satisfied the television news rule that "If it bleeds, it leads." But today they have second thoughts: viewers should have been warned about the graphic scenes. Next, the editors and producers listen to reporters across the country, hoping that one of them has a strong opening story to keep Canadians watching rather than going to bed. Plenty of good news, they agree, but no great lead stories.

The relatively quiet day is turned upside down at 5 p.m. when employees learn that in a few hours Alberta premier Ralph Klein will call an election. "It's not supposed to happen like this!" calls out a frantic producer who is on the telephone to CBC reporter Kelly Crowe. Crowe is in Calgary, but Klein will announce the election in Edmonton. Crowe asks whether to book a high-priced flight but the producer decides: "Can we afford not to go there? I say just get on a plane and go!"

Crowe discovers that all flights are booked, so she decides to hop in her car and speed up the highway to Edmonton. She arrives one hour before news time and still needs to interview people and prepare a script. Another problem appears: CBC's Edmonton studio has a power failure. Producers in Toronto start thinking about Plan B — having Peter Mansbridge mention the election while old footage is shown. It isn't a good option because "The National's" main competitor, "CTV News," is aired later and will get the whole story live.

Five minutes before airtime, Crowe's material has not arrived, so editors scramble to rewrite teleprompters for Plan B. Peter Mansbridge is seated at his studio desk, ready to go on air. Then, a satellite feed comes to life with Crowe's footage and voice-over. Two people cobble it together and rush the segment in place just a minute before airtime.

A producer counts down on her stopwatch. On cue, Peter Mansbridge announces: "Tonight: Albertans are going to the polls!"[1]

Decision making A conscious process of making choices among one or more alternatives with the intention of moving toward some desired state of affairs.

Hundreds of decisions are made each day by producers and directors at "The National." **Decision making** is a conscious process of making choices among one or more alternatives with the intention of moving toward some desired state of affairs.[2] It involves recognizing a problem or opportunity, looking for alternative ways to deal with the situation, and ensuring that the selected choice is implemented and fulfils the intended objectives. This process is fraught with the perceptual, communication, and team dynamics problems that were described in previous chapters.

This chapter explores the process of individual and team decision making in organizations. We begin by looking at each step in the general decision-making model. Then, we examine the model more critically, by identifying the individual and team dynamics that impede effective decision making. We also examine ways to improve decision making. The latter part of the chapter looks at creativity in decision making, including specific team structures that support the creative process and minimize some of the team-dynamics problems described earlier in the chapter.

A General Model of Decision Making

How do people make decisions? The best place to start to answer this question is the general model of decision making shown in Exhibit 11.1.[3] As we shall see, people do not really make decisions this systematically, but the model provides a useful template for our discussion of the topic. To some extent, we should also strive to follow this model.[4]

When Albert Einstein was asked how he would save the world in one hour, he replied that he would spend the first 55 minutes defining the problem and the last five minutes solving it. Problem identification is the first step in decision making and,

EXHIBIT 11.1: General Model of Decision Making

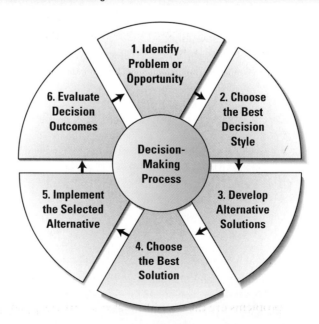

arguably, the most important step. A problem is a deviation between the current and desired situation. It is the gap between "what is" and "what ought to be." This deviation or gap is a *symptom* of more fundamental root causes in the organization. We need to correctly identify the problem in order to choose the best solution. This occurs by understanding the underlying causes of the symptom(s) that catches our attention. The decision process is then directed toward changing the root causes so that the symptoms are reduced or eliminated.[5]

The second step in decision making is to determine the most appropriate decision style.[6] One important question is whether this is a **programmed** or **nonprogrammed decision**.[7] A programmed decision follows standard operating procedures. There is no need to explore alternative solutions because the optimal solution has been identified and documented in the past. For example, when customers call General Electric's (GE) Answer Centre, operators key in the problem and a computer database of 1.5 million issues provides the best solution for the client.[8] In contrast, new, complex, or ill-defined problems require nonprogrammed decisions. In these cases, decision makers must search for alternatives and possibly develop a unique solution. As problems reappear, however, programmed decision routines are formed. In this respect, programmed decisions drive out nonprogrammed decisions because we strive for predictable, routine situations.

The third step in the general decision model is to develop a list of possible solutions to the problem.[9] This usually begins by searching for ready-made solutions, such as practices that have worked well on similar problems. If an acceptable solution cannot be found, decision makers try to design a custom-made solution or modify an existing one. The fourth step involves choosing one of the available alternatives. In a purely rational process, this would involve identifying all factors against which the alternatives are judged, assigning weights that reflect the importance of those factors, rating each alternative on those factors, and calculating each alternative's total value from the ratings and factor weights.[10]

In the fifth step, decision makers must rally employees and mobilize sufficient resources to translate their decisions into action. They must consider the motivation, ability, and role perceptions of employees implementing the solution, as well as situational contingencies to facilitate its implementation (Chapter 2). The last step in the decision model involves evaluating whether the gap has narrowed between "what is" and "what ought to be." Ideally, this information should come from systematic benchmarks so that relevant feedback is objective and easily observed.

Individual Problems in Decision Making

The general model of decision making seems so logical, yet it is rarely observed in organizations. Decision makers experience a number of personal limitations that make it difficult to identify problems, choose the best solution, and evaluate decision outcomes.

Problems with Identifying Problems

Problems and opportunities do not announce themselves. Rather, they are defined by the decision maker. Unfortunately, people are not perfectly efficient or neutral thinking machines, so problems and opportunities are often misdiagnosed. The two main problems are the decision maker's imperfect perceptions and diagnostic skills.

Programmed decision The process whereby decision makers follow standard operating procedures to select the preferred solution without the need to identify or evaluate alternative choices.

Nonprogrammed decision The process applied to unique, complex, or ill-defined situations whereby decision makers follow the full decision-making process, including a careful search for and/or development of unique solutions.

Perceptual biases

People define problems based on their perceptions, values, and assumptions. Unfortunately, selective attention mechanisms, such as perceptual defense (Chapter 6), can cause relevant information to be subconsciously screened out. A second concern is that employees, clients, and others with vested interests can influence the decision maker's perceptions so that they are more or less likely to perceive a problem or opportunity. Thus, decision making is frequently marked by politics and negotiation.[11]

A broader perceptual problem is that people see problems or opportunities through their **mental models** (Chapter 6).[12] These working models of the world help us to make sense of our environment, but they also perpetuate assumptions that blind us to new realities. As we see in Perspective 11.1, narrow mental models are the source of several famous missed opportunities.

Mental models The broad world-views or "theories-in-use" that people rely on to guide their perceptions and behaviours.

Poor diagnostic skills

Perceptual problems block our ability to diagnose problems effectively. People want to make sense of situations, so they quickly define problems based on stereotypes and other unsubstantiated information.[13] At CBC and other newsrooms, employees fail to see problems (such as public complaints about showing seals being bludgeoned)

PERSPECTIVE 11.1

Famous Missed Opportunities

Mental models create a road map for us to follow through life. Unfortunately, this cognitive map may leave out emerging perspectives and trends, resulting in costly decision-making errors. Here are a few famous missed opportunities.

- In the 1970s, Thomas Bata, Sr., then CEO of Toronto-based Bata Ltd., was approached by a visitor who asked for credit to finance his fledgling running shoe company. Even as head of the world's largest footwear company, Bata decided to reject the invitation because he was skeptical about extending credit to a stranger. The visitor was the founder of Reebok International Ltd., which today is one of the leading names in athletic footwear. Meanwhile, Bata Ltd. is still struggling to secure a niche in this highly profitable sector of the footwear business.
- In 1972, several Hollywood studios rejected the script for a low-budget movie called *American Graffiti* to be produced by a new film director, George Lucas. Universal Studios initially rejected the script on the grounds that it was commercially unacceptable, but later changed its mind. *American Graffiti* became one of the highest-grossing movies of all time. In spite of Lucas's first success,

Universal and other studios rejected the director's next project, a sci-fi movie. Twentieth Century Fox reluctantly provided some development money, but Lucas had to raise most of the money for the project himself. The project left Lucas financially broke and dispirited, but at least he kept the picture rights. His film, *Star Wars*, was a monumental success, as were its sequels.

- *The Wealthy Barber* has sold almost one million copies, making it one of Canada's top-selling trade books ever. Yet author David Chilton marketed the book himself during its first year of publication after it was rejected by several publishers. The publishers didn't think a story about three people visiting a local barber for financial advice would get much interest.
- In 1962, Brian Epstein approached Decca Records with a demo of a new rock group he was managing. The Decca executive refused to sign the group, saying, "Groups with guitars are on their way out." Epstein's demo was rejected by three other record companies before EMI Records agreed to sign the group, known as The Beatles. The rest is history!

Source: E. Roseman, "How David Chilton Became a Wealthy Author," *Globe & Mail*, February 18, 1995, p. B20; R. Collison, "How Bata Rules Its World," *Canadian Business*, September 1990, p. 28; L. J. Peter, *Why Things Go Wrong* (New York: Bantam, 1984), pp. 147, 148, 150; and D. Frost and M. Deakin, *I Could Have Kicked Myself* (London: André Deutsch, 1982), pp. 98, 123.

because they lack time to fully consider the consequences of their actions. Others define problems poorly because the situation is complex or emotionally charged.

Another common diagnostic error is the tendency to define problems in terms of their solutions. Someone who says, "The problem is that we need more control over our suppliers," has fallen into this trap. The tendency to focus on solutions is based on our need to reduce uncertainty; however, it can short-circuit the problem-identification stage of decision making.[14]

Problems with Choosing the Best Solution

For many years, decision making was studied mainly by economists who made several assumptions about how decision makers choose among alternatives. They assumed that decision makers make choices based on well-articulated and agreed-on organizational goals. They also assumed that decision makers are rational thinking machines who efficiently and simultaneously process facts about all alternatives and the consequences of those alternatives. Finally, these theorists assumed that decision makers always choose the alternative with the highest pay-off.

Today, even the economists have cast off these unrealistic assumptions.[15] Instead, they are embracing a more behaviourist perspective that assumes decision makers have a limited capacity to digest and analyze information. For the past 40 years, organizational behaviour researchers have debunked several economic assumptions about decision making in organizations, as we see in Exhibit 11.2.

EXHIBIT 11.2: Traditional Economic Assumptions Versus Organizational Behaviour Findings About Choosing Decision Alternatives

Economic Assumptions	Organizational Behaviour Findings
Decision makers choose the alternative with highest payoff (maximization)	Decision makers choose the alternative that is good enough (satisficing)
Decision makers evaluate all alternatives simutaneously	Decision makers evaluate alternatives sequentially
Decision makers use goals that are clear, compatible, and agreed-upon	Decision makers use goals that are ambiguous, in conflict, and lack consensus
Decision makers can process information about all alternatives and their outcomes	Decision makers have limited information-processing abilities
Decision makers process factual information	Decision makers process perceptually distorted information
Decision makers evaluate alternatives against a set of absolute standards	Decision makers evaluate alternatives against an implicit favourite alternative

Problems with goals

To choose the best solution, we need to have clear goals. These goals identify "what ought to be" and, therefore, provide a goal-post against which each alternative is evaluated. In reality, though, organizational goals are often ambiguous or in conflict with each other. The problem is compounded when organizational members disagree over the relative importance of these goals.[16] It is also doubtful that all decisions are based on organizational objectives; some decisions are made to satisfy the decision maker's personal goals even when they are incompatible with the organization's goals.

Problems with information processing

We are not perfect decision-making machines. One problem is that personal biases typically distort the selection and interpretation of information. Thus, people do not make perfectly rational decisions because they never have perfectly accurate information. Second, people have limited information-processing capabilities and, therefore, engage in a limited search for and evaluation of alternatives.[17]

Third, decision makers typically look at alternatives sequentially rather than examine all alternatives at the same time. As a new alternative comes along, it is immediately compared to an implicit favourite.[18] Even when decision makers seem to be evaluating all the choices at the same time, they likely have had an implicit favourite long before the decision is formally made. Moreover, people subconsciously distort information to make their implicit favourite come out the winner in most comparisons.[19]

Problems with maximization

Rather than select the best alternative, decision makers tend to select the alternative that is satisfactory or "good enough." In other words, they **satisfice** rather than maximize. What constitutes a good enough solution depends on the availability of satisfactory alternatives. Standards rise when satisfactory alternatives are easily found, and fall when few are available.[20] Satisficing fits in with the fact that decision makers tend to evaluate alternatives sequentially. They evaluate one alternative at a time against the implicit favourite and eventually select one that is good enough to satisfy their needs or preferences.

Satisficing The tendency to select a solution that is satisfactory or "good enough" rather than optimal or "the best."

Problems with Evaluating Decision Outcomes

Decision makers aren't completely honest with themselves when evaluating the effectiveness of their decisions. Two significant concerns are postdecisional justification and escalation of commitment.

Postdecisional justification

Suppose that you are job hunting and receive several good offers. There is a good chance that you will subconsciously distort information so that the chosen offer seems more favourable, while the rejected offers look less favourable. You might selectively look for more information that supports your decision. You might forget about negative attributes of the chosen job and focus on its positive features. This tendency to inflate the quality of the selected alternative and deflate the quality of the discarded alternatives is known as **postdecisional justification**.[21] It is an ego-defense mechanism that makes us more comfortable with our decisions, particularly where we must select from several favourable alternatives.

Postdecisional justification gives decision makers an excessively optimistic evaluation of their decisions, but only until they receive very clear and undeniable information

Postdecisional justification A perceptual phenomenon whereby decision makers justify their choices by subconsciously inflating the quality of the selected option and deflating the quality of the discarded options.

to the contrary. Unfortunately, postdecisional justification inflates the decision maker's initial evaluation of the decision, so reality often comes as a painful shock when objective feedback is finally received.

Escalation of Commitment

Ontario Hydro's Darlington nuclear power generating station had an initial cost estimate of $2 billion. The project now costs more than $14 billion — and costs continue to escalate. If the project had been cancelled in the early 1980s, Ontario Hydro would have saved $10 billion — one-third of the company's entire debt load today. Ontario Hydro officials and the Ontario government knew that the project was out of control. Worse, they had information that Canadians wouldn't need the energy generated from the station when (or if) it was completed. Yet they continued to pour more money into the project.

Escalation of commitment Repeating an apparently bad decision or allocating more resources to a failing course of action.

This tendency to repeat bad decisions or invest more resources into a failing course of action is known as **escalation of commitment**.[22] Along with the Darlington project, there are numerous escalation of commitment examples in Canada. Canadian banks seem to throw good money after bad in large transactions, such as Olympia & York's Canary Wharf project a few years ago. Governments have also sunk millions of dollars into ill-fated projects ranging from cucumber greenhouses in Newfoundland to meat-packing plants in Alberta. These large projects are particularly vulnerable to escalation of commitment because of their long development time. "Once you commit to them, there's very little you can do to reverse that commitment," admits a former Ontario Hydro CEO.[23]

Courtesy of Ontario Hydro.

Ontario Hydro's Darlington nuclear power generating station is a classic example of escalation of commitment. Its original cost estimate of $2 billion ballooned to more than $14 billion. If the project had been cancelled in the early 1980s, Ontario Hydro would have avoided one-third of the company's entire debt load today.

Causes of escalating commitment

Why are people led deeper and deeper into failing projects? One reason is that decision makers subconsciously screen out or explain away negative information that threatens their self-esteem. This is mainly due to perceptual defense. Investment in poor decisions continues because the person doesn't perceive any problems with the current situation. A related explanation is that decision makers typically receive ambiguous information about the consequences of their decisions, at least in the early stages. Serious problems initially look like random errors along the trend line to success. In other words, decision makers see the negative evidence, but it doesn't initially scream out that the decision was a flop.

Escalation of commitment also occurs because of image management (Chapter 12).[24] People who are personally identified with the decision tend to persist because this demonstrates confidence in their own decision-making ability. From the decision maker's perspective, this shows leadership — "staying the course" in spite of what critics say about the project. From another perspective, however, this is simply the decision maker's way of saving face — looking good to avoid the embarrassment of admitting past errors. People in Mexico and some Asian cultures tend to have a stronger emphasis on saving face than in Canada, so escalation of commitment is probably more common in those societies.[25]

Finally, even when decision makers realize that a project will not be successful, they persist because the costs of ending the project are high or unknown. Terminating a major project may involve large financial penalties or produce a bad image to contractors. Many government projects also have political costs. When former Ontario premier David Peterson was asked why the Ontario government didn't stop the Darlington project in the early 1980s, he explained: "I don't think anybody can look at a situation with . . . $7 billion in the ground and just cavalierly write it off."[26] In other words, terminating the Darlington project after this large expense may have been political suicide to the Ontario government.

Team Problems in Decision Making

Employees rarely make decisions alone. For example, editors and producers of CBC's "The National" meet several times each day to identify problems and opportunities, choose among the available options, and evaluate the previous day's decisions. As we learned in Chapter 10, involving others in decisions has several advantages, such as improved decision quality and acceptance. However, team dynamics can also get in the way of good decisions. In this section, we look at the main problems people face when they make decisions in group settings.

Time Constraints

When Fred Tomczyk became CEO of London Life Insurance Co., one of his first actions was to cut the size of the executive committee from 35 to just 12 people. External consultants concluded that the larger committee had become unwieldy and "an ineffective decision making group." With so many people, meetings were taking too long and London Life's senior executives couldn't agree on issues quickly enough.[27]

There's a saying that "committees keep minutes and waste hours." This reflects the fact that teams take longer than individuals to make decisions.[28] Unlike individuals, teams require extra time to organize, coordinate, and socialize. As London Life learned, the larger the group, the more time required to make a decision. Team members need time to learn about each other and build rapport. They need to manage an imperfect communication process to develop sufficient understanding of each other's ideas. They also need to coordinate roles and rules of order within the decision process. As for teams that want to reach consensus rather than vote on the best solution, one critic offered the following advice: "Bring pajamas — you could be doing this all night."[29]

Another time constraint found in most team structures is that only one person can speak at a time.[30] This problem, known as **production blocking**, causes participants to forget what they wanted to say by the time it is their turn to speak. Team members who rehearse their lines while waiting might ignore what others are saying, even though their statements could trigger more creative ideas. These process losses, which were described in Chapter 9, cause teams to take much longer than individuals to make a decision.

Evaluation Apprehension

Individuals are reluctant to mention ideas that may seem silly or not directly applicable because they believe (often correctly) that other team members are silently evaluating them. This **evaluation apprehension** is based on the individual's desire to create

Production blocking A time constraint in meetings due to the procedural requirement that only one person may speak at a time.

Evaluation apprehension The reluctance to mention ideas to others that seem silly or peripheral in order to create a favourable self-presentation and maintain social esteem.

a favourable self-presentation and his or her need for social esteem. It is most common when the meeting is attended by someone with higher status or expertise, or when members formally evaluate each other's performance throughout the year. Evaluation apprehension is a problem when the group wants to generate creative ideas, because these thoughts often sound bizarre or lack logic when presented. Unfortunately, many potentially valuable ideas are never presented to the group because these creative thoughts initially seem ridiculous and a waste of time.

Conformity to Peer Pressure

Chapter 9 described how cohesiveness leads individual members to conform to the team's norms. This control keeps the group organized around common goals, but it may also cause team members to suppress their dissenting opinions about discussion issues, particularly when a strong team norm is related to the issue. When someone does state a point of view that violates the majority opinion, other members might punish the violator or try to persuade the person that the opinion is incorrect. According to a recent survey, nearly 50 percent of managers give up in team decisions because they experience pressure from others to conform to the team's decision.[31] Conformity can also be subtle. To some extent, we depend on the opinions that others hold to validate our own views. If co-workers don't agree with us, we begin to question our own opinions even without overt peer pressure.[32]

Groupthink

Groupthink The tendency of highly cohesive groups to value consensus at the price of decision quality by avoiding conflict and withholding their dissenting opinions.

Groupthink is the tendency of highly cohesive groups to value consensus at the price of decision quality.[33] Groupthink is based on conformity, but goes far beyond it. There are strong social pressures on individual members to maintain harmony by avoiding conflict and disagreement. They suppress doubts about decision alternatives preferred by the majority or group leader. Team members want to maintain this harmony because their self-identity is enhanced by membership in a powerful decision-making body that speaks with one voice.[34] Team harmony also helps members cope with the stress of making crucial top-level decisions.

Along with high cohesiveness, groupthink is most likely to occur when the team is isolated from outsiders, the team leader is opinionated (rather than remaining impartial), the team is under stress due to an external threat, the team has experienced recent failures or other decision-making problems, and the team lacks clear guidance from corporate policies or procedures.

Several symptoms of groupthink have been identified and are summarized in Exhibit 11.3. In general, teams overestimate their invulnerability and morality, become close-minded to outside and dissenting information, and experience several pressures toward consensus.

Most research on groupthink has analyzed policy decisions that turned into fiascos. The best-known example of groupthink is NASA's space shuttle *Challenger* explosion in 1986.[35] The technical cause of the explosion that killed all seven crew members was a faulty O-ring seal that did not withstand the freezing temperatures the night before launch. However, a government commission pointed to a faulty decision-making process as the primary cause of the disaster. Key decision makers at NASA experienced many groupthink symptoms. They were under intense pressure to launch due to previous delays and promises of the space shuttle program's success. Information about O-ring problems was withheld to avoid conflict. Engineers raised concerns about the O-rings before the launch, but they were criticized for this.

EXHIBIT 11.3: Symptoms of Groupthink

Groupthink Symptom	Description
Illusion of Invulnerability	The team feels comfortable with risky decisions because possible weaknesses are suppressed or glossed over.
Assumption of Morality	There is such an unquestioned belief in the inherent morality of the team's objectives that members do not feel the need to debate whether their actions are ethical.
Rationalization	Underlying assumptions, new information, and previous actions that seem inconsistent with the team's decision are discounted or explained away.
Stereotyping Outgroups	The team stereotypes or oversimplifies the external threats upon which the decision is based, and "enemies" are viewed as purely evil or moronic.
Self-censorship	Team members suppress their doubts in order to maintain harmony.
Illusion of Unanimity	Self-censorship results in harmonious behaviour, so individual members believe that they alone have doubts; silence is automatically perceived as evidence of consensus.
Mindguarding	Some members become self-appointed guardians to prevent negative or inconsistent information from reaching the team.
Pressuring Dissenters	Members who happen to raise their concerns about the decision are pressured to fall into line and be more loyal to the team.

Source: Based on I. L. Janis, *Groupthink: Psychological Studies of Policy Decisions and Fiascoes*, 2nd ed. (Boston: Houghton Mifflin, 1982), p. 244.

Group Polarization

Group polarization The tendency for teams to make more extreme decisions (either more risky or more risk-averse) than the average team member would if making the decision alone.

Group polarization refers to the tendency of teams to make more extreme decisions than individuals working alone.[36] Exhibit 11.4 shows how the group polarization process operates. Individuals form initial preferences when given several alternatives. Some of these choices are riskier than others, and the average member's opinion leans one way or the other. Through open discussion, members become comfortable with more extreme positions when they realize that their views are also held by others. Persuasive arguments favouring the dominant position convince doubtful members and help form a consensus around the extreme option. Finally, because the final decision is made by the team, individuals feel less personally responsible for the decision consequences.

Group polarization explains why groups make more *extreme* decisions than the average individual, but there is also evidence that teams usually make *riskier* decisions. Why does this occur? When given the choice between a certain alternative and a risky one, individuals tend to initially prefer the risky option because the certain loss is viewed as more unpleasant than a more severe but less certain loss. This occurs even when the probability of success is extremely low, because people also tend to inflate the likelihood that they will beat the odds in a risky situation. For example, they tend to think, "This strategy might be unsuccessful 80 percent of the time, but it will work for me!" Thus, team members are more likely to favour the risky option.[37]

An extreme choice — whether risky or risk-averse — is sometimes the correct solution to a problem or opportunity, but group polarization explains why some executive

EXHIBIT 11.4: The Group Polarization Process

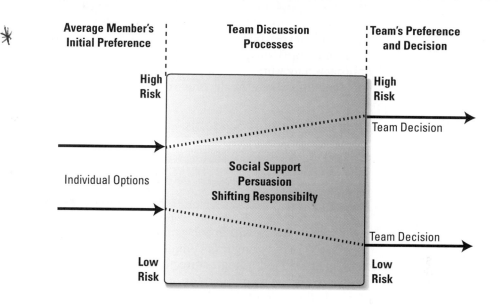

teams unwisely gamble assets and develop overoptimistic forecasts of success. Under some conditions, senior executives might support a "bet your company" solution in which most corporate assets are allocated to an investment with little probability of success. At the other extreme, teams whose members generally favour risk-averse solutions will suffer from inaction and stagnation. They will continually miss windfall opportunities and be ill-prepared for environmental changes.

Improving Decision Making

With so many individual and team problems, you might think that decision making is best performed by rolling dice! Fortunately, there are a number of ways to minimize, if not overcome, these barriers to effective decision making.

The first step is to make people aware of the problems described above so that they manage them to some extent. Awareness may sensitize decision makers to their perceptual errors and the need for more careful diagnosis of the situation. By recognizing how mental models restrict a person's understanding of the world, decision makers learn to openly consider other perspectives of reality. Similarly, by discussing the situation with colleagues, decision makers can eventually discover blind spots in their problem identification and evaluation.[38]

At least two strategies should be considered to minimize escalation of commitment and postdecisional justification. The most effective strategy is to separate decision choosers from decision implementers. This minimizes the problem of saving face because the person responsible for implementation and evaluation would not be concerned about saving face if the project were cancelled. In support of this recommendation, a recent study found that banks were more likely to take action against bad loans when the executive responsible had left.[39] In other words, problem loans were effectively managed when someone else took over the portfolio.

The other escalation of commitment strategy is to establish a preset level at which the decision is abandoned or reevaluated.[40] This is similar to a stop-loss order in the stock market, whereby the stock is sold if it falls below a certain price. The problem with this solution is that conditions are often so complex that it is difficult to identify an appropriate point at which to abandon a project. However, this approach may work if a stopping point can be determined and it is established by someone other than the decision maker.

Decision Support Systems

A variety of structures and systems can help minimize some decision-making problems. Decision support systems have become very sophisticated. Some software programs engage in "data mining" in which information is quickly retrieved from huge databases. This gives decision makers the information they need more quickly. For instance, analysts at Canadian National use data mining technologies to identify meaningful patterns within a few minutes. In the past, this would have required days or even weeks of poring over computer printouts.[41]

Other DSS technologies directly assist the decision process, such as by helping people who are searching for more diverse alternatives or by guiding them through the rational decision model more carefully.[42] At SmithKline Beecham's Canadian headquarters, executives improve their decisions through the "executive dashboard" — software based on Excel spreadsheets that continuously monitors sales, budgets, and other key corporate performance indicators.[43] Great Lakes Power Ltd. has introduced DSS technology to improve the reliability and accuracy of decisions. As Perspective 11.2 describes, DSS technology helps the Sault Ste.

PERSPECTIVE 11.2

Great Lakes Power Uses Technology for More Accurate Decisions

Great Lakes Power Ltd. distributes electrical energy to 11,500 customers located within a 5,000 square mile area around Sault Ste. Marie, Ontario. To maintain safe working conditions, Great Lakes crews regularly inspect the 25,000 or more electrical poles to make sure they are functioning properly and standing up to the elements. It's a job that's not taken lightly.

For several years, hydro poles were evaluated using a paper-based survey that left plenty of room for personal bias. For example, one inspector might think a tree is encroaching on a line while another inspector might think the tree is not a threat.

"If you took two reviewers and they went and looked at the same pole, they could come back with two different scores," admits Dan Richards, distribution technician at Great Lakes. "The consistency wasn't acceptable, especially

with the number of poles we were looking at." The paperwork was also becoming a headache for administrative staff.

To solve these problems, Great Lakes formed a cross-functional task force representing line crews, distribution engineering, and supervisors. After considering the options, the team selected Which & Why, a decision support software (DSS) tool from Montreal-based Arlington Software Corp. Now, pole inspection data are keyed into the DSS system and results are displayed graphically. This allows supervisors to determine more easily which poles deserve the highest maintenance priority.

"All the groups that were affected were represented and we came to consensus on all the issues," says Richards. "If you don't build a team atmosphere and everyone agrees to it, it's going to fail."

Source: Adapted from S. Wintrob, "Utility Empowers Line Crews," *Computing Canada*, March 28, 1996, p. 36.

Marie distributor of electrical power to more accurately decide whether hydro poles need maintenance work.

Improving Team Dynamics

Team dynamics problems may be reduced in a number of ways. One approach is to ensure that neither the team leader nor any other participant dominates the process. This limits the adverse effects of conformity and lets other team members generate more ideas.[44] Another practice is to maintain an optimal team size. The group should be large enough that members possess the collective knowledge to resolve the problem, yet small enough that the team doesn't consume too much time or restrict individual input.[45]

Finally, groupthink, group polarization, and other team-dynamics problems may be minimized by introducing more effective team structures. We will describe four team structures later in the chapter. Along with improving team dynamics, these structures potentially support more creative decision making, which we discuss next.

Creativity in Decision Making

Henry Yuen wanted to record a baseball game on TV while out of town, but the scientist had problems setting his VCR properly. While venting his anger, Yuen had an idea. "I thought that taping a program should be as easy as dialing a telephone," he says. So he and co-inventor Daniel Kwoh set out to develop a system that makes VCR recording as simple as dialing a telephone. Today, most VCR owners enjoy the fruits of Yuen's creative inspiration. It's called VCR Plus. Users simply punch in the appropriate number from the TV guide listing and the system does the rest.[46]

Creativity The capability to develop an original product, service, or idea that makes a socially recognized contribution.

Creativity refers to developing an original product, service, or idea that makes a socially recognized contribution. Creativity has been romanticized by some consultants as a special function of the brain's right hemisphere. It isn't. This myth is based on pseudosciences of the 1800s that have been proven incorrect in scientific research.[47] Others view creativity as something separate from regular decision making. Although there are unique features of creativity that we discuss in this section, creativity is really part of most nonprogrammed decisions. We use the creative process to find problems, identify alternatives, and implement solutions. Creativity is not something we save for special occasions.

Creativity Model

Scholars are still struggling to understand the creative process, but they generally agree that the model presented in Exhibit 11.5 provides a reasonable representation.[48]

EXHIBIT 11.5: Model of Creativity in Decision Making

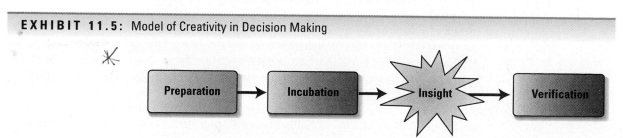

1. *Preparation* Creativity is not a passive activity; rather, we gather the necessary information and concentrate on the problem or issue. For example, people are usually more creative when they take the problem apart and closely analyze each component.

2. *Incubation* This is the stage of reflective thought. We put the problem aside (sometimes out of frustration), but our mind is still working on it subconsciously. This stage is usually aided by working (or playing) on an unrelated object or event.

3. *Insight* At some point during the incubation stage, we become aware of a unique idea. These flashes of inspiration are fleeting and can be lost quickly if not documented. In other words, creative thoughts don't keep a particular schedule; they might come to you at any time of day or night. Many great ideas have been lost because the individual did not write them down at the moment of inspiration.

4. *Verification* Insights are merely rough ideas. Their usefulness still requires verification through conscious evaluation and experimentation. This is similar to the evaluating decision outcomes stage in the decision-making model described earlier in the chapter.

The flashes of inspiration identified in the creativity model are usually derived from a unique combination of previous information. For instance, Henry Yuen's inspiration for VCR Plus came from associating VCR programming with making a telephone call. The creativity of this idea is that we don't normally think of VCRs in terms of telephone activities. This represents a special feature of creativity, known as **divergent thinking**. Divergent thinking involves reframing the problem in a unique way and generating different approaches to the issue. For example, one test of divergent thinking is to identify as many uses of an object as possible. Divergent thinkers are able to break away from the known uses to completely different applications. Some of the creative strategies we describe later encourage divergent thinking.

Divergent thinking The ability to reframe problems in a unique way and generate different approaches to the issue.

Conditions for Creativity

Minnesota Mining & Manufacturing Co. (3M) generates 30 percent of its annual revenues from products developed within the past four years.[49] To accomplish this, 3M has learned to find creative people and put them in an environment that encourages innovation. In other words, 3M has learned that creativity is a function of both the person and the situation.

Some people are inherently more creative than others. This is why 3M carefully screens out applicants with less creative potential. "When it comes to creativity, [some people] can't get out of the box," says 3M Canada manager Jim McSheffrey. Research has found that creative people have strong artistic and intellectual values, tolerance of ambiguity, need for achievement, and self-confidence. People can be creative throughout their lives, although the highest level of creativity tends to occur between the ages of 30 and 40.[50]

In addition to hiring creative people, organizations need to provide jobs and work environments that foster creativity.[51] Jobs should give employees enough freedom in deciding how to accomplish tasks and solve problems. Employees perform better when assigned creative goals and evaluated on their creative output, but they should be buffered from tight deadlines. At Nintendo, the Japanese game maker, designers are given free rein of their time to develop new products. "We never put a time limit on the development of products," explains Nintendo president Hiroshi Yamauchi. "We have

"There, there! Two, maybe three floors down. Someone has an <u>idea</u>!"

kept quiet even when [designers] go to see a movie or play during work."[52]

Supportive leadership is another critical feature for creativity and innovation. Supervisors, team leaders, and others should encourage risk taking by ensuring that employees aren't punished for behaving or thinking differently. They should reinforce the notion that errors are part of the learning process. Creativity results from trial and error, not from getting it right every time or else!

Cross-pollination of ideas is another key ingredient for creativity. This occurs when employees work on divergent projects rather than focusing their career in one product or service area. IDEO, an industrial design firm, encourages employees to consider how features of one product they've worked on might be relevant to another. For instance, while designing a quieter fan for a computer system, designers might recall how they designed a quieter vacuum cleaner a few months earlier. One IDEO designer likes to bring toys to development meetings because toy designs spark ideas about how to make skin staplers, computer cases, and other innovations.[53]

Cross-pollination also occurs when people with diverse skills and knowledge throughout the organization interact and share information with each other.[54] Bell Labs gives its scientists a lot of freedom, but it insists that they eat lunch together because this forces them to schmooze, cross-pollinate, and breed ideas. 3M takes a different approach. It holds corporatewide trade shows where employees learn about projects in other areas of the organization. 3M also holds Technical Forums in each geographic area to "encourage free and active interchange of information and the cross-fertilization of ideas."[55]

Creativity Training

Some people are naturally more creative than others, but creativity can also be learned to some extent.[56] Creativity-training programs help participants in three ways. First, some training activities make people aware that their creativity is stifled by the existing mental models that guide their thinking (Chapter 6). Saying that something isn't logical simply means that it doesn't fit our mental model. This awareness encourages program participants to question their logic and avoid closing their minds to ideas that don't fit existing mental models.

Second, some creativity-training activities encourage participants to spend more time understanding the problem or opportunity and, in particular, redefining it in unique ways. Current research particularly emphasizes problem finding in the creative process.[57] In one creativity exercise, participants read a case, identify the main problem, and then compare their problem definition with others in the class. They discover that the same incident can be viewed in several ways.[58]

Divergent thinking strategies

A third function of creativity training is to teach people various divergent thinking strategies. One method, called morphological analysis, involves listing different dimensions of a system and the elements of each dimension, then looking at each combination. This encourages people to carefully examine combinations that initially seem nonsensical.

Officials from the Canadian government fisheries department used morphology to find new opportunities for Canadian water resources. They drew a three-dimensional grid and then identified different resources in their jurisdiction (fish, shellfish, plants, etc.), different uses of the resource (sport, export product, sightseeing, etc.), and different benefits (employment, nutrition, etc.). The group then looked at all combinations of the three dimensions and were able to identify new challenges and opportunities for the industry.[59]

Another divergent thinking strategy is to use metaphors to compare the situation with something else so that it is seen in a different light.[60] A telephone company used this approach to find ways to reduce damage to its pay telephones. Program participants were asked to think of a telephone booth as some other object that protects — such as a bank vault or medicine capsule. Then they looked at features of these other objects that might protect telephone booths. Notice that this is similar to the incubation stage of creativity, in which decision makers put the problem in the back of their heads while focusing on a divergent object or event.

Aside from training programs, companies have experimented with different team structures to improve creativity as well as the general decision-making process. The next section introduces the most popular structures: constructive controversy, brainstorming, electronic brainstorming, and nominal group technique.

Team Structures for Creativity and Decision Making

Traditionally, team members meet face-to-face to suggest solutions and debate alternatives. Discussion is usually unstructured, ideas are generated and evaluated simultaneously, and there is a tendency to search for solutions before the problem is clearly understood. Consequently, traditional team structures are often marred by evaluation apprehension, production blocking, groupthink, and other problems described earlier. To minimize these problems, four alternative techniques have been proposed: constructive controversy, brainstorming, nominal group technique, and electronic brainstorming.

Constructive Controversy

Constructive controversy
Any situation in which team members debate their different opinions regarding a problem or issue in a way that minimizes socio-emotional conflict.

Constructive controversy occurs when team members debate their different perceptions about an issue in a way that minimizes socio-emotional conflict. Through dialogue, participants learn about other points of view, which encourages them to re-examine their basic assumptions about a problem and its possible solution. Constructive controversy is *constructive* because the discussion minimizes socio-emotional conflict while discussing differences. This can occur if participants focus on facts rather than people and avoid statements that threaten the esteem and well-being of other team members.[61]

How do we generate constructive controversy? First, decision-making groups should be heterogeneous.[62] They should be diverse with respect to gender, age, ethnicity, career experiences, educational backgrounds, and other relevant dimensions. Second, these heterogeneous team members need to meet often enough to allow meaningful discussion over contentious issues. The team's diversity won't generate constructive controversy if the team leader makes most of the decisions alone. Only through dialogue can team members better understand different perspectives, generate more creative ideas, and improve decision quality.

Third, effective teams generate constructive controversy when individual members take on different discussion roles. Some participants are action-oriented, others are moderates who insist on reviewing details, one or two might be stabilizers who minimize dysfunctional conflict in the group, and so on. Some people should be **devil's advocates** — team members who challenge others to explain the logic of their preferences and who identify problems with that logic. Some scholars recommend a formal process whereby half the group takes on the devil's advocate role during discussion.[63] However, some individuals naturally tend to fill this role without any special arrangement. Randy Powell, described in Perspective 11.3, is certainly an example of this. Powell diplomatically disagreed with the CEO of Campbell Soup Co. Ltd. and was respected for his different perspective of the issues.

Devil's advocates People who challenge others to explain the logic of their preferences and who identify problems with that logic

---

PERSPECTIVE 11.3

Mavericks Like Randy Powell Create Constructive Controversy

Randy Powell doesn't like to follow the crowd. Instead, the former Campbell Soup marketer (now president of S. C. Johnson and Son, Ltd.) believes that differences of opinion should be heard and appreciated.

"Groupthink can happen," warns Powell. "What the senior person says tends to rule. I have always believed I should speak for what I believe to be true."

Powell demonstrated his penchant for constructive controversy early in his career — in fact, just one month after being hired as a brand manager at Campbell Soup Ltd. in Toronto. He had been assigned to Prego spaghetti sauce products and, during the brand review, Campbell's CEO concluded that Prego was losing out to price-cutting competitors. Powell mustered his courage and said that he disagreed with the veteran marketer. He explained that Prego's line needed more variety and advertising budget. The CEO accepted Powell's reasoning.

Later, Powell's supervisor approached him and confided: "I wanted to say that, but I just didn't have the courage to step in front of [the CEO]." By the end of the day, more than a dozen colleagues congratulated Powell for speaking up.

Some time later, Campbell's CEO sent Powell and 40 other executives to a week-long New Age management session. Powell soon concluded that the consultants were off-base with their "planning back from the future" stuff. Between sessions, most of the other Campbell's executives confided that they felt the same way. The consultants heard about the dissent on the fourth day and dramatically asked participants whether they were in or out. Those who said "Out" had to leave immediately.

As the consultants went around the room, every executive who privately grumbled about the session said "In."

Chris Wahl. Used with permission.

Randy Powell demonstrated a penchant for constructive controversy early in his career.

Powell was third from last. "I believed it could be political suicide to go against [the CEO] on an issue he believed to be true," Powell recalls. Every one before him had agreed to stay in. Still, when it was his turn, Powell said "Out" and left the room.

The next day, the CEO called Powell into his office and told him that he respected his decision, even if he disagreed. Two months later, at 31 years of age, Powell was promoted to vice-president of sales.

Source: Adapted from S. Silcoff, "The Sky's Your Limit," *Canadian Business*, April 1997, pp. 58–66.

Lastly, constructive controversy is more likely to occur when the decision is viewed from several angles. Team members should consider the effectiveness of the preferred choice under different scenarios, rather than just one or two. Before buying another company, for instance, an executive team should consider the wisdom of this decision if the economy stumbles, the government changes, a supply shortage occurs, and so on. Taking different angles also means comparing the preferred alternative against many choices, not only one or two limited options. To identify these varied alternatives, effective teams engage in some form of brainstorming, which we discuss next.

Think like children → no boundaries

Brainstorming

Brainstorming A freewheeling, face-to-face meeting in which team members generate as many alternative solutions to the problem as possible, piggyback on the ideas of others, and avoid evaluating anyone's ideas during the idea-generation stage.

In the 1950s, advertising executive Alex Osborn wanted to find a better way for teams to generate creative ideas.[64] Osborn's solution, called **brainstorming**, requires team members to abide by four rules that encourage divergent thinking and minimize evaluation apprehension:

1. *No criticism*   The most important rule in brainstorming is that no one should criticize any ideas that are presented. This rule should ensure that more suggestions are presented and team members are less reluctant to offer new ideas.

2. *Encourage freewheeling*   Wild and strange ideas are welcomed because these become the seeds of divergent thinking in the creative process.

3. *Piggyback ideas*   Team members are encouraged to combine and improve on the ideas already presented because this encourages the synergy of team processes (Chapter 10).

4. *Encourage many ideas*   Brainstorming is based on the idea that quality increases with the number of ideas presented. This relates to the notion that divergent thinking occurs after traditional ideas have been exhausted. Therefore, the group should think of as many as possible solutions and go well beyond the traditional solutions to a problem.

Brainstorming is widely used, but it is not a perfect solution for creativity and decision making. One problem is that brainstorming rules do not completely remove evaluation apprehension because employees still know that others are silently evaluating the quality of their ideas. Production blocking and related time constraints prevent all ideas from being presented. In fact, individuals working alone usually produce more potential solutions to a problem than if they work together using the brainstorming method.

On a more positive note, brainstorming rules minimize dysfunctional conflict among members and improve the team's focus on the required task. Brainstorming participants also interact and participate directly, thereby increasing decision acceptance and team cohesiveness. We also need to consider that mature groups may overcome evaluation apprehension and leverage the subtle benefits of face-to-face communication. For example, there is some evidence that effective brainstorming sessions create emotional contagion (Chapter 8). Specifically, team members share feelings of optimism and excitement that may encourage a more creative climate. Clients are often involved in brainstorming sessions, so this emotional contagion may produce higher customer satisfaction than if people are working alone on the product.[65]

Electronic Brainstorming

Electronic brainstorming
Using computer software, several people enter ideas at any time on their computer terminals. Each participant can have the computer list a random sample of anonymous ideas generated by other people at the session to aid in thinking up new ideas.

CIBC, IBM Canada, Ontario Hydro, and other Canadian firms have built specially designed meeting rooms for small groups to participate in **electronic brainstorming**. With the aid of groupware (special computer software for groups), electronic brainstorming lets participants share ideas while minimizing the team-dynamics problems inherent in traditional brainstorming sessions.[66] Individuals can enter ideas at any time on their computer terminal. These ideas are posted anonymously and randomly on the screens of all participants. A central convenor monitors the entire input to ensure that participants stay focused on the issue.

Electronic brainstorming sessions typically take place in a room with up to a few dozen computer terminals. However, participants could be located in different places and attend the "meeting" at different times if the technology is available. The individual's computer screen looks similar to Exhibit 11.6, although this varies with the software used. The statements shown on the upper part of the screen represent a random selection of ideas developed by the group. The individual can look at other ideas already developed by pressing the appropriate function key or mouse command. The lower part of the screen provides space for the individual to type in a new idea.

Effectiveness of electronic brainstorming

The greatest benefit of electronic brainstorming is that it significantly reduces the problem of production blocking. Participants are able to document their ideas whenever they occur, rather than wait their turn to communicate.[67] This process also supports creative synergy because participants can easily develop new ideas from those

EXHIBIT 11.6: Computer Screen of an Electronic Brainstorming Session

PREVIOUS IDEAS

- SUPPLIER COULD PHONE US EVERY FEW HOURS
- HOOK UP OUR COMPUTER TO THE SUPPLIER'S COMPUTER
- HAVE INVENTORY NEEDS CONTINUOUSLY TRANSMITTED TO SUPPLIER
- BECOME OUR OWN SUPPLIER

ENTER NEW IDEA
- MOVE THE SUPPLIER TO OUR LOCATION

Press F10 to see other ideas and enter new ideas

Press Alt/F9 to exit

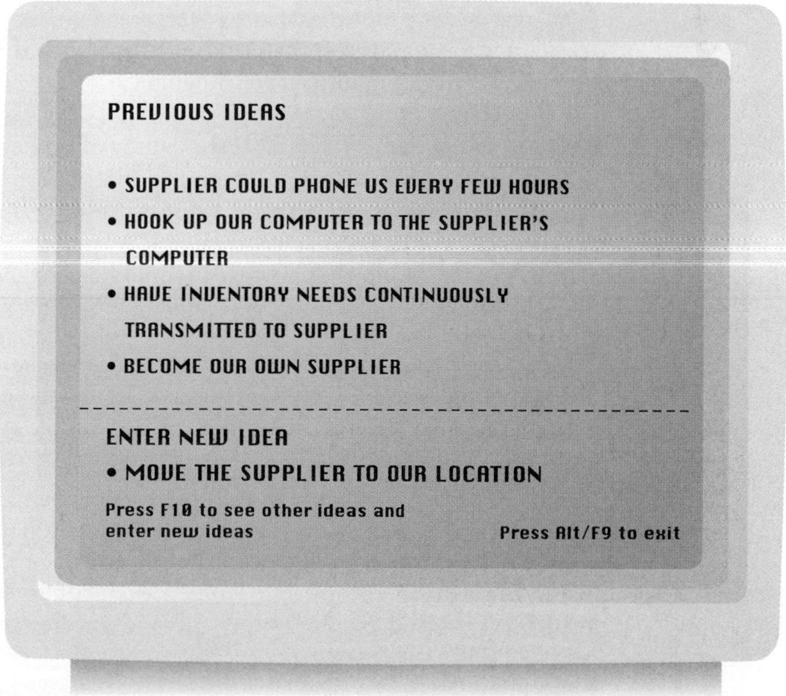

IBM Canada's Decision Support Centre provides the technology and setting for electronic brainstorming. The centre claims that participants can increase team decision-making productivity by 50 percent.

generated by other people. Electronic brainstorming also minimizes the problem of evaluation apprehension because ideas are posted anonymously. "If we had to attach our names to our suggestions, I think people would be less forthcoming," insists an engineer at aircraft manufacturer Boeing Co.[68]

Electronic brainstorming is far more efficient than traditional team decision making because there is little socializing. A study of 64 electronic brainstorming groups at aircraft manufacturer Boeing Co. found that total meeting time was reduced by 71 percent.[69] Following an electronic brainstorming session on the company's budget, a vice-president of Royal LePage explained, "We garnered a substantial amount of information in one session that normally would have required a day or two on each of the subjects." Overall, electronic brainstorming generates more ideas than traditional brainstorming and participants seem to be more satisfied, motivated, and confident in the decision-making exercise than in other team structures.[70]

Despite these advantages, electronic brainstorming is perhaps too structured and technology-bound for most people. Some critics note that the additional number of ideas generated through electronic brainstorming is not enough to justify its cost. Another concern is that organizational participants are generally less enthusiastic about electronic brainstorming sessions than are students who participate in research samples.[71] It would seem odd, for example, to advise clients that they conduct an electronic brainstorm rather than talk to each other. This reflects the fact that electronic brainstorming removes face-to-face conversation and the unexplored benefits (such as emotional contagion and social bonding) that may exist through that communication medium. Lastly, we must consider the political dynamics of electronic brainstorming. Some people may feel threatened by the honesty of some statements and by their inability to control the discussion.

Nominal Group Technique

Nominal group technique A structured team decision-making technique whereby members independently write down ideas, describe and clarify them to the group, and then independently rank or vote on them.

Nominal group technique is a variation of traditional brainstorming that tries to combine individual efficiencies with team dynamics.[72] The method is called *nominal* because participants form a group *in name only* during two stages of decision making. This process, shown in Exhibit 11.7, first involves the individual, then the group, and finally the individual again.

After the problem is described, team members silently and independently write down as many solutions as they can. During the group stage, participants describe their solutions to the other team members, usually in a round-robin format. As with brainstorming, there is no criticism or debate, although members are encouraged to ask for clarification of the ideas presented. In the final stage, participants silently and independently rank order or vote on each proposed solution. Rank ordering is preferred because this forces each person to carefully review all of the alternatives presented.[73] Nominal group technique prefers voting or ranking over reaching consensus to avoid dysfunctional conflict that comes with debate.

St. Joseph's Hospital in London, Ontario, applied nominal group technique when choosing demonstration projects for its quality management program. Team members developed ideas individually, the group discussed and further developed these ideas, and then they were chosen by vote.[74]

Nominal group technique tends to produce more and better quality ideas than do traditional interacting groups.[75] Due to its high degree of structure, nominal group technique tends to maintain a high task orientation and relatively low potential for conflict within the team. However, team cohesiveness is generally lower in nominal decisions because the structure minimizes social interaction. Production blocking and evaluation apprehension still occur to some extent.

EXHIBIT 11.7: Nominal Group Technique Process

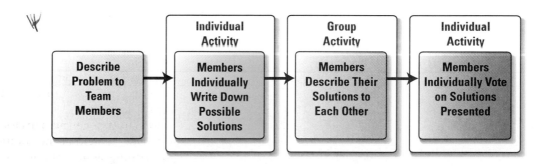

Chapter Summary

- Decision making is a conscious process of making choices among one or more alternatives with the intention of moving toward some desired state of affairs. This involves identifying problems and opportunities, choosing the best decision style, developing alternative solutions, choosing the best solution, implementing the selected alternative, and evaluating decision outcomes.

- People have trouble identifying problems due to perceptual biases and poor diagnostic skills. They have difficulty choosing the best solution because organizational goals are ambiguous or in conflict, they do not process information fully or objectively, and they tend to satisfice rather than maximize. Postdecisional justification and escalation of commitment make it difficult for people to evaluate the outcomes of their decisions.

- When working with others, decisions are impeded by time constraints, evaluation apprehension, conformity to peer pressure, groupthink, and group polarization.

- Individual and team problems with decision making may be minimized by becoming aware of these problems, separating decision choosers from those responsible for implementation and evaluation, improving team dynamics, and using decision support systems.

- Creativity refers to developing an original product, service, or idea that makes a socially recognized contribution. The four creativity stages are preparation, incubation, insight, and verification. Creativity is a function of both the person and the situation. Creativity training programs make people aware of limited mental models, the importance of spending time thinking about the problem, and specific strategies to think differently about a problem or issue.

- Three team structures that potentially improve creativity and team decision making are brainstorming, electronic brainstorming, and nominal group technique.

Discussion Questions

1. A school district is experiencing very high levels of teacher absenteeism. Describe three reasons why school district administrators might not realize that a problem exists or why they are unable to identify the root cause(s) of the high absenteeism.

2. A management consultant is hired by a manufacturing firm to determine the best North American site for its next plant. The consultant has had several meetings with the company's senior executives regarding the factors to consider when making its recommendation. Discuss three problems that might prevent the consultant from choosing the best site location.

3. In the late 1970s, the premier of British Columbia announced that the province would host a transportation exhibition in 1986 with a modest budget of only $78 million. On at least two occasions, administrators recommended cancelling the

exposition due to cost overruns and labour troubles, but the government decided to continue with the project. But by the end of Expo '86, the budget exceeded $1.5 billion with a deficit of $300 million. Using your knowledge of escalation of commitment, discuss four reasons why the government might have been motivated to continue with the project.

4. Production blocking is often identified as a problem in team decision making. Describe production blocking and identify a team structure that minimizes this problem.

5. Ancient Book Company has a problem with new book projects. Even when it is apparent to others that a book is far behind schedule and may not have much public interest, development editors are reluctant to terminate contracts with authors whom they have signed. The result is that development editors invest more time on these projects than on more fruitful projects. As a form of escalation of commitment, describe two methods that Ancient Book Company can use to minimize this problem.

6. Describe the four stages of the creative process.

7. A senior executive committee wants to make better decisions by practising constructive controversy. Identify four things that the group must do to increase constructive controversy.

8. Moncton Widget Corp. wants to use brainstorming with its employees and customers to identify new uses for it widget technology. Advise Moncton Widget's president about the rules to follow for this session.

Chapter Case

Eastern Province Light and Power*

I work as a systems and procedures analyst for the Eastern Province Light and Power Company. The systems and procedures department analyzes corporate policies, procedures, forms, equipment, and methods to simplify and standardize operations. We apply "organized common sense" to develop new practices and to improve old ones.

Requests for analysis of organizational problems are submitted to the systems and procedures department by persons of department head or higher status. Our manager places projects in line for consideration and assigns them to an analyst on the basis of availability; projects are accepted and assigned on the FIFO (first in–first out) method. Projects must undergo analysis, design,

and implementation before a change in procedure is realized. What follows is a description of a problem assigned to me. I am in the midst of investigating it right now.

The Problem
For some time, management had been concerned with the inventory-carrying charges that accrue when material is stored in company warehouses. Not only is there a cost attached to carrying inventory for future use, but there are additional related costs such as labour to handle the inventory, warehouse usage in terms of square feet taken up in storage, and clerical time used to account for materials flowing into and out of inventory. One

type of material stored is office supplies — pens, writing pads, forms, stationery, envelopes, and dozens of similar items. A desire to reduce the costs of storing these items prompted the head of the department of purchasing and material control to submit a request for study by systems and procedures.

The request came in the required written form. It described the current procedures, estimated their costs, and invited us to explore ways of changing the procedures to reduce costs. In brief, at the time the study request was submitted, purchases of office supplies were made through 11 vendors. The items were stored in a common warehouse area and disbursed to using departments as requested. As is customary, I convened a meeting of the requesting manager and others who seemed most directly involved in the problem.

The First Meeting

I opened the meeting by summarizing the present procedures for purchasing and storing office supplies and the estimated costs associated with these problems. I explained that we were meeting to explore ways of reducing these costs. I suggested we might try to generate as many ideas as we could without being too critical of them, and then proceed to narrow the list by criticizing and eliminating the ideas with obvious weaknesses.

Just as soon as I finished my opening remarks, the head of purchasing and material control said that we should conduct a pilot study in which we would contract with one of the regular vendors to supply each involved department directly, eliminating company storage of any inventory. The vendor would continue to sell us whatever we usually purchased from it, but would sell and deliver the items to various departments instead of to our central purchasing group. A pilot study with one vendor would indicate how such a system would work with all vendors of office supplies. If it worked well we could handle all office supplies this way.

She went on to explain that she had already spoken to the vice-president to whom she (and, through intermediate levels, the rest of us) reported and that he recognized the potential savings that would result. She also said that she had

gone over the idea with the supervisor of stores (who reported to her) and that he agreed. She wanted to know how long it would take me to carry out the pilot study. I looked at a few faces to see if anybody would say anything, but nobody did. I said I didn't know. She said, "Let's meet in a week when you've come up with a proposal." The meeting ended without anything else of any real substance being said.

I felt completely frustrated. She was the highest-ranking person in the meeting. She had said what she wanted and, if her stature wasn't enough, she had invoked the image of the vice-president being in agreement with her. Nobody, including me, had said anything. No idea other than hers was even mentioned, and no comments were made about it.

I decided that I would work as hard as I could to study the problem and her proposed pilot study before the next meeting and come prepared to give the whole thing a critical review.

Between Meetings

I talked to my boss about my feeling that it seemed as though I was expected to rubber-stamp the pilot study idea. I said that I wished he would come to the next meeting. I also said that I wanted to talk to some people close to the problem, some clerks in stores, some vendors, and some buyers in purchasing to see if I could come up with any good ideas or find any problems in the pilot study area. He told me to learn all I could and that he would come to the next meeting.

My experience with other studies had taught me that sometimes the people closest to the work had expertise to contribute, so I found one stores clerk, two buyers, and two vendor sales representatives to talk to. Nobody had spoken to any of them about the pilot study and the general plan it was meant to test. This surprised me a little. Each one of these people had some interesting things to say about the proposed new way of handling office supplies. A buyer, for example, thought it would be chaotic to have 17 different departments ordering the same items. She thought we might also lose out on some quantity discounts, and it would mean 17 times the paperwork. A vendor said he didn't think any vendor would like the idea because it would increase the number of contacts necessary to sell the amount that could be sold now through one contact — the buyer in the purchasing department. A stores clerk said it might be risky to depend on a vendor to maintain inventories at adequate levels. He said, "What if a vendor failed to supply us with, say, enough mark-sensing tools for our meter readers one month, thereby causing them to be unable to complete their task and our company to be unable to get its monthly billings out on time?"

The Second Meeting

Armed with careful notes, I came to the next meeting prepared to discuss these and other criticisms. One of the stores clerks had even agreed to attend so that I could call on him for comments. But when I looked around the conference room, everyone was there except the stores clerk. The head of purchasing and material control said she had talked to the clerk and could convey any of his ideas so she had told him it wasn't necessary for him to come.

I pointed out that the stores clerk had raised a question about the company's ability to control inventory. He had said that we now have physical control of inventory, but the proposal involved making ourselves dependent on the vendor's maintaining adequate inventory. The head of purchasing and material control said, "Not to worry. It will be in the vendor's own interest to keep us well supplied." No one, including my boss, said anything.

I brought up the subject of selecting a vendor to participate in the pilot study. My boss mentioned that I had told him some vendors might object to the scheme because the additional contacts would increase their costs of sales. The head of purchasing and material control said, "Any vendor would be interested in doing business with a company as big as Eastern Province Light and Power." No further comments were made.

I mentioned that it was the practice of the systems and procedures staff to estimate independently the costs and benefits of any project before undertaking it, and also to have the internal auditing department review the proposal. I said we would need to go ahead with those steps. I asked the head of purchasing and material control to give me the name of somebody in her area I should contact to get the costs of the present system. She said that it really didn't seem necessary to go through all the usual steps in this case since she had already submitted an estimate. Besides, it was only going to be a pilot study. She said, "I think we can all agree on that and just move ahead now with the designation of a vendor." She looked around the table and nobody said anything. She said, "Fine. Let's use Moore Business Forms." Nobody said anything. She then said to me, "OK, let's get back together after you've lined things up."

---

*D. R. Hampton, *Contemporary Management* (New York: McGraw Hill, 1981). Used with permission.

Experiential Exercise #1

Hopping Orange Exercise

Purpose: To help students understand the dynamics of creativity and team problem solving.

Instructions: You will be placed in teams of six students. One student serves as the official timer for the team and must have a watch, preferably with stopwatch timer. The instructor will give each team an orange (or similar object) with a specific task involving use of the orange. (The objective is easily understood and nonthreatening, and will be described by the instructor at the beginning of the exercise.) Each team will have a few opportunities to achieve the objective more efficiently.

Experiential Exercise #2

Creativity Brainbusters Exercise

Purpose: To help students understand the dynamics of creativity and team problem solving.

Instructions: This exercise may be completed alone or in teams of three or four people, although the latter is more fun. If teams are formed, students who already know the solutions to these problems should identify themselves and serve as silent observers. When finished (or time is up), the instructor will review the solutions and discuss the implications of this exercise. In particular, be prepared to discuss what you needed to solve these puzzles and what may have prevented you from solving them quickly (or at all).

1. *Roman Numeral Problem*
Below is the Roman numeral 9. Add one single line to create a 6.

IX

2. *Nine Dot Problem*
Below are nine dots. Without lifting your pencil, draw no more than four straight lines that pass through all nine dots.

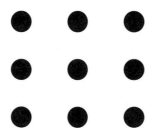

3. *Nine Dot Problem Revisited*
Referring to the nine dot exhibit above, describe how, without lifting your pencil, you could pass a pencil line through all dots with three (3) or fewer straight lines.

4. *Word Search*
In the following line of letters, cross out five letters so that the remaining letters, without altering their sequence, spell a familiar English word.

FCIRVEEALTETITVEERS

CHAPTER 12

Organizational Power and Politics

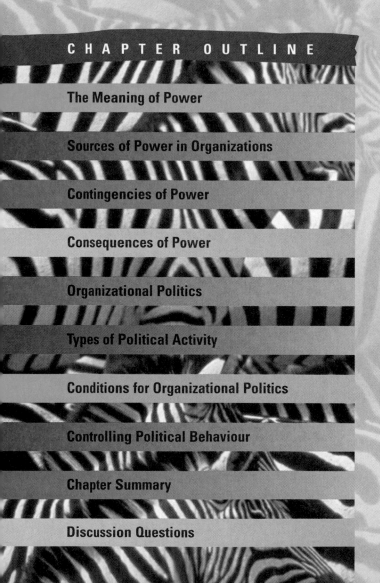

CHAPTER OUTLINE

The Meaning of Power

Sources of Power in Organizations

Contingencies of Power

Consequences of Power

Organizational Politics

Types of Political Activity

Conditions for Organizational Politics

Controlling Political Behaviour

Chapter Summary

Discussion Questions

LEARNING OBJECTIVES

After reading this chapter, you should be able to:

- Define the meaning of power and counter-power.

- Describe the five bases of power in organizations.

- Explain how information relates to power in organizations.

- List four ways to increase power through non-substitutability.

- Discuss the role of power in sexual harassment.

- Summarize the advantages and disadvantages of organizational politics.

- List seven types of political activity found in organizations.

Organizational politics and backstabbing have plagued Intercontinental Packers Ltd. "It was a really ugly situation," admits Fred Mitchell (shown above).

Saskatoon's peaceful prairie life has been disrupted by the Wild West antics at Intercontinental Packers Ltd. (Intercon). Lawsuits, alleged death threats, and corporate politics among its owners, the Mitchell family, have plagued Intercon, which is one of Canada's largest meat-processing companies.

Fred Mitchell stepped down as Intercon's president in the late 1980s when he became deathly ill with cystic fibrosis. Fred's mother, brother, and sister pressured him to place his shares of Intercon into a family trust. Miraculously, Fred recovered and returned as Intercon's CEO in 1991.

But when Fred tried to get his shares back, the other Mitchells refused. Instead, according to Fred, they conspired to strip him of his power. In 1994, his relatives secretly ordered Intercon's senior managers to begin reporting to them instead of Fred. Fred also learned that the family cut off his bonuses and took back his company credit card. Without much power, Fred resigned and his brother, Chip, took over. "I was pushed out," Fred complains. "They ganged up on me — I can't believe my mother and brother and sister would do that."

Fred sued to regain control of Intercon. The other Mitchells sued Fred, claiming that he manipulated creditors and senior management to increase his power. Another lawsuit claimed that Fred's sister, Camille, made death threats against his wife, Lu-Anne. "We certainly know what hell is like," confides Lu-Anne.

Weary from the legal battles, the Mitchells agreed in 1996 to mend fences by having Fred manage Intercontinental with his brother and mother. But the truce didn't last long. Within a year, the family concluded that the only solution was to split the business. Fred and his wife run the pork-processing business in Saskatoon, while his brother, mother, and sister own the beef-processing plant in Moose Jaw. "It was a really ugly situation," admits Fred Mitchell. "We've just had a complete division."[1]

P ower and politics exist in every organization. Some writers suggest that power and politics are ingrained in every decision and action.[2] Power is necessary to coordinate organizational activities, but it might also serve personal objectives that threaten the organization's survival. Moreover, organizations are rapidly changing the distribution of power. Hierarchies are being replaced by flatter structures with empowered employees.[3] Information that was once closely guarded by secretive department heads is now widely available to those who need it. These changes require a careful understanding of the dynamics of power and politics in organizations, which is the focus of this chapter.

We begin by defining power and presenting a basic model depicting the dynamics of power in organizational settings. We then discuss the five bases of power, as well as information as a power base. Next, we look at the contingencies necessary to translate those sources into meaningful power. The latter part of the chapter examines the dynamics of organizational politics, including the various types of political activity, the conditions that encourage organizational politics, and the ways that it can be controlled.

The Meaning of Power

Power The capacity of a person, team, or organization to influence others.

Power is the capacity of a person, team, or organization to influence others.[4] Power is not the act of changing others' attitudes or behaviour; it is only the *potential* to do so. People frequently have power they do not use; they might not even know they have power.

The most basic prerequisite of power is that one party believes he or she is dependent on the other for something of value.[5] This relationship is shown in Exhibit 12.1, where Person A has power over Person B by controlling something that Person B needs to achieve his or her goals. You might have power over others by controlling a desired job assignment, useful information, or even the privilege of being associated with you! These dependency relationships are an inherent part of organizational life because work is divided into specialized tasks and the organization has limited resources with which to accomplish its goals. Also, power is ultimately a perception, so people might gain power simply by convincing others that they have something of value. Thus, power exists when others believe that you control resources that they want.[6]

EXHIBIT 12.1: Dependence in the Power Relationship

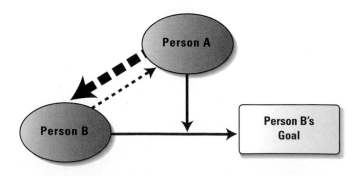

Although power requires dependence, it is more accurate to say that the parties are interdependent. One party may be more dependent than the other, but the relationship exists only when both parties have something of value to the other. Exhibit 12.1 shows a thinner dotted line to illustrate the weaker party's (Person B) power over the dominant participant (Person A). This **counterpower**, as it is known, is strong enough to maintain Person A's participation in the exchange relationship. For example, managers have power over subordinates by controlling their job security and promotional opportunities, but employees have counterpower by controlling the ability to work productively and thereby create a positive impression of the supervisor to that person's boss. Counterpower motivates managers to apply their power judiciously, so that the relationship is not broken.

Counterpower The capacity of a person, team, or organization to keep a more powerful person or group in the exchange relationship.

A Model of Power in Organizations

Power involves more than just dependence. As we see in Exhibit 12.2, the model of power includes both power sources and contingencies. It indicates that power is derived from five sources: legitimate, reward, coercive, expert, and referent. But tapping into one or more of these power bases only leads to increased power under certain conditions. These contingencies of power include the employee's or department's substitutability, centrality, discretion, and visibility. Finally, as we will discuss later, the type of power applied affects the type of influence the powerholder has over the other person or work unit.

Sources of Power in Organizations

More than 30 years ago, French and Raven listed five sources of power within organizations: legitimate, reward, coercive, expert, and referent.[7] Researchers have studied these five power bases and searched for others. For the most part, French and Raven's list remains intact. The first three power bases are derived from characteristics of the powerholder's position, whereas the latter two are derived from the powerholder's own characteristics.[8]

EXHIBIT 12.2: A Model of Power Within Organizations

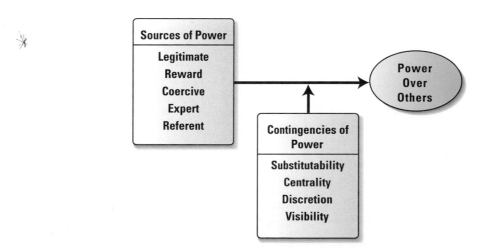

Legitimate Power

Legitimate power The capacity to influence others through formal authority; that is, the perceived right to direct certain behaviours of people in other positions.

Legitimate power is the perceived right to influence certain behaviours of others. It is an *agreement* among organizational members that people in certain roles can request certain behaviours of others. Legitimate power determines the degree of discretion someone has in decision making. In other words, you have a certain amount of legitimate power in the decisions you make, and this discretion is agreed upon by the employees affected by those decisions.[9]

What determines the amount of someone's legitimate power? The person's position is a major factor. Employees mutually agree that people in some jobs have more authority over them than others. The amount of legitimate power vested in a job also varies across cultures. In Korea and other cultures with high power distance, for instance, employees give superiors a great deal of legitimate power.[10] This results in more obedience to authority than we tend to find in Canada.

Some companies have a corporate culture in which individual discretion is valued more than respect for authority. For instance, it is not unusual for a 3M scientist to continue working on a project after being told by superiors to stop working on it. The 3M culture supports an entrepreneurial spirit, which includes ignoring your boss's authority from time to time.[11] The same action in the Canadian Forces, on the other hand, may result in immediate dismissal!

Executives are not the only ones with legitimate power. Employees have the right to ask supervisors and others for assistance or information that will help them per-

---

PERSPECTIVE 12.1

The Power of Peer Pressure

Jen, an employee at a Bay Street brokerage firm, gave up her membership at a Toronto health club. It wasn't the workout or the trouble getting there. Rather, she couldn't take the guilt that co-workers made her feel when she left for the exercise class. "I would go for an hour and fifteen minutes a week," says Jen (not her real name). "But every time I walked out the door, I felt this huge cloud of disapproval, like I was shirking my responsibilities or something."

Peer pressure has always existed in organizations, but some companies are now using it to replace supervisors in controlling employee behaviour. Corel Corp. has been able to stay lean by using teams rather than supervisors to monitor employees. Michael Copeland, CEO of the software company, calls this "the self-correcting phenomenon." In other words, noncontributors are kept in line by the colleagues they see every day instead of by some higher authority.

NUMMI, the joint venture with General Motors and Toyota in California, was one of the early organizations to realize that teams use peer pressure to control their members. "People try to meet the team's expectations," says one NUMMI worker, "and under peer pressure they end up pushing themselves too hard."

The idea that employees pressure their colleagues to work harder does not sit well with labour unions. "Teamwork leads to competition between teams, speed-up, and peer pressure within teams," warns Mumir Khalid, a union leader at McDonnell Douglas Canada. "It also leads to team members reprimanding fellow workers if they are absent or can't keep up for any reason."

Many employees at CAMI Automotive Inc. in Ingersoll, Ontario, would agree with Khalid's statement. When the automobile plant opened in the late 1980s, only 19 percent of employees thought that teams forced workers to exert pressure on one another. But in a more recent survey, 44 percent felt that teams are used as a control system to boost attendance and job performance.

Source: Based on T. Tillson, "Corel Inside Out," *Canadian Business*, Spring 1997, pp.58–62; G. Macdonald, "When Workouts and Work Collide," *Globe & Mail*, October 24, 1995, p. B13; "The Trouble with Teams," *Economist*, January 1995, p. 61; D. Robertson, J. Rinehart, C. Huxley, and the CAW Research Group at CAMI, "Team Concept and *Kaizen*: Japanese Production Management in a Unionized Canadian Auto Plant," *Studies in Political Economy* 39 (Autumn 1992), pp. 77–107; W. List, "CAW Rejects Concept of Work Teams as Not in Workers' Interest," *Globe & Mail*, October 23, 1989, p. B3.

form their jobs.[12] These rights may exist in formal job descriptions or informal rules of conduct. More broadly, Canadian society has an informal rule of reciprocity ("I did that for you, so you should feel obligated to help me") that gives people legitimate power over others who owe them a favour.[13]

Legitimate power can be very strong, because those receiving the order suspend judgment and let the powerholder guide their behaviour. This was demonstrated in a study in which an unknown doctor telephoned a request to several nurses working at their stations. The doctor asked each nurse to give a certain patient in that ward 20 milligrams of Astrogen. This drug was not on the hospital's approved list and hospital rules required a written order (rather than a telephone call) for all such requests. Moreover, the Astrogen was locked in a special cabinet and the bottle carried a label saying that the daily dose should not exceed 10 milligrams per day. Yet 59 percent of the nurses tried to comply with the unknown doctor's order! (They were stopped on their way to the patient's room.)[14] These nurses suspended judgment and placed the doctor's legitimate power above hospital rules and other warnings.

Reward Power

Reward power The capacity to influence others by controlling the allocation of rewards valued by them and the removal of negative sanctions.

Coercive power The capacity to influence others through the ability to apply punishment and remove rewards affecting these people.

Reward power exists for those who control the allocation of rewards valued by others and the removal of negative sanctions (i.e., negative reinforcement). Managers have formal authority that gives them power over the distribution of organizational rewards such as pay, promotions, time off, vacation schedules, and work assignments. Employees may have reward power by extolling praise and extending personal benefits within their discretion to other co-workers. As organizations delegate responsibility and authority, work teams gain reward power over their members. In some organizations, subordinates have reward power over their bosses through the use of 360 degree performance feedback.

Coercive Power

Coercive power, the ability to apply punishment and remove rewards (i.e., extinction), is another source of power. Managers have coercive power through their authority to reprimand, demote, and fire employees. Labour unions might use coercive power tactics, such as withholding services, to influence management in collective agreement negotiations. Clients use coercive power by threatening to take their business elsewhere unless certain improvements occur. For instance, investment analysts are reluctant to give negative reviews of stocks representing their major clients (such as banks) because those clients have threatened to take their underwriting business to other investment houses.[15]

Team members sometimes apply sanctions, ranging from sarcasm to ostracism, to ensure that co-workers conform to team norms. As we see in Perspective 12.1, organizations are leveraging this peer pressure to improve work attendance and

© 1992 Farcus Cartoons/dist. by Universal Press Syndicate   WAISGLASS/COULTHART

"Seeing you brought the gun, Norman, why don't *you* start the meeting?"

performance, particularly in team-based structures where there are no supervisors to watch output.

Expert Power

Expert power The capacity to influence others by possessing knowledge or skills that they want.

Expert power exists when an individual or subunit depends on others for valued information. Employees with unique knowledge or skills may be very powerful if the organization depends on this expertise to achieve organizational objectives such as operating complex equipment. For instance, civilians working at Canada's Department of National Defence have acquired a lot of power because they know how to operate the bureaucracy. Military personnel are rotated around various Canadian Forces bases, so they are dependent on the civilians for their expertise as the corporate memory.[16] Some employees acquire expert power by networking with co-workers to maintain a current knowledge of organizational events. These people are well known for their "inside" information that may help others.[17]

Referent Power

Referent power The capacity to influence others by virtue of the admiration of and identification with the powerholder.

People have **referent power** when others identify with them, like them, or otherwise respect them. This form of power usually develops slowly and is largely a function of the person's interpersonal skills. Referent power is usually associated with organizational leaders, but subordinates may have referent power over their boss. *Charisma* is another concept that we associate with leaders. Charisma is often defined as a form of interpersonal attraction whereby followers develop a respect for and trust in the charismatic individual. Although charisma is similar to referent power in some respects, it is sufficiently different that scholars are now exploring how this concept uniquely relates to power in organizations.[18]

Information and Power

Information plays an important role in organizational power.[19] One type of information power is based on control over the flow and interpretation of data given to others. In traditional hierarchies, specific employees or departments are given legitimate power to serve as gatekeepers, and selectively distribute valued information. The other type of information power refers to the individual's or subunit's ability to cope with organizational uncertainties. This is a variation of expert power that has become a central concept in the literature on organizational power. Let's look more closely at these two aspects of information power.

Control over information flow

Many employees have power by controlling the flow of information that others need. This right to control information flow is found in more bureaucratic firms and is usually accorded to certain work units or people in specific positions. The wheel formation in Exhibit 12.3 depicts this highly centralized control over information flow. The information gatekeeper in the middle of this configuration can influence others through the amount and type of information they receive.

As you can imagine, the centralized information control structure is incompatible with learning-organization and team-based organization concepts. Instead, these

EXHIBIT 12.3: Power Through the Control of Information

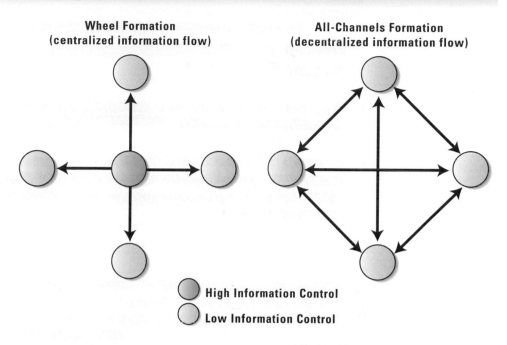

Wheel Formation
(centralized information flow)

All-Channels Formation
(decentralized information flow)

High Information Control

Low Information Control

emerging views call for the all-channel communication structure in which all employees have relatively equal access to information. This allows employees and self-directed work teams to make better decisions. However, the all-channel network may seem chaotic in larger, more structured organizations, so there is a tendency to slip back into the wheel pattern.[20]

Employees and work units are reluctant to give up control over information because it threatens their power base. This happened at the Canadian Imperial Bank of Commerce (CIBC) when it introduced white-collar teams in cheque-processing centres across Canada. Some employees in these centres feared that they would lose control of the information that maintained their power in the organization. "We recognize that information, turf, and ego are huge issues that we have to deal with," says Berkley Emmons, CIBC's director of performance improvement. "It takes a long time to break this down."[21]

Coping with uncertainty

Organizations are open systems that interact with their environments by receiving inputs and transforming them into outputs (Chapter 1). This process involves varying degrees of uncertainty; that is, a lack of information about future events.[22] Uncertainty interferes with the organization's ability to carry out routine activities. Consider the troubles that Canadian steel producers would face if they did not know where to find tomorrow's supply of raw materials or how much demand will exist for their products next week. They could not plan production, arrange long-term contracts with suppliers, or adjust their product lines to satisfy future customer needs. Thus, to operate more efficiently and ensure continued survival, organizations need to cope with environmental uncertainties.[23]

Individuals and their work units gain power by being able to cope with uncertainties related to important organizational goals. Coping includes any activity that effectively deals with environmental uncertainties affecting the organization. In their study of Canadian breweries and container companies, Hinings and his colleagues identified three general strategies to help organizations cope with uncertainty:[24]

- *Prevention*   The most effective strategy is to prevent environmental changes and variations from occurring. For example, financial experts acquire power by preventing the organization from experiencing a cash shortage or defaulting on loans.

- *Forecasting*   The next best strategy is to be able to predict environmental changes or variations. In this respect, marketing specialists gain power by predicting changes in consumer preferences.

- *Absorption*   People and subunits also gain power by absorbing or neutralizing the impact of environmental shifts as they occur. A classic example is the ability of maintenance crews to come to the rescue when machines break down and the production process stops.

Contingencies of Power

Access to one or more sources of power will influence other people or departments only under certain conditions. The four most important contingencies of power in organizations are substitutability, centrality, discretion, and visibility.[25] Keep in mind that these are not sources of power; rather, they determine the extent to which a power base will influence others.

Substitutability

Substitutability The extent to which those dependent on a resource have alternative sources of supply of the resource or can use other resources that would provide a reasonable substitute.

Substitutability refers to the availability of alternatives. Power is strongest when someone has a monopoly over a valued resource. Conversely, power decreases as the number of alternative sources of the critical resource increases. Substitutability refers not only to other sources that offer the resource, but also to substitutions of the resource itself. For instance, labour unions are weakened when companies introduce technologies that replace the need for their union members. At one time, a strike by telephone employees would have shut down operations, but computerized systems and other technological innovations now ensure that telephone operations continue during labour strikes and reduce the need for telephone operators during normal operations. Technology is a substitute for employees and, consequently, reduces union power.[26]

How do people and work units increase their power through nonsubstitutability? There are several ways, although not all of them are ethical. We describe some of them here for your information — not necessarily for you to practise.

- *Controlling tasks*   Professions have legislation preventing outsiders from performing certain tasks within their domain. Lawyers keep paralegals out of certain activities, and doctors keep nurses, midwives, and others away from certain interventions. Chartered accountants require public corporations to use their services in audits.

- *Controlling knowledge*   Professions restrict access to the knowledge of their work domain, such as through restricted enrolment in educational programs. Knowledge is also restricted on the job. Several years ago, maintenance workers in a French tobacco-processing plant had become very powerful because they controlled the knowledge required to repair the tobacco machines.[27] The maintenance manuals had mysteriously disappeared and the machines had been redesigned enough that only the maintenance staff knew how to fix them if they broke down (which they often did). Knowing the power of nonsubstitutability, maintenance staff carefully avoided documenting the repair procedures and didn't talk to production employees about their trade knowledge.

- *Controlling labour*   Aside from their knowledge resource, people gain power by controlling the availability of their labour. Labour unions attempt to organize as many people as possible within a particular trade or industry so that employers have no other source of labour supply.[28] When unionized workers produce almost all of a particular product or service in a society, the union has an easier time increasing wages. The current fight against outsourcing — having outside companies perform some of the work — is partly based on concerns about losing jobs, but it is also a fight against losing union power through substitutability. The union's power during a strike is significantly weakened when the employer can continue production through these outside contractors.

- *Differentiation*   Differentiation occurs when an individual or work unit claims to have a unique resource — such as raw materials or knowledge — that the organization would want. By definition, the uniqueness of this resource means that no one else has it. The tactic here isn't so much to show the nonsubstitutability of the resource, but to make organizational leaders believe that the resource is unique. Some people claim that consultants use this tactic. They take skills and knowledge that many consulting firms can provide and wrap them into a package (with the latest buzzwords, of course) so that it looks like a service that no one else can offer.

Canadian Auto Workers' (CAW) president Buzz Hargrove visits strikers at the General Motors plant in Oshawa. Union members took over the plant to prevent the company from outsourcing some of its production to nonunion labour. Outsourcing reduces the union's power from nonsubstitutability.

✓Centrality

Centrality The degree and nature of interdependence between the powerholder and others.

Employees and departments have more power as their centrality increases. **Centrality** refers to the degree and nature of interdependence between the powerholder and others.[29] There are two dimensions of centrality. One dimension refers to *how many* people are affected by your actions. An organization's finance department, for instance, may have considerable power because its budget activities affect virtually every other department in the organization. In contrast, employees in a branch office may affect very few people in the organization.

The other dimension of centrality refers to *how quickly* people are affected by your actions. Just-in-time inventory systems — where parts or raw materials are delivered to customers when they are needed rather than stockpiled — have given labour unions more power for this reason. With just-in-time, inventory is so low that a strike by employees at one supplier can quickly paralyze the operations of customers who depend on those parts. How quickly people are affected by your actions also depends on timing. As Perspective 12.2 describes, the Major League Baseball Players' Association applied this form of centrality by going on strike at a time that had the greatest impact on the club owners.

✓Discretion

The freedom to exercise judgment — to make decisions without referring to a specific rule or receiving permission from someone else — is another important contingency

---

PERSPECTIVE 12.2

Centrality and Power in a Major League Baseball Strike

Timing is everything in labour disputes. When a labour union needs to take strike action to put pressure on the employer, it wants to have as much power as possible so that its members are off the job for the shortest time possible. By threatening strike action at a critical time, the union increases centrality and, therefore, its power over the employer.

The Major League Baseball Players' Association knows all about centrality and power in labour disputes. A few years ago, the association made the unprecedented announcement that its members would go on strike in September unless club owners came up with an acceptable proposal to replace the existing contract. The players carefully timed the proposed strike so that the World Series would be threatened. A September strike would have cost the players only one-sixth of their salaries, whereas the owners could have lost several hundred million dollars in television revenue from the playoffs and World Series.

Paul Molitor, a Toronto Blue Jay and member of the players' association subcommittee, explains why a players' strike in late summer is better than one in December when

the contract normally ends: "If we strike next spring, there's nothing stopping [the club owners] from letting us go until next June or July because they don't have that much at stake except for gate receipts. I hate to say it, but the only time you can hurt them and get them to negotiate seriously is to have the possibility of a work stoppage this fall."

The baseball strike was avoided that year because the baseball club owners didn't want to suffer severe financial losses. The next year, the players repeated their strategy by going on strike in late August. Unfortunately, the owners resisted their demands and after several weeks of failed negotiations, announced that the World Series was cancelled.

Why did the power of centrality not work for the players the second time? The answer is that the players wanted to alter the owners' financial control of the industry by removing salary caps and introducing revenue sharing with the players. The baseball club owners were willing to lose millions of dollars rather than let this happen. Although timing increases power in labour disputes, even this power has its limits.

Source: Based on J. Deacon, "No Runs, No Hits, Just Errors," *Maclean's*, September 26, 1994, p. 32; "Huge Pitch about to Come," *Calgary Herald*, August 9, 1993, p. D1.

of power in organizations. Consider the plight of first-line supervisors. It may seem that they have legitimate power over employees, but this power is often curtailed by specific rules. They must administer programs developed from above and follow specific procedures in their implementation. They administer rewards and punishments, but must abide by precise rules regarding their distribution. Indeed, supervisors are often judged not on their discretionary skills, but on their ability to follow prescribed rules and regulations. This lack of discretion makes supervisors largely powerless even though they may have access to some of the power bases described earlier in the chapter.[30]

Visibility

Power does not flow to unknown people in the organization. Rather, employees gain power by communicating their sources of power to others. If someone has unique knowledge to help others do their job better, that person's knowledge will yield power only when others are aware of it.

Visibility increases with the number of people with whom you interact in the company. Thus, employees become more visible — and tend to have more successful careers — by taking people-oriented jobs that require extensive contacts rather than isolated technical positions. Similarly, visibility increases with the amount of face-to-face contact rather than less personal forms of communication. People further increase their visibility by introducing themselves to senior management and by being assigned to important task forces. Along with the valuable learning experience, these committees let you work closely with, and get noticed by, senior people in the organization.

People often use public symbols as subtle (and not-so-subtle) cues to make their power sources known to others.[31] Professionals display their educational diplomas and awards on office walls to remind visitors of their expertise. Many senior executives still rely on the size of their office and related status symbols to show their legitimate power in the organization. Even the clothing we wear communicates power. Medical professionals wear white coats with a stethoscope around their necks to symbolize their legitimate and expert power in hospital settings. One Canadian study reported that women who wear jackets are initially perceived as having more legitimate and expert power than women without jackets.[32]

Another way to increase visibility is through mentoring — the process of learning the ropes of organizational life from a senior person within the company. Mentors give protégés more visible and meaningful work opportunities, and open doors for them to meet more senior people in the organization. Mentors also teach these newcomers political skills and tactics supported by the organization's senior decision makers.[33]

Consequences of Power

We use power to influence others, but the type of influence depends on the power source used.[34] Coercive power is generally the least desirable source because it generates *resistance* by the person or department being influenced. In other words, the targetted person tends to oppose the influence attempt and actively tries to avoid carrying it out. Applying coercive power also reduces trust between the parties and increases employee dissatisfaction. Resistance and distrust also occur when other power bases are used arrogantly or in a manipulative way.

Reward and legitimate power tend to produce *compliance*, whereby people are motivated to implement the powerholder's request for purely instrumental reasons.

You will consciously agree to perform an extra task if your boss gives you a bonus for performing that task, but you aren't enthusiastic about it and will certainly do no more than is necessary to receive the reward. *Commitment* is the strongest form of influence, whereby people identify with the powerholder's request and are motivated to implement it even when there are no extrinsic benefits for doing so. Commitment is the most common consequence of expert and referent power. For instance, employees will follow a charismatic leader and do more than is asked because this power base evokes commitment rather than compliance or resistance.

Power also affects the powerholder. As we learned in Chapter 3, some people have a strong need for power and are motivated to acquire it for personal or organizational purposes. These individuals are more satisfied and committed to their jobs when they have increased responsibility, authority, and discretion.[35] However, you should also be warned that people who acquire too much power often abuse their position to better their personal interests and to gain more power.[36] Powerful employees tend to use their influence more often than is necessary, devalue their less powerful co-workers, and reduce their interpersonal associations with them. They also use their power to acquire more power. If unchecked, powerful employees eventually become even more powerful. In short, there appears to be some truth in Lord Acton's well-known statement that "Power tends to corrupt; absolute power corrupts absolutely."[37]

Sexual Harassment: An Abuse of Power

On her first day as secretary at a Vancouver construction company, Joan asked her boss why he hired her. "I either had to hire you or ask you out," he replied. That was the first of several sexual harassment incidents, including leering, calls to her home, and unwanted comments at work about her looks. "I was in tears so many times," recalls the 31-year-old single mother. One time, the manager put his arms around Joan in the photocopy room and wouldn't let her go for some time. After two months, Joan angrily told her boss, "There will never be anything between you and me and I want you to leave me alone." She was fired the next day.[38]

Harassment Unwelcome conduct that detrimentally affects the work environment or leads to adverse job-related consequences for the victims of harassment.

In Chapter 6, we defined **harassment** as unwelcome conduct that detrimentally affects the work environment or leads to adverse job-related consequences for the victims of harassment.[39] The Supreme Court of Canada has concluded that sexual harassment — the most often reported form of workplace harassment — covers a variety of behaviours, ranging from posting pornographic material, leering, and making unwanted sexual comments, to unwanted touching and demanding sexual favours.[40] Statistics Canada reports that nearly one in four women has been sexually harassed on the job. As shown in Exhibit 12.4, most incidents involved inappropriate comments about the woman's body or sexual activities. However, 18 percent of Canadian women who reported sexual harassment were threatened with job loss if they did not engage in a sexual relationship.[41]

Recall from Chapter 6 that harassment is caused by two conditions: the harasser's power and the harasser's prejudices that arise from stereotyping. The issue of prejudice was covered earlier, so let's look more closely at how power is related to sexual harassment. The literature almost always explains sexual harassment in terms of the harasser's power over the victim.[42] This power relationship takes several forms. The most obvious abuse of power occurs when people in higher-level jobs use their position to gain sexual favours from others. This seems to have occurred to Joan at the Vancouver construction company.

EXHIBIT 12.4: Incidents of Workplace Sexual Harassment Against Canadian Women

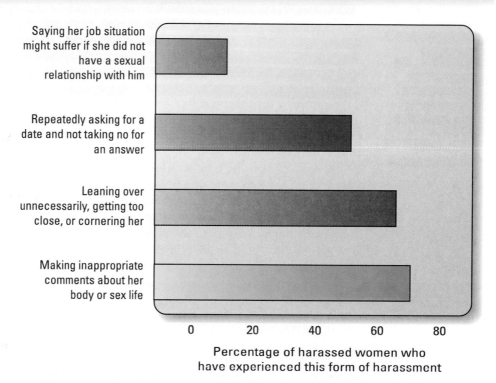

Percentage of harassed women who
have experienced this form of harassment

Saying her job situation might suffer if she did not have a sexual relationship with him

Repeatedly asking for a date and not taking no for an answer

Leaning over unnecessarily, getting too close, or cornering her

Making inappropriate comments about her body or sex life

Source: Based on information in H. Johnston, "Work-Related Sexual Harassment," *Perspectives on Labour and Income*, Winter 1994, pp. 9–12.

Co-workers also abuse their power in ways that cause sexual harassment. Everyone holds coercive and reward power that could potentially be abused to gain sexual favours. For example, an employee might refuse to help a female co-worker unless she agreed to a date.[43] Subordinates abuse power in a more subtle way, by threatening the dynamics of the work relationship. Suppose an employee makes an inappropriate sexual comment to his female supervisor. The supervisor may feel threatened because the comment is offensive, yet she needs to maintain harmony in the working relationship. Supervisors are reluctant to reprimand the harassing subordinate because this disrupts the work dynamic entrusted to the supervisor.

An important characteristic of many sexual harassment incidents is that men are often unaware that their power is causing harassment. They usually view a comment about a co-worker's figure or allure as a compliment. The female co-worker, on the other hand, feels threatened because the situation is awkward and any response may cause the harasser to use his power against her. In short, many men simply don't realize they are harassers, or that they have abused their power in the organization.[44]

Organizational Politics

Organizational politics is a concept that everyone seems to understand until they are asked to define it. Many of us believe that political behaviour is the shady side of organizational life in which people are manipulated without their consent and sometimes without their knowledge. But a more accurate view is that political behaviour

Organizational politics
Attempts to influence others using discretionary behaviours for the purpose of promoting personal objectives; discretionary behaviours are neither explicitly prescribed nor prohibited by the organization and are linked to one or more power bases.

sometimes makes a valuable contribution to organizational effectiveness. People need to be good politicians, particularly as they reach higher levels in the corporation.[45]

We define **organizational politics** as attempts to influence others using discretionary behaviours to promote personal objectives.[46] Organizational politics is the exercise of power to get one's own way, including the acquisition of more power, often at the expense of others. People rely on behaviours that are neither explicitly prescribed nor prohibited by the organization and are linked to one or more power bases.

Consider the situation at Bow Valley Industries Inc., described in Perspective 12.3. The company was eventually able to introduce a computer network that gave employees more open access to information, but not before departments tried to scuttle the development of the new computer system because it threatened their power base. Some people tried to stall the process, whereas others questioned the competence of those who wanted the new system. A few tried to opt out of the process altogether. These actions certainly were not encouraged or sanctioned by the company, but neither were they prohibited. Rather, these informal behaviours fall somewhere between acceptable and unacceptable. As you can see, political behaviours usually occur under conditions of organizational conflict, a topic that we discuss more fully in the next chapter.[47]

PERSPECTIVE 12.3

Organizational Politics at Bow Valley

On a cold January afternoon, employees from Bow Valley Energy Inc. (now part of Renaissance Energy Ltd.) gathered in the company's computer room in downtown Calgary. In silence, they watched a man wearing a black executioner's outfit approach the company's old mainframe computer and throw the switch. The computer died, along with all the applications that ran it.

The event was a symbolic ending to Bow Valley's mainframe era. But to senior management, it was also the end — or so they hoped — to several months of organizational politics. Before that day, Bow Valley's information resided in accounting, land administration, reserves management, well administration, and other departments throughout the organization. Information was power at Bow Valley, and that information power was jealously guarded by the departments that held it.

When Bow Valley's CEO announced that the company would introduce a new computer system allowing information to flow more freely, many people feared that their power base would disappear. Tempers flared in meetings, entire departments opted out of the process, and managers were accused of grandstanding. "It was really unpleasant," winced one manager as he recalls the verbal barrages a few months earlier.

Today, information that previously resided in one department or another is now widely accessible. If someone

Chris Beegen. Courtesy of *Oilweek*.

Switching to a more open computer information network stirred up organizational politics at Bow Valley Energy Inc.

needs a colour map, for example, it can be retrieved from the central server without the person having to go through the map department.

"Philosophically, you have to accept that you are not owners of the data," explains Dr. Gary Moore, the former University of Calgary business professor brought in to transform Bow Valley's information system. "You are stewards of the data on behalf of the corporation. People will buy into that — until they have to give up control."

Source: C. Motherwell, "Bow Valley Uncaps a Well of Knowledge," *Globe & Mail*, January 18, 1994, p. B26; H. Hanley, "A Struggle for Strategic Control," I.T. *Magazine* 25 (December 1993), pp. 2–6; A. Morrall, "A Cause for Celebration," *Oilweek*, May 17, 1993, p. 8; and "Re-engineering Valley," *Economist*, May 1, 1993, p. 68.

Organizational Politics: Good or Bad?

Peter Redman, *Financial Post.* Used with permission.

Michael McCain, Wallace McCain's son, was in the middle of organizational politics between Wallace and co-founder Harrison McCain. "Blocking [Michael] and undermining him is constantly on your mind," Wallace wrote to Harrison during the battle for control of the firm. Eventually, Wallace, Michael, and others on Wallace's side of the family left the giant New Brunswick food company to run a meat-processing company in Toronto.

You might think that all political activities in organizations are bad because they serve the individual's interest, but this is not necessarily so. Political tactics can help organizations achieve their objectives where traditional influence methods may fail. A manager might use politics to influence an important organizational strategy that, in the long run, may be good for the organization. Research scientists and idea champions often build coalitions and rely on other political tactics to help their ideas gain acceptance so that the company provides enough funding to bring these ideas to market.[48] Political actions are also used by individuals to acquire more power. This, again, may be good or bad for the organization, depending on the circumstances.

Although some political behaviours are beneficial, others may be very harmful to the organization.[49] Some political behaviours reduce interpersonal trust and, in the long term, can hurt the firm's profitability, customer service, and employee satisfaction. Moreover, organizational politics potentially wastes time — about 20 percent of an executive's time, according to one source.[50]

The problems with organizational politics are clearly evident in our opening story about Intercontinental Packers Ltd. in Saskatoon. The Mitchell family's tactics to gain or regain control of the company disrupted the company's operations and distracted employees from their work. Similar organizational politics occurred at McCain Foods Ltd., the New Brunswick–based food manufacturer. The two founding brothers, Wallace and Harrison McCain, had accused each other of using political tactics to strengthen their heirs' positions in the company.

When Wallace McCain appointed his son Michael as chief executive officer of McCain USA, Harrison allegedly took steps to limit Michael's authority. "Blocking him and undermining him is constantly on your mind," Wallace wrote to Harrison. Meanwhile, Wallace apparently reduced the authority of Harrison's son, Peter. At one point, Peter wrote to Wallace: "[This] is just another depressingly familiar example of the nepotism and political maneuvering [I] have come to expect from you. You set me up." As in the Intercon situation, the McCain brothers eventually went separate ways. Harrison retained control of McCain's; Wallace left to take over another large Canadian food company. And just as Intercon's financial health faltered during the political turmoil, so did McCain's.[51]

The ethics of organizational politics

Just as a political tactic can be helpful or harmful to the organization, so can it be either ethical or unethical to society. To determine the moral standing of a particular political behaviour, we need to ask the three questions described below. Notice that these questions correspond to the ethical values discussed in Chapter 7. A political behaviour is ethical only if it satisfies all three moral principles.[52]

1. *Utilitarian rule*   Does the political tactic provide the greatest good for the greatest number of people? If it mainly benefits the individual and possibly harms the welfare of others, then the political behaviour is inappropriate. Recall the Bow Valley events described in Perspective 12.3. If Bow Valley's new computer system is good for customers and shareholders, then employees who lose power should not try to scuttle the change effort.

2. *Individual rights rule*   Does the political tactic violate anyone's legal or moral rights? If the political activity threatens another person's privacy, free speech, due process, or other rights, then it should not be used even if the results might be beneficial to a larger audience. For example, even if an incompetent senior executive is undermining shareholder wealth and employee job satisfaction, this does not justify wiretapping his or her telephone for embarrassing evidence that would force the executive to quit.

3. *Distributive justice rule*   Does the political activity treat all parties fairly? If the political behaviour benefits those who are better off at the expense of those who are already worse off, then the activity is unethical. For example, it would be unethical for a manager to take personal credit for a subordinate's project and receive the financial benefits resulting from that performance.

Types of Political Activity

What political tactics are used in organizational settings? There are many, but organizational behaviour scholars have conveniently grouped most of them into the seven categories illustrated in Exhibit 12.5.[53]

Attacking or Blaming Others

Not long ago, senior management at the Canadian Wheat Board in Winnipeg was deciding whether to replace its mainframe with a client/server system of microcomputers. During this tense time, the mainframe and microcomputer experts in the information systems department engaged in a heated battle of political infighting by openly bad-mouthing each other.[54] The mainframe employees would tell anyone who listened that microcomputer systems were inadequate, while the microcomputer people would point to their mainframe colleagues as the source of many evils in the company.

EXHIBIT 12.5: Types of Political Behaviour in Organizations

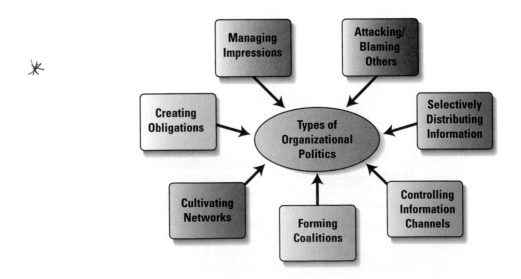

The information systems employees at the Canadian Wheat Board were engaging in one of the most direct forms of political behaviour: attacking and blaming others. They applied the proactive strategy by attempting to give rivals a bad impression in the eyes of decision makers. A more reactive approach is for employees to dissociate themselves from undesirable situations by transferring blame to others (called *scapegoating*), distancing themselves from the event, or using excuses to form an external attribution of the cause of the problem.[55]

Selectively Distributing Information

For several years, the CEO of a major pharmaceutical company asked Graef Crystal, a compensation consultant, to compare the CEO's base pay and bonus with that of other industry leaders. Each year, Crystal's letter indicated that the CEO's pay was approximately in the top 25 percent. Each year, the CEO passed the letter on to the board of directors. But one year, Crystal decided it was more appropriate to look at total compensation, including the CEO's long-term stock options. According to the new calculations, the CEO's total pay was higher than almost everyone else in similar-size companies. Crystal submitted the letter but didn't hear back from the company. A few months later, Crystal happened to meet the human resources vice-president who routinely received these letters for the CEO. When asked what the CEO did with the letter, the executive replied: "He threw it in the wastebasket!"[56]

As we see from this incident, information is a political tool as well as a source of power. People strategically manage the distribution of information to shape perceptions, limit the potential performance of rivals, or further increase their power base. The pharmaceutical company CEO threw out Graef Crystal's letter because he didn't want the board of directors to see that he was overpaid! Similarly, employees have been known to manipulate the data used to determine their pay rates.[57] For example, they might overstate the number of employees under their supervision, embellish the difficulty of their work, or strategically time the completion of certain assignments around performance review times. These data manipulation tactics represent a form of selectively distributing information.

Information politics also involves hoarding information so that it is unavailable to others. For many years, the CIBC was known as a hotbed of information politics. One CEO at the bank was notorious for locking up vital client files while he was away so that no other executive would gain power from knowledge of those important clients. A more dramatic example of information politics occurred in the mid-1980s, when CIBC's chairman and CEO decided to promote another CIBC executive to the CEO role. The chairman had planned to remain as head of the board for another three years, but the new CEO apparently had other plans. Soon after his promotion, the new CEO removed the chairman's name from certain circulation lists so that the chairman no longer received the information so vital to his position. The chairman had lost power, so he retired one year after the new CEO's appointment.[58]

Controlling Information Channels

Through legitimate power, some people can control the interactions among employees as well as the topics of those discussions. Managers might discourage people in different work units from talking directly to each other because this might threaten the manager's power or reveal damaging information. Similarly, committee leaders might organize meeting agendas to suit their personal interests. If leaders want to avoid a decision on a particular topic, they might place the issue near the bottom of the agenda so that the committee either doesn't get to it or is too fatigued to make a final judgment.

Forming Coalitions

When Hill and Knowlton Canada's president stepped down, the influential public relations firm began a rough period of political sparring and uncertainty. Two executives actively wanted the top job and had different agendas for the company's future. Senior vice-president Jo-Anne Polak describes the situation: "The fact of the matter is that both individuals had their own, not necessarily camps, but their own supporters and friends," she says, choosing words carefully. "That's natural when you've worked in a company like this for as long as both of them did. But nobody knew which side would come out ahead. . . That was tough for people, because nobody knew how they fit into the situation."[59]

Coalition **An informal group that attempts to influence people outside the group by pooling the resources and power of its members.**

Hill and Knowlton Canada experienced a form of political behaviour known as a coalition. In Chapter 9, we explained that a **coalition** is an informal group that attempts to influence people outside the group by pooling the resources and power of its members. A coalition usually forms when two people agree on common objectives that they cannot achieve alone — such as getting a particular person promoted to run the company. Coalition formation pools the power of several people toward a common objective that each member is unable to influence alone. By demonstrating their strength in numbers, coalitions also create a sense that an issue has broad appeal and therefore deserves legitimate support.[60]

However, coalitions have adverse side effects. One concern is that they put pressure on others to change, thereby creating compliance rather than commitment to the change.[61] A second concern is that employees who line up behind a losing proposition may suffer in the long run. At Hill and Knowlton Canada, for example, several employees who backed the losing executive left the company within the year. "When you firmly position yourself and firmly support one person," explains Jo-Anne Polak, "if the company takes a different direction, then you're less comfortable with it."

Cultivating Networks

"It's not what you know, but who you know that counts!" This often-heard (and usually annoying) statement reflects the philosophy behind another political tactic known as **networking**. Networking refers to cultivating social relationships with others to accomplish one's goals. By forming a trust network, people receive valuable information that increases their expert power in the organization.[62] Networking also nurtures allies and sponsors, thereby making it easier to get approval for projects and other initiatives. Finally, networking helps employees increase their referent power, and this may lead to more favourable decisions by others in the network.

Networking **Cultivating social relationships with others for the purpose of accomplishing one's goals.**

Networking is a natural part of the informal organization, yet it can create a formidable barrier to those who are not actively connected to it. Women have difficulty getting into senior management because they are usually excluded from powerful networks.[63] One reason for this exclusion may be that women are unaware of the importance of networks for career advancement. Another explanation is that men (still the dominant powerholders in most organizations) don't feel as comfortable networking with women as they do with other men. But perhaps the most important reason is that men don't realize that their informal networks shut women out from information and decision making. Edwina Woodbury, senior vice-president and chief financial officer for Avon Products, Inc., sums up the problem: "It's there all the time," she said. "How many business conversations [and] business decisions are made in the men's room or on golf day?"[64]

Creating Obligations

Earlier in the chapter we noted that legitimate power can exist through the norm of reciprocity. The obligation to help someone who has once helped you is a deeply embedded norm in Canadian society. It is also a frequently used political tactic.[65] For example, an employee who has helped someone might later ask that person to put in a good word or support them on a promotion. The indebted co-worker is more likely to agree to this than if there is no debt to repay. Some organizational politicians are able to leverage these debts for a greater return than whatever was given initially.

Managing Impressions

Impression management
The practice of actively shaping our public images.

Impression management is the practice of actively shaping our public images.[66] Many impression management activities are done routinely to satisfy the basic norms of social behaviour. Others are political tactics because they are used deliberately to get one's way. Some political tactics described earlier — including blaming others, filtering information, and increasing the visibility of one's power base — are forms of impression management. Another well-known impression management tactic is to manage your appearance and behaviour so that others develop a desired image of you.[67] For example, the way we dress is part of the impression management process.

Employees use a variety of impression management tactics to receive more favourable performance appraisal reviews.[68] For example, those who are often out of the office might put in more "face time" prior to the annual appraisal. Other people perform their best work around the time the boss is considering merit increases.

Conditions for Organizational Politics

Organizational politics flourish under the right conditions.[69] One such condition is scarce resources. When budgets are slashed, people rely on political tactics to safeguard their resources and maintain the status quo. Another important condition is the existence of complex and ambiguous rules in resource allocation decisions. This occurs because decision makers are given more discretion over resource allocation, so potential recipients of those resources use political tactics to influence the factors that should be considered in the decision. Finally, political tactics are more common if they are tolerated or actually reinforced by the organization.[70] If left unchecked, organizational politics can take on a life of its own and the company becomes paralyzed. Political activity becomes self-reinforcing unless the conditions supporting political behaviour are altered.

Personal Characteristics

A person's personality and values can influence his or her likelihood of engaging in organizational politics.[71] In Chapter 3 we learned that some people have a strong personal need for power. They seek power for its own sake, and use political tactics to acquire more power. People with a high internal locus of control are more likely than those with a high external locus of control to engage in political behaviours to shape the world around them. This does not mean that internals are naturally political; rather, they are more likely to use influence tactics when political conditions are present because, unlike externals, they feel very much in charge of their own destiny.

Machiavellian values
The belief that deceit is a natural and acceptable way to influence others.

Some people have strong **Machiavellian values**. Machiavellianism is named after Niccolo Machiavelli, the 16th-century Italian philosopher who wrote the well-known treatise about political behaviour, *The Prince*. People with high Machiavellian values believe that deceit is a natural and acceptable way to influence others. They seldom trust co-workers and frequently use power to manipulate others toward their own personal goals, even when these goals are unfavourable to the organization. In particular, these people tend to use cruder influence tactics, such as bypassing one's boss or being assertive.[72]

Gender differences in organizational politics

When Gil Amelio suddenly left as Apple Computer's CEO in 1997, he sent a letter to employees identifying the things he claims to have achieved during his tenure. Apple executive vice-president Ellen Hancock stepped down at the same time. When interviewed, she mainly thanked Apple employees for the opportunity to work with them and for their support in getting the company turned around.[73]

Amelio was mainly pushed out by Apple's board of directors whereas Hancock voluntarily left, but their actions might also reflect differences in the way men and women approach organizational politics. According to some sources, men are more likely than women to use direct impression management tactics.[74] Like Amelio, most men are comfortable advertising their achievements and taking personal credit for successes of others reporting to them. Women are more reluctant to force the spotlight on themselves, preferring instead to share the credit with others.

Men and women also seem to differ in assigning blame.[75] Research suggests that women are well known for apologizing — personally taking blame — even when the problems are not caused by them. Men are more likely to assign blame and less likely to assume it. In fact, some men try to turn their errors into achievements by appearing as the white knight to save the day. This difference is consistent with our discussion of gender communication (Chapter 8), namely, that men tend to communicate and behave in ways that support their status and power.[76]

If they don't rely on blaming or impression management, then which political tactics do women tend to use? According to some writers, women don't use any political tactics very well in organizations, and this has limited their promotional opportunities.[77] If anything, women probably use more indirect impression management as well as forms of networking and coalition building. Of course, we must be careful not to generalize gender differences too much. Some women are very agile corporate politicians, and some men are politically inept in organizations.

Controlling Political Behaviour

The conditions that fuel organizational politics also give us some clues about how to control dysfunctional political activities. When resources are necessarily scarce, companies should formalize the organization; that is, introduce rules and regulations to specify the use of those resources.[78] Reward systems can be introduced that encourage information sharing. Information systems should be redesigned to avoid the wheel pattern that centralizes information power in the hands of a few people. Team norms and organizational values can eventually be restructured so they reject political tactics that interfere with organizational effectiveness. One strategy is to forewarn employees about political tactics so that people are exposed when trying to practise them. Finally, companies can try to hire people with low Machiavellianism and personal need for power.

Chapter Summary

- Power is the capacity to influence others. It exists when one party perceives that he or she is dependent on the other for something of value. However, the dependent person must also have counterpower to maintain the relationship.

- There are five power bases: legitimate (formal authority), reward (positive and negative reinforcement), coercive (punishment and extinction), expert (knowledge), and referent (charisma and attraction). Information plays an important role in organizational power. Employees gain power by controlling the flow of information that others need, and by being able to cope with uncertainties related to important organizational goals.

- Power bases are leveraged into actual power only under four conditions: individuals and subunits are more powerful when they are nonsubstitutable; quickly affect many others (centrality); have considerable discretion; and are visible.

- Power is applied to influence others, but the type of influence depends on the power source. Coercive power tends to produce resistance; reward and legitimate power result in compliance; expert and referent power produce commitment. People with a high need for power feel more satisfied and committed to their jobs when they have power, but many people tend to abuse their power when given too much of it.

- Harassment is an abuse of power as well as evidence of prejudice. This power abuse occurs from subordinates and co-workers, not just supervisors and higher-ranking people. Men are often unaware that their power causes sexual harassment.

- Organizational politics attempt to influence others using discretionary behaviours that promote personal objectives. People tend to have an unfavourable view of organizational politics, but some political activities benefit the organization. Still, we must always consider the ethical implications of political behaviours.

- There are many types of organizational politics. The most common tactics include attacking or blaming others, selectively distributing information, controlling information channels, forming coalitions, cultivating networks, creating obligations, and managing impressions.

- Organizational politics is more prevalent when scarce resources are allocated using complex and ambiguous decisions, and when the organization tolerates or rewards political behaviour. Individuals with a high need for personal power, an internal locus of control, and a Machiavellian personality have a high propensity to use political tactics. Women are less likely than men to use organizational politics, particularly direct impression management and blaming tactics, to get ahead in their career.

Discussion Questions

1. What role does counterpower play in the power relationship?

2. You have just been hired as a brand manager of soda biscuits for a large Canadian consumer products company. Your job mainly involves encouraging the advertising and production groups to promote and manufacture your product more effectively. These departments aren't under your direct authority, although company procedures indicate that they must complete certain tasks requested by brand managers. Describe the sources of power you can use to ensure that the advertising and production departments will help you make and sell soda biscuits more effectively.

3. Suppose you have formal authority to allocate performance bonuses to your employees. What contingencies must exist before this source of power will translate into actual power?

4. What two organizational behaviour concepts influence harassment in the workplace?

5. Power does not flow to unknown people in the organization. Discuss three types of activities that will increase the visibility of your power without appearing to be a disrespectful political tactic.

6. The author of a popular press business book recently wrote: "Office politics is a demotivator that must be eliminated." He argues that when companies allow politics to determine who gets ahead, employees put their energy into political behaviour rather than job performance. Discuss the author's comments about organizational politics.

7. How might employees use (or misuse) information as a political tactic?

8. How do men and women tend to differ in their use of organizational politics?

Chapter Case

Analyzing Political Behaviour in Organizations

Incident 1: Seeking a Better Career Opportunity

Jill Pettroci, an engineering supervisor for an Ontario municipality, wanted a more challenging job in the organization. She mentioned this to her immediate supervisor a few times over the past year, but he was ambiguous and somewhat evasive about her chances of promotion. One day, a recruitment firm telephoned Jill to ask whether she was interested in a more senior management position with another Ontario municipality. Jill told the recruiter that she needed a few days before deciding to attend an interview, even though she really had no interest in leaving her current employer. During those days, Jill casually mentioned the conversation to the vice-president of human resources and explained that she hoped for a more senior job here. As Jill predicted, the VP talked to her immediate supervisor who, in turn, suddenly told Jill that she would probably receive a promotion within the next few months.

Incident 2: The Politics of Sweet Success

James Tadki's research group at Canadian Beer Ltd. identified a new sugar substitute that requires another year of laboratory work before market feasibility can be assured. Tadki believed the patent could be easily licensed to food manufacturers, but the research director felt that it deviated from the company's core business (beer) and therefore shouldn't receive more funding. Rather than watch the innovation die in the laboratory, Tadki quietly mentioned the matter to his friends throughout the company, some of whom worked with the manufacturing vice-president (the research director's boss). Tadki also "happened" to meet the company president and manufacturing VP at a golf course and briefly mentioned the issue. In reality, Tadki learned about their tee-off time from a secretary and made a point of playing golf at that time with a neighbour who belongs to the club. None of these activities were known to the research director, who was later surprised to hear the manufacturing VP suggest that Tadki's work may be valuable to the company.

Discussion Questions (for both incidents)

1. What political tactics did Jill and James use in these incidents?

2. Assess the ethical justification of these political tactics using the three ethical criteria described in this chapter.

3. What would you have done differently than the people in these incidents?

Experiential Exercise

Power Relations in a Loonie Organization*

Purpose: This exercise is designed to help you to understand some of the power dynamics that occur across hierarchical levels in organizations.

Instructions: This exercise works best with a class of 50 people or more with a session lasting one hour or longer. It also works best when there is a secluded office, an adjoining room (with a door between them), and a large nearby hallway. Students are also asked to make a small financial sacrifice — usually contributing a one dollar coin (loonie) each.

After submitting their financial contribution to the instructor, students are divided into three groups by the instructor. Five people (the instructor may vary this number slightly) are put into the top group and assigned to a small closed office. They receive two-thirds of the money given to the instructor. Approximately 10 students (or twice as many as the top group) are assigned to the middle group and assigned to the adjoining office. The middle group receives the other one-third of the money. The remaining students (at least 20 people) are put into the lower group and are sent into the hallway or other moderately large space near the two closed offices. Students are given five minutes to read the rules and group tasks presented below. The exercise should take at least 30 or 40 minutes with another 20 to 30 minutes for post-exercise discussion. Representatives from each group will be asked to answer the questions below to the class during the post-exercise discussion phase.

Rules: Members of the top group are free to enter the space of either the middle or lower groups and to communicate whatever they wish, whenever they wish. Members of the middle group may enter the space of the lower group whenever they wish, but must request permission to enter the top group's space. The top group can refuse the middle group's request. Members of the lower group are not allowed to disturb the top group in any way unless specifically invited by members of the top group. The lower group does have the right to knock on the door of the middle group and request permission to communicate with them. The middle group can refuse the lower group's request.

Tasks: The top group's task is responsibility for the organization's overall effectiveness, deciding how to use its money, and learning from the exercise. The middle group's task is to assist the top group in its responsibility for the organization's overall effectiveness, and to decide how to use the middle group's money. The lower group's task is to identify its resources, decide how best to contribute to the organization's effectiveness, and how to contribute to the learning process.

Post-Exercise Discussion Questions: What can we learn from this exercise about power in organizational hierarchies? How is this exercise similar to relations in real organizations? How did students in each group feel about the amount of power they held? How did they exercise their power in relations with the other groups?

*This exercise is based on ideas in B. Oshry, *Power and Position* (Boston: Power and Systems, 1979); and L. Bolman and T. Deal, "A Simple — But Powerful — Power Simulation," *Exchange* 4 (Summer 1979), pp. 38–42.

CHAPTER 13

Organizational Conflict and Negotiation

CHAPTER OUTLINE

What Is Conflict?

Consequences of Organizational Conflict

Sources of Conflict in Organizations

Interpersonal Conflict Management Styles

Structural Approaches to Conflict Management

Resolving Conflict Through Negotiation

Third-Party Conflict Resolution

Chapter Summary

Discussion Questions

LEARNING OBJECTIVES

After reading this chapter, you should be able to:

- Distinguish task-related from socio-emotional conflict.

- Discuss the positive and negative consequences of conflict.

- Identify six sources of organizational conflict.

- Outline the five interpersonal styles of conflict management.

- Summarize six structural approaches to managing conflict.

- Outline four situational influences on negotiations.

- Describe four objectives of third-party dispute resolution.

- Discuss the preferred third-party intervention strategy in organizations.

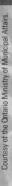

The Ontario government's Subsidies Management Branch overcame intense conflict among its employees by help-ing them form a better understanding of each other and their common goals.

During Paul Hallson's first day of employment with the Ontario government's Subsidies Management Branch (SMB), he realized that the place was riddled with conflict. The first thing he noticed was that employees didn't speak to each other — except to shout. "At one point, a vicious argument broke out over the photocopier, which was next to my workstation," he recalls. Later, Hallson felt the window beside him rattle. "It had been hit by a heavy computer printout report that one staff member had thrown at another."

Coincidentally, Roberta Veley became SMB's director on the same day that Paul Hallson joined. She also has vivid memories of the problems in that department. "That first week, two male staff members came into my office and broke into tears," she recalls. "It was clear that a way had to be found to get people to care more about themselves and their colleagues," she says.

Veley believed that the employees had to take charge of the change. So, with a consul-tant's help, SMB staff organized a retreat where they led sessions to better understand each other. One session, called Recognizing the Value of Each Others' Jobs, helped to clarify their dependent relationships. Another session, Shaping Our Future, began the process of estab-lishing a common set of objectives for SMB staff.

Over the year, the physical workplace was spruced up so that employees were prouder to work there. SMB staff attended an Outward Bound team-building retreat in the woods, where they learned the value of depending on each other. These conflict management and team development interventions have significantly improved relations among SMB staff. "The truth is, we have come an amazingly long way," Veley acknowledges.[1]

C onflict may occur anywhere two or more people interact with each other. It can either energize the organization or wear it down and degenerate into organizational politics. This chapter looks at the dynamics of conflict in organizational settings. We begin by defining conflict, describing the conflict cycle, and discussing the consequences and sources of conflict in organizational settings. Five conflict management styles are then described, followed by a discussion of the structural approaches to conflict management. The last two sections of the chapter introduce two important types of procedures for resolving conflict: negotiation and third-party resolution.

What Is Conflict?

Conflict The process in which one party perceives that its interests are being opposed or negatively affected by another party.

Conflict is a process in which one party perceives that its interests are being opposed or negatively affected by another party.[2] Conflict is a perception, so it begins when someone *believes* that another might obstruct his or her efforts. This may be a mild disagreement between two people regarding the best choice in a decision. Or it may be the foundation of an all-out war between two nations.

Task-Related Versus Socio-Emotional Conflict

Conflict is not always bad, so we need to find ways to allow (or even encourage) mild forms of conflict without having it escalate into an emotional battle among employees or corporate divisions. The key is to keep conflict task-related, and to prevent it from escalating to a socio-emotional state.[3] When conflict is task-related, the parties view the conflict experience as something separate from them. It is an object "out there" that must be addressed. This conflict is potentially healthy and valuable because it makes people rethink their perspectives of reality. As long as the conflict remains focused on the issue, new ideas may emerge and the conflict remains controlled.

Unfortunately, conflict often becomes personal. Rather than focusing on the issue, each party starts to see the other person as the problem. Their differences are viewed as personal attacks rather than attempts to resolve an issue. The discussion becomes emotionally charged, so that perceptual biases are introduced and information processing is impeded.

Conflict escalation cycle

The conflict process is often described as a series of conflict episodes that potentially link together into an escalation cycle or spiral.[4] One party communicates to the other party in a way that creates a perception of conflict. The second party's response may alert the first party to the conflicting relationship. If the conflict remains task-related, both parties may resolve the conflict through logical analysis. However, the communication process has enough ambiguity that an interaction may trigger an emotional response and set the stage for socio-emotional conflict.

The perceptual process then adopts an "us-them" frame of reference, so that the other party's actions are more likely to receive a negative interpretation. These distorted beliefs and emotions reduce the motivation to communicate with the other side. Unfortunately, the parties then rely more on stereotypes to reinforce their image of the other side. These conditions make it more difficult to discover common ground and resolve the conflict.[5] As we shall learn in this chapter, some structural conditions increase the likelihood of conflict escalation. Employees who are more confrontational and less diplomatic also tend to escalate conflict.[6]

Consequences of Organizational Conflict

Conflict management
Interventions that alter the level and form of conflict in ways that maximize its benefits and minimize its dysfunctional consequences.

There is a natural tendency to suppress conflict. While suppression may be appropriate for socio-emotional conflict, task-related conflict should be encouraged under some conditions.[7] Thus, **conflict management** refers to interventions that alter the level and form of conflict in ways that maximize its benefits and minimize its dysfunctional consequences.

It has been said that if two people agree, one of them is unnecessary. This means that conflict is good (potentially) and that agreement is redundant. This is the concept of constructive controversy that was introduced in Chapter 11. Task-related conflict helps people to recognize problems, identify a variety of solutions, and better understand the issues involved.[8] Conflict is a catalyst for change and improved decision making. It occurs when people raise new perspectives of issues and these emerging views are debated.[9] For example, Telus Corporation, Alberta's largest telephone company, encourages constructive controversy in meetings so that solutions are critically evaluated and dominant employees do not overwhelm the process.

Conflict between groups or organizations potentially improves team dynamics within those units. Teams increase their cohesiveness and task orientation when they face an external threat. Under conditions of moderate conflict, this motivates team members to work more efficiently toward these goals, thereby increasing the team's productivity.

There is, of course, a darker side to conflict in organizations. When managed poorly, conflict encourages organizational politics by motivating people to attack or undermine the activities of their adversaries. For example, one study of conflict episodes at a Canadian engineering firm reported that conflict caused employees to ignore valuable advice, avoid communicating with some co-workers, and disregard design flaws so that co-workers would look incompetent.[10] Perspective 13.1 describes

Courtesy of Telus Corporation.

Telus Corporation, Alberta's largest telephone company, uses constructive controversy to debate new ideas. Constructive controversy is a form of task-related conflict, because it encourages team members to discuss different options more fully and think more carefully about the consequences of their decisions.

PERSPECTIVE 13.1

Revenge of the Andons: Conflict at CAMI and Subaru-Isuzu

The General Motors–Suzuki plant (CAMI) in Ingersoll, Ontario, and the Subaru-Isuzu plant in the United States were supposed to be models of cooperative labour-management relations. Instead, understaffing and the stress of continuous improvement (*kaizen*) have created battlefields of industrial conflict. "[Managers] want complete control over us as people and it's come to the point where we're starting to realize this and we're rebelling," says Teresa Parsons, a production associate at the CAMI plant.

Employees are hitting back with andons — the yellow and red cords at each workstation that management provided to improve productivity. When an employee pulls the yellow andon, a repetitive song starts playing and the workstation number is lighted on a large board above the assembly line. This alerts the team leader that help is needed at that station. The red andon cord stops the entire assembly line, so employees are discouraged from pulling it unless a team leader is not available to solve the problem with the line moving.

At CAMI, employees rebelled against understaffing by frequently pulling the red andons. "One of the things we did out at the CAMI plant . . . was to get people to pull those damn andon cords," explains Rob Pelletier, a former CAMI employee. "If you're short [of] people, stop the line. They put those cords there, not us."

For example, one CAMI team was understaffed because management refused to replace an injured employee. In retaliation, the team started pulling the red andons whenever they got behind a little. "They pulled that cord 87 times in one day," says Pelletier. "The new person was on that line the next day."

Similar conflicts occur at the Subaru-Isuzu automobile plant, but one production team discovered how to stop the assembly line without management tracing their location. Whenever one team member fell behind and no team leader or group leader was in sight, the group executed its secret strategy and the entire car line stopped. This gave everyone an opportunity to catch up or take a break. It was also entertaining to watch management trying in desperation to find the source of the line stoppage. On one shift, the team stopped the line several times for a total of 20 minutes!

Source: L. Graham, "Yosh!" *Across the Board* 32 (October 1995), pp. 37–41; J. Rinehart, C. Huxley, and D. Robertson, "Worker Commitment and Labour Management Relations Under Lean Production at CAMI," *Relations Industrielles* 49 (1994), pp. 750–75; Canadian Auto Workers, *Working Lean: Challenging Work Reorganization* (Video) (Toronto: CAW, 1993).

the adverse consequences of conflict at the CAMI automobile plant in Ingersoll, Ontario, and the Subaru-Isuzu plant in the United States. This conflict often results in frustration, job dissatisfaction, and stress. Unbridled conflict may cause employees to escape from the situation through turnover or absenteeism.[11]

Sources of Conflict in Organizations

What are the main sources of conflict in organizations? We often hear that employees have conflicting personalities, but this explains relatively few disputes. More often, conflict germinates and flourishes under the six conditions identified in Exhibit 13.1. In a given situation, more than one of these six factors may be contributing to conflict.

Goal Incompatibility

At the Consumers Packaging plant in Bramalea, Ontario, production employees are divided into the "hot end" and "cold end" of the production process. The hot end

EXHIBIT 13.1: Sources of Conflict in Organizations

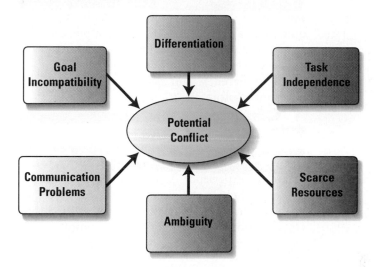

forms the glass containers that make their way down the line to the cold end, where they are packed for shipment. The cold-end employees receive bonuses for minimizing the number of customer complaints and returns, so they weed out jars that don't meet high standards. This doesn't sit well with the hot-end employees, however, because they earn bonuses based on their output and rejection rate. The fewer bottles rejected by employees at the cold end, the fatter the bonuses of employees at the hot end.[12]

As you might imagine, the cool-end and hot-end employees don't always get along with each other. Hot-end employees complain that their cold-end co-workers are too fussy about product quality. Cold-end employees don't like the hot-end employees questioning their quality control decisions. The conflict in this situation is due to goal incompatibility. The more the cold-end employees try to achieve their goal, the more their actions interfere with the goals of the hot-end employees. Notice that conflict due to incompatible goals is strengthened when the opposing parties receive financial rewards for their goal achievement.[13] This further entrenches the perceived conflict because employees are more motivated to pursue their own goals.

Differentiation

When Japan's Mitsui Bank and Taiyo Kobe Bank merged to form Sakura Bank, the new entity was supposed to be more efficient and have more economic clout. It did not work out that way. The managements of the two banks refused to work together, even on basic operational matters. One American banker who did business with Sakura soon after the merger recalls working separately with representatives from each of the former banks rather than together. The merged staff wouldn't even get together on their own to iron out differences of opinion, so the American had to act as a middleman. "They wouldn't even sit down in the same room together," complains the American banker.[14]

Sakura Bank experienced conflict primarily due to differentiation. Differentiation occurs when employees hold divergent beliefs and attitudes due to their unique backgrounds, experiences, or training. Mergers create this form of conflict because they bring together people with divergent corporate cultures. Employees fight over the "right way" to do things. This often results in the loss of valuable talent as professionals quit to escape the conflict. For example, after National Bank of Canada acquired investment firm Lévesque Beaubien Geoffrion Inc., 10 of Lévesque's 25 investment bankers — including all of its senior people — left the company. Most of these people apparently quit because they disagreed with National's executives about Lévesque's future directions.[15]

Differentiation partly explains why the potential for conflict is higher in a multicultural workforce.[16] Employees from different cultural backgrounds have difficulty understanding or accepting each other's beliefs and values toward organizational decisions and events. Differentiation also explains why many organizations experience conflict among its technical and professional employees. Through their specialized training and career patterns, these people learn to see problems in a particular way and have difficulty understanding other perspectives. Organizations unwittingly fuel this employee conflict by hiring people for their technical knowledge and encouraging them to become even more specialized.

Task Interdependence

Task interdependence
The degree to which the task requires collective action. High task interdependence exists when team members must share inputs or outcomes, or need to interact while executing their work.

Conflict tends to increase with the level of **task interdependence**. Recall from Chapter 9 that task interdependence exists when a work activity requires collective action. Under these conditions, employees must share common inputs to their individual tasks, need to interact in the process of executing their work, or receive outcomes (such as rewards) that are partly determined by the performance of others.[17] The higher the level of task interdependence, the greater the risk of conflict because there is a greater chance that each side will disrupt or interfere with the other side's goals.[18] Exhibit 13.2 illustrates the three levels of task interdependence.[19]

EXHIBIT 13.2: Levels of Task Interdependence

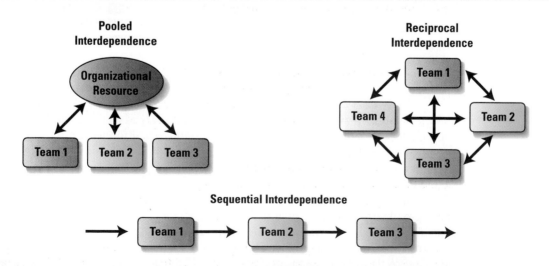

Source: Based on J. D. Thompson, *Organizations in Action* (New York: McGraw-Hill, 1967), pp. 54–56.

- *Pooled interdependence* This is the weakest form of interdependence (other than independence), in which work units operate independently except for reliance on a common resource or authority. Students experience this level of interdependence when they are lined up at the laser printers trying to get their assignments done just before a class deadline. The same thing happens in organizations. Corporate divisions must share scarce resources provided by headquarters, thereby increasing potential conflict.

- *Sequential interdependence* This occurs where the output of one person or unit becomes the direct input for another person or unit. This interdependent linkage is found in fish processing plants. Fish are handled by the slitter, then passed to the gutter, who then pass their work to the slimers, who then send their work to the grader.[20]

- *Reciprocal interdependence* This is the highest level of interdependence, in which work output is exchanged back and forth among individuals or work units. This relationship exists between bus drivers and maintenance crews in virtually every Canadian transit authority. Drivers are dependent on the maintenance crews to keep the buses in good repair, whereas the maintenance crews are dependent on the drivers to operate the vehicles wisely so that their work is minimized.

Scarce Resources

Scarce resources generate conflict because scarcity motivates people to compete with others who also need those resources to achieve their objectives.[21] Division leaders and plant managers sometimes experience this conflict over allocation of budgets because there is rarely enough money to meet everyone's needs.

Ambiguity

Ambiguity breeds conflict because the uncertainty increases the risk that one party intends to interfere with the other party's goals. The ambiguity encourages political tactics and, in some cases, employees enter a free-for-all battle to win decisions in their favour. When rules exist, on the other hand, everyone knows what to expect from each other and have agreed to abide by those rules.

Communication Problems

As we noted in the conflict escalation process, ineffective communication typically triggers the conflict cycle. When one party communicates its disagreement in an arrogant way, opponents are more likely to heighten their perception of the conflict. Arrogant behaviour also sends a message that the party intends to be competitive rather than cooperative. This may lead the other party to reciprocate with a similar conflict management style.[22]

Conflict also escalates when the parties limit the amount of communication with each other. This explains (along with differentiation, described earlier) why conflict is more likely to occur in a multicultural workforce. People tend to feel uncomfortable or awkward interacting with co-workers from different cultures, so they are less motivated to engage in dialogue with them. This is one reason that minorities are often excluded from key organizational information and are less willing to disclose their own ideas and opinions to others.[23] With limited communication, people rely more on stereotypes to fill in missing information. They also tend to misunderstand each other's verbal and nonverbal signals, further escalating the conflict.

Interpersonal Conflict Management Styles

Win-win orientation A person's belief that the parties will find a mutually beneficial solution to their conflict.

Win-lose orientation A person's belief that the conflicting parties are drawing from a fixed pie, so his or her gain is the other person's loss.

Based on their initial experiences and personal dispositions, some people enter a conflict with a **win-win orientation**. This is the perception that the parties will find a mutually beneficial solution to their disagreement. They believe that the resources at stake are expandable rather than fixed if the parties work together to find a creative solution to their problem. Other people enter a conflict with a **win-lose orientation**. They adopt the belief that the parties are drawing from a fixed pie, so the more one party receives, the less the other party will receive.

Conflict tends to escalate when the parties develop a win-lose orientation because they rely on power and politics to gain advantage. A win-lose orientation may occasionally be appropriate when the conflict really is over a fixed resource, but few organizational conflicts are due to perfectly opposing interests with fixed resources. To varying degrees, the opposing groups can gain by believing that their positions aren't perfectly opposing and that creative solutions are possible.

Adopting a win-win or win-lose orientation influences the way we approach the conflict, including our actions toward the other person. Researchers have categorized five interpersonal styles of approaching the other party in a conflict situation. As we see in Exhibit 13.3, each approach can be placed in a two-dimensional grid reflecting the person's motivation to satisfy his or her own interests (called *assertiveness*) and to satisfy the other party's interests (called *cooperativeness*).[24] Collaboration is the only style that represents a purely win-win orientation. The other four styles represent variations of the win-lose approach.[25] For effective conflict management, we should learn to apply different conflict management styles to different situations.[26]

EXHIBIT 13.3: Interpersonal Conflict Management Styles

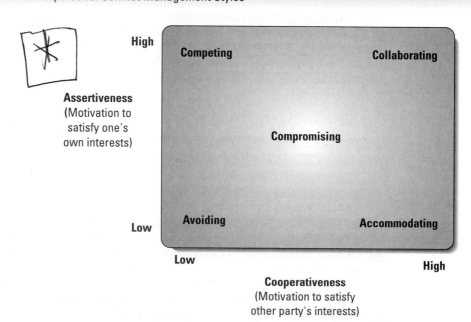

Source: Based on T. L. Ruble and K. Thomas, "Support For a Two-Dimensional Model of Conflict Behavior," *Organizational Behavior and Human Performance* 16 (1976), p. 145. Reprinted with permission.

- *Collaborating*   Collaboration tries to resolve the conflict through problem solving. It is best when the parties do not have perfectly opposing interests and when they have enough trust and openness to share information. Collaborating is usually desirable because organizational conflicts are rarely win-lose situations. There is usually some opportunity for mutual gain if the parties search for creative solutions.[27]

- *Avoiding*   Avoiding tries to smooth over or avoid conflict situations altogether. For example, some employees will rearrange their work area or tasks to minimize interaction with certain co-workers.[28] This may be appropriate where the issue is trivial, or as a temporary tactic to cool down heated disputes. However, conflict avoidance should not be a long-term solution, because it increases the other party's frustration.

- *Competing*   Competing tries to win the conflict at the other's expense. This style has the strongest win-lose orientation because it has the highest level of assertiveness and lowest level of cooperativeness. Competing may be necessary where you know you are correct, the dispute requires a quick solution, and the other party would likely take advantage of more cooperative strategies. However, the competing style is usually inappropriate because organizational relationships rarely involve complete opposition.

- *Accommodating*   Accommodating involves giving in completely to the other side's wishes, or at least cooperating with little or no attention to your own interests. This style may be appropriate when your original position is wrong, the other party has substantially more power, or the issue is not as important to you as to the other party. On the other hand, accommodating behaviours may give the other side unrealistically high expectations, thereby motivating them to seek more from you in the future. In the long run, accommodating may produce more conflict rather than resolve it.

- *Compromising*   Compromising tries to reach a middle ground with the other party. You look for a position in which your losses are offset by equally valued gains. This style may be best when there is little hope for mutual gain through problem solving, both parties have equal power, and both are under time pressure to settle their differences. However, compromise is rarely a final solution and may cause the parties to overlook options for mutual gain.

Cultural and Gender Differences in Conflict Management Styles

Although the conflict style we choose is partly influenced by the type of dispute, it is also affected by personal characteristics, including cultural background. Culture determines the values and interests that define conflict. Cultural values cause some people to perceive a conflict where others do not. Moreover, even where two people from different cultures perceive the same conflict, their conflict management style may differ. This is because conflict styles must be consistent with the person's personal and cultural value system.[29]

People from collectivist cultures — where group goals are valued more than individual goals — tend to collaborate or avoid conflict more than people in individualistic cultures. This likely occurs because those with collectivist values are motivated to maintain harmonious relations. People from individualistic cultures are more likely to compromise or be competitive.[30]

Some writers suggest that men and women often rely on different conflict management styles.[31] Generally, women tend to pay more attention than men to the relationship between the parties. Consequently, they rely more often on a collaborative style in business settings, and are more willing to compromise to protect the relationship. Men tend to be more competitive and take a short-term orientation to the relationship. We must be cautious about these observations, however, because gender has a weak influence on conflict management style.

Structural Approaches to Conflict Management

The conflict management styles described above focus on how to approach the other party in a conflict situation, but conflict management also involves altering the underlying structural causes of potential conflict identified in Exhibit 13.4. Although this section discusses ways to reduce conflict, keep in mind that conflict management sometimes calls for the introduction of conflict. This occurs mainly by reversing the strategies described below.[32]

Emphasizing Superordinate Goals

Superordinate goal A common objective held by conflicting parties that is more important than their conflicting departmental or individual goals.

A potentially valuable way to minimize conflict, particularly when it is caused by differentiation, is to focus everyone on a superordinate goal. **Superordinate goals** are common interests held by conflicting parties that are more important than the departmental or individual goals on which the conflict is based. Employees often lose sight of their common goals and, instead, emphasize their differences. These may be conflicting departmental goals or competing personal values and beliefs. By emphasizing superordinate goals, these differences become less important and conflict is reduced.[33]

Superordinate goals might be framed by corporate leaders, or they may occur naturally by threats from the external environment. Consider the experience of Canadian Airlines International (CAI), described in Perspective 13.2. CAI was formed from several airline mergers, resulting in "colour-coded conflict" as employees continued to identify with their original airline. But when CAI's financial health faltered and a merger with arch rival Air Canada seemed likely, CAI's employees put aside their differences and fought for their independence.

Reducing Differentiation

Emphasizing superordinate goals may reduce conflict, but it doesn't remove the differences on which the conflict is based. To reduce differentiation, some companies

---

EXHIBIT 13.4: Structural Approaches to Conflict Management

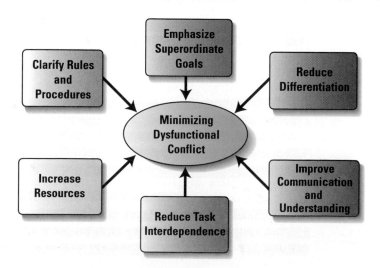

PERSPECTIVE 13.2

Colour-Coded Conflict at Canadian Airlines International

Canadian Airlines International (CAI) is the result of five airlines that merged over six years. These airlines had energetic leaders who established distinct operating procedures and demanded absolute loyalty from their employees. When the airlines merged into CAI, employees continued their allegiance to their former airline by identifying themselves with its colour — blue for Pacific Western, orange for Canadian Pacific, yellow for Nordair, and so on. This differentiation produced a level of conflict among CAI employees that hurt morale and customer service.

Sidney Fattedad, a CAI director and former executive, describes the colour-coded conflicts that permeated the organization: "Coffee circles began to form around colour codes rather than work groups, and prospective transferees were asked what colour they came from. In some areas, colour heritage decided a promotion, explained a botch-up, or was offered as a reason why things couldn't change."

CAI's colour-coded conflict ended in 1992 when the company was forced by its high debt load to enter merger talks with Air Canada. CAI's employees may have come from different airlines, but they were from entrepreneurial companies that viewed Air Canada as their main rival. These common values sparked an immediate collective reaction to news of the merger talks. CAI employees formed a rescue team that developed an employee concession and investment proposal to avoid the Air Canada merger.

Even when the proposal was developed and received government support, the rescue team faced another formidable challenge — getting the six unions representing CAI's workforce to set aside their past conflicts and agree on the plan. Some of the union leaders had fought with each other

The colour-coded conflict of Canadian Airlines International ended when a proposed merger with Air Canada created superordinate goals for employees.

over past violations on picket lines and in grievances, so they were very defensive and guarded in their discussions. As one union official recalls: "There was a lot of mistrust and negative body language during the first few meetings. It took a lot of late nights and bad pizza to build a bond."

The union leaders eventually agreed to the employee plan and the Air Canada merger was averted. Now that CAI is putting its financial house in order, most employees have replaced their colour-coded conflict with talk about working together to ensure the airline's success. As one flight attendant remarked: "I just want to say this is my airline. I'm proud."

Sources: S. O. Fattedad, "Behind the Scenes at Canadian Airlines," *CGA Magazine*, June 1993, pp. 30–33, 75, 76; D. McMurdy, "A New Way of Saving Jobs," *Maclean's*, September 20, 1993, pp. 18–20; C. Motherwell, "Loyal Employees Airline's Foundation," *Globe & Mail*, November 30, 1992, pp. B1, B7; and C. Cattaneo, "Flying to the Rescue," *Calgary Herald*, August 30, 1992, pp. B1, B2.

develop a generalist, rather than specialist, career orientation within the organization. Many Japanese companies follow this strategy by moving employees around to different jobs, departments, and regions.[34]

W. L. Gore and Associates, which makes everything from Gore-Tex to high-tech cables, moves employees around to different teams so that they maintain a common perspective of the organization and its values. This rotation occurred after it became apparent that employees were paying too much attention to their original team. "You can get a little too focused on your own team and forget the good of the whole company," admits one of Gore's team members.[35]

Reducing differentiation can be as simple as relaxing dress codes so that employees and managers wear more similar clothing. This strategy helped to improve employee-management relations at Chrysler Canada's Windsor plant. "One of our first changes was relaxing the dress code," explains Chrysler Canada manager Adrian Vido. "Although this may seem insignificant, it did make a difference. Our supervisors and managers were viewed by the workers as less 'different' without suits and ties!"[36]

Improving Communication and Understanding

Dialogue A process of conversation among team members in which they learn about each other's personal mental models and assumptions, and eventually form a common model for thinking within the team.

Direct communication can minimize conflict so that people develop a better understanding of each other's work environments and resource limitations. Some companies introduce **dialogue** meetings, in which the disputing parties discuss their differences. In Chapter 9, we learned that dialogue helps the two sides understand each other's mental models and fundamental assumptions so that they can create a common thinking process and mental models for the team.[37]

Dialogue can occur informally, simply by giving the parties more opportunity to interact with each other. Dufferin Aggregates, a large gravel quarry in Milton, Ontario, reduced dysfunctional conflict between its supervisors and employees in this way. Supervisors were on a different shift-rotation schedule than employees, so a particular supervisor didn't spend much time with his or her employees. By aligning the supervisors' shift schedule with their employees, the two groups communicated more often and developed better understanding. "By teaming up the foremen with the specific work crews, they all started to understand each other," says John Beck, Dufferin's mine manager. "Over the past year, we have actually experienced better labour relations."[38]

Intergroup mirroring

Intergroup mirroring A structured conflict management intervention in which the parties discuss their perceptions of each other and look for ways to improve their relationship by correcting misperceptions.

When relations between two or more work teams or departments are openly hostile, it may be advisable to introduce **intergroup mirroring** with the assistance of a trained facilitator.[39] The basic objective is for the conflicting groups to express their perceptions, discuss their differences, and then work out strategies to improve the relationship. The process is unique, because both sides share their images of themselves and each other so that distortions and misunderstandings are revealed and ultimately corrected.

Intergroup mirroring is usually a multi-day retreat that begins with the parties identifying and prioritizing their relationship problems. Next, the two groups separately list three sets of perceptions. One list describes the group's perception of itself. The second list describes how the group perceives the other group. The third list describes the group's beliefs about how the other group perceives it. The "mirroring" activity in intergroup mirroring occurs when the two sides meet again to exchange their perceptions of each other. After discussing these perceptions, the two sides jointly review their relationship problems, usually in small groups that combine both sides. Finally, the participants establish goals and action plans to correct their perceptual distortions and establish more favourable relationships in the future. This typically includes future meetings that review and evaluate progress.

Mutual gain bargaining applies some of the principles of intergroup mirroring to minimize dysfunctional conflict during labour-management negotiations.

Reducing Task Interdependence

Reducing the level of interdependence between the parties can avoid or minimize dysfunctional conflict. If cost-effective, this might occur simply by dividing the shared resource so that each party has exclusive use of part of it. Sequentially or reciprocally interdependent jobs might be combined so that they form a pooled interdependence.

For example, rather than having one employee serve customers and another operate the cash register, each employee could handle both customer activities alone.

Another strategy is to introduce buffers between employees in sequentially or reciprocally interdependent tasks. Just-in-time practices tend to remove inventory buffers, so companies need to identify the optimal level to minimize both costs and the risk of conflict. Some companies use human buffers — coordinators who minimize conflict among highly interdependent work units.[40] Mobil Oil relied on this strategy when it integrated its upstream (drilling) and downstream (processing and marketing) workforce in various global regions. These two groups, which have significantly different perspectives of the oil business, had previously worked fairly independently. Mobil's reorganization created a reciprocal interdependence, so coordination councils were set up in each region to minimize conflict when this reorganization occurred.[41]

Increasing Resources

An obvious way to reduce conflict due to resource scarcity is to increase the amount of resources available. Corporate decision makers quickly dismiss this solution because of the costs involved. However, they need to carefully compare these costs with the costs of dysfunctional conflict arising out of resource scarcity.

Clarifying Rules and Procedures

Some conflicts arise from ambiguous decision rules regarding the allocation of scarce resources. Consequently, these conflicts can be minimized by establishing rules and procedures. This strategy was used when conflicts emerged (Perspective 13.3) between

---

PERSPECTIVE 13.3

Armstrong and Booz Allen Sort Out Their Differences

Armstrong Worldwide, Inc. didn't expect so much conflict when the flooring and building materials company brought in consultants from Booz Allen & Hamilton, Inc. to implement a client/server network. "[These conflicts] created a large amount of stress and some turnover for us," says Robyn Alspach, Armstrong's information systems development manager.

Armstrong discovered three sources of conflict during the contract with Booz Allen. First, although Armstrong had no plans to outsource its information systems activities, employees in that area were worried that they would be replaced by consultants. To some extent, this made them reluctant to give the consultants information about Armstrong's operations. "They think, 'Everything could get outsourced, so why should I share with them?'" Alspach explains.

A second source of conflict is who should lead the project — the people at Armstrong or Booz Allen? Booz Allen was given the leadership role, but this decision simply added

to the tension. The problem was that Armstrong's information systems people would be responsible for the system long after the consultants from Booz Allen were gone, so they felt somewhat trapped by the consultants' power.

Scheduling was a third major source of conflict. Booz Allen consultants preferred working 12-hour days, Monday through Thursday, then flying home on Friday. This didn't sit well with Armstrong's people, who lived nearby and therefore favoured a traditional schedule.

Armstrong and Booz Allen tried to minimize these conflicts by spelling out as much as possible in the contract about each party's responsibilities and roles. Issues that were unclear or overlooked in the contract were clarified by joint discussion between two senior executives at the companies. With the benefit of hindsight, Robyn Alspach offers the following advice: "You have to plan for the potential conflicts up front, then you have a better chance of resolving them amicably."

Source: Adapted from E. Horwitt, "Knowledge, Knowledge, Who's Got the Knowledge," *Computerworld*, April 8, 1996, pp. 80, 81, 84.

information systems people at Armstrong World Industries and consultants from Booz Allen & Hamilton, Inc. The two companies ultimately reached a clearer agreement in their relationship that minimized conflicts arising from ambiguity and goal incompatibility.

Clarifying rules can also help two parties when there are scarce resources. If two departments are fighting over the use of a new laboratory, a schedule might be established that allocates the lab exclusively to each team at certain times of the day or week. In some respects, the schedule reduces resource interdependence by dividing it among those who need it to fulfil their goals. This approach also reduces the need for direct contact between the parties, thereby minimizing the likelihood of episodes that might further escalate conflict.

Resolving Conflict through Negotiation

Negotiation Any attempt by two or more conflicting parties to resolve their divergent goals by redefining the terms of their interdependence.

Negotiation occurs whenever two or more conflicting parties attempt to resolve their divergent goals by redefining the terms of their interdependence.[42] In other words, people negotiate when they think that discussion can produce a more satisfactory arrangement (at least for them) in their exchange of goods or services. Employees negotiate with their supervisors over next month's work assignments, suppliers negotiate with purchasing managers over the sale and delivery schedules of their product, and union representatives negotiate with management over changes to the collective agreement.

Some writers suggest that negotiations are more successful when the parties adopt a collaborative style, whereas others caution that this conflict management style is sometimes costly.[43] We know that any win-lose style (competing, accommodating, etc.) is unlikely to produce the optimal solution, because the parties have not shared information necessary to discover a mutually satisfactory solution. On the other hand, we must be careful about adopting an openly collaborative style until mutual trust has been established. The concern is that information is power, so information sharing gives the other party more power to leverage a better deal if the opportunity occurs. Skilled negotiators often adopt a *cautiously* collaborative style at the outset by sharing information slowly and determining whether the other side will reciprocate. In this respect, they try to establish trust with the other party.[44] They switch to one of the win-lose styles only when it becomes apparent that a win-win solution is not possible or the other party is unwilling to share information with a cooperative orientation.

Bargaining Zone Model of Negotiations

The negotiation process moves each party along a continuum with an area of potential overlap called the *bargaining zone*.[45] Exhibit 13.5 displays one possible bargaining zone situation. This linear diagram illustrates a purely win-lose situation — one side's gain will be the other's loss. However, the bargaining zone model can also be applied to situations in which both sides potentially gain from the

Negotiation occurs all around us in organizational settings. At this *Globe & Mail* meeting, editors negotiate with each other for line space and the priority of items that should appear in tomorrow's newspaper. These people negotiate to resolve their divergent goals by redefining the terms of their interdependence.

EXHIBIT 13.5: Bargaining Zone Model of Negotiations

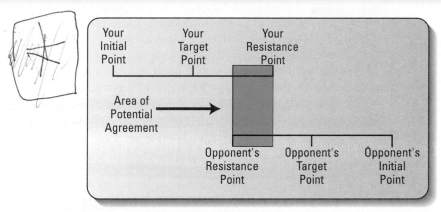

negotiations. As this model illustrates, the parties typically establish three main nego-tiating points. The *initial* offer point is the team's opening offer to the other party. This may be its best expectation or a pie-in-the-sky starting point. The *target point* is the team's realistic goal or expectation for a final agreement. The *resistance point* is the point beyond which the team will not make further concessions.

The parties begin negotiations by describing their initial offer point for each item on the agenda. In most cases, the participants know that this is only a starting point that will change as both sides offer concessions. In win-lose situations, neither the target nor resistance points are revealed to the other party. However, people try to discover the other side's resistance point because this knowledge helps them determine how much they can gain without breaking off negotiations.

In purely win-win settings, on the other hand, the objective is to find a creative solution that keeps both parties close to their initial offer points. They can hopefully find an arrangement by which each side loses relatively little value on some issues and gains significantly more on other issues. For example, a supplier might want to delay delivery dates, whereas delivery times are not important to the business customer. If the parties share this information, they can quickly agree to a delayed delivery sched-ule, thereby costing the customer very little and gaining the supplier a great deal. On other items (financing, order size, etc.), the supplier might give something with min-imal loss even though it is a significant benefit to the business customer.

Situational Influences on Negotiations

What makes some negotiations work more smoothly than others? What factors influence the negotiation outcomes? In this section, we briefly describe four situational factors and four negotiator behaviours that provide some answers to these questions. Four of the most important situational factors are location, physical setting, time, and audience.

Location
It is easier to negotiate on your own turf because you are familiar with the negotiating environment and are able to maintain comfortable routines.[46] Also, there is no need to cope with travel-related stress or depend on others for resources during the negotia-tion. Of course, you can't walk out of negotiations as easily when its your own turf, but this is usually a minor issue.

Considering these strategic benefits of home turf, many negotiators agree to neutral territory. Increasingly, computer technology is making it possible for two distant groups to negotiate without a location or, more correctly, by remaining at their own location.[47] However, electronic messages are subject to misinterpretation and conflict can easily escalate if the parties engage in flaming (Chapter 8). Even videoconferencing is seldom used in negotiations because it does not adequately capture the subtle nonverbal cues that negotiators rely on for feedback about their offers and counteroffers. Negotiation requires high media richness due to the complexity and ambiguity of issues, so face-to-face meetings are usually required at some point.

Physical setting

The physical setting can be very important in negotiations.[48] Some high-level government negotiators have even refused to negotiate unless the negotiation table is set up in a particular way. People who sit face-to-face are more likely to develop a win-lose orientation toward the conflict situation. When a win-win orientation is preferred, both parties should disperse their representatives around a circular table and meet in an informal setting. The physical distance between the parties and formality of the setting can also influence the parties' orientation toward each other and the disputed issues.

Time passage and deadlines

Time passage and deadlines are two important factors in negotiations. The more time people invest in negotiations, the stronger is their commitment to reaching an agreement. This increases the motivation to resolve the conflict, but it also results in the escalation of commitment problems described in Chapter 11. For example, the more time put into negotiations, the stronger the tendency to make unwarranted concessions so that the negotiations do not fail.

Time deadlines may be useful to the extent that they motivate the parties to complete negotiations. However, time deadlines may become a liability when exceeding deadlines is costly.[49] Negotiators make concessions and soften their demands more rapidly as the deadline approaches. Moreover, time pressure inhibits a collaborative conflict management style because the parties have less time to exchange information or present flexible offers.

Skilled negotiators try to keep their own time limits flexible. For example, one Brazilian company invited a group of Americans to negotiate a contract the week before Christmas. The Brazilians knew that the Americans would want to return to the United States by Christmas, so they delayed agreement until the last minute to extract more concessions from their visitors. The final agreement definitely favoured the Brazilians.[50]

Audience characteristics

Most negotiators have audiences — anyone with a vested interest in the negotiation outcomes, such as senior management, other team members, or even the general public. Negotiators tend to act differently when their audience observes the negotiation or has detailed information about the process, compared to situations in which the audience only sees the end results.[51] When the audience has direct surveillance over the proceedings, negotiators tend to be more competitive, less willing to make concessions, and more likely to engage in political tactics against the other party.[52] This "hard-line" behaviour shows the audience that the negotiator is working for their interests. With their audience watching, negotiators also have more interest in saving face. Sometimes, audiences are drawn into the negotiations by acting as a source of indirect appeals. The general public often takes on this role when groups negotiate with the provincial or federal governments.[53]

Negotiator Behaviours

Negotiator behaviour plays an important role in resolving conflict. Four of the most important behaviours are planning and goal setting, gathering information, communicating effectively, and making concessions.

- *Planning and goal setting*   Research consistently reports that people have more favourable negotiation results when they plan and set goals.[54] In particular, negotiators should carefully think through their initial offer, target, and resistance points.

- *Gathering information*   Effective negotiators spend more time listening than talking during negotiations. They gather information by listening closely to the other party and asking them for details of their position.[55] Some people negotiate in teams and make each member responsible for listening intently to specific issues related to their expertise. This potentially improves the information-gathering process, although it also introduces problems with coordinating among several people.[56] With more information about the opponent's interests and needs, negotiators are better able to discover low-cost concessions or proposals that will satisfy the other side.

- *Communicating effectively*   Earlier in the chapter, we noted that poor communication often triggered conflict escalation. That certainly applies to negotiations, where both sides listen closely to each other for hidden meaning.[57] Studies report that effective negotiators communicate in a way that maintains effective relationships between the parties. Specifically, they tend to (1) discuss issues rather than people, (2) avoid making irritating statements such as "I think you'll agree that this is a generous offer," and (3) use effective persuasion tactics by managing the content of their messages (Chapter 8).[58] In general, they try to avoid escalating the conflict.

- *Making concessions*   Concessions are important because they (1) enable the parties to move toward the area of potential agreement, (2) symbolize each party's motivation to bargain in good faith, and (3) tell the other party of the relative importance of the negotiating items.[59] How many concessions should you make? This varies with the other party's expectations and the level of trust between you. For instance, Chinese negotiators are wary of people who change their position during negotiations. Similarly, Russian negotiators tend to view making concessions as a sign of weakness rather than a sign of trust.[60] Generally, the best strategy is to be moderately tough and give just enough concessions to communicate sincerity and motivation to resolve the conflict.[61] Being too tough can undermine relations between the parties; giving too many concessions implies weakness and encourages the other party to use power and resistance.

Third-Party Conflict Resolution

Third-party conflict resolution Any attempt by a relatively neutral person to help the parties resolve their differences.

Most of this chapter has focused on people directly involved in a conflict, yet many disputes in organizational settings are resolved with the assistance of a third party. **Third-party conflict resolution** is any attempt by a relatively neutral person to help the parties resolve their differences. This may range from formal labour arbitration to informal managerial interventions to resolve disagreements among employees.

There are at least four objectives in third-party conflict resolution.[62] One objective is *efficiency*. Those who take the third-party role try to resolve the dispute quickly and with minimum expenditure of organizational resources. Second, the conflict resolution should be *effective*, meaning that the process should find the best long-term solution which will correct the underlying causes of the conflict. Third, this process should have outcome fairness, which ensures that the parties feel that the solution provided by the third-party intervention is fair. Although outcome fairness is similar to effectiveness, they are not the same because people sometimes think that a solution is fair even though it does not work well in the long term.

Finally, third-party conflict resolution should ensure that the parties feel that the dispute resolution process is fair, whether or not the outcome is favourable to them. This objective, known as **procedural fairness**, is particularly important when the third party makes a binding decision to resolve the dispute. In these situations, procedural fairness increases when the third party isn't biased (e.g., doesn't have a vested interest toward one party), is well informed about the facts of the situation, and has listened to all sides of the dispute. It also increases when the decision can be appealed to a higher authority and the third party applies existing policies consistently.[63]

Procedural fairness
Perceptions of fairness regarding the dispute resolution process, whether or not the outcome is favourable to the person.

Types of Third-Party Intervention

There are generally three types of third-party dispute resolution activities: mediation, arbitration, and inquisition. As Exhibit 13.6 illustrates, these activities can be classified by their level of control over the process and control over the decision.[64]

EXHIBIT 13.6: Types of Third-Party Intervention

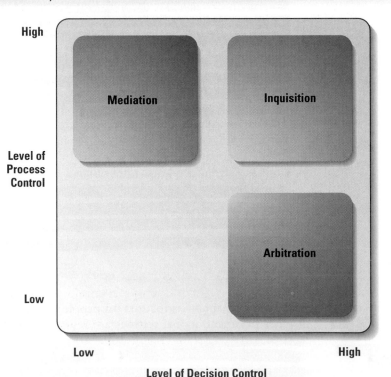

- *Mediation*   Mediators have high control over the intervention process. In fact, their main purpose is to manage the process and context of interaction between the disputing parties. However, the parties still make the final decision about how to resolve their differences. Thus, mediators have little or no control over the conflict resolution decision. Some organizations, including MacMillan Bloedel and DuPont Canada Ltd. have an ombuds officer to mediate conflicts between management and employees, such as allegations of employment discrimination.[65]

- *Arbitration*   Arbitrators make a binding decision on the conflicting parties and, consequently, have high control over the final decision. However, arbitrators have low process control because the process is largely determined by existing due process rules.[66] Canadian labour laws give unionized employees the right to arbitration hearings in most disputes. A few companies also offer arbitration to disputes between management and nonunionized employees. Coors Brewing Co. has a peer tribunal arbitration process.[67]

- *Inquisition*   Inquisitors control all discussion about the conflict. Like arbitrators, they have high decision control because they choose the form of conflict resolution. However, they also have high process control because they choose which information to examine, how to examine it, and generally decide how the conflict resolution process will be handled.

Choosing the Best Third-Party Intervention Strategy

Team leaders, managers, and co-workers regularly intervene in disputes between employees and departments. Sometimes they adopt a mediator role; other times they serve as arbitrators. However, research suggests that people in positions of authority (e.g., managers) usually adopt an inquisitional approach whereby they dominate the intervention process as well as make a binding decision.[68] Managers like the inquisition approach because it is consistent with the decision-oriented nature of managerial jobs, gives them control over the conflict process and outcome, and tends to resolve disputes efficiently.

However, the inquisitional approach to third-party conflict resolution is usually the least effective in organizational settings.[69] One problem is that managers who take an inquisitional role tend to collect limited information about the problem using this approach, so their imposed decision may produce an ineffective solution to the conflict. Moreover, employees tend to think that the procedures and outcomes of inquisitions are unfair because they have little control over this approach.

Which third-party intervention is most appropriate in organizations? The answer partly depends on the situation. However, for everyday disputes between two employees, the mediation approach is usually best because this gives employees more responsibility for resolving their own disputes. The third-party representative merely establishes an appropriate context for conflict resolution. Although not as efficient as other strategies, mediation potentially offers the highest level of employee satisfaction with the conflict process and outcomes.[70] When employees cannot resolve their differences, arbitration seems to work best because the predetermined rules of evidence and other processes create a higher sense of procedural fairness. Moreover, arbitration is preferred where the organization's goals should take priority over individual goals.

Chapter Summary

- Conflict is the process in which one party perceives that its interests are being opposed or negatively affected by another party. When conflict is task-related, the parties view the conflict experience as something separate from them. Conflict is much more difficult to resolve when it rises to a socio-emotional state of tension. The conflict process often escalates through a series of episodes, and shifts from task-related to socio-emotional.

- Conflict management maximizes the benefits and minimizes the dysfunctional consequences of conflict. Conflict is beneficial for introducing new ideas, making people think more fully about issues, and increasing cohesiveness (when conflict is with another group.) The main problems with conflict are that it encourages organizational politics and may lead to job dissatisfaction and turnover.

- Conflict tends to increase under conditions of goal incompatibility, differentiation, task interdependence, scarce resources, ambiguity, and communication problems. Conflict is more common in a multicultural workforce because of greater differentiation and communication problems among employees.

- There are basically five interpersonal conflict management styles: avoiding, competing, accommodating, compromising, and collaborating. Collaborating is the only style that represents a purely win-win orientation — the belief that the parties will find a mutually beneficial solution to the conflict. The four other conflict management styles adopt some variation of a win-lose orientation — the belief that one party will lose if the other wins. Women and people from collectivist cultures tend to use a collaborative or avoidance style more than men and people from individualistic cultures.

- Structural approaches to conflict management include emphasizing superordinate goals, reducing differentiation, improving communication and understanding, reducing task interdependence, increasing resources, and clarifying rules and procedures. These elements can also be altered to stimulate conflict.

- Negotiation occurs whenever two or more conflicting parties attempt to resolve their divergent goals by redefining the terms of their interdependence. Negotiations are influenced by several situational factors, including location, physical setting, time passage and deadlines, and audience. Important negotiator behaviours include planning and goal setting, gathering information, communicating effectively, and making concessions.

- Third-party conflict resolution is any attempt by a relatively neutral person to help the parties resolve their differences. The main objectives are to resolve the dispute efficiently and effectively, and to ensure that the parties feel that the process and outcome of dispute resolution are fair. The three main forms of third-party dispute resolution are mediation, arbitration, and inquisition. Managers tend to use an inquisitional approach, although mediation and arbitration are more appropriate, depending on the situation.

Discussion Questions

1. Distinguish task-related from socio-emotional conflict and explain where these two forms fit into the conflict escalation cycle.

2. The president of Creative Toys Inc. read about cooperation in Japanese companies and has vowed to bring this same philosophy to the company. The goal is to avoid all conflict so that employees work cooperatively and are happier at Creative Toys. Discuss the merits and limitations of the president's policy.

3. Conflict among managers emerged soon after a Swedish company was bought by a French company. The Swedes perceived the French management as hierarchical and arrogant, whereas the French thought the Swedes were naive, cautious, and lacking an achievement orientation. Describe an intergroup mirroring intervention that would reduce dysfunctional conflict in this situation. What conditions might make the intergroup mirroring process difficult here?

4. Identify three levels of interdependence and give an organizational example for each.

5. Jane has just been appointed purchasing manager of Canadian Widget Ltd. The previous purchasing manager, who recently retired, was known for his "winner-take-all" approach to suppliers. He continually fought for more discounts and was skeptical about any special deals that suppliers proposed. A few suppliers refused to do business with Canadian Widget, but senior management was confident that the former purchasing manager's approach minimized the company's costs. Jane wants to try a more collaborative approach to working with suppliers. Will her approach work? How should she adopt a more collaborative approach in future negotiations with suppliers?

6. Suppose that Canadian Airlines International did not have a financial crisis that helped employees overcome past differences. Describe two other ways that the company could reduce employee conflict through superordinate goals.

7. Discuss two effects of time on negotiations.

8. Managers tend to use an inquisitional approach to resolving disputes between employees and departments. Describe the inquisitional approach and discuss its appropriateness in organizational settings.

Chapter Case

Maelstrom Communications

Sales manager Roger Todd was fuming. Thanks to, as he put it, "those nearsighted addleheads in service," he had nearly lost one of his top accounts. When told of Todd's complaint, senior service representative Ned Rosen retorted, "That figures. Anytime Mr. Todd senses even the remotest possibility of a sale, he immediately promises the customer the world on a golden platter. We can't possibly provide the service they request under the time constraints they give us and do an acceptable job."

Feelings of this sort were common in the departments both Roger and Ned worked for at Maelstrom Communications. Sales and service, the two dominant functions in the company, never saw eye to eye on anything, it seemed. The problems dated well back in the history of the company, even before Roger or Ned were hired some years ago.

Maelstrom Communications is a franchised distributionship belonging to a nationwide network of communications companies that sell products such as intercom, paging, sound, and interconnect telephone systems. Maelstrom competes directly with the Bell System companies in the telephone hardware market. Equipment installation and maintenance service are an integral part of the total package Maelstrom offers.

Modern telephone system hardware is highly sophisticated and few, if any, system users have the technological know-how to do their own equipment servicing. An excellent service record is crucial to the success of any company in the field. After the direct sale of a Maelstrom system, the sales force maintains contacts with customers. There is nothing the salespeople dislike so much as hearing that a customer hasn't received the type of service promised at the time of sale. On the other hand, service technicians complain of being hounded by the salespeople whenever a preferred customer needs a wire spliced. As Ned Rosen put it, "I can't remember the last time a service request came through that *wasn't* an emergency from a preferred customer."

Maelstrom's owner and president, Al Whitfield, has a strong sales background and views sales as the bread-and-butter department of the company. He is in on all major decisions and has final say on any matter brought to his attention. He spends most of his time working with sales and marketing personnel, and rarely concerns himself with the day-to-day activities of the service department unless a major problem of some sort crops up.

Next in line in Maelstrom's corporate hierarchy is the vice-president in charge of production, Lawrence Henderson. Henderson is responsible for the acquisition and distribution of all job-related equipment and materials and for the scheduling of all service department activities. His sympathies lie primarily with the service department.

Each week Whitfield, Henderson, and all members of the sales force hold a meeting in Maelstrom's conference room. The sales personnel present their needs to Henderson so that equipment can be ordered and jobs scheduled. Service requests reported to salespeople from customers are also relayed to Henderson at this point. Once orders for service have been placed with production, sales personnel receive no feedback on the disposition of them (unless a customer complains to them directly) other than at these weekly meetings. It is common for a salesperson to think all is well with his or her accounts when, in fact, they are receiving delayed service or none at all. When an irate customer phones the sales representative to complain, it sets in motion the machinery that leads to disputes such as the one between Roger Todd and Ned Rosen.

It has become an increasingly common occurrence at Maelstrom for sales personnel to go to Henderson to complain when their requests are not met by the service department. Henderson has exhibited an increasing tendency to side with the service department and to tell the salespeople that existing service department priorities must be adhered to and that any sales requests will have to wait for rescheduling. At this point, a salesperson's only recourse is to go to Whitfield, who invariably agrees with the salesperson and instructs Henderson to take appropriate action. All of this is time-consuming and only serves to produce friction between the president and the vice-president in charge of production.

Discussion Questions

1. What situational conditions have created the conflict in this case?

2. What actions should the organization take to manage the conflict more effectively?

Source: Written by Daniel Robey in collaboration with Todd Anthony. Used with permission.

Experiential Exercise

Ugli Orange Role Play

Purpose: This exercise is designed to help you understand the dynamics of interpersonal and intergroup conflict as well as the effectiveness of negotiation strategies under specific conditions.

Instructions: The instructor will divide the class into an even number of teams of three people each, with one participant left over for each team formed (e.g., six observers if there are six teams). One-half of the teams will take the role of Dr. Roland and the other half will be Dr. Jones. Teams will receive the appropriate materials from the instructor. Members within each team are given 10 minutes to learn their roles and decide negotiating strategy. After reading their roles and discussing strategy, each Dr. Jones team is matched with a Dr. Roland team to conduct negotiations.

Observers will receive observation forms from the instructor, and two observers will be assigned to watch the paired teams during prenegotiations and subsequent negotiations. At the end of the negotiations, the observers will describe the process and outcomes in their negotiating session. The instructor will then invite the negotiators to describe their experiences and the implications for conflict management.

Source: This exercise was developed by Dr. Robert J. House.

CHAPTER 14

Organizational Leadership

CHAPTER OUTLINE

Perspectives of Leadership

Trait Perspective of Leadership

Behavioural Perspective of Leadership

Contingency Perspective of Leadership

Transformational Perspective of Leadership

Romance Perspective of Leadership

Gender Issues in Leadership

Chapter Summary

Discussion Questions

LEARNING OBJECTIVES

After reading this chapter, you should be able to:

- List seven traits identified with effective leaders.

- Describe people-oriented and task-oriented leadership styles.

- Outline the path-goal theory of leadership.

- Contrast transactional with transformational leadership.

- Describe the four features of transformational leadership.

- Explain why leaders are given too much credit or blame for organizational events.

- Discuss similarities and differences in the leadership styles of women and men.

Christina Gold has a visionary leadership style that energized the workforce and brought profitability back to Avon Products, Inc.

Christina Gold has helped bring Avon Products, Inc. back to life. Raised in Montreal, Gold ascended from an inventory clerk in 1970 to Avon Canada's top job by 1990. James Preston, Avon's chairman and CEO in New York, noticed Gold's impressive leadership in Canada and asked her to "work your magic here." She was put in charge of North American operations and, more recently, global direct selling.

Along with keen intelligence and a strong work ethic, Gold is known for her integrity and ability to build employee commitment. "Christina has this sincerity, this warmth, this charisma that reps trust and respect," says a senior Avon executive.

Gold stays close to Avon's 8,000 employees and 400,000 contract sales reps. She writes in a monthly newsletter, goes out with reps on sales calls, and attends all of Avon's sales conventions in North America. "She has a unique talent to motivate people to achieve greater results," says Sandy Mountford, an Avon rep in Calgary who now heads the company's largest U.S. division.

Christina Gold's leadership has paid off for Avon's shareholders as well as for the company's employees and customers. "[Christina Gold] almost single-handedly turned around an ailing U.S. business," says a leading New York investment analyst. "Her visionary approach at revitalizing the representatives and adding new business categories should provide positive momentum for the company."[1]

mistake of focusing too much on the physical appearance and abstract personality traits of leaders. Instead, the emerging view is that effective leaders have a few common values and abilities. The current popularity of competency-based executive selection and development indicates that many organizations support the trait perspective of leadership.[8] As we learned in Chapter 2, **competencies** are the underlying characteristics of people that lead to superior performance.[9] Competency-based executive selection and development takes the view that effective executives possess a common set of abilities, values, personality characteristics, and other traits.

Competencies The abilities, individual values, personality traits, and other characteristics of people that lead to superior performance.

The recent leadership literature identifies seven traits that are characteristic of effective leaders. These traits are listed in Exhibit 14.2 and briefly described below.[10]

- *Drive*   This refers to the inner motivation that leaders possess to pursue their goals. Leaders have a high need for achievement (Chapter 3). You can see this trait in Terry Matthews through his unwavering tenacity and energy to make Newbridge Networks Corp. a global leader in its industry.

- *Leadership motivation*   This is the person's need for socialized power (described in Chapter 3). Leaders want to use their power bases to influence their team or organization and make it successful.

- *Integrity*   This refers to the leader's truthfulness and tendency to translate words into deeds. Several large-scale studies have reported that followers consistently identify integrity as the most important leadership trait. Leaders will only have followers when trust is maintained through the leader's integrity.[11]

- *Self-confidence*   Leaders believe in their leadership skills and ability to achieve objectives. They also use impression management tactics (Chapter 12) to convince followers of their confidence. Terry Matthews's confidence was apparent when he invested in Newbridge long before a market existed. And when short-sellers (investors betting the company's stock would fall) predicted the company's demise

---

EXHIBIT 14.2: Seven Traits of Effective Leaders

Leadership Trait	Description
Drive	The leader's inner motivation to pursue goals.
Leadership motivation	The leader's need for socialized power to accomplish team or organizational goals.
Integrity	The leader's truthfulness and tendency to translate words into deeds.
Self-confidence	The leader's belief in his/her own leadership skills and ability to achieve objectives.
Intelligence	The leader's above-average cognitive ability to process enormous amounts of information.
Knowledge of the business	The leader's understanding of the company's environment to make intuitive decisions.
Self-monitoring personality	The leader's sensitivity to situational cues and ability to adapt his/her own behaviour appropriately.

Source: Based on information in S. A. Kirpatrick and E. A. Locke, "Leadership: Do Traits Matter?" *Academy of Management Executive* 5 (May 1991), pp. 48–60; S. J. Zaccaro, R. J. Foti, and D.A. Kenny, "Self-Monitoring and Trait-Based Variance in Leadership: An Investigation of Leader Flexibility Across Multiple Group Situations," *Journal of Applied Psychology* 76 (1991), pp. 308–15.

a few years ago, Matthews instilled confidence in employees that Newbridge would overcome its financial obstacles.

- *Intelligence* Leaders have above-average cognitive ability to process enormous amounts of information. Leaders aren't necessarily geniuses; rather, they have superior ability to analyze alternate scenarios and identify potential opportunities.

- *Knowledge of the business* Leaders need to know the business environment in which they operate so that they have an intuitive understanding of which decisions to make and whose ideas make sense for the organization's survival and success. Matthews has demonstrated this trait from his astute knowledge of the telecommunications hardware industry.

- *Self-monitoring personality* Effective leaders have a strong self-monitoring personality (Chapter 6) so that they are sensitive to situational cues and can readily adapt their own behaviour appropriately. Recent studies have found that high self-monitors are more likely to emerge as informal leaders in small groups.[12] Moreover, the contingency leadership perspective described later in the chapter assumes that effective leaders are high self-monitors so they can adjust their behaviour to match the situation.[13]

Limitations of the Trait Perspective of Leadership

Although the trait perspective of leadership is popular in organizations and has some research support, we must not assume that everyone with the traits listed above are great leaders. Leadership scholars warn that traits only indicate leadership *potential*, not leadership *performance*. People with these traits aren't necessarily effective leaders until they have mastered the necessary leadership behaviours.

A related concern is that the trait perspective implies a universal approach to leadership. It suggests that leaders must have all these traits and that they are useful in every situation. This is probably a false assumption; leadership is far too complex to have a universal list of traits that apply to every condition. Some traits might not be important all the time, although researchers have not yet explored this aspect of traits.

A third limitation of the trait approach is that traits might only influence our perception that someone is a leader, not whether the individual really makes a difference to the organization's success.[14] People who exhibit integrity, self-confidence, and other traits are called leaders because they act like leaders. Moreover, some traits are subjective enough that they may really be due to the follower's stereotype of leadership rather than the leader's actual characteristics. For example, we might see a successful person, call that person a leader, and then attribute to that person several unobservable traits that we consider essential for great leaders. We will discuss this perceptual distortion more fully toward the end of the chapter. At this point, you should be aware that our knowledge of leadership traits may be partly due to perceptual distortions.

Behavioural Perspective of Leadership

In the 1940s and 1950s, scholars from Ohio State University launched an intensive research investigation to answer the question: What behaviours make leaders effective? Questionnaires were administered to subordinates, asking them to rate their supervisors on a large number of behaviours. These studies, along with similar research at the University of Michigan, distilled two clusters of leadership behaviours from more than 1,800 leadership behaviour items.[15]

One cluster represented people-oriented behaviours. This included showing mutual trust and respect for subordinates, demonstrating a genuine concern for their needs, and having a desire to look out for their welfare. People-oriented leaders listen to employee suggestions, do personal favours for employees, support their interests when required, and treat employees as equals. Craig Weatherup, CEO of PepsiCo Inc., has a reputation for favouring this leadership style. He encourages executives to spend time with their families. He has called spouses of executives kept away from home on special projects to thank them for their support. And when PepsiCo laid off some people, Weatherup invited those who complained to meetings where he patiently explained why the cutbacks were necessary.[16]

The other cluster of leader behaviours identified by researchers represented a task-oriented leadership style and included behaviours that define and structure work roles. Task-oriented leaders assign employees to specific tasks, clarify their work duties and procedures, ensure that they follow company rules, and push them to reach their performance capacity. For example, Paul Giannelia applied the task-oriented style as project director of Strait Crossing Development Inc. during construction of the Confederation Bridge linking Prince Edward Island with the mainland. "The tough schedule made it hard to keep everyone focused," he admits. "I had to be the benevolent dictator while being the head cheerleader."[17]

After identifying the two clusters of leader behaviour, researchers associated them with specific measures of leadership effectiveness. The early studies concluded that people-oriented leadership is associated with higher job satisfaction, as well as lower absenteeism, grievances, and turnover among subordinates. Job performance is lower than for employees with task-oriented leaders.[18] Task-oriented leadership, on the other hand, is associated with lower job satisfaction as well as higher absenteeism and turnover among subordinates. However, this leadership style seems to increase productivity and team unity. Canadian university students apparently value task-oriented instructors because they want clear course objectives and well-prepared lectures that abide by the course objectives.[19]

The "Hi-Hi" Leadership Hypothesis

Behavioural leadership scholars initially thought that people-oriented and task-oriented leadership were at opposite ends of a behaviour spectrum. In other words, they believed that a strong task-oriented leader was necessarily a weak people-oriented leader. But researchers later concluded that these styles are independent of each other. Some people are high or low on both styles, others are high on one style and low on the other, and most are somewhere in between.

With the revised assumption that leaders could be both people-oriented and task-oriented, behavioural leadership scholars hypothesized that the most effective leaders exhibit high levels of both types of behaviour. This became known as the **"hi-hi" leadership hypothesis**.[20] Effective leaders, it was thought, should have a high people-oriented style and a high task-oriented style.

A popular leadership program that grew out of the "hi-hi" leadership hypothesis is the **Leadership Grid®**. Participants begin by assessing their own leadership style on the Grid (see Exhibit 14.3), then develop skills to move toward the best leadership style. *Authority-compliance managers* (9, 1) try to maximize productivity through power and authority. *Country club managers* (1, 9) focus on developing good feelings among employees even when production suffers. *Middle-of-the-road managers* (5, 5) try to maintain the status quo by adopting a middle-of-the-road approach. *Impoverished managers*

Hi-hi leadership hypothesis A proposition stating that effective leaders exhibit high levels of both people-oriented and task-oriented behaviours.

Leadership Grid® A leadership model developed by Blake and Mouton that assesses an individual's leadership effectiveness in terms of his or her concern for people and for production.

EXHIBIT 14.3: The Leadership Grid® Figure

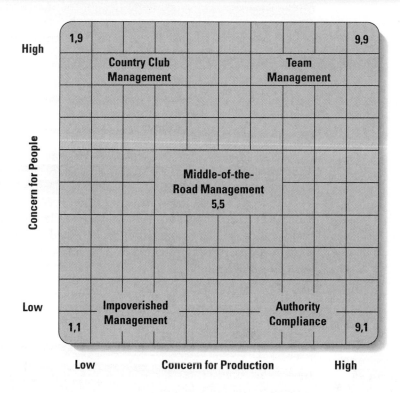

Source: The Leadership Grid Figure from *Leadership Dilemmas — Grid Solutions*, by Robert R. Blake and Anne Adams McCanse (Houston: Gulf Publishing Company), p. 29. © Copyright 1991, by Scientific Methods, Inc. Reproduced by permission of the owners.

(1, 1) do the minimum required to fulfil their leadership role and keep their job. According to the model, the best leadership style is *team management* (9, 9), in which leaders rely on commitment, participation, and conflict resolution to seek results.

When the Leadership Grid® was first introduced, it adopted the "hi-hi" leadership hypothesis; namely, that leaders are most effective when they have both a high concern for people and a high concern for production (i.e., team management). While still aiming participants for this ideal level, the most recent version of the Leadership Grid® program states that effective leaders have the *capacity* for high levels of both dimensions, but they should choose appropriate levels of both dimensions for the specific situation.[21] This revision adopts the contingency perspective, which we discuss later in the chapter.

Limitations of the Behavioural Leadership Perspective

The Leadership Grid® probably distanced itself from the hi-hi leadership hypothesis for the same reasons that scholars have moved away from the behavioural perspective of leadership.[22] One concern is that studies supporting the hi-hi leadership hypothesis relied on very subjective questionnaire items, so it was easy for stereotyping and other biases to falsely link effective leaders with high levels of both styles.[23] Followers may have concluded that someone is a great leader and this positive halo caused them to rate the leader highly on the people-oriented and task-oriented items in the questionnaire.

Contemporary leadership scholars have also moved away from the behavioural perspective because it is a universal approach. It ignores the possibility that the best leadership style may depend on the situation.[24] This severely limits the predictive value of the behavioural perspective, so it has been largely set aside in favour of contingency theories of leadership, which we describe next.

Contingency Perspective of Leadership

The contingency perspective of leadership is based on the idea that the most appropriate leadership style depends on the situation. Most (although not all) contingency leadership theories assume that effective leaders must be both insightful and flexible.[25] They must be able to adapt their behaviours and styles to the immediate situation. This isn't easy to do, however. As we see in Perspective 14.1, leaders typically have a preferred style. It takes considerable effort for leaders to learn when and how to alter their styles to match the situation. As we noted earlier, leaders must have a high self-monitoring personality so they can diagnose the circumstances and match their behaviours accordingly.

Path-Goal Theory of Leadership

Path-goal leadership theory A contingency theory of leadership based on expectancy theory of motivation that includes four leadership styles as well as several employee and situational contingencies.

Several contingency theories have been proposed over the years, but **path-goal leadership theory** has withstood scientific critique better than the others. The theory has its roots in the expectancy theory of motivation (Chapter 3). Martin Evans had incorporated expectancy theory into his study of how leader behaviours influence employee perceptions of expectancies (paths) between employee effort and performance (goals). Based on these findings and earlier leadership research, Robert House proposed path-goal theory as a contingency leadership model.[26]

PERSPECTIVE 14.1

The Trials of Practising Contingency Leadership

Sue Miller is struggling to become a more participative leader. The president of Merisel Canada, Inc., the Toronto-based distributor of computer hardware and software, was promoted through the ranks for her ability to take charge and get things done. "I just did my job so damn well people couldn't help but notice," she says. "Now I have to learn a whole new set of skills."

Miller is not alone. One of the most difficult challenges for most managers is to learn to adapt their leadership style to the situation. Like Miller, many have been promoted for their ability to achieve difficult objectives and to use directive- or achievement-oriented styles to increase employee performance. But although the achievement-oriented style potentially works well for subordinates at all levels, the directive style is usually inappropriate when the subordinate is a skilled manager with several years of experience.

Meanwhile, Miller is still working at being a more effective leader by adjusting her style to the situation. At an executive meeting, Miller started to tell the vice-president of finance to put a new credit procedure in place: "Will you designate . . . " Miller stopped in mid-sentence to change her style to a more participative tone: "Do you think it would be a good idea if we were to designate . . .?"

Source: Adapted from J. Allan, "When Women Set the Rules," *Canadian Business*, April 1991, pp. 40–43.

Path-goal theory states that effective leaders influence employee satisfaction and performance by making their need satisfaction contingent on effective job performance. Thus, leaders strengthen the performance-to-outcome expectancy and valences of those outcomes by ensuring that employees who perform their jobs well have a higher degree of need fulfilment than employees who perform poorly. Second, path-goal theory states that effective leaders strengthen the effort-to-performance expectancy by providing the information, support, and other resources necessary to help employees complete their tasks.[27] Notice that this theory emphasizes relations between two people — a supervisor and a subordinate — rather than the leader's effect on an entire work unit. This makes path-goal theory mainly a dyadic (two-person) theory of leadership.

As Exhibit 14.4 illustrates, path-goal theory considers four leadership styles and several contingency factors leading to three indicators of leader effectiveness.

Leadership styles

Path-goal theory suggests that leaders motivate and satisfy employees in a particular situation by adopting one or more of the four leadership styles described below:[28]

- *Directive* These are clarifying behaviours that provide a psychological structure for subordinates. The leader clarifies performance goals, the means to reach those

EXHIBIT 14.4: Path-Goal Leadership Theory

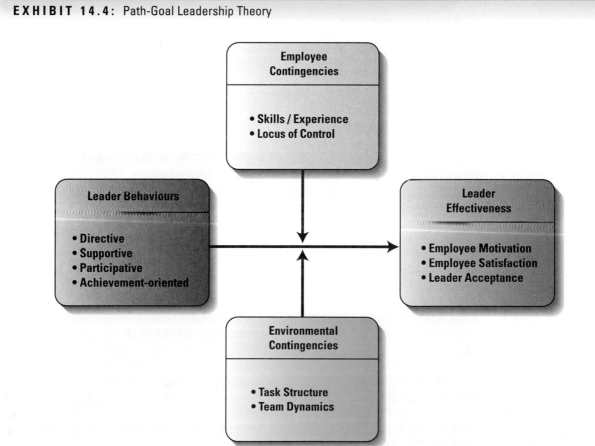

goals, and the standards against which performance will be judged. Directive leadership also includes judicious use of rewards and disciplinary actions. It is the same as task-oriented leadership described earlier and echoes the discussion in Chapter 2 on the importance of clear role perceptions in employee performance.

- *Supportive*   These behaviours provide psychological support for subordinates. The leader is friendly and approachable; makes the work more pleasant; treats all employees with equal respect; and shows concern for the status, needs, and well-being of employees. Supportive leadership is the same as the people-oriented leadership described earlier and reflects the benefits of social support to help employees cope with stressful situations (Chapter 5).

- *Participative*   These behaviours encourage and facilitate subordinate involvement in decisions beyond their normal work activities. The leader consults with employees, asks for their suggestions, and takes these ideas into serious consideration before making a decision. Participative leadership relates to the employee involvement concepts and issues described in Chapter 10.

- *Achievement-oriented*   These behaviours encourage employees to reach their peak performance. The leader sets challenging goals, expects employees to perform at their highest level, continuously seeks improvement in employee performance, and shows a high degree of confidence that employees will assume responsibility and accomplish challenging goals. Achievement-oriented leadership applies goal-setting theory (Chapter 3) as well as positive expectations in self-fulfilling prophecy (Chapter 6).

The path-goal model contends that effective leaders are capable of selecting the most appropriate behavioural style (or styles) for that situation. Leaders might simultaneously use more than one style at a time. For example, they might be both supportive and participative in a specific situation.

Contingencies of Path-Goal Theory

As a contingency theory, path-goal theory states that each of these four leadership styles will be effective in some situations but not in others. The path-goal leadership model specifies two sets of situational variables that moderate the relationship between a leader's style and effectiveness: (1) employee characteristics and (2) characteristics of the employee's work environment. Several contingencies have already been studied within the path-goal framework, and the model is open for more variables in the future.[29] However, we will examine only four contingencies here (see Exhibit 14.5).

Skill and experience

A combination of directive and supportive leadership is best for employees who are (or perceive themselves to be) inexperienced and unskilled. Directive leadership gives subordinates information about how to accomplish the task, whereas supportive leadership helps them cope with the uncertainties of unfamiliar work situations. Directive leadership is detrimental when employees are skilled and experienced because it introduces too much supervisory control. Instead, these employees should receive participative and achievement-oriented leadership because employees have the necessary knowledge to meet the demands of autonomy and challenging goals.

EXHIBIT 14.5: Selected Contingencies of Path-Goal Theory

	Directive	Supportive	Participative	Achievement-oriented
Employee Contingencies				
Skill-Experience	Low	Low	High	High
Locus of Control	External	External	Internal	Internal
Environmental Contingencies				
Task Structure	Nonroutine	Routine	Nonroutine	???*
Team Dynamics	Negative norms	Low cohesion	Positive norms	???*

*Question marks indicate that the contingency has not yet been studied.

Locus of control

Locus of control A personality trait referring to the extent to which people believe what happens to them is within their control; those who feel in control of their destiny have an internal locus, whereas those who believe that life events are due mainly to fate or luck have an external locus of control.

Recall from Chapter 6 that people with an internal **locus of control** believe that they have control over their work environment. Consequently, these employees prefer participative and achievement-oriented leadership styles and may become frustrated with a directive style. In contrast, people with an external locus of control believe that their performance is due more to luck and fate, so they tend to be more satisfied with directive and supportive leadership.

Task structure

Directive leadership should be adopted when the task is nonroutine because this style minimizes role ambiguity that tends to occur in these complex work situations (particularly for inexperienced employees).[30] This style is ineffective when employees have routine and simple tasks because the manager's guidance serves no purpose and may be viewed as unnecessarily close control. Employees in highly routine and simple jobs may require supportive leadership to help them cope with the tedious nature of the work and lack of control over the pace of work. Participative leadership is preferred for employees performing nonroutine tasks because the lack of rules and procedures gives them more discretion to achieve challenging goals. This style is ineffective for employees in routine tasks because they lack discretion over their work.

Team dynamics

Cohesive teams with performance-oriented norms act as a substitute for most leader interventions. High team cohesiveness substitutes for supportive leadership, whereas performance-oriented team norms substitute for directive and achievement-oriented leadership. Thus, when team cohesiveness is low, leaders should use the supportive style. Leaders should apply a directive style to counteract team norms that oppose the team's formal objectives. For example, the team leader may need to use legitimate power if team members have developed a norm to "take it easy" rather than get a project completed on time.

Recent Extensions of Path-Goal Theory

In one of the few attempts to expand path-goal theory, Robert House recently proposed elements that apply to the work unit and organization rather than just dyadic relations between a supervisor and employee.[31] The extended model includes leader behaviour styles and contingencies of the path-goal model just described, but it adds a few leader styles that were not previously considered. Some of the newly proposed leadership styles include:

- *Value-based*   Value-based leader behaviours include articulating a vision of the future, displaying passion for this vision, demonstrating self-confidence in the attainment of the vision, communicating the vision, and acting in ways consistent with the vision. This is the same as the transformational leadership perspective that is described later in the chapter.

- *Representation and networking*   This leadership style includes representing the work unit and networking with others. Networking is an important political activity (Chapter 12) that legitimizes the work unit and maintains positive influences on other areas of the organization.

- *Interaction facilitation*   This leadership style includes maintaining collaboration and positive interactions among members of the work unit, as well as emphasizing the importance of interaction and teamwork.

Evaluating Path-Goal Theory

Path-goal theory is the predominant contingency theory of leadership and has a number of strengths. One advantage of this theory is that most of its contingencies refer to specific conditions (e.g., employee abilities, task structure) so that it is relatively easy to identify conditions in which a specific style is preferred. Moreover, several original contingencies have been tested and have reasonably strong research support.[32] Another advantage is that path-goal theory can be amended by adding more contingency variables as they are identified through research.[33] For example, the locus of control contingency was added a few years after the original model was introduced. Lastly, path-goal theory emphasizes the dyadic (two-person) relationship between leader and subordinate, whereas previous perspectives tended to consider the leader's effect on the entire work unit or organization.[34]

Research supports many elements of the path-goal leadership model, but it still requires considerable work and clarification. One problem is that although the theory was introduced more than 25 years ago, several contingencies and leadership styles have received relatively little scholarly investigation.[35] For example, you probably noticed that some cells in Exhibit 14.5 have question marks. This is because we do not yet know how those leadership styles apply to those contingencies. The recently expanded model adds new leadership styles and contingencies, but they have not yet been tested.

Another concern is that as path-goal theory expands, the model may become too complex for practical use. Although the expanded model provides a closer representation of the complexity of leadership, it may become too cumbersome for training people in leadership styles. Few people would be able to remember all the contingencies and appropriate leadership styles for those contingencies. In spite of these limitations, path-goal theory remains the most complete and robust contingency leadership theory.

Other Contingency Theories

Several other contingency leadership theories have been proposed over the years. Some overlap with the path-goal model in terms of leadership styles, but most use simpler and more abstract contingencies. For example, one contingency model that is popular among training consultants relies on subordinate "readiness" as the only contingency factor to determine which of four leadership styles to apply.[36] Although it may be convenient to have only one contingency variable, this lack of complexity explains why the theory lacks research support.[37]

A few leadership theories emphasize contingencies that have not yet been explored by path-goal researchers. One contingency, presented by Canadian scholar Bill Reddin, is organizational climate. Specifically, he suggests that leaders need to adjust their style to the type of relations between employees and management. Another contingency factor that leaders should consider is situational control; that is, the degree of power and influence that the leader possesses in a particular situation.

Changing the situation to match the style

Most contingency leadership theories assume that leaders can change their style to match a given situation. However, at least one prominent scholar has argued that leadership style is related to the individual's personality and, consequently, is relatively stable over time.[38] Leaders might be able to alter their style temporarily, but they tend to use a preferred style in the long term.

If leadership style is influenced by a person's personality, then organizations should engineer the situation to fit the leader's dominant style rather than expect leaders to change their style with the situation. A directive leader might be assigned inexperienced employees who need direction rather than seasoned people who work less effectively under a directive style. Alternatively, companies might transfer supervisors to workplaces where their dominant style fits best. For instance, directive leaders might be parachuted into work teams with counterproductive norms, whereas leaders who prefer a supportive style might be sent to departments in which employees face work pressures and other stressors.

Leadership substitutes

Leadership substitutes
Characteristics of the employee, task, or organization that either limit the leader's influence or make it unnecessary.

So far, we have looked at theories that recommend using different leadership styles in various situations. But one theory, called **leadership substitutes**, identifies contingencies that either limit the leader's ability to influence subordinates or make that particular leadership style unnecessary. When substitute conditions are present, employees are effective without a formal leader who applies a particular style. Some conditions substitute for task-oriented leadership, whereas others substitute for people-oriented leadership. For example, gainsharing reward systems keep employees directed toward organizational goals, so they probably replace or reduce the need for task-oriented leadership.[39]

As organizations shift toward flatter, team-based structures, we are seeing increasing use of co-workers as a substitute for the formal work-unit leader. Co-workers instruct new employees, thereby providing directive leadership. Co-workers provide social support, which helps to reduce stress among fellow employees (Chapter 5). Teams with norms that support organizational goals may substitute for achievement-oriented leadership, because employees encourage (or pressure) co-workers to stretch their performance levels.

Many elements of the leadership substitutes model are similar to contingencies in the path-goal leadership model. As an example, the leadership substitute model states that skilled and experienced employees replace task-oriented (directive) leadership. Similarly, path-goal theory states that directive leadership is unnecessary — and possibly dysfunctional — when employees are skilled and experienced. Although many aspects of the leadership substitutes model require further refinement, there is general support for the overall notion that some conditions neutralize or substitute for leadership styles.[40]

Transformational Perspective of Leadership

When Ted Pattenden became president of National Rubber, the air in the plant was so bad that employees couldn't see across it. The Toronto-based manufacturer of recycled rubber products also had a narrow product focus, broken equipment, and a terrible work accident record. Pattenden soon articulated a new vision for the company, one that would expand the firm's product lines and bring new hope to employees for a better workplace. Pattenden demonstrated his sincerity and integrity toward that vision by introducing ventilation systems and training programs that improved worker health and safety. He held regular all-employee meetings to communicate the importance of a safe and healthy work environment, as well as the need for employee involvement to turn the company around. It was a slow process, but Pattenden's persuasiveness and consistency paid off. "Leadership is an emotional thing," says Pattenden. "If you are going to lead people, you have to have some sort of emotional link to them."[41]

Transformational leadership A leadership perspective that explains how leaders change teams or organizations by creating, communicating, and modelling a vision for the organization or work unit, and inspiring employees to strive for that vision.

Ted Pattenden is a **transformational leader**. Through his vision and actions, he turned National Rubber from a money-losing company with a dismal safety record into a profitable firm with high safety standards and employees who are proudly involved in the company's success. Transformational leaders are agents of change. They develop a vision for the organization or work unit, inspire and collectively bond employees to that vision, and give them a "can-do" attitude that makes the vision achievable.[42]

Transformational leaders such as Timothy Eaton, H. R. MacMillan, Elizabeth Arden, and Samuel Cunard dot the landscape of Canadian history. Today, transformational leaders may be found in all types of organizations, and at all levels of the enterprise. At the beginning of this chapter, we described how Christina Gold's optimism and vision revitalized a demoralized sales force at Avon Products, Inc. Isadore Sharp built Toronto-based Four Seasons Hotels Inc. into the largest and most successful luxury hotel chain in the world. Terry Matthews, who was described earlier in the chapter, has built one of Canada's most successful high-technology companies. Each of these leaders defined a vision for the organization, communicated that vision, and built employee commitment to it.

Courtesy of T. Eaton Company.

Timothy Eaton, founder of the T. Eaton Company, was an entrepreneur and transformational leader who dramatically improved customer and employee relations in Canada during the 1800s. He introduced the unheard-of idea that customers should have their money refunded if they don't like what they bought. He criticized other employers who made employees work six full days each week, and set an example by closing his business so that employees could be with their families on Saturday afternoons.

Transformational versus Transactional Leadership

Transformational leadership is different from **transactional leadership**. Transactional leadership is about helping organizations achieve their current objectives more efficiently, such as by linking job performance to valued rewards and ensuring that employees have the resources they need to get the job done.[43] The contingency and behavioural theories described earlier adopt the transactional perspective because they focus on leader behaviours that improve employee performance and satisfaction. In contrast, transformational leaders change the organization's culture and strategies so that they have a better

Transactional leadership Leadership that helps organizations achieve their current objectives more efficiently by linking job performance to valued rewards and ensuring that employees have the resources needed to get the job done.

fit with the surrounding environment.[44] They are change agents who energize and direct employees to a new set of corporate values and behaviours. For example, Ted Pattenden instilled the importance of a safe work environment and employee involvement at National Rubber. Neither employees nor managers had placed much emphasis on these ideas before Pattenden's arrival.

Organizations need both transactional and transformational leadership. Transactional leadership improves organizational efficiency, whereas transformational leadership steers organizations onto a better course of action. Unfortunately, too many leaders get trapped in the daily managerial activities that represent transactional leadership.[45] They lose touch with the transformational aspect of effective leadership. Without transformational leaders, organizations stagnate and eventually become seriously misaligned with their environments.

Transformational versus Charismatic Leadership

Another important distinction is between transformational and charismatic leadership. These concepts create some controversy and confusion among experts.[46] A few writers use the words *charismatic* and *transformational* leadership interchangeably, as if they are the same thing.[47] Others view charismatic leadership mainly as leadership based on personal identification of followers with the leader. This latter interpretation is more consistent with the traditional notion of charisma. As we described in Chapter 12, charisma is a form of interpersonal attraction whereby followers develop a respect for and trust in the charismatic individual. Charisma is similar, but not identical, to referent power.[48]

Charismatic leaders certainly use transformational behaviours to change organizations, but the charismatic leadership concept extends beyond behaviours to personal traits that are not yet clearly understood. The remainder of this section will focus on transformational leadership because it offers more specific behavioural implications.

Is Matthew Barrett (centre) a charismatic or transformational leader? Many people say he is both. The Bank of Montreal CEO gains much support from his personal charisma. But his success is due to more than charm. By establishing and communicating a new vision, Barrett has transformed the Bank of Montreal into a leader of electronic services, employment equity, and other important issues in the financial industry.

Features of Transformational Leadership

There are several descriptions of transformational leadership, but most include the four features illustrated in Exhibit 14.6. These features include creating a strategic vision, communicating the vision, modelling the vision, and building commitment toward the vision.

Creating a strategic vision

Transformational leaders are the brokers of dreams.[49] They shape a strategic vision of a realistic and attractive future that bonds employees together and focuses their energy toward a superordinate organizational goal.[50] Visions represent the substance of transformational leadership. They reflect a future for the company or work unit that is ultimately accepted and valued by organizational members. Strategic visions might originate with the leader, but they are just as likely to emerge from employees, clients, suppliers, or other constituents. They typically begin as abstract ideas that become progressively clearer through critical events and discussions with staff about strategic and operational plans.[51]

There is some evidence that visions are the most important part of transformational leadership.[52] Visions offer the motivational benefits of goal setting, but they are more than mundane goals. Visions are compelling future states that bond employees and motivate them to strive for those objectives. Visions are typically described in a way that distinguishes them from the current situation, yet makes the goal both appealing and achievable.

Communicating the vision

If vision is the substance of transformational leadership, then communicating that vision is the process. Effective leaders are able to communicate meaning and elevate the importance of the visionary goal to employees.[53] They frame messages around a grand purpose with emotional appeal that captivates employees and other corporate stakeholders. Framing establishes a common mental model of the future state.[54] Recall from Chapter 6 that mental models are "theories-in-use" — our assumptions and interpretations about the world around us that guides our everyday behaviours and decisions. Through framing, transformational leaders help to establish a common mental model so that the group or organization will act collectively. For example, George Cohen, the ebullient CEO of McDonald's Canada, used framing to achieve his vision of McDonald's in Russia. Cohen viewed his mission not as selling hamburgers in foreign countries, but as making the world a better place through "hamburger diplomacy."[55]

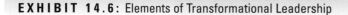

EXHIBIT 14.6: Elements of Transformational Leadership

Transformational leaders also bring their visions to life through symbols, metaphors, stories, and other vehicles that transcend plain language.[56] Metaphors borrow images of other experiences, thereby creating richer meaning of the vision that has not yet been experienced. Samuel Cunard built his Halifax-based Cunard Steamship Lines during the 1800s by constantly communicating his vision of an "ocean railway." This metaphor referred to his belief that ships could transport people across the Atlantic Ocean just as safely and on schedule as trains could transport people across Canada. The ocean-railway metaphor reflected the values of safety and reliability that were easily accepted by employees during an age when ocean travel was a risky business.[57]

Modelling the vision
Transformational leaders not only talk about a vision, they enact it. They "walk the talk" by stepping outside the executive suite and doing things that symbolize the vision.[58] Walking the talk includes altering meeting agendas, office locations, executive schedules, and other mundane events so that they are consistent with the vision and its underlying values. If Canadian executives fail as transformational leaders, walking the talk seems to be the most likely reason. According to a recent survey, Canadian employees give executives low ratings in their ability to walk the talk.[59]

Along with walking the talk, transformational leaders are reliable and persistent in their actions. They stay on course, thereby legitimizing the vision and providing further evidence that they can be trusted. Walking the talk and staying on course are two important features of transformational leaders, because employees and other stakeholders are executive watchers who look for evidence that the leader's vision is sincere.[60]

Building commitment toward the vision
Transforming a vision into reality requires employee commitment. Transformational leaders build this commitment in several ways. Their words, symbols, and stories build a contagious enthusiasm that energizes people to adopt the vision as their own. Leaders demonstrate a "can-do" attitude by enacting their vision and staying on course. Their persistence and consistency reflect an image of honesty, trust, and integrity. Finally, leaders build commitment by involving employees in the process of shaping the organization's vision.

Evaluating the Transformational Leadership Perspective

Organizational behaviour studies report that transformational leaders do make a difference. Subordinates are more satisfied and have higher affective organizational commitment under transformational leaders. They also perform their jobs better and tend to demonstrate more organizational citizenship behaviours.[61] One recent study of a Canadian bank reported that organizational commitment and financial performance may have increased in branches where the branch manager completed a transformational leadership training program.[62]

Transformational leadership is currently the most popular leadership perspective, but it faces a number of challenges. One problem is that some transformational leadership writers define this concept in terms of the leader's success.[63] They suggest that leaders are transformational when they successfully bring about change rather than whether they engage in certain behaviours we call transformational. A related concern is that qualitative studies of transformational leaders only investigate people who are successful. A better strategy is to compare successful with unsuccessful leaders and distinguish their use of transformational behaviours.

A third problem is that the transformational leadership model still implies a universal rather than contingency approach to leadership. Only very recently have writers begun to explore the idea that transformational leadership is more appropriate or effective in some situations than in others.[64] For instance, transformational leadership is probably more appropriate when organizations need to adapt than when environmental conditions are stable. Transactional leadership would be more suitable, on the other hand, when the organization requires greater efficiency. Preliminary evidence suggests that the general concept of transformational leadership is relevant and appropriate across cultures. However, there may be specific elements of transformational leadership, such as the way visions are formed and communicated, that are more appropriate in North America than in other cultures.[65]

Lastly, we need to remember that establishing and communicating a broad corporate vision does not replace the practical value of hard goals and results. The problem is determining how and when to reduce the transformational leader's lofty ideals to measurable progress. Sir David Simon, chairman of British Petroleum, recently echoed this concern: "I'm not too happy about this floating in vision territory," he says. "I like to know the how and the what. I am very nervous of visions that end in superlatives (the 'we will be best' type) — I like deliverables."[66]

Romance Perspective of Leadership

The trait, behaviour, contingency, and transformational leadership perspectives make the basic assumption that leaders "make a difference." Leaders seem to influence the organization's success, but maybe not as much as we would like to believe. Some leadership experts now suggest that three perceptual processes cause people to inflate the importance of leadership in explaining organizational events. These processes, collectively called the "romance of leadership," include attribution errors, stereotyping, and the need for situational control.[67]

Attributing Leadership

Actor-observer error An attribution error whereby people tend to attribute their own actions more to external factors and the behaviour of others more to internal factors.

People have a strong need to attribute the causes of events around them so they can feel more confident about how to control them in the future. As we described in Chapter 6, the **actor-observer error** is a common perceptual bias in this attribution process. Actor-observer error is the tendency to believe that events associated with other people are due to their own motivation and ability rather than to situational contingencies. In the context of leadership, the actor-observer error causes employees to believe that organizational events are due more to the motivation and ability of their leaders than to environmental conditions. Leaders are given credit or blame for the company's success or failure because employees do not readily see the external forces that also influence these events. Leaders reinforce this belief by taking credit for organizational successes.[68]

Stereotyping Leadership

There is some evidence that people rely on leadership stereotypes to make sense of organizational events. Almost everyone has a set of shared expectations regarding what an effective leader should look and act like.[69] These preconceived ideas influence perceptions about whether someone is an effective leader. By relying on these stereotypes, employees and other stakeholders evaluate a leader's effectiveness more on his or her appearance and actions than on actual outcomes. Part of the reason this occurs is that the outcome of a leader's actions may not be known for months or years. Consequently, employees depend on immediate information to decide whether the leader is effective. If the leader fits the mould, then employees are more confident that the leader is effective.

Need for Situational Control

A third perceptual distortion of leadership suggests that people want to believe leaders make a difference. There are two basic reasons for this belief.[70] First, leadership is a useful way for us to simplify life events. It is easier to explain organizational successes and failures in terms of the leader's ability than by analyzing a complex array of other forces. For example, there are usually many reasons why a company fails to change quickly enough in the marketplace, yet we tend to simplify this explanation to the notion that the company president or some other corporate leader was ineffective. Second, there is a strong tendency in Canada and other Western societies to believe that life events are generated more from people than from uncontrollable natural forces.[71] This illusion of control is satisfied by believing that events result from the rational actions of leaders. In short, employees feel better believing that leaders make a difference, so they actively look for evidence that this is so.

The romance perspective of leadership questions the importance of leadership, but it also provides valuable advice to improve leadership effectiveness. This approach highlights the fact that leadership is a perception of followers as much as it is the actual behaviours and characteristics of people calling themselves leaders. Potential leaders must be sensitive to this fact, understand what followers expect, and act accordingly. Individuals who do not make an effort to fit leadership prototypes will have more difficulty bringing about necessary organizational change.[72]

Gender Issues in Leadership

When Anne McCall-Simms recently became general manager of Toronto's SkyDome Hotel, she brought to the job a more participative leadership style. McCall-Simms holds quarterly staff meetings as well as breakfast meetings each month with employees from different work units. "If [employees] are given opportunities to provide input, they come up with amazing suggestions for improving service," says McCall-Simms. "I get my own energy from many of these activities."[73]

As one of the first female general managers at Canadian Pacific Hotels, Anne McCall-Simms seems to bring a leadership style to SkyDome Hotel that is more participative than the styles of male general managers who preceded her. The question that currently interests many organizational behaviour scholars is whether McCall-Simms and other female executives really do lead any differently from their male counterparts. As we read in Perspective 14.2, this question has also sparked debate among executives.

Colin McConnell. Used with permission of the *Toronto Star*.

Anne McCall-Simms brought a more participative leadership style when she became SkyDome Hotel's general manager. "We have quarterly meetings that are fun and morale-boosting," says McCall-Simms. "I also meet a different group of staff members each month for breakfast. We call them our Group of Seven meetings."

PERSPECTIVE 14.2

Do Women Lead Differently?

When Carol Stephenson became manager of a Bell Canada telephone switching centre, she discovered that her new boss did not believe that women could lead the all-male workforce at the facility. "He was a crusty old plant manager," Stephenson recalls. "At first he wouldn't even talk to me. But after one week he called me into his office to tell me this was no job for a woman."

Fortunately, Stephenson ignored his advice and applied a leadership style that came naturally to her. She consulted with the employees and learned that they had been overmanaged. So she gave them the much-needed autonomy to apply their skills. "I was delighted because my job had become so much easier. And even my crusty boss was pleased."

Now, as CEO of Stentor (the alliance of Canada's telephone companies), Carol Stephenson believes that women have skills and dispositions that are well suited to the emerging leadership in today's workplace. "The corporate world is changing," she explains. "More and more there's a need to develop alliances. Knowledge workers require a new approach to employee management. The result is that the feminine style of leadership is valued more than ever before."

With more women taking over leadership positions in Canada, people are asking whether they lead differently than their male counterparts. Some female leaders, such as Stephenson, claim that they are more people-oriented. They are better listeners and conciliators. Moreover, she notes, women have not learned the command-and-control leadership style that has become less appropriate in today's corporate Canada.

Other female executives agree that leadership styles are changing, but they don't think men and women lead differently. "The gender angle is simply not a big deal with me," says Bobbie Gaunt, CEO of Ford Motor Co. of Canada Ltd. "I'm a CEO who happens to be a woman, not a woman who happens to be a CEO." Susan Insley, who manages a Honda plant in Ohio, agrees. "If there are differences in how a male or female would run this plant," explains Insley, "I believe the differences would be based on the person and the skills they bring to the job, not their gender."

Source: C. Stephenson, "The Female Model of Leadership," *Canadian Speeches* 10 (March 1997), pp. 59–64; G. Keenan, "Ford Boss No Stranger to Cars," *Globe & Mail*, April 19, 1997, p. B5; K. Gay, "Female CEOs Take Hammer to the Glass Ceiling," *Financial Post*, April 16, 1994, p. S14; B. S. Moskal, "Glass Ceiling, Beware!" *Industry Week*, April 18, 1994, pp. 13–15.

Several writers argue that women have an interactive style that includes more people-oriented and participative leadership.[74] They suggest that women exhibit more affiliation and attachment, cooperativeness, nurturance, and emotionality to their leadership roles. They further assert that these qualities make women particularly well suited to leadership roles at a time when companies are adopting a stronger emphasis on teams and employee involvement. These arguments are consistent with sex-role stereotypes; namely, that men tend to be more task-oriented, whereas women are more people-oriented.

Are these stereotypes true? Do women adopt high people-oriented and low task-oriented leadership styles? The answer, according to recent literature reviews, is that these stereotypes of female leaders are mostly false. Leadership studies in field settings have generally found that male and female leaders do not differ in their levels of task-oriented or people-oriented leadership. The main explanation why men and women do not differ on these styles is that real-world jobs require similar behaviour from male and female job incumbents.[75]

One leadership style that women do adopt more readily than their male counterparts is participation. Scholars explain that women are possibly more participative because their upbringing has made them more egalitarian and less status-oriented. There is also some evidence that women have somewhat better interpersonal skills than men, and this translates into their relatively greater use of the participative leadership style. Finally, women might be more participative because subordinates expect them to be so, based on their own sex stereotypes. If a female manager tries to be more autocratic, subordinates are more likely to complain (or use some other power base) because they expect the female manager to be participative.[76]

A disturbing finding is that people evaluate female leaders slightly less favourably than equivalent male leaders, and this difference is almost completely due to sex stereotype bias. Specifically, women are evaluated negatively when they adopt a stereotypically male leadership style (i.e., autocratic) and occupy traditionally male-dominated positions. Men also tend to give female leaders lower ratings than do other women. Moreover, male subordinates have lower acceptance of female supervisors as role models.[77] These negative evaluations suggest that women "pay the price" for entering traditionally male leadership jobs and for adopting a male-stereotypic leadership style.[78] It also lends further support to our earlier point on why women adopt a more participative style.

The debate regarding leadership differences between men and women isn't over yet. Meanwhile, we should be careful about perpetuating the apparently false assumption that women leaders are less task-oriented or more people-oriented. By holding these assumptions, many corporate decision makers have shifted women into staff roles — such as human resources, public relations, and customer service — and out of line management jobs that most frequently lead to senior management positions.

Moreover, our implicit assumptions about how female leaders should act may lead to unfair negative evaluations of them under conditions in which the leader must adopt a stereotypically male style. This is consistent with our discussion in the previous section on the romance of leadership. Leaders must be sensitive to the fact that followers have expectations about how leaders should act, and negative evaluations may go to leaders who deviate from those expectations.

Chapter Summary

- Although leadership is difficult to define, it is often described as the process of influencing people and providing an environment for them to achieve team or organizational objectives. Leaders use power and persuasion to motivate followers, and arrange the work environment so that followers do the job more effectively.

- The trait perspective tries to identify the characteristics of effective leaders. Recent writing suggests that leaders have drive, leadership motivation, integrity, self-confidence, above-average intelligence, knowledge of the business, and a high self-monitoring personality.

- The behavioural perspective of leadership identifies two clusters of leader behaviour — people-oriented and task-oriented. This perspective includes the "hi-hi" leadership hypothesis, meaning that the most effective leaders exhibit high levels of both types of behaviours. This hypothesis has since been cast into doubt.

- The contingency perspective of leadership takes the view that effective leaders diagnose the situation and adapt their style to fit that situation. The path-goal model is the prominent contingency theory that identifies four leadership styles and several contingencies relating to the characteristics of the employee and the situation. A recent extension of path-goal theory adds more leader styles and moves the model from a dyadic to a team and organizational level.

- Transformational leaders create a strategic vision, communicate that vision through framing and the use of metaphors, model the vision by "walking the talk" and acting consistently, and build commitment toward the vision. This contrasts with transactional leadership, which involves linking job performance to valued rewards and ensuring that employees have the resources needed to get the job done. The contingency and behavioural perspectives adopt the transactional view of leadership.

- According to the romance perspective, people inflate the importance of leadership through attribution, stereotyping, and fundamental needs for human control.

- Women generally do not differ from men in the degree of people-oriented or task-oriented leadership. However, female leaders more often adopt a participative style. Recent reviews also suggest that people evaluate female leaders slightly less favourably than equivalent male leaders, but this is mainly due to sex stereotype biases.

Discussion Questions

1. Northern Lights Industrials Ltd. wants to develop a competencies approach to executive selection. Which leadership perspective mainly applies to this practice? Also, based on leadership research, identify four "competencies" that Northern Lights will probably identify in effective executives.

2. What leadership styles does the behavioural perspective identify, and what is the hypothesized relationship between these styles?

3. Your employees are skilled and experienced customer service representatives who perform nonroutine tasks, such as solving unique customer problems or special needs with the company's equipment. Use path-goal theory to identify the most appropriate leadership style(s) you should use in this situation. Be sure to fully explain your answer and discuss why other styles are inappropriate.

4. Discuss the accuracy of the following statement: "Contingency theories don't work because they assume leaders can adjust their style to the situation. In reality, people have a preferred leadership style that they can't easily change."

5. What role does communication play in transformational leadership?

6. Transformational leadership is currently the most popular perspective of leadership. However, it is far from perfect. Discuss three concerns with transformational leadership.

7. Why do people tend to give leaders too much credit or blame for organizational outcomes?

8. You hear two people debating the merits of women as leaders. One person claims that women make better leaders than men because women are more sensitive to their employees' needs and involve them in organizational decisions. The other person counters that although these leadership styles may be increasingly important, most women have trouble gaining acceptance as leaders when they face tough situations in which a more autocratic style is required. Discuss the accuracy of the comments made in this discussion.

Chapter Case

Leadership in Whose Eyes?

Two senior managers — John Waisglass and Sammi Intar — are discussing Tegan Upton, the company president who joined the organization last year. Waisglass says: "I think Upton is great. She has given us a clearer sense of what we want to be as an organization. I feel much better about working here since she took over. Haven't you noticed the difference? Upton is visible and approachable. She's listened to everyone's ideas and pulled them into something that we can aim for. Upton also does what she says. Remember in one of our first meetings with her that we agreed to spend more time with our clients? Soon after, Upton was personally calling on clients and sending out production people with sales staff to hear about any customer complaints. I was skeptical at first, thinking that Upton's actions were temporary. But she's maintained this focus. And I now hear employees throughout the company using that buzzword of hers — "reality-based action" — meaning that our actions must be consistent with the customer's needs. She's great!"

Sammi Intar replies: "I don't know, John. I want to believe that Upton is a great leader for this company, but I can't. She doesn't look the part. Just listen to her. She sounds like Mickey Mouse with a cold. And the way she walks into a room doesn't look to me like someone who should be running a $30-million business. I've heard a few clients notice this — not many, mind you, just a few. They seem to shrug it off, pointing to some good things that our company has done for them since she took over. But my clients can go elsewhere if they have to. For me, this company is a career. Even though Upton has been doing some good things and our results have been good, I get very concerned about the future with her in charge."

Discussion Question

1. John Waisglass and Sammi Intar are relying on two different perspectives of leadership in their judgment of Tegan Upton. Describe these two perspectives using specific comments to illustrate the features of each model.

Experiential Exercise

Leadership Diagnostic Analysis

Purpose: To help students learn about the different path-goal leadership styles and to learn when to apply each style.

Instructions: The exercise begins with students individually writing down two incidents in which someone has been an effective manager or leader over them. The leader and situation might be from work, a sports team, a student work group, or any other setting where leadership might emerge. For example, students might describe how their supervisor in a summer job pushed them to reach higher performance goals than they would have done otherwise. Each incident should state the actual behaviours that the leader used, not just general statements (e.g., "My boss sat down with me and we agreed on specific targets and deadlines, then he said several times over the next few weeks that I was capable of reaching those goals."). Each incident requires only two or three sentences.

After everyone has written down their two incidents, the instructor will form small groups (typically between 4 or 5 students). Each team will answer the following questions for each incident presented in that team:

1. Which path-goal theory leadership style(s) (i.e., directive, supportive, participative, or achievement-oriented) did the leader apply in this incident?

2. Ask the person who wrote the incident about the conditions that made this leadership style (or these styles, if more than one was used) appropriate in this situation. The team should list these contingency factors clearly and, where possible, connect them to the contingencies described in path-goal theory. (Note: The team might identify path-goal leadership contingencies that are not described in the book. These, too, should be noted and discussed.)

After the teams have diagnosed the incidents, each team will describe to the entire class its most interesting incident as well as its diagnosis of that incident. Other teams will critique the diagnosis. Any leadership contingencies not mentioned in the textbook should also be presented and discussed.

Practice Session For Part 4

The true-false, multiple-choice, and written-answer questions presented here are based on information in Part 4 of this book (Chapters 9 to 14). These questions can help test your knowledge of material in these chapters. If your instructor uses the test bank for this textbook, these questions also give you an opportunity to practise for examinations in this course. The answers to these questions are found in Appendix C.

True-False

1. T   F   Skunkworks are teams organized around traditional departments.

2. T   F   Heterogeneous teams are generally more effective than homogeneous teams on complex projects and problems requiring innovative solutions.

3. T   F   The Canadian government discouraged employee involvement in industry until it became popular in the 1970s.

4. T   F   Most labour union leaders have been strong supporters of most employee involvement initiatives.

5. T   F   Production blocking is more likely to occur in an electronic brainstorming session than in a traditional brainstorming session.

6. T   F   Counterpower maintains the stronger party's participation with the weaker party in the exchange relationship.

7. T   F   The accommodating style of conflict management creates the risk of giving the other party unrealistically high expectations about what they can receive in the relationship.

8. T   F   Contemporary leadership scholars have moved away from the behavioural perspective of leadership partly because it assumes a universal rather than contingency approach.

Multiple-Choice

1. Team cohesiveness can usually be strengthened by: (a) ensuring that the team has at least ten members at all times; (b) making it relatively easy to become a team member; (c) creating or sensitizing the team to an external threat to its existence or goal accomplishment; (d) ensuring that team members perform independent tasks; (e) doing c and d only.

2. Quality management does NOT specifically focus on: (a) continuously improving work processes; (b) satisfying needs through time off and generous benefits; (c) encouraging employee involvement; (d) preventing defects; (e) measuring performance.

3. Which of the following statements about evaluation apprehension in team settings is FALSE? (a) Evaluation apprehension increases the individual's motivation to share his or her ideas; (b) Evaluation apprehension is more likely to occur when team members formally evaluate each other's performance throughout the year; (c) Evaluation apprehension is based on the individual's desire to create a favourable self-presentation and need for social esteem; (d) Evaluation apprehension occurs when employees believe that other team members are silently evaluating them; (e) Evaluation apprehension is most common when the meeting is attended by someone with higher status or expertise.

4. Employees are more likely to be creative when: (a) they have a high degree of autonomy in their job; (b) risk-taking is strongly discouraged; (c) their jobs are in jeopardy when they make mistakes; (d) they are given tight deadlines to complete their tasks; (e) only b and c occur.

5. Lee, a loans officer at Canbank Corp., often arrives late for work. Lee's manager would normally dismiss someone in this situation. However, the manager tolerates Lee's behaviour (with the occasional reminder and warning) because Lee is one of the best people in the bank to secure new loans. In this situation, Lee has: (a) referent power; (b) counterpower; (c) legitimate power; (d) delinquent power; (e) no power over the manager.

6. Negotiations are more effective when: (a) the parties do not set any goals for completing the negotiations; (b) neither party gives concessions; (c) both parties listen closely to the other party to understand their needs; (d) participants frequently tell each other that they are getting a "good deal" or a "fair settlement"; (e) both a and c occur.

7. Path-Goal theory states that leaders should apply the directive style when: (a) the employee has an external locus of control; (b) the employee lacks some of the skills necessary to perform the job; (c) the employee lacks experience in the job; (d) all of the above; (e) none of the above.

8. Leaders who create a strategic vision of change and bring about that change through communication and commitment are: (a) transactional; (b) transformational; (c) directive; (d) hi-hi; (e) none of the above.

Written-Answer Questions

1. In 1912, a British chemist called on the president of a Yorkshire textile mill to offer his formula for rayon. The president decided to reject the offer, saying: "It will never catch on — the public will never accept artificial silks." Today, rayon is an immensely popular material in the textile industry. Discuss the decision-making problem that caused the textile mill president to miss this opportunity.

2. Susan Chu wants her marketing team to develop more creative ways to assess the advertising agencies they use in product promotions. In the past, she simply called the group together for their ideas. Susan heard about brainstorming and wants to try that process instead. Describe the brainstorming process and describe two problems or limitations of brainstorming.

3. Jim Smith has special education and experience in a new system of bond trading, and was hired recently by the director of bond trading at CanCorp. Investments for that purpose. The director was enthusiastic about Jim's knowledge of bond trading and was eager to have him working in Toronto where all bond trading occurs. However, the company needed Jim to begin the first few months of his employment in Vancouver to fill in a staff shortage of retail traders there. A few months after Jim began his job in Vancouver, the director of bond trading left the company and was replaced by another director who was not familiar with Jim's skills or the emerging bond-trading system that Jim knew about. Meanwhile, the new director of bond trading had hired three more bond traders in Toronto who were well-trained in current bond-trading practices. Diagnose Jim's power over the new director in this situation, including his power base(s) and contingencies of power.

PART 5

Organizational Processes

CHAPTER 15
Organizational Change and Development

CHAPTER 16
Organizational Culture

CHAPTER 17
Employment Relationship and Career Dynamics

CHAPTER 18
Organizational Structure and Design

Organizational Change and Development

CHAPTER OUTLINE

Forces for Change

Resistance to Change

Supporting Organizational Change

Organization Development

Emerging Trends in Organization Development

Effectiveness of Organization Development

Chapter Summary

Discussion Questions

LEARNING OBJECTIVES

After reading this chapter, you should be able to:

- Describe six reasons why people resist organizational change.

- Diagram force field analysis.

- Discuss five strategies to minimize resistance to change.

- Describe how to diffuse successful organizational change projects.

- Outline the action research approach to organization development.

- Compare incremental with quantum organizational change.

- Discuss four ethical dilemmas facing organization development.

Canadian National Railways has experienced more change over the past few years than almost any other Canadian organization. CEO Paul Tellier pressured senior executives and lower-level employees to transform the former government-owned Crown corporation into a profit-driven, customer-oriented company.

Soon after becoming CEO of Canadian National Railways (CN), Paul Tellier paid a visit to CN's largest customer, General Motors of Canada. The visit went well until a CN employee who works at the General Motors site picked Tellier up in a Ford. When Tellier grilled his senior executives about this incident, one executive naively replied: "What's wrong with that?" Ten weeks later, the executive was gone.

Paul Tellier radically transformed CN from a money-losing Canadian government Crown corporation into a privatized "profit-driven, customer-oriented company." He instilled a better customer focus (no more Fords driven around General Motors sites) and negotiated new labour contracts so that CN could become more cost-competitive. "We're all in this together and it has to change," Tellier said to labour leaders when he first became CEO. "Every one of us has to be an agent of change."

Tellier drove the change effort from both the top and bottom of the organization. "When I came here, I started applying pressure from the top," Tellier explains. He challenged his senior vice-presidents in weekly interrogations and dumped several executives who were not aligned with his vision of CN's future. Tellier also used a "bubbling-up process" by convincing employees that the company needed to be more cost-competitive. For example, employees agreed to simplify work rules, blur job duties, and introduce a gainsharing plan on the Northern Quebec Internal Short Line in order to keep the line running.

"It's only the beginning," Tellier predicts. "I don't think many companies in Canada — if any — have changed as much as we have in the past three years. And I think we have to change as much, if not more, in the next three years."[1]

The speed of corporate change today is enough to leave anyone breathless. Canadian National Railways was a money-losing millstone around the Canadian government's neck before Paul Tellier took the reins. Petro-Canada, another privatized Crown corporation, has been transformed into an aggressive oil producer that is gaining respect in Alberta's oil patch. Magna International, the Canadian automobile parts company, was given up for dead in the early 1990s. Now it's the world's leading auto-parts supplier. On the other side of the coin, Novell practically owned the computer network market a few years ago; now it's struggling to survive. So is Apple, the company that brought user-friendliness to personal computers.[2]

This chapter examines the effective management of change in organizations. We begin by considering some of the more significant forces for organizational change and the forces resisting change. Next, a general model is presented that considers these opposing forces and proposes ways to effectively manage the change process. The latter part of this chapter introduces the field of organization development (OD). In particular, we review the OD process, emerging OD interventions, and issues relating to OD effectiveness.

Forces for Change

As we learned at the beginning of the book, organizations are open systems that need to remain compatible with their external environments. But these environments are constantly changing, so organizations must recognize these shifts and respond accordingly to survive and remain effective. Successful organizations monitor their environments and take appropriate steps to maintain a compatible fit with the new external conditions. Rather than resisting change, employees in successful companies embrace change as an integral part of organizational life.

Canadian organizations are rapidly changing as they face an increasingly global marketplace. Competitors are just as likely to be located in Japan, Germany, Mexico, or the United States as somewhere else in Canada.[3] The North American Free Trade Agreement (NAFTA) has opened Canada's competitive environment with the United States, Mexico, and possibly some South American countries. Emerging trading blocs in Europe, Asia, and other areas of the world add to the intense competitive pressures Canadian firms now face. The Canadian government has fuelled competition by deregulating airlines, trucking, telecommunications, and other industries.[4] "It's a whole new, aggressive world out there," says the president of Neilson-Cadbury, Canada's leading candy-manufacturing company. "Change — rapid change — has become the way of life."[5]

While Canadian firms adjust to external economic shifts, they are also adapting to Canada's emerging workforce. Canadians entering the labour force today are far more diverse than workers a few decades ago. They are also more educated and expect more involvement and interesting work. These changes have put pressure on organizational leaders to alter work practices and embrace more diverse views.

Computer Technology and Organizational Change

The speed of change has been lubricated by emerging computer-based technologies. Some computer systems have drastically compressed work processes. Consider Iona Appliances, the Welland, Ontario, designer and manufacturer of vacuum cleaners. Iona's engineers previously required a week to draft and model a single component. They can now do the same thing with a 3-D computer-aided design system in just two

hours.[6] This has dramatically sped up the product development process and increased production flexibility.

Computer technologies have also made it easy and inexpensive for companies to transfer information.[7] Computer networks have been set up with suppliers for just-in-time delivery of parts and resources. Major clients are hooked up to the organization's product database for direct ordering and delivery. Employees use Intranet systems to directly access job-related information, bypassing supervisors who previously served as conduits.

Computer systems and other technologies have significantly reduced employment levels and changed the skill requirements of remaining employees. At Canadian National Railways, for instance, a single employee standing beside the track with a remote-control system can operate a six-ton train engine in the marshalling yard. This technology alone has replaced nearly 300 locomotive engineers.[8] Although some technological change reduces employee skill requirements, studies suggest that job quality typically improves and skill requirements increase.[9]

Resistance to Change

No matter how noble the cause, most organizational change efforts are resisted by employees, managers, clients, or other stakeholders.[10] Resistance to change can take many forms: passive noncompliance, complaints, absenteeism, turnover, or collective action (e.g., strikes, walkouts). Resistance is often an important symptom that problems exist, but this is even more reason to understand why resistance occurs and to prevent it wherever possible. Resistance is not an irrational act; it stems from a logical motivation to maintain the status quo rather than comply with new behaviour patterns. The main reasons that people typically resist change are direct costs, saving face, fear of the unknown, breaking routines, incongruent organizational systems, and incongruent team dynamics, as Exhibit 15.1 illustrates.[11]

EXHIBIT 15.1: Forces Resisting Organizational Change

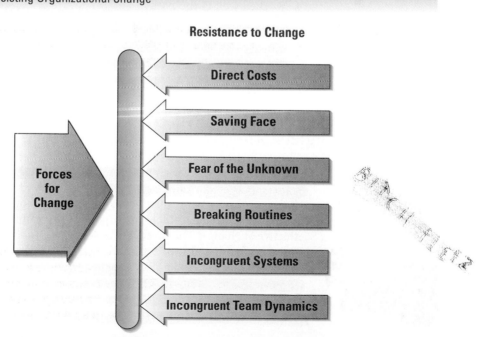

- *Direct costs*   People resist change whenever they believe the new state of affairs will have higher direct costs or lower benefits than the existing situation. For instance, as described in Chapter 12, some employees at Bow Valley Energy Inc. resisted change because they believed that they would lose power over the information that maintained their status in the organization.

- *Saving face*   Some people resist change as a political strategy to "prove" that the decision is wrong or that the change agent is incompetent. For example, senior management in a manufacturing firm bought a computer system other than the one recommended by the information systems department. Soon after the system was in place, several information systems employees let minor implementation problems escalate to demonstrate that senior management had made a poor decision.

- *Fear of the unknown*   Change is resisted because it involves facing uncertainty. Employees might worry about lacking the necessary skills or losing valued work arrangements after the transition.

- *Breaking routines*   In Chapter 1, we said that along with organizational learning, companies need to "unlearn."[12] This means that employees need to abandon the routines and behavioural habits that are no longer appropriate. Unfortunately, people are creatures of habit. They like to maintain routine role patterns that make life more predictable and less troublesome.[13] Consequently, many people resist organizational changes that force them to abandon old ways and to invest time and energy learning new role patterns.

- *Incongruent organizational systems*   Rewards, selection, training, and other control systems ensure that employees maintain desired role patterns. Yet the organizational systems that maintain stability also discourage employees from adopting new ways.[14] The implication, of course, is that organizational systems must be altered to fit the desired change. Unfortunately, control systems can be difficult to change, particularly when they have supported role patterns that worked well in the past.[15]

- *Incongruent team dynamics*   As we learned in Chapter 9, work teams develop and enforce conformity to a set of norms that guide behaviour. However, conformity to existing team norms may discourage employees from accepting organizational change. Change agents need to recognize and alter team norms that conflict with the desired changes.

Supporting Organizational Change

Force field analysis A model that helps change agents diagnose the forces that drive and restrain proposed organizational change.

Only 20 percent of Canadian employees believe that their organizations are very good at managing organizational change. And only 3 percent of representatives from Canadian firms gave themselves excellent ratings on most of the strategies for assessing corporate change.[16] How can organizations minimize resistance and become more effective at change? The best place to start is by understanding the dynamics of change through a long-established model called **force field analysis**.

As shown in Exhibit 15.2, one side of the force field model represents the *driving forces* that push organizations toward a new state of affairs. The other side represents the *restraining forces* that try to maintain the status quo. Stability occurs when the driving and restraining forces are roughly in equilibrium; that is, they are of approximately

EXHIBIT 15.2: Force Field Analysis Model

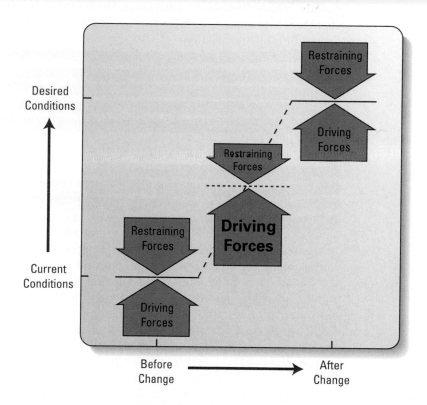

equal strength in opposite directions. Change occurs when the driving forces are stronger than the restraining forces. This perspective of organizational change provides a very useful way to diagnose the situation before beginning the change process.[17]

The central idea behind the force field model is that effective change begins by **unfreezing** the current situation and ends by **refreezing** it. Unfreezing means that the change agent produces a disequilibrium between the driving and restraining forces. Refreezing introduces systems and conditions that reinforce and maintain the new role patterns and prevent the organization from slipping back into the old way of doing things.

Unfreezing the Status Quo

To move the organization to a future state, change agents need to unfreeze the status quo by creating a disequilibrium between the driving and restraining forces. The approach used too often is to increase the driving forces. This occurs when change agents put direct pressure on employees to change. They threaten those who do not actively support the change effort and they complain that employees aren't living up to the company's standards. For instance, a former CEO of the Canadian Imperial Bank of Commerce tried to bring about change by referring to people as "middle management mush." In another example, a former CEO of Southam Inc. belittled employees in a failed attempt to bring about change.

Generally, increasing the driving forces alone rarely brings about meaningful change because the restraining forces often adjust to counterbalance the driving

Unfreezing The first part of the change process whereby the change agent produces a disequilibrium between the driving and restraining forces.

Refreezing The latter part of the change process in which systems and conditions are introduced that reinforce and maintain the desired behaviours.

forces, rather like the coils of a mattress. The harder management pushes for new procedures without employee acceptance, the stronger employees tend to resist these changes. This antagonism threatens the change effort by producing tension and conflict within the organization.

Rather than increasing the driving forces, change agents need to focus more on reducing the restraining forces. This occurs by re-aligning the four elements in the model of individual behaviour presented in Chapter 2. Specifically, change is more likely to occur when employees are motivated to change, possess the requisite abilities, have clear role perceptions, and have supportive situational contingencies.

Creating an urgency for change

Change efforts often fail because the change agent does not convince employees that there is an urgency for change. In other words, employees must be motivated to change. They must believe that the status quo is less acceptable than transforming the organization into an unknown future state. One corporate leader did this by commissioning and making public the first-ever customer satisfaction survey, knowing that the results would be terrible. Another CEO engineered a significant accounting loss so that shareholders would pressure the company to become more efficient.[18]

Power Computing, the Macintosh-clone manufacturer recently purchased by Apple Computer, created an urgency for change by directly showing employees that customer service problems were hurting the company. Joel Kocher, Power Computing's chief operating officer, read a harsh customer complaint letter at a meeting with employees. Then, to everyone's surprise, he brought the customer into the meeting to explain the problem. "We actually brought the customer to the meeting, to personalize it for every single person in the room," says Kocher. "And it was very, very interesting to see the metamorphosis that occurred within the context of these several hundred people when you actually had a customer talking about how their foul-up had hurt this person and hurt their business."[19]

Along with motivating employees — creating an urgency for change — corporate leaders reduce the restraining forces by making employees aware of their new roles, and they provide the skills, knowledge, and resources needed to execute those role patterns. These conditions are mainly established through communication, training, employee involvement, and stress management. Exhibit 15.3 outlines six ways to overcome employee resistance. Communication, training, employee involvement, and stress management try to reduce the restraining forces and, if feasible, should be attempted first.[20] However, negotiation and coercion are necessary for people who will clearly lose something from the change and when the speed of change is critical.

Communication

To remain competitive, Bonas Machine Company had to introduce a team-based production system with quality management practices. But before it could begin the change process, the British weaving-machine manufacturer arranged several information sessions to convince employees that these changes were necessary. Employees learned that the company's major Swiss competitor had developed a similar product that would affect Bonas's market share unless productivity increased. Guest speakers described how Japanese firms used efficient quality management practices that would threaten Bonas's survival unless applied here. Bonas's employees also heard how other companies in the area had gone out of business due to their lack of production flexibility.[21]

EXHIBIT 15.3: Methods for Dealing with Resistance to Change

Strategy	Example	When Used	Problems
Communication	Customer complaint letters shown to employees.	When employees don't feel an urgency for change, or don't know how the change will affect them.	Time-consuming and potentially costly.
Training	Employees learn how to work in teams as company adopts a team-based structure.	When employees need to break old routines and adopt new role patterns	Time-consuming and potentially costly.
Employee Involvement	Company forms task force to recommend new customer service practices.	When the change effort needs more employee commitment, some employees need to save face, and/or employee ideas would improve decisions about the change strategy.	Very time-consuming. Might also lead to conflict and poor decisions if employees' interests are incompatible with organizational needs.
Stress Management	Employees attend sessions to discuss their worries about the change.	When communication, training, and involvement do not sufficiently ease employee worries.	Time-consuming and potentially expensive. Some methods may not reduce stress for all employees.
Negotiation	Employees agree to replace strict job categories with multi-skilling in return for increased job security.	When employees will clearly lose something of value from the change and would not otherwise support the new conditions. Also necessary when the company must change quickly.	May be expensive, particularly if other employees want to negotiate their support. Also tends to produce compliance but not commitment to the change.
Coercion	Company president tells managers to "get on board" the change or leave.	When other strategies are ineffective and the company needs to change quickly.	Can lead to more subtle forms of resistance, as well as long-term antagonism with the change agent.

Communication is the highest priority and first strategy required for any organizational change. Although time-consuming and costly, communication reduces the restraining forces by providing the previously mentioned sense of urgency or motivation to change.[22] Bonas employees were more willing to change after they realized that the company's future was less certain. Similarly, employees at CEMEX, the Mexican-based cement company, were more receptive to change after they learned about the competitive advantages its main rivals enjoyed in foreign markets.[23] Along with motivating employees to change, communication keeps employees informed about what to expect from the change effort. This can potentially reduce fear of the unknown and develop team norms that are more consistent with the change effort.[24]

Training

Training is necessary for most change efforts so that employees learn the required skills and knowledge under the new conditions. For example, after Bonas Machine Company employees learned about the need for change, the company provided extensive training in quality management techniques, as well as leadership and coaching skills for team leaders and managers. Without this training, employees would have experienced more stress and uncertainty regarding the future state that Bonas's management was trying to create. Training is time-consuming, but it lets people learn new role patterns more easily and, consequently, tends to minimize resistance to breaking routines.

Employee involvement

Employee involvement creates a sense of ownership of the change process, thereby minimizing problems of saving face and fear of the unknown.[25] It also helps companies make better decisions about the type of change needed and provides a means for employees to better understand the change activities. Bell Canada actively relied on employee involvement to implement its Zero Waste Program. Task force members represented different parts of the organization and served as role models for the change effort. This helped other employees learn and feel more comfortable with ways to reduce environmental waste in their building.

More recently, Bell Canada improved customer satisfaction and sales performance at its Consumer Answer Centre by involving employees in the change process. An investigative team of employees surveyed customers and visited call centres in several industries to find out how to change Bell Canada's centre. "One of the most important lessons we learned was about involvement," concludes Tom Band, Bell Canada's regional manager who oversaw the change. "Gaining the commitment of an employee's hands and head can be ineffective unless the heart is also involved."[26]

Courtesy of Bell Canada.

Employee involvement helped Bell Canada change wasteful behaviour. The telecommunications company's Zero Waste Program was designed and steered by a task force of respected employees who served as role models for the change effort.

Bell Canada relied on indirect employee involvement to bring about change. However, direct involvement of all employees is both desirable and possible, even in fairly large organizations. As we read in Perspective 15.1, Richmond Savings Credit Union found a way to involve all of its 400 employees in the change process of redirecting the financial institution's objectives and action plans.

Stress management

Stress is a common problem in organizational change.[27] Communication, training, and employee involvement can reduce some of the tension, but companies also need to introduce stress management practices to help employees cope with the changes. Labatt Breweries recognized the need for stress management during a corporate restructuring. "[Labatt] had systems in place from day one to help people cope with the stress of the change," recalls the general manager of Labatt's Newfoundland operations. These systems included "rap sessions" in which employees shared their thoughts and concerns with Labatt's senior managers.[28]

PERSPECTIVE 15.1

Richmond Savings Gets Everyone Involved in Change

With the help of some logistical planning, Richmond Savings, Canada's third-largest credit union, was able to involve all of its 400 employees — from part-time office workers to senior executives — in a six-day meeting to create a new vision for the financial institution.

To keep operations running, half of the employees attended sessions on Tuesday and Wednesday, and the other half attended on Thursday and Friday. During these sessions, employees were organized into groups of eight people with maximum diversity regarding their branch, title, gender, and ethnic background.

Each session began with outside speakers talking about Richmond Savings' customers and reputation as well as changes in the financial services industry. Next, each group reached a consensus on the corporate objectives arising from these presentations. Using Post-it notes and felt pens, each group then discussed action plans for each objective. Everyone at the session then voted on the best of the action plans.

Richmond Savings' executives met on Saturday to review the objectives and action plans that employees had prepared during the previous four days. On Sunday, the executives met with all of the credit union's 400 employees to

Richmond Savings used a unique approach to involve all 400 of its employees in organizational change strategy sessions.

explain what they had changed and why. "It was a tremendous experience," says Richmond Savings CEO Kirk Lawrie. "Something you remember for a very long time."

According to a subsequent survey, this employee involvement process for organizational change was a success. All of the employees surveyed understood the company's objectives and 91 percent knew how they could help make these plans a reality.

Source: Adapted from T. McCallum, "Vision 2001: Staying Ahead of the Competition," *Human Resource Professional*, November 1996, pp. 25–26.

Negotiation

Organizational change is, in large measure, a political activity.[29] People have vested interests and apply their power to ensure that the emerging conditions are consistent with their personal values and needs. Consequently, negotiation may be necessary for employees who will clearly lose out from the change activity. This negotiation offers certain benefits to offset some of the cost of the change.

Consider the experience of GE Capital Fleet Services in Richmond Hill, Ontario. When the company removed two levels of management, it faced serious resistance from supervisors who worried that they would lose their status. After several months, senior management negotiated with the supervisors and eventually created an intermediate manager position to overcome this resistance. "In our case, the decision to delayer was non-negotiable," recalls a GE Capital manager. "As time was subsequently to show, however, we should have been prepared to negotiate on the number of layers to be eliminated."[30]

Coercion

We often hear about recently hired company presidents who threaten then dismiss executives who do not adopt their new vision. As described in the opening story to the chapter, CN's Paul Tellier removed several executives for this reason. Ted Pattenden, CEO of Toronto-based National Rubber, replaced his entire management team because they were not in tune with the changes he wanted to make. These are not isolated examples. One survey reported that two-thirds of senior management in large U.S. firms were replaced by the time the businesses were revived.[31]

Dismissals and other forms of coercion represent ways of increasing the driving forces for change. As mentioned earlier, this is a risky strategy because increasing the driving forces usually causes the restraining forces to increase in response. Moreover, as a form of punishment, coercion may produce an adverse emotional reaction (Chapter 2). Those who are threatened may comply, but they aren't likely to embrace the change. Those who survive the rash of dismissals either become overly cautious or engage in organizational politics to keep their jobs.

At the same time, coercion may be necessary when speed is essential and other tactics are ineffective. For example, it may be necessary to remove several members of an executive team who have internalized a misaligned corporate culture and are unwilling or unable to change. This is also a radical form of organizational "unlearning" (Chapter 1) because when executives leave, they take with them knowledge of the organization's past routines. This potentially opens up opportunities for new practices to take hold.[32]

Refreezing the Desired Conditions

After unfreezing and changing the previous conditions, we need to refreeze them so that people do not slip back into their old work practices.[33] Refreezing occurs when organizational systems and team dynamics are reconfigured so that they support the desired changes. Reward systems must be altered to reinforce the new behaviours and attitudes rather than previous practices. Information and support must be continuously transmitted to reaffirm the new practices. New feedback systems must be introduced and existing ones recalibrated to focus on the new priorities and performance goals. Organizational systems and structures shape employee values and behaviours. Consequently, these elements need to be re-aligned so that they stabilize or refreeze the desired future state.[34]

This refreezing process was applied by Pratt & Whitney Canada (P&W) when its Longueuil, Quebec, plant changed from long runs of a few jet engines to a short-run synchronous process (i.e., making only a few units of many types of engines).[35] P&W introduced measures and rewards that emphasized customer needs and minimized inventory costs because these goals are priorities in the short-run synchronous process. At the same time, P&W reduced or removed measures and rewards of production efficiency and standardization that supported the long-run process. Without these systems changes, P&W's employees probably would have slipped back into their previous goals and behaviours.

Diffusion of Change

There is fairly strong support for the idea that organizational transformations should begin with pilot projects. The reason is that pilot projects are more flexible and less risky than centralized organizationwide programs.[36] Consider the experience of Schneider Corp., described in Perspective 15.2. The Kitchener, Ontario, meat-processing company lost valuable time and effort by trying to change the entire organization at the same time. When the transformation was successfully tested as a pilot project in the smoke-

---

house, the employees in this area became disciples who diffused the change to other parts of the organization.

The question, of course, is how do we successfully diffuse the results of the pilot project? Richard Walton, who has studied the diffusion of work restructuring programs at Alcan Aluminum and other companies, offers several recommendations for the effective diffusion of change.[37] Generally, diffusion is more likely to occur when the pilot project is successful within one or two years and receives visibility (e.g., favourable news media coverage). These conditions tend to increase top-management support for the change program as well as persuade other managers to introduce the change effort in their operations. Successful diffusion also depends on labour union support and active involvement in the diffusion process.

Another important condition is that the diffusion strategy isn't described too abstractly, because this makes the instructions too vague to introduce the change elsewhere. Neither should the strategy be stated too precisely, because it might not seem relevant to other areas of the organization. Finally, without producing excessive turnover in the pilot group, people who have worked under the new system should be moved to other areas of the organization. These employees bring their knowledge and commitment of the change effort to work units that have not yet experienced it.

Organization Development

Organization development (OD) A planned systemwide effort, managed from the top with the assistance of a change agent, that uses behavioural science knowledge to improve organizational effectiveness.

Action research A data-based, problem-oriented process that diagnoses the need for change, introduces the OD intervention, and then evaluates and stabilizes the desired changes.

Force field analysis and the diffusion of change explain the main dynamics of change that occur every day in organizations. However, there is an entire field of study, called **organization development (OD),** that tries to understand how to manage planned change in organizations. OD is a planned systemwide effort, managed from the top with the assistance of a change agent, that uses behavioural science knowledge to improve organizational effectiveness.[38]

OD relies on many of the organizational behaviour concepts described in this book, such as team dynamics, perceptions, job design, and conflict management. OD also takes a systems perspective, because it recognizes that organizations have many interdependent parts and must adapt to their environments. Thus, OD experts try to ensure that all parts of the organization are compatible with the change effort, and that the change activities help the company fit its environment.[39]

Most OD activities rely on **action research** as the primary blueprint for planned change. As depicted in Exhibit 15.4, action research is a data-based, problem-oriented

---

EXHIBIT 15.4: The Action Research Approach to Organization Development

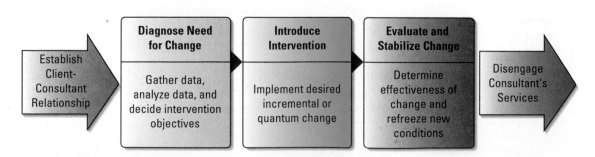

| Establish Client-Consultant Relationship | **Diagnose Need for Change** — Gather data, analyze data, and decide intervention objectives | **Introduce Intervention** — Implement desired incremental or quantum change | **Evaluate and Stabilize Change** — Determine effectiveness of change and refreeze new conditions | Disengage Consultant's Services |

process that diagnoses the need for change, introduces the OD intervention, and then evaluates and stabilizes the desired changes.[40]

Action research is a highly participative process, involving the client throughout the various stages.[41] It typically includes an action research team consisting of people affected by the organizational change who have the power to facilitate it. This participation is a fundamental philosophy of OD, but it also increases commitment to the change process and provides valuable information to conduct organizational diagnosis and evaluation. Let's look at the main elements of the action research process.

The Client-Consultant Relationship

Change agent A person who possesses enough knowledge and power to guide and facilitate the change effort. This may be a member of the organization or an external consultant.

Organizational change requires a **change agent** — a manager, consultant, labour union official, or anyone else who possesses enough knowledge and power to guide and facilitate the change effort. External consultants with special training in the behavioural sciences and previous experience in OD techniques are sometimes hired as change agents. A few large Canadian firms employ internal OD consultants to assist change activities in the company. However, we must keep in mind that change agents are usually line managers and team leaders who serve as champions to keep the change effort on track.

Change agents first need to determine the client's readiness for change, and whether people are motivated to participate in the process, are open to meaningful change, and possess the abilities to complete the process. They watch out for people who enter the process with preconceived answers before the situation is fully diagnosed, or who intend to use the change effort to their personal advantage (e.g., closing down a department or firing a particular employee). Change agents also need to establish their power base in the client relationship.[42] Effective consultants rely on expertise and perhaps referent power to have any influence on the participants (see Chapter 12 for a discussion of the various power bases). However, they *should not* use reward, legitimate, or coercive power, because these bases may weaken trust and neutrality in the client-consultant relationship.

Change agents need to agree with their clients on the most appropriate role in the relationship.[43] This might range from providing technical expertise on a specific change activity to facilitating the change process. Many OD experts prefer the latter role, commonly known as **process consultation**.[44] Process consultation involves helping the organization solve its own problems by making it aware of organizational processes, the consequences of those processes, and the means by which they can be changed. Rather than providing expertise about the content of the change — such as how to introduce continuous-improvement teams — process consultants help participants learn how to solve their own problems by guiding them through the change process.[45]

Process consultation A method of helping the organization solve its own problems by making it aware of organizational processes, the consequences of those processes, and the means by which they can be changed.

Diagnose the Need for Change

Action research is a problem-oriented activity that carefully diagnoses the problem (or opportunity) through systematic analysis of the situation. *Organizational diagnosis* involves gathering and analyzing data about an ongoing system. This stage is important because if organizational diagnosis is incorrect, subsequent steps will likely be wasted effort.[46]

Various data collection methods are available, but the consultant needs to consider the advantages and disadvantages of each method.[47] Interviews are common, because OD consultants can build rapport with the client, explore specific issues spontaneously, and cover a range of subjects. However, they are susceptible to perceptual bias and are expensive in large client groups. Questionnaires allow the consultant to collect and quantify information from many people relatively easily and inexpensively, although they are more impersonal and inflexible than interviews. Direct observation can be used when small teams are involved, but this method is too time-consuming in large work units. Secondary data, such as monthly productivity records and union grievance reports, represent an unobtrusive source of diagnostic information, although they may be too politically sensitive and expensive to retrieve.

The consultant typically organizes and interprets the data, then presents it to the client to identify symptoms, problems, and possible solutions. The data analysis also motivates participants to support the change intervention because it allows them to see the need for change. The data analysis should be neutral and descriptive to avoid perceptual defensiveness. The information should also relate to factors over which participants have control.

Along with gathering and analyzing data, the diagnostic process involves agreeing on specific prescriptions for action, including the appropriate change method and the schedule for these actions. This process, known as *joint action planning*, ensures that everyone knows what is expected of them and that standards are established to properly evaluate the process after the transition.[48]

Introduce the OD Intervention

The OD process includes several interventions, including the consultant's entry into the relationship and the diagnostic process. Nevertheless, the focal intervention involves altering specific system variables identified in the organizational diagnosis and planning stages. These changes might alter tasks, strategic organizational goals, system controls (e.g., rewards), attitudes, or interpersonal relationships.

An important issue during implementation is the degree of change that should occur. **Incremental change** is an evolutionary strategy because the organization fine-tunes the existing organization and takes small steps toward the change effort's objectives.[49] Continuous improvement (Chapter 10) usually applies incremental change because it attempts to make small improvements to existing work processes. Organizational change experts usually recommend incremental change because it produces less resistance and involves less risk. It is less threatening and stressful to employees because they have time to adapt to the new conditions. Moreover, any problems in the intervention can be corrected while the change process is occurring, rather than afterwards.[50]

Quantum change is a revolutionary strategy because the organization breaks out of its existing ways and moves toward a totally different configuration of systems and structures. Quantum change is necessary when environmental shifts occur suddenly or leaders have delayed action until the situation is critical.[51] Some writers now argue that companies need more "re-engineering" (quantum change) rather than incremental tinkering to survive in this rapidly changing environment. Others advise us that bold changes face less employee resistance than small, incremental changes.[52]

Although re-engineering and other forms of quantum change are sometimes necessary, they also present risks. One problem is that quantum change usually

Incremental change An evolutionary approach to change in which existing organizational conditions are fine-tuned and small steps are taken toward the change effort's objectives.

Quantum change A revolutionary approach to change in which the organization breaks out of its existing ways and moves toward a totally different configuration of systems and structures.

includes the costly task of altering organizational systems and structures. Many costs, such as getting employees to learn completely different roles, are not apparent until the change process has started. Another problem is that quantum change is usually traumatic and rapid, so change agents rely more on coercion and negotiation rather than employee involvement to build support for the change effort.[53]

Evaluate and Stabilize Change

OD interventions can be very expensive, so it makes sense that we should measure their effectiveness. To evaluate an OD intervention, we need to recall its objectives that were developed during the organizational diagnosis and action planning stages. But even when these goals are clearly stated, the effectiveness of an OD intervention might not be apparent for several years. It is also difficult to separate the effects of the intervention from external factors (e.g., improving economy, introduction of new technology).

If the intervention has the desired effect, the change agent and participants need to stabilize the new conditions. This is essentially the same as the refreezing process described above. Organizational systems and team dynamics are aligned with the desired conditions so that people do not slide back into old practices. For example, reward and communication systems are redesigned so that they support the new values and behaviours.

Emerging Trends in Organization Development

Organization development includes any planned change intended to make a firm more effective. In theory, this means that OD covers almost every area of organizational behaviour, as well as many aspects of strategic and human resource management. In practice, OD consultants have favoured one perspective and level of intervention more than others at various periods in OD's history.

When the field of OD emerged in the 1940s and 1950s, OD practitioners focused almost exclusively on interpersonal and small-group dynamics. Few OD interventions were involved with macro-level organizationwide changes. The field was equated with T-groups, encounter groups, and other forms of sensitivity training. **Sensitivity training** is an unstructured and agendaless session in which a small group of people meet face-to-face, often for a few days, to learn more about themselves and their relations with others.[54] Learning occurs as participants disclose information about themselves and receive feedback from others during the session.

Sensitivity training An unstructured and agendaless session in which participants become more aware through their interactions of how they affect others and how others affect them.

Today, the reverse is true.[55] OD interventions are now mostly aimed at improving service quality, corporate restructuring, and organizational learning. They are typically organizationwide, affecting organizational systems and structures, with less emphasis on individual emotions and values. OD practitioners pay more attention to productivity, customer service, product or service quality, and related business outcomes.[56] And although surveys suggest that OD consultants still value their humanistic roots, there is also increasing awareness that the field's values have shifted to a more bottom-line focus.

There are numerous OD interventions, such as job design (Chapter 4), team building (Chapter 9), intergroup mirroring (Chapter 13), and changing organizational culture (Chapter 16). In this section, we briefly discuss two emerging OD interventions: parallel learning structures and appreciative inquiry.

Parallel Learning Structures

Executives at Europcar wanted to make its vehicle rental process more customer-friendly and efficient. But as Europe's second-largest vehicle rental company, Europcar operated as a set of independent fiefdoms in each country. The only way to change this dispersed organization was to create a parallel learning structure in the form of a task force that represented these far-reaching and independent units. The Greenway Project, as it was called, brought together 100 representatives from Europcar's operations across the continent to design and implement a better car rental process. In spite of opposition from turf-protective country managers, the Greenway Project made significant progress over its 18-month mandate. More important, its proposals were much easier to implement as its members returned to their countries.[57]

Parallel learning structure A highly participative social structure constructed alongside (i.e., parallel to) the formal organization with the purpose of increasing the organization's learning.

The Greenway Project relied on a form of organization development intervention known as a parallel learning structure. **Parallel learning structures** are highly participative arrangements composed of people from most levels of the organization who follow the action research model to produce meaningful organizational change. They are social structures developed alongside the formal hierarchy with the purpose of increasing the organization's learning.[58] Ideally, parallel learning structure participants are sufficiently free from the constraints of the larger organization that they may solve organizational issues more effectively.

The Greenway Project served as a parallel learning structure because it operated alongside the existing organization. It involved representatives from various countries and work units of Europcar. The group established a new way of operating the organization. In fact, the entire structure established a precedent by acting as a pan-European unit. By separating the intervention from the traditional hierarchy, Europcar was able to instill new attitudes, role patterns, and work behaviours to the larger organization more effectively.

Appreciative Inquiry

The action research process described earlier in the chapter is based on the traditional problem-solving model. OD participants focus on problems with the existing organizational system and identify ways to correct those problems. Unfortunately, this deficiency model of the world — in which something is wrong that must be fixed — emphasizes the negative dynamics of the group or system rather than its positive opportunities.

Appreciative inquiry An organization development intervention that directs the group's attention away from its own problems and focuses participants on the group's potential and positive elements.

Appreciative inquiry tries to break out of the problem-solving mentality by reframing relationships around the positive and the possible. It takes the view that organizations are creative entities in which people are capable of building synergy beyond their individual capabilities. To avoid dwelling on the group's own shortcomings, the process usually directs its inquiry toward a successful organization with similar characteristics. This external focus becomes a form of behavioural modelling, but it also increases open dialogue by redirecting the group's attention away from its own problems. Appreciative inquiry is especially useful when participants are aware of their "problems" or already suffer from enough negativity in their relationships. The positive orientation of appreciative inquiry enables groups to overcome these negative tensions and build a more hopeful perspective of their future by focusing on what is possible.

Exhibit 15.5 outlines the four main stages of appreciative inquiry.[59] The process begins with *appreciating* — identifying the positive elements of the observed organization. For instance, participants might interview members of the other organization to discover its fundamental strengths. As participants discuss their findings, they shift into the *envisioning* stage by considering what might be possible in an ideal organization. By

EXHIBIT 15.5: The Appreciative Inquiry Process

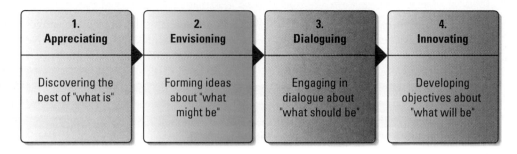

1. Appreciating	2. Envisioning	3. Dialoguing	4. Innovating
Discovering the best of "what is"	Forming ideas about "what might be"	Engaging in dialogue about "what should be"	Developing objectives about "what will be"

Source: Based on F. J. Barrett and D. L. Cooperrider, "Generative Metaphor Intervention: A New Approach for Working with Systems Divided by Conflict and Caught in Defensive Perception," *Journal of Applied Behavioral Science* 26 (1990), p. 229.

directing their attention to another organization and its ideal state, participants feel safer revealing their hopes and aspirations than if they were discussing their own organization.

As participants make their private thoughts public to the group, the process shifts into the third stage, called *dialoguing*. **Dialogue**, which we introduced in Chapter 9, is a long-term process in which participants listen with selfless receptivity to each others' models and assumptions and eventually form a collective model for thinking within the team.[60] As this model takes shape, group members shift the focus back to their own organization. In the final stage of appreciative inquiry, called *innovating*, participants establish specific objectives and direction for their own organization based on their model of what should be.

Dialogue A process of conversion among team members in which they learn about each other's personal models and assumptions, and eventually form a common model for thinking within the team.

Chrysler Canada practised a form of appreciative inquiry by beginning each "working together" meeting with a success story. "We had found that too often we would dwell on our mistakes and failures, subsequently spiralling around them," says Chrysler Canada manager Adrian Vido. Writing success stories helped Chrysler's managers see themselves and their colleagues in a more positive and optimistic light. At first, people were hard-pressed to think of successes, but they eventually realized that these gems of experience existed every day in their part of the operation.[61]

Courtesy of Chrysler Canada.

Chrysler Canada practised a form of appreciative inquiry by beginning each "working together" meeting with a success story. These anecdotes helped the plant managers see themselves and their colleagues in a more positive and optimistic light. Rather than dwelling on past problems, the group refocused around images of a positive future state.

Effectiveness of Organization Development

Is organization development effective? Considering the incredible range of organization development interventions, answering this question is not easy. Nevertheless, a few studies have generally reported that some OD interventions have a moderately positive effect on employee productivity and attitudes. According to some reviews, team building and intergroup mirroring produce the most favourable results when a single intervention is applied.[62] Others report that self-directed work teams are very effective.[63] One of the most consistent findings is that OD is most effective when it includes two or more types of interventions.

Cross-Cultural Concerns with OD

One significant concern with OD techniques originating from North America is that they conflict with cultural values in other countries.[64] Some scholars argue that OD in North America assumes a particular model of change that is different than organizational change philosophies held by people in other cultures.[65] The North American model of change is linear, as shown earlier in the force field analysis, and is punctuated by tension and conflict. Until recently, OD practitioners also embraced a humanistic approach with intergroup mirroring, sensitivity training, and other interpersonal interventions. These practices are based on assumptions that open dialogue and conflict based on direct communication are good for individuals and organizations.

However, the linear and open conflict assumptions about change are not held in cultures with high power distance, saving face, and collectivism (high need to maintain harmony). Instead, people in some countries work well with Confucian assumptions; namely, that change is a natural cyclical process with harmony and equilibrium as the objectives.[66] This does not mean that OD is ineffective elsewhere. Rather, it suggests that the field needs to develop a more contingency-oriented perspective with respect to the values of participants.

Ethical Concerns with OD

The field of organization development also faces ethical concerns with respect to some interventions.[67] One ethical concern is that OD interventions potentially increase management's power by inducing compliance and conformity in organizational members. This power shift occurs because OD initiatives create uncertainty and reestablish management's position in directing the organization. Moreover, because OD is a systemwide activity, it requires employee participation rather than allowing individuals to get involved voluntarily. Indeed, one of the challenges of OD consultants is to "bring onside" those who are reluctant to engage in the process.

A second ethical concern is that OD activities may threaten the individual's privacy rights. The action research model is built on the idea of collecting information from organizational members, yet this requires employees to provide personal information that they may not want to divulge. The scientific nature of the data collection exercise may mislead employees into believing that their information is confidential when, in reality, senior management can sometimes identify opinions of individual employees.[68]

Some OD interventions, such as sensitivity training, further threaten individual privacy rights by requiring participants to reveal their private lives. OD activities at

TransAlta Utilities Corp., the Calgary-based electrical utility, were widely criticized because they seemed to violate individual privacy rights. Complaints presented to the Alberta Public Utilities Board stated that the consultants hired by TransAlta made employees publicly criticize each other, change their physical appearance, dance with members of the same sex, and reveal their personal lives to co-workers.[69]

A third ethical concern with some OD interventions is that they undermine the individual's self-esteem. The unfreezing process requires participants to disconfirm their existing beliefs, sometimes including their own competence at certain tasks or interpersonal relations. Sensitivity training and intergroup mirroring may involve direct exposure to personal critique by co-workers as well as public disclosure of one's personal limitations and faults. The OD interventions at TransAlta seem to threaten self-esteem as well as individual privacy. A more extreme example, however, apparently occurred at SaskTel. As we read in Perspective 15.3, the Regina-based telecommunications company brought in consultants whose OD tactics allegedly included public ridicule and control over employees who participated in the project.

A fourth ethical dilemma facing OD consultants is their role in the client relationship. Generally, they should occupy "marginal" positions with the clients they are serving. This means that they must be sufficiently detached from the organization to maintain objectivity and avoid having the client become too dependent on them.[70] However, this can be a difficult objective to satisfy due to the politics of organizational change. OD consultants and clients have their own agendas, and these are not easily resolved without moving beyond the marginal positions that change agents should ideally attain.

PERSPECTIVE 15.3

Organization Development Behind Closed Doors at SaskTel

It all seemed quite normal on the surface. A group of SaskTel employees and managers would form a cross-functional team under the guidance of Symmetrix, a U.S. consulting firm. Beneath this facade, however, was an organization development intervention that may have wandered over the line of ethical conduct.

Symmetrix used a "greenhouse approach" by isolating the SaskTel employees in an office suite with paper taped over its glass walls so that no one could see inside. Participants were quarantined in small cubicles and were prevented from talking to each other. Moreover, Symmetrix refused to give reasons for assignments or why employees had to work long hours with tight deadlines at various times.

The project was supposed to last six weeks. Instead, it ended one year later, after participants united and forced

SaskTel to get rid of Symmetrix. Of the 20 SaskTel employees who were involved in the project, nearly half took stress leave. The employees' union hired a University of Regina professor to evaluate and expose problems with the Symmetrix project. That report, along with internal documents, shocked SaskTel's board.

Participants complained that Symmetrix consultants manipulated them. "There was always a manipulative pressure on the group to submit," says Gord Young, a SaskTel installer who participated in the Symmetrix project.

"Team members regularly received insults in front of the group," recalls Kathryn Markus, a seven-year SaskTel manager. "The isolation, long hours, and purposeless activity left me feeling abandoned, betrayed, and frightened." Markus hasn't worked since she left the project.

Source: Adapted from S. Parker, Jr., "SaskTel Dials the Wrong Number," *Western Report*, February 26, 1996, pp. 14–17.

Chapter Summary

- Organizations face numerous forces for change because they are open systems that need to adapt to changing environments. Some current environmental dynamics include increasing global competition, deregulation, workforce changes, and innovations in computer technology.

- Almost all organizational change efforts face one or more forms of employee resistance. The main reasons that people resist change are direct costs, saving face, fear of the unknown, breaking routines, incongruent organizational systems, and incongruent team dynamics.

- The force field analysis model proposes that change occurs when the driving forces are stronger than the restraining forces. The model advocates unfreezing the status quo mainly by reducing the resisting forces. Six ways to overcome resistance include communication, training, employee involvement, stress management, negotiation, and coercion. After the organizational change, it is necessary to refreeze the desired state so that employees do not slip back into their previous role patterns. Pilot projects need to be diffused throughout the organization to ensure their success.

- Organization development (OD) is a planned systemwide effort, managed from the top with the assistance of a change agent that uses behavioural science knowledge to improve organizational effectiveness. Planned change is based on the action research model, which calls for organizational diagnosis and action planning, implementation, and evaluation of the intervention's effect on the system involved. Change agents need to determine the readiness for change, establish their power base in the client relationship, and understand their appropriate role in the change process. An important issue in choosing an intervention is whether change should be evolutionary (incremental change) or revolutionary (quantum change).

- When OD emerged during the 1940s, practitioners emphasized humanistic interventions, such as sensitivity training. OD interventions today are more involved in macro-level organizationwide changes, such as improving service quality, corporate restructuring, and organizational learning. Two emerging OD interventions are parallel learning structures and appreciative inquiry. Parallel learning structures are social structures developed alongside the formal hierarchy with the purpose of increasing the organization's learning. Appreciative inquiry focuses participants on the positive and possible rather than on problems within the group.

- OD activities, particularly those with multiple types of interventions, have a moderately positive effect on employee productivity and attitudes. However, there are some cross-cultural concerns with OD interventions. Moreover, there are ethical concerns with some OD interventions, including increasing management's power over employees, threatening individual privacy rights, undermining individual self-esteem, and making clients dependent on the OD consultant.

Discussion Questions

1. Use force field analysis to describe the dynamics of organizational change at Canadian National.

2. According to the force field analysis model, what is the best strategy to move the status quo to a desired state?

3. Senior management of a large multinational corporation is planning to restructure the organization. Currently, the organization is decentralized around geographical areas so that the executive responsible for each area has considerable autonomy over manufacturing and sales. The new structure will transfer power to the executives responsible for different product groups. The executives responsible for each geographic area will no longer be responsible for manufacturing in their area but will retain control over sales activities. Describe two types of resistance senior management might encounter from this organizational change.

4. Read the organizational change intervention at Richmond Savings Credit Union (Perspective 15.1). Then explain how this intervention reduced resistance to change by altering some or all of the elements in the individual behaviour model described in Chapter 2.

5. Web Circuits Ltd. is a Montreal-based manufacturer of computer circuit boards for high-technology companies. Senior management wants to introduce value-added management practices to reduce production costs and remain competitive. A consultant has recommended that the company start with a pilot project in one department and, when successful, diffuse these practices to other areas of the organization. Discuss the merits of this recommendation and identify three conditions (other than the pilot project's success) that would make diffusion of the change effort more successful.

6. Outline the organization development process based on the action research model.

7. Describe appreciative inquiry, and explain how it differs from traditional OD interventions.

8. Describe three ethical problems that may arise from organization development activities.

Chapter Case

Eastern Provincial Insurance Corporation

Eastern Provincial Insurance corporation (EPIC) is a Crown corporation formed 10 years ago to provide all automobile insurance in the province. Last year, the provincial government (through EPIC's board of directors) hired a new president and gave her a mandate for organizational renewal. To fulfil this mandate, the new president replaced three vice-presidents. Jim Leon was hired as vice-president of Claims, EPIC's largest division with 600 unionized employees, 20 managers, and 4 regional directors.

Jim immediately met with all claims managers and directors, and visited the 20 claims centres throughout the province. This was a formidable task for an outsider, but his strong interpersonal skills and uncanny ability to remember names and ideas helped him through the process. Through these visits and discussions, Jim discovered that the division had been managed in a relatively authoritarian, top-down manner. He could also see the aftermath of the month-long strike from the previous year. Morale was very low and employee-management relations were guarded. High workloads and isolation (adjusters work in tiny cubicles) were two other common complaints. Several managers acknowledged that the high turnover among claims adjusters was partly due to these conditions.

Following discussions with EPIC's president, Jim decided to make morale and management style his top priority. He initiated a divisional newsletter with a tear-off feedback form for employees to register their comments. He announced an open-door policy in which any Claims Division employee could speak to him directly and confidentially without going first to the immediate supervisor. Jim also fought organizational and contractual barriers to initiate a flex-time program so that employees could design work schedules around their needs. This program later became a model for other areas of EPIC.

One of Jim's most pronounced symbols of change was the "Claims Management Credo" outlining the philosophy that every claims manager would follow. At his first meeting with the complete claims management team, Jim presented a list of what he thought were important philosophies and actions of effective managers. The management group was asked to select and prioritize items from this list. They were told that the resulting list would be the division's management philosophy and all managers would be held accountable for abiding by its principles. Most claims managers were uneasy about this process, but they also understood that the organization was under government pressure to change its style and that Jim was using this exercise to demonstrate his leadership.

The claims managers developed a list of 10 items, such as encouraging teamwork, fostering a trusting work environment, setting clear and reasonable goals, and so on. The list was circulated to senior management in the organization for their comment and approval, and sent back to all claims managers for their endorsement. Once this was done, a copy of the final document was sent to every claims division employee. Jim also announced plans to follow up with an annual survey to evaluate each claims manager's performance. This concerned the managers, but most of them believed that the credo exercise was a result of Jim's initial enthusiasm and that he would be too busy to introduce a survey after settling into the job.

One year after the credo had been distributed, Jim announced that the first annual survey would be conducted. All unionized employees in the Claims Division would complete the survey and return it confidentially to the union steward in their centre. The stewards would send the completed forms to EPIC's information systems division for processing. The survey asked the extent to which the manager had lived up to each of the 10 items in the credo. Each form also provided space for comments.

Claims managers were surprised that a survey would be conducted, but they were even more worried about Jim's statement that the results would be shared with employees. What "results" would employees see? Who would distribute these results? What happens if a manager gets poor ratings from subordinates? "We'll work out the details later," said Jim in response to these questions. "Even if the survey results aren't great, the information will give us a good baseline for next year's survey."

The Claims Division survey had a high response rate. In some centres, every employee completed and returned a form. The Information Systems Division processed the surveys and produced reports for each claims manager. Each manager's report showed an average score for each of the 10 items as well as how many employees rated the manager at each level of the five-point scale. The reports also included every comment made by employees at that centre.

No one was prepared for the results of the first survey. Most managers received moderate or poor ratings on the 10 items. Very few managers averaged above 3.0 (out of a 5-point scale) on more than a couple of items. This suggested that, at best, employees were ambivalent about whether their claims centre manager had abided by the 10 management philosophy items. The comments were even more devastating than the ratings. Comments ranged from mildly disappointed to extremely critical of their claims manager. Employees also described their long-standing frustration with EPIC, high workloads, and isolated working conditions. Several people bluntly stated that they were skeptical about the changes that Jim had promised. "We've heard the promises before, but now we've lost faith," wrote one claims adjuster.

The survey results were sent to each claims manager, the regional director, and executive members of the union representing claims centre employees. Jim instructed managers to discuss the survey data and comments with their regional manager and directly with employees. The managers went into shock when they realized that the discussion reports included personal comments. Some managers went to their regional director to complain that revealing these personal comments would ruin their careers. Many directors sympa-

thized, but the union executive had the results, so they were already available to employees. It would be impossible to ask the union leaders to return the reports or keep them confidential because this might look like management had something to hide and wanted to keep the union out of the process.

When Jim heard about these concerns, he agreed that the results were lower than expected and that the comments should not have been shown to employees. After discussing the situation with his directors, he decided that the discussion meetings between claims managers and their employees should proceed as planned. To delay or withdraw the reports would undermine the credibility and trust that Jim was trying to develop with unionized employees. However, each discussion meeting would be attended by the regional director to control or avoid any direct confrontations that might otherwise emerge between claims managers and their employees.

Although many of these meetings went smoothly, a few created harsh feelings between managers and their employees. The source of some comments were easily identified by their content, and this created a few delicate moments in several sessions. A few months after these meetings, two claims managers quit and three others asked for transfers back to unionized positions in EPIC. Meanwhile, Jim wondered how to manage this process more effectively, particularly since employees expected another survey the following year.

Discussion Questions

1. What symptoms exist in this case to suggest that something has gone wrong?

2. What are the root causes that have led to these symptoms?

3. What actions should the company take to correct these problems?

CHAPTER SIXTEEN

Organizational Culture

CHAPTER OUTLINE

What Is Organizational Culture?

Organizational Culture and Performance

Communicating Organizational Culture

Merging Organizational Cultures

Strengthening Organizational Culture

Chapter Summary

Discussion Questions

LEARNING OBJECTIVES

After reading this chapter, you should be able to:

• Explain why strong organizational cultures don't necessarily perform better.

• Distinguish between an organization's dominant culture and its subcultures.

• List four types of artifacts through which corporate culture is communicated.

• Compare and contrast four strategies for merging organizational cultures.

• Explain how organizations may strengthen their corporate culture.

Robert Schad, founder and CEO of Husky Injection Molding Systems Ltd., walks with staff naturopath Ruth Anne Baron. Schad has created a successful company based on a "healthy culture."

H usky Injection Molding Systems Ltd. has a corporate culture like no other. The Bolton, Ontario, firm has become one of the world's leading manufacturers of plastic molding machines by valuing employee and environmental well-being and by expecting dedication from its 1,700 employees in return.

Artifacts of this "healthy culture" are apparent throughout Husky's headquarters and manufacturing "campus." Books on wildlife greet visitors in the foyer. The gardens around the company's four buildings are pesticide-free. The company is years ahead of government standards on recycling. The manufacturing area is almost spotless. Forklifts are electric, not gas-powered.

A new building houses a professional fitness centre as well as a clinic with a part-time doctor, naturopath, industrial nurse, and physiotherapist. The company subsidizes meals selected by the naturopath. Coffee costs 85 cents but herbal tea is free. You can't get doughnuts — they were cut from the menu a few years ago, along with all other fried foods. Husky banned smoking long ago. Time clocks were removed in the 1960s. An employee council ensures that the company acts on suggestions and complaints.

Robert Schad, Husky's visionary founder and CEO, is the driving force behind the company's powerful culture. "A healthy employee really is a better employee and a happier employee," he says. "And a healthy employee is also a more productive employee."

This corporate culture has paid off for Husky. The company's products are respected around the world. Absenteeism and turnover are less than half the industry average. Workers' compensation claims are so low that Husky receives a rebate each year on its premiums.

"Husky is one of the most remarkable companies I've come across," says Jim Collins, a management consultant who has studied exceptional companies. "What makes Husky unusual is that it has a very strong value system, and it lives it consistently, brings it to life in its buildings, its employees, and its products."[1]

H usky Injection Molding Systems Ltd. has a distinctive organizational culture that is apparent to anyone who visits the firm. This chapter examines
the meaning of organizational culture, including the issues of culture content and strength. This is followed by a discussion of the relationship
between organizational culture and corporate performance. Next, ways of communicating organizational culture are identified. Then we turn to the issue of mergers and
corporate culture. The last section of the chapter examines specific strategies for
maintaining a strong organizational culture.

What Is Organizational Culture?

Organizational culture
The basic pattern of shared
assumptions, values, and
beliefs governing the way
employees within an
organization think about
and act on problems and
opportunities.

Organizational culture is the basic pattern of shared assumptions, values, and beliefs
considered to be the correct way of thinking about and acting on problems and opportunities facing an organization.[2] Culture operates unconsciously, serving as an automatic pilot that directs employee attitudes and behaviour. Organizational culture is,
therefore, a deeply embedded form of social control whereby individuals abide by cultural prescriptions shared with others within the organization. It is the emotional
landscape of work organizations.

Organizational culture is shaped by critical events in the organization's history,
the organization's founder and subsequent leaders, the industry in which the organization operates, and cultural values of the larger society.[3] Employees are motivated to
internalize the organization's dominant culture because it fulfils their need for social
identity. By sharing common values with others in the organization, employees experience a sense of personal meaning and connection with co-workers. In other words,
organizational culture is part of the "social glue" that bonds people together and
makes them feel part of the organizational experience.[4]

EXHIBIT 16.1: The Visible and Hidden Elements of Organizational Culture

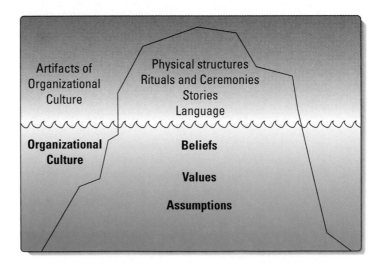

Artifacts of Organizational Culture

We cannot directly see an organization's cultural assumptions and values. As depicted in Exhibit 16.1, these core elements lie beneath the surface of organizational behaviour. Values are closer to the surface because people are aware of them, whereas assumptions lie much deeper because employees take them for granted. For instance, employees at Husky Injection Molding Systems Ltd. know that employee well-being is a dominant value, yet they probably don't even question the deeper assumption that healthy employees are productive employees.

Artifacts The observable symbols and signs of an organization's culture, including its physical structures, ceremonies, language, and stories.

Although we can't see the assumptions or values that represent an organization's culture, we can look for indirect evidence of them through **artifacts**. Artifacts are the observable symbols and signs of an organization's culture, such as its physical structures, ceremonies, language, and stories.[5] They maintain and transmit shared meanings and perceptions of reality within the organization.

Consider DuPont's safety culture in Perspective 16.1. Artifacts of safety include physical workplace designs, rituals (holding handrails), and stories (such as the popular joke about DuPont employees). The safety culture is also found in the language of employees, such as the safety jargon they use and how often they refer to safety issues.

DuPont's safety culture is easy to see, but this isn't typical. Artifacts are often quite difficult to decipher when we are trying to identify an organization's dominant values for the first time. Artifacts are subtle and often ambiguous indicators of culture, so we need to examine many artifacts and search for common themes through these diverse pieces of evidence.[6]

PERSPECTIVE 16.1

DuPont Canada's Fanatical Safety Culture

Dennis Hamilton was getting impatient with the journalist who didn't seem to "get it." But the human resource manager at DuPont Canada's textile plant in Kingston, Ontario, wasn't going to give up. Before Hamilton would end the interview, the journalist would understand DuPont's passionate belief in safety.

"Safety is the way we view our world," explains Hamilton (again). "It is built into DuPont that safety makes for superb business and it is the right and moral thing to do."

Safety isn't just a program or a legal requirement at DuPont Canada. It's the company's cultural imperative. In fact, the company is positively fanatical about safety. "If you don't believe passionately in safety, it doesn't happen," Hamilton explains. "We will stop anything for safety."

You can't escape the fact that DuPont Canada's safety culture really does exist. Three people tell the journalist at different times to hold on to the banisters when climbing the stairs. Safety posters are everywhere. Full protective clothing is required — no exceptions. Most employee terminations are due to unsafe behaviours. The culture is even reinforced with friendly jokes that people around Kingston make about DuPont employees: "How can you identify a group of DuPont employees at a dance? They're the ones wearing safety glasses!"

DuPont's safety culture waned for a short time in the 1980s, but it came back with a vengeance when accident rates crept up. Dennis Hamilton believes the cultural value is here to stay. "You can't pluck safety out of our culture," says Hamilton. "It has tentacles everywhere."

Source: "A Magnificent Obsession," *Canadian Occupational Safety*, January/February 1997, pp. 23–24; T. Van Alphen, "DuPont Gives Work Safety Top Priority," *Canadian Press Newswire*, April 21, 1997.

Organizational Culture Content

Organizations differ in their cultural content; that is, their relative ordering of beliefs and values.[7] In the opening story to this chapter, we learned that the top belief at Husky Injection Molding Systems is healthy employees. Other organizational cultures might emphasize technological efficiency, customer service, employee welfare, or maximizing profits. Here are a few other companies and their apparent dominant values:

*   *Smith Packaging Ltd.*   With 130 employees, Smith Packaging is a young, entrepreneurial firm in Mississauga, Ontario — it has to be in the highly competitive business of manufacturing corrugated items and shipping supplies. "Our culture is the key," explains a senior executive. "If somebody is satisfied with the status quo, that's not acceptable."[8]

*   *Davies, Ward, and Beck*   The Toronto law firm of Davies, Ward, and Beck emphasizes hard-driving performance with a focus on big-name commercial contracts. "They're all completely driven maniacs," says one observer of the Toronto legal community. "I don't know if anybody works quite as hard as the people at Davies. They've got little couches so you don't ever have to go home." Another observer adds: "Either you are a Davies person or you won't last two weeks there."[9]

*   *Rocky Mountain Bicycle Company*   Rocky Mountain's employees don't just make bikes; they almost live on them. This "cyclist culture" is evident throughout the firm's New Westminster, British Columbia, plant. Most employees wear bicycle shorts at work. In the lunch room, they show off raw patches where skin had been left behind on some mountain trail. "Most of the people here are avid cyclists," explains Rocky Mountain CEO Grayson Bain.[10]

*   *Value Health Sciences*   Value Health Sciences is a leading applied health services research company, providing software that helps medical professionals in their diagnoses. The company expects a lot from its employees, but it also instills a culture that values community. This is a culture that supports the psychological bond among employees and generates a feeling of being a second home. "We mourn together, we celebrate births together, we take care of one another," says co-founder Leslie D. Michelson. "We really care about one another."[11]

Entrepreneurial. Hard-driving. Sports-oriented. Family-oriented. How many corporate cultural values are there? No one knows for certain. There are dozens of individual and cross-cultural values, so there are likely as many organizational values. Some writers and consultants have attempted to classify organizational cultures into a few categories with catchy labels such as "clubs" and "fortresses." Although these typologies might reflect the values of a few organizations, they oversimplify the diversity of cultural values in Canadian businesses. Worse, they tend to distort rather than clarify our attempts to diagnose corporate culture.

Another concern is that it is very difficult to identify an organization's cultural content. As noted earlier, organizational culture requires painstaking assessment of many artifacts. Some suggest extracting organizational values from the narratives of everyday life in the organization.[12] Others survey employees, observe workplace behaviour, and study written documents. We probably need to do all of these things to accurately assess an organization's culture. The process is very much like an anthropological investigation of a new society. Although we try to present accurate examples in this book, we should remain cautious about media statements on a company's culture. Most often, these statements are based on no more than a journalist's quick scan or the company's own public relations pronouncements.

Strength of Corporate Culture

You have probably heard someone say that a particular organization has a strong corporate culture. The strength of an organization's culture refers to how many employees in the organization accept the dominant values; how strongly, deeply, and intensely they believe in these values; and how long these values have dominated in the organization.

Strong corporate cultures exist when the dominant values are held by most employees across all subunits. The values are also institutionalized through well-established artifacts. In other words, it is difficult to change the culture because the existing artifacts are plentiful and support the cultural values. Lastly, strong cultures are long-lasting and can often be traced back to the beliefs established by the company's founder.[13] In contrast, companies have weak cultures when the dominant values are short-lived, poorly communicated, and held mainly by a few people at the top of the organization.

Organizational Culture and Performance

Should companies have a strong culture? Several writers think so. They claim that firms with strong cultures are better managed and have superior financial performance over the long term than those with weak cultures.[14] This makes sense if we consider that culture is a form of social control guiding both decisions and behaviour.[15] A strong corporate culture also creates common bonds among employees, resulting in more efficient communication and higher levels of cooperation. Finally, a strong culture makes it easier for employees to make sense of organizational events and understand what is expected of them.

However, the relationship between cultural strength and organizational performance is not as simple as we might initially think. In fact, recent studies have found only a modestly positive relationship between the organization's cultural strength and its economic performance. One reason for the weak relationship is that a strong culture increases organizational performance only when the cultural content is appropriate for the organization's environment.[16] Companies that operate in a highly competitive environment would be better served with a culture that engenders efficiency. Companies in environments that require dedicated employees will be more successful with an employee-oriented culture. When a firm's culture does not fit its environment, on the other hand, employees have difficulty anticipating and responding to the needs of the company's dominant stakeholders.

A second problem is that a company's culture might be so strong that employees blindly focus on the mental model shaped by that culture. Recall from Chapter 6 that mental models frame our perceptions and actions. When an organization's culture intensely emphasizes customer service, for example, employees tend to see problems as customer service problems, even though some are really problems about efficiency or technology. Thus, strong cultures might cause decision makers to overlook or incorrectly define subtle misalignments between the organization's activities and the changing environment.[17]

Finally, the stronger the culture, the more it suppresses dissenting values. In the long term, this prevents organizations from nurturing new cultural values that should become dominant values as the environment changes. For this reason, corporate leaders need to recognize that healthy organizations have subcultures with dissenting values that may produce dominant values in the future. Let's look more closely at this subcultural perspective of organizational culture.

Organizational Subcultures

When discussing organizational culture, we are actually referring to the *dominant culture*; that is, the themes shared most widely by the organization's members. However, organizations also consist of subcultures located throughout their various subunits.[18] Some subcultures enhance the dominant culture by espousing parallel assumptions, values, and beliefs; others are countercultures because they directly oppose the organization's core values.

Countercultures may irritate some corporate leaders, but they serve two important functions. First, as mentioned earlier, companies eventually need to replace their dominant values with ones that are more appropriate for the changing environment. Subcultures are the spawning grounds for these emerging values that keep the firm aligned with the needs of its dominant stakeholders. Companies that try to subdue their subcultures may be less able to replace cultural values that no longer fit the environment.

The second reason we should respect the existence of subcultures is that they maintain the organization's standards of performance and ethical behaviour. Employees who belong to countercultural groups are an important source of surveillance and critique over the dominant order.[19] They encourage constructive controversy and more creative thinking about how the organization should interact with its environment. Strong cultures can cause people to act blindly, whereas subcultures ensure that corporate activities do not violate wider societal values of ethical behaviour. Thus, while maintaining a reasonably strong dominant culture, leaders also need to support the organization's subcultures.

Overall, subcultures represent an important part of the organizational culture dynamics. They are the source of tension or "contested terrain" as current organizational values give way to new ones. Subcultures try to legitimize the emerging values, and use a variety of power sources and influence tactics to accomplish these changes.[20]

Graham Harrop. Used with permission.

Communicating Organizational Culture

Artifacts are an important part of our discussion of organizational culture because they are the means by which culture is communicated.[21] Artifacts come in many forms, but they may be generally classified into four broad categories: organizational stories, rituals and ceremonies, language, and physical structures and space.

Organizational Stories

In Chapter 2 we described how Rick Boomer, head porter at the Empress Hotel in Victoria, British Columbia, went out of his way to deliver 100 pieces of luggage that a tour of guests had left behind.[22] Boomer rented a truck, took the luggage across Georgia Strait to Vancouver, then drove up to the guests' next destination in Whistler. After a short nap, Boomer returned to Victoria in time for his next work shift. This story illustrates organizational citizenship behaviour, but it also communicates the corporate culture found at the Empress and other properties owned by Canadian Pacific Hotels and Resorts Ltd.

Stories about past corporate incidents serve as powerful social prescriptions of "the way things should (or should not) be done around here." They provide human realism to individual performance standards and use role models to demonstrate that organizational objectives are attainable. The Empress story, for instance, shows employees that there are no limits to customer service and that regular people can make this happen. Stories are most effective at communicating the organization's culture when they are told to employees throughout the company, when the stories describe real people, when employees believe that the stories are true, and when the stories are prescriptive — they describe how things are to be done (or not to be done) in the organization.[23]

Rituals The programmed routines of daily organizational life that dramatize the organization's culture.

Ceremonies Deliberate and usually dramatic displays of organizational culture, such as celebrations and special social gatherings.

Gala dinners and other formal reward ceremonies are artifacts that represent Nortel's performance-oriented corporate culture. The company has been a leader in sales incentives and special rewards for employees who stand out as performance achievers.

Rituals and Ceremonies

Do you attend a school where most of the instructors insist on being called "Mr./Ms.," "Doctor," or "Professor"? Or at your institution is everyone on a first-name basis, at least after the first meeting? How people address each other reflects the values held in that organization, such as its power distance (Chapter 7) and respect for status.[24] It is one form of artifact called a ritual. **Rituals** are the programmed routines of daily organizational life that dramatize the organization's culture. Along with naming, rituals include such activities as how meetings are conducted, how visitors are greeted, how often senior executives visit subordinates, and how much time employees take for lunch.

Ceremonies are more formal artifacts than rituals. Ceremonies are planned activities conducted specifically for the benefit of an audience. This would include publicly rewarding (or punishing) employees or celebrating the launch of a new product or newly won contract.[25] For example, Nortel has a strong performance-oriented culture. This is reflected in the flashy awards dinners and exotic trips it offers to its top sales performers each year.

Courtesy of Northern Telecom.

Organizational Language

IBM Canada has a problem. It's trying to change its corporate culture from the private business club mentality to a set of values that puts IBM employees closer to the customer. The company changed its dress code (no ties), dumped its private golf course, and is bringing in new people rather than just promoting from within. The problem? Long-time IBM staff can't seem to drop the old acronyms that distance them from the customers they serve. They routinely drop gibberish like DPDCE (Data Processing Division, Customer Engineering) and CRM (customer relationship management).[26]

IBM's language may be keeping employees attached to the company's previous set of cultural values. In Chapter 8, language was described as an important element in transmitting and sustaining shared values. Specifically, people adopt metaphors and other special vocabularies that represent their perspective of reality.[27] IBM Canada implicitly holds on to a technical "club" value set through its use of acronyms. Other companies strengthen their culture through metaphors and unique phrases like "laying pipe."

The Royal Bank of Canada's culture may be represented in the design of its headquarters building in Toronto. The solid-looking building with unusually rich, gold-coated windows symbolizes the company's undeniable image of financial security and strength.

Courtesy of Royal Bank of Canada.

Physical Structures and Space

Anyone who walks along Front and Yonge Streets in Toronto can't help noticing the solid-looking building with unusually rich, reflective windows. This is the Royal Bank of Canada's headquarters, and it symbolizes the company's undeniable image of financial security and strength. Indeed, the building literally glistens with 2,500 ounces of gold coating on its mirror-glass exterior, ostensibly for climate control within the building, but also to convey a deeper meaning.[28] (Some people half-jokingly suggest that if there was ever a run on the bank, Royal Bank could simply start melting its windows!)

Physical structures and spaces, such as Royal Bank's gleaming gold-plated building, often symbolize the company's underlying values and beliefs.[29] The size, shape, location, and age of buildings might suggest the organization's emphasis on teamwork, risk aversion, flexibility, or any other set of values.

Office design represents another relevant artifact. Organizational cultures that emphasize hierarchy tend to carefully measure offices so that higher officials have larger spaces and more expensive furniture. Procter & Gamble Canada, for instance, has a well-defined protocol for office size, furniture, and carpeting according to the person's position in the organization. Contrast this with the office and building design of Upper Canada Brewing, which is described in Perspective 16.2.

P E R S P E C T I V E   1 6 . 2

Transmitting Cultural Values Through Building Design

Upper Canada Brewing Company is different. Just walk into its executive offices on Atlantic Avenue in Toronto and you can see that the premium microbrewery has a corporate culture quite different from Molson's and other big-league beer companies.

The executive offices are located in a post-and-beam-ceilinged warehouse with workspaces divided up by panelled Muskoka-pine screens. Upper Canada's president, Frank Heaps, sits behind a pine desk in a doorless office. The only barrier between visitors and Heaps is the black Labrador retriever sprawled across the hall. The setting nicely symbolizes the values that Upper Canada Brewing is trying to communicate for its premium beer products, such as down-home originality, authentic Bavarian tradition, and quality.

In another country and another industry, British Petroleum's (BP) building and office design is also aligned with the corporate values its employees should adopt. A few years ago, BP's chairperson decided that the best way to get rid of the company's hierarchical and bureaucratic culture was to move from its 35-story headquarters building in London, England, to a structure that more closely represented an open, efficient, and egalitarian value system. BP's new headquarters at 1 Finsbury Circus has open space and few closed offices. A few people do get their own offices at Finsbury Circus, but strictly on the basis of need rather than status.

"We were trying to reflect two aspects," explains BP's manager in charge of the relocation. "One was a flatter, less hierarchical society and, two, a more open arrangement of interchanging information and being more aware of what's going on around you inside the company. That really means that you do two things: first, you don't give everybody an office in which they can shut the door and pretend there's no one else around, and, second, you keep the place as open-plan as possible."

Source: "Camp Brewski," *Toronto Life*, January 1996, pp. 37–38; A. Oakley, "The Company Character Revealed in Design," *Management Today*, February 1993, p. 83.

Merging Organizational Cultures

Bombardier Inc., the Montreal-based transportation-vehicle manufacturer, has acquired several companies over the years. Along with a careful study of the other firm's financial and market strength, Bombardier's executives determine whether their corporate cultures are compatible. An organization's values and beliefs aren't found at the bottom of a financial statement, so Bombardier executives conduct a personal diagnosis and evaluation of the situation. "When we look at a possible acquisition," says Bombardier president Raymond Royer, "the first thing we look at in-house is whether or not we share the same values."[30]

Bombardier is the exception. Most mergers and acquisitions are decided almost entirely from a financial or marketing perspective. Little consideration is given to differences in the organizational cultures of the companies involved. Yet attempting to merge two organizations with distinct values and beliefs could result in a cultural collision that threatens the success of an otherwise strategically compatible merger.[31] Consider the disaster that occurred when Novell Inc. acquired WordPerfect Corp. Although WordPerfect suffered from Microsoft Corporation's incredible marketing savvy, it was also buffeted by intense cultural value conflicts with its new owners. Novell sold WordPerfect to Corel Corp. two years later, but both WordPerfect and Novell had near-death experiences from their temporary merger.[32]

To minimize the risk of a postmerger culture clash, a bicultural audit that diagnoses cultural relations between the companies should be conducted.[33] A bicultural audit begins with interviews, questionnaires, focus groups, and observation of cultural artifacts to identify cultural differences between the merging companies. Next, the audit data are analyzed to determine which differences between the two firms will result in conflict and which cultural values provide common ground on which to build a cultural foundation in the merged organization. The final stage of the bicultural audit involves identifying strategies and preparing action plans to bridge the two organizations' cultures.

Strategies to Merge Different Organizational Cultures

In some cases, the bicultural audit results in a decision to end merger talks because the two cultures are too different to merge effectively. However, even with substantially different cultures, two companies may form a workable union if they apply the appropriate merger strategy. The four main strategies for merging different corporate cultures are integration, deculturation, assimilation, and separation (see Exhibit 16.2).[34]

Assimilation
Assimilation occurs when employees at the acquired company willingly embrace the cultural values of the acquiring organization. This tends to occur when the acquired company has a weak culture that is dysfunctional, whereas the acquiring company's culture is strong and focused on clearly defined values. Assimilation has minimal culture clash because employees have mostly rejected the dominant values of their firm. Usually, this rejection means that the acquired organization has a weak culture at the time of the merger.

EXHIBIT 16.2: Strategies for Merging Different Organizational Cultures

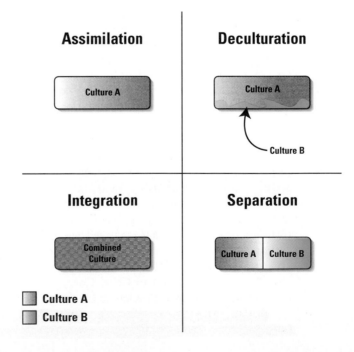

Deculturation

Assimilation is, unfortunately, rare. Employees usually resist organizational change, particularly when they include throwing away personal and cultural values. Under these conditions, the acquiring company usually applies a deculturation strategy by imposing its culture and practices on the acquired organization. The acquiring firm strips away artifacts and reward systems that support the old culture. People who cannot adopt the acquiring company's culture are often terminated.

This happened when Anderson Exploration Ltd. acquired Home Oil Co. Ltd. Both oil firms have headquarters in Calgary, but they are different in every other way. Home Oil valued status and splendour, with a bit of extravagance thrown in. The firm had an executive dining room, two floors of executive offices, a small fleet of planes, and expensive art. Not anymore. Anderson's founder, J. C. Anderson, replaced Home Oil's belief system with the efficient and lean cultural values that dominate Anderson Exploration. "They had a culture, we had a culture," says Anderson with characteristic bluntness. "Ours worked, theirs didn't. At the end of the day, we've got to have this combined organization being a lot closer to our culture."[35]

Integration

Abitibi-Price Inc. and Stone Consolidated Corp. recently merged companies with the understanding that they will bring together the best of both cultures. As Perspective 16.3 describes, this will be challenging, but then, almost any merger that applies the integration strategy is challenging. The integration strategy involves combining the two cultures into a new composite culture that preserves the best features of the previous cultures. The process is slow and potentially risky because there are many forces preserving the existing cultures. Integration is most

---

PERSPECTIVE 16.3

Abitibi and Stone Consolidated Merge Cultures Through Integration

When Abitibi-Price Inc. and Stone-Consolidated Corp. decided to become one mega–pulp and paper firm, their respective cultures were near the top of the list of things to consider. "I think you should have to do due diligence on culture," explains Stone's CEO, James Doughan.

The problem is that the corporate cultures at Abitibi and Stone are different. Abitibi CEO Ronald Oberlander talks a lot about teamwork and inclusiveness. He wants to set up employee discussion groups to receive feedback about the merger. Abitibi's employees work in funky, colourful offices at Toronto's Queen's Quay Terminal.

Stone employees embrace lean, practical values. The company is downright stingy compared to Abitibi. Doughan is worried that asking employees for their feedback might raise their expectations too much. Stone's offices are, well, traditional — an office tower in downtown Montreal.

The two CEOs downplay the differences in their corporate cultures, but recognize that each firm has a few unique, even conflicting, values. The solution, they say, is to bring together the best values from both companies.

"I've been through a number of acquisitions and mergers," says James Doughan, "and what you find is that you never end up with one culture. Two cultures emerge. You always end up getting something from both."

Source: J. MacFarland, "An Unusual Team, on Paper," *Globe & Mail*, February 19, 1997, pp. B1, B11; G. MacDonald, "What Happens After the Deal is Done," *Globe & Mail*, February 20, 1997, p. B14.

effective when the two companies have relatively weak cultures, or when their cultures include several overlapping values. Integration also works best when people realize that their existing cultures are ineffective and are, therefore, motivated to adopt a new set of dominant values.

Separation

Finally, some mergers adopt a separation strategy, in which the merging companies agree to remain distinct entities with minimal exchange of culture or organizational practices. In other words, the two companies are sufficiently independent that the acquired firm can maintain its existing culture. Separation is most appropriate when the two merging companies are in unrelated industries because, as noted earlier, the most appropriate cultural values tend to differ with industry. Unfortunately, the acquiring company usually wants to control managerial decisions by imposing its own cultural values, so few mergers result in a long-lasting separation strategy.

Strengthening Organizational Culture

Whether merging two cultures or reshaping the firm's existing values, corporate leaders need to understand how to strengthen weak organizational cultures. As we warned earlier, strong cultures increase organizational effectiveness only if the cultural content fits the external environment and the culture is not so strong that it drives out dissenting views. With these concerns in mind, let's examine the five strategies in Exhibit 16.3 to strengthen organizational culture.

EXHIBIT 16.3: Strategies for Strengthening Organizational Culture

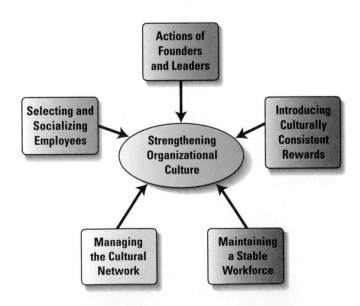

Actions of Founders and Leaders

Founders have a major effect on organizational culture because, from the very beginning, they establish the organization's purpose and lay down its basic philosophy for interaction with the external environment.[36] We can certainly see the powerful influence of living founders such as Robert Schad at Husky Injection Molding Systems Ltd. (see opening story to this chapter), Anita Roddick at The Body Shop, and Frank Stronach at Magna International. The founder's cultural imprint often remains with the organization for many years after other leaders take over the company's direction. For example, Eaton's well-known emphasis on customer satisfaction was established by Timothy Eaton soon after his first store opened in 1869.[37]

By communicating and enacting their vision of the future, transformational leaders strengthen organizational culture.[38] Cultural values are particularly reinforced when leaders behave in ways that are consistent with the vision ("walking the talk"). Four Seasons Hotels founder Isadore Sharp maintains a strong quality service culture by ensuring that managers are consistent with this cultural standard. "Employees watch their managers and take their cues from them, so our managers have to act as role models," says Sharp. "We made changes at the very top — head-office senior executives, hotel general managers — until those whom others would imitate were setting the proper standard. The message got through and superior service became our competitive edge."[39]

Introducing Culturally Consistent Rewards

Reward systems can strengthen corporate culture when they are consistent with cultural values.[40] For example, Microsoft Corporation uses stock options, new job opportunities, and competition between project groups to strengthen its culture, known as "The Microsoft Way." The Microsoft Way includes working late at night and on weekends to ensure that the company's products dominate the market. Another example is the Canadian federal government, in which a performance appraisal system for senior government administrators was introduced so that they would maintain a common set of cultural values across government departments.[41]

Maintaining a Stable Workforce

An organization's culture is embedded in the minds of its employees. Organizational stories are rarely written down; rituals and celebrations do not usually exist in procedural manuals; organizational metaphors are not found in corporate directories. Thus, organizations depend on a stable workforce to communicate and reinforce the dominant beliefs and values. The organization's culture can literally disintegrate during periods of high turnover or rapid expansion because employees have not sufficiently learned the ways to do things around the organization.[42] For this reason, some organizations try to keep their culture intact by moderating employment growth and correcting turnover problems.

Managing the Cultural Network

Organizational culture is learned, so an effective network of cultural transmission is necessary to strengthen the company's underlying assumptions, values, and beliefs.

According to Max De Pree, CEO of furniture manufacturer Herman Miller Inc., every organization needs "tribal storytellers" to keep the organization's history and culture alive.[43] The cultural network exists through the organizational grapevine, but it can be further supported by providing opportunities for frequent interaction among employees so that stories may be shared and rituals reenacted. Senior executives must tap into the cultural network, sharing their own stories and creating new ceremonies and other opportunities to demonstrate shared meaning. Company magazines and other media can also strengthen organizational culture by communicating cultural values and beliefs more efficiently.

Selecting and Socializing Employees

Another way to strengthen an organization's culture is to hire people whose own beliefs and values are consistent with that culture. This strategy also increases employee satisfaction and organizational commitment because new hires with values compatible to the corporate culture adjust more quickly to the organization.[44] Shell Canada Ltd. and Anchor Hocking carefully select people with a deeply ingrained team orientation, to ensure that a team-based culture is perpetuated at their new plants.[45]

Organizational socialization The process by which individuals learn the values, expected behaviours, and social knowledge necessary to assume their roles in the organization.

Organizations also maintain strong cultures through the effective socialization of new employees. **Organizational socialization** refers to the process by which individuals learn the values, expected behaviours, and social knowledge necessary to assume their roles in the organization.[46] By communicating the company's dominant values, job candidates and new hires are more likely to internalize these values quickly and deeply.

Newcomers learn about the organization's culture through recruiting literature, orientation programs, and informal interactions with other employees. Companies that describe "the way things are done around here" during recruitment help applicants decide whether they identify with or reject the company's culture. This strategy also reduces employee turnover because selected employees are less likely to experience conflict with the organization's dominant values after they are hired.[47] Organizational socialization is an important topic within the employment relationship, so we will discuss it more fully in the next chapter.

Chapter Summary

- Organizational culture is the basic pattern of shared assumptions, values, and beliefs that govern behaviour within a particular organization. Artifacts are the observable symbols and signs of an organization's culture.

- Companies with strong cultures generally perform better than those with weak cultures, but only when the cultural content is appropriate for the organization's environment. Also, the culture should not be so strong that it drives out dissenting values that may form emerging values for the future.

- In addition to the dominant culture, organizations have subcultures. Some enhance the dominant culture by espousing parallel assumptions, values, and beliefs. Countercultures have values that oppose the organization's core values. Subcultures help organizations because they are the source of emerging values that replace aging core values. Moreover, countercultural group members provide a surveillance function to maintain ethical standards and promote creative thinking.

- Artifacts communicate an organization's culture. They include organizational stories, rituals and ceremonies, language, and physical structures and space.

- Mergers should include a bicultural audit to diagnose the compatibility of the two organizational cultures. The four main strategies for merging different corporate cultures are integration, deculturation, assimilation, and separation.

- An organization's culture may be strengthened through the actions of founders and leaders. Culture is also strengthened by introducing culturally consistent rewards, maintaining a stable workforce, managing the cultural network, and selecting and socializing employees.

Discussion Questions

1. Superb Consultants Inc. have submitted a proposal to analyze the cultural values of your organization. The proposal states that Superb has developed a revolutionary new survey to tap the company's true culture. The survey takes just 10 minutes to complete and accurate results can be based on a small sample of employees. Discuss the merits and limitations of this proposal.

2. Some people suggest that the most effective organizations have the strongest cultures. What do we mean by the "strength" of organizational culture, and what possible problems are there with a strong organizational culture?

3. Identify four types of artifacts used to communicate organizational culture. Why are artifacts used for this purpose?

4. Acme Ltd. is planning to acquire Beta Corp., which operates in a different industry. Acme's culture is entrepreneurial and fast-paced, whereas Beta employees value slow, deliberate decision making by consensus. Which merger strategy would you recommend to minimize culture shock when Acme acquires Beta? Explain your answer.

5. Under what conditions is assimilation likely to occur when two companies merge. Your answer should clearly describe the assimilation strategy.

6. Explain how transformational leadership strengthens corporate culture.

◆ Chapter Case ◆

Hillton's Transformation

Twenty years ago, Hillton was a small city (about 30,000 residents) that served as a suburb to one of Canada's largest metropolitan areas. The municipality treated employees like family and gave them a great deal of autonomy in their work. Everyone in the organization, including the labour unions, implicitly agreed that the leaders and supervisors of the organization should rise through the ranks based on their experience. Few people were ever hired from the outside into middle or senior positions. The rule of employment at Hilton was to learn the job skills, maintain a reasonably good work record, and wait your turn for promotion.

Hillton initially grew slowly, then more rapidly as a suburb. As the population grew, so did the municipality's workforce, to keep pace with the increasing demand for municipal services. This meant that employees were promoted fairly quickly and were almost assured guaranteed employment. In fact, until recently, Hilton had never laid off any employees. The organization's culture could be described as one of entitlement and comfort. Neither the elected councilors nor city manager bothered the department managers about their work. There were few cost controls because Hillton's growth placed more emphasis on keeping up with the population expansion. The public became somewhat more critical of the city's poor service, including road construction at inconvenient times and the apparent lack of respect some employees showed toward taxpayers.

During these expansion years, Hillton placed most of its money into "outside" (also called "hard") municipal services. These included road-building, utility construction and maintenance, fire and police protection, recreational facilities, and land-use control. This emphasis occurred because an expanding population demanded more of these services and most of Hillton's senior people came from the outside services group. For example, Hillton's city manager for many years was a road development engineer. The "inside" workers (taxation, community services,

etc.) tended to have less seniority and their departments were given less priority.

As commuter and road systems developed, Hillton attracted more upwardly mobile professionals into the community. Some infrastructure demands continued, but now these suburban dwellers wanted more of the "soft" services, such as libraries, social activities, and community services. They also began complaining about the way the municipality was managed. The population had more than tripled by the early 1990s, and it was increasingly apparent that the organization needed more corporate planning, information systems, organization development, and cost control systems. In various ways, residents voiced their concerns that the municipality was not providing the quality of management that they would expect from a city of its size.

In 1993, a new mayor and council replaced most of the previous incumbents, mainly on the platform of improving the municipality's management structure. The new council gave the city manager, along with two other senior managers, an early retirement buyout package. Rather than promoting from the lower ranks, council decided to fill all three positions with qualified candidates from large municipal corporations elsewhere in Canada. The following year, several long-term managers left Hillton and at least half of those positions were filled by people from outside the organization.

In less than two years, Hillton had hired eight senior or department managers from other municipalities who played a key role in changing the organization's value system. These eight managers became known (often with negative connotations) as the "professionals." They worked closely with one another to change the way middle- and lower-level managers had operated for many years. They brought in a new computer system and emphasized cost controls where managers previously had complete autonomy. Promotions were increasingly based more on merit than seniority.

These managers frequently announced in meetings and newsletters that municipal employees must provide superlative customer service, and that Hillton will become one of the most customer-friendly places for citizens and those who do business with the municipality. To this end, these managers were quick to support the public's increasing demand for more "soft" services, including expanded library services and recreational activities. And when population growth recently flattened out for a few years, the city manager and other professionals gained council support to lay off a few of the outside workers due to lack of demand for hard services.

One of the most significant changes was that the "outside" departments no longer held dominant positions in city management. Most of the "professional" managers had worked exclusively in administrative and related inside jobs. Two had Master of Business Administration degrees. This led to some tension between the professional managers and the older outside managers.

Even before the layoffs, managers of outside departments resisted the changes more than others. These managers complained that their employees with the highest seniority were turned down for promotions. They argued for more budget and

warned that infrastructure problems would cause liability problems. Informally, these outside managers were supported by the labour union representing outside workers. The labour union tried to bargain for more job guarantees, whereas the union representing inside workers focused more on improving wages and benefits. Leaders of the outside union made several statements in the local media that the city had "lost its heart" and that the public would suffer from the actions of the new professionals.

Discussion Questions

1. Contrast Hillton's earlier corporate culture with the emerging set of cultural values.

2. Considering the difficulty in changing organizational culture, why does Hillton's management seem to be successful at this transformation?

3. Identify two other strategies that the city might consider to entrench the new set of corporate values.

© Copyright 1998. Steven L. McShane. This case is a slightly fictionalized account of actual events in a Canadian municipality.

Experiential Exercise

Organizational Culture Assessment Exercise

Purpose: This exercise is designed to help you understand the meaning of organizational culture, as well as the ways that organizational culture may be identified.

Long Version Instructions: This exercise has a short and long version. The short version is completed entirely in class (see below). The long version requires library work before class.

Step 1:   During the class prior to the exercise, students form teams and the instructor assigns the name of an organization to each team. The organization should be one that is well-known and frequently cited in print media.

Step 2:   Students are expected to search for recent articles that describe events in the organization. Several computer indexes (Canadian Business and Current Affairs, ABII/UMI) provide quick identification of these articles and often provide the entire article on-line. Students scan articles to find evidence of the organization's dominant values along the dimensions listed in the organizational culture assessment scale presented below. These examples should be brought to class as "artifacts" of the company's cultural values.

Step 3:   In class, team members compare their findings and complete the scale below. Team members should first complete the form individually, then compare results and reach a consensus.

Step 4:   Each team presents its results to the class, including a review of the artifacts supporting their organizational culture assessment. If several teams are assigned the same organization, the instructor may ask each team to provide its assessment of only one scale item so that others have an opportunity to participate. Other teams will be asked to comment and compare their results of that scale with the assessment given by the presenting team.

Short Version Instructions: The short version is completed entirely in class.

Step 1:   At the beginning of class, students form teams and the instructor assigns the name of an organization that is well known to the team. This may be a company that receives a lot of publicity, the college/university that students are attending, a major employer in the community, or an organization where several team members are employed.

Step 2:   Team members individually complete the organizational culture assessment form presented below. Team members then compare their results and reach a consensus. During this process, they should try to identify specific incidents that support their assessment.

Step 3: Each team presents its results to the class, including a review of recalled incidents supporting their organizational culture assessment. If several teams are assigned the same organization, the instructor may ask each team to provide its assessment of only one scale item so that others have an opportunity to participate. Other teams will be asked to comment and compare their results of that scale item with the assessment given by the presenting team.

ORGANIZATIONAL CULTURE ASSESSMENT SCALE

Name of Organization: _____

This Organization Values:								This Organization Values:
Employee Output	1	2	3	4	5	6	7	Employee Well-being
Mutual Support	1	2	3	4	5	6	7	Survival of the Fittest
Job Status	1	2	3	4	5	6	7	Equality
Order	1	2	3	4	5	6	7	Creative Chaos
Customer Needs	1	2	3	4	5	6	7	Customer Chequebook
Corporate Publicity	1	2	3	4	5	6	7	Corporate Anonymity
Safety and Environment	1	2	3	4	5	6	7	Efficiency at All Cost
Teamwork	1	2	3	4	5	6	7	Individualism
Aggressiveness	1	2	3	4	5	6	7	Civility
Constructive Conflict	1	2	3	4	5	6	7	Conflict Avoidance

CHAPTER 17

Employment Relationship and Career Dynamics

CHAPTER OUTLINE

The Psychological Contract

Organizational Socialization

Stages of Socialization

Managing the Socialization Process

Organizational Careers

Contingent Workforce

Chapter Summary

Discussion Questions

LEARNING OBJECTIVES

After reading this chapter, you should be able to:

- Discuss the different types of psychological contract.

- Identify three types of trust in organizational settings.

- Describe the stages of organizational socialization.

- Explain how socialization agents potentially assist new employees.

- Identify three conditions that would encourage lateral career development.

- Explain why the contingent workforce is growing in Canada.

- Discuss the issues surrounding job performance of contingent workers.

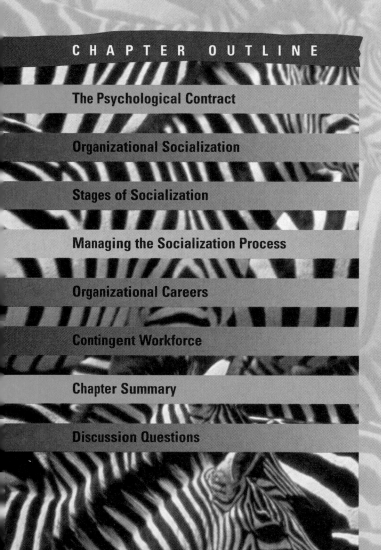

After a management career in Canada's banking industry, Robert Smythe has become a "free agent" in the contingent workforce.

Hal Savage has been a busy guy lately — busy turning down jobs that others would kill for. For the past six years, the 52-year-old ex-journalist has been setting up telemarketing operations and re-organizing customer service departments at Bell Canada, Labatt Breweries, RJR MacDonald, and many other firms.

Savage isn't a job hopper. He's one of the growing number of professionals who prefer working as "free agents" in the contingent workforce. Savage initially arranged contracts on his own, but found it a nuisance to work on one project while marketing himself for the next assignment. So he signed up with Kelly Services Canada Ltd. "I don't have to spend money advertising and getting the word out that I'm available," he explains.

Robert Smythe became a free agent when his former employer, Royal Trust, was merged with Royal Bank of Canada, making his executive position redundant. Smythe contacted an executive search agency who helped him land a contract position as chief information officer at Canadian Satellite Communications Inc. (Cancom). The arrangement works well for both. Cancom was able to have an experienced executive for a limited time, and Smythe gets more flexibility and variety of work than he did as a permanent employee.

Robert Smythe still feels the lure of permanent employment, but he is willing to wait for the right opportunity. Besides, he realizes that traditional careers and employment relationships have changed. "Some people have a need to have corporations look after their welfare," he says. "But that doesn't exist anymore. It's gone."[1]

H al Savage and Robert Smythe are part of the growing trend toward free agent careers, in which employees contract their time and competencies to different companies. The opening story paints a glowing picture of contingent work, but most people in this segment of the labour force would rather have permanent jobs. As we will find out in this chapter, contingent work may offer some economic benefits, but an organizational behaviour perspective reveals hidden costs, too.

Before exploring the contingent labour force and other emerging career trends, we need to understand certain basic features of all employment relationships. This chapter begins with the most fundamental element: the psychological contract. We consider the type of contracts, how contracts change, and the importance of trust in employment relationships. Next, we examine the process of employee socialization, including the stages of socialization and specific socialization strategies. We then turn to the topic of career development, including career stages and the emerging trend toward lateral career movement. The chapter concludes with a detailed look at the dynamics and implications of the contingent workforce.

The Psychological Contract

Cindy Fisher feels betrayed by her employer, Northern Telecom (Nortel). The single mother believed management at the Bramalea, Ontario, plant when they said that everyone was family and that teamwork would keep the plant competitive. Now, Nortel is shutting down the plant, putting Fisher and many others out of work. "They've certainly brought me to the reality of what I can expect in the working world," Fisher warns. "You shouldn't rely on your employers for security."[2]

Psychological contract
The employer's and employee's perceived mutual obligations about their exchange relationship.

Cindy Fisher and some other employees at Nortel's Bramalea plant believe that their **psychological contract** has been violated. The psychological contract is a set of perceived mutual obligations about the employer's and employee's exchange relationship. It consists of implicit understandings or assumptions about what the employee should contribute to and receive from the organization.[3] These are perceived mutual obligations because employees naturally presume that the company holds the same set of beliefs about the relationship. For example, Cindy Fisher and other Nortel employees believed they would have job security in exchange for encouraging teamwork, and they thought their employer held the same expectations.[4]

Everyone forms a psychological contract when they are employed or have a contractual relationship with an organization. Even when people sign a formal employment contract, they hold assumptions about the relationship that are not explicitly stated in that written contract. Psychological contracts reduce uncertainty about the environment in which we operate, satisfy our need to know what to expect, and give us a sense of control over our destiny. The psychological contract also provides a set of guidelines to direct our behaviour.[5]

Types of Psychological Contracts

As Exhibit 17.1 illustrates, psychological contracts can be viewed along a continuum from transactional to relational.[6] *Transactional contracts* are primarily short-term economic exchanges. Responsibilities are precisely defined and the individual has more self-interest than consideration for the organization's well-being. People hired for a short time tend to have transactional contracts. *Relational contracts,* on the other

---

EXHIBIT 17.1: Types of Psychological Contracts in Employment

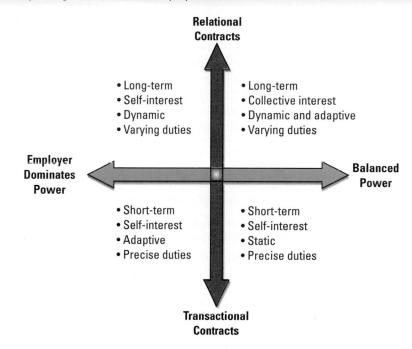

Source: Based on information in J. McLean Parks and D. L. Kidder, "'Till Death Us do Part...' Changing Work Relationships in the 1990s," In C. L. Cooper and D. M. Rousseau (eds.) *Trends in Organizational Behaviour*, Vol. 1 (Chichester, U.K.: Wiley, 1994), pp. 112–36.

hand, are rather like marriages; they are long-term attachments in which parties do not expect precise and perfectly reciprocal exchanges in the short run. Instead, expectations are fuzzy and the parties are willing to let the relationship evolve over time. Permanent employees are more likely to believe they have a relational contract. Not surprisingly, organizational citizenship behaviours are more likely to prevail under relational than transactional contracts.

Exhibit 17.1 also shows that contracts vary with the employer's relative power in the relationship. When the employer has greater power, employees feel less voluntariness in the relationship and, consequently, are less likely to engage in organizational citizenship behaviour. In relational contracts, the employer's greater power is somewhat hidden because applying this power weakens the relationship. In transactional contracts, the employer's power is directly seen by deliberate and specific alterations to the contract. Consider the recent incident in which Bell Canada outsourced its telephone-line installation and maintenance business as a spin-off company. The employer significantly altered the previous psychological contract, including a 29 percent pay cut and loss of job security, because of its significant power advantage. Employees accepted jobs in the spin-off company because there isn't much demand elsewhere for telephone installers.[7]

Trust and the Psychological Contract

Trust Positive expectations about another party's intentions and actions toward us in risky situations.

Any relationship — including an employment relationship — depends on a certain degree of trust between the parties.[8] Recall from Chapter 7 that **trust** occurs when we have positive expectations about another party's intentions and actions toward us in risky situations. High trust occurs when the other party's actions affect you, but you believe they will not adversely affect your needs.

In an employment relationship, people identify with and feel obliged to work for an organization only when they trust its leaders. There are three types of trust, each representing a different level and form of relationship.[9]

- *Calculus-based trust*   This minimal level of trust refers to an expected consistency of behaviour based on deterrence. Each party believes that the other will deliver on its promises because punishments will be administered if they fail. For example, most Canadians trust their employer enough to expect a paycheque at the end of the work period because they believe the company will face government sanctions if payment isn't received.

- *Knowledge-based trust*   Knowledge-based trust is grounded on the other party's predictability. This predictability develops from meaningful communication and past experience. The better you know senior management's past actions, the more accurately you can predict what they will do in the future.

- *Identification-based trust*   This third type of trust is based on mutual under-standing. Identification occurs when one party thinks like, feels like, and responds like the other party. High-performance teams exhibit this level of trust. To some extent, employees can have a high level of identification-based trust in organizations with strong cultures. By identifying with the company's dominant values, employees understand what to expect and what is expected of them.

Calculus-based trust is the weakest of the three because it is easily broken by a violation of expectations and the subsequent application of sanctions against the violating party. It is difficult to develop a strong level of trust based on the threat of punishment if one party fails to deliver its promises. Generally, a relational contract cannot be sustained with only calculus-based trust.

Knowledge-based trust is more stable than calculus-based trust because it is developed over time. Suppose an employer hires someone from outside the company rather than promotes from within, as it almost always did in the past. A trusting employee "knows" that this is probably an exception because it deviates from the employer's past actions.

Identification-based trust is the most robust of all three. Because the individual identifies with the organization (or any other party), the employee is more likely to forgive transgressions. Moreover, we are reluctant to acknowledge a violation of this high-level trust because it strikes at the heart of our self-image.

Trust is important in the employment relationship because it affects the type of psychological contract. When employees experience psychological contract violations, they lose trust in the employer and are less likely to engage in organizational citizenship behaviours.[10] If violations continue, the loss of trust shifts the employee's psychological contract from open and dynamic to precise and static. In other words, loss of trust moves the psychological contract from relational to transactional.

Psychological Contract Dynamics

Psychological contracts evolve over time, particularly for people in relational contracts. These changes are typically mutual accommodations to the existing contract. The parties believe the original contract is still in place and has minor additions or modifications. How much change to the original contract can occur, yet still maintain this sense of continuity? The answer depends on the flexibility of the employer and employee, which is largely determined by the degree of trust between them.[11]

In contrast to accommodation, people occasionally experience transformations in their psychological contract. These transformations occur when one party — usually the employer — wants to create a radically different psychological contract. Some elements of the original contract usually remain, but the fundamental components are sufficiently different that the parties believe they are entering into a new relationship.

Petro-Canada has dramatically transformed the psychological contracts for most of its employees, as Perspective 17.1 describes. As with many other firms, the Calgary-based oil company is replacing the "job-for-life" contract to a "new deal" based on **employability**. The old contract was based on the belief that if you are loyal to the company, the company will be loyal to you.[12] Employees could expect lifelong career progression through the ranks with ever-increasing salaries.

Employability The "new deal" employment relationship in which the job is viewed as a temporary event, so employees are expected to keep pace with changing competency requirements and shift to new projects as demand requires.

PERSPECTIVE 17.1

Rethinking the Psychological Contract at Petro-Canada

Wishart Robson is remarkably calm for someone whose job security is at risk . . . again. The environment, health, and safety manager thought he had a long-term career with Petro-Canada, until he was laid off in the mid-1980s. He was rehired two years later and since then has survived half a dozen downsizings at the Calgary-based oil company. "It's not pleasant anticipating change," says Robson, "but once you've been through it a number of times, you find ways to manage it."

Petro-Canada has been transformed from a sleepy government-owned Crown corporation into an efficient enterprise. A series of layoffs reduced the company's workforce from nearly 10,000 in the mid-1980s to 6,000 today. Employees who didn't lose their jobs during this transformation have redefined their psychological contract from a "job-for-life" to survival of the fittest.

"What we're trying to do," says Petro-Canada vice-president Roy Legge, "is switch the emphasis to development opportunities and employability, as opposed to just switching from one job to another and the employment-for-life kind of mode that a lot of companies had 10 years ago."

Now Petro-Canada's senior executives want to push the change further by focusing on the company's core competencies: finding, producing, and selling oil. Wishart Robson and other non-core employees will be placed into strategic business units that provide shared services, or will be laid off and rehired on short-term contracts. The company has already outsourced its printing services.

Ian Tomlinson. Used with permission of the *Globe & Mail*.

To remain competitive, Petro-Canada rewrote the psychological contract from loyalty-based to employability-based.

Accountants, health and safety managers, secretaries, and human resource advisers may be next. Petro-Canada hopes to cut another 10 percent of its workforce through these actions.

Source: B Jang, "On the Firing Line Again," *Globe & Mail*, June 20, 1995, p. B14; G. Pearson, "New Look in Development of Tomorrow's Executive," *Canadian HR Reporter*, December 5, 1994, pp. 13–14.

Under the employability agreement, employees are expected to keep pace with changing competency requirements and shift to new projects as demand requires. Employees must learn that a job is only a temporary event, not a life-raft in a sea of unemployment. Consequently, they must learn to continually develop the skills that make them ideal candidates for new work opportunities when their current tasks are completed.

How do companies change the psychological contract? Mainly, they follow the organizational change model that we learned about in Chapter 15. In particular, companies need to develop a readiness for change and clearly communicate the new expectations to employees. Some firms have dramatically symbolized the shift from job-for-life to employability by making employees reapply for their own jobs. This occurred at Consumers Gas Co. Ltd. when the Toronto-based utility cut supervisory positions. To ensure that remaining employees were not complacent, all supervisors had to reapply for the fewer positions.[13] Although this action may symbolize the transformed psychological contract, it also creates stress and possible resentment. In the long term, the best way to accurately form a psychological contract is through effective socialization of new employees, which we describe next.

Organizational Socialization

Markham Stouffville Hospital has won some of the highest awards in Canada for quality and service in a health care facility. Located north of Toronto, the community hospital relies heavily on formal socialization of employees to ensure that quality standards and values are maintained. "You don't just rely on training," advises Markham Stouffville Hospital president Marilyn Bruner. "You need a whole socialization process."[14]

Organizational socialization The process by which individuals learn the values, expected behaviours, and social knowledge necessary to assume their roles in the organization.

Organizational socialization refers to the process by which individuals learn the values, expected behaviours, and social knowledge necessary to assume their roles in the organization.[15] It is a process of both learning and change. Organizational socialization is a learning process because newcomers try to make sense of the organization's physical arrangements, psychological contract, and cultural values. They learn about what is expected of them, how they fit into the organization, and what they should expect to receive in return for their effort, loyalty, and job performance.[16]

To develop a cognitive map of their new work environment, newcomers need to find reliable sources of information. Job applicants receive some objective information during the recruiting process, such as how much they are paid, where they work, and what tasks they will perform. But new employees are heavily dependent on co-workers for soft information, such as who has power, what is expected of newcomers, and how employees really get ahead in the organization.[17]

Organizational socialization is also a process of change because individuals need to adapt to their new work environment.[18] They develop new work roles, adopt new team norms, and practise new behaviours. To varying degrees, newcomers also acquire the values and assumptions of the organization's dominant culture as well as the local subculture. Some people quickly internalize the company's culture; a few others rebel against these attempts to change their mental models and values. Ideally, newcomers adopt a level of creative individualism in which they accept the essential elements of the organization's culture and team norms, yet maintain a healthy individualism that challenges the allegedly dysfunctional elements of organizational life.

Socialization is a continuous process, beginning long before the first day of employment and continuing throughout a person's career within the company. However, it is most intense when people cross organizational boundaries, such as when they first join a company, move to a new department or regional branch office, get transferred to (or back from) an international assignment, or get promoted to a higher level in the firm. For each of these transitions, employees need to learn about and adjust to an entirely new work context, as well as learn role-specific behaviours.[19]

Stages of Socialization

The organizational socialization process can be divided into three stages: pre-employment socialization, encounter, and role management (see Exhibit 17.2). These stages parallel the individual's transition from outsider, to newcomer, and then to insider.[20]

Stage 1: Pre-Employment Socialization

Think back to the months and weeks before you began working in a new job (or attending a new school). You actively searched for information about the company, formed expectations about working there, and felt some anticipation about fitting into that environment. The pre-employment socialization stage encompasses all of the learning and adjustment that occurs prior to the first day of work in a new position.

Recent evidence suggests that much of the socialization adjustment process occurs prior to the first day of work.[21] This is not an easy process, however. Individuals are outsiders, so they must rely on friends, employment interviews, recruiting literature, and other indirect information to form expectations about what it is like to work in the organization. The employer also forms a set of expectations about the job applicant, such as the unique skills and vitality that he or she will bring to the organization.

Conflicts when exchanging information
Job applicants and employers need an open exchange of accurate information during pre-employment socialization to ensure that they form the same psychological contract. Unfortunately, as Exhibit 17.3 illustrates, four conflicts make it difficult for both parties to send or receive accurate information.[22]

EXHIBIT 17.2: Stages of Organizational Socialization

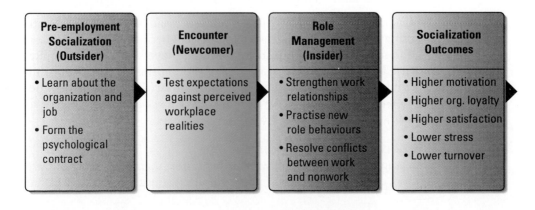

Pre-employment Socialization (Outsider)	Encounter (Newcomer)	Role Management (Insider)	Socialization Outcomes
• Learn about the organization and job • Form the psychological contract	• Test expectations against perceived workplace realities	• Strengthen work relationships • Practise new role behaviours • Resolve conflicts between work and nonwork	• Higher motivation • Higher org. loyalty • Higher satisfaction • Lower stress • Lower turnover

EXHIBIT 17.3: Information Exchange Conflicts During Pre-employment Socialization

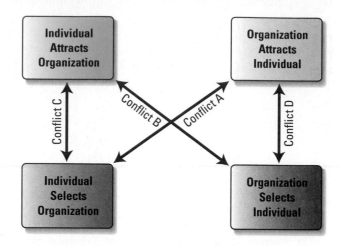

Source: L. W. Porter, E. E. Lawler III, and J. R. Hackman, *Behavior in Organizations* (New York: McGraw-Hill, 1975), p. 134. Reprinted by permission.

- *Conflict A* This occurs between the employer's need to attract qualified applicants and the applicant's need for complete information to make accurate employment decisions. Many firms use a "flypaper" approach by describing only the positive aspects of the job and company, causing applicants to accept job offers on the basis of incomplete or false expectations.

- *Conflict B* This occurs between the applicant's need to look attractive to employers and the organization's need for complete information to make accurate selection decisions. The problem is that applicants sometimes emphasize favourable employment experiences and leave out less favourable events in their careers. This provides employers with inaccurate data, thereby distorting their expectations of the job candidate and weakening the quality of organizational selection decisions.

- *Conflict C* This occurs when applicants avoid asking important career-decision questions because the questions convey an unfavourable image. For instance, applicants usually don't like to ask about starting salaries and promotion opportunities because it makes them sound greedy or overaggressive. Yet, unless the employer presents this information, applicants might fill in the missing information with false assumptions that produce an inaccurate psychological contract.

- *Conflict D* This occurs when employers avoid asking certain questions or avoid using potentially valuable selection devices because they might put the organization in a bad light. For instance, some employers refuse to use aptitude or ability tests because they don't want to give the impression that the organization treats employees like mice running through a maze. Unfortunately, without the additional information, employers may form a less accurate opinion of the job candidate's potential as an employee.

Postdecisional justification

Both employers and job applicants further distort their perceptions of the psychological contract through the process of postdecisional justification (Chapter 11). After the decision to accept employment has been made, new hires subconsciously increase the importance of favourable elements of the job and justify or completely forget about some negative elements. At the same time, they negatively distort the image of job offers that they turned down. Employers often distort their expectations of new hires in the same way. The result is that both parties develop higher expectations of each other than they will actually experience during the encounter stage.

Stage 2: Encounter

The first day on the job typically marks the beginning of the encounter stage of organizational socialization. During this stage, newcomers test their prior expectations with the perceived realities. According to recent evidence, most come to the conclusion that the employer has violated the psychological contract.[23] For instance, the majority of new hires in one study reported more negative than positive first-day experiences. These critical incidents included unprofessional orientation sessions, beginning work immediately without adequate instruction, and being assigned menial work. In some cases, new employees arrived to discover that their supervisor and co-workers had forgotten they were starting that day!

Reality shock The gap between pre-employment expectations and the perceived organizational reality that employees experience as they enter a new work situation.

Most negative experiences reflect the company's failure to recognize the importance of employee socialization. To some extent, these experiences are amplified by overoptimistic expectations that newcomers form during the pre-employment socialization stage. Whatever the cause, newcomers usually experience some degree of **reality shock** when they realize that their expectations about the employment relationship have not been met. Reality shock is the gap between what is and what ought to be. It is a specific application of discrepancy theory (Chapter 7) in which the perceived reality falls significantly short of the newcomer's pre-employment expectations. Reality shock might occur on the first day of work, or it may be more subtle, such as eventually realizing that the company's emphasis on profits over safety is at odds with the newcomer's own values.

Reality shock can be stressful for most people, particularly when they have made a significant investment or sacrifice to join the organization (such as moving to another city or turning down other potentially good jobs). Reality shock impedes the socialization process because the newcomer's energy is directed toward managing the stress rather than learning and accepting organizational knowledge and roles.[24]

Stage 3: Role Management

During the role management stage in the socialization process, employees settle in as they make the transition from newcomers to insiders. They strengthen relationships with co-workers and supervisors, practise new role behaviours, and adopt attitudes and values consistent with their new position and organization.

Role management also involves resolving the conflicts between work and non-work activities. In particular, employees must redistribute their time and energy between work and family, reschedule recreational activities, and deal with changing perceptions and values in the context of other life roles. They must address any discrepancies between their existing values and those emphasized by the organizational culture. New self-identities are formed that are more compatible with the work environment.

was in trouble. Current practices succeeded in producing a more flexible workforce, and there was some evidence that using contingent workers increased profitability. However, these practices created unanticipated problems that become apparent as the percentage of contingent workers increased.

One problem was that few people wanted contingent employment. Most were seeking full-time permanent work and were using their contingent position as a stepping stone to those jobs at Quantor. The result was that many contract workers remained for the entire two-year maximum period and beyond. The company was reluctant to apply the task force's recommendation of not renewing contracts beyond two years because of the perceived arbitrariness of this action as well as loss of knowledge to the organization. Several contract-staff members asked the company for an employee-paid benefit package (benefits are mainly employer-paid for permanent employees). However, Quantor rejected this because it would add further permanence to their employment relationship.

Quantor's managers also began to complain about the company policy that contingent workers could not be offered permanent employment. They appreciated the opportunity to select permanent employees based on observations of their performance in on-contract or on-call positions. Quantor's task force had warned against this practice because it might create inequities and raise false expectations about the likelihood of permanent employment. Managers acknowledged this risk, but they were frustrated by the inability to permanently hire good contract staff.

The third problem was that Quantor's treatment of contingent workers was incompatible with its organizational culture. Quantor had a strong culture based on the philosophy of employee well-being. The company had a generous benefits package, supportive leadership, and a belief system that made employees a top priority in corporate decisions. The company did not treat contingent workers

in a way that was consistent with this philosophy. Yet if Quantor treated contingent workers the same as permanent staff members, then flexibility would be lost. For example, managers would continue renewing contract workers even when their employment was not essential, and be reluctant to schedule on-call people at awkward times.

Quantor's team orientation was also incompatible with its use of contingent workers. Permanent staff members frequently gathered to discuss organizational and group decisions. Contingent workers were not invited to these team activities because they might be working at Quantor for only a few more months. This barrier created some awkward moments for managers as contingent workers continued working while permanent employees went to meetings and team sessions.

As these problems intensified, senior management formed another task force to reexamine Quantor's contingent-workforce policy. The company needed contingent workers, but it was increasingly apparent that the current practices were not working.

Discussion Questions

1. Identify the problems that Quantor experienced with its contingent-workforce practices. Also identify other possible contingent-workforce problems that have not been explicitly mentioned in this case.

2. Discuss the problems with contingent workers at Quantor in terms of the psychological contract and organizational commitment.

3. What alternative strategies might allow Quantor to include a contingent workforce with fewer problems?

Experiential Exercise

Organizational Socialization Diagnostic Exercise

Purpose: To help students understand the socialization strategies that organizations should use for new employees, and to learn about the impediments to forming an accurate psychological contract.

Instructions: The instructor will form small teams of three or four students. Each member will describe one particularly memorable positive or negative experience encountered when entering an organization. (Students without employment experience can describe their entry into a school, volunteer group, or other organization.) For example, the person might describe how he or she was greeted during the first day of work, how the company kept him or her informed before the first day of work, how the company did (or didn't) tell the person about negative aspects of the work or job context.

Based on these experiences, the team will develop a list of strategies that companies should use to improve the socialization process. Some experiences will reflect effective management of the socialization process. Other experiences will indicate what companies have done ineffectively, so the team must identify strategies to avoid those problems.

When the list of strategies has been developed, each team describes one of the incidents its members have experienced and then describes what corporate socialization strategy was (or should have been) used to make this experience effective. This process can be repeated until the most significant anecdotes and their implications have been presented. The class will discuss common elements among experiences presented (e.g., unrealistic job previews, problems adjusting to new values, violations of the psychological contract) and strategies companies should follow to make the socialization process more effective.

CHAPTER 18

Organizational Structure and Design

CHAPTER OUTLINE

Division of Labour and Coordination

Elements of Organizational Structure

Traditional Forms of Departmentation

Emerging Forms of Departmentation

Contingencies of Organizational Design

Chapter Summary

Discussion Questions

LEARNING OBJECTIVES

After reading this chapter, you should be able to:

- Describe the two fundamental requirements of organizational structures.

- Explain why firms can have flatter structures than previously believed.

- Compare the functional structure with the divisional structure.

- Explain why multinational firms have difficulty selecting the best form of departmentation.

- Describe four features of team-based organizational structures.

- Identify four contingencies of organizational design.

Northern Telecom has changed its organizational structure at least three times over the past decade. Its most recent structural transformation focuses employees more on customers than on products.

As one of the world's leading telecommunications manufacturers, Northern Telecom (Nortel) continually revised its organizational structure to keep the company aligned with a changing environment. A decade ago, Nortel was divided into three geographic business units (Canada, United States, and World Trade), with each area responsible for its own marketing, manufacturing, and most product development.

This arrangement worked fine in the days of telephone monopolies. But Nortel's structure created inefficiencies and product fragmentation as the telecommunications industry globalized. In the early 1990s, Nortel reorganized around a hybrid structure with three product groups responsible for global product development and four geographically based subsidiaries responsible for marketing and manufacturing.

This arrangement didn't last long. In the latter part of the 1990s, Northern Telecom again reorganized, this time around four client-based divisions (Public Carrier Networks, Wireless Networks, Broadband Networks, and Enterprise Networks) and two geographical groups (North America and World Trade). The new structure reflects an evolution in the telecommunications market toward clients rather than just geographic regions. It encourages Nortel's employees to focus on the client's complete telecommunications needs rather than on a specific product.

"Nortel's new structure reinforces the tie-in with the market and with our customers," explains Clarence Chandran, president of Nortel's Public Carrier Networks group. "The point is: we don't just sell switches, we sell total network solutions — solutions that enable our customers to be successful in their own businesses."[1]

Organizational structure
The division of labour as well as the patterns of coordination, communication, work flow, and formal power that direct organizational activities.

Organizational design
The creation and modification of organizational structures.

There is something of a revolution occurring in how organizations are structured. Nortel and many other companies are throwing out the old organizational charts and experimenting with new designs that will hopefully improve coordination, information flow, and employee focus on critical objectives. **Organizational structure** refers to the division of labour as well as the patterns of coordination, communication, work flow, and formal power that direct organizational activities.[2] An organizational structure reflects its culture and power relationships.[3] Our knowledge of this subject provides the basic tools to engage in **organizational design**; that is, to create and modify organizational structures.

We begin this chapter by considering the two fundamental processes in organizational structure: division of labour and coordination. This is followed by a detailed investigation of the four main elements of organizational structure: span of control, centralization, formalization, and departmentation. The latter part of the chapter examines the contingencies of organizational design, including organizational size, technology, external environment, and strategy.

Division of Labour and Coordination

All organizational structures include two fundamental requirements: the division of labour into distinct tasks and the coordination of that labour so that employees are able to accomplish common goals.[4] Recall from Chapter 1 that organizations are groups of people who work interdependently toward some purpose.[5] When people collectively accomplish goals, they tend to divide the work into manageable chunks, particularly when there are many different tasks to perform. They also introduce various coordinating mechanisms to ensure that everyone is working effectively toward the same objectives.

Division of Labour

Job specialization The result of division of labour, in which each job now includes a narrow subset of the tasks required to complete the product or service.

Division of labour refers to the subdivision of work into separate jobs assigned to different people. As we learned in Chapter 4, subdivided work leads to **job specialization** because each job now includes a narrow subset of the tasks necessary to complete the product or service. Assembling a satellite at Spar Aerospace, for example, requires thousands of specific tasks that are divided among hundreds of people. Tasks are also divided vertically, such as having supervisors coordinate work while employees perform the work.

Work is divided into specialized jobs because it increases work efficiency.[6] Job incumbents can master their tasks quickly because work cycles are very short. Less time is wasted changing from one task to another. Training costs are reduced because employees require fewer physical and mental skills to accomplish the assigned work. Finally, job specialization makes it easier to match people with specific aptitudes or skills to the jobs for which they are best suited.

Coordinating Work Activities

When work is divided among people, we need a coordinating mechanism to ensure that everyone works in concert.[7] Supervisors traditionally coordinate work among employees in their work unit. However, as we shall learn, there are limits to how many employees can be "coordinated" by a supervisor, at least where direct supervision is really necessary.

Informal communication is a coordinating mechanism in all organizations.[8] This includes sharing information on mutual tasks as well as forming common mental models so that employees synchronize work activities using the same mental road map.[9] At one time, scholars thought that coordination through informal communication was limited to small firms and work units. However, emerging electronic communication technologies have expanded the ability of this coordinating mechanism to operate in large organizations, even when the work-unit members are scattered around the globe.

Standardization is the third means of coordination. Some firms introduce formal instructions and job descriptions. Others use goals and product or service output indicators (e.g., customer satisfaction, production efficiency) to focus and coordinate employee work effort. When work activities are too complex to standardize through procedures or goals, companies often coordinate work effort by extensively training employees or hiring people who have learned precise role behaviours from educational programs. In hospital operating rooms, surgeons, nurses, and other operating-room professionals coordinate their work more through training than through goals or company rules.

Elements of Organizational Structure

There are four basic elements of organizational structure. This section introduces three of them: span of control, centralization, and formalization. The fourth element — departmentation — is presented in the next section.

Span of Control

Span of control The number of people directly reporting to a supervisor.

Span of control refers to the number of people directly reporting to the next level in the hierarchy. Early theorists prescribed a relatively narrow span of control, typically no more than 20 employees per supervisor and 6 supervisors per manager. These prescriptions were based on the assumption that managers simply cannot monitor and control any more subordinates closely enough.

Today, we know better. According to a recent survey, the best-performing production plants in the United States currently assign 31 employees per supervisor, on average. This is a much higher span of control than early scholars had recommended. Yet these operations plan to stretch this span further. Over the next few years, the same companies plan to further widen the span of control to an average of 75 employees per supervisor.[10]

What's the secret here? Did past scholars miscalculate the optimal span of control? The answer is that early scholars thought in terms of Fredrick Taylor's scientific management model (Chapter 4). They believed that employees should "do" the work, whereas supervisors and other management personnel should monitor employee behaviour and make most of the decisions. This division of labour limited the span of control. It isn't possible to *directly supervise* 75 people. It is possible, however, to have 75 subordinates grouped into several self-directed work teams. This arrangement lets employees manage themselves, thereby releasing supervisors from the time-consuming tasks of monitoring behaviour.

The underlying principle here is that the span of control depends on the presence of other coordinating principles.[11] Self-directed work teams replace direct supervision with informal communication and specialized knowledge. This also explains why dozens of surgeons and other medical professionals may report to the head surgeon in a major hospital. The head surgeon doesn't engage in much direct supervision because the unit's work is coordinated by the specialized training of its staff.

Span of control can also widen when employees in the unit perform similar tasks or have routine jobs. When people perform similar tasks, the unit is coordinated by

"That reminds me... Harris, they want to see you in Personnel."

standardized work processes or outputs, so there is less need for hands-on supervision. When tasks are routine, work processes can also be standardized and less time is required to discuss exceptional cases with subordinates.

Tall and flat structures

One of Paul Tellier's first tasks as head of Canadian National was to slash the transportation company's bureaucratic hierarchy from ten levels to just five. Air Canada, Domtar Inc., Labatt Breweries, and other companies have also introduced flatter organizational structures. IDEO, a leading industrial design firm, claims to have a completely flat organizational structure — no management layers.[12]

Delayering — moving from a tall to flat structure — has become popular in executive boardrooms because it potentially increases organizational productivity by cutting overhead costs. Moreover, delayering shifts companies from direct supervision to standardization and other more efficient coordinating mechanisms.

The average span of control within the organization determines the number of hierarchical levels required. As shown in Exhibit 18.1, a tall structure has many hierarchical levels, each with a relatively narrow span of control, whereas a flat structure has few levels, each with a wide span of control.[13] Early writers recommended a relatively

EXHIBIT 18.1: Span of Control and Tall/Flat Structures

**Tall Structure/
Narrow Span of Control**

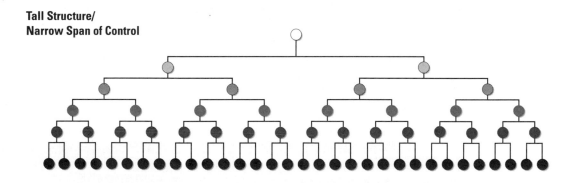

**Flat Structure/
Wide Span of Control**

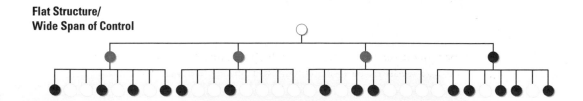

narrow span of control, so they necessarily prescribed many hierarchical levels. In the 1950s, Peter Drucker, a preeminent management thinker, questioned those perspectives by saying that companies should have no more than seven hierarchical levels. In the 1980s, popular management writer Tom Peters challenged management to cut the number of layers to three within a facility and to five within the entire organization.[14] As companies stretch the span of control, they will continue to move toward a flatter organizational structure.

Centralization and Decentralization

Centralization The degree to which formal decision authority is held by a small group of people, typically those at the top of the organizational hierarchy.

Centralization means that formal decision authority is held by a small group of people, typically those at the top of the organizational hierarchy. Most organizations begin with centralized structures, as the founder makes most of the decisions and tries to direct the business toward a personal vision. But as organizations grow, they become more complex. Work activities are divided into more specialized functions, a broader range of products or services is introduced, and operations expand into different regions or countries. Under these conditions, the founder and senior management lack the necessary time and expertise to process all the decisions that significantly influence the business.[15] Consequently, growing organizations become *decentralized*; that is, they disperse decision authority throughout the organization.

Along with increasing complexity, organizations decentralize because employees demand more control over their work lives. As we learned in Chapter 4, empowerment potentially increases job enrichment, which can lead to improved work motivation and job satisfaction. Empowerment occurs through decentralization. A Canadian study has also reported that centralized companies have more labour relations problems than do firms with decentralized structures.[16]

Although organizational complexity and employee needs push for decentralization, other forces push for centralization. Managers try to gain decision-control during times of turbulence and organizational crisis; however, when the problems are over, decision-making power does not quickly return to the lower levels. Senior executives push for centralization to increase their organizational power over organizational activities.

Centralization may reduce costs if, as noted above, it doesn't reduce local flexibility too much. This is the main reason that companies are moving toward shared services — centralizing human resources, accounting, and other support functions in one unit rather than scattering them around different divisions or countries. For instance, many companies have centralizing hardware, software, and other information technology resources to improve coordination and operating efficiencies.[17] Similarly, Compaq Computers centralized its European operations by replacing freestanding business units in each European country with a single distribution and administrative unit for the continent. This significantly increased efficiency by reducing duplication.[18]

Formalization

Formalization The degree to which organizations standardize behaviour through rules, procedures, formal training, and related mechanisms.

Have you ever wondered why a McDonald's hamburger in Saanich, British Columbia, tastes the same as one in St. John's, Newfoundland? The reason is formalization. **Formalization** is the degree to which organizations standardize behaviour through rules, procedures, formal training, and related mechanisms.[19] McDonald's Restaurants of Canada Ltd. has a formalized structure because it prescribes every activity in explicit detail. Each McDonald's franchise must dole out five perfect drops of mustard on each hamburger. A quarter-ounce of onions and two pickles — three if they're small — are used per sandwich. Drink cups are filled with ice up to a point just below the arches on their sides. Take-out bags are folded exactly twice. Cooking and bagging fries are explained in 19 steps. The strict rules even prescribe what colour nail polish employees can wear.[20]

Older companies tend to become more formalized because work activities become routinized, making them easier to document into standardized practices. Larger companies formalize as a coordinating mechanism because direct supervision and informal communication among employees do not operate as easily. External influences, such as government safety legislation and strict accounting rules, also encourage formalization.

Problems with formalization

Formalization may increase efficiency, but it can also create problems. Rules and procedures reduce organizational flexibility, so employees follow prescribed behaviours even when the situation clearly calls for a customized response. Some work rules become so convoluted that organizational efficiency would decline if they were actually followed as prescribed. Indeed, labour unions sometimes call work-to-rule strikes, in which their members closely follow the formalized rules and procedures established by an organization. This tactic increases union power because the company's productivity falls significantly when employees follow the rules that are supposed to guide their behaviour.

Another concern is that although employees with very strong security needs and a low tolerance for ambiguity like working in highly formalized organizations, others become alienated and feel powerless in these structures. Finally, rules and procedures have been known to take on a life of their own in some organizations. They become the focus of attention rather than the organization's ultimate objectives of producing a product or service and serving its dominant stakeholders.

Mechanistic Versus Organic Structures

Mechanistic structure An organizational structure with a narrow span of control and high degrees of formalization and centralization.

Organic structure An organizational structure with a wide span of control, very little formalization, and highly decentralized decision making.

The three elements of organizational structure described so far — span of control, centralization, and formalization — are sometimes grouped into two distinct forms known as *mechanistic* and *organic structures*.[21] A **mechanistic structure** has high degrees of formalization and centralization. It is characterized by many rules and procedures, limited decision making at lower levels, large hierarchies of people in specialized roles, and vertical rather than horizontal communication flows. Tasks are rigidly defined and are altered only when sanctioned by higher authorities. An **organic structure** is just the opposite. It usually has very little formalization and highly decentralized decision making. Communication flows in all directions with little concern for the formal hierarchy. Tasks are fluid, adjusting to new situations and organizational needs.

Traditional Forms of Departmentation

Span of control, centralization, and formalization are important elements of organizational structure, but most people think about organizational charts when the discussion of organizational structure arises. The organizational chart represents the

Departmentation An element of organizational structure specifying how employees and their activities are grouped together, such as by function, product, geographic location, or some combination.

fourth element in the structuring of organizations, called **departmentation**. Departmentation specifies how employees and their activities are grouped together. It is a fundamental strategy for coordinating organizational activities, as it influences organizational behaviour in the following ways:[22]

- Departmentation establishes a system of common supervision among positions and units within the organization. It establishes formal work teams, as we learned in Chapter 9. Departmentation typically determines which positions and units must share resources. Thus, it establishes interdependencies among employees and subunits (Chapter 13).

- Departmentation usually creates common measures of performance. Members of the same work team, for example, share common goals and budgets, giving the company standards against which to compare subunit performance.

- Departmentation encourages coordination through informal communication among people and subunits. With common supervision and resources, members within each configuration typically work near each other, so they can use frequent and informal interaction to get the work done.

There are almost as many organizational charts as there are businesses, but we can identify four pure types of departmentation: simple, functional, divisional, and matrix. Few companies fit exactly into any of these categories, but they represent a useful framework for discussing more complex hybrid forms of departmentation. This section also introduces two emerging forms of departmentation: team-based and network structures.

Simple Structure

L&M Highland Outfitters Ltd. manufactures leather Highland pipe bags, drum slings, and related merchandise which are sold to Scotland, United States, Australia, and other countries. President Joe MacLean and secretary-treasurer Peggie MacLean directly manage production and sales at the Dartmouth, Nova Scotia, firm which employs nine people.[23] L&M Highland Outfitters, along with most small businesses, has a *simple structure*. Although there is some hierarchy (the MacLeans oversee the others), employees are not rigidly organized into departments. The MacLeans employ only a few people and offer only one distinct product or service.

In simple structures, employees are grouped into broadly defined roles because there are insufficient economies of scale to assign them to specialized roles. Simple structures are flexible, yet they usually depend on the owner's direct supervision to coordinate work activities. Consequently, this structure is very difficult to operate under complex conditions. As L&M Highland Outfitters grows, for instance, the MacLeans will need to add professionals to their staff to coordinate more specialized roles.

Christopher Reardon. Used with permission.

L&M Highland Outfitters Ltd. of Dartmouth, Nova Scotia, employs nine people to manufacture leather Highland pipe bags, drum slings, and related merchandise. Even though its products are sold to Scotland, United States, Australia, and other countries, president Joe MacLean and secretary-treasurer Peggie MacLean use a simple organizational structure to directly manage production and sales.

Functional Structure

A **functional structure** organizes employees around specific skills or other resources. Employees with marketing expertise are grouped into a marketing unit, those with production skills are located in manufacturing, engineers are found in product development, and so on. Organizations with functional structures are typically centralized to coordinate their activities effectively. Coordination through standardization of work processes is the most common form of coordination used in a functional structure. Most organizations use functional structures at some level or at some time in their development.

Advantages and disadvantages

An important advantage of functional structures is that they foster professional identity and clarify career paths. They permit greater specialization so that the organization has expertise in each area. Direct supervision is easier because managers have backgrounds in that functional area and employees approach them with common problems and issues. Finally, functional structures create common pools of talent that typically serve everyone in the organization. This creates an economy of scale that would not exist if functional specialists were spread over different parts of the organization.[24]

Functional structures also have limitations. Because people are grouped together with common interests and backgrounds, these designs promote differentiation among functions. For this reason, functional structures tend to have higher dysfunctional conflict and poorer coordination with other work units. A related concern is that functional structures tend to emphasize subunit goals over superordinate organizational goals. Engineers, for example, tend to give lower priority to the company's product or service than to the goals of the engineering department. A third concern is that functional structures perpetuate specialization at the expense of more holistic management. Unless managers are transferred from one function to the next, they fail to develop a broader understanding of the business. Together, these problems require substantial formal controls and coordination when functional structures are used.

Divisional Structure

A **divisional structure** groups employees around outputs, clients, or geographic areas. Divisional structures are sometimes called *strategic business units* (SBUs) because they are normally more autonomous than functional structures and may operate as subsidiaries rather than departments of the enterprise.

Exhibit 18.2 illustrates the three pure forms of divisional structure. *Product/service structures* organize work around distinct outputs. Exhibit 18.2(a) displays the product structure at Moore Corp. Ltd., including forms and print management, labels and label systems, and customer communication services.[25]

Geographic structures, such as the one adopted by Mobil Oil, establish organizational groupings around different locations. Exhibit 18.2(b) illustrates part of the geographic design at Toronto-based Bata Limited. The world's largest footwear company has divisions in Canada, Europe, Africa, South America, the Far East, and four other global regions.[26]

EXHIBIT 18.2: Three Types of Divisional Structure

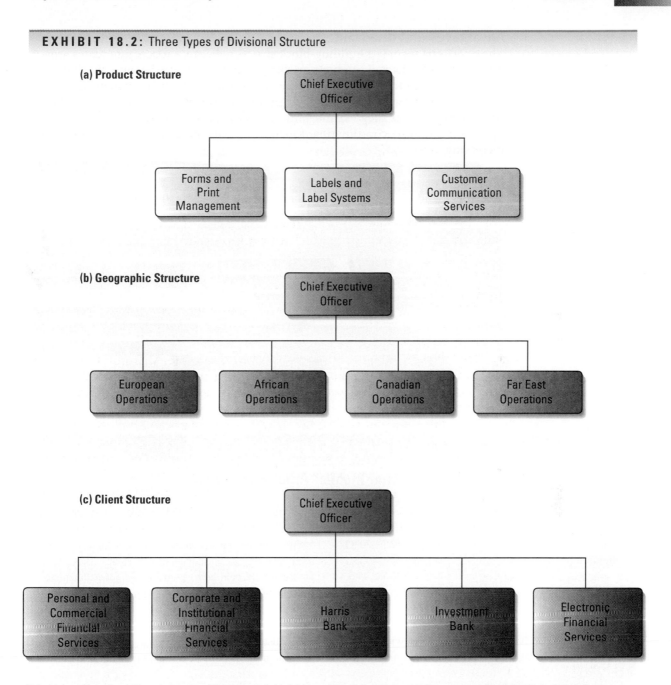

(a) Product Structure

(b) Geographic Structure

(c) Client Structure

Note: (a) shows Moore Corp. Ltd.'s product structure; (b) shows several global divisions of Bata Limited; (c) shows the five customer divisions of the Bank of Montreal.

Client structures organize work activities around specific customers. Canadian financial institutions have adopted a stronger market orientation and are reorganizing their operations around specific client groups to reflect this new emphasis, as in Exhibit 18.2(c). For example, the Bank of Montreal reorganized its business into five strategic business units: Personal and Commercial Financial Services; Corporate and Institutional Financial Services; Harris Bank; Investment Banking; and Electronic Financial Services.

Advantages and disadvantages

The divisional form is a building-block structure because it accommodates growth relatively easily. Related products or clients can be added to existing divisions with little need for additional learning, whereas increasing diversity may be accommodated by sprouting a new division. Organizations typically reorganize around divisional structures as they expand into distinct products, services, and domains of operation because coordinating functional units becomes too unwieldy with increasing diversity.[27]

The main advantage of divisional structures is that they give employees more flexibility and output focus than in functional structures. As Perspective 18.1 describes, Mobil Oil switched to geographically based business units for these reasons. Corporate divisions have self-contained resources, so decision making is delegated further down the hierarchy and the unit can be more flexible to client needs. Accountability increases because each division's goals and output measures are easier to identify and measure. Divisionalized business units also tend to place more emphasis on clients and product quality because divisional goals and output measures are now directly related to these factors.

In spite of their popularity, divisional structures increase the risk of duplication and underutilization of resources. Another concern is that divisional structures might reduce cooperation across groups because employees identify more with their own division than with the company as a whole. Microsoft Corporation has worked to overcome this problem, resulting in greater compatibility in its Microsoft Office software package. Previously, Excel programmers didn't share

---

PERSPECTIVE 18.1

Creating "Mini-Mobils" Around the World

For many years, Mobil Oil organized employees into upstream and downstream operations. The upstream people explored oil and produced it. The downstream people refined and marketed the oil to customers. The company also had three global divisions, but they had limited control and were responsible for diverse geopolitical regions.

It was increasingly clear that this mainly functional structure was inappropriate for Mobil's global operations. A unit that wanted to do something in Eastern Europe would have to request permission through at least two other levels of management before the issue reached Mobil's headquarters in Fairfax, Virginia. Then it would have to work with functional units to get the job done.

CEO Lucio Noto wanted to create a structure that would "better focus our entrepreneurial talent on seizing new business opportunities." His solution was to establish a strong geographic divisional structure that put people closer to key markets with tighter links to the company's global headquarters. Eleven regional units — affectionately known as "mini-Mobils" — were established, with each operating as an independent business. These business units provided both upstream and downstream customer needs in their market and reported directly to Mobil's headquarters.

For example, Mobil's Europe and Consortium of Independent States business unit offers business partners a complete package. It works with the consortium to get the oil out, then arranges with Mobil's partners to develop a market for it. In effect, the division manages the entire process from the ground to the customer.

"When you talk to one person," explains a Mobil Oil executive, "that person has a perception of all of Mobil's operations in that region, whereas before, you'd find that people had a very specific functional focus."

Source: Adapted from J. S. DeMott, "The Key Issue: Managing Bigness," *Worldbusiness*, September/October 1996, pp. 30–33.

ideas or resources with their counterparts in the Word or PowerPoint™ groups. It took direct intervention by Bill Gates to convince employees in each product group to cooperate.[28] Finally, although division autonomy is a potential advantage, it may reduce top management's control over the entire organization. Unless control mechanisms are introduced, the organization's senior management group might not be aware of a division's deviation from organizational standards or objectives until it is too late.

Matrix Structure

MacDonald Dettwiler & Associates Ltd. (MDA) offers customized computer systems development for meteorological systems, space and defence, geological information systems, and aviation. However, the Richmond, British Columbia, computer systems development firm also does mainly contract work, so a traditional divisionalized structure doesn't make the best use of engineers with specialized knowledge. Instead, project teams in each product group receive employees from several functional departments. MDA's employees are temporarily assigned to these teams, but report directly to the head of their functional department as well as to the project team leader.

Matrix structure A type of departmentation that overlays a divisionalized structure (typically a project team) with a functional structure.

MacDonald Dettwiler uses a **matrix structure** in which a divisionalized structure (typically a project team) is overlaid with a functional structure. Most matrix structures involve temporarily assigning employees to a specific project team, usually for no longer than a couple of years. These employees belong to a permanent functional unit, typically known as a "home" department, to which they return

The matrix structure at MacDonald Dettwiler & Associates Ltd. combines engineering functions with four product groups: meteorological systems, space and defence, geological information systems, and aviation. Engineering specialists are assigned to project teams in the product groups, but also report to their functional departments. Matrix structures potentially increase ambiguity and conflict, but they also adapt to client needs more easily than functional or divisional structures.

Courtesy of MacDonald Dettwiler & Associates Ltd.

when a project is completed. The result is that employees have two bosses within the matrix structure — the project manager and the functional manager. The relative degree of supervisory authority of these two managers depends on the specific matrix configuration and duties of these managers.[29]

Exhibit 18.3 depicts a simplified matrix structure consisting of three functional departments that provide specialists to the two project teams. (MacDonald Dettwiler's matrix structure is more complex than this.) Cossette Communication Inc. relies on a matrix structure to serve its clients. While most advertising and public relations agencies keep employees in their functional silos, Cossette integrates employees across departments into specific client groups. For example, the Quebec City–based firm has client teams for Saturn, Bombardier, Bell Mobility, McDonald's, and several other accounts. Each cross-functional team includes employees from public relations, advertising, market research, and graphic design departments, depending on the client's needs.[30]

Advantages and disadvantages

Matrix structures usually optimize the use of resources and expertise, making them ideal for project-based organizations with fluctuating workloads.[31] When properly managed, they improve communication efficiency, project flexibility, and innovation compared to purely functional designs. Matrix structures focus technical specialists on the goals of serving clients and creating marketable products. Yet, by maintaining a link to their functional unit, employees are able to interact and coordinate with others in their technical speciality. For example, MacDonald, Dettwiler's 20 engineers

EXHIBIT 18.3: A Simplified Matrix Structure

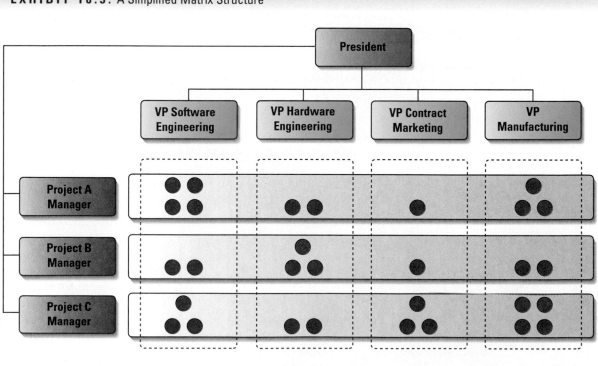

● **Team Member**

specializing in user-interface technology are assigned to various project teams across the company's four business units, but their engineering manager ensures that they develop products that look alike.

Matrix structures can be valuable, but they also tend to generate conflict, organizational politics, and stress.[32] Senior management must maintain a proper balance of power between project leaders and functional managers. Project leaders must have a general management orientation and conflict resolution skills to coordinate people with diverse backgrounds. Otherwise, dysfunctional conflict may arise among team members due to their diverse backgrounds and perspectives. Project leaders also need good negotiation skills to get the people they need from the functional managers. Employees who feel comfortable in structured bureaucracies tend to have difficulty adjusting to the relatively fluid nature of matrix structures. Stress is a common symptom of poorly managed matrix structures because employees must cope with two managers who have potentially divergent needs and expectations.

Hybrid Structure

As companies grow and become global entities, very few adopt a purely functional or divisional structure. Instead, they combine some parts of each design into a hybrid structure. Research suggests that multinational corporations need to develop structures and systems that maintain some balance of power and effectiveness across functional, product, and geographic groups.[33] In other words, they must ensure that functional managers do not dominate product managers, product managers do not dominate regional managers, and so forth. As we learned at the beginning of the chapter, Northern Telecom has been grappling with this issue by reconfiguring its structure around products, geographic areas, and clients. Nortel has also introduced emerging structures (team-based and networks) which we discuss next.

Emerging Forms of Departmentation

All organizations include one or more of the previously described forms of departmentation. However, due to changes in the workforce and information technology, two new forms of departmentation are emerging: team-based and network structures. Although they typically exist within or in conjunction with traditional departmentation, team-based and network structures have unique features and someday may become the dominant structural design in some industries.

Team-Based (Lateral) Structure

When Eastman Kodak Co. spun off its chemical division into a separate company called Eastman Chemical Co., it reorganized the operation into the shape of a pizza with pepperoni sprinkled over it. Each pepperoni represents a cross-functional team responsible for managing a business, a geographic area, or a core competence in a specific technology or area. GE Canada's plant in Bromont, Quebec, has a similar structure. But when Bromont's employees decided to draw their team-based design, they produced a three-dimensional shape of a large sphere with several bubbles inside.[34]

Courtesy of GE Canada.

When GE Canada designed its plant in Bromont, Quebec, there wasn't an organizational chart that it could copy. Bromont relies completely on teams to get the work done, rather than a traditional hierarchy, so employees at the aircraft engine plant drew a structure that reflected its uniqueness. Instead of boxes and lines, Bromont's organizational chart consists of a three-dimensional sphere with several bubbles inside.

Team-based organizational structure
A type of departmentation with a flat span of control and relatively little formalization, consisting of self-directed work teams responsible for various work processes.

Eastman Chemical and GE Canada in Bromont are two examples of the **team-based organizational structure** that we introduced in Chapter 9. Some writers call it a *lateral structure* because, with few organizational levels, it is very flat (like a pizza). Others refer to it as a *circle structure* (similar to Bromont's sphere) because senior management becomes an outer casing that serves the free-floating team units within.[35] The team-based organization is also known as a *cluster structure* because it is composed of a cluster of teams. Exhibit 18.4 illustrates two of these perspectives of team-based organizations.

No matter what name is used or how it is drawn, the team-based structure has a few features that distinguish it from other organizational forms. First, it is based on self-directed work teams rather than individuals as the basic building block of organizations. This means that work is assigned to teams rather than to specific employees and that these teams exist throughout the organization, not just in the production area (where self-directed work teams are traditionally found).

A second feature is that the team-based structure organizes most teams around work processes, such as making a specific product or serving a specific client group. Very few employees are grouped into functional specialties (e.g., legal, human resources). The San Diego Zoo provides a good example of this. The zoo replaced most of its 50 functional departments (horticulture, maintenance, animal keeping, etc.) with teams assigned to different bioclimate exhibit areas. Thus, the team assigned to the Gorilla Tropics area takes care of the animals, plants, maintenance, construction, and several other functional activities. Although members tend to retain their expertise, they typically work together on various tasks within the exhibit area.[36]

A third distinguishing feature of team-based organizations is that they have a very flat span of control, usually with no more than two or three management levels. As we explained in Chapter 9, team-based organizations typically have no first-

EXHIBIT 18.4: Two Perspectives of a Team-Based (Lateral) Structure

Perspective A

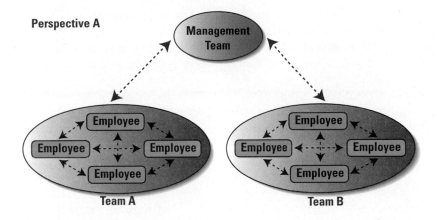

Perspective B

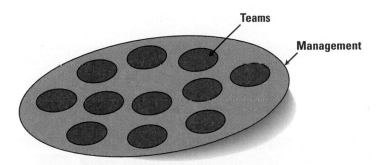

line supervisors. Instead, most supervisory activities are delegated to the team by having members take turns as the coordinator.

Finally, the team-based organization has very little formalization. Virtually all day-to-day decisions are made by team members rather than someone further up the organizational hierarchy. Teams are given relatively few rules about how to organize their work. Instead, management controls focus on output goals, such as the volume and quality of product or service, or productivity improvement targets for the work process.

Team-based structures are usually found within larger divisionalized forms. For example, GE Canada's Bromont plant is organized around a team-based structure, but it is part of GE Canada's larger product divisions. However, a few innovative (and daring!) companies are experimenting with a team-based structure from the top to the bottom of the organization. One example is Oticon Holding A/S, the Danish hearing aid manufacturer mentioned in Chapter 9. As we describe in Perspective 18.2, Oticon is a highly flexible organization with almost no hierarchy. The company's CEO calls it a "spaghetti organization" because it is a chaotic interconnection of people working freely on different projects.

PERSPECTIVE 18.2

Oticon Holding A/S Turns to Spaghetti

Oticon Holding A/S has been transformed from a sleepy Danish hearing aid manufacturer to nimble trendsetter. Oticon's secret is a radical organizational structure that replaced departments with project teams pursued by interested employees. A hundred or so projects exist at any one time, and most people work on several projects at once. This is an open-market system where project leaders compete for resources, and employees compete for a place on desirable projects.

Ars Kolind, Oticon's president, likes to call this structure "the spaghetti organization" — a continuously changing chaotic tangle of human relationships. "To keep a company alive, one of the jobs of top management is to keep it dis-organized," Kolind declares approvingly.

The spaghetti organization replaced formal communication with informal dialogue. Incoming mail is scanned into a network computer system and then shredded. Anyone can access almost any document; project teams are encouraged to share knowledge by tapping into each other's files. Everyone walks around with mobile telephones clipped to their waists.

The most obvious feature of Oticon's new structure is the office design that supports it. The new building (a refurbished soft-drink plant) is an open space filled with uniform workstations. Each person has a computer and a birch desk on wheels — an "organization of 1,000 birch trees," as Kolinds likes to call it. This allows any employee to move his or her "office" anywhere else in the building in just five minutes.

The spaghetti structure has significantly improved creativity and knowledge sharing. Oticon is now a leader in hearing aid technology and has gained in market share and profitability. In spite of the chaos, employees seem better off, not burned out. "There's a paradox here," Kolind says. "We're developing products twice as fast as anybody else. But when you look around, you see a very relaxed atmosphere. We're not fast on the surface; we're fast underneath."

Source: P. Labarre "This Organization is Dis-Organization," *Fast Company* (on-line), Issue 3 (1997); "The Revolution at Oticon: Creating a 'Spaghetti' Organization," *Research-Technology Management* 39 (September–October 1996), p. 54; P. LaBarre, "The Dis-organization of Oticon," *Industry Week*, July 18, 1994, pp. 22–28.

Advantages and disadvantages

One of the main benefits of team-based organizations is that they empower employees and reduce reliance on a hierarchy of managers.[37] Employees with high growth-need strength are more motivated and satisfied with this arrangement, and the company reduces overhead costs. Because employees need to work across functions, team-based structures potentially improve communication and cooperation across traditional boundaries. With greater autonomy, this structure also allows quicker and more informed decision making.

These benefits are partly (or sometimes completely!) offset by several documented problems with team-based structures. One concern is that this structure is more costly to maintain. Teamwork takes more effort to coordinate than the old command-and-control hierarchical system. Employees may experience more stress due to increased ambiguity in their roles. Team leaders also experience more stress due to increased conflict, loss of functional power, and unclear career progression ladders.

Network Structure

Wellness Innovations Corp. conceived of and sells the Thumper Mini-Pro, a $299 hand-held therapeutic massage device. The product may not be glamorous, but Wellness Innovations' organizational design is an emerging form that is highly flexible and efficient. Rather than doing everything in-house, Wellness outsources a lot of its work to Baranti Group Inc. "We're their virtual R&D and their virtual manufacturing company," explains Barry Papoff, Baranti's president.[38]

Wellness Innovation Corp. is one of the many companies with a network structure. A **network structure** is an alliance of several organizations for the purpose of creating a product or serving a client.[39] Typically, several satellite organizations are beehived around a "hub" or "core" firm. As illustrated in Exhibit 18.5, a network structure might have an entire product or service designed, manufactured, marketed, delivered, and sold by subcontracting firms located anywhere around the world.

Some networks exist as coalitions to legitimize their objectives.[40] The United Way fits this type of network because it provides small charities with visibility and status. More often, networks exist because this structure offers certain economic efficiencies compared to having all activities performed in-house by different departments. In particular, the core firm relies on satellite firms for their expertise and greater efficiency at providing specific services. As the core company for the Thumper Mini-Pro, Wellness Innovation focuses on its core competency (marketing) and outsources other functions to Baranti Group and other firms.

Network organizations are becoming more common as firms focus on their core competencies and outsource non-core activities. In some cases, the satellite firms were once departments of the core firm. "The traditional idea of the unit of

Network structure An alliance of several organizations for the purpose of creating a product or serving a client.

EXHIBIT 18.5: A Network Structure

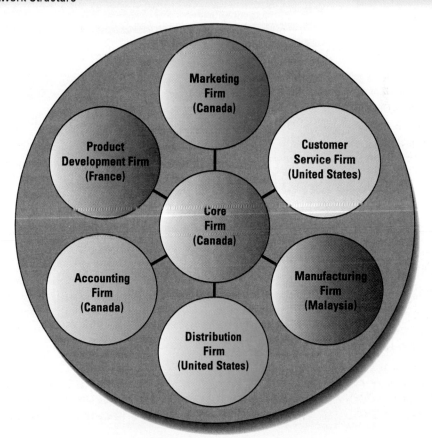

business has always been the company," explains Jayson Myers, chief economist at the Alliance of Manufacturers and Exporters Canada. "Now, it's the network, going beyond one company and encompassing all its suppliers and many of its customers."[41]

Virtual corporations and affiliate networks

Virtual corporation An extreme form of network structure in which almost every activity is distributed to satellite organizations in the network.

Take the network organization to its extreme and you would have a **virtual corporation**. Virtual corporations exist in name, but almost everything beyond the initial contact is farmed out to satellite organizations. Information flows easily and openly between the core firm and its satellites.[42] In most cases, just-in-time linkages connect suppliers with the core company and its clients.

Consider Emergex Planning Inc., described in Perspective 18.3. Emergex forms new alliances with outside companies — some of them are associates, others are independent vendors — whenever it begins a new project. The client's requirements shape the project team that, in turn, shapes Emergex's structure for that project. Emergex is almost a virtual corporation because it is able to change alliances to fit client needs.

Affiliate networks Network organizations where the satellite companies have a special affiliation with the core firm. The satellites may have been spun-off departments from the core firm, or the core firm may be a major investor in the satellite.

Some network organizations are formed when the core firm spins off or "seeds" satellite firms. These are known as **affiliate networks**. They represent network organizations where the satellites have a special affiliation with the core company. Newbridge Networks Corp., of Kanata, Ontario, has affiliate networks with nearly a dozen affiliate companies that support Newbridge's products. For instance, Newbridge provided venture capital to CrossKeys Systems Corp., which makes software that complements Newbridge's line of telecommunications network products.[43]

Newbridge relies on joint ventures with entrepreneurs, but other affiliate networks consist of divisions that have been spun off into separate companies. Basically, the core firm becomes the primary shareholder, but the division is a separate corporate entity. This disaggregates the business so that the spun-off firms can be more nimble in the marketplace.

PERSPECTIVE 18.3

The Network Structure of Emergex Planning Inc.

When MacMillan Bloedel's Powell River Division wanted to develop a comprehensive emergency preparedness plan, it called Emergex Planning Inc. in Vancouver for help. Tully Waisman, an emergency preparedness consultant and Emergex's only full-time employee, quickly pulled together three full-time professionals to handle the complex project.

Emergex Planning is the ultimate network organization — an alliance of companies that temporarily join forces to make a product or serve a client. Emergex is composed of 14 independent consulting firms (called *associates*) that provide resources when specific projects require their assistance. Every time Emergex takes on a new contract, Waisman and the associates name a team and project manager. They often subcontract some work to outside specialists or companies

near the client's site. "You only get the people you need for the length of time you need them," explains an Emergex associate.

Why would several independent consulting firms work together through Emergex? The answer is that some of their clients need work that requires diverse expertise. Emergex serves as a contractor of emergency services. Few firms could afford to keep this depth and variety of talent in-house, so Emergex's network organizational structure is a logical choice. Emergex's associates include a former Vancouver police chief who does security assessments, a public relations firm that draws up crisis management plans, an emergency training specialist, an architect, a facilities planning firm, and several others.

Source: Based on "The Un-Corporation," *BC Business*, November 1993, pp. 10–11.

Advantages and disadvantages

Flexibility is the main advantage of network structures. If a product or service is no longer in demand, the core firm can wind down operations as contracts end. If the company wants to shift into a different type of product or service, it forms new alliances with other firms offering the appropriate resources. Because network structures depend on markets rather than hierarchies to create products and services, they potentially make better use of skills and technology. The core firm becomes globally competitive as it shops worldwide for subcontractors with the best people and the best technology at the best price. It is not saddled with the same resources used for previous products or services.

A potential disadvantage of network structures is that they expose the core firm to the same market forces used to get the best resources. Other companies may bid up the price for subcontractors in any functional area, whereas the short-term cost would be lower if the company hired its own employees to provide this function. Another problem is that although information technology makes worldwide communication much easier, it will never replace the degree of control that organizations have when manufacturing, marketing, and other functions are in-house. The core firm can use arm's-length incentives and contract provisions to maintain the subcontractor's quality, but these actions are relatively crude compared to those used to maintain performance of in-house employees.

Contingencies of Organizational Design

Organizational theorists and practitioners are interested not only in the elements of organizational structure, but also in the contingencies that determine or influence the optimal design. In this section, we introduce four contingencies of organizational design: size, technology, environment, and strategy.

Organizational Size

Larger organizations have considerably different structures than smaller organizations.[44] As the number of employees increases, job specialization increases due to a greater division of labour. Larger firms also have more elaborate coordinating mechanisms to manage the greater division of labour. They are more likely to use standardization of work processes and outputs to coordinate work activities. These coordinating mechanisms create an administrative hierarchy and greater formalization. Informal communication is used less often as a coordinating mechanism as organizations get larger. However, emerging computer technologies and increased emphasis on empowerment have caused informal communication to regain its importance in large firms.[45]

Larger organizations also tend to be more decentralized. As noted earlier in the chapter, neither founders nor senior managers have sufficient time or expertise to process all the decisions that significantly influence the business as it grows. Therefore, decision-making authority is pushed down to lower levels, where incumbents are able to cope with the narrower range of issues under their control.[46]

Technology

Based on the open systems model (Chapter 1), we know that an organization's structure needs to be aligned with its dominant technology. Two important technological contin-

gencies that influence the best type of organizational structure are the variety and analyzability of work activities.[47] *Variety* refers to the number of exceptions to standard
procedure that can occur in the team or work unit. *Analyzability* refers to the extent
that the transformation of input resources to outputs can be reduced to a series of
standardized steps.

Some jobs are routine, meaning that employees perform the same tasks all of
the time and rely on set rules (standard operating procedures) when exceptions do
occur. Almost everything is predictable. These situations, such as automobile assembly lines, have high formalization and centralization as well as standardization of
work processes.

When employees perform tasks with high variety and low analyzability, they apply
their skills to unique situations with little opportunity for repetition. Research project
teams operate under these conditions. These situations call for an organic structure,
one with low formalization, highly decentralized decision-making authority, and
coordination mainly through informal communication among team members.

High-variety and high-analyzability tasks have many exceptions to routines, but
these exceptions can usually be resolved through standard procedures. Engineering
work units experience these conditions. Work units that fall into this category should
use an organic structure, but it is possible to have somewhat greater formalization and
centralization due to the analyzability of problems.

Skilled tradespeople tend to work in situations with low variety and low analyzability. Their tasks involve few exceptions, but the problems that arise are difficult to
resolve. This situation allows more centralization and formalization than in a purely
organic structure, but coordination must include informal communication among the
skilled employees so that unique problems can be resolved.

External Environment

The best structure for an organization is a function of its external environment. The
external environment includes anything outside the organization, including most
stakeholders (e.g., clients, suppliers, government), resources (e.g., raw materials,
human resources, information, finances), and competitors. Four relatively distinct
characteristics of external environments influence the type of organizational structure
best suited to a particular situation: dynamism, complexity, diversity, and hostility.[48]

- *Dynamic versus routine environments* Dynamic environments have a high rate of
change, leading to novel situations and a lack of identifiable patterns. Organic
structures are better suited to this type of environment so that the organization
can adapt more quickly to changes.[49] Network and team-based structures seem to
be most effective in dynamic environments because they usually have these features. In contrast, stable environments are characterized by regular cycles of activity and steady changes in supply and demand for inputs and outputs. Events are
more predictable, enabling the firm to apply rules and procedures. Thus, more
mechanistic structures tend to work best under these conditions.

- *Complex versus simple environments* Complex environments have many elements, whereas simple environments have few things to monitor. For instance, a
multinational corporation has a complex environment because it has many stakeholders. Decentralized structures seem to be better suited to complex environments because these subunits are close to their local environment and are able to
make more informed choices.

- *Diverse versus integrated environments* Organizations located in diverse environments have a greater variety of products or services, clients, and regions. In contrast, an integrated environment has only one client, product, and geographic area. The more diversified the environment, the more the firm needs to use a divisionalized form aligned with that diversity. If it sells a single product around the world, a geographic divisionalized form would align best with the firm's geographic diversity. As we saw with Nortel at the beginning of the chapter, global firms with several products and client groups have a continuous dilemma as to which form of diversity is most important.

- *Hostile versus munificent environments* Firms located in a hostile environment face resource scarcity and more competition in the marketplace. Hostile environments are typically dynamic ones because they reduce the predictability of access to resources and demand for outputs. Organic structures tend to be best in hostile environments. However, when the environment is extremely hostile — such as a severe shortage of supplies or lower market share — organizations tend to temporarily centralize so that decisions can be made more quickly and executives feel more comfortable being in control.[50] Ironically, centralization may result in lower-quality decisions during organizational crises because top management has less information, particularly when the environment is complex.

Organizational Strategy

Organizational strategy
The way the organization positions itself in its setting in relation to its stakeholders given the organization's resources, capabilities, and mission.

Strategic choice The idea that an organization interacts with its environment rather than being totally determined by it.

Although size, technology, and environment influence the optimal organizational structure, these contingencies do not necessarily determine structure. Instead, there is increasing evidence that corporate leaders formulate and implement strategies that shape both the characteristics of these contingencies as well as the organization's resulting structure. **Organizational strategy** refers to the way the organization positions itself in its setting in relation to its stakeholders, given the organization's resources, capabilities, and mission.[51] The idea that an organization interacts with its environment rather than being totally determined by it is known as **strategic choice**.[52] In other words, organizational leaders take steps to define and manipulate their environments rather than let the organization's fate be entirely determined by external influences.

The notion of strategic choice can be traced back to the work of Alfred Chandler in the early 1960s.[53] Chandler's proposal was that structure follows strategy. He observed that organizational structures follow the growth strategy developed by the organization's decision makers. Moreover, he noted that organizational structures change only after decision makers decide to do so. This recognizes that the link between structure and the contingency factors described earlier is mediated by organizational strategy.

Chandler's thesis that structure follows strategy has become the dominant perspective of business policy and strategic management. An important aspect of this view is that organizations can choose the environments in which they want to operate. Some businesses adopt a *differentiation strategy* by bringing unique products to the market or attracting clients who want customized goods and services. They try to distinguish their outputs from those provided by other firms through marketing, providing special services, and innovation. Others adopt a *cost leadership strategy*, in which they maximize productivity and are, thereby, able to offer popular products or services at a competitive price.[54]

The type of organizational strategy selected leads to the best organizational structure to adopt.[55] Organizations with a cost leadership strategy should adopt a mechanistic, functional structure with high levels of job specialization and standardized work processes. This is similar to the routine technology category described earlier because they maximize production and service efficiency. A differentiation strategy, on the other hand, requires more customized relations with clients, so the technology would either be engineering- or craft-oriented. A matrix or team-based structure with less centralization and formalization is most appropriate here so that technical specialists are able to coordinate their work activities more closely with the client's needs. Overall, it is now apparent that organizational structure is influenced by size, technology, and environment, but the organization's strategy may reshape these elements and loosen their connection to organizational structure.

Chapter Summary

- Organizational structure refers to the division of labour as well as the patterns of coordination, communication, work flow, and formal power that direct organizational activities. All organizational structures divide labour into distinct tasks and coordinate that labour to accomplish common goals. The primary means of coordination are informal communication, direct supervision, and various forms of standardization.

- The four basic elements of organizational structure include span of control, centralization, formalization, and departmentation. The recent trend is toward flatter, decentralized structures with less formalization. In other words, many firms are trying to be more organic than mechanistic.

- Departmentation specifies how employees and their activities are grouped together. Organizations usually begin as simple structures, then develop into functional, divisionalized, matrix, or hybrid forms. A functional structure organizes employees around specific skills or other resources. A divisional structure groups employees around outputs, clients, or geographic areas. A matrix structure typically overlays a product-based divisional structure with a functional structure. Most larger organizations adopt a hybrid structure that includes some combination of functional, divisionalized, and/or matrix grouping.

- Two emerging forms of departmentation are team-based and network structures. A team-based structure is very flat with low formalization that organizes self-directed teams around work processes rather than functional specialties. A network structure is an alliance of several organizations for the purpose of creating a product or serving a client. Virtual corporations are network structures that can quickly reorganize themselves to suit the client's requirements.

- The best organizational structure depends on the firm's size, technology, and environment. Generally, larger organizations are decentralized and more formalized, with greater job specialization and elaborate coordinating mechanisms. The work unit's technology—including variety of work and analyzability of problems — influences whether to adopt an organic or mechanistic structure. We need to consider whether the external environment is dynamic, complex, diverse, and hostile.

- Although size, technology, and environment influence the optimal organizational structure, these contingencies do not necessarily determine structure. Rather, organizational leaders formulate and implement strategies to define and manipulate their environments. These strategies, rather than the other contingencies, directly shape the organization's structure.

Discussion Questions

1. Why are organizations moving toward flatter structures?

2. Canadian Widgets Ltd. makes widgets in every Canadian province because each jurisdiction has unique regulations governing the manufacturing and selling of this product. The company makes four types of widgets, each type to be sold to different types of clients. For example, one widget design is sold exclusively to automobile-repair shops, whereas another is used mainly in hospitals. Client expectations and needs are similar throughout Canada (i.e., they don't vary by province). The Canadian government has announced that it intends to break down interprovincial barriers, including the unnecessary regulatory and manufacturing restrictions on widgets. Deregulation would allow Canadian Widgets to manufacture and distribute its widgets from any Canadian location. If this occurs, how might Canadian Widgets reorganize its manufacturing and distribution operations to maximize efficiency yet keep in touch with its markets?

3. Why don't all organizations group people around product-based divisions?

4. What must top management, functional managers, and project managers do to make a matrix structure more effective?

5. Many companies claim to have a team-based organization, yet relatively few have actually adopted this form of departmentation. Describe four structural features that would suggest that a company has adopted a team-based organizational structure.

6. What is a network structure? Why do some writers believe that a network structure is an effective design for global competition?

7. Explain how environmental dynamism, complexity, diversity, and hostility influence organizational structure.

8. What do we mean by "structure follows strategy"?

Chapter Case

The Rise and Fall of PMC AG*

Founded in 1930, PMC AG is a German manufacturer of high-priced sports cars. During the early years, PMC was a small consulting engineering firm that specialized in solving difficult automotive-design problems for clients. At the end of World War II, however, the son of PMC's founder decided to expand the business beyond consulting engineering. He was determined that PMC would build its own precision automobiles.

In 1948, the first PMC prototypes rolled out of the small manufacturing facility. Each copy was handmade by highly skilled craftspeople. For several years, parts and engines were designed and built by other companies and assembled at the PMC plant. By the 1960s, however, PMC had begun to design and build its own parts.

PMC grew rapidly during the 1960s to mid-1980s. The company designed a completely new car in the early 1960s, launched a lower-priced model in 1970, and added a mid-priced model in 1977. By the mid-1980s, PMC had become very profitable as its name became an icon for wealthy entrepreneurs and jetsetters. In 1986, the year of highest production, PMC sold 54,000 cars. Nearly two-thirds of these were sold in North America.

PMC's Structure

PMC's organizational structure expanded with its success. During the early years, the company consisted only of an engineering department and a production department. By the 1980s, employees were divided into more than 10 functional departments representing different stages of the production process as well as upstream (e.g., design, purchasing) and downstream (e.g., quality control, marketing) activities. Employees worked exclusively in one department. It was almost considered mutiny for an employee to voluntarily move into another department.

PMC's production staff were organized into a traditional hierarchy. Front-line employees reported to work-group leaders, who reported to supervisors, who reported to group supervisors in each area. Group supervisors reported to production managers, who reported to production directors, who reported to PMC's executive vice-president of manufacturing. At one point nearly 20 percent of production staff members were involved in supervisory tasks. In the early 1990s, for example, there were 48 group supervisors, 96 supervisors, 162 work-group leaders supervising about 2,500 front-line production employees.

PMC's Craft Tradition

PMC had a long tradition and culture that supported craft expertise. This appealed to Germany's skilled workforce because it gave employees an opportunity to test and further develop their skills. PMC workers were encouraged to master long work cycles, often as much as 15 minutes per unit. Their ideal was to build as much as possible alone. For example, a few masters were able to assemble an entire engine. Their reward was to personally sign their name on the completed component.

The design engineers worked independently of the production department, with the result that production employees had to adjust to fit the available parts. Rather than being a nuisance, the production employees viewed this as a challenge that would further test their well-developed craft skills. Similarly, manufacturing engineers occasionally redesigned the product to fit manufacturing capabilities.

To improve efficiency, a moving track assembly system was used until 1977. Even then, the emphasis on craft skill was apparent. Employees were encouraged to quickly put all the parts on the car, knowing that highly skilled troubleshooting craftspeople would discover and repair defects after the car came off the line. This was much more costly and time-consuming than assembling the vehicle correctly the first time, but it provided yet another challenging set of tasks for skilled craftspeople. And to support their position, PMC vehicles were known for their few defects by the time they were sold to customers.

The End of Success?

PMC sports cars filled a small niche in the automobile market for those who wanted a true sports car just tame enough for everyday use. PMCs were known for their superlative performance based on excellent engineering technology, but they were also becoming very expensive. Japanese sports cars were not quite in the same league as a PMC, but the cost of manufacturing the Japanese vehicles was a small fraction of the cost of manufacturing a vehicle at PMC.

This cost inefficiency hit PMC's sales during the late 1980s and early 1990s. First, the German currency appreciated against the U.S. dollar, which made PMC sports cars even more expensive in the North American market. By 1990, PMC was selling half the number of cars it sold four years earlier. Then, the North American recession hit, further driving down PMC sales. In 1993, PMC sold just 14,000 vehicles, compared to 54,000 in 1987. And although sales rebounded to 20,000 by 1995, the high price tag put PMCs out of reach of many potential customers. It was clear to PMC's found-

ing family that changes were needed, but they weren't sure where to begin.

Discussion Questions

1. Describe PMC's organizational structure in terms of the four organizational design features.

2. Describe an organizational structure that, in your opinion, would reduce costs and improve production efficiency at PMC.

3. This case touches on quality management issues (Chapter 10). Identify some quality management practices that PMC should consider to improve its competitiveness.

---

*The company name and some details of actual events have been altered to provide a fuller case discussion.

Source: Written by Steven L. McShane based on information from several sources about "PMC."

Practice Session For Part 5

The true-false, multiple-choice, and written-answer questions presented here are based on information in Part 5 of this book (Chapters 15 to 18). These questions can help test your knowledge of material in these chapters. If your instructor uses the test bank for this textbook, these questions also give you an opportunity to practise for examinations in this course. The answers to these questions are found in Appendix C.

True-False

1. T F According to force field analysis, the most effective way to bring about change is to increase the driving forces.

2. T F OD consultants should rely on coercive and possibly legitimate power in their relationship with clients.

3. T F The organizational culture content in most companies can be classified into one of five categories (club, fortress, etc.)

4. T F An organization's culture tends to weaken during periods of high turnover or rapid hiring.

5. T F The contingent workforce is growing mainly because employers want a more flexible workforce.

6. T F Realistic job previews reduce employee turnover and increase organizational commitment by helping applicants develop more accurate pre-employment expectations.

7. T F Departmentation shapes informal communication patterns among employees.

8. T F Most team-based structures organize teams around functional departments rather than work processes.

Multiple-Choice

1. As CEO of a mid-sized Canadian trust company, you believe that the company needs to introduce certain innovative bank practices to remain competitive. However, you believe the marketing employees who normally recommend these ideas will resist this idea because they didn't think of it. Which of the following strategies would best minimize resistance due to saving face? (a) communication; (b) employee involvement; (c) stress management; (d) negotiation; (e) coercion.

2. ABC Corp. wants to bring about change through a task force composed of people from most levels of the organization. The group will follow the action research model and operate alongside the formal hierarchy. This organization process is known as: (a) increasing the driving forces; (b) sensitivity training; (c) appreciative inquiry; (d) process consultation; (e) parallel learning structure.

3. A weak corporate culture: (a) should be avoided at all costs; (b) is beneficial when the firm's dominant values are inconsistent with the external environment; (c) is beneficial when there are no counterculural values in the organization; (d) should be avoided when the firm's dominant values are inconsistent with the external environment; (e) is neither beneficial nor harmful to an organization's success.

4. When employees at the acquired company willingly embrace the cultural values of the acquiring organization, the merger strategy is known as: (a) deculturation; (b) separation; (c) integration; (d) countercultural; (e) assimilation.

5. Lateral career development occurs when: (a) all employees at the same level of the organization follow the same career path; (b) employees work for other organizations to receive the career that they want; (c) employees follow through exploration, establishment, and other career stages within the same job; (d) employees work in different jobs across the organization rather than moving through the hierarchy; (e) employees move into different anchors throughout their working lives rather than keep the same career anchor.

6. Organizational socialization is best described as a process of: (a) learning and change; (b) replacing the psychological contract with a more formal employment contract; (c) power and politics; (d) moving from exploration to midcareer transition; (e) moving to a new organization.

7. Low formalization and high decentralization are characteristics of: (a) all organizations; (b) older organizations with strict government regulations; (c) organizations in crisis; (d) mechanistic organizational structures; (e) none of the above.

8. CanCorp Ltd. has seven departments: production, marketing, engineering, sales, accounting, human resources, and legal. Which form of department does this organization have? (a) functional; (b) divisional; (c) matrix; (d) virtual; (e) team-based.

Written-Answer Questions

1. Tuff Bolt, Inc., a manufacturer of nails and other construction materials, has a strong corporate culture that emphasizes high individual achievement and high individual rewards for successful employees. The CEO of Tuff Bolt recently read that companies with strong cultures are not much more effective than companies with weak cultures. The CEO has called you to find out why a strong culture isn't always good. Answer the CEO's question with three explanations.

2. Describe the three pure types of divisional structure and identify the most important factor to consider when choosing which of these to organize around.

Additional Cases

Case 1 Arctic Mining Consultants

Case 2 A Window on Life

Case 3 Cantron Ltd.

Case 4 Jersey Dairies Ltd.

Case 5 Pamela Jones, Former Banker

Case 6 Perfect Pizzeria

Case 7 Treetop Forest Products Ltd.

Case 8 Western Agencies Ltd.

— Case 1 —

Arctic Mining Consultants*

Tom Parker enjoyed working outdoors. At various times in the past, he worked as a ranch hand, high steel rigger, headstone installer, prospector, and geological field technician. Now 43, Parker is a geological field technician and field coordinator with Arctic Mining Consultants. He has specialized knowledge and experience in all nontechnical aspects of mineral exploration, including claim staking, line cutting and grid installation, soil sampling, prospecting, and trenching. He is responsible for hiring, training, and supervising field assistants for all of Arctic Mining Consultants' programs. Field assistants are paid a fairly low daily wage (no matter how long they work, which may be up to 12 hours or more) and are provided meals and accommodation. Many of the programs are operated by a project manager who reports to Parker.

Parker sometimes acts as a project manager, as he did on a job that involved staking 15 claims near Eagle Lake, British Columbia. He selected John Talbot, Greg Boyce, and Brian Millar, all of whom had previously worked with him, as the field assistants. To stake a claim, the project team marks a line with flagging tape and blazes along the perimeter of the claim, cutting a claim post every 500 metres (called a "length"). The 15 claims would require almost 100 kilometres of line in total. Parker had budgeted seven days (plus mobilization and demobilization) to complete the job. This meant that each of the four stakers (Parker, Talbot, Boyce, and Millar) would have to complete a little over seven "lengths" each day. The following is a chronology of the project.

Day 1 The Arctic Mining Consultants crew assembled in the morning and drove to Eagle Lake, from where they were flown by helicopter to the claim site. On arrival, they set up tents at the edge of the area to be staked, and agreed on a rota for cooking duties. After supper, they pulled out the maps and discussed the job — how long it would take, the order in which the areas were to be staked, possible helicopter landing spots, and areas that might be more difficult to stake.

Parker pointed out that with only a week to complete the job, everyone would have to average seven and a half lengths per day. "I know that is a lot," he said, "but you've all staked claims before and I'm confident that each of you is capable of it. And it's only for a week. If we get the job done in time, there's a $100 bonus for each man." Two hours later, Parker and his crew members had developed what seemed to be a workable plan.

Day 2 Millar completed six lengths, Boyce six lengths, Talbot eight, and Parker eight. Parker was not pleased with Millar's or Boyce's production. However, he didn't make an issue of it, thinking that they would develop their "rhythm" quickly.

Day 3 Millar completed five and a half lengths, Boyce four, and Talbot seven. Parker, who was nearly twice as old as the other three, completed eight lengths. He also had enough time remaining to walk over and check the quality of stakes that Millar and Boyce had completed, then walk back to his own area for helicopter pick-up back to the tent site.

That night Parker exploded with anger. "I thought I told you that I wanted seven and a half lengths a day!" he shouted at Boyce and Millar. Boyce said that he was slowed down by unusually thick underbrush in his assigned area. Millar said that he had done his best and would try to pick up the pace. Parker did not mention that he had inspected their work. He explained that as far as he was concerned, the field assistants were supposed to finish their assigned area for the day, no matter what.

Talbot, who was sharing a tent with Parker, talked to him later. "I think that you're being a bit hard on them, you know. I know that it has been more by luck than anything else that I've been able to do my quota. Yesterday I only had five lengths done after the first seven hours and there was only an hour before I was supposed to be picked up. Then I hit a patch of really open bush, and was able to do three lengths in 70 minutes. Why don't I take Millar's area tomorrow and he can have mine? Maybe that will help."

"Conditions are the same in all of the areas," replied Parker, rejecting Talbot's suggestion. "Millar just has to try harder."

Day 4   Millar did seven lengths and Boyce completed six and a half. When they reported their production that evening, Parker grunted uncommunicatively. Parker and Talbot did eight lengths each.

Day 5   Millar completed six lengths, Boyce six, Talbot seven and a half, and Parker eight. Once again Parker blew up, but he concentrated his diatribe on Millar. "Why don't you do what you say you are going to do? You know that you have to do seven and a half lengths a day. We went over that when we first got here, so why don't you do it? If you aren't willing to do the job then you never should have taken it in the first place!"

Millar replied by saying that he was doing his best, that he hadn't even stopped for lunch, and that he didn't know how he could possibly do any better. Parker launched into him again: "You have got to work harder! If you put enough effort into it, you will get the area done!"

Later Millar commented to Boyce, "I hate getting dumped on all the time! I'd quit if it didn't mean that I'd have to walk 50 miles to the highway. And besides, I need the bonus money. Why doesn't he pick on you? You don't get any more done than me; in fact, you usually get less done. Maybe if you did a bit more he wouldn't be so bothered about me."

"I only work as hard as I have to," Boyce replied.

Day 6   Millar raced through breakfast, was the first one to be dropped off by the helicopter, and arranged to be the last one picked up. That evening the production figures were Millar eight and a quarter lengths, Boyce seven, and Talbot and Parker eight each. Parker remained silent when the field assistants reported their performance for the day.

Day 7   Millar was again the first out and last in. That night, he collapsed in an exhausted heap at the table, too tired to eat. After a few moments, he announced in an abject tone, "Six lengths. I worked like a dog all day and I only got a lousy six lengths!" Boyce completed five lengths, Talbot seven, and Parker seven and a quarter.

Parker was furious. "That means we have to do a total of 34 lengths tomorrow if we are to finish this job on time!" With his eyes directed at Millar, he added: "Why is it that you never finish the job? Don't you realize that you are part of a team, and that you are letting the rest of the team down? I've been checking your lines and you're doing too much blazing and wasting too much time making picture-perfect claim posts! If you worked smarter, you'd get a lot more done!"

Day 8   Parker cooked breakfast in the dark. The helicopter dropoffs began as soon as morning light appeared on the horizon. Parker instructed each assistant to complete eight lengths and, if they finished early, to help the others. Parker said that he would finish the other ten lengths. Helicopter pickups were arranged for one hour before dark.

By noon, after working as hard as he could, Millar had only completed three lengths. "Why bother," he thought to himself, "I'll never be able to do another five lengths before the helicopter comes, and I'll catch the same amount of abuse from Parker for doing six lengths as for seven and a half." So he sat down and had lunch and a rest. "Boyce won't finish his eight lengths either, so even if I did finish mine, I still wouldn't get the bonus. At least I'll get one more day's pay this way."

That night, Parker was livid when Millar reported that he had completed five and a half lengths. Parker had done ten and a quarter lengths, and Talbot had completed eight. Boyce proudly announced that he'd finished seven and a half lengths, but sheepishly added that Talbot had helped him with some of it. All that remained were the two and a half lengths that Millar had not completed.

The job was finished the next morning and the crew demobilized. Millar never worked for Arctic Mining Consultants again, despite being offered work several times by Parker. Boyce sometimes does staking for Arctic, and Talbot works full-time with the company.

— Case 2 —

A Window on Life*

For Gilles LaCroix, there is nothing quite as beautiful as a handcrafted wood-framed window. LaCroix's passion for windows goes back to his youth in St. Jean, Quebec, where he was taught how to make residential windows by an elderly carpenter. He learned about the characteristics of good wood, the best tools to use, and how to choose the best glass from local suppliers. LaCroix apprenticed with the carpenter in his small workshop and, when the carpenter retired, was given the opportunity to operate the business himself.

LaCroix hired his own apprentice as he built up business in the local area. His small operation soon expanded as the quality of windows built by LaCroix Industries Ltd. became better known. Within eight years, the company employed nearly 25 people and the business had moved to larger facilities to accommodate the increased demand from southern Quebec. In these early years, LaCroix spent most of his time in the production shop, teaching new apprentices the unique skills that he had mastered and applauding the journeymen for their accomplishments. He would constantly repeat the point that LaCroix products had to be of the highest quality because they gave families a "window on life."

After 15 years, LaCroix Industries employed over 200 people. A profit-sharing program was introduced to give employees a financial reward for their contribution to the organization's success. Due to the company's expansion, headquarters had to be moved to another area of town, but the founder never lost touch with the workforce. Although new apprentices were now taught entirely by the master carpenters and other craftspeople, LaCroix would still chat with plant and office employees several times each week.

When a second work shift was added, LaCroix would show up during the evening break with coffee and boxes of doughnuts and discuss how the business was doing and how it became so successful through quality work. Production employees enjoyed the times when he would gather them together to announce new contracts with developers from Montreal and Toronto. After each announcement, LaCroix would thank everyone for making the business a success. They knew that LaCroix quality had become a standard of excellence in window manufacturing across Canada.

It seemed that almost every time he visited, LaCroix would repeat the now well-known phrase that LaCroix products had to be of the highest quality because they provided a window on life to so many families. Employees never grew tired of hearing this from the company founder. However, it gained extra meaning when LaCroix began posting photos of families looking through LaCroix windows. At first, LaCroix would personally visit developers and homeowners with a camera in hand. Later, as the "window on life" photos became known by developers and customers, people would send in photos of their own families looking through elegant front windows made by LaCroix Industries. The company's marketing staff began using this idea, as well as LaCroix's famous phrase, in their advertising. After one such marketing campaign, hundreds of photos were sent in by satisfied customers. Production and office employees took time after work to write personal letters of thanks to those who had submitted photos.

As the company's age reached the quarter-century mark, LaCroix, now in his mid-fifties, realized that the organization's success and survival depended on expansion into the United States. After consulting with employees, LaCroix made the difficult decision to sell a majority share to Build-All Products, Inc., a conglomerate with international marketing expertise in building products. As part of the agreement, Build-All brought in a vice-president to oversee production operations while LaCroix spent more time meeting with developers around North America. LaCroix would return to the plant and office at every opportunity, but often this would be only once a month.

Rather than visiting the production plant, Jan Vlodoski, the new production vice-president, would rarely leave his office in the company's downtown headquarters. Instead, production orders were sent to supervisors by memorandum. Although product quality had been a priority throughout the company's history, less attention had been paid to inventory controls. Vlodoski introduced strict inventory guidelines and outlined procedures on using supplies for each shift. Goals were established for supervisors to meet specific inventory targets. Whereas previously employees could have tossed out several pieces of warped wood, they would now have to justify this action, usually in writing.

Vlodoski also announced new procedures for purchasing production supplies. LaCroix Industries had highly trained purchasing staff who worked closely with senior craftspeople when selecting suppliers, but Vlodoski wanted to bring in Build-All's procedures. The new purchasing methods removed production leaders from the decision process and, in some cases, resulted in trade-offs that LaCroix's employees would not have made earlier. A few employees quit during this time, saying that they did not feel comfortable about producing a window that would not stand the test of time. However, unemployment was high in St. Jean, so most staff members remained with the company.

After one year, inventory expenses decreased by approximately 10 percent, but the number of defective windows returned by developers and wholesalers had increased markedly. Plant employees knew that the number of defective windows would increase, as they used somewhat lower-quality materials to reduce inventory costs. However, they heard almost no news about the seriousness of the problem until Vlodoski sent a memo to all production staff saying that quality must be maintained. During the latter part of the first year under Vlodoski, a few employees had the opportunity to personally ask LaCroix about the changes and express their concerns. LaCroix apologized, saying that due to his travels to new regions, he had not heard about the problems, and that he would look into the matter.

Exactly 18 months after Build-All had become majority shareholder of LaCroix Industries, LaCroix called together five of the original staff in the plant. The company founder looked pale and shaken as he said that Build-All's actions were inconsistent with his vision of the company and, for the first time in his career, he did not know what to do. Build-All was not pleased with the arrangement either. Although LaCroix windows still enjoyed a healthy market share and were competitive for the value, the company did not quite provide the minimum 18 percent return on equity that the conglomerate expected. LaCroix asked his long-time companions for advice.

— Case 3 —

Cantron Ltd.*

Cantron Ltd., a Canadian manufacturer of centralized vacuum systems, was facing severe cash-flow problems due to increasing demand for its products and rapid expansion of production facilities. Steve Heinrich, Cantron's founder and majority shareholder, flew to Germany to meet with management of Rohrtech GMB to discuss the German company's willingness to become majority shareholder of Cantron in exchange for an infusion of much-needed cash. A deal was struck whereby Rohrtech would become majority shareholder while Heinrich would remain as Cantron's president and general manager. One of Rohrtech's senior executives would become the chairperson of Cantron's board of directors, and Rohrtech would appoint two other board members.

This relationship worked well until Rohrtech was acquired by a European conglomerate a couple of years later and the new owner wanted more precise financial information and controls placed on its holdings, including Cantron. Heinrich resented this imposition and refused to provide the necessary information. Within another two years, relations between Rohrtech and Cantron had soured to the point where Heinrich refused to let Rohrtech representatives into the Cantron plant. He also instituted legal proceedings to regain control of the company.

According to Canadian law, any party who possesses over two-thirds of a company's shares may force the others to sell their shares. Heinrich owned 29 percent of Cantron's shares, whereas Rohrtech owned 56 percent. The remaining 15 percent of Cantron shares were held by Jean Parrot, Cantron's head of operations in Quebec. Parrot was a long-time manager at Cantron and remained on the side-lines throughout most of the legal battle between Rohrtech and Heinrich. However, Parrot finally agreed to sell his shares to Rohrtech, thereby legally forcing Heinrich to give up his shares. When Heinrich's bid for control failed, Rohrtech purchased all remaining shares, and Cantron's board of directors (now dominated by Rohrtech) dismissed Heinrich as president and general manager a month later. The board immediately appointed Parrot as Cantron's new president.

Searching for a New General Manager

Several months before Heinrich's departure, the chairman of Cantron's board of directors received instructions from Rohrtech to hire a management consulting firm in Toronto to identify possible out-side candidates for the position of general manager at Cantron. The successful candidate would be hired after the conflict with Heinrich had ended (presum-ably with Heinrich's departure). The general man-ager would report to the president (the person eventually replacing Heinrich) and would be responsible for day-to-day management of the com-pany. Rohrtech's management correctly believed that most of Cantron's current managers were loyal to Heinrich and, by hiring an outsider, the German firm would gain more inside control over its Canadian subsidiary.

More than 50 candidates applied for the general manager position, and three candidates were inter-viewed by Cantron's chairman and another Rohrtech representative. One of these candidates, Kurt Devine, was vice-president of sales at an industrial packaging firm in Toronto and, at 52 years old, was looking for one more career challenge before retirement. The Rohrtech representatives explained the current situ-ation and said that they were offering stable employ-ment after the problem with Heinrich was resolved so that the general manager could help settle Cantron's problems. When Devine expressed his concern about rivalry with internal candidates, the senior Rohrtech manager stated: "We have a book-keeper, but he is not our choice. The sales manager is capable, but he is located in New York and doesn't want to move to Canada."

One week after Heinrich's dismissal and the appointment of Parrot as president, Cantron's chair-man invited Devine to a meeting at a posh Toronto hotel attended by the chairman, another Rohrtech manager on Cantron's board of directors, and Parrot. The chairman explained the recent events at Cantron and formally invited Devine to accept the position of vice-president and general manager of the company. After discussing salary and details about job duties, Devine asked the others whether he had their support as well as the support of Cantron's employees. The two Rohrtech representa-tives said yes, while Parrot remained silent. When the chairman left the room to get a bottle of wine to toast the new general manager, Devine asked Parrot how long he had known about the decision to hire him. Parrot replied, "Just last week when I became president. I was surprised . . . I don't think I would have hired you."

Confrontation with Tom O'Grady

Devine began work at Cantron in early November and, within a few weeks, noticed that the president and two other Cantron managers were not giving him the support he needed to accomplish his work. For example, Parrot would call the salespeople almost daily, yet rarely speak with Devine unless the general manager approached him first. The vice-president of sales acted cautiously toward Devine. But it was Tom O'Grady, the vice-president of finance and administration, who seemed to resent Devine's presence the most. O'Grady had been pro-moted from the position of controller in October and now held the highest rank at Cantron below Devine. After Heinrich was dismissed, Cantron's board of directors had placed O'Grady in charge of day-to-day operations until Devine took over.

Devine depended on O'Grady for information because O'Grady had more knowledge than anyone else about many aspects of the business outside of Quebec. However, O'Grady provided incomplete information on many occasions and would com-pletely refuse to educate the general manager on some matters. O'Grady was also quick to criticize many of Devine's decisions and made indirect state-ments to Devine about his inappropriateness as a general manager. He also mentioned how he and other Cantron managers didn't want the German company (Rohrtech) to interfere with their company.

Devine would later learn about other things O'Grady had said and done to undermine his posi-tion. For example, O'Grady actively spoke to office staff and other managers about the problems with

Devine, and encouraged them to tell the president about their concerns. Devine overhead O'Grady telling another manager that Devine's memoranda were a "complete joke" and that "Devine didn't know what he was talking about." On one occasion, O'Grady let Devine send out incorrect information about the organization's structure even though O'Grady knew that it was incorrect "just to prove what an idiot Rohrtech had hired."

Just six weeks after joining Cantron, Devine confronted O'Grady with his concerns. O'Grady was candid with the general manager, saying that everyone felt that Devine was a "plant" by Rohrtech and was trying to turn Cantron into a branch office of the German company. He said that some employees would quit if Devine did not leave, because they wanted Cantron to maintain its independence from Rohrtech. In a later meeting with Devine and Parrot, O'Grady repeated these points and added that Devine's management style was not appropriate for Cantron. Devine responded that he had not received any support from Cantron since the day he had arrived, even though Rohrtech had sent explicit directions to Parrot and other Cantron managers that he was to have complete support in managing the company's daily operations. Parrot told the two men that they should work together and that, of course, Devine was the more senior person.

Decision by Cantron's Board of Directors
As a member of Cantron's board of directors, Parrot made sure that the matter of Devine was dis-

cussed and that the board invite O'Grady to repeat his story. Based on this testimony, the board decided to remove Devine from the general manager job and give him a special project instead. O'Grady was immediately named acting general manager. The chairman and other Rohrtech representatives on Cantron's board were disappointed that events did not unfold as they had hoped, but they agreed to remove Devine rather than face the mass exodus of Cantron managers that Parrot and O'Grady had warned about.

Less than one year after his appointment, Devine attended a morning meeting of Cantron's board of directors to present his interim report on the special project. The board agreed to give Devine until mid-June to complete the project. However, the board recalled Devine into the boardroom in the afternoon and Parrot bluntly asked Devine why he didn't turn in his resignation. Devine replied: "I can't think of a single reason why I should. I will not resign. I joined your company six months ago as a challenge. I have not been allowed to do my job. My decision to come here was based on support from Rohrtech and on a great product." The next day, Parrot came to Devine's office with a letter of dismissal signed by the chairman of Cantron's board of directors.

—— Case 4 ——

Jersey Dairies Ltd.*

Jersey Dairies Ltd. faced increasing competition that threatened its dominant market share in Eastern Ontario's "Golden Triangle." Senior management at the 300-employee dairy food processing company decided that the best way to maintain or increase market share was to take the plunge into total quality management (TQM). Jersey hired consultants to educate management and employees about the TQM process, and sent several managers

to TQM seminars. A steering team of managers and a few employees visited other TQM companies throughout North America.

To strengthen the company's TQM focus, Jersey president Tina Stavros created a new position called vice-president of quality, and hired James Alder into that position. Alder, who had previously worked as a TQM consultant at a major consulting firm, was enthusiastic about implementing a complete TQM program. One of Alder's first accomplishments was convincing management to give every employee in the organization several days of training in quality measurement (e.g., Pareto diagrams), structured problem solving, and related TQM practices. Jersey's largely unskilled workforce had difficulty learning this material, so the training took longer than expected and another round was required one year later.

Alder worked with production managers to form continuous improvement (CI) teams — groups of employees who looked for ways to cut costs, time, and space throughout the work process. Although Alder was enthusiastic about CI teams, most supervisors and employees were reluctant to get involved. Supervisors complained that the CI teams were "asking too many questions" about activities in their department. Less than one-quarter of the production areas formed CI teams because employees thought TQM was a fancy way for management to speed up the work. This view was reinforced by some of management's subsequent actions, such as setting higher production targets and requiring employees to complete the tasks of those who were absent from work.

To gain more support for TQM, Jersey president Tina Stavros spoke regularly to employees and supervisors about how TQM was their answer to beating the competition and saving jobs. Although these talks took her away from other duties, she wanted every employee to know that their primary objective was to improve customer service and production efficiency in the company. To encourage more involvement in the CI teams, Stavros and Alder warned employees that they must support the TQM program to save their jobs. To further emphasize this message, the company placed large signs throughout the company's production facilities that said, "Our Jobs Depend on Satisfied Customers" and "Total Quality: Our Competitive Advantage."

Alder and Stavros agreed that Jersey's suppliers must have a strong commitment toward the TQM philosophy, so Jersey's purchasing manager was told to get suppliers "on board" or find alternative sources. Unfortunately, the purchasing manager preferred a more collegial and passive involvement with suppliers, so he was replaced a few months later. The new purchasing manager informed suppliers that they should begin a TQM program immediately because Jersey would negotiate for lower prices in the next contracts and would evaluate their bids partly based on their TQM programs.

Twenty months after Jersey Dairies began its TQM journey, Tina Stavros accepted a lucrative job offer from a large food products company in the United States. Jersey Dairies promoted its vice-president of finance, Thomas Cheun, to the president's job. The board of directors was concerned about Jersey's falling profits over the previous couple of years and wanted Cheun to strengthen the bottom line. Although some CI teams did find cost savings, these were mostly offset by higher expenses. The company had nearly tripled its training budget and had significantly higher paid-time-off costs as employees took these courses. A considerable sum was spent on customer surveys and focus groups. Employee turnover was higher, mainly due to dissatisfaction with the TQM program. Just before Stavros left the company, she received word that several employees had contacted the Commercial Food Workers Union about organizing Jersey's nonunion production workforce.

A group of suppliers asked for a confidential meeting in which they told Cheun to reconsider the TQM demands on them. They complained that their long-term relationships with Jersey were being damaged and that other dairies were being more realistic about price, quality, and delivery requirements. Two major suppliers bluntly stated that they might decide to end their contracts with Jersey rather than agree to Jersey's demands.

Almost two years after Jersey Dairies began TQM, Thomas Cheun announced that James Alder was leaving Jersey Dairies, that the position of vice-president of quality would no longer exist, and that the company would end several TQM initiatives begun over the previous two years. Instead, Jersey Dairies Ltd. would use better marketing strategies and introduce new technologies to improve its competitive position in the marketplace.

Case 5

Pamela Jones, Former Banker

Pamela Jones enjoyed banking. She had taken a battery of personal aptitude and interest tests that suggested she might like and do well in either banking or librarianship. Because the job market for librarians was poor, she applied for employment with a large chartered bank, the Bank of Winnipeg (B. of W.), and was quickly accepted.

Her early experiences in banking were almost always challenging and rewarding. She was enrolled in the bank's management development program because of her education (a B.A. in languages and some postgraduate training in business administration), her previous job experience, and her obvious intelligence and drive.

During her first year in the training program, Pamela attended classes on banking procedures and policies, and worked her way through a series of low-level positions in her branch. She was repeatedly told by her manager that her work was above average. Similarly, the training officer who worked out of the main office and coordinated the development of junior officers in the program frequently told Pamela that she was "among the best three" of her cohort of 20 trainees.

Although she worked hard and frequently encountered discrimination from senior bank personnel (as well as customers) because of her sex, Pamela developed a deep-seated attachment to banking in general, and to her bank and branch in particular. She was proud to be a banker and proud to be a member of the Bank of Winnipeg.

After one year in the management development program, however, Pamela found she was not learning anything new about banking or the B. of W. She was shuffled from one job to another at her own branch, cycling back over many positions several times to help meet temporary problems caused by absences, overloads, and turnover. Turnover — a rampant problem in banking — amazed Pamela. She couldn't understand, for many months, why so many people started careers "in the service" of banking, only to leave after one or two years.

After her first year, the repeated promises of moving into her own position at another branch started to sound hollow to Pamela. The training officer claimed that there were no openings suitable for her at other branches. On two occasions when openings did occur, the manager of each of the branches in question rejected Pamela, sight unseen, presumably because she hadn't been in banking long enough.

Pamela was not the only unhappy person at her branch. Her immediate supervisor, George Burns, complained that, because of the bank's economy drive, vacated customer service positions were left unfilled. As branch accountant, Burns was responsible for day-to-day customer service. As a result, he was unable to perform the duties of his own job. The manager told Burns several times that customer service was critical, but Burns would have to improve his performance on his own job. Eventually, George Burns left the bank to work for a trust company, earning $70 a month more for work similar to the work he had been performing at the B. of W. This left Pamela in the position of having to supervise the same tellers who had trained her only a few months earlier. Pamela was amazed at all the mistakes the tellers made, but found it difficult to do much to correct their poor work habits. All disciplinary procedures had to be administered with the approval of head office.

After several calls to her training officer, Pamela was finally transferred to her first "real" position in her own branch. Still keen and dedicated, Pamela would soon lose her enthusiasm.

At her new branch, Pamela was made "assistant accountant." Her duties included the supervision of the seven tellers, some customer service, and a great deal of paperwork. The same economy drive that she had witnessed at her training branch resulted in the failure to replace customer service personnel. Pamela was expected to pick up the slack at the front desk, neglecting her own work. Her tellers seldom balanced their own cash, so Pamela stayed late almost every night to find their errors. To save on overtime, the manager sent the tellers home while Pamela stayed late, first to correct the tellers' imbalances, then to finish her own paperwork. He told Pamela that as an officer of the bank, she was expected to stay until the work of her subordinates, and her own work, was satisfactorily completed. Pamela realized that most of her counterparts in other B. of W. branches were willing to give this sort of dedication; therefore, she rationalized, so should she. This situation lasted six months with little sign of change in sight.

One day, Pamela learned from a phone conversation with a friend at another branch that she would be transferred to Hope, British Columbia, to fill an opening that had arisen. Pamela's husband was a professional, employed by a large corporation in Vancouver. His company did not have an office in Hope; moreover, his training was very specialized, so that he could probably find employment only in large cities anyway.

Accepting transfers was expected of junior officers who wanted to get ahead. Pamela inquired at head office and learned that the rumour was true. Her training officer told her, however, that Pamela could decline the transfer if she wished, but he couldn't say how soon her next promotion opportunity would come along.

Depressed, annoyed, disappointed, and frustrated, Pamela quit the bank.

Source: C. C. Pinder, *Work Motivation* (Glenview, Ill.: Scott, Foresman, 1984), pp. 317–18. Used with permission of the author.

--- Case 6 ---

Perfect Pizzeria

Perfect Pizzeria in Southville, deep in southern Illinois, is the second-largest franchise of the chain in the United States. The headquarters is located in Phoenix, Arizona. Although the business is prospering, it has employee and managerial problems.

Each operation has one manager, an assistant manager, and from two to five night managers. The managers of each pizzeria work under an area supervisor. There are no systematic criteria for being a manager or becoming a manager trainee. The franchise has no formalized training period for the manager. No college education is required. The managers for whom the case observer worked during a four-year period were relatively young (ages 24 to 27), and only one had completed college. They came from the ranks of night managers, assistant managers, or both. The night managers were chosen for their ability to perform the duties of the regular employees. The assistant managers worked a two-hour shift during the luncheon period five days a week to gain knowledge about bookkeeping and management. Those becoming managers remained at that level unless they expressed interest in investing in the business.

The employees were mostly college students, with a few high school students performing the less challenging jobs. Because Perfect Pizzeria was located in an area with few job opportunities, it had a relatively easy task of filling its employee quotas. All the employees, with the exception of the manager, were employed part time. Consequently, they earned only the minimum wage.

The Perfect Pizzeria system is devised so that food and beverage costs and profits are set up according to a percentage. If the percentage of food unsold or damaged in any way is very low, the manager gets a bonus. If the percentage is high, the manager does not receive a bonus; rather, the manager receives only a normal salary.

There are many ways in which the percentage can fluctuate. Because the manager cannot be in the store 24 hours a day, some employees make up for their paycheques by helping themselves to the food. When a friend comes in to order a pizza, extra ingredients are put on the friend's pizza. Occasional nibbles by 18 to 20 employees throughout the day at the meal table also raise the percentage figure. An occasional bucket of sauce may be spilled or a pizza accidentally burned. Sometimes the wrong size of pizza may be made.

In the event of an employee mistake or a burned pizza by the oven person, the expense is supposed to come from the individual. Because of peer pressure, the night manager seldom writes up a bill for the erring employee. Instead, the establishment takes the loss and the error goes unnoticed until the end of the month when the inventory is taken. That's when the manager finds out that the percentage is high and that there will be no bonus.

In the present instance, the manager took retaliatory measures. Previously, each employee was entitled to a free pizza, salad, and all the soft drinks the person could drink for every 6 hours of work. The manager raised this figure from 6 to 12 hours of work. However, the employees had received these 6-hour benefits for a long time. Therefore, they simply took advantage of the situation whenever the manager or the assistant was not in the building. Although theoretically the night managers had complete control of the operation in the evenings, they did not command the respect that the manager or assistant manager did. That was because night managers received the same pay as the regular employees, could not reprimand other employees, and were basically the same age or sometimes even younger than the other employees.

Thus, apathy grew within the pizzeria. There seemed to be a further separation between the manager and his workers, who started out to be a closely knit group. The manager made no attempt to alleviate the problem because he felt it would iron itself out. Either the employees who were dissatisfied would quit or they would be content to put up with the new regulations. As it turned out, there was a rash of employee dismissals. The manager had no problem filling the vacancies with new workers, but the loss of key personnel was costly to the business.

With the large turnover, the manager found he had to spend more time in the building, supervising and sometimes taking the place of inexperienced workers. This was in direct violation of the franchise regulation, which stated that a manager would act as a supervisor and at no time take part in the actual food preparation. Employees were not placed under strict supervision with the manager working alongside them. The operation no longer worked smoothly because of differences between the remaining experienced workers and the manager concerning the way in which a particular function should be performed.

Within a two-month period, the manager was again free to go back to his office and leave his subordinates in charge of the entire operation. During this two-month period, in spite of the differences between experienced workers and the manager, the unsold/damaged food percentage had returned to the previous low level and the manager received a bonus each month. The manager felt that his problems had been resolved and that conditions would remain the same, since the new personnel had been properly trained.

It didn't take long for the new employees to become influenced by the other employees. Immediately after the manager had returned to his supervisory role, the unsold/damaged food percentage began to rise. This time the manager took a bolder step. He cut out any benefits that the employees had — no free pizzas, salads, or drinks. With the job market at an even lower ebb than usual, most employees were forced to stay. The appointment of a new area supervisor made it impossible for the manager to "work behind the counter," because the supervisor was centrally located in Southville.

The manager tried still another approach to alleviate the rising unsold/damaged food percentage problem and maintain his bonus. He placed a notice on the bulletin board, stating that if the percentage remained at a high level, a lie detector test would be given to all employees. All those found guilty of taking or purposely wasting food or drinks would be immediately terminated. This did not have the desired effect on the employees because they knew that if they were subjected to the test, all would be found guilty and the manager would have to dismiss all of them. This would leave him in a worse situation than ever.

Even before the following month's percentage was calculated, the manager knew it would be high. He had evidently received information from one of the night managers about the employees' feelings toward the notice. What he did not expect was that the percentage would reach an all-time high. That is the state of affairs at the present time.

Source: J. E. Dittrich and R. A. Zawacki, *People and Organizations* (Plano, Texas: Business Publications, 1981), pp. 126–28. Used by permission of McGraw-Hill/Irwin.

Case 7

Treetop Forest Products Ltd.*

Treetop Forest Products Ltd. is a sawmill operation located along the Fraser River near the British Columbia coast. The mill is owned by an international forest products company, but operates autonomously. It was built in 1979, and completely updated with new machinery in 1990. Treetop receives raw logs from the upper Fraser Valley area for cutting and planing into building-grade lumber, mostly 2-by-4 and 2-by-6 pieces of standard lengths. Higher-grade logs leave Treetop's sawmill department in their finished form and are sent directly to the packaging department. The remaining 40 percent of sawmill output are cuts from lower-grade logs, requiring further work by the planing department.

Treetop has 1 general manager, 16 supervisors and support staff, and 180 unionized employees. The unionized employees are paid an hourly rate specified in the collective agreement, whereas management and support staff are paid a monthly salary. The mill is divided into six operating departments: boom, sawmill, planer, packaging, shipping, and maintenance. The sawmill, boom, and packaging departments operate a morning shift starting at 6:00 a.m. and an afternoon shift starting at 2:00 p.m. Employees in these departments rotate shifts every two weeks. The planer and shipping departments operate only morning shifts. Maintenance employees work the night shift (starting at 10:00 p.m.).

Each department, except for packaging, has a supervisor on every work shift. The planer supervisor is responsible for the packaging department on the morning shift, and the sawmill supervisor is responsible for the packaging department on the afternoon shift. However, the packaging operation is housed in a separate building from the other departments, so supervisors seldom visit the packaging department. This is particularly true for the afternoon shift because the sawmill supervisor is the farthest distance from the packaging building.

Packaging Quality

Ninety percent of Treetop's product is sold on the international market through Westboard Co., a large marketing agency. Westboard represents all forest products mills owned by Treetop's parent

company as well as several other clients in the region. The market for building-grade lumber is very price competitive because there are numerous mills selling a relatively undifferentiated product. However, some differentiation does occur in product packaging and presentation. Buyers will look closely at the packaging when deciding whether to buy from Treetop or another mill.

To encourage its clients to package their products better, Westboard sponsors a monthly package quality award. The marketing agency samples and rates its clients' packages daily, and the sawmill with the highest score at the end of the month is awarded a plaque. Package quality is a combination of how the lumber is piled (e.g., defects turned in), where the bands and dunnage are placed, how neatly the stencil and seal are applied, the stencil's accuracy, and how neatly and tightly the plastic wrap is attached.

Treetop Forest Products won Westboard's packaging quality award several times over the past few years, and received high ratings in the months that it didn't win. However, the mill's ratings have started to decline over the past couple of years, and several clients have complained about the appearance of the finished product. A few large customers switched to competitors' lumber, saying that the decision was based on the substandard appearance of Treetop's packaging when it arrived in their lumber yard.

Bottleneck in Packaging

The planing and sawmilling departments have significantly increased productivity over the past couple of years. The sawmill operation recently set a new productivity record on a single day. The planer operation has increased productivity to the point where last year it reduced operations to just one (rather than two) shifts per day. These productivity improvements are due to better operator training, fewer machine breakdowns, and better selection of raw logs. (Sawmill cuts from high-quality logs usually do not require planing work.)

Productivity levels in the boom, shipping, and maintenance departments have remained constant. However, the packaging department has recorded decreasing productivity over the past couple of years, with the result that a large backlog of finished product is typically stockpiled outside the packaging building. The morning shift of the packaging department is unable to keep up with the combined production of the sawmill and planer departments, so the unpackaged output is left for the afternoon shift. Unfortunately, the afternoon shift packages even less product than the morning shift, so the backlog continues to build. The backlog adds to Treetop's inventory costs and increases the risk of damaged stock.

Treetop has added Saturday overtime shifts as well as extra hours before and after the regular shifts for the packaging department employees to process this backlog. Last month, the packaging department employed 10 percent of the workforce but accounted for 85 percent of the overtime. This is frustrating to Treetop's management because time and motion studies recently confirmed that the packaging department is capable of processing all of the daily sawmill and planer production without overtime. Moreover, with employees earning one and a half or two times their regular pay on overtime, Treetop's cost competitiveness suffers.

Employees and supervisors at Treetop are aware that people in the packaging department tend to extend lunch by 10 minutes and coffee breaks by 5 minutes. They also typically leave work a few minutes before the end of shift. This abuse has worsened recently, particularly on the afternoon shift. Employees who are temporarily assigned to the packaging department also seem to participate in this time loss pattern after a few days. Although they are punctual and productive in other departments, these temporary employees soon adopt the packaging crew's informal schedule when assigned to that department.

Case 8

Western Agencies Ltd.*

Western Agencies Ltd. is a manufacturers' agent representing Stanfields, McGregors, and several other men's fashion manufacturers in Western Canada and the Pacific Northwest of the United States. Jack Arthurs began his employment at Western as a warehouse worker in 1962. In 1965, he became a sales representative and was given responsibility for the company's business in the interior region of British Columbia. In 1973, he was transferred back to Vancouver and assigned several large accounts, including all Eaton's stores in the Lower Mainland.

Over the years, Arthurs bought shares in the company and, by 1979, held nearly one-third of the company's issued nonvoting shares. He also enjoyed a special status with the company founder and president, Mr. A. B. Jackson. Arthurs was generally considered Jackson's "number 1 man" and the president frequently sought Arthurs's ideas on various company policies and practices.

In 1980, the senior Mr. Jackson retired as president of Western Agencies and his son, C. D. Jackson, became president. C. D. Jackson was seven years younger than Arthurs and had begun his career in the warehouse under Arthurs's direct supervision. Arthurs had no illusions of becoming president of Western, saying that he had neither the education nor the skills for the job. However, he did expect to continue his special position as the top salesperson in the company, although this was not directly discussed with the new president.

Until 1987, Arthurs had an unblemished performance record as a sales representative. He had built up numerous accounts and was able to service these clients effectively. But Arthurs's performance began to change for the worse when Eaton's changed its buying procedures and hired a new buyer for Western Canada. Arthurs disliked Eaton's new procedures and openly complained to the retailer's new buyer and to her superiors. The

Eaton's buyer resented Arthurs's behaviour and finally asked her boss to call Western Agencies to have Arthurs replaced. The Eaton's manager advised Jackson of the problem and suggested that another salesperson should be assigned to the Eaton's account. Jackson was aware of the conflict and had advised Arthurs a few months earlier that he should be more cooperative with the Eaton's buyer. Following the formal complaint, Jackson assigned another salesperson to Eaton's and gave Arthurs the Hudson's Bay account in exchange. Jackson did not mention the formal complaint from Eaton's and, in fact, Arthurs believed that the account switch was due to an internal reorganization for the benefit of other salespeople employed at Western Agencies Ltd.

At about this time, several employees noticed that Arthurs was developing a negative attitude toward his clients and Jackson. He was increasingly irritable and rude to customers, and was making derogatory comments to Jackson. Arthurs even advised some of the younger employees that they should leave Western Agencies Ltd. and get into a sensible business. A phenomenon known as "pulling an Arthurs" became a topic of discussion around the office, whereby Arthurs would leave the office to go home midafternoon after announcing that he had had enough. Co-workers also noticed that Arthurs was becoming increasingly forgetful. He was often unable to remember stock numbers, colour codes, product lines, packaging modes, and other information essential for serving clients efficiently and completing orders accurately. These problems were subtle in 1987, but became quite pronounced and embarrassing over the next three years.

In May 1989, Arthurs and Jackson had a conflict relating to the purchase of a new company car. According to Jackson, Arthurs presented him with a quotation for a car which, in Jackson's view, included $2,500 in unnecessary options. Jackson informed Arthurs of his concerns and instructed him to find a car worth $13,000 instead of $16,000. Jackson then left town on business and when he returned was distressed to find that Arthurs had made his proposed car purchase with almost all of the unnecessary options. Jackson issued the cheque to pay for the car, but also included a note to Arthurs saying that he had lost confidence in the

sales representative. It was about this time that Jackson contemplated firing Arthurs, but decided instead to be a "nice guy" and overlook the matter.

At the end of 1989, Jackson decided to reassign the North Vancouver independent accounts from Arthurs to another Western Agencies salesperson because the existing accounts had shown minimal growth and no new accounts were being added. Arthurs acknowledged that he had no time to find new accounts, but he denied Jackson's allegation that he was inadequately servicing the existing retailers in that area. At least one retailer later stated that Arthurs serviced his account well. Moreover, the salesperson assigned this territory added only a couple new accounts over the next two years.

In early 1990, the vice-president of marketing for Fields Stores called Jackson to say that Arthurs was not providing satisfactory service and that action should be taken if Western wanted to keep the Fields account. Arthurs had handled the Fields account for four or five years and there had been no problems until a new Fields buyer arrived. The new buyer complained that Arthurs was not providing sufficient promotional advice and assistance. She also expected Arthurs to take inventory counts, a practice that Arthurs resented and did not feel was properly part of his job. This was not the only retailer who expected Arthurs to count inventory, but Arthurs let them, as well as Jackson, know that he was an account builder, not an inventory stock counter. Eventually, the Fields buyer did not want to deal with Arthurs at all. In March 1990, matters were brought to a head when the Fields buyer and Arthurs had a major disagreement and Arthurs was not allowed back into any Fields stores. At this point, Jackson personally took over the Fields account and sales volume doubled within a few months.

A few months later, Western Agencies suffered several embarrassments over Arthurs's mishandling of the Work Wear World account. Arthurs had landed the Work Wear account a few years earlier when it was a small retailer with only two stores, but the company had subsequently grown into a regional chain of 10 stores. Problems began when Arthurs persuaded the Work Wear buyer to purchase a new line of stock by promising a manufacturer's allowance on an older line of goods. Arthurs had no authority to do this and, when the manufacturer refused to provide the allowance, Jackson had to personally explain that the allowance promise could not be honoured.

In late 1990, Arthurs mistakenly tripled a stock order for three of Work Wear's stores. This error was discovered when the second shipment arrived, and Jackson instructed Arthurs to take immediate steps to cancel the third order. Arthurs failed to do so and Work Wear wound up with three times the inventory it had ordered. Work Wear's buyer subsequently gave Jackson the dis-tinct impression that he should remove Arthurs from the account or risk losing Work Wear's business altogether.

For Jackson, Work Wear World's complaint was the last straw. In the spring of 1991, based on the series of incidents since 1987, Arthurs was dismissed from his job at Western Agencies Ltd.

---

*© Copyright 1991. Steven L. McShane. This case is based on actual events described in a Canadian court case. Only the dates and names of the main parties have been changed.

Theory Building and the Scientific Method

Theory A general set of propositions that describes interrelationships among several concepts.

People need to make sense of their world, so they form theories about the way the world operates. A **theory** is a general set of propositions that describes interrelationships among several concepts. We form theories for the purpose of predicting and explaining the world around us.[1] What does a good theory look like? First, it should be stated as clearly and simply as possible so that the concepts can be measured and there is no ambiguity regarding the theory's propositions. Second, the elements of the theory must be logically consistent with each other, because we cannot test anything that doesn't make sense. Finally, a good theory provides value to society; it helps people understand their world better than without the theory.[2]

Theory building is a continuous process that typically includes the inductive and deductive stages shown in Exhibit A.1.[3] The inductive stage draws on personal experience to form a preliminary theory, whereas the deductive stage uses the scientific method to test the theory.

The inductive stage of theory building involves observing the world around us, identifying a pattern of relationships, and then forming a theory from these personal observations. For example, you might casually notice that new employees want their supervisor to give direction, whereas this leadership style irritates long-service employees. From these observations, you form a theory about the effectiveness of directive leadership. (See Chapter 14 for a discussion of this leadership style.)

Theory Testing: The Deductive Process

Hypotheses Statements making empirically testable declarations that certain variables and their corresponding measures are related in a specific way proposed by a particular theory.

Once a theory has been formed, we shift into the deductive stage of theory building. This process includes forming hypotheses, defining and measuring constructs, and testing hypotheses (see Exhibit A.1). **Hypotheses** make empirically testable declarations that certain variables and their corresponding measures are related in a specific way proposed by the theory. For instance, to find support for the directive leadership theory described earlier, we need to form and then test a specific hypothesis from that theory. One such hypothesis might be: "New employees are more satisfied with supervisors who exhibit a directive rather than nondirective leadership style." Hypotheses are indispensable tools of scientific research because they provide the vital link between the theory and empirical verification.

Defining and measuring constructs

Hypotheses are testable only if we can define and then form measurable indicators of the concepts stated in those hypotheses. Consider the hypothesis in the previous paragraph about new employees and directive leadership. To test this hypothesis, we first need to define the concepts, such as "new employees," "directive leadership," and "supervisor." These are known as **constructs** because they are abstract ideas constructed by the researcher that can be linked to observable information. Organizational behaviour scholars developed the construct called *directive leadership* to help them understand the different effects that leaders have over followers. We can't directly see, taste, or smell directive leadership; instead, we rely on indirect indicators that it exists, such as observing someone giving directions, maintaining clear performance standards, and ensuring that procedures and practices are followed.

As you can see, defining constructs well is very important because these definitions become the foundation for finding or developing acceptable measures of those constructs. We can't measure directive leadership if we only have a vague idea about what this concept means. The better the definition is, the better our chances of applying a measure that adequately represents that construct. However, even with a good definition, constructs can be difficult to measure because the empirical representation must capture several elements in the definition. A measure of directive leadership must be able to identify not only people who give directions, but also those who maintain performance standards and ensure that procedures are followed.

Constructs Abstract ideas constructed by researchers that can be linked to observable information.

EXHIBIT A.1: The Theory Building Process

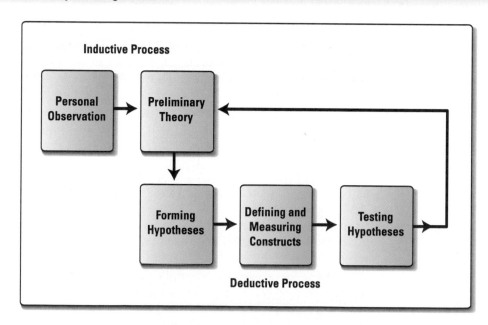

Testing hypotheses

The third step in the deductive process is to collect data for the empirical measures of the variables. Following our directive leadership example, we might conduct a formal survey in which new employees indicate the behaviour of their supervisors and their attitudes toward their supervisor. Alternatively, we might design an experiment in which people work with someone who applies either a directive or nondirective leadership style. When the data have been collected, we can use various procedures to statistically test our hypotheses.

A serious concern in theory building is that some researchers might inadvertently find support for their theory simply because they use the same information used to form the theory during the inductive stage. Consequently, the deductive stage must collect new data that are completely independent of the data used during the inductive stage. For instance, you might decide to test your theory of directive leadership by studying employees in another organization. Moreover, the inductive process may have relied mainly on personal observation, whereas the deductive process might use survey questionnaires. By studying different samples and using different measurement tools, we minimize the risk of conducting circular research.

Using the Scientific Method

Scientific method A set of principles and procedures that help researchers to systematically understand previously unexplained events and conditions.

Earlier, we said that the deductive stage of theory building follows the scientific method. The **scientific method** is a systematic, controlled, empirical, and critical investigation of hypothetical propositions about the presumed relationships among natural phenomena.[4] There are several elements to this definition, so let's look at each one.

First, scientific research is systematic and controlled because researchers want to rule out all but one explanation for a set of interrelated events. To rule out alternative explanations, we need to control them in some way, such as by keeping them constant or removing them entirely from the environment.

Second, we say that scientific research is empirical because researchers need to use objective reality — or as close as we can get to it — to test theory. They measure observable elements of the environment, such as what a person says or does, rather than rely on their own subjective opinion to draw conclusions. Moreover, scientific research analyzes these data using acceptable principles of mathematics and logic.

Finally, scientific research involves critical investigation. This means that the study's hypotheses, data, methods, and results are openly described so that other experts in the field can properly evaluate this research. It also means that scholars are encouraged to critique and build on previous research. Eventually, the scientific method encourages the refinement and then the replacement of a particular theory with one that better suits our understanding of the world.

Selected Issues in Organizational Behaviour Research

There are many issues to consider in theory building, particularly when we use the deductive process to test hypotheses. Some of the more important issues are sampling, causation, and ethical practices in organizational research.

Sampling in Organizational Research

When finding out why things happen in organizations, we typically gather information from a few sources and then draw conclusions about the larger population. If we survey several employees and determine that older employees are more loyal to their company, then we would like to generalize this statement to all older employees in our population, not just those whom we surveyed. Scientific inquiry generally requires researchers to engage in **representative sampling** — that is, sampling a population in such a way that we can extrapolate the results of that sample to the larger population.

Representative sampling
Sampling a population in such a way that we can extrapolate the results of that sample to the larger population.

One factor that influences representativeness is whether the sample is selected in an unbiased way from the larger population. Let's suppose that you want to study organizational commitment among employees in your organization. A casual procedure might result in sampling too few employees from the head office and too many located elsewhere in the country. If head office employees actually have higher loyalty than employees located elsewhere, then the biased sampling would cause the results to underestimate the true level of loyalty among employees in the company. If you repeat the process again next year but somehow overweight employees from the head office, the results might wrongly suggest that employees have increased their organizational commitment over the past year. In reality, the only change may be the direction of sampling bias.

How do we minimize sampling bias? The answer is to randomly select the sample. A randomly drawn sample gives each member of the population an equal probability of being chosen, so there is less likelihood that a subgroup within that population dominates the study's results.

The same principle applies to random assignment of subjects to groups in experimental designs. If we want to test the effects of a team development training program, we need to randomly place some employees in the training group and randomly place others in a group that does not receive training. Without this random selection, each group might have different types of employees, so we wouldn't know whether the training explains the differences between the two groups. Moreover, if employees respond differently to the training program, we couldn't be sure that the training program results are representative of the larger population. Of course, random sampling does not necessarily produce a perfectly representative sample, but we do know that this is the best approach to ensure unbiased selection.

The other factor that influences representativeness is sample size. Whenever we select a portion of the population, there will be some error in our estimate of the population values. The larger the sample, the less error will occur in our estimate. Let's suppose that you want to find out how employees in a 500-person firm feel about smoking in the workplace. If you asked 400 of those employees, the information would provide a very good estimate of how the entire workforce in that organization feels. If you survey only 100 employees, the estimate might deviate more from the true population. If you ask only 10 people, the estimate could be quite different from what all 500 employees feel.

Notice that sample size goes hand in hand with random selection. You must have a sufficiently large sample size for the principle of randomization to work effectively. In our example of attitudes toward smoking, we would do a poor job of random selection if our sample consisted of only 10 employees from the 500-person organization. The reason is that these 10 people probably wouldn't capture the diversity of employees throughout the organization. In fact, the more diverse the population, the larger the sample size should be, to provide adequate representation through random selection.

Causation in Organizational Research

Theories present notions about relationships among constructs. Often, these propositions suggest a causal relationship, namely, that one variable has an effect on another variable. When discussing causation, we refer to variables as being independent or dependent. Independent variables are the presumed causes of dependent variables, which are the presumed effects. In our earlier example of directive leadership, the main independent variable (there might be others) would be the supervisor's directive or nondirective leadership style, because we presume that it causes the dependent variable (satisfaction with supervision).

In laboratory experiments (described later), the independent variable is always manipulated by the experimenter. In our research on directive leadership, we might have subjects (new employees) work with supervisors who exhibit directive or nondirective leadership behaviours. If subjects are more satisfied under the directive leaders, then we would be able to infer an association between the independent and dependent variables.

Researchers must satisfy three conditions to provide sufficient evidence of causality between two variables.[5] The first condition of causality is that the variables are empirically associated with each other. An association exists whenever one measure of a variable changes systematically with a measure of another variable. This condition of causality is the easiest to satisfy because there are several well-known statistical measures of association. A research study might find, for instance, that heterogeneous groups (in which members come from diverse backgrounds) produce more creative solutions to problems. This might be apparent because the measure of creativity (such as number of creative solutions produced within a fixed time) is higher for teams that have a high score on the measure of group heterogeneity. They are statistically associated or correlated with each other.

The second condition of causality is that the independent variable precedes the dependent variable in time. Sometimes, this condition is satisfied through simple logic. In our group heterogeneity example, it doesn't make sense to say that the number of creative solutions caused the group's heterogeneity because the group's heterogeneity existed before it produced the creative solutions. In other situations, however, the temporal relationship among variables is less clear. One example is the ongoing debate about job satisfaction and organizational commitment. Do companies develop more loyal employees by increasing their job satisfaction, or do changes in organizational loyalty cause changes in job satisfaction? Simple logic does not answer these questions; instead, researchers must use sophisticated longitudinal studies to build up evidence of a temporal relationship between these two variables.

The third requirement for evidence of a causal relationship is that the statistical association between two variables cannot be explained by a third variable. There are many associations that we quickly dismiss as being causally related. For example, there is a statistical association between the number of storks in an area and the birth rate in that area. We know that storks don't bring babies, so something else must cause the association between these two variables. The real explanation is that both storks and birth rates have a higher incidence in rural areas.

In other studies, the third variable effect is less apparent. Many years ago, before polio vaccines were available, a study in the United States reported a surprisingly strong association between consumption of a certain soft drink and the incidence of polio. Was polio caused by drinking this pop, or did people with polio have an unusual craving for this beverage? Neither. Both polio and consumption of the soft drink were caused by a third variable: climate. There was a higher incidence of polio in the summer months and in warmer climates, and people drink more liquids in these climates.[6] As you can see from this example, researchers have a difficult time supporting causal inferences because third variable effects are sometimes difficult to detect.

Ethics in Organizational Research

Organizational behaviour researchers need to abide by the ethical standards of the society in which the research is conducted. One of the most important ethical considerations is the individual subject's freedom to participate in the study. For example, it is inappropriate to force employees to fill out a questionnaire or attend an experimental intervention for research purposes only. Moreover, researchers have an obligation to tell potential subjects about any potential risks inherent in the study so that participants can make an informed choice about whether or not to be involved.

Finally, researchers must be careful to protect the privacy of those who participate in the study. This usually includes letting people know when they are being studied, as well as guaranteeing that their individual information will remain confidential (unless publication of identities is otherwise granted). Researchers maintain anonymity through careful security of data. The research results usually aggregate data in numbers large enough that they do not reveal the opinions or characteristics of any specific individual. For example, we would report the average absenteeism of employees in a department rather than state the absence rates of each person. When sharing data with other researchers, it is usually necessary to specially code each case so that individual identities are not known.

Research Design Strategies

So far, we have described how to build a theory, including the specific elements of empirically testing that theory within the standards of scientific inquiry. But what are the different ways to design a research study so that we get the data necessary to achieve our research objectives? There are many strategies, but they mainly fall under three headings: laboratory experiments, field surveys, and observational research.

Laboratory Experiments

Laboratory experiment
Any research study in which independent variables and variables outside the researcher's main focus of inquiry can be controlled to some extent.

A **laboratory experiment** is any research study in which independent variables and variables outside the researcher's main focus of inquiry can be controlled to some extent. Laboratory experiments are usually located outside the everyday work environment, such as a classroom, simulation lab, or any other artificial setting in which the researcher can manipulate the environment. Organizational behaviour researchers sometimes conduct experiments in the workplace (called *field experiments*) in which the independent variable is manipulated. However, the researcher has less control over the effects of extraneous factors in field experiments than in laboratory situations.

Advantages of laboratory experiments

There are many advantages of laboratory experiments. By definition, this research method offers a high degree of control over extraneous variables that would otherwise confound the relationships being studied. Suppose we wanted to test the effects of directive leadership on the satisfaction of new employees. One concern might be that employees are influenced by how much leadership is provided, not just the type of leadership style. An experimental design would allow us to control how often the supervisor exhibited this style so that this extraneous variable does not confound the results.

A second advantage of lab studies is that the independent and dependent variables can be developed more precisely than in a field setting. For example, the researcher can ensure that supervisors in a lab study apply specific directive or nondirective behaviours, whereas real-life supervisors would use a more complex mixture of leadership behaviours. By using more precise measures, we are more certain that we are measuring the intended construct. Thus, if new employees are more satisfied with supervisors in the directive leadership condition, we are more confident that the independent variable was directive leadership rather than some other leadership style.

A third benefit of laboratory experiments is that the independent variable can be distributed more evenly among participants. In our directive leadership study, we can ensure that approximately half of the subjects have a directive supervisor, whereas the other half have a nondirective supervisor. In natural settings, we might have trouble finding people who have worked with a nondirective leader and, consequently, we couldn't determine the effects of this condition.

Disadvantages of laboratory experiments

With these powerful advantages, you might wonder why laboratory experiments are the least appreciated form of organizational behaviour research.[7] One obvious limitation of this research method is that it lacks realism and, consequently, the results might be different in the real world. One argument is that laboratory experiment subjects are less involved than their counterparts in an actual work situation. This is sometimes true, although many lab studies have highly motivated participants. Another criticism is that the extraneous variables controlled in the lab setting might produce a different effect of the independent variable on the dependent variables. This might also be true, but remember that the experimental design controls variables in accordance with the theory and its hypotheses. Consequently, this concern is really a critique of the theory, not the lab study.

Finally, there is the well-known problem that participants are aware they are being studied and this causes them to act differently than they normally would. Some participants try to figure out how the researcher wants them to behave and then deliberately try to act that way. Other participants try to upset the experiment by doing just the opposite of what they believe the researcher expects. Still others might act unnaturally simply because they know they are being observed. Fortunately, experimenters are well aware of these potential problems and are usually (although not always) successful at disguising the study's true intent.

Field Surveys

Field survey Any research design in which information is collected in a natural environment.

Field surveys collect and analyze information in a natural environment — an office, factory, or other existing location. The researcher takes a snapshot of reality and tries to determine whether elements of that situation (including the attitudes and behaviours of people in that situation) are associated with each other as hypothesized. Everyone does some sort of field research. You might think that people from some provinces are better drivers than others, so you "test" your theory by looking at the way people with out-of-province licence plates drive. Although your methods of data collection might not satisfy scientific standards, this is a form of field research because it takes information from a naturally occurring situation.

Advantages and disadvantages of field surveys

One advantage of field surveys is that the variables often have a more powerful effect than they would in a laboratory experiment. Consider the effect of peer pressure on the behaviour of members within the team. In a natural environment, team members would form very strong cohesive bonds over time, whereas a researcher would have difficulty replicating this level of cohesiveness and corresponding peer pressure in a lab setting.

Another advantage of field surveys is that the researcher can study many variables simultaneously, thereby permitting a fuller test of more complex theories. Ironically, this is also a disadvantage of field surveys because it is difficult for the researcher to contain his or her scientific inquiry. There is a tendency to shift from deductive hypothesis testing to more inductive exploratory browsing through the data. If these two activities become mixed together, the researcher can lose sight of the strict covenants of scientific inquiry.

The main weakness with field surveys is that it is very difficult to satisfy the conditions for causal conclusions. One reason is that the data are usually collected at one point in time, so the researcher must rely on logic to decide whether the independent variable really preceded the dependent variable. Contrast this with the lab study in which the researcher can usually be confident that the independent variable was applied before the dependent variable occurred. Increasingly, organizational behaviour studies use longitudinal research to provide a better indicator of temporal relations among variables, but this is still not as precise as the lab setting. Another reason causal analysis is difficult in field surveys is that extraneous variables are not controlled as they are in lab studies. Without this control, there is a higher chance that a third variable might explain the relationship between the hypothesized independent and dependent variables.

Observational Research

In his book *The Creative Edge*, journalist Randy Scotland provides a rich account of life in the fast lane at Toronto advertising agency Vickers & Benson Advertising Ltd.[8] To collect his qualitative data, Scotland regularly visited the advertising agency's offices for almost one year, observing the comings and goings of people and events. Scotland's use of observational research was quite appropriate for his research objectives because this method generates a wealth of descriptive accounts about the drama of human existence in organizations. It is a useful vehicle for learning about the complex dynamics of people and their activities.

Participant observation takes the observation method one step further by having the observer take part in the organization's activities. This experience gives the researcher a fuller understanding of the activities compared to just watching others participate in those activities.

In spite of its intuitive appeal, observational research has a number of weaknesses. The main problem is that the observer is subject to the perceptual screening and organizing biases that we discuss in Chapter 6. There is a tendency to overlook the routine aspects of organizational life, even though they may prove to be the most important data for research purposes. Instead, observers tend to focus on unusual information, such as activities that deviate from what the observer expects. Because observational research usually records only what the observer notices, valuable information is often lost.

Another concern, particularly with participant observation, is that the researcher's presence and involvement may influence the people being studied. This can be a problem in short-term observations, but in the long term people tend to return to their usual behaviour patterns. With ongoing observations, such as Randy Scotland's study of Vickers & Benson Advertising Ltd., employees eventually forget that they are being studied.

Finally, observation is usually a qualitative process, so it is more difficult to empirically test hypotheses with the data. Instead, observational research provides rich information for the inductive stages of theory building. It helps us to form ideas about the way things work in organizations. We begin to see relationships that lay the foundation for new perspectives and theory. We must not confuse this inductive process of theory building with the deductive process of theory testing.

Vroom-Jago Decision Tree

The Vroom-Jago model guides decision makers through the chararteristics of a problem (called *problem attributes*) to determine the most appropriate level of employee involvement for that problem. There are five levels of employee involvement specified in the model. They are:

AI: You make the decision alone with no employee involvement.

AII: Subordinates provide information that you request, but they don't offer recommendations and they might not be aware of the problem.

CI: You describe the problem to relevant subordinates individually, getting their information and recommendations. You make the final decision, which does not necessarily reflect the advice that subordinates have provided.

CII: You describe the problem to subordinates in a meeting, in which they discuss information and recommendations. You make the final decision, which does not necessarily reflect the advice that subordinates have provided.

GII: You describe the problem to subordinates in a meeting. They discuss the problem and make a decision that you are willing to accept and implement if it has the entire team's support. You might chair this session, but you do not influence the team's decision.

The Vroom-Jago model consists of four decision trees. Two trees pertain to decisions affecting a team of employees, whereas the other two focus on individual problems. Within each pair, one emphasizes time efficiency and the other emphasizes employee development. Exhibit B.1 describes the time-driven decision tree for team issues, because it is most frequently used in organizational settings. It consists of eight problem attributes that distinguish the characteristics of each decision situation. Each problem attribute is phrased as a question, and the appropriate answer directs the decision maker along a different path in the decision tree.

The decision maker begins at the left side of the decision tree and must first decide whether the problem has a high- or low-quality dimension. Most decisions have a quality requirement because some alternatives are more likely than others to achieve organizational objectives. However, where all of the alternatives are equally good (or bad), the decision maker would select the low-importance route in the decision tree. The decision maker would then be asked whether subordinate commitment is important to the decision. This process continues until the path leads to the recommended participation level, ranging from AI to GII.

EXHIBIT B.1: Vroom-Jago Time-Driven Decision Tree

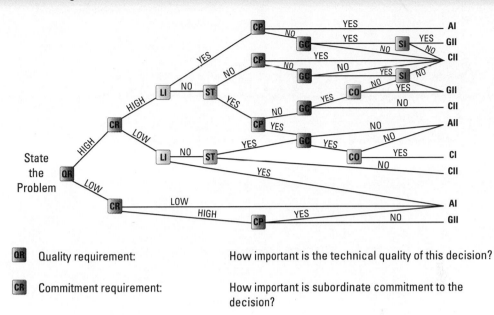

QR	Quality requirement:	How important is the technical quality of this decision?
CR	Commitment requirement:	How important is subordinate commitment to the decision?
LI	Leader's information:	Do you have sufficient information to make a high-quality decision?
ST	Problem structure:	Is the problem well structured?
CP	Commitment probability:	If you make the decision yourself, is it reasonably certain that your subordinate(s) would be committed to the decision?
GC	Goal congruence:	Do subordinates share the organizational goals to be attained in solving this problem?
CO	Subordinate conflict:	Is conflict among subordinates over preferred solutions likely?
CO	Subordinate information:	Do subordinates have sufficient information to make a high-quality decision?

Source: V. H. Vroom and A. G. Jago, *The New Leadership: Managing Participation in Organizations* (Englewood Cliffs, N.J.: Prentice Hall, 1988), p. 184. © 1987 V. H. Vroom and A. G. Jago. Used with permission of the authors.

Answers to Practice Session Questions

Practice Session Answers for Part 1

True-False	Multiple-Choice
1. F	1. B
2. F	2. B
3. T	

Written Answer

1. One way that organizational behaviour can potentially benefit students is by satisfying their need to predict and understand events in organizations. This field also helps students to adopt more accurate theories of reality. This includes testing the accuracy of the theories they have used implicitly in the past, as well as learning new theories that clarify how organizations operate. Lastly, organizational behaviour knowledge teaches students how to control organizational events.

Practice Session Answers for Part 2

True-False	Multiple-Choice
1. F	1. B
2. T	2. C
3. T	3. C
4. F	4. A
5. T	5. B
6. T	6. C

Written Answers

1. *(Note: This incident is based on an actual experience. The senior government official proceeded with the job enrichment, allegedly with the minister's approval, the inspectors complained loudly, and the official eventually left the department.)*

   There are two important issues that we should consider before this job enrichment intervention begins. First, we need to determine how "enriched" the inspector jobs are before the change. The deputy minister is assuming that the current jobs need enrichment so that employees will be more motivated by the work, yet there is no evidence that the jobs offer a low level of motivation. Thus, the deputy minister should measure the level of job enrichment and interview job incumbents about their feelings toward this intervention.

   The second — and somewhat related — issue is whether the individual differences support a job enrichment intervention. The deputy minister should determine whether job incumbents have a high growth need strength. Even if the jobs offer little motivation, they might be appropriate for the needs of these employees. The deputy minister should also be certain that employees are reasonably satisfied with their work environment. Finally, it is important to ensure that employees have the requisite skills and knowledge to master the additional challenges of the proposed enriched job, or that they are capable of learning the necessary skills and knowledge for those tasks.

2. The accuracy of this statement depends on the situation. Participation in goal setting increases performance when (a) employees need to have higher goal commitment, and/or when (b) employee knowledge will improve goal quality. However, participation will not improve performance where employees accept and are committed to assigned goals and where those who decide the assigned goals have sufficient information to develop high-quality goals.

Practice Session Answers for Part 3

True-False

1. T
2. F
3. T
4. T
5. T
6. F

Multiple-Choice

1. C
2. B
3. A
4. B
5. D
6. D

Written Answers

1. Although an employment interview is not the best way to measure a person's emotional intelligence (EI), there are a few indicators to observe. To answer this question, you should consider the five dimensions of EI and discuss indicators of each. Self-awareness and managing emotions might be apparent by the applicant's ability to avoid unfavourable emotions when discussing sensitive or potentially emotionally charged issues. For the motivating yourself dimension, the

applicant might be asked about how he or she gets things accomplished, and then listen for incidents of self-set goals and delayed self-reinforcement. Empathy can be indicated by listening to the applicant respond as you describe a recent incident at work. For handling emotions, you might ask the applicant to describe a situation in which a customer or co-worker was getting too angry or upset, and ask what they did.

2. Actor-observer error causes people to see the behaviours of others caused mainly by internal factors such as ability and motivation, whereas they are more sensitive to the influence of external factors (situational contingencies) on their own behaviour. In the case of a co-worker showing up late for work, actor-observer error would increase the degree to which co-workers thought the employee lacked motivation to come to work and to downplay the role of external causes, such as car troubles or unusual traffic congestion.

Practice Session Answers for Part 4

True-False	Multiple-Choice
1. F	1. C
2. T	2. B
3. F	3. A
4. F	4. A
5. F	5. B
6. T	6. C
7. T	7. D
8. T	8. B

Written Answers

1. This incident illustrates how narrow or inappropriate mental models create a barrier to identifying problems and opportunities. In this incident, the textile company president had a mental model that created a false assumption that customers wanted real silk rather than the lower-priced and more versatile rayon. This mental model was based on the president's past experience with the marketplace.

2. Brainstorming requires team members to abide by four rules that encourage divergent thinking and minimize evaluation apprehension. First, no one should criticize any ideas that are presented. Second, wild and strange ideas are encouraged. Third, team members should combine and improve on the ideas already presented. Fourth, the group should think of as many solutions as possible and go well beyond the traditional solutions to a problem. One problem/limitation of brainstorming is that there is still some evaluation apprehension (concern over what others think of them when giving crazy ideas). The second problem is that production blocking still exists because only one person speaks at a time.

3. Jim mainly has expert power through his special knowledge and experience. He may have some legitimate power if there is, say, a letter of hire referring to the transfer. Jim's expert power is limited because he lacks visibility and centrality. Moreover, although Jim's knowledge is apparently unique, he is highly substitutable with people who have skill and experience in more traditional bond trading.

Practice Session Answers for Part 5

True-False	Multiple-Choice
1. F	1. B
2. F	2. E
3. F	3. B
4. T	4. E
5. T	5. D
6. T	6. A
7. T	7. E
8. F	8. A

Written Answers

1. Strong cultures aren't necessarily better for organizations, because the cultural content may be inappropriate for the environment. Another concern is that a company's culture might be so strong that employees blindly focus on the mental model shaped by that culture. Lastly, strong cultures tend to suppress dissenting values. In the long term, this prevents organizations from nurturing new cultural values that might emerge as dominant values as the environment changes.

2. The three pure types of divisionalization are geographic, product, and client. Geographic divisional forms are organized around global regions, such as North America, Europe, Asia, etc. They also include divisions divided by regions within a country. Product divisions organize people around specific product groups, such as widgets, bumpers, and consulting services. Client divisions are organized around a particular type of customer group, such as government, education, manufacturers, etc. The main factor to consider when choosing a divisional form is where employees should focus their attention. This was described in the Nortel example (opening story to Chapter 18). Nortel has moved toward a client structure because it believes that a successful firm focuses employees on clients rather than on regions or products.

GLOSSARY

*The number(s) after each definition indicates the chapter in which the term is defined.

Ability The natural aptitudes and learned capabilities required to successfully complete a task. (2)

Action learning A form of on-site, experiential-based learning in which participants investigate an organizational problem or opportunity and possibly implement their solution. (2)

Action research A data-based, problem-oriented process that diagnoses the need for change, introduces the OD intervention, and then evaluates and stabilizes the desired changes. (15)

Actor-observer error An attribution error whereby people tend to attribute their own actions more to external factors, and the behaviour of others more to internal factors. (6) (14)

Affiliate networks Network organizations where the satellite companies have a special affiliation with the core firm. The satellites may have been spun-off departments from the core firm, or the core firm may be a major investor in the satellite. (18)

Agency theory An economic theory that assumes company owners (principals) and employees (agents) have different goals and interests, so rewards and other control systems are required to align the agent's goals with those of the principals. (4)

Appreciative inquiry An organization development intervention that directs the group's attention away from its own problems and focuses participants on the group's potential and positive elements. (15)

Artifacts The observable symbols and signs of an organization's culture, including its physical structures, ceremonies, language, and stories. (16)

Attitudes The cluster of beliefs, assessed feelings, and behavioural intentions toward an object. (7)

Attribution process A perceptual process whereby we interpret the causes of behaviour in terms of the person (internal attributions) or the situation (external attributions). (6)

Autonomy The degree to which a job gives employees the freedom, independence, and discretion to schedule their work and determine the procedures to be used to complete the work. (4)

Behaviourism A perspective that focuses entirely on behaviour and observable events, rather than on a person's thoughts. (2)

Benchmarking A systematic and ongoing process of improving performance by measuring a product, service, or process against a partner that has mastered it. (10)

"Big Five" personality dimension The five abstract personality dimensions under which most personality traits are represented. They are extroversion, agreeableness, conscientiousness, emotional stability, and openness to experience. (6)

Brainstorming A freewheeling, face-to-face meeting in which team members generate as many alternative solutions to the problem as possible, piggyback on the ideas of others, and avoid evaluating anyone's ideas during the idea-generation stage. (11)

Career anchor A person's self-image of his or her abilities, motivations, and interests relating to a particular career orientation. (17)

Career A sequence of work-related experiences that people participate in over the span of their working lives. (17)

Centrality The degree and nature of interdependence between the powerholder and others. (12)

Centralization The degree to which formal decision authority is held by a small group of people, typically those at the top of the organizational hierarchy. (18)

Ceremonies Deliberate and usually dramatic displays of organizational culture, such as celebrations and special social gatherings. (16)

Change agent A person who possesses enough knowledge and power to guide and facilitate the change effort. This may be a member of the organization or an external consultant. (15)

Coalition An informal group that attempts to influence people outside the group by pooling the resources and power of its members. (9) (12)

Coercive power The capacity to influence others through the ability to apply punishment and remove rewards affecting these people. (12)

Cognitive dissonance A state of anxiety that occurs when an individual's beliefs, attitudes, intentions, and behaviours are inconsistent with one another. (7)

Cohesiveness   The degree of attraction that members feel toward their team and their motivation to remain members. (9)

Communication   The process by which information is transmitted and understood between two or more people. (8)

Competencies   The abilities, individual values, personality traits, and other characteristics of people that lead to superior performance. (2) (4) (14)

Concurrent engineering   The integration and concurrent development of a product or service and its associated processes, usually guided by a cross-functional team. (10)

Conflict   The process in which one party perceives that its interests are being opposed or negatively affected by another party. (13)

Conflict management   Interventions that alter the level and form of conflict in ways that maximize its benefits and minimize its dysfunctional consequences. (13)

Conscientiousness   A "Big Five" personality dimension that characterizes people who are careful, dependable, and self-disciplined. (6)

Constructive controversy   Any situation in which team members debate their different opinions regarding a problem or issue in a way that minimizes socio-emotional conflict. (11)

Constructs   Abstract ideas constructed by researchers that can be linked to observable information. (Appendix A)

Content theories of motivation   Theories that explain the dynamics of employee needs, such as why people have different needs at different times. (3)

Contingency approach   The idea that a particular action may have different consequences in different situations; that no single solution is best in all circumstances. (1)

Contingent work   Any job in which the individual does not have an explicit or implicit contract for long-term employment, or one in which the minimum hours of work can vary in a nonsystematic way. (17)

Continuous reinforcement   A schedule that reinforces behaviour every time it occurs. (2)

Counterpower   The capacity of a person, team, or organization to keep a more powerful person or group in the exchange relationship. (12)

Creativity   The capability to develop an original product, service, or idea that makes a socially recognized contribution. (11)

Cross-functional teams   Groups that overlay a more permanent structure, usually functional departments. (9)

Decision making   A conscious process of making choices among one or more alternatives with the intention of moving toward some desired state of affairs. (11)

Departmentation   An element of organizational structure specifying how employees and their activities are grouped together, such as by function, product, geographic location, or some combination. (18)

Devil's advocates   People who challenge others to explain the logic of their preferences and who identify problems with that logic. (11)

Dialogue   A process of conversation among team members in which they learn about each other's mental models and assumptions, and eventually form a common model for thinking within the team. (9) (13) (15)

Discrepancy theory   A theory that partly explains job satisfaction and dissatisfaction in terms of the gap between what a person expects to receive and what is actually received. (7)

Divergent thinking   The ability to reframe problems in a unique way and generate different approaches to the issue. (11)

Divisional structure   A type of departmentation that groups employees around outputs, clients, or geographic areas. (18)

Effort-to-performance (E→P) expectancy   An individual's perceived probability that a particular level of effort will result in a particular level of performance. (3)

Electronic brainstorming   Using computer software, several people enter ideas at any time on their computer terminals. Each participant can have his or her computer list a random sample of anonymous ideas generated by other people at the session to aid in thinking up new ideas. (11)

Emotional contagion   The automatic and subconscious tendency to mimic and synchronize our nonverbal behaviours with other people. (8)

Emotional intelligence   The ability to monitor your own and others' emotions, to discriminate among them, and to use the information to guide your thinking and actions. (7)

Emotional labour   The effort, planning, and control needed to express organizationally desired emotions during interpersonal transactions. (7) (8)

Emotions   Feelings experienced toward an object, person, or event that create a state of readiness. (7)

Empathy   A person's ability to understand and be sensitive to the feelings, thoughts, and situation of others. (6)

Employability The "new deal" employment relationship in which the job is viewed as a temporary event, so employees are expected to keep pace with changing competency requirements and shift to new projects as demand requires. (17)

Employee assistance programs (EAPs) Counselling services that help employees cope with personal or organizational stressors and adopt more effective coping mechanisms. (5)

Employee involvement The degree that employees share information, knowledge, rewards, and power throughout the organization. (10)

Employee share ownership plan (ESOP) A reward system that encourages employees to buy shares of the company. (4)

Empowerment The feeling of control and self-efficacy that emerges when people are given power in a previously powerless situation. (4)(10)

Environmental scanning Receiving information from the external and internal environments so that more effective strategic decisions can be made. (1)

Equity theory A process motivation theory that explains how people develop perceptions of fairness in the distribution and exchange of resources. (3) (7)

ERG theory Alderfer's content motivation theory of three instinctive needs arranged in a hierarchy, in which people progress to the next higher need when a lower one is fulfilled, and regress to a lower need if unable to fulfil a higher need. (3)

Escalation of commitment Repeating an apparently bad decision or allocating more resources to a failing course of action. (11)

Ethical values Beliefs about whether certain actions are good or bad, directing them to what is virtuous and right. (7)

Evaluation apprehension The reluctance to mention ideas to others that seem silly or peripheral in order to create a favourable self-presentation and maintain social esteem. (11)

Existence needs A person's physiological and physically related safety needs, such as the need for food, shelter, and safe working conditions. (3)

Expectancy theory A process motivation theory stating that work effort is directed toward behaviours that people believe will lead to desired outcomes. (3)

Expert power The capacity to influence others by possessing knowledge or skills that they want. (12)

Extinction Occurs when the removal or withholding of a consequence decreases the frequency or future probability of the behaviour preceding that event. (2)

Extroversion A "Big Five" personality dimension that characterizes people who are outgoing, talkative, sociable, and assertive. (6) (7)

Family-friendly workplaces Organizations that try to minimize work-family time conflict by offering flexible work arrangements, job sharing, telework, family leave, and childcare facilities. (5)

Feedback Any information that people receive about the consequences of their behaviour. (2)

Field survey Any research design in which information is collected in a natural environment. (Appendix A)

Fixed interval schedule A schedule that reinforces behaviour after it has occurred for a fixed period of time. (2)

Fixed ratio schedule A schedule that reinforces behaviour after it has occurred a fixed number of times. (2)

Flaming Sending an emotionally charged electronic mail message. (8)

Force field analysis A model that helps change agents diagnose the forces that drive and restrain proposed organizational change. (15)

Formalization The degree to which organizations standardize behaviour through rules, procedures, formal training, and related mechanisms. (18)

Frustration-regression process Process whereby people who are unable to satisfy a higher need become frustrated and regress to the next lower need level. (3)

Functional structure A type of departmentation that organizes employees around specific skills or other resources. (18)

Gainsharing plans A reward system usually applied to work teams that distributes bonuses to team members based on the amount of cost reductions and increased labour efficiency in the production process. (4) (10)

General adaptation syndrome A model of the stress experience, consisting of three stages: alarm reaction, resistance, and exhaustion. (5)

Goal setting The process of motivating employees and clarifying their role perceptions by establishing performance objectives. (3)

Goals The immediate or ultimate objectives that employees are trying to accomplish from their work effort. (3)

Grafting The process of acquiring knowledge by hiring individuals or buying entire companies. (1)

Grapevine The organization's informal communication network that is formed and maintained by social relationships rather than by the formal reporting relationships. (8)

Group polarization The tendency for teams to make more extreme decisions (either more risky or more risk averse) than the average team member would if making the decision alone. (11)

Groupthink The tendency of highly cohesive groups to value consensus at the price of decision quality by avoiding conflict and withholding their dissenting opinions. (11)

Growth needs A person's self-esteem through personal achievement as well as self-actualization. (3)

Halo effect A perceptual error whereby our general impression of a person, usually based on one prominent characteristic, biases our perception of other characteristics of that person. (6)

Harassment Unwelcome conduct that detrimentally affects the work environment or leads to adverse job-related consequences for the victims of harassment. (6) (12)

Heterogeneous teams Formal or informal groups whose members have diverse personal characteristics and backgrounds. (9)

Hi-hi leadership hypothesis A proposition stating that effective leaders exhibit high levels of both people-oriented and task-oriented behaviours. (14)

Homogeneous teams Formal or informal groups whose members have similar technical expertise, ethnicity, experiences, or values. (9)

Hypotheses Statements making empirically testable declarations that certain variables and their corresponding measures are related in a specific way proposed by a particular theory. (Appendix A)

Implicit learning The experiential phenomenon of acquiring information about relationships in the environment without any conscious attempt to do so. (2) (3)

Impression management The practice of actively shaping our public images. (12)

Incremental change An evolutionary approach to change in which existing organizational conditions are fine-tuned and small steps are taken toward the change effort's objectives. (15)

Individualism-collectivism The degree that people value their individual versus group goals. Collectivists respect and value their membership in the group to which they belong, whereas individualists tend to give low priority to group interests. (7) (10)

Informal group Two or more people who group together primarily to meet their personal (rather than organizational) needs. (9)

Information overload A condition in which the volume of information received by an employee exceeds that person's ability to process it effectively. (8)

Inoculation effect A persuasive communication strategy of warning listeners that others will try to influence them in the future and that they should be wary about the opponent's arguments. (8)

Intellectual capital The knowledge that resides in an organization, including its human, organizational, and customer capital. (1) (2)

Intergroup mirroring A structured conflict management intervention in which the parties discuss their perceptions of each other and look for ways to improve their relationship by correcting misperceptions. (13)

Jargon Technical language of a particular occupational group or recognized words with specialized meaning in specific organizations or social groups. (8)

Job burnout The process of emotional exhaustion, depersonalization, and reduced personal accomplishment resulting from prolonged exposure to stress. (5)

Job characteristics model A job design model that relates five core job dimensions to three psychological states and several personal and organizational consequences. (4)

Job design The process of assigning tasks to a job and distributing work throughout the organization. (4)

Job enlargement Increasing the number of tasks employees perform within their job. (4)

Job enrichment Assigning responsibility for scheduling, coordinating, and planning work to employees who actually make the product or provide the service. (4)

Job evaluation Systematically evaluating the worth of jobs within the organization by measuring their required skill, effort, responsibility, and working conditions. Job evaluation results create a hierarchy of job worth. (4)

Job feedback The degree to which employees can tell how well they are doing based on direct sensory information from the job itself. (4)

Job rotation Moving employees from one job to another for short periods of time. (4)

Job satisfaction A person's attitude (beliefs, assessed feelings, and behavioural intentions) regarding the job and work context. (7)

Job specialization The result of division of labour in which each job now includes a narrow subset of the tasks required to complete the product or service. (4) (18)

Johari Window A model of personal and interpersonal understanding that encourages disclosure and feedback to increase the open area and reduce the blind, hidden, and unknown areas of oneself (6)

Laboratory experiment Any research study in which independent variables and variables outside the researcher's main focus of inquiry can be controlled to some extent. (Appendix A)

Lateral career development The view that career success occurs when employees fulfil their personal needs in different jobs across the organization rather than by moving through the organizational hierarchy. (17)

Leadership Grid® A leadership model developed by Blake and Mouton that assesses an individual's leadership effectiveness in terms of his or her concern for people and concern for production. (14)

Leadership substitutes Characteristics of the employee, task, or organization that either limit the leader's influence or make it unnecessary. (14)

Leadership The process of influencing people and providing an environment for them to achieve team or organizational objectives. (14)

Lean production The practice of continuously pushing for more output with less human effort, less equipment, less time, and less space. (5)

Learning A relatively permanent change in behaviour (or behaviour tendency) that occurs as a result of a person's interaction with the environment. (2)

Legitimate power The capacity to influence others through formal authority; that is, the perceived right to direct certain behaviours of people in other positions. (12)

Locus of control A personality trait referring to the extent that people believe what happens to them is within their control; those who feel in control of their destiny have an internal locus, whereas those who believe that life events are due mainly to fate or luck have an external locus of control. (6) (14)

Machiavellian values The belief that deceit is a natural and acceptable way to influence others. (12)

Management-by-objectives (MbO) A formal, participative goal-setting process in which organizational objectives are cascaded down to work units and individual employees. (3)

Masculinity-femininity The degree to which people value assertiveness, competitiveness, and materialism (masculinity) versus relationships and the well-being of others (femininity). (7)

Matrix structure A type of departmentation that overlays a divisionalized structure (typically a project team) with a functional structure. (18)

Mechanistic structure An organizational structure with a narrow span of control and high degrees of formalization and centralization. (18)

Media richness The data-carrying capacity of a communication medium; the volume and variety of information that it can transmit. (8)

Mental imagery Mentally practising a task and visualizing its successful completion. (4)

Mental models The broad world-views or "theories-in-use" that people rely on to guide their perceptions and behaviours. (6) (11)

Methods-time measurement The process of systematically observing, measuring, and timing the smallest physical movements to identify more efficient work behaviours. (4)

Moods Emotional states that are not directed toward anything in particular. (7)

Motivation The internal forces that affect the direction, intensity, and persistence of a person's voluntary choice of behaviour. (2) (3)

Needs Deficiencies that energize or trigger behaviours to satisfy those needs. (3)

Needs hierarchy theory Maslow's content motivation theory of five instinctive needs arranged in a hierarchy, whereby people are motivated to fulfil a higher need as a lower one becomes gratified. (3)

Negative affectivity (NA) The tendency to experience negative emotional states. (7)

Negative reinforcement Occurs when the removal or termination of a consequence increases or maintains the frequency or future probability of the behaviour preceding that event. (2)

Negotiation Any attempt by two or more conflicting parties to resolve their divergent goals by redefining the terms of their interdependence. (13)

Network structure An alliance of several organizations for the purpose of creating a product or serving a client. (18)

Networking   Cultivating social relationships with others for the purpose of accomplishing one's goals. (12)

Nominal group technique   A structured team decision-making technique whereby members independently write down ideas, describe and clarify them to the group, and then independently rank or vote on them. (11)

Nonprogrammed decision   The process applied to unique, complex, or ill-defined situations whereby decision makers follow the full decision-making process, including a careful search for and/or development of unique solutions. (11)

Nonterritorial offices   Office arrangements in which employees work at any available workstation and are not assigned to specific desks, offices, or workspaces. (8)

Norms   Informal rules and expectations that groups establish to regulate the behaviour of their members. (9)

Open systems   Organizations and other entities with interdependent parts that work together to continually monitor and transact with the external environment. (1)

Organic structure   An organizational structure with a wide span of control, very little formalization, and highly decentralized decision making. (18)

Organization development (OD)   A planned systemwide effort, managed from the top with the assistance of a change agent, that uses behavioural science knowledge to improve organizational effectiveness. (15)

Organizational behaviour   The study of what people think, feel, and do in and around organizations. (1)

Organizational behaviour modification   A theory that explains learning in terms of the antecedents and consequences of behaviour. (2)

Organizational citizenship   Employee behaviours that extend beyond the usual job duties. They include avoiding unnecessary conflicts, helping others without selfish intent, gracefully tolerating occasional impositions, being involved in organizational activities, and performing tasks that extend beyond normal role requirements. (2) (7)

Organizational commitment   A complex attitude pertaining to the strength of an individual's identification with and involvement in a particular organization; includes a strong belief in the organization's goals, as well as a motivation to work for and remain a member of the organization. (7)

Organizational culture   The basic pattern of shared assumptions, values, and beliefs governing the way employees within an organization think about and act on problems and opportunities. (16)

Organizational design   The creation and modification of organizational structures. (18)

Organizational learning   An organization's capacity to acquire, disseminate, and apply knowledge for its survival and success. (1) (2)

Organizational memory   The storage and preservation of the organization's knowledge (i.e., its intellectual capital). (1)

Organizational politics   Attempts to influence others using discretionary behaviours for the purpose of promoting personal objectives; discretionary behaviours are neither explicitly prescribed nor prohibited by the organization and are linked to one or more power bases. (12)

Organizational socialization   The process by which individuals learn the values, expected behaviours, and social knowledge necessary to assume their roles in the organization. (16) (17)

Organizational strategy   The way the organization positions itself in its setting in relation to its stakeholders given the organization's resources, capabilities, and mission. (18)

Organizational structure   The division of labour as well as the patterns of coordination, communication, work flow, and formal power that direct organizational activities. (18)

Organizations   Groups of people who work interdependently toward some purpose. (1)

Parallel learning structure   A highly participative social structure constructed alongside (i.e., parallel to) the formal organization with the purpose of increasing the organization's learning. (15)

Path-goal leadership theory   A contingency theory of leadership based on expectancy theory of motivation that includes four leadership styles as well as several employee and situational contingencies. (14)

Perception   The process of selecting, organizing, and interpreting information in order to make sense of the world around us. (6)

Perceptual defense   A defensive psychological process that involves subconsciously screening out large blocks of information that threaten the person's beliefs and values. (6)

Perceptual grouping   The perceptual organization process of placing people and objects into recognizable and manageable patterns or categories. (6)

Performance-to-outcome (P→O) expectancy   An individual's perceived probability that a specific behaviour or performance level will lead to specific outcomes. (3)

Personality   The relatively stable pattern of behaviours and consistent internal states that explain a person's behavioural tendencies. (6)

Persuasive communication   The process of having listeners accept rather than just understand the sender's message. (8)

Positive affectivity (PA)   The tendency to experience positive emotional states. (7)

Positive reinforcement   Occurs when the introduction of a consequence increases or maintains the frequency or future probability of the behaviour preceding that event. (2)

Postdecisional justification   A perceptual phenomenon whereby decision makers justify their choices by subconsciously inflating the quality of the selected option and deflating the quality of the discarded options. (11)

Power   The capacity of a person, team, or organization to influence others. (12)

Power distance   The extent that people accept unequal distribution of power in a society. (7) (10)

Prejudice   Negative emotions toward people belonging to a particular stereotyped group based on inaccurate perceptions about people in that group. (6)

Primacy effect   A perceptual error in which we quickly form an opinion of people based on the first information we receive about them. (6)

Procedural fairness   Perceptions of fairness regarding the dispute resolution process, whether or not the outcome is favourable to the person. (13)

Process consultation   A method of helping the organization solve its own problems by making it aware of organizational processes, the consequences of those processes, and the means by which they can be changed. (15)

Process losses   Resources (including time and energy) expended toward team development and maintenance rather than the task. (9)

Process theories of motivation   Theories that describe the processes through which need deficiencies are translated into behaviour. (3)

Production blocking   A time constraint in meetings due to the procedural requirement that only one person may speak at a time. (11)

Profit sharing   A reward system in which a designated group of employees receives a share of corporate profits. (4)

Programmed decision   The process whereby decision makers follow standard operating procedures to select the preferred solution without the need to identify or evaluate alternative choices. (11)

Projection   A perceptual error in which we tend to believe that other people hold the same beliefs and attitudes that we do. (6)

Psychological contract   The employer and employee's perceived mutual obligations about their exchange relationship. (17)

Punishment   Occurs when the introduction of a consequence decreases the frequency or future probability of the behaviour preceding that event. (2)

Quality   The value that the end user perceives from the product or service, including satisfying customer needs or expectations and conforming to a standard. (10)

Quality circles   Small teams of employees who meet for a few hours each week to identify quality and productivity problems, propose solutions to management, and monitor the implementation and consequences of these solutions in their work area. (10)

Quantum change   A revolutionary approach to change in which the organization breaks out of its existing ways and moves toward a totally different configuration of systems and structures. (15)

Realistic job previews   Giving job applicants a realistic balance of positive and negative information about the job and work context. (17)

Reality shock   The gap between pre-employment expectations and the perceived organizational reality that employees experience as they enter a new work situation. (17)

Recency effect   A perceptual error in which the most recent information dominates our perception about the person. (6)

Referent power   The capacity to influence others by virtue of the admiration of and identification with the powerholder. (12)

Refreezing   The latter part of the change process in which systems and conditions are introduced that reinforce and maintain the desired behaviours. (15)

Relatedness needs   A person's need to interact with other people, receive public recognition, and feel secure around people (i.e., interpersonal safety). (3)

Representative sampling   Sampling a population in such a way that we can extrapolate the results of that sample to the larger population. (Appendix A)

Reward power The capacity to influence others by controlling the allocation of rewards valued by them and the removal of negative sanctions. (12)

Rituals The programmed routines of daily organizational life that dramatize the organization's culture. (16)

Role ambiguity Uncertainty about job duties, performance expectations, level of authority, and other job conditions. (5)

Role conflict A situation whereby people experience competing demands, such as having job duties that are incompatible with personal values, or receiving contradictory messages from different people. (5)

Role perceptions A person's beliefs about what behaviours are appropriate or necessary in a particular situation, including the specific tasks that make up the job, their relative importance, and the preferred behaviours to accomplish those tasks. (2)

Satisfaction-progression process A process whereby people become increasingly motivated to fulfil a higher need as a lower need is gratified. (3)

Satisficing The tendency to select a solution that is satisfactory or "good enough" rather than optimal or "the best." (11)

Scientific management The process of systematically determining how work should be partitioned into its smallest possible elements and how the process of completing each task should be standardized to achieve maximum efficiency. (4)

Scientific method A set of principles and procedures that help researchers to systematically understand previously unexplained events and conditions. (1) (Appendix A)

Selective attention The process of filtering (selecting and screening out) information received by our senses. (6)

Self-directed work team (SDWT) A work group that completes an entire piece of work requiring several interdependent tasks and has substantial autonomy over the execution of these tasks. (9) (10)

Self-efficacy A person's belief that he or she has the ability, motivation, and situational contingencies to complete a task successfully. (2) (3) (6)

Self-fulfilling prophecy A phenomenon in which an observer's expectations of someone causes that person to act in a way consistent with the observer's expectation. (6)

Self-leadership The process of influencing oneself to establish the self-direction and self-motivation needed to perform a task. This includes personal goal setting, constructive thought patterns, designing natural rewards, self-monitoring, and self-reinforcement. (4)

Self-monitoring A personality trait referring to the extent that people are sensitive to situational cues and can readily adapt their own behaviour appropriately. (6) (7)

Self-serving bias A perceptual error whereby people tend to attribute their own success to internal factors and their failures to external factors. (6)

Self-talk Talking to yourself about your own thoughts or actions, for the purpose of increasing self-efficacy and navigating through the decisions required to get the job done effectively. (4)

Sensitivity training An unstructured and agendaless session in which participants become more aware through their interactions of how they affect others and how others affect them. (15)

Shaping The strategy of initially reinforcing crude approximations of the ideal behaviour, then increasing reinforcement standards until only the ideal behaviour is rewarded. (2)

Situational contingencies Environmental conditions beyond the employee's immediate control that constrain or facilitate employee behaviour and performance. (2)

Skill variety The extent to which a job requires employees to use different skills and talents to complete a variety of work activities. (4)

Skill-based pay (SBP) Pay structures in which employees earn higher pay rates with the number of skill modules they have mastered, even though they perform only some of the mastered tasks in a particular job. (4)

Skunkwork A cross-functional team of employees borrowed from several functional areas of the organization to develop new products, services, or procedures, usually in isolation from the organization and without the normal restrictions. (9)

Social identity theory A model that explains self-perception and social perception in terms of our unique characteristics (personal identity) as well as membership in various social groups (social identity). (6)

Social learning theory A theory stating that learning mainly occurs by observing others and then modelling the behaviours that lead to favourable outcomes and avoiding behaviours that lead to punishing consequences. (2)

Social loafing The situation in which people perform at a lower level when working in groups than when alone. (9)

Sociotechnical design A theory stating that every work site consists of a social system and a technological system, and that organizations are most effective when the two systems are compatible with each other. (10)

Span of control The number of people directly reporting to a supervisor. (18)

Stereotyping The process of using a few observable characteristics to assign people to a preconceived social category, and then assigning less observable traits to those persons based on their membership in the group. (6)

Strategic choice The idea that an organization interacts with its environment rather than being totally determined by it. (18)

Stress An individual's adaptive response to a situation that is perceived as challenging or threatening to the person's well-being. (5)

Stressor Any environmental condition that places a physical or emotional demand on the person. (5)

Substitutability The extent to which those dependent on a resource have alternative sources of supply of the resource or can use other resources that would provide a reasonable substitute. (12)

Superordinate goal A common objective held by conflicting parties that is more important than their conflicting departmental or individual goals. (13)

Synergy A condition in which the interaction of two or more people produces higher quality and quantity of solutions than if these people worked alone on the problem. (10)

Tacit knowledge Subtle information, acquired through observation and experience, that is not clearly understood and therefore cannot be explicitly communicated. (2)

Task identity The degree to which a job requires completion of a whole or identifiable piece of work. (4)

Task interdependence The degree to which a task requires collective action. High task interdependence exists when team members must share inputs or outcomes, or need to interact while executing their work. (9) (13)

Task performance Goal-directed activities that are under the individual's control. (2)

Task significance The degree to which the job has a substantial impact on the organization and/or larger society. (4)

Team Two or more people who interact and mutually influence each other to achieve common goals. (9)

Team-based organizational structure A type of departmentation with a flat span of control and relatively little formalization, consisting of self-directed work teams responsible for various work processes. (18)

Team-based structure A type of departmentation with a flat span of control and relatively little formalization, consisting of self-directed work teams responsible for various work processes. (9)

Team building Any formal intervention directed toward improving the development and functioning of a work team. (9)

Team effectiveness The extent to which the team achieves its objectives, achieves the needs and objectives of its members, and sustains itself over time. (9)

Theory A general set of propositions that describes interrelationships among several concepts. (Appendix A)

Third-party conflict resolution Any attempt by a relatively neutral person to help the parties resolve their differences. (13)

360-degree feedback Performance feedback is received from a full circle of people around the employee. (2)

Transactional leadership Leadership that helps organizations achieve their current objectives more efficiently by linking job performance to valued rewards and ensuring that employees have the resources needed to get the job done. (14)

Transformational leadership A leadership perspective that explains how leaders change teams or organizations by creating, communicating, and modelling a vision for the organization or work unit, and inspiring employees to strive for that vision. (14)

Trust Positive expectations about another party's intentions and actions toward us in risky situations. (7) (17)

Type A behaviour pattern A behaviour pattern of people with high risk of premature coronary heart disease; Type As tend to be impatient, lose their temper, talk rapidly, and interrupt others. (5)

Type B behaviour pattern A behaviour pattern of people with low risk of coronary heart disease; Type Bs tend to work steadily, take a relaxed approach to life, and be even-tempered. (5)

Uncertainty avoidance The degree to which people tolerate ambiguity (low uncertainty avoidance) or feel threatened by ambiguity and uncertainty (high uncertainty avoidance). (7)

Unfreezing The first part of the change process whereby the change agent produces a disequilibrium between the driving and restraining forces. (15)

Utilitarianism A moral principle stating that decision makers should seek the greatest good for the greatest number of people when choosing among alternatives. (7)

Valence The anticipated satisfaction or dissatisfaction that an individual feels toward an outcome. (3)

Values Stable, long-lasting beliefs about what is important to the individual. (7)

Variable interval schedule A schedule that reinforces behaviour after it has occurred for a variable period of time around some average. (2)

Variable ratio schedule A schedule that reinforces behaviour after it has occurred a varying number of times around some average. (2)

Virtual corporation An extreme form of network structure in which almost every activity is distributed to satellite organizations in the network. (18)

Virtual teams Cross-functional teams that operate across space, time, and organizational boundaries with members who communicate mainly through electronic technologies. (9)

Visible leadership A management practice of having frequent face-to-face communication with employees so that managers are better informed about employee concerns and organizational activities. (8)

Win-lose orientation A person's belief that the conflicting parties are drawing from a fixed pie, so his or her gain is the other person's loss. (13)

Win-win orientation A person's belief that the parties will find a mutually beneficial solution to their conflict. (13)

Notes

CHAPTER 1

1 "Top Concurrent-Engineering Efforts Earn Kudos," *Machine Design*, May 22, 1997, pp. 20–23; B. Robertson, "New Buses Offer the Luxury of a Stately Ocean Liner," *Winnipeg Free Press*, November 23, 1996, p. A4; B. Robertson, "Growing Motor Coach Industries Riding High," *Winnipeg Free Press*, November 23, 1996, p. B12.

2 L. E. Greiner, "A Recent History of Organizational Behavior," in *Organizational Behavior*, ed. S. Kerr (Columbus, Ohio: Grid, 1979), pp. 3–14.

3 B. Bergman, "One of a Kind," *Maclean's*, March 3, 1997, pp. 30–31; P. Crow, "A Grand Day," *Oil & Gas Journal*, June 2, 1997, p. 33.

4 R. N. Stern and S. R. Barley, "Organizations as Social Systems: Organization Theory's Neglected Mandate," *Administrative Science Quarterly* 41 (1996), pp. 146–62; D. Katz and R. L. Kahn, *The Social Psychology of Organizations* (New York: Wiley, 1966), Chapter 2.

5 J. Pfeffer, *New Directions for Organization Theory* (New York: Oxford University Press, 1997), pp. 7–9.

6 Etzioni, *Modern Organizations*, p. 1.

7 P. R. Lawrence, "Historical Development of Organizational Behavior," in *Handbook of Organizational Behavior*, ed. L. W. Lorsch (Englewood Cliffs, N.J.: Prentice Hall, 1987), pp. 1–9; D. S. Pugh, "Modern Organizational Theory: A Psychological and Sociological Study," *Psychological Bulletin* 66 (1966), pp. 235–51. For a contrary view of the role of practicality in OB research, see A. P. Brief and J. M. Dukerich, "Theory in Organizational Behaviour: Can It Be Useful?" *Research in Organizational Behaviour* 13 (1991), pp. 327–52.

8 "Canada's Changing Face," *Maclean's*, December 30, 1996, pp. 38–39; V. M. Esses and R. C. Gardner, "Multiculturalism in Canada: Context and Current Status," *Canadian Journal of Behavioural Science* 28 (July 1996), pp. 145–52; C. L. Taylor, *Dimensions of Diversity in Canadian Business* (Ottawa: Conference Board of Canada, 1995).

9 M. Gibb-Clark, "Canadian Workers Satisfied but Anxious," *Globe & Mail*, October 8, 1996, p. B13.

10 J. A. Conger, "How Generational Shifts Will Transform Organizational Life," in F. Hesselbein, M. Goldsmith and R. Beckhard (eds.), *The Organization of the Future* (San Francisco: Jossey-Bass, 1997), pp. 17–24.

11 J. King, "All Work, No Play? Gen X-ers: No Way," *Computerworld*, May 5, 1997, pp. 1–2.

12 T. McCallum, "Between Successes: Finding Work in HR-again," HR *Professional*, September 1996, pp. 13-15.

13 M. G. Evans, H. P. Gunz, H. P., and R. M. Jalland, "The Aftermath of Downsizing: A Cautionary Tale of Restructuring and Careers," *Business Horizons* 39 (March 1996), pp. 62–66; J. Laabs, "Employee Commitment," *Personnel Journal*, August 1996, pp. 58–66; C. C. Heckscher, *White-Collar Blues: Management Loyalties In An Age of Corporate Restructuring* (New York: BasicBooks, 1995).

14 S. B. Gould, K. J. Weiner, and B. R. Levin, *Free Agents: People and Organizations Creating a New Working Community* (San Francisco: Jossey-Bass, 1997).

15 For several examples, see: R. S. Wellins, W. C. Byham, and G. R. Dixon, *Inside Teams* (San Francisco: Jossey-Bass, 1994).

16 "How Bombardier Created Sleek Global Express," *Computing Canada*, February 3, 1997, pp. 1, 6.

17 J. Lipnack and J. Stamps, *Virtual Teams: Reaching Across Space, Time, and Organizations with Technology* (New York: John Wiley & Sons, 1997), pp. 5–8.

18 Lipnack and Stamps, *Virtual Teams*, pp. 25–33.

19 M. N. Zald, "More Fragmentation? Unfinished Business in Linking the Social Sciences and the Humanities," *Administrative Science Quarterly* 41 (1996), pp. 251–61.

20 C. Hardy, "The Contribution of Political Science to Organizational Behavior," in J. W. Lorsch (ed.) *Handbook of Organizational Behavior* (Englewood Cliffs, N.J.: Prentice Hall, 1987), pp. 96–108.

21 J. Pfeffer, *New Directions for Organization Theory: Problems and Prospects* (New York: Oxford University Press, 1997), p. 192–93.

22 T. S. Kuhn, *The Structure of Scientific Revolutions* (Chicago: University of Chicago Press, 1970).

23 H. L. Tosi and J. W. Slocum, Jr., "Contingency Theory: Some Suggested Directions," *Journal of Management* 10 (1984), pp. 9–26.

24 D. M. Rousseau and R. J. House, "Meso Organizational Behavior: Avoiding Three Fundamental Biases," in C. J. Cooper and D. M. Rousseau (eds.), *Trends in Organizational Behavior*, Vol. 1, (Chichester, U.K.: John Wiley & Sons, 1994), pp. 13–30.

25 P. M. Senge, "Leading Learning Organizations: The Bold, the Powerful, and the Invisible," in F. Hesselbein, M. Goldsmith, and R. Beckhard (eds.), *The Leader of the Future* (San Francisco: Jossey-Bass, 1996), pp. 41–57.

26 A. Waring, *Practical Systems Thinking* (Boston: International Thomson Business Press, 1997); K. Ellis et al., (eds.), *Critical Issues in Systems Theory and Practice* (New York: Plenum, 1995); P. M. Senge, *The Fifth Discipline: The Art and Practice of the Learning Organization* (New York: Doubleday Currency, 1990), Chapter 4; F. E. Kast and J. E. Rosenweig, "General Systems Theory: Applications for Organization and Management," *Academy of Management Journal*, 1972, pp. 447–65.

27 C. Knight, "Sectoral Skills Council," *Learning in the Workplace* (*Canadian HR Reporter Supplement*), May 22, 1995, pp. L10–L11.

28 Cited in: A. T. Young, "Ethics in Business," *Vital Speeches of the Day* 58 (September 15, 1992), pp. 725–30.

29 K. Noble, "How to Salvage a Corporate Basket-Case," *Globe & Mail*, February 17, 1997, p. B8.

30 T. A. Stewart, *Intellectual Capital: The New Wealth of Organizations* (New York: Currency/Doubleday, 1997); H. Saint-Onge, "Tacit Knowledge: The Key to the Strategic Alignment of Intellectual Capital," *Strategy & Leadership* 24 (March/April 1996), pp. 10–14; G. Petrash, "Dow's Journey to a Knowledge Value Management Culture," *European Management Journal* 14 (August 1996), pp. 365–73.

31 S. Edwards, "The Brain Gain, " *CA Magazine*, April 1997, pp. 20–25.

32 There is no complete agreement on the meaning of organizational learning. The definition presented here is based on the following sources: R. P. Mai, *Learning Partnerships* (Chicago: Irwin, 1996), Chapter 1; G. Huber, "Organizational Learning: The Contributing Processes and Literature," *Organizational Science* 2 (1991), pp. 88–115; P. M. Senge, *The Fifth Discipline: The Art and Practice of the Learning Organization* (New York: Doubleday Currency, 1990), pp. 3–5.

33 F. Luthans, M. J. Rubach, and P. Marsnik, "Going Beyond Total Quality: The Characteristics, Techniques, and Measures of Learning Organizations," *International Journal of Organizational Analysis* 3 (1995), pp. 24–44.

34 Several models of the organizational learning process are effectively summarized in: P. L. Moen, *An Exploratory Study of the Communication System and Practices of Learning Organizations*. Unpublished MBA project (Burnaby, B.C.: Simon Fraser University, April 1996); E. C. Nevis, A. J. DiBella, and J. M. Gould, "Understanding Organizations as Learning Systems," *Sloan Management Review* 36 (Winter 1995), pp. 73–85; Huber "Organizational Learning," *Organizational Science*.

35 N. M. Dixon, *Organizational Learning* (Ottawa: Conference Board of Canada, 1994), p. 9.

36 R. Karpinski, "Microsoft Buys Vermeer Technologies," *CommunicationsWeek*, January 22, 1996, p. 29; P. Keefe, "PC Software Pioneer Ends Missionary Work," *Computerworld*, October 5, 1987, pp. 41, 48.

37 Huber, "Organizational Learning," *Organizational Science*.

38 C. W. Wick and L. S. Leon, "From Ideas to Actions: Creating a Learning Organization." *Human Resource Management* 34 (Summer 1995), pp. 299–311; D. Ulrich, T. Jick, and M. Von Glinow, "High Impact Learning: Building and Diffusing Learning Capability," *Organizational Dynamics* 22 (Autumn 1993), pp. 52–66. This is similar to "synthetic learning" described in D. Miller, "A Preliminary Typology of Organizational Learning: Synthesizing the Literature," *Journal of Management* 22 (1996), pp. 485–505.

39 Dixon, *Organizational Learning*, p. 7.

40 G. S. Richards, S. C. and Goh, "Implementing Organizational Learning: Toward a Systematic Approach," *The Journal of Public Sector Management* (Autumn 1995), pp. 25–31.

41 P. LaBarre, "The Rush on Knowledge," *Industry Week*, February 19, 1996, pp. 53–56.

42 I. Nonaka and H. Takeuchi, *The Knowledge-Creating Company; How Japanese Companies Create the Dynamics of Innovation* (New York: Oxford University Press, 1995).

43 A. Walmsley, "The Brain Game," *Report on Business Magazine*, April 1993, pp. 36–46.

44 W. D. Hitt, "The Learning Organization: Some Reflections on Organizational Renewal," *Leadership & Organization Development Journal* 16 (8) (1995), pp. 17–25.

45 J. Kurtzman, "A Mind is a Terrible Thing to Waste," *Chief Executive*, April 1996, p. 20.

46 M. S. Darling, "Building the Knowledge Organization," *Business Quarterly*, Winter 1996, pp. 61–66.

47 M. E. McGill and J. W. Slocum, Jr., "Unlearn the Organization," *Organizational Dynamics* 22 (2) (1993), pp. 67–79.

CHAPTER 2

1   A. Czarnecki, "Customer Service Training: More Than an 'Event,'" *Learning for the Workplace* (*Canadian HR Reporter* Supplement), May 20, 1996, pp. L4–L7; N. Winter, "Connecting Compensation, Corporate Strategy," *Canadian HR Reporter*, September 23, 1996, p. 10; C. J. Clark, "Safety, Service are 'Make or Break'," *Canadian HR Reporter*, February 26, 1996, pp. 14–15.

2   Cited in A. Haasen, "Opel Eisenach GMBH — Creating a High-Productivity Workplace," *Organizational Dynamics* 24 (Winter 1996), pp. 80–85.

3   C. C. Pinder, *Work Motivation* (Glenview, Ill.: Scott, Foresman, 1984), pp. 7–10; and E. E. Lawler III, *Motivation in Work Organizations* (Monterey, Calif.: Brooks/Cole, 1973), pp. 2–5.

4   L. M. Spencer and S. M. Spencer, *Competence at Work: Models for Superior Performance* (New York: Wiley, 1993).

5   P. Benimadhu, "Adding Value Through Diversity: An Interview with Bernard F. Isautier," *Canadian Business Review* 22 (Spring 1995), pp. 6–11.

6   J. R. Edwards, "Person-Job Fit: A Conceptual Integration, Literature Review, and Methodological Critique," *International Review of Industrial and Organizational Psychology* 6 (1991), pp. 283–357; J. E. Hunter and R. F. Hunter, "Validity and Utility of Alternative Predictors of Job Performance," *Psychological Bulletin* 96 (1984), pp. 72–98.

7   J. W. Johnson, "Linking Employee Perceptions of Service Climate to Customer Satisfaction," *Personnel Psychology* 49 (1996), pp. 831–51; A. Sharma and D. Sarel, "The Impact of Customer Satisfaction Based Incentive Systems on Salespeople's Customer Service Response: An Empirical Study," *Journal of Personal Selling & Sales Management* 15 (Summer 1995), pp. 17–29; R. A. Guzzo, R. D. Jette, and R. A. Katzell, "The Effects of Psychologically Based Intervention Programs on Worker Productivity: A Meta-Analysis," *Personnel Psychology* 38 (1985), pp. 275–91.

8   "Crew's Disastrous Response Mars Report on Ferry Safety," *Vancouver Sun*, January 9, 1997, p. B3.

9   S. P. Brown and R. A. Peterson, "The Effect of Effort on Sales Performance and Job Satisfaction," *Journal of Marketing* 58 (April 1994), pp. 70–80; D. N. Behrman and W. D. Perreault, Jr., "A Role Stress Model of the Performance and Satisfaction of Industrial Salespersons," *Journal of Marketing* 48 (1984), pp. 9–21.

10 S. B. Bacharach and P. Bamberger, "Beyond Situational Constraints: Job Resources Inadequacy and Individual Performance at Work," *Human Resource Management Review* 5 (1995), pp. 79–102; K. F. Kane (ed.), "Special Issue: Situational Constraints and Work Performance," *Human Resource Management Review* 3 (Summer 1993), pp. 83–175.

11 S. L. Rynes, "Applicant Attraction Strategies: An Organizational Perspective," *Academy of Management Review* 15 (1990), pp. 286–310.

12 R. Ray, "The Net is Growing Up Fast as a Corporate Hiring Tool," *Globe & Mail*, October 22, 1996, pp. C1, C10.

13 M. Salter, "Digital's Can-Do Canadians," *Canadian Business* (May 1995, Technology Edition), p. 60; J. Zeidenberg, "Chalk One Up for Quality," *Globe & Mail*, October 12, 1993, pp. C1, C8.

14 R. W. Griffeth and P. W. Hom, "The Employee Turnover Process," *Research in Personnel and Human Resource Management* 13 (1995), pp. 245–93; D. Irvine and M. G. Evans, "Job Satisfaction and Turnover Among Nurses: Integrating Research Findings Across Studies," *Nursing Research* 44 (1995), pp. 246–53; M. J. Withey and W. H. Cooper, "Predicting Exit, Voice, Loyalty, and Neglect," *Administrative Science Quarterly* 34 (1989), pp. 521–39.

15 S. J. Hartman, A. C. Yrle, and A. R. Yrle, "Turnover in the Hotel Industry: Is There a Hobo Phenomenon at Work?" *International Journal of Management* 13 (1996), pp. 340–48; T. A. Judge and S. Watanabe, "Is the Past Prologue? A Test of Ghiselli's Hobo Syndrome," *Journal of Management* 21 (1995), pp. 211–29.

16 "Devco Warns of Layoffs Over Absenteeism," *Globe & Mail*, July 14, 1993, p. B10.

17 S. Whitaker, "Absenteeism Costs Economy \$12 Billion a Year," *Montreal Gazette*, March 22, 1997, p. G1; E. Akyeampong, "Work Absence Rates, 1995," *Perspectives on Labour & Income* 8 (Fall 1996), pp. S1–S11.

18 D. F. Colemen and N. V. Schaefer, "Weather and Absenteeism," *Canadian Journal of Administrative Sciences* 7, no. 4 (1990), pp. 35–42; S. R. Rhodes and R. M. Steers, *Managing Employee Absenteeism* (Reading, Mass.: Addison-Wesley, 1990).

19 R. D. Hackett and P. Bycio, "An Evaluation of Employee Absenteeism as a Coping Mechanism Among Hospital Nurses," *Journal of Occupational & Organizational Psychology* 69 (December 1996), pp. 327–38; J. J. Bardsley and S. R. Rhodes, "Using the Steers-Rhodes (1984) Framework to Identify Correlates of Employee Lateness," *Journal of Business & Psychology* 10 (Spring 1996), pp. 351–65; R. G. Ehrenberg,

R. A. Ehrenberg, D. I. Rees, and E. L. Ehrenberg, "School District Leave Policies, Teacher Absenteeism, and Student Achievement," *Journal of Human Resources* 26 (Winter 1991), pp. 72–105; I. Ng, "The Effect of Vacation and Sick Leave Policies on Absenteeism," *Canadian Journal of Administrative Sciences* 6 (December 1989), pp. 18–27; V. V. Baba and M. J. Harris, "Stress and Absence: A Cross-Cultural Perspective," *Research in Personnel and Human Resources Management,* Supplement 1 (1989), pp. 317–37.

20 J. P. Campbell, R. A. McCloy, S. H. Oppler, and C. E. Sager, "A Theory of Performance," in N. Schmitt, W. C. Borman, and Associates (eds.), *Personnel Selection in Organizations* (San Francisco: Jossey-Bass, 1993), pp. 35–70.

21 S. T. Hunt, "Generic Work Behavior: An Investigation into the Dimensions of Entry-Level, Hourly Job Performance," *Personnel Psychology* 49 (1996), pp. 51–83.

22 Czarnecki, "Customer Service Training: More Than an 'Event'".

23 P. M. Podsakoff, M. Ahearne, and S. B. MacKenzie, "Organizational Citizenship Behavior and the Quantity and Quality of Work Group Performance," *Journal of Applied Psychology* 82 (1997), pp. 262–70; D. W. Organ, "The Motivational Basis of Organizational Citizenship Behavior," *Research in Organizational Behavior* 12 (1990), pp. 43–72. The discussion of altruism is also based on R. N. Kanungo and J. A. Conger, "Promoting Altruism as a Corporate Goal," *Academy of Management Executive* 7, no. 3 (1993), pp. 37–48.

24 C. I. Barnard, *The Functions of the Executive* (Cambridge, Mass.: Harvard University Press, 1938), pp. 83–84; and D. Katz and R. L. Kahn, *The Social Psychology of Organizations* (New York: Wiley, 1966), pp. 337–40.

25 K. Mark, "No More Pink Slips," *Human Resource Professional,* November 1996, pp. 21–23.

26 Organ, "The Motivational Basis of Organizational Citizenship Behavior," pp. 60–63.

27 Kanungo and Conger, "Promoting Altruism as a Corporate Goal," p. 42.

28 D. M. Harris and R. L. DeSimone, *Human Resource Development* (Fort Worth, Texas: Harcourt Brace, 1994), p. 54; B. Bass and J. Vaughn, *Training in Industry: The Management of Learning* (Belmont, Calif.: Wadsworth, 1966), p. 8; W. McGehee and P. W. Thayer, *Training in Business and Industry* (New York: Wiley, 1961), pp. 131–34.

29 S. MacLaurin, "A Real-Life Communications Model," *Training & Development Journal,* March 1991, pp. 79–80.

30 There is no complete agreement on the meaning of organizational learning. The definition presented here is based on the following sources: R. P. Mai, *Learning Partnerships* (Chicago: Irwin, 1996), Chapter 1; G. Huber, "Organizational Learning: The Contributing Processes and Literature," *Organizational Science* 2 (1991), pp. 88–115; P. M. Senge, *The Fifth Discipline: The Art and Practice of the Learning Organization* (New York: Doubleday Currency, 1990), pp. 3–5.

31 I. Nonaka and H. Takeuchi, *The Knowledge-Creating Company* (New York: Oxford University Press, 1995); R. K. Wagner and R. J. Sternberg, "Practical Intelligence in Real-World Pursuits: The Role of Tacit Knowledge," *Journal of Personality and Social Psychology* 49 (1985), pp. 436–58.

32 M. J. Kerr, "Tacit Knowledge as a Predictor of Managerial Success: A Field Study," *Canadian Journal of Behavioural Science* 27 (1995), pp. 36–51.

33 R. G. Miltenberger, *Behavior Modification: Principles and Procedures* (Pacific Grove, Calif.: Brooks/Cole, 1997); H. P. Sims and P. Lorenzi, *The New Leadership Paradigm: Social Learning and Cognition in Organizations* (Newbury Park, Calif.: Sage, 1992), Part II.

34 F. Luthans and R. Kreitner, *Organizational Behavior Modification and Beyond* (Glenview, Ill.: Scott, Foresman, 1985), pp. 85–88; and T. K. Connellan, *How to Improve Human Performance* (New York: Harper & Row, 1978), pp. 48–57.

35 Miltenberger, *Behavior Modification,* Chapters 4–6.

36 Luthans and Kreitner, *Organizational Behavior Modification and Beyond,* pp. 53–54.

37 T. C. Mawhinncy and R. R. Mawhinney, "Operant Terms and Concepts Applied to Industry," in *Industrial Behavior Modification: A Management Handbook,* eds. R. M. O'Brien, A. M. Dickinson, and M. P. Rosow (New York: Pergamon Press, 1982), p. 117; and R. Kreitner, "Controversy in OBM: History, Misconceptions, and Ethics," in *Handbook of Organizational Behavior Management,* ed. L. W. Frederiksen (New York: Wiley, 1982), pp. 76–79.

38 Butterfield et al., "Punishment from the Manager's Perspective"; L. K. Trevino, "The Social Effects of Punishment in Organizations: A Justice Perspective," *Academy of Management Review* 17 (1992), pp. 647–76.

39 B. S. Klaas and H. N. Wheeler, "Managerial Decision Making about Employee Discipline: A Policy-Capturing Approach," *Personnel Psychology* 43 (1990), pp. 117–34.

40 K. D. Butterfield, L. K. Trevino, and G. A. Ball, "Punishment from the Manager's Perspective: A Grounded Investigation and Inductive Model," *Academy of Management Journal* 39 (1996), pp. 1479–1512; G. Eden, "Progressive Discipline: An Oxymoron?" *Relations Industrielles* 47 (1992), pp. 511–27; Luthans and Kreitner, *Organizational Behavior Modification and Beyond,* pp. 139–44; J. M. Beyer and H. M. Trice,

"A Field Study of the Use and Perceived Effects of Discipline in Controlling Work Performance," *Academy of Management Journal* 27 (1984), pp. 743–64.

41 D. N. Campbell, R. L. Fleming, and R. C. Grote, "Discipline without Punishment — at Last," *Harvard Business Review* 63 (July–August 1985), pp. 162–74; and P. Johnson, "Discipline without Punishment," *Financial Times of Canada*, April 20, 1981, pp. H16–H17.

42 G. P. Latham and V. L. Huber, "Schedules of Reinforcement: Lessons from the Past and Issues for the Future," *Journal of Organizational Behavior Management* 13 (1992), pp. 125–49.

43 Miltenberger, *Behavior Modification*, Chapter 10; L. Grant and E. Evans, *Principles of Behavior Analysis* (New York: HarperCollins, 1994); Pinder, *Work Motivation*, p. 198.

44 J. Austin, M. L. Kessler, J. E. Riccobono, and J. S. Bailey, "Using Feedback and Reinforcement to Improve the Performance and Safety of a Roofing Crew" *Journal of Organizational Behavior Management* 16 (1996), pp. 49–75; T. LaFleur and C. Hyten "Improving the Quality of Hotel Banquet Staff Performance," *Journal of Organizational Behavior Management* 15 (1995), pp. 69–93; D. H. B. Welsh, F. Luthans, and S. M. Sommer, "Managing Russian Factory Workers: The Impact of U.S.-based Behavioral and Participative Techniques," *Academy of Management Journal* 36 (February 1993), pp. 58–79.

45 G. A. Merwin, J. A. Thomason, and E. E. Sanford, "A Methodological and Content Review of Organizational Behavior Management in the Private Sector: 1978–1986," *Journal of Organizational Behavior Management* 10 (1989), pp. 39–57.

46 P. Drucker, *Management: Tasks, Responsibilities, Practices* (N.Y.: Harper & Row, 1974).

47 Latham and Huber, "Schedules of Reinforcement," pp. 132–33.

48 Pinder, *Work Motivation*, pp. 230–32; T. C. Mawhinney, "Philosophical and Ethical Aspects of Organizational Behavior Management: Some Evaluative Feedback," *Journal of Organizational Behavior Management* 6 (Spring 1984), pp. 5–31; and F. L. Fry, "Operant Conditioning in Organizational Settings: Of Mice or Men?" *Personnel* 51 (July–August 1974), pp. 17–24.

49 L. Csoka, *Closing the Human Performance Gap: A Research Report* (New York: Conference Board, 1994).

50 A. A. Shikdar and B. Das, "A Field Study of Worker Productivity Improvements," *Applied Ergonomics* 26 (1995), pp. 21–27; L. M. Sama and R. E. Kopelman, "In Search of a Ceiling Effect on Work Motivation: Can Kaizen Keep Performance 'Risin'?" *Journal of Social Behavior & Personality* 9 (1994), pp. 231–237.

51 M. D. Cooper and R. A. Phillips, "Reducing Accidents Using Goal Setting and Feedback: A Field Study," *Journal of Occupational & Organizational Psychology* 67 (1994) pp. 219–40; K. N. Wexley and G. P. Latham, *Developing and Training Human Resources in Organizations*, 2nd ed. (New York: HarperCollins, 1991), pp. 77–80.

52 R. Waldersee and F. Luthans, "The Impact of Positive and Corrective Feedback on Customer Service Performance," *Journal of Organizational Behavior* 15 (1994), pp. 83–95; P. K. Duncan and L. R. Bruwelheide, "Feedback: Use and Possible Behavioral Functions," *Journal of Organizational Behavior Management* 7 (Fall 1985), pp. 91–114; J. Annett, *Feedback and Human Behavior* (Baltimore: Penguin, 1969).

53 R. McDonald, "Transition to PowerPC: RAM Doubler 1.5" *TidBITS*, #236, July 25, 1994 (Web-zine: http://king.tidbits.com).

54 R. Brillinger, "The Many Faces of 360-Degree Feedback," *Canadian HR Reporter*, December 16, 1996, pp. 20–21; P. Jay, "What Goes Around, Comes Around," *Workplace News* 2 (October 1996), p. 3; M. Marchetti, "Pepsi's New Generation of Employee Feedback," *Sales & Marketing Management*, August 1996, pp. 38–39; C. Kapel, "Performing with Abandon," *Human Resource Professional*, June 1996, pp. 16–18.

55 M. London and J. W. Smither, "Can Multisource Feedback Change Perceptions of Goal Accomplishment, Self-Evaluations, and Performance-Related Outcomes? Theory-Based Applications and Directions for Research," *Personnel Psychology* 48 (1995), pp. 803–39. For discussion of multi-source feedback, see: M. Edwards and A. Ewan, *360 Feedback: The Powerful New Model for Employee Assessment & Performance Improvement* (New York: AMACOM, 1996); D. Antonioni, "Designing an Effective 360-Degree Appraisal Feedback Process," *Organizational Dynamics*, Autumn 1996, pp. 24–38.

56 R. Y. Bergstrom, "Cells in Steel Country," *Production*, February 1995, pp. 51–54; C. Hilborn, "Those Upwardly Mobile Machines," *Canadian Business*, October 1993, pp. 117–22.

57 D. M. Herold, R. C. Linden, and M. L. Leatherwood, "Using Multiple Attributes to Assess Sources of Performance Feedback," *Academy of Management Journal*, 1987, pp. 826–35.

58 M. London, "Giving Feedback: Source-Centered Antecedents and Consequences of Constructive and Destructive Feedback," *Human Resource Management Review* 5 (1995), pp. 159–88; D. Antonioni, "The Effects of Feedback Accountability on 360–Degree Appraisal Ratings," *Personnel Psychology* 47 (1994), pp. 375–90; S. J. Ashford and G. B. Northcraft, "Conveying More (or Less) Than We Realize: The Role of Impression Management in Feedback Seeking," *Organizational Behavior and Human Decision Processes* 53 (1992), pp. 310–34; E. W. Morrison and R. J. Bies, "Impression Management in the Feedback-Seeking Process: A Literature Review and Research Agenda," *Academy of Management Review* 16 (1991), pp. 522–41.

59 G. B. Northcraft and S. J. Ashford, "The Preservation of Self in Everyday Life: The Effects of Performance Expectations and Feedback Context on Feedback Inquiry," *Organizational Behavior and Human Decision Processes* 47 (1990), pp. 42–64.

60 R. D. Pritchard, P. L. Roth, S. D. Jones, and P. G. Roth, "Implementing Feedback Systems to Enhance Productivity: A Practical Guide," *National Productivity Review* 10 (Winter 1990–1991), pp. 57–67.

61 P. M. Posakoff and J. Fahr, "Effects of Feedback Sign and Credibility on Goal Setting and Task Performance," *Organizational Behavior and Human Decision Processes* 44 (1989), pp. 45–67.

62 R. D. Guzzo and B. A. Gannett, "The Nature of Facilitators and Inhibitors of Effective Task Performance," *Facilitating Work Effectiveness*, eds. F. D. Schoorman and B. Schneider (Lexington, Mass.: Lexington Books, 1988), p. 23; and R. C. Linden and T. R. Mitchell, "Reactions to Feedback: The Role of Attributions," *Academy of Management Journal*, 1985, pp. 291–308.

63 S. Robinson and E. Weldon, "Feedback Seeking in Groups: A Theoretical Perspective," *British Journal of Social Psychology* 32 (1993), pp. 71–86; S. J. Ashford and L. L. Cummings, "Feedback as an Individual Resource: Personal Strategies of Creating Information," *Organizational Behavior and Human Performance* 32 (1983), pp. 370–98; and S. J. Ashford, "Feedback Seeking in Individual Adaptation: A Resource Perspective," *Academy of Management Journal* 29 (1986), pp. 465–87.

64 S. Bryant, "Electronic Surveillance in the Workplace," *Canadian Journal of Communication* 20 (1995), pp. 505–21; E. Kallman, "Electronic Monitoring of Employees: Issues and Guidelines," *Journal of Systems Management* 44, no. 6 (June 1993), pp. 17–21; and R. Grant and C. Higgins, "Monitoring Service Workers via Computer: The Effect on Employees, Productivity, and Service," *National Productivity Review*, Spring 1989, pp. 101–12.

65 R. Grant, "Work Monitored Electronically," *HRMagazine*, May 1992, pp. 81–86.

66 R. Fulford, "Tolerating Electronic Sweatshops," *Globe & Mail*, December 14, 1994, p. A12.

67 Bryant, "Electronic Surveillance in the Workplace" *Canadian Journal of Communication*; K. A. Jenero and L. D. Mapes-Riordan, "Electronic Monitoring of Employees and the Elusive 'Right to Privacy,'" *Employee Relations Law Journal* 18 (Summer 1992), pp. 71–102.

68 A. Walmsley, "The Brain Game," *Report on Business Magazine*, April 1993, pp. 36–45.

69 International Labour Organization. *Conditions of Work Digest: Monitoring and Surveillance in the Workplace* 12(1) (Geneva: International Labour Office, 1993).

70 D. Lyon, *The Electronic Eye: The Rise of the Surveillance Society* (Minneapolis, Minn.: University of Minnesota Press, 1994); B. P. Niehoff and R. H. Moorman, "Justice as a Mediator of the Relationship Between Methods of Monitoring and Organizational Citizenship Behavior," *Academy of Management Journal* 36 (1993), pp. 527–56; J. Chalykoff and T. A. Kochan, "Computer-Aided Monitoring: Its Influence on Employee Job Satisfaction and Turnover," *Personnel Psychology* 42 (1989), pp. 807–34.

71 A. Bandura, *Social Foundations of Thought and Action: A Social Cognitive Theory* (Englewood Cliffs, N.J.: Prentice Hall, 1986).

72 A. Pescuric and W. C. Byham, "The New Look of Behavior Modeling," *Training & Development* 50 (July 1996), pp. 24–30; H. P. Sims, Jr., and C. C. Manz, "Modeling Influences on Employee Behavior," *Personnel Journal*, January 1982, pp. 58–65.

73 G. Goldberg, "Matter over Mind," *Occupational Health & Safety Canada* 7 (March–April 1991), pp. 56–63.

74 A. Bandura, *Self-Efficacy: The Exercise of Control* (W. H. Freeman & Co., 1996); M. E. Gist and T. R. Mitchell, "Self-Efficacy: A Theoretical Analysis of Its Determinants and Malleability," *Academy of Management Review* 17 (1992), pp. 183–211; R. F. Mager, "No Self-Efficacy, No Performance," *Training* 29 (April 1992), pp. 32–36.

75 A. Bandura, "Self-Efficacy Mechanism in Human Agency," *American Psychologist* 37 (1982), pp. 122–47.

76 L. K. Trevino, "The Social Effects of Punishment in Organizations: A Justice Perspective," *Academy of Management Review* 17 (1992), pp. 647–76; M. E. Schnake, "Vicarious Punishment in a Work Setting," *Journal of Applied Psychology* 71 (1986), pp. 343–45.

77 A. W. Logue, *Self-Control: Waiting Until Tomorrow for What You Want Today* (Engelwood Cliffs, N.J.: Prentice Hall, 1995); A. Bandura, "Self-Reinforcement: Theoretical and Methodological Considerations," *Behaviorism* 4 (1976), pp. 135–55.

78 C. A. Frayne, "Improving Employee Performance Through Self-Management Training," *Business Quarterly* 54 (Summer 1989), pp. 46–50.

79 International Forest Products Limited. *1995 Environmental Report* (Vancouver: Company, 1996), p. 7.

80 L. J. Perelman, "Kanban to Kanbrain," *Forbes ASAP*, June 6, 1994, pp. 85–95.

81 R. P. DeShon and R. A. Alexander, "Goal Setting Effects on Implicit and Explicit Learning of Complex Tasks," *Organizational Behavior and Human Decision Processes* 65 (1996), pp. 18–36; C. A. Seger, "Implicit Learning," *Psychological Bulletin* 115 (1994), pp. 163–96.

82 A. C. Edmondson, "Learning from Mistakes is Easier Said than Done: Group and Organizational Influences on the Detection and Correction of Human Error," *Journal of Applied Behavioral Science* 32

(1996), pp. 5–28; C. D'Andrea-O'Brien and A. F. Buono, "Building Effective Learning Teams: Lessons from the Field," *SAM Advanced Management Journal* 61 (April 1996), pp. 4–9.

83 G. Dutton "Enhancing Creativity," *Management Review*, November 1996, p. 44–46.

84 C. Charney, "Self-directed Peer Training in Teams," *Journal for Quality & Participation* 19 (October 1996), pp. 34–37.

85 M. Meehan and J. Jarvis, "A Refreshing Angle on Staff Education," *People Management*, July 1996, pp. 38–39; P. Froiland, "Action Learning: Taming Real Problems in Real Time," *Training*, January 1994, pp. 27–34.

CHAPTER 3

1 R. Williamson, "Motivation on the Menu," *Globe & Mail*, November 24, 1995, p. B7.

2 C. C. Pinder, *Work Motivation* (Glenview, Ill.: Scott, Foresman, 1984), pp. 7–10; and E. E. Lawler III, *Motivation in Work Organizations* (Monterey, Calif.: Brooks/Cole, 1973), pp. 2–5.

3 D. J. McNerney, "Creating a Motivated Workforce," *HR Focus* (August 1996), pp. 1, 4–6.

4 D. K. Foot, *Boom, Bust, and Echo* (Toronto: Macfarlane Walter & Ross, 1996), Chapter 4; B. Tulgan, *Managing Generation X: How to Bring Out the Best in Young Talent* (Oxford: Capstone, 1996).

5 A. H. Maslow, "A Theory of Human Motivation," *Psychological Review* 50 (1943), pp. 370–96; A. H. Maslow, *Motivation and Personality* (New York: Harper & Row, 1954).

6 M. A. Wahba and L. G. Bridwell, "Maslow Reconsidered: A Review of Research on the Need Hierarchy Theory," *Organizational Behavior and Human Performance* 15 (1976), pp. 212–40.

7 C. P. Alderfer, *Existence, Relatedness, and Growth* (New York: The Free Press, 1972).

8 J. P. Wanous and A. A. Zwany, "A Cross-Sectional Test of Need Hierarchy Theory," *Organizational Behavior and Human Performance* 18 (1977), pp. 78–97.

9 D. C. McClelland, *The Achieving Society* (New York: Van Nostrand Reinhold, 1961).

10 J. Langan-Fox and S. Roth, "Achievement Motivation and Female Entrepreneurs," *Journal of Occupational and Organizational Psychology* 68 (1995), pp. 209–18.

11 D. C. McClelland, "Retrospective Commentary," *Harvard Business Review* (January–February 1995), pp. 138–139.

12 D. C. McClelland and D. H. Burnham, "Power Is the Great Motivator," *Harvard Business Review* (January–February 1995), pp. 126–39 (reprinted from 1976); D. C. McClelland and R. Boyatzis, "Leadership Motive Pattern and Long-Term Success in Management," *Journal of Applied Psychology* 67 (1982), pp. 737–43.

13 D. C. McClelland and D. G. Winter, *Motivating Economic Achievement* (New York: The Free Press, 1969); and D. Miron and D. C. McClelland, "The Impact of Achievement Motivation Training on Small Business," *California Management Review* 21 (1979), pp. 13–28.

14 A. Kohn, *Punished by Rewards* (N.Y.: Houghton Mifflin, 1993).

15 D. A. Nadler and E. E. Lawler, "Motivation: A Diagnostic Approach," in *Perspectives on Behavior in Organizations*, 2nd ed., ed. J. R. Hackman, E. E. Lawler III, and L. W. Porter (New York: McGraw-Hill, 1983), pp. 67–78; and V. H. Vroom, *Work and Motivation* (New York: Wiley, 1964).

16 K. Lewin, "Psychology of Success and Failure," *Occupations* 14 (1936), pp. 926–30.

17 Lawler's version of expectancy theory is described in: J. P. Campbell, M. D. Dunnette, E. E. Lawler, and K. E. Weick, *Managerial Behavior, Performance, and Effectiveness* (New York: McGraw-Hill, 1970), pp. 343–48; E. E. Lawler, *Motivation in Work Organizations* (Monterey, Calif.: Brooks/Cole, 1973), Chapter 3; and Nadler and Lawler, "Motivation: A Diagnostic Approach," pp. 67–78.

18 Nadler and Lawler, "Motivation: A Diagnostic Approach," pp. 70–73.

19 Lawler, *Motivation in Work Organizations*, pp. 53–55.

20 K. A. Karl, A. M. O'Leary-Kelly, and J. J. Martoccio, "The Impact of Feedback and Self-Efficacy on Performance in Training," *Journal of Organizational Behavior* 14 (1993), pp. 379–94; T. Janz, "Manipulating Subjective Expectancy through Feedback: A Laboratory Study of the Expectancy-Performance Relationship," *Journal of Applied Psychology* 67 (1982), pp. 480–85.

21 J. B. Fox, K. D. Scott, and J. M. Donohoe, "An Investigation into Pay Valence and Performance in a Pay-for-Performance Field Setting," *Journal of Organizational Behavior* 14 (1993), pp. 687–93.

22 W. Van Eerde and H. Thierry, "Vroom's Expectancy Models and Work-Related Criteria: A Meta-Analysis," *Journal of Applied Psychology* 81 (1996), pp. 575–86; T. R. Mitchell, "Expectancy Models of Job Satisfaction, Occupational Preference and Effort: A Theoretical, Methodological, and Empirical Appraisal," *Psychological Bulletin* 81 (1974), pp. 1053–77.

23 D. D. Baker, R. Ravichandran, and D. M. Randall, "Exploring Contrasting Formulations of Expectancy Theory," *Decision Sciences* 20 (1989), pp. 1–13; Vroom, *Work and Motivation*, pp. 14–19.

24 K. C. Snead and A. M. Harrell, "An Application of Expectancy Theory to Explain a Manager's Intention to Use a Decision Support System," *Decision Sciences* 25 (1994), pp. 499–513; M. E. Tubbs, D. M. Boehne, and J. G. Dahl, "Expectancy, Valence, and Motivational Force Functions in Goal-Setting Research: An

Empirical Test," *Journal of Applied Psychology* 78 (1993), pp. 361–73; J. A. Shepperd, "Productivity Loss in Performance Groups: A Motivation Analysis." *Psychological Bulletin* 113 (January 1993), pp. 67–81; T. P. Summers and W. H. Hendrix, "Development of a Turnover Model that Incorporates a Matrix Measure of Valence-Instrumentality-Expectancy Perceptions," *Journal of Business & Psychology* 6 (1991), pp. 227–45; Pinder, *Work Motivation: Theory, Issues, and Applications,* pp. 144–47.

25 K. Cox, "Hospital Merger Bears Fruit," *Globe & Mail,* February 17, 1997, pp. A1, A6; S LeBrun, "Massive Medical Merger Spawns Staff Survey," *Canadian HR Reporter,* December 2, 1996, p. 6.

26 J. S. Adams, "Toward an Understanding of Inequity," *Journal of Abnormal and Social Psychology* 67 (1963), pp. 422–36; R. T. Mowday, "Equity Theory Predictions of Behavior in Organizations," in *Motivation and Work Behavior,* 5th ed., ed. R. M. Steers and L. W. Porter (New York: McGraw-Hill, 1991), pp. 111–31.

27 G. Blau, "Testing the Effect of Level and Importance of Pay Referents on Pay Level Satisfaction," *Human Relations* 47 (1994), pp. 1251–268; C. T. Kulik and M. L. Ambrose, "Personal and Situational Determinants of Referent Choice," *Academy of Management Review* 17 (1992), pp. 212–37; J. Pfeffer, "Incentives in Organizations: The Importance of Social Relations," in *Organization Theory: From Chester Barnard to the Present and Beyond,* ed. O. E. Williamson (New York: Oxford University Press, 1990), pp. 72–97.

28 T. P. Summers and A. S. DeNisi, "In Search of Adams' Other: Reexamination of Referents Used in the Evaluation of Pay," *Human Relations* 43 (1990), pp. 497–511.

29 C. Varcoe, "SaskPower's Raises," *Leader Post (Saskatoon),* February 1, 1997, p. A1.

30 J. S. Adams, "Inequity in Social Exchange," in *Advances in Experimental Psychology,* ed. L. Berkowitz (New York: Academic Press, 1965), pp. 157–89.

31 J. Barling, C. Fullagar, and E. K. Kelloway, *The Union and Its Members: A Psychological Approach* (New York: Oxford University Press, 1992).

32 L. Greenberg and J. Barling, "Employee Theft," in C. L. Cooper and D. M. Rousseau (eds.) *Trends in Organizational Behavior* 3 (1996), pp. 49–64.

33 J. Greenberg, "Cognitive Reevaluation of Outcomes in Response to Underpayment Inequity," *Academy of Management Journal* 32 (1989), pp. 174–84; E. Hatfield and S. Sprecher, "Equity Theory and Behavior in Organizations," *Research in the Sociology of Organizations* 3 (1984), pp. 94–124.

34 Cited in *Canadian Business,* February 1997, p. 39.

35 R. Folger and R. A. Baron, "Violence and Hostility at Work: A Model of Reactions to Perceived Injustice," in G. R. VandenBos and E. Q. Bulatao (eds.), *Violence on the Job: Identifying Risks and Developing Solutions* (Washington: American Psychological Association, 1996); J. Greenberg, "Stealing in the Name of Justice: Informational and Interpersonal Moderators of Theft Reactions to Underpayment Inequity," *Organizational Behavior and Human Decision Processes* 54 (1993), pp. 81–103; R. D. Bretz, Jr. and S. L. Thomas, "Perceived Equity, Motivation, and Final-Offer Arbitration in Major League Baseball," *Journal of Applied Psychology* 77 (1993), pp. 280–87.

36 R. P. Vecchio and J. R. Terborg, "Salary Increment Allocation and Individual Differences," *Journal of Organizational Behaviour* 8 (1987), pp. 37–43.

37 "Volvo's New Man," *Fortune,* March 8, 1993, p. 135.

38 For recent research on the effectiveness of goal setting, see: K. H. Doerr and T. R. Mitchell, "Impact of Material Flow Policies and Goals on Job Outcomes," *Journal of Applied Psychology* 81 (1996), pp. 142–52; A. A. Shikdar and B. Das, "A Field Study of Worker Productivity Improvements." *Applied Ergonomics* 26 (February 1995), pp. 21–27; M. D. Cooper and R. A. Phillips, "Reducing Accidents Using Goal Setting and Feedback: A Field Study," *Journal of Occupational & Organizational Psychology* 67 (1994), pp. 219–40.

39 T. H. Poister and G. Streib, "MBO in Municipal Government: Variations on a Traditional Management Tool," *Public Administration Review* 55 (1995), pp. 48–56.

40 E. A. Locke and G. P. Latham, *A Theory of Goal Setting and Task Performance* (Englewood Cliffs, N.J.: Prentice Hall, 1990); A. J. Mento, R. P. Steel, and R. J. Karren, "A Meta-analytic Study of the Effects of Goal Setting on Task Performance: 1966–1984," *Organizational Behavior and Human Decision Processes* 39 (1987), pp. 52–83; M. E. Tubbs, "Goal-setting: A Meta-analytic Examination of the Empirical Evidence," *Journal of Applied Psychology* 71 (1986), pp. 474–83.

41 I. R. Gellatly and J. P. Meyer, "The Effects of Goal Difficulty on Physiological Arousal, Cognition, and Task Performance," *Journal of Applied Psychology* 77 (1992), pp. 694–704; A. Mento, E. A. Locke, and H. Klein, "Relationship of Goal Level to Valence and Instrumentality," *Journal of Applied Psychology* 77 (1992), pp. 395–405.

42 S. Sherman, "Stretch Goals: The Dark Side of Asking for Miracles," *Fortune* 132 (November 13, 1995), pp. 231–32.

43 S. K. Yearta, S. Maitlis, and R. B. Briner, "An Exploratory Study of Goal Setting in Theory and Practice: A Motivational Technique that Works?" *Journal of Occupational and Organizational Psychology* 68 (1995), pp. 237–52.

44 M. E. Tubbs, "Commitment as a Moderator of the Goal-Performance Relation: A Case for Clearer Construct Definition," *Journal of Applied Psychology* 78 (1993), pp. 86–97.

45 H. J. Klein, "Further Evidence of the Relationship Between Goal setting and Expectancy Theory," *Organizational Behavior and Human Decision Processes* 49 (1991), pp. 230–57.

46 "Keeping an Eye on Government," *Canadian Press Newswire*, March 31, 1996.

47 G. P. Latham, D. C. Winters, and E. A. Locke, "Cognitive and Motivational Effects of Participation: A Mediator Study," *Journal of Organizational Behavior* 15 (1994), pp. 49–63.

48 J. Chowdhury, "The Motivational Impact of Sales Quotas on Effort," *Journal of Marketing Research* 30 (1993), pp. 28–41; Locke and Latham, *A Theory of Goal Setting and Task Performance*, Chapters 6 and 7; E. A. Locke, G. P. Latham, and M. Erez, "The Determinants of Goal Commitment," *Academy of Management Review* 13 (1988), pp. 23–39.

49 P. M. Wright, "Goal Setting and Monetary Incentives: Motivational Tools that Can Work Too Well," *Compensation and Benefits Review*, (May–June, 1994), pp. 41–49.

50 F. M. Moussa, " Determinants and Process of the Choice of Goal Difficulty," *Group & Organization Management* 21 (1996), pp. 414–38.

51 R. P. DeShon and R. A. Alexander, "Goal Setting Effects on Implicit and Explicit Learning of Complex Tasks," *Organizational Behavior and Human Decision Processes* 65 (1996), pp. 18–36; A. M. Saks, R. R. Haccoun, and D. Laxer, "Transfer Training: A Comparison of Self-Management and Relapse Prevention Interventions," *Administrative Sciences Association of Canada Proceedings, Human Resources Division* 17 (9) (1996), pp. 81–91.

52 G. Audia, K. G. Brown, A. Kristof-Brown, and E. A. Locke, "Relationship of Goals and Microlevel Work Processes to Performance on a Multipath Manual Task," *Journal of Applied Psychology* 81, (1996), pp. 483–97.

53 N. J. Adler, *International Dimensions of Organizational Behavior*, 3rd ed. (Cincinnati: South-Western, 1997), Chapter 6; G. Hofstede, "Motivation, Leadership, and Organization: Do American Theories Apply Abroad?" *Organizational Dynamics*, Summer 1980, pp. 42–63.

54 A. Sagie, D. Elizur, and H. Yamauchi, "The Structure and Strength of Achievement Motivation: A Cross-Cultural Comparison," *Journal of Organizational Behavior* 17 (September 1996), pp. 431–44; D. Elizur, I. Borg, R. Hunt, and I. M. Beck, "The Structure of Work Values: A Cross Cultural Comparison," *Journal of Organizational Behavior* 12 (1991), pp. 21–38.

55 N. A. Boyacigiller and N. J. Adler, "The Parochial Dinosaur: Organizational Science in a Global Context," *Academy of Management Review* 16 (1991), pp. 262–90; Adler, *International Dimensions of Organizational Behavior*, 3rd ed., Chapter 6.

56 D. H. B. Welsh, F. Lthans, and S. M. Sommer, "Managing Russian Factory Workers: The Impact of U.S.-Based Behavioral and Participative Techniques," *Academy of Management Journal* 36 (1993), pp. 58–79; T. Matsui and I. Terai, "A Cross-Cultural Study of the Validity of the Expectancy Theory of Motivation," *Journal of Applied Psychology* 60 (1979), pp. 263–65.

57 K. I. Kim, H.-J. Park, and N. Suzuki, "Reward Allocations in the United States, Japan, and Korea: A Comparison of Individualistic and Collectivistic Cultures," *Academy of Management Journal* 33 (1990), pp. 188–98.

CHAPTER 4

1 "Case Study: On Tour with Hewlett-Packard," *Adnews Insight*, August 1995. (From Web site: http://www.interlog.com/~adnews/)

2 S. L. McShane and B. Redekop, "Compensation Management and Canadian Wrongful Dismissal: Lessons from Litigation," *Relations Industrielles* 45 (1990), pp. 357–80.

3 M. C. Bloom and G. T. Milkovich, "Issues in Managerial Compensation Research," in C. L. Cooper and D. M. Rousseau (eds.), *Trends in Organizational Behavior*, Vol. 3 (Chicester, U.K.: John Wiley & Sons, 1996), pp. 23–47.

4 S. Desker-Shaw, "Revving Up Asia's Workers," *Asian Business* 32 (February 1996), pp. 41–44.

5 For a discussion of LTD, see R. N. Kanungo and M. Mendonca, *Compensation: Effective Reward Management* (Toronto: Butterworths, 1992), pp. 328–33.

6 F. S. Hills, T. J. Bergmann, and V. G. Scarpello, *Compensation Decision Making* (Fort Worth, Texas: Dryden, 1994, pp. 316–18; L. R. Gomez-Mejia and D. B. Balkin, *Compensation, Organizational Strategy, and Firm Performance* (Cincinnati: South-Western, 1992), pp. 40–41.

7 R. Thériault, *Mercer Compensation Manual: Theory and Practice* (Boucherville, Que.: G. Morin Publisher, 1992), p. 75–78; Kanungo and Mendonca, *Compensation: Effective Reward Management*, p. 247.

8   M. Gunderson and R. E. Robb, "Equal Pay for Work of Equal Value: Canada's Experience," *Advances in Industrial and Labor Relations* 5 (1991), pp. 151–68; and S. L. McShane, "Two Tests of Direct Gender Bias in Job Evaluation Ratings," *Journal of Occupational Psychology* 63 (1990), pp. 129–40.

9   F. F. Reichheld, *The Loyalty Effect* (Boston: Harvard Business School Press, 1996), p. 137; M. Quaid, *Job Evaluation: The Myth of Equitable Assessment* (Toronto: University of Toronto Press, 1993).

10 L. M. Spencer and S. M. Spencer, *Competence at Work: Models for Superior Performance* (New York: Wiley, 1993).

11 N. Winter, "Competencies Help Create New Culture," *Canadian HR Reporter*, April 22, 1996, p. 6.

12 C. Kapel, "Pay and Competencies," *Human Resource Professional*, September 1996, pp. 25–27; D. Hofrichter, "Broadbanding: A 'Second Generation' Approach," *Compensation & Benefits Review* 25 (September/October 1993), pp. 53–58.

13 E. E. Lawler, III, "From Job-Based to Competency-Based Organizations," *Journal of Organizational Behavior* 15 (1994), pp. 3–14; R. L. Bunning, "Models for Skill-Based Pay Plans," *HR Magazine* 37 (February 1992), pp. 62–64; and G. E. Ledford, Jr., "The Design of Skill-Based Pay Plans," in *The Compensation Handbook*, eds. M. L. Rock and L. A. Berger (New York: McGraw-Hill, 1991), pp. 199–217.

14 E. E. Lawler, III, G. E. Ledford, Jr., and L. Chang, "Who Uses Skill-Based Pay, and Why," *Compensation and Benefits Review* 25 (March–April 1993), pp. 22–26.

15 E. E. Lawler, III, "Competencies: A Poor Foundation for The New Pay," *Compensation & Benefits Review*, November/December 1996, pp. 20, 22–26.

16 G. G. Nasmith, *Timothy Eaton* (Toronto: McClelland & Stewart, 1923), p. 91; and P. C. Newman, *Caesars of the Wilderness* (Toronto: Viking, 1987), p. 121.

17 Kanungo and Mendonca, *Compensation: Effective Reward Management*, Chapter 8.

18 E. B. Peach and D. A. Wren, "Pay for Performance from Antiquity to the 1950s," *Journal of Organizational Behavior Management*, 1992, pp. 5–26.

19 J. Heinzl, "A Knack for Knit Earnings," *Globe & Mail*, September 21, 1993, p. B26.

20 G. Pearson, "Looking for More Discretionary Effort? A Little Recognition Can Go a Long Way," *Canadian HR Reporter*, July 15, 1996, pp. 19–20; B. Nelson, *1001 Ways to Reward Employees* (New York: Workman Publishing, 1994), p. 118.

21 D. G. Shaw and C. E. Schneier, "Team Measurement and Rewards: How Some Companies are Getting It Right," *Human Resource Planning* (1995), pp. 34–49.

22 "Health Care Diaper," *BC Business*, October 1993, p. 38.

23 J. Schofield, "Hope for Higher Pay," *Maclean's*, November 25, 1996, pp. 100–101; C. Knight, "'Normal' is Hairier Than Ever," *Canadian HR Reporter*, January 29, 1996, pp. 1, 2. For a recent discussion of gainsharing, see: C. Cooper and B. Dyck, "Improving the Effectiveness of Gainsharing: The Role of Fairness and Participation," *Administrative Science Quarterly* 37 (1992), pp. 471–90.

24 T. H. Wagar and R. J. Long, "Profit Sharing in Canada: Incidence and Predictors," *1995 ASAC Conference, Human Resources Division* 16 (9) (1995), pp. 97–105. For a recent example of profit sharing, see: S. G. Ogden, "Profit Sharing and Organizational Change," *Accounting, Auditing, & Accountability Journal* 8 (1995), pp. 23–47.

25 D. Tyson, *Profit Sharing in Canada* (Toronto: John Wiley & Sons, 1996); J. Chelius and R. S. Smith, "Profit Sharing and Employment Stability," *Industrial and Labor Relations Review* 43 (1990), pp. 256s–73s.

26 R. J. Long, "The Incidence and Nature of Employee Profit Sharing and Share Ownership in Canada," *Relations Industrielles* 47 (1992), pp. 463–86.

27 D. Flavelle, "The Bosses' Sun," *Toronto Star*, August 3, 1996, pp. C1, C2; M. Gunderson, J. Sack, J. McCartney, D. Wakely, and J. Eaton, "Employee Buyouts in Canada," *British Journal of Industrial Relations* 33 (September 1995), pp. 417–42.

28 A. Kohn, *Punished by Rewards* (Boston: Houghton Mifflin, 1993).

29 Nelson, *1001 Ways to Reward Employees*, p. 148.

30 M. E. Enzle, E. F. Wright, and I. M. Redondo, "Cross-Task Generalization of Intrinsic Motivation Effects," *Canadian Journal of Behavioural Science* 28 (1996), pp. 19–26.

31 V. Scarpello and F. F. Jones, "Why Justice Matters in Compensation Decision Making," *Journal of Organizational Behavior* 17 (May 1996), pp. 285–99; T. J. Keefe, G. R. French, and J. L. Altmann, "Incentive Plans Can Link Employee and Company Goals," *Compensation and Benefits Review*, (January–February 1994), pp. 27–33; E. L. Pavlik and A. Belkaoui, *Determinants of Executive Compensation* (New York: Quorum, 1991); K. M. Eisenhardt, "Agency Theory: An Assessment and Review," *Academy of Management Review* 14 (1989), pp. 57–74.

32 Towers Perrin Inc., *Towers Perrin Workplace Index: How Canadian Employees Really Feel About their Work* (Toronto: Towers Perrin, 1996).

33 K. M. Bartol and D. C. Martin, "When Politics Pays: Factors Influencing Managerial Compensation Decisions," *Personnel Psychology* 43 (1990), pp. 599–614.

34 M. Stevenson, "Be Nice for a Change," *Canadian Business*, November 1993, pp. 81–85.

35 R. Wageman, "Interdependence and Group Effectiveness," *Administrative Science Quarterly* 40 (1995), pp. 145–80.

36 H. Syedain, "The Rewards of Recognition," *Management Today*, May 1995, pp. 72–74.

37 D. R. Spitzer, "Power Rewards: Rewards That Really Motivate," *Management Review*, May 1996, pp. 45–50.

38 J. W. Medcof, "The Effect of Extent of Use and Job of the User upon Task Characteristics," *Human Relations* 42 (1989), pp. 23–41; R. J. Long, *New Office Information Technology: Human and Managerial Implications* (London: Crom Helm, 1987).

39 "Groups Want Pay Equity Rolled into Employment Standards," *Canadian HR Reporter*, May 6, 1996, pp. 1, 10.

40 M. Hequet, "Worker Involvement Lights Up Neon," *Training*, June 1994, pp. 23–29.

41 A. Smith, *The Wealth of Nations* (London: Dent, 1910).

42 M. A. Campion, "Ability Requirement Implications of Job Design: An Interdisciplinary Perspective," *Personnel Psychology* 42 (1989), pp. 1–24; H. Fayol, *General and Industrial Management*, trans. C. Storrs (London: Pitman, 1949); E. E. Lawler III, *Motivation in Work Organizations* (Monterey, Calif.: Brooks/Cole, 1973), Chapter 7.

43 C. R. Littler, "Taylorism, Fordism, and Job Design," in *Job Design: Critical Perspectives on the Labour Process*, eds. D. Knights, H. Willmott, and D. Collinson (Aldershot, U.K.: Gower Publishing, 1985), pp. 10–29; F. W. Taylor, *The Principles of Scientific Management* (New York: Harper & Row, 1911).

44 Cited in H. Mintzberg, *The Structuring of Organizations* (Englewood Cliffs, N.J.: Prentice Hall, 1979), p. 74.

45 "Postal Jobs Taking a Hike," *Ottawa Sun*, April 6, 1997; A. A. Shikdar and B. Das, "A Field Study of Worker Productivity Improvements," *Applied Ergonomics* 26 (1995), pp. 21–27; W. J. Duncan, *Great Ideas in Management* (San Francisco: Jossey-Bass, 1989), Chapter 4.

46 R. Fulford, "Firm Management," *Saturday Night*, September 1983, pp. 42–48, 52.

47 E. E. Lawler, III, *High-Involvement Management* (San Francisco: Jossey-Bass, 1986), Chapter 6; and C. R. Walker and R. H. Guest, *The Man on the Assembly Line* (Cambridge, Mass.: Harvard University Press, 1952).

48 D. F. Coleman, "Job Characteristics and Work Alienation at Multiple Levels of Analysis," *1996 ASAC Proceedings, Organizational Behaviour Division* 17 (5) (1996), pp. 1–10; J. W. Rhinehart, *The Tyranny of Work*, 2nd ed. (Don Mills: HBJ Canada, 1987); R. Kanungo, *Work Alienation: An Integrative Approach* (New York: Praeger, 1982); M. Seeman, "On the Meaning of Alienation," *American Sociological Review* 24 (1959), pp. 783–91; and R. Blauner, *Alienation and Freedom: The Factory Worker and His Industry* (Chicago: University of Chicago Press, 1964).

49 W. F. Dowling, "Job Redesign on the Assembly Line: Farewell to Blue-Collar Blues?" *Organizational Dynamics*, Autumn 1973, pp. 51–67; and Lawler, *Motivation in Work Organizations*, p. 150.

50 M. Keller, *Rude Awakening* (New York: Harper Perennial, 1989), p. 128.

51 M. Sczech and D. Attenello, "NationsBank Reengineers to Achieve Leadership in International Services," *National Productivity Review* 14 (Spring 1995), pp. 89–96; C. S. Wong and M. A. Campion, "Development and Test of a Task Level Model of Motivational Job Design," *Journal of Applied Psychology* 76 (1991), pp. 825–37.

52 F. Herzberg, B. Mausner, and B.B. Snyderman, *The Motivation to Work*, (New York: Wiley, 1959).

53 R. M. Steers and L. W. Porter, *Motivation and Work Behavior*, 5th ed. (New York: McGraw-Hill, 1991), p. 413.

54 J. R. Hackman and G. Oldham, *Work Redesign* (Reading, Mass.: Addison-Wesley, 1980).

55 G. Johns, J. L. Xie, and Y. Fang, "Mediating and Moderating Effects in Job Design," *Journal of Management* 18 (1992), pp. 657–76.

56 P. E. Spector, "Higher-Order Need Strength as a Moderator of the Job Scope — Employee Outcome Relationship: A Meta Analysis," *Journal of Occupational Psychology* 58 (1985), pp. 119–27.

57 P. Osterman, "How Common is Workplace Transformation and Who Adopts It?" *Industrial and Labor Relations Review* 47 (1994), pp. 173–88.

58 J. Wells, "Winning Colours," *Report on Business Magazine*, July 1992, pp. 26–35.

59 "Cross-Trained Employees," *Food Management*, June 1996, pp. 32, 35.

60 W. List, "Under the Gun About Safety," *Globe & Mail*, January 4, 1994, p. B14. Also see: C. Gannage "Union Women in the Garment Industry Respond to New Managerial Strategies," *Canadian Journal of Sociology* 20 (1995), pp. 469–95.

61 H. Enchin, "Video Players," *Globe & Mail*, December 6, 1994, p. B22.

62 J. Mansell, *An Inventory of Innovative Work Arrangement in Ontario* (Toronto: Ontario Ministry of Labour, 1978), pp. 66–68; and P. P. Schoderbek and W. E. Reif, *Job Enlargement: Key to Improved Performance* (Ann Arbor, Mich.: University of Michigan, 1969).

63 N. G. Dodd and D. C. Ganster, "The Interactive Effects of Variety, Autonomy, and Feedback on Attitudes and Performance," *Journal of Organizational Behavior* 17 (1996), pp. 329–47; M. A. Campion and C. L. McClelland, "Follow-up and Extension of the Interdisciplinary Costs and Benefits of Enlarged Jobs," *Journal of Applied Psychology* 78 (1993), pp. 339–51.

64 R. W. Griffin, *Task Design: An Integrative Approach* (Glenview, Ill: Scott Foresman, 1982); J. R. Hackman, G. Oldham, R. Janson, and K. Purdy, "A New Strategy for Job Enrichment," *California Management Review* 17(4) (1975), pp. 57–71.

65 J. A. Conger and R. N. Kanungo, "The Empowerment Process: Integrating Theory and Practice," *Academy of Management Review* 13 (1988), pp. 471–82.

66 R. C. Liden and S. Arad, "A Power Perspective of Empowerment and Work Groups: Implications for Human Resource Management Research," *Research in Personnel and Human Resource Management* 14 (1996), pp. 205–51; G. M. Spreitzer, "Psychological Empowerment in the Workplace: Dimensions, Measurement, and Validation," *Academy of Management Journal* 38 (1995), pp. 1442-465; J. Gandz, "The Employee Empowerment Era," *Business Quarterly*, Autumn 1990, p. 75.

67 J. Godard, "When Do Workplace Reform Programs Appear to Work? Some Preliminary Findings," paper presented at the Organizational Practices and the Changing Employment Relationship Conference, University of British Columbia, October 18–19, 1996; M. S. Darling, "Empowerment: Myth or Reality?" *Canadian Speeches* 10 (April 1996) pp. 48–54; A. J. H. Thorlakson and R. P. Murray, "An Empirical Study of Empowerment in the Workplace" *Group & Organization Management* 21 (March 1996), pp. 67–83.

68 "Highland Valley Triumphs Employee Empowerment," *Canadian Mining Journal* 116 (June 1995), pp. 6–15.

69 For an excellent application of client relationship job enrichment, see: Sczech and Attenello, "NationsBank Reengineers to Achieve Leadership in International Services."

70 L. R. Comeau, "Re-engineering for a More Competitive Tomorrow," *Canadian Business Review*, Winter 1994, pp. 51–52.

71 P. Osterman, "How Common is Workplace Transformation and Who Adopts It?"; R. J. Long, "Patterns of Workplace Innovation," *Relations Industrielles* 44 (1989), pp. 805–26.

72 Y. Fried and G. R. Ferris, "The Validity of the Job Characteristics Model: A Review and Meta-analysis," *Personnel Psychology* 40 (1987), pp. 287–322; and B. T. Loher, R. A. Noe, N. L. Moeller, and M. P. Fitzgerald, "A Meta-analysis of the Relation of Job Characteristics to Job Satisfaction," *Journal of Applied Psychology* 70 (1985), pp. 280–89.

73 D. E. Bowen and E. E. Lawler, III, "The Empowerment of Service Workers: What, Why, How, and When," *Sloan Management Review*, Spring 1992, pp. 31–39; and C. A. Sales, E. Levanoni, and R. Knoop, "Employee Performance as a Function of Job Orientation and Job Design," *Relations Industrielles* 44 (1989), pp. 409–20.

74 Johns et al., "Mediating and Moderating Effects in Job Design," pp. 672–73; and R. W. Griffin, "Toward an Integrated Theory of Task Design," *Research in Organizational Behavior* 9 (1987), pp. 79–120.

75 J. B. Cunningham, "A Look at Four Approaches to Work Design," *Optimum* 20(1) (1989/90), pp. 39–55.

76 W. Westley, *Quality of Working Life: The Role of the Supervisor* (Ottawa: Labour Canada, 1981).

77 P. Kraft, "To Control and Inspire: US Management in the Age of Computer Information Systems and Global Production," in M. Wardell, P. Meiksins, and T. Steiger (eds.), *Labor and Monopoly Capital in the Late Twentieth Century: The Braverman Legacy and Beyond* (Albany, NY: SUNY Press, in press); A. C. Frost, "Labour-Management Collaboration Over the Redesign of Work: The Impact of Alternative Approaches," paper presented at the Organizational Practices and the Changing Employment Relationship Conference, University of British Columbia, October 18–19, 1996; J. Rinehart, "Improving the Quality of Working Life Through Job Redesign: Work Humanization or Work Rationalization?" *Canadian Review of Sociology and Anthropology* 23 (1986), pp. 507–30; and C. Pinder, *Work Motivation* (Glenview, Ill.: Scott, Foresman, 1984), pp. 257–58.

78 "Bodies for Hire — The Contracting Out Debate," *Workplace Change* (Australia), April 1996, pp. 1–3.

79 Campion, "Ability Requirement Implications of Job Design: An Interdisciplinary Perspective," p. 20; and R. B. Dunham, "Relationships of Perceived Job Design Characteristics to Job Ability Requirements and Job Value," *Journal of Applied Psychology* 62 (1977), pp. 760–63.

80 R. Martin and T. D. Wall, "Attentional Demand and Cost Responsibility as Stressors in Shopfloor Jobs," *Academy of Management Journal* 32 (1989), pp. 69–86; and D. P. Schwab and L. L. Cummings, "Impact of Task Scope on Employee Productivity: An Evaluation Using Expectancy Theory," *Academy of Management Review* 1 (1976), pp. 23–35.

81 C. P. Neck and C. C. Manz, "Thought Self-Leadership: The Impact of Mental Strategies Training on Employee Cognition, Behavior, and Affect," *Journal of Organizational Behavior* 17 (1996), pp. 445–67.

82 C. C. Manz and H. P. Sims, Jr. *Superleadership: Leading Others to Lead Themselves* (Englewood Cliffs, N.J.: Prentice Hall, 1989); C. C. Manz, "Self-Leadership: Toward an Expanded Theory of Self-Influence Processes in Organizations," *Academy of Management Review* 11 (1986), pp. 585–600.

83 A. M. Saks, R. R. Haccoun, and D. Laxer, "Transfer Training: A Comparison of Self-Management and Relapse Prevention Interventions," *ASAC 1996 Conference Proceedings, Human Resources* 17 (9) (1996), pp. 81–91; M. E. Gist, A. G. Bavetta, and C. K. Stevens, "Transfer Training Method: Its Influence on Skill Generalization, Skill Repetition, and Performance Level," *Personnel Psychology* 43 (1990), pp. 501–23.

84 H. P. Sims, Jr. and C. C. Manz, *Company of Heroes: Unleashing the Power of Self-Leadership* (New York: Wiley, 1996).

85 A. Morin, "Self-Talk and Self-Awareness: On the Nature of the Relation," *Journal of Mind and Behavior* 14 (1993), pp. 223–34; C. P. Neck and C. C. Manz, "Thought Self-Leadership: The Influence of Self-Talk and Mental Imagery on Performance," *Journal of Organizational Behavior* 13 (1992), pp. 681–99.

86 Neck and Manz, "Thought Self-Leadership: The Impact of Mental Strategies Training on Employee Cognition, Behavior, and Affect."

87 V. D. Mayo and J. Tanaka-Matsumi, "Think Aloud Statements and Solutions of Dysphoric Persons on a Social Problem-Solving Task," *Cognitive Therapy and Research* 20 (1996), pp. 97–113.

88 Early scholars seem to distinguish mental practice from mental imagery, whereas recent literature combines mental practice with visualizing positive task outcomes within the meaning of mental imagery. For recent discussion of this concept, see: C. P. Neck, G. L. Stewart, and C. C. Manz, "Thought Self-Leadership as a Framework for Enhancing the Performance of Performance Appraisers," *Journal of Applied Behavioral Science* 31 (September 1995), pp. 278–302; W. P. Anthony, R. H. Bennett, III, E. N. Maddox, and W. J. Wheatley, "Picturing the Future: Using Mental Imagery to Enrich Strategic Environmental Assessment," *Academy of Management Executive* 7 (2) (1993), pp. 43–56.

89 J. E. Driscoll, C. Cooper, and A. Moran, "Does Mental Practice Enhance Performance?" *Journal of Applied Psychology* 79 (1994), pp. 481–92.

90 Manz, "Self-Leadership: Toward an Expanded Theory of Self-Influence Processes in Organizations."

91 A. W. Logue, *Self-Control: Waiting Until Tomorrow for What You Want Today* (Englewood Cliffs, N.J.: Prentice Hall, 1995).

92 A. M. Saks and B. E. Ashforth, "Proactive Socialization and Behavioral Self-Management," *Journal of Vocational Behavior* 48 (1996), pp. 301–23; Neck and Manz, "Thought Self-Leadership: The Impact of Mental Strategies Training on Employee Cognition, Behavior, and Affect."

93 S. Ming and G. L. Martin, "Single-Subject Evaluation of a Self-Talk Package for Improving Figure Skating Performance," *Sport Psychologist* 10 (1996), pp. 227–38.

94 G. L. Stewart, K. P. Carson, and R. L. Cardy, "The Joint Effects of Conscientiousness and Self-Leadership Training on Employee Self-Directed Behavior in a Service Setting," *Personnel Psychology* 49 (1996), pp. 143–64.

CHAPTER 5

1 "Work Causes Teacher Intense Pain," *Canadian Press Newswire*, October 2, 1996; R. Turner, "Stressed-out Teachers Can't Make the Grade," *Winnipeg Free Press*, September 20, 1996, pp. A1, A2; R. Turner, "Teachers Pushed to the Edge," *Winnipeg Free Press*, September 20, 1996, p. A6

2 C. Dawson, "Study Shows Teachers Stressed," *Calgary Herald,* May 30, 1996, p. B2; "Stressed to the Max," *Benefits Canada* 20 (March 1996), pp. 29–33.

3 Stress costs are based on personal communication with Dr. Richard Earle, Canadian Institute of Stress, in 1990, and a 1996 estimate of $150–$300 billion cost in the United States. For other information on stress costs, see: C. Nolan, "Stressed to the Max," *Benefits Canada*; "The Stress Mess," *B.C. Business Magazine* (December 1995), pp. 20–27; Cross-National Collaborative Group, "The Changing Rate of Major Depression: Cross-National Comparisons," JAMA: *The Journal of the American Medical Association* 268 (December 2, 1992), pp. 3098–105.

4 C. Walker, "Workplace Stress," *Canadian Dimension*, August 1993, pp. 29–32; "It's a Jungle Out There! Why Stress in the 1990s is a Whole Different Animal," *Canadian Occupational Safety* 32 (July/August 1994), pp. 14–17.

5 R. J. Burke and T. Weir, "Coping with the Stress of Managerial Occupations," in *Current Concerns in Occupational Stress*, eds. C. L. Cooper and R. Payne (London: Wiley, 1980), pp. 299–335; M. T. Matteson and J. M. Ivancevich, *Managing Job Stress and Health* (New York: The Free Press, 1982); and J. C. Quick and J. D. Quick, *Organizational Stress and Prevention Management* (New York: McGraw-Hill, 1984).

6 S. Sauter and L. R. Murphy (eds.), *Organizational Risk Factors for Job Stress* (Washington, D.C.: American Psychological Association, 1995); M. Jamal, "Job Stress and Job Performance Controversy: An Empirical Assessment," *Organizational Behavior and Human Performance* 33 (1984), pp. 1–21.

7 H. Selye, *Stress without Distress* (Philadelphia: J. B. Lippincott, 1974).

8 Quick and Quick, *Organizational Stress and Prevention Management*, p. 3.

9 S. Melamed and S. Bruhis, "The Effects of Chronic Industrial Noise Exposure on Urinary Cortisol, Fatigue, and Irritability: A Controlled Field Experiment," *Journal of Occupational and Environmental Medicine* 38 (1996), pp. 252–56.

10 M. Siegall and L. L. Cummings, "Stress and Organizational Role Conflict," *Genetic, Social, and General Psychology Monographs* 12 (1995), pp. 65–95; E. K. Kelloway and J. Barling, "Job Characteristics, Role Stress and Mental Health," *Journal of Occupational Psychology* 64 (1991), pp. 291–304; R. L. Kahn, D. M. Wolfe, R. P. Quinn, J. D. Snoek, and R. A. Rosenthal, *Organizational Stress: Studies in Role Conflict and Ambiguity* (New York: Wiley, 1964).

11 A. Kristof, "Person-Organization Fit: A Integrative Review of Its Conceptualizations, Measurement, and Implications," *Personnel Psychology* 49 (1996) pp. 1–50; B. E. Ashforth and R. H. Humphrey, "Emotional Labor in Service Roles: The Influence of Identity," *Academy of Management Review* 18 (1993), pp. 88–115.

12 Siegall and Cummings, "Stress and Organizational Role Conflict."

13 J. Barling, C. Fullagar, and E. K. Kelloway, *The Union and Its Members: A Psychological Approach* (Oxford, U.K.: Oxford University Press, 1992), Chapter 6.

14 A. M. Saks and B. E. Ashforth, "Proactive Socialization and Behavioral Self-Management." *Journal of Vocational Behavior* 48 (1996), pp. 301–23; D. L. Nelson and C. Sutton, "Chronic Work Stress and Coping: A Longitudinal Study and Suggested New Directions," *Academy of Management Journal* 33 (1990), pp. 859–69.

15 "Overworked and Under-Appreciated in the Okanagan," *British Columbia Report*, May 13, 1996, p. 27.

16 R. Karasek and T. Theorell, *Healthy Work: Stress, Productivity, and the Reconstruction of Working Life* (New York: Basic Books, 1990).

17 J. P. Womack and D. T. Jones, *Lean Thinking* (New York: Simon & Schuster, 1996).

18 J. MacFarland, "Many are Called, But What are the Choices: Working in New Brunswick's 1-800 Call Centres," *New Maritimes* 14 (July/August 1996), pp. 10–19.

19 J. Barling, I. Dekker, C. A. Loughlin, E. K. Kelloway, C. Fullagar, and D. Johnson, "Prediction and Replication of the Organizational and Personal Consequences of Workplace Sexual Harassment," *Journal of Managerial Psychology* 11 (5) (1996), pp. 4–25; "Female Mounties Sexually Harassed," *Globe & Mail*, September 27, 1996, p. A6; J. Carlisle, "Sexual Harassment is Now a Health and Safety Issue," *Financial Post*, July 9, 1996; H. Johnson, "Work-Related Sexual Harassment," *Perspectives on Labour and Income*, Winter 1994, pp. 9–12; A. Picard, "Plagued by Racist Taunts, Teacher Awarded $10,000," *Globe & Mail*, April 14, 1993, p. A4.

20 B. L. Galperin, "Impact of Privatization on Stress in Different Cultures," *Proceedings of the Annual ASAC Conference, International Business Division* 17 (8) (1996), pp. 8–16; P. H. Mirvis and M. L. Marks, *Managing the Merger: Making It Work* (Englewood Cliffs, N.J.: Prentice Hall, 1992), Chapter 5.

21 S. Lewis and C. L. Cooper, "Balancing the Work/Home Interface: A European Perspective," *Human Resource Management Review* 5 (1995), pp. 289–305; L. Duxbury, C. Higgins, and C. Lee, "The Impact of Job Type and Family Type on Work-Family Conflict and Perceived Stress: A Comparative Analysis," *Proceedings of the Annual ASAC Conference, Human Resources Division* 14 (9) (1993), pp. 21–30; K. J. Williams and G. M. Alliger, "Role Stressors, Mood Spillover, and Perceptions of Work-Family Conflict in Employed Parents," *Academy of Management Journal* 37 (1994), pp. 837–68.

22 "Flex More, Worry Less," *Canadian HR Reporter*, August 12, 1996, pp. 1, 8.

23 J. E. Fast and J. A. Frederick, "Working Arrangements and Time Stress," *Canadian Social Trends*, Winter 1996, pp. 14–19; L. Duxbury, C. Lee, C. Higgins, and S. Mills, "Time Spent in Paid Employment," *Optimum 23* (Autumn 1992), pp. 38–45; M. Jamal and V. V. Baba, "Shiftwork and Department-Type Related to Job Stress, Work Attitudes and Behavioral Intentions: A Study of Nurses," *Journal of Organizational Behavior* 13 (1992), pp. 449–64.

24 C. S. Rogers, "The Flexible Workplace: What Have We Learned?" *Human Resource Management* 31 (Fall 1992), pp. 183–99; L. E. Duxbury and C. A. Higgins, "Gender Differences in Work-Family Conflict," *Journal of Applied Psychology* 76 (1991), pp. 60–74; and A. Hochschild, *The Second Shift* (New York: Avon, 1989).

25 M. P. Leiter and M. J. Durup, "Work, Home, and In-Between: A Longitudinal Study of Spillover," *Journal of Applied Behavioral Science* 32 (1996), pp. 29–47; W. Stewart and J. Barling, "Fathers' Work Experiences Effect on Children's Behaviors via Job-Related Affect and Parenting Behaviors," *Journal of Organizational Behavior* 17 (1996), pp. 221–32; C. A. Beatty, "The Stress of Managerial and Professional Women: Is the Price too High?" *Journal of Organizational Behavior* 17 (1996), pp. 233–51. Also see: C. Higgins, L. Duxbury, and R. Irving, "Determinants and Consequences of Work-Family Conflict," *Organizational Behavior and Human Decision Processes* 51 (February 1992), pp. 51–75; R. J. Burke and C. A. McKeen, "Work and Family: What We Know and What We Need to Know," *Canadian Journal of Administrative Sciences* 5 (December 1988), pp. 30–40.

26 A. S. Wharton and R. J. Erickson, "Managing Emotions on the Job and at Home: Understanding the Consequences of Multiple Emotional Roles," *Academy of Management Review* 18 (1993), pp. 457–86; and S. E. Jackson and C. Maslach, "After-Effects of Job-Related Stress: Families as Victims," *Journal of Occupational Behaviour* 3 (1982), pp. 63–77.

27 International Labour Office, *World Labour Report* (Geneva: ILO, 1993), Chapter 5; "High-Anxiety Occupations," *Globe & Mail*, March 23, 1993, p. A9; "Stress Test," *Globe & Mail*, August 11, 1992, p. B20; Karasek and Theorell, *Healthy Work.*

28 A. O'Leary and S. Brown, "Self-Efficacy and the Physiological Stress Response," in J. E. Maddux (ed.). *Self-Efficacy, Adaptation, and Adjustment : Theory, Research, and Application* (New York : Plenum Press, 1995.)

29 K. R. Parkes, "Personality and Coping as Moderators of Work Stress Processes: Models, Methods and Measures," *Work & Stress* 8 (April 1994) pp. 110–129; S. J. Havlovic and J. P. Keenen, "Coping with Work Stress: The Influence of Individual Differences," in P. L. Perrewé (ed.). Handbook on Job Stress [Special Issue], *Journal of Social Behavior and Personality* 6 (1991), pp. 199–212.

30 B. C. Long and S. E. Kahn (eds.), *Women, Work, and Coping : A Multidisciplinary Approach to Workplace Stress* (Montreal : McGill-Queen's University Press, 1993); E. R. Greenglass, R. J. Burke, and M. Ondrack, "A Gender-Role Perspective of Coping and Burnout," *Applied Psychology: An International Review* 39 (1990), pp. 5–27; and T. D. Jick and L. F. Mitz, "Sex Differences in Work Stress," *Academy of Management Review* 10 (1985), pp. 408–20.

31 M. Friedman and R. Rosenman, *Type A Behavior and Your Heart* (New York: Knopf, 1974). For a more recent discussion, see K. R. Parkes, "Personality and Coping as Moderators of Work Stress Processes: Models, Methods and Measures." *Work & Stress* 8 (April 1994) pp. 110–129.

32 M. Jamal and V. V. Baba, "Type A Behavior, Its Prevalence and Consequences Among Women Nurses: An Empirical Examination," *Human Relations* 44 (1991), pp. 1213–228; and T. Kushnir and S. Melamed, "Work-Load, Perceived Control and Psychological Distress in Type A/B Industrial Workers," *Journal of Organizational Behavior* 12 (1991), pp. 155–68.

33 M. Jamal, "Type A Behavior and Job Performance: Some Suggestive Findings," *Journal of Human Stress* 11 (Summer 1985), pp. 60–68; and C. Lee, P. C. Earley, and L. A. Hanson, "Are Type A's Better Performers?" *Journal of Organizational Behavior* 9 (1988), pp. 263–69.

34 E. Greenglass, "Type A Behaviour and Occupational Demands in Managerial Women," *Canadian Journal of Administrative Sciences* 4 (1987), pp. 157–68.

35 M. Jamal and B. Jamal, "Job Stress Among Muslim Immigrants in North America: Moderating Effects of Religiosity," *Stress Medicine* 9 (1993), pp. 145–151.

36 "The Yuppie Flu," *Benefits Canada* 21 (January 1997), p. 17; C. Nair, F. Colburn, D. McLean, and A. Petrasovits, "Cardiovascular Disease in Canada," *Statistics Canada Health Reports* 1(1) (1989), pp. 1–22.

37 Jamal, "Job Stress and Job Performance Controversy: An Empirical Assessment;" S. J. Motowidlo, J. S. Packard, and M. R. Manning, "Occupational Stress: Its Causes and Consequences for Job Performance," *Journal of Applied Psychology* 71 (1986), pp. 618–29; and G. Keinan, "Decision Making under Stress: Scanning of Alternatives under Controllable and Uncontrollable Threats," *Journal of Personality and Social Psychology* 52 (1987), pp. 638–44.

38 R. D. Hackett and P. Bycio, "An Evaluation of Employee Absenteeism as a Coping Mechanism Among Hospital Nurses," *Journal of Occupational & Organizational Psychology* 69 (December 1996) pp. 327–38; V. V. Baba and M. J. Harris, "Stress and Absence: A Cross-Cultural Perspective," *Research in Personnel and Human Resources Management*, Supplement 1 (1989), pp. 317–37.

39 B. Came, "Publish and Perish," *Maclean's*, June 20, 1994, p. 15. For a recent example of co-worker violence, see: "Three Pressmen Charged with Assault and Intimidation" *Ottawa Citizen*, May 4, 1996.

40 E. Wright, "Workplace Trauma, The Day After," *Canadian HR Reporter*, February 24, 1997, pp. 20–21; E. Newton, "Clear Policy, Active Ear Can Reduce Violence," *Canadian HR Reporter*, February 26, 1996, pp. 16–17; "Looking Out for Trouble," *Occupational Health & Safety*, 11(March/April 1995) pp. 34–37; D. Anfuso, "Deflecting Workplace Violence," *Personnel Journal*, October 1994, pp. 66–68.

41 "Violence Caused by Workplace Failures," *Occupational Health & Safety* 12 (September/October 1996), p. 15

42 R. T. Lee and B. E. Ashforth, "A Meta-analytic Examination of the Correlates of the Three Dimensions of Job Burnout," *Journal of Applied Psychology* 81 (1996) pp. 123–33; R. J. Burke, "Toward a Phase Model of Burnout: Some Conceptual and Methodological Concerns," *Group and Organization Studies* 14 (1989), pp. 23–32; and C. Maslach, *Burnout: The Cost of Caring* (Englewood Cliffs, N.J.: Prentice Hall, 1982).

43 C. L. Cordes and T. W. Dougherty, "A Review and Integration of Research on Job Burnout," *Academy of Management Review* 18 (1993), pp. 621–56.

44 R. T. Lee and B. E. Ashforth, "A Further Examination of Managerial Burnout: Toward an Integrated Model," *Journal of Organizational Behavior* 14 (1993), pp. 3–20.

45 "Where Employee Health Comes First," *Globe & Mail*, March 3, 1995, p. C6.

46 Siegall and Cummings, "Stress and Organizational Role Conflict," *Genetic, Social, & General Psychology Monographs*; Havlovic and Keenen, "Coping with Work Stress: the Influence of Individual Differences."

47 T. Newton, J. Handy, and S. Fineman, *Managing Stress: Emotion and Power at Work* (Newbury Park, Calif.: Sage, 1995); "It's a Jungle Out There!" *Canadian Occupational Safety* 32 (July/August 1994), pp. 14–17

48 N. Terra, "The Prevention of Job Stress by Redesigning Jobs and Implementing Self-Regulating Teams," in L. R. Murphy (ed.), *Job Stress Interventions* (Washington, D.C.: American Psychological Association, 1995); T. D. Wall and K. Davids, "Shopfloor Work Organization and Advanced Manufacturing Technology," *International Review of Industrial and Organizational Psychology* 7 (1992), pp. 363–98; Karasek and Theorell, *Healthy Work.*

49 R. Burke, "Accommodating Work and Family: A Stalled Revolution," *Human Resources Professional,* November 1996, pp. 17–19, 29.

50 D. J. McNerney, "Contingent Workers: Companies Refine Strategies," *HRFocus,* October 1996, pp. 4–6; B. S. Watson, "Share and Share Alike," *Management Review,* October 1995; T. McCallum, "The Old 'Seven to Three,'" *Human Resources Professional,* June 1995, pp. 12–14.

51 "Home-Office Workers Need Special Discipline," *Financial Post,* October 12/14, 1996 p. H5; "Business Plugs into Telecommuting: Bringing Work to People Rather than People to Work," *Modern Purchasing* 37 (June 1995), pp. 19–23.

52 B. Livesey, "Provide and Conquer," *Report on Business Magazine,* March 1997, pp. 34–44; K. Mark, "Balancing Work and Family," *Canadian Banker,* January-February 1993, pp. 22–24; Bureau of Municipal Research, *Work-Related Day Care — Helping to Close the Gap* (Toronto: BMR, 1981).

53 K. Hein, "Cigna Offers Employees 'Fast Break' Stress Relief," *Incentive* (July 1996) p. 6.

54 "Buying Time," *Benefits Canada* 20 (September 1996) pp. 19–22; C. Cornell, "Loving It and Leaving It," *Human Resources Professional,* April 1991, pp. 19–22.

55 "Asian Nations Graded for Stress," *Daily Commercial News,* April 25, 1996 p. B1; J. M. Brett, L. K. Stroh, and A. H. Reilly, "Job Transfer," *International Review of Industrial and Organizational Psychology* 7 (1992), pp. 323–62.

56 A. M. Saks and B. E. Ashforth, "Proactive Socialization and Behavioral Self-Management." *Journal of Vocational Behavior* 48 (1996), pp. 301-23; M. Waung, "The Effects of Self-Regulatory Coping Orientation on Newcomer Adjustment and Job Survival," *Personnel Psychology* 48 (1995), pp. 633–50; J. E. Maddux (ed.), *Self-Efficacy, Adaptation, and Adjustment : Theory, Research, and Application* (New York: Plenum Press, 1995.)

57 E. P. Lima, "The Human Element," *Air Transport World* 32 (February 1995), pp. 55–61.

58 A. S. Sethi, "Meditation for Coping with Organizational Stress," in *Handbook of Organizational Stress Coping Strategies,* A. S. Sethi and R. S. Schuler (Cambridge, Mass.: Ballinger, 1984), pp. 145–65; and Matteson and Ivancevich, *Controlling Work Stress,* pp. 160–66.

59 J. Steed, "Healthy, Wealthy, and Wise," *Toronto Star,* January 5, 1997, pp. F1, F5; "Life Skills," *Benefits Canada,* 19 (February 1995), p. 17.

60 L. E. Falkenberg, "Employee Fitness Programs: Their Impact on the Employee and the Organization," *Academy of Management Review* 12 (1987), pp. 511–22; and R. J. Shephard, M. Cox, and P. Corey, "Fitness Program Participation: Its Effect on Workers' Performance," *Journal of Occupational Medicine* 23 (1981), pp. 359–63.

61 S. MacDonald and S. Wells, "The Prevalence and Characteristics of Employee Assistance, Health Promotion and Drug Testing Programs in Ontario," *Employee Assistance Quarterly* 10 (1994), pp. 25–60; R. Loo and T. Watts, "A Survey of Employee Assistance Programs in Medium and Large Canadian Organizations," *Employee Assistance Quarterly* 8 (1993), pp. 65–71.

62 J. M. George, T. F. Reed, K. A. Ballard, J. Colin, and J. Fielding, "Contact with AIDS Patients as a Source of Work-Related Distress: Effects of Organizational and Social Support," *Academy of Management Journal* 36 (1993), pp. 157–71; and S. L. Dolan, M. R. van Ameringen, and A. Arsenault, "Personality, Social Support and Workers' Stress," *Relations Industrielles* 47 (1992), pp. 125–39.

63 S. L. Dolan and P. Zeilig, "Occupational Stress, Emotional Exhaustion, and Propensity to Quit amongst Female Accountants: The Moderating Role of Mentoring," *Proceedings of the Annual ASAC Conference, Human Resources Division* 15(9) (1994), pp. 124–33.

64 J. S. House, *Work Stress and Social Support* (Reading, Mass.: Addison-Wesley, 1981); S. Cohen and T. A. Wills, "Stress, Social Support, and the Buffering Hypothesis," *Psychological Bulletin* 98 (1985), pp. 310–57.

65 S. Schachter, *The Psychology of Affiliation* (Stanford, Calif.: Stanford University Press, 1959).

CHAPTER 6

1 D. McCauley, "Women Chefs: Shattering the Glass Ceiling," *Foodservice and Hospitality,*" January 1996, pp. 25–30.

2 Plato, *The Republic,* trans. D. Lee (Harmondsworth, England: Penguin, 1955), Part VII, Section 7.

3 S. F. Cronshaw and R. G. Lord, "Effects of Categorization, Attribution, and Encoding Processes on Leadership Perceptions," *Journal of Applied Psychology* 72 (1987), pp. 97–106.

4   R. H. Fazio, D. R. Roskos-Ewoldsen, and M. C. Powell, "Attitudes, Perception, and Attention," in P. M. Niedenthal and S. Kitayama (eds.), *The Heart's Eye: Emotional Influences in Perception and Attention* (San Diego, Calif.: Academic Press, 1994), pp. 197–216.

5   D. Goleman, *Vital Lies, Simple Truths: The Psychology of Deception* (New York: Touchstone, 1985); M. Haire and W. F. Grunes, "Perceptual Defenses: Processes Protecting an Organized Perception of Another Personality," *Human Relations* 3 (1950), pp. 403–12.

6   C. N. Macrae and G. V. Bodenhausen, "The Dissection of Selection in Person Perception: Inhibitory Processes in Social Stereotyping," *Journal of Personality & Social Psychology* 69 (1995), pp. 397–407; J. P. Walsh, "Selectivity and Selective Perception: An Investigation of Managers' Belief Structures and Information Processing," *Academy of Management Journal* 31 (1988), pp. 873–96; D. C. Dearborn and H. A. Simon, "Selective Perception: A Note on the Departmental Identification of Executives," *Sociometry* 21 (1958), pp. 140–44.

7   R. Mead, *Cross-Cultural Management Communication* (Chichester, U.K.: John Wiley & Sons, 1992), Chapter 8.

8   C. Argyris and D. A. Schön, *Organizational Learning II.* (Reading, Mass.: Addison–Wesley, 1996); D. Nicolini and M. B. Meznar, "The Social Construction of Organizational Learning: Conceptual and Practical Issues in the Field," *Human Relations* 48 (1995), pp. 727–46; P. M. Senge, *The Fifth Discipline: The Art and Practice of the Learning Organization* (New York: Doubleday Currency, 1990), Chapter 10; P. N. Johnson-Laird, *Mental Models* (Cambridge: Cambridge University Press, 1984).

9   V. L. Shalin and G. V. Prabhu, "A Cognitive Perspective on Manual Assembly," *Ergonomics* 39 (1996), pp. 108–127; P. Nystrom and W. Starbuck, "To Avoid Organizational Crises, Unlearn," *Organizational Dynamics* 12 (Winter 1984), pp. 53–65.

10 I. Mitroff, *Break-Away Thinking* (New York: John Wiley & Sons, 1988).

11 B. E. Ashforth and F. Mael, "Social Identity Theory and the Organization," *Academy of Management Review* 14 (1989), pp. 20–39; H. Tajfel, *Social Identity and Intergroup Relations* (Cambridge: Cambridge University Press, 1982).

12 K. E. Weick, *Sensemaking in Organizations* (Thousand Oaks, Calif.: Sage, 1995), p. 20.

13 W. G. Stephan and C. W. Stephan, *Intergroup Relations* (Boulder, Col.: Westview, 1996), Chapter 1; L. Falkenberg, "Improving the Accuracy of Stereotypes within the Workplace," *Journal of Management* 16 (1990), pp. 107–18; D. L. Hamilton, S. J. Sherman, and C. M. Ruvolo, "Stereotype-Based Expectancies: Effects on Information Processing and Social Behavior," *Journal of Social Issues* 46 (1990), pp. 35–60.

14 C. N. Macrae, A. B. Milne, and G. V. Bodenhausen, "Stereotypes as Energy-Saving Devices: A Peek Inside the Cognitive Toolbox," *Journal of Personality and Social Psychology* 66 (1994), pp. 37–47; S. T. Fiske, "Social Cognition and Social Perception," *Annual Review of Psychology* 44 (1993), pp. 155–94.

15 C. Stangor and L. Lynch, "Memory for Expectancy-Congruent and Expectancy-Incongruent Information: A Review of the Social and Social Development Literatures," *Psychological Bulletin* 111 (1992), pp. 42–61; C. Stangor, L. Lynch, C. Duan, and B. Glass, "Categorization of Individuals on the Basis of Multiple Social Features," *Journal of Personality and Social Psychology* 62 (1992), pp. 207–18.

16 D. L. Stone and A. Colella, "A Model of Factors Affecting the Treatment of Disabled Individuals in Organizations," *Academy of Management Review* 21 (1996), pp. 352–401.

17 M. J. Monteith, "Self-Regulation of Prejudiced Responses: Implications for Progress in Prejudice-Reduction Efforts," *Journal of Personality and Social Psychology* 65 (1993), pp. 469–85.

18 M. E. Heilman, "Sex Stereotypes and their Effects in the Workplace: What We Know and What We Don't Know," *Journal of Social Behavior & Personality* 10 (1995) pp. 3–26.

19 P. M. Buzzanell, "Reframing the Glass Ceiling as a Socially Constructed Process: Implications for Understanding and Change," *Communication Monographs* 62 (December 1995), pp. 327–54.

20 L. Everett, D. Thorne, and C. Danehower, "Cognitive Moral Development and Attitudes Toward Women Executives," *Journal of Business Ethics* 15 (November 1996), pp. 1227–235; J. M. Norris and A. M. Wylie, "Gender Stereotyping of the Managerial Role Among Students in Canada and the United States," *Group & Organization Management* 20 (1995), pp. 167–82; R. J. Burke, "Canadian Business Students' Attitudes Towards Women as Managers," *Psychological Reports* 75 (1994), pp. 1123–129; S. Coate and G. C. Loury, "Will Affirmative-Action Policies Eliminate Negative Stereotypes?" *American Economic Review* 83 (1993), pp. 1220–240; C. L. Owen and W. D. Todor, "Attitudes Toward Women as Managers: Still the Same," *Business Horizons* 36 (March–April 1993), pp. 12–16.

21 V. E. Schein and R. Mueller, "Sex Role Stereotyping and Requisite Management Characteristics: A Cross Cultural Look," *Journal of Organizational Behavior* 13 (1992), pp. 439–47; O. C. Bremmer, J. Tomkiewicz, and V. E. Schein, "The Relationship Between Sex Role Stereotypes and Requisite Management Characteristics Revisited," *Academy of Management Journal* 32 (1989), pp. 662–69.

22 Janzen and Governeau v. Platy Enterprises Ltd. (1989) *Canadian Human Rights Reporter* 10, D/6205 at p. D/6227.

23 S. I. Paish and A. A. Alibhai, *Act, Don't React: Dealing With Sexual Harassment in Your Organization* (Vancouver: Western Legal Publications, 1996).

24 D. E. Terpstra, "The Effects of Diversity on Sexual Harassment: Some Recommendations on Research," *Employee Responsibilities and Rights Journal* 9 (1996), pp. 303–13; J. A. Bargh and P. Raymond, "The Naive Misuse of Power: Nonconscious Sources of Sexual Harassment," *Journal of Social Issues* 51 (1995) pp. 85–96; R. A. Carr, "Addicted to Power: Sexual Harassment and the Unethical Behaviour of University Faculty," *Canadian Journal of Counselling* 25 (1991), pp. 447–61.

25 S. P. Phillips and M. S. Schneider, "Sexual Harassment of Female Doctors by Patients," *New England Journal of Medicine* 329 (1993), pp. 1936–939.

26 J. Barling, I. Dekker, C. A. Loughlin, E. K. Kelloway, C. Fullagar, and D. Johnson, "Prediction and Replication of the Organizational and Personal Consequences of Workplace Sexual Harassment," *Journal of Managerial Psychology* 11 (5) (1996), pp. 4–25; "Female Mounties Sexually Harassed," *Globe & Mail*, September 27, 1996, p. A6; J. Carlisle, "Sexual Harassment is Now a Health and Safety Issue," *Financial Post*, July 9, 1996; H. Johnson, "Work-Related Sexual Harassment," *Perspectives on Labour and Income*, Winter 1994, pp. 9–12; A. Picard, "Plagued by Racist Taunts, Teacher Awarded $10,000," *Globe & Mail*, April 14, 1993, p. A4.

27 S. T. Fiske and P. Glick, "Ambivalence and Stereotypes Cause Sexual Harassment: A Theory with Implications for Organizational Change," *Journal of Social Issues* 51 (1995), pp. 97–115; K. Deaux, "How Basic Can you Be? The Evolution of Research on Gender Stereotypes," *Journal of Social Issues* 51 (1995) pp. 11–20.

28 H. H. Kelley, *Attribution in Social Interaction* (Morristown, N.J.: General Learning Press, 1971).

29 J. D. Ford, "The Effects of Causal Attributions on Decision Makers' Responses to Performance Downturns," *Academy of Management Review* 10 (1985), pp. 770–86; M. J. Martinko and W. L. Gardner, "The Leader/Member Attribution Process," *Academy of Management Review* 12 (1987), pp. 235–49.

30 B. Bemmels, "Attribution Theory and Discipline Arbitration," *Industrial and Labor Relations Review* 44 (April 1991), pp. 548–62.

31 J. M. Crant and T. S. Bateman, "Assignment of Credit and Blame for Performance Outcomes," *Academy of Management Journal* 36 (1993), pp. 7–27; M. G. Evans and L. T. Brown, "The Role of Attributions in the Performance Evaluation Process," *Proceedings of the Annual ASAC Conference, Organizational Behaviour Division* 10, Part 7 (1989), pp. 31 38.

32 J. Martocchio and J. Dulebohn, "Performance Feedback Effects in Training: The Role of Perceived Controllability," *Personnel Psychology* 47 (1994), pp. 357–73; D. R. Norris and R. E. Niebuhr, "Attributional Influences on the Job Performance–Job Satisfaction Relationship," *Academy of Management Journal* 27 (1984), pp. 424–31.

33 H. J. Bernardin and P. Villanova, "Performance Appraisal," in *Generalizing from Laboratory to Field Settings,* ed. E. A. Locke (Lexington, Mass.: Lexington Books, 1986), pp. 43–62; and S. G. Green and T. R. Mitchell, "Attributional Processes of Leader-Member Interactions," *Organizational Behavior and Human Performance* 23 (1979), pp. 429–58.

34 J. R. Bettman and B. A. Weitz, "Attributions in the Board Room: Causal Reasoning in Corporate Annual Reports," *Administrative Science Quarterly* 28 (1983), pp. 165–83.

35 P. Rosenthal and D. Guest, "Gender Difference in Managers' Causal Explanations for Their Work Performance: A Study in Two Organizations," *Journal of Occupational & Organizational Psychology* 69 (1996) pp. 145–51.

36 For a summary of cross cultural attribution research, see: Stephan and Stephan, *Intergroup Relations,* pp. 124–25.

37 "The Motive Isn't Money," *Profit* 14 (Spring 1995) pp. 20–29.

38 J. M. Darley and K. C. Oleson, "Introduction to Research on Interpersonal Expectations," in *Interpersonal Expectations: Theory, Research, and Applications* (Cambridge, U.K.: Cambridge University Press, 1993), pp. 45–63; D. Eden, *Pygmalion in Management* (Lexington, Mass.: Lexington, 1990); and L. Jussim, "Self-Fulfilling Prophecies: A Theoretical and Integrative Review," *Psychological Review* 93 (1986), pp. 429–45.

39 Similar models are presented in R. H. G. Field and M. G. Evans, "Pygmalion at Work: Manager Expectation Effects on Travel Agency Outcomes," *Proceedings of the Annual ASAC Conference, Organizational Behaviour Division* 14(5) (1993), pp. 102–11; R. H. G. Field and D. A. Van Seters, "Management by Expectations (MBE): The Power of Positive Prophecy," *Journal of General Management* 14 (Winter 1988), pp. 19–33; and D. Eden, "Self-Fulfilling Prophecy as a Management Tool: Harnessing Pygmalion," *Academy of Management Review* 9 (1984), pp. 64–73.

40 M. J. Harris and R. Rosenthal, "Mediation of Interpersonal Expectancy Effects: 31 Meta-Analyses," *Psychological Bulletin* 97 (1985), pp. 363–86.

41 D. Eden, "Interpersonal Expectations in Organizations," *in Interpersonal Expectations: Theory, Research, and Applications* (Cambridge, U.K.: Cambridge University Press, 1993), pp. 154–78.

42 A. Bandura, *Self-Efficacy: The Exercise of Control* (W. H. Freeman & Co., 1996); M. E. Gist and T. R. Mitchell, "Self-Efficacy: A Theoretical Analysis of Its Determinants and Malleability," *Academy of Management Review* 17 (1992), pp. 183–211.

43 P. D. Blanck, "Interpersonal Expectations in the Courtroom: Studying Judges' and Juries' Behavior," in *Interpersonal Expectations: Theory, Research, and Applications* (Cambridge, U.K.: Cambridge University Press, 1993), pp. 64–87; J. B. Rosser, Jr., "Belief: Its Role in Economic Thought and Action," *American Journal of Economics & Sociology* 52 (1993), pp. 355–68; R. Rosenthal and L. Jacobson, *Pygmalion in the Classroom: Teacher Expectation and Student Intellectual Development* (New York: Holt, Rinehart, & Winston, 1968).

44 J. S. Livingston, "Retrospective Commentary," *Harvard Business Review* 66 (September–October 1988), p. 125.

45 For a review of organizational studies of self-fulfilling prophecy, see: Eden, "Interpersonal Expectations in Organizations," in *Interpersonal Expectations: Theory, Research, and Applications.*

46 D. Eden and A. B. Shani, "Pygmalion Goes to Boot Camp: Expectancy, Leadership, and Trainee Performance," *Journal of Applied Psychology* 67 (1982), pp. 194–99.

47 S. Oz and D. Eden, "Restraining the Golem: Boosting Performance by Changing the Interpretation of Low Scores," *Journal of Applied Psychology* 79 (1994), pp. 744–54; D. Eden, "OD and Self-Fulfilling Prophecy: Boosting Productivity by Raising Expectations," *Journal of Applied Behavioral Science* 22 (1986), pp. 1–13.

48 W. H. Cooper, "Ubiquitous Halo," *Psychological Bulletin* 90 (1981), pp. 218–44; and K. R. Murphy, R. A. Jako, and R. L. Anhalt, "Nature and Consequences of Halo Error: A Critical Analysis," *Journal of Applied Psychology* 78 (1993), pp. 218–25.

49 S. Kozlowski, M. Kirsch, and G. Chao, "Job Knowledge, Rate Familiarity, Conceptual Similarity, and Halo Error: An Exploration," *Journal of Applied Psychology* 71 (1986), pp. 45–49; and H. C. Min, "Country Image: Halo or Summary Construct?" *Journal of Marketing Research* 26 (1989), pp. 222–29.

50 W. K. Balzer, and L. M. Sulsky, "Halo and Performance Appraisal Research: A Critical Examination," *Journal of Applied Psychology* 77 (1992), pp. 975–85; and H. J. Bernardin and R. W. Beatty, *Performance Appraisal: Assessing Human Behavior at Work* (Boston: Kent, 1984).

51 T. Hill, P. Lewicki, M. Czyzewska, and A. Boss, "Self-Perpetuating Development of Encoding Biases in Person Perception," *Journal of Personality and Social Psychology* 57 (1989), pp. 373–87; C. L. Kleinke, *First Impressions: The Psychology of Encountering Others* (Englewood Cliffs, N.J.: Prentice Hall, 1975).

52 D. D. Steiner and J. S. Rain, "Immediate and Delayed Primacy and Recency Effects in Performance Evaluation," *Journal of Applied Psychology* 74 (1989), pp. 136–42; R. L. Heneman and K. N. Wexley, "The Effects of Time Delay in Rating and Amount of Information Observed in Performance Rating Accuracy," *Academy of Management Journal* 26 (1983), pp. 677–86.

53 G. G. Sherwood, "Self-Serving Biases in Person Perception: A Re-examination of Projection as a Mechanism of Defense," *Psychological Bulletin* 90 (1981), pp. 445–59.

54 Bank of Montreal, The Task Force on the Advancement of Women in the Bank, *Report to Employees* (Toronto: Bank of Montreal, November 1991).

55 G. Flynn, "Bank of Montreal Satisfies Customers by Satisfying Employees," *Workforce* 76 (February 1997), pp. 46-47; H. Kluge, "Reflections on Diversity: Cultural Assumptions," *Vital Speeches of the Day* 63 (January 1, 1997), pp. 171–75; A. Rossett and T. Bickham, "Diversity Training: Hope, Faith, and Cynicism," *Training*, January 1994, pp. 40–46; and K. Foss, "Keeping Harmony in Race Relations," *Financial Times of Canada*, July 6–12, 1992, p. 17.

56 M. G. Fine, *Building Successful Multicultural Organizations* (Westport, Conn.: Quorum, 1995), pp. 114–16.

57 M. M. Starcevich, S. J. Stowell, and R. S. Yamahiro, "An Unusual Day of Development," *Training and Development Journal* 40 (March 1986), pp. 45–48.

58 G. Egan, *The Skilled Helper: A Model for Systematic Helping and Interpersonal Relating* (Belmont, Calif.: Brooks/Cole, 1975); and D. B. Fedor and K. M. Rowland, "Investigating Supervisor Attributions of Subordinate Performance," *Journal of Management* 15 (1989), pp. 405–16.

59 L. Beamer, "Learning Intercultural Communication Competence," *Journal of Business Communication* 29 (1992), pp. 285–303; and D. Landis and R. W. Brislin (eds.), *Handbook of Intercultural Training* (New York: Pergamon, 1983).

60 S. Silcoff, "The Sky's Your Limit," *Canadian Business*, April 1997, p. 62.

61 T. W. Costello and S. S. Zalkind, *Psychology in Administration: A Research Orientation* (Englewood Cliffs, N.J.: Prentice Hall, 1963), pp. 45–46.

62 J. Luft, *Group Processes* (Palo Alto, Calif.: Mayfield Publishing, 1984). For a variation of this model, see J. Hall, "Communication Revisited," *California Management Review* 15 (Spring 1973), pp. 56–67.

63 L. C. Miller and D. A. Kenny, "Reciprocity of Self-Disclosure at the Individual and Dyadic Levels: A Social Relations Analysis," *Journal of Personality and Social Psychology* 50 (1986), pp. 713–19.

64 R. Laver, "A Jury System for Jobs," *Maclean's*, August 5, 1996, p. 45.

65   M. Maccoby, "Teams Need Open Leaders," *Research-Technology Management* 38 (January 1995), pp. 57–59.

66   M. Beaugé, "Riding the Wave," *Business in Vancouver*, April 8–14, 1997, pp. 10–11.

67   R. T. Hogan, "Personality and Personality Measurement," in M. D. Dunnette and L. M. Hough (eds.) *Handbook of Industrial and Organizational Psychology*, 2nd ed., Vol. 2 (Palo Alto, Calif.: Consulting Psychologists Press, 1991), pp. 873–919. Also see: W. Mischel, *Introduction to Personality* (New York: Holt, Rinehart, & Winston, 1986).

68   H. M. Weiss and S. Adler, "Personality and Organizational Behavior," *Research in Organizational Behavior* 6 (1984), pp. 1–50.

69   W. Revelle, "*Personality Processes*" *Annual Review of Psychology* 46 (1995), pp. 295–328.

70   This historical review and the trait descriptions in this section are discussed in: R. J. Schneider and L. M. Hough, "Personality and Industrial/Organizational Psychology," *International Review of Industrial and Organizational Psychology* 10 (1995), pp. 75–129; M. K. Mount and M. R. Barrick, "The Big Five Personality Dimensions: Implications for Research and Practice in Human Resources Management," *Research in Personnel and Human Resources Management* 13 (1995), pp. 153–200; J. M. Digman, "Personality Structure: Emergence of the Five-Factor Model," *Annual Review of Psychology* 41 (1990), pp. 417–40.

71   J. M. Howell and C. A. Higgins, "Champions of Change: Identifying, Understanding, and Supporting Champions of Technological Innovations," *Organizational Dynamics*, Summer 1990, pp. 40–55; B. M. Bass, *Stogdill's Handbook of Leadership: A Survey of Theory and Research*, 3rd ed. (New York: Free Press, 1990); J. L. Holland, *Making Vocation Choices: A Theory of Careers* (Englewood Cliffs, N.J.: Prentice Hall, 1973).

72   R. M. Guion and R. F. Gottier, "Validity of Personality Measures in Personnel Selection," *Personnel Psychology* 18 (1965), pp. 135–64. Also see: N. Schmitt, R. Z. Gooding, R. D. Noe, and M. Kirsch, "Meta-Analyses of Validity Studies Published Between 1964 and 1982 and the Investigation of Study Characteristics," *Personnel Psychology* 37 (1984), pp. 407–22.

73   R. D. Gatewood and H. S. Feild, *Human Resource Selection,* 3rd ed. (Fort Worth, Tex.: Harcourt Brace and Company, 1994), Chapter 15.

74   P. G. Irving, "On the Use of Personality Measures in Personnel Selection," *Canadian Psychology* 34 (April 1993), pp. 208–14; R. P. Tett, D. N. Jackson, and M. Rothstein, "Personality Measures as Predictors of Job Performance: A Meta-Analytic Review," *Personnel Psychology* 44 (1991), pp. 703–42.

75   I. R. Gellatly, "Dispositional Determinants of Task Performance: Focus on the Big Five Factor of Conscientiousness," *Proceedings of the Annual ASAC Conference, Human Resources Division* 17 (9) (1996), pp. 43–52; M. K. Mount, M. R. Barrick, and J. P. Strauss, "Validity of Observer Ratings of the Big Five Personality Factors," *Journal of Applied Psychology* 79 (1994), pp. 272–80.

76   K. P. Carson and G. L. Stewart, "Job Analysis and the Sociotechnical Approach to Quality: A Critical Examination," *Journal of Quality Management* 1 (1996), pp. 49–64; Mount and Barrick, "The Big Five Personality Dimensions," pp. 177–78.

77   For discussion of bandwidth-fidelity issue in personality measurement for selecting job applicants, see *Journal of Organizational Behavior* 17 (November 1996), pp. 607–55.

78   R. Zemke, "Second Thoughts about the MBTI," *Training*, April 1992, pp. 42–47.

79   H. A. Simon, *Administrative Behavior* (New York: The Free Press, 1957), p. xv.

80   J. M. Howell and B. J. Avolio, "Transformational Leadership, Transactional Leadership, Locus of Control, and Support for Innovation: Key Predictors of Consolidated-Business-Unit Performance," *Journal of Applied Psychology* 78 (1993), pp. 891–902; S. D. Saleh and K. Desai, "An Empirical Analysis of Job Stress and Job Satisfaction of Engineers," *Journal of Engineering & Technology Management* 7 (July 1990), pp. 37–48; P. E. Spector, "Behavior in Organizations as a Function of Employee's Locus of Control," *Psychological Bulletin* 91 (1982), pp. 482–97; and P. J. Andrisani and C. Nestel, "Internal-External Control as a Contributor to and Outcome of Work Experience," *Journal of Applied Psychology* 61 (1976), pp. 156–65.

81   D. Miller and J.-M. Toulouse, "Chief Executive Personality and Corporate Strategy and Structure in Small Firms," *Management Science* 32 (1986), pp. 1389–409; and D. Miller, M. F. R. Ket de Vries, and J.-M. Toulouse, "Top Executive Locus of Control and Its Relationship to Strategy-Making, Structure, and Environment," *Academy of Management Journal* 25 (1982), pp. 237–53.

82   M. Snyder, *Public Appearances/Private Realities: The Psychology of Self-Monitoring* (New York: W. H. Freeman, 1987); and R. S. Adamson, R. J. Ellis, G. Deszca, and T. F. Cawsey, "Self-Monitoring and Leadership Emergence," *Proceedings of the Annual ASAC Conference, Organizational Behaviour Division* 5, Part 5 (1984), pp. 9–15.

83   S. J. Zaccaro, R. J. Foti, and D. A. Kenny, "Self-Monitoring and Trait-Based Variance in Leadership: An Investigation of Leader Flexibility Across Multiple Group Situations," *Journal of Applied Psychology* 76 (1991), pp. 308–15; and T. F. Cawsey, G. Deszca, R. J. Ellis, and R. S. Adamson, "Self-Monitoring and Interview Success," *Proceedings of the Annual ASAC Conference, Organizational Behaviour Division* 7, Part 5 (1986), pp. 29–37.

CHAPTER 7

1   P. Verburg, "The Little Airline That Could," *Canadian Business*, April 1997, pp. 34–40; A. Daniels, "The Jokes are Free," *Vancouver Sun*, May 17, 1996, pp. A1, A8.

2   B. E. Ashforth and R. H. Humphrey, "Emotion in the Workplace: A Reappraisal," *Human Relations* 48 (1995), pp. 97–125.

3   For a fuller discussion of specific emotions, see: R. Pekrun and M. Frese, "Emotions in Work and Achievement," *International Review of Industrial and Organizational Psychology* 7 (1992), pp. 153–200.

4   This definition is based on material in H. M. Weiss and R. Cropanzano, "Affective Events Theory: A Theoretical Discussion of the Structure, Causes, and Consequences of Affective Experiences at Work," *Research in Organizational Behavior* 18 (1996), pp. 1–74; S. Kitayama and P. M. Niedenthal, "Introduction," in P. M. Niedenthal and S. Kitayama, *The Heart's Eye: Emotional Influences in Perception and Attention* (San Diego, Calif.: Academic Press, 1994), pp. 6–7.

5   K. Oatley and J. M. Jenkins, "Human Emotions: Function and Dysfunction," *Annual Review of Psychology* 43 (1992), pp. 55–85.

6   J. M. George and A. P. Brief, "Motivational Agendas in the Workplace: The Effects of Feelings on Focus of Attention and Work Motivation," *Research in Organizational Behavior* 18 (1996), pp. 75–109; J. M. George, "Mood and Absence," *Journal of Applied Psychology* 74 (1989), pp. 317–24.

7   T. A. Judge, E. A. Locke, and C. C. Durham, "The Dispositional Causes of Job Satisfaction: A Core Evaluations Approach," *Research in Organizational Behavior* 19 (1997), pp. 151–88; A. P Brief, A. H. Butcher, and L. Roberson, "Cookies, Disposition, and Job Attitudes: The Effects of Positive Mood-Inducing Events and Negative Affectivity on Job Satisfaction in a Field Experiment," *Organizational Behavior and Human Decision Processes* 62 (1995), pp. 55–62; J. M. George, "The Role of Personality in Organizational Life: Issues and Evidence," *Journal of Management* 18 (1992), pp. 185–213.

8   J. Schaubroeck, D. C. Ganster, and B. Kemmerer, "Does Trait Affect Promote Job Attitude Stability?," *Journal of Organizational Behavior* 17 (1996), pp. 191–96; R. D. Arvey, B. P. McCall, T. L. Bouchard, and P. Taubman, "Genetic Differences on Job Satisfaction and Work Values," *Personality and Individual Differences* 17 (1994), pp. 21–33; B. M. Staw and J. Ross, "Stability in the Midst of Change: A Dispositional Approach to Job Attitudes," *Journal of Applied Psychology* 70 (1985), pp. 469–80.

9   J. M. Olson and M. P. Zama, "Attitudes and Attitude Change," *Annual Review of Psychology* 44 (1993), pp. 117–54; C. C. Pinder, *Work Motivation: Theory, Issues, and Applications* (Glenview, Ill.: Scott, Foresman & Co., 1984), p. 82; M. Fishbein and I. Ajzen, *Belief, Attitude, Intention, and Behavior* (Reading, Mass.: Addison-Wesley, 1975).

10 Weiss and Cropanzano, "Affective Events Theory."

11 M. D. Zalesny and J. K. Ford, "Extending the Social Information Processing Perspective: New Links to Attitudes, Behaviors, and Perceptions," *Organizational Behavior and Human Decision Processes* 52 (1992), pp. 205–46; G. Salancik and J. Pfeffer, "A Social Information Processing Approach to Job Attitudes and Task Design," *Administrative Science Quarterly* 23 (1978), pp. 224–53.

12 For a full discussion of several theories on this topic, see: K. T. Strongman, *The Psychology of Emotion: Theories of Emotion in Perspective*, 4th ed. (Chichester, U.K.: John Wiley & Sons, 1996), Chapter 6.

13 M. R. Klinger and A. G. Greenwald, "Preferences Need No Inference?: The Cognitive Basis of Unconscious Mere Exposure Effects," in Niedenthal and Kitayama (eds.), *The Heart's Eye*, pp. 67–85.

14 D. M. Irvine and M. G. Evans, "Job Satisfaction and Turnover Among Nurses: Integrating Research Findings Across Studies," *Nursing Research* 44 (1995), pp. 246–53.

15 Pinder, *Work Motivation*, pp. 88–89.

16 Weiss and Cropanzano, "Affective Events Theory," pp. 52–57.

17 L. Festinger, *A Theory of Cognitive Dissonance* (Evanston, Ill.: Row, Peterson, 1957); and G. R. Salancik, "Commitment and the Control of Organizational Behavior and Belief," in *New Directions in Organizational Behavior*, eds. B. M. Staw and G. R. Salancik (Chicago: St. Clair, 1977), pp. 1–54.

18 Weiss and Cropanzano, "Affective Events Theory."

19 E. A. Locke, "The Nature and Causes of Job Satisfaction," in *Handbook of Industrial and Organizational Psychology*, ed. M. Dunnette (Chicago: Rand McNally, 1976), pp. 1297–350.

20 M. Gibb-Clark, "Workers Pinpoint Bosses' Flaws," *Globe & Mail*, October 18, 1996, p. B12.

21 S. Ross, "Most Workers in Canada, U.S. Feel Work Fulfilling, Survey Says," *Globe & Mail*, November 7, 1995, p. B4.

22 J. McFarland, "Canadian Workers Rank High in Happiness," *Globe & Mail*, September 5, 1996, p. B13.

23 E. E. Lawler III, *Motivation in Work Organizations* (Belmont, Calif.: Wadsworth, 1973), pp. 66–69, 74–77.

24 D. B. McFarlin and R. W. Rice, "The Role of Facet Importance as a Moderator in Job Satisfaction Processes," *Journal of Organizational Behavior* 13 (1992), pp. 41–54.

25 M. Kerr, "Developing a Corporate Culture for the Maximum Balance Between the Utilization of Human Resources and Employee Fulfillment in Canada," *Canada-United States Law Journal* 22 (1996), pp. 169–76.

26 R. D. Hackett and P. Bycio, "An Evaluation of Employee Absenteeism as a Coping Mechanism Among Hospital Nurses," *Journal of Occupational & Organizational Psychology* 69 (December 1996), pp. 327–38; J. Barling, "The Prediction, Psychological Experience, and Consequences of Workplace Violence," in G. R. VandenBos and E. Q. Bulatao, *Violence on the Job* (Washington, D.C.: American Psychological Association, 1996), pp. 29–49; R. P. Tett and J. P. Meyer, "Job Satisfaction, Organizational Commitment, Turnover Intention, and Turnover: Path Analyses Based on Meta-Analytical Findings," *Personnel Psychology* 46 (1993), pp. 259–93; P. Y. Chen and P. E. Spector, "Relationships of Work Stressors with Aggression, Withdrawal, Theft and Substance Use: An Exploratory Study," *Journal of Occupational & Organizational Psychology* 65 (1992), pp. 177–84; E. K. Kelloway and J. Barling, "Job Characteristics, Role Stress and Mental Health," *Journal of Occupational Psychology* 64 (1991), pp. 291–304.

27 A. Toulin, "Civil Servants Scramble to Get Buyouts," *Financial Post*, July 15, 1995, p. 3

28 S. D. Bluen, "The Psychology of Strikes," *International Review of Industrial and Organizational Psychology* 9 (1994), pp. 113–45; J. Barling, C. Fullagar, K. Kelloway, and K. McElvie, "Union Loyalty and Strike Propensity," *Journal of Social Psychology* 132 (1992), pp. 581–90; I. Ng, "Predictors of Strike Voting Behaviour: The Case of University Faculty," *Journal of Labor Research* 12 (1991), pp. 121–34; and S. L. McShane, "Sources of Attitudinal Union Militancy," *Relations Industrielles* 40 (1985), pp. 284–302.

29 J. Greenberg, "Employee Theft as a Reaction to Underpayment Inequity: The Hidden Cost of Pay Cuts," *Journal of Applied Psychology* 75 (1990), pp. 561–68.

30 G. Allen, "Issues of Trust," *Maclean's*, November 23, 1992, pp. 16–18.

31 P. Y. Chen and P. E. Spector, "Relationships of Work Stressors with Aggression, Withdrawal, Theft and Substance Use: An Exploratory Study," *Journal of Occupational & Organizational Psychology* 65 (1992), pp. 177–84.

32 B. M. Staw and S. G. Barsade, "Affect and Managerial Performance: A Test of the Sadder-but-Wiser vs. Happier-and-Smarter Hypotheses," *Administrative Science Quarterly* 38 (1993), pp. 304–31; M. T. Iaffaldano and P. M. Muchinsky, "Job Satisfaction and Job Performance: A Meta-Analysis," *Psychological Bulletin* 97 (1985), pp. 251–73; D. P. Schwab and L. L. Cummings, "Theories of Performance and Satisfaction: A Review," *Industrial Relations* 9 (1970), pp. 408–30.

33 E. E. Lawler III and L. W. Porter, "The Effect of Performance on Job Satisfaction," *Industrial Relations* 7 (1967), pp. 20 28.

34 C. D. Fisher and E. A. Locke, "The New Look in Job Satisfaction Research and Theory," in Cranny et al. (eds.), *Job Satisfaction*, pp. 165–94; P. M. Podsakoff, S. B. MacKenzie, and C. Hui, "Organizational Citizenship Behaviors and Managerial Evaluations of Employee Performance: A Review and Suggestions for Future Research," *Research in Personnel and Human Resources Management* 11 (1993), pp. 1–40; D. W. Organ, "The Motivational Basis of Organizational Citizenship Behavior," *Research in Organizational Behavior* 12 (1990), pp. 43–72.

35 S. H. Shapoff, "Why Corning Breathes TQM," *Financial Executive* 12 (November–December 1996), pp. 26–28; R. Hallowell, L. A. Schlesinger, and J. Zornitsky, "Internal Service Quality, Customer and Job Satisfaction: Linkages and Implications for Management," *Human Resource Planning* 19 (2) (1996), pp. 20–31; A. Payne, *Advances in Relationship Marketing* (London: Kogan Page, 1995), pp. 46–48.

36 S. Franklin, *The Heroes: A Saga of Canadian Inspiration* (Toronto: McClelland & Stewart, 1967), pp. 53–59.

37 J. P. Meyer, "Organizational Commitment," *International Review of Industrial and Organizational Psychology* 12 (1997), pp. 175–228.

38 T. E. Becker, R. S. Billings, D. M. Eveleth, and N. L. Gilbert, "Foci and Bases of Employee Commitment: Implications for Job Performance," *Academy of Management Journal* 39 (1996), pp. 464–82.

39 R. T. Mowday, L. W. Porter, and R. M. Steers, *Employee Organization Linkages: The Psychology of Commitment, Absenteeism, and Turnover* (New York: Academic Press, 1982).

40 R. D. Hackett, P. Bycio, and P. A. Hausdorf, "Further Assessments of Meyer and Allen's (1991) Three-Component Model of Organizational Commitment," *Journal of Applied Psychology* 79 (1994), pp. 15–23; M. Withey, "Antecedents of Value Based and Economic Organizational Commitment," *Proceedings of the Annual ASAC Conference, Organizational Behaviour Division* 9, Part 5 (1988), pp. 124–33.

41 F. F. Reichheld, *The Loyalty Effect* (Boston: Harvard Business School Press, 1996), Chapter 4.

42 Meyer, "Organizational Commitment," pp. 203–15; R. Karambayya, "Good Organizational Citizens Do Make a Difference," *Proceedings of the Annual ASAC Conference, Organizational Behaviour Division* 11, Part 5 (1990), pp. 110–19; J. P. Meyer, S. V. Paunonen, I. R. Gellatly, R. D. Goffin, and D. N. Jackson, "Organizational Commitment and Job Performance: It's the Nature of the Commitment That Counts," *Journal of Applied Psychology* 74 (1989), pp. 152–56.

43 S. Rubin, "Scenes From a Marriage," *Financial Post*, February 8, 1997, p. 9.

44 A. A. Luchak and I. R. Gellatly, "Employer-Sponsored Pensions and Employee Commitment," *Proceedings of the Annual ASAC Conference, Human Resource Management Division* 17 (9) (1996), pp. 64–71; L. M. Shore and S. J. Wayne, "Commitment and Employee Behavior: Comparison of Affective

Commitment and Continuance Commitment with Perceived Organizational Support," *Journal of Applied Psychology* 78 (1993), pp. 774–80; Meyer et al., "Organizational Commitment and Job Performance: It's the Nature of the Commitment That Counts."

45 P. C. Newman, *The Canadian Establishment* (Toronto: McClelland & Stewart, 1975), p. 183.

46 S. Haggett, "Motivating Employees a Leader's Greatest Challenge," *Financial Post*, May 8, 1993, p. 23; D. MacArthur, "Springtime: Four Seasons Growth Goes Global," *Globe & Mail*, May 18, 1991, p. F6.

47 Angus Reid Interactive, "Loyalty At Work," Angus Reid Group/Bloomberg Business News Poll, Press Release, October 17, 1996 (www.angusreid.com); D. Israelson, "Job Slashing Sets Workers Sizzling," *Toronto Star*, March 16, 1996, pp. B1, B3; P. Houston, "The Smartest Ways to Build Loyalty," *Working Woman* 17 (April 1992), pp. 72–74, 100, 101. For an analysis of declining work ethic and loyalty in Canada, see: A. J. Ali and A. Azim, "Work Ethic and Loyalty in Canada," *Journal of Social Psychology* 135 (1995), pp. 31–37.

48 J. Laabs, "Employee Commitment," *Personnel Journal*, August 1996, pp. 58–66; C. C. Heckscher, *White-Collar Blues: Management Loyalties in an Age of Corporate Restructuring* (New York: BasicBooks, 1995).

49 T. Nhan, "Some Companies Have a Mission, But Does the Staff?" *Calgary Herald*, September 30, 1995, p. D8.

50 J. P. Meyer and N. J. Allen, *Commitment in the Workplace: Theory, Research, and Application* (Thousand Oaks, Calif.: Sage, 1997), Chapter 4.

51 E. W. Morrison and S. L. Robinson, "When Employees Feel Betrayed: A Model of How Psychological Contract Violation Develops," *Academy of Management Review* 22 (1997), pp. 226–56.

52 K. Mark, "No More Pink Slips," *Human Resources Professional*, November 1996, pp. 21–23; Shore and Wayne, "Commitment and Employee Behavior"; D. M. Rousseau and J. M. Parks, "The Contracts of Individuals and Organizations," *Research in Organizational Behavior* 15 (1993), pp. 1–43; and D. J. Koys, "Human Resource Management and a Culture of Respect: Effects on Employees' Organizational Commitment," *Employee Responsibilities and Rights Journal* 1 (1988), pp. 57–68.

53 D. M. Noer, *Healing the Wounds* (San Francisco: Jossey-Bass, 1993); and S. Ashford, C. Lee, and P. Bobko, "Content, Causes, and Consequences of Job Insecurity: A Theory-Based Measure and Substantive Test," *Academy of Management Journal* 32 (1989), pp. 803–29.

54 J. Aspery, "British Companies Meet the Challenge of Change," *IABC Communication World* 7 (December 1990), pp. 39–41.

55 V. V. Baba and R. Knoop, "Organizational Commitment and Independence Among Canadian Managers," *Relations Industrielles* 42 (1987), pp. 325–44; and W. L. Weber, J. J. Marshall, and G. H. Haines, "Modelling Commitment and Its Antecedents: An Empirical Study," *Canadian Journal of Administrative Sciences* 6 (1989), pp. 12–23.

56 R. J. Lewicki and B. B. Bunker, "Developing and Maintaining Trust in Work Relationships," in R. M. Kramer and T. R. Tyler (eds.), *Trust in Organizations: Frontiers of Theory and Research* (Thousand Oaks, Calif.: Sage, 1996), pp. 114–39; S. L. Robinson, "Trust and Breach of the Psychological Contract," *Administrative Science Quarterly* 41 (1996), pp. 574–99; B. S. Frey, "Does Monitoring Increase Work Effort? The Rivalry with Trust and Loyalty," *Economic Inquiry* 31 (1993), pp. 663–70; J. K. Butler, Jr., "Toward Understanding and Measuring Conditions of Trust: Evolution of a Conditions of Trust Inventory," *Journal of Management* 17 (1991), pp. 643–63; J. M. Kouzes and B. Z. Posner, *The Leadership Challenge* (San Francisco: Jossey-Bass, 1987), pp. 146–52.

57 J. McFarland, "How Domtar Workers Added $20-Million to Profit," *Globe & Mail*, October 20, 1995, p. B9.

58 J. A. Morris and D. C. Feldman, "The Dimensions, Antecedents, and Consequences of Emotional Labor," *Academy of Management Review* 21 (1996), pp. 986–1010; B. E. Ashforth and R. H. Humphrey, "Emotional Labor in Service Roles: The Influence of Identity," *Academy of Management Review* 18 (1993), pp. 88–115.

59 S. Fish and F. Jamerson (eds.), *Inside the Mouse: Work and Play at Disney World*, (Durham, N.C.: Duke University Press, 1995); R. I. Sutton, "Maintaining Norms about Expressed Emotions: The Case of Bill Collectors," *Administrative Science Quarterly* 36 (1991), pp. 245–68.

60 Cited in R. Buck, "The Spontaneous Communication of Interpersonal Expectations," in *Interpersonal Expectations: Theory, Research, and Applications* (Cambridge, U.K.: Cambridge University Press, 1993), pp. 227–41.

61 P. K. Adelmann "Emotional Labor as a Potential Source of Job Stress," in S. Sauter and L. R. Murphy (eds.), *Organizational Risk Factors for Job Stress* (Washington, D.C.: American Psychological Association, 1995), Chapter 24.

62 W. G. Stephen and C. W. Stephen, *Intergroup Relations* (Boulder, Col.: Westview, 1996), pp. 120–21; M. Montagu-Pollock "Look Within for Expertise" *Asian Business*, January 1995; Ashforth and Humphrey, "Emotional Labor in Service Roles: The Influence of Identity," *Academy of Management Review*, p. 91;

M. H. Bond, *Beyond the Chinese Face: Insights from Psychology* (Hong Kong: Oxford University Press, 1991).

63 G. Pitts, "Hotel Chain Hires for Attitude," *Globe & Mail*, June 3, 1997, p. B13; R. Henkoff, "Finding, Training, and Keeping the Best Service Workers," *Fortune*, (October 3, 1994), pp. 110–22.

64 J. D. Mayer and P. Salovey, "The Intelligence of Emotional Intelligence," *Intelligence* 17 (1993), pp. 433–42.

65 A. Sagie and D. Elizur, "Work Values: A Theoretical Overview and a Model of Their Effects," *Journal of Organizational Behavior* 17 (1996), pp. 503–14; W. H. Schmidt and B. Z. Posner, *Managerial Values in Perspective* (New York: American Management Association, 1983).

66 P. McDonald and J. Gandz, "Getting Value from Values," *Organizational Dynamics* (Winter 1992), pp. 64–77.

67 M. Rokeach, *The Nature of Human Values* (New York: The Free Press, 1973); and F. Kluckhorn and F. L. Strodtbeck, *Variations in Value Orientations* (Evanston, Ill.: Row, Peterson, 1961).

68 S. Day, "Mexico's Business Bottlenecks," *Financial Times of Canada*, May 8–14, 1993, p. 7.

69 K. L. Newman and S. D. Nolan, "Culture and Congruence: The Fit Between Management Practices and National Culture," *Journal of International Business Studies* 27 (1996), pp. 753–79; G. Hofstede, "Cultural Constraints in Management Theories," *Academy of Management Executive* 7 (1993), pp. 81–94; G. Hofstede, *Culture's Consequences: International Differences in Work-Related Values* (Beverly Hills, Calif.: Sage, 1980).

70 Stephen and C. W. Stephen, *Intergroup Relations*, pp. 119–21; J. A. Wagner III, "Studies of Individualism-Collectivism: Effects of Cooperation in Groups," *Academy of Management Journal* 38 (1995), pp. 152–72.

71 M. Erez and P. Christopher Earley, *Culture, Self-Identity, and Work* (New York: Oxford University Press, 1993), pp. 126–27.

72 Erez and Earley, *Culture, Self-Identity, and Work*, p. 127.

73 H. C. Jain, J. Normand, and R. N. Kanungo, "Job Motivation of Canadian Anglophone and Francophone Hospital Employees," *Canadian Journal of Behavioural Science* 11 (1979), pp. 160–63.

74 L. Redpath and M. O. Nielson, "Crossing the Cultural Divide Between Traditional Native Values and Non-Native Management Ideology," *Proceedings of the Annual ASAC Conference, Organizational Theory Division* 15 (12) (1994), pp. 70–79; I. Chapman, D. McCaskill, and D. Newhouse, *Management in Contemporary Aboriginal Organizations* (Peterborough, Ont.: Trent University, 1992), Administrative Studies Working Paper Series #92-04.

75 Leslie Goodson, "Doing the Right Thing," *Human Resources Professional*, March 1996, pp. 21–22.

76 M. E. MacPherson, *Shopkeepers to a Nation: The Eatons* (Toronto: McClelland & Stewart, 1963); and G. G. Nasmith, *Timothy Eaton* (Toronto: McClelland & Stewart, 1923).

77 J. DeMont, "Passing the Westray Buck," *Maclean's*, June 10, 1996, pp. 18–20; "The Kickback Boom and How to Fight It," *Canadian Business* 64 (November 1991), pp. 78–81.

78 W. H. Shaw and V. Barry, *Moral Issues in Business*, 5th ed. (Belmont, Calif.: Wadsworth, 1992), Chapters 1–3; and M. G. Velasquez, *Business Ethics*, 2nd ed. (Englewood Cliffs, N.J.: Prentice Hall, 1988), Chapter 2.

79 M. K. Nyaw and I. Ng, "A Comparative Analysis of Ethical Beliefs: A Four Country Study," *Journal of Business Ethics* 13 (1994), pp. 543–55.

80 B. Irvine and L. Lindsay, "Corporate Ethics and the Controller," *CMA Magazine* 67 (December 1993), pp. 23–26; J. Gandz and F. G. Bird, "Designing Ethical Organizations," *Business Quarterly* 54 (Autumn 1989), pp. 108–12; and D. Olive, *Just Rewards: The Case for Ethical Reform in Business* (Toronto: Key Porter, 1987).

81 Olive, *Just Rewards*, p. 125.

82 Goodson, "Doing the Right Thing," *Human Resources Professional*.

CHAPTER 8

1 C. Knight, "There's Nothing Like the Truth," *Canadian HR Reporter*, February 26, 1996, pp. 11, 12, 19.

2 L. E. Penley, E. R. Alexander, I. E. Jernigan, and C. L. Henwood, "Communication Abilities of Managers: The Relationship to Performance," *Journal of Management* 17 (1991), pp. 57–76; H. Mintzberg, *The Nature of Managerial Work* (New York: Harper & Row, 1973); E. T. Klemmer and F. W. Snyder, "Measurement of Time Spent Communicating," *Journal of Communication* 22 (June 1972), pp. 142–58.

3 C. Downs, P. Clampitt, and A. L. Pfeiffer, "Communication and Organizational Outcomes," in *Handbook of Organizational Communication*, eds. G. Goldhaber and G. Barnett (Norwood, N.J.: Ablex, 1988), pp. 171–211; and H. C. Jain, "Supervisory Communication and Performance in Urban Hospitals," *Journal of Communication* 23 (1973), pp. 103–17.

4 V. L. Shalin, and G. V. Prabhu, "A Cognitive Perspective on Manual Assembly," *Ergonomics* 39 (1996), pp. 108–27; I. Nonaka and H. Takeuchi, *The Knowledge-Creating Company* (New York: Oxford University Press, 1995).

554

5   "We are the World," *CIO* 9 (August 1996), p. 24.

6   R. J. Burke and D. S. Wilcox, "Effects of Different Patterns and Degrees of Openness in Superior–Subordinate Communication on Subordinate Satisfaction," *Academy of Management Journal* 12 (1969), pp. 319–26; R. T. Mowday, L. W. Porter, and R. M. Steers, *Employee-Organization Linkages* (New York: Academic Press, 1982).

7   L. K. Lewis and D. R. Seibold, "Communication During Intraorganizational Innovation Adoption: Predicting User's Behavioral Coping Responses to Innovations in Organizations," *Communication Monographs* 63 (2), (1996), pp. 131–57.

8   C. E. Shannon and W. Weaver, *The Mathematical Theory of Communication* (Urbana, Ill: University of Illinois Press, 1949). For a more recent discussion, see: K. J. Krone, F. M. Jablin, and L. L. Putnam, "Communication Theory and Organizational Communication: Multiple Perspectives," in *Handbook of Organizational Communication: An Interdisciplinary Perspective*, ed. F. M. Jablin, L. L. Putnam, K. H. Roberts, and L. W. Porter (Newbury Park, Calif.: Sage, 1987), pp. 18–40.

9   S. Axley, "Managerial and Organizational Communication in Terms of the Conduit Metaphor," *Academy of Management Review* 9 (1984), pp. 428–37.

10 M. J. Glauser, "Upward Information Flow in Organizations: Review and Conceptual Analysis," *Human Relations* 37 (1984), pp. 613–43.

11 L. Larwood, "Don't Struggle to Scope Those Metaphors Yet," *Group and Organization Management* 17 (1992), pp. 249–54; and L. R. Pondy, P. J. Frost, G. Morgan, and T. C. Dandridge (eds.), *Organizational Symbolism* (Greenwich, Conn.: JAI Press, 1983).

12 M. Kaeter, "Quality through Clarity," *Quality*, May 1993, pp. 19–22.

13 M. Siconolfi, "Firms Freeze Out Stock Bashers," *Globe & Mail*, August 3, 1995, p. B8.

14 A. Markham, "Designing Discourse: A Critical Analysis of Strategic Ambiguity and Workplace Control," *Management Communication Quarterly* 9 (1996), pp. 389–421; Larwood, "Don't Struggle to Scope Those Metaphors Yet;" R. Mead, *Cross-Cultural Management Communication* (Chichester, U.K.: John Wiley & Sons, 1990), pp. 130–37; E. M. Eisenberg, "Ambiguity as a Strategy in Organizational Communication," *Communication Monographs* 51 (1984), pp. 227–42; R. Daft and J. Wiginton, "Language and Organization," *Academy of Management Review* 4 (1979), pp. 179–91.

15 G. Morgan, *Images of Organization*, 2nd ed. (Thousand Oaks, Calif.: Sage, 1997); L. L. Putnam, Nelson Phillips, and P. Chapman, "Metaphors of Communication and Organization," in S. R. Clegg, C. Hardy, and W. R. Nord (eds.), *Handbook of Organization Studies* (London: Sage, 1996), pp. 373–408.

16 A. G. Schick, L. A. Gordon, and S. Haka, "Information Overload: A Temporal Approach," *Accounting, Organizations & Society* 15 (1990), pp. 199–220; K. Alesandrini, *Survive Information Overload* (Homewood, Ill.: Business One-Irwin, 1993).

17 Schick et al., "Information Overload," pp. 209–14; C. Stohl and W. C. Redding, "Messages and Message Exchange Processes," in *Handbook of Organizational Communication: An Interdisciplinary Perspective*, ed. Jablin et al., pp. 451–502.

18 B. Crosariol, "Yours Truly.com," *Globe & Mail*, June 28, 1997, pp. C1, C8.

19 J. Wells, "Rogers in Retreat," *Maclean's*, May 20, 1996, pp. 36–37.

20 L. Porter and K. Roberts, "Communication in Organizations," in *Handbook of Industrial and Organizational Psychology*, ed. M. Dunnette (Chicago: Rand McNally, 1976), pp. 1553–589.

21 J. H. E. Andriessen, "Mediated Communication and New Organizational Forms," *International Review of Industrial and Organizational Psychology* 6 (1991), pp. 17–70.

22 J. Hunter and M. Allen, "Adaptation to Electronic Mail," *Journal of Applied Communication Research*, August 1992, pp. 254–74; M. Culnan and M. L. Markus, "Information Technologies," in *Handbook of Organizational Communication: An Interdisciplinary Perspective*, ed. Jablin et al., pp. 420–43.

23 D. A. Adams, P. A. Todd, and R. R. Nelson, "A Comparative Evaluation of the Impact of Electronic and Voice Mail on Organizational Communication," *Information & Management* 24 (1993), pp. 9–21.

24 C. S. Saunders, D. Robey, and K. A. Vaverek, "The Persistence of Status Differentials in Computer Conferencing," *Human Communications Research* 20 (1994), pp. 443–72.

25 M. Gooderham, "Electronic Messages Burying Workers," *Globe & Mail*, May 14, 1997, p. A9; H. Schachter, "Slaves to the New Economy," *Canadian Business*, April 1996, pp. 86–92.

26 D. Asbrand, "E-mail 'Flame' Messages Can Ignite Office Angst," *InfoWorld*, December 6, 1993, p. 74; J. Scott, "The Etiquette of Email," *Vancouver Sun*, October 2, 1993, p. B3; J. Goode and M. Johnson, "Putting Out the Flames: The Etiquette of Email," *Online*, November 1991, pp. 61–65.

27 A. D. Shulman, "Putting Group Information Technology in its Place: Communication and Good Work Group Performance," In Clegg et al. (eds.), *Handbook of Organization Studies*, pp. 373–408.

28 "Technology a Source of Stress," *Canadian Press Newswire*, January 30, 1997.

29 P. Bordia "Face-To-Face Versus Computer-Mediated Communication: A Synthesis of the Experimental Literature," *Journal of Business Communication* 34 (January 1997), pp. 99–120.

30 J. Shoesmith, "Bank of Montreal Takes HR off Big Iron," *Computing Canada*, October 10, 1996, p. 28; A. Yeung, W. Brockbank, and D. Ulrich, "Lower Cost, Higher Value: Human Resource Function in Transformation," *Human Resource Planning* (1995) pp. 1–16.

31 L. Lester, "Web TV Nears," *Globe & Mail* (supplement), April 28, 1997, p. 7; D. Thomas, "Desktop Conferencing Gains in Popularity," *Financial Post*, December 2, 1995, p. 46.

32 G. Arnault, "Imaging Cuts the Paper Chase," *Globe & Mail*, October 17, 1995, p. C2; J. Chevreau, "Lotus Notes 'Bring Competitors Together,'" *Financial Post*, March 12, 1994, p. 5.

33 T. E. Harris, *Applied Organizational Communication: Perspectives, Principles, and Pragmatics* (Hillsdale, N.J.: Lawrence Erlbaum Associates, 1993), Chapter 5; A. Mehrabian, *Silent Messages*, 2nd ed. (Belmont, Calif.: Wadsworth, 1981).

34 J. A. Morris and D. C. Feldman, "The Dimensions, Antecedents, and Consequences of Emotional Labor," *Academy of Management Review* 21 (1996), pp. 986–1010.

35 B. Reiss, "Under that Smiling, Calm Exterior is a Graduate Deltoid," *Smithsonian* 24 (November 1994), pp. 88–97.

36 B. Parkinson, *Ideas and Realities of Emotion* (London: Routledge, 1995), pp. 182–83; E. Hatfield, J. T. Cacioppo, and R. L. Rapson, *Emotional Contagion* (Cambridge, U.K.: Cambridge University Press, 1993).

37 R. L. Daft, R. H. Lengel, and L. K. Tevino, "Message Equivocality, Media Selection, and Manager Performance: Implications for Information Systems," *MIS Quarterly* 11 (1987), pp. 355–66.

38 R. H. Lengel and R. L. Daft, "The Selection of Communication Media as an Executive Skill," *Academy of Management Executive* 2 (1988), pp. 225–32; G. Huber and R. L. Daft, "The Information Environments of Organizations," in *Handbook of Organizational Communication: An Interdisciplinary Perspective*, ed. Jablin et al., pp. 130–64; ; R. L. Daft and R. H. Lengel, "Information Richness: A New Approach to Managerial Behavior and Organization Design," *Research in Organizational Behavior* 6 (1984), pp. 191–233.

39 R. E. Rice, "Task Analyzability, Use of New Media, and Effectiveness: A Multi-Site Exploration of Media Richness," *Organization Science* 3 (1992), pp. 475–500; J. Fulk, C. W. Steinfield, J. Schmitz, and J. G. Power, "A Social Information Processing Model of Media Use in Organizations," *Communication Research* 14 (1987), pp. 529–52.

40 D. Stork and A. Sapienza, "Task and Human Messages over the Project Life Cycle: Matching Media to Messages," *Project Management Journal* 22 (December 1992), pp. 44–49.

41 M. McLuhan, *Understanding Media: The Extensions of Man* (New York: McGraw-Hill, 1964).

42 S. B. Sitkin, K. M. Sutcliffe, and J. R. Barrios-Choplin, "A Dual-Capacity Model of Communication Media Choice in Organizations," *Human Communication Research* 18 (June 1992), pp. 563–98; J. Schmitz and J. Fulk, "Organizational Colleagues, Media Richness, and Electronic Mail: A Test of the Social Influence Model of Technology Use," *Communication Research* 18 (1991), pp. 487–523.

43 B. Schneider, S. D. Ashworth, A. C. Higgs, and L. Carr, "Design, Validity, and Use of Strategically Focused Employee Attitude Surveys," *Personnel Psychology* 49 (1996), pp. 695–705; T. Geddie, "Surveys are a Waste of Time...Until You Use Them," *Communication World*, April 1996, pp. 24–26; D. M. Saunders and J. D. Leck, "Formal Upward Communication Procedures: Organizational and Employee Perspectives," *Canadian Journal of Administrative Sciences* 10 (1993), pp. 255–68.

44 B. W. Little, "Employee Surveys: An Effective Agenda for Change," *Canadian Forest Industries* (August–September 1992), pp. 32–34.

45 K. Mark, "No More Pink Slips," *Human Resources Professional*, November 1996, pp. 21–23; R. V. Lindahl, "Automation Breaks the Language Barrier," *HRMagazine*, 41 (March 1996), pp. 79–83; S. Haggett, "Motivating Employees a Leader's Greatest Challenge," *Financial Post*, May 8, 1993, p. 23.

46 R. Bonanno, "Canada Trust's Video News Program Keeps Employees Tuned-In," *Canadian HR Reporter*, October 8, 1993, p. 16.

47 R. Bonanno, "Bell Canada: Answering Its Employees' Calls," *Canadian HR Reporter*, June 25, 1993, p. 16; C. McGoon, "Putting the Employee Newsletter On-Line," *IABC Communication World* 9 (March 1992), pp. 16–18.

48 "Camp Collegiality," *Maclean's*, December 12, 1994 p. 44–45.

49 M. Young and J. E. Post, "Managing to Communicate, Communicating to Change: How Leading Companies Communicate with Employees," *Organizational Dynamics* 22 (Summer 1993), pp. 31–43.

50 P. Currie, "CEO has Unique View of Where Fault Lies," *London Free Press*, April 10, 1995 (reprinted in Canadian Press Newswire).

51 Young and Post, "Managing to Communicate, Communicating to Manage," pp. 31–43; C. Kapel, "Look Who's Talking," *Human Resources Professional*, October 1991, pp. 9–11.

52 M. Maruyama, *Mindscapes in Management* (Aldershot, U.K.: Dartmouth, 1994), pp. 33–34.

53 S. LeBrun, "Workscape as Cityscape," *Canadian HR Reporter*, June 16, 1997, p. 7; G. Levitch, "Pizzas and Piazzas: Workplace of the Future," *Globe & Mail*, October 12, 1996, p. C7.

54 B. Nelson, "Appreciate Employees to Get Best Results," *Canadian Manager*, Summer 1996, pp. 11–12.

55 C. G. Johnston and C. R. Farquhar, *Empowered People Satisfy Customers* (Ottawa: Conference Board of Canada, 1992), p. 12; and "Top-Level Togetherness Speeds Communication," *Financial Post*, July 11, 1988, p. 15.

56 A. Goldman, "Implications of Japanese Total Quality Control for Western Organizations: Dimensions of an Intercultural Hybrid," *Journal of Business Communication* 30 (1993), pp. 29–47; and J. P. Womack, D. T. Jones, and D. Roos, *The Machine That Changed the World* (New York: Rawson, 1990), p. 79.

57 J. Kroho, Jr., "What Makes an Office Work," *Across the Board*, May 1993, pp. 16–23; T. Peters, *Liberation Management: Necessary Disorganization for the Nanosecond Nineties* (New York: Knopf, 1992), pp. 379–80; T. H. Walker, "Designing Work Environments that Promote Corporate Productivity," *Site Selection and Industrial Development*, April 1992, pp. 8–10.

58 G. M. Dault, "Flowing with the Transparent Office," *Globe & Mail*, October 12, 1996, p. C7; J. Macht, "When the Walls Come Tumbling Down," *Inc. Technology* 17 (September 1995), pp. 70–72; F. Becker, "A Workplace by Any Other Name: The Unassigned Office," *Facilities Design & Management* 12 (July 1993), pp. 50–53.

59 C. Knight, "Gone Virtual," *Canadian HR Reporter*, December 16, 1996, pp. 24, 26; P. LaBarre, "The Dis-Organization of Oticon," *Industry Week*, July 18, 1994, pp. 23–28.

60 T. Davis, "The Influence of the Physical Environment in Offices," *Academy of Management Review* 9 (2) (1984), pp. 271–83; and S. B. Bacharach and M. Aitken, "Communications in Administrative Bureaucracies," *Academy of Management Journal* 20 (1977), pp. 365–77.

61 A. Minnick and K. Pischke-Winn, "Work Redesign: Making It a Reality," *Nursing Management*, October 1996, pp. 61–65.

62 M. Gibb-Clark, "Most Job Losers Find Out Second-Hand," *Globe & Mail*, April 14, 1993, pp. B1, B4; J. Mishra, "Managing the Grapevine," *Public Personnel Management* 19 (Summer 1990), pp. 213–28.

63 G. Kreps, *Organizational Communication* (White Plains, N.Y.: Longman, 1986), pp. 202–6; W. L. Davis and J. R. O'Connor, "Serial Transmission of Information: A Study of the Grapevine," *Journal of Applied Communication Research* 5 (1977), pp. 61–72; K. Davis, "Management Communication and the Grapevine," *Harvard Business Review* 31 (September–October 1953), pp. 43–49.

64 R. L. Rosnow, "Inside Rumor: A Personal Journey," *American Psychologist* 46 (May 1991), pp. 484–96; C. J. Walker and C. A. Beckerle, "The Effect of State Anxiety on Rumor Transmission," *Journal of Social Behavior & Personality* 2 (August 1987), pp. 353–60.

65 N. Fitzgerald, "Spread the Word," *The Accountant's Magazine* 97 (February 1993), pp. 32–33.

66 D. Krackhardt and J. R. Hanson, "Informal Networks: The Company Behind the Chart," *Harvard Business Review* 71 (July–August 1993), pp. 104–11; H. Mintzberg, *The Structuring of Organizations* (Englewood Cliffs, N.J.: Prentice Hall, 1979), pp. 46–53.

67 M. Noon and R. Delbridge, "News from Behind My Hand: Gossip in Organizations," *Organization Studies* 14 (1993), pp. 23–36.

68 E. Innes and L. Southwick-Trask, *Turning It Around* (Toronto: Fawcett Crest, 1990), p. 124.

69 For a review of the main issues on cultural diversity in Canadian organizations, see the series of articles edited by R. J. Burke, "Managing an Increasingly Diverse Workforce," *Canadian Journal of Administrative Sciences* 8 (1991). Also see: C. M. Solomon, "Managing Today's Immigrants," *Personnel Journal*, February 1993, pp. 57–65; T. Cox, Jr., "The Multicultural Organization," *Academy of Management Executive* 5 (May 1991), pp. 34–47.

70 J. Christensen-Hughes, "Cultural Diversity: The Lesson of Toronto's Hotels," *Cornell H. R. A. Quarterly*, April 1992, pp. 78–87.

71 Mead, *Cross-Cultural Management Communication*, pp. 161–62; and J. V. Hill and C. L. Bovée, *Excellence in Business Communication* (New York: McGraw-Hill, 1993), Chapter 17.

72 H. Yamada, *American and Japanese Business Discourse: A Comparison of Interaction Styles* (Norwood, N.J.: Ablex, 1992), p. 34.

73 "E-mail, Bloody E-mail," *Training*, January 1996, p. 12.

74 R. Axtell, *Gestures: The Do's and Taboos of Body Language around the World* (New York: Wiley, 1991); P. Harris and R. Moran, *Managing Cultural Differences* (Houston: Gulf, 1987); and P. Ekman, W. V. Friesen, and J. Bear, "The International Language of Gestures," *Psychology Today*, May 1984, pp. 64–69.

75 H. Yamada, *Different Games, Different Rules* (New York: Oxford University Press, 1997), pp. 76–79; H. Yamada, *American and Japanese Business Discourse*, Chapter 2; D. Tannen, *Talking from 9 to 5* (New York: Avon, 1994), pp. 96–97; D. C. Barnlund, *Communication Styles of Japanese and Americans: Images and Realities* (Belmont, Calif.: Wadsworth, 1988).

76 J. Allan, "When Women Set the Rules," *Canadian Business*, April 1991, pp. 40–43.

77 M. Crawford, *Talking Difference: On Gender and Language* (Thousand Oaks, Calif.: Sage, 1995), pp. 41–44; Tannen, *Talking from 9 to 5*; D. Tannen, *You Just Don't Understand: Men and Women in Conversation* (New York: Ballentine Books, 1990); S. Helgesen, *The Female Advantage: Women's Ways of Leadership* (New York: Doubleday, 1990).

78 G. H. Graham, J. Unruh, and P. Jennings, "The Impact of Nonverbal Communication in Organizations: A Survey of Perceptions," *Journal of Business Communication* 28 (1991), pp. 45–61; J. Hall, "Gender Effects in Decoding Nonverbal Cues," *Psychological Bulletin* 68 (1978), pp. 845–57.

79 This stereotypic notion is prevalent throughout J. Gray, *Men Are From Mars, Women Are From Venus* (New York: HarperCollins, 1992). For a critique of this view see: Crawford, *Talking Difference*, Chapter 4.

80 P. Tripp-Knowles "A Review of the Literature on Barriers Encountered by Women in Science Academia," *Resources for Feminist Research* 24 (Spring/Summer 1995), pp. 28–34.

81 Cited in K. Davis and J. W. Newstrom, *Human Behavior at Work: Organizational Behavior*, 7th ed. (New York: McGraw-Hill, 1985), p. 438.

82 J. Brownell, *Building Active Learning Skills* (Englewood Cliffs, N.J.: Prentice Hall, 1986); A. Mikalachki, "Does Anyone Listen to the Boss?" *Business Horizons*, March–April 1982, pp. 34–39.

83 S. Trenholm, *Persuasion and Social Influence* (Englewood Cliffs, N.J.: Prentice Hall, 1989); W. J. McGuire, "Attitudes and Attitude Change," in *Handbook of Social Psychology*, 3rd ed., vol. 2, eds. G. Lindzey and E. Aronson (New York: Random House, 1985), pp. 233–346; and P. Zimbardo and E. B. Ebbeson, *Influencing Attitudes and Changing Behavior* (Reading, Mass.: Addison-Wesley, 1969).

84 J. Cooper and R. T. Coyle, "Attitudes and Attitude Change," *Annual Review of Psychology* 35 (1984), pp. 395–426; and N. MacLachlan, "What People Really Think About Fast Talkers," *Psychology Today* 113 (November 1979), pp. 112–17.

85 D. B. Freeland, "Turning Communication into Influence," *HR Magazine* 38 (September 1993), pp. 93–96; and M. Snyder and M. Rothbart, "Communicator Attractiveness and Opinion Change," *Canadian Journal of Behavioural Science* 3 (1971), pp. 377–87.

86 E. Aronson, *The Social Animal* (San Francisco: W. H. Freeman, 1976), pp. 67–68; and R. A. Jones and J. W. Brehm, "Persuasiveness of One- and Two-Sided Communications as a Function of Awareness that There Are Two Sides," *Journal of Experimental Social Psychology* 6 (1970), pp. 47–56.

87 D. G. Linz and S. Penrod, "Increasing Attorney Persuasiveness in the Courtroom," *Law and Psychology Review* 8 (1984), pp. 1–47; R. B. Zajonc, "Attitudinal Effects of Mere Exposure," *Journal of Personality and Social Psychology Monograph* 9 (1968), pp. 1–27; and R. Petty and J. Cacioppo, *Attitudes and Persuasion: Classic and Contemporary Approaches* (Dubuque, Iowa: W. C. Brown, 1981).

88 Zimbardo and Ebbeson, *Influencing Attitudes and Changing Behavior*.

89 M. Zellner, "Self-Esteem, Reception, and Influenceability," *Journal of Personality and Social Psychology* 15 (1970), pp. 87–93.

CHAPTER 9

1 K. Dorrell, "The Right Stuff," *Plant*, December 16, 1996, pp. 18–19; D. Jones, "Robo-Shop," *Report on Business Magazine*, March 1994, pp. 54–62; L. Gutri, "Pratt & Whitney Employees Don't Want to Be Managed: Teams Demand Leadership," *Canadian HR Reporter*, May 2, 1988, p. 8; J. Todd, "Firm Fashions Workplace for High-Tech Era," *Montreal Gazette*, December 12, 1987, p. B4.

2 C. Charney, "Self-Directed Peer Training in Teams," *Journal for Quality & Participation* 19 (October 1996), pp. 34–37; W. J. Crawley, B. J. Mekechuk, and G. K. Oickle, "Powering Up For Change," *CA Magazine*, June/July 1995, pp. 33–38; J. Terrett, "New Plant Gears Up for the Future," *Modern Purchasing* 34 (March 1992), pp. 16–18.

3 R. M. McIntyre, E. Salas, "Measuring and Managing for Team Performance: Emerging Principles from Complex Environments," in R. A. Guzzo, E. Salas, and Associates (eds.), *Team Effectiveness and Decision Making in Organizations* (San Francisco: Jossey Bass, 1995), pp. 9–45; S. A. Mohrman, S. G. Cohen, and A. M. Mohrman, Jr., *Designing Team-Based Organizations: New Forms for Knowledge Work* (San Francisco: Jossey-Bass, 1995), pp. 39–40; D. Cartwright and A. Zander (eds.), *Group Dynamics: Research and Theory*, 3rd ed. (New York: Harper & Row, 1968); M. E. Shaw, *Group Dynamics*, 3rd ed. (New York: McGraw-Hill, 1981), p. 8.

4 G. E. Huszczo, *Tools for Team Excellence* (Palo Alto, Calif.: Davies-Black, 1996), pp. 9–15; R. Likert, *New Patterns of Management* (New York: McGraw-Hill, 1961), pp. 106–8.

5 B. Little, "A Factory Learns to Survive," *Globe & Mail*, May 18, 1993, p. B22.

6 Mohrman, Cohen, and Mohrman, Jr., *Designing Team-Based Organizations*, p. 6; J. H. Shonk, *Team-Based Organizations: Developing a Successful Team Environment* (Homewood, Ill: Business Irwin One, 1992).

7 G. McKay, *Increasing the Power of Self-Managing Work Teams Through Effective Human Resource Management Strategies*. Unpublished MBA project (Burnaby, B.C.: Simon Fraser University, December 1992); S. Fife, "The Total Quality Muddle," *Report on Business Magazine*, November 1992, pp. 64–74.

8 Mohrman, Cohen, and Mohrman, Jr., *Designing Team-Based Organizations*, Chapter 2; R. S. Wellins, W. C. Byham, and G. R. Dixon, *Inside Teams* (San Francisco: Jossey-Bass, 1994), pp. 9–10.

9 A. Morris and S. Thomas, "A Med/Surg Nursing Record: Convenient, Adequate — And Accepted," *Nursing Management* 23 (May 1992), pp. 68–72.

10   T. Peters, *Thriving on Chaos* (New York: Knopf, 1987), pp. 211–18; T. Kidder, *Soul of a New Machine* (Boston: Little, Brown, 1981); T. Peters and N. Austin, *A Passion for Excellence* (New York: Random House, 1985), Chapters 9, 10.

11   L. Iacocca and W. Novak, *Iacocca* (New York: Bantam, 1984), Chapter 6.

12   J. Lipnack and J. Stamps, *Virtual Teams: Reaching Across Space, Time, and Organizations with Technology* (New York: John Wiley & Sons, 1997), pp. 5–8; D. J. Armstrong and P. Cole, "Managing Distances and Differences in Geographically Distributed Work Groups," in S. E. Jackson and M. N. Ruderman (eds.), *Diversity in Work Teams: Research Paradigms for a Changing Workplace* (Washington, D.C.: American Psychological Association, 1995), pp. 187–215.

13   J. Rendleman, "Grumman Embraces SMDS Nationwide," *Communications Week*, June 2, 1997, p. 1.

14   A. Savoie, "Les Groupes Informels dans les Organisations: Cadre General d'Analyse," *Canadian Psychology* 34 (1993), pp. 79–97.

15   W. B. Stevenson, J. L. Pearce, and L. W. Porter, "The Concept of 'Coalition' in Organization Theory and Research," *Academy of Management Review* 10 (1985), pp. 256–68; Shaw, *Group Dynamics*, pp. 105–10.

16   B. E. Ashforth and F. Mael, "Social Identity Theory and the Organization," *Academy of Management Review* 14 (1989), pp. 20–39; L. N. Jewell and H. J. Reitz, *Group Effectiveness in Organizations* (Glenview, Ill.: Scott, Foresman, 1981).

17   A. S. Tannenbaum, *Social Psychology of the Work Organization* (Belmont, Calif.: Wadsworth, 1966), p. 62; S. Schacter, *The Psychology of Affiliation* (Stanford, Calif.: Stanford University Press, 1959), pp. 12–19.

18   For a summary of several models, see: P. S. Goodman, E. Ravlin, and M. Schminke, "Understanding Groups in Organizations," *Research in Organizational Behavior* 9 (1987), pp. 121–73.

19   Mohrman, Cohen, and Mohrman, Jr., *Designing Team-Based Organizations*, pp. 58–65; J. E. McGrath, "Time, Interaction, and Performance (TIP): A Theory of Groups," *Small Group Research* 22 (1991), pp. 147–74; G. P. Shea and R. A. Guzzo, "Group Effectiveness: What Really Matters?," *Sloan Management Review* 27 (1987), pp. 33–6.

20   "Team Incentives Prominent Among 'Best-Practice' Companies," *Quality* 35 (April 1996), p. 20. For discussion of the role of rewards in team dynamics, see: A. Barua, C. H. S. Lee, and A. B. Whinston, "Incentives and Computing Systems for Team-Based Organizations," *Organization Science* 6 (1995), pp. 487–504; R. L. Heneman and C. von Hippel, "Balancing Group and Individual Rewards: Rewarding Individual Contributions to the Team," *Compensation & Benefits Review* 27 (July–August, 1995), pp. 63–68.

21   P. Bordia "Face-To-Face Versus Computer-Mediated Communication: A Synthesis of the Experimental Literature," *Journal of Business Communication* 34 (January 1997), pp. 99–120; A. D. Shulman, "Putting Group Information Technology in its Place: Communication and Good Work Group Performance," in S. R. Clegg, C. Hardy, and W. R. Nord (eds.), *Handbook of Organization Studies* (London: Sage, 1996), pp. 357–74; J. E. McGrath and A. B. Hollingshead, *Groups Interacting with Technology*, (Thousand Oaks, Calif.: Sage, 1994).

22   M. A. Campion, E. M. Papper, and G. J. Medsker, "Relations Between Work Team Characteristics and Effectiveness: A Replication and Extension," *Personnel Psychology* 49 (1996), pp. 429–52; S. Worchel and S. L. Shackelford, "Groups Under Stress: The Influence of Group Structure and Environment on Process and Performance," *Personality & Social Psychology Bulletin* 17 (1991), pp. 640–47; E. Sundstrom, K. P. De Meuse, and D. Futrell, "Work Teams: Applications and Effectiveness," *American Psychologist* 45 (1990), pp. 120–33.

23   R. C. Liden, S. J. Wayne, and L. K. Bradway, "Task Interdependence as a Moderator of the Relation Between Group Control and Performance," *Human Relations* 50 (1997), pp. 169–81; R. Wageman, "Interdependence and Group Effectiveness," *Administrative Science Quarterly* 40 (1995), pp.145–80; M. A. Campion, G. J. Medsker, and A. C. Higgs, "Relations Between Work Group Characteristics and Effectiveness: Implications for Designing Effective Work Groups," *Personnel Psychology* 46 (1993), pp. 823–50; M. N. Kiggundu, "Task Interdependence and the Theory of Job Design," *Academy of Management Review* 6 (1981), pp. 499–508.

24   J. R. Katzenbach and D. K. Smith, *The Wisdom of Teams: Creating the High-Performance Organization* (Boston: Harvard University Press, 1993), pp. 45–47; and G. Stasser, "Pooling of Unshared Information During Group Discussion," in *Group Process and Productivity*, ed. S. Worchel, W. Wood, and J. A. Simpson (Newbury Park, Calif.: Sage, 1992), pp. 48–67.

25   R. S. Wellins, W. C. Byham, and G. R. Dixon, *Inside Teams: How 20 World-Class Organizations are Winning Through Teamwork* (San Francisco: Jossey-Bass, 1994), pp. 94–95.

26   J. Zeidenberg, "HR and the Innovative Company," *Human Resources Professional* (June 1996), pp. 12–15; "New Anchor Hocking Plant Incorporates 'Socio-Tech' Work Environment Philosophy," *Business Wire*, October 19, 1995; P. C. Earley, "East Meets West Meets Mideast: Further Explorations of Collectivistic and Individualistic Work Groups," *Academy of Management Journal* 36 (1993), pp. 319–48.

27 R. Klimoski and R. G. Jones, "Staffing for Effective Group Decision Making: Key Issues in Matching People and Teams," in Guzzo, Salas, and Associates (eds.), *Team Effectiveness and Decision Making in Organizations*, pp. 291–332; Mohrman, Cohen, and Mohrman, Jr., *Designing Team-Based Organizations*, pp. 248–54; A. P. Hare, *Handbook of Small Group Research*, 2nd ed. (New York: The Free Press, 1976), pp. 12–15.

28 C. D'Andrea-O'Brien and A. F. Buono, "Building Effective Learning Teams: Lessons from the Field," *SAM Advanced Management Journal* 61 (Summer 1996), pp. 4–9.

29 J. E. McGrath, J. L. Berdahl, and H. Arrow, "Traits, Expectations, Culture, and Clout: The Dynamics of Diversity in Work Groups," in Jackson and Ruderman (eds.), *Diversity in Work Teams*, pp. 17–45.

30 S. M. Colarelli and A. L. Boos, "Sociometric and Ability-Based Assignment to Work Groups: Some Implications for Personnel Selection," *Journal of Organizational Behavior* 13 (1992), pp. 187–96; D. G. Ancona and D. F. Caldwell, "Demography and Design: Predictors of New Product Team Performance," *Organization Science* 3 (1992), pp. 321–41; and J. K. Murnighan and D. Conlon, "The Dynamics of Intense Work Groups: A Study of British String Quartets," *Administrative Science Quarterly* 36 (1991), pp. 165–86.

31 B. Daily, A. Wheatley, S. R. Ash, and R. L. Steiner, "The Effects of a Group Decision Support System on Culturally Diverse and Culturally Homogeneous Group Decision Making," *Information & Management* 30 (1996), pp. 281–89; W. E. Watson, K. Kumar, and L. K. Michaelson, "Cultural Diversity's Impact on Interaction Process and Performance: Comparing Homogeneous and Diverse Task Groups," *Academy of Management Journal* 36 (1993), pp. 590–602; C. Kirchmeyer and J. McLellan, "Managing Ethnic Diversity: Utilizing the Creative Potential of a Diverse Workforce to Meet the Challenges of the Future," *Proceedings of the 1990 ASAC Conference, Organizational Behaviour Division* 11, Part 5 (1990), pp. 120–29.

32 B. W. Tuckman and M. A. C. Jensen, "Stages of Small-Group Development Revisited," *Group and Organization Studies* 2 (1977), pp. 419–42. For a humorous and somwhat cynical discussion of team dynamics through these stages, see: H. Robbins and M. Finley, *Why Teams Don't Work* (Princeton, N.J.: Peterson's/Pacesetters, 1995), Chapter 21.

33 Likert, *New Patterns of Management*, pp. 172–77.

34 J. A. Cannon-Bowers, S. I. Tannenbaum, E. Salas, and C. E. Volpe, "Defining Competencies and Establishing Team Training Requirements," in Guzzo, Salas, and Associates (eds.), *Team Effectiveness and Decision Making in Organizations*, pp. 333–80.

35 C. Argyris, *Interpersonal Competence and Organizational Effectiveness* (Homewood, Ill.: Irwin, 1962).

36 G. Amelio and W. Simon, *Profit from Experience* (New York: Van Nostrand Reinhold, 1996).

37 D. L. Miller, "Synergy in Group Development: A Perspective on Group Performance," *Proceedings of the Annual ASAC Conference, Organizational Behaviour Division* 17, Part 5 (1996), pp. 119–28; S. Worchel, D. Coutant-Sassic, and M. Grossman, "A Developmental Approach to Group Dynamics: A Model and Illustrative Research," in *Group Process and Productivity*, ed. Worchel et al., pp. 181–202; C. J. G. Gersick, "Time and Transition in Work Teams: Toward a New Model of Group Development," *Academy of Management Journal* 31 (1988), pp. 9–41.

38 D. C. Feldman, "The Development and Enforcement of Group Norms," *Academy of Management Review* 9 (1984), pp. 47–53; L. W. Porter, E. E. Lawler, and J. R. Hackman, *Behavior in Organizations* (New York: McGraw-Hill, 1975), pp. 391–94.

39 I. R. Gellatly, "Individual and Group Determinants of Employee Absenteeism: Test of a Causal Model," *Journal of Organizational Behavior* 16 (1995), pp. 469–85; G. Johns, "Absenteeism Estimates by Employees and Managers: Divergent Perspectives and Self-Serving Perceptions," *Journal of Applied Psychology* 79 (1994), pp. 229–39.

40 B. Latané, "The Psychology of Social Impact," *American Psychologist* 36 (1981), pp. 343–56; and C. A. Kiesler and S. B. Kiesler, *Conformity* (Reading, Mass.: Addison-Wesley, 1970).

41 Porter, Lawler, and Hackman, *Behavior in Organizations*, pp. 399–401.

42 L. Coch and J. R. P. French, Jr., "Overcoming Resistance to Change," *Human Relations* 1 (1948), pp. 512–32.

43 Feldman, "The Development and Enforcement of Group Norms," pp. 50–52.

44 Katzenbach and Smith, *The Wisdom of Teams*, pp. 121–23.

45 K. L. Bettenhausen and J. K. Murnighan, "The Development of an Intragroup Norm and the Effects of Interpersonal and Structural Challenges," *Administrative Science Quarterly* 36 (1991), pp. 20–35.

46 D'Andrea-O'Brien and Buono, "Building Effective Learning Teams," *SAM Advanced Management Journal*.

47 R. S. Spich and K. Keleman, "Explicit Norm Structuring Process: A Strategy for Increasing Task-Group Effectiveness," *Group & Organization Studies* 10 (March 1985), pp. 37–59.

48 D. I. Levine, "Piece Rates, Output Restriction, and Conformism," *Journal of Economic Psychology* 13 (1992), pp. 473–89.

49 D. Vinokur-Kaplan, "Treatment Teams that Work (and Those that Don't): An Application of Hackman's Group Effectiveness Model to Interdisciplinary Teams in Psychiatric Hospitals," *Journal of Applied Behavioral Science* 31 (1995), pp. 303–27; Shaw, *Group Dynamics,* pp. 213–26; Goodman et al., "Understanding Groups in Organizations," pp. 144–46.

50 B. E. Ashforth and R. H. Humphrey, "Emotion in the Workplace: A Reappraisal," *Human Relations* 48 (1995), pp. 97–125; P. R. Bernthal and C. A. Insko, "Cohesiveness Without Groupthink: The Interactive Effects of Social and Task Cohesiveness," *Group and Organization Management* 18 (1993), pp. 66–87.

51 A. Lott and B. Lott, "Group Cohesiveness as Interpersonal Attraction: A Review of Relationships with Antecedent and Consequent Variables," *Psychological Bulletin* 64 (1965), pp. 259–309.

52 C. Kirchmeyer, "Demographic Similarity to the Work Group: A Longitudinal Study of Managers at the Early Career Stage," *Journal of Organizational Behavior* 16 (1995), pp. 67–83.

53 S. E. Jackson, "Team Composition in Organizational Settings: Issues in Managing an Increasingly Diverse Work Force," in *Group Process and Productivity,* ed. Worchel et al., pp. 138–73; J. Virk, P. Aggarwal, and R. N. Bhan, "Similarity versus Complementarity in Clique Formation," *Journal of Social Psychology* 120 (1983), pp. 27–34.

54 J. A. Alexander, R. Lichtenstein, K. Jinnett, T. A. D'Aunno, and E. Ullman, "The Effects of Treatment Team Diversity and Size on Assessments of Team Functioning," *Hospital & Health Services Administration* 41 (1996), pp. 37–53.

55 M. B. Pinto, J. K. Pinto, and J. E. Prescott, "Antecedents and Consequences of Project Team Cross-Functional Cooperation," *Management Science* 39 (1993), pp. 1281–296; W. Piper, M. Marrache, R. Lacroix, A. Richardson, and B. Jones, "Cohesion as a Basic Bond in Groups," *Human Relations* 36 (1983), pp. 93–108.

56 S. B. Gould, K. J. Weiner, and B. R. Levin, *Free Agents: People and Organizations Creating a New Working Community* (San Francisco: Jossey-Bass, 1997), pp. 158–60.

57 O. Harari, "Open the Doors, Tell the Truth," *Management Review* 84 (January 1995), pp. 33–35; P. LaBarre, "The Dis-organization of Oticon," *Industry Week,* July 18, 1994, pp. 22–28.

58 J. E. Hautaluoma and R. S. Enge, "Early Socialization into a Work Group: Severity of Initiations Revisited," *Journal of Social Behavior & Personality* 6 (1991), pp. 725–48; E. Aronson and J. Mills, "The Effects of Severity of Initiation on Liking for a Group," *Journal of Abnormal and Social Psychology* 59 (1959), pp. 177–81.

59 B. Mullen and C. Copper, "The Relation Between Group Cohesiveness and Performance: An Integration," *Psychological Bulletin* 115 (1994), pp. 210–27; Shaw, *Group Dynamics,* p. 215.

60 B. Carroll, "Team Competition Spurs Continuous Improvement at Motorola," *National Productivity Review* 14 (Autumn 1995), pp. 1–9.

61 J. M. McPherson and P. A. Popielarz, "Social Networks and Organizational Dynamics," *American Sociological Review* 57 (1992), pp. 153–70; Piper et al., "Cohesion as a Basic Bond in Groups," pp. 93–108.

62 C. A. O'Reilly III, D. F. Caldwell, and W. P. Barnett, "Work Group Demography, Social Integration, and Turnover," *Administrative Science Quarterly* 34 (1989), pp. 21–37.

63 R. D. Banker, J. M. Field, R. G. Schroeder, and K. K. Sinha, "Impact of Work Teams on Manufacturing Performance: A Longitudinal Study," *Academy of Management Journal* 39 (1996), pp. 867–90; Mullen and Copper, "The Relation Between Group Cohesiveness and Performance," *Psychological Bulletin;* C. R. Evans and K. L. Dion, "Group Cohesion and Performance: A Meta-Analysis," *Small Group Research* 22 (1991), pp. 175–86.

64 Robbins and Finley, *Why Teams Don't Work,* Chapter 20; "The Trouble with Teams," *Economist,* January 14, 1995, p. 61; A. Sinclair, "The Tyranny of Team Ideology," *Organization Studies* 13 (1992), pp. 611–26.

65 B. Dumaine, "The Trouble with Teams," *Fortune,* September 5, 1994, pp. 86–92.

66 I. D. Steiner, *Group Process and Productivity* (New York: Academic Press, 1972).

67 D. Dunphy and B. Bryant, "Teams: Panaceas or Prescriptions for Improved Performance?," *Human Relations* 49 (1996), pp. 677–99.

68 M. Erez and A. Somech, "Is Group Productivity Loss the Rule or the Exception? Effects of Culture and Group-Based Motivation," *Academy of Management Journal* 39 (1996), pp. 1513–537; S. J. Karau and K. D. Williams, "Social Loafing: A Meta-Analytic Review and Theoretical Integration," *Journal of Personality and Social Psychology* 65 (1993), pp. 681–706; J. M. George, "Extrinsic and Intrinsic Origins of Perceived Social Loafing in Organizations," *Academy of Management Journal* 35 (1992), pp. 191–202; R. Albanese and D. D. Van Fleet, "Rational Behavior in Groups: The Free-Riding Tendency," *Academy of Management Review* 10 (1985), pp. 244–55.

69 Erez and Somech, "Is Group Productivity Loss the Rule or the Exception? Effects of Culture and Group-Based Motivation," pp. 1513–537; P. C. Earley, "Social Loafing and Collectivism: A Comparison of the U.S. and the People's Republic of China," *Administrative Science Quarterly* 34 (1989), pp. 565–81.

70 T. A. Judge and T. D. Chandler, "Individual-level Determinants of Employee Shirking," *Relations Industrielles* 51 (1996), pp. 468–86; J. M. George, "Asymmetrical Effects of Rewards and Punishments: The Case of Social Loafing," *Journal of Occupational and Organizational Psychology* 68 (1995), pp. 327–38; R. E. Kidwell and N. Bennett, "Employee Propensity to Withhold Effort: A Conceptual Model to Intersect Three Avenues of Research," *Academy of Management Review* 19 (1993), pp. 429–56; J. A. Shepperd, "Productivity Loss in Performance Groups: A Motivation Analysis," *Psychological Bulletin* 113 (1993), pp. 67–81.

71 W. G. Dyer, *Team Building: Issues and Alternatives*, 2nd ed. (Reading, Mass.: Addison-Wesley, 1987); and S. J. Liebowitz and K. P. De Meuse, "The Application of Team Building," *Human Relations* 35 (1982), pp. 1–18.

72 E. Sundstrom, K. P. De Meuse, and D. Futrell, "Work Teams: Applications and Effectiveness," *American Psychologist* 45 (1990), p. 128; M. Beer, *Organizational Change and Development: A Systems View* (Santa Monica, Calif.: Goodyear, 1980), pp. 143–46.

73 Beer, *Organizational Change and Development*, p. 145.

74 D. Morley, "Team Building: Changing Managerial Attitudes and Behaviour in a Quality Environment," *Optimum* 22 (3) (1991/92), pp. 17–24.

75 J. J. Laabs, "Team Training Goes Outdoors," *Personnel Journal*, June 1991, pp. 56–63.

76 Robbins and Finley, *Why Teams Don't Work*, Chapter 17.

77 M. J. Brown, "Let's Talk About It, Really Talk About It," *Journal for Quality & Participation* 19 (6) (1996) pp. 26–33; E. H. Schein, "On Dialogue, Culture, and Organizational Learning," *Organizational Dynamics* (Autumn 1993), pp. 40–51; and P. M. Senge, *The Fifth Discipline* (New York: Doubleday Currency, 1990), pp. 238–49.

78 G. Coetzer, *A Study of the Impact of Different Team Building Techniques on Work Team Effectiveness*, unpublished MBA research project (Burnaby, B.C.: Simon Fraser University, 1993).

79 T. G. Cummings and C. G. Worley, *Organization Development & Change*, 6th ed. (Cincinnati: South-Western, 1997), pp. 218–19; P. F. Buller and C. H. Bell, Jr., "Effects of Team Building and Goal Setting on Productivity: A Field Experiment," *Academy of Management Journal* 29 (1986), pp. 305–28.

80 C. J. Solomon, "Simulation Training Builds Teams Through Experience," *Personnel Journal* 72 (June 1993), pp. 100–6.

81 R. W. Woodman and J. J. Sherwood, "The Role of Team Development in Organizational Effectiveness: A Critical Review," *Psychological Bulletin* 88 (1980), pp. 166–86; Sundstrom et al., "Work Teams: Applications and Effectiveness," p. 128.

82 Huszczo, *Tools for Team Excellence*, pp. 50–58.

83 P. McGraw, "Back from the Mountain: Outdoor Management Development Programs and How to Ensure the Transfer of Skills to the Workplace," *Asia Pacific Journal of Human Resources* 31 (Spring 1993), pp. 52–61; G. E. Huszczo, "Training for Team Building," *Training and Development Journal* 44 (February 1990), pp. 37–43.

84 R. W. Boss and H. L. McConkie, "The Destructive Impact of a Positive Team-Building Intervention," *Group & Organization Studies* 6 (1981), pp. 45–56.

CHAPTER 10

1 P. A. Thorpe, "Concurrent Engineering: The Key to Success in Today's Competitive Environment," *IIE Solutions*, October 1995, pp. 10–13; W. Lilley, "Road Warrior: Following a Reorganization and Changes to Design," *Western Commerce & Industry Magazine*, 46 (January 1995), pp. 12–35.

2 E. E. Lawler, "Far From the Fad Crowd," *People Management* (October 24, 1996), pp. 38–40.

3 G. C. McMahon and E. E. Lawler, III, "Effects of Union Status on Employee Involvement: Diffusion and Effectiveness," *Research in Organizational Change and Development* 8 (1995), pp. 47–76; V. H. Vroom and A. G. Jago, *The New Leadership: Managing Participation in Organizations* (Englewood Cliffs, N.J.: Prentice Hall, 1988), p. 15.

4 P. S. McInnis, "Teamwork for Harmony: Labour-Management Production Committees and the Postwar Settlement in Canada," *Canadian Historical Review* 77 (September 1996), pp. 317–52.

5 R. Dubin, "Union-Management Co-operation and Productivity," *Industrial and Labor Relations Review* 2 (1949), pp. 195–209; W. R. Dymond, "Union-Management Cooperation at the Toronto Factory of Lever Brothers Limited," *Canadian Journal of Economics and Political Science* 10 (February 1947), pp. 26–67.

6 R. Chalmers, "Workers Rescue Doomed Plant," *Calgary Herald*, January 16, 1995, p. C1; D. Roberts, "A Long Way from Cambodia," *Globe & Mail*, July 5, 1994, p. B18; D. Scott, "Hard to Beat," *Canadian Mining Journal* 114 (June 1993), pp. 12–14.

7 D. I. Levine, *Reinventing the Workplace* (Washington, D.C.: Brookings, 1995), Chapter 3; M. N. Lam, "Forms of Participation: A Comparison of Preferences Between Chinese Americans and American Caucasians," *Canadian Journal of Administrative Sciences* 3 (June 1986), pp. 81–98; D. V. Nightingale,

"The Formally Participative Organization," *Industrial Relations* 18 (1979), pp. 310–21; E. A. Locke and D. M. Schweiger, "Participation in Decision-Making: One More Look," *Research in Organizational Behavior* 1 (1979), pp. 265–339.

8   B. R. Gordon, "Employee Involvement in the Enforcement of the Occupational Safety and Health Laws of Canada and the United States," *Comparative Labor Law Journal* 15 (1994), pp. 527–60.

9   Levine, *Reinventing the Workplace*, pp. 47–48.

10 "Republic Steels Remakes Workplace Through ESOP," *Employee Benefit Plan Review* 51 (July 1996), pp. 48–50.

11 S. O. Fattedad, "Behind the Scenes at Canadian Airlines," *CGA Magazine*, June 1993, pp. 30–33, 75, 76; D. McMurdy, "A New Way of Saving Jobs," *Maclean's*, September 20, 1993, pp. 18–20.

12 R. C. Liden and S. Arad, "A Power Perspective of Empowerment and Work Groups: Implications for Human Resources Management Research," *Research in Personnel and Human Resources Management* 14 (1996), pp. 205–51; R. C. Ford and M. D. Fottler, "Empowerment: A Matter of Degree," *Academy of Management Executive* 9 (August 1995), pp. 21–31; R. W. Coye and J. A. Belohlav, "An Exploratory Analysis of Employee Participation," *Group & Organization Management* 20 (1995), pp.4–17; Vroom and Jago, *The New Leadership*.

13 N. S. Bruning and P. R. Liverpool, "Membership in Quality Circles and Participation in Decision Making," *Journal of Applied Behavioral Science* 29 (March 1993), pp. 76–95; S. D. Saleh, Z. Guo, and T. Hull, "The Use of Quality Circles in the Automobile Parts Industry," *Proceedings of the Annual ASAC Conference, Organizational Behaviour Division* 9, Part 5 (1988), pp. 95–104.

14 G. Davidson, "Quality Circles Didn't Die — They Just Keep Improving," CMA *Magazine*, February 1995, p. 6.

15 P. E. Rossler and C. P. Koelling, "The Effect of Gainsharing on Business Performance at a Papermill," *National Productivity Review* 12 (Summer 1993), pp. 365–82; C. R. Gowen, III, "Gainsharing Programs: An Overview of History and Research," *Journal of Organizational Behavior Management* 11 (2) (1990), pp. 77–99; F. G. Lesieur (ed.), *The Scanlon Plan: A Frontier in Labor-Management Cooperation* (Cambridge, Mass.: MIT Press, 1958).

16 J. Case, "Opening the Books," *Harvard Business Review* 75 (March-April 1997), pp. 118–27; T. R. V. Davis, "Open-Book Management: Its Promise and Pitfalls," *Organizational Dynamics* (Winter 1997), pp. 7–20; J. Case, *Open Book Management: The Coming Business Revolution* (New York: Harper Business, 1995).

17 P. Robertson and S. Matthews, "Like an Open Book," *CA Magazine*, May 1997, pp. 33–35.

18 G. MacDonald, "An Open-Book Approach to Motivation," *Globe & Mail*, March 31, 1997, p. B9.

19 S. A. Mohrman, S. G. Cohen, and A. M. Mohrman, Jr., *Designing Team-Based Organizations: New Forms for Knowledge Work* (San Francisco: Jossey-Bass, 1995); Lawler, *High-Involvement Management*, Chapters 11 and 12; L. C. Plunkett and R. Fournier, *Participative Management: Implementing Empowerment* (New York: Wiley, 1991).

20 R. Robertson, "Pain Relief," *Materials Management and Distribution*, April 1997.

21 S. G. Cohen, G. E. Ledford, Jr., and G. M. Spreitzer, "A Predictive Model of Self-Managing Work Team Effectiveness," *Human Relations* 49 (1996), pp. 643–76.

22 P. S. Goodman, R. Devadas, and T. L. G. Hughson, "Groups and Productivity: Analyzing the Effectiveness of Self-Managing Teams," in *Productivity in Organizations*, ed. J. P. Campbell, R. J. Campbell, and Associates (San Francisco: Jossey-Bass, 1988), pp. 295–327.

23 D. Tjosvold, *Teamwork for Customers* (San Francisco: Jossey-Bass, 1993); J. Dibbs, "Organizing for Empowerment," *Business Quarterly* 58 (Autumn 1993), pp. 97–102; D. E. Bowen and E. E. Lawler, III, "The Empowerment of Service Workers: What, Why, How, and When," *Sloan Management Review* (Spring 1992), pp. 31–39; K. Foss, "A Better Kind of Keeping House in Banff," *Foodservice and Hospitality* 25 (May 1992), pp. 36–37.

24 E. L. Trist, G. W. Higgin, H. Murray, and A. B. Pollock, *Organizational Choice* (London: Tavistock, 1963).

25 C. C. Manz and G. L. Stewart, "Attaining Flexible Stability by Integrating Total Quality Management and Socio-technical Systems Theory," *Organization Science* 8 (1997), pp. 59–70; K. P. Carson and G. L. Stewart, "Job Analysis and the Sociotechnical Approach to Quality: A Critical Examination," *Journal of Quality Management* 1 (1996), pp. 49–65; J. B. Cunningham, "A Look at Four Approaches to Work Design," *Optimum* 20 (1) (1989–90), pp. 39–55; H. F. Kolodny, C. P. Johnston, and W. Jeffrey, *Quality of Working Life: Job Design and Sociotechnical Systems*, rev. ed. (Ottawa: Supply and Services Canada, 1985).

26 N. Herrick, *Joint Management and Employee Participation* (San Francisco: Jossey-Bass, 1990); T. Rankin and J. Mansell, "Integrative Collective Bargaining and New Forms of Work Organization," *National Productivity Review* 5 (4) (1986), pp. 338–47; N. Halpern, "Sociotechnical System Design: The Shell Sarnia Experience," in *Quality of Working Life: Contemporary Cases*, eds. J. B. Cunningham and T. H. White (Ottawa: Supply and Services Canada, 1984), pp. 31–75.

27 P. S. Adler and R. E. Cole, "Designed for Learning: A Tale of Two Auto Plants," *Sloan Management Review* 34 (Spring 1993), pp. 85–94; O. Hammarström and R. Lansbury, "The Art of Building a Car:

The Swedish Experience Re-examined," *New Technology, Work and Employment* 2 (Autumn 1991), pp. 85–90; J. P. Womack, D. T. Jones, and D. Roos, *The Machine that Changed the World* (New York: MacMillan, 1990). For more favourable evaluations of Volvo's plants, see: I. Magaziner and M. Patinkin, *The Silent War* (New York: Random House, 1988); P. G. Gyllenhammar, *People at Work* (Reading, Mass.: Addison-Wesley, 1977).

28 R. Likert, *New Patterns of Management* (New York: McGraw-Hill, 1961); D. McGregor, *The Human Side of Enterprise* (New York: McGraw-Hill, 1960); C. Argyris, *Personality and Organization* (New York: Harper & Row, 1957).

29 J. A. Wagner, III, C. R. Leana, E. A. Locke, and D. M. Schweiger, "Cognitive and Motivational Frameworks in U.S. Research on Participation: A Meta-Analysis of Primary Effects," *Journal of Organizational Behavior* 18 (1997), pp. 49–65; G. P. Latham, D. C. Winters, and E. A. Locke, "Cognitive and Motivational Effects of Participation: A Mediator Study," *Journal of Organizational Behavior* 15 (1994), pp. 49–63; Cotton, *Employee Involvement*, Chapter 8; S. J. Havlovic, "Quality of Work Life and Human Resource Outcomes," *Industrial Relations*, 1991, pp. 469–79; K. I. Miller and P. R. Monje, "Participation, Satisfaction, and Productivity: A Meta-Analytic Review," *Academy of Management Journal* 29 (1986), pp. 727–53.

30 Cited in M. S. Darling, "Learning How to Use Intellectual Assets to Make Economic Magic" *Canadian Speeches* 10 (October 1996), pp. 43–51.

31 K. T. Dirks, L. L. Cummings, and J. L. Pierce, "Psychological Ownership in Organizations: Conditions Under Which Individuals Promote and Resist Change," *Research in Organizational Change and Development* 9 (1996), pp. 1–23; L. Coch and J. R. P. French, Jr., "Overcoming Resistance to Change," *Human Relations* 1 (1948), pp. 512–32.

32 C. L. Cooper, B. Dyck, and N. Frohlich, "Improving the Effectiveness of Gainsharing: The Role of Fairness and Participation," *Administrative Science Quarterly* 37 (1992), pp. 471–90.

33 A. Sagie and M. Koslowsky, "Organizational Attitudes and Behavior as a Function of Participation in Strategic and Tactical Change Decisions: An Application of Path-Goal Theory," *Journal of Organizational Behavior* 15 (1994), pp. 37–47.

34 J. A. Conger and R. N. Kanungo, "The Empowerment Process: Integrating Theory and Practice," *Academy of Management Review* 13 (1988), pp. 471–82.

35 A. Bandura, *Self-Efficacy: The Exercise of Control* (W. H. Freeman & Co., 1996); M. E. Gist and T. R. Mitchell, "Self-Efficacy: A Theoretical Analysis of Its Determinants and Malleability," *Academy of Management Review* 17 (1992), pp. 183–211; R. F. Mager, "No Self-Efficacy, No Performance," *Training* 29 (April 1992), pp. 32–36.

36 C. C. Manz, "Self-Leading Work Teams: Moving Beyond Self-Management Myths," *Human Relations* 45 (1992), pp. 1119–140; N. Bayloff and E. M. Doherty, "Potential Pitfalls in Employee Participation," *Organizational Dynamics* 17 (1989), pp. 51–62; V. H. Vroom, *Some Personality Determinants of the Effects of Participation* (Englewood Cliffs, N.J.: Prentice Hall, 1960).

37 The limits of employee involvement for improving employee satisfaction are discussed in: J. A. Wagner, III, C. R. Leana, E. A. Locke, and D. Schweiger, "Cognitive and Motivational Frameworks in U.S. Research on Participation: A Meta-Analysis of Primary Effects," *Journal of Organizational Behavior* (1997), pp. 49–65; V. Smith, "Employee Involvement, Involved Employees: Participative Work Arrangements in a White-Collar Service Occupation," *Social Problem* 43 (May 1996), pp. 166–79; D. J. Glew, A. M. O'Leary-Kelly, R. W. Griffin, and D. D. Van Fleet, "Participation in Organizations: A Preview of the Issues and Proposed Framework for Future Analysis," *Journal of Management* 21 (1995), pp. 395–421.

38 Vroom and Jago, *The New Leadership*, pp. 151–52.

39 A. Haasen, "Opel Eisenach GMBH — Creating a High-Productivity Workplace," *Organizational Dynamics* 24 (January 1996), pp. 80–85; T. Murakami, "Introducing Team Working — A Motor Industry Case Study from Germany," *Industrial Relations Journal* 26 (1995), pp. 293–305; R. S. Wellins, W. C. Byham, and G. R. Dixon, *Inside Teams* (San Francisco: Jossey-Bass, 1994), pp. 262–71.

40 C. Pavett and T. Morris, "Management Styles Within A Multinational Corporation: A Five Country Comparative Study," *Human Relations* 48 (1995), pp. 1171–191; M. Erez and P. C. Earley, *Culture, Self-Identity, and Work* (New York: Oxford University Press, 1993), pp. 104–12.

41 L. Redpath and M. O. Nielson, "Crossing the Cultural Divide Between Traditional Native Values and Non-Native Management Ideology," *Proceedings of the Annual ASAC Conference, Organizational Theory Division* 15, Part 12 (1994), pp. 70–79; I. Chapman, D. McCaskill, and D. Newhouse, *Management in Contemporary Aboriginal Organizations* (Peterborough, Ont.: Trent University, 1992), Administrative Studies Working Paper Series 92–04.

42 D. Kramer, "How National Rubber Bounced Back from the Edge of Disaster," *Canadian Occupational Safety* 34 (November–December 1996), pp. 16–17.

43 D. I. Levine, *Reinventing the Workplace* (Washington, D.C.: Brookings, 1995), pp. 63–66, 86; C. C. Manz, D. E. Keating, and A. Donnellon, "Preparing for an Organizational Change to Employee Self-Management: The Managerial Transition," *Organizational Dynamics* 19 (Autumn 1990), pp. 15–26.

44 K. Mark, "Team Power," *Canadian HR Reporter*, October 18, 1989, p. 8.

45 G. T. Fairhurst, S. Green, and J. Courtright, "Inertial Forces and the Implementation of a Socio-Technical Systems Approach: A Communication Study," *Organization Science* 6 (1995), pp. 168–85; Manz et al., "Preparing for an Organizational Change to Employee Self-Management," pp. 23–25.

46 G. McKay, *Increasing the Power of Self-Managing Work Teams Through Effective Human Resource Management Strategies*, unpublished MBA project (Burnaby, B.C.: Simon Fraser University, December 1992).

47 I. Goll and N. B. Johnson, "The Influence of Environmental Pressures, Diversification Strategy, and Union/Nonunion Setting on Employee Participation," *Employee Responsibilities and Rights Journal* 10 (1997), pp. 141–54.

48 H. Allerton "The TEAM Act," *Training & Development* 50 (October 1996), p. 9; R. King, "Dupont Plant Settles Worker Team Dispute," *Plastics News*, May 27, 1996, p. 8; G. C. Armas "Plant's Worker Teams Ignite Debate," *St. Louis Post-Dispatch*, February 10, 1996, p. 6A.

49 F. Pomeroy, "Workplace Change: A Union Perspective," *Canadian Business Review* 22 (Summer 1995), pp. 17–19; Levine, *Reinventing the Workplace*, pp. 66–69; A. Verma and T. A. Kochan, "Two Paths to Innovations in Industrial Relations: The Case of Canada and the United States," *Labor Law Journal*, 1990, pp. 601–7; M. Parker and J. Slaughter, *Choosing Sides: Unions and the Team Concept* (Boston: South End Press, 1988); T. A. Kochan, H. C. Katz, and R. B. McKersie, *The Transformation of American Industrial Relations* (New York: Basic Books, 1986), Chapters 6 and 7.

50 M. Stevenson, "Be Nice for a Change," *Canadian Business*, November 1993, pp. 81–85.

51 E. Cohen-Rosenthal, "Sociotechnical Systems and Unions: Nicety or Necessity," *Human Relations* 50 (May 1997), pp. 585–604; R. E. Allen and K. L. Van Norman, "Employee Involvement Programs: The Noninvolvement of Unions Revisited," *Journal of Labor Research* 17 (Summer 1996), pp. 479–95; B. Gilbert, "The Impact of Union Involvement on the Design and Introduction of Quality of Working Life," *Human Relations* 42 (1989), pp. 1057–78; T. A. Kochan, H. C. Katz, and R. B. McKersie, *The Transformation of American Industrial Relations* (New York: Basic Books, 1986), pp. 238–45.

52 E. Trapunski, "Quality Is the Magic Word for Corporate Slogans," *Globe & Mail*, October 26, 1993, p. B26. The slogans belong to Ford Motor Co. of Canada, Motorola Canada, and Xerox Canada Ltd., respectively.

53 For discussions on the meaning of quality and total quality management, see A. Rao et al., *Total Quality Management: A Cross Functional Perspective* (New York: John Wiley & Sons, 1996), Chapter 2; M. Zairi and P. Leonard, *Practical Benchmarking: The Complete Guide* (London: Chapman & Hall, 1994), pp. 14–21; W. H. Schmidt and J. P. Finnigan, *The Race Without a Finish Line* (San Francisco: Jossey-Bass, 1992); B. Brocka and M. S. Brocka, *Quality Management: Implementing the Best Ideas of the Masters* (Homewood, Ill.: Business One-Irwin, 1992), Chapter 1; C. R. Farquhar and C. G. Johnston, *Total Quality Management: A Competitive Imperative* (Ottawa: Conference Board of Canada, 1990), Chapter 1.

54 K. Ferdows and A. De Meyer, "Lasting Improvements in Manufacturing Performance: In Search of a New Theory," *Journal of Operations Management* 9 (April 1990), pp. 168–94; see also Rao et al., *Total Quality Management*, pp. 9–12.

55 M. V. Uzumeri, "ISO 9000 and Other Metastandards: Principles for Management Practice?" *Academy of Management Executive* 11 (February 1997), pp. 21–36.

56 "Cutting Car Trouble: QS-9000 Standards Designed to Reduce Probability of Faulty Products," *Financial Post Daily*, August 23, 1996 p. 15.

57 S. Bourette, "Schools Adopt 'Quality' Philosophy," *Globe & Mail*, March 27, 1997, p. C6; "ISO 9000 is Passport to Foreign Business," *Globe & Mail* (Supplement), December 16, 1996, p. S1.

58 "Souper Duper!" *Canadian Packaging* 47 (November 1994), pp. 8–10.

59 "Learning from an Auto Process," *Computing Canada*, December 19, 1996, p. 30; "Navigating the Road to QS 9000," *Plant*, July 15, 1996, p. 23.

60 D. L. Goetsch and S. B. Davis, *Introduction to Total Quality*, 2nd ed. (Upper Saddle River, N.J.: Prentice Hall, 1997), Chapter 7; M. E. Milakovich, *Improving Service Quality* (Delray Beach, Fl.: St. Lucie Press, 1995), pp. 16–23; R. L. Flood, *Beyond TQM* (Chichester, U.K.: John Wiley & Sons, 1993).

61 R. Hallowell, L. A. Schlesinger, and J. Zornitsky, "Internal Service Quality, Customer and Job Satisfaction: Linkages and Implications for Management," *Human Resource Planning* 19 (2) (1996), pp. 20–31.

62 D. McGarry, "Can Canada Emulate Xerox Record: Success, Setback, Comeback," *Canadian Speeches* 9 (October 1995), pp. 44–49.

63 R. D. Banker, J. M. Field, R. G. Schroeder, and K. K. Sinha, "Impact of Work Teams on Manufacturing Performance: A Longitudinal Study," *Academy of Management Journal* 39 (1996), pp. 867–90.

64 C. G. Johnston and C. R. Farquhar, *Empowered People Satisfy Customers* (Ottawa: Conference Board of Canada, 1992).

65 L. D. Fredendall and T. L. Robbins, "Modeling the Role of Total Quality Management in the Customer Focused Organization," *Journal of Managerial Issues* 7 (Winter 1995), pp. 403–19.

66 J. P. Womack and D. T Jones, *Lean Thinking* (New York: Simon & Schuster, 1996), pp. 90–91.

67 R. Y. Bergstrom, "Probing the Softer Side of Steelcase," *Production* (November 1994), pp. 52–54.

68 K. Shapansky, "How Fact-Based Management Works for Xerox," *CMA Magazine* (January 1995), pp. 20–22.

69 E. Heinrich, "Keeping the Minivan in the Fast Lane," *Financial Post*, September 9, 1995, pp. 6–7.

70 T. J. McCoy, *Creating An 'Open Book' Organization* (New York: AMACOM 1966), Chapters 6 and 7; R. Y. Bergstrom, "Cells in Steel Country," *Production*, February 1995, pp. 50–54.

71 E. A. Locke and V. K. Jain, "Organizational Learning and Continuous Improvement," *International Journal of Organizational Analysis* 3 (January 1995), pp. 45–68.

72 P. B. Crosby, *The Eternally Successful Organization* (New York: McGraw-Hill, 1988); P. B. Crosby, *Quality Is Free* (New York: McGraw-Hill, 1979).

73 M. E. Raynor, "Doing Everything Right the First Time Pays Off Handsomely at Cadet Uniform Service," *National Productivity Review* 11 (Summer 1992), pp. 347–53.

74 Milakovich, *Improving Service Quality*, Chapter 6.

75 McGarry, "Can Canada Emulate Xerox Record?"

76 D. Kramer, "Small is Beautiful," *Plant Engineering and Maintenance* 19 (June 1996), pp. 38–43.

77 M. Zairi and P. Leonard, *Practical Benchmarking: The Complete Guide* (London: Chapman & Hall, 1994); E. F. Glanz and L. K. Dailey, "Benchmarking," *Human Resource Management* 31 (Spring/Summer 1992), pp. 9–20.

78 C. Frank, "From the Rust Belt to the Baldrige Award," *Journal for Quality and Participation*, 19 (December 1996), pp. 46–51.

79 R. K. Reger, L. T. Gustafson, S. M. DeMarie, and J. V. Mullane, "Reframing the Organization: Why Implementing Total Quality is Easier Said than Done," *Academy of Management Review* 19 (1994), pp. 565–84.

80 M. L. Swink, J. C. Sandvig, and V. A. Mabert, "Customizing Concurrent Engineering Processes: Five Case Studies," *Journal of Product Innovation Management* 13 (1996), pp. 229–44; W. I. Zangwill, *Lightning Strategies for Innovation: How the World's Best Firms Create New Products* (New York: Lexington, 1993); J. V. Owen, "Concurrent Engineering," *Manufacturing Engineering* 109 (November 1992), pp. 69–73.

81 L. Terrett, "New Plant Gears Up for the Future," *Modern Purchasing* 34 (March 1992), pp. 16–18; J. Zeidenberg, "New Focus for Old Strategy," *Globe & Mail*, October 1, 1991, p. B28.

82 K. Mark, "All in One Go," *Canadian Business* (Special Technology Issue), Spring 1994, pp. 39–43

83 R. Reed, D. J. Lemak, and J. C. Montgomery, "Beyond Process: TQM Content and Firm Performance," *Academy of Management Review* 21 (1996), pp. 173–202; R. C. Hill, "When the Going Gets Rough: A Baldrige Winner on the Line," *Academy of Management Executive* 7 (August 1993), pp. 75–79; M. M. Steeples, *The Corporate Guide to the Malcolm Baldrige National Quality Award*, 2nd ed. (Homewood, Ill.: Business One-Irwin, 1993), pp. 293–99.

84 M. Brown, D. Hitchcock, and M. Willard, *Why TQM Fails and What to do About It* (Burr Ridge, Ill: Irwin, 1994).

85 C. R. Harris, "The Evolution of Quality Management: An Overview of the TQM Literature," *Canadian Journal of Administrative Sciences* 12 (June 1995), pp. 95–105; C. S. Fleisher and J. R. Nickel, "Attempting TQM in Organizational Staff Areas: TQM as Managerial Innovation in Corporate Public Affairs," *Canadian Journal of Administrative Sciences* 12 (June 1995), pp. 116–27; R. M. Grant, R. Shani, and R. Krishnan, "TQM's Challenge to Management Theory and Practice," *Sloan Management Review* (Winter 1994), pp. 25–35.

86 G. Chaisson, "Seal of Approval," *Marketing Magazine*, April 29, 1996, p. 29.

CHAPTER 11

1 Adapted from D. Saunders, "If it Bleeds, It Leads," *Globe & Mail*, February 15, 1997, pp. C1, C2.

2 F. A. Shull, Jr., A. L. Delbecq, and L. L. Cummings, *Organizational Decision Making* (New York: McGraw-Hill, 1970), p. 31. Also see: J. G. March, "Understanding How Decisions Happen in Organizations," in Z. Shapira (ed.), *Organizational Decision Making* (New York: Cambridge University Press, 1997), pp. 9–32.

3 This model is adapted from several sources: H. Mintzberg, D. Raisinghani, and A. Théorét, "The Structure of 'Unstructured' Decision Processes," *Administrative Science Quarterly* 21 (1976), pp. 246–75; H. A. Simon, *The New Science of Management Decision* (New York: Harper & Row, 1960); C. Kepner and B. Tregoe, *The Rational Manager* (New York: McGraw-Hill, 1965); W. C. Wedley and R. H. G. Field, "A Predecision Support System," *Academy of Management Review* 9 (1984), pp. 696–703.

4 J. W. Dean, Jr. and M. P. Sharfman, "Does Decision Process Matter? A Study of Strategic Decision-Making Effectiveness," *Academy of Management Journal* 39 (1996), pp. 368–96.

5 P. F. Drucker, *The Practice of Management* (New York: Harper & Brothers, 1954), pp. 353–57.

6   Wedley and Field, "A Predecision Support System," p. 696; Drucker, *The Practice of Management*, p. 357; and L. R. Beach and T. R. Mitchell, "A Contingency Model for the Selection of Decision Strategies," *Academy of Management Review* 3 (1978), pp. 439–49.

7   I. L. Janis, *Crucial Decisions* (New York: The Free Press, 1989), pp. 35–37; Simon, *The New Science of Management Decision*, pp. 5–6.

8   I. Nonaka and H. Takeuchi, *The Knowledge-Creating Company* (New York: Oxford University Press, 1995), p. 69.

9   Mintzberg, Raisinghani, and Théorét, "The Structure of 'Unstructured' Decision Processes," pp. 255–56.

10 B. Fischhoff and S. Johnson, "The Possibility of Distributed Decision Making," in Shapira, *Organizational Decision Making*, pp. 216–37.

11 J. E. Dutton, "Strategic Agenda Building in Organizations," in Shapira, *Organizational Decision Making*, pp. 81–107; M. Lyles and H. Thomas, "Strategic Problem Formulation: Biases and Assumptions Embedded in Alternative Decision-Making Models," *Journal of Management Studies* 25 (1988), pp. 131–45; I. I. Mitroff, "On Systematic Problem Solving and the Error of the Third Kind," *Behavioral Science* 9 (1974), pp. 383–93.

12 P. M. Senge, *The Fifth Discipline: The Art and Practice of the Learning Organization* (New York: Doubleday Currency, 1990), Chapter 10.

13 M. Basadur, "Managing the Creative Process in Organizations," in M. A. Runco (ed.), *Problem Finding, Problem Solving, and Creativity* (Norwood, N.J.: Ablex Publishing, 1994), pp. 237–68.

14 P. C. Nutt, "Preventing Decision Debacles," *Technological Forecasting and Social Change* 38 (1990), pp. 159–74.

15 J. Conlisk, "Why Bounded Rationality?" *Journal of Economic Literature* 34 (1996), pp. 669–700; W. B. MacLeod, "Decision, Contract, and Emotion: Some Economics for a Complex and Confusing World," *Canadian Journal of Economics* 29 (1996), pp. 788–810; B. L. Lipman, "Information Processing and Bounded Rationality: A Survey," *Canadian Journal of Economics* 28 (1995), pp. 42–67.

16 L. T. Pinfield, "A Field Evaluation of Perspectives on Organizational Decision Making," *Administrative Science Quarterly* 31 (1986), pp. 365–88.

17 H. A. Simon, *Administrative Behavior*, 2nd ed. (New York: The Free Press, 1957), pp. xxv, 80–84; and J. G. March and H. A. Simon, *Organizations* (New York: Wiley, 1958), pp. 140–41.

18 P. O. Soelberg, "Unprogrammed Decision Making," *Industrial Management Review* 8 (1967), pp. 19–29; and H. A. Simon, "A Behavioral Model of Rational Choice," *Quarterly Journal of Economics* 69 (1955), pp. 99–118.

19 J. E. Russo, V. H. Medvec, and M. G. Meloy, "The Distortion of Information During Decisions," *Organizational Behavior & Human Decision Processes* 66 (1996), pp. 102–10.

20 H. A. Simon, *Models of Man: Social and Rational* (New York: Wiley, 1957), p. 253.

21 R. N. Taylor, *Behavioral Decision Making* (Glenview, Ill.: Scott, Foresman, 1984), pp. 163–66.

22 D. R. Bobocel and J. P. Meyer, "Escalating Commitment to a Failing Course of Action: Separating the Role of Choice and Justification," *Journal of Applied Psychology* 79 (1994), pp. 360–63; G. Whyte, "Escalating Commitment in Individual and Group Decision Making: A Prospect Theory Approach," *Organizational Behavior and Human Decision Processes* 54 (1993), pp. 430–55; G. Whyte, "Escalating Commitment to a Course of Action: A Reinterpretation," *Academy of Management Review* 11 (1986), pp. 311–21.

23 J. Lorinc, "The Politics of Power," *Canadian Business*, March 1993, pp. 41–42; J. Lorinc, "Power Failure," *Canadian Business*, November 1992, pp. 50–58.

24 F. D. Schoorman and P. J. Holahan, "Psychological Antecedents of Escalation Behavior: Effects of Choice, Responsibility, and Decision Consequences," *Journal of Applied Psychology* 81 (1996), pp. 786–93.

25 D. K. Tse, K. Lee, I. Vertinsky, and D. A. Wehrung, "Does Culture Matter? A Cross-Cultural Study of Executives' Choice, Decisiveness, and Risk Adjustment in International Marketing," *Journal of Marketing* 52 (1988), pp. 81–95.

26 S. McKay, "When Good People Make Bad Choices," *Canadian Business*, February 1994, pp. 52–55.

27 J. Partridge, "London Life Overhauling Management," *Globe & Mail*, February 15, 1997, p. B3.

28 V. H. Vroom and A. G. Jago, *The New Leadership* (Englewood Cliffs, N.J.: Prentice Hall, 1988), pp. 28–29.

29 H. Robbin and M. Finley, *Why Teams Don't Work* (Princeton, N.J.: Peterson's/Pacesetters, 1995), p. 42

30 R. B. Gallupe, W. H. Cooper, M. L. Grisé, and L. M. Bastianutti, "Blocking Electronic Brainstorms," *Journal of Applied Psychology* 79 (1994), pp. 77–86; M. Diehl and W. Stroebe, "Productivity Loss in Idea-Generating Groups: Tracking Down the Blocking Effects," *Journal of Personality and Social Psychology* 61 (1991), pp. 392–403.

31 P. W. Mulvey, J. F. Veiga, P. M. Elsass, "When Teammates Raise a White Flag," *Academy of Management Executive* 10 (February 1996), pp. 40–49.

32 S. Plous, *The Psychology of Judgment and Decision Making* (Philadelphia: Temple University Press, 1993), pp. 200–2.

33 I. L. Janis, *Crucial Decisions* (New York: Free Press, 1989), pp. 56–63; and I. L. Janis, *Groupthink: Psychological Studies of Policy Decisions and Fiascoes*, 2nd ed. (Boston: Houghton Mifflin, 1982).

34 M. E. Turner and A. R. Pratkanis, "Threat, Cohesion, and Group Effectiveness: Testing a Social Identity Maintenance Perspective on Groupthink," *Journal of Personality and Social Psychology* 63 (1992), pp. 781–96.

35 G. Moorhead, R. Ference, and C. P. Neck, "Group Decision Fiascoes Continue: Space Shuttle Challenger and a Revised Groupthink Framework," *Human Relations* 44 (1991), pp. 539–50; and Janis, *Crucial Decisions*, pp. 76–77.

36 C. McGarty, J. C. Turner, M. A. Hogg, B. David, and M. S. Wetherell, "Group Polarization as Conformity to the Prototypical Group Member," *British Journal of Social Psychology* 31 (1992), pp. 1–20; D. Isenberg, "Group Polarization: A Critical Review and Meta-analysis," *Journal of Personality and Social Psychology* 50 (1986), pp. 1141–151; and D. G. Myers and H. Lamm, "The Group Polarization Phenomenon," *Psychological Bulletin* 83 (1976), pp. 602–27.

37 D. Kahneman and A. Tversky, "Prospect Theory: An Analysis of Decision under Risk," *Econometrica* 47 (1979), pp. 263–91.

38 P. C. Nutt, *Making Tough Decisions* (San Francisco: Jossey-Bass, 1989).

39 B. M. Staw, K. W. Koput, and S. G. Barsade "Escalation at the Credit Window: A Longitudinal Study of Bank Executives' Recognition and Write-Off of Problem Loans," *Journal of Applied Psychology* 82 (1997), pp. 130–42.

40 W. Boulding, R. Morgan, and R. Staelin, "Pulling the Plug to Stop the New Product Drain," *Journal of Marketing Research* 34 (1997), pp. 164–76; I. Simonson and B. M. Staw, "De-escalation Strategies: A Comparison of Techniques for Reducing Commitment to Losing Courses of Action," *Journal of Applied Psychology* 77 (1992), pp. 419–26.

41 G. Arnault, "Proper Tools Can Yield Nuggets of Information," *Globe & Mail*, October 15, 1995, p. C11.

42 A. Rangaswamy and G. L. Lilien, "Software Tools for New Product Development," *Journal of Marketing Research* 34 (1997), pp. 177–85.

43 "Tracking Vital Signs," *Canadian Business*, April 1997 (Middle Supplement).

44 Janis, *Crucial Decisions*, pp. 244–49.

45 F. A. Schull, A. L. Delbecq, and L. L. Cummings, *Organizational Decision Making* (New York: McGraw-Hill, 1970), pp. 144–49.

46 A. MacKensie "Innovate or Be Damned," *Asian Business* (January 1995).

47 T. Hines, "Left Brain/Right Brain Mythology and Implications for Management and Training," *Academy of Management Review* 12 (1987), pp. 600–6.

48 B. Kabanoff and J. R. Rossiter, "Recent Developments in Applied Creativity," *International Review of Industrial and Organizational Psychology* 9 (1994), pp. 283–324.

49 M. J. Kiernan, "Get Innovative or Get Dead," *Business Quarterly* 61 (Autumn 1996), pp. 51–58; J. Zeidenberg, "HR and the Innovative Company," *Human Resources Professional* 13 (June 1996), pp. 12–15; T. A. Stewart, "3M Fights Back," *Fortune*, February 5, 1996, pp. 9–99.

50 J. S. Dacey, "Peak Periods of Creative Growth Across the Lifespan," *Journal of Creative Behavior* 23 (1989), pp. 224–47; and F. Barron and D. M. Harrington, "Creativity, Intelligence, and Personality," *Annual Review of Psychology* 32 (1981), pp. 439–76.

51 G. R. Oldham and A. Cummings, "Employee Creativity: Personal and Contextual Factors at Work," *Academy of Management Journal* 39 (1996), pp. 607–34; C. E. Shalley, "Effects of Coaction, Expected Evaluation, and Goal Setting on Creativity and Productivity," *Academy of Management Journal* 38 (1995), pp. 483–503; R. M. Burnside, "Improving Corporate Climates for Creativity," in *Innovation and Creativity at Work*, eds. M. A. West and J. L. Farr (Chichester, U.K.: Wiley, 1990), pp. 265–84.

52 C. M. Farkus and P. DeBacker, *Maximum Leadership* (New York: Henry Holt and Company, 1996), pp. 154–55.

53 R. I. Sutton and A. Hargadon, "Brainstorming Groups in Context: Effectiveness in a Product Design Firm," *Administrative Science Quarterly* 41 (1996), pp. 685–718.

54 T. M. Amabile, R. Conti, H. Coon, J. Lazenby, and M. Herron, "Assessing the Work Environment for Creativity," *Academy of Management Journal* 39 (1996), pp. 1154–184; R. W. Woodman, J. E. Sawyer, and R. W. Griffin, "Toward a Theory of Organizational Creativity," *Academy of Management Review* 18 (1993), pp. 293–321; and T. M. Amabile, "A Model of Creativity and Innovation in Organizations," *Research in Organizational Behavior* 10 (1988), pp. 123–67.

55 G. Dutton, "Enhancing Creativity," *Management Review* (November 1996), pp. 44–46.

56 B. Kabanoff and P. Bottiger, "Effectiveness of Creativity Training and Its Relation to Selected Personality Factors," *Journal of Organizational Behavior* 12 (1991), pp. 235–48; and L. H. Rose and H. T. Lin, "A Meta-Analysis of Long-Term Creativity Training Programs," *Journal of Creative Behavior* 18 (1984), pp. 11–22.

57   S. Z. Dudek and R. Côté, "Problem Finding Revisited," in Runco (ed.), *Problem Finding, Problem Solving, and Creativity*, pp. 130–50.

58   M. Basadur, G. B. Graen, and S. G. Green, "Training in Creative Problem Solving: Effects on Ideation and Problem Finding and Solving in an Industrial Research Organization," *Organizational Behavior and Human Performance* 30 (1982), pp. 41–70.

59   F. D. Barret, "Management by Creativity and Innovation," *Business Quarterly*, Summer 1970, pp. 64–72.

60   W. J. J. Gordon, *Synectics: The Development of Creative Capacity* (New York: Harper & Row, 1961).

61   A. C. Amason, "Distinguishing the Effects of Functional and Dysfunctional Conflict on Strategic Decision Making: Resolving a Paradox for Top Management Teams," *Academy of Management Journal* 39 (1996), pp. 123–48; G. Katzenstein, "The Debate on Structured Debate: Toward a Unified Theory," *Organizational Behavior and Human Decision Processes* 66 (1996), pp. 316–32; D. Tjosvold, *Team Organization: An Enduring Competitive Edge* (Chichester, U.K.: Wiley, 1991).

62   K. M. Eisenhardt, J. L. Kahwajy, and L. J. Bourgeois, III "Conflict and Strategic Choice: How Top Management Teams Disagree," *California Management Review* 39 (Winter 1997), pp. 42–62.

63   J. S. Valacich and C. Schwenk, "Structuring Conflict In Individual, Face-To-Face, and Computer-Mediated Group Decision Making: Carping Versus Objective Devil's Advocacy," *Decision Sciences* 26 (1995), pp. 369–93; D. M. Schweiger, W. R. Sandberg, and P. L. Rechner, "Experiential Effects of Dialectical Inquiry, Devil's Advocacy, and Consensus Approaches to Strategic Decision Making," *Academy of Management Journal* 32 (1989), pp. 745–72.

64   A. F. Osborn, *Applied Imagination* (New York: Scribner, 1957).

65   Sutton and Hargadon, "Brainstorming Groups in Context," *Administrative Science Quarterly*; P. B. Paulus and M. T. Dzindolet "Social Influence Processes in Group Brainstorming," *Journal of Personality and Social Psychology* 64 (1993), pp. 575–86; B. Mullen, C. Johnson, and E. Salas, "Productivity Loss in Brainstorming Groups: A Meta-Analytic Integration." *Basic and Applied Psychology* 12 (1991), pp. 2–23.

66   Gallupe et al., "Blocking Electronic Brainstorms;" J. Blackwell, "You, Too, Can Be An Einstein," *Canadian Business*, May 1993, pp. 66–69; and C. Leitch, "Big Blue Staff Let It All Hang Out — On-Line," *Globe & Mail*, February 26, 1992, p. B18.

67   P. Bordia "Face-To-Face Versus Computer-Mediated Communication: A Synthesis of the Experimental Literature," *Journal of Business Communication* 34 (1997), pp. 99–120; J. S. Valacich, A. R. Dennis, and T. Connolly, "Idea Generation in Computer-Based Groups: A New Ending to an Old Story," *Organizational Behavior and Human Decision Processes* 57 (1994), pp. 448–67; R. B. Gallupe, W. H. Cooper, M. L. Grisé, and L. M. Bastianutti, "Blocking Electronic Brainstorms," *Journal of Applied Psychology* 79 (1994), pp. 77–86.

68   M. Schrage, "Anonymous E-mail Fans Flames of Corporate Conflict," *Computerworld* (June 9, 1997), p. 33.

69   W. M. Bulkeley, " 'Computerizing' Dull Meetings Is Touted as an Antidote to the Mouth that Bored," *The Wall Street Journal*, January 28, 1992, pp. B1, B2.

70   B. Daily, A. Wheatley, S. R. Ash, and R. L. Steiner, "The Effects of a Group Decision Support System on Culturally Diverse and Culturally Homogeneous Group Decision Making," *Information & Management* 30 (1996), pp. 281–89; R. B. Gallupe, A. R. Dennis, W. H. Cooper, J. S. Valacich, L. M. Bastianutti, and J. F. Nunamaker, Jr., "Electronic Brainstorming and Group Size," *Academy of Management Journal* 35 (June 1992), pp. 350–69; and R. B. Gallupe, L. M. Bastianutti, and W. H. Cooper, "Unblocking Brainstorms," *Journal of Applied Psychology* 76 (1991), pp. 137–42.

71   Kabanoff and Rossiter, "Recent Developments in Applied Creativity," pp. 283–324.

72   A. L. Delbecq, A. H. Van de Ven, and D. H. Gustafson, *Group Techniques for Program Planning: A Guide to Nominal Group and Delphi Processes* (Middleton, Wis.: Green Briar Press, 1986).

73   A. B. Hollingshead, "The Rank-Order Effect In Group Decision Making," *Organizational Behavior and Human Decision Processes* 68 (1996), pp. 181–93.

74   P. Hassen, *Rx for Hospitals: New Hope for Medicare in the Nineties* (Toronto: Stoddart, 1993), p. 117.

75   S. Frankel, "NGT + MDS: An Adaptation of the Nominal Group Technique for Ill-Structured Problems," *Journal of Applied Behavioral Science* 23 (1987), pp. 543–51; and D. M. Hegedus and R. Rasmussen, "Task Effectiveness and Interaction Process of a Modified Nominal Group Technique in Solving an Evaluation Problem," *Journal of Management* 12 (1986), pp. 545–60.

CHAPTER 12

1   P. Waldie, "Deal Ends Mitchells' Family Feud," *Globe & Mail*, July 5, 1997, p. B1; P. Waldie, "A Family Buries the Cleaver," *Globe & Mail*, October 31, 1996, pp. B1, B6; "Slicing up the Intercon Empire," *Western Report*, June 10, 1996 pp. 28–30; S. D. Driedger, "High Noon in Saskatoon," *Maclean's*, April 29, 1996, pp. 46–47; P. Waldie, "Family Fights Over Control of Major Saskatchewan Firm," *Globe & Mail*, March 27, 1996, pp. B1, B28; "Saskatoon's Homegrown Dynasty" *Western Report*, March 18, 1996, p. 16.

2   R. Farson, *Management of the Absurd*, (New York: Simon & Schuster, 1996), Chapter 13; R. M. Cyert and J. G. March, *A Behavioral Theory of the Firm* (Englewood Cliffs, N.J.: Prentice Hall, 1963).

3   R. C. Liden and S. Arad, "A Power Perspective of Empowerment and Work Groups: Implications for Human Resources Management Research," *Research in Personnel and Human Resource Management* 14 (1996), pp. 205–51.

4   For a discussion of the definition of power, see: J. Pfeffer, *New Directions in Organizational Theory* (New York: Oxford University Press, 1997), Chapter 6; J. Pfeffer, *Managing with Power* (Boston: Harvard Business University Press, 1992), pp. 17, 30; H. Mintzberg, *Power In and Around Organizations* (Englewood Cliffs, N.J.: Prentice Hall, 1983), Chapter 1.

5   A. M. Pettigrew, *The Politics of Organizational Decision-Making* (London: Tavistock, 1973); R. M. Emerson, "Power-Dependence Relations," *American Sociological Review* 27 (1962), pp. 31–41; R. A. Dahl, "The Concept of Power," *Behavioral Science* 2 (1957), pp. 201–18.

6   D. J. Brass and M. E. Burkhardt, "Potential Power and Power Use: An Investigation of Structure and Behaviour," *Academy of Management Journal* 36 (1993), pp. 441–70; K. M. Bartol and D. C. Martin, "When Politics Pays: Factors Influencing Managerial Compensation Decisions," *Personnel Psychology* 43 (1990), pp. 599–614.

7   P. P. Carson and K. D. Carson, "Social Power Bases: A Meta-Analytic Examination of Interrelationships and Outcomes," *Journal of Applied Social Psychology* 23 (1993), pp. 1150–169; P. Podsakoff and C. Schreisheim, "Field Studies of French and Raven's Bases of Power: Critique, Analysis, and Suggestions for Future Research," *Psychological Bulletin* 97 (1985), pp. 387–411; J. R. P. French and B. Raven, "The Bases of Social Power," in D. Cartwright (ed.), *Studies in Social Power* (Ann Arbor, Mich.: University of Michigan Press, 1959), pp. 150–67.

8   G. Yukl and C. M. Falbe, "Importance of Different Power Sources in Downward and Lateral Relations," *Journal of Applied Psychology* 76 (1991), pp. 416–23.

9   C. Hardy and S. R. Clegg, "Some Dare Call It Power," in S. R. Clegg, C. Hardy, and W. R. Nord (eds.), *Handbook of Organization Studies* (London: Sage, 1996), pp. 622–41.

10   R. P. Kearny, *Warrior Worker* (New York: Henry Holt & Co., 1991), pp. 69–74.

11   I. Nonaka and H. Takeuchi, *The Knowledge-Creating Company* (New York: Oxford University Press, 1995), pp. 138–39. Quotation originally found in G. Pinchot, III, *Intrapreneuring* (New York: Harper & Row, 1985), p. 208.

12   G. A. Yukl, *Leadership in Organizations*, 3rd ed. (Englewood Cliffs, N.J.: Prentice Hall, 1994), p. 13.

13   B. H. Raven, "The Bases of Power: Origins and Recent Developments," *Journal of Social Issues* 49 (1993), pp. 227–51.

14   D. Koulack, "When It's Healthy to Doubt the Doctor," *Globe & Mail*, February 17, 1993, p. A20.

15   M. Siconolfi, "Firms Freeze Out Stock Bashers," *Globe & Mail*, August 3, 1995, p. B8.

16   J. Sallot, "New Chief of Forces Must Rebuild their Morale," *Globe & Mail*, October 12, 1996, pp. A1, A6.

17   S. Finkelstein, "Power in Top Management Teams: Dimensions, Measurement, and Validation," *Academy of Management Journal* 35 (1992), pp. 505–38; D. Krackhardt, "Assessing the Political Landscape: Structure, Cognition, and Power in Organizations," *Administrative Science Quarterly* 35 (1990), pp. 342–69.

18   J. D. Kudisch and M. L. Poteet, "Expert Power, Referent Power, and Charisma: Toward the Resolution of a Theoretical Debate," *Journal of Business & Psychology* 10 (Winter 1995), pp. 177–95.

19   Yukl and Falbe, "Importance of Different Power Sources in Downward and Lateral Relations."

20   D. J. Brass, "Being in the Right Place: A Structural Analysis of Individual Influence in an Organization," *Administrative Science Quarterly* 29 (1984), pp. 518–39; N. M. Tichy, M. L. Tuchman, and C. Frombrun, "Social Network Analysis in Organizations," *Academy of Management Review* 4 (1979), pp. 507–19; H. Guetzkow and H. Simon, "The Impact of Certain Communication Nets upon Organization and Performance in Task-Oriented Groups," *Management Science* 1 (1955), pp. 233–50.

21   J. Schilder, "Secret Agents," *Human Resources Professional* (January 1993), pp. 23–25.

22   D. J. Hickson, C. R. Hinings, C. A. Lee, R. E. Schneck, and J. M. Pennings, "A Strategic Contingencies. Theory of Intraorganizational Power," *Administrative Science Quarterly* 16 (1971), pp. 216–27.

23   J. D. Thompson, *Organizations in Action* (New York: McGraw-Hill, 1967); and Cyert and March, *A Behavioral Theory of the Firm*.

24   C. R. Hinings, D. J. Hickson, J. M. Pennings, and R. E. Schneck, "Structural Conditions of Intraorganizational Power," *Administrative Science Quarterly* 19 (1974), pp. 22–44.

25   Hickson et al., "A Strategic Contingencies Theory of Intraorganizational Power"; Hinings et al., "Structural Conditions of Intraorganizational Power"; R. M. Kanter, "Power Failure in Management Circuits," *Harvard Business Review* (July–August 1979), pp. 65–75.

26   E. Zureik, V. Mosco, and C. Lochhead, "Telephone Workers' Reaction to the New Technology," *Relations Industrielles* 44 (1989), pp. 507–31; S. McGovern, "Strikes Don't Stop Employers Cold Any More," *Montreal Gazette*, September 24, 1988, p. C1.

27   M. Crozier, *The Bureaucratic Phenomenon* (London: Tavistock, 1964).

28   M. Gunderson and D. Hyatt, "Union Impact on Compensation, Productivity, and Management of the Organization," in *Union-Management Relations in Canada*, 3rd ed., M. Gunderson and A. Ponak (eds.) (Don Mills, Ont.: Addison-Wesley, 1995), pp. 311–37.

29   Brass and Burkhardt, "Potential Power and Power Use," pp. 441–70; Hickson et al., "A Strategic Contingencies Theory of Intraorganizational Power," pp. 219–21; J. D. Hackman, "Power and Centrality in the Allocation of Resources in Colleges and Universities," *Administrative Science Quarterly* 30 (1985), pp. 61–77.

30   Kanter, "Power Failure in Management Circuits," p. 68; B. E. Ashforth, "The Experience of Powerlessness in Organizations," *Organizational Behavior and Human Decision Processes* 43 (1989), pp. 207–42; J. W. Medcof, "The Power Motive and Organizational Structure: A Micro-Macro Connection," *Canadian Journal of Administrative Sciences* 2 (1985), pp. 95–113.

31   Raven, "The Bases of Power," pp. 237–39.

32   L. E. Temple and K. R. Loewen, "Perceptions of Power: First Impressions of a Woman Wearing a Jacket," *Perceptual and Motor Skills* 76 (1993), pp. 339–48.

33   B. R. Ragins, "Diversified Mentoring Relationships in Organizations: A Power Perspective," *Academy of Management Review* 22 (1997), pp. 482–521; G. R. Ferris, D. D. Frink, D. P. S. Bhawuk, J. Zhou, and D. C. Gilmore, "Reactions of Diverse Groups to Politics in the Workplace," *Journal of Management* 22 (1996), pp. 23–44; C. A. McKeen and R. J. Burke, "Mentor Relationship in Organizations: Issues, Strategies, and Prospects for Women," *Journal of Management Development* 8 (1989), pp. 33–42.

34   C. M. Falbe and G. Yukl, "Consequences for Managers of Using Single Influence Tactics and Combinations of Tactics," *Academy of Management Journal* 35 (1992), pp. 638–52; A. R. Elangovan, "Perceived Supervisor-Power Effects on Subordinate Work Attitudes and Behaviour," *Proceedings of the Annual ASAC Conference, Organizational Behaviour Division* 11, Part 5 (1990), pp. 80–89.

35   J. W. Medcof, P. A. Hausdorf, and M. W. Piczak, "Opportunities to Satisfy the Need for Power in Managerial and Nonmanagerial Jobs," *Proceedings of the Annual ASAC Conference, Personnel and Human Resources Division* 12, Part 8 (1991), pp. 80–87.

36   D. Kipnis, *The Powerholders* (Chicago: University of Chicago Press, 1976); G. R. Salancik and J. Pfeffer, "The Bases and Use of Power in Organizational Decision Making: The Case of a University," *Administrative Science Quarterly* 19 (1974), pp. 453–73.

37   G. E. G. Catlin, *Systematic Politics* (Toronto: University of Toronto Press, 1962), p. 71.

38   D. Ward, "Drawing the Line," *Vancouver Sun*, April 8, 1995, p. B3.

39   Janzen and Governeau v. Platy Enterprises Ltd. (1989) 10, *Canadian Human Rights Reporter*, D/6205 at p. D/6227.

40   S. I. Paish and A. A. Alibhai, *Act, Don't React: Dealing With Sexual Harassment in Your Organization* (Vancouver: Western Legal Publications, 1996).

41   H. Johnson, "Work-Related Sexual Harassment," *Perspectives on Labour and Income* (Winter 1994), pp. 9–12.

42   D. E. Terpstra, "The Effects of Diversity on Sexual Harassment: Some Recommendations on Research," *Employee Responsibilities and Rights Journal* 9 (1996), pp. 303–13; J. A. Bargh and P. Raymond, "The Naive Misuse of Power: Nonconscious Sources of Sexual Harassment," *Journal of Social Issues* 51 (1995), pp. 85–96; R. A. Carr, "Addicted to Power: Sexual Harassment and the Unethical Behaviour of University Faculty," *Canadian Journal of Counselling* 25 (1991), pp. 447–61.

43   R. A. Thacker and G. R. Ferris, "Understanding Sexual Harassment in the Workplace: The Influence of Power and Politics with the Dyadic Interaction of Harasser and Target," *Human Resource Management Review* 1 (1991), pp. 23–37.

44   T. L. Tang and S. L. McCollum, "Sexual Harassment in the Workplace," *Public Personnel Management* 25 (1996), pp. 53–58; Bargh and Raymond, "The Naive Misuse of Power: Nonconscious Sources of Sexual Harassment," pp. 85–96.

45   T. H. Davenport, R. G. Eccles, and L. Prusak, "Information Politics," *Sloan Management Review* (Fall 1992), pp. 53–65; Pfeffer, *Managing with Power*, Chapter 17; C. Kirchmeyer, "Organizational Politics from the Manager's Point of View: An Exploration of Beliefs, Perceptions, and Actions," *Proceedings of the Annual ASAC Conference, Organizational Behaviour Division* 9, Part 5 (1988), pp. 57–66.

46   K. M. Kacmar and G. R. Ferris, "Politics at Work: Sharpening the Focus of Political Behavior in Organizations," *Business Horizons* 36 (July–August 1993), pp. 70–74; A. Drory and T. Romm, "The Definition of Organizational Politics: A Review," *Human Relations* 43 (1990), pp. 1133–154; and P. J. Frost and D. C. Hayes, "An Exploration in Two Cultures of a Model of Political Behavior in Organizations," in *Organizational Influence Processes*, eds. R. W. Allen and L. W. Porter (Glenview, Ill.: Scott, Foresman, 1983), pp. 369–92.

47   P. J. Frost, "Power, Politics, and Influence," in *Handbook of Organizational Communication: An Interdisciplinary Perspective*, ed. F. M. Jablin, L. L. Putnam, K. H. Roberts, and L. W. Porter (Newbury Park, Calif.: Sage, 1987), pp. 503–48.

48 P. J. Frost and C. P. Egri, "Influence of Political Action on Innovation: Part I," *Leadership and Organizational Development Journal* 11(1) (1990), pp. 17–25; P. J. Frost and C. P. Egri, "Influence of Political Action on Innovation: Part II," *Leadership and Organizational Development Journal* 11 (2) (1990), pp. 4–12.

49 P. Kumar and R. Ghadially, "Organizational Politics and Its Effects on Members of Organizations," *Human Relations* 42 (1989), pp. 305–14.

50 Time spent managing organizational politics is from an Accountemps survey. See: "A Waste of Time," *Manitoba Business*, October 1994, p. 9.

51 P. Waldie, "Turmoil Hit McCain Bottom Line," Globe & Mail, January 10, 1997 pp. B1, B6; M. MacIsaac, "Picking Up the Pieces," *Canadian Business* (March 1995), pp. 29–44; M. Woloschuk, *The Real Story of the McCain Feud* (Toronto: Seal, 1995).

52 M. Velasquez, D. J. Moberg, and G. F. Cavanaugh, "Organizational Statesmanship and Dirty Politics: Ethical Guidelines for the Organizational Politician," *Organizational Dynamics* 11 (1983), pp. 65–79.

53 R. W. Allen, D. L. Madison, L. W. Porter, P. A. Renwick, and B. T. Mayes, "Organizational Politics: Tactics and Characteristics of Its Actors," *California Management Review* 22 (Fall 1979), pp. 77–83; V. Murray and J. Gandz, "Games Executives Play: Politics at Work," *Business Horizons*, December 1980, pp. 11–23.

54 A. LaPlante, "Rightsizing Angst," *Forbes ASAP*, June 7, 1993, p. 100.

55 B. E. Ashforth and R. T. Lee, "Defensive Behavior in Organizations: A Preliminary Model," *Human Relations* 43 (1990), pp. 621–48.

56 G. S. Crystal, *In Search of Excess* (New York: W. W. Norton & Co., 1991), pp. 12–13.

57 N. Gupta and G. D. Jenkins, Jr., "The Politics of Pay," *Compensation and Benefits Review* 28 (March–April 1996), pp. 23–30.

58 S. Gittins, "Retirement No Life of Leisure for ex-CEOs," *Financial Post,* February 13, 1989, p. 17. Also see: R. McQueen, *The Money Spinners* (Toronto: Macmillan, 1983), Chapter 4.

59 "Coming Through Slaughter: Q&A with H&K," *Adnews Insight* (1996).

60 E. A. Mannix, "Organizations as Resource Dilemmas: The Effects of Power Balance on Coalition Formation in Small Groups." *Organizational Behavior and Human Decision Processes* 55 (1993), pp. 1–22; A. T. Cobb, "Toward the Study of Organizational Coalitions: Participant Concerns and Activities in a Simulated Organizational Setting," *Human Relations* 44 (1991), pp. 1057–79; W. B. Stevenson, J. L. Pearce, and L. W. Porter, "The Concept of 'Coalition' in Organization Theory and Research," *Academy of Management Review* 10 (1985), pp. 256–68.

61 Falbe and Yukl, "Consequences for Managers of Using Single Influence Tactics and Combinations of Tactics," pp. 638–52.

62 D. Krackhardt and J. R. Hanson, "Informal Networks: The Company Behind the Chart," *Harvard Business Review* 71 (July–August 1993), pp. 104–11; and R. E. Kaplan, "Trade Routes: The Manager's Network of Relationships," *Organizational Dynamics* (Spring 1984), pp. 37–52.

63 R. J. Burke and C. A. McKeen, "Women in Management," *International Review of Industrial and Organizational Psychology* 7 (1992), pp. 245–83; B. R. Ragins and E. Sundstrom, "Gender and Power in Organizations: A Longitudinal Perspective," *Psychological Bulletin* 105 (1989), pp. 51–88.

64 "Balancing Briefcase and Baby," *Daily Commercial News*, March 4, 1996 p. B1.

65 A. R. Cohen and D. L. Bradford, "Influence Without Authority: The Use of Alliances, Reciprocity, and Exchange to Accomplish Work," *Organizational Dynamics* 17 (3) (1989), pp. 5–17.

66 R. A. Giacalone and P. Rosenfeld (eds.), *Applied Impression Management* (Newbury Park, Calif.: Sage, 1991); and J. T. Tedeschi (ed.), *Impression Management Theory and Social Psychological Research* (New York: Academic Press, 1981).

67 W. L. Gardner, III, "Lessons in Organizational Dramaturgy: The Art of Impression Management," *Organizational Dynamics* (Summer 1992), pp. 33–46; R. C. Liden and T. R. Mitchell, "Ingratiatory Behaviors in Organizational Settings," *Academy of Management Review* 13 (1988), pp. 572–87; and A. MacGillivary, S. Ascroft, and M. Stebbins, "Meritless Ingratiation," *Proceedings of the Annual ASAC Conference, Organizational Behaviour Division* 7, Part 7 (1986), pp. 127–35.

68 A. Rao and S. M. Schmidt, "Upward Impression Management: Goals, Influence Strategies, and Consequences," *Human Relations* 48 (1995), pp. 147–67.

69 C. Hardy, *Strategies for Retrenchment and Turnaround: The Politics of Survival* (Berlin: Walter de Gruyter, 1990), Chapter 14; S. C. Goh and A. R. Doucet, "Antecedent Situational Conditions of Organizational Politics: An Empirical Investigation," *Proceedings of the Annual ASAC Conference, Organizational Behaviour Division* 7, Part 5 (1986), pp. 77–86; J. Gandz and V. V. Murray, "The Experience of Workplace Politics," *Academy of Management Journal* 23 (1980), pp. 237–51.

70 G. R. Ferris, G. S. Russ, and P. M. Fandt, "Politics in Organizations," in R. A. Giacalone and P. Rosenfeld (eds.), *Impression Management in the Organization* (Hillsdale, N.J.: Erlbaum, 1989), pp. 143–70; H. Mintzberg, "The Organization as Political Arena," *Journal of Management Studies* 22 (1985), pp. 133–54.

71 R. J. House, "Power and Personality in Complex Organizations," *Research in Organizational Behavior* 10 (1988), pp. 305–57; L. W. Porter, R. W. Allen, and H. L. Angle, "The Politics of Upward Influence in Organizations," *Research in Organizational Behavior* 3 (1981), pp. 120–22.

72 S. M. Farmer, J. M. Maslyn, D. B. Fedor, and J. S. Goodman, "Putting Upward Influence Strategies in Context," *Journal of Organizational Behavior* 18 (1997), pp. 17–42; P. E. Mudrack, "An Investigation into the Acceptability of Workplace Behaviors of a Dubious Ethical Nature," *Journal of Business Ethics* 12 (1993), pp. 517–24; and R. Christie and F. Geis, *Studies in Machiavellianism* (New York: Academic Press, 1970).

73 K. Ryer, "Hancock Speaks," *MacWeek* (On-Line), July 11, 1997; "Amelio Says His Good-byes," *Macworld Daily* (On-Line), July 11, 1997.

74 D. Tannen, *Talking From 9 to 5* (New York: Avon, 1995), pp. 137–41, 151–52.

75 Tannen, *Talking From 9 to 5* , Chapter 2.

76 M. Crawford, *Talking Difference: On Gender and Language* (Thousand Oaks, Calif.: Sage, 1995), pp. 41–44; D. Tannen, *You Just Don't Understand: Men and Women in Conversation* (New York: Ballantine Books, 1990); S. Helgesen, *The Female Advantage: Women's Ways of Leadership* (New York: Doubleday, 1990).

77 S. Mann, "Politics and Power in Organizations: Why Women Lose Out," *Leadership & Organization Development Journal* 16 (1995), pp. 9–15; L. Larwood, and M. M. Wood "Training Women for Management: Changing Priorities," *Journal of Management Development* 14 (1995), pp. 54–65. A recent popular press book even serves as a guide for women to learn organizational politics. See: H. Rubin, *The Princessa: Machiavelli For Women*, (New York: Doubleday/Currency, 1996).

78 G. R. Ferris et. al., "Perceptions of Organizational Politics: Prediction, Stress-Related Implications, and Outcomes," *Human Relations* 49 (1996), pp. 233–63.

CHAPTER 13

1 S. McKay, "Building Morale: The Key to Successful Change," *Nonprofit World* 13 (May–June 1995), pp. 40–46.

2 J. A. Wall and R. R. Callister, "Conflict and Its Management," *Journal of Management* 21 (1995), pp. 515–58; D. Tjosvold, *Working Together to Get Things Done* (Lexington, Mass.: Lexington, 1986), pp. 114–15.

3 A. C. Amason, "Distinguishing the Effects of Functional and Dysfunctional Conflict on Strategic Decision Making: Resolving a Paradox for Top Management Teams," *Academy of Management Journal* 39 (1996), pp. 123–48; K. A. Jehn, "A Multimethod Examination of the Benefits and Detriments of Intragroup Conflict," *Administrative Science Quarterly* 40 (1995), pp. 256–82.

4 G. Wolf, "Conflict Episodes," in *Negotiating in Organizations*, eds. M. H. Bazerman and R. J. Lewicki (Beverly Hills, Calif.: Sage, 1983), pp. 135–40; L. R. Pondy, "Organizational Conflict: Concepts and Models," *Administrative Science Quarterly* 12 (1967), pp. 296–320.

5 H. Witteman, "Analyzing Interpersonal Conflict: Nature of Awareness, Type of Initiating Event, Situational Perceptions, and Management Styles," *Western Journal of Communications* 56 (1992), pp. 248–80; F. J. Barrett and D. L. Cooperrider, "Generative Metaphor Intervention: A New Approach for Working with Systems Divided by Conflict and Caught in Defensive Perception," *Journal of Applied Behavioral Science* 26 (1990), pp. 219–39.

6 Wall and Callister, "Conflict and Its Management," pp. 526–33.

7 Amason, "Distinguishing the Effects of Functional and Dysfunctional Conflict on Strategic Decision Making"; D. Nightingale, "Conflict and Conflict Resolution," in G. Strauss, R. Miles, C. Snow, and A. Tannenbaum (eds.), *Organizational Behavior: Research and Issues* (Belmont, Calif.: Wadsworth, 1976), pp. 141–64.

8 L. L. Putnam, "Productive Conflict: Negotiation as Implicit Coordination," *International Journal of Conflict Management* 5 (1994), pp. 285–99; D. Tjosvold, *The Conflict-Positive Organization* (Reading, Mass.: Addison-Wesley, 1991); R. A. Baron, "Positive Effects of Conflict: A Cognitive Perspective," *Employee Responsibilities and Rights Journal* 4 (1991), pp. 25–36.

9 K. M. Eisenhardt, J. L. Kahwajy, and L. J. Bourgeois, III, "Conflict and Strategic Choice: How Top Management Teams Disagree," *California Management Review* 39 (Winter 1997), pp. 42–62; J. K. Bouwen and R. Fry, "Organizational Innovation and Learning: Four Patterns of Dialog Between the Dominant Logic and the New Logic," *International Studies of Management and Organizations* 21 (1991), pp. 37–51.

10 T. Janz and D. Tjosvold, "Costing Effective vs. Ineffective Work Relationships," *Canadian Journal of Administrative Sciences* 2 (1985), pp. 43–51.

11 R. R. Blake and J. S. Mouton, *Solving Costly Organizational Conflicts* (San Francisco: Jossey-Bass, 1984).

12 D. Evans, "Team Players," *Canadian Business* (August 1991), pp. 28–31.

13 R. E. Walton and J. M. Dutton, "The Management of Conflict: A Model and Review," *Administrative Science Quarterly* 14 (1969), pp. 73–84.

14 N. McGrath, P. Janssen, and D. Hulme, "Scheming Workers Can Ruin Business," *Asian Business* (September 1995).

15 B. Critchley, "Lévesque Beaubien's Brain Drain," *Financial Post*, October 17, 1996, p. 5

16 K. Labich, "Making Diversity Pay," *Fortune*, September 9, 1996, pp. 177–80; C. Kirchmeyer, "Demographic Similarity to the Work Group: A Longitudinal Study of Managers at the Early Career Stage," *Journal of Organizational Behavior* 16 (1995), pp. 67–83.

17 R. C. Liden, S. J. Wayne, and L. K. Bradway, "Task Interdependence as a Moderator of the Relation Between Group Control and Performance," *Human Relations* 50 (1997), pp. 169–82; R. Wageman, "Interdependence and Group Effectiveness," *Administrative Science Quarterly* 40 (1995), pp.145–80; M. A. Campion, G. J. Medsker, and A. C. Higgs, "Relations Between Work Group Characteristics and Effectiveness: Implications for Designing Effective Work Groups," *Personnel Psychology* 46 (1993), pp. 823–50; M. N. Kiggundu, "Task Interdependence and the Theory of Job Design," *Academy of Management Review* 6 (1981), pp. 499–508.

18 P. C. Earley and G. B. Northcraft, "Goal Setting, Resource Interdependence, and Conflict Management," in *Managing Conflict: An Interdisciplinary Approach*, ed. M. A. Rahim (New York: Praeger, 1989), pp. 161–70.

19 J. D. Thompson, *Organizations in Action* (New York: McGraw-Hill, 1967), pp. 54–56.

20 K. H. Doerr, T. R. Mitchell, and T. D. Klastorin, "Impact of Material Flow Policies and Goals on Job Outcomes," *Journal of Applied Psychology* 81 (1996), pp. 142–52.

21 W. W. Notz, F. A. Starke, and J. Atwell, "The Manager as Arbitrator: Conflicts over Scarce Resources," in *Negotiating in Organizations,* eds. Bazerman and Lewicki, pp. 143–64.

22 R. A. Baron, "Reducing Organizational Conflict: An Incompatible Response Approach," *Journal of Applied Psychology* 69 (1984), pp. 272–79.

23 C. Kirchmeyer and J. McLellan, "Capitalizing on Ethnic Diversity: An Approach to Managing the Diverse Workgroups of the 1990s," *Canadian Journal of Administrative Sciences* 8 (June 1991), pp. 72–79; E. J. Mighty, "Valuing Workforce Diversity: A Model of Organizational Change," *Canadian Journal of Administrative Sciences* 8 (June 1991), pp. 64–70.

24 K. W. Thomas, "Conflict and Conflict Management," in *Handbook of Industrial and Organizational Psychology*, ed. M. D. Dunnette (Chicago: Rand McNally, 1976), pp. 889–935. For similar models see: R. R. Blake and J. S. Mouton, *The Managerial Grid* (Houston: Gulf Publications, 1964); M. A. Rahim, "A Measure of Styles of Handling Interpersonal Conflict," *Academy of Management Journal* 26 (1983), pp. 368–76.

25 R. J. Lewicki and J. A. Litterer, *Negotiation* (Homewood, Ill.: Irwin, 1985), pp. 102–6.

26 K. W. Thomas, "Toward Multi-Dimensional Values in Teaching: The Example of Conflict Behaviors," *Academy of Management Review* 2 (1977), pp. 484–90.

27 Tjosvold, *Working Together to Get Things Done*, Chapter 2; D. W. Johnson, G. Maruyama, R. T. Johnson, D. Nelson, and S. Skon, "Effects of Cooperative, Competitive, and Individualistic Goal Structures on Achievement: A Meta-Analysis," *Psychological Bulletin* 89 (1981), pp. 47–62; R. J. Burke, "Methods of Resolving Superior-Subordinate Conflict: The Constructive Use of Subordinate Differences and Disagreements," *Organizational Behavior and Human Performance* 5 (1970), pp. 393–441.

28 Jehn, "A Multimethod Examination of the Benefits and Detriments of Intragroup Conflict," p. 276.

29 M. A. Rahim and A. A. Blum (eds.), *Global Perspectives on Organizational Conflict*, (Westport, Conn.: Praeger, 1995); M. Rabie, *Conflict Resolution and Ethnicity*, (Westport, Conn.: Praeger, 1994).

30 S. M. Elsayed-Ekhouly and R. Buda, "Organizational Conflict: A Comparative Analysis of Conflict Styles Across Cultures," *International Journal of Conflict Management* 7 (1996), pp. 71–81; D. K. Tse, J. Francis, and J. Walls, "Cultural Differences in Conducting Intra- and Inter-Cultural Negotiations: A Sino-Canadian Comparison," *Journal of International Business Studies* 25 (1994), pp. 537–55; S. Ting-Toomey et al., "Culture, Face Management, and Conflict Styles of Handling Interpersonal Conflict: A Study in Five Cultures," *International Journal of Conflict Management* 2 (1991), pp. 275–91.

31 L. Karakowsky, "Toward an Understanding of Women and Men at the Bargaining Table: Factors Affecting Negotiator Style and Influence in Multi-Party Negotiations," *Proceedings of the Annual ASAC Conference, Women in Management Division*, (1996), pp. 21–30; W. C. King, Jr. and T. D. Hinson, "The Influence of Sex and Equity Sensitivity on Relationship Preferences, Assessment of Opponent, and Outcomes in a Negotiation Experiment," *Journal of Management* 20 (1994), pp. 605–24; R. Lewicki, J. Litterer, D. Saunders, and J. Minton (eds.), *Negotiation: Readings, Exercises, and Cases* (Homewood, Ill.: Irwin, 1993).

32 E. Van de Vliert, "Escalative Intervention in Small Group Conflicts," *Journal of Applied Behavioral Science* 21 (Winter 1985), pp. 19–36.

33 M. B. Pinto, J. K. Pinto, and J. E. Prescott, "Antecedents and Consequences of Project Team Cross-Functional Cooperation," *Management Science* 39 (1993), pp. 1281–297; M. Sherif, "Superordinate Goals in the Reduction of Intergroup Conflict," *American Journal of Sociology* 68 (1958), pp. 349–58.

34 M. Zimmerman, *How to Do Business with the Japanese* (New York: Random House, 1985), pp. 170, 200; W. G. Ouchi, *Theory Z* (New York: Avon, 1982), pp. 25–32.

35 "American Factories Halt Their Assembly Lines," *Globe & Mail*, January 7, 1995, p. D4.

36 A. Vido, "Chrysler and Minivans: Are We There Yet?" *CMA Magazine*, November 1993, pp. 11–16.

37 W. N. Isaacs, "Taking Flight: Dialogue, Collective Thinking, and Organizational Learning," *Organizational Dynamics* (Autumn 1993), pp. 24–39; E. H. Schein, "On Dialogue, Culture, and Organizational Learning," *Organizational Dynamics* (Autumn 1993), pp. 40–51; P. M. Senge, *The Fifth Discipline* (New York: Doubleday Currency, 1990), pp. 238–49.

38 G. A. Peer, "Operations Team at Huge Ontario Quarry Gears Up for the Future," *Heavy Construction News*, November 1996, pp. 8–11.

39 Blake and Mouton, *Solving Costly Organizational Conflicts*, Chapter 6; R. R. Blake and J. S. Mouton, "Overcoming Group Warfare," *Harvard Business Review*, November–December 1984, pp. 98–108.

40 P. R. Lawrence and J. W. Lorsch, *Organization and Environment* (Homewood, Ill.: Irwin, 1969).

41 J. S. DeMott, "The Key Issue: Managing Bigness," *Worldbusiness* (September/October 1996), pp. 30–33.

42 D. G. Pruitt and P. J. Carnevale, *Negotiation in Social Conflict* (Buckingham, U.K.: Open University Press, 1993), p. 2; and J. A. Wall, Jr., *Negotiation: Theory and Practice* (Glenview, Ill.: Scott, Foresman, 1985), p. 4.

43 For a critical view of collaboration in negotiation, see: J. M. Brett, "Managing Organizational Conflict," *Professional Psychology: Research and Practice* 15 (1984), pp. 664–78.

44 R. E. Fells, "Developing Trust in Negotiation," *Employee Relations* 15 (1993), pp. 33–45.

45 R. Stagner and H. Rosen, *Psychology of Union-Management Relations* (Belmont, Calif.: Wadsworth, 1965), pp. 95–96, 108–10; and R. E. Walton and R. B. McKersie, *A Behavioral Theory of Labor Negotiations: An Analysis of a Social Interaction System* (New York: McGraw-Hill, 1965), pp. 41–46.

46 J. W. Salacuse and J. Z. Rubin, "Your Place or Mine? Site Location and Negotiation," *Negotiation Journal* 6 (January 1990), pp. 5–10; and Lewicki and Litterer, *Negotiation*, pp. 144–46.

47 B. C. Herniter, E. Carmel, and J. F. Nunamaker, Jr., "Computers Improve Efficiency of the Negotiation Process," *Personnel Journal*, April 1993, pp. 93–99.

48 Lewicki and Litterer, *Negotiation*, pp. 146–51; and B. Kniveton, *The Psychology of Bargaining* (Aldershot, U.K.: Avebury, 1989), pp. 76–79.

49 Pruitt and Carnevale, *Negotiation in Social Conflict*, pp. 59–61; and Lewicki and Litterer, *Negotiation*, pp. 151–54.

50 N. J. Adler, *International Dimensions of Organizational Behavior*, 2nd ed. (Belmont, Calif.: Wadsworth, 1991), p. 191.

51 B. M. Downie, "When Negotiations Fail: Causes of Breakdown and Tactics for Breaking the Stalemate," *Negotiation Journal*, April 1991, pp. 175–86.

52 Pruitt and Carnevale, *Negotiation in Social Conflict*, pp. 56–58; and Lewicki and Litterer, *Negotiation*, pp. 215–22.

53 V. V. Murray, T. D. Jick, and P. Bradshaw, "To Bargain or Not to Bargain? The Case of Hospital Budget Cuts," in *Negotiating in Organizations*, eds. Bazerman & Lewicki, pp. 272–95.

54 R. L. Lewicki, A. Hiam, and K. Olander, *Think Before you Speak: The Complete Guide to Strategic Negotiation* (New York : John Wiley & Sons, 1996); G. B. Northcraft and M. A. Neale, "Joint Effects of Assigned Goals and Training on Negotiator Performance," *Human Performance* 7 (1994), pp. 257–72.

55 M. A. Neale and M. H. Bazerman, *Cognition and Rationality in Negotiation* (New York: Free Press, 1991), pp. 29–31; and L. L. Thompson, "Information Exchange in Negotiation," *Journal of Experimental Social Psychology* 27 (1991), pp. 161–79.

56 L. Thompson, E. Peterson, and S. E. Brodt, "Team Negotiation: An Examinaton of Integrative and Distributive Bargaining," *Journal of Personality and Social Psychology* 70 (1996), pp. 66–78; Lewicki and Litterer, *Negotiation*, pp. 177–80; and Adler, *International Dimensions of Organizational Behavior*, 2nd ed., pp. 190–91.

57 L. L. Putnam and M. E. Roloff (eds.), *Communication and Negotiation* (Newbury Park, Calif.: Sage, 1992).

58 L. Hall (ed.), *Negotiation: Strategies for Mutual Gain* (Newbury Park, Calif.: Sage, 1993); and D. Ertel, "How to Design a Conflict Management Procedure that Fits Your Dispute," *Sloan Management Review* 32 (Summer 1991), pp. 29–42.

59 Lewicki and Litterer, *Negotiation*, pp. 89–93.

60 P. Brethour, "Toronto Firm Takes to Heart Cultural Lessons," *Globe & Mail*, August 30, 1996, p. B6; Adler, *International Dimensions of Organizational Behavior*, 2nd ed., pp. 180–81.

61 Kniveton, *The Psychology of Bargaining*, pp. 100–101; J. Z. Rubin and B. R. Brown, *The Social Psychology of Bargaining and Negotiation* (New York: Academic Press, 1976), Chapter 9; and Brett, "Managing Organizational Conflict," pp. 670–71.

62 B. H. Sheppard, R. J. Lewicki, and J. W. Monton, *Organizational Justice: The Search for Fairness in the Workplace* (New York: Lexington, 1992).

63 R. Folger and J. Greenberg, "Procedural Justice: An Interpretive Analysis of Personnel Systems," *Research in Personnel and Human Resources Management* 3 (1985), pp. 141–83.

64 L. L. Putnam, "Beyond Third Party Role: Disputes and Managerial Intervention," *Employee Responsibilities and Rights Journal* 7 (1994), pp. 23–36; A. R. Elangovan, "Managerial Third-Party Intervention: Cognitive Biases and Heuristics," *Proceedings of the Annual ASAC Conference, Organizational Behaviour Division* 14, Part 5 (1993), pp. 92–101; Sheppard et al., *Organizational Justice.*

65 "An Ombudsperson Can Improve Management-Labor Relations," *Personnel Journal* (August 1993), p. 62; M. Crawford, "The New Office Etiquette," *Canadian Business* (May 1993), pp. 22–31.

66 M. A. Neale and M. H. Bazerman, *Cognition and Rationality in Negotiation* (New York: The Free Press, 1991), pp. 140–42.

67 D. K. Denton, "Behind the Curve," *Business Horizons* 36 (July–August 1993), pp. 1–4; Crawford, "The New Office Etiquette," p. 31; S. L. McShane, "Conflict Resolution Practices for Nonunion Employees," *Human Resources Management in Canada* (January 1991), pp. 35, 527–36.

68 B. H. Sheppard, "Managers as Inquisitors: Lessons from the Law," in M. Bazerman and R. J. Lewicki (eds.), *Bargaining Inside Organizations* (Beverly Hills, Calif.: Sage, 1983), pp. 193–213.

69 Tjosvold, *The Conflict-Positive Organization,* pp. 112–13; R. Karambayya and J. M. Brett, "Managers Handling Disputes: Third Party Roles and Perceptions of Fairness," *Academy of Management Journal* 32 (1989), pp. 687–704.

70 J. P. Meyer, J. M. Gemmell, and P. G. Irving, "Evaluating the Management of Interpersonal Conflict in Organizations: A Factor-Analytic Study of Outcome Criteria," *Canadian Journal of Administrative Sciences* 14 (1997), pp. 1–13.

CHAPTER 14

1   R. Siklos, "Canadian in Running for Top Job at Avon," *Financial Post,* June 5, 1997, p. 22; "Ding Dong: Profit Calling," *Financial Post,* May 22, 1996 p. 11; P. Wisenthal, "Sweet Smell of Success," *Montreal Gazette,* March 13, 1995 pp. E1, E2; J. Quinn, "Avon's New Face," *Incentive,* June 1994, pp. 26–30; C. H. Deutsch, "Avon's Montreal Recruit has Gold Touch with Reps," *Globe & Mail,* April 5, 1994, p. B10.

2   R. Farson, *Management of the Absurd* (New York: Simon & Schuster, 1996), Chapter 28; P. C. Drucker, "Forward," in F. Hesselbein et al., *The Leader of the Future* (San Francisco, Calif.: Jossey-Bass, 1997); R. A. Barker, "How Can We Train Leaders if We Do Not Know What Leadership Is?" *Human Relations* 50 (1997), pp. 343–62.

3   J. M. Burns, *Leadership* (New York: Harper & Row, 1978), p. 2.

4   D. Miller, M. F. R. Ket de Vries, and J. M. Toulouse, "Top Executive Locus of Control and Its Relationship to Strategy-Making, Structure, and Environment," *Academy of Management Journal* 25 (1982), pp. 237–53; S. Withane, "Leadership Influence on Organizational Reorientations: A Strategic Choice Model," *Proceedings of the Annual ASAC Conference, Organizational Behaviour Division* 7, Part 5 (1986), pp. 218–27; and P. Selznick, *Leadership in Administration* (Evanston, Ill.: Row, Peterson, 1957), p. 37.

5   C. A. Beatty, "Implementing Advanced Manufacturing Technologies: Rules of the Road," *Sloan Management Review* (Summer 1992), pp. 49–60; J. M. Howell and C. A. Higgins, "Champions of Technological Innovation," *Administrative Science Quarterly* 35 (1990), pp. 317–41.

6   J. P. Souque and J. Warda, "A Winning Formula," *Canadian Business Review* (Summer 1996), pp. 7–13; A. Kainz, "Newbridge Touch Spans Globe," *Montreal Gazette,* June 19, 1993, pp. D1, D2; D. Girard, "High-Flying Newbridge Called a Global Success Story," *Toronto Star,* April 18, 1993, pp. H1, H5; J. Bagnall, "Smart, Scrappy, Innovative, and Profitable: Newbridge Networks Shows How It's Done," *Financial Times of Canada,* August 3, 1992, pp. 10–12; F. Misutka, "Newbridge: Choking on Its Own Success?" *Canadian Business* 63 (November 1990), pp. 90–95; and J. Stackhouse, "Second Empire," *Report on Business Magazine* (October 1990), pp. 72–77.

7   R. M. Stogdill, *Handbook of Leadership* (New York: The Free Press, 1974), Chapter 5.

8   For example, see: S. Edwards, "How Campbell Soup Develops Global Leaders," *Canadian HR Reporter,* September 23, 1996, pp. 17–18; G. Pearson, "New Look in Development of Tomorrow's Executive," *Canadian HR Reporter,* December 5, 1994, pp. 13–14.

9   L. M. Spencer and S. M. Spencer, *Competence at Work: Models for Superior Performance* (New York: Wiley, 1993).

10 The first six traits are described in S. A. Kirkpatrick and E. A. Locke, "Leadership: Do Traits Matter?" *Academy of Management Executive* 5 (May 1991), pp. 48–60.

11 J. M. Kouzes and B. Z. Posner, *Credibility: How Leaders Gain and Lose It, Why People Demand It* (San Francisco: Jossey-Bass, 1993).

12 S. J. Zaccaro, R. J. Foti, and D. A. Kenny, "Self-Monitoring and Trait-Based Variance in Leadership: An Investigation of Leader Flexibility Across Multiple Group Situations," *Journal of Applied Psychology* 76 (1991), pp. 308–15; G. H. Dobbins, W. S. Long, E. J. Dedrick, and T. C. Clemons, "The Role of Self-Monitoring and Gender on Leader Emergence: A Laboratory and Field Study," *Journal of Management* 16 (1990), pp. 609–18; and R. J. Ellis and R. S. Adamson, "Antecedents of Leadership Emergence," *Proceedings of the Annual ASAC Conference, Organizational Behaviour Division* 7, Part 5 (1986), pp. 49–57.

13 R. S. Adamson, R. J. Ellis, G. Deszca, and T. F. Cawsey, "Self-Monitoring and Leadership Emergence," *Proceedings of the Annual ASAC Conference, Organizational Behaviour Division* 5, Part 5 (1984), pp. 9–15.

14 R. G. Lord and K. J. Maher, *Leadership and Information Processing: Linking Perceptions and Performance* (Cambridge, Mass.: Unwin Hyman, 1991).

15 G. A. Yukl, *Leadership in Organizations*, 3rd ed. (Englewood Cliffs, N.J.: Prentice Hall, 1994), pp. 53–75; R. Likert, *New Patterns of Management* (New York: McGraw-Hill, 1961).

16 N. Deogun, "Does Pepsi Need a Tyrant at the Top?" *Globe & Mail*, March 20, 1997, p. B13.

17 "A Conversation with Paul Giannelia," *Initiative Media Special Feature Supplement*, April 1997.

18 A. K. Korman, "Consideration, Initiating Structure, and Organizational Criteria — A Review," *Personnel Psychology* 19 (1966), pp. 349–62; and E. A. Fleishman, "Twenty Years of Consideration and Structure," in *Current Developments in the Study of Leadership*, eds. E. A. Fleishman and J. C. Hunt (Carbondale, Ill.: Southern Illinois University Press, 1973), pp. 1–40.

19 V. V. Baba, "Serendipity in Leadership: Initiating Structure and Consideration in the Classroom," *Human Relations* 42 (1989), pp. 509–25.

20 R. L. Kahn, "The Prediction of Productivity," *Journal of Social Issues* 12 (2) (1956), pp. 41–49; P. Weissenberg and M. H. Kavanagh, "The Independence of Initiating Structure and Consideration: A Review of the Evidence," *Personnel Psychology* 25 (1972), pp. 119–30; Stogdill, *Handbook of Leadership*, Chapter 11.

21 R. R. Blake and A. A. McCanse, *Leadership Dilemmas — Grid Solutions* (Houston: Gulf Publishing Company, 1991); and R. R. Blake and J. S. Mouton, "Management by Grid Principles or Situationalism: Which?" *Group and Organization Studies* 7 (1982), pp. 207–10.

22 L. L. Larson, J. G. Hunt, and R. N. Osborn, "The Great Hi-Hi Leader Behavior Myth: A Lesson from Occam's Razor," *Academy of Management Journal* 19 (1976), pp. 628–41; and A. K. Korman, "Consideration, Initiating Structure, and Organizational Criteria — A Review," *Personnel Psychology* 19 (1966), pp. 349–62.

23 G. N. Powell and D. A. Butterfield, "The 'High-High' Leader Rides Again!" *Group & Organization Studies* 9 (1984), pp. 437–50.

24 S. Kerr, C. A. Schriesheim, C. J. Murphy, and R. M. Stogdill, "Towards a Contingency Theory of Leadership Based Upon the Consideration and Initiating Structure Literature," *Organizational Behavior and Human Performance* 12 (1974), pp. 62–82.

25 R. Tannenbaum and W. H. Schmidt, "How to Choose a Leadership Pattern," *Harvard Business Review*, May–June 1973, pp. 162–80.

26 M. G. Evans, "The Effects of Supervisory Behavior on the Path-Goal Relationship," *Organizational Behavior and Human Performance* 5 (1970), pp. 277–98; M. G. Evans, "Extensions of a Path-Goal Theory of Motivation," *Journal of Applied Psychology* 59 (1974), pp. 172–78; R. J. House, "A Path-Goal Theory of Leader Effectiveness," *Administrative Science Quarterly* 16 (1971), pp. 321–38.

27 R. J. House and T. R. Mitchell, "Path-Goal Theory of Leadership," *Journal of Contemporary Business*, Autumn 1974, pp. 81–97.

28 R. J. House, "Path-Goal Theory of Leadership: Lessons, Legacy, and a Reformulated Theory," *Leadership Quarterly* 7 (1996), pp. 323–52.

29 J. C. Wofford and L. Z. Liska, "Path-Goal Theories of Leadership: A Meta-Analysis," *Journal of Management* 19 (1993), pp. 857–76; and J. Indvik, "Path-Goal Theory of Leadership: A Meta-Analysis," *Academy of Management Proceedings*, 1986, pp. 189–92.

30 R. T. Keller, "A Test of the Path-Goal Theory of Leadership with Need for Clarity as a Moderator in Research and Development Organizations," *Journal of Applied Psychology* 74 (1989), pp. 208–12.

31 House, "Path-Goal Theory of Leadership: Lessons, Legacy, and a Reformulated Theory."

32 Wofford and Liska, "Path-Goal Theories of Leadership: A Meta-Analysis;" Yukl, *Leadership in Organizations*, pp. 102–4; and Indvik, "Path-Goal Theory of Leadership: A Meta-Analysis."

33 R. J. House and M. L. Baetz, "Leadership: Some Empirical Generalizations and New Research Directions," *Research in Organizational Behavior* 1 (1979), pp. 341–423.

34 J. M. Jermier, "The Path-Goal Theory of Leadership: A Subtextural Analysis," *Leadership Quarterly* 7 (1996), pp. 311–16.

35 C. A. Schriesheim and L. L. Neider, "Path-Goal Leadership Theory: The Long and Winding Road," *Leadership Quarterly* 7 (1996), pp. 317–21.

36 P. Hersey and K. H. Blanchard, *Management of Organizational Behavior: Utilizing Human Resources*, 5th ed. (Englewood Cliffs, N.J.: Prentice Hall, 1988).

37 W. Blank, J. R. Weitzel, and S. G. Green, "A Test of the Situational Leadership Theory," *Personnel Psychology* 43 (1990), pp. 579–97; and R. P. Vecchio, "Situational Leadership Theory: An Examination of a Prescriptive Theory," *Journal of Applied Psychology* 72 (1987), pp. 444–51.

38 F. E. Fiedler, *A Theory of Leadership Effectiveness* (New York: McGraw-Hill, 1967); and F. E. Fiedler and M. M. Chemers, *Leadership and Effective Management* (Glenview, Ill.: Scott, Foresman, 1974).

39 T. H. Wagar, and R. J. Long, "Profit Sharing in Canada: Incidence and Predictors," *1995 ASAC Conference, Human Resources Division* 16 (9) (1995), pp. 97–105.

40 P. M. Podsakoff, B. P. Niehoff, S. B. MacKenzie, and M. L. Williams, "Do Substitutes Really Substitute for Leadership? An Empirical Examination of Kerr and Jermier's Situational Leadership Model," *Organizational Behavior and Human Decision Processes* 54 (1993), pp. 1–44.

41 D. Kramer, "How National Rubber Bounced Back from the Edge of Disaster," *Canadian Occupational Safety*, November–December 1996, pp. 15–16.

42 J. M. Howell and B. J. Avolio, "Transformational Leadership, Transactional Leadership, Locus of Control, and Support for Innovation: Key Predictors of Consolidated-Business-Unit Performance," *Journal of Applied Psychology* 78 (1993), pp. 891–902; J. A. Conger and R. N. Kanungo, "Perceived Behavioural Attributes of Charismatic Leadership," *Canadian Journal of Behavioural Science* 24 (1992), pp. 86–102; J. Seltzer and B. M. Bass, "Transformational Leadership: Beyond Initiation and Consideration," *Journal of Management* 16 (1990), pp. 693–703.

43 B. J. Avolio and B. M. Bass, "Transformational Leadership, Charisma, and Beyond," in J. G. Hunt, H. P. Dachler, B. R. Baliga, and C. A. Schriesheim (eds.), *Emerging Leadership Vistas* (Lexington, Mass.: Lexington Books, 1988), pp. 29–49.

44 W. Bennis and B. Nanus, *Leaders: The Strategies for Taking Charge* (New York: Harper & Row, 1985), p. 21; A. Zaleznik, "Managers and Leaders: Are They Different?" *Harvard Business Review* 55 (5) (1977), pp. 67–78.

45 W. Bennis, *An Invented Life: Reflections on Leadership and Change* (Reading, Mass.: Addison-Wesley, 1993); D. Tjosvold and M. M. Tjosvold, *The Emerging Leader* (New York: Lexington, 1993), p. 25.

46 B. S. Pawar and K. K. Eastman, "The Nature and Implications of Contextual Influences on Transformational Leadership: A Conceptual Examination," *Academy of Management Review* 22 (1997), pp. 80–109.

47 J. A. Conger and R. N. Kanungo, "Toward a Behavioral Theory of Charismatic Leadership in Organizational Settings," *Academy of Management Review* 12 (1987), pp. 637–47; R. J. House, "A 1976 Theory of Charismatic Leadership," in J. G. Hunt and L. L. Larson (eds.), *Leadership: The Cutting Edge*, (Carbondale, Ill.: Southern Illinois University Press, 1977), pp. 189–207.

48 J. D. Kudisch and M. L. Poteet, "Expert Power, Referent Power, and Charisma: Toward the Resolution of a Theoretical Debate," *Journal of Business & Psychology* 10 (Winter 1995), pp. 177–95.

49 L. Sooklal, "The Leader as a Broker of Dreams," *Organizational Studies* (1989), pp. 833–55.

50 J. M. Stewart, "Future State Visioning — A Powerful Leadership Process," *Long Range Planning* 26 (December 1993), pp. 89–98; Bennis and Nanus, *Leaders*, pp. 27 – 33, 89; J. M. Kouzes and B. Z. Posner, *The Leadership Challenge* (San Francisco: Jossey-Bass, 1987), Chapter 5.

51 T. J. Peters, "Symbols, Patterns, and Settings: An Optimistic Case for Getting Things Done," *Organizational Dynamics* 7 (Autumn 1978), pp. 2–23.

52 S. A. Kirkpatrick and E. A. Locke (1996). "Direct and Indirect Effects of Three Core Charismatic Leadership Components on Performance and Attitudes," *Journal of Applied Psychology* 81 (1996), pp. 36–51.

53 J. A. Conger, "Inspiring Others: The Language of Leadership," *Academy of Management Executive* 5 (February 1991), pp. 31–45.

54 G. T. Fairhurst and R. A. Sarr, *The Art of Framing: Managing the Language of Leadership* (San Francisco, Calif.: Jossey-Bass, 1996).

55 L. Black, "Hamburger Diplomacy," *Report on Business Magazine* 5 (August 1988), pp. 30–36.

56 Fairhurst and Sarr, *The Art of Framing*, Chapter 5; J. Pfeffer, "Management as Symbolic Action: The Creation and Maintenance of Organizational Paradigms," *Research in Organizational Behavior* 3 (1981), pp. 1–52.

57 S. Franklin. *The Heroes: A Saga of Canadian Inspiration* (Toronto: McClelland and Stewart, 1967), p. 53.

58 N. H. Snyder and M. Graves, "Leadership and Vision," *Business Horizons* 37 (1) (1994), pp. 1–7; P. Tommerup, "Stories About an Inspiring Leader," *American Behavioral Scientist* 33 (1990), pp. 374–85; and D. E. Berlew, "Leadership and Organizational Excitement," in *Organizational Psychology: A Book of Readings*, eds. D. A. Kolb, I. M. Rubin, and J. M. McIntyre (Englewood Cliffs, N.J.: Prentice Hall, 1974).

59 C. Knight, "Canada, U.S. Share Similar Leadership Concerns," *Canadian HR Reporter*, May 5, 1997, pp. 1, 3.

60 Bennis and Nanus, *Leaders*, pp. 43–55; Kouzes and Posner, *Credibility: How Leaders Gain and Lose It, Why People Demand It*.

61 P. Bycio, R. D. Hackett, and J. S. Allen, "Further Assessments of Bass's (1985) Conceptualization of Transactional and Transformational Leadership," *Journal of Applied Psychology* 80 (1995), pp. 468–78; W. L. Koh, R. M. Steers, and J. R. Terborg, "The Effects of Transformational Leadership on Teacher Attitudes and Student Performance in Singapore," *Journal of Organizational Behavior* 16 (1995), pp. 319–33; Howell and Avolio, "Transformational Leadership, Transactional Leadership, Locus of Control, and Support for Innovation."

62 J. Barling, T. Weber, and E. K. Kelloway, "Effects of Transformational Leadership Training on Attitudinal and Financial Outcomes: A Field Experiment," *Journal of Applied Psychology* 81 (1996), pp. 827–32.

63 A. Bryman, "Leadership in Organizations," in S. R. Clegg, C. Hardy, and W. R. Nord (eds.), *Handbook of Organization Studies* (Thousand Oaks, Calif.: Sage, 1996), pp. 276–92.

64 Pawar and Eastman, "The Nature and Implications of Contextual Influences on Transformational Leadership."

65 K. Boehnke, A. C. DiStefano, J. J. DiStefano, and N. Bontis, "Leadership for Extraordinary Performance," *Business Quarterly* 61 (Summer 1997), pp. 56–63.

66 M. Johnson, "Taking the Lid Off Leadership," *Management Review*, November 1996, pp. 59–61.

67 R. J. Hall and R. G. Lord, "Multi-level Information Processing Explanations of Followers' Leadership Perceptions," *Leadership Quarterly* 6 (1995), pp. 265–87; R. Ayman, "Leadership Perception: The Role of Gender and Culture," in M. M. Chemers and R. Ayman (eds.), *Leadership Theory and Research: Perspectives and Directions*, (San Diego, Calif.: Academic Press, 1993), pp. 137–66; J. R. Meindl, "On Leadership: An Alternative to the Conventional Wisdom," *Research in Organizational Behavior* 12 (1990), pp. 159–203.

68 G. R. Salancik and J. R. Meindl, "Corporate Attributions as Strategic Illusions of Management Control," *Administrative Science Quarterly* 29 (1984), pp. 238–54; and J. M. Tolliver, "Leadership and Attribution of Cause: A Modification and Extension of Current Theory," *Proceedings of the Annual ASAC Conference, Organizational Behaviour Division* 4, Part 5 (1983), pp. 182–91.

69 S. F. Cronshaw and R. G. Lord, "Effects of Categorization, Attribution, and Encoding Processes on Leadership Perceptions," *Journal of Applied Psychology* 72 (1987), pp. 97–106; J. W. Medcof and M. G. Evans, "Heroic or Competent? A Second Look," *Organizational Behavior and Human Decision Processes* 38 (1986), pp. 295–304; A. de Carufel and S. C. Goh, "Implicit Theories of Leadership: Strategy, Outcome, and Precedent," *Proceedings of the Annual ASAC Conference, Organizational Behaviour Division* 8, Part 5 (1987), pp. 47–55.

70 Meindl, "On Leadership: An Alternative to the Conventional Wisdom," p. 163.

71 J. Pfeffer, "The Ambiguity of Leadership," *Academy of Management Review* 2 (1977), pp. 102–12; and Yukl, *Leadership in Organizations*, pp. 265–67.

72 Cronshaw and Lord, "Effects of Categorization, Attribution, and Encoding Processes on Leadership Perceptions," pp. 104–5.

73 D. Layton, "SkyDome's Head Coach," *Toronto Star*, November 24, 1996, pp. E1, E3.

74 S. H. Appelbaum and B. T. Shapiro, "Why Can't Men Lead Like Women?" *Leadership and Organization Development Journal* 14 (1993), pp. 28–34; J. B. Rosener, "Ways Women Lead," *Harvard Business Review* 68 (November–December 1990), pp. 119–25; and J. Grant, "Women as Managers: What They Can Offer to Organizations," *Organization Dynamics* (Winter 1988), pp. 56–63.

75 G. N. Powell, "One More Time: Do Female and Male Managers Differ?" *Academy of Management Executive* 4 (August 1990), pp. 68–75; K. K. Lush and M. J. Withey, "Gender as a Moderator in the Path-Goal Theory of Leadership," *Proceedings of the Annual ASAC Conference, Organizational Behaviour Division* 11, Part 5 (1990), pp. 140–49; and G. H. Dobbins and S. J. Platts, "Sex Differences in Leadership: How Real Are They?" *Academy of Management Review* 11 (1986), pp. 118–27.

76 A. H. Eagly and B. T. Johnson, "Gender and Leadership Style: A Meta-Analysis," *Psychological Bulletin* 108 (1990), pp. 233–56.

77 M. Javidan, B. Bemmels, K. S. Devine, and A. Dastmalchian, "Superior and Subordinate Gender and the Acceptance of Superiors as Role Models," *Human Relations* 48 (1995), pp. 1271–284.

78 A. H. Eagly, S. J. Karau, and M. G. Makhijani, "Gender and the Effectiveness of Leaders: A Meta-Analysis," *Psychological Bulletin* 117 (1995), pp. 125–45; M. E. Heilman and C. J. Block, "Sex Stereotypes: Do They Influence Perceptions of Managers?" *Journal of Social Behavior & Personality* 10 (1995), pp. 237–52; R. L. Kent and S. E. Moss, "Effects of Sex and Gender Role on Leader Emergence," *Academy of Management Journal* 37 (1994), pp. 1335–346; A. H. Eagly, M. G. Makhijani, and B. G. Klonsky, "Gender and the Evaluation of Leaders: A Meta-Analysis," *Psychological Bulletin* 111 (1992), pp. 3–22.

CHAPTER 15

1 P. Kaihla, "Back on the Rails," *Maclean's*, January 13, 1997, pp. 36–38; G. Welty, "Can Labor Agreements be Brought into the 20th (and 21st) Century?" *Railway Age*, May 1997, p. 9; K. Leger, "A Fine Way to Run a Railroad," *Financial Post*, December 23, 1995, pp. 6–7; M. Hallman, "Changing Tracks," *Financial Post*, February 3, 1993, pp. S16–S17.

2 T. Brusse, "Second-Quarter Losses Cast Doubt over Novell's Future," *InfoWorld*, June 9, 1997, p. 58.

3 K. Ohmae, *The Borderless World* (New York: HarperBusiness, 1990); and Economic Council of Canada, *Transitions for the 90s* (27th Annual Review) (Ottawa: Supply and Services Canada, 1990), Chapter 1.

4 B. Crosariol, "War of the Wires," *Report on Business Magazine*, May 1994, pp. 32–46.

5 S. McKay, "The Challenge of Change," *Financial Post Magazine*, April 1992, pp. 43–46.

6   "Iona Slashes Design Cycle Time with CAD," *Design Engineering*, January 1997.

7   D. Tapscott and A. Laston, *Paradigm Shift* (New York: McGraw-Hill, 1993); W. H. Davidow and M. S. Malone, *The Virtual Corporation* (New York: HarperBusiness, 1992).

8   Kaihla, "Back on the Rails," *Maclean's*, p. 37–38.

9   R. J. Long, "New Information Technology and Employee Involvement," *Proceedings of the Annual ASAC Conference, Organizational Behaviour Division* 14, Part 5 (1993), pp. 161–70; R. J. Long, "The Impact of New Office Information Technology on Job Quality of Female and Male Employees," *Human Relations* 46 (1993), pp. 939–61; J. W. Medcof, "The Effect of Extent of Use of Information Technology and Job of the User upon Task Characteristics," *Human Relations* 42 (1989), pp. 23–41.

10 C. Hardy, *Strategies for Retrenchment and Turnaround: The Politics of Survival* (Berlin: Walter de Gruyter, 1990), Chapter 13.

11 D. A. Nadler, "The Effective Management of Organizational Change," in *Handbook of Organizational Behavior*, ed. J. W. Lorsch (Englewood Cliffs, N.J.: Prentice Hall, 1987), pp. 358–69; and D. Katz and R. L. Kahn, *The Social Psychology of Organizations*, 2nd ed. (New York: Wiley, 1978).

12 M. E. McGill and J. W. Slocum, Jr., "Unlearn the Organization," *Organizational Dynamics* 22 (2) (1993), pp. 67–79.

13 R. Katz, "Time and Work: Toward an Integrative Perspective," *Research in Organizational Behavior* 2 (1980), pp. 81–127.

14 D. Nicolini, and M. B. Meznar, "The Social Construction of Organizational Learning: Conceptual and Practical Issues in the Field," *Human Relations* 48 (1995), pp. 727–46.

15 D. Miller, "What Happens after Success: The Perils of Excellence," *Journal of Management Studies* 31 (1994), pp. 325–58.

16 J. McHutchion, "Managing Change Gets Frowns in Business Survey," *Toronto Star*, March 23, 1996, p. C8.

17 K. Lewin, *Field Theory in Social Science* (New York: Harper & Row, 1951).

18 J. P. Kotter, "Leading Change: Why Transformation Efforts Fail," *Harvard Business Review*, March–April 1995, pp. 59–67.

19 A. Gore, "Joel Kocher: Power COO Says It's Time to Evolve," *MacUser*, April 1997 (on-line).

20 J. P. Kotter and L. A. Schlesinger, "Choosing Strategies for Change," *Harvard Business Review*, March–April 1979, pp. 106–14.

21 "Organisational Change in Bonas Machine Company," *IRS Employment Review*, June 1996, pp. 5–10.

22 R. M. D'Aprix, *Communicating for Change: Connecting the Workplace with the Marketplace* (San Francisco, Calif.: Jossey-Bass, 1996).

23 "CEMEX: A New Foundation," *CEO Brief* (Supplement to *Chief Executive*), July 25, 1995, pp. 10–11.

24 V. D. Miller and J. R. Johnson, "Antecedents to Willingness to Participate in a Planned Organizational Change," *Journal of Applied Communication Research* 22 (1994), pp. 59–80; L. C. Caywood and R. P. Ewing, *The Handbook of Communications in Corporate Restructuring and Takeovers* (Englewood Cliffs, N.J.: Prentice Hall, 1992).

25 K. T. Dirks, L. L. Cummings, and J. L. Pierce, "Psychological Ownership in Organizations: Conditions Under Which Individuals Promote and Resist Change," *Research in Organizational Change and Development* 9 (1996), pp. 1–23; K. D. Dannemiller and R. W. Jacobs, "Changing the Way Organizations Change: A Revolution of Common Sense," *Journal of Applied Behavioral Science* 28 (1992), pp. 480–98.

26 "Partners in Honing High-Quality Customer Service Skills," *Training* 34 (January 1997), p. S23–S26.

27 P. H. Mirvis and M. L. Marks, *Managing the Merger* (Englewood Cliffs, N.J.: Prentice Hall, 1992); R. J. Burke, "Managing the Human Side of Mergers and Acquisitions," *Business Quarterly* (Winter 1987), pp. 18–23.

28 S. McKay, "The Challenge of Change," *Financial Post Magazine*, April 1992, pp. 43–46.

29 R. Greenwood and C. R. Hinings, "Understanding Radical Organizational Change: Bringing Together the Old and the New Institutionalism," *Academy of Management Review* 21 (1996), pp. 1022–54.

30 J. Dibbs, "Organizing for Empowerment," *Business Quarterly* 58 (Autumn 1993), pp. 97–102.

31 J. Lublin, "Curing Sick Companies Better Done Fast," *Globe & Mail*, July 25, 1995, p. B18.

32 Nicolini and Meznar, "The Social Construction of Organizational Learning."

33 T. G. Cummings and E. F. Huse, *Organization Development and Change*, 4th ed. (St. Paul, Minn.: West, 1989), pp. 477–85; P. Goodman and J. Dean, "Creating Long-Term Organizational Change," in *Change in Organizations*, ed. P. Goodman and Associates (San Francisco: Jossey-Bass, 1982), pp. 226–79; W. W. Burke, *Organization Development: A Normative View* (Reading, Mass.: Addison-Wesley, 1987), pp. 124–25.

34 R. Greenwood and C. R. Hinings, "Understanding Strategic Change: The Contribution of Archetypes," *Academy of Management Journal* 36 (1993), pp. 1052–81.

35 W. K. Beckett and K. Dang, "Synchronous Manufacturing: New Methods, New Mind-Set," *Journal of Business Strategy*, January–February 1992, pp. 53–56.

36 M. Beer, R. A. Eisenstat, and B. Spector, *The Critical Path to Corporate Renewal* (Boston, Mass.: Harvard Business School Press, 1990).

37 R. E. Walton, *Innovating to Compete: Lessons for Diffusing and Managing Change in the Workplace* (San Francisco: Jossey-Bass, 1987); Beer et al., *The Critical Path to Corporate Renewal*, Chapter 5; and R. E. Walton, "Successful Strategies for Diffusing Work Innovations," *Journal of Contemporary Business* (Spring 1977), pp. 1–22.

38 R. Beckhard, *Organization Development: Strategies and Models* (Reading, Mass.: Addison-Wesley, 1969), Chapter 2. Also see Cummings and Huse, *Organization Development and Change*, pp. 1–3.

39 Burke, *Organization Development*, pp. 12–14.

40 W. L. French and C. H. Bell, Jr., *Organization Development: Behavioral Science Interventions for Organization Improvement*, 4th ed. (Englewood Cliffs, N.J.: Prentice Hall, 1990), Chapter 8. For a recent discussion of action research model, see J. B. Cunningham, *Action Research and Organization Development* (Westport, Conn.: Praeger, 1993).

41 A. B. Shani and G. R. Bushe, "Visionary Action Research: A Consultation Process Perspective," *Consultation: An International Journal* 6 (1) (1987), pp. 3–19.

42 M. L. Brown, "Five Symbolic Roles of the Organizational Development Consultant: Integrating Power, Change, and Symbolism," *Proceedings of the Annual ASAC Conference, Organizational Behaviour Division* 14, Part 5 (1993), pp. 71–81; D. A. Buchanan and D. Boddy, *The Expertise of the Change Agent: Public Performance and Backstage Activity* (New York: Prentice Hall, 1992); L. E. Greiner and V. E. Schein, *Power and Organization Development: Mobilizing Power to Implement Change* (Reading, Mass.: Addison-Wesley, 1988).

43 D. F. Harvey and D. R. Brown, *An Experiential Approach to Organization Development*, 5th ed. (Upper Saddle River, N.J.: Prentice Hall, 1996), Chapter 4.

44 M. Beer and E. Walton, "Developing the Competitive Organization: Interventions and Strategies," *American Psychologist* 45 (February 1990), pp. 154–61.

45 E. H. Schein, *Process Consultation: Its Role in Organization Development* (Reading, Mass.: Addison-Wesley, 1969).

46 For a case study of poor diagnosis, see M. Popper, "The Glorious Failure," *Journal of Applied Behavioral Science* 33 (March 1997), pp. 27–45.

47 D. Nadler, *Feedback and Organization Development: Using Data-Based Methods* (Reading, Mass.: Addison-Wesley, 1977); and J. A. Waters, P. F. Salipante, Jr., and W. W. Notz, "The Experimenting Organization: Using the Results of Behavioral Science Research," *Academy of Management Review* 3 (1978), pp. 483–92.

48 Beer, *Organization Change and Development*, pp. 101–2.

49 D. A. Nadler, "Organizational Frame Bending: Types of Change in the Complex Organization," in R. H. Kilmann, T. J. Covin, and Associates (eds.), *Corporate Transformation: Revitalizing Organizations for a Competitive World* (San Francisco: Jossey-Bass, 1988), pp. 66–83.

50 J. M. Kouzes and B. Z. Posner, *The Leadership Challenge* (San Francisco: Jossey-Bass, 1988), Chapter 10; and C. Lindblom, "The Science of Muddling Through," *Public Administration Review* 19 (1959), pp. 79–88.

51 C. R. Hinings and R. Greenwood, *The Dynamics of Strategic Change* (Oxford, U.K.: Basil Blackwell, 1988), Chapter 6; D. Miller and P. H. Friesen, "Structural Change and Performance: Quantum versus Piecemeal-Incremental Approaches," *Academy of Management Journal* 25 (1982), pp. 867–92.

52 R. E. Farson, Richard Evans, *Management of the Absurd: Paradoxes in Leadership* (New York : Simon & Schuster, 1996), Chapter 20; M. Hammer and J. Champy, *Reengineering the Corporation: A Manifesto for Business Revolution* (New York: HarperBusiness, 1993).

53 P. A. Strassmann, "The Hocus-Pocus of Reengineering," *Across the Board* 31 (June 1994), pp. 35–38.

54 Cummings and Huse, *Organization Development and Change*, pp. 158–61.

55 A. H. Church and W. W. Burke, "Practitioner Attitudes About the Field of Organization Development," *Research in Organizational Change and Development* 8 (1995), pp. 1–46.

56 A. H. Church, W. W. Burke, and D. F. Van Eynde, "Values, Motives, and Interventions of Organization Development Practitioners," *Group and Organization Management* 19 (1994), pp. 5–50; and N. J. Adler, "The Future of Organization Development in Canada," *Canadian Journal of Administrative Sciences* 1 (1984), pp. 122–32. Also see R. J. Long, "Patterns of Workplace Innovation in Canada," *Relations Industrielles* 44 (1989), pp. 805–24.

57 R. T. Pascale, "Europcar's 'Greenway' Reengineering Project," *Planning Review* (May/June 1994), pp. 18–19.

58 E. M. Van Aken, D. J. Monetta, and D. S. Sink, "Affinity Groups: The Missing Link in Employee Involvement," *Organization Dynamics* 22 (Spring 1994), pp. 38–54; and G. R. Bushe and A. B. Shani, *Parallel Learning Structures* (Reading, Mass.: Addison-Wesley, 1991).

59 F. J. Barrett and D. L. Cooperrider, "Generative Metaphor Intervention: A New Approach for Working with Systems Divided by Conflict and Caught in Defensive Perception," *Journal of Applied Behavioral Science* 26 (1990), pp. 219–39.

60 G. R. Bushe and G. Coetzer, "Appreciative Inquiry as a Team-Development Intervention: A Controlled Experiment," *Journal of Applied Behavioral Science* 31 (1995), pp. 13–30; L. Levine, "Listening with Spirit and the Art of Team Dialogue," *Journal of Organizational Change Management* 7 (1994), pp. 61–73.

61 A. Vido, "Chrysler and Minivans: Are we There Yet?" *CMA Magazine* (November 1993), pp. 11–16.

62 G. A. Neuman, J. E. Edwards, and N. S. Raju, "Organizational Development Interventions: A Meta-Analysis of Their Effects on Satisfaction and Other Attitudes," *Personnel Psychology* 42 (1989), pp. 461–89; and R. A. Guzzo, R. D. Jette, and R. A. Katzell, "The Effects of Psychologically Based Intervention Programs on Worker Productivity: A Meta-Analysis," *Personnel Psychology* 38 (1985), pp. 275–91.

63 R. J. Long, "The Effects of Various Workplace Innovations on Productivity: A Quasi-Experimental Study," *Proceedings of the Annual ASAC Conference, Personnel and Human Resources Division* 11, Part 9 (1990), pp. 98–107.

64 C-M. Lau, "A Culture-Based Perspective of Organization Development Implementation," *Research in Organizational Change and Development* 9 (1996), pp. 49–79.

65 T. C. Head and P. F. Sorenson, "Cultural Values and Organizational Development: A Seven-Country Study," *Leadership and Organization Development Journal* 14 (1993), pp. 3–7; J. M. Putti, "Organization Development Scene in Asia: The Case of Singapore," *Group and Organization Studies* 14 (1989), pp. 262–70; and A. M. Jaeger, "Organization Development and National Culture: Where's the Fit?" *Academy of Management Review* 11 (1986), pp. 178–90.

66 R. J. Marshak, "Lewin Meets Confucius: A Review of the OD Model of Change," *Journal of Applied Behavioral Science* 29 (1993), pp. 395–415.

67 C. M. D. Deaner, "A Model of Organization Development Ethics," *Public Administration Quarterly* 17 (1994), pp. 435–46; and M. McKendall, "The Tyranny of Change: Organizational Development Revisited," *Journal of Business Ethics* 12 (February 1993), pp. 93–104.

68 G. A. Walter, "Organization Development and Individual Rights," *Journal of Applied Behavioral Science* 20 (1984), pp. 423–39.

69 D. Stamps, "Over the Line?" *Training* 33 (January1996), pp. 56–64; L. Sillars, "TransAlta Does Damage Control on BDA," *Western Report*, February 6, 1995, pp. 18–19; S. Parker, Jr., "TransAlta Prepares for the New Age," *Western Report*, January 16, 1995, pp. 15–16; L. Ludwick, "TransAlta's Attempt to 'Change' Workers Backfires," *Financial Post*, January 14, 1995, p. 3.

70 Burke, *Organization Development*, pp. 149–51; and Beer, *Organization Change and Development*, pp. 223–24.

CHAPTER 16

1 J. Steed, "Healthy, Wealthy, Wise" *Toronto Star*, January 5, 1997 pp. F1, F5; D. Menzies, "What Do You Mean There are No More Donuts?" *Financial Post Magazine* (December 1996), p. 10; "Husky Team is Right on Track," *Canadian Packaging* 49 (September 1996), p. A50; "Healthy, Wealthy and Wise," *Canadian Occupational Safety* 33 (November/December 1995), pp. 12–13.

2 E. H. Schein, "What Is Culture?" in *Reframing Organizational Culture*, eds. P. J. Frost, L. F. Moore, M. R. Louis, C. C. Lundberg, and J. Martin (Beverly Hills, Calif.: Sage, 1991), pp. 243–53; A. Williams, P. Dobson, and M. Walters, *Changing Culture: New Organizational Approaches* (London, U.K.: Institute of Personnel Management, 1989).

3 For the effect of industry on organizational culture, see J. A. Chatman and K. A. Jehn, "Assessing the Relationship Between Industry Characteristics and Organizational Culture: How Different Can You Be?" *Academy of Management Journal* 37 (1994), pp. 522–53.

4 B. Ashforth and F. Mael, "Social Identity Theory and the Organization," *Academy of Management Review* 14 (1989), pp. 20–39.

5 M. O. Jones, *Studying Organizational Symbolism: What, How, Why?* (Thousand Oaks, Calif.: Sage, 1996).

6 A. Furnham and B. Gunter, "Corporate Culture: Definition, Diagnosis, and Change," *International Review of Industrial and Organizational Psychology* 8 (1993), pp. 233–61; E. H. Schein, "Organizational Culture," *American Psychologist*, February 1990, pp. 109–19; J. S. Ott, *The Organizational Culture Perspective* (Pacific Grove, Calif.: Brooks/Cole, 1989), Chapter 2; W. J. Duncan, "Organizational Culture: 'Getting a Fix' on an Elusive Concept," *Academy of Management Executive* 3 (1989), pp. 229–36.

7 A. de Carufel, "Changing 'Corporate Culture' in the Public Sector: Lessons from Two Canadian Case Studies," *Proceedings of the Annual ASAC Conference, Organizational Behaviour Division* 8, Part 5 (1987), pp. 37–46; J. P. Siegel, "Searching for Excellence: Company Communications as Reflections of Culture," *Proceedings of the Annual ASAC Conference, Organizational Behaviour Division* 5, Part 5 (1984), pp. 1–8.

8 "Smith Packaging Ltd.," *Financial Post*, December 16, 1995, p. 40.

9 G. McLaughlin, "Corporate Cults," *Financial Post Magazine*, November 1993, pp. 118–23

10 G. Shaw, "Hard Work Takes the Skin Right Off Their Bodies, but Rocky Mountain's Bike Builders Like That," *Vancouver Sun*, July 6, 1993, pp. D1, D2; "Rocky Mountain's Bikes Win 'Almost a Cult Following,'" *Calgary Herald*, July 27, 1992, p. C2.

11 M. Groves, "Corporate Currents," *Los Angeles Times* (on-line), July 6, 1997.

12 J. C. Meyer, "Tell Me a Story: Eliciting Organizational Values from Narratives," *Communication Quarterly* 43 (1995), pp. 210–24.

13 G. S. Saffold, III, "Culture Traits, Strength, and Organizational Performance: Moving Beyond 'Strong' Culture," *Academy of Management Review* 13 (1988), pp. 546–58; Williams et al., *Changing Culture*, pp. 24–27.

14 C. Siehl and J. Martin, "Organizational Culture: A Key to Financial Performance?" in *Organizational Climate and Culture*, ed. B. Schneider (San Francisco, Calif.: Jossey-Bass, 1990), pp. 241–81; J. B. Barney, "Organizational Culture: Can It Be a Source of Sustained Competitive Advantage?" *Academy of Management Review* 11 (1986), pp. 656–65; V. Sathe, *Culture and Related Corporate Realities* (Homewood, Ill.: Irwin, 1985), Chapter 2; T. E. Deal and A. A. Kennedy, *Corporate Cultures* (Reading, Mass.: Addison-Wesley, 1982), Chapter 1.

15 C. A. O'Reilly and J. A. Chatman, "Culture as Social Control: Corporations, Cults, and Commitment," *Research in Organizational Behavior* 18 (1996), pp. 157–200.

16 J. P. Kotter and J. L. Heskett, *Corporate Culture and Performance* (New York: Free Press, 1992); G. G. Gordon and N. DiTomasco, "Predicting Corporate Performance from Organizational Culture," *Journal of Management Studies* 29 (1992), pp. 783–98; D. R. Denison, *Corporate Culture and Organizational Effectiveness* (New York: Wiley, 1990).

17 E. H. Schein, "On Dialogue, Culture, and Organizational Learning," *Organization Dynamics*, Autumn 1993, pp. 40–51.

18 S. Sackmann, "Culture and Subcultures: An Analysis of Organizational Knowledge," *Administrative Science Quarterly* 37 (1992), pp. 140–61; J. Martin and C. Siehl, "Organizational Culture and Counterculture: An Uneasy Symbiosis," *Organizational Dynamics*, Autumn 1983, pp. 52–64; Ott, *The Organizational Culture Perspective*, pp. 45–47; Deal and Kennedy, *Corporate Cultures*, pp. 138–39.

19 A. Sinclair, "Approaches to Organizational Culture and Ethics," *Journal of Business Ethics* 12 (1993), pp. 63–73.

20 For discussions of organizational culture and power, see: B. White, "Power and Culture in Organizational Change: Implications for the Concept of Diversity," *Proceedings of the Annual ASAC Conference, Organizational Theory Division*, 18 (22) (1997), pp. 80–87.

21 M. O. Jones, *Studying Organizational Symbolism: What, How, Why?* (Thousand Oaks, Calif.: Sage, 1996); J. S. Pederson and J. S. Sorensen, *Organisational Cultures in Theory and Practice* (Aldershot, England: Gower, 1989), pp. 27–29.

22 A. Czarnecki, "Customer Service Training: More Than an 'Event,'" *Learning for the Workplace* (*Canadian HR Reporter Supplement*), May 20, 1996, pp. L4–L7.

23 R. Zemke, "Storytelling: Back to a Basic," *Training* 27 (March 1990), pp. 44–50; A. L. Wilkins, "Organizational Stories as Symbols Which Control the Organization," in *Organizational Symbolism*, eds. L. R. Pondy, P. J. Frost, G. Morgan, and T. C. Dandridge (Greenwich, Conn.: JAI Press, 1984), pp. 81–92; J. Martin and M. E. Powers, "Truth or Corporate Propaganda: The Value of a Good War Story," in *Organizational Symbolism*, eds. Pondy et al., pp. 93–107.

24 D. A. Morand, "What's in a Name? An Exploration of the Social Dynamics of Forms of Address in Organizations," *Management Communication Quarterly* 9 (1996), pp. 422–51.

25 J. M. Beyer and H. M. Trice, "How an Organization's Rites Reveal Its Culture," *Organizational Dynamics* 15(4) (1987), pp. 5–24; L. Smirchich, "Organizations as Shared Meanings," in *Organizational Symbolism*, eds. Pondy et al., pp. 55–65.

26 T. Tillson, "Be It Ever so Humble," *Canadian Business Technology Issue*, 1995, pp. 27–32.

27 L. A. Krefting and P. J. Frost, "Untangling Webs, Surfing Waves, and Wildcatting," in *Organizational Culture*, eds., P. J. Frost, L. F. Moore, M. R. Louis, C. C. Lundberg, and J. Martin (Beverly Hills, Calif.: Sage, 1985), pp. 155–68.

28 P. Young, "Monuments to Money," *Maclean's*, November 26, 1990, pp. 72–73.

29 J. M. Kouzes and B. Z. Posner, *The Leadership Challenge* (San Francisco: Jossey-Bass, 1995), pp. 230–31.

30 D. Estok, "Putting a Bloom on Intangibles," *Financial Post 500*, Summer 1990, pp. 56–61.

31 G. A. Walter, "Culture Collisions in Mergers and Acquisitions," in *Organizational Culture*, eds. Frost et al., pp. 301–14; A. F. Buono and J. L. Bowditch, *The Human Side of Mergers and Acquisitions* (San Francisco, Calif.: Jossey-Bass, 1989), Chapter 6; Schein, *Organizational Culture and Leadership*, pp. 33–36.

32 D. Clark, "Sadder but Wiser, Novell Refocuses," *Globe & Mail*, January 12, 1996, p. B4.

33 M. Raynaud and M. Teasdale, "Confusions and Acquisitions: Post-Merger Culture Shock and Some Remedies," IABC *Communication World* (May/June 1992), pp. 44–45.

34 A. R. Malekazedeh and A. Nahavandi, "Making Mergers Work by Managing Cultures," *Journal of Business Strategy* (May/June 1990), pp. 55–57.

35 S. Feschuk, "Lean, Mean Anderson Trims Home Oil's Fat," *Globe & Mail*, October 17, 1995, p. B8.

36 E. H. Schein, "The Role of the Founder in Creating Organizational Culture," *Organizational Dynamics* 12 (1) (Summer 1983), pp. 13–28.

37 G. G. Nasmith, *Timothy Eaton* (Toronto: McClelland & Stewart, 1923); M. E. MacPherson, *Shopkeepers to a Nation: The Eatons* (Toronto: McClelland & Stewart, 1963).

38 E. H. Schein, *Organizational Culture and Leadership* (San Francisco, Calif.: Jossey-Bass, 1985), Chapter 10; T. J. Peters, "Symbols, Patterns, and Settings: An Optimistic Case for Getting Things Done," *Organizational Dynamics* 7 (2) (Autumn 1978), pp. 2–23.

39 I. Sharp, "Quality for All Seasons," *Canadian Business Review* 17 (1) (Spring 1990), p. 22.

40 J. Kerr and J. W. Slocum, Jr., "Managing Corporate Culture Through Reward Systems," *Academy of Management Executive* 1 (May 1987), pp. 99–197; Williams et al., *Changing Cultures*, pp. 120–24; K. R. Thompson and F. Luthans, "Organizational Culture: A Behavioral Perspective," in *Organizational Climate and Culture*, ed. Schneider, pp. 319–44.

41 M. Meyer, "Culture Club," *Newsweek*, July 11, 1994, pp. 38–42; J. Bourgault, S. Dion, and M. Lemay, "Creating a Corporate Culture: Lessons from the Canadian Federal Government," *Public Administration Review* 53 (1993), pp. 73–80.

42 W. G. Ouchi and A. M. Jaeger, "Type Z Organization: Stability in the Midst of Mobility," *Academy of Management Review* 3 (1978), pp. 305–14; K. McNeil and J. D. Thompson, "The Regeneration of Social Organizations," *American Sociological Review* 36 (1971), pp. 624–37.

43 M. De Pree, *Leadership Is an Art* (East Lansing, Mich.: Michigan State University Press, 1987).

44 A. L. Kristof, "Person-Organization Fit: An Integrative Review of Its Conceptualizations, Measurement, and Implications," *Personnel Psychology* 49 (1996), pp. 1–49; J. A. Chatman, "Matching People and Organizations: Selection and Socialization in Public Accounting Firms," *Administrative Science Quarterly* 36 (1991), pp. 459–84.

45 J. Zeidenberg, "HR and the Innovative Company," *Human Resources Professional*, June 1996, pp. 12–15; "New Anchor Hocking Plant Incorporates 'Socio-Tech' Work Environment Philosophy," *Business Wire*, October 19, 1995.

46 J. Van Maanen, "Breaking In: Socialization to Work," in *Handbook of Work, Organization, and Society*, ed. R. Dubin (Chicago: Rand McNally, 1976), p. 67.

47 C. A. O'Reilly, III, J. Chatman, and D. F. Caldwell, "People and Organizational Culture: A Profile Comparison Approach to Assessing Person-Organization Fit," *Academy of Management Journal* 34 (1991), pp. 487–516.

CHAPTER 17

1 S. LeBrun, "Supertemps to the Rescue," *Canadian HR Reporter*, March 10, 1997, pp. 19–22; R. Scotland, "Wanted: Top-Notch Hired Guns," *Financial Post*, September 16, 1995, p. 13.

2 T. Van Alphen, "'Whirlwind' of Corporate Restructuring Leaves Families, Communities Uprooted," *Toronto Star*, August 10, 1996, p. A17.

3 E. W. Morrison and S. L. Robinson, "When Employees Feel Betrayed: A Model of How Psychological Contract Violation Develops," *Academy of Management Review* 22 (1997), pp. 226–56.

4 S. L. Robinson, M. S. Kraatz, and D. M. Rousseau, "Changing Obligations and the Psychological Contract: A Longitudinal Study," *Academy of Management Journal* 37 (1994), pp. 137–52; D. M. Rousseau and J. M. Parks, "The Contracts of Individuals and Organizations," *Research in Organizational Behavior* 15 (1993), pp. 1–43.

5 L. M. Shore and L. E. Tetrick, "The Psychological Contract as an Explanatory Framework in the Employment Relationship," in C. L. Cooper and D. M. Rousseau (eds.), *Trends in Organizational Behaviour*, Vol. 1 (Chichester, U.K.: Wiley, 1994), pp. 91–109.

6 J. McLean Parks and D. L. Kidder, "'Till Death Us do Part...' Changing Work Relationships in the 1990s," in C. L. Cooper and D. M. Rousseau (eds.), *Trends in Organizational Behaviour*, Vol. 1 (Chichester, U.K.: Wiley, 1994), pp. 112–36.

7 G. Ip, "Outsourcing Becoming a Way of Life for Firms," *Globe & Mail*, October 2, 1996, p. B8.

8 S. L. Robinson, "Trust and Breach of the Psychological Contract," *Administrative Science Quarterly* 41 (1996), pp. 574–99.

9 R. J. Lewicki and B. B. Bunker, "Developing and Maintaining Trust in Work Relationships," in R. M. Kramer and T. R. Tyler (eds.), *Trust in Organizations: Frontiers of Theory and Research* (Thousand Oaks, Calif.: Sage, 1996), pp. 114–39.

10 S. L. Robinson and E. W. Morrison, "Psychological Contracts and OCB: The Effect of Unfulfilled Obligations on Civic Virtue Behaviour," *Journal of Organizational Behavior* 16 (1995), pp. 289–98.

11 D. M. Rousseau, "Changing the Deal While Keeping the People," *Academy of Management Executive* 10 (February 1996), pp. 50–61.

12 P. Herriot and C. Pemberton, *New Deals: The Revolution in Managerial Careers* (John Wiley & Sons, 1995), Chapter 3; W. H. Whyte, *The Organization Man* (New York: Simon & Schuster, 1956), p. 129.

13 C. Leitch, "Consumers' to Reduce Staff," *Globe & Mail*, May 13, 1997, p. B9.

14 A. Czarnecki, "Customer Service Training: More Than an 'Event,'" *Learning for the Workplace* (*Canadian HR Reporter* Supplement), May 20, 1996, pp. L4–L7; "Markham Stouffville Hospital Wins 1995 Canada Award For Excellence," *Canada NewsWire*, October 3, 1995.

15 J. Van Maanen, "Breaking In: Socialization to Work," in *Handbook of Work, Organization,* and Society, ed. R. Dubin (Chicago: Rand McNally, 1976), p. 67.

16 E. F. Holton, III, "New Employee Development: A Review and Reconceptualization," *Human Resource Development Quarterly* 7 (Fall 1996), pp. 233–52; G. T. Chao, A. O'Leary-Kelly, S. Wolf, H. J. Klein, and P. D. Gardner, "Organizational Socialization: Its Content and Consequences," *Journal of Applied Psychology* 79 (1994), pp. 450–63.

17 C. A. Young and C. C. Lundberg, "Creating a Good First Day on the Job," *Cornell Hotel and Restaurant Administration Quarterly* 37 (December 1996), pp. 26–33.

18 B. E. Ashforth and A. M. Saks, "Socialization Tactics: Longitudinal Effects on Newcomer Adjustment," *Academy of Management Journal* 39 (1996), pp. 149–78; C. D. Fisher, "Organizational Socialization: An Integrative View," *Research in Personnel and Human Resources Management* 4 (1986), pp. 101–45; and N. Nicholson, "A Theory of Work Role Transitions," *Administrative Science Quarterly* 29 (1984), pp. 172–91.

19 C. C. Pinder and K. G. Schroeder, "Time to Proficiency Following Job Transfers," *Academy of Management, Journal* 30 (1987), pp. 336–53; and N. J. Adler, *International Dimensions of Organizational Behavior,* 2nd ed. (Belmont, Calif.: Wadsworth, 1991), Chapter 8.

20 Van Maanen, "Breaking In," pp. 67–130; L. W. Porter, E. E. Lawler, III, and J. R. Hackman, *Behavior in Organizations* (New York: McGraw-Hill, 1975), pp. 163–67; and D. C. Feldman, "The Multiple Socialization of Organization Members," *Academy of Management Review* 6 (1981), pp. 309–18.

21 Ashforth and Saks, "Socialization Tactics"; T. N. Bauer and S. G. Green, "Effect of Newcomer Involvement in Work-Related Activities: A Longitudinal Study of Socialization," *Journal of Applied Psychology* 79 (1994), pp. 211–23.

22 Porter et al., *Behavior in Organizations,* Chapter 5.

23 Young and Lundberg, "Creating a Good First Day on the Job," pp. 26–33; S. L. Robinson and D. M. Rousseau, "Violating the Psychological Contract: Not the Exception but the Norm," *Journal of Organizational Behavior* 15 (1994), pp. 245–59.

24 M. R. Louis, "Surprise and Sensemaking: What Newcomers Experience in Entering Unfamiliar Organizational Settings," *Administrative Science Quarterly* 25 (1980), pp. 226–51; and D. L. Nelson, "Organizational Socialization: A Stress Perspective," *Journal of Occupational Behaviour* 8 (1987), pp. 311–24.

25 Morrison and Robinson, "When Employees Feel Betrayed," p. 251.

26 J. A. Breaugh, *Recruitment: Science and Practice* (Boston: PWS-Kent, 1992), Chapter 7; J. P. Wanous, *Organizational Entry,* 2nd ed. (Reading, Mass.: Addison–Wesley, 1992), Chapter 3; and A. M. Saks and S. F. Cronshaw, "A Process Investigation of Realistic Job Previews: Mediating Variables and Channels of Communication," *Journal of Organizational Behavior* 11 (1990), pp. 221–36.

27 J. P. Wanous and A. Colella, "Organizational Entry Research: Current Status and Future Directions," *Research in Personnel and Human Resources Management* 7 (1989), pp. 59–120.

28 C. Ostroff and S. W. J. Koslowski, "Organizational Socialization as a Learning Process: The Role of Information Acquisition," *Personnel Psychology* 45 (1992), pp. 849–74; N. J. Allen and J. P. Meyer, "Organizational Socialization Tactics: A Longitudinal Analysis of Links to Newcomers' Commitment and Role Orientation," *Academy of Management Journal* 33 (1990), pp. 847–58; F. M. Jablin, "Organizational Entry, Assimilation, and Exit," in F. M. Jablin, L. L. Putnam, K. H. Roberts, and L. W. Porter (eds.), *Handbook of Organizational Communication* (Beverly Hills, Calif.: Sage, 1987), pp. 679–740.

29 E. W. Morrison, "Newcomer Information Seeking: Exploring Types, Modes, Sources, and Outcomes," *Academy of Management Journal* 36 (1993), pp. 557–89; Fisher, "Organizational Socialization," pp. 135–36; Porter et al., *Behavior in Organizations,* pp. 184–86.

30 S. L. McShane, "Effect of Socialization Agents on the Organizational Adjustment of New Employees" Paper presented at the Annual Conference of the Western Academy of Management, Big Sky, Montana, March 1988.

31 W. F. Whyte, *Organization Man* (New York: Simon & Schuster, 1956).

32 B. O'Reilly, "The New Deal: What Companies and Employees Owe One Another," *Fortune*, June 13, 1994, pp. 44–52.

33 J. Lyon, "How Safe is Your Job?" *Canadian Banker,* (February 1997), pp. 12–15.

34 M. B. Arthur, D. T. Hall, and B. S. Lawrence, "Generating New Directions in Career Theory: The Case for a Transdisciplinary Approach," in *Handbook of Career Theory,* ed. M. B. Arthur, D. T. Hall, and B. S. Lawrence (Cambridge, England: Cambridge University Press, 1989), pp. 7–25.

35 M. B. Arthur, "The Boundaryless Career: A New Perspective for Organizational Inquiry," *Journal of Organizational Behavior* 15 (1994), pp. 295–306.

36 D. T. Hall, *Careers in Organizations* (Glenview, Ill.: Scott, Foresman, 1976), pp. 93–97; T. McAteer-Early, "Career Development and Health-Related Complaints: Development of a Measuring Instrument," *Proceedings of the Annual ASAC Conference, Personnel and Human Resources Division* 12, Part 8 (1991), pp. 70–79; and R. J. Burke and E. R. Greenglass, "Career Orientations, Satisfaction and Health: A Longitudinal Study," *Canadian Journal of Administrative Sciences* 7 (September 1990), pp. 19–25.

37 E. H. Schein, "Career Anchors Revisited: Implications for Career Development in the 21st Century," *Academy of Management Executive* 10 (November 1996), pp. 80–88; R. P. Bourgeois and T. Wils, "Career Concepts, Personality and Values of Some Canadian Workers," *Relations Industrielles* 42 (1987), pp. 528–43.

38 Hall, *Careers in Organizations*, Chapter 3; and J. H. Greenhaus, *Career Management* (Chicago, Ill.: Dryden, 1987), Chapter 5.

39 For example, see: D. T. Hall, "Protean Careers of the 21st Century," *Academy of Management Executive* 10 (November 1996), pp. 8–16.

40 B. Kaye and C. Farren, "Up is Not the Only Way," *Training & Development* 50 (February 1996), pp. 48–53.

41 E. Innes, J. Lyon, and J. Harris, *100 Best Companies to Work For in Canada* (Toronto: HarperCollins, 1990), p. 46.

42 D. T. Hall and J. Richter, "Career Gridlock: Baby Boomers Hit the Wall," *Academy of Management Executive* 4 (August 1990), pp. 7–22.

43 M. G. Evans, H. P. Gunz, H. P., and R. M. Jalland, "The Aftermath of Downsizing: A Cautionary Tale of Restructuring and Careers," *Business Horizons* 39 (March 1996), pp. 62–66.

44 M. Gibb-Clark, "How Statscan Spreads the Jobs Around," *Globe & Mail*, March 28, 1997, p. B9.

45 T. Degler, "Career Planning Joins Outplacement to Facilitate Employee Transition," *Canadian HR Reporter*, July 18, 1994, pp. 8–9; and S. Caudron, "Apple Computer Leaves No Stone Unturned in Employee Career Management," *Personnel Journal* 73 (April 1994), p. 64E.

46 D. Luckow, "Moving Up by Moving Sideways," *Financial Times of Canada*, April 10–16, 1993, pp. 19–20.

47 Facts about Manpower, Inc. are from its Web site: www.manpower.com

48 A. E. Polivka, "Contingent and Alternative Work Arrangements, Defined," *Monthly Labor Review* 119 (October 1996), pp. 3–10. For further discussion of the meaning of contingent work, see: S. Nollen and H. Axel, *Managing Contingent Workers* (New York: AMACOM, 1996), pp. 4–9.

49 P. Booth, *Contingent Work: Trends, Issues, and Challenges for Employers* (Ottawa: Conference Board of Canada, 1997).

50 Booth, *Contingent Work*, p. 5; von Hippel, Mangum, Greenberger, Heneman, and Skoglind, "Temporary Employment," pp. 100–101.

51 P. Gombu and D. Smith, "Day in the Life of a Temp Worker, *Toronto Star*, August 31, 1996, pp. A1, A16.

52 "Goodbye Cleaner, Hello Contractor," *Financial Post*, April 10, 1996, p. 6.

53 C. von Hippel, S. L. Mangum, D. B. Greenberger, R. L. Heneman, and J. D. Skoglind, "Temporary Employment: Can Organizations and Employees Both Win?" *Academy of Management Executive* 11 (February 1997), pp. 93–104; A. E. Polivka, "Into Contingent and Alternative Employment: By Choice?" *Monthly Labor Review* 119 (October 1996), pp. 55–74; "Temporary Jobs Replacing Careers," *Canadian Press Newswire*, February 25, 1996.

54 S. B. Gould, K. J. Weiner, and B. R. Levin, *Free Agents: People and Organizations Creating a New Working Community* (San Francisco: Jossey-Bass, 1997); von Hippel, Mangum, Greenberger, Heneman, and Skoglind, "Temporary Employment," *Academy of Management Executive*, pp. 94–96; W. J. Byron, S. J., "Coming to Terms with the New Corporate Contract," *Business Horizons*, January–February 1995, pp. 8–15.

55 S. J. Hartman, A. C. Yrle, and A. R. Yrle, "Turnover in the Hotel Industry: Is There a Hobo Phenomenon at Work?" *International Journal of Management* 13 (1996), pp. 340–48; T. A. Judge and S. Watanabe, "Is the Past Prologue? A Test of Ghiselli's Hobo Syndrome," *Journal of Management* 21 (1995), pp. 211–29.

56 J. Pfeffer, *New Directions in Organizational Theory* (New York: Oxford University Press, 1997), pp. 18–20.

57 K. M. Beard and J. R. Edwards, "Employees at Risk: Contingent Work and the Psychological Experience of Contingent Workers," in C. L. Cooper and D. M. Rousseau (eds.), *Trends in Organizational Behavior*, Vol. 2 (Chichester, U.K.: Wiley, 1995), pp. 109–26.

58 Beard and Edwards, "Employees at Risk," *Trends in Organizational Behavior*, Vol. 2, pp. 118–19.

59 D. Nye, "Not Made in Heaven," *Across the Board* 33 (October 1996), pp. 41–46.

60 "Bodies for Hire — The Contracting Out Debate," *Workplace Change* (Australia), April 1996, pp. 1–3.

61 D. J. McNerney, "Contingent Workers: Companies Refine Strategies," *HRFocus*, October 1996, pp. 1, 4–6.

62 D. M. Rousseau and C. Libuser, "Contingent Workers in High Risk Environments," *California Management Review* 39 (Winter 1997), pp. 103–23; J. Greenwald, "Temporary Workers Increase Unknown Risks," *Business Insurance*, June 3, 1996, p. 45.

63 "Four Arrested as Campus "Theft Ring" is Exposed," *Simon Fraser News*, September 5, 1996.

64 D. C. Feldman and H. I. Doerpinghaus, "Managing Temporary Workers: A Permanent HRM Challenge." *Organizational Dynamics* 23 (Fall 1994), pp. 49–63.

65 A. M. Saks, P. E. Mudrack, and B. E. Ashforth, "The Relationship Between the Work Ethic, Job Attitudes, Intentions to Quit, and Turnover for Temporary Service Workers," *Canadian Journal of Administrative Sciences* 13 (1996), pp. 226–36.

66 Scotland, "Wanted: Top-Notch Hired Guns," p. 13.

CHAPTER 18

1 B. Rayner, "Life's Getting Complex," *Electronic Business Today*, December 1996; "A World of Networks: Building the Foundation for the Future," *Telesis*, October 1995; "Nortel Splits Operating Roles," *Globe & Mail*, December 23, 1993, p. B3; and L. Surtees, "Power Shifts at Northern Telecom," *Globe & Mail*, February 14, 1991, pp. B1, B2.

2 A. G. Bedeian and R. F. Zammuto, *Organizations: Theory and Design* (Hinsdale, Ill.: Dryden, 1991), pp. 117–18.

3 S. Ranson, R. Hinings, and R. Greenwood, "The Structuring of Organizational Structure," *Administrative Science Quarterly* 25 (1980), pp. 1–14.

4 H. Mintzberg, *The Structuring of Organizations* (Englewood Cliffs, N.J.: Prentice Hall, 1979), pp. 2–3.

5 D. Katz and R. L. Kahn, *The Social Psychology of Organizations* (New York: Wiley, 1966), Chapter 2.

6 H. Fayol, *General and Industrial Management*, trans. C. Storrs (London: Pitman, 1949); E. E. Lawler, III, *Motivation in Work Organizations* (Monterey, Calif.: Brooks/Cole, 1973), Chapter 7; and M. A. Campion, "Ability Requirement Implications of Job Design: An Interdisciplinary Perspective," *Personnel Psychology* 42 (1989), pp. 1–24.

7 Material in this section is based on Mintzberg, *The Structuring of Organizations*, pp. 2–8.

8 C. Downs, P. Clampitt, and A. L. Pfeiffer, "Communication and Organizational Outcomes," in *Handbook of Organizational Communication*, ed. G. Goldhaber and G. Barnett (Norwood, N.J.: Ablex, 1988), pp. 171–211; and H. C. Jain, "Supervisory Communication and Performance in Urban Hospitals," *Journal of Communication* 23 (1973), pp. 103–17.

9 V. L. Shalin and G. V. Prabhu, "A Cognitive Perspective on Manual Assembly" *Ergonomics* 39 (1996), pp. 108–127; I. Nonaka and H. Takeuchi, *The Knowledge-Creating Company* (New York: Oxford University Press, 1995).

10 J. H. Sheridan, "Lessons from the Best," *Industry Week*, February 20, 1995, pp. 13–22.

11 D. D. Van Fleet and A. G. Bedeian, "A History of the Span of Management," *Academy of Management Review* 2 (1977), pp. 356–72; Mintzberg, *The Structuring of Organizations*, Chapter 8; and D. Robey, *Designing Organizations*, 3rd ed. (Homewood, Ill.: Irwin, 1991), pp. 255–59.

12 G. Welty, "A Work in Progress," *Railway Age* (August 1996); R. Y. Bergstrom, "Okay, So You're Not Having Fun Yet, But Who Said You Would?" *Production*, May 1994, p. 16; J. Lorinc, "Managing When There's No Middle," *Canadian Business* (June 1991), pp. 86–94.

13 Mintzberg, *The Structuring of Organizations*, p. 136.

14 T. Peters, *Thriving on Chaos* (New York: Knopf, 1987), p. 359.

15 A. Dastmalchian and M. Javidan, "Centralization and Organizational Context: An Analysis of Canadian Public Enterprises," *Canadian Journal of Administrative Sciences* 4 (1987), pp. 302–19.

16 A. Dastmalchian and P. Blyton, "Organizational Structure, Human Resource Practices and Industrial Relations," *Management Decision* 30 (6), 1992, pp. 109–15.

17 E. M. von Simson, "The Recentralization of IT," *Computerworld*, December 18, 1995, pp. SS1–SS7.

18 "Compaq Centralises to Cut Costs," *Business Europe* 33 (January 8, 1993), pp. 6–7.

19 Mintzberg, *The Structuring of Organizations*, Chapter 5.

20 C. Davies, "1990 Strategy Session," *Canadian Business*, January 1990, pp. 49–50; G. Morgan, *Creative Organization Theory: A Resourcebook* (Newburg Park, Calif.: Sage, 1989), pp. 271–73; and K. Deveny, "Bag Those Fries, Squirt that Ketchup, Fry that Fish," *Business Week* (October 13), 1986, p. 86.

21 T. Burns and G. Stalker, *The Management of Innovation* (London: Tavistock, 1961).

22 Mintzberg, *The Structuring of Organizations*, p. 106.

23 Mintzberg, *The Structuring of Organizations*, Chapter 17.

24 Robey, *Designing Organizations*, pp. 186–89.

25 S. McKay, "A Paper Tiger in the Paperless World," *Canadian Business* (April 1996), pp. 25–29.

26 R. Collison, "How Bata Rules the World," *Canadian Business* (September 1990), pp. 28–34.

27 Robey, *Designing Organizations*, pp. 191–7; and Bedeian and Zammuto, *Organizations: Theory and Design*, pp. 162–68.

28 S. Hamm, "Office Politics," *PCWeek Inside* (April 18, 1994), pp. A1, A4.

29 H. F. Kolodny, "Managing in a Matrix," *Business Horizons* (March–April 1981), pp. 17–24; and S. M. Davis and P. R. Lawrence, *Matrix* (Reading, Mass.: Addison-Wesley, 1977).

30 "Cossette Communications Inc.," *Financial Post*, December 16, 1995, p. 21.

31 K. Knight, "Matrix Organization: A Review," *Journal of Management Studies* (May 1976), pp. 111–30.

32 H. Denis, "Matrix Structures, Quality of Working Life, and Engineering Productivity," *IEEE Transactions on Engineering Management* EM-33 (August 1986), pp. 148–56; and J. L. Brown and N. M. Agnew, "The Balance of Power in a Matrix Structure," *Business Horizons* (November–December 1982), pp. 51–54.

33 C. A. Bartlett and S. Ghoshal, "Managing Across Borders: New Organizational Responses," *Sloan Management Review* (Fall 1987), pp. 43–53.

34 J. A. Byrne, "Congratulations. You're Moving to a New Pepperoni," *Business Week* (December 20, 1993), pp. 80–81; and C. G. Johnston and C. R. Farquhar, *Empowered People Satisfy Customers* (Ottawa: Conference Board of Canada, 1992).

35 J. B. Rieley, "The Circular Organization: How Leadership Can Optimize Organizational Effectiveness," *National Productivity Review* 13 (Winter 1993/1994), pp. 11–19; J. R. Galbraith, *Competing with Flexible Lateral Organizations* (Reading, Mass.: Addison-Wesley, 1994); J. A. Byrne, "The Horizontal Corporation," *Business Week*, December 20, 1993, pp. 76–81; R. Tomasko, *Rethinking the Corporation* (New York: AMACOM, 1993); and D. Quinn Mills (with G. Bruce Friesen), *Rebirth of the Corporation* (New York: Wiley, 1991), pp. 29–30.

36 T. A. Stewart, "The Search for the Organization of Tomorrow," *Fortune* (May 18, 1992), pp. 93–98.

37 W. F. Joyce, V. E. McGee, J. W Slocum Jr., "Designing Lateral Organizations: An Analysis of the Benefits, Costs, and Enablers of Nonhierarchical Organizational Forms," *Decision Sciences* 28 (Winter 1997), pp. 24.

38 G. Ip, "Outsourcing Becoming a Way of Life for Firms," *Globe & Mail*, October 2, 1996, p. B8.

39 R. E. Miles and C. C. Snow, "The New Network Firm: A Spherical Structure Built on a Human Investment Philosophy," *Organizational Dynamics* 23(4) (1995), pp. 5–18; R. E. Miles and C. C. Snow, "Causes of Failure in Network Organizations," *California Management Review* 34 (Summer 1992), pp. 53–72; H. F. Kolodny, "Some Characteristics of Organizational Designs in New/High Technology Firms," in *Organizational Issues in High Technology Management*, eds. L. R. Gomez-Mejia and M. W. Lawless (Greenwich, Conn.: JAI Press, 1990), pp. 165–76.

40 H. Kerwood, "Where Do Just-in-Time Manufacturing Networks Fit? A Typology of Networks and a Framework for Analysis," *Human Relations* 48 (1995), pp. 927–50.

41 Ip, "Outsourcing Becoming a Way of Life for Firms."

42 L. Fried, *Managing Information Technology in Turbulent Times* (New York: John Wiley and Sons, 1995); R. Nagel and D. Allen, "Virtual Winners," *International Management* 48 (June 1993), p. 64; and W. H. Davidow and M. S. Malone, *The Virtual Corporation* (New York: HarperBusiness, 1992).

43 "Newbridge Nurtures Affiliates Under its Wing," *Financial Post*, March 13, 1996, p. 10.

44 Mintzberg, *The Structuring of Organizations*, Chapter 13; and D. S. Pugh and C. R. Hinings (eds.), *Organizational Structure: Extensions and Replications* (Farnborough, U.K.: Lexington Books, 1976).

45 T. A. Stewart, *Intellectual Capital: The New Wealth of Organizations* (New York: Doubleday/Currency, 1997), Chapter 10.

46 Robey, *Designing Organizations*, p. 102.

47 C. Perrow, "A Framework for the Comparative Analysis of Organizations," *American Sociological Review* 32 (1967), pp. 194–208.

48 Mintzberg, *The Structuring of Organizations*, Chapter 15.

49 Burns and Stalker, *The Management of Innovation*; P. R. Lawrence and J. W. Lorsch, *Organization and Environment* (Homewood, Ill.: Irwin, 1967); and D. Miller and P. H. Friesen, *Organizations: A Quantum View* (Englewood Cliffs, N.J.: Prentice Hall, 1984), pp. 197–98.

50 Mintzberg, *The Structuring of Organizations*, p. 202.

51 R. H. Kilmann, *Beyond the Quick Fix* (San Francisco: Jossey-Bass, 1984), p. 38.

52 J. Child, "Organizational Structure, Environment, and Performance: The Role of Strategic Choice," *Sociology* 6 (1972), pp. 2–22.

53 A. D. Chandler, *Strategy and Structure* (Cambridge, Mass.: MIT Press, 1962).

54 M. E. Porter, *Competitive Strategy* (New York: The Free Press, 1980).

55 D. Miller, "Configurations of Strategy and Structure," *Strategic Management Journal* 7 (1986), pp. 233–50.

APPENDIX A

1 Kerlinger, *Foundations of Behavioral Research* (New York: Holt, Rinehart, & Winston, 1964), p. 11.

2 J. B. Miner, *Theories of Organizational Behavior* (Hinsdale, Ill.: Dryden, 1980), pp. 7–9.

3 Ibid. pp. 6–7.

4 Kerlinger, *Foundations of Behavioral Research*, p. 13.

5 P. Lazarsfeld, *Survey Design and Analysis* (New York: The Free Press, 1955).

6 This example is cited in D. W. Organ and T. S. Bateman, *Organizational Behavior*, 4th ed. (Homewood, Ill.: Irwin, 1991), p. 42.

7 Ibid., p. 45

8 R. Scotland, *The Creative Edge: Inside the Ad Wars* (Toronto: Viking, 1994).

360-degree corrective feedback, 45

A-B-C model, 38
Ability
    aptitudes, 31
    defined, 31
    job design and, 94, 100
    leadership and, 364
    matching job requirements with,
        31, 63, 67
    self-fulfilling prophecy effect on,
        156–157
    subordinates and leadership style,
        371
    tacit skills and knowledge, 31
    team members, 240–241
    technological change and, 392
Absenteeism
    bonuses to minimize, 90
    Canadian rates of, 35
    causes of, 35
    cost of, 35
    equity theory and, 73
    job satisfaction and, 182
    strategies to reduce, 35
    stress and, 126–127
    team norms and, 243
Acquisitions. See Mergers and
        acquisitions
Action learning, 50
Action research, 402, 403
Actor-observer error, 155, 378
Affiliate network, 478
Agency theory, 92
Alderfer's ERG theory, 61–62
Appreciative inquiry, 406–407
Aptitudes, 31
Arbitration, 355
Artifacts, 419
Assertiveness, 344
Assimilation, 426
Attitude surveys. See Employee
        surveys
Attitudes. See also Job satisfaction;
        Organizational commitment
    behaviour and, 176–177
    beliefs, 175, 176–177
    business ethics, 176
    cognitive dissonance, 177–178
    components of, 176
    conflict cycle and, 338

defined, 175
    feelings, 175, 176–177
    importance of, 174–176
    intentions, 175, 177
    job satisfaction, 178–182
    model of, 176–177
    organizational commitment,
        182–186
    personality and, 175
    prejudicial, 153
    selective perception and, 147
Attribution theory, 155–156, 378
Autonomous work teams. See Self-
        directed work teams
Autonomy, 99, 102

Bargaining zone model, 350–351
Behaviour. See also Absenteeism; Job
        performance; Organizational cit-
        izenship behaviours; Turnover
    model of, 30–36, 394–395
    types of work-related, 33–36
Behaviour modification. See
        Organizational behaviour
        modification
Behavioural aspect of leadership,
        365–368
Behavioural modelling, 48–49, 377,
        406–407
    See also Social learning theory
Behaviourism, 38–39
Beliefs, 175, 176–177
Benchmarking, 276
Big Five personality dimensions, 165
Bonuses, 90
Bootlegging, 235
Brainstorming, 302–303
Broadbanding, 88
Building design. See Physical work
        environment
Burnout, 127
Business ethics
    attitudes, 175
    distributive justice principle, 328
    individual rights principle, 328
    monitoring employee perfor-
        mance, 47–48
    organizational behaviour modifi-
        cation and, 48
    organizational behaviour research
        and, 510

organizational citizenship behaviours
        and, 35–36
    organizational commitment, 183
    organizational development and,
        408–409
    organizational politics and, 327
    privacy and, 408–409, 510
    reward systems and, 86–87
    stereotyping and, 151–154
    subcultures and, 422
    substitutability and, 320–321
    utilitarianism principle, 327
    values and, 188, 191–192

Canada Awards for Business
        Excellence, 271
Career(s)
    anchor, 448
    boundaryless, 451
    conflict and, 342, 346
    defined, 447–448
    disengagement, 449
    effectiveness of, 448
    emerging issues, 451
    lateral career development, 450–451
    self-assessments, 451
    stages, 448–449
    stress of balancing with family life,
        122–124
    values and, 189
Causation in organizational behaviour
        research, 509–510, 512
Centrality, 322
Centralization, 465
Ceremonies, 423
Change. See Organizational change
Change agent, 402–403, 409
Charisma, 318, 375
Closure (perceptual interpretation), 150
Coalition, 236–237, 330
Codetermination, 264
Coercive power, 317, 323, 397, 400
Cognitive dissonance, 177–178
Cohesiveness
    causes of, 245–248
    conflict and, 339
    consequences of, 247–248
    defined, 245
    entry costs and, 247
    external competition/challenges
        and, 247

leadership style and, 373
member interaction and, 245–248
member similarity and, 246–247
team performance and, 247, 248
team size and, 247
Collaboration, 344
Collectivism-individualism, 189, 190,
    240–241, 250, 269
Commissions, 89
Commitment, 324
    See also Escalation of commitment;
        Organizational commitment
Committee(s). *See* Decision making;
    Teams
Communication
    ambiguity, 202
    barriers to effective, 202–204
    channels, 200–210, 221
    choosing the best medium, 208–210
    conflict and, 343, 348
    conversational overlaps, 217
    coordination, 200
    creativity and, 298
    cross-cultural and, 216–217
    defined, 200
    departmentation and, 467
    downward, 210–211
    effective listening, 219–220
    electronic mail, 205, 352
    emotional labour, 208
    employee magazines, 211, 430
    employee surveys, 210
    feedback in, 201
    filtering, 202
    functions of, 200
    gender differences in, 217–219
    grapevine, 214–216
    improving interpersonal, 219–220
    information overload, 203–204
    jargon, 320–321
    language, 202, 216–217, 424
    media, 200–210, 221
    media richness, 209–210
    model of, 200–201
    negotiations and, 353
    nonverbal, 207–208, 216–217
    organizational change and, 396
    organizational culture and, 423, 430
    organizational politics and, 329
    perception and, 201–202
    perceptual errors in, 202
    persuasive, 220–221
    power and, 318–319
    stress and, 129
    symbolic meaning of medium, 210
    teams, 239
    transformational leadership and,
        376

upward, 210
    verbal, 204–205, 221
    visible management, 211–213
    written, 204–205, 221
Comparison other, 71
Competencies, 31
Competency-based rewards, 88–89
Competitive benchmarking, 276
Compliance, 323
Computer technology and organiza-
    tional behaviour, 9
Concurrent engineering, 277, 278
Conflict. *See also* Conflict manage-
    ment; Negotiation(s); Third-
    party conflict resolution
    ambiguity and, 343
    careers and, 342, 346
    communication and, 343
    consequences of, 339–340
    costs of dysfunctional, 339
    cycle, 338
    defined, 338
    differentiation, 341–342, 346,
        467–468
    episodes, 338
    goal incompatibility, 340–341
    organizational socialization, in,
        444
    organizational structure and,
        467–468, 470
    resource scarcity, 343
    sources of, 340–343
    stimulating, 350
    superordinate goals, 468
    task interdependence, 342–343
    team composition and, 240–241
    value differences and, 189
    win-lose orientation, 344, 351, 352
    win-win orientation, 344, 351, 352
Conflict management. *See also*
    Conflict; Negotiation(s); Third-
    party conflict resolution
    accommodating style, 345
    arbitration, 355
    avoiding style, 345
    clarifying rules and procedures,
        349–350
    collaborating style, 345
    communication and, 348
    competing style, 345
    compromising style, 345
    constructive controversy and, 300
    defined, 339
    dialogue, 348
    differentiation and, 346
    duplicating resources, 348
    increasing resources, 349
    inquisition, 355

intergroup mirroring, 348
    interpersonal styles, 344–346, 350
    job design and, 346, 348
    mediation, 355
    negotiation, 350–351
    peer tribunals, 355
    perceptions and, 348
    relations by objectives, 348
    social activities and, 348
    structural approaches, 346–350
    superordinate goals, 346
    task interdependence and, 348–349
    third-party conflict resolution,
        353–355
    win-lose orientation, 344, 351, 352
    win-win orientation, 344, 351, 352
Conformity, 243–244, 293
Conscientiousness, 166
Constructive controversy, 300, 339
Constructs, 506
Content theories of motivation. *See
    also* Motivation
    cross-cultural relevance of, 78
    defined, 60
    ERG theory, 61–62
    learned needs theory, 62–63
    needs hierarchy theory, 60–61
    practical implications, 63–64
Contingency approach, 11
Contingent workforce, 451
    adjustment, 455
    concerns, 454
    types, 453
Continuous improvement, 121, 273,
    392
Continuous reinforcement schedule, 41
Contract work, 451
Cooperativeness, 344
Coordination, 200, 462–463, 479
Corporate culture. *See* Organizational
    culture
Counterpower, 315
Creativity, 297
    brainstorming and, 302–303
    conditions for, 298
    defined, 297
    evaluation apprehension and,
        292–293
    improving, 299
    model of, 298–299
    perceptual grouping and, 151
    team composition and, 240–241
Creativity Edge, The, 512
Cross-cultural management. *See*
    International business;
    Multicultural work force
Cross-functional teams, 50
Customer capital, 14

Customer service
   burnout and, 126–127
   employee feedback and, 47–48
   formalization and, 465–466
   improving interpersonal relations
      in, 163
   internal versus external customers,
      273
   job enrichment and, 104
   role perceptions and, 32
   stress and, 130
   total quality management and,
      271, 273

Decentralization, 465
Decision making. *See also* Employee
      involvement; Team(s)
   advantages of consensus in, 302
   barriers to effective, 289
   brainstorming, 302–303
   choosing the best decision style,
      286–287
   choosing the best solution, 267, 287
   conflict and, 339–340
   constructive controversy, 300, 339
   creative, 298–300
   creativity, 297
   decentralization and, 465
   defined, 286
   developing alternatives, 267, 287
   devil's advocacy, 301
   economic assumptions about, 289
   electronic brainstorming, 303–305
   escalation of commitment, 291
   ethical. *See* Business ethics
   evaluation apprehension in team,
      292–293
   function of communication in, 200
   general model, 286–287
   group polarization in team, 294–295
   groupthink in team, 292
   identifying problems, 267,
      287–288, 289
   improving team, 295–297
   intuitive, 364
   mental models, 288
   model of, 286–287
   nominal group technique, 305
   nonprogrammed, 287
   organizational politics and, 332
   perceptual defense, 288, 291
   postdecisional justification, 290,
      444–445
   potential benefits of team,
      266–268, 292
   problems with team, 292–295
   production blocking in team, 292
   programmed, 287

   satisficing, 290
   symptoms and causes, 286, 289
   team building and, 253
   time constraints in team, 292
   Vroom-Jago model, 514–515
Decision Support System, 296
Deculturation, 427
Delayering, 464
Departmentation
   client structure, 469
   consequences of, 467
   defined, 467
   divisional structure, 468
   functional structure, 468
   geographic structure, 468
   hybrid structure, 473
   matrix structure, 471–473
   network structure, 476–479
   product structure, 468
   simple structure, 467
   strategic business units, 469
Dependent variables, 508
Depersonalization, 128
Devil's advocacy, 301
Dialogue
   appreciative inquiry and, 406–407
   conflict management and, 348
   team building and, 251
Differentiation, 341–342, 467–468
Diffusion of change, 401–402
Direction, 31
Discipline defined, 92
Disclosure, 163
Discrepancy theory, 179–180
Discretion, 322–323, 465
Discrimination
   cultural diversity awareness train-
      ing and, 145, 160, 163
   employment, 145, 151–154
   old boys' networks and, 330, 332
   pay, 87–88
Distress, 118
   See also Stress
Distributive justice, 35, 192, 328
Divergent thinking, 298
Division of labour, 95, 462
   See also Job specialization
Divisional organizational structure, 468
Downsizing and organizational
      memory, 17–19
Downward communication, 210–211
Drug/alcohol abuse and job satisfac-
      tion, 182

Effort, 65
Effort-to-performance expectancy, 65,
      67–68, 157, 369
Electronic brainstorming, 303–305

Electronic mail, 205, 352
Emotional contagion, 208
Emotional exhaustion, 127
Emotional intelligence, 188
Emotional labour, 186
   communication, 208
Emotions, 174, 186
Empathy, 160–161, 188, 219
Employability, 441
Employee assistance programs, 132,
      132–133
Employee involvement. *See also*
      Decision making; Self-directed
      work team; Teams(s)
   barriers to, 268–270
   codetermination, 264
   decision commitment, 268
   decision quality and, 266–268
   defined, 260
   employee development through, 268
   empowerment and, 268
   flatter organizational structures
      and, 464
   forms of, 260–261
   goal setting, in, 45
   job satisfaction and, 268
   leadership and, 370
   levels of, 262
   organizational change and, 398
   organizational commitment and,
      185
   organizational development and,
      402
   potential benefits of, 266–268
   quality circles, 262
   self-directed work teams, 264–266
   team decision making methods,
      295–297
   total quality management, 275
Employee loyalty. *See* Organizational
      commitment
Employee magazines, 211, 430
Employee motivation. *See* Motivation
Employee performance. *See* Job per-
      formance
Employee selection. *See* Selection
Employee share ownership plans
      (ESOPs), 91
Employee surveys, 183, 210
Empowerment, 102, 266, 268, 465
Encounter groups, 405
Encounter stage of organizational
      socialization, 446
Entrepreneurs, 62–63
Environmental scanning, 16
Equity theory
   comparison other, 71
   consequences of inequity, 71–73

defined, 70
example of, 73
job satisfaction and, 179–180
model of, 70–73
outcome/input ratio, 70
overreward equity, 71
practical implications of, 73
third-party conflict resolution and,
    353–354
underreward inequity, 71
ERG theory, 61–62
Escalation of commitment
    causes of, 291–292
    defined, 291
    negotiation deadlines and, 352
Ethical values, 191–192
Ethics. See Business ethics
Eustress, 118
    See also Stress
Evaluation apprehension, 292
Expectancy theory
    accuracy of, 69
    cross-cultural relevance of, 78
    defined, 64
    effort-to-performance expectancy,
        65, 67–68
    model of, 65–66
    path-goal leadership theory, 369
    performance-to-outcome
        expectancy, 65, 69
    practical implications, 66–69
    valence, 66
Experience, 50
Expert power, 318, 325, 331
External environment
    complex, 480–481
    diverse, 481
    dynamic, 480
    hostile, 481
    open systems and, 11–13
    organizational culture and, 422
    organizational structure and,
        480–481
    team effectiveness and, 238–239
Extinction, 39
Extroversion, 165

Family-friendly workplaces, 129
Feedback
    360-degree, 45
    active versus passive, 45
    characteristics of effective, 46–47
    communication model, in, 201
    corrective, 45
    customers, from, 104
    defined, 44–45
    frequency of, 46
    goal setting and, 47

importance of, 44–45
interpersonal relations, in, 163
job itself, from the, 100
monitoring employees, 47–48
need fulfillment and, 47
open systems and, 12
organizational change and, 400
role perception and, 32
sources of, 45
upward, 210
Field experiment, 510
Field survey, 511–512
Figure/ground principle, 148
Filtering, 202, 288
Fitness/lifestyle programs, 132
Fixed interval schedule, 41, 42
Fixed ratio schedule, 41, 42
Flaming (in e-mail), 206
Flexible work arrangements and
    stress, 130
Force field analysis, 394, 396
Formal work teams, 232–234
    See also Team(s)
Formalization, 465–466
Free agents, 8
Frustration-regression process, 61
Functional organizational structure,
    468

Gainsharing, 90, 263
Gender, 217–219
    See also Women
General adaptation syndrome, 119
Generation X, 7
Glass ceiling, 153
Goal setting
    characteristics of effective goals,
        75–76
    defined, 74
    feedback in, 45
    leadership and, 370
    negotiations and, 353
    participation in, 45
    personal, 105–106
    team building and, 252
Goals. See also Goal setting
    conflict and, 340–341
    decision making and, 290
    defined, 74
    difficulty of, 76–77
    organizational, 5
    stated versus actual, 5
    superordinate, 346, 468
    team membership and, 236–237
    total quality management and, 275
    types of, 75
Gold of the Desert Kings, 252–253
Grafting, 16

Grapevine communications, 214–216
Group decision support systems
    (groupware), 352
Group polarization, 294–295
Groups. See Team(s)
Groupthink, 293
Growth need strength, 100

Halo effect, 158
Harassment, 153, 324–325
    cultural diversity awareness train-
        ing, 145
    stress, 121–122
Health (physical and emotional). See
    also Safety
    job satisfaction and, 182
    stress and, 126
Heterogeneous teams, 240–241
Hi-hi leadership hypothesis, 366,
    366–367
Hobo phenomenon, 35
Homogeneous teams, 240–241
Horizontal communication, 215
Horizontal job specialization. See Job
    specialization
Human capital, 14
Hybrid organization structure, 473
Hypotheses, 505

Implicit learning, 50, 77
Impression management
    evaluation apprehension and,
        292–293
    feedback seeking and, 47
    leadership and, 364, 379
    organizational politics and, 331
Incremental change, 404
Independent variables, 508
Individual behaviour. See Behaviour
Individual rights, 192
Individualism-collectivism, 189, 190,
    240–241, 230, 269
Inequity. See Equity theory
Influence. See Organizational politics;
    Power
Informal groups, 236–237
    See also Team(s)
Information overload, 203–204, 329
Inoculation effect, 221
Inquisitional conflict management,
    355
Integration, 427
Integrity and leadership, 364
Intellectual capital, 14, 37
Intensity, 31
Intentions, 175, 177
Intergroup mirroring, 348, 408
Internal labour market, 70

International business
  centralization and, 465
  communication across cultures,
    216, 216–217
  competition, 392
  decentralization and, 465
  employee involvement and, 270
  legitimate power and, 316
  managing stress during foreign
    assignments, 131
  motivation theories and, 77–78
  negotiations and, 352, 354
  North American Free Trade
    Agreement, 392
  organization development inter-
    ventions in, 408
  perceptual differences, 147
  reward system in United kingdom,
    94
  values across cultures, 189
Interpersonal process, 251
Interpersonal relations, 162–163,
  219–220
Intrarole conflict, 121
Intuition
  developing, 299
  leadership and, 364
ISO 9000 series quality standard,
  271–272

Jargon, 202, 320–321
Job burnout. See Burnout
Job characteristics model, 98–100
Job design
  ability and, 94, 100
  autonomy, 102
  conflict management and, 346, 348
  defined, 94
  empowerment, 102
  job characteristics model, 98–100
  job enlargement, 101
  job enrichment, 102–103, 250
  job rotation, 100–101, 346
  job specialization and, 95–98
  motivation and, 98–104
  obstacles to, 104–105
  person-job matching and, 31
  scientific management and, 96–97
  self-directed work teams and,
    264–266
  self-efficacy, 102
  work efficiency and, 95–97
Job enlargement, 101
Job enrichment, 102–103, 250
Job evaluation, 87
Job performance. See also Productivity
  dimensions of, 35
  emotions and, 174

  job satisfaction and, 182
  leadership and, 362
  model of, 30–36, 394–395
  organizational commitment and,
    183
  performance standards, 35
  personality and, 166
  reward systems based on, 89–94
  self-fulfilling prophecy effect on,
    156–157
  stress and, 126–127
  team member composition and,
    240–241
  type A/type B behaviour pattern
    and, 125–126
Job rotation, 100–101, 346
Job satisfaction
  absenteeism and, 35
  attribution theory and, 155
  Canada, in, 179
  consequences of, 179–182
  defined, 178
  discrepancy theory and, 179–180
  employee involvement and, 268
  equity theory and, 179–180
  facets of, 179
  job design and, 100
  model of, 179–180
  overall, 179
  valences based on, 66
Job security, 184
Job sharing and stress, 130
Job specialization
  advantages of, 95
  defined, 95
  horizontal versus vertical, 95, 96
  job performance and, 97–98
  organizational structure and, 462
  problems with, 97–98
  reducing social loafing through,
    250
  scientific management and, 95–97
Job status-based rewards, 87–88
Johari Window, 162–163
Just-in-time inventory systems, 322
Justice. See Distributive justice; Equity
  theory; Procedural fairness

Kaizen, 121–122, 273–275
Knowledge. See Ability

Laboratory experiment, 510–511
Labour unions. See also Unionization
  centrality and, 322, 323
  diffusion of change and, 402
  employee involvement and, 270
  job design and, 97, 104–105
  job satisfaction and strikes, 181

  negotiating through computer
    technology, 352
  relations by objectives, 348
  rewards systems and, 86–87
  substitutability and, 321
  third party conflict resolution and,
    355
  use of coercive power, 317
  work-to-rule strikes, 466
Language, 202
Lateness, 35
Law of effect, 37
Leadership
  achievement-oriented, 370
  attribution and, 378
  behavioural perspective, 365–368
  communication and, 202
  contingency perspective and,
    368–373
  defined, 362
  directive, 369
  gender issues in, 379–380
  hi-hi leadership hypothesis,
    366–367
  integrity, 364
  Leadership Grid (Reg), 366–368
  locus of control and, 167
  motivation, 364
  organizational culture and, 429
  participative, 370, 380–381
  path-goal theory, 368–372
  people-oriented style, 365–368,
    370, 380–381
  perceptions and, 378–381
  personality and, 166, 167
  perspectives of, 362
  romance perspective of, 378–381
  self-confidence, 364
  self-directed work teams and, 269
  self-monitoring and, 365, 366
  stereotyping and, 366, 369,
    378–379, 380–381
  substitutes, 373
  supportive, 370
  task-oriented style, 365–368, 370,
    380–381
  team decision making, 295
  trait perspective, 363–365
  transactional, 374–375
  transformational perspective,
    374–378
  visible management, 211–212
  Vroom-Jago model, 514–515
  See also Employee involvement
Leadership Grid (Reg), 366–368
Lean production practices, 121
Learned capabilities, 31
Learned helplessness, 128

Learning. *See also* Organizational
    behavioural modification; Social
    learning theory
    action, 50
    defined, 36–37
    feedback and, 45
    implicit, 50, 77
    needs, 62–63
    OB modification, 38–48
    organizational, 37
    organizational socialization and,
        443
    social learning theory and, 48–51
    total quality management and, 276
Legitimate power, 316, 323
Listening, 219–220, 353
Locus of control, 167, 331, 371
Long-term disability insurance,
    86–87, 127–128
Loyalty. *See* Organizational commit-
    ment

Machiavellianism, 331
Management by objective, 74
Managerial Grid (Reg). *See* Leadership
    Grid (reg)
Masculinity-femininity value, 190
Maslow's needs hierarchy theory,
    60–61, 78
Matrix structure, 471–473
Mechanistic organizational structure,
    466, 479–480
Media richness, 209–210
Mediation, 355
Membership-based rewards, 87
Mental imagery, 107
Mental models, 149, 288
    appreciative inquiry and, 407
    creativity training and, 299
    decision making and, 288
    organizational culture and, 425–426
    perceptions, 149
    stressors, as
Mentoring, 323
Mergers and acquisitions
    organizational change and, 392
    organizational culture and, 425–426
    stressors, as, 122
Merit pay plans, 90
Methods-time measurement, 97
Monitoring employee performance,
    47–48
Moods, 175
Moral rights. *See* Business ethics
Morale. *See* Job satisfaction
Motivation, 188
    attitudes and, 175
    attribution theory and, 155

basic framework of, 60
content theories, 60–64, 78
cross-cultural relevance of theo-
    ries, 77–78
defined, 31
drive, 364
equity theory and, 70–73
ERG theory, 61–62
expectancy theory, 64–69, 78
feedback, 73–77
goal setting and feedback, 73–77
goal-setting, 105–106
job design and, 98–104
leadership, 364
learned needs theory, 62–63, 78
mental imagery, 107
natural rewards, 107–108
needs, 60
needs hierarchy theory, 60–61, 78
process theories, 60, 64–78
self-leadership, 105
self-monitoring, 108
self-reinforcement, 108
self-talk, 106
team members, of, 240–241
Multicultural work force
    communication across cultures,
        216–217, 345
    concessions in negotiations and, 354
    conflict and, 342, 345
    cultural diversity awareness train-
        ing, 160, 163
    employee involvement and,
        268–269
    employment discrimination, 154
    informal groups and, 235
    motivation theories and, 77–78
    organization development and, 408
    perceptual differences and, 147
    reward systems and, 94
    values and, 189
Multiskilled work force, 88, 101

National culture. *See* International
    business; Multicultural work
    force
Natural work units, 103
Needs
    achievement, 62, 63, 298, 364
    affiliation, 62, 237
    belongingness, 61
    deficiency, 60
    defined, 60
    esteem, 61
    existence, 61
    growth, 60, 61, 100
    learning, 62–63
    physiological, 61

power, 62, 63, 324, 364
relatedness, 61, 200
reward systems and, 93
safety, 61
self-actualization, 61
team membership and, 237
valences based on, 66
Needs hierarchy theory, 60–61, 78
Negative affectivity, 175
Negative reinforcement, 40
Negotiation(s)
    audience effects, 352
    bargaining zone model, 350–351
    communication skills, 353
    concessions in, 353
    defined, 350
    gathering information, 353
    goal setting, 353
    location, 351
    negotiator behaviours, 353
    organizational change and, 397,
        400
    physical setting, 352
    situational influences on, 351
    time factor, 352
    win-win versus win-lose orienta-
        tion, 351, 352
Network organization structure,
    476–479
    affiliate network, 478
Networks, 318, 330
Noise, 201
    See also Communication
Nominal group technique, 305
Nonterritorial offices, 213
Nonverbal communication, 207–208
    See also Communication
Norms
    changing, 244–245
    conformity to, 243–244
    defined, 243–244
    development of, 244–245
    effect on team performance,
        243–244, 248
    leadership style and, 373
    organizational politics and, 331
    reciprocity, 316, 331
North American Free Trade
    Agreement, 392

Observational research, 512–513
Office design. *See* Physical work envi-
    ronment
Open book management, 263
Open system defined, 12
Operant conditioning. *See*
    Organizational behaviour
    modification

Organic organizational structure, 466,
    479–480
Organization development. *See also*
    Organizational change
    action research, 402, 403
    appreciative inquiry, 406–407
    change agent, 402–403, 409
    data collection, 404
    defined, 402
    dialogue, 251, 348, 407
    effectiveness of, 408
    ethics of, 408–409
    evaluating interventions, 405
    incremental change, 404
    intergroup mirroring, 348
    intervention, 404–405
    joint action planning, 404
    Leadership Grid (Reg), 366–368
    organizational diagnosis, 403–404
    parallel learning structures, 406
    process consultation, 403
    quantum change, 404
    sensitivity training, 405
    team building, 250–253
    See also Team building
Organizational behaviour
    common sense and, 5
    computer technology, 9
    contingency approach, 11
    defined, 4
    effect of changing labour force on,
        392–393
    emerging trends, 6–8
    influence of departmentation on,
        466
    levels of analysis, 11
    maturing of discipline, 11
    multidisciplinary field, as a, 9–10
    multiple levels, 11
    open systems, 11–12
    other disciplines and, 9–10
    personality and, 166
    reasons for studying, 5–6
    research in, 505–513
    systems perspective, 11–13
    teams, 8
    value of theory and research in, 9
Organizational behaviour modifica-
    tion. *See also* Discipline;
    Punishment; Reward systems
    A-B-C model, 38
    behaviourism and, 38–39
    contingencies of reinforcement,
        39–41
    defined, 38
    ethical problems with, 48
    law of effect, 37
    limitations of, 43–44

    practice of, 43
    schedules of reinforcement, 41–43
    shaping behaviour, 43
    steps in implementing, 43
Organizational behaviour research.
    See also Theory building
    causation, 509–510, 512
    dependent variables, 508
    ethics in, 510
    field experiment, 510
    field survey, 511–512
    hypotheses, 505
    independent variables, 508
    laboratory experiment, 510–511
    observational research, 512–513
    participant observation, 512–513
    research designs, 510–511
    sampling, 508
    scientific method, 5, 11, 507
    theory building, 505–506
Organizational capital, 14
Organizational careers. *See* Career(s)
Organizational change. *See also*
    Organization development
    champions of, 166
    coercion and, 396, 400
    communication and, 396
    competition and, 392
    diffusion of, 401–402
    employee involvement and, 398
    force field analysis, 394
    forces for, 392–393
    government legislation and, 392
    incremental versus quantum,
        404–405
    legislation and, 392
    managing, 394–402
    mergers/acquisitions and, 392
    model of individual behaviour
        and, 395–396
    negotiation and, 397, 400
    population changes and, 392–393
    refreezing the desired conditions,
        400–401
    resistance to, 393–394
    stress management and, 397, 399
    technological change and, 392
    training and, 398, 399
    unfreezing the status quo, 395–396
Organizational citizenship behaviours
    defined, 36
    job satisfaction and, 182
    organizational commitment and,
        182
    types of, 35–36
Organizational commitment
    affective, 183
    business ethics and, 182

    consequences of, 183
    continuance, 183
    decline of, 184
    defined, 182
    increasing, 184–186
    normative, 183
    power and, 324
    realistic job previews, 446
Organizational comprehension, 185
Organizational culture
    artifacts, 419
    assimilation, 426
    ceremonies, 423
    communicating, 423
    content of, 420, 421, 422
    cultural network and, 429–430
    deculturation, 427
    defined, 418
    founders, 429
    grapevine communications and,
        214–216
    integration, 427
    language, 424
    leadership and, 429
    mergers/acquisitions and, 425–426
    organizational effectiveness and,
        421
    organizational socialization and,
        430
    physical work environment, 424
    reward systems and, 429
    rituals, 423
    role perceptions and, 32
    selecting employees and, 430
    separation, 428
    strength of, 421
    strengthening, 428–430
    subcultures, 422
    work force stability and, 429
Organizational design, 462
Organizational effectiveness
    competency-based rewards
        and, 89
    formalization and, 466
    job enrichment and, 104–105
    learning organization and, 38
    organizational culture and, 421
    performance-based rewards and,
        92
    sociotechnical design and, 265
    training and, 31
    transformational leadership and,
        374–375
Organizational environment and
    teams, 238–239
Organizational goals. *See* Goals
Organizational knowledge, 13–19
    dissemination, 17

environmental scanning, 16
experimentation, 16
grafting, 16
learning, 13–16
organizational memory, 17–19
utilization, 17
Organizational learning, 15, 37
Organizational Man, 449
Organizational memory, 17–19
Organizational politics
   attacking and blaming others,
     328–329
   coalitions, 330
   communication channels, 329
   conditions for, 331
   conflict and, 339, 344
   controlling, 332
   decision making and, 286, 331
   defined, 325–326
   filtering upward information, 202
   impression management, 331
   information distribution, 329
   job status-based rewards and, 87
   Machiavellianism, 331
   networking, 318
   norm of reciprocity, 331
   norms and, 331
   organizational effectiveness and, 328
   performance-based rewards and, 92
   personal characteristics and, 331
   scapegoating, 328–329
   scarce resources, 331
   types of political activity, 328–329
Organizational power. *See* Power
Organizational socialization
   agents, 446–447
   conflicts during, 444
   defined, 430, 442
   encounter stage of, 445, 446
   managing, 446–447
   organizational culture and, 430
   organizational transitions and, 443
   postdecisional justification and,
     444–445
   pre-employment stage of, 443–445
   psychological contract, 438
   realistic job previews, 446
   reality shock, 446
   role management stage of, 445
   stages of, 443–445
   stress and, 446
Organizational strategy, 481–482
Organizational structure. *See also*
   Departmentation
   age of organization and, 466
   centralization, 465
   client structure, 468
   contingencies of design, 479–482

coordination, 462–463
decentralization, 465
defined, 462
departmentation, 466–473
division of labour, 462
divisional structure, 468
external environment and,
   480–481
formalization, 465–466
functional structure, 468
geographic structure, 469
hybrid structure, 473
information power and, 318
matrix structure and, 471–473
mechanistic, 466, 479–480
network structure, 476–479
organic, 466, 479–480
organizational design, 462
organizational strategy and,
   481–482
power and, 465
product structure, 468
simple structure, 467
size of organization and, 463, 465,
   473, 479
span of control, 463–464
standardization, 463
tall versus flat, 464
team-based (lateral), 264, 450,
   473–476
technology and, 479–481
virtual corporation, 478
Organizations
   defined, 4–5
   effectiveness of. *See* Organizational
     effectiveness
   open systems perspective, 11–13
Outcome/input ratio, 70
Outsourcing, 451
Outward Bound, 251

Parallel learning structure, 406
Parallel processing teams. *See*
   Concurrent engineering
Participant observation, 512–513
Participation. *See* Employee involve-
   ment
Participative management, 260
Path-goal leadership theory
   contingency factors, 371
   defined, 369
   evaluation of, 373
   leadership styles, 369–370
Pay. *See* Reward systems
Pay discrimination, 87–88
Perception(s)
   actor-observer error, 155
   attribution theory, 155–156

closure, 150
communication and, 201–202
conflict and, 339, 348
defined, 146
empathy, 160–161, 163
errors in, 151–159
figure/ground principle, 148
halo effect, 158
impression management and, 331
improving accuracy of, 160–163
Johari Window, 162–163
leadership and, 378–381
mental models, 149
model of, 146, 147
organizing/interpreting information, 148
perceptual defense, 147, 288, 291
perceptual grouping principles, 148
primacy effect, 158–159
projection error, 159
recency effect, 159
selective attention, 146–147
self-efficacy, 157
self-fulfilling prophecy, 156–157
self-serving bias, 155
sharing, 162
stereotyping, 151–154, 345
stress management and, 131–132
Perceptual defense, 147, 288, 291
Performance. *See* Job performance
Performance appraisal(s)
   attribution theory and, 155
   figure/ground effect and, 148
   halo effect and, 158
   recency effect and, 159
   reward systems and, 92
Performance standard, 35
Performance-based rewards, 89–94
Performance-to-outcome expectancy,
   65, 69, 369
Person-job matching
   job redesign and, 31
   motivational implications of, 63, 67
   personality and, 166
   selection and, 31
   stress and, 125, 131
   training and, 31
Person-role conflict, 120
Personality
   attitudes and, 175
   defined, 164
   formation of, 164–165
   leadership and, 363, 366, 373
   limitations, 166–167
   locus of control, 167, 331
   Machiavellianism, 331
   performance and, 166
   person-job matching and, 166

self-monitoring, 167, 188
Type A/Type B behaviour pattern, 125–126
Persuasive communication
   audience characteristics, 221
   changing team norms and, 244–245
   communication medium, 221
   communicator characteristics, 220
   defined, 220
   group polarization and, 294–295
   inoculation effect, 221
   message content, 221
Physical work environment
   job status-based rewards and, 87
   negotiations and, 352
   organizational culture and, 424
   stress and, 120
   team effectiveness and, 237–238
Piece rate, 89
Platform teams. *See* Concurrent engineering
Politics. *See* Organizational politics
Pooled interdependence, 343
Positive affectivity, 175
Positive reinforcement, 39
Postdecisional justification, 290, 444–445
Power
   abuse of, 324–325
   centrality, 322
   centralization and, 465
   charisma, 318
   coercive, 317, 324, 397, 400
   communication networks and, 318–319
   consequences of, 323–325
   contingencies of, 320–323
   coping with uncertainty, 319–320
   counterpower, 315
   defined, 314
   discretion, 322–323
   expert, 318
   information, 318–320, 350
   interdependence and, 315
   legitimate, 316, 323
   model of, 315
   need for, 62
   organizational development and, 403, 408
   organizational structure and, 465
   referent, 318
   reward, 316, 323–325
   scarce resources, 314–315
   sources of, 315–320
   substitutability, 320–321
   visibility, 323
Power distance, 189, 190, 269

Pre-employment stage of organizational socialization, 443–445
Prejudice, 153
Primacy effect, 158–159, 245
Prince, The, 331
Privatization and stress, 122
Problem solving. *See* Decision making
Procedural fairness, 354
Process consultation, 403
Process losses, 249
Process theories of motivation
   cross-cultural relevance of, 77–78
   defined, 60
   equity theory, 70–73
   expectancy theory, 64–69
   goal setting and feedback, 73–77
Production blocking, 292
Productivity
   job design and, 95–97, 101, 104–105
   training and, 31
   transactional leadership and, 374–375
Profit sharing plans, 91
Programmed decisions, 287
Projection error, 159
Psychological contract, 438
   dynamics of, 440–442
   trust, 439–440
Punishment
   coercive power and, 317
   contrasted with negative reinforcement, 40–41
   defined, 39–40
   discipline and, 93
   organizational change strategy, 397, 400
Pygmalion effect. *See* Self-fulfilling prophecy

Quality. *See* Quality management
Quality circles, 262
Quality management
   benchmarking, 276
   competency-based rewards and, 88–89
   competitive benchmarking and, 276
   continuous improvement and, 273–275
   continuous learning and, 276
   defect prevention and, 275
   defined, 271
   employee involvement and, 275
   kaizen and, 273–275
   limitations of, 278–279
   performance measurement and, 275–276
   principles of, 271-275
   self-directed work teams, 273
Quantum change, 404

Realistic job previews, 446
Reality shock, 446
Recency effect, 159
Reciprocal interdependence, 343
Recruitment, 33–34
Reengineering, 404–405
Referent power, 318
Refreezing, 395, 400–401
Reinforcement. *See* Organizational behaviour modification
Relations by objectives, 348
Relaxation and meditation, 132
Resistance point, 351
Resistance to change. *See also* Organization development; Organizational change
   job design and, 104–105
   job status-based rewards and, 87
   model, 394
   overcoming, 394–402
   power and, 323–325
   sources of, 394
Reward power, 316, 323–325
Reward systems
   agency theory, 92
   attribution theory and, 155
   bonuses, 90
   broadbanding, 88
   business ethics and, 86–87
   commissions, 89
   competency-based, 88–89
   employee share ownership plans (ESOPs), 91
   flexible, 63
   gainsharing plans, 91
   hiring bonuses, 34
   job satisfaction and, 182
   job status-based, 87–88
   membership-based, 87
   merit pay plans, 90
   motivational effects of, 63–64, 69
   objectives of, 86, 87
   office space, 88
   organizational behaviour modification and, 43
   organizational change and, 400
   organizational culture and, 429
   organizational stakeholders' influence on, 86
   pay discrimination, 88
   pension plans, 87
   performance-based, 89–94
   piece rate, 89
   positive reinforcement contrasted with, 39
   problems with, 87, 88, 89, 92–94
   profit sharing plans, 91
   seniority-based, 87

skill-based pay, 88–89
team effectiveness and, 239
team norms and, 245
Rights of the individual, 192
Risky-shift phenomenon. *See* Group
polarization
Rituals, 423
Role
ambiguity, 121–122, 371
conflict, 120, 122–124
defining through team building, 251
management during organizational socialization, 445
perceptions, 30, 32, 369
team development and, 241–242
Role conflict, 120
Romance perspective of leadership,
378–381

Safety
feedback and, 48
job rotation and, 101
joint health and safety committees,
261
need for, 61
OB modification and, 43
stress and, 127, 129
team norms and, 244
Sampling, 508
Satisfaction-progression process, 61
Satisficing, 290
Scientific management, 95–97
Scientific method, 11, 507
Selection
ability and, 31
attitudes of applicants and, 175
managing stress through, 131
personality and, 166
reducing social loafing through, 250
values and, 189
Selective attention
defined, 146
object characteristics and, 146–147
Selective perception
decision making problems and,
288
perceiver characteristics and, 147
situational characteristics and,
148
Self-actualization, 61
Self-directed work teams, 8, 234
defined, 264
effectiveness of, 266, 408
information-based power and,
318–320
leadership and, 362
management resistance to, 269
Shell Canada, at, 265–266

sociotechnical design and, 265
team-based organizational structure and, 473–476
Self-efficacy, 49, 76, 102, 127, 157
stress, 125, 131–132
Self-employment, 8
Self-esteem
job satisfaction and, 180
persuasive communication and,
221
self-fulfilling prophecy effect on,
157
stress and, 125
Self-fulfilling prophecy, 156–157
Self-leadership, 105
goal-setting, 105–106
mental imagery, 107
motivation, 105
natural rewards, 107–108
self-monitoring, 108
self-reinforcement, 108
self-talk, 106
Self-managing work teams. *See* Self-
directed work teams
Self-monitoring personality, 167, 188,
365, 366
Self-reinforcement, 49, 108
Self-serving bias, 155
Self-talk, 106
stress, 131
Seniority-based rewards, 87
Sensitivity training, 405
Separation, 428
Sequential interdependence, 343
Sexual harassment. *See* Harassment
Shaping behaviour, 43
Simple organization structure, 467
Situational contingencies, 30, 33, 92,
177
Skill variety, 99
Skill(s). *See* Ability
Skill-based work, 88–89
Skunkworks, 235
Social bonding, 421
Social identity theory, 149
Social learning theory
behavioural modelling, 48–49
defined, 48
learning behavioural consequences, 49–51
self-efficacy, 49
self-reinforcement, 49
Social loafing, 249–250
Social support
group polarization and, 294–295
leadership and, 370
socialization agents and, 446
stress and, 133

team membership and, 237
Sociotechnical design, 265
Span of control, 463–464
Stabilization zone, 131
Stakeholders
decision making and, 286
formalization and, 465
reward systems and, 86
Status
gender differences and, 217–219
reward systems and, 87–88
selective perception and, 147
team membership and, 237
Stereotyping
conflict and, 345
ethical issues with, 153–154
leadership and, 366, 369, 378–379,
380–381
problems with, 152
process, 151–152
Strategic business units, 468
Strategic choice, 481
Stress. *See also* Stress management
childcare facilities, 130
consequences of, 126–127
coronary heart disease in Canada
and, 126
costs of, 118
defined, 118
family-leave programs, 130
flexible work arrangements, 130
general adaptation syndrome, 119
grapevine communication and,
214–216
individual differences in, 125
interpersonal stressors, 121–122
job sharing, 130
managing, 128–133
mergers and, 392, 400
model of, 120–121
occupations and, 124–125
organizational stressors and, 122
physical environment, 120
prevalence of in Canada, 118
privatization, 122
reality shock and, 446
removing stressors, 129
role-related stressors, 120–123
self-efficacy, 125, 131–132
self-talk, 131
sexual harassment, 121–122
stressors, 120–126
team membership and, 237
telework, 130
Type A/Type B behaviour pattern,
125–126
types of stressors, 120–126
work-family stressors, 122–124

Stress management
  changing stress perceptions, 131–132
  employee counselling, 132–133
  fitness/lifestyle programs, 132
  organizational change and, 397, 399
  relaxation and meditation, 132
  removing stressor, 129
  social support, 133, 446
  withdrawing from stressor, 131–132
Stressor, 120
Subcultures, 422
Substitutability, 320–321
Subsystems, 11
  See also Systems theory
Superordinate goals, 346, 468
Synergy, 267
Systems theory
  learning organization and, 38
  model, 11–13
  organizational change and, 392

T-groups, 405
Tacit knowledge, 38
Tacit skills and knowledge, 31, 49
Target point, 351
Task
  characteristics, 121
  force, 235
  identity, 99
  interdependence. See Task interde-
    pendence
  performance, 35
  significance, 99
  specialization. See Job specialization
  structure, 371
Task interdependence
  conflict and, 342, 348–349
  departmentation and, 467
  performance-based rewards and, 92
  pooled, 343
  power and, 315
  reciprocal, 343
  reducing, 348–349
  sequential, 343
  social loafing and, 250
  team effectiveness and, 239
Task performance, 35
Team building
  defined, 250
  effectiveness of, 253, 408
  Outward Bound, 251
  simulation games and, 252, 253
  types of, 251–253
Team(s)
  adjourning, 242
  advantages of decision making in,
    292
  brainstorming, 302–303

coalition, 236–237, 330
cohesiveness, 245–248, 339, 373
  See also Cohesiveness
communication, 239
composition of, 240–241
concurrent engineering, 277
conformity, 243–244, 293
constructive controversy, 300, 339
cross-functional, 50
decision making in, 292–295
defined, 232
departmentation and, 467
development, 241–242
devil's advocacy, 301
diversity, 240–241
effectiveness, 238
electronic brainstorming, 303–305
evaluation apprehension in,
    292–293
formal, 232–234
forming, 241–242
goals, 236–238
group polarization, 294–295
groupthink, 293
heterogenous versus homoge-
    neous, 240–241
individual goals in, 236–238
informal groups, 236–237
interacting, 302
model of team effectiveness,
    237–238, 239
multicultural work force and, 235
nominal group technique, 305
norming, 242
norms, 243–244, 248, 316, 331, 373
  See also Norms
organizational behaviour, 8
organizational environment,
    238–239
organizational structure and, 234,
    264, 450, 474
performing, 242
physical work environment and,
    237–238
process losses, 249
production blocking in, 292
reasons for joining, 236–237
resistance to change and, 394
reward systems for, 90–91
roles in, 241–242
self-directed, 8, 264–266
self-managing, 474
size, 240, 250
skunkworks, 235
social loafing, 249–250
social support in, 237–238
  sociotechnically-designed, 265
  storming, 242

task characteristics, 239
task force, 235
time constraints in decision mak-
    ing, 292
types of, 232–237
virtual, 235–236
Vroom-Jago model, 514–515
Team-based organizational structure,
    234, 264, 450, 474
Team-based structure, 234
Technology
  champions, 362
  organizational behaviour, 9
  organizational structure and,
    479–481
  substitutability, 320
Telework, 130
Theft, 181
Theory building
  constructs, 505–506
  deductive, 505–506
  hypotheses, 505–506
  inductive, 507
  scientific method, 507
  theory, 505
Third-party conflict resolution
  arbitration, 355
  inquisition, 355
  mediation, 355
  objectives of, 353–355
  peer tribunals, 355
  procedural fairness and, 353–355
  types of, 355
Time and motion study, 96
Total quality management. See Quality
    management
Training
  Canadian levels of, 31
  competency-based rewards and,
    88–89
  creativity, 299
  job performance and, 31
  organizational change and, 398, 399
  organizational citizenship behav-
    iours, 35–36
  person-job matching and, 31
  productivity and, 31
  social learning theory and, 48–51
Trait perspective of leadership, 363–365
Transactional leadership, 374–375
Transformational leadership
  behavioural modelling and, 377
  charisma and, 375
  defined, 374
  elements of, 376
  model of, 377
  organizational culture and, 429
  transactional versus, 374–375

Trust
  calculus-based, 440
  conflict management and, 345
  identification-based, 440
  knowledge-based, 440
  leadership and, 364
  organizational commitment and, 185
  persuasive communication and, 220
  psychological contract, 439–440
  team building and, 251
Turnover
  benefits of minimizing, 34
  causes of, 34–35
  conflict and, 339
  equity theory and, 73
  job satisfaction and, 181
  organizational commitment and, 183
  seniority-based rewards and, 87
  ways to increase, 35
Type A/Type B behaviour pattern, 125–126

Uncertainty
  avoidance, 189, 190
  coping with, as a power source, 319–320
  organizational politics and, 331
Unfreezing, 394–402

Unionization, 409
  equity theory and, 71
  job satisfaction and, 181
  job specialization and, 97
Unprogrammed decisions, 287
Upward communications, 210
Utilitarianism, 192, 327

Valence, 66
Values
  aboriginal, 190–191
  creativity and, 298
  decision making and, 288
  defined, 188
  importance of, 188
  individualism-collectivism, 189, 190, 240–241, 250, 269
  Machiavellianism, 331
  masculinity-femininity, 190
  power distance, 189, 190, 269
  uncertainty avoidance, 189, 190
Variable interval schedule, 41, 42
Variable ratio schedule, 41, 42, 43
Verbal communication, 204–205, 221
Vertical job specialization. See Job specialization
Vesting in pension plans, 87
Virtual corporation, 478
Virtual teams, 235–236
Visibility, 323
Visible management, 211–212

Vision
  appreciative inquiry and, 407
  leadership and, 374–378
Vroom-Jago model, 514–515
Win-lose orientation, 344, 351, 352
Win-win orientation, 344, 351, 352

Women
  communication differences with men, 217–219
  employment discrimination against, 153–154
  labour force changes in, 392
  leadership and, 380–381
  networks and, 330, 332
  stressor of being a "supermom", 122–124
Work attendance. See Absenteeism
Work attitudes. See Attitudes
Work overload/underload, 121
Work schedules, 123
Work-related behaviour. See Behaviour
Work-related values. See Values
Worker alienation, 97
World Series (baseball), 322
Written communication, 204–205, 221

Zero Waste program (Bell Canada), 33, 398, 400

NAME INDEX

Aberlee, C., 211
Adams, D.A., 554n
Adams, J.S., 537n
Adamson, R.S., 549n, 575n, 576n
Adelmann, P.K., 552n
Adler, N.J., 538n, 574n, 580n, 584n
Adler, P.S., 562n
Adler, S., 549n
Adsetts, P., 103
Aggarwal, P., 560n
Agnew, N.M., 587n
Ahearne, M., 533n
Aitken, M., 556n
Ajzen, L., 550n
Akyeampong, E., 532n
Albanese, R., 560n
Albert, T., 7, 8
Alderfer, C.P., 61, 62, 77, 78, 536n
Alesandrini, K., 554n
Alexander, E.R., 553n
Alexander, J.A., 560n
Alexander, R.A., 535n, 538n
Ali, A.J., 552n
Alibhai, A.A., 547n, 570n
Allan, J., 368, 556n
Allen, D., 587n
Allen, G., 551n
Allen, J.S., 577n
Allen, M., 554n
Allen, N.J., 552n, 584n
Allen, R.E., 564n
Allen, R.W., 570n, 571n, 572n
Allen, S., 164, 165
Allentuck, A., 274
Allerton, H., 564n
Alliger, G.M., 543n
Alspach, R., 349
Altmann, J.L., 539n
Amabile, T.M., 567n
Amason, A.C., 568n, 572n
Ambrose, M.L., 537n
Amelio, G., 242, 332, 559n
Ancona, D.G., 559n
Anderson, J.C., 427
Andriessen, J.H.E., 554n
Andrisani, P.J., 549n
Anfuso, D., 544n
Angle, H.L., 572n
Anhalt, R.L., 548n
Annett, J., 534n
Anthony, T., 358

Anthony, W.P., 542n
Antonioni, D., 534n
Appelbaum, S.H., 578n
Arad, S., 541n, 562n, 569n
Arden, E., 374
Argyris, C., 546n, 559n, 563n
Armas, G.C., 564n
Armstrong, D.J., 558n
Arnault, G., 555n, 567n
Aronson, E., 557n, 560n
Arrow, H., 559n
Arsenault, A., 545n
Arthur, M.B., 584n
Arvey, R.D., 550n
Asbrand, D., 554n
Ascroft, S., 571n
Ash, S.R., 559n, 568n
Ashford, S.J., 534n, 535n, 552n
Ashforth, B.E., 542n, 543n, 544n,
    545n, 546n, 550n, 552n, 558n,
    560n, 570n, 571n, 581n, 584n,
    586n
Ashworth, S.D., 555n
Aspery, J., 14, 552n
Attenello, D., 540n, 541n
Atwell, J., 573n
Audia, G., 538n
Austin, C., 122
Austin, J., 534n
Austin, N., 558n
Avolio, B.J., 549n, 577n
Axel, H., 585n
Axley, S., 554n
Axtell, R., 556n
Ayman, R., 578n
Azim, A., 552n

Baba, V.V., 533n, 543n, 544n, 552n,
    576n
Bacharach, S.B., 532n, 556n
Baetz, M.L., 576n
Bagnall, J., 37, 575n
Bailey, J.S., 534n
Bain, G., 420
Baker, D.D., 536n
Baliga, B.R., 577n
Balkin, D.B., 538n
Ball, G.A., 533n
Ballard, K.A., 545n
Balthazard, C., 14
Balzer, W.K., 548n

Bamberger, P., 532n
Band, T., 398
Bandura, A., 535n, 548n, 563n
Banker, R.D., 560n, 564n
Bardsley, J.J., 532n
Bargh, J.A., 547n, 570n
Barker, R.A., 575n
Barley, S.R., 530n
Barling, J., 537n, 543n, 547n, 551n,
    578n
Barnard, C.I., 533n
Barnard, R., 64
Barnett, G., 553n, 586n
Barnett, W.P., 560n
Barney, J.B., 582n
Barnlund, D.C., 556n
Baron, R.A., 417, 537n, 572n, 573n
Barret, F.D., 568n
Barrett, F.J., 407, 572n, 580n
Barrett, M., 74, 375
Barrick, M.R., 549n
Barrios-Choplin, J.R., 555n
Barron, F., 567n
Barry, V., 553n
Barsade, S.G., 551n, 567n
Bartlett, C.A., 587n
Bartol, K.M., 540n, 569n
Barua, A., 558n
Basadur, M., 566n, 568n
Bass, B.M., 533n, 549n, 577n
Bastianutti, L.M., 566n, 568n
Bata, T., Sr., 288
Bateman, T.S., 547n, 587n
Bauer, T.N., 584n
Bavetta, A.G., 542n
Bayloff, N., 563n
Bazerman, M.H., 572n, 574n, 575n
Beach, L.R., 566n
Beamer, L., 548n
Bear, J., 556n
Beard, K.M., 585n
Beatty, C.A., 543n, 575n
Beatty, R.W., 548n
Beauge, M., 549n
Beck, I.M., 538n
Beck, J., 348
Becker, F., 556n
Becker, T.E., 551n
Beckerle, C.A., 556n
Beckett, W.K., 579n
Beckhard, R., 530n, 531n, 580n

Beddoe, C., 173
Bedeian, A.G., 586n
Beer, M., 561n, 579n, 580n, 581n
Behrman, D.N., 532n
Belkaoui, A., 539n
Bell, C.H., Jr., 561n, 580n
Belohlav, J.A., 562n
Bemmels, B., 547n, 578n
Benimadhu, P., 532n
Bennett, N., 561n
Bennett, R.H., III, 542n
Bennis, W., 577n
Bentley, D., 211
Berdahl, J.L., 559n
Berger, L.A., 539n
Bergman, B., 530n
Bergmann, T.J., 538n
Bergstrom, R.Y., 534n, 565n, 586n
Berkowitz, L., 537n
Berlew, D.E., 577n
Bernacchi, J., 3
Bernardin, H.J., 547n, 548n
Bernthal, P.R., 560n
Bertin, D., 401
Bessette, G., 276
Bettenhausen, K.L., 559n
Bettman, J.R., 547n
Beyer, J.M., 582n
Beyer, M., 533n
Bhan, R.N., 560n
Bhawuk, D.P.S., 570n
Bickham, T., 548n
Bies, R.J., 534n
Billings, R.S., 551n
Bird, F.G., 553n
Black, L., 577n
Blackwell, J., 568n
Blackwell, R., 74
Blake, R.R., 366, 367, 572n, 573n, 574n, 576n
Blanchard, K.H., 576n
Blanck, P.D., 548n
Blank, W., 576n
Blau, G., 537n
Blauner, R., 540n
Block, C.J., 578n
Bloom, M.C., 538n
Bluen, S.D., 551n
Blum, A.A., 573n
Blyton, P., 586n
Bobko, P., 552n
Bobocel, D.R., 566n
Boddy, D., 580n
Bodenhausen, G.V., 546n
Boehne, D.M., 537n
Boehnke, K., 578n
Bogyo, T.J., 413
Bolman, L., 335

Bonanno, R., 555n
Bond, M.H., 553n
Bontis, N., 578n
Boomer, R., 35, 36, 423
Boos, A.L., 559n
Booth, P., 585n
Bordia, P., 554n, 558n, 568n
Borg, I., 538n
Borman, W.C., 533n
Boss, A., 548n
Boss, R.W., 561n
Bottiger, P., 567n
Bouchard, T.L., 550n
Boulding, W., 567n
Bourette, S., 564n
Bourgault, J., 583n
Bourgeois, L.J., III, 568n, 572n
Bourgeois, R.P., 585n
Bouwen, J.K., 572n
Bovee, C.L., 556n
Bowditch, J.L., 582n
Bowen, D.E., 541n, 562n
Boyacigiller, N.A., 538n
Boyatzis, R., 536n
Bradford, D.L., 571n
Bradshaw, P., 574n
Bradway, L.K., 558n, 573n
Brass, D.J., 569n, 570n
Breaugh, J.A., 584n
Brehm, J.W., 557n
Bremmer, O.C., 546n
Brenneman, R., 154
Brethour, P., 574n
Brett, B.M., 545n
Brett, J.M., 574n, 575n
Bretz, R.D., Jr., 537n
Bridwell, L.G., 536n
Brief, A.P., 530n, 550n
Brillinger, R., 534n
Briner, R.B., 538n
Brislin, R.W., 548n
Brocka, B., 564n
Brocka, M.S., 564n
Brockbank, W., 555n
Brockhouse, G., 204
Brodt, S.E., 574n
Brown, B.R., 574n
Brown, D.R., 580n
Brown, J.L., 587n
Brown, K.G., 538n
Brown, L.T., 547n
Brown, M., 565n
Brown, M.J., 561n
Brown, M.L., 580n
Brown, S., 544n
Brown, S.P., 532n
Brownell, J., 557n
Bruhis, S., 542n

Bruner, M., 442
Bruning, N.S., 562n
Brusse, T., 578n
Bruwelheide, L.R., 534n
Bryant, B., 560n
Bryant, S., 535n
Bryman, A., 578n
Buchanan, D.A., 580n
Buck, R., 552n
Buda, R., 573n
Bulatao, E.Q., 537n, 551n
Bulkeley, W.M., 568n
Buller, P.F., 561n
Bunker, B.B., 552n, 583n
Bunning, R.L., 539n
Buono, A.F., 536n, 559n, 582n
Burke, R.J., 542n, 543n, 544n, 545n, 546n, 554n, 556n, 570n, 571n, 573n, 579n, 585n
Burke, W.W., 579n, 580n, 581n
Burkhardt, M.E., 569n, 570n
Burman, T., 285
Burnham, D.H., 536n
Burns, G., 186
Burns, J.M., 575n
Burns, T., 586n, 587n
Burnside, R.M., 567n
Bushe, G.R., 580n, 581n
Butcher, A.H., 550n
Butler, J.K., Jr., 552n
Butterfield, D.A., 576n
Butterfield, K.D., 533n
Buzzanell, P.M., 546n
Bycio, P., 532n, 544n, 551n, 577n
Byham, W.C., 530n, 535n, 557n, 558n, 563n
Byrne, J.A., 587n
Byron, W.J., 585n

Cacioppo, J.T., 555n, 557n
Caldwell, D.F., 559n, 560n, 583n
Caldwell, J., 199
Callister, R.R., 572n
Came, B., 544n
Campbell, D.N., 534n
Campbell, J.P., 533n, 536n, 562n
Campbell, R.J., 562n
Campion, M.A., 540n, 541n, 558n, 573n, 586n
Cannon-Bowers, J.A., 559n
Cardy, R.L., 542n
Carlisle, J., 543n, 547n
Carmel, E., 574n
Carnevale, P.J., 574n
Caropreso, F., 218
Carr, L., 555n
Carr, R.A., 547n, 570n
Carroll, B., 560n

Carroll, P., 11, 12
Carson, K.D., 569n
Carson, K.P., 542n, 549n, 562n
Carson, P.P., 569n
Carter, L., 50
Cartwright, D., 557n, 569n
Case, J., 562n
Casgrain, T., 14
Catlin, G.E.G., 570n
Cattaneo, C., 347
Caudron, S., 585n
Cavanaugh, G.E., 571n
Cawsey, T.F., 549n, 576n
Caywood, L.C., 579n
Chaisson, G., 565n
Chalmers, R., 561n
Chalykoff, J., 535n
Champy, J., 580n
Chan, A., 154
Chandler, A.D., 481, 587n
Chandler, T.D., 561n
Chandran, C., 461
Chang, L., 539n
Chao, G., 548n
Chao, G.T., 584n
Chapman, I., 553n, 563n
Chapman, P., 554n
Charney, C., 557n
Charney, G., 536n
Chartrand, B.L., 266
Chatman, J.A., 581n, 582n, 583n
Chelius, J., 539n
Chemers, M.M., 576n, 578n
Chen, P.Y., 551n
Chevreau, J., 555n
Child, J., 587n
Chilton, D., 288
Chisholm, P., 123
Chowdhury, J., 538n
Chown, R., 90
Christensen-Hughes, J., 556n
Christie, K., 123
Christie, R., 572n
Church, A.H., 212, 580n
Clampitt, P., 553n, 586n
Clark, C.J., 29, 532n
Clark, D., 582n
Clegg, S.R., 554n, 558n, 569n, 578n
Cleghorn, J., 74
Clemons, T.C., 575n
Coate, S., 546n
Cobb, A.T., 571n
Coch, L., 244, 559n, 563n
Coetzer, G., 561n, 581n
Cohen, A.R., 571n
Cohen, G., 376
Cohen, S., 545n
Cohen, S.G., 557n, 558n, 559n, 562n

Cohen-Rosenthal, E., 564n
Colarelli, S.M., 559n
Colburn, F., 544n
Cole, P., 558n
Cole, R.E., 562n
Colella, A., 546n, 584n
Coleman, D.F., 532n, 540n
Colin, J., 545n
Collins, E., 152
Collinson, D., 540n
Collison, R., 288, 586n
Comeau, L.R., 104, 541n
Condit, P., 248
Conger, J.A., 530n, 533n, 541n, 563n, 577n
Conlisk, J., 566n
Conlon, D., 559n
Connellan, T.K., 39, 533n
Connolly, T., 568n
Conti, R., 567n
Cook, J., 274
Coon, H., 567n
Cooper, C., 539n, 542n
Cooper, C.J., 531n
Cooper, C.L., 439, 538n, 542n, 543n, 563n, 583n, 585n
Cooper, J., 557n
Cooper, M.D., 534n, 537n
Cooper, W.H., 532n, 548n, 566n, 568n
Cooperrider, D.L., 407, 572n, 580n
Copeland, M., 317
Copper, C., 560n
Cordes, C.L., 544n
Corey, P., 545n
Cornell, C., 545n
Costello, T.W., 548n
Cote, R., 568n
Courtwright, J., 564n
Coutant-Sassic, D., 559n
Covin, T.J., 580n
Cox, K., 44, 537n
Cox, M., 545n
Cox, T., Jr., 556n
Coye, R.W., 562n
Coyle, R.T., 557n
Crant, J.M., 547n
Crawford, M., 556n, 557n, 572n, 575n
Crawley, W.J., 557n
Critchley, B., 573n
Cronshaw, S.F., 545n, 578n, 584n
Cropanzano, R., 174, 550n
Crosariol, B., 554n, 578n
Crosby, P.B., 272, 565n
Crow, P., 530n
Crowe, K., 285
Crowley, W., 236
Crozier, M., 570n
Crystal, G.S., 74, 329, 571n

Csoka, L., 534n
Culnan, M., 554n
Cummings, A., 567n
Cummings, L.L., 535n, 541n, 543n, 544n, 551n, 563n, 565n, 567n, 579n
Cummings, T.G., 561n, 579n, 580n
Cunard, S., 182, 183, 374, 377
Cunningham, J.B., 541n, 562n, 580n
Currie, P., 555n
Cushing, C., 145
Cyert, R.M., 569n
Czarnecki, A., 532n, 533n, 582n, 584n
Czyzewska, M., 548n

D'Andrea-O'Brien, C., 536n, 559n
D'Aprix, R.M., 579n
D'Aunno, T.A., 560n
Dacey, J.S., 567n
Dachler, H.P., 577n
Daft, R.L., 209, 554n, 555n
Dahl, J.G., 537n
Dahl, T.A., 569n
Dailey, L.K., 565n
Daily, B., 559n, 568n
Dal Monte, R., 178
Dalglish, B., 123
Dandridge, T.C., 554n, 582n
Danehower, C., 546n
Dang, K., 579n
Daniels, A., 550n
Dannemiller, K.D., 579n
Darley, J.M., 547n
Darling, M.S., 532n, 541n, 563n
Dary, E., 211, 212
Das, B., 534n, 537n, 540n
Dastmalchian, A., 578n, 586n
Dault, G.M., 556n
Davenport, T.H., 570n
David, B., 567n
Davidow, W.H., 579n, 587n
Davids, K., 545n
Davidson, G., 562n
Davies, C., 586n
Davis, K., 556n, 557n
Davis, S.B., 564n
Davis, S.M., 586n
Davis, T., 556n
Davis, T.R.V., 562n
Dawson, C., 542n
Day, S., 553n
De Backer, P., 450
de Carufel, A., 581n
De Meuse, K.P., 558n, 561n
De Meyer, A., 564n
De Pree, M., 430, 583n
Deacon, J., 322
Deakin, M., 288

Deal, T.E., 335, 582n
Dean, J., 579n
Dean, J.W., Jr., 565n
Deaner, C.M.D., 581n
Dearborn, D.C., 546n
Deaux, K., 547n
DeBacker, P., 567n
Dedrick, E.J., 575n
Degler, T., 585n
Dekker, I., 543n, 547n
Delbecq, A.L., 565n, 567n, 568n
Delbridge, R., 556n
Delenea, W., 262
DeMarie, S.M., 565n
DeMont, J., 553n
DeMott, J.S., 470, 574n
Denis, H., 587n
DeNisi, A.S., 537n
Denison, D.R., 582n
Dennis, A.R., 568n
Denton, D.K., 575n
Deogun, N., 576n
DeRosa, W., 204
Desai, K., 549n
DeShon, R.P., 535n, 538n
DeSimone, R.L., 533n
Desker-Shaw, S., 538n
Deszca, G., 549n, 576n
Deutsch, C.H., 575n
Devadas, R., 562n
Deveny, K., 586n
Devine, K.S., 578n
Dibbs, J., 562n, 579n
DiBella, A.J., 531n
Dickinson, A.M., 533n
Diehl, M., 566n
Digman, J.M., 549n
Dion, K.L., 560n
Dion, S., 583n
Dirks, K.T., 563n, 579n
DiStefano, A.C., 578n
DiStefano, J.J., 578n
DiTomasco, N., 582n
Dittrich, J.E., 502
Dixon, G.R., 530n, 557n, 558n, 563n
Dixon, N.M., 531n
Dobbins, G.H., 575n, 578n
Dobson, P., 581n, 582n, 583n
Dodd, N.G., 541n
Dodds, D.W., 401
Doerpinghaus, H.I., 586n
Doerr, K.H., 537n, 573n
Doherty, E.M., 563n
Dolan, S.L., 545n
Donnellon, A., 563n
Donnelly, J.H., 119, 256
Donohoe, J.M., 536n
Dorrell, K., 557n

Doughan, J., 427
Dougherty, T.W., 544n
Dowling, W.F., 540n
Downie, B.M., 574n
Downs, C., 553n, 586n
Dreidger, S.M., 568n
Driscoll, J.E., 542n
Driscoll, T.P., 224
Drory, A., 570n
Drouillard, P., 90
Drucker, P., 74, 465, 534n
Drucker, P.C., 575n
Drucker, P.F., 565n, 566n
Duan, C., 546n
Dubin, R., 561n
Dudek, S.Z., 568n
Dukerich, J.M., 530n
Dulebohn, J., 547n
Dumaine, B., 560n
Duncan, P.K., 534n
Duncan, W.J., 540n, 581n
Dunham, R.B., 541n
Dunnette, M.D., 536n, 549n, 550n,
    573n
Dunphy, D., 560n
Durham, C.C., 550n
Durup, M.J., 543n
Dutton, G., 536n, 567n
Dutton, J.E., 566n
Dutton, J.M., 572n
Duxbury, L., 543n
Dyck, B., 539n, 563n
Dyer, B., 37
Dyer, W.G., 561n
Dymond, W.R., 561n
Dzindolet, M.T., 568n

Eade, R., 18
Eagly, A.H., 578n
Earley, P.C., 544n, 553n, 558n, 560n,
    563n, 573n
Eastman, K.K., 577n, 578n
Eaton, J., 539n
Eaton, T., 89, 192, 374, 429
Ebbeson, E.B., 557n
Eccles, R.G., 570n
Eden, D., 547n, 548n
Eden, G., 533n
Edmondson, A.C., 536n
Edwards, J.E., 581n
Edwards, J.R., 532n, 585n
Edwards, M., 534n
Edwards, S., 531n, 575n
Egan, G., 548n
Egri, C.P., 571n
Ehrenberg, E.L., 533n
Ehrenberg, R.A., 533n
Ehrenberg, R.G., 532n

Einstein, A., 286
Eisenberg, E.M., 554n
Eisenhardt, K.M., 539n, 568n, 572n
Eisenstat, R.A., 579n, 580n
Ekman, P., 556n
Elangovan, A.R., 570n, 575n
Elizur, D., 538n, 553n
Ellis, K., 531n
Ellis, R.J., 549n, 575n, 576n
Elsass, P.M., 566n
Elsayed-Ekhouly, S.M., 573n
Emerson, R.M., 569n
Emmons, B., 319
Enchin, H., 540n
Enge, R.S., 560n
Enzle, M.E., 539n
Epstein, B., 288
Erez, M., 538n, 553n, 560n, 563n
Erickson, R.J., 543n
Ertel, D., 574n
Esses, V.M., 530n
Estok, D., 212, 582n
Evans, C.R., 560n
Evans, D., 572n
Evans, E., 534n
Evans, M.G., 368, 530n, 532n, 547n,
    550n, 576n, 578n, 585n
Evans, R., 580n
Eveleth, D.M., 551n
Everett, L., 546n
Ewan, A., 534n
Ewing, R.P., 579n

Fahr, J., 535n
Fairhurst, G.T., 564n, 577n
Falbe, C.M., 569n, 570n, 571n
Falkenberg, L.E., 545n, 546n
Fandt, P.M., 571n
Fang, Y., 540n
Farkas, C.M., 450, 567n
Farmer, S.M., 572n
Farquhar, C.R., 204, 556n, 561n, 587n
Farr, J.L., 567n
Farren, C., 585n
Farson, R.E., 569n, 575n, 580n
Fast, J.E., 543n
Fattedad, S.O., 347, 562n
Fayol, H., 540n, 586n
Fazio, R.H., 546n
Fedor, D.B., 548n, 572n
Feild, H.S., 549n
Feldman, D.C., 552n, 555n, 559n,
    584n, 586n
Feldman, J.M., 161
Fellegi, I., 451
Fells, R.E., 574n
Fennell, T., 74
Ferdows, K., 564n

Ference, R., 567n
Ferris, G.R., 541n, 570n, 571n, 572n
Feschuk, S., 582n
Festinger, L., 550n
Fiedler, F.E., 576n
Field, J.M., 560n, 564n
Field, R.H.G., 547n, 565n, 566n
Fielding, J., 545n
Fife, S., 557n
Filmon, G., 3
Fine, M.G., 548n
Fineman, S., 545n
Finkelstein, S., 569n
Finlayson, J., 154
Finley, M., 559n, 560n, 561n, 566n
Finnigan, J.P., 564n
Fischoff, B., 566n
Fish, S., 552n
Fishbein, M.M., 550n
Fisher, A., 64
Fisher, C.D., 438, 551n, 584n
Fiske, S.T., 546n, 547n
Fitzgerald, M.P., 541n
Fitzgerald, N., 556n
Flavelle, D., 539n
Fleisher, C.S., 565n
Fleishman, E.A., 576n
Fleming, R.L., 534n
Fleury, T., 107
Flood, A., 74
Flood, R.L., 564n
Flynn, G., 548n
Folger, R., 537n, 574n
Fonseca, R., 12
Foot, D.K., 536n
Ford, J.D., 547n
Ford, J.K., 550n
Ford, R.C., 562n
Foss, K., 548n, 562n
Foti, R.J., 364, 549n, 575n
Fottler, M.D., 562n
Fournier, R., 562n
Fox, J.B., 536n
Francis, J., 573n
Frank, C., 565n
Frankel, S., 568n
Franklin, S., 551n, 577n
Franssen, M., 64, 65
Frayne, C.A., 535n
Fredendall, L.D., 564n
Frederick, J.A., 543n
Frederiksen, L.W., 533n
Freeland, D.B., 557n
Freidman, M., 544n
French, G.R., 539n
French, J.R.P., 244, 315, 559n, 563n, 569n
French, W.L., 580n

Frese, M., 550n
Frey, B.S., 552n
Fried, L., 587n
Fried, Y., 541n
Friesen, G.B., 587n
Friesen, P.H., 580n, 587n
Friesen, W.V., 556n
Frink, D.D., 570n
Frohlich, N., 563n
Froiland, P., 536n
Frombrun, C., 569n
Frost, A.C., 541n
Frost, D., 288
Frost, P.J., 554n, 570n, 571n, 581n, 582n
Fry, F.L., 534n
Fry, R., 572n
Fulford, R., 535n, 540n
Fulk, J., 555n
Fullagar, C., 537n, 543n, 547n, 551n
Furnham, A., 581n
Futrell, D., 558n, 561n

Gadacz, O., 161
Galbraith, J.R., 587n
Gallupe, R.B., 566n, 568n
Galperin, B.L., 543n
Galt, V., 185
Gandz, J., 541n, 553n, 571n
Gannage, C., 540n
Gannett, B.A., 535n
Ganster, D.C., 541n, 550n
Gardner, P.D., 584n
Gardner, R.C., 530n
Gardner, W.L., 547n
Gardner, W.L., III, 571n
Gates, W., 204, 471
Gatewood, R.D., 549n
Gay, K., 380
Geddie, T., 555n
Geis, F., 572n
Gellatly, I.R., 537n, 549n, 551n, 559n
Gemmell, M., 575n
George, J.M., 545n, 550n, 560n, 561n
Gersick, C.J.G., 559n
Ghadially, R., 571n
Ghoshal, S., 587n
Giacalone, R.A., 571n
Gibb-Clark, M., 185, 530n, 550n, 556n, 585n
Gibbon, A., 74, 161
Gibbons, R., 74
Gibson, J.L., 119, 256
Gilbert, B., 564n
Gilbert, N.L., 551n
Gilmore, D.C., 570n
Girard, D., 575n
Gist, M.E., 535n, 542n, 548n, 563n

Gittins, S., 571n
Glanz, E.F., 565n
Glass, B., 546n
Glauser, M.J., 554n
Glew, D.J., 563n
Glick, P., 547n
Godard, J., 541n
Godfrey, P, 205
Goetsch, D.L., 564n
Goffin, R.D., 551n
Goh, S.C., 578n
Gold, C., 361, 362, 374
Goldberg, G., 535n
Goldhaber, G., 553n, 586n
Goldman, A., 556n
Goldsmith, M., 530n, 531n
Goleman, D., 546n
Goll, I., 564n
Gombu, P., 585n
Gomez-Mejia, L.R., 538n, 587n
Goode, J., 554n
Gooderham, M., 554n
Gooding, R.Z., 549n
Goodman, J.S., 572n
Goodman, P., 579n
Goodman, P.S., 558n, 560n, 562n
Goodson, L., 553n
Gordon, B., 145
Gordon, B.R., 562n
Gordon, G.G., 582n
Gordon, L.A., 554n
Gordon, W.J.J., 568n
Gore, A., 579n
Gottier, R.F., 549n
Gould, J.M., 531n
Gould, S.B., 530n, 560n, 585n
Gourley, G., 218
Gowen, C.R., III, 562n
Graen, G.B., 568n
Graham, G.H., 557n
Graham, L., 340
Grant, J., 578n
Grant, L., 534n
Grant, R., 535n
Grant, R.M., 565n
Graves, M., 577n
Gray, J., 557n
Green, S., 564n
Green, S.G., 547n, 568n, 576n, 584n
Greenberg, J., 551n, 574n
Greenberg, L., 537n
Greenberger, D.B., 585n
Greenglass, E., 544n
Greenglass, E.R., 544n, 585n
Greenhaus, J.H., 585n
Greenwald, A.G., 550n
Greenwald, J., 585n
Greenwood, R., 579n, 580n, 586n

Greiner, L.E., 530n, 580n
Grenke, D., 271
Griffeth, R.W., 532n
Griffin, R.W., 541n, 563n, 567n
Grise, M.L., 566n, 568n
Grossman, M., 559n
Grote, R.C., 534n
Groves, M., 582n
Grunes, W.F., 546n
Guest, D., 547n
Guest, R.H., 540n
Guetzkow, H., 569n
Guion, R.M., 549n
Gunderson, M., 539n, 570n
Gunter, B., 581n
Gunz, H.P., 530n, 585n
Guo, Z., 562n
Gupta, N., 571n
Gustafson, D.H., 568n
Gustafson, L.T., 565n
Gutner, T., 161
Gutri, L., 557n
Guzzo, R.A., 532n, 557n, 558n, 559n, 581n
Guzzo, R.D., 535n
Gyll, S., 73
Gyllenhammar, P.G., 563n

H.L. Tosi, 531n
Haasen, A., 532n, 563n
Haberbusch, J., 163
Haccoun, R.R., 538n, 542n
Hackett, R.D., 532n, 544n, 551n, 577n
Hackman, J.D., 570n
Hackman, J.R., 98, 99, 112, 444, 536n, 540n, 541n, 559n, 584n
Haggett, S., 552n, 555n
Haier, B., 448
Haines, G.H., 552n
Haire, M., 546n
Haka, S., 554n
Hall, D.T., 584n, 585n
Hall, J., 548n, 557n
Hall, L., 574n
Hall, R.J., 578n
Hallman, M., 578n
Hallowell, R., 551n, 564n
Hallson, P., 337
Halpern, N., 562n
Hamilton, D., 419
Hamilton, D.L., 546n
Hamm, S., 586n
Hammarstrom, O., 562n
Hammer, M., 580n
Hampton, D.R., 309
Hancock, E., 332
Handy, J., 545n
Hanley, H., 326

Hanson, J.R., 556n, 571n
Hanson, L.A., 544n
Harari, O., 560n
Hardy, C., 531n, 554n, 558n, 569n, 571n, 578n, 579n
Hare, A.P., 559n
Hargadon, A., 567n, 568n
Hargrove, B., 321
Harrell, A.M., 537n
Harrington, D.M., 567n
Harris, C.R., 565n
Harris, D.M., 533n
Harris, J., 585n
Harris, M.J., 533n, 544n, 547n
Harris, P., 556n
Harris, T.E., 555n
Hartman, S.J., 532n, 585n
Harvey, D.F., 580n
Hassen, P., 568n
Hatfield, E., 537n, 555n
Hausdorf, P.A., 551n, 570n
Hautaluoma, J.E., 560n
Havlovic, S.J., 544n, 563n
Hayes, D.C., 570n
Head, T.C., 581n
Heaps, F., 425
Heard, L., 145
Heckscher, C.C., 552n
Hecksher, C.C., 530n
Hegedus, D.M., 568n
Heilbronn, F.S., 133
Heilman, M.E., 546n, 578n
Hein, K., 545n
Heinrich, E., 204, 565n
Heinzl, J., 539n
Helgesen, S., 556n, 572n
Hendrix, W.H., 537n
Heneman, R.L., 548n, 558n, 585n
Henkoff, R., 553n
Henwood, C.L., 553n
Hequet, M., 540n
Herniter, B.C., 574n
Herold, D.M., 534n
Herrick, N., 562n
Herriot, P., 583n
Herron, M., 567n
Hersey, P., 576n
Herzberg, F., 98, 540n
Heskett, J.L., 582n
Hesselbein, F., 530n, 531n, 575n
Hiam, A., 574n
Hickson, D.J., 569n, 570n
Higgin, G.W., 562n
Higgins, C., 535n, 543n
Higgins, C.A., 549n, 575n
Higgs, A.C., 555n, 558n, 573n
Hilborn, C., 534n
Hill, J.V., 556n

Hill, R.C., 565n
Hill, T., 548n
Hills, F.S., 538n
Hines, T., 567n
Hinings, C.R., 569n, 579n, 580n, 586n, 587n
Hinson, T.D., 573n
Hitchcock, D., 565n
Hitt, W.D., 531n
Hochschild, A., 543n
Hoffman, L., 184
Hofrichter, D., 539n
Hofstede, G., 190, 538n, 553n
Hogan, R.T., 549n
Hogg, M.A., 567n
Holahan, P.J., 566n
Holland, J.L., 549n
Hollingshead, A.B., 558n, 568n
Holton, E.F., III, 584n
Hom, P.W., 532n
Horwitt, E., 349
Hough, L.M., 549n
House, J.S., 545n
House, R.J., 359, 368, 371, 531n, 572n, 576n, 577n
Houston, P., 162, 552n
Hovey, B., 103
Howell, J.M., 549n, 575n, 577n
Huber, G., 531n, 533n, 555n
Huber, V.L., 534n
Hughson, T.L.G., 562n
Hui, C., 551n
Hull, T., 562n
Hulme, D., 572n
Hulse, R., 206
Humphrey, R.H., 543n, 550n, 552n, 560n
Hunt, J.G., 576n, 577n
Hunt, R., 538n
Hunt, S.T., 533n
Hunter, J., 554n
Hunter, J.E., 532n
Hunter, R.F., 532n
Huse, E.F., 579n, 580n
Huszczo, G.E., 557n, 561n
Huxley, C., 122, 317, 340
Hyatt, D., 570n
Hyten, C., 534n

Iacocca, L., 235, 558n
Iaffaldano, M.T., 551n
Indvik, J., 576n
Ingram, H., 162
Innes, E., 556n, 585n
Insko, C.A., 560n
Ip, G., 583n, 587n
Irvine, B., 553n

Irvine, D., 532n
Irvine, D.M., 550n
Irving, P.G., 549n, 575n
Irving, R., 543n
Isaacs, W.N., 574n
Isautier, B.F., 7
Isdell, N., 51
Isenberg, D., 567n
Israelson, D., 552n
Ivancevich, J.M., 119, 139, 256, 542n, 545n
Ivany, T., 44

Jablin, F.M., 554n, 570n, 584n
Jackson, D.N., 549n, 551n
Jackson, S.E., 543n, 558n, 559n, 560n
Jacobs, B., 57
Jacobs, R.W., 579n
Jacobson, L., 548n
Jacobson, S., 186
Jaeger, A.M., 581n, 583n
Jago, A.G., 282, 514, 515, 561n, 562n, 563n, 566n
Jain, H.C., 553n, 586n
Jain, V.K., 565n
Jako, R.A., 548n
Jalland, H.P., 530n, 585n
Jalland, R.M., 530n, 585n
Jamal, B., 544n
Jamal, M., 542n, 543n, 544n
Jamerson, F., 552n
Jang, B., 441
Janis, I.L., 294, 566n, 567n
Janson, R., 541n
Janssen, P., 133, 572n
Janz, T., 536n, 572n
Jarvis, J., 536n
Javidan, M., 578n, 586n
Jay, P., 534n
Jeffrey, W., 562n
Jehn, K.A., 572n, 573n, 581n
Jenero, K.A., 535n
Jenkins, G.D., Jr., 571n
Jenkins, J.M., 550n
Jennings, P., 557n
Jensen, M.A.C., 559n
Jermier, J.M., 576n
Jernigan, I.E., 553n
Jette, R.D., 532n, 581n
Jewell, L.N., 558n
Jick, T.D., 531n, 544n, 574n
Jinnett, K., 560n
Johannson, S., 117, 118, 126, 128, 129
Johns, G., 540n, 541n, 559n
Johnson, B.C., 568n
Johnson, B.T., 578n
Johnson, D., 283, 543n, 547n

Johnson, D.W., 573n
Johnson, F., 283
Johnson, H., 543n, 547n, 570n
Johnson, J.R., 579n
Johnson, J.W., 532n
Johnson, M., 554n, 578n
Johnson, N.B., 564n
Johnson, P., 534n
Johnson, R., 454
Johnson, R.T., 573n
Johnson, S., 566n
Johnson-Laird, P.N., 546n
Johnston, C.G., 204, 266, 556n, 564n, 587n
Johnston, C.P., 562n
Johnston, H., 325
Jones, B., 560n
Jones, D., 557n
Jones, D.T., 122, 543n, 556n, 563n, 565n
Jones, F.F., 539n
Jones, M.O., 581n, 582n
Jones, R.A., 557n
Jones, R.G., 559n
Jones, S.D., 535n
Joyce, W.F., 587n
Judge, T.A., 532n, 550n, 561n, 585n
Jussim, L., 547n

Kabanoff, B., 567n, 568n
Kacmar, K.M., 570n
Kaeter, M., 554n
Kahn, R.L., 530n, 533n, 543n, 576n, 579n, 586n
Kahn, S.E., 544n
Kahneman, D., 567n
Kahwajy, J.L., 568n, 572n
Kaihla, P., 578n, 579n
Kainz, A., 575n
Kallman, E., 535n
Kam, A., 252
Kane, K.F., 532n
Kanke, B., 59
Kanter, R.M., 569n, 570n
Kanungo, R.N., 533n, 538n, 539n, 540n, 541n, 553n, 563n, 577n
Kapel, C., 534n, 539n, 555n
Kaplan, R.E., 571n
Karakowsky, L., 573n
Karambayya, R., 551n, 575n
Karasek, R., 543n, 544n
Karau, S.J., 560n, 578n
Karl, K.A., 536n
Karpinski, R., 531n
Karren, R.J., 537n
Kast, F.E., 531n
Katz, D., 530n, 533n, 579n, 586n
Katz, H.C., 564n

Katz, R., 579n
Katzell, R.A., 532n, 581n
Katzenbach, J.R., 558n, 559n
Katzenstein, G., 568n
Kavanagh, M.H., 64, 576n
Kaye, B., 585n
Kearny, R.P., 569n
Keating, D.E., 563n
Keefe, P., 531n
Keefe, T.J., 539n
Keenan, G., 380
Keenen, J.P., 544n
Keinan, G., 544n
Keleman, K., 559n
Keller, M., 540n
Keller, R.T., 576n
Kelley, H.H., 547n
Kelloway, E.K., 537n, 543n, 547n, 551n, 578n
Kemmerer, B., 550n
Kennedy, A.A., 582n
Kenny, D.A., 364, 548n, 549n, 575n
Kent, R.L., 578n
Kepner, C., 565n
Kerlinger,, 587n
Kerr, J., 583n
Kerr, M., 550n
Kerr, M.J., 533n
Kerr, R., 95
Kerr, S., 530n, 576n
Kerwood, H., 587n
Kessler, M.L., 534n
Ket de Vries, M.F.R., 549n, 575n
Khalid, M., 317
Kidder, D.L., 439, 583n
Kidder, T., 558n
Kidwell, R.E., 561n
Kiernan, M.J., 567n
Kiesler, C.A., 559n
Kiesler, S.B., 559n
Kiggundu, M.N., 558n, 573n
Killough, R., 103
Kilmann, R.H., 580n, 587n
Kim, K.I., 538n
King, J., 530n
King, W.C., Jr., 573n
King, W.L.M., 260
Kingston, A., 123
Kipnis, D., 570n
Kirchmeyer, C., 559n, 560n, 570n, 573n
Kirkpatrick, S.A., 364, 575n, 577n
Kirsch, M., 548n, 549n
Kirson, D., 174
Kitayama, S., 546n, 550n
Klaas, B.S., 533n
Klastorin, T.D., 573n
Klein, H.J., 537n, 538n, 584n

Klein, R., 285
Kleinke, C.L., 548n
Klemmer, E.T., 553n
Klimoski, R., 559n
Klinger, M.R., 550n
Klonsky, B.G., 578n
Kluckhorn, F., 553n
Kluge, H., 161
Knebl, L., 272
Knight, C., 103, 212, 531n, 539n, 553n, 556n, 577n
Knight, K, 587n
Knights, D., 540n
Kniveton,, 574n
Knoop, R., 541n, 552n
Ko, W., 152
Kochan, T.A., 535n, 564n
Kocher, J., 396
Koelling, C.P., 562n
Koh, W.L., 577n
Kohn, A., 92, 93, 536n, 539n
Kolb, D.A., 577n
Kolind, A., 476
Kolodny, H.F., 562n, 586n, 587n
Kopelman, R.E., 534n
Koput, K.W., 567n
Korman, A.K., 576n
Koslowski, S.W.J., 584n
Koslowsky, M., 563n
Kotter, J.P., 579n, 582n
Koulack, D., 569n
Kouzes, J.M., 552n, 575n, 577n, 580n, 582n
Koys, D.J., 552n
Kozlowski, S., 548n
Kraatz, M.S., 583n
Krackhardt, D., 556n, 569n, 571n
Kraft, P., 122, 541n
Kramer, D., 563n, 565n, 577n
Kramer, R.M., 552n, 583n
Krefting, L.A., 582n
Kreitner, R., 39, 533n
Kreps, G., 556n
Krishnan, R., 565n
Kristof, A.L., 543n, 583n
Kristof-Brown, A., 538n
Kroho, J., Jr., 556n
Krone, K.J., 554n
Kudisch, J.D., 569n, 577n
Kuhn, T.S., 531n
Kulik, C.T., 537n
Kumagai, N., 450
Kumar, K., 559n
Kumar, P., 571n
Kupcis, A., 185
Kurtzman, J., 531n
Kushnir, T., 544n

Laabs, J., 530n, 552n
Laabs, J.J., 561n
Labarre, P., 476, 531n, 556n
Labich, K., 573n
Lacroix, R., 560n
LaFleur, T., 534n
Lam, M.N., 561n
Lamm, H., 567n
Landis, D., 548n
Landry, Y., 173
Lane, C., 217
Langan-Fox, J., 536n
Lansbury, R., 562n
LaPlante, A., 571n
Larson, J.R., Jr., 53
Larson, L.L., 576n, 577n
Larwood, L., 554n, 572n
Laston, A., 579n
Latane, B., 559n
Latham, G.P., 534n, 537n, 538n, 563n
Lau, C.-M., 581n
Laver, R., 548n
Lawler, E.E., 65, 536n, 561n
Lawler, E.E., III, 95, 181, 444, 532n, 536n, 539n, 540n, 541n, 550n, 551n, 559n, 561n, 562n, 584n, 586n
Lawless, M.W., 587n
Lawrence, B.S., 584n
Lawrence, P.R., 530n, 574n, 586n, 587n
Lawrie, K., 399
Laxer, D., 538n, 542n
Layton, D., 578n
Lazarsfeld, P., 587n
Lazenby, J., 567n
Leana, C.R., 563n
Leatherwood, M.L., 534n
Lebeter, D., 504
LeBlanc, A., 128, 129, 130
LeBrun, S., 537n, 555n, 583n
Leck, J.D., 555n
Ledford, G.E., Jr., 539n, 562n
Lee, C., 543n, 544n, 552n
Lee, C.A., 569n, 570n
Lee, C.H.S., 558n
Lee, K., 566n
Lee, R.T., 544n
Lee, T.E., 571n
Leger, K., 578n
Legge, R., 441
Leitch, C., 568n, 584n
Leiter, M.P., 543n
Lemak, D.J., 565n
Lemay, M., 583n
Lengel, R., 209
Lengel, R.H., 555n
Leon, L.S., 531n

Leonard, P., 564n, 565n
Lesieur, F.G., 562n
Lester, L., 555n
Levanoni, E., 541n
Levin, B.R., 530n, 560n, 585n
Levine, D.I., 559n, 561n, 563n, 564n
Levine, L., 581n
Levine, R.D., 562n
Levitch, G., 555n
Lewicki, P., 548n
Lewicki, R.J., 552n, 572n, 573n, 574n, 575n, 583n
Lewin, K., 65, 536n, 579n
Lewis, L.K., 552n, 554n
Lewis, S., 543n
Libuser, C., 585n
Lichtenstein, R., 560n
Liden, R.C., 541n, 558n, 562n, 569n, 571n, 573n
Liebowitz, S.J., 561n
Likert, R., 559n, 563n, 576n
Lilien, G.L., 567n
Lima, E.P., 14, 545n
Lin, H.T., 567n
Lindahl, R.V., 555n
Lindblom, C., 580n
Linden, R.C., 534n, 535n
Lindsay, L., 553n
Lindzey, G., 557n
Linz, D.G., 557n
Lipman, B.L., 566n
Lipnack, J., 236, 530n, 558n
Liska, L.Z., 576n
List, W., 317, 540n
Litterer, J.A., 573n, 574n
Little, B.W., 555n, 557n
Littler, C.R., 540n
Liverpool, P.R., 562n
Livesey, B., 545n
Livingston, J.S., 548n
Lochhead, C., 569n
Locke, E.A., 361, 537n, 538n, 550n, 551n, 562n, 563n, 565n, 575n, 577n
Loewen, K.R., 570n
Logue, A.W., 535n, 542n
Loher, B.T., 541n
London, M., 534n
Long, B.C., 544n
Long, R.J., 539n, 540n, 541n, 576n, 579n, 580n, 581n
Long, W.S., 575n
Loo, R., 545n
Lord, R.G., 545n, 576n, 578n
Lorenzi, P., 533n
Lorinc, J., 566n, 586n
Lorsch, J.W., 530n, 531n, 574n, 579n, 587n

Lott, A., 560n
Lott, B., 560n
Loughlin, C.A., 543n, 547n
Louis, M.R., 581n, 582n, 584n
Loury, G.C., 546n
Lublin, J., 579n
Lucas, G., 288
Luchak, A.A., 551n
Luckow, D., 585n
Ludwick, L., 581n
Luft, J., 162, 548n
Lundberg, C.C., 581n, 582n, 584n
Lush, K.K., 578n
Luthans, F., 39, 531n, 533n, 534n, 538n, 583n
Lyles, M., 566n
Lynch, L., 546n
Lyon, D., 535n
Lyon, J., 585n
Lyon, L., 584n

Mabert, V.A., 565n
MacArthur, D., 552n
MacCarthy, D., 185
Maccoby, M., 549n
MacDonald, E., 257
MacDonald, G., 64
Macdonald, G., 317
MacDonald, G., 427, 562n
MacDonald, S., 545n
MacFarland, J., 427, 543n
MacGillivary, A., 571n
Macher, K., 14
Machiavelli, N., 331
Macht, J., 556n
MacIsaac, M., 571n
MacKensie, A., 567n
MacKenzie, S.B., 533n, 551n, 577n
MacLachlan, N., 557n
MacLaurin, S., 533n
MacLean, J., 467
MacLean, P., 467
MacLeod, W.B., 566n
MacMillan, H.R., 374
MacPherson, M.E., 553n, 583n
Macrae, C.N., 546n
Maddox, E.N., 542n
Maddux, J.E., 57, 544n, 545n
Madison, D.L., 571n
Mael, F., 546n, 558n, 581n
Magaziner, I., 563n
Mager, R.F., 535n, 563n
Maher, K.J., 576n
Mahood, C., 33
Mai, R.P., 531n, 533n
Maitlis, S., 538n
Makhijani, M.G., 578n
Malec, W., 161

Malekazedeh, A.R., 582n
Malone, M.S., 579n, 587n
Mangum, S.L., 585n
Mann, S., 572n
Manning, M.R., 544n
Mannix, E.A., 571n
Mansbridge, P., 285
Mansell, J., 540n, 562n
Manz, C.C., 114, 535n, 541n, 542n, 562n, 563n, 564n
Mapes-Riordan, L.D., 535n
March, J.G., 565n, 566n, 569n
Marchetti, M., 534n
Mark, K., 533n, 545n, 552n, 555n, 564n, 565n
Markham, A., 554n
Marks, M.L., 543n, 579n
Markus, K., 409
Markus, M.L., 554n
Marrache, M., 560n
Marshak, R.J., 581n
Marshall, J.J., 552n
Marsnik, P., 531n
Martin, D.C., 540n, 569n
Martin, G.L., 542n
Martin, J., 581n, 582n
Martin, R., 541n
Martinko, M.J., 547n
Martocchio, J., 547n
Martoccio, J.J., 536n
Maruyama, G., 573n
Maruyama, M., 555n
Masini, B., 85
Maslach, C., 543n, 544n
Maslow, A.H., 61, 62, 77, 78, 536n
Maslyn, J.M., 572n
Massa, D., 269
Matsui, T., 538n
Matteson, M.T., 139, 542n, 545n
Matthews, S., 562n
Matthews, T., 363, 364, 374
Mausner, B., 540n
Mawhinney, R.R., 533n
Mawhinney, T.C., 533n, 534n
Maxwell, M., 74
Mayer, J.D., 553n
Mayes, B.T., 571n
Mayo, V.D., 542n
McAteer-Early, T., 585n
McCabe, D., 130
McCain, H., 327
McCain, M., 327
McCain, W., 327
McCall, B.P., 550n
McCall-Simms, A., 379
McCallum, T., 399, 530n, 545n
McCandless, M., 217
McCanse, A.A., 367, 576n

McCartney, J., 539n
McCaskill, D., 553n, 563n
McCauley, D., 545n
McClelland, C.L., 541n
McClelland, D.C., 62, 63, 77, 78, 536n
McCloy, R.A., 533n
McCollum, S.L., 570n
McConkie, H.L., 561n
McCoy, T.J., 565n
McDonald, P., 553n
McDonald, R., 534n
McElvie, K., 551n
McFarland, J., 74, 550n, 552n
McFarlin, D.B., 550n
McGarry, D., 273, 452, 564n, 565n
McGarty, C., 567n
McGee, V.E., 587n
McGehee, W., 533n
McGill, M.E., 532n, 579n
McGoon, C., 555n
McGovern, S., 569n
McGrath, J.E., 558n, 559n
McGrath, N., 572n
McGraw, P., 561n
McGregor, D., 563n
McGuire, W.J., 557n
McHutchion, J., 579n
McInnis, P.S., 561n
McIntyre, J.M., 577n
McIntyre, R.M., 557n
McKay, G., 557n, 564n
McKay, S., 566n, 572n, 578n, 579n, 586n
McKeen, C.A., 543n, 570n, 571n
McKendall, M., 581n
McKersie, R.B., 564n, 574n
McLaughlin, G., 581n
McLean, D., 544n
McLellan, J., 559n, 573n
McLuhan, M., 149, 210, 555n
McMahon, G.C., 561n
McMurdy, D., 347, 562n
McNeil, K., 583n
McNeill, M., 274
McNerney, D.J., 536n, 545n, 585n
McPherson, J.M., 560n
McQueen, R., 571n
McShane, S.L., 23, 81, 83, 111, 136, 170, 196, 413, 433, 435, 447, 458, 485, 492, 494, 496, 498, 504, 506, 538n, 539n, 551n, 575n, 584n
McSheffrey, J., 298
McWilliams, K., 212
Mead, R., 546n, 556n
Medcof, J.W., 540n, 570n, 578n, 579n
Medsker, G.J., 558n, 573n
Medvec, V.H., 566n
Meehan, M., 536n

Mehrabian, A., 555n
Meiksins, P., 122, 541n
Meindl, J.R., 578n
Mekechuk, B.J., 557n
Melamed, S., 542n, 544n
Meloy, M.G., 566n
Mendonca, M., 538n, 539n
Mento, A.J., 537n
Menzies, D., 252, 581n
Mercandante, B., 57
Merwin, G.A., 534n
Meyer, J.C., 582n
Meyer, J.P., 537n, 551n, 552n, 566n, 575n, 584n
Meyer, M., 583n
Meznar, M.B., 546n, 579n
Michaelson, L.K., 559n
Michaud, Y., 74
Michelson, L.D., 420
Mighty, E.J., 573n
Mikalachki, A., 557n
Milakovich, M.E., 564n, 565n
Miles, R.E., 572n, 587n
Milkovich, G.T., 538n
Miller, D., 531n, 549n, 579n, 580n, 587n
Miller, D.L., 559n
Miller, J.L., 186
Miller, J.M., 575n
Miller, K.I., 563n
Miller, L.C., 548n
Miller, S., 368
Miller, T., 152
Miller, V.D., 579n
Mills, D.Q., 587n
Mills, J., 33, 560n
Mills, S., 543n
Milne, A.B., 546n
Miltenberger, R.G., 533n, 534n
Min, H.C., 548n
Miner, J.B., 587n
Ming, S., 542n
Minish, K., 117, 118
Minnick, A., 556n
Minton, J., 573n
Mintzberg, H., 540n, 556n, 565n, 566n, 569n, 571n, 586n, 587n
Miron, D., 536n
Mirvis, P.H., 543n, 579n
Mischel, W., 549n
Mishra, J., 556n
Misutka, F., 575n
Mitchell, F., 313
Mitchell, T.R., 53, 535n, 536n, 537n, 547n, 548n, 563n, 566n, 571n, 573n, 576n
Mitroff, I.I., 546n, 566n
Mitz, L.F., 544n

Moberg, D.J., 571n
Moeller, N.L., 541n
Moen, P.L., 531n
Mohrman, A., 557n, 558n, 559n, 562n
Mohrman, A.M., Jr., 557n, 558n, 559n, 562n
Molitor, P., 322
Monetta, D.J., 580n
Monje, P.R., 563n
Montagu-Pollock, M., 552n
Monteith, M.J., 546n
Montgomery, J.C., 565n
Monton, J.W., 574n
Moore, G., 326
Moore, L.F., 581n, 582n
Moorhead, G., 567n
Moorman, R.H., 535n
Moran, A., 542n
Moran, R., 556n
Morand, D.A., 582n
More, N., 178
Morgan, C., 105
Morgan, G., 554n, 582n, 586n
Morgan, R., 567n
Morin, A., 542n
Morley, D., 561n
Morrell, A., 326
Morris, A., 557n
Morris, J.A., 552n, 555n
Morris, T., 563n
Morrison, E.W., 534n, 552n, 583n, 584n
Mosco, V., 569n
Moskal, B.S., 380
Moss, S.E., 578n
Motherwell, C., 266, 326, 347
Motowidlo, S.J., 544n
Mount, M.K., 549n
Mountford, S., 361
Moussa, F.M., 538n
Mouton, J.S., 366, 572n, 573n, 574n, 576n
Mowday, R.T., 537n, 551n, 554n
Muchinsky, P.M., 551n
Mudrack, P.E., 572n, 586n
Mueller, H., 264
Mueller, R., 546n
Mullane, J.V., 565n
Mullen, B., 560n, 568n
Mulvey, P.W., 566n
Murakami, T., 563n
Murnighan, J.K., 559n
Murphy, C.J., 576n
Murphy, K.R., 548n
Murphy, L.R., 542n, 552n
Murray, H., 562n
Murray, R.P., 541n
Murray, V.V., 571n, 574n

Myers, D.G., 567n
Myers, J., 478

Nadler, D.A., 536n, 579n, 580n
Nagel, R., 587n
Nahavandi, A., 582n
Nair, C., 544n
Nanus, B., 577n
Nasmith, G.G., 539n, 553n, 583n
Neale, M.A., 574n, 575n
Neale, T., 492
Neck, C.P., 541n, 542n, 567n
Neider, L.L., 576n
Nelson, B., 539n, 555n
Nelson, D., 573n
Nelson, D.L., 543n, 584n
Nelson, R.R., 554n
Nestel, C., 549n
Neuman, G.A., 581n
Nevis, E.C., 531n
Newhouse, D., 553n, 563n
Newman, K.L., 553n
Newman, P.C., 552n
Newstrom, J.W., 557n
Newton, E., 544n
Newton, T., 545n
Ng, I., 533n, 553n
Nhan, T., 552n
Nicholson, N., 584n
Nickel, J.R., 565n
Nicolini, D., 546n, 579n
Niebuhr, R.E., 547n
Niedenthal, P.M., 546n, 550n
Niehoff, B.P., 535n, 577n
Nielson, M.O., 553n, 563n
Nightingale, D., 572n
Nightingale, D.V., 561n
Noble, K., 531n
Noe, R.A., 541n
Noe, R.D., 549n
Noer, D.M., 552n
Nolan, C., 542n
Nolan, S.D., 553n
Nollen, S., 585n
Nonaka, I., 531n, 533n, 553n, 566n, 569n, 586n
Noon, M., 556n
Nord, W.R., 554n, 558n, 578n
Normand, J., 553n
Norris, D.R., 547n
Norris, J.M., 546n
Northcraft, G.B., 534n, 535n, 573n, 574n
Noto, L., 470
Notz, W.W., 573n, 580n
Novak, W., 558n
Nunamaker, J.F., Jr., 568n, 574n
Nutt, P.C., 566n, 567n

Nyaw, M.K., 553n
Nye, D., 585n
Nystrom, P., 546n

O'Brien, R.M., 533n
O'Connor, C., 174
O'Connor, J.R., 556n
O'Leary, A., 544n
O'Leary-Kelly, A.M., 536n, 563n, 584n
O'Reilly, B., 584n
O'Reilly, C.A., 560n, 582n, 583n
Oakley, A., 425
Oatley, K., 550n
Oberlander, R., 427
Ogden, S.G., 539n
Ohmae, K., 578n
Oickle, G.K., 557n
Olander, K., 574n
Oldham, G.R., 98, 99, 112, 540n, 541n, 567n
Oleson, K.C., 547n
Olive, D., 553n
Olson, J.M., 550n
Ondrack, M., 544n
Oppler, S.H., 533n
Organ, D.W., 533n, 551n, 587n
Osborn, A.F., 302, 568n
Osborn, R.N., 576n
Oshry, B., 335
Osterman, P., 540n, 541n
Ostroff, C., 584n
Ott, J.S., 581n
Ouchi, W.G., 583n
Owen, C.L., 546n
Owen, J.V., 565n
Oz, S., 548n

Packard, J.S., 544n
Paish, S.I., 570n
Paish, S.J., 547n
Papoff, B., 477
Papper, E.M., 558n
Park, H.-J., 538n
Parker, M., 564n
Parker, S., Jr., 409, 581n
Parkes, K.R., 544n
Parkinson, B., 555n
Parks, J.M., 439, 552n, 583n
Parsons, T., 340
Partridge, J., 566n
Pascale, R.T., 580n
Patinkin, M., 563n
Paton, J., 91
Paton, T., 191
Pattenden, T., 374, 375, 400
Paulus, P.B., 568n
Paunonen, S.V., 551n
Pavett, C., 563n

Pavlik, E.L., 539n
Pawar, B.S., 577n, 578n
Pawley, D., 275
Pawluk, C., 173, 179
Payne, A., 551n
Payne, R., 542n
Peach, E.B., 539n
Pearce, J.L., 558n, 571n
Pearce, P., 257
Pearson, G., 441, 539n, 575n
Pederson, J.S., 582n
Peer, G.A., 574n
Pekrun, R., 550n
Pelletier, R., 122, 340
Pemberton, C., 583n
Pender, T., 95
Penley, L.E., 553n
Penner, C., 59
Pennings, J.M., 569n
Penrod, S., 557n
Perelman, L.J., 535n
Perreault, W.D., Jr., 532n
Perrewe, P.L., 544n
Perrow, C., 587n
Pescuric, A., 535n
Peter, L.J., 288
Peters, T., 465, 556n, 558n, 586n
Peters, T.J., 577n, 583n
Peterson, D., 292
Peterson, E., 574n
Peterson, R.A., 532n
Petrash, G., 531n
Petrasovits, A., 544n
Pettigrew, A.M., 569n
Petty, R., 557n
Pfeffer, J., 530n, 531n, 537n, 550n, 569n, 570n, 578n, 585n
Pfeiffer, A.L., 553n, 586n
Phillips, N., 554n
Phillips, R.A., 534n, 537n
Phillips, S.P., 547n
Picard, A., 543n, 547n
Piczak, M., 226
Piczak, M.W., 570n
Pierce, J.L., 563n, 579n
Pinchot, G., III, 569n
Pinder, C.C., 500, 532n, 534n, 536n, 537n, 541n, 550n, 584n
Pinfield, L.T., 566n
Pinto, J.K., 560n, 573n
Pinto, M.B., 560n, 573n
Piper, W., 560n
Pischke-Winn, K., 556n
Pitts, G., 553n
Plato, 74, 146, 545n
Platts, S.J., 578n
Plous, S., 566n
Plunkett, L.C., 562n

Podsakoff, P.M., 533n, 535n, 551n, 569n, 577n
Poister, T.H., 537n
Polak, J., 330
Polivka, A.E., 585n
Pollock, A.B., 562n
Pomeroy, F., 564n
Ponak, A., 570n
Pondy, L.R., 554n, 572n, 582n
Popielarz, P.A., 560n
Popper, M., 580n
Porter, L.W., 444, 536n, 537n, 540n, 551n, 554n, 558n, 559n, 570n, 571n, 572n, 584n
Porter, M.E., 587n
Posner, B.Z., 552n, 553n, 575n, 577n, 580n, 582n
Post, J.E., 555n
Poteet, M.L., 569n, 577n
Powell, G.N., 576n, 578n
Powell, M.C., 546n
Powell, R., 301
Power, J.G., 555n
Powers, M.E., 582n
Prabhu, G.V., 546n, 553n, 586n
Pratkanis, A.R., 567n
Prentice, L., 145
Prentice-Dunn, S., 57
Prescott, J.E., 560n, 573n
Preston, J., 361
Pritchard, R.D., 535n
Pruitt, D.G., 574n
Prusak, L., 570n
Prystay, C., 252
Pugh, D.S., 530n, 587n
Pulleyn, I., 7
Purdy, K., 541n
Putnam, L.L., 554n, 570n, 572n, 574n, 575n, 584n
Putti, J.M., 581n

Quick, J.C., 542n
Quick, J.D., 542n
Quinn, J., 575n
Quinn, R.P., 543n

Rabie, M., 573n
Ragins, B.R., 570n, 571n
Rahim, M.A., 573n
Rain, J.S., 548n
Raisinghani, D., 565n, 566n
Raju, N.S., 581n
Randall, D.M., 536n
Rangaswamy, A., 567n
Rankin, T., 562n
Ranson, S., 586n
Rao, A., 564n, 571n
Rapson, R.L., 555n

Rasmussen, R., 568n
Raven, B., 569n
Raven, B.H., 315, 569n, 570n
Ravichandran, R., 536n
Ravlin, E., 558n
Ray, R., 532n
Raymond, P., 547n, 570n
Raynaud, M., 582n
Rayner, B., 586n
Raynor, M.E., 565n
Rechner, P.L., 568n
Reddin, W., 373
Redding, W.C., 554n
Redekop, B., 538n
Redondo, I.M., 539n
Redpath, L., 553n, 563n
Reed, R., 565n
Reed, T.F., 545n
Rees, D.I., 533n
Reger, R.K., 565n
Reichheld, F.F., 95, 539n
Reichhold, F.F., 551n
Reif, W.E., 540n
Reilly, A.H., 545n
Reiss, B., 555n
Reitz, H.J., 558n
Rendleman, J., 558n
Renwick, P.A., 571n
Revelle, W., 549n
Rhinehart, J.W., 540n
Rhodes, S.R., 532n
Riccobono, J.E., 534n
Rice, R.E., 555n
Rice, R.W., 550n
Richards, D., 296
Richards, G.S., 531n
Richardson, A., 560n
Richter, J., 585n
Rieley, J.B., 587n
Rinehart, J., 122, 317, 340, 541n
Robb, R.E., 539n
Robbin, H., 566n
Robbins, H., 559n, 560n, 561n
Robbins, T.L., 564n
Roberson, L., 550n
Roberts, D., 561n
Roberts, K.H., 554n, 570n, 584n
Robertson, B., 530n
Robertson, D., 122, 317, 340
Robertson, P., 562n
Robey, D., 358, 554n, 586n, 587n
Robinson, S., 535n
Robinson, S.L., 552n, 583n, 584n
Robson, W., 441
Rock, M.L., 539n
Roddick, A., 429
Rogers, C.S., 543n
Rogers, R.W., 57

Rokeach, M., 553n
Roloff, M.E., 574n
Romm, T., 570n
Roos, D., 556n, 563n
Rose, L.H., 567n
Roseman, E., 288
Rosen, H., 574n
Rosener, J.B., 578n
Rosenfeld, P., 571n
Rosenman, R., 544n
Rosenthal, R., 547n, 548n
Rosenthal, R.A., 543n
Rosenweig, J.E., 531n
Roskos-Ewoldsen, D.R., 546n
Rosnow, R.L., 556n
Rosow, M.P., 533n
Ross, D., 259
Ross, J., 550n
Ross, S., 550n
Rosser, J.B., Jr., 548n
Rossett, A., 548n
Rossiter, J.R., 567n, 568n
Rossler, P.E., 562n
Roszell, J., 259
Roth, P.G., 535n
Roth, P.L., 535n
Roth, S., 536n
Rothbart, M., 557n
Rothstein, M., 549n
Rousseau, D.M., 439, 531n, 538n, 552n, 583n, 584n, 585n
Rowland, K.M., 548n
Royer, R., 425
Rubach, M.J., 531n
Rubin, H., 572n
Rubin, I.M., 577n
Rubin, J.Z., 574n
Rubin, S., 551n
Ruble, T.L., 344
Ruderman, M.N., 558n, 559n
Runco, M.A., 566n, 568n
Russ, G.S., 571n
Russo, J.E., 566n
Ruvolo, C.M., 546n
Ryer, K., 572n
Rynes, S.L., 532n

Sack, J., 539n
Sackmann, S., 582n
Saffold, G.S., III, 582n
Sager, C.E., 533n
Sagie, A., 538n, 553n, 563n
Saint-Onge, H., 531n
Saks, A.M., 538n, 542n, 543n, 545n, 584n, 586n
Salacuse, J.W., 574n
Salancik, G.R., 550n, 570n, 578n
Salas, E., 557n, 559n, 568n

Saleh, S.D., 549n, 562n
Sales, C.A., 541n
Salipante, P.F., 580n
Sallot, J., 569n
Salovey, P., 553n
Salter, M., 37, 532n
Sama, L.M., 534n
Sandberg, W.R., 568n
Sandvig, J.C., 565n
Sanford, E.E., 534n
Sapienza, A., 555n
Sarasan, S., 133
Sarel, D., 532n
Sarr, R.A., 577n
Sathe, V., 582n
Saunders, C.S., 554n
Saunders, D., 565n, 573n
Saunders, D.M., 555n
Sauter, S., 542n, 552n
Savage, H., 437, 438, 453
Savoie, A., 558n
Sawyer, J.E., 567n
Scarpello, V.G., 538n, 539n
Schachter, H., 554n
Schacter, S., 545n, 558n
Schad, R., 417, 429
Schaefer, N.V., 532n
Schaubroeck, J., 550n
Schein, E.H., 561n, 574n, 580n, 581n, 582n, 583n, 585n
Schein, V.E., 546n, 580n
Scheller, M., 185
Schenck, R.E., 569n
Schick, A.G., 554n
Schilder, J., 44, 569n
Schipper, L., 205
Schlesinger, L.A., 551n, 564n, 579n
Schmidt, S.M., 571n
Schmidt, W.H., 553n, 564n, 576n
Schminke, M., 558n
Schmitt, N., 533n, 549n
Schmitz, J., 555n
Schnake, M.E., 535n
Schneider, B., 535n, 555n
Schneider, M.S., 547n
Schneider, R.J., 549n
Schneier, C.E., 539n
Schoderbek, P.P., 540n
Schoeder, R.G., 560n
Schofield, J., 539n
Schon, D.A., 546n
Schoorman, F.D., 535n, 566n
Schrage, M., 568n
Schreisheim, C.A., 569n
Schriesheim, C.A., 576n, 577n
Schroeder, K.G., 584n
Schroeder, R.G., 564n
Schuler, R.S., 545n

Schull, F.A., 567n
Schwab, D.P., 541n, 551n
Schwartz, J., 174
Schweiger, D.M., 562n, 563n, 568n
Schwenk, C., 568n
Scotland, R., 512, 513, 583n, 586n, 587n
Scott, D., 561n
Scott, D.B., 401
Scott, J., 554n
Scott, K.D., 536n
Sczech, M., 540n, 541n
Seeman, M., 540n
Seger, C.A., 535n
Seibold, D.R., 554n
Seiling, R., 94
Seltzer, J., 577n
Selye, H., 119, 542n
Selznick, P., 575n
Senge, P.M., 531n, 533n, 546n, 561n, 566n, 574n
Sethi, A.S., 545n
Shackelford, S.L., 558n
Shalin, V.L., 546n, 553n, 586n
Shalley, C.E., 567n
Shani, A.B., 548n, 580n
Shani, R., 565n
Shannon, C.E., 554n
Shapansky, K., 565n
Shapira, Z., 566n
Shapiro, B.T., 578n
Shapiro, I., 191
Shapiro, Z., 565n
Shapoff, S.H., 551n
Sharfman, M.P., 565n
Sharma, A., 532n
Sharman, P.A., 274
Sharp, I., 187, 374, 429, 583n
Shaver, P., 174
Shaw, D., 274
Shaw, D.G., 539n
Shaw, G., 581n
Shaw, M.E., 557n, 558n
Shaw, W.H., 553n
Shea, G.P., 558n
Shephard, R.J., 545n
Sheppard, B.H., 574n, 575n
Shepperd, J.A., 537n, 561n
Sherer, M., 57
Sheridan, J.H., 586n
Sherif, M., 573n
Sherman, S., 538n
Sherman, S.J., 546n
Sherwood, G.G., 548n
Sherwood, J.J., 561n
Shikdar, A.A., 534n, 537n, 540n
Shoesmith, J., 555n
Shonk, J.H., 557n

Shore, L.M., 551n, 552n, 583n
Shull, F.A., Jr., 565n
Shulman, A.D., 554n, 558n
Siconolfi, M., 554n, 569n
Siegall, M., 543n, 544n
Siegel, J.P., 581n
Siehl, C., 582n
Siklos, P., 575n
Silcoff, S., 301, 548n
Sillars, L., 581n
Simon, D., 378
Simon, H., 569n
Simon, H.A., 167, 546n, 549n, 565n, 566n
Simon, W., 559n
Simonson, I., 567n
Simpson, J.A., 558n
Sims, H.P., 533n
Sims, H.P., Jr., 535n, 541n, 542n
Sinclair, A., 560n, 582n
Sinha, K.K., 560n, 564n
Sink, D.S., 580n
Sitkin, S.B., 555n
Skoglind, J.D., 585n
Skon, S., 573n
Slangerup, J., 36
Slaughter, J., 564n
Slocum, J.W., Jr., 531n, 532n, 579n, 583n, 587n
Smirchich, L., 582n
Smith, A., 95, 96, 540n
Smith, D., 585n
Smith, D.K., 156, 157, 558n, 559n
Smith, R.S., 539n
Smith, V., 563n
Smither, J.W., 534n
Smythe, R., 437, 438, 453
Snead, K.C., 537n
Snoek, J.D., 543n
Snow, C.C., 572n, 587n
Snyder, F.W., 553n
Snyder, M., 549n, 557n
Snyder, N.H., 577n
Snyderman, B.B., 540n
Sobol, Y., 37
Soelberg, P.O., 566n
Solomon, C.J., 561n
Solomon, C.M., 556n
Somech, A., 560n
Sommer, S.M., 534n, 538n
Sooklal, L., 577n
Sorensen, J.S., 582n
Sorenson, P.F., 581n
Souque, J.P., 575n
Southwick-Trask, L., 556n
Spector, B., 579n, 580n
Spector, P.E., 540n, 549n, 551n
Spencer, L.M., 532n, 539n, 575n

Spencer, S.M., 532n, 539n, 575n
Spich, R.S., 559n
Spitzer, D.R., 95, 540n
Sprecher, S., 537n
Spreitzer, G.M., 541n, 562n
Stackhouse, J., 575n
Staelin, R., 567n
Stagner, R., 574n
Stalker, G., 586n, 587n
Stamps, D., 581n
Stamps, J., 236, 530n, 558n
Stang, D., 123
Stangor, C., 546n
Starbuck, W., 546n
Starcevich, M.M., 548n
Starke, F.A., 573n
Stasser, G., 558n
Staw, B.M., 550n, 551n, 567n
Stebbins, M., 571n
Steed, J., 545n, 581n
Steel, R.P., 537n
Steeples, M.M., 565n
Steers, R.M., 532n, 537n, 540n, 551n, 554n, 577n
Steiger, T., 122, 541n
Steiner, D.D., 548n
Steiner, I.D., 560n
Steiner, R.L., 559n, 568n
Steinfield, C.W., 555n
Stephen, C.W., 546n, 552n, 553n
Stephen, W.G., 546n, 552n, 553n
Stephenson, C., 380
Stern, R.N., 530n
Sternberg, R.J., 533n
Stevens, C.K., 542n
Stevenson, M., 540n, 564n
Stevenson, W.B., 558n, 571n
Stewart, G.L., 542n, 549n, 562n
Stewart, J.M., 577n
Stewart, T.A., 531n, 567n, 587n
Stewart, W., 543n
Stogdill, R.M., 575n, 576n
Stohl, C., 554n
Stone, D.L., 546n
Stork, D., 555n
Stowell, S.J., 548n
Strang, M., 95
Strassmann, P.A., 580n
Strauss, G., 572n
Strauss, J.P., 549n
Streib, G., 537n
Strodtbeck, F.L., 553n
Stroebe, W., 566n
Stroh, L.K., 545n
Stronach, F., 429
Strongman, K.T., 550n
Sulsky, L.M., 548n
Summers, T.P., 537n

Sundstrom, E., 558n, 561n, 571n
Sung-Won, C., 161
Surtees, L., 586n
Sutcliffe, K.M., 555n
Sutton, C., 543n
Sutton, R.I., 552n, 567n, 568n
Suzuki, N., 538n
Swink, M.L., 565n
Syedain, H., 540n

Tajfel, H., 546n
Takeuchi, H., 531n, 533n, 553n, 566n, 569n, 586n
Tanaka-Matsumi, J., 542n
Tang, T.L., 570n
Tannen, D., 556n, 572n
Tannenbaum, A., 572n
Tannenbaum, A.S., 558n
Tannenbaum, R., 576n
Tannenbaum, S.I., 559n
Tapscott, D., 579n
Taubman, P., 550n
Taylor, C.L., 530n
Taylor, F.W., 96, 97, 540n
Taylor, R.N., 566n
Teasdale, M., 582n
Tedeschi, J.T., 571n
Tellier, P., 391, 392, 400, 464
Temple, L.E., 570n
Terai, I., 538n
Terborg, J.R., 537n, 577n
Terpstra, D.E., 547n, 570n
Terra, N., 545n
Terrett, J., 557n
Terrett, L., 565n
Tetrick, L.E., 583n
Tett, R.P., 549n, 551n
Thacker, R.A., 570n
Thanakit, P., 133
Thayer, P.W., 533n
Theorell, T., 543n, 544n
Theoret, A., 565n, 566n
Theriault, R., 539n
Thierry, H., 536n
Thomas, D., 555n
Thomas, H., 566n
Thomas, K., 344
Thomas, K.W., 573n
Thomas, S., 557n
Thomas, S.L., 537n
Thomason, J.A., 534n
Thompson, G., 257
Thompson, J.D., 342, 569n, 573n, 583n
Thompson, K.R., 583n
Thompson, L.L., 574n
Thorlakson, A.J.H., 541n
Thorne, D., 546n

Thorpe, P.A., 561n
Tichy, N.M., 569n
Tillson, T., 317, 582n
Ting-Toomey, S., 573n
Tjosvold, D., 562n, 568n, 572n, 573n, 575n, 577n
Tjosvold, M.M., 577n
Todd, J., 557n
Todd, P.A., 554n
Todor, W.D., 546n
Tolliver, J.M., 578n
Tomasko, R., 587n
Tomczyk, F., 292
Tomkiewicz, J., 546n
Tommerup, P., 577n
Toulin, A., 551n
Toulouse, J.-M., 549n, 575n
Trapunski, E., 564n
Tregoe, B., 565n
Trenholm, S., 557n
Trevino, L.K., 533n, 535n, 555n
Trice, H.M., 533n, 582n
Tripp-Knowles, P., 557n
Trist, E.L., 265, 562n
Tse, D.K., 566n, 573n
Tubbs, M.E., 537n, 538n
Tuchman, M.L., 569n
Tuckman, B.W., 241, 242, 559n
Tulgan, B., 64, 536n
Turner, J.C., 133, 567n
Turner, M.E., 567n
Turner, R., 542n
Tversky, A., 567n
Tyler, T.R., 552n, 583n
Tyson, D., 539n

Ullman, E., 560n
Ulrich, D., 531n, 555n
Unruh, J., 557n
Uzumeri, M.V., 564n

Valacich, J.S., 568n
Van Aken, E.M., 580n
Van Alphen, T., 419, 583n
van Ameringen, M.R., 545n
Van de Ven, A.H., 568n
Van de Vliert, E., 573n
Van Eerde, W., 536n
Van Eynde, D.F., 580n
Van Fleet, D.D., 560n, 563n, 586n
Van Maanen, J., 583n, 584n
Van Norman, K.L., 564n
Van Seters, D.A., 547n
Van Zante, H., 5
VandenBos, G.R., 537n, 551n
Varcoe, C., 537n
Vaughn, J., 533n
Vaverek, K.A., 554n

Vecchio, R.P., 537n, 576n
Veiga, J.F., 566n
Velasquez, M., 571n
Velasquez, M.G., 553n
Veley, R., 337
Verberg, P., 550n
Verma, A., 564n
Vertinsky, I., 566n
Vido, A., 204, 348, 407, 574n, 581n
Villanova, P., 547n
Vinokur-Kaplan, D., 560n
Virk, J., 560n
Vogl, A.J., 74
Vollenhoven, A., 252
Volpe, C.E., 559n
Von Glinow, M., 531n
von Hippel, C., 558n, 585n
von Simson, E.M., 586n
Vroom, V.H., 65, 282, 514, 515, 536n, 561n, 562n, 563n, 566n

Wagar, T.H., 539n, 576n
Wageman, R., 540n, 558n, 573n
Wagner, J.A., III, 553n, 563n
Wagner, R.K., 533n
Wahba, M.A., 536n
Wahl, Q., 275
Waisman, T., 478
Wakefield, T., 274
Wakely, D., 539n
Waldersee, R., 534n
Waldie, P., 568n, 571n
Waldner, M., 266
Walker, C., 118, 542n
Walker, C.J., 556n
Walker, C.R., 540n
Walker, T.H., 556n
Wall, J.A., 572n
Wall, J.A., Jr., 574n
Wall, T.D., 541n, 545n
Walls, J., 573n
Walmsley, A., 531n, 535n
Walsh, J.P., 546n
Walter, G.A., 581n, 582n
Walters, M., 581n, 582n, 583n
Walton, R.E., 402, 572n, 574n, 580n
Wanous, J.P., 536n, 584n
Ward, A., 17
Ward, D., 570n
Warda, J., 575n
Wardell, M., 122, 541n
Waring, A., 531n
Watanabe, S., 532n, 585n
Waters, J.A., 580n
Watson, B.S., 545n
Watson, W.E., 559n
Watts, T., 545n
Waung, M., 545n

Wayne, S.J., 551n, 552n, 558n, 573n
Weatherup, C., 366
Weaver, W., 554n
Weber, T., 578n
Weber, W.L., 552n
Wedley, W.C., 565n, 566n
Wehrung, D.A., 566n
Weick, K.E., 536n, 546n
Weiner, K.J., 530n, 585n
Weir, T., 542n
Weiss, H.M., 174, 549n, 550n
Weitz, B.A., 547n
Weitzel, J.R., 576n
Weldon, E., 535n
Welland, R., 206
Wellins, R.S., 530n, 557n, 558n, 563n
Wells, J., 540n, 554n
Wells, S., 545n
Welsh, D.H.B., 534n, 538n
Welty, G., 586n
West, M.A., 567n
Westley, W., 541n
Wetherell, M.S., 567n
Wexley, K.N., 534n, 548n
Wharton, A.S., 543n
Wheatley, A., 559n, 568n
Wheatley, W.J., 542n
Wheeler, H.N., 533n
Whinston, A.B., 558n
Whitaker, S., 532n
White, B., 582n
White, J.B., 204
White, T.H., 562n
Whyte, G., 566n
Whyte, W.F., 447, 583n, 584n
Wick, C.W., 531n
Wiener, K.J., 560n
Wiginton, J., 554n
Wilcox, D.S., 554n
Wilkins, A.L., 582n
Willard, M., 565n

Williams, A., 581n, 582n, 583n
Williams, K.D., 560n
Williams, K.J., 543n
Williams, M.L., 577n
Williamson, O.E., 537n
Williamson, R., 536n
Willmott, H., 540n
Wills, T.A., 545n
Wils, T., 585n
Winter, D.G., 536n
Winter, N., 532n, 539n
Winters, D.C., 538n, 563n
Wintrob, S., 296
Wisenthal, P., 575n
Withane, S., 575n
Withey, M.J., 532n, 551n, 578n
Witteman, H., 572n
Wofford, J.C., 576n
Wolf, G., 572n
Wolf, S., 584n
Wolfe, D.M., 543n
Woloschuk, M., 571n
Womack, J.P., 122, 543n, 556n, 563n, 565n
Wong, C.S., 540n
Wong, J., 66, 67, 69
Wood, M.M., 572n
Wood, W., 558n
Woodbury, E., 330
Woodman, R.W., 561n, 567n
Woods, D., 97
Worchel, S., 558n, 559n
Worley, C.G., 561n
Wren, D.A., 539n
Wressell, P., 231
Wright, E., 544n
Wright, E.F., 539n
Wright, P.M., 538n
Wylie, A.M., 546n

Xie, J.L., 540n

Yamada, H., 556n
Yamahiro, R.S., 548n
Yamauchi, H., 298, 538n
Yearta, S.K., 538n
Yeung, A., 555n
Young, A.T., 531n
Young, C.A., 584n
Young, M., 555n
Young, P., 582n
Yrle, A.C., 532n, 585n
Yrle, A.R., 532n, 585n
Yuen, H., 297
Yukl, G., 570n, 571n
Yukl, G.A., 569n, 576n

Zaccaro, S.J., 364, 549n, 575n
Zairi, M., 564n, 565n
Zajonc, R.B., 557n
Zald, M.N., 530n
Zalesney, M.D., 550n
Zaleznik, A., 577n
Zalkind, S.S., 548n
Zama, M.P., 550n
Zammit, F., 29, 30
Zammuto, R.F., 586n
Zander, A., 557n
Zangwill, W.I., 565n
Zawacki, R.A., 502
Zeidenberg, J., 532n, 558n, 565n, 567n, 583n
Zeilig, P., 545n
Zellner, M., 557n
Zemke, R., 549n, 582n
Zhou, J., 570n
Zimbardo, P., 557n
Zimmerman, M., 573n
Zornitsky, J., 551n, 564n
Zureik, E., 569n
Zwany, A.A., 536n

COMPANY INDEX

3H Communications, 279
3M, 213, 298–299, 316

ABB. *See* Asea Brown Boveri
ABII/UMI, 434
Abitibi-Price Inc., 427
AGF (mutual funds), 207
AGI, 213
Air Canada, 48, 187, 346, 347, 464
Alberta Public Utilities Board, 409
Alcan Aluminum, 133, 402
Alcan Cable, 276
Algoma Steel Inc., 91, 261, 262
Alliance of Manufacturers and
    Exporters of Canada, 478
America West Airlines, 108
American Express, 86
Amoco Canada, 87, 263
Anchor Hocking, 240
Ancol Ltd., 23
Anderson Exploration Ltd., 427
Apple Computer, 50, 207, 332, 392,
    396, 451
Arctic Mining Consultants, 491
Arlington Software Corp., 296
Armstrong World Industries Inc,
    247–248
Armstrong World Industries Inc., 350
Armstrong Worldwide Inc., 349
Asea Brown Boveri (Canada), 232, 277
AT&T, 211, 279
Ault Foods, 17, 207
Avcorp Aerostructures, 252
Avon Products Inc., 330, 361–362, 374

B. C. Transit, 446
Banff Springs Hotel, 265
Bank of Montreal, 35, 74, 152, 160,
    207, 211, 375, 469
Bank of Winnipeg, 498
Baranti Group Inc., 477
Bata Limited, 288, 468–469
Battlefords Credit Union, 207
Bayer Inc., 264
BC Ferries, 32
BC Gas, 45
BC Telecom, 132, 211, 216
Bell Canada, 7, 33, 88, 192, 380,
    398–399, 437, 439
Bell Labs, 299
Bell Mobility, 472

Bell Sygma, 88
Bell-Northern Research Ltd., 36
Binney and Smith, 100
Boba Restaurant, 145
Body Shop Canada, The, 64, 65
Boeing 777, 273
Boeing Inc., 248, 273, 304
Bombardier, 472
Bombardier Inc., 9, 425
Bonas Machine Company, 396–398
Booz Allen & Hamilton Inc., 349–350
Bow Valley Energy Inc., 326, 327, 394
BP. *See* British Petroleum
British Airways, 14, 185
British Columbia Transit Authority,
    446
British Petroleum, 378, 425
British Steel, 133
Britvic, 51
Buckman Labs, 9
Build-All Products Inc., 493
BusNews Inc., 22

Cadet Uniform Services, 184, 187, 275
CAE Electronics, 199–200, 210, 212,
    263
CAI. *See* Canadian Airlines
    International
Calgary Flames, 107
Calsonic North America, 217
CAMI Automotive Inc., 122, 317, 340
CAMI. *See* CAMI Automotive Inc.
Campbell Soup Co. Ltd., 90–91, 94,
    217, 301
Canada Post Corp., 97, 184, 252, 453
Canada Trust, 211
Canadian Airlines International, 262,
    263, 346, 347
Canadian Auto Workers, 118, 122,
    129, 321
Canadian Broadcasting Corporation,
    101–102, 285, 288, 292
Canadian Business, 434
Canadian Coast Guard, 99
Canadian Forces, 316
Canadian Imperial Bank of
    Commerce, 14, 16, 74, 87, 130,
    160, 161, 207, 212, 303, 319, 329,
    395, 451
Canadian National Railways, 296,
    391–393, 400, 464

Canadian Occidental Petroleum Ltd.,
    7, 31
Canadian Pacific, 347
Canadian Pacific Hotels & Resorts
    Ltd., 29–30, 379, 423
Canadian Rolling Mills, 452
Canadian Satellite Communications
    Inc., 437
Canadian Spring Waters Co. Ltd., 164
Canadian Tire, 192
Canadian Wheat Board, 328–329
Cancom, 437
CanCorp Ltd., 489
Canon, 200
CanOxy. *See* Canadian Occidental
    Petroleum Corp.
Cantron Ltd., 494
Cape Breton Development Corp., 35
Carpenter Technology, Inc., 45
Caterpillar, 185
Cathay Pacific Airlines, 187
CAW. *See* Canadian Auto Workers
CBC. *See* Canadian Broadcasting
    Corporation
CEMEX, 397
Champion Road Machinery Ltd., 212,
    259–260, 277
Chateau Frontenac, 161
Chez Toi (cooking school), 145
Chrysler Corp., 75, 95, 204, 205, 272,
    275, 348, 407
Cigna Corp., 131
City of Calgary, 22
City of Ottawa, 18
City of Saskatoon, 66–67, 69
City of Toronto, 131
Citytv, 102
CN Tower, 12
Coca-Cola Company, 51, 217, 218,
    252
Colgate Palmolive, 122, 160
Compaq Computers, 206, 465
Concordia University, 127
Connectix, Inc., 45
Consumers Gas Co. Ltd., 45, 90, 163,
    442
Consumers Packaging, 340
Continental Airlines, 90, 161
Coors Brewing Co., 355
Corel Corp., 317, 425
Cornell University, 207

Corning Glass, 182, 213
Cossette Communications Inc., 472
Crayola, 100
CrossKeys Systems Corp., 478
CTV, 285
Cunard Steamship Lines, 182, 377
Current Affairs, 434

D-Code Inc., 64
Davies, Ward and Beck, 420
Decca Records, 288
Deloitte & Touche, 123
Delta Airlines, 187, 208
Department of National Defence, 318
Detroit Diesel, 3
Devco. *See* Cape Breton Development
    Corp.
Digital Equipment Corporation, 34,
    160, 240, 244
Dominion Insurance, 216
Domtar, 186
Domtar Inc., 464
Donnelly Mirrors, 95
Dufferin Aggregates, 348
Dufferin Game Room Store Ltd., 103
DuPont Canada Ltd., 8, 261, 270, 355,
    419, 450

Eagle's Flight Inc., 253
Earl Industries Inc., 186
Eastern Province Light and Power
    Company, 307
Eastern Provincial Insurance
    Corporation, 412
Eastman Chemical Co., 473–474
Eastman Kodak Co., 473
Eaton's, 192, 374, 429, 505
Edper Group Ltd., 14
EDS. *See* Electronic Data Systems
    Corp.
Edson Packaging Machinery Ltd., 185
Efco Corp., 270
Einblau & Associates, 252
Electronic Data Systems Corp., 7
Emergex Planning Inc., 478
EMI Records, 288
Empress Hotel, 35, 423
Europcar, 406
External Affairs, 181

Federal Express, 36, 160, 184, 210, 279
Fields Stores, 503
Financial Post, 205
Finning International, 185
Fletcher Challenge, 211
Florida Power and Light, 276
FNGP. *See* Freudenberg-NOK General
    Partnership

Ford Motor Company, 235, 271, 272,
    380, 455
Forethought Inc., 16
Four Seasons Hotels, 184, 187, 374,
    429
Freudenberg-NOK General
    Partnership, 273
Frito-Lay, 41
Frontpage, 16

GE Canada, 8, 88, 234, 240, 473–475
GE Capital Fleet Services, 265, 400
General Electric, 75, 287
General Electric Canada, 269
General Motors, 31, 97, 213, 272, 317,
    321, 340, 391, 451
Global Express, 9
Globe & Mail, 350
GO-train, 133
Gould Shawmut Ltd., 12
Great Lakes Power Ltd., 296
Great West Life Assurance Co., 280
Group 4 CPS Limited, 455
GTE Canada, 102
Gusher Drilling Company, 456

Health Care Diaper, 91
Herman Miller Inc., 74, 430
Hewlett-Packard (Canada) Ltd.,
    85–86, 128–130, 207
Hibernia Management and
    Development Co., 4–5
Highland Valley Copper, 103
Hill and Knowlton Canada, 330
Home Oil Co. Ltd., 427
Honeywell Ltd., 232
Hospital for Sick Children, 212
Hudson's Bay Company, 89
Hughes Aircraft of Canada, 191–192
Hughes Space & Communication Co.,
    17
Human Resources Development
    Canada, 251
Humpty Dumpty, 452
Husky Injection Molding Systems
    Ltd., 130, 132, 417–420, 429
Hyundai Motor Co., 161

IBM, 86, 184, 189–190, 451
IBM Canada, 303, 304, 424
IDEO, 299, 464
Imperial Oil Ltd., 153, 154, 160, 192
Inco Ltd., 95, 266
Industrial Accident Prevention
    Association, 132
Insurance Corporation of British
    Columbia, 68
Intercontinental Packers Ltd., 313, 327

International Forest Products, 50
International Woodworkers Union,
    270
Iona Appliances, 392
Israeli Defence Force, 157

James MacLaren Industries, 210
Jersey Dairies Ltd., 496
Joe Fortes Seafood Restaurant, 59

Kanke Seafood Restaurants Ltd., 59,
    74
Kao Corp., 37
Kao Infosystems Canada Inc., 37
Kellogg's, 105, 454
Kelly Services Canada Ltd., 437
Kitchen Overall & Shirt Company, 260
KPMG, 452

L&M Highland Outfitters Ltd., 467
Labatt Breweries, 132, 178, 399, 437,
    464
LaCroix Industries Ltd., 493
Lever Brothers, 260
Levesque Beaubien Geoffrion Inc.,
    342
Levi Strauss, 133
LINK Inc., 194
Litton Systems Canada Ltd., 269
Lola Restaurant, 145
London Life Insurance Co., 292
Lotus Notes, 235

MacDonald Dettwiler & Associates
    Ltd., 471–472
MacMillan Bloedel, 91, 93, 355, 478
Maelstrom Communications, 357
Magna International, 392, 429
Major League Baseball Players'
    Association, 322
Manitoba Telephone System, 261
Manpower Inc., 451
Marine Atlantic, 43–44
Maritime Life, 123
Markham Stouffville Hospital, 442
Mattel, 452
McCain Foods Ltd., 327
McCain USA, 327
McDonald's, 133, 187, 376, 447,
    465–466
McDonnell Douglas Canada, 317
McGregor's, 502
MCI. *See* Motor Coach Industries
McMaster University, 226
Memorial Medical Centre, 101
Merisel Canada Inc., 368
Microsoft Corporation, 16, 64, 204,
    277, 425, 429, 470

Minnesota Mining & Manufacturing Co. *See* 3M
Mitel Corp., 34
Mitsui Bank, 341
Mitsui Group, 450
Mobil Oil, 349, 468, 470
Mohawk College, 226
Moore Corp. Ltd., 468–469
Motor Coach Industries, 3, 4, 8
Motorola, 236
Mustang, 235

NASA, 17–18
NASA. *See* National Aeronautic and Space Administration
Nate's Deli, 156
National Aeronautic and Space Administration, 293
National Bank of Canada, 74, 130, 342
National Rubber, 269, 374, 375, 400
National Sea Products Ltd., 97
National Semiconductor, 242
NCR Canada, 102
Neilson-Cadbury, 392
Neon, 95
Nesel Fast Freight Inc., 212
New Coke, 51
Newbridge Networks Corp., 363–364, 478
Nintendo, 298
Nissan Group, 217
Noram Canada Ltd., 135
Nordair, 347
Nortel, 34, 45, 181, 207, 213, 246, 438, 461, 473 *See also* Northern Telecom
Northern Chicken Ltd., 280
Northern Lights Industrials Ltd., 382
Northern Telecom, 14, 88, 181, 207, 213, 438, 451, 461, 473 *See also* Nortel
Northrup Grumman, 235
Norwest Soil Research ltd., 263
Nova Scotia Government Employees Union, 70
Nova Scotia Power Inc., 104, 232
Novell Inc., 392, 425
NUMMI, 317
Nupath Foods Ltd., 169

Ohio State University, 365
Oki Poki Designs Inc., 189
Olympia & York, 291
Ontario Hotel/Motel Association, 94
Ontario Hydro, 185, 291, 303
Opel, 31, 268
Oticon Holding A/S, 213, 246, 475–476

Ottawa Sun, 91
Outward Bound, 251

Pacific Western, 347
Palliser Furniture Ltd., 260
Pan Restaurant, 145
PanCanadian Petroleum, 266
Peak Adventures International, 252
Pepsi-Cola Company, 45, 63, 164
PepsiCo. Inc., 366
Perfect Pizzeria, 499
Petro-Canada, 392, 441, 452
Pfizer Inc., 240
Placer Dome, 260, 261
PMC AG, 484
Power Computing, 396
PowerPoint, 16
Pratt & Whitney, 231, 234, 238, 260–261, 278–279, 401
Precision Metalcraft Inc., 213
Prego, 301
Price Waterhouse Limited, 16, 207
Procter & Gamble, 48, 87, 424
Public Works Canada, 453
PWA Corp., 262, 263

Qantas Aitlines, 132
Quantor Corp. Ltd., 457
Queen Elizabeth II Health Sciences Centre, 70

RBC Dominion Securities, 183
RCMP. *See* Royal Canadian Mounted Police
Reebok International Ltd., 288
Renaissance Energy Ltd., 326
Republic Steel, 261
Richardson Greenshields, 183
Richmond Savings Credit Union, 399
Riverdale Hopsital, 130
RJR MacDonald, 437
Rocky Mountain Bicycle Company, 420
Rogers Communications, 91
Royal Bank of Canada, 34, 64, 74, 130, 170–171, 424, 437, 454
Royal Bank of Scotland, 215–216
Royal Canadian Mounted Police, 121, 183, 455
Royal LePage, 304
Royal Trust, 437
Royal York Hotel, 29–30

S. C. Johnson and Son Ltd., 301
Sakura Bank, 341
San Diego Zoo, 474
SaskTel, 409
Saturn, 472

Schneider Corp., 260, 401
Scott's Restaurants Inc., 162
Shell Canada Ltd., 87, 88, 240, 264, 265
Shell Chemicals, 8, 265
Shell Oil, 11
Sigma (mine), 260
Simon Fraser University, 455
SkyDome, 12
SkyDome Hotel, 379
Smith Packaging Ltd., 420
SmithKline Beecham, 296
Snap-On Tools of Canada Ltd., 101
Sobey Stores, 164
Southam Inc., 395
Spar Aerospace, 462
Sparkling Spring Water Ltd., 164
St. Joseph's Hospital, 305
St. Luke's Medical Center, 214–216
Standard Aero Ltd., 47, 250, 274
Stanfield's, 502
Steelcase, 274
Steelfab Ltd., 80–81
Stentor, 380
Stone Consolidated Corp., 427
Strait Crossing Development Inc., 366
Stratton Knitting Mills, 89
Subsidies Management Branch, 337
Sun Microsystems Canada Ltd., 184, 235, 236, 240
Sunnybrook Health Science Centre, 191, 235
Supreme Court of Canada, 153
Suzuki, 340
Swedbank, 163
Symmetrix, 409

T. Eaton Company. *See* Eaton's
Taiyo Kobe Bank, 341
Tavistock Institute, 265
TBWA Chiat/Day, 213, 214, 246
TD Bank, 448
TD Greenline, 48
Telus Corporation, 339
Tennessee Valley Authority, 161
Texas Instruments, 268
Thomas J. Lipton, 272
Toronto Blue Jays, 322
Toronto Dominion Bank, 448
Toronto Sun Publishing Co., 91, 131, 205
Toyota Motor Company, 95, 122, 213, 273, 317
TransAlta Utilities Corp., 409
Treetop Forest Products Ltd., 501
Tuff Bolt Inc., 489
Twentieth Century Fox, 288

Unheard Of Restaurant, 145
United Brotherhood of Carpenters, 270
United Way, The, 477
Universal Studios, 288
University Hospital, 91
University of Alberta Hospitals, 48
University of Calgary, 82, 326
University of Michigan, 365
University of New Brunswick, 149–150
University of Prince Edward Island, 82
Upper Canada Brewing, 424–425

Value Health Sciences, 420
VanCity. *See* Vancouver City Savings Credit Union

Vancouver City Savings Credit Union, 51, 232
VCR Plus, 297–298
Vermeer Technologies Corp., 16
Vetements Ltee, 110
Vickers & Benson Advertising Ltd., 512–513
Victoria General Hospital, 70
VISA, 130
Volvo, 73, 266

W. L. Gore and Associates, 347
Wacker Siltronic Corp., 202
Walt Disney World, 186
Wascana Energy Inc., 263
Web Circuits Ltd., 411
Wellness Innovations Corp., 476–477

Western Agencies Ltd., 502
Westinghouse Canada, 88
WestJet Airlines, 173–174, 179
Westray, 192
Windsor Factory Supply, 262
Woods Gordon, 97
WordPerfect Corp., 425
Work Wear World, 503
Workers Temporary Help Ltd., 452
Workers' Compensation Board of British Columbia, 127
Workers' Compensation Board of Ontario, 127

Xerox, 16, 45, 94, 236, 273, 275–277

York Knitting Mills, 97

cut here

STUDENT REPLY CARD

In order to improve future editions, we are seeking your comments on
Canadian Organizational Behaviour, Third Edition, by McShane.
Please answer the following questions and return this form via Business Reply Mail.
Your opinions matter. Thank you in advance for sharing them with us!

Name of your college or university: _____

Major program of study: _____

Course title: _____

Were you required to buy this book?   yes _____ no _____

Did you buy this book new or used?   new _____ used _____ ($_____)

Do you plan to keep or sell this book?   keep _____ sell _____

Is the order of topic coverage consistent with what was taught in your course?

cut here

fold here

Are there chapters or sections of this text that were not assigned for your course?
Please specify:

Were there topics covered in your course that are not included in this text?
Please specify:

What did you like most about this text?

What did you like least?

If you would like to say more, we'd love to hear from you. Please write to us at the
address shown on the reverse of this card.

cut here

fold here

cut here

Att.: Senior Sponsoring Editor
College Division
McGRAW-HILL RYERSON LIMITED
300 WATER STREET
WHITBY ON   L1N 9Z9